Fodor's 2008

AUSTRALIA

Where to Stay and Eat for All Budgets

Must-See Sights and Local Secrets

Ratings You Can Trust

Fodor's Travel Publications   New York, Toronto, London, Sydney, Auckland
www.fodors.com

FODOR'S AUSTRALIA 2008

Editor: Margaret Kelly, Adam Taplin, Mark Sullivan

Editorial Production: Bethany Cassin Beckerlegge, Astrid deRidder

Editorial Contributors: Roger Allnutt, Melanie Ball, Caroline Gladstone, Graham Hodgson, Victoria Patience, and Merran White

Maps & Illustrations: David Lindroth Inc., Mapping Specialists, cartographers; Bob Blake and Rebecca Baer, *map editors*

Design: Fabrizio LaRocca, *creative director*; Guido Caroti, Siobhan O'Hare, *art directors*; Ann McBride, *designer*; Melanie Marin, *senior picture editor*; Moon Sun Kim, *cover designer*

Cover Photo (Aboriginal Bark Painting): Ken Welsh/Alamy

Production/Manufacturing: Angela McLean

COPYRIGHT

ISBN 978–1–4000–1811–6

ISSN 1095–2675

SPECIAL SALES

This book is available at special discounts for bulk purchases for sales promotions or premiums. Special editions, including personalized covers, excerpts of existing books, and corporate imprints, can be created in large quantities for special needs. For more information, write to Special Markets/Premium Sales, 1745 Broadway, MD 6-2, New York, New York 10019, or e-mail specialmarkets@randomhouse.com.

AN IMPORTANT TIP & AN INVITATION

Although all prices, opening times, and other details in this book are based on information supplied to us at press time, changes occur all the time in the travel world, and Fodor's cannot accept responsibility for facts that become outdated or for inadvertent errors or omissions. So **always confirm information when it matters,** especially if you're making a detour to visit a specific place. Your experiences—positive and negative—matter to us. If we have missed or misstated something, **please write to us.** We follow up on all suggestions. Contact the Australia editor at editors@fodors.com or c/o Fodor's at 1745 Broadway, New York, NY 10019.

PRINTED IN THE UNITED STATES OF AMERICA

10 9 8 7 6 5 4 3 2 1

Be a Fodor's Correspondent

Your opinion matters. It matters to us. It matters to your fellow Fodor's travelers, too. And we'd like to hear it. In fact, we need to hear it.

When you share your experiences and opinions, you become an active member of the Fodor's community. That means we'll not only use your feedback to make our books better, but we'll publish your names and comments whenever possible. Throughout our guides, look for "Word of Mouth," excerpts of your unvarnished feedback.

Here's how you can help improve Fodor's for all of us.

Tell us when we're right. We rely on local writers to give you an insider's perspective. But our writers and staff editors—who are the best in the business—depend on you. Your positive feedback is a vote to renew our recommendations for the next edition.

Tell us when we're wrong. We're proud that we update most of our guides every year. But we're not perfect. Things change. Hotels cut services. Museums change hours. Charming cafés lose charm. If our writer didn't quite capture the essence of a place, tell us how you'd do it differently. If any of our descriptions are inaccurate or inadequate, we'll incorporate your changes in the next edition and will correct factual errors at fodors.com immediately.

Tell us what to include. You probably have had fantastic travel experiences that aren't yet in Fodor's. Why not share them with a community of like-minded travelers? Maybe you chanced upon a beach or bistro or B&B that you don't want to keep to yourself. Tell us why we should include it. And share your discoveries and experiences with everyone directly at fodors.com. Your input may lead us to add a new listing or highlight a place we cover with a "Highly Recommended" star or with our highest rating, "Fodor's Choice."

Give us your opinion instantly at our feedback center at www.fodors.com/feedback. You may also e-mail editors@fodors.com with the subject line "Australia Editor." Or send your nominations, comments, and complaints by mail to Australia Editor, Fodor's, 1745 Broadway, New York, NY 10019.

You and travelers like you are the heart of the Fodor's community. Make our community richer by sharing your experiences. Be a Fodor's correspondent.

Tim Jarrell, Publisher

CONTENTS

CLOSE UPS

CONTENTS

MAPS

ABOUT THIS BOOK

Our Ratings

Sometimes you find terrific travel experiences and sometimes they just find you. But usually the burden is on you to select the right combination of experiences. That's where our ratings come in.

As travelers we've all discovered a place so wonderful that its worthiness is obvious. And sometimes that place is so unique that superlatives don't do it justice: you just have to be there to know. These sights, properties, and experiences get our highest rating, **Fodor's Choice**, indicated by orange stars throughout this book.

Black stars highlight sights and properties we deem **Highly Recommended**, places that our writers, editors, and readers praise again and again for consistency and excellence.

By default, there's another category: any place we include in this book is by definition worth your time, unless we say otherwise. And we will.

Disagree with any of our choices? Care to nominate a place or suggest that we rate one more highly? Visit our feedback center at www.fodors.com/feedback.

Budget Well

Hotel and restaurant price categories from ¢ to $$$$ are defined in the opening pages of each chapter. For attractions, we always give standard adult admission fees; reductions are usually available for children, students, and senior citizens. Want to pay with plastic? **AE, D, DC, MC, V** following restaurant and hotel listings indicate whether American Express, Discover, Diners Club, MasterCard, and Visa are accepted.

Restaurants

Unless we state otherwise, restaurants are open for lunch and dinner daily. We mention dress only when there's a specific requirement and reservations only when they're essential or not accepted—it's always best to book ahead.

Hotels

Hotels have private bath, phone, TV, and air-conditioning and operate on the European Plan (aka EP, meaning without meals), unless we specify that they use the Continental Plan (CP, with a Continental breakfast), Breakfast Plan (BP, with a full breakfast), or Modified American Plan (MAP, with breakfast and dinner) or are all-inclusive (AI, including all meals and most activities). We always list facilities but not whether you'll be charged an extra fee to use them, so when pricing accommodations, find out what's included.

Many Listings

★	Fodor's Choice
★	Highly recommended
🔲	Physical address
✛	Directions
⚬	Mailing address
☎	Telephone
🖷	Fax
⊕	On the Web
✎	E-mail
🎫	Admission fee
☉	Open/closed times
Ⓜ	Metro stations
▭	Credit cards

Hotels & Restaurants

🏨	Hotel
↵	Number of rooms
☖	Facilities
❋	Meal plans
✕	Restaurant
♙	Reservations
↘	Smoking
⌂	BYOB
✕🏨	Hotel with restaurant that warrants a visit

Outdoors

🏌	Golf
⛺	Camping

Other

☺	Family-friendly
⇨	See also
✉	Branch address
☞	Take note

WHAT'S WHERE

SYDNEY 	Sydney, one of the most naturally beautiful cities in the world, blends beachside cool with corporate capitalism and Victorian-era colonial architecture. When Australians are looking for big-city living, they automatically think of Sydney. Arts, tourism, and Asian business interests thrive here. Beaches surround the city, and while most tourist itineraries stay focused around Sydney Harbour, much of the city's vitality is in the residential suburban neighborhoods to its south, east, and north. The eastern suburbs in particular are home to some of the city's most dynamic restaurants, thriving nightlife, and fashion-forward shopping.
NEW SOUTH WALES 	Although Sydney may be the ultimate urban experience south of Hong Kong, southeastern Australia displays virtually all of the continent's rural and coastal variations: historic towns, mountain ranges, dramatic beaches, and world-class vineyards. The Blue Mountains rise 3,500 feet out of a eucalyptus-laden forest to the west of the city. Sprinkled with quaint towns full of bed-and-breakfasts and charming shops, the mountain range is a great one-night getaway from Sydney. Oenophiles will want to check out the Hunter Valley wine region. Beach bums will find their way to the hippie-cum-surfer community of Byron Bay, which is the easternmost point in Australia. The national parks around the south end of New South Wales are great places to see examples of native flora and fauna without getting too far from the urban center.
CANBERRA & THE A.C.T. 	Everyone loves to hate Canberra, the nation's spacious and immaculately landscaped capital city. At the time of Canberra's founding, the government had hoped to create a neutral capital to end the ongoing rivalry between Sydney and Melbourne. They placed Canberra at an almost-perfect midpoint between the two cities—in the Australian Capital Territory (A.C.T.)—where mountain ranges and rivers dominate the landscape. A functional aesthetic permeates the city, which planners built around Parliament and the needs of a seat of government. Not only does Canberra showcase myriad Australian national monuments, it has a thriving arts scene as well.

MELBOURNE 	European sophistication fills Melbourne, Australia's most European city. With its cobblestone streets, tramways, and café culture, you can feel what a palpable impact the tremendous wave of post–World War II European immigrants had on Melbourne. The historic city center, with its narrow lanes and alleys, feels more like London than Sydney. More Greeks live in Melbourne than anywhere outside of Athens, and sizable Italian and Jewish immigrant communities are present as well, making for an ethnically and culturally diverse population. These influences also contribute to the city's incredible restaurant scene. You'll find much more delicious, diverse, and affordable cuisine here than in Sydney. Melbourne's shopping can't be beat anywhere else in Australia, with Chapel Street and Bridge Road boasting outposts of every major Australian designer. Art and culture are highly prized here and the ultramodern Arts Complex is an aesthete's delight.
VICTORIA 	The Victorian countryside has much natural and unpretentious charm. The Southern Ocean coastline and the famous Great Ocean Road attract many visitors. Dotted by spectacular natural rock formations—don't miss the Twelve Apostles—the drive also takes you through some quaint beach towns and famous surf spots. It's so close to Antarctica the weather can be on the frosty side, and Victoria's wildlife denizens are more ice dwellers than desert creatures. Phillip Island's fairy penguins draw a fair amount of tourism, and you may also spot seals and sea lions along the coast. Wineries and getaway spots also abound here, as do historic towns and lush national parks. All are ample reason to tear yourself away from the city and explore a little bit.
TASMANIA 	From Freycinet Peninsula to the wilds of South West National Park, Tasmania's intoxicating natural beauty testifies to Australia's topographic diversity. It looks and feels very different from the iconic Australia of kangaroos, Outback, and barbies. Tasmania looks more like the Lake District of England than a part of Australia. Since it lies so close to Antarctica, temperatures drop quite low here—you'll see more Ugg boots than flip-flops. The island is separated from the southeast coast of Australia by the Bass Strait, and the most interesting way to journey here is via the *Spirit of Tasmania* overnight ship, which departs from Sydney and Melbourne. Hikers will love the rich wilderness here, while quaint shops and tea rooms are distractions for non-outdoorsy types. Don't miss the numer-

WHAT'S WHERE

	ous small museums and historic sites that exhibit remnants of the island's volatile days as a penal colony. One arcane law in Tasmania still prohibits kite flying, which convicts once used as a means of escape.
QUEENSLAND 	Name your pleasure (or poison) and you'll find it in Queensland. The state has actively promoted tourism, and such areas as the Gold Coast in the south and Cairns in the north have exploded into mini-Miamis, complete with high-rise buildings, casinos, and beachfront amusements. North of Brisbane is the quieter Sunshine Coast, where you can kick back on nearly deserted beaches or take four-wheel-drive expeditions into beautiful rain forests. Pavement pounders will enjoy vastly underrated Brisbane, a river city with outstanding public works, a thriving arts scene, great restaurants, and easy access to the family-friendly adventure parks of Dreamworld and Movie World.
THE GREAT BARRIER REEF 	The crown jewel of the Gold Coast is the 2,600-km-long (1,616-mi-long) Great Barrier Reef. More than 3,000 individual reefs and 900 islands make up this vast aquatic universe. There are countless ways to experience this quickly disappearing natural wonder, not least of which include diving, snorkeling, and sailing.
ADELAIDE & SOUTH AUSTRALIA 	Most Aussies know Adelaide as a city filled with churches, and it has also become home to some of the most politically progressive people in the nation. Citizens have campaigned hard to ensure a high quality of life in this well-planned, picturesque capital. Adelaide has many charms, including its famous biennial festival of the arts. To experience all of Australia's best and most typical natural and cultural phenomena in one spot, explore South Australia. From nature-rich Kangaroo Island to the quirky Outback mining town of Coober Pedy, South Australia boasts diverse natural environments and landscapes. Be sure to take a tour of the renowned wine country, and then unwind on a Murray River cruise.

PERTH & WESTERN AUSTRALIA 	Those who make it to the "undiscovered country" of Australia's largest state are stunned by its sheer diversity. Relax on beautiful beaches, wonder at coastal formations in Nambung National Park, or swim with dolphins at Monkey Mia or Ningaloo Reef Marine Park. Explore the goldfields east of Perth or the historic towns, wineries, and seaside parks of the South West. The city of Perth itself has a laid-back, welcoming air. With its marinas and strong navy presence, it feels a bit like the San Diego of Australia.
THE RED CENTRE 	The Red Centre is the heart and soul of Australia. For tens of thousands of years Aboriginal people have occupied this vast desert territory named for the deep color of its soil. Aboriginal traditions revolve around Uluru, also known as Ayers Rock. Enormous monoliths that rise out of the desert like a dream, Uluru and neighboring Kata Tjuta have a profoundly otherworldly quality about them. Many sacred sites among Red Centre's mountain ranges, gorges, dry riverbeds, and spinifex plains also figure prominently in Aboriginal tradition. At the center of the region lies Alice Springs, Australia's only desert city, a one-horse town that caters to the tourists who come through each year on their visit to the center of the country. The climate here can be harsh and forbidding. Temperatures are sweltering in summer and drop below freezing at night in winter, which means you should choose the time of year you plan to visit very carefully. Tourists flock to the Red Centre despite its remoteness, so expect to pay a lot of money for meals and accommodation in the spots around these famous desert sites.
DARWIN, THE TOP END & THE KIMBERLEY 	From Darwin Harbour to the rocky domes and towers of Purnululu National Park, the Top End and the Kimberley's landforms are stunning and diverse. Besides being breathtakingly beautiful, this area in northern Australia holds many examples of ancient Aboriginal rock art. Crocodile Dundee hailed from here, but wildlife lovers should resist the temptation to go hunting. Kakadu National Park attracts among the highest volume of tourists of anywhere in Australia, though some prefer the smaller Litchfield National Park, with its waterfalls and sandstone mountain creations. Darwin and Broome—both far closer to Asia than to any Australian cities—host the most racially diverse populations of the nation.

Australia

Timor Sea

Darwin

Katherine

INDIAN OCEAN

Kununurra

KIMBERLEY REGION

Broome Derby   Great Northern Hwy.   Halls Creek

NORTHERN

TANAMI DESERT WILDLIFE SANCTUARY

Port Hedland

Dampier

GREAT SANDY DESERT

RUDALL RIVER NATIONAL PARK

Exmouth

KARIJINI NATIONAL PARK

Tom Price   Newman

Tropic of Capricorn

Uluru (Ayers Rock)

Carnarvon

WESTERN AUSTRALIA

BROWNE RANGE NATURE RESERVE

Monkey Mia

Meekatharra

GREAT VICTORIA DESERT

Coober Pe

Geraldton

NAMBUNG NATIONAL PARK

New Norcia

Kalgoorlie

GREAT VICTORIA DESERT NATURE RESERVE

Perth

Merredin

Coolgardie

NULLARBOR   PLAIN

Fremantle

Narrogin

Eyre Hwy.

Bunbury
Busselton

Esperance

Great Australian Bight

Margaret River

Albany

SOUTHERN OCEAN

Bass Strait

King Island

Burnie   Launceston

St. Marys

Strahan   TASMANIA

Hobart   Port Arthur

0   400 miles

0   400 kilometers

Arafura Sea

KAKADU NATIONAL PARK

ARNHEM LAND

Gulf of Carpentaria

Weipa

PAPUA NEW GUINEA

Coral Sea

CAPE YORK PENINSULA

Laura

Cooktown

Coral Sea Islands

Port Douglas

Mareeba

Cairns

Innisfail

GREAT

Burketown

Normanton

Georgetown

Ingham

BARRIER

TERRITORY

1

QUEENSLAND

GREAT

Townsville

Ayr

REEF

Tennant Creek

Mt. Isa

Cloncurry

66

Hughenden

DIVIDING

Mackay

Bruce Hwy.

Alice Springs

Bedourie

Longreach

66

Emerald

Blackwater

Rockhampton

RANGE

Gladstone

Birdsville

Windorah

71

Charleville

54

Roma

Kingaroy

Dalby

Nambour

1

Brisbane

Oodnadatta

Lake Eyre

Cunnamulla

71

Toowoomba

Warwick

SOUTH AUSTRALIA

Marree

Lake Torrens

FLINDERS RANGES NATIONAL PARK

Goondiwindi

Mitchell Hwy.

Moree

Lismore

Pacific Hwy.

Bourke

NEW SOUTH WALES

Walgett

Armidale

Grafton

Coffs Harbour

Ceduna

Port Augusta

32

Broken Hill

71

Nyngan

Kempsey

Port Macquarie

Port Pirie

Dubbo

1

EYRE PENINSULA

Renmark

Sturt Hwy.

Mildura

Hay

Orange

Bathurst

Cowra

Young

Newcastle

Port Lincoln

Adelaide

VICTORIA

Shepparton

Murray R.

Albury

Canberra

Sydney

Wollongong

Kangaroo Island

Bordertown

Bendigo

Seymour

Cooma

Bega

Mt. Gambier

Ballarat

Colac

Melbourne

Orbost

Bairnsdale

Portland

Geelong

Sale

Warrnambool

Wonthaggi

King Island

Bass Strait

Flinders Island

TASMANIA
(SEE INSET)

QUINTESSENTIAL AUSTRALIA

Go Bush

Aussies love to take some of their ample holiday time each year to go bush. When they refer to the bush, they can mean a scrubby patch of ground a few kilometers outside the city, or they can mean the vast, sprawling desert Outback. In most cases it's a way to describe getting out of the daily routine of the city and getting in touch with the natural landscape of this incredibly geographically and topographically diverse country.

With 80% of its population living on eastern shores, and with all of its major cities (except Canberra) situated along the coast, most of Australia's interior is wild, wonderful, and virtually empty. Whether you find yourself watching the sun rise (or set) over Uluru, taking a camel trek through the Kimberley, or sleeping under the stars in a swag (traditional Australian camping kit), there are countless ways to go bush and see Australia's most natural, rural, and stunning sights.

Swimming Between the Flags

Australians love their beaches as much as they love their barbies, and that's a good thing, because stunning beaches line the country's coast. Put on your bathers or your cossie (slang for bathing suit) and slather on some sunblock. The damage to the ozone layer is more apparent in Australia than elsewhere in the world, and one in three Australians ultimately develops skin cancer.

Australian beaches are patrolled by volunteer members of the Surf Lifesaving Association (SLSC), who post red and yellow flags to demarcate the safest areas to swim on any beach. Formed in 1907, the tan, buff lifesavers make the team on *Baywatch* look like amateurs—it is said that no one has ever drowned when swimming in the areas that they patrol.

Aussies refer to authentic or genuine things as *fair dinkum*. Here are a few ways to experience Australia like the locals do.

Of course, these hunky heroes can't be everywhere all the time, so use caution when swimming on those picturesque deserted beaches you're bound to come across in your travels. The undertow can be strong and dangerous.

Aussie! Aussie! Aussie! Oy! Oy! Oy!

From world-class sporting events like the Australian Open to national obsessions like the Australian Football League Grand Final, Aussies love their sports. And they have a lot to choose from, including cricket matches, regattas, and surfing competitions. The calendar is full of sporting events that give Aussies good reason to drink a cold beer and gather with mates to barrack for (cheer on) their favorite team.

Aussie Rules Football enjoys perhaps the greatest popularity. This rough-and-tumble sport, played without padding, uses what looks like an American football through four 25-minute quarters. Rugby League Football, a 13-a-side game that is played internationally, rivals Aussie Rules in popularity, though Australians dominate it. Cricket test matches are the sport of summer, though much less happens during these games than in footy matches. Spectators get to soak up the sun and drink a lot of beer while watching the Australians duel international teams in test matches that can go for one to five days.

The Barbie

Paul Hogan, aka Crocodile Dundee, showed the world laid-back Australian hospitality by inviting visitors to say "G'day" then throw another shrimp on the barbie, or barbecue. But it's unlikely you'll find shrimp on a barbie in Australia. What you will find is Aussies cooking up steak, sausages (often called snaggers), beef, chicken, and lamb on gas grills all

QUINTESSENTIAL AUSTRALIA

over the country. Most butchers sell pre-cut packs of meat to take directly to the barbie from the shop.

Barbies are so ubiquitous in Australia that almost every public park or beach will have a barbie area set up for people to come and grill at will. The tools required for "doing a barbie" the traditional Aussie way are newspaper and butter. The newspaper helps wipe the barbie clean from the previous grilling, and butter greases it back up again before putting the meat on. Sometimes an onion instead of a newspaper is used to clean off the grill—a slightly more hygienic system.

Australia Day

This national holiday, observed on January 26, commemorates the day in 1788 when Colonel Arthur Phillip took formal possession of the colony of New South Wales, becoming its governor. Australians celebrate with brash, proud expressions of Australian spirit, much as an American would on July 4th. Barbecues are held, fireworks are launched, and boat races are staged around the country, though the main Australia Day celebrations take place around Sydney Harbour. The harbor fills with historic and modern ships, and the Australia Day Regatta—the oldest continuous regatta in the world—takes place.

Some know Australia Day as a Day of Mourning. Many Aborigines feel that celebrations of Australia Day ignore the oppression suffered by Australia's native people. Whatever one's thoughts on the matter might be, Australia Day does present a framework for dialogue about the Aboriginal experience in today's Australia.

WHEN TO GO

Australia is in the Southern Hemisphere, so the seasons are reversed. It's winter Down Under during the American and European summer.

The ideal time to visit the north, particularly the Northern Territory's Kakadu National Park, is early in the dry season (around May). Birdlife remains profuse on the drying floodplains, and waterfalls are still spectacular and accessible. The Dry (April–October) is also a good time to visit northern Queensland's beaches and rain forests. You can swim off the coast without fear of dangerous stinging box jellyfish, which infest ocean waters between November and March. In rain forests, heat and humidity are lower than later in the year, and crocodile viewing is at its prime, as the creatures tend to bask on riverbanks rather than submerge in the colder water.

During school holidays, Australians take to the roads in droves. The busiest period is mid-December to the end of January, which is the equivalent of the U.S. and British summer break.

Climate

Australia's climate is temperate in southern states, particularly in coastal areas, and tropical in Australia's far north. The Australian summer north of the Tropic of Capricorn is a steam bath. From September through November (the Australian spring), or from February through April (late summer–autumn), southern regions are generally sunny and warm, with only occasional rain in Sydney, Melbourne, and Adelaide. Perth and the south of Western Australia are at their finest in springtime, when wildflowers blanket the land.

Forecasts Weather Channel Connection
(☎900/932–8437 95¢ per min from a Touch-Tone phone ⊕www.weather.com).

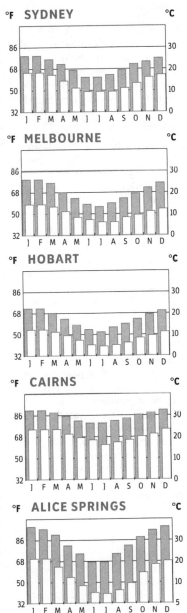

IF YOU LIKE

Beautiful Beaches

Whether you want to sun-bake, see or be seen, or try body- or board-surfing in the white-capped waves, Australia has an abundance of beautiful beaches. Miles and miles of pristine sand line the coastline, where you can sunbathe in solitary splendor.

- **Bondi Beach.** On the edge of the Tasman Sea, Bondi Beach is the most famous perhaps in all of Australia. Don't miss the Cliff Walk from Bondi to Bronte Beach, either. This breathtaking path will take you along a string of eastern beaches all at once, while trawling the dramatic cliffs that line the coast.

- **Queensland's Gold Coast.** This 70-km (43-mi) stretch of beach features clean sand washed by warm, moderate surf. Beach bums know to head north to the islands of the Great Barrier Reef for less-crowded, tropical beaches, however.

- **Whitehaven.** The Whitsunday Islands are home to a beautiful near-deserted arc of coast which has some of the whitest, most powdery sand on earth. Fringing the Indian Ocean between Perth and South Fremantle are 19 wide beaches with good breaks, but head down to the south coast for a dip in the crystal-clear waters of the deserted, sandy white beaches around Margaret River.

Wine

Australian wines are among the best in the world, a judgment that international wine shows consistently reinforce. Australians are very proud of their wine. You'll be hard-pressed to find anything but Australian wines on the menus at most places, so take this opportunity to expand your palate beyond the export brands you may have tried at home, like Rosemount, Jacob's Creek, and Penfolds.

- **Hunter Valley.** The largest grape-growing area in New South Wales, Hunter Valley has more than 120 wineries and a reputation for producing excellent wines. Expect some amazing semillons and cabernets.

- **South Australia.** The Barossa Valley, about an hour's drive northeast of Adelaide, produces some of Australia's most famous syrah (or shiraz, as they call it Down Under). You might recognize the Penfolds label, a famous shiraz producer here. In the nearby Clare Valley, German immigrants planted Riesling many decades ago and today the grape has met with great success there.

- **Margaret River.** In Western Australia the Margaret River region produces just 1% of the country's total wine output. Yet 25% of Australia's premium and ultrapremium wines come from this small area. Margaret River's Bordeaux-like climate helps producers grow excellent cabernet-merlot blends, since these grapes originally came from that region.

- **Yarra Valley.** More than 70 wineries fill the floor of the Yarra Valley, where pinot noir thrives.

Incredible Wildlife

Australia's diverse habitats are home to countless strange and amazing creatures.

- **Koalas and Kangaroos.** No trip to Australia would be complete without an encounter with Australia's iconic animals: kangaroos and koala bears. The Lone Pine Koala Sanctuary in Brisbane is one of many wildlife parks around Australia that let you take a picture with a cuddly koala or hand-feed a pack of kangaroos.

- **Birds.** Australia has many wild and wonderful creatures of the nonmarsupial variety. The water holes at Kakadu National Park in the Northern Territory attract more than 280 species of birds, plus crocodiles, the ubiquitous creatures of Australia's Top End. The much friendlier, cuter, and fluffier fairy penguins draw nighttime crowds at Philip Island in Victoria.

- **Camels.** Don't be surprised if you catch the eye of a camel wandering the desert of the Red Centre. These are descendants of dromedaries brought over from Afghanistan in the 20th century.

- **Creatures of the Deep.** The Great Barrier Reef gets plenty of attention for underwater wildlife, but Western Australia has two phenomenal spots of its own. The dolphins at Shark Bay in Monkey Mia, Western Australia, can be hand-fed. Ningaloo Reef, off the Exmouth Peninsula, is home to humpback whales and whale sharks.

Water Sports

With 36,735 km (22,776 mi) of coast bordering two oceans and four seas, Australians spend a good deal of their time in and on the water. Opportunities abound for scuba diving, snorkeling, surfing, waterskiing, and windsurfing. Prime diving season is September–December and mid-March–May.

- **Diving.** Avid divers will want to visit the island resorts of the Great Barrier Reef, which provide upscale resort accommodation and access to some of the country's top diving spots. Cod Hole, off the reef of Lizard Island, ranks highly among them. You can do a one-day dive certification course, or if flippers and oxygen tanks aren't your speed, opt for snorkeling off the beaches of the islands.

- **Sailing.** Sailors love the Whitsunday Islands, a group of 74 islands. Almost all the islands in this group are national parks, and only seven have resorts on them, making this an ideal spot to drop anchor and moor for a few days, or to try a vacation on a live-aboard boat or yacht. Farther north in the area around Cairns, diving expeditions are a specialty, with carriers like Quicksilver and Tusa Dive organizing day trips to the reef for diving and snorkeling.

GREAT ITINERARIES

HIGHLIGHTS OF AUSTRALIA

Starting in Sydney, this tour surveys the misty heights of Tasmania's Cradle Mountain, the hauntingly spiritual Uluru monolith, the steamy wetlands of Kakadu, the central deserts, and the northern rain forests. It finishes in Cairns, a good jumping-off point for exploring the top of Queensland.

Days 1 to 3: Sydney

On Day 1, start at Circular Quay, the heart of Sydney Harbour, and walk up through the Rocks to the base of the Harbour Bridge. Come back around for a tour of the Opera House and Royal Botanic Gardens. The next day, take a ferry to Taronga Zoo or Manly for views of all of Sydney from the water, then go out to one of the trendy neighborhoods in the eastern suburbs for dinner. Day 3 could be spent beachside at Bondi or at one of the museums near Hyde Park. ⇨ *Exploring Sydney and Beaches in Chapter 1.*

Day 4: Blue Mountains

Stop at Wentworth Falls for a view across the Jamison Valley and the National Pass trail, then go through Katoomba to Echo Point for the Three Sisters, which take their name from an Aboriginal legend involving a witch doctor and a mythical monster. Have tea and scones at a tea room in Leura. Continue along Cliff Drive to Blackheath, with its great hiking and antiques shops. ⇨ *The Blue Mountains in Chapter 2.*

Days 5 to 9: Tasmania

Spend the first afternoon strolling Hobart's waterfront. The following day, drive to Port Arthur and explore the penal settlement there, which, after establishment in 1830, housed the colony's worst offend-

ers. On Day 7, head for Freycinet National Park and hike to Wineglass Bay; then overnight in Launceston. Finish off with two days of hiking in Cradle Mountain–Lake St. Clair National Park before driving back to Hobart for your final night. ⇨ *Hobart, Port Arthur, Freycinet National Park & East-Coast Resorts, and Launceston in Chapter 6.*

Days 10 and 11: Uluru

Fly into Alice Springs to experience Uluru (Ayers Rock), a monolith that resonates with mystical force. Watch the sun rise or set here, then spend the rest of the day exploring Kata Tjuta (the Olgas), a series of 36 gigantic rock domes hiding a maze of fascinating gorges and crevasses. Drive out to Watarrka National Park to see Kings Canyon on Day 11. ⇨ *Uluru and Kata Tjuta in Chapter 10.*

Day 12: Kakadu

Fly into Darwin and head for Kakadu National Park, the jewel of the Top End. Beginning east of Darwin, and covering some 19,800 square km (7,645 square mi), the park protects a large system of unspoiled rivers and creeks, as well as a rich Aboriginal heritage that extends back to the earliest days of humankind.

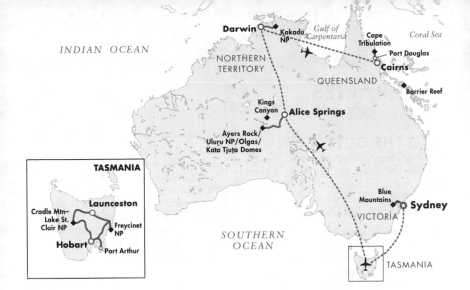

Some of the artwork here is believed to survive from as long as 20,000 years ago. Stay in the park or overnight in Darwin, a town full of historical sights.

Days 13 to 15: Cairns

Fly into Cairns and rent a car to drive north through the Top End of Queensland and take a day trip out to the Great Barrier Reef on Day 13. This marine park, otherwise known as the Blue Outback, is a diving mecca that thousands of species of sea life, turtles, and birds call home. The following two days you can spend exploring the surrounding rain forest and taking a four-wheel-drive tour to Cape Tribulation. ⇨*North from Cairns in Chapter 7.*

By Public Transportation

Daily flights depart from Sydney to Hobart (2 hours), from Hobart to Alice Springs via Melbourne (4 hours), from Alice Springs to Darwin (2 hours), and from Darwin to Cairns (3 hours, 45 minutes). From each hub you can rent a car or join a tour to get around.

TIPS & LOGISTICS

■ Although most Sydney attractions are located around the Harbour and the Central Business District, this area closes down after 6 PM during the week, and becomes a virtual ghost town (except for tourists) on the weekend.

■ The weather on this itinerary varies in extremes, regardless of the time of year you travel. The desert blazes in summer and goes down to freezing temperatures in winter.

■ One operating company has a monopoly on all accommodations and food options around Uluru, so save up for your trip to this region. Although there are differences in the range of accommodations, you'll be spending most of your time out of your hotel room, so choose one of the lower-end price options.

GREAT ITINERARIES

INTO THE OUTBACK

In the stark, stunning Outback, a little imagination takes you back to a time when Earth was created by the giant ancestral beings from whom the Aboriginal people trace their lineage.

Days 1 and 2: Adelaide

Begin the day with a visit to the Central Market area and a tour of the historic buildings along North Terrace. Learn about Aboriginal culture at Tandanya Aboriginal Culture Institute. Later head down to Glenelg, an exciting waterfront district of restaurants and bars, for dinner by the sea. Spend the next day touring the wineries of McLaren Vale, a half-hour drive south. Don't forget to bring back some shiraz for your friends at home! ⇨ *Adelaide and Barossa Region in Chapter 9.*

Days 3 to 5: Flinders Ranges National Park

From Adelaide, drive or join a four-wheel-drive tour via Port Augusta to Flinders Ranges and its towering crimson hills. This ruggedly beautiful area north of Adelaide holds Aboriginal cave paintings and fossil remains from when the area was an ancient seabed. Take time to ascend St. Mary's Peak at Wilpena Pound, an 80-square-km (31-square-mi) bowl ringed by quartzite hills. ⇨ *The Outback in Chapter 9.*

Days 6 and 7: Alice Springs

Spend the afternoon shopping at the Todd Mall for Aboriginal art in the galleries or go out to Emily and Jessie Gap National Park in the eastern MacDonnell Ranges. The next day, head down to Uluru (Ayers Rock) in time for sunset. ⇨ *Alice Springs and Side Trips from Alice Springs in Chapter 10.*

Days 8 and 9: Uluru

Take time to wonder at the magnificent Uluru (Ayers Rock) and then head out to visit Kata Tjuta (the Olgas) and hike through the Valley of the Winds, an 8-km (5-mi) long cleft between the two giant rocks. Take an Aboriginal guided tour learning about indigenous culture and lifestyle. If you have the extra time, consider heading west to Kings Canyon in Watarrka National Park for an additional day or two. ⇨ *Uluru and Kata Tjuta in Chapter 10.*

Days 10 to 12: Kakadu

Kick back and enjoy the warm climate, abundant wildlife, and sandstone caves. When Aborigines camped here aeons ago they daubed the walls with ocher, clay, and charcoal. Ubirr is one place where the paintings are quite impressively displayed. ⇨ *Kakadu National Park in Chapter 11.*

By Public Transportation

Flights depart daily from Adelaide to Alice Springs (2 hours), Alice Springs to Darwin (2 hours), and Darwin back to Adelaide (4½ hours). Use these cities as bases—either rent a car or take day tours of the sights mentioned.

Darwin

Kakadu NP

Gulf of Carpentaria

Coral Sea

NORTHERN TERRITORY

INDIAN OCEAN

MacDonnell Ranges

Alice Springs

Ayers Rock/
Uluru NP/Olgas/
Kata Tjuta Domes

SOUTH
AUSTRALIA

Flinders
Ranges NP

St. Mary's Peak/
Wilpena Pound

Port Augusta

Adelaide

Barossa
Valley

Sydney

SOUTHERN
OCEAN

TIPS & LOGISTICS

■ The faint of heart will want to avoid driving in the Outback. Although major roads are paved, they tend to have only one lane going in any direction, which means passing someone requires you to veer into the oncoming traffic lane—a maneuver best left for absolutely necessary situations.

■ Amenities on long-distance drives are few and far between, so make sure to travel with plenty of water, some snacks, and on very long Outback drives, extra gasoline in your car just in case.

■ Should your car break down, never leave your vehicle. Turn on the hazard lights and wait by your car—someone will surely come along.

GREAT ITINERARIES

TROPICAL WONDERS

Take a stab at finding Nemo when you visit the Great Barrier Reef, which may have been destroyed by erosion by the next time you visit. Few reefs are more full of life than this one.

Day 1: Brisbane

Explore the Queensland capital's city center and the South Bank Parklands, cooling off in a dip in one of the spectacularly landscaped public pools. Have dinner in one of trendy Fortitude Valley's hip restaurants. ⇨ *Brisbane in Chapter 7.*

Days 2 and 3: The Sunshine Coast

Drive through the dramatic Glass House mountains, visit Steve Irwin's Australia Zoo, and then stay in Noosa, where Australia's low-key sophisticates take their beachside holidays. ⇨ *Sunshine Coast & Airlie Beach in Chapter 7.*

Days 4 and 5: Fraser Island

Fly to Hervey Bay and take a ferry to Fraser Island to join a four-wheel-drive tour of rocky headlands, the rusting wreck of the *Maheno,* and towering sand dunes. In the interior are paperbark swamps, freshwater lakes, and forests of brush box trees. ⇨ *Fraser Island in Chapter 7.*

Days 6 and 7: Heron Island

Back at Hervey Bay, fly to Gladstone and then head on to this Great Barrier Reef island, where you can spend your time diving or bird-watching. ⇨ *Mackay–Capricorn Islands in Chapter 8.*

Days 8 to 10: Cairns

Fly from Gladstone to Cairns and spend the first day at the pool or beachside in this tropical capital; be sure to hit the night markets after dusk. Devote one day to a snorkeling or diving trip out to the Great Barrier Reef. Check out the stun-

ning beach enclave of Palm Cove and the World Heritage–listed drive up to Port Douglas on the next day. ⇨ *Cairns and North from Cairns in Chapter 7.*

Days 11 to 13: Cape Tribulation

Keep driving north from Port Douglas to this area of untamed beaches and rain forests. Stop for hiking, horseback riding, and beachcombing, then take a guided crocodile-spotting cruise. Head north to Cooktown for your final day. ⇨ *North from Cairns in Chapter 7.*

Day 13: Cooktown

North from Cape Tribulation, the rough Bloomfield Track and numerous river crossings make the four-wheel-drive journey to Cooktown an adventure. Stop along the way at the spectacular Mossman Gorge, and have a pint and a meal at Ironbar in Port Douglas. ⇨ *North from Cairns in Chapter 7.*

By Public Transportation

Fly from Brisbane to Hervey Bay (1 hour), where car ferries chug to Fraser Island from River Heads and Inskip Point. Daily flights connect Hervey Bay with Gladstone (1 hour), and it's a two-hour boat trip or 25-minute helicopter ride from there to Heron Island. Daily flights link Gladstone to Cairns (1 hour), where you can rent a car to tour Port Douglas and the north. In each region, the best way to get around is to rent a four-wheel-drive vehicle or join a tour.

TIPS & LOGISTICS

■ There's a reason Crocodile Hunter Steve Irwin made Queensland his base. Crocs love the area around the mid and top end of the state. Although crocodile attacks on humans are relatively rare, the risk nonetheless remains great. Beaches around Cairns may be closed for crocodile sightings, and travelers should never wander on unpatrolled beaches, no matter how scenic, especially not at night.

■ Other natural dangers lurk around these beautiful parts, and jellyfish rank among the most prevalent. So ubiquitous are these creatures that most beaches are rendered unswimmable between November and March, the height of the summer tourist season.

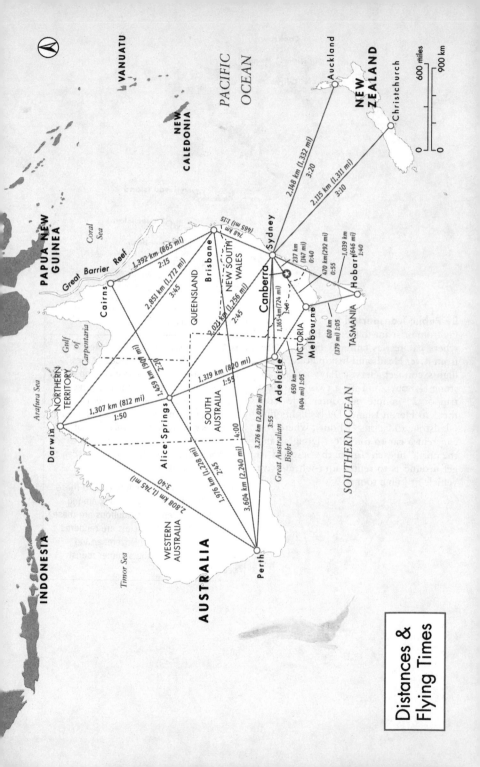

Distances &
Flying Times

Sydney

WORD OF MOUTH

"If I can manage the Sydney Harbour Bridge climb, virtually anyone can. It is done at a very leisurely pace. The total experience lasts about 3½ hours, of which you are only climbing up for about 30 minutes with plenty of breaks. Seriously, if you can walk a mile you will have no trouble with the bridge climb. It's worth every penny—but you'll needs lots of them, because it's not cheap."

–Walter_Walltotti

"Another way of seeing the city is by catching a ferry from Circular Quay to Manly. The views are amazing!"

–Nire 79

Updated
by Caroline
Gladstone

SYDNEY BELONGS TO THE EXCLUSIVE club of world cities that generate a sense of excitement from the air. Even at the end of a marathon flight across the Pacific, there's renewed vitality in the cabin as the plane circles the city, crossing the branching fingers of the harbor, where thousands of yachts are suspended on the dark water and the sails of the Opera House glisten in the distance. Endowed with dazzling beaches and a sunny Mediterranean climate, its setting alone guarantees Sydney a place among the most beautiful cities on the planet.

At 4 million people, Sydney is the biggest and most cosmopolitan city in Australia. Take a taxi from Sydney Airport and chances are that the driver won't say "G'day" with the accent you might expect. A wave of immigration in the 1950s has seen the Anglo-Irish immigrants who made up the city's original population enriched by Italians, Greeks, Turks, Lebanese, Chinese, Vietnamese, Thais, and Indonesians. This intermingling has created a cultural vibrancy and energy—and a culinary repertoire—that was missing only a generation ago.

Sydneysiders, as locals are known, embrace their harbor with a passion. Indented with numerous bays and beaches, Sydney Harbour is the presiding icon for the city, and for urban Australia. Captain Arthur Phillip, commander of the 11-ship First Fleet, wrote in his diary when he first set eyes on the harbor on January 26, 1788: "We had the satisfaction of finding the finest harbor in the world, in which a thousand ships of the line may ride in the most perfect security." It was not an easy beginning, however. Pushing inland, Australia's first settlers were confronted with harsh, foreign terrain that few of them possessed skills to navigate. They were the first round of wretched inmates (roughly 800) flushed from overcrowded jails in England and sent halfway around the globe to serve their sentences.

Sydney has long since outgrown the stigma of its convict origins, but the passage of time has not tamed its rebellious spirit. Sydney's panache and appetite for life are unchallenged in the Australian context. A walk among the scantily clad sunbathers at Bondi Beach or through the buzzing nightlife districts of Kings Cross and Oxford Street provides ample evidence.

Although a visit to Sydney is an essential part of an Australian experience, the city is no more representative of Australia than Los Angeles is of the United States. Sydney has joined the ranks of the great cities whose characters are essentially international. What Sydney offers are style, sophistication, and good—no, great—looks; an exhilarating prelude to the continent at its back door.

EXPLORING SYDNEY

Sydney is a giant, stretching nearly 97 km (60 mi) from top to bottom and about 55 km (34 mi) across. The harbor divides the city into northern and southern halves, with most of the headline attractions on the south shore. Most tourists spend their time on the harbor's south side, within an area bounded by Chinatown in the south, Harbour

Bridge in the north, Darling Harbour to the west, and the beaches and coastline to the east. North of Harbour Bridge lie the important commercial center of North Sydney and leafy but somewhat bland suburbs. Ocean beaches, Taronga Zoo, Ku-ring-gai Chase National Park, and great shopping in the village of Mosman are the most likely reasons to venture north of the harbor.

Within a few hours' drive of Sydney are the World Heritage–listed Blue Mountains and the renowned Hunter Valley vineyards. Although both these spots are worthy of an overnight stay, they're also close enough to visit on day trips from the city.

WHEN TO VISIT

The best times to visit Sydney are in late spring and early fall. The spring months of October and November are pleasantly warm, although the ocean is slightly cool for swimming. The midsummer months of December through February are typically hot and humid, February being quite rainy. In the early-autumn months of March and April, weather is typically stable and comfortable, outdoor city life is still in full swing, and the ocean is at its warmest. Even the coolest winter months of July and August typically stay mild and sunny, with average daily maximum temperatures in the low 60s.

> ### CULTURAL CRUISING
>
> There are many ways to cruise around Sydney Harbour, but only one with an Aboriginal perspective. The *Deerubbin*, a former torpedo recovery vessel, is owned by the Tribal Warrior Association, an organization committed to empowering Aboriginal people. After departing Circular Quay, the boat heads to an island where you are treated to a traditional welcoming ceremony. Back on board, you are shown cultural landmarks, fishing spots, and ancient rock carvings. The two-hour cruises cost A$55 per person and depart Tuesday to Saturday at 12:45 PM. ☎ 02/9699–3491 ⊕ www.tribalwarrior.org.

SYDNEY HARBOUR

Captain Arthur Phillip, commander of the first European fleet to sail here and the first governor of the colony, called Sydney Harbour "in extent and security, very superior to any other that I have ever seen." Two centuries later, few would dispute that the harbor is one of nature's extraordinary creations.

Fodor's Choice ★ Officially titled Port Jackson, the harbor is in its depths a river valley carved by the Parramatta and Lane Cove rivers and the many creeks that flow in from the north. Several pockets of land are now protected within **Sydney Harbour National Park,** 958 acres of separate foreshores and islands, most of them on the north side of the harbor. To see the best areas, put on your walking shoes and head out on the many well-marked trails. The Hermitage Foreshore Walk skirts through bushland around Vaucluse's Nielsen Park, with sensational views and a fine beach backed by shady parkland. On the north side of the harbor, Bradleys Head and Chowder Head Walk is a 5-km (3-mi) stroll that starts from Taronga Zoo Wharf. The most inspiring trail is the 9½-km

GREAT ITINERARIES

You really need three days in Sydney to see the essential city center, while six days would give you time to explore the beaches and inner suburbs. A stay of 10 days would allow trips outside the city and give you time to explore a few of Sydney's lesser-known delights.

IF YOU HAVE 3 DAYS

Start with an afternoon Sydney Harbour Explorer cruise for some of the best views of the city. Follow with a tour of the Rocks, the nation's birthplace, and take a sunset walk up onto the **Sydney Harbour Bridge.** The following day, take a Sydney Explorer tour to the famous **Sydney Opera House** and relax in the afternoon in the **Royal Botanic Gardens, Domain South,** and **Domain North** parks. On the third day, explore the city center, with another spectacular panorama from the **Sydney Tower.** Include a walk around Macquarie Street, a living reminder of Sydney's colonial history, and the contrasting experience of futuristic Darling Harbour, with its museums, aquarium, cafés, and lively shops.

IF YOU HAVE 6 DAYS

Follow the three-day itinerary above, then visit Kings Cross, Darlinghurst, and Paddington on the fourth day. You could continue to **Bondi,** Australia's most famous beach. The next day, catch the ferry to **Manly** to visit its beach and the historic Quarantine Station. From here, take an afternoon bus tour to the northern beaches, or return to the city to shop or visit museums and galleries. Options for the last day include a trip to wildlife or national park, **Taronga Zoo,** or the **Sydney Olympic Park** west of the city.

IF YOU HAVE 10 DAYS

Follow the six-day itinerary above, and then travel beyond the city by rental car or with an organized tour. Take day trips to the Blue Mountains, Hunter Valley, **Ku-ring-gai Chase National Park,** the Hawkesbury River, or the historic city of Parramatta to Sydney's west. Or travel on the Bondi Explorer bus to **Vaucluse** or the charming harborside village of **Watsons Bay.** You could take a boat tour to the historic harbor island of **Fort Denison,** play a round of golf, or just shop or relax on the beach.

(6-mi) Manly Scenic Walkway, which joins the Spit Bridge with Manly by meandering along sandstone headlands, small beaches, and pockets of rain forest, and past Aboriginal sites and the historic Grotto Point Lighthouse. From Cadman's Cottage you can take day tours of Fort Denison and Goat Island, which have significant colonial buildings. From Circular Quay you can board a cruise to Shark Island on weekends. The other two islands in the harbor park—Rodd and Clark—are recreational reserves that can be visited with permission from the New South Wales National Parks and Wildlife Service.

WHAT TO SEE

⑩ Castlecrag. Walter Burley Griffin, an associate of Frank Lloyd Wright, founded this calm, prestigious Middle Harbour suburb after he designed the layout for Canberra. In 1924, after working on the national capital and in Melbourne, the American architect moved to Sydney and built

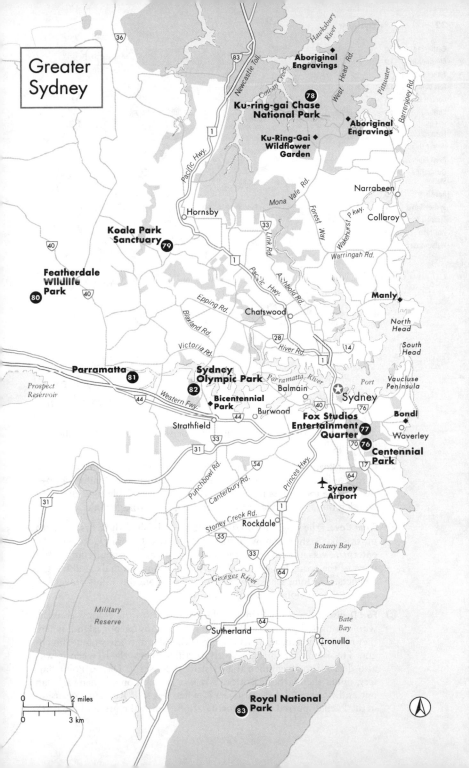

Greater Sydney

36

83

Newcastle Toll

Hawkesbury River

Aboriginal Engravings

West Head Rd.

78

Ku-ring-gai Chase National Park

Cowan Creek

Pittwater

Barrenjoey Rd.

Ku-Ring-Gai Wildflower Garden

Aboriginal Engravings

Pacific Hwy.

1

Mona Vale Rd.

Narrabeen

Forest Way

Hornsby

33

Link Rd.

Wakehurst Pkwy.

Collaroy

40

Koala Park Sanctuary **79**

Warringah Rd.

1

Pacific Hwy.

Featherdale Wildlife Park **80**

40

Epping Rd.

Archbold Rd.

Manly

North Head

Blaxland Rd.

Chatswood

28

South Head

Victoria Rd.

River Rd.

1

14

Parramatta **81**

Prospect Reservoir

44

Western Fwy.

Sydney Olympic Park **82**

Parramatta River

Balmain

Port

Vaucluse Peninsula

Bicentennial Park

Burwood

40

Sydney ☆

76

Bondi

Strathfield

44

Fox Studios Entertainment Quarter **77**

Waverley

33

31

54

70 **76**

Centennial Park

Punchbowl Rd.

Canterbury Rd.

Princes Hwy.

17

64

31

Stoney Creek Rd.

Rockdale

✈ **Sydney Airport**

1

55

Botany Bay

33

64

Georges River

Bate Bay

Military Reserve

64

Sutherland

Cronulla

0   2 miles

0   3 km

Royal National Park **83**

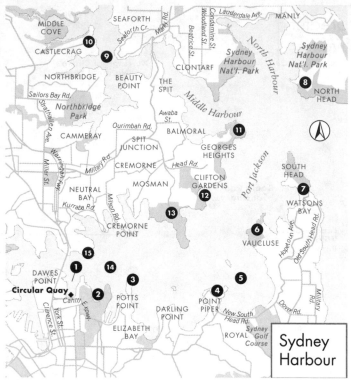

Sydney Harbour

a number of houses that are notable for their harmony with the surrounding bushland.

🔟2 **Chowder Bay.** In the 19th century the American whalers who anchored here would collect oysters from the rocks and make shellfish soup—which gave the bay its name. Its location is identifiable by a cluster of wooden buildings at water's edge and twin oil-storage tanks.

2 **Farm Cove.** The original convict-settlers established their first gardens on this bay's shores, now home to the **Royal Botanic Gardens.** The enterprise was not a success: the soil was too sandy for agriculture, and most of the crops fell victim to pests, marauding animals, and hungry convicts. The long seawall was constructed from the 1840s onward to enclose the previously swampy foreshore.

14 **Fort Denison.** For a brief time in the early days of the colony, convicts who committed petty offenses were kept on this harbor island, where they existed on a meager diet that gave the island its early name: Pinchgut. The island was progressively fortified from 1841, when it was also decided to strengthen the existing defenses at Dawes Point Battery, under the Harbour Bridge. Work was abandoned when cash ran out and not completed until 1857, when fears of Russian expansion in the Pacific spurred further fortification. Today the firing of the fort's

cannon signals not an imminent invasion, but merely the hour—one o'clock. The National Parks and Wildlife Service runs tours to Fort Denison lasting 2½ to 3 hours. Tours depart from Cadman's Cottage, 110 George Street, the Rocks. ⊠*Sydney Harbour* ☎*02/9247–5033* ⊕*www.npws.nsw.gov.au/parks/metro/harbour/shfortdenison.html* ☞*A$22* ⊗*Tours Wed.–Sun. at 11:45* AM.

❸ Garden Island. Although it's still known as an "island," this promontory was connected with the mainland in 1942. During the 1941–45 War of the Pacific, Australia's largest naval base and dockyard was a frontline port for Allied ships. Part of the naval base is now open to the public. This small park area has superb views of the Opera House and glimpses of the dockyard facilities, including the largest shipyard crane in the southern hemisphere. Access to the site is via ferry from Circular Quay. Garden Island was used when the *Queen Mary 2* docked here in 2007, as the Overseas Passenger Terminal at Circular Quay was not long enough to accommodate the mighty ocean liner.

⓯ Kirribilli. Residences of this attractive suburb opposite the city and Opera House have million-dollar views—and prices to match. Two of Sydney's most important mansions stand here. The more modest of the two is **Kirribilli House,** which is the official Sydney home of the prime minister and not open to the public. Next door and far more prominent is **Admiralty House** (☎*02/9955–4095*)—the Sydney residence of the governor-general, the Queen's representative in Australia. This impressive residence is occasionally open for inspection. Both houses can be seen during harbor cruises.

❾ Middle Harbour. Except for the yachts moored in the sandy coves, the upper reaches of Middle Harbour are almost exactly as they were when the first Europeans set eyes on Port Jackson more than 200 years ago. Tucked away in idyllic bushland are tranquil suburbs just a short drive from the city.

⑪ Middle Head. Despite its benign appearance today, Sydney Harbour once bristled with armaments. In the mid-19th century, faced with expansionist European powers hungry for new colonies, the authorities erected artillery positions on the headlands to guard harbor approaches. At Middle Head you can still see the rectangular gun emplacements set into the cliff face; however, the guns have never been fired at an enemy.

❹ Point Piper. The majestic Gatsbyesque houses in this harborside suburb are prized addresses for Sydney's rich and famous. This was once the Sydney neighborhood of Tom Cruise and Nicole Kidman, and the record for the suburb's—and Australia's—most expensive house is still held by Altona, which fetched A$28.5 million when it sold in 2002.

❽ Quarantine Station. From the 1830s onward, ship passengers who arrived with contagious diseases were isolated on this outpost in the shadow of North Head until pronounced free of illness. You can access the station only as part of a guided tour; there's a guided tour that departs from Manly Wharf and a three-hour evening ghost tour (the station reputedly has its fair share of specters) that departs from the visitor center at the Quarantine Station. The ghost tour includes supper, and reservations are essential. Both tours are led by rangers from the National Parks and Wildlife Service, caretakers of the site. ⊠ *North Head, Manly* ☎ *02/9247–5033* ⊕ *www.q-station.com.au* ☜ *Basic tour A$25, ghost tour A$34* ⊙ *Basic tour Mon., Wed., Fri., and weekends at 1:10 PM; Ghost Tour Wed., Fri., and weekends 7:30 PM, 8 PM in Dec. and Jan.*

❺ **Rose Bay.** This large bay was once a base for the Qantas flying boats that provided the only passenger air service between Australia and America and Europe. The last flying boat departed from Rose Bay in the 1960s, but the "airstrip" is still used by floatplanes on scenic flights connecting Sydney with the Hawkesbury River and the Central Coast. It's a popular place for joggers who pound the pavement of New South Head Road, which runs along the bay.

❶ **Sydney Cove.** Bennelong Point and the Sydney Opera House to the east and Circular Quay West and the Rocks to the west enclose this cove, which was named after Lord Sydney, the British home secretary at the time the colony was founded. The settlement itself was to be known as New Albion, but the name never caught on. Instead, the city took its name from this tiny bay.

⓭ **Taronga Zoo.** In Sydney's zoo, in a natural bush area on the harbor's
Ⓒ north shore, lives an extensive collection of Australian fauna, includ-
★ ing everybody's favorite marsupial, the koala. The zoo has taken great care to create spacious enclosures that simulate natural habitats. The hillside setting is steep in parts, and a complete tour can be tiring, but you can use the map distributed free at the entrance gate to plan a leisurely route. The views of the harbor are stunning. Use of children's strollers (the basic model) is free. The best way to get here from the city is by ferry from Circular Quay or Darling Harbour. From Taronga Wharf a bus or the cable car will take you up the hill to the main entrance. The ZooPass, a combined ferry-zoo ticket (A$39) is available at Circular Quay. You can also stay overnight at the zoo in what's billed as the "wildest slumber party in town." The "Roar and Snore" program includes a night tour, two behind-the-scenes tours, dinner, breakfast, and tent accommodation for A$165 per person. ⊠ *Bradleys Head Rd., Mosman* ☎ *02/9969–2777* ⊕ *www.zoo.nsw.gov.au* ☜ *A$32* ⊙ *Daily 9–5.*

❻ **Vaucluse.** The palatial homes in this glamorous harbor suburb provide a glimpse of Sydney's high society. The small beaches at Nielsen Park and Parsley Bay are safe for swimming and provide wonderful views. Both beaches are packed with families in summer. The suburb takes its name from the 1803 **Vaucluse House,** one of Sydney's most illustrious remaining historic mansions. The 15-room Gothic Revival house and its lush gardens, managed by the Historic Houses Trust, are open to the public. The tea rooms, built in the style of an Edwardian conservatory, are a popular spot for lunch and afternoon tea on weekends. The house is one of the stops on the Bondi Explorer bus. ⊠ *Wentworth Rd., Vaucluse*

☎02/9388–7922 ⊕*www.hht.nsw.*
gov.au ✉*A$8* ⊙*House Tues.–Sun.*
10–4:30, grounds daily 10–5.

❼ Watsons Bay. Established as a military base and fishing settlement in the colony's early years, Watsons Bay is a charming suburb that has held on to its village ambience, despite the exorbitant prices paid for tiny cottages here. In comparison to Watsons Bay's tranquil harborside, the side that faces the ocean is dramatic and tortured, with the raging sea dashing itself against the sheer, 200-foot sandstone cliffs of The Gap. When the sun shines, the 15-minute cliff-top stroll along South Head Walkway between The Gap and the **Macquarie Lighthouse** affords some of Sydney's most inspiring views. Convict-architect Francis Greenway (jailed for forgery) designed the original lighthouse here, Australia's first, in 1818. ✉*Old South Head Rd., Vaucluse.*

MOVIES UNDER THE STARS

The best place for outdoor movies is at **Mrs. Macquarie's Point** (⊕ *www.stgeorgeopenair.com.au*). At the Royal Botanic Gardens, it screens films from mid-January to mid-February. Every now and then a flying fox whizzes past the huge screen that hangs over Sydney Harbour. **Centennial Park** (⊕ *www.moonlight.com.au*) is where film buffs relax on rugs or rented beanbags. It's the only time you're allowed in the park after sunset. Movies run from early January to mid-March. **Bondi Beach** (⊕ *www.bondiopenair.com. au*) screens movies at the 1928 Pavilion.

THE ROCKS & SYDNEY HARBOUR BRIDGE

The Rocks is the birthplace not just of Sydney, but of modern Australia. Here the 11 ships of the First Fleet, the first of England's 800-plus ships carrying convicts to the penal colony, dropped anchor in 1788, and this stubby peninsula enclosing the western side of Sydney Cove became known simply as The Rocks.

The first crude wooden huts erected by the convicts were followed by simple houses made from mud bricks cemented together by a mixture of sheep's wool, straw, and mud. The rain soon washed this rough mortar away, and no buildings in The Rocks survive from the earliest settlement. Most of the architecture dates from the Victorian era, by which time Sydney had become a thriving port. Warehouses lining the waterfront were backed by a row of tradesmen's shops, banks, and taverns, and above them, ascending Observatory Hill, rose a tangled mass of alleyways lined with the cottages of seamen and wharf laborers. By the late 1800s all who could afford to had moved out of the area, and it was widely regarded as a rough, tough, squalid part of town. As late as 1900, bubonic plague swept through The Rocks, prompting the government to offer a bounty for dead rats in an effort to exterminate their disease-carrying fleas.

It's only since the 1970s that the Rocks has become appreciated for its historic significance, and extensive restoration has transformed the area. Here you can see the evolution of a society almost from its inception to the present, and yet the Rocks is anything but a stuffy tutorial. History stands side by side with shops, cafés, and museums.

Begin at Circular Quay, the lively waterfront area where Sydney's ferry, bus, and train systems converge. Walk towards the Harbour Bridge via Circular Quay West, climbing the stairs leading to George Street. (20) Continue down the hill and steps on the right to **Campbells Cove** and its warehouses. The waterfront restaurants and cafés are a pleasant spot for a drink or meal, although you pay for the view. Continue up George Street toward the Sydney Harbour Bridge until you are directly beneath (22) the bridge's massive girders. Walk under the bridge to **Dawes Point Park** for excellent views of the harbor, including the Opera House and the small island of Fort Denison. Now turn your back on the bridge and walk south and west, via Lower Fort Street. Explore Argyle Place and (28) continue walking south, past the **Sydney Observatory**. While you're in the neighborhood, be sure and pick up brochures and city information (32) at the **Sydney Visitor Centre at the Rocks,** on the corner of Argyle and Play-(34) fair streets. Turn right at **Nurses Walk**, another of the area's historic and atmospheric backstreets, then left into Surgeons Court, and left again onto George Street. On the left is the handsome sandstone facade of the former Rocks Police Station, now a crafts gallery. From this point, Circular Quay is only a short walk away.

WHAT TO SEE

(30) **Argyle Cut.** Argyle Street, which links Argyle Place and George Street, is dominated by the Argyle Cut and its massive walls. In the days before the cut was made, the sandstone ridge here was a major barrier to traffic crossing between Circular Quay and Millers Point. In 1843 convict work gangs hacked at the sandstone with hand tools for 2½ years before the project was abandoned due to lack of progress. Work restarted in 1857, when drills, explosives, and paid labor completed the job. On the lower side of the Cut an archway leads to the **Argyle Stairs,** which begin the climb from Argyle Street up to the Sydney Harbour Bridge walkway. There's a spectacular view from the South East Pylon.

(25) **Argyle Place.** With all the traditional requirements of an English green— a pub at one end, a church at the other, and grass in between—this charming enclave in the suburb of Millers Point is unusual for Sydney. Argyle Place is lined with 19th-century houses and cottages on its northern side and overlooked by Observatory Hill to the south.

NEED A BREAK? While in the west end of Argyle Place, consider the liquid temptations of the **Lord Nelson** (⊠ *19 Kent St., at Argyle St., Millers Point, the Rocks* ☏ *02/9251–4044* ⊕ *www.lordnelson.com.au*), Sydney's oldest hotel, which has been licensed to serve alcohol since 1841. The sandstone pub has its own brewery on the premises. One of its specialties is Quayle Ale, named after the former U.S. vice president, who "sank a schooner" (drank a beer) here during his 1989 visit to Australia.

③ Argyle Stores. These solid sandstone warehouses date from the late 1820s and now house chic gift and souvenir shops, clothes boutiques, and cafés. ✉*12–20 Argyle St., opposite Harrington St., The Rocks.*

⑱ Cadman's Cottage. Sydney's oldest building, completed in 1816, has a history that outweighs its modest dimensions. John Cadman was a convict who was sentenced for life to New South Wales for stealing a horse. He later became superintendent of government boats, a position that entitled him to live in the upper story of this house. The water once practically lapped at Cadman's doorstep, and the original seawall still stands at the front of the house. The small extension on the side of the cottage was built to lock up the oars of Cadman's boats, since oars would have been a necessity for any convict attempting to escape by sea. The upper floor of Cadman's Cottage is now a National Parks and Wildlife Service bookshop and information center for Sydney Harbour National Park. ✉*110 George St., The Rocks* ☎*02/9247–8861* ⊕*www.cityofsydney.nsw.gov.au* ⊙*Tues.–Sun. 10–4:30.*

⑳ Campbell's Cove. Robert Campbell was a Scottish merchant who is sometimes referred to as the "father of Australian commerce." Campbell broke the stranglehold that the British East India Company exercised over seal and whale products, which were New South Wales's only exports in those early days. The cove's atmospheric sandstone **Campbell's Storehouse,** ✉*Campbell's Storehouse, 7–27 Circular Quay West, The Rocks* ☎*No phone)* built from 1838 onward, now houses waterside restaurants. The pulleys that were used to hoist cargoes still hang on the upper level of the warehouses. The cove is also the mooring for Sydney's fully operational tall ships—including the HMAV *Bounty,* an authentic replica of the original 18th-century vessel—which conducts theme cruises around the harbor.

㉟ Customs House. The last surviving example of the elegant sandstone buildings that once ringed Circular Quay, this former customs house now features an amazing model of Sydney under a glass floor. You can walk over the city's skyscrapers, all of which are illuminated by meters of fiber-optic lights. There's an excellent two-level library and plenty of art galleries. The rooftop Café Sydney, the standout in the clutch of restaurants and cafés in this late-19th-century structure, overlooks Sydney Cove. The building stands close to the site where the British flag was first raised on the shores of Sydney Cove in 1788. ✉*Customs House Sq., Alfred St., Circular Quay* ☎*02/9242–8592.*

㉒ Dawes Point Park. The wonderful views of the harbor (and since the 1930s, the Harbour Bridge) have made this park and its location noteworthy for centuries. Named for William Dawes, a First Fleet marine officer and astronomer who established the colony's first basic observatory nearby in 1788, this park was also once the site of a fortification known as Dawes Battery. The cannons on the hillside pointing toward the Opera House came from the ships of the First Fleet.

Harrington Street area. The small precinct around this street forms one of the Rocks' most interesting areas. Many old cottages, houses, and warehouses here have been converted into hotels. Between Harrington

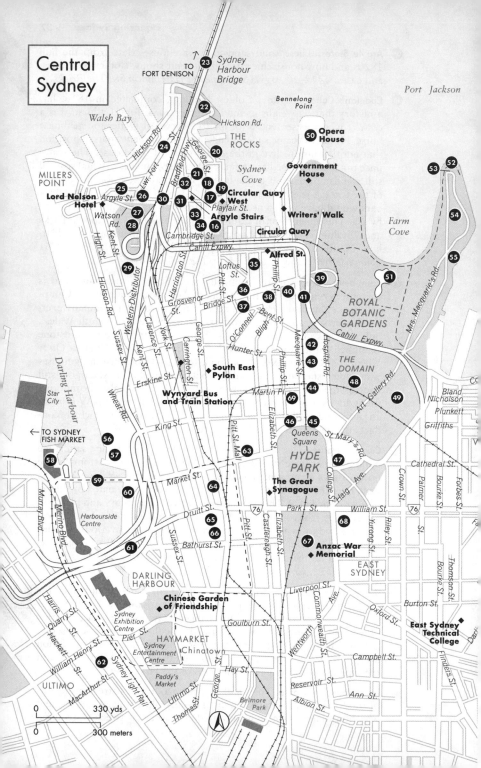

Central Sydney

Port Jackson

To Fort Denison
23
Sydney Harbour Bridge

22

Walsh Bay

Hickson Rd.

THE ROCKS

Bennelong Point

50 Opera House

24

Sydney Cove

Government House

MILLERS POINT

25
26
Lord Nelson Hotel

Argyle St.

Watson Rd.

27
28

20
21 **18**
32
30 **31**
33
34 **16**

19 Circular Quay West
17
Playfair St.
Argyle Stairs
Cambridge St.
Circular Quay

Writers' Walk

Farm Cove

53 **52**

54

High St.

29

Hickson Rd.

Sussex St.

Western Distributor

Kent St.

Cahill Expwy.
Loftus St.
35
Alfred St.
39

51

ROYAL BOTANIC GARDENS

55

Mrs. Macquarie's Rd.

Darling Harbour

Star City

TO SYDNEY FISH MARKET

Clarence St.

York St.

George St.

Harrington St.

Grosvenor St.
Bridge St.
36
37
O'Connell St.
Bent St.
Bligh St.
Hunter St.

38
40
41

Macquarie St.

Phillip St.

Cahill Expwy.

THE DOMAIN

42
43

Hospital Rd.

48

Art Gallery Rd.

Bland
Nicholson
Plunkett
Griffiths

Carrington St.
Erskine St.

South East Pylon

Wynyard Bus and Train Station

King St.

Martin Pl.
44
69

Elizabeth St.

49

Crown St.

Cathedral St.

Palmer St.

Bourke St.

Forbes St.

56
57

58

Merino Blvd.

59

Market St.

64

63

46
45
Queens Square

St. Mary's Rd.

HYDE PARK

47

College St.

Thomson St.

Bourke St.

Harbourside Centre

Druitt St.

65
66

Pitt St.
Castlereagh St.

76

The Great Synagogue

Park St.

William St.

68

EAST SYDNEY

60

61

Sussex St.

Bathurst St.

67 Anzac War Memorial

Yurong St.

Riley St.

Haig Ave.

Liverpool St.

Burton St.

Oxford St.

East Sydney Technical College

DARLING HARBOUR

Chinese Garden of Friendship

Sydney Exhibition Centre
Pier St.

HAYMARKET

Sydney Entertainment Centre

Chinatown

Goulburn St.

Commonwealth St.

Wentworth Ave.

Campbell St.

Harris St.

Quarry St.

Hackett St.

William Henry St.

62

ULTIMO

MacArthur St.

Sydney Light Rail

Paddy's Market

Ultimo Rd.

George St.

Hay St.

Thomas St.

Belmore Park

Reservoir St.

Albion St.

Ann St.

Flinders St.

0 — 330 yds
0 — 300 meters

Garden
Island
Naval
Dockyard

Woolloomooloo Bay

POTTS
POINT

Billyard
Ave.

Elizabeth
Bay

Wylde St.

Challis
Ave.

Wharf Roadway

Victoria St.

Cowper

Brougham St.

McElhone St.

Dowling St.

71
70
72

BEARE
PARK

Onslow

Greenknowe

Hughes St.

Orwell St.

Eliz. Bay Rd.

ELIZABETH
BAY

WOOLLOOMOOLOO

Darlinghurst

RUSHCUTTERS
BAY PARK

KINGS
CROSS

Kings

Cross Rd.

76

Farrell Ave.

St.

McLachlan Ave.

Neild Ave.

DARLINGHURST
Surrey

Womerah Ave.

Liverpool St.

11

Liverpool

Stephen St.

Brown St.

Goodhope

Glenmore Rd.

73

Barcom Ave.

Boundary St.

Liverpool

Glenmore Rd.

Darlinghurst Rd.

Victoria St.

Hopewell St.

Glenmore St.

Shadforth St.

Heeley St.

Royal Hotel ◆

75

PADDINGTON

Greens
Rd.

Oxford St.

74

Street and George Street are some historical and creatively named alleyways to explore, including Nurses Walk and Suez Canal.

㉖ Holy Trinity Church. Every morning, redcoats would march to this 1840 Argyle Place church from Dawes Point Battery (now Dawes Point Park), and it became commonly known as the Garrison Church. As the regimental plaques and colors around the walls testify, the church still retains a close military association. The tattered ensign on the left wall was carried into battle by Australian troops during the Boer War, in which many Australians enlisted to help Great Britain in its war with South Africans of Dutch ancestry. ⊠*Argyle Pl., The Rocks* ☎*02/9247–1268* ⊙*Daily 9–5.*

HISTORIC WATERING HOLES

You're sure to get involved in a singalong when bands take to the stage at the historic **Hero of Waterloo** (⊠*81 Lower Fort St.* ☎*02/9252–4553*). The pub has a maze of cellars and tunnels said to be used by smugglers in Sydney's early days. You can get a close-up view of climbers on the Harbour Bridge from a bar stool at the aptly named **Harbour View Hotel** (⊠*18 Lower Fort St., at Cumberland St.* ☎*02/9254–4111*). The view from the roof of the **Glenmore** (⊠*96 Cumberland St.* ☎*02/9247–4792*) is inspirational.

㉔ Lower Fort Street. At one time the handsome Georgian houses along this street, originally a rough track leading from the Dawes Point Battery to Observatory Hill, were among the best addresses in Sydney. Elaborate wrought-iron lacework still graces many of the facades.

⑯ Museum of Contemporary Art. This ponderous art deco building houses one of Australia's most important collections of modern art, as well as two significant collections of Aboriginal art. There's no permanent collection, but the program of continually changing exhibits has included works by such luminaries as Andy Warhol, Roy Lichtenstein, Cindy Sherman, and Tracey Moffat. ⊠*140 George St., The Rocks* ☎*02/9245–2400* ⊕*www.mca.com.au* ✉*Free* ⊙*Daily 10–5.*

㉞ Nurses Walk. Cutting across the site of the colony's first hospital, Nurses Walk acquired its name at a time when "Sydney" and "sickness" were synonymous. Many of the 736 convicts who survived the voyage from Portsmouth, England, aboard the First Fleet's 11 ships arrived suffering from dysentery, smallpox, scurvy, and typhoid. A few days after he landed at Sydney Cove, Governor Phillip established a tent hospital to care for the worst cases. Subsequent convict boatloads had even higher rates of death and disease.

NEED A BREAK? The Gumnut Café (⊠*28 Harrington St., The Rocks* ☎*02/9247–9591*), in the 1830 sandstone residence of blacksmith William Reynolds, serves delicious salads, pasta dishes, sandwiches, rolls, and cakes. The best tables are in the shady back garden. Reservations are necessary at lunch.

㉗ Observatory Hill. The city's highest point, at 145 feet, was known originally as Windmill Hill, since the colony's first windmill occupied this breezy spot. Its purpose was to grind grain for flour, but soon after it was built the canvas sails were stolen, the machinery was damaged in a storm, and the foundations cracked. The signal station at the top of the hill was built in 1848. This later became an astronomical observatory, hence the current name. This is a great place for a picnic with a view.

⑲ Overseas Passenger Terminal. Busy **Circular Quay West** is dominated by this multilevel steel-and-glass port terminal, which is often used by visiting cruise ships. There are several excellent waterfront restaurants in the terminal, all with magnificent harbor views. Even if you're not dining in the terminal, it's worth taking the escalator to the upper deck for a good view of the harbor and Opera House.

㉙ S.H. Ervin Gallery. This gallery, in the architecturally impressive 1856 National Trust Centre, concentrates on Australian art and architecture from a historical perspective. The changing exhibitions are of a consistently high standard and have shown the work of such well-known Australian artists as Lloyd Rees, Sidney Nolan, Hans Heysen, and Russell Drysdale. The gallery has a bookshop, and there's an outstanding gift shop next door. ✉ *National Trust Centre, Observatory Hill, Watson Rd., Millers Point* ☎ *02/9258–0178* ⊕ *www.nsw.nationaltrust.org. au/ervin.html* ▣ *A$6* ⊙ *Tues.–Sun. 11–5, weekends noon–5.*

㉝ Suez Canal. So narrow that two people can't walk abreast, this alley acquired its name before drains were installed, when rainwater would pour down its funnel-like passageway and gush across George Street. Lanes such as this were once the haunt of the notorious late-19th-century Rocks gangs, when robbery was rife in the area.

㉓ Sydney Harbour Bridge. Sydney's iron colossus, Harbour Bridge was a monumental engineering feat when it was completed in 1932. The roadway is supported by the arch, not by the massive stone pylons, which were added for aesthetic rather than structural reasons. The 1,650-foot-long bridge is 160 feet wide and contains two sets of railway tracks, eight road lanes, a bikeway, and a footpath on both sides. Actor Paul Hogan worked for several years as a rigger on the bridge, long before he earned international fame as the star of *Crocodile Dundee*. Sydneysiders love of Harbour Bridge was displayed in earnest on March 18, 2007, when 200,000 people walked across to commemorate its 75th anniversary.

Fodor'sChoice There are several ways to experience the bridge and its spectacular views.
★ The first is to follow the walkway from its access point near the Argyle Stairs to the **South East Pylon** (☎ *02/9240–1100*). This structure houses a display on the bridge's construction, and you can climb the 200 steps to the lookout and its unbeatable harbor panorama. The fee is A$8.50 and the display is open daily 10–5. Another (more expensive) option—not for those afraid of heights—is the **BridgeClimb tour** (☎ *02/8274–7777*), which takes you on a guided walking tour to the very top of Harbour Bridge, 439 feet above sea level. The cost ranges from A$165 to A$200 per person, depending on which tour you select. The third option is to walk to the midpoint of the bridge to take in the views free of charge, but be sure to take the eastern footpath, which overlooks the Sydney

Opera House. Access is via the stairs on Cumberland Street, close to the Shangri-La Hotel.

28 Sydney Observatory. Originally a signaling station for communicating with ships anchored in the harbor, this handsome building on top of Observatory Hill is now an astronomy museum. Within its sandstone walls, hands-on displays—including constellation charts, talking computers, and games—illustrate principles of astronomy. During evening observatory shows you can tour the building, watch videos, and get a close-up view of the universe through a 16-inch mirror telescope. Reservations are required for the evening show. Times vary depending on the season. ✉ *Watson Rd., Millers Point* ☎ *02/9241-3767* ⊕ *www.sydneyobservatory.com.au* 🖃 *Museum free, daytime show A$7, evening show A$15* ☉ *Daily 10–5.*

32 Sydney Visitor Centre at the Rocks. The center relocated to this former warehouse site (near the popular Löwenbräu Keller, where many tourists gather for a beer) in December 2005, and is known as the Rocks Centre. The ultramodern interior is packed with information including free city maps and brochures, and the friendly staff sells SydneyPasses and books tours, hotel rooms, and bus travel. The Rocks Discovery Museum is next door and can be accessed from the center. ✉ *The Rocks Centre, Argyle and Playfair Sts., The Rocks* ☎ *02/9240–8788* ⊕ *www.sydneyvisitorcentre.com* ☉ *Daily 9:30–5:30.*

Upper George Street. The restored warehouses and Victorian terrace houses that line this part of George Street make this a charming section of the Rocks. The covered **Rocks Market** takes place here on weekends.

21 Westpac Banking Museum. This museum on a lane off George Street displays a collection of coins from the earliest days of the colony of New South Wales. ✉ *6–8 Playfair St., The Rocks* ☎ *02/9251-1419* 🖃 *Free* ☉ *Weekdays 9–noon and 1–4.*

17 William Bligh statue. Although history may have painted him as a tyrant, Captain William Bligh of HMS *Bounty* fame was perhaps more unlucky than cruel. In 1806, almost two decades after the infamous mutiny on the ship he commanded, Bligh became governor of New South Wales. Two years later he faced his second mutiny. Bligh had made himself unpopular with the soldiers of the New South Wales Corps, commonly known as the Rum Corps, who were the real power in the colony. When he threatened to end their lucrative monopoly on the liquor trade, he was imprisoned during the Rum Rebellion. He spent the next two years as a captive until his successor, Lachlan Macquarie, arrived. Ironically, the statue's gaze frequently rests on HMAV *Bounty,* a replica of Bligh's ship, as it sails around the harbor on charter cruises.

DOMAIN, MACQUARIE STREET & HYDE PARK

Some of Sydney's most notable Victorian-era public buildings, as well as one of its finest parks, can be found in this area. In contrast to the simple, utilitarian stone convict cottages of the Rocks, these buildings

Building Sydney

Descended from Scottish clan chieftains, Governor Lachlan Macquarie was an accomplished soldier and a man of vision. Macquarie, who was governor from 1810 to 1821, was the first governor to foresee a role for New South Wales as a free society rather than an open prison. He laid the foundations for that society by establishing a plan for the city, constructing significant public buildings, and advocating that reformed convicts be readmitted to society.

Macquarie's policies of equality may seem perfectly reasonable today, but in the early 19th century they marked him as a radical. When his vision of a free society threatened to blur distinctions between soldiers, settlers, and convicts, Macquarie was forced to resign. He was later buried on his Scottish estate, his gravestone inscribed with the words "the Father of Australia."

Macquarie's grand plans for the construction of Sydney might have come to nothing were it not for Francis Greenway. Trained as an architect in England, where he was convicted of forgery and sentenced to 14 years in New South Wales, Greenway received a ticket of prison leave from Macquarie In 1814 and set to work transforming Sydney. Over the next few years he designed lighthouses, hospitals, convict barracks, and many other government buildings, several of which remain to bear witness to his simple but elegant eye. Greenway was eventually even depicted on one side of the old A$10 notes, which went out of circulation early in the 1990s. Only in Australia, perhaps, would a convicted forger occupy pride of place on the currency.

were constructed at a time when Sydney was experiencing a long period of prosperity, thanks to the gold rushes of the mid-19th century and an agricultural boom. The sandstone just below the surface of many coastal areas proved an ideal building material—easily honed into the ornamentation so fashionable during the Victorian era.

WHAT TO SEE

49 **Art Gallery of New South Wales.** Apart from Canberra's National Gallery, this is the best place to explore the evolution of European-influenced Australian art, as well as the distinctly different concepts that underlie Aboriginal art. All the major Australian artists of the last two centuries are represented in this impressive collection. The entrance level, where large windows frame spectacular views of the harbor, exhibits 20th-century art. Below, in the gallery's major extensions, the Yiribana Gallery displays one of the nation's most comprehensive collections of Aboriginal and Tor-

ART AND ANGST

If you like a bit of controversy with your culture, head to the Art Gallery of New South Wales to view the finalists in the annual **Archibald Prize** (⊕www. thearchibaldprize.com.au). Each year since 1921, the competition has attracted plenty of drama as everyone debates the merits of the winners. Prizes are announced in early March, and the exhibition hangs until mid-May.

res Strait Islander art. ⊠ *Art Gallery Rd., The Domain* ☎ *02/9225–1700* ⊕ *www.artgallery.nsw.gov.au* ⊡ *Free, fee for special exhibits* ⊘ *Thurs.–Tues. 10–5, Wed. 10–9.*

㊽ Domain South. Laid out by Governor Macquarie in 1810 as his own personal "domain" and originally including what is now the Royal Botanic Gardens, this large park is a tranquil area at the city's eastern edge. Office workers flock here for lunchtime recreation, and the park holds free outdoor concerts during the Festival of Sydney in January.

㊶ Garden Palace Gates. These gates are all that remain of the Garden Palace, a massive glass pavilion that was erected for the Sydney International Exhibition of 1879 and destroyed by fire three years later. On the arch above the gates is a depiction of the Garden Palace's dome. Stone pillars on either side of the gates are engraved with Australian wildflowers. ⊠ *Macquarie St. between Bridge and Bent Sts., Macquarie Street.*

㊵ History House. You're welcome to visit History House, the home of the Royal Australian Historical Society, and its collection of books and other materials. Note the balconies and the Corinthian columns, all made from iron, a style which was just becoming popular when this building was constructed in 1872. ⊠ *133 Macquarie St., Macquarie Street* ☎ *02/9247–8001* ⊡ *Library A$5* ⊘ *Weekdays 9:30–4:30.*

㊺ Hyde Park Barracks. Before Governor Macquarie arrived, convicts were left to roam freely at night. Macquarie was determined to establish law and order, and in 1819 he commissioned convict-architect Francis Greenway to design this restrained, classically Georgian-style building. Today the Barracks houses compelling exhibits that explore behind the scenes of the prison. For example, a surprising number of relics from this period were preserved by rats, which carried away scraps of clothing and other artifacts for their nests beneath the floorboards. A room on the top floor is strung with hammocks, exactly as it was when the building housed convicts. ⊠ *Queens Sq., Macquarie St., Macquarie Street* ☎ *02/9223–8922* ⊕ *www.hht.nsw.gov.au* ⊡ *A$10* ⊘ *Daily 9:30–5.*

▪ **NEED A BREAK?**

On a sunny day the courtyard tables of the **Hyde Park Barracks Café** (⊠ *Queens Sq., Macquarie St., Macquarie Street* ☎ *02/9361–6288*) provide one of the city's finest places to enjoy an outdoor lunch. The café serves light, moderately priced meals, salads, and open sandwiches, with an extensive Australian wine list.

㊲ Lands Department. The figures occupying the niches at the corners of this 1890 sandstone building are early Australian explorers and politicians. James Barnet's building stands among other fine Victorian structures in the neighborhood. ⊠ *Bridge St. near intersection of Macquarie Pl., Macquarie Street.*

㊱ Macquarie Place. This park, once a site of ceremonial and religious importance to Aboriginal people, contains a number of important monuments, including the obelisk formerly used as the point from which all distances from Sydney were measured. On a stone plinth at the bottom of the park is the anchor of HMS *Sirius,* flagship of the First Fleet, which struck a reef and sank off Norfolk Island in 1790. The bronze statue with his hands on his hips represents Thomas Mort, who in 1879 became the first to export refrigerated cargo from Australia. The implications of this shipment were enormous. Mutton, beef, and dairy products suddenly became valuable export commodities, and for most of the following century agriculture dominated the Australian economy. ⊠ *Bridge St., between Gresham and Loftus Sts., City Center.*

Macquarie Street. Sydney's most elegant boulevard was shaped by Governor Macquarie, who from 1810 until he was ousted in 1821 planned the transformation of the cart track leading to Sydney Cove into a stylish street of dwellings and government buildings. An occasional modern high-rise breaks up the streetscape, but many of the 19th-century architectural delights here escaped demolition.

48 Museum of Sydney. This museum, built on the site of the original Government House, documents Sydney's early period of European colonization. Aboriginal culture, convict society, and the gradual transformation of the settlement at Sydney Cove are woven into an evocative portrayal of life in the country's early days. A glass floor in the lobby reveals the foundations of the original structure. One of the most intriguing exhibits, however, is outside: the striking Edge of the Trees sculpture, the first collaborative public artwork in Sydney between an Aboriginal and a European artist. ⊠ *Bridge and Phillip Sts., Macquarie Street* ☎ *02/9251–5988* ⊕ *www.hht.nsw.gov.au* ⊠ *A$10* ⊙ *Daily 9:30–5.*

Near the Museum of Sydney, at the intersection of Bridge and Phillip streets, is an imposing pair of sandstone buildings. The most impressive view of the mid-19th-century **Treasury Building,** now part of the Hotel Inter-Continental, is from Macquarie Street. The **Chief Secretary's Building**—designed by James Barnet, who also designed the Lands Department—stands opposite the Treasury Building. Note the buildings' similarities, right down to the figures in the corner niches.

46 St. James Church. Begun in 1822, the colonial Georgian–style St. James is Sydney's oldest surviving church, and another fine Francis Greenway design. Now lost among the skyscrapers, the church's tall spire once served as a landmark for ships entering the harbor. Enter through the door in the Doric portico. Plaques commemorating Australian explorers and administrators cover the interior walls. Free guided tours are given weekdays at 2:30 PM. Lunchtime concerts are presented every Wednesday from late February to late December. ⊠ *Queens Sq., 173 King St., Hyde Park* ☎ *02/9232–3022* ⊙ *Daily 9–5.*

42 State Library of New South Wales. This large complex is based around the Mitchell and Dixson libraries, which make up the world's largest collection of Australiana. Enter the foyer through the classical portico to see one of the earliest maps of Australia, a copy in marble mosaic of a map made by Abel Tasman, the Dutch navigator, in the mid-17th century. Through the glass doors lies the vast Mitchell Library reading room, but you need a reader's ticket (establishing that you are pursuing legitimate research) to enter. You can, however, take a free escorted tour Tuesday at 11 and Thursday at 2. The Shakespeare Room is open to the public Tuesday 10 AM–4 PM. Inquire at the reception desk of the general reference library on Macquarie Street. ⊠ *Macquarie St. off Bent St., Macquarie Street* ☎ *02/9273–1414* ⊕ *www.sl.nsw.gov.au* ☻ *Weekdays 9–9, Fri. 9–6, weekends 11–5 (Mitchell Library closed Sun.).*

43 State Parliament House. The simple facade and shady verandas of this Greenway-designed 1816 building, formerly the Rum Hospital, typify Australian colonial architecture. From 1829, two rooms of the old hospital were used for meetings of the executive and legislative councils, which had been set up to advise the governor. These advisory bodies grew in power until New South Wales became self-governing in the 1840s, at which time Parliament occupied the entire building. The Legislative Council Chamber—the upper house of the parliament, identifiable by its red color scheme—is a prefabricated cast-iron structure that was originally intended to be a church on the goldfields of Victoria.

State Parliament generally sits between mid-February and late May, and again between mid-September and late November. You can visit the public gallery and watch the local version of the Westminster system of democracy in action. When parliament is not sitting, you can take a free escorted tour or walk around at your leisure and view the large collection of portraits and paintings. You must reserve ahead for tours and to sit in the public gallery. ⊠ *Macquarie St. across from Martin Pl., Macquarie Street* ☎ *02/9230–2111* ⊕ *www.parliament.nsw.gov.au* ☻ *Weekdays 9–5; hrs vary when Parliament is in session—call ahead.*

39 Sydney Conservatorium of Music. Providing artistic development for talented young musicians, this institution hosts free lunchtime concerts on Wednesday, jazz on Sunday, and other musical events. The conservatory's turreted building was originally the stables for nearby Government House. The construction cost caused a storm among Governor Macquarie's superiors in London and eventually helped bring about the downfall of both Macquarie and the building's architect, Francis Greenway. ⊠ *Conservatorium Rd. off Macquarie St., Macquarie Street* ☎ *02/9351–1222.*

44 Sydney Hospital. Completed in 1894 to replace the main Rum Hospital building, this institution offered an infinitely better medical option. By all accounts, admission to the Rum Hospital was only slightly preferable to death itself. Convict nurses stole patients' food, and abler patients stole from the weaker. The kitchen sometimes doubled as a mortuary, and the table was occasionally used for operations.

In front of the hospital is a bronze figure of a boar. This is *Il Porcellino,* a copy of a statue that stands in Florence, Italy. According to the inscription, if you make a donation in the coin box and rub the boar's nose, "you will be endowed with good luck." Sydney citizens seem to be a superstitious bunch, because the boar's nose is very shiny indeed. ⊠ *Macquarie St. at Martin Pl., Macquarie Street* ☎ *02/9382–7111.*

THE OPERA HOUSE & THE DOMAIN NORTH

Bordering Sydney Cove, Farm Cove, and Woolloomooloo Bay, this section of Sydney includes the iconic Sydney Opera House, as well as extensive and delightful harborside gardens and parks.

The colony's first farm was established here in 1788, and the botanical gardens were laid out in 1816. The most dramatic change to the area occurred in 1959, however, when ground was broken on the site for the Sydney Opera House at Bennelong Point. This promontory was originally a small island, then the site of 1819 Fort Macquarie, later a tram depot, and finally the Opera House, one of the world's most striking modern buildings. The area's evolution is an eloquent metaphor for Sydney's own transformation.

BACK A WINNER

Sydney residents love a day at the races. You'll find the veteran punters (gamblers) mixing with newcomers at **Royal Randwick** (⊕ *www.ajc.com.au*), a racetrack run by the Australian Jockey Club. Races are held most Saturdays, but the big events—where everyone dons their best outfit—take place around Easter when the Australian Derby, the Doncaster Cup, and the Sydney Cup are run over the weeklong Autumn Carnival.

WHAT TO SEE

Andrew (Boy) Charlton Pool. This heated saltwater swimming pool overlooking the navy ships tied up at Garden Island has become a local favorite. Complementing its stunning location is a radical design in glass and steel. The pool also has a chic terrace café above Woolloomooloo Bay. ✉ *Mrs. Macquarie's Rd., Domain North, The Domain* 🕿 *02/9358–6686* ⊕ *www.abcpool.org* 🎟 *A$5.20* 🕙 *Daily 6 AM–7 PM.*

Domain North. The northern part of the Domain adjoins the Royal Botanic Gardens and extends from Mrs. Macquarie's Point to the Cahill Expressway. Surrounded by Farm Cove and Woolloomooloo Bay, this is a pleasant, harbor-fringed park.

Government House. Completed in 1843, this Gothic-Revival building in the Royal Botanic Gardens served as the residence of the Governor of New South Wales—who represents the British crown in local matters—until the government handed it back to the public in 1996. Prominent English architect Edward Blore designed the two-story building without ever having set foot in Australia. The sandstone house's restored stenciled ceilings are its most impressive feature. Paintings hanging on the walls bear the signatures of some of Australia's best-known artists. You are free to wander on your own around Government House's gardens, which lie within the Royal Botanic Gardens, but you must join a guided tour to see the house's interior. ✉ *Royal Botanic Gardens, The Domain* 🕿 *02/9931–5200* 🎟 *Free* 🕙 *Tours Fri.–Sun. every ½ hr 10:30–3.*

⑤ Mrs. Macquarie's Chair. During the early 1800s, Elizabeth Macquarie often sat on the point in the Domain at the east side of Farm Cove, at the rock where a seat has been hewn in her name.

⑤ Mrs. Macquarie's Point. The inspiring views from this point combine with the shady lawns to make this a popular place for picnics. The views are best at dusk, when the setting sun silhouettes the Opera House and the Harbour Bridge.

⑤ Royal Botanic Gardens. More than 80 acres of sweeping green lawns, ★ groves of indigenous and exotic trees, duck ponds, greenhouses, and some 45,124 types of plants—many of them in bloom—grace these gardens. The elegant property, which attracts strollers and botany enthusiasts from all over the country, is a far cry today from what it once was: a failed attempt by convicts of the First Fleet to establish a farm. Though their early attempts at agriculture were disastrous, the efforts of these first settlers are acknowledged in the Pioneer Garden, a sunken garden built in their memory.

Among the many other feature gardens on the property are the Palm Grove—home to some of the oldest trees in Sydney, the Begonia Garden, and the Rare and Threatened Plants Garden. Not to be missed is a cutting from the famous Wollemi Pine, a plant thought to be extinct until it was discovered in a secluded gully in the Wollemi National Park in the Blue Mountains in 1994. Plants throughout the gardens have various blooming cycles, so no matter what time of year you visit, there are sure to be plenty of flowers. The gardens include striking sculptures and hundreds of species of birds (along with a large colony of flying foxes, also known as fruit bats). There are spectacular views over the harbor and the Opera House from the two lovely restaurants.

Tours leave from the visitor center, near the Art Gallery of New South Wales. There are also maps available for a variety of themed, self-guided walks. ⊠ *Domain North, The Domain* ☎ *02/923–8111, 02/9231–8125 weekends* ⊕ *www.rbgsyd.nsw.gov.au* ⊠ *Free* ☉ *Royal Botanic Gardens daily dawn–dusk; tours at 10:30* AM.

⑤ Sydney Opera House. Sydney's most famous landmark had such a long
Fodor's Choice and troubled construction phase that it's almost a miracle that the
★ building was ever completed. In 1954 the state premier appointed a committee to advise the government on the building of an opera house. The site chosen was Bennelong Point (named after an early Aboriginal inhabitant), which was, until that time, occupied by a tram depot. The premier's committee launched a competition to find a suitable plan, and a total of 233 submissions came in from architects the world over. One of them was a young Dane named Joern Utzon.

His plan was brilliant, but it had all the markings of a monumental disaster. The structure was so narrow that stages would have minuscule wings, and the soaring "sails" that formed the walls and roof could not be built by existing technology.

Nonetheless, Utzon's dazzling, dramatic concept caught the judges' imagination, and construction of the giant podium began in 1959.

From the start, the contractors faced a cost blowout; the building that was projected to cost A$7 million and take four years to erect would eventually require A$102 million and 15 years. Construction was financed by an intriguing scheme. Realizing that citizens might be hostile to the use of public funds for the controversial project, the state government raised the money through the Opera House Lottery. For almost a decade, Australians lined up to buy tickets, and the Opera House was built without depriving the state's hospitals or schools of a single cent.

Initially it was thought that the concrete exterior of the building would have to be cast in place, which would have meant building an enormous birdcage of scaffolding at even greater expense. Then, as he was peeling an orange one day, Utzon had a flash of inspiration. Why not construct the shells from segments of a single sphere? The concrete ribs forming the skeleton of the building could be prefabricated in just a few molds, hoisted into position, and joined together. These ribs are clearly visible inside the Opera House, especially in the foyers and staircases of the Concert Hall.

In 1966 Utzon resigned as Opera House architect and left Australia, embittered by his dealings with unions and the government. He has never returned to see his masterpiece. A team of young Australian architects carried on, completing the exterior one year later. Until that time, however, nobody had given much thought to the *interior*. The shells created awkward interior spaces, and conventional performance areas were simply not feasible. It's a tribute to the architectural team's ingenuity that the exterior of the building is matched by the aesthetically pleasing and acoustically sound theaters inside.

Guided one-hour tours depart at frequent intervals from the tour office, on the lower forecourt level, daily between 9 and 5. A two-hour backstage tour departs daily at 7 AM. Call in advance. ⊠ *Bennelong Point, Circular Quay* ☎ *02/9250–7111* ⊕ *www.soh.nsw.gov.au* ⊠ *General tour A$26, backstage tour A$140.*

DARLING HARBOUR

Until the mid-1980s this horseshoe-shape bay on the city center's western edge was a wasteland of disused docks and railway yards. Then, in an explosive burst of activity the whole area was redeveloped and opened in time for Australia's bicentenary in 1988. Now there's plenty to take in at the Darling Harbour complex: the National Maritime Museum, the Sydney Aquarium, Sydney Wildlife World, and the gleaming Exhibition Centre, whose masts and spars recall the square-riggers that once berthed here. At the harbor's center is a large park shaded by palm trees. Waterways and fountains lace the complex together.

The Powerhouse Museum is within easy walking distance of the harbor, and immediately to the south are Chinatown and the Sydney Entertainment Centre. The Star City entertainment complex, based around the Star City Casino, lies just to the west of Darling Harbour.

WHAT TO SEE

 Australian National Maritime Museum.
The six galleries of this soaring, futuristic building tell the story of Australia and the sea. In addition to figureheads, model ships, and brassy nautical hardware, there are antique racing yachts and the jet-powered *Spirit of Australia*, current holder of the world water speed record, set in 1978. The USA Gallery displays objects from such major U.S. collections as the Smithsonian Institution and was dedicated by President George Bush Sr. on New Year's Day 1992. An outdoor section showcases numerous vessels moored at the museum's wharves, including the HMAS *Vampire*, a World War II destroyer. ✉ *Wharf 7, Maritime Heritage Centre, 2 Murray St., Darling Harbour* ☎ *02/9298–3777* ⊕ *www.anmm.gov.au* ✑ *Free* ⊙ *Daily 9:30–5.*

> ### VILLAGE VIBE
>
> If you're seeking a taste of village life, take a ferry to Balmain. The left-of-center community spirit makes it one of Sydney's special places. On the western side of the harbor, Balmain is home to narrow streets, sandstone cottages, and good pubs, including one that welcomes dogs at the **London Hotel** (✉ *234 Darling St.* ☎ *02/9555–1377*). To get here, take the ferry from Circular Quay to Balmain Wharf and connect with buses that climb up Darling Street hill.

Chinatown. Bounded by the Entertainment Centre, George Street, Goulburn Street, and Paddy's Market, this neighborhood takes your senses on a galloping tour of the Orient. Within this compact grid are aromatic restaurants, traditional apothecaries, Chinese grocers, clothing boutiques, and shops selling Asian-made electronics. The best way to get a sense of the area is to take a stroll along Dixon Street, now a pedestrian mall with a Chinese Lion Gate at either end.

Sydney's Chinese community was first established here in the 1800s, in the aftermath of the gold rush that originally drew many Chinese immigrants to Australia. By the 1920s the area around Dixon Street was a thriving Chinese enclave, although the fear and hostility that many white Australians felt toward the "Yellow Peril" gave it the status of a ghetto. Chinatown was redeveloped in the 1970s, by which time Australians had overcome much of their racial paranoia and embraced the area's liveliness, multiculturalism, and food. These days, most of Sydney comes here regularly to dine, especially on weekends for dim sum lunches (called *yum cha*).

Chinese Garden of Friendship. Chinese prospectors came to the Australian goldfields as far back as the 1850s, and the nation's long and enduring links with China are symbolized by this tranquil walled enclave, the largest garden of its kind outside China. Designed by Chinese landscape architects, the garden includes bridges, lakes, waterfalls, sculptures, and Cantonese-style pavilions. The garden is a welcome refuge from sightseeing and the perfect place for a refreshing cup of tea from the café. ✉ *Darling Harbour* ☎ *02/9281–6863* 🎟 *A$6* ⊙ *Daily 9:30–5.*

60 Cockle Bay Wharf. Fueling Sydney's addiction to fine food, most of this sprawling waterfront complex is dedicated to gastronomy. This is also the site of Sydney's biggest nightclub, Home. If you have a boat you can dock at the marina—and avoid the hassle of parking a car in one of the city's most congested centers. ⊠ *201 Sussex St., Darling Harbour* ☎ *02/9269–9800* ⊕ *www.cocklebaywharf.com.*

61 LG IMAX Theatre. Both in size and impact, this eight-story-tall movie screen is overwhelming. One-hour presentations take you on astonishing, wide-angle voyages of discovery under the oceans and to the summit of the world's highest mountains. ⊠ *Southern Promenade, Darling Harbour* ☎ *02/9281–3300* ⊕ *www.imax.com.au* ☑ *A$18* ☉ *Daily 10–10.*

62 Powerhouse Museum. Learning the principles of science is a painless process with this museum's stimulating, interactive displays ideal for all ages. Exhibits in the former 1890s electricity station that once powered Sydney's trams include a whole floor of working steam engines, space modules, airplanes suspended from the ceiling, state of the art computer gadgetry, and a 1930s art deco–style movie-theater auditorium. ⊠ *500 Harris St., Ultimo* ☎ *02/9217–0111* ⊕ *www.phm.gov.au* ☑ *A$10* ☉ *Daily 10–5.*

59 Pyrmont Bridge. Dating from 1902, this is the world's oldest electrically operated swing-span bridge. The structure once carried motor traffic, but it's now a walkway that links Darling Harbour with Cockle Bay. The monorail runs above the bridge, but the center span still swings open to allow tall-masted ships into Cockle Bay, which sits at the bottom of the horseshoe-shape shore.

57 Sydney Aquarium. The larger and more modern of Sydney's public aquariums presents a fascinating view of the underwater world, with saltwater crocodiles, giant sea turtles, and delicate, multicolor fish. Excellent displays highlight Great Barrier Reef marine life and Australia's largest river system, the Murray-Darling. The marine mammal sanctuary and touch pool are favorites with children. Two show-stealing transparent tunnels give a fish's-eye view of the sea, while sharks and stingrays glide overhead. Although the adult admission price is high, family tickets are a good value, and prices are lower if you buy online. ⊠ *Aquarium pier, 1–5 Wheat Rd., Darling Harbour* ☎ *02/8251–7800* ⊕ *www.sydney-aquarium.com.au* ☑ *A$27.50* ☉ *Daily 9 AM–10 PM.*

56 Sydney Wildlife World. Sydney's newest major attraction brings 6,000 native Australian animals right to the heart of Sydney. Kangaroos, koalas, and dozens of other species come together under the one huge roof—in nine separate habitats—next door to the Sydney Aquarium. A huge wire-mesh dome covers Flight Canyon, an aviary where dozens of birds fly freely overhead as you stroll the 1-km (½-mi) walkway. You'll find koalas in Gum Tree Gully, and endangered bilbies, together with other nocturnal creatures, in the After Dark habitat. The Lush Canopy rain forest habitat is home to the cassowary and red-legged pademelons (a type of kangaroo), while giant cockroaches and other creepy crawlies can be found in Spineless Wonders. Each day you can watch a different animal being fed (including the snakes). Twice-daily bird training demonstrations take place at 11 and 3. ⊠ *Aquarium Pier, Wheat Rd., Darling Harbour* ☎ *02/9262-2385* ⊕ *www.sydney-wildlifeworld.com.au* ⊠ *A$28.50* ☉ *Daily 9-10.*

■ **OFF THE BEATEN PATH**

Sydney Fish Market. Second in size only to Tokyo's giant Tsukiji fish market, Sydney's is a showcase for the riches of Australia's seas. Just a five-minute drive from the city (and with its own stop on the Metro Light Rail network), the market is a great place to sample sushi, oysters, octopus, spicy Thai and Chinese fish dishes, and fish-and-chips at the waterfront cafés overlooking the fishing fleet. It's open daily from 7 AM to about 5. ⊠ *Pyrmont Bridge Rd. at Bank St., Pyrmont West* ☎ *02/9004-1100* ⊕ *www.sydneyfishmarket.com.au.*

> ## BOATING BLISS
>
> A great way to pamper your body and soul simultaneously is to take a Massage and Beauty Cruise on Sydney Harbour. Choose between an hour-long massage or facial aboard the luxury catamaran *Olympic Spirit* (⊕ *www.massageandbeautycruise.com.au*). The pampering starts with a welcome glass of champagne, followed by brunch or afternoon tea. While women love these weekend-only jaunts, couples come as well.

SYDNEY CITY CENTER

Shopping is the main reason to visit Sydney's city center, but there are several buildings and other places of interest among the office blocks, department stores, and shopping centers.

WHAT TO SEE

68 **Australian Museum.** The strength of this natural-history museum, a well-respected academic institution, is its collection of plants, animals, geological specimens, and cultural artifacts from the Asia-Pacific region. Particularly notable are the collections of artifacts from Papua New Guinea and from Australia's Aboriginal peoples. The museum also has an ever-changing array of fascinating temporary exhibitions, such as the popular "Eaten Alive: The World of Predators." There's an excellent shop and a lively café. ⊠ *6 College St., near William St., Hyde Park* ☎ *02/9320-6000* ⊕ *www.amonline.net.au* ⊠ *A$10* ☉ *Daily 9:30-5.*

67 **Hyde Park.** Declared public land by Governor Phillip in 1792 and used for the colony's earliest cricket matches and horse races, this area was turned into a park in 1810. The gardens are formal, with fountains, statuary, and tree-lined walks, and its tranquil lawns are popular with office workers at lunchtime. In the southern section of Hyde Park (near Liverpool Street) stands the 1934 art deco **Anzac Memorial** (☎ *02/9267-7668*), a tribute to the Australians who died in military service during World War I, when the acronym ANZAC (Australian and New Zealand Army Corps) was coined. The 120,000 gold stars inside the dome represent each man and woman of New South Wales who served. The lower level exhibits war-related photographs. It's open daily 9-4:30. ⊠ *Elizabeth, College, and Park Sts., Hyde Park.*

■ **NEED A BREAK?**

Stop in the Marble Bar (✉ *Hilton Sydney, 259 Pitt St., City Center* ☎ *02/9265–6094* ☉ *Closed Sun.*) to experience a masterpiece of Victorian extravagance. The 1890 bar was formerly in another building that was constructed on the profits of the horse-racing track, thus establishing the link between gambling and majestic public architecture that has its modern-day parallel in the Sydney Opera House. Threatened with demolition in the 1970s, the whole bar was moved—marble arches, color-glass ceiling, elaborately carved woodwork, paintings of voluptuous nudes, and all—to its present site. By night the basement bar serves as a backdrop for live music.

69 **Martin Place.** Sydney's largest pedestrian precinct, flanked by banks, offices, and shopping centers, is the hub of the central business district. There are some grand buildings here—including the beautifully refurbished Commonwealth Bank and the 1870s Venetian Renaissance–style General Post Office building with its 230-foot clock tower (now a Westin hotel). Toward the George Street end of the plaza the simple 1929 cenotaph war memorial commemorates Australians who died in World War I. Weekdays from about 12:30, the amphitheater near Castlereagh Street hosts free lunchtime concerts with sounds from all corners of the music world, from police bands to string quartets to rock-and-rollers. ✉ *Between Macquarie and George Sts., City Center.*

64 **Queen Victoria Building (QVB).** Originally the city's produce market, this huge 1898 sandstone structure was handsomely restored with sweeping staircases, enormous stained-glass windows, and the 1-ton Royal Clock, which hangs from the glass roof. The clock chimes the hour from 9 AM to 9 PM with four tableaux: the second shows Queen Elizabeth I knighting Sir Frances Drake; the last ends with an executioner chopping off King Charles I's head. The complex includes more than 200 boutiques, those on the upper floors generally more upscale and exclusive. The basement level has several inexpensive dining options. ✉ *George, York, Market, and Druitt Sts., City Center* ☎ *02/9264–9209* ☉ *Daily 8 AM–10 PM.*

66 **St. Andrew's Cathedral.** The foundation stone for Sydney's Gothic Revival Anglican cathedral—the country's oldest—was laid in 1819, although the original architect, Francis Greenway, fell from grace soon after work began. Edmund Blacket, Sydney's most illustrious church architect, was responsible for its final design and completion—a whopping 50 years later in 1868. Notable features of the sandstone construction include ornamental windows depicting Jesus's life and a great east window with images relating to St. Andrew. ✉ *Sydney Sq., George and Bathurst Sts., next to Town Hall, City Center* ☎ *02/9265–1661* ☉ *Weekdays 10:30–3:30, Sun. for services only 8:30 AM, 10:30 AM, 6:30 PM; tours by arrangement.*

47 **St. Mary's Cathedral.** The first St. Mary's was built here in 1821, but fire destroyed the chapel. Work on the present cathedral began in 1868. The spires weren't added until 2000, however. St. Mary's has some particularly fine stained-glass windows and a terrazzo floor in the crypt, where exhibitions are often held. The cathedral's large rose window was imported from England.

At the front of the cathedral stand statues of Cardinal Moran and Archbishop Kelly, two Irishmen who were prominent in Australia's Roman Catholic Church. Due to the high proportion of Irish men and women in the convict population, the Roman Catholic Church was often the voice of the oppressed in 19th-century Sydney, where anti-Catholic feeling ran high among the Protestant rulers. Australia's first cardinal, Patrick Moran, was a powerful exponent of Catholic education and a diplomat who did much to heal the rift between the two faiths. By contrast, Michael Kelly, his successor as head of the church in Sydney, was excessively pious and politically inept; Kelly and Moran remained at odds until Moran's death in 1911. ⊠ *College and Cathedral Sts., Hyde Park* ☎ *02/9220–0400* ☞ *Tour free* ☉ *Weekdays 6:30* AM*–6:30* PM*, Sat. 8–7:30, Sun. 6:30* AM*–7:30* PM*; tour Sun. at noon.*

63 **Sydney Tower.** Short of taking a scenic flight, a visit to the top of this 1,000-foot golden-turret-topped spike is the best way to see Sydney's spectacular layout. This is the city's tallest building, and the views from its indoor observation deck encompass the entire Sydney metropolitan area of more than 1,560 square km (600 square mi). You can often see as far as the Blue Mountains, more than 80 km (50 mi) away. The tower is home to OzTrek, which takes you "high above" Sydney's major attractions. However, the real adrenaline rush comes from Sky-Walk, a guided walk around the outside of the golden turret some 880 feet above the city. Walkers are attached to the tower's superstructure by harness lines and wear special all-weather suits. For those who work up an appetite, the building houses two restaurants in the turret. ⊠ *100 Market St., between Pitt and Castlereagh Sts., City Center* ☎ *02/9333–9222* ⊕ *www.skywalk.com.au* ☞ *Observation tower and OzTrek A$24, Skywalk A$109–A$149* ☉ *Sun.–Fri. 9* AM*–10:30* PM*, Sat. 9* AM*–11:30* PM*.*

65 **Sydney Town Hall.** Sydney's most ornate Victorian building—an elaborate sandstone structure—has some grand interior spaces, especially the vestibule and large Centennial Hall, and a massive 8,000-pipe Grand Organ, one of the world's most powerful, which is used for lunchtime concerts. Mingle with locals on the marble steps of the front entrance. Call for details of building tours. ⊠ *George and Druitt Sts., City Center* ☎ *02/9275–9333 general inquiries, 02/4285–5686 for tour information* ⊕ *www.cityofsydney.nsw.gov.au* ☞ *Free* ☉ *Weekdays 8:30–6.*

THE EASTERN SUBURBS

Sydney's eastern suburbs are truly the people's domain. They stretch from the mansions of the colonial aristocracy and the humble laborers' cottages of the same period to the modernized terrace houses of Paddington, one of Sydney's most charming suburbs and one of its most desirable. This tour also passes through Kings Cross and Darlinghurst, the country's best-known nightlife districts; visits a genteel colonial

1

mansion in Elizabeth Bay; and takes you to the acclaimed Sydney Jewish Museum.

WHAT TO SEE

⑦ Arthur McElhone Reserve. On the doorstep of Elizabeth Bay House, this is one of the city's welcome havens. The little park has tree ferns, a gushing stream, a stone bridge over a carp pond, and views over the harbor. ⊠ *Onslow and Billyard Aves., Elizabeth Bay* ☒ *Free* ⊙ *Daily dawn–dusk.*

⑦ Beare Park. With its pleasant harbor views, this waterfront park is a favorite recreation spot among Elizabeth Bay locals. The adjoining wharf is often busy with sailors coming and going to their yachts, moored out in the bay. ⊠ *Ithaca Rd., Elizabeth Bay* ☒ *Free* ⊙ *Daily dawn–dusk.*

Elizabeth Bay. Much of this densely populated but still-charming harborside suburb was originally part of the extensive Elizabeth Bay House grounds. Wrought-iron balconies and French doors on some of the older apartment blocks give the area a Mediterranean flavor. During the 1920s and 1930s this was a fashionably bohemian quarter, and it remains a favorite among artists and writers.

⑦ Elizabeth Bay House. Regarded in its heyday as the "finest house in the colony," this 1835–39 mansion retains little of its original furniture, although the rooms have been restored in Georgian style. The most striking feature is an oval-shaped salon with a winding staircase, naturally lighted by glass panels in the domed roof. The view, from the front-facing windows across Elizabeth Bay, is stunning. ⊠ *7 Onslow Ave., Elizabeth Bay* ☎ *02/9356–3022* ⊕ *www.hht.net.au* ☒ *A$8* ⊙ *Tues.–Sun. 10–4:30.*

❚ OFF THE BEATEN PATH

Harry's Café de Wheels. The attraction of this all-day dockyard food stall is not so much the delectable meat pies and coffee served as it is the clientele. Famous opera singers, actors, and international rock stars have been spotted here rubbing shoulders with shift workers and taxi drivers. This "pie cart" has been a Sydney institution since 1945, when the late Harry "Tiger" Edwards set up his van to serve sailors from the nearby Garden Island base. Drop in any time from 7 AM to the wee hours for a Tiger Pie, made with mushy peas, mashed potatoes, and gravy. ⊠ *1 Cowper Wharf Rd., Woolloomooloo* ☎ *02/9357–3074* ⊕ *www.harryscafedewheels.com.au.*

Paddington. Most of this suburb's elegant two-story terrace houses were built during the 1880s, when the colony experienced a long period of economic growth following the gold rushes that began in the 1860s. The balconies are trimmed with decorative wrought iron, sometimes known as Paddington lace, which initially came from England and later from Australian foundries. Rebuilt and repainted, the now-stylish Paddington terrace houses give the area its characteristic, villagelike charm. Today an attractive, renovated terrace home will cost at least A$1 million.

75 Shadforth Street. Built at about the same time as Elizabeth Bay House, the tiny stone houses in this street were assembled to house the workers who built and serviced the Victoria Barracks.

The Royal Hotel (⊠ *237 Glenmore Rd., Paddington* ☏ *02/9331-2604*) is an enjoyable Victorian pub with leather couches and stained-glass windows. It's a good place to stop for something cool to drink. The top floor has a balcony restaurant that's popular on sunny afternoons.

> **SHEER LUNACY**
>
> What's that brightly-lit face on the harbor's edge? It's Sydney's most treasured icon, **Luna Park** (⊕ *lunaparksydney.com*). A trip to Luna Park is a nostalgic adventure for most Sydneysiders who flocked there as kids. You can walk through the giant mouth and wander around for free, or buy tickets for the fairground rides like the authentic 1930s funhouse called Coney Island. Ferries run here from Circular Quay.

73 ★ Sydney Jewish Museum. Artifacts, interactive displays, and audiovisual displays chronicle the history of Australian Jews and commemorate the 6 million killed in the Holocaust. Exhibits are brilliantly arranged on eight levels, which lead upward in chronological order, from the handful of Jews who arrived with the First Fleet in 1788 to the 30,000 concentration-camp survivors who came after World War II—one of the largest populations of Holocaust survivors to be found anywhere. A 40-minute guided tour starts every day at noon. ⊠ *148 Darlinghurst Rd., Darlinghurst* ☏ *02/9360-7999* ⊕ *www.sydneyjewishmuseum. com.au* ⊡ *A$10* ⊙ *Sun.–Thurs. 10–4, Fri. 10–2.*

74 Victoria Barracks. Built by soldiers and convicts from 1841 on to replace the colony's original Wynyard Barracks—and still occupied by the army—this vast building is an excellent example of Regency-style architecture. Behind the 740-foot-long sandstone facade is mostly a parade ground, where an army band performs most Thursdays at 10 AM. In the former military prison on the parade grounds is the **Army Museum,** with exhibits covering Australia's military history from the early days of the Rum Corps to the Malayan conflict of the 1950s. Free tours of the barracks take place Thursday at 10 AM sharp (it's the army!), and include a tour of the museum (mid-February to late November). The museum is open on Sunday for those who don't want to take a tour, but you'll have to pay A$2. ⊠ *Oxford St. at Oatley Rd., Paddington* ☏ *02/9339-3303* ⊡ *Tours free, museum only A$2* ⊙ *Museum Thurs. 10–12:30, Sun. 10–3.*

GREATER SYDNEY

The Sydney area has numerous attractions that are well away from the inner suburbs. These include historic townships, the Sydney 2000 Olympics site, national parks where you can experience the Australian bush, and wildlife and theme parks that appeal to children.

Other points of interest are the Bondi and Manly beaches; the historic city of Parramatta, founded in 1788 and located 26 km (16 mi) to the west; and the magnificent Hawkesbury River, which winds its way around the city's western and northern borders. The waterside suburb of Balmain has pubs and restaurants, an atmospheric Saturday flea market, and backstreets full of character.

Each of the sights below could easily fill the better part of a day. If you're short on time, try a tour company that combines visits within a particular area—for example, a day trip west to the Olympic Games site, Australian Wildlife Park, and the Blue Mountains.

WHAT TO SEE

76 Centennial Park. More than 500 acres of palm-lined avenues, groves of Moreton Bay figs, paperbark tree–fringed lakes, and cycling and horse-riding tracks make this a popular park and Sydney's favorite workout circuit. In the early 1800s the marshy land at the lower end provided Sydney with its fresh water. The park was proclaimed in 1888, the centenary of Australia's founding as a colony. The Centennial Park Café is often crowded on weekends, but a mobile canteen between the lakes in the middle of the park serves snacks and espresso. Bikes and blades can be rented from the nearby Clovelly Road outlets, on the eastern side of the park. The Moonlight Cinema screens movies during the summer months. ⊠ *Oxford St. at Centennial Ave., Centennial Park* ⊕ *www. cp.nsw.gov.au* ⊙ *Daily dawn–dusk.*

80 Featherdale Wildlife Park. This is the place to see kangaroos, dingoes, wallabys, and echidnas (and even feed some of them) in native bush settings 14 km (9 mi) west of Sydney. You can have your picture taken with a koala for free. The daily crocodile feeding sessions are very popular. ⊠ *217 Kildare Rd., Doonside* ☎ *02/9622–1644* ⊕ *www.featherdale. com.au* ☒ *A$19* ⊙ *Daily 9–5.*

77 Fox Studios Entertainment Quarter. Australia's largest movie-production facility offers an entertainment quarter comprising restaurants, cafés, bars, movie theaters, and a retail center, as well as Wednesday and Saturday produce markets and a Sunday flea market. At Lollipop's Playland, children can ride the merry-go-round and play on the trampolines. ⊠ *Driver Ave., Centennial Park, Moore Park* ☎ *02/9383–4333* ⊕ *www.eqmoorepark.com.au* ☒ *Free* ⊙ *Daily 10* AM–*11* PM.

79 Koala Park Sanctuary. At this private park on Sydney's northern outskirts you can feed a kangaroo or cuddle a koala. (Koala presentations are daily at 10:20, 11:45, 2, and 3.) The sanctuary also has dingoes, wombats, emus, and wallaroos. There are sheep-shearing and boomerang-throwing demonstrations. ⊠ *84 Castle Hill Rd., West Pennant Hills* ☎ *02/9484–3141* ⊕ *www.koalaparksanctuary. com.au* ☒ *A$19* ⊙ *Daily 9–5.*

78 Ku-ring-gai Chase National Park. Nature hikes here lead past rock engravings and paintings by the Guringai Aboriginal tribe, the area's original inhabitants for whom the park is named. Created in the 1890s, the park mixes large stands of eucalyptus trees with moist, rain-forest-filled gullies where swamp wallabies, possums, goannas, and other creatures roam. The delightful trails are mostly easy or moderate, including the compelling 3-km (2-mi) Garigal Aboriginal Heritage Walk at West Head, which takes in ancient rock-art sites. From Mt. Ku-ring-gai train station you can walk the 3-km (2-mi) Ku-ring-gai Track to Appletree Bay, while the 30-minute, wheelchair-accessible Discovery Trail is an excellent introduction to the region's flora and fauna. Leaflets on all of the walks are available at the park's entry stations and from the Wildlife Shop at Bobbin Head.

The park is 24 km (15 mi) north of Sydney. Railway stations at Mt. Ku-ring-gai, Berowra, and Cowan, close to the park's western border, provide access to walking trails. On Sunday, for example, you can walk from Mt. Ku-ring-gai station to Appletree Bay and then to Bobbin Head, where a bus can take you to the Turramurra rail station. By car, take the Pacific Highway to Pymble. Then turn into Bobbin Head Road or continue on the highway to Mt. Colah and turn off into the park on Ku-ring-gai Chase Road. You can also follow the Pacific Highway to Pymble and then drive along the Mona Vale Road to Terry Hills and take the West Head turnoff.

Camping in the park is permitted only at the **Basin** (☏*02/9974–1011*) on Pittwater (near Palm Beach). Sites with access to barbecues and picnic tables must be booked in advance. The rate is A$10 per night. Supplies can be purchased in Palm Beach. For more information on the park, contact Ku-ring-gai Chase National Park Visitors Centre. ✉*Box 834, Hornsby, 2077* ☏*02/9472–8949* ⊕*www. nationalparks.nsw.gov.au.*

❽❶ Parramatta. This bustling satellite city 24 km (16 mi) west of Sydney
★ is one of Australia's most historic precincts. Its origins as a European settlement are purely agrarian. The sandy, rocky soil around Sydney Cove was too poor to feed the fledgling colony, so Governor Phillip looked to the banks of the Parramatta River for the rich alluvial soil they needed. In 1789, just a year after the first convicts-cum-settlers arrived, Phillip established Rosehill, an area set aside for agriculture. The community developed as its agricultural successes grew, and several important buildings survive as outstanding examples of the period. The two-hour Harris Park Heritage Walk, which departs from the RiverCat Ferry Terminal, connects the key historic sites and buildings. The ferry departs at frequent intervals from Sydney's Circular Quay, and is a relaxing, scenic alternative to the drive or train ride from the city.

The site of the first private land grant in Australia, **Experiment Farm** was settled in 1789 by James Ruse, a former convict who was given 1½ acres by Governor Phillip on condition that he become self-sufficient—a vital experiment if the colony was to survive. Luckily for Phillip, his gamble paid off. The bungalow, with its wide verandas, was built by colonial surgeon John Harris in the 1830s; it contains a fine collection of Australian colonial furniture, and the cellar now houses an exhibition on the life and work of James Ruse. The surrounding ornamental garden is most beautiful in early summer, when the floral perfumes are strongest. ✉*9 Ruse St., Harris Park, Parramatta* ☏*02/9635–5655* ⊕*www.nsw.nationaltrust.org.au* ▨*A$6*

⊙ *Tues.–Fri. 10:30–3:30, weekends 11–3:30.* On the bank of the Parramatta River, **Old Government House** is Australia's oldest surviving public building, and a notable work from the Georgian period. Built by governors John Hunter and Lachlan Macquarie, the building has been faithfully restored in keeping with its origins, and contains the nation's most significant collection of early Australian furniture. In the 260-acre parkland surrounding the house are Governor Brisbane's bathhouse and observatory and the Government House Dairy. ⊠ *Parramatta Park, Parramatta* ☎ *02/9635–8149* ⊕ *www.nsw.nationaltrust.org. au* ☜ *A$8; $10 combined ticket with Experiment Farm* ⊙ *Weekdays 10–4, weekends 10:30–4.* The oldest European building in Australia, **Elizabeth Farm** was built by John and Elizabeth Macarthur in 1793. With its simple but elegant lines and long, shady verandas, the house became a template for Australian farmhouses that survives to the present day. It was here, too, that the merino sheep industry began, since the Macarthurs were the first to introduce the tough Spanish breed to Australia. Although John Macarthur has traditionally been credited as the father of Australia's wool industry, it was Elizabeth who largely ran the farm while her husband pursued his official and more-lucrative unofficial duties as an officer in the colony's Rum Corps. Inside are personal objects of the Macarthur family, as well as a re-creation of their furnishings. ⊠ *70 Alice St., Rosehill* ☎ *02/9635–9488* ⊕ *www. hht.net.au/museums* ☜ *A$8* ⊙ *Daily 10–5.*

Royal National Park. Established in 1879 on the coast south of Sydney, the Royal has the distinction of being the first national park in Australia and the second in the world, after Yellowstone National Park in the United States. Several walking tracks traverse the grounds, most of them requiring little or no hiking experience. The Lady Carrington Walk, a 10-km (6-mi) trek, is a self-guided tour that crosses 15 creeks and passes several historic sites. Other tracks take you along the coast past beautiful wildflower displays and through patches of rain forest. You can canoe the Port Hacking River upstream from the Audley Causeway; rentals are available at the Audley boat shed on the river. The Illawarra–Cronulla train line stops at Loftus, Engadine, Heathcote, Waterfall, and Otford stations, where most of the park's walking tracks begin. There are three campsites in the park. ⊠ *Royal National Park Visitor Centre, 35 km (22 mi) south of Sydney via Princes Hwy. to Farnell Ave., south of Loftus, or McKell Ave. at Waterfall* ☊ *Box 44, Sutherland, 1499* ☎ *02/9542–0648, 02/9542–0666 National Parks and Wildlife Service district office* ⊕ *www.nationalparks.nsw.gov.au* ☜ *A$11 per vehicle per day, overnight camping A$3–A$8* ⊙ *Daily 7:30 AM–8:30 PM.*

🔵 **Sydney Olympic Park.** The center of the 2000 Olympic and Paralympic Games lies 14 km (8½ mi) west of the city center. Sprawling across 1,900 acres on the shores of Homebush Bay, the site is a series of majestic stadiums, arenas, and accommodation complexes. Among the park's sports facilities are an aquatic center, archery range, tennis center, and the centerpiece: the 85,000-seat Telstra Olympic Stadium. Since the conclusion of the 2000 Games it has been used for major sporting events like the 2003 Rugby World Cup. The Explore interactive stadium tour, costing A$27.50 per person, takes you behind the scenes to sit in the media room and have your photo taken on the winners' dais. The Games Trail walking tour, A$20 per person, includes a stop at the Cauldron where the Olympic flame burned.

Don't miss the adjacent **Bicentennial Park**, made up of 247 acres of swamps, lakes, and parks dotted with picnic grounds and bike trials. The area, a former quarry, was developed to commemorate Australia's Bicentennial celebrations in 1988. There's a visitor center outlining the history of the park, as well as an upscale restaurant (Bel Parco) and café (Lillies on the Park). The most scenic and relaxing way to get to Sydney Olympic Park is to take the RiverCat from Circular Quay to Homebush Bay. You can also take a train from Central Station, Sydney, to Olympic Park. ⊠ *1 Herb Elliot Ave., Homebush Bay* ☎ *02/9714–7888, 02/8765–2300 for tours, 02/9763–7530 for restaurants* ⊕ *www.sydneyolympicpark.nsw. gov.au* ⊙ *Daily during daylight hrs.*

> ## RUN FOR YOUR LIFE
>
> Pack your jogging shoes for the biggest foot race in the country. **City to Surf** (⊕ *city2surf.sunherald.com.au*) attracts more than 50,000 people each August—some taking it very seriously, others donning a gorilla suit or fairy outfit. The race starts at Hyde Park and winds through the eastern suburbs 14 km (9 mi) to Bondi Beach, via the notorious "Heartbreak Hill" at Rose Bay. For some reason, it never rains on the second Sunday in August.

BEACHES

Sydney is paradise for beach-lovers. Within the metropolitan area there are more than 30 ocean beaches, all with golden sand and rolling surf, as well as several more around the harbor with calmer water for safe swimming. If your hotel is on the harbor's south side, the logical choice for a day at the beach is the southern ocean beaches between Bondi and Coogee. On the north side of the harbor, Manly is easily accessible by ferry, but beaches farther north involve a longer trip by car or public transportation.

Lifeguards are on duty at most of Sydney's ocean beaches during summer months, and flags indicate whether a beach is being patrolled. "Swim between the flags" is an adage that is drummed into every Australian child, with very good reason: the undertow can be very dangerous. If you get into difficulty, don't fight the current. Breathe evenly, stay calm, and raise one arm above your head to signal the lifeguards.

Although there's no shortage of sharks inside and outside the harbor, the risk of attack is very low. These species are not typically aggressive toward humans, and shark nets protect many Sydney beaches. A more-common hazard is jellyfish, known locally as bluebottles, which inflict a painful sting—with a remote risk of more-serious complications (including severe allergic reactions). The staff at most beaches will supply a spray-on remedy to help relieve the pain, which generally lasts about 24 hours. Many beaches will post warning signs when bluebottles are present, but you can also determine the situation yourself by looking for the telltale bright-blue, bubblelike jellies washed up along the waterline.

Topless sunbathing is common at all Sydney beaches, but full nudity is permitted only at a couple of locations, including Lady Jane Beach, close to Watsons Bay on the south side of the harbor.

Details of how to reach the beaches by bus, train, or ferry are provided below, but some of the city's harbor and southern beaches are also on the Bondi Explorer bus route. These are Nielsen Park, Camp Cove, Lady Jane, Bondi, Bronte, Clovelly, and Coogee.

Numbers in the margin correspond to beaches on the Sydney Beaches map.

INSIDE THE HARBOR

⑨⓪ Balmoral. This 800-yard-long, rarely crowded beach—among the best of
★ the inner-harbor beaches—is in one of Sydney's most exclusive northern suburbs. There's no surf, but it's a great place to learn to windsurf (sailboard rentals are available). The Esplanade, which runs along the back of the beach, has a handful of upscale restaurants, as well as several snack bars and cafés that serve award-winning fish-and-chips. In summer you can catch performances of Shakespeare on the Beach. You could easily combine a trip to Balmoral with a visit to Taronga Zoo. To reach Balmoral, take the ferry from Circular Quay to Taronga Zoo and then board Bus 238. ⊠ *Raglan St., Balmoral.*

⑨② Camp Cove. Just inside South Head, this crescent-shape beach is where Sydney's fashionable people come to see and be seen. The gentle slope and calm water make it a safe playground for children. A shop at the northern end of the beach sells salad rolls and fresh fruit juices. The grassy hill at the southern end of the beach has a plaque to commemorate the spot where Captain Arthur Phillip, the commander of the First Fleet, first set foot inside Port Jackson. Parking is limited; arrive by car after 10 on weekends, and keep in mind it's a long walk to the beach. Take Bus 324 or 325 from Circular Quay. ⊠ *Cliff St., Watsons Bay.*

⑨① Lady Jane. Lady Jane—officially called Lady Bay—is the most accessible of the nude beaches around Sydney. It's also a popular part of Sydney's gay scene. Only a couple of hundred yards long and backed by a stone wall, the beach has safe swimming with no surf. From Camp Cove, follow the path north and then descend the short, steep ladder leading down the cliff face to the beach.

⑨③ Nielsen Park. By Sydney standards, this beach at the end of the Vaucluse Peninsula is small, but behind the sand is a large, shady park that's ideal for picnics. The headlands at either end of the beach are especially popular for their magnificent views across the harbor. The beach is protected by a semicircular net, so don't be deterred by the beach's correct name, Shark Bay. The shop and café behind the beach sell drinks, snacks, and meals. Parking is often difficult on weekends.

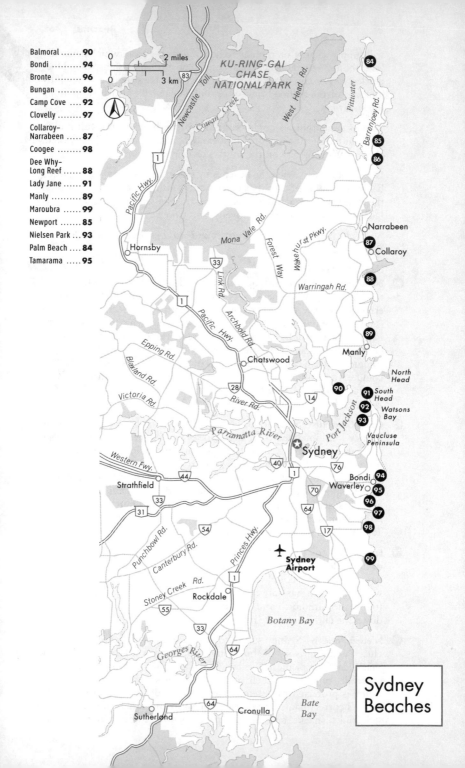

Sydney
Beaches

Historic Greycliffe House—built in 1840 and now used as National Park offices—is in the park, while the more-elaborate and stately Vaucluse House is a 10-minute walk away. Take Bus 325 from Circular Quay. ⊠ *Greycliffe Ave. off Vaucluse Rd., Vaucluse.*

SOUTH OF THE HARBOR

94 Bondi. Wide, wonderful Bondi (pronounced *bon*-dye) is the most famous and most crowded of all Sydney beaches. It has something for just about everyone, and the droves that flock here on a sunny day give it a bustling, carnival atmosphere unmatched by any other Sydney beach. Facilities include toilets, showers, and a kiosk on the beach that rents out sun lounges, beach umbrellas, and even swimsuits. Cafés, ice-cream outlets, and restaurants line Campbell Parade, which runs behind the beach. Families tend to prefer the calmer waters of the northern end of the beach. Surfing is popular at the south end, where a path winds along the sea-sculpted cliffs to Tamarama and Bronte beaches. Take Bus 380, 382, or the new 333 all the way from Circular Quay, or take the train from the city to Bondi Junction and then board Bus 380, 382, or 333. ⊠ *Campbell Parade, Bondi Beach.*

Fodor's Choice
★

> ### CUTE COSSIES
>
> Finding great bathing suits (or cossies, as they're called in Sydney) can be a dilemma. If you want a perfectly fitting cossie—and a matching sarong—that you'll wear for years, check out **The Big Swim** (⊠ *74 Campbell Parade, Bondi Beach* ☎ *02/9365-4456*). This Bondi Beach favorite stocks women's cossies for all shapes and sizes. Check out the Australian brand, Jets, which has a huge selection of terrific designs.

96 Bronte. If you want an ocean beach that's close to the city, has both sand and grassy areas, and offers a terrific setting, this one is hard to beat. A wooded park of palm trees and Norfolk Island pines surrounds Bronte. The park includes a playground and sheltered picnic tables, and excellent cafés are in the immediate area. The breakers can be fierce, but swimming is safe in the sea pool at the southern end of the beach. Take Bus 378 from Central Station, or take the train from the city to Bondi Junction and then board Bus 378. ⊠ *Bronte Rd., Bronte.*

★

97 Clovelly. Even on the roughest day it's safe to swim at the end of this long, keyhole-shape inlet, which makes it a popular family beach. There are toilet facilities but no snack bars or shops in the immediate area. This is also a popular snorkeling spot that usually teems with tropical fish. Take Bus 339 from Argyle Street, Millers Point (the Rocks), or Wynyard bus station; Bus 341 from Central Station; or a train from the city to Bondi Junction, then board Bus 329. ⊠ *Clovelly Rd., Clovelly.*

★

98 Coogee. A reef protects this lively beach (pronounced *kuh*-jee), creating calmer swimming conditions than those found at its neighbors. A grassy headland overlooking the beach has an excellent children's playground. Cafés in the shopping precinct at the back of the beach sell ice cream, pizza, and the ingredients for picnics. Take Bus 373 from Circular Quay or Bus 372 from Central Station. ⊠ *Coogee Bay Rd., Coogee.*

CLOSE UP

Surf Lifesaving Clubs

In 2007 the Australian Surf Lifesaving Association celebrated its 100-year anniversary. The world's first Surf Lifesaving club was formed at Bondi Beach on February 21, 1907. Other clubs formed in quick secession, and today there are more than 300 clubs in Australia, with 36 in Sydney and 129 in New South Wales.

In the last century, more than 500,000 swimmers have been rescued from patrolled beaches around the country and more than 1 million swimmers have received first aid.

Lifesavers are Australian icons; volunteers undertake their five-hour beach patrols on a rostered basis during the summer season from September to April. In addition to the thousands of volunteers across Australia, there are also permanent, paid lifeguards who are employed by the local councils and are on duty year-round.

Lifesavers arrive at the beach bright and early, check the beach conditions, erect the red and yellow flags to indicate the safe swimming areas, and keep an eye on swimmers throughout their patrol. It's easy to spot a surf lifesaver—he or she wears the bright red-and-yellow cap, and matching red-and-yellow uniform.

Bondi Beach lifesavers are the busiest in Australia. Each year about 2.5 million people come for a swim: some 2,500 rescues took place in 2005. The worst day in Bondi's history was February 6, 1938, known as Black Sunday. Lifesavers plucked 300 people from the huge surf. Five lives were lost.

It's not all work for Surf Lifesaving clubs. They hold competitions and surf carnivals throughout the summer months at numerous beaches. Events include surf swims, crew boat races (man-powered by oarsmen), surf ski races, and the macho-named "iron man" races where men (and women in separate events) perform all manner of endurance tests. Surf Lifesaving clubs opened their doors to women and children several decades ago.

—Caroline Gladstone

99 Maroubra. Extending for 1 km (½ mi), this expansive beach is the longest in the eastern suburbs. Board riders say it has the region's best surf. Though not as sophisticated as other eastern suburbs beachside towns, the stretch of sand is a good place to escape the excesses of Bondi and Coogee. Take Bus 395 from Central Station or Bus 396 from Circular Quay. ⊠ *Marine Parade, Maroubra.*

95 Tamarama. This small, fashionable beach—aka "Glam-a-rama"—is one
★ of Sydney's prettiest, but the rocky headlands that squeeze close to the sand on either side make it less than ideal for swimming. The sea is often hazardous here, and surfing is prohibited. A café in the small park behind the beach sells sandwiches, fresh juices, and fruit whips. Take the train from the city to Bondi Junction and then board Bus 391, or walk for 10 minutes along the cliffs from the south end of Bondi Beach. ⊠ *Tamarama Marine Dr., Tamarama.*

1

NORTH OF THE HARBOR

86 **Bungan.** If you *really* want to get away from it all, this is the beach for you. Very few Sydneysiders have discovered Bungan, and those who have would like to keep it to themselves. As well as being relatively empty, this wide, attractive beach is one of the cleanest, due to the prevailing ocean currents. Access to the beach involves a difficult hike down a wooden staircase, and there are no facilities. Take Bus 184 or 190 from the Wynyard bus stand near Wynyard Station (City Center). ⊠ *Beach Rd. off Barrenjoey Rd., Mona Vale.*

87 **Collaroy–Narrabeen.** This is actually one beach that passes through two suburbs. Its main attractions are its size—it's almost 3 km (2 mi) long— and the fact that it's always possible to escape the crowds here. The shops are concentrated at the southern end of the beach. Take Bus 155 or 157 from Manly or Bus 182, 184, 189, or 190 from the Wynyard bus station. ⊠ *Pittwater Rd., Narrabeen.*

88 **Dee Why–Long Reef.** Separated from Dee Why by a narrow channel, Long Reef Beach is remoter and much quieter than its southern neighbor. However, Dee Why has better surfing conditions, a big sea pool, and several good restaurants. To get here take Bus 136 from Manly. ⊠ *The Strand, Dee Why.*

89 **Manly.** The Bondi Beach of the north shore, Manly caters to everyone
Fodor$Choice except those who want to get away from it all. On sunny days Sydney-
★ siders, school groups, and travelers from around the world crowd the 2-km-long (1¼-mi-long) sweep of white sand and take to the waves to swim and ride boards. The beach is well equipped with changing and toilet facilities and lockers. The promenade that runs between the Norfolk Island pines is great for people-watching and rollerblading. Cafés, souvenir shops, and ice-cream parlors line the nearby shopping area, the Corso. Manly also has several nonbeach attractions including Oceanworld, an aquarium about 200 yards from the ferry wharf. The ferry ride from the city makes a day at Manly feel more like a holiday than just an excursion to the beach. Take a ferry or JetCat from Circular Quay. From the dock at Manly the beach is a 10-minute walk. ⊠ *Steyne St., Manly.*

85 **Newport.** With its backdrop of Norfolk Island pines, this broad sweep of sand is one of the finest northern beaches. Although the relaxed town of Newport is known for its bodysurfing, it has one of the best selections of cafés and take-out shops of any Sydney beach, and there's a shopping center within easy walking distance. To get there, go to the Wynyard bus interchange on Carrington Street (City Center)—just across the road from Wynyard Railway Station—and take Bus 189 or 190 to Newport. ⊠ *Barrenjoey Rd., Newport.*

84 **Palm Beach.** The golden sands of Palm Beach run along one side of a peninsula separating the large inlet of Pittwater from the Pacific Ocean. Bathers can easily cross from the ocean side to Pittwater's calm waters and sailboats, and you can take a circular ferry trip around this waterway from the wharf on the Pittwater side. The view from the lighthouse at the northern end of the beach is well worth the walk. Nearby shops and cafés sell light snacks and meals. Take Bus 190 from Wynyard bus station. ✉ *Ocean Rd., Palm Beach.*

WHERE TO EAT

Sydney's dining scene is as sunny and cosmopolitan as the city itself, and there are diverse and exotic culinary adventures to suit every appetite. Mod-Oz (modern-Australian) cooking flourishes, fueled by local produce and guided by Mediterranean and Asian techniques. Look for such innovations as tuna tartare with flying-fish roe and wasabi; emu prosciutto; five-spice duck; shiitake mushroom pie; and sweet turmeric barramundi curry. A meal at Tetsuya's, Claude's, or Rockpool constitutes a crash course in this dazzling culinary language. A visit to the city's fish markets at Pyrmont, just five minutes from the city center, will also tell you much about Sydney's diet. Look for rudderfish, barramundi, blue-eye, kingfish, John Dory, ocean perch, and parrot fish, as well as Yamba prawns, Balmain and Moreton Bay bugs (shovel-nose lobsters), sweet Sydney rock oysters, mud crab, spanner crab, yabbies (small freshwater crayfish), and marrons (freshwater lobsters).

There are many expensive and indulgent restaurants in the city center, but the real dining scene is in the inner city, eastern suburbs, and inner-western suburbs of Leichhardt and Balmain. Neighborhoods like Surry Hills, Darlinghurst, Paddington, and beachside suburb Bondi are dining destinations unto themselves. Plus, you're more likely to find a restaurant that will serve on a Sunday night in one of these places than in the central business district—which can become a bit of a ghost town after offices close during the week and on weekends. Circular Quay and the Rocks are always lively, and the Overseas Passenger Terminal (on the opposite side of the harbor from the Opera House) has several top-notch restaurants with stellar views.

Surry Hills is a delight for diners with adventurous taste buds and limited budgets. Crown Street is lined with ethnic and gourmet restaurants where you can get a delicious meal for between A$20 and A$30. The restaurants in Darlinghurst are similarly diverse, though they tend to be a bit trendier and more expensive. Oxford Street in Paddington offers great upscale dining options as well as pub fare, and Bondi, which used to be a tourist trail of fast-food chains and cheap take-out joints, is now home to some of the most famous and beloved restaurants in the city.

Although most Sydney restaurants are licensed to serve alcohol, the few that aren't usually allow you to bring your own bottle (BYO). Reservations are generally required, although some restaurants don't take bookings at all. Lunch hours are from around noon to 2:30; dinner is served between 7 and 10:30. The 10% Goods and Services Tax (GST) is already incorporated in the prices, but a 10% tip is customary for exemplary service. If you bring your own wine, a corkage fee often applies. Expect a 10% service surcharge on weekends and holidays. Smoking is prohibited inside all restaurants throughout New South Wales.

WHAT IT COSTS IN AUSTRALIAN DOLLARS					
	$$$$	$$$	$$	$	¢
AT DINNER	over A$65	A$46–A$65	A$36–A$45	A$25–A$35	under A$25

Prices are for a main course at dinner.

THE ROCKS & CIRCULAR QUAY

CAFÉS

¢ ✕ **Costi's Famous Fish Café.** This casual café—in the heart of the Rocks—has market-fresh fish and seafood at very reasonable prices. Favorites such as battered fish-and-chips, barbecued octopus, and oysters (mornay, Kilpatrick, or Asian steamed), can be had for under A$12, while a Cajun fish-fillet burger is a steal at A$6.95. There's an array of salads, as well as fresh fish and lobsters to take home and cook on the barbie. ✉91 George St., The Rocks ☎02/9247–7110 ⟁Reservations not accepted ▤AE, MC, V.

JAPANESE

$$$$ ✕ **Galileo.** The gracious, salon-style look of the Observatory Hotel's dining room has become a hot spot, thanks to the innovative, Franco-Japanese fusion cuisine of chef Haru Inukai. Start with the amazing trio of duck terrine (duck confit, duck breast, and foie gras), before moving onto the chef's popular signature dish, spatchcock à la Haru. The seven-course tasting menu (A$115) is also a favorite with the locals. ✉89–113 Kent St., City Center ☎02/9256–2215 ▤AE, DC, MC, V ✣No lunch.

$$$$ ✕ **Yoshii.** The eponymous restaurant of Sydney's finest sushi chef, Ryuichi Yoshii, has a Zen-like decor that feels just like Japan. Lunchtime bento boxes start at A$38, but serious sushi fans book the special sushi menus (from A$45 at lunch). For the full Yoshii experience, order the set dinner menu (A$110–A$120), which, if you're lucky, may include roasted duck. ✉115 Harrington St., The Rocks ☎02/9247–2566 ⟁Reservations essential ▤AE, DC, MC, V ✣Closed Sun. No lunch Mon. and Sat.

MODERN AUSTRALIAN

$$$$ ✕ **Rockpool.** A meal at Rockpool is a crash course in what Mod-Oz cooking is all about, conducted in a glamorous, long dining room with a catwalklike ramp. Chefs Neil Perry and Khan Danis weave Thai, Chinese, Mediterranean, and Middle Eastern influences into their repertoire with effortless flair and originality. Prepare to be amazed by the lobster tagine with spice-stuffed dates, eggplant salad, and couscous. Try to snag one of the limited portions of slow-roasted aged beef with anchovy-spice butter, spinach puree, and potato and cabbage gratin. Don't miss the date tart for dessert. Tasting menus (including a vegetarian menu) are also available (A$150–$A175). ✉107 George St., The Rocks, 2000 ☎02/9252–1888 ⟁Reservations essential ▤AE, DC, MC, V ✣Closed Sun. and Mon. No lunch.

Fodor's Choice
★

$$$ ✕ **Aria.** With windows overlooking the Opera House and Harbour Bridge, Aria could easily rest on the laurels of its location. Instead,
★

chef Matthew Moran creates a menu of extraordinary dishes that may be your best meal in the antipodes. (Be warned: the bill will have you reeling!) Make a reservation before you even get on the plane, and let your mouth begin to water for the double-cooked sweet pork belly and the aged beef fillet in béarnaise sauce. The wine list is superb, as is the service. Even the warm rolls with butter are memorable. ⊠ *1 Macquarie St., East Circular Quay* ☎ *02/9252–2555* ⊟ *AE, DC, MC, V* ⊘ *No lunch weekends.*

$$$ ✕ **Guillaume at Bennelong.** Chef Guillaume Brahimi rattles the pans at possibly the most superbly situated dining room in town. Tucked into the side of the Opera House, the restaurant affords views of Sydney Harbour Bridge and the city lights. Brahimi's creations soar: try the fresh ink papardelle with seared Queensland scallops, roasted Moreton Bay bug, and blue swimmer crab meat in a tomato-and-coriander broth, or the Kangaroo Island chicken on Chinese cabbage with ravioli of duck foie gras and a veal jus. Better yet, work your way through the nine-course degustation menu ($80). ⊠ *Bennelong Point, Circular Quay* ☎ *02/9241–1999* ⚲ *Reservations essential* ⊟ *AE, DC, MC, V* ⊘ *Closed Sun. No lunch Sat.–Wed.*

$$–$$$ ✕ **Quay.** In his take on Mod-Oz cuisine, chef Peter Gilmore masterfully
★   crafts such dishes as crisp-skinned Murray cod with brown butter; baby squid filled with potato puree, flowering chive, and spring onions; and slow-braised White Rocks veal with lentils. Desserts are sublime— the five-textured Valrhona chocolate cake may make you weak at the knees—and the wine list fits the flavors of the cuisine perfectly. Glass walls afford wonderful views of the bridge and Opera House, right at your fork's tip. ⊠ *Upper Level, Overseas Passenger Terminal, West Circular Quay, The Rocks* ☎ *02/9251–5600* ⚲ *Reservations essential* ⊟ *AE, DC, MC, V* ⊘ *No lunch Sat.–Mon.*

$$ ✕ **Altitude.** The lure of this decadent restaurant, perched high above Sydney Harbour on the 36th floor of the luxurious Shangri-La Hotel, is the view through the floor-to-ceiling windows, but the food is equally impressive. Chef Michael Kean, formerly with London's exclusive Dorchester Hotel, has concocted an enticing menu of Mod-Oz dishes with a definite European influence. The venison and scallop brochette is exquisitely juicy, and if you love seafood you'll find it difficult to choose between the Tasmanian salmon, baby barramundi, or steamed kingfish wrapped in a basil and prawn jacket. For a special occasion, gather a dozen friends to dine in the opulent, egg-shaped private dining room. On the weekends the adjoining bar attracts a crowd that loves the thumping music, so it might be a good idea to beat it early or join in the fun. ⊠ *Shangri-La Hotel, 176 Cumberland St., The Rocks* ☎ *02/9250– 6123* ⚲ *Reservations essential* ⊟ *AE, DC, MC, V* ⊘ *Closed Sun. No lunch Mon.–Sat.*

$–$$ ✕ **harbourkitchen & bar.** Dramatic harbor and Opera House views are democratically shared by this one-size-fits-all restaurant and its attendant bar. The food rivals the views of the Opera House and is best described as Modern Rustic, with a produce-driven menu revolving around the rotisserie and wood-fired grill. The extensive menu includes dishes such as swordfish with *caponata* (eggplant relish), anchovy butter, and zucchini blossoms. ✉ *Park Hyatt Sydney, 7 Hickson Rd., Circular Quay* ☎ *02/9256–1661* ⚖ *Reservations essential* 🖵 *AE, DC, MC, V.*

$ ✗ **Wharf Restaurant.** At one time only the Wharf's proximity to the Sydney Theatre Company (they share Pier 4) attracted diners, but with the restaurant now in the hands of two of Sydney's legendary chefs, Aaron Ross and Tim Pak Poy, the emphasis is firmly on the food. Fish dominates the menu, befitting the restaurant's name and locale, and there is a theme of Japanese-Western fusion in the flavoring: the kingfish is wrapped in prosciutto with daikon and shiitake broth; the salt-and-pepper squid is served with cucumber, mint, and red-pepper relish. You can see Sydney Harbour Bridge from some tables, but it's North Sydney and the ferries that provide the real show. Meal times and sizes are flexible to accommodate theatergoers. ✉ *End of Pier 4, Hickson Rd., Walsh Bay* ☎ *02/9250–1761* ⚖ *Reservations essential* 🖵 *AE, DC, MC, V* ⊘ *Closed Sun.*

THAI

$–$$ ✗ **Sailors Thai.** Sydney's most exciting and authentic Thai food comes
★ from this glamorously restored restaurant in the Old Sailors Home. Downstairs, business types rub shoulders with sightseers and hard-core shoppers, devouring delicious red curries and salads fragrant with lime juice and fish sauce. Upstairs is the Sailors Thai Canteen (no reservations accepted), a casual noodle bar where long, communal zinc tables groan with *som dtam* (shredded papaya salad) and pad thai (rice noodles stir-fried with shrimp, egg, peanuts, and chili). ✉ *106 George St., The Rocks* ☎ *02/9251–2466* ⚖ *Reservations essential* 🖵 *AE, DC, MC, V* ⊘ *Closed Sun.*

CITY CENTER AREA

CHINESE

¢–$ ✗ **BBQ King.** You can find better basic Chinese food elsewhere in town,
★ but for duck and pork, barbecue-loving Sydneysiders know that this is the place to come. The poultry hanging in the window are the only decor at this small Chinatown staple, where the food is so fresh you can almost hear it clucking. Barbecued pork is the other featured dish, and the suckling pig is especially delicious. It's open until late at night, when the average customers are large groups of mates sprawled at the Formica tables feeding their drunken munchies, or Chinatown chefs kicking back after a day in the kitchen. The service is brusque (some say downright rude), but it's all part of the low-budget charm. ✉ *18–20 Goulburn St., Haymarket* ☎ *02/9267–2586 or 02/9267–2433* 🖵 No credit cards.

¢–$ ✗ **Golden Century.** For two hours—or as long as it takes for you to consume delicately steamed prawns, luscious mud crab with ginger and shallots, and *pipis* (triangular clams) with black bean sauce—you might as well be in Hong Kong. This place is heaven for seafood-lovers, with wall-to-wall fish tanks filled with crab, lobster, abalone, and schools of barramundi, parrotfish, and coral trout. You won't have to ask if the food is fresh: most of it is swimming around you as

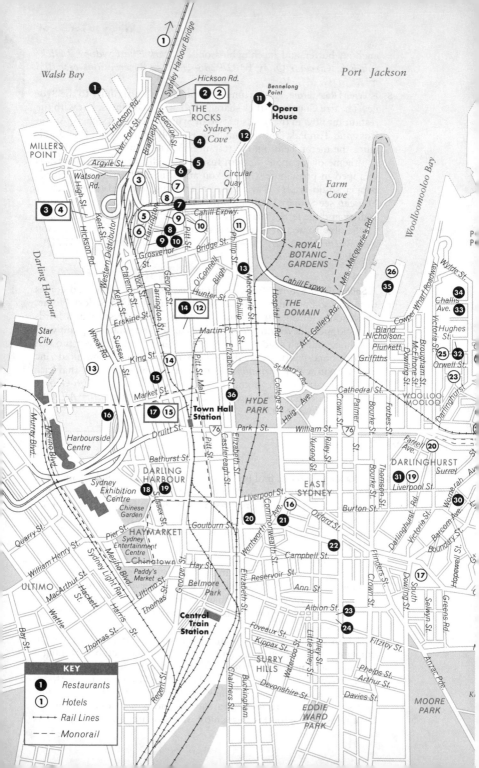

Where to Stay & Eat in Sydney

Garden
Island
Naval
Dockyard

POTTS
POINT

Elizabeth
Bay

Billyard
Ave.

BEARE
PARK

Rushcutters
Bay

Greenknowe

ELIZABETH
BAY

Eliz. Bay Rd.

Onslow

Yarranabbe Rd.

Darling Point Rd.

New Beach Rd.

Mona Rd.

Green Oaks Ave.

KINGS
CROSS

RUSHCUTTERS
BAY
PARK

Kings Cross Rd.

New South Head Rd.

McLachlan Ave.

Neild Ave.

Rd.

Cascade St.

Glenmore

Stephen St.

Brown St.

Goodhope

Glenmore Rd.

Shadforth

Brown St.

Gurner St.

Heeley

Broughton St.

Union St.

William St.

Sutherland Ave.

Harris St.

Hargrave St.

Taylor St.

PADDINGTON

Oxford St.

Paddington St.

Underwood St.

Renny St.

Oatley Rd.

Oxford St.

Jersey Rd.

Queen St.

Moore Park Rd.

Leinster St.

Sydney
Football
Stadium

Kippax
Lake

Driver Ave.

Clapton Rd.

TO
BONDI
BEACH

0 ____ 330 yds
0 ____ 300 meters

Restaurants ▼

Altitude	8
Aria	12
Bambini Trust	36
BBQ King	20
Bécasse	15
bills	30
Billy Kwong	23
Bistro Moncur	27
Buon Ricordo	29
Claude's	26
Costi's Famous Fish Café	7
Est	10
Fishface	31
Forty One	13
Four in Hand	28
Fratelli Paradiso	33
Galileo	3
glass brasserie	17
Golden Century	18
Goods Organic	22
Guillaume at Bennelong	11
harbourkitchen & bar	2
Hugo's Bar Pizza	32
Longrain	21
Lotus	34
The Malaya	16
Marque	24
Otto	35
Prime	14
Quay	4
Rockpool	6
Sailor's Thai	5
Tetsuya's	19
Wharf Restaurant	1
Yoshii	9

Hotels ▼

Blacket Hotel	14
BLUE Sydney	26
The Chelsea	21
De Vere Hotel	24
Four Seasons Hotel Sydney	9
Harbour Rocks Hotel	7
Hilton Sydney	15
Hotel 59 & Cafe	22
Hotel Inter-Continental Sydney	11
The Hughenden	18
Kirketon	20
Medina Grand Harbourside	13
Medusa	19
Observatory Hotel	4
Park Hyatt Sydney	2
Quay West Suites Sydney	5
Regents Court	23
Rendezvous Stafford Hotel Sydney	3
The Russell	8
Sebel Manly Beach	1
Shangri-La Hotel Sydney	6
Sullivans Hotel	17
Swiss Grand Resort & Spa	27
Sydney Harbour Marriott	10
Victoria Court Sydney	25
Westin Sydney	12
Y Hotel Hyde Park	16

you eat. The atmosphere is no-frills, and the noise level can be deafening, but the food is worth it. Supper is served late evenings from 10 PM until 4 AM. ⊠ *393–399 Sussex St., Haymarket* ☎ *02/9212–3901* ⊟ *AE, DC, MC, V.*

FRENCH

$–$$

FodorsChoice

★

✕ **Bécasse.** Foodies followed this award-winning French restaurant when it moved to more-sophisticated digs in the city center. It retained its tradition of an open kitchen, which was popular with diners. Inventive, flavorful cuisine with excellent service accompanies the clink of silverware against dinner plates here. The night always starts with an *amuse bouche,* which may be smoked haddock with red cabbage, or demitasse of potato-and-bacon soup, followed by mains such as roast loin of venison. Whatever your choice, you'll want to join the fan club. ⊠ *204 Clarence St., City Center, 2000* ☎ *02/9283–3440* ⚠ *Reservations essential* ⊟ *AE, MC, V* ⊘ *Closed Mon. and Tues. No lunch.*

MALAYSIAN

¢–$

★

✕ **The Malaya.** The cocktails are lethal, the view is captivating, and the food is extraordinary at this modern-Asian restaurant on King Street Wharf. Signature dishes include beef Rendang (Indonesian-style beef curry), and marinated, sticky-sweet and crunchy Szechuan eggplant that's so good it may just be the food of the gods. Try one of the four set menus (for a minimum of three people) for a true feast on the extensive menu's flavor combinations. ⊠ *39 Lime St., King Street Wharf, Darling Harbour* ☎ *02/9279–1170* ⊟ *AE, DC, MC, V.*

MODERN AUSTRALIAN

$$$$

★

✕ **Forty One.** The view east over the harbor is glorious, the private dining rooms are plush, and Dietmar Sawyere's Asian-influenced classical food is top-notch. The set-price three-course dinner menu (A$125) might include steamed Western Australian yabby tails with asparagus and bread sauce, and espresso parfait with dark chocolate and Grand Marnier sauce for dessert. The vegetarian menu, with the likes of Ossau Iraty sheep's-milk cheese on a salad of apples, dates, celeriac, and walnuts, is sublime. There is also a six-course tasting menu (A$140–A$200) with wine pairings. Arrive early and sip champagne before dinner, and take in the glorious views from the attached lounge. ⊠ *Level 42, Chifley Tower, 2 Chifley Sq., City Center* ☎ *02/9221–2500* ⚠ *Reservations essential* ⊟ *AE, DC, MC, V* ⊘ *Closed Sun. No lunch Mon. and Sat.*

$$$$

FodorsChoice

★

✕ **Tetsuya's.** It's worth getting on the waiting list—there's *always* a waiting list—to sample the unique blend of Western and Japanese-French flavors crafted by Sydney's most applauded chef, Tetsuya Wakuda. The serene, expansive dining room's unobtrusive Japanese aesthetic leaves the food as the true highlight. Confit of ocean trout served with unpasteurized ocean-trout roe and double-cooked, deboned spatchcock with braised daikon and bread sauce are signature items from the pricey set menu (A$180 for nine courses) that changes often and never fails to dazzle. Views of a Japanese garden—complete with bonsai and a waterfall—make this place feel miles from the city center. ⊠ *529 Kent St.,*

Australian Cuisine: What, Where & Why

CLOSE UP

1

Australia simply didn't have time to sit back and wait for a homegrown cuisine to evolve in the traditional way. So we borrowed an Anglo-Saxon way of eating that had little to do with where, what, or who we happened to be. We learned, of necessity, to include what was in our natural larder.

The incredibly vast landmass of Australia means that somewhere in the country is a microclimate that is suitable for producing whatever we feel like eating, from the tropical fruit and sugarcane fields of northern Queensland to the grazing pastures and citrus groves of the temperate Riverina and Riverland areas, to the cool-climate dairy products of Victoria and Tasmania. It also didn't take us too long to realize that a country surrounded by water is a country surrounded by oysters, clams, crabs, lobsters, prawns, and fish.

The next great influence came from the southern Europeans who came to this country as refugees after World War II. Many were Spaniards, Greeks, and Italians, people who had lived with coastal breezes in their veins and whose lives and foods had been warmed by the Mediterranean sun.

But the emergence of a truly identifiable Australian way of eating came when we finally realized in the late 1970s that it was actually Asia's doorstep we were on, and not England's. These Asian and Mediterranean influences, together with a continual drive for superior produce and a spirit of experimentation, are the major factors that continue to define Australian cuisine. Key dishes can immortalize indigenous produce, such as rare-roasted kangaroo with baby beets, or steamed barramundi with soy and ginger. At the same time, they can totally transform more universal ingredients such as char-grilled Atlantic salmon with preserved lemon and couscous.

But Australian cuisine is no slammed-together grab bag of fusion techniques or ingredients. It's brash, easygoing, big-flavored, fresh, and thoroughly natural. It's Japanese-born Tetsuya Wakuda's impossibly silky ocean trout confit with trout roe and konbu seaweed at Tetsuya's in Sydney, or Malaysian native Cheong Liew's bravely conceived braised chicken with sea scallops, veal sweetbreads, roasted fennel, and black moss at the Grange restaurant in Adelaide.

This is the sort of cooking that has made Australia a modern culinary force, and stamped Sydney as one of the three current food capitals of the world, along with New York and London. Let the academics ponder if it is a true cuisine or just a lifestyle. The rest of us will do the only sensible thing: head off to a great Australian restaurant and make up our own minds.

—Terry Durack

City Center, 2000 ☎*02/9267–2900* ♣*Reservations essential* ▱*AE, DC, MC, V* ⊘*Closed Sun. and Mon. No lunch Tues.–Fri.*

$$
★ ✕**Est.** This elegant, pillared dining room is the perfect setting for showing off chef Peter Doyle's modern, light touch with Mod-Oz cuisine. Anything Doyle cooks with scallops is divine; the crisp-skin John Dory fillet is also a sure bet, as is the lamb with sautéed spinach and eggplant caviar. The warm caramelized peach tart with peach-pistachio-nougat ice cream will test any dieter's resolve. ✉*Establishment Hotel, 252*

George St., City Center ☎02/9240–3010 ⚖Reservations essential ☰AE, DC, MC, V ⊘Closed Sun. No lunch Sat.

$–$$ ✗**glass brasserie.** Well-known Sydney chef Luke Mangan is at the helm of this stunning restaurant in the Hilton Sydney. The 40-foot floor-to-ceiling glass wall provides a perfect view of the stately, historic Queen Victoria Building next door. This 240-seat restaurant has become a favorite for business lunches, while after-hour diners start with a cocktail from the hip Zeta Bar. The Mod-Oz menu includes upscale appetizers such as salmon gravlax and Wagu steak tartare, and mains like the signature mustard-crusted sirloin. The restaurant has its own "master of wine," 1 of only 14 in Australia and 247 in the world, who has assembled a selection of more than 10,000 bottles. ⊠Hilton Sydney, 488 George St., City Center ☎02/9265–6065 ☰AE, DC, MC, V.

$ ✗**Bambini Trust.** It's hidden behind huge black doors in one of the city's historic sandstone buildings, but once you're inside you'd swear you were in Paris. Dark wood paneling, black-and-white photographs, and mirrors bearing the day's specials in flowing script lend a bistro feel. The fare is a little French, a little more Italian, and a fair sprinkling of Mod-Oz. Owners Angela and Michael Potts, who have run cafés for years, love their truffles; you'll find them mixed with the duck liver pâté and swirled with the potato mash that accompanies the barramundi fillets. The Italian ice cream or the chocolate and almond tart are a lovely way to round off a meal. A pre- or post meal drink in the marble-lined, chandelier-adorned Bambini Wine Room is a must. ⊠185 Elizabeth St., City Center ☎02/9283–7098 ☰AE, DC, MC, V ⊘Closed Sun.

STEAK

$–$$$ ✗**Prime.** Steak houses in Sydney were once old-fashioned affairs where men in dark suits scoffed down copious quantities of cheap red wine and charred red meat. Now, inspired by the likes of Smith & Wollensky and Maloney & Porcelli in New York, this subterranean diner elevates the image of the Aussie steak. The result is an elegant restaurant in what was once the staff canteen for the General Post Office. As well as serving some of the best steaks in town, Prime also has knockout seafood tortellini and poached barramundi with clams. The oysters are also superb. ⊠1 Martin Pl., City Center ☎02/9229–7777 ⚖Reservations essential ☰AE, DC, MC, V ⊘Closed Sun. No lunch Sat.

DARLINGHURST, KINGS CROSS & WOOLLOOMOOLOO

CAFÉS

¢–$ ✗**bills.** Named after celebrity chef and cookbook author Bill Granger,
Fodor'sChoice this sunny corner café is so addictive it should come with a health
★ warning. It's a favorite hangout of everyone from local nurses to semi-disguised rock stars, and you never know who you might be sitting next to at the newspaper-strewn communal table. If you're not interested in the creaminess of what must be Sydney's best scrambled eggs, try the ricotta hotcakes with honeycomb butter. Lunch choices include spring-onion pancakes with gravlax and the most famous steak sandwich in town. Dinner selections are similarly gourmet comfort food, like the chicken fricassee entrée. ⊠433 Liverpool St., Darlinghurst, 2010

1

☎02/9360–9631 ☱AE, MC, V ⓎBYO ⊗No dinner Sun. ✉352
Crown St., Surry Hills ☎02/9360–4762 ☱AE, MC, V.

¢ ✗**Goods Organic.** This friendly organic café and food store is the perfect
place to stop for a wholesome salad, chicken pie, or ragout of organic
goat and brown rice, while shopping in nearby trendy Darlinghurst. All
of the produce on the shelves, ingredients used in the meals, and tea and
coffee were grown on organic or biodynamic farms. Even the spring
water is flavored with organic mint leaves. Here's a place you can happily (and healthily!) browse for an hour or two. ✉253 Crown St.,
Darlinghurst ☎02/9357–6690 ☱MC, V ⊗Closed Sun. No dinner.

ITALIAN

$$ ✗**Otto.** Few restaurants have the magnetic pull of Otto, a place where
radio shock jocks sit side by side with fashion-magazine editors and
foodies. Yes, it's a scene. But fortunately it's a scene with good Ital-
ian food and waiters who have just enough attitude to make them a
challenge worth conquering. The homemade pastas are very good, the
slow-roasted duck with green lentils a benchmark, and the selection of
Italian wines expensive but rarely matched this far from Milan. Next
door is a sister restaurant, Nove Cucina, offering pizzas and dishes from
Otto's menu at lower prices. ✉Wharf at Woolloomooloo, 8 Cowper
Wharf Rd., Woolloomooloo ☎02/9368–7488 ⚓Reservations essen-
tial ☱AE, DC, MC, V ⊗Closed Mon.

PIZZA

¢–$ ✗**Hugo's Bar Pizza.** Hugo's is one of the hippest bars in Sydney, so when
it launched a pizzeria it had a built-in clientele queuing up for a seat at
its tiny tables with leather settees. Unless you're friends with the own-
ers, you should be prepared to wait, and wait, and wait to get into this
hot spot on bar- and club-lined Bayswater Road. Nurse an expensive
cocktail or overpriced beer while you wait to sink your teeth into the
gourmet thin-crust pizzas, which are absolutely worth every second
that you've stood in line. Everything is fresh, flavorful, and crispy; try
the pork-belly pie served on a slab of wood. The restaurant is so dimly
lighted no one will be able to tell if you've got sauce on your face.
✉19 Bayswater Rd., Kings Cross ☎02/9332–1227 ⚓Reservations
not accepted ☱AE, DC, MC, V ⊗No lunch.

SEAFOOD

¢–$ ✗**Fishface.** Get here early, score one of the tiny tables, and you'll be
★ able to dig into some of the most scrumptious seafood in Australia. The
best sashimi-grade fish in the country—which is as good as it comes—is
served up here to discerning locals. Menu highlights include the pea
and yabby (freshwater crayfish) soup, and the tuna, always served rare
and moist. The fish-and-chips redefine the nation's favorite take-out
order. Reservations aren't accepted after 7 PM. ✉132 Darlinghurst Rd.,
Darlinghurst ☎02/9332–4803 ☱MC, V ⓎBYO, corkage fee A$4.50
⊗Closed Sun. No lunch.

PADDINGTON & WOOLLAHRA

AUSTRALIAN

$ ✗**Four in Hand.** At this cute, popular little pub in Paddington, chef Colin Fassnidge makes a splash with dishes such as the kingfish carpaccio with crab and grapefruit salad. The two-course lunches Friday to Sunday (A$39) are popular with diners. ⊠*105 Sutherland St., Paddington* ☎*02/9362-1999* ⊟*AE, DC, MC, V* ⊘*No lunch Mon.–Thurs.*

FRENCH

$$$$ ✗**Claude's.** This tiny, unprepossessing restaurant proves that good
Fodor'sChoice things really do come in small packages. This was the first restaurant to
★ serve Australia's cultivated black truffles, and that interest in broadening the palates of its diners continues under the leadership of Singaporean chef-owner Chui Lee Lu. With an emphasis on East-West fusion, dishes like the Burgundy-style sautéed freshwater crayfish and guinea fowl are masterly delights, while the champagne violet bomb is a dessert with impact. ⊠*10 Oxford St., Woollahra, 2025* ☎*02/9331–2325* ⌂*Reservations essential* ⊟*AE, MC, V* ⌂*BYO, corkage fee A$15* ⊘*Closed Sun. and Mon. No lunch.*

$–$$ ✗**Bistro Moncur.** Archetypically loud and proud, this bistro in the Woollahra Hotel spills over with happy-go-lucky patrons—mostly locals from around the leafy suburb of Woollahra—who don't mind waiting a half hour for a table. The best dishes are inspired takes on Parisian fare, like the grilled Sirloin Café de Paris and the Bistro Moncur pure pork sausages with potato puree and Lyonnaise onions. There is a focus on fresh, high-quality ingredients—even the coffee at the end of the meal comes from a fancy espresso machine. ⊠*Woollahra Hotel, 116 Queen St., Woollahra* ☎*02/9363–2519* ⌂*Reservations not accepted* ⊟*AE, DC, MC, V* ⊘*No lunch Mon.*

ITALIAN

$$–$$$ ✗**Buon Ricordo.** Walking into this happy, bubbly place is like turning
Fodor'sChoice up at a private party in the backstreets of Naples. Host, chef, and
★ surrogate uncle Armando Percuoco invests classic Neapolitan and Tuscan techniques with inventive personal touches to produce such dishes as warmed figs with Gorgonzola and prosciutto, truffled egg pasta, and scampi with saffron sauce and black-ink risotto. The fettuccine *al tartufovo*, with eggs, cream, and Reggiano cheese, is legendary. Everything comes with Italian-style touches that you can see, feel, smell, and taste. Leaving the restaurant feels like leaving home, especially if you've partaken of the wonderful six-course degustation menu (A$115). ⊠*108 Boundary St., Paddington, 2021* ☎*02/9360–6729* ⌂*Reservations essential* ⊟*AE, DC, MC, V* ⊘*Closed Sun. and Mon. No lunch Tues.–Thurs.*

POTTS POINT

ITALIAN

¢–$$ ✗**Fratelli Paradiso.** Fratelli (meaning "brothers") is run by the Paradiso
★ family, whose Italian heritage shows in everything from the *bomba* (like a donut) served in their adjoining bakery to the friendly service. Arrive

1

early to find local devotees sipping their morning constitutional caffeine along with rice pudding, or join the buzz of lunchtime diners. Dinner choices include the mouthwatering penne with a veal ragu, while the zucchini-flower-and-fontina risotto is the stuff local legends are built on. ⊠*12–16 Challis Ave., Potts Point* ☎*02/9357–1744* ⚒*Reservations not accepted* ☰*AE, DC, MC, V* ⊘*No dinner weekends.*

MODERN AUSTRALIAN

$ ✕**Lotus.** With its fabulous back bar and pencil-thin diners, the food probably doesn't have to be as good as it is at this ultracool inner-city restaurant. Located on leafy Challis Avenue, just past where the riff-raff of Kings Cross gives way to the urban chic of Potts Point, Lotus is a study in cool. Start with the twice-baked Gruyère soufflé before moving on to the fennel-spiced pork cutlet. Punctuate each course with an inventive, and potent, cocktail, and turn your evening meal into a big night out. ⊠*22 Challis Ave., Potts Point* ☎*02/9326–9000* ⚒*Reservations not accepted* ☰*AE, DC, MC, V* ⊘*Closed Sun. and Mon. No lunch.*

SURRY HILLS

CHINESE

¢–$$ ✕**Billy Kwong.** Locals rub shoulders while eating no-fuss Chinese food
★ at TV chef Kylie Kwong's trendy drop-in restaurant. Kwong prepares the kind of food her family cooks, with Grandma providing not just the inspiration but also the recipes. Even the dumplings are made by specialty chefs from Shanghai. If you have a big appetite, indulge in a variety of dishes with Kylie's banquet (A$75). Although the table you're occupying is probably being eyed by the next set of adoring fans, staffers never rush you. But you could always play nice and ask for the bill through your last mouthful of scallops with XO sauce or steamed wontons. ⊠*3/355 Crown St., Surry Hills* ☎*02/9332–3300* ⚒*Reservations not accepted* ☰*AE, MC, V* ⦿*BYO, corkage fee A$5* ⊘*Closed Mon. No lunch.*

FRENCH

$$–$$$ ✕**Marque.** Chef Mark Best insists on exemplary service and great food at this elegant Surry Hills restaurant. Few chefs approach French flavors with such passion and dedication (and stints alongside three-star demigods Alain Passard in Paris and Raymond Blanc in England haven't done any harm either). Best's roast South Australian jewfish with potato anglaise and shallot confit is a triumph, while the beetroot tart with fresh horseradish sauce turns the humble vegetable into a tantalizing treat. The eight-course tasting menu (A$125) will transport you to foodie heaven. ⊠*355 Crown St., Surry Hills* ☎*02/9332–2225* ⚒*Reservations essential* ☰*AE, DC, MC, V* ⊘*Closed Sun. No lunch.*

THAI

¢–$$$ ✕**Longrain.** Start with a cool cocktail in the minimalist bar, where
★ Sydney's high life gathers around low-slung tables. Then make for the dining room, where the hip crowd jostles for a position at one of three

giant wooden communal tables—it might be trendy, but the food is terrific. Chef Martin Boetz aimed to make this restaurant a leader among Sydney's Thai spots, and managed to score a double whammy: a smoldering bar scene and an outstanding eatery. His duck, venison, tuna, beef shin, and pork hock each marry style with substance. Reservations are not accepted for dinner. ⊠ *85 Commonwealth St., Surry Hills* ☎ *02/9280–2888* ⊟ *AE, DC, MC, V* ⊘ *Closed Sun. No lunch weekends.*

BONDI BEACH & EASTERN SUBURBS

ITALIAN

$$–$$$
Fodor'sChoice
★ ✕**Icebergs Dining Room and Bar.** The fashionable and famous (including celebrities like Mick Jagger) just adore perching like seagulls over the swimming pool at the south end of Australia's most famous beach. The bar is a scene unto itself, with a tasty menu of bar snacks like polenta chips and oysters, and killer cocktails like the Icebergs T—a proprietary mix of vodka, Nocello, crushed mint, and chilled black tea. Once you move into the restaurant and situate yourself on a low-back suede seat, check your reflection in the frosted glass and prepare to indulge in sophisticated Italian creations like Livornese-style fish stew and grilled quail with grape salad. ⊠ *1 Notts Ave., Bondi Beach, 2026* ☎ *02/9365–9000* ⌂ *Reservations essential* ⊟ *AE, DC, MC, V* ⊘ *Closed Mon.*

¢–$
✕**North Bondi Italian Food.** This popular spot is more casual and less expensive than Icebergs (both are owned by stylish restaurateur Maurice Terzini), yet the trendy interior and great balcony overlooking the beach are sure to dazzle. The broad menu has more than 60 dishes (appetizers, entrées, and desserts) and is best described as home-style Italian. The restaurant does not accept reservations, so arrive early to snag a table. ⊠ *118–120 Ramsgate Ave., North Bondi* ☎ *02/9300–4400* ⌂ *Reservations not accepted* ⊟ *AE, DC, MC, V* ⊘ *No lunch Mon. and Tues.*

MODERN AUSTRALIAN

¢–$
✕**Swell.** When you finish the famous Bondi to Bronte coastal cliff walk, this is a great place for a meal. By day it's a casual café, but at night it becomes more formal, thanks to white linen tablecloths and tea lights. The salt-and-pepper squid with tamari and chili makes a great light lunch (or appetizer at dinner). When the sun goes down, order a cocktail while you decide between the crisp-skinned salmon with crab-stuffed zucchini blossoms, the pan-roasted spatchcock, or one of the fresh seafood dishes from the daily specials. Don't forget to listen for the surf lapping 100 yards away. ⊠ *465 Bronte Rd., Bronte* ☎ *02/9386–5001* ⊟ *AE, MC, V.*

SEAFOOD

$$
Fodor'sChoice
★ ✕**Pier.** With its wraparound harbor views and shipshape good looks, this wharf restaurant is a great place to enjoy Australia's finest seafood. (Some well-known foodies even say it's the best in the country.) Chef Greg Doyle knows his fish, and manages to reach beyond the

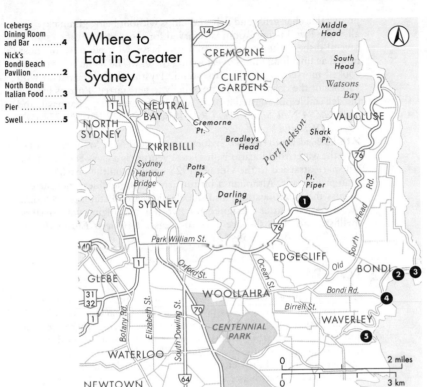

Where to
Eat in Greater
Sydney

predictable char-grills and fish-and-chips without being gimmicky. The all-white Pier Tasting Room is reserved for those who want to sample several dishes. The space is casual yet classy, with white stools positioned against long tables overlooking the bay. The menu has raw and cooked morsels, oysters, and sashimi. Try the chilled gazpacho with yabbies or the crispy skinned pork belly to get started. Entrées include the delectable pot-roasted lobster with Kaffir lime leaf, Thai basil, and chili. ⊠ *594 New South Head Rd., Rose Bay, 2029* ☎ *02/9327–6561* ▭ *AE, DC, MC, V.*

¢–$ ✕ **Nick's Bondi Beach Pavilion.** Sydney restaurateur Nick Manettas likes to grab the waterfront locations; his latest venture is a glass-encased modern space attached to the vintage-1928 pavilion on the beach's pedestrian promenade. Although a bit touristy for some diners, no one can dismiss the great location, and the classic seafood staples—including the three-tied platter (designed for two diners) bulging with oysters, shellfish, and crayfish—are sure to please. ⊠ *Queen Elizabeth Dr., Bondi Beach* ☎ *02/9365–4122* ▭ *AE, DC, MC.*

WHERE TO STAY

From grand hotels with white-glove service to tucked-away bed-and-breakfasts, there's lodging to fit all styles and budgets in Sydney. The best addresses in town are undoubtedly at the Rocks, where the tranquil setting and harbor views are right near major cultural attractions, restaurants, shops, and galleries. The area around Kings Cross is another major hotel district, as well as a backpacker magnet. Keep in mind, however, that this is also the city's major nightlife district, and the scene can get pretty raucous after sunset.

WHAT IT COSTS IN AUSTRALIAN DOLLARS				
$$$$	**$$$**	**$$**	**$**	**¢**
FOR TWO PEOPLE	over A$450	A$301–A$450	A$201–A$300	A$150–A$200	under A$150

Prices are for two people in a standard double room in high season, including tax and service, based on the European Plan (with no meals) unless otherwise noted.

THE ROCKS & CIRCULAR QUAY

$$$$ ▦ **Observatory Hotel.** More English country manor than inner-city
Fodor's Choice   hotel, this gorgeous property feels like a decadent, luxurious sanctuary. The spacious rooms, with their Venetian- and Asian-inspired decor, have mahogany furnishings, antique reproductions, and plush fabrics. The spectacular indoor pool is surrounded by marble and potted palms, with a fresco of a starry night on the ceiling. You can have a drink and check your e-mail with the Wi-Fi in the Globe Bar, Galileo Restaurant, lounge, and lobby. The hotel's single weakness is its lack of views, but that's like saying the Mona Lisa's single weakness is her crooked smile. ⊠ *89–113 Kent St., The Rocks, 2000* ☎ *02/9256–2222* 🖷 *02/9256–2233* ⊕ *www.observatoryhotel.com.au* ⟿ *79 rooms, 21 suites* ᕤ *In-room: safe, VCR, Wi-Fi. In-hotel: restaurant, room ser-*

★

vice, bar, pool, gym, concierge, laundry service, public Wi-Fi, parking (fee), no-smoking rooms ▭AE, DC, MC, V ⍩BP.

$$$$
Fodor's Choice
★

▢▢**Park Hyatt Sydney.** Moored in the shadow of Harbour Bridge, the Park Hyatt is the first choice for visiting celebrities (a minor irony, considering that the thousands who cross the bridge each day get a bird's-eye view of the guests lazing about the hotel's rooftop pool). Rooms here are decorated with reproductions of classical statuary, contemporary bronzes, and Australian artwork. Nearly all the spacious, elegant rooms have balconies and views of the Opera House. This is also the only hotel in Australia with full-time personal butler service in all rooms. Excellent Australian cuisine awaits at the restaurant. ✉7 Hickson Rd., Circular Quay, 2000 ☎02/9241–1234 ✆02/9256–1555 ⊕www.sydney.park.hyatt.com ⬫122 rooms, 36 suites ♿In-room: safe, ethernet. In-hotel: restaurant, room service, bars, pool, gym, spa, concierge, laundry service, Wi-Fi, parking (fee), no-smoking rooms ▭AE, DC, MC, V.

$$$$

▢▢**Quay West Suites Sydney.** Bordering the Rocks and the central business and shopping district, this statuesque tower combines the space and comforts of an apartment with the amenities of a five-star hotel. Luxurious one- and two-bedroom units, all on the eighth floor or higher, each have a lounge, dining room, full kitchen, and laundry. All apartments have either harbor or city views, and some of the more expensive Harbour View Suites have balconies. Round-the-clock room service, a glamorous health club, and a trendy restaurant and bar add even more panache. ✉98 Gloucester St., The Rocks, 2000 ☎02/9240–6000 ✆02/9240–6060 ⊕www.mirvachotels.com.au ⬫121 suites ♿In-room: safe, kitchen, VCR, dial-up. In-hotel: restaurant, room service, bar, pool, gym, concierge, laundry service, public Internet, parking (fee), no-smoking rooms ▭AE, DC, MC, V.

$$$–$$$$
★

▢▢**Four Seasons Hotel Sydney.** Although it's the oldest of Sydney's elite hotels, continual upgrades and refinement have kept this landmark a favorite. Silk furnishings, mahogany timbers, marble bathrooms, and warm hues create opulence in the large rooms (those above the 20th floor have better views). Thoughtful touches for business travelers are everywhere, including enormous room safes that can easily accommodate your laptop, and mobile phones for rent. Executive Club rooms on Level 32 come with extras like meeting rooms and complimentary breakfasts. The spa offers treatments, like the frangipani wrap, that marry exotic ingredients with Australian Aboriginal healing formulas. ✉199 George St., Circular Quay, 2000 ☎02/9238–0000 ✆02/9251–2851 ⊕www.fourseasons.com/sydney ⬫417 rooms, 114 suites ♿In-room: safe, ethernet. In-hotel: restaurant, room service, bar, pool, gym, spa, concierge, laundry service, public Internet, parking (fee), no-smoking rooms ▭AE, DC, MC, V.

$$$–$$$$
★

▢▢**Hotel Inter-Continental Sydney.** This sleek, sophisticated hotel rises from the sandstone facade of the historic Treasury Building. It's also near the harbor and within easy walking distance of Circular Quay, the Opera House, and the central business district. North-facing rooms overlook Harbour Bridge, while those on the eastern side of the hotel overlook the Royal Botanic Gardens. Rooms have window seats for taking in the views, as well as remote-controlled blinds to tune out the bright Sydney sunshine. The decor features brown-and-white suede—including funky checkered, padded headboards on the beds. Four executive floors have separate check-in, complimentary breakfast and cocktails, meeting rooms, and access to the wonderful views of the rooftop lounge on the 32nd floor. The Mediterranean-inspired Mint restaurant and bar downstairs are major hot spots. ⊠*117 Macquarie St., Circular Quay, 2000* ☎*02/9253–9000* 🖷*02/9240–1240* ⊕*www. intercontinental.com* ⇆*475 rooms, 28 suites* ⟁*In-room: safe, dial-up. In-hotel: 3 restaurants, room service, bar, pool, gym, spa, concierge, laundry service, public Wi-Fi, parking (fee), no-smoking rooms* ▤*AE, DC, MC, V.*

$$$–$$$$ 🏨 **Shangri-La Hotel Sydney.** Towering above Walsh Bay from its prime
★ position alongside the Sydney Harbour Bridge, this sleek hotel is *the* place for a room with a view. North-facing rooms overlooking the water are the best; views on the other sides—Darling Harbour, the city, or the eastern suburbs—are less impressive. Rooms are large, modestly opulent, and decorated in pleasing autumnal colors. With a private bar and lounge, the Horizon Club floor offers impeccable service, with a purser to look after your needs. Altitude restaurant and the adjacent Blu Horizon bar on the 36th floor provide terrific views of Sydney Harbour, especially in the evening. Look for deals on one-night stays over weekends. ⊠*176 Cumberland St., The Rocks, 2000* ☎*02/9250–6000* 🖷*02/9250–6250* ⊕*www.shangri-la.com/eng/hotel/index.asp* ⇆*531 rooms, 32 suites* ⟁*In-room: safe, ethernet. In-hotel: 3 restaurants, room service, bars, pool, gym, spa, concierge, laundry service, public Internet, parking (fee), no-smoking rooms* ▤*AE, DC, MC, V.*

$$–$$$ 🏨 **Harbour Rocks Hotel.** Formerly a wool-storage facility, this four-story hotel provides good value for its location, although its historic character is confined to the exterior of the 150-year-old building. Tidy rooms are modestly furnished in the style of British hotels from the 1980s, with a color scheme in red and cream and overstuffed armchairs and settees. Top-floor rooms on the east side afford glimpses of Circular Quay and the Opera House, while the penthouse suite is a secluded little gem with fantastic views. The restaurant is called Lanes—so named because the terrace has a view over the intriguing back lanes of The Rocks. ⊠*34–52 Harrington St., The Rocks, 2000* ☎*02/8220–9999* 🖷*02/8220–9998* ⊕*www.harbourrocks.com. au* ⇆*55 rooms* ⟁*In-room: safe. In-hotel: restaurant, bar, laundry service, no-smoking rooms* ▤*AE, DC, MC, V* ⦿|*BP.*

$$–$$$ 🏨 **Sydney Harbour Marriott.** This modern high-rise hotel on the harbor's edge is a minute's walk from Circular Quay, a two-minute stroll from the Rocks, and a short distance from Pitt Street's best shopping. Many rooms have harbor views, with the best vistas from the executive rooms on the top five floors and the executive lounge on the 30th floor. A drink in the historic Customs Bar is always a lively affair, while Icon's restaurant is popular not only for its seafood buffet but the wine buffet, where A$17 means a bottomless glass of wine with dinner. ⊠*30 Pitt St., City Center, 2000* ☎*02/9259–7000* 🖷*02/9251–1122* ⊕*www. Marriott.com.au/sydm* ⇆*508 rooms, 42 suites* ⟁*In-room: VCR, eth-*

1

ernet. *In-hotel: 2 restaurants, room service, bar, pool, gym, laundry service, parking (fee), no-smoking rooms* 🖃*DC, MC, V.*

$$ 🖭**The Russell.** For charm, character, and central location, it's hard to beat this ornate Victorian hotel. No two rooms are the same, but all have fresh flowers, down pillows, and Gilchrist & Soames toiletries. The spacious double rooms at the front have views of Circular Quay. There are also somewhat quieter standard-size double rooms overlooking Nurses Walk or opening onto an inner courtyard. Ceiling fans and windows allow for a breeze in all rooms, and the rooftop garden is a delight, especially in the evening. This historic building has four floors but no elevator; winding corridors and the steep, narrow staircase to the reception desk can be challenging for those with impaired mobility. ✉*143A George St., The Rocks, 2000* 🕾*02/9241–3543* 🖷*02/9252–1652* ⊕*www.therussell.com.au* ⇖*26 rooms, 16 with bath; 1 suite; 1 apartment* ⟁*In-room: no a/c. In-hotel: restaurant, no elevator* 🖃*AE, DC, MC, V* ⑩*CP.*

$–$$ 🖭**Rendezvous Stafford Hotel Sydney.** Situated in the heart of the historic Rocks precinct, the lodging has a boutique-hotel style. The accommodations are a stone's throw from the attractions around Circular Quay, and several rooms have large picture windows with spectacular views of the Opera House. (The terrace restaurant has a similar view.) If you hanker for something a little different—and more charming—seven historic two-story houses are available. Each has a bedroom and bathroom upstairs, and lounge (with sofa bed) and kitchen downstairs. The houses are ideal for families or extended vacationers. ✉*75 Harrington St., The Rocks, 2000* 🕾*02/9251–6711* 🖷*02/9251–3458* ⊕*www.rendezvoushotels.com/sydney* ⇖*59 apartments, 7 terrace houses* ⟁*In-room: safe, kitchen, VCR, ethernet. In-hotel: pool, gym, spa, laundry service, public Wi-Fi, parking (fee)* 🖃*AE, DC, MC, V.*

CITY CENTER

$$$$ 🖭**Westin Sydney.** The Westin hotel chain is renowned for its heavenly
★ beds—in Sydney it offers heavenly service, too. The staff here is cool, efficient, capable, and stylish as at a boutique hotel, but without the hipper-than-thou attitude. Located on stately Martin Place in the center of Sydney's central business district, the hotel's 31-story building incorporates the ornate, Victorian-era shell of Sydney's former General Post Office. Heritage Rooms, in the original building, have soaring ceilings, tall windows, and opulent decor. High-design Tower Rooms have stainless steel, aquamarine glass, and floor-to-ceiling windows for panoramic city views. ✉*1 Martin Pl., City Center, 2000* 🕾*02/8223–1111* 🖷*02/8223–1222* ⊕*www.westin.com.au* ⇖*370 rooms, 51 suites* ⟁*In-room: safe, ethernet. In-hotel: 2 restaurants, room service, bar, pool, gym, concierge, laundry service, public Internet, public Wi-Fi, parking (fee), no-smoking rooms* 🖃*AE, DC, MC, V.*

$$–$$$ 🖭**Hilton Sydney.** At this landmark hotel in downtown Sydney, you enter a spacious, light-filled lobby displaying a stunning four-story sculpture. Among the five different room types are 31 relaxation rooms divided into three zones: relaxation space, spa bathroom, and work

zone. Whirlpool baths, body-jet showers, and the latest electronic wizardry are just some of the features. The glass brassiere, run by well-known Sydney chef Luke Mangan, and trendy bar Zeta, designed by New Yorker Tony Chi, are hip places to eat and meet. The circa-1890 Marble Bar also attracts a crowd. The hotel is home to LivingWell, the largest hotel-based health club in Australia, offering group fitness, yoga, and Pilates classes, as well as a plethora of pampering treatments. *⊠488 George St., City Center, 2000 ☎02/9265–2000 🌐www.hiltonsydney.com.au ⇨550 rooms, 27 suites ☝In-room: DVD, Wi-Fi. In-hotel: restaurant, pool, gym, spa ▭AE, DC, MC, V.*

$$–$$$ **Medina Grand Harbourside.** A Darling Harbour setting, balconies with water views, and moderate rates make Medina Grand Harbourside a great choice for families who want apartment-style lodgings within walking distance of Sydney's major attractions. Large, bright studios and one-bedroom units approximate the look of a more stylish hotel, with bold-color velour couches and chairs. Most bathrooms lack tubs, but all apartments have kitchenettes with full cooking facilities. Book online for discounts. *⊠55 Shelley St., King St. Wharf, Darling Harbour, 2000 ☎02/9249–7000 🖷02/9249–6900 🌐www.medinaapartments.com.au ⇨114 apartments ☝In-room: safe, kitchen, ethernet. In-hotel: restaurant, room service, pool, gym, laundry service, parking (fee), no-smoking rooms ▭AE, DC, MC, V.*

$$ **Blacket Hotel.** A study in minimalist chic, this small hotel in a former bank building has been on Sydney's hot list since its debut in 2001. From the moment you step into the fashionably dim, charcoal-and-off-white reception area, the setting delivers the requisite degree of cool. Its great location, at the corner of busy George Street, ensures a steady stream of repeat corporate clientele. Rates are low, as is the price of the continental breakfast (A$7.50). The one- and two-bedroom apartments and loft suites all have kitchenettes, whirlpool tubs, and washing machines. Those wanting to sample the city's nightlife need only take the elevator down to the Privilege Bar, deep within the old bank vault. *⊠70 King St., City Center, 2000 ☎02/9279–3030 🖷02/9279–3020 🌐www.theblacket.com ⇨26 rooms, 5 suites, 9 apartments ☝In-room: kitchen (some). In-hotel: restaurant, bar, public Wi-Fi, parking (fee) ▭AE, DC, MC, V.*

¢ ★ **Y Hotel Hyde Park.** Comfortable, affordable lodgings in a prime city location means that rooms here are often booked months in advance. Dorms with shared bathrooms sleep four, while the family, deluxe, and corporate rooms include a fruit platter, daily newspaper, French-press coffeemaker, and toiletries. Studios have a kitchenette, in-room safe, and Internet connection. *⊠5–11 Wentworth Ave., near corner of Hyde Park and Oxford St., City Center, 2010 ☎02/9264–2451 🖷02/9285–6288 🌐www.yhotel.com.au ⇨11 dorm rooms with shared baths, 6 studios, 104 rooms ☝In-room: no phone (some), refrigerator (some), no TV (some), ethernet (some). In-hotel: restaurant, no-smoking rooms ▭AE, DC, MC, V 🍴BP.*

1

PADDINGTON & WOOLLAHRA

¢–$$ ⚏**The Hughenden.** This cozy, friendly converted Victorian mansion is ideal for those who steer clear of big city hotels. Built by a pioneering doctor in the late 19th century (and now owned by an artist-writer couple), the property has loads of character. Writers' groups meet here regularly, there's high tea on winter weekends, and special events (like Australia Day and Melbourne Cup) are always celebrated. Rooms are decorated in a modern-country style. Just across the road is Veronica's, a three-story terraced house popular with families (from A$358 a night). After enjoying the made-to-order breakfast, you can relax on the porch or stroll across the well-manicured lawns of this Anglophile's dream estate. The prestigious eastern suburbs address is close to the great shops of Oxford Street, Centennial Park, and trendy Paddington, while the city and the eastern beaches are just 10–15 minutes away by public transportation. ⊠*14 Queen St., Woollahra, 2025* ☎*02/9363–4863* 🖶*02/9362–0398* ⊕*www.hughendenhotel. com.au* ⤴*36 rooms* ♿*In-room: dial-up. In-hotel: restaurant, bar, parking (no fee), no-smoking rooms, some pets allowed (fee)* ⊟*AE, DC, MC, V* ❢⃝*BP.*

$ ⚏**Sullivans Hotel.** Set on a quiet stretch in the trendy shopping pre-
★   cinct of Paddington, this small, friendly, family-run hotel has simple accommodations at an outstanding price. Garden rooms overlook an Italianate central courtyard and pool; the corner rooms, Numbers 116, 216, and 316, are the largest and quietest. Triple-glazed windows mean rooms overlooking bustling Oxford Street aren't bombarded by traffic noise. Those on the third floor have harbor views. Extras include free in-house movies. The location, close to shops, restaurants, and nightlife, is a 15-minute walk from the city center. ⊠*21 Oxford St., Darlinghurst, Paddington, 2021* ☎*02/9361–0211* 🖶*02/9360–3735* ⊕*www.sullivans.com.au* ⤴*64 rooms* ♿*In-room: refrigerator, dial-up. In-hotel: restaurant, pool, bicycles, public Wi-Fi, public Internet, parking (no fee)* ⊟*AE, DC, MC, V.*

EAST OF THE CITY

$$$$ ⚏**BLUE Sydney.** This ultra-hip hotel, part of the prestigious Taj Hotel
★   group of India, occupies a former warehouse. Guests love the authentic structures of the former wharf (pulleys, giant trusses, and brontosaurus-like machinery) and its location (a stone's throw from the Opera House). The lobby is dominated by the hip Water Bar, one of Sydney's places to see and be seen. Guest rooms, which have a light, bright, cappuccino color scheme, are arranged like the cabins on a luxury liner, rising in tiers on the outside of the central cavity. There are five restaurants in the adjoining wharf complex. *Wharf at Woolloomooloo* ⊠*Cowper Wharf Rd., Woolloomooloo, 2011* ☎*02/9331–9000* 🖶*02/9331–9031* ⊕*www.tajhotels.com* ⤴*100 rooms, 36 suites* ♿*In-room: safe, VCR, ethernet. In-hotel: restaurant, bar, pool, gym, concierge, laundry service, public Internet, parking (fee), no-smoking rooms* ⊟*AE, DC, MC, V.*

$$–$$$ ⊞**Medusa.** If you're tired of the standard traveler's rooms, this reno-
★   vated Victorian terrace house may be just the tonic. Having under-
gone a massive conversion into 21st-century cool, it sports a decorating
scheme of brash colors—blues, yellows, and creams splashed against
reds—and furnishings (platform beds, chaise longues, and so on) that
might have come direct from a Milan design gallery. Every room is
slightly different, and each has a kitchenette. Behind the glamour is a
comfortable, well-run hotel with friendly, attentive staff. This is one
of the few city hotels that welcomes guests' dogs. ⊠*267 Darlinghurst
Rd., Darlinghurst, 2010* ☎*02/9331–1000* 🖷*02/9380–6901* ⊕*www.
medusa.com.au* ⇘*18 rooms* ⌂*In-room: safe, kitchen. In-hotel: bar,
no elevator, public Wi-Fi, some pets allowed* ⊟*AE, DC, MC, V.*

$$ ⊞**Kirketon.** The small hotel is elevated to an art form in this stylish,
intricately designed building. Striking glass doors at the entryway take
you into a minimalist foyer, which then leads to coffee-and-cream-color
guest rooms that are a study in simplicity. Furnishings blend 1950s
classics with European imports, although the relentless pursuit of style
sometimes intrudes into the comfort zone (for example, rooms lack
comfortable chairs). If you don't mind suffering slightly for fashion's
sake, though, there's no better address. Tech junkies will appreciate
the wireless Internet access throughout the hotel, and fitness fanatics
can utilize free passes to a nearby gym. ⊠*229 Darlinghurst Rd., Dar-
linghurst, 2010* ☎*02/9332–2011* 🖷*02/9332–2499* ⊕*www.kirketon.
com.au* ⇘*40 rooms* ⌂*In-room: safe, kitchen, dial-up, Wi-Fi. In-hotel:
restaurant, bar, no elevator, concierge, no-smoking rooms, public Wi-Fi*
⊟*AE, DC, MC, V.*

$$ ⊞**Regents Court.** Known for its contemporary style, this boutique hotel
★   is one of Sydney's best-kept secrets. The mood is intimate yet relaxed,
and the location in a cul-de-sac in Potts Point is quiet. Each room has
its own well-equipped kitchenette, and many have an extra pull-down
bed in addition to the queen-size bed. There's always an artist or writer
in residence, and you're bound to meet someone for an interesting
chat in the comfy ground-floor guest lounge while making yourself
a coffee or sipping on complimentary wine. There are a host of good
restaurants nearby, but experienced patrons head upstairs to eat take-
out meals and watch the sun set amid the glorious rooftop gardens.
⊠*18 Springfield Ave., Potts Point, Kings Cross, 2011* ☎*02/9358–
1533* 🖷*02/9358–1833* ⊕*www.regentscourt.com.au* ⇘*30 rooms*
⌂*In-room: kitchen, DVD. In-hotel: concierge, laundry service, public
Internet, parking (fee)* ⊟*AE, DC, MC, V.*

¢–$ ⊞**The Chelsea.** The motto of this beautiful guesthouse is "Come home
Fodor'sChoice   to the Chelsea"—and it won't be long before you're wishing it were
★   *your* home. Occupying adjoining Victorian houses on a quiet, leafy
street between Darlinghurst and Rushcutters Bay, this B&B is luxurious and warmly inviting. Rooms are either deluxe, done in a French
provincial style with fireplaces and frosted glass bathrooms, or smaller
and more contemporary, with shared facilities. Room 13 has a private
courtyard with a fancy fountain; Room 7 is the largest of the contemporary units, with iron-trellised windows. The four rooms without private facilities are a great value (A$94 a night), and are only steps away

from two shared bathrooms. You can use the modern, well-equipped kitchen to do your own cooking—although a Continental breakfast is included. ⊠*49 Womerah Ave., Darlinghurst, 2010* ☏*02/9380–5994* 🖷*02/9332–2491* ⊕*www.chelseaguesthouse.com.au* ☎*13 rooms; 9 with bath* ⚙*In-hotel: restaurant, no elevator, public Internet, no-smoking rooms* ⊟*AE, DC, MC, V* ⓄⓁ*CP.*

¢-$ 🖥**De Vere Hotel.** "Simply comfortable and affordable" is the slogan at this 1920s-style hotel at the leafy end of Potts Point, and it's hard to disagree on either count. Location and price are also major draws of this friendly hotel that has a mini-facelift every year to keep it looking neat. Rooms are spacious; some standard accommodations have balconies, while the studio apartments include kitchenettes. Good standby rates are available through the Internet. ⊠*46 Macleay St., Potts Point, Kings Cross, 2011* ☏*02/9358–1211* 🖷*02/9358–4685* ⊕*www.devere. com.au* ☎*100 rooms* ⚙*In-room: kitchen (some). In-hotel: restaurant, laundry service, parking (fee)* ⊟*AE, DC, MC, V.*

¢-$ 🖥**Hotel 59 & Cafe.** In its character as well as its dimensions, this friendly B&B on a quiet part of a bar- and club-lined street is reminiscent of a European *pensione*. Simple, tastefully outfitted rooms come with high-quality beds and linens, as well as wooden blinds over the windows. Access to the four floors of rooms is via a small staircase, and there is no elevator. Despite its proximity to the heart of Kings Cross, the hotel has a relaxed, serene atmosphere. There's a two-night minimum stay; book online for cheaper rates. ⊠*59 Bayswater Rd., Kings Cross, 2011* ☏*02/9360–5900* 🖷*02/9360–1828* ⊕*www.hotel59.com.au* ☎*9 rooms* ⚙*In-hotel: restaurant, no elevator* ⊟*MC, V* ⓄⓁ*BP.*

¢-$ 🖥**Victoria Court Sydney.** A small, smart hotel on a Potts Point street lined with budget accommodations, the Victoria Court is appealing for more than just its reasonable rates. Hand-painted tiles and etched-glass doors recall the hotel's Victorian ancestry, yet the rooms come with the modern blessings of en suite bathrooms and comfortable beds. Most rooms have marble fireplaces, some have four-poster beds, and a few have balconies overlooking Victoria Street. The leafy courtyard is the perfect place to have breakfast and read the morning paper. ⊠*122 Victoria St., Potts Point, Kings Cross, 2011* ☏*02/9357–3200* 🖷*02/9357–7606* ⊕*www.victoriacourt.com.au* ☎*25 rooms* ⊟*AE, DC, MC, V* ⓄⓁ*CP.*

BONDI BEACH & MANLY

$$$ 🖥**Sebel Manly Beach.** On a secluded corner of the main beachside drag at Manly, this boutique hotel is one of the best places to stay at this busy tourist mecca. The hotel is a mixture of studios and one- and two-bedroom suites, all with private balconies; the more spacious accommodations have hot tubs, kitchenettes, and high-tech goodies. Will and Toby's, the new restaurant, serves until midnight. ⊠*8–13 S. Steyne, Manly, 2037* ☏*02/9552–1141* 🖷*02/9692–9462* ⊕*www. mirvachotels.com.au* ☎*83 rooms* ⚙*In-room: kitchen (some), ethernet. In-hotel: restaurant, room service, bar, pools, laundry facilities, parking (fee)* ⊟*AE, DC, MC, V* ⓄⓁ*CP.*

$$$ ⊞ **Swiss Grand Resort & Spa.** With the beach just across the road, a rooftop pool, and a relaxing day spa, a stay at the Swiss Grand makes it easy to forget that you're just 15 minutes away from the action of Sydney. Ask for one of the 65 beachfront rooms, as the rest face the sometimes-noisy side streets of this crowded beachside suburb. The hotel, which resembles a huge wedding cake, is often buzzing with wedding parties on weekends, so look out for the good selection of inexpensive package deals for families and couples at other times. ⊠ *Campbell Parade at Beach Rd., Bondi Beach, 2026* ☎ *02/9365–5666* ⊜ *02/9365–5330* ⊕ *www.swissgrand.com.au* ⤴ *203 suites* ⟑ *In-hotel: 3 restaurants, bars, pools, gym, spa, public Internet, parking (no fee)* ⊟ *AE, DC, MC, V.*

> ## A SEA OF TALENT
>
> A steel whale's tail sticking out of the ocean and retro kettles cunningly disguised as penguins strapped to a huge rock being lashed by waves are some of the imaginative artworks that have wowed visitors to the annual show called **Sculpture by the Sea** (⊕ *www.sculpturebythesea. com.au*). Since 1996, artists from 15 countries have positioned their sculptures on and under rocky outcrops and on hilltops along the much-trodden Bondi to Bronte Coastal Walk. This free exhibition, which runs for two weeks beginning in late October, attracts thousands of visitors.

NIGHTLIFE & THE ARTS

THE ARTS

Nothing illustrates the dynamism of Sydney's arts scene better than its live theater. Some of the hottest names in Hollywood received their first taste of stardom in Sydney: Nicole Kidman got her first onstage kiss here; Guy Pearce rocked out in *Grease*; and Russell Crowe notched up a total of 416 Sydney performances in the *Rocky Horror Show*—including the role of Dr. Frank N. Furter. At the root of these successes is a powerful, pithy theatrical tradition that has produced many talented Australian writers, directors, and performers. And though Sydney's contemporary theater pays tribute to the giants of drama, it's also driven by distinctly Australian themes: multiculturalism, relating to the troubled relations between Aboriginal and white Australia, and the search for national identity, characterized by the famous Australian irreverence.

Dance, music, and the visual arts are celebrated with equal enthusiasm. At their best, Sydney's artists and performers bring a new slant to the arts, one that reflects the unique qualities of their homeland and the city itself. Standouts on the Sydney arts scene include the Sydney Dance Company, the Museum of Contemporary Arts, the Sydney Opera House, and Belvoir Street Theatre. The most comprehensive listing of upcoming events is in the Metro section of the *Sydney Morn-*

ing Herald, published on Friday. On other days, browse through the entertainment section of the paper.

Ticketek Phone Box Office (☎*13–2849* ⊕*http://premier.ticketek.com. au*) is the major ticket reservations agency, covering most shows and performances.

BALLET, OPERA & CLASSICAL MUSIC

Fodor's Choice **Sydney Opera House** (⊠*Bennelong Point, Circular Quay* ☎*02/9250–*
★ *7777* ⊕*www.soh.nsw.gov.au*) showcases all the performing arts in its five theaters, one of which is devoted to opera. The Australian Ballet, the Sydney Dance Company, and the Australian Opera Company also call the Opera House home. The complex includes two stages for theater and the 2,700-seat Concert Hall, where the Sydney Symphony Orchestra and the Australian Chamber Orchestra perform. The box office is open Monday to Saturday 9 to 8:30.

DANCE

Bangarra Dance Theatre (⊠*Pier 4, 5 Hickson Rd., The Rocks* ☎*02/9251–5333* ⊕*www.bangarra.com.au*), an Aboriginal dance company, stages productions based on contemporary Aboriginal social themes, often to critical acclaim.

★ **Sydney Dance Company** (⊠*The Wharf, Pier 4, Hickson Rd., The Rocks* ☎*02/9221–4811* ⊕*www.sydneydance.com.au*) is an innovative contemporary dance troupe with an international reputation from its many years under acclaimed director Graeme Murphy. The company generally performs at the Opera House when it's in town.

THEATER

Belvoir Street Theatre (⊠*25 Belvoir St., Surry Hills* ☎*02/9699–3444* ⊕*www.belvoir.com.au*) has two stages that host innovative and challenging political and social drama. The smaller downstairs space is the home of "B Sharp," Company B's lineup of brave new Australian works. The theater is a 10-minute walk from Central Station.
Capitol Theatre (⊠*13 Campbell St., Haymarket* ☎*02/9320–5000* ⊕*www.capitoltheatre.com.au*), a century-old city landmark, was redone with such modern refinements as fiber-optic ceiling lights that twinkle in time to the music. The 2,000-seat theater specializes in Broadway blockbusters.
Lyric Theatre (⊠*20–80 Pyrmont St., Pyrmont, Darling Harbour* ☎*02/9777–9000* ⊕*www.starcity.com.au*), at the Star City Casino complex, is one of Sydney's most spectacular performing-arts venues. Despite its size, there's no better place to watch big-budget musicals. Every seat in the lavishly spacious, 2,000-seat theater is a good one. The **SWB Stables Theatre** (⊠*10 Nimrod St., Kings Cross* ☎*02/9361–3817 or 1300/406776* ⊕*www.griffintheatre.com.au*) is home of the Griffin Theatre Company, which specializes in new Australian writing.
State Theatre (⊠*49 Market St., City Center* ☎*02/9373–6655* ⊕*www. statetheatre.com.au*) is the grande dame of Sydney theaters. It operates as a cinema in June each year when it hosts the two-week-long Sydney Film Festival; at other times the space hosts local and international

performers. Built in 1929 and restored to its full-blown opulence, the theater has a vaulted ceiling, mosaic floors, marble columns and statues, and brass and bronze doors. A highlight of the magnificent theater is the 20,000-piece chandelier that is supposedly the world's second largest, which actor Robin Williams once likened to "one of Imelda Marcos's earrings."

Wharf Theatre (⊠*Pier 4, Hickson Rd., The Rocks* ☎*02/9250–1777* ⊕*sydneytheatre.com.au*), on a redeveloped wharf in the shadow of Harbour Bridge, hosts the Sydney Theatre Company, one of Australia's most original and highly regarded performing groups. Contemporary British and American plays and the latest offerings from leading Australian playwrights such as David Williamson and Nick Enright are the main attractions.

NIGHTLIFE

"Satan made Sydney," wrote Mark Twain, quoting a citizen of the city, and to some there can be no doubt that Satan was the principal architect behind Kings Cross. Strictly speaking, Kings Cross refers to the intersection of Victoria Street and Darlinghurst Road, although the name "The Cross" applies to a much wider area. Essentially, it is a ½-km (¼-mi) stretch of trendy bars and clubs, seedy sports bars, betting venues, strip clubs, and massage parlors. The area is buzzing with backpackers checking in and out of hostels and checking their e-mail for most of the day, while farther down Bayswater Road and Victoria Street, urban hipsters lounge at classy cafés on tree-lined streets. The real action starts at 10 PM, and runs hot for most of the night.

Sydneysiders in search of late-night action are more likely to head for Oxford Street, between Hyde Park and Taylor Square, where the choice ranges from pubs to the hottest dance clubs in town. Oxford Street is also the nighttime focus for Sydney's large gay scene. Another nightlife district runs along Cockle Bay Wharf in Darling Harbour; the bars, restaurants, and nightclubs here are especially popular during the summer months. Nightlife in the Rocks is focused on the pubs along George Street, which attract a boisterous crowd. Several Spanish restaurants along the west side of Liverpool Street, just before Darling Harbour, serve delicious food and stay open late for salsa dancing.

The *Sydney Morning Herald*'s daily entertainment section is the most informative guide to the city's pubs and clubs. For club-scene coverage—who's been seen where and what they were wearing—pick up a free copy of *Beat,* available at just about any Oxford Street café or via the Internet (⊕*www.beat.com.au*). The CitySearch Web site (⊕*www.sydney.citysearch.com.au*) is another weekly source of entertainment information.

All bars and clubs listed here are open daily unless noted. Entry is free unless we list a cover charge.

1

BARS & DANCE CLUBS

★ A former School of the Arts building, **Arthouse** (⊠ *275 Pitt St., City Center* ☏ *02/9284–1200*) has been renovated into a modern, belle epoque–style hot spot, with four bars and a restaurant spread over three cavernous floors. Art is the focus here, whether it's visual—life-drawing classes are given in the space—aural, or comestible, and there is a full-time curator dedicated to programming events and installing exhibitions.

★ **Bambini Wine Room** (⊠ *185 Elizabeth St., City Centre* ☏ *02/928–7098*) is a sparkling little jewel box encased by marble-clad walls and topped with lovely chandeliers. You can sip cocktails and any number of fine wines late into the night and feast on affordable bar snacks.

★ The **Beach Road Hotel** (⊠ *71 Beach Rd., Bondi Beach* ☏ *02/9130–7247*), a Bondi institution, is famous for its Sunday Sessions, when locals come to drink and dance all day in one of several pub rooms. You can snack on a sausage grilled right out front or dine on Italian food on the back patio and settle in for a long night of partying like a Sydneysider.

Blu Horizon Bar (⊠ *176 Cumberland St., The Rocks* ☏ *02/9250–6013*) has the view! Situated on the 36th floor of the Shangri-La Hotel, this is a sophisticated place to relax after work or enjoy a late-night drink while taking in the sweeping views of Sydney Harbour and the Opera House. Get here early for a ringside seat.

★ With its primo waterside location at the northern end of King Street Wharf, and famous mussels from its open kitchen, **Bungalow 8** (⊠ *8 The Promenade, King Street Wharf* ☏ *02/9299–4660*) invites a night of posing and partying. This is the place to be seen bobbing your head to the spinning of several ultracool resident DJs. Tuesday is especially packed for the all-you-can-eat mussel extravaganza.

FodorsChoice
★ **Hemmesphere** (⊠ *Level 4, 252 George St., City Center* ☏ *02/9240–3040*) is where Sydney's hippest pay homage to cocktail culture from low, leather divans. The mood is elegant, sleek, and cultish, and the guest list is usually sprinkled with whichever glitterati happen to be in town. Club members, who pay A$1,500 a year, get priority. It's closed Sunday and Monday.

FodorsChoice
★ **Home** (⊠ *Cockle Bay Wharf, 101 Wheat Rd., Darling Harbour* ☏ *02/9266–0600*), Sydney's largest nightclub, is a three-story colossus that holds up to 2,000 party animals. The main dance floor has an awesome sound system, and the top-level terrace bar is the place to go when the action becomes too frantic. Outdoor balconies provide the essential oxygen boost. Arrive early or prepare for a long wait. It's open Thursday to Sunday 10 PM–4 AM, with a cover charge of up to A$20.

Hugo's Lounge (⊠ *Level 1, 33 Bayswater Rd., Kings Cross* ☏ *02/9357–4411*) is the place that transformed Kings Cross from a seedy crossroads of sex shops and smut to a must-be-seen-here destination for Sydney's beautiful people. Red lamps are a nod to the neighborhood's skin trade, but the deep couches, opulent ottomans, and decadent cocktail menu are purely upmarket. Closed Monday.

Jimmy Liks (⊠ *188 Victoria St., Potts Point* ☏ *02/8354–1400*), a small, sexy Asian street-food restaurant, serves up drink concoctions with exotic flavors—like lemongrass martinis and "twisted and tasty" iced teas accented with basil—which you can sip under a honeycomb-like lantern that flatters with its golden light.

Fodor's Choice ★ **Le Panic** (⊠20 *Bayswater Rd., Kings Cross* ☎02/9368–0763) is the perfect combination of bar and dance club. With its sleek, gentlemen's-club ambience and private back room, it's a great space for hanging out with a group. The dance floor is small and suitably crowded, though not people-keep-bumping-into-me crowded, thanks to a rotating list of visiting DJs spinning in various styles. It's a major pickup scene for beautiful people who don't get their groove on until late—the action usually doesn't start until 11 PM. It's open Thursday to Monday, and there's sometimes a cover charge.

Fodor's Choice ★ **Mars Lounge** (⊠16 *Wentworth Ave., Surry Hills* ☎02/9267–6440) takes its music as seriously as it takes its list of lethal cocktails, including the Marslide, with malt chocolate, Baileys, butterscotch, and cream. DJs spin everything from funk to fusion, and each night has a different theme, like Thursday's combination of good food and soulful music. Closed Monday and Tuesday; no cover.

For a northern Sydney landmark, **The Oaks** (⊠118 *Military Rd., Neutral Bay* ☎02/9953–5515) encapsulates the very best of the modern pub. The immensely popular watering hole is big and boisterous, with a beer garden, a restaurant, and several bars offering varying levels of sophistication. It's packed on Friday and Saturday nights.

Fodor's Choice ★ Perched beneath the concourse of the Opera House and at eye level with Sydney Harbour, **Opera Bar** (⊠*Sydney Opera House, Circular Quay* ☎02/9247–1666) has the best location in all of Sydney. Cozy up for a drink in the enclosed bar area or grab a waterside umbrella table and take in the glimmering skyline. Live music plays under the stars nightly. The bar has a full menu, though the attraction here is the scenery, not the cuisine.

★ A cross between a swinging '60s London nightspot and the back lot of a James Bond film, the small, groovy **Peppermint Lounge** (⊠281 *Victoria St., Potts Point* ☎02/9356–6634) has a mod mood, and, naturally, martinis. Tuck into an octagonal red-lighted booth surrounded by frosted glass and try one of the more than 70 libations on offer. It's open Wednesday to Saturday until midnight.

The mood of the inner-city **Soho Bar** (⊠*Piccadilly Hotel, 171 Victoria St., Kings Cross* ☎02/9358–6511), a major celeb hangout, is relaxed and funky. Its poolroom is rated one of the city's finest.

★ **Tank** (⊠3 *Bridge La., City Center* ☎02/9240–3094) is the grooviest and best looking of all Sydney's nightclubs, with a polar-cool clientele and a slick dress code rigidly enforced at the door. Finding the door can be tricky (painted in shades of blue), but you'll know you're there when you're standing in a grungy lane off Bridge Street, near the George Street corner. The cover charge is A$20, and you'll continue to shell out as much for drinks all evening. The interior is plush and relaxed, despite its space-capsule setting, and the techno music thumps. It's open until 5 AM on Friday and Saturday.

COMEDY CLUBS

Sydney's Comedy Store (✉ *Fox Studios Entertainment Quarter, Bent St. off Driver Ave., Centennial Park* ☎ *02/9357–1419* ⊕ *www.comedystore.com.au*), the city's oldest comedy club, is found in this plush 300-seat theater in a huge movie-production facility. The difficult-to-find theater is at the rear of the complex, close to the parking lot. Shows are Tuesday–Saturday at 8 PM, and admission runs A$15 to A$30.

GAY & LESBIAN BARS & CLUBS

Most of the city's gay and lesbian venues are along Oxford Street, in Darlinghurst. The free *Sydney Star Observer,* available along Oxford Street, has a roundup of Sydney's gay and lesbian goings-on, or check the magazine's Web site (⊕ *www.ssonet.com.au*). A monthly free magazine, *Lesbians on the Loose,* lists events for women, and the free *SX* (⊕ *www.sxnews.com.au*) lists bars and events.

★ **ARQ** (✉ *16 Flinders St., Darlinghurst* ☎ *02/9380–8700*), Sydney's biggest, best looking, and funkiest gay nightclub, attracts a clean-cut crowd who like to whip off their shirts as soon as they hear the beat. (Some women head here, too.) There are multiple dance floors, a bar, and plenty of chrome and sparkly lighting. It's open from 9 PM until whenever Friday through Sunday, with a cover charge of A$10 to A$20.

Midnight Shift (✉ *85 Oxford St., Darlinghurst* ☎ *02/9360–4463*) is Sydney's hard-core party zone, a living legend on the gay scene for its longevity and its take-no-prisoners approach. If anything, the upstairs nightclub is a little quieter than the ground-floor bars, where most of the leather-loving men go to shoot pool. Opening hours are daily from about midday to 6 AM.

Though the look, music, and decor of the **Newtown Hotel** (✉ *174 King St., Newtown* ☎ *02/9557–1329*) do not approach the gloss and sophistication of Paddington's glamorous gay scene, you can't beat the laid-back attitudes and the bawdy drag shows. The pub also has special women's nights, but they vary from week to week. Open daily until late. It's about 4 km (2½ mi) west of the city.

JAZZ CLUBS

Avery's Bar (✉ *389 Pitt St., City Center* ☎ *02/8268–1888*), located in the Avillion Hotel, is an intimate nightspot offering jazz Wednesday to Friday. Happy-hour drinks and free nibbles are available 5 to 7 every night.

★ **The Basement** (✉ *29 Reiby Pl., Circular Quay* ☎ *02/9251–2797*) is a Sydney legend, the city's premier venue for top local and international

---

HAVE A GAY OLD TIME

If you're in Sydney in late February and early March, you'll think the whole city has gone gay. The Sydney Gay and Lesbian Mardi Gras parade, which celebrates its 30th anniversary in 2008, is one of Australia's major events. Dozens of floats covered with buff dancers make their way from College Street, near St. Mary's Cathedral, up Oxford Street to Taylor's Square. Thousands of spectators lining the route make this one of the city's biggest parties.

jazz, rock, and blues musicians. Dinner is also available. Expect a cover charge starting at $A20.

PUBS WITH MUSIC

Empire Hotel (✉ *103A Parramatta Rd., [corner of Johnson St.], Annandale* ☎ *02/9557–1701*) calls itself the Sydney home of the blues, though it also has roots music and a bit of rock thrown in on Wednesday to Sunday night. The Sydney Blues Society holds its open jam sessions here on the last Sunday afternoon of every month. Some nights are free, other have a cover charge of A$5 to A$15. It's 3½ km (2 mi) west of the city center.

Mercantile Hotel (✉ *25 George St., The Rocks* ☎ *02/9247–3570*), in the shadow of Harbour Bridge, is Irish and very proud of it. Fiddles, drums, and pipes rise above the clamor in the bar, and lilting accents rejoice in song seven nights a week. There's no cover charge.

Rose, Shamrock and Thistle (✉ *193 Evans St., Rozelle* ☎ *02/9810–2244*), popularly known as the Three Weeds, is a friendly, boisterous pub 5 km (3 mi) from the city center. It's one of the best places to hear live music. Thursday to Saturday there's a moderate cover charge of A$5 to A$10.

SPORTS & THE OUTDOORS

Given its climate and its taste for the great outdoors, it's no surprise that Sydney is addicted to sports. In the cooler months rugby dominates the sporting scene, although these days the Sydney Swans, the city's flag bearer in the national Australian Rules Football competition, attract far bigger crowds. In summer, cricket is the major spectator sport, and nothing arouses more passion than international test cricket games—especially when Australia plays against England, the traditional enemy. Sydney is well equipped with athletic facilities, from golf courses to tennis courts, and water sports come naturally on one of the world's greatest harbors. **Ticketek Phone Box Office** (☎ *13–2849* ⊕ *www.premier. ticketek.com.au*) is the place to buy tickets for major sports events.

AUSTRALIAN RULES FOOTBALL

A fast, demanding game in which the ball can be kicked or punched between teams of 22 players, Australian Rules Football has won a major audience in Sydney, even though the city has only one professional team—the Sydney Swans—compared to the dozen that play in Melbourne—the home of the sport. **Sydney Cricket Ground** (✉ *Moore Park Rd., Centennial Park, Paddington* ☎ *02/9360–6601* ⊕ *www.scgt. nsw.gov.au*) hosts games April to September.

BICYCLING

Sydney's favorite cycling track is Centennial Park's Grand Parade, a 3¾-km (2¼-mi) cycle circuit around the perimeter of this grand, gracious eastern suburbs park.

Centennial Park Cycles (✉ *50 Clovelly Rd., Randwick, Centennial Park* ☎ *02/9398–5027* ✉ *Grand Dr., Centennial Park*) rents bicycles for around A$15 per hour, A$40 per day.

Clarence Street Cyclery (⊠*104 Clarence St., City Center* ☎*02/9299–4962* ⊕*www.cyclery.com.au*) is a major store for all cycling needs.

BOATING & SAILING

EastSail (⊠*D'Albora Marine, New Beach Rd., Rushcutters Bay, Darling Point* ☎*02/9327–1166* ⊕*www.eastsail.com.au*) rents bareboat sailing and motored yachts from about A$465 per half day. Skippers' rates are around A$50 per hour.

Northside Sailing School (⊠*Spit Rd., the Spit, Mosman* ☎*02/9969–3972* ⊕*www.northsidesailing.com.au*) at Middle Harbour teaches dinghy sailing to individuals and children's groups. You can learn the ropes on a three-hour, one-on-one private lesson from A$130.

Sydney Harbour Kayaks (⊠*3/25 Spit Rd., Mosman* ☎*02/9960–4389*) rents one- and two-person kayaks. The location beside Spit Bridge offers calm water for novices, as well as several beaches and idyllic coves. Prices per hour start from A$20 for a one-person kayak to A$30 for a double.

CRICKET

Cricket is Sydney's summer sport, and it's often played at the beach as well as in parks throughout the nation. For Australians, the pinnacle of excitement is the Ashes, when the national cricket team takes the field against the English. It happens every other summer and the two nations take turns hosting the event. The next Ashes series in Australia is December 2008–January 2009. Cricket season runs from October through March. International test series games are played at the **Sydney Cricket Ground** (⊠*Moore Park Rd., Centennial Park, Paddington* ☎*02/9360–6601* ⊕*www.scgt.nsw.gov.au*).

HIKING

Fine walking trails can be found in the national parks in and around Sydney, especially in **Royal National Park, Ku-ring-gai Chase National Park,** and **Sydney Harbour National Park,** all of which are close to the city. The **Bondi to Bronte Coast Walk** is a lovely 3½-km (2-mi) cliff walk, popular with just about everyone in the eastern suburbs. It's dotted with signage explaining the flora and Aboriginal history, and the area is the venue for the hugely popular Sculpture by the Sea outdoor art display (held every October and November). The **Federation Cliff Walk** from Dover Heights (just north of Bondi Beach) to Vaucluse, and on to Watson's Bay, winds past some of Sydney's most exclusive suburbs. At Diamond Bay you can soak in great views of the 20-million-year-old sandstone cliffs from the steps and boardwalks.

RUGBY

Known locally as footy, rugby is Sydney's winter addiction. This is a fast, gutsy, physical game that bears some similarities to North American football, although the action is more constant and the ball cannot be passed forward. The season falls between April and September. **Aussie Stadium** (⊠*Moore Park Rd., Centennial Park, Paddington* ☎*02/9360–6601* ⊕*www.scgt.nsw.gov.au*) is the home stadium of the Sydney Roosters. Other games are played at Telstra Stadium (Sydney Olympic Park) and stadiums throughout the suburbs.

SCUBA DIVING

Dive Centre Manly (✉ *10 Belgrave St., Manly* ☎ *02/9977–4355* ⊕ *www. divesydney.com*), at the popular north Sydney beach, runs all-inclusive shore dives each day, which let you see weedy sea dragons and other sea creatures. PADI certification courses are also available. The cost for two shore dives starts at A$95.

Pro Dive (✉ *Shop 8, the Clock Tower, 55 Harrington St., The Rocks* ☎ *1800/820820* ⊕ *www.prodive.com.au*) is a PADI operator conducting courses and shore- or boat-diving excursions around the harbor and city beaches. Some of the best dive spots—with coral, rock walls, and lots of colorful fish, including "Bazza" the grouper—are close to the eastern suburb beaches of Clovelly and Coogee, where Pro Dive has an office. The company also has a center in Manly. A four-hour boat dive with an instructor or dive master costs around A$189, including rental equipment; a three-day learn-to-dive course is A$395.

SURFING

All Sydney surfers have their favorite breaks, but you can usually count on good waves on at least one of the city's ocean beaches. **Surfcam** (⊕ *www.surfcam.com.au*) has surf reports and weather details.

Lets go Surfing (✉ *128 Ramsgate Ave., North Bondi* ☎ *02/9365–1800* ⊕ *www.letsgosurfing.com.au*) is a complete surfing resource for anyone who wants to hang five with confidence. Lessons are available for all ages, and you can rent or buy boards and wet suits. The basic three-class package of two-hour Surf Easy lessons costs A$155.

Manly Surf School (✉ *North Steyne Surf Club, Manly Beach, Manly* ☎ *02/9977–6977* ⊕ *www.manlysurfschool.com*) conducts courses for adults and children, and provides all equipment, including wet suits. Adults can join a two-hour group lesson (four per day) for A$50. Private instruction costs A$80 per hour.

Rip Curl (✉ *82 Campbell Parade, Bondi Beach* ☎ *02/9130–2660*) has a huge variety of boards and surfing supplies. It's conveniently close to Bondi Beach.

SWIMMING

Sydney has many heated Olympic-size swimming pools, some of which go beyond the basic requirements of a workout. Many Aussies, however, prefer to do their "laps" in the sea off Bondi and Manly.

Andrew (Boy) Charlton Pool (✉ *Mrs. Macquarie's Rd., Domain North, The Domain* ☎ *02/9358–6686*) isn't just any heated Olympic-size salt-water pool. Its stunning outdoor location overlooking the ships at Garden Island, its radical glass-and-steel design, and its chic terrace café above Woolloomooloo Bay make it an attraction unto itself. Admission is A$5.20 and it's open October–April, daily 6 AM–7 PM.

Cook and Phillip Park Aquatic and Fitness Centre (✉ *College St., City Center* ☎ *02/9326–0444*) includes wave, hydrotherapy, children's, and Olympic-size pools in a stunning, high-tech complex on the eastern edge of the city center near St. Mary's Cathedral. There's also a complete fitness center and classes. Admission is A$6 and it's open weekdays 6 AM–10 PM, weekends 7 AM–8 PM.

TENNIS

Cooper Park Tennis Centre (⊠ *Off Suttie Rd., Cooper Park, Bellevue Hill* ☎ *02/9389–9259*) is a complex of eight synthetic-grass courts in a park surrounded by an expansive area of native bushland, about 5 km (3 mi) east of the city center. Weekday court fees are A$22 per hour from 7 AM to 5 PM and A$27

per hour from 6 AM to 10 PM. On Saturday they are A$26 until 5 and A$27 afterward; Sunday A$26 until 1 and A$18 afterwards.
Parklands Sports Centre (⊠ *Lang Rd. at Anzac Parade, Moore Park, Centennial Park* ☎ *02/9662–7033* ⊕ *www.cp.nsw.gov.au/aboutus/sports. htm*) has 11 courts in a shady park approximately 2½ km (1½ mi) from the city center. The weekday cost is A$16.50 per hour 9–5 and A$22 per hour 5 PM–10:30 PM; it's A$22 per hour 8 AM–6 PM on weekends.

WINDSURFING

Balmoral Windsurfing, Kite Surfing, Sailing, and Kayak School (⊠ *The Esplanade, Balmoral Beach* ☎ *02/9960–5344* ⊕ *www.sailboard.net.au*) runs classes from its base at this north-side harbor beach. Kite-surfing, sailing, and kayaking lessons are also available. Kite-surfing lessons start from A$99, windsurfing from A$175, sailing from A$195.
Rose Bay Aquatic Hire (⊠ *1 Vickery Ave., Rose Bay* ☎ *02/9371–7036*) rents motorboats, kayaks, catamarans, and Lasers. The cost is from A$35 per hour for a Laser and A$40 per hour for a catamaran; some sailing experience is required to rent these boats. Kayaks are also available for rent from A$20 per hour for a single; motorboat rentals cost A$30 per hour for the first two hours, then A$15 per hour.

SHOPPING

Sydney's shops vary from those with international cachet (Tiffany's, Louis Vuitton) to Aboriginal art galleries, opal shops, craft bazaars, and weekend flea markets. If you're interested in buying genuine Australian products, look carefully at the labels. Stuffed koalas and didgeridoos made anywhere but in Australia are a standing joke.

Business hours are usually about 9 or 10 to 6 on weekdays; on Thursday stores stay open until 9. Shops are open Saturday 9–5 and Sunday 11–5. Prices include the Goods and Services Tax (GST).

DEPARTMENT STORES

David Jones (⊠ *Women's store, Elizabeth and Market Sts., City Center* ⊠ *Men's store, Castlereagh and Market Sts., City Center* ☎ *02/9266–5544* ⊕ *www.davidjones.com.au*), or "Dee Jays," as it's known locally,

is the city's largest department store, with a reputation for excellent service and high-quality goods. Clothing by many of Australia's finest designers is on display here, and the store also sells its own fashion label at reasonable prices. The basement level of the men's store is a fabulous food hall with international treats.
Myer (⊠*George and Market Sts., City Center* ☎*02/9238–9111* ⊕*www.gracebros.com.au*), opposite the Queen Victoria Building, is the place to shop for clothing and accessories by Australian and international designers.

FLEA MARKETS

Balmain Market (⊠*St. Andrew's Church, Darling St., Balmain*), in a leafy churchyard less than 5 km (3 mi) from the city, has a rustic quality that makes it a refreshing change from city-center shopping. Crafts, handmade furniture, plants, bread, toys, tarot readings, and massages are among the offerings at the 140-odd stalls. Inside the church hall you can buy international snacks, from Indian samosas to Indonesian satays to Australian meat pies. The market runs 8:30 to 4 on Saturday.

Fodor'sChoice **Paddington Bazaar** (⊠*St. John's Church, Oxford St., Paddington*), more
★ popularly known as Paddington Market, is a busy churchyard bazaar with more than 100 stalls crammed with clothing, plants, crafts, jewelry, and souvenirs. Distinctly New Age and highly fashion conscious, the market is an outlet for a handful of avant-garde clothing designers. It also acts as a magnet for buskers and some of the area's flamboyant and entertaining characters. It's open Saturday 10 to 4.

Paddy's Market (⊠*9–13 Hay St., Haymarket*) is a huge fresh produce and flea market held under the Market City complex near the Sydney Entertainment Centre in the Chinatown precinct. There has been a market on this site since 1834, and much of the historic exterior remains. The Metro Light Rail, Explorer bus, and Monorail stop at the door. It's open Thursday to Sunday 9 to 5.

The Rocks Market (⊠*Upper George St. near Argyle St., The Rocks*), a sprawling covered bazaar, transforms the upper end of George Street into a multicultural collage of music, food, arts, crafts, and entertainment. It's open weekends 10 to 5.

SHOPPING CENTERS & ARCADES

Birkenhead Point (⊠*Victoria Rd. near the Iron Cove Bridge, Drummoyne* ☎*02/9181–3922*) is a factory outlet with more than 100 clothing, shoe, and housewares stores. Situated on the western shores of Iron Cove about 7 km [4 mi] west of Sydney, it's a great place to shop for discounted labels including Alannah Hill, Witchery, Bendon (Elle Macpherson's lingerie range), and Table Eight. Take Bus 506 or Bus 507 from Circular Quay or Town Hall, or a ferry from Circular Quay.

Oxford Street, Paddington's main artery (from South Dowling Street east to Queen Street, Woollahra), is dressed to thrill. Lined with boutiques, home-furnishings stores, and Mediterranean-inspired cafés, it's a perfect venue for watching the never-ending fashion parade.

1

Pitt Street Mall (⊠ *Between King and Market Sts.*, *City Center*), at the heart of Sydney's shopping area, includes the Mid-City Centre, Centrepoint Arcade, Imperial Arcade, Skygarden, Myer, and the charming and historic Strand Arcade—six multilevel shopping plazas crammed with more than 450 shops, from mainstream clothing stores to designer boutiques.

Queen Victoria Building (⊠ *George, York, Market, and Druitt Sts.*, *City Center* ☏ *02/9264–9209*) is a splendid Victorian building with more than 200 boutiques, cafés, and antiques shops. The building is open 24 hours, so you can window-shop even after the stores have closed.

SPECIALTY STORES

ABORIGINAL ART

Aboriginal art includes historically functional items, such as boomerangs, wooden bowls, and spears, as well as paintings and ceremonial implements that testify to a rich culture of legends and dreams. Although much of this artwork remains strongly traditional in essence, the tools and colors used in Western art have fired the imaginations of many Aboriginal artists. Works on canvas are now more common than works on bark, for example. Although the two most prolific sources of Aboriginal art are Arnhem Land and the Central Desert Region (close to Darwin and Alice Springs, respectively), much of the best work finds its way into the galleries of Sydney.

Aboriginal Dreamtime Fine Art Gallery (⊠ *Shop 8, 199 George St., Circular Quay* ☏ *02/9241–2953*) has a large collection of didgeridoos, sculpture, paintings, and craftwork.

Coo-ee Aboriginal Art (⊠ *31 Lamrock Ave., Bondi Beach* ☏ *02/9300–9233*), open by appointment, exhibits and sells high-end Aboriginal paintings, sculptures, and limited-edition prints.

Gavala (⊠ *Shop 131, Harbourside Centre, Darling Harbour* ☏ *02/9213–7232* ⊕ *www.gavala.com.au*) brings you art and artifacts directly from Aboriginal artists. There's a large selection of paintings, boomerangs, didgeridoos, books, music, and clothing such as scarves and sarongs.

Hogarth Galleries (⊠ *7 Walker La., Paddington* ☏ *02/9360–6839* ⊕ *www. aboriginalartcentres.com*) showcases quality contemporary Aboriginal artworks from around the country.

BOOKS

Ariel Booksellers (⊠ *42 Oxford St., Paddington* ☏ *02/9332–4581* ⊠ *103 George St., The Rocks* ☏ *02/9241–5622* ⊕ *www.arielbooks.com.au*) is a large, bright browser's delight and the place to go for literature, pop culture, and anything avant garde. It also has a fine selection of art books. Both branches are open daily 9 AM–midnight.

Dymocks (⊠ *424 George St., City Center* ☏ *02/9235–0155* ⊕ *www. dymocks.com.au*), a big, bustling bookstore packed to its gallery-level coffee shop, is the place to go for all literary needs. It's open Monday to Wednesday and Friday 9 to 6:30, Thursday 9 to 9, Saturday 9 to 6, and Sunday 10 to 5.

The Travel Bookshop (⌧*Shop 3, 175 Liverpool St., Hyde Park* ☎*02/9261–8200*) carries Sydney's most extensive selection of maps, guides, armchair-travel books, and histories.

BUSH APPAREL & OUTDOOR GEAR

Mountain Designs (⌧*499 Kent St., City Center* ☎*02/9267–3822* ⊕*www.mountaindesigns.com.au*), in the middle of Sydney's "Rugged Row" of outdoor specialists, sells camping and climbing hardware and dispenses the advice necessary to keep you alive and well in the wilderness.

Paddy Pallin (⌧*507 Kent St., City Center* ☎*02/9264–2685* ⊕*www.paddypallin.com.au*) is the first stop for serious bush adventurers heading for the Amazon, Annapurna, or wild Australia. Maps, books, and mounds of gear are tailored especially for the Australian outdoors.

★ **R. M. Williams** (⌧*389 George St., City Center* ☎*02/9262–2228* ⊕*www.rmwilliams.com.au*) is the place to go for the complete bush look, with accessories such as Akubra hats, Drizabone riding coats, plaited kangaroo-skin belts, moleskin trousers, and their classic men's boots.

CLOTHING

Artwear by Lara S (⌧*77½ George St., City Center* ☎*02/9247–3668*) carries cutting-edge Australian and New Zealand designer fashions. Owner Lara Shaya stocks small collections of clothes for every occasion, as well as a range of accessories.

Belinda (⌧*8 and 14 Transvaal Ave., Double Bay* ☎*02/9328–6288 or 02/9327–8199* ⊕*www.belinda.com.au*) is where Sydney's female fashionistas go when there's a dress-up occasion looming. From her namesake store that scores high marks for innovation and imagination, former model Belinda Seper sells nothing but the very latest designs off the catwalks.

Collette Dinnigan (⌧*33 William St., Paddington* ☎*02/9360–6691* ⊕*www.collettedinnigan.com.au*), one of the hottest names on Australia's fashion scene, has dressed Nicole Kidman, Cate Blanchett, and Sandra Bullock. Her Paddington boutique is packed with sensual, floating, negligee-inspired fashions crafted from silks, chiffons, and lace in soft pastel colors accented with hand-beading and embroidery. Her clothes are also available at the David Jones women's store in the city center.

Country Road (⌧*142–144 Pitt St., City Center* ☎*02/9394–1818* ⊕*www.countryroad.com.au*) stands somewhere between Ralph Lauren and Timberland, with an all-Australian assembly of classic, countrified his 'n' hers, plus an ever-expanding variety of soft furnishings in cotton and linen for the rustic retreat.

Marcs (⌧*Shop 288, Mid-City Centre, Pitt Street Mall, City Center* ☎*02/9221–5575* ⊕*www.marcs.com.au*) is located somewhere close to Diesel-land in the fashion spectrum, with a variety of clothing, footwear, and accessories for the fashion-conscious. Serious shoppers should look for the Marcs Made in Italy sub-label for that extra touch of style and craftsmanship.

Orson & Blake (⌧*83–85 Queen St., Woollahra* ☎*02/9326–1155*) is a virtual gallery dedicated to great modern design, with eclectic housewares, fashions, handbags, and accessories. There's even a coffee shop where you can mull over your purchases.

Scanlan & Theodore (⊠*122 Oxford St., Paddington* ☎*02/9380–9388*) is the Sydney outlet for one of Melbourne's most distinguished fashion houses. Designs take their cues from Europe, with superbly tailored women's knitwear, suits, and stylishly glamorous evening wear.

CRAFTS

Collect (⊠*88 George St., The Rocks* ☎*02/9247–7984* ⊕*www.object. com.au*) sells beautiful glass, wood, and ceramic creations. **Object** (⊠*415 Bourke St., Surry Hills* ☎*02/9361–4511*), its gallery in inner-city Surry Hills, displays a larger selection of Australian-made crafts.

MUSIC

Birdland Records (⊠*231 Pitt St., City Center* ☎*02/9267–6881* ⊕*www. birdland.com.au*) has an especially strong selection of jazz, blues, African, and Latin American music, as well as an authoritative staff ready to lend some assistance. It's open Monday to Wednesday and Friday 10 to 5:30, Thursday 10 to 7:30, and Saturday 9 to 4:30.

Folkways (⊠*282 Oxford St., Paddington* ☎*02/9361–3980*) sells Australian bush, folk, and Aboriginal recordings. The store is open Monday to Wednesday 10 to 6, Thursday 9 to 8, Friday 9 to 6, Saturday 10 to 6, and Sunday 11 to 6.

OPALS & JEWELRY

Australia has a virtual monopoly on the world's supply of opals. The least expensive of these fiery gemstones are triplets, which consist of a thin shaving of opal mounted on a plastic base and covered by a plastic, glass, or quartz crown. Doublets are a slice of mounted opal without the capping. The most expensive stones are solid opals, which cost anywhere from a few hundred dollars to a few thousand. You can pick up opals at souvenir shops all over the city, but if you want a valuable stone you should visit a specialist. Sydney is also a good hunting ground for other jewelry, from the quirky to the gloriously expensive.

Dinosaur Designs (⊠*Shop 77, Strand Arcade, George St., City Center* ☎*02/9223–2953* ⊠*339 Oxford St., Paddington* ☎*02/9361–3776* ⊕*www.dinosaurdesigns.com.au*) sells luminous bowls, plates, and vases, as well as fanciful jewelry crafted from resin and Perspex in eye-popping color combinations from both locations.

Hathi Jewellery (⊠*19 Playfair St., The Rocks* ☎*02/9252–4328*) has a beautiful collection of handmade jewelry including earrings, necklaces, and bracelets. Most pieces are one of a kind.

★ **Makers Mark** (⊠*72A Castlereagh St., City Center* ☎*02/9231–6800* ⊕*www.makersmark.com.au*) has a gorgeous collection of handmade designer jewelry and objects by some of Australia's finest artisans.

The National Opal Collection (⊠*176 Pitt St. Mall, City Center* ☎*02/9233–8844* ⊕*www.gemtec.com.au*) is the only Sydney opal retailer with total ownership of its entire production process—mines, workshops, and showroom—making prices very competitive. In the Pitt Street showroom you can see artisans at work cutting and polishing the stones. Hours are weekdays 9 to 6 and weekends 10 to 4.

★ **Paspaley Pearls** (⊠*2 Martin Pl., City Center* ☏*02/9232–7633* ⊕*www. paspaleypearls.com*) derives its exquisite jewelry from pearl farms near the remote Western Australia town of Broome. Prices start high and head for the stratosphere, but if you're serious about a high-quality pearl, this gallery requires a visit.

Percy Marks Fine Gems (⊠*60 Elizabeth St., City Center* ☏*02/9233–1355* ⊕*www.percymarks.com.au*) has an outstanding collection of high-quality Australian gemstones, including dazzling black opals, pink diamonds, and pearls from Broome.

Rox Gems and Jewellery (⊠*Shop 31, Strand Arcade, George St., City Center* ☏*02/9232–7828* ⊕*www.rox.com.au*) sells serious one-off designs, at the cutting edge of lapidary chic, that can be spotted on some exceedingly well-dressed wrists.

SOUVENIRS

ABC Shops (⊠*Queen Victoria Bldg., 455 George St., City Center* ☏*02/9286–3726* ⊕*www.shop.abc.net.au*), the retail arm of Australia's national broadcaster, sells an offbeat collection of things Australian in words, music, and print. It's an unfailing source of inspiration for gifts and souvenirs.

Australian Geographic (⊠*Shop C15A, Centrepoint, Market and Pitt Sts., City Center* ☏*02/9231–5055*) is a virtual museum crammed with games, puzzles, experiments, and environmental science that promises endless fascination for the inquisitive mind.

T-SHIRTS & BEACHWEAR

Done Art and Design (⊠*123 George St., The Rocks* ☏*02/9251–6099* ⊕*www.done.com.au*) sells the striking artworks of prominent artist Ken Done, who catches the sunny side of Sydney with vivid colors and bold brushstrokes. His shop also carries practical products with his distinctive designs, including bed linens, sunglasses, beach towels, beach and resort wear, and T-shirts.

Mambo (⊠*80 Campbell Parade, Bondi Beach* ☏*02/9365–2255* ⊕*www.mambo.com.au*) has designs inspired by bold beach colors and culture. The shirts, T-shirts, board shorts, and accessories are loud and funky—not for those who prefer their apparel understated.

Rip Curl (⊠*105 George St., The Rocks* ☏*02/9252–4551*), the well-known Australian surfing company that has been making surfboards since 1967, sells gear from this flagship store. The two levels are packed with the latest board shorts, surf clothes, wet suits, swimsuits, T-shirts, and accessories. It also makes ski and adventure clothing.

SYDNEY ESSENTIALS

TRANSPORTATION

BY AIR

Sydney's main airport is Kingsford–Smith International, 8 km (5 mi) south of the city. Luggage carts are available in the baggage area of the international terminal. You can convert your money to Australian currency at the Travelex offices in both the arrival and departure areas.

These are open daily from about 5 AM to 10 PM or later, depending on flight times.

Tourism New South Wales has two information counters in the arrival level of the international terminal. One provides free maps and brochures and handles general inquiries. The other books accommodations and tours, and sells travel insurance. Both counters are open daily from approximately 6 AM to 11 PM.

Kingsford–Smith's domestic and international terminals are 3 km (2 mi) apart. To get from one terminal to the other, you can take a taxi for about A$12 or use the Airport Shuttle Bus for A$4.

TRANSFERS AirportLink rail service reaches the city in 13 minutes. Trains depart every 5 to 10 minutes during peak hours and at least every 15 minutes at other times. A one-way fare is A$12; a group ticket (three people) costs A$27. The link meshes with the suburban rail network at Central Station and Circular Quay Station. You take an escalator down to the platform, but, even so, taking the train can be a bit difficult for travelers with anything more than light luggage. Trains do not have adequate stowage facilities, and for two traveling together a taxi is more convenient and costs only slightly more.

Taxis are available outside the terminal buildings. It's about A$35 to city hotels, and A$31 to Kings Cross.

A chauffeured limousine to the city hotels costs about A$80. Waiting time is charged at the rate of A$72 per hour. Astra Chauffeured Limousines has reliable services.

Airport Kingsford–Smith International Airport (☎ 02/9667–9111 ⊕ www. sydneyairport.com.au).

Airlines Air Canada (☎ 1300/655767). Air France (☎ 1300/399–0190). Air New Zealand (☎ 13–2476). Air Pacific (☎ 1800/230150). Austrian Airlines (☎ 18/064–2438). British Airways (☎ 1300/767177). Cathay Pacific (☎ 13–1747). Emirates (☎ 133/303777). Garuda (☎ 1300/365330). Japan Airlines (☎ 02/9272–1111). Jetstar (☎ 13–1538). Malaysia Airlines (☎ 13–2627). Pacific Blue (☎ 13–1645). Qantas (☎ 13–1313). Regional Express Airlines (☎ 13–1713). Singapore Airlines (☎ 13–1011). Thai Airways (☎ 1300/651960). United Airlines (☎ 13–1777). Virgin Blue (☎ 13–6789).

Transfers AirportLink (☎ 13–1500 ⊕ www.airportlink.com.au). Astra Chauffeured Limousines (☎ 1800/819797 ⊕ www.astralimousines.com.au). Transport Info Line (City Rail) (☎ 13–1500).

BY BOAT

Cunard, Holland America Line, Princess Cruises, and P&O cruise ships call frequently at Sydney as part of their South Pacific and around-the-world itineraries. Passenger ships generally berth at the Overseas Passenger Terminal at Circular Quay. The terminal sits in the shadow of the Harbour Bridge, close to many of the city's major attractions and the bus, ferry, and train networks. Otherwise, passenger ships berth at the Darling Harbour Passenger Terminal (also called Wharf 8 Darling Harbour), a short walk from the city center.

International cruise ships call at Sydney during the warmer months (from November to March), while P&O Australia has two, locally based cruise ships that travel year-round from Sydney to the Pacific islands on 7- to 14-day round-trip itineraries. The Sydney Ports authority has details of all ships calling at Sydney.

There is no finer introduction to the city than a trip aboard one of the commuter ferries that ply Sydney Harbour. The hub of the ferry system is Circular Quay, and ferries dock at the almost 30 wharves—which span the length and breadth of the harbor—between about 6 AM and 11:30 PM. One of the most popular sightseeing trips is the Manly ferry, a 30-minute journey from Circular Quay that provides glimpses of harborside mansions and the sandstone cliffs and bushland along the north shore. On the return journey, consider taking the speedy JetCat, which skims the waves in an exhilarating 15-minute trip back to the city. But be warned: passengers are not allowed on deck, and views are obscured.

The one-way Manly ferry fare is A$6, and the JetCat costs A$7.90. Fares for shorter inner-harbor journeys start at A$4.80. You can also buy economical ferry-and-entrance-fee passes, available from the Circular Quay ticket office, to such attractions as Taronga Zoo and Sydney Aquarium.

The sleek RiverCat ferries travel west from Circular Quay as far as Parramatta. These ferries are used overwhelmingly by commuters, although they also provide a useful and practical connection to Homebush Bay, site of Sydney Olympic Park. A one-way fare to Olympic Park is A$6.

A fun, fast, but somewhat expensive way to get around is by water taxi. (Circular Quay to Watsons Bay, for example, costs A$65 for two people.) Companies including Harbour Taxi Boats, Taxis Afloat, and Water Taxis Combined operate to and from practically anywhere on Sydney Harbour that has wharf or steps access. Watertours runs a taxi shuttle between Darling Harbour and the Opera House for A$15 one way, A$25 return. Mini-tours of the harbor in the little yellow taxi boats begin at A$15 per person for 30 minutes.

Cruise Ships Crystal Cruises (☎ *02/8247-7100*). **Cunard** (☎ *13-2469*). **Darling Harbour Passenger Terminal (Wharf 8 Darling Harbour)** (☎ *02/9296-4999* ⊕ *www.sydneyports.com.au*). **Holland America Line** (☎ *02/8296-7072*). **Overseas Passenger Terminal** (☎ *02/9299-5868*). **P&O** (☎ *13-2469*). **Princess Cruises** (☎ *13-2469*). **Sydney Ports** (☎ *02/9296-4999* ⊕ *www.sydneyports.com.au*).

Ferries Transport Info Line (ferries) (☎ *13-1500* ⊕ *www.sydneyferries.info*).

Water Taxis Harbour Taxi Boats (☎ *02/9555-1155*). **Taxis Afloat** (☎ *02/9555-3222*). **Water Taxis Combined** (☎ *02/9555-8888*). **Watertours** (☎ *02/9211-7730*).

BY BUS
Greyhound Australia and Murrays bus services are available to all major cities from Sydney. Firefly Express caters mainly to backpackers. You can purchase tickets for long-distance buses from travel agents, by

1

telephone, or at bus terminals. Approximate travel times by bus are: Sydney to Canberra, 4 hours; Sydney to Melbourne, 11 hours; Sydney to Brisbane, 11 hours; Sydney to Adelaide, 13 hours. The main terminal is the Central Station (Eddy Avenue) terminus, just south of the city center. Lockers are available in the terminal.

Contacts Central Station (☎ *02/9379–1777* ⊕ *www.cityrail.info*). **Firefly Express** (☎ *1300/730740* ⊕ *www.fireflyexpress.com.au*). **Greyhound Australia** (☎ *13–1499* ⊕ *www.greyhound.com.au*). **Murrays** (☎ *13–2251* ⊕ *www.murrays.com.au*).

Bus travel in Sydney is rather slow because of the city's congested streets and undulating terrain. Fares are calculated by the number of city sections traveled. The minimum two-section bus fare (A$1.70) applies to trips throughout the inner-city area. You would pay the minimum fare, for example, for a ride from Circular Quay to Kings Cross, from Park Street to Oxford Street in Paddington, or from Bondi Junction railway station to Bondi Beach. Tickets may be purchased from the driver, who will compute the fare based on your destination (Bus 333, running from Circular Quay to Bondi Beach, only accepts passengers who have pre-paid tickets or a travel pass.) Discounted fares are available in several forms, including Travelten passes (valid for 10 journeys), which start at A$13.60 and are available from bus stations and most newsstands. You can also buy TravelPasses, which provide unlimited travel for one week on buses, ferries, and trains in various zones. The cheapest is the A$32 Red TravelPass. It covers most of the areas visitors would want to see, with the exception of Manly and Sydney Olympic Park.

Contact Transport Info Line (☎ *13–1500* ⊕ *www.sydneybuses.info*).

BY CAR
With the assistance of a good road map or street directory, you shouldn't have too many problems driving in and out of Sydney, thanks to a decent freeway system. Keep in mind that Australia is almost as large as the continental United States. In computing your travel times for trips between Sydney and the following cities, allow for an average speed of about 85 kph (53 mph). The main roads to and from other state capitals are: the 1,027-km (642-mi) Pacific Highway (Highway 1) north to Brisbane; the 290-km (181-mi) M5 southwest to Canberra, and 893 km (558 mi) southwest to Melbourne via the M5 and Hume Highway; also the 1,038-km (644-mi) Princes Highway (Highway 1) south to the New South Wales south coast and Melbourne. Adelaide is 1,422 km (889 mi) away west via the Hume and Sturt (Highway 20) highways, and Perth is a long and rather tedious 4,136-km (2,585-mi) drive west via Adelaide. You can check distances on the Australian Explorer ⊕ *www.australianexplorer.com*.

Driving a car around Sydney is not recommended. Close to the city the harbor inlets plus the hilly terrain equal few straight streets. Parking space is limited, and both parking lots and parking meters are expensive. If you do decide to drive, ask your car-rental agency for a street directory or purchase one from a newsstand.

If you rent from a major international company, expect to pay about A$85 per day for a medium-size automatic and about A$75 for a standard compact. However, if you go with a local operator, such as Bayswater, you might pay as little as A$23 per day for a one-year-old vehicle. Some of these discount operators restrict travel to within a 50-km (30-mi) radius of the city center, and one-way rentals are not possible. A surcharge applies if you pick up your car from the airport.

Contacts Avis (☏ 13–6333). **Bayswater** (☏ 02/9360–3622). **Budget** (☏ 13–2727). **Hertz** (☏ 13–3039). **Thrifty** (☏ 13–6139).

BY MONORAIL & TRAM

Sydney Monorail is one of the fastest, most relaxing forms of public transportation in the city, but its use is limited to travel between the city center, Darling Harbour, and Chinatown. The fare is A$4 one way. The A$8 Day Pass is a better value if you intend to use the monorail to explore. You can purchase tickets at machines in the monorail stations. Monorails run every three to five minutes, generally from 7 AM to 10 PM, and until midnight on Friday and Saturday. Stations are identified by a large white M against a black background.

The Sydney Light Rail, a tram, is identifiable by signs with a large black M against a white background, and is a limited system that provides a fast, efficient link between Central Station, Darling Harbour, the Star City casino and entertainment complex, Sydney fish markets, and the inner-western suburbs of Glebe and Lilyfield. The modern, air-conditioned trams operate at 10- to 30-minute intervals, 24 hours a day. One-way tickets are A$3 to A$4, and the Day Pass is a comparatively good value at A$8.50. You can purchase tickets at machines in Light Rail stations or on board the trams.

Contact Metro Monorail and Light Rail (☏ 02/9285–5600 ⊕ www.metromonorail.com.au).

BY TAXIS & LIMOUSINE

Taxis are a relatively economical way to cover short to medium distances in Sydney. A 3-km (2-mi) trip from Circular Quay to the eastern suburbs costs around A$16. Drivers are entitled to charge more than the metered fare if the passenger's baggage exceeds 55 pounds, if the taxi has been booked by telephone, or if the passenger crosses the Harbour Bridge, where a toll is levied. Fares are 10% higher between 10 PM and 5 AM, when the numeral "2" will be displayed in the tariff indicator on the meter. At all other times, make sure the numeral "1" is displayed. Taxis are licensed to carry four passengers. Most drivers will accept payment by American Express, Diners Club, MasterCard, and Visa, although a 10% surcharge is applied. Taxis can be hailed on the street, boarded at a taxi stand, or booked by phone. Taxi stands can be found outside most bus and railway stations, as well as outside the larger hotels. Complaints should be directed to Taxi Cab Complaints.

Chauffeur-driven limousines are available for trips around Sydney. At your request, the driver will give commentary on the major sights. Limousines can be rented for approximately A$80 per hour.

Limousine Company **Astra Chauffeured Limousines** (☎ *1800/819797*).

Taxi Companies **ABC Taxis** (☎ *13–2522*). **Taxi Cab Complaints** (☎ *1800/648478*). **Taxis Combined Services** (☎ *02/8332–8888*).

BY TRAIN

The main terminal for long-distance and intercity trains is Central Station, about 2 km (1 mi) south of the city center. Two daily services (morning and evening) operate between Sydney and Melbourne; the trip takes about 11 hours. Two *Explorer* trains make the four-hour trip to Canberra daily. The overnight *Brisbane XPT* makes the 15-hour Sydney–Brisbane journey every day. Call the state rail authority, Countrylink, between 6:30 AM and 10 PM daily for information about fares and timetables, or check the Countrylink Web site. The *Indian-Pacific* (operated by Great Southern Railways) leaves Sydney on Wednesday and Saturday afternoons for Adelaide (26 hours) and Perth (64 hours).

Tickets for long-distance train travel can be purchased from Countrylink Travel Centres at Central Station, Circular Quay, Wynyard Station, and Town Hall Station. Countrylink has several passes that are a good value: the Backtracker Pass allows unlimited travel between Sydney and Melbourne (and back to Brisbane), and includes a return trip to the Blue Mountains and one day with unlimited travel on Sydney buses, trains, and ferries. Passes are available for 14 days and one, three, and six months, starting at A$220.

Contacts **Central Station** (✉ *Eddy Ave., City South*). **City Rail** (☎ *13–1500* ⊕ *www.cityrail.nsw.gov.au*). **Countrylink Travel Centres** (✉ *Eddy Ave., Central Station, City South* ✉ *Shop W6/W7, Alfred St., Circular Quay* ✉ *Shop W15, Wynyard Concourse, Wynyard Station, City Center* ✉ *Lower level, Queen Victoria Bldg., George and Park Sts., Town Hall Station, City Center* ☎ *13–2232* ⊕ *www.countrylink. info*). **Great Southern Railways** (☎ *13–2147* ⊕ *www.gsr.com.au*). **Metro Light Rail** (☎ *02/8584–5250* ⊕ *www.metromonorail.com.au*).

CONTACTS & RESOURCES

BANKS & EXCHANGE SERVICES

Any bank will exchange traveler's checks and most foreign currencies. ATMs are ubiquitous in airports, shopping malls, and tourist areas. Cirrus and Plus cards are accepted at most ATMs, but check with your bank to make sure that you can access your funds overseas and that you have a four-digit PIN. Banks can be found in all areas where you are likely to shop, including the city center, Kings Cross, Paddington, Double Bay, Bondi Beach, and Darling Harbour.

Banks **ANZ** (✉ *365 George St., City Center* ☎ *13–1314*). **Commonwealth Bank** (✉ *254 George St., City Center* ☎ *02/9241–6855*). **Westpac Bank** (✉ *60 Martin Pl., City Center* ☎ *13–2032*).

CONSULATES

Contacts **British Consulate General** (✉ *Level 16, Gateway Bldg., 1 Macquarie Pl., Circular Quay* ☎ *02/9247–7521*). **Canadian Consulate General** (✉ *Level*

5, 111 Harrington St., The Rocks ☎*02/9364-3000*). **New Zealand Consulate General** (✉*Level 10, 55 Hunter St., City Center* ☎*02/9223-0223*). **United States of America Consulate General** (✉*Level 59, 19-29 Martin Pl., City Center* ☎*02/9373-9200*).

DISCOUNTS & DEALS

For the price of admission to two or three top attractions, the Smart-Visit Card (available from the Sydney Visitor Centre in the Rocks and several other locations) gets you into 40 Sydney sights and attractions—including the Opera House, Sydney Aquarium, and Koala Park Sanctuary. Several different cards are available, including single-day and weekly cards. Cards may also include public transportation. Prices start at A$65 for a single-day adult card without transportation.

A SydneyPass is a good value if you have limited time and want to do a lot of travel on public transportation. The pass allows unlimited travel on public buses, harbor ferries, and on most suburban train services. It also includes the AirportLink rail service, the guided Sydney Explorer and Bondi Explorer buses, and any of the three sightseeing cruises operated by the State Transit Authority. A three-day pass is A$110; five-day, A$145; seven-day, A$165. Purchase passes from the Tourism New South Wales counter on the ground floor of the international airport terminal or from the driver of any Explorer bus.

A TravelPass allows unlimited travel aboard buses, ferries, and trains (but not the light-rail system) within designated areas of the city for a week or more. A useful pass is the weeklong Red TravelPass (A$32), which covers the city and eastern suburbs and inner-harbor ferries. (Ferries to Manly and Sydney Olympic Park cost extra.) TravelPasses are available from railway and bus stations and from most newsagents on bus routes. Contact the Transport Info Line for all state-government-run transportation.

Contacts SmartVisit Card (☎*02/9247-6611 or 1300/661711* ⊕*www.seesydneycard.com*). **SydneyPass** (☎*13-1500* ⊕*www.sydneypass.info*). **Transport Info Line** (☎*13-1500* ⊕*www.sydneybuses.info*). **TravelPass** (☎*13-1500* ⊕*www.131500.com.au*).

EMERGENCIES

Dial **000** for an ambulance, the fire department, or the police. Dental Emergency Information Service provides names and numbers for nearby dentists. It's available only after 7 PM daily. Royal North Shore Hospital is 7 km (4½ mi) northwest of the city center. St. Vincent's Public Hospital is 2½ km (1½ mi) east of the city center.

Your best bets for a late-night pharmacy are the Kings Cross and Oxford Street (Darlinghurst) areas, or ask reception for information if staying in a major hotel in the city. Since Sydney's overnight pharmacies work on a rotating basis, call the Pharmacy Guild for 24-hour advice and referrals to the nearest open outlet.

Dentist Dental Emergency (☎*02/9211-2224*).

Hospitals Royal North Shore Hospital (✉ *Pacific Hwy., St. Leonards* ☎ *02/9926–7111*). **St. Vincent's Public Hospital** (✉ *Victoria and Burton Sts., Darlinghurst* ☎ *02/8382–1111*).

Pharmacies Pharmacy Guild (☎ *02/9966–8377*).

Police Bondi Beach (✉ *77 Gould St., Bondi Beach* ☎ *02/9365–9699*). **City Central** (✉ *192 Day St., Darlinghurst* ☎ *02/9265–6499*). **Kings Cross** (✉ *1–15 Elizabeth Bay Rd., Kings Cross* ☎ *02/8356–0099*). **Manly** (✉ *3 Belgrave St., Manly* ☎ *02/9977–9499*). **The Rocks** (✉ *132 George St., The Rocks* ☎ *02/8220–6399*).

MAIL, SHIPPING & THE INTERNET

If you need business services, such as faxing, using a computer, photocopying, typing, or translation services during your trip, plan to stay in a hotel with a business center, since their services are normally available only to guests. Post offices often have fax services and one-hour photo processing.

DHL and Federal Express both ship internationally overnight.

Internet Cafés Global Gossip (✉ *415 Pitt St., City Center* ☎ *02/9281–6890* ✉ *61–65 Darlinghurst Rd., Kings Cross* ☎ *02/9326–9777*). **Phone Net Café** (✉ *73–75 Hall St., Bondi Beach* ☎ *02/9365–0681*). **Surfnet Internet Cafe** (✉ *54 Spring St., Bondi Junction* ☎ *02/9386–4066*).

Post Offices General Post Office (✉ *1 Martin Pl., City Center* ☎ *13–1318* ⊕ *www.australiapost.com.au*). **Glebe Post Office** (✉ *181A Glebe Point Rd., Glebe* ☎ *13–1318*). **Kings Cross Post Office** (✉ *Shop 501–502, Kingsgate Hotel, Victoria and William Sts., Kings Cross* ☎ *13–1318*).

Overnight Shipping Services DHL (☎ *13–1406* ⊕ *www.dhl.com.au*). **Federal Express** (☎ *13–2610* ⊕ *www.fedex.com.au*).

SIGHTSEEING TOURS

Dozens of tour operators lead guided trips through Sydney and the surrounding areas. Options include shopping strolls, tours of the Sydney fish markets, and rappelling the waterfalls of the Blue Mountains. The Sydney Visitor Centre and other booking and information centers can provide you with many more suggestions and recommendations. Most suburban shopping plazas have a travel agency—in addition to the many general and specialist travel agents in the city center.

Fodor'sChoice ★ The Sydney Harbour Explorer cruise, run by Captain Cook Cruises, allows you to hop on and off at the Opera House, Watsons Bay, Taronga Zoo, and Darling Harbour. Explorer cruises (A$29) depart daily from Circular Quay at 9:45 AM, 10:45 AM, and then every two hours. The best introductory trip to Sydney Harbour is Captain Cook's 2½-hour Coffee Cruise, which follows the southern shore to Watsons Bay, crosses to the north shore to explore Middle Harbour, and returns to Circular Quay. Coffee cruises (A$44) depart daily at 10 and 2:15. Dinner, sunset, and showtime cruises are also available, and all cruises depart from Wharf 6, Circular Quay.

The Sydney Ferries Corporation runs several Harboursights cruises at lower costs than those of privately operated cruises. Light refreshments are for sale on board. All cruises depart from Wharf 4 at the Circular Quay terminal. The Morning Harbour Cruise (A$18) takes in the major sights of the harbor to the east of the city. The one-hour journey begins daily at 10:30. The Afternoon Harbour Cruise (A$24) is a leisurely 2½-hour tour that takes in the scenic eastern suburbs and affluent Middle Harbour. Cruises leave weekdays at 1 and weekends at 12:30. The 1½-hour Evening Harbour Lights Cruise (A$22) takes you into Darling Harbour for a nighttime view of the city from the west, then passes the Garden Island naval base to view the Opera House and Kings Cross. Tours depart Monday through Saturday at 8 PM.

Harbour Jet offers high-speed jet-boat tours of the harbor, racing around at 75 kph (47 mph) per hour and performing 270-degree spins. Trips range from 35 minutes to 1½ hours and begin at A$60 per person.

Contacts Captain Cook Cruises (02/9206–1122 ⊕ www.captaincook.com. au/sydney). **Harbour Jet** (02/9698–2110 or 1300/887373 ⊕ www.harbourjet. com). **Sydney Ferries Corporation** (13–1500 ⊕ www.sydneyferries.info).

The Sydney Explorer bus, which makes a 35-km (22-mi) circuit of all the major attractions, including the Rocks, Kings Cross, Darling Harbour, Chinatown, and across Harbour Bridge to Milsons Point, is a great way to see the city. Ticket holders can board or leave the bus at any of the 27 stops along the route and catch any following Explorer bus. The bright red buses follow one another every 20 minutes, and the service operates from 8:40 AM daily. The last bus to make the circuit departs from Circular Quay at 5:20 PM. If you choose to stay on board for the entire circuit, the trip takes around two hours.

The Bondi Explorer bus runs a guided bus tour of the eastern suburbs. The blue bus begins its 30-km (19-mi) journey at Circular Quay and travels through Kings Cross, Double Bay, Vaucluse, and Watsons Bay to the Gap, then returns to the city via Bondi, Bronte, and Coogee beaches; Centennial Park; and Oxford Street. You can leave the bus at any of its 19 stops and catch a following bus, or remain on board for a round-trip of about 90 minutes. Buses follow one another at 30-minute intervals beginning at 8:45 AM. The last bus departs from Circular Quay at 4:15 PM.

Tickets for both Explorer buses, valid for one day, cost A$39 and can be purchased on board or from the Sydney Visitor Centre at Darling Harbour and The Rocks. A two-day combined pass for both buses, which can be used within an eight-day period, is A$68. The tickets also include travel on all regular Sydney buses that operate within the area covered by Explorer buses.

Sydney Day Tours, AAT Kings, Great Sights, and Grayline run half-day tours covering the city, Darling Harbour, and Bondi Beach (A$44 to A$57).

Several bus companies run day trips in and around the Sydney region, reaching as far as the Blue Mountains, the Hunter Valley wine region, Canberra, wildlife parks, and the 2000 Olympics site at Homebush

Bay. AAT Kings, Great Sights, and Murrays both have a 24-hour information and reservation service.

Contacts AAT Kings (☎*1300/556100*). **Explorer Buses** (☎*13–1500* ⊕*www. sydneybuses.info*). **Grayline** (☎*1300/858687*). **Great Sights** (☎*1300/850850*). **Murrays Australia** (☎*13–2251*). **Sydney Day Tours** (☎*02/9251–6101* ⊕*www. sydneydaytours.com.au*).

Mount 'n Beach Safaris is a four-wheel-drive operator that arranges soft adventures to areas of outstanding beauty around Sydney. The company's Blue Mountains 4WD Wildlife Discovery gives you the chance to see koalas and kangaroos, enjoy morning tea in the bush, take in the scenic highlights of the Blue Mountains, lunch at a historic pub, and return to Sydney in time for a performance at the Opera House. Their Best of Hunter Wines & Dolphins tour of the Hunter Valley wine-growing district and the aquatic playground of Port Stephens is a two-day option.

Contact Mount 'n Beach Safaris (☎*02/9439–3010* ⊕*www.mountnbeach safaris.com.au*).

A flight on Sydney Seaplanes is a wonderful way to see the Sydney sights and soar over the beaches. Short flights taking in the harbor, Bondi Beach, and Manly cost from A$120 per person. A trip to the Hawkesbury River (including a gourmet lunch when you're on land) costs A$460. The seaplanes take off from Rose Bay.

BridgeClimb is a unique tour that affords the ultimate view of the harbor and city center from Sydney Harbour Bridge. The hugely popular tours last for 3½ hours and cost from A$190 per person. Tours depart from 5 Cumberland Street, the Rocks. Twilight climbs and night climbs are also available.

Easyrider Motorbike Tours conducts exciting chauffeur-driven (you ride as a passenger) Harley-Davidson tours to the city's landmarks and beaches, the Blue Mountains, and Kangaroo Valley. A two-hour tour is A$190 per person, and a full-day excursion starts at about A$400.

Bonza Bikes lets you see the best Sydney sights without having to worry about heavy traffic. The half-day Classic Sydney Bike Ride cruises past the Opera House, winds around the harbor, and offers the chance to take in the foliage in the Sydney Botanic Gardens and sights at Darling Harbour. Some trips include lunch and go over Harbour Bridge, with prices starting from A$70 for a half-day (bike and helmet included).

Local gardening guru Graham Ross runs popular jacaranda cruises in early November each year. You'll see the beautiful purple flowering trees planted on the shores of the harbor. The three-hour cruise (A$49) takes in the city's sights with fascinating commentary on history and horticulture. Phone or check the Web, as dates change each year.

The Cadi Jam Ora First Encounters is a tour of the Royal Botanic Gardens' display of plants that were growing before Europeans arrived on Sydney's shores in 1788. An Aboriginal guide explains the plants and their uses.

You can go whale-watching from Sydney Harbour with Bass and Flinders Cruises and Captain Cook Cruises. Boats leave from Sydney Harbour in the winter months and venture a few kilometers outside Sydney Heads to see southern right whales making their way up and down the New South Wales coast.

Contacts Bass and Flinders (☎ *02/9583-1199* ⊕ *www.bassflinders.com. au*). **Bonza Bikes** (☎ *02/9331-1175* ⊕ *www.bonzabikes.com*). **BridgeClimb** (☎ *02/8274-7777* ⊕ *www.bridgeclimb.com.au*). **Cadi Jam Ora First Encounters** (☎ *02/9231-1811* ⊕ *www.rbgsyd.nsw.gov.au*). **Captain Cook Cruises** (☎ *02/9206-1122* ⊕ *www.captaincook.com.au/sydney*). **Easyrider Motorbike Tours** (☎ *02/9247-2477 or 1300/882065* ⊕ *www.easyrider.com.au*). **Ross Garden Tours** (☎ *1800/809348* ⊕ *www.rosstours.com*). **Sydney Seaplanes** (☎ *9388-1978 or 1300/732752* ⊕ *www.seaplanes.com.au*).

The Rocks Walking Tours will introduce you to Sydney's European settlement site, with an emphasis on the neighborhood buildings and personalities of the convict period. The 1½-hour tour costs A$19 and involves little climbing. Tours leave weekdays at 10:30, 12:30, and 2:30 (in January 10:30 and 2:30 only), and weekends at 11:30 and 2.

You can literally drink in Sydney's history during the Rocks Pub Tour, where you wander the narrow streets of the Rocks with a guide and stop in for drinks at three pubs. You will hear the stories of hard times in the early days of Sydney and learn about its colorful characters. The 1¾-hour tours depart from Cadman's Cottage on George Street (near the Museum of Contemporary Art) at 5 PM on Monday, Wednesday, Friday, and Saturday. The cost is A$34.50.

The dark alleyways of the Rocks can be scary, and the Rocks Ghost Tours makes sure people are suitably spooked as the guides, dressed in long black cloaks and carrying lanterns, regale them with stories of the murders and other nasty goings-on in the early days of the colony. Tours depart nightly at 6:45 (April–October) and 7:45 (November–March) from Cadman's Cottage and cost A$34.

Kings Cross has been the haunt of bohemians, criminals, and ladies of the evening for many decades. The Crimes and Passion walking tour, run by Bounce Walking Tours, takes you alongside streets where notorious villains plied their trade. Tours depart from Circular Quay on Thursday and Saturday at 5 PM (November–March) and 1 PM (April–October) and cost A$40. The 2½-hour tour includes a drink in a local bar.

Contacts The **Crimes and Passions Walking Tour** (☎ *02/9328-5917* ⊕ *www. bouncewalkingtours.com*). The **Rocks Ghost Tours** (☎ *1300/731971* ⊕ *www. ghosttours.com.au*). The **Rocks Pub Tour** (☎ *02/9240-8788 or 1800/067676* ⊕ *www.therockspubtour.com*). The **Rocks Walking Tours** (✉ *23 Playfair St., The Rocks* ☎ *02/9247-6678* ⊕ *www.rockswalkingtours.com.au*).

TELEPHONES

The telephone code for Sydney and New South Wales is 02. If you're calling a New South Wales number that is a nonlocal call, dial 02 before the eight-digit local number. You can make interstate and international calls from any telephone.

TRAVEL AGENCIES
The following travel agencies can help you arrange tours and excursions.

Contacts American Express Travel Shop (✉ *105 Pitt St., City Center* ☎ *02/9236–4216*). **Australian Travel Specialists (ATS)** (✉ *Alfred St. and Wharf 6, Circular Quay* ☎ *02/9211–3192* ⊕ *www.atstravel.com.au*). **Flight Centre** (✉ *Shop 509, Kingsgate Centre, Darlinghurst Rd., Kings Cross* ☎ *02/9368–0688* ✉ *2/255 Elizabeth St., Hyde Park, City Center* ☎ *02/9202–3600* ⊕ *www.flightcentre.com.au*). **STA Travel** (✉ *855 George St., City Center* ☎ *02/9212–1255* ⊕ *www.statravel.com.au*). **Student Flights** (✉ *55–73 Oxford St., Darlinghurst* ☎ *02/8255–6144*). **YHA Travel Centre** (✉ *422 Kent St., City Center* ☎ *02/9261–1111* ⊕ *www.yha.com.au*).

VISITOR INFORMATION
There are information kiosks throughout the city, including Circular Quay (corner of Alfred and Pitt streets), Martin Place (at the corner of Elizabeth Street), and Town Hall (corner of George and Bathurst streets).

Countrylink, the state rail authority, is a good source of Sydney and New South Wales travel information.

The Sydney Visitor Centre is the major source of information, brochures, and maps for Sydney and New South Wales. There are two locations: the Rocks and Darling Harbour. The Tourism New South Wales Web site also has accommodation and food guides, maps, and what's on.

Contacts Countrylink (✉ *Shop W15, Wynyard Concourse, Wynyard Station, City Center* ☎ *13–2829* ⊕ *www.countrylink.info*). **Sydney Visitor Centre** (✉ *Level 2, the Rocks Centre, Argyle and Playfair Sts., The Rocks* ✉ *33 Wheat Rd., near IMAX Theatre, Darling Harbour* ☎ *02/9240–8788* ⊕ *www.sydneyvisitorcentre.com*). **Tourism New South Wales** (⊕ *www.sydneyaustralia.com*).

New South Wales

WORD OF MOUTH

"[If you like] to cuddle in front of the fire, drink mulled wine, eat fantastic stodgy food like baked puddings and...pot roasts, be able to hike to your heart's content without getting hot and uncomfortable and to get out there in nature's wilds and enjoy yourself...there is nowhere better than the Blue Mountains within a two-hour drive from Sydney."

—lizF

Updated
by Caroline
Gladstone

2

FOR MANY TRAVELERS, SYDNEY *IS* New South Wales, and they look to the other, less-populous states for Australia's famous wilderness experiences. There may be no substitute for Queensland's Great Barrier Reef or the Northern Territory's Kakadu National Park, but New South Wales has many of Australia's natural wonders within its borders. High on the list are the World Heritage areas of Lord Howe Island and the subtropical rain forests of the North Coast, as well as desert Outback, the highest mountain peaks in the country, lush river valleys, warm seas, golden beaches, and some of Australia's finest vineyards.

Today, with approximately 6.7 million people, New South Wales is Australia's most populous state. Although this is crowded by Australian standards, it's worth remembering that New South Wales is larger than every U.S. state except Alaska. In the state's east, a coastal plain reaching north to Queensland varies in width from less than a mile to almost 160 km (100 mi). This plain is bordered to the west by a chain of low mountains known as the Great Dividing Range, which tops off at about 7,300 feet in the Snowy Mountains in the state's far south. On this range's western slopes is a belt of pasture and farmland. Beyond that are the western plains and Outback, an arid, sparsely populated region that takes up two-thirds of the state.

EXPLORING NEW SOUTH WALES

New South Wales covers a large area that can broadly be divided into six popular regions. The Blue Mountains lie to the west of Sydney, while the Southern Highlands and South Coast stretch to the south, and the Hunter Valley is north of the capital. The North Coast is exactly where its name suggests, while Lord Howe Island is 700 km (435 mi) northeast of Sydney, a distant offshore environment of its own. At the state's south edge are the Snowy Mountains, part of the Great Dividing Range, which parallels the New South Wales coastline from the northern state of Queensland to the southern state of Victoria.

ABOUT THE RESTAURANTS

Dining varies dramatically throughout New South Wales, from superb city-standard restaurants to average country-town fare. As popular weekend retreats for well-heeled Sydneysiders, the Blue Mountains and Southern Highlands have a number of fine restaurants and cozy tea rooms that are perfect for light lunches or afternoon teas. In the Hunter Valley several excellent restaurants show off the region's fine wines. And although the Snowy Mountains area isn't gastronomically distinguished, the succulent trout makes a standout meal.

WHAT IT COSTS IN AUSTRALIAN DOLLARS					
	$$$$	$$$	$$	$	¢
AT DINNER	over A$50	A$36–A$50	A$21–A$35	A$10–A$20	under A$10

Prices are per person for a main course at dinner.

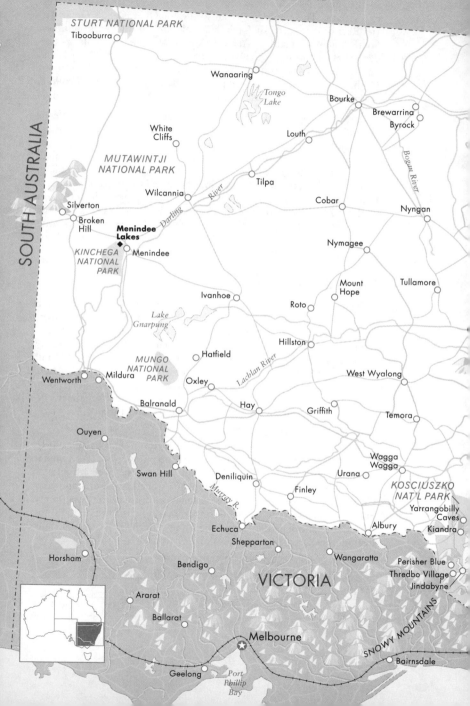

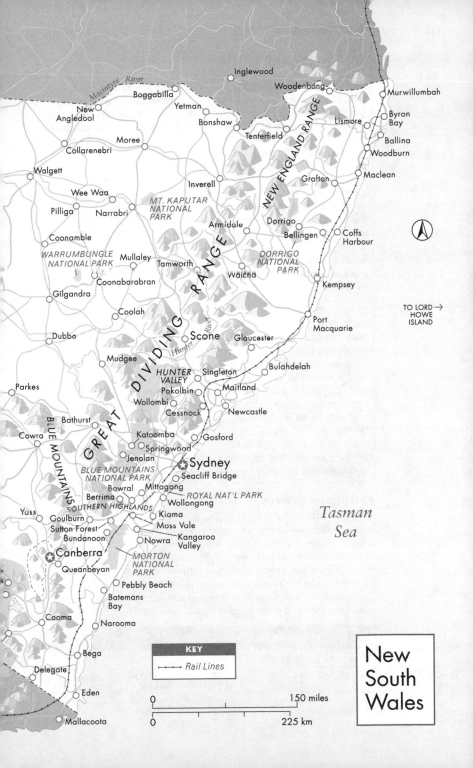

Macintyre River

Inglewood

Woodenbong

Murwillumbah

Boggabilla

Yetman

Lismore

Byron
Bay

New
Angledool

Bonshaw

Ballina

Tenterfield

Woodburn

Moree

Collarenebri

Maclean

Walgett

Inverell

Grafton

NEW ENGLAND RANGE

Wee Waa

MT. KAPUTAR
NATIONAL
PARK

Pilliga

Narrabri

Armidale

Dorrigo

Coonamble

Bellingen

Coffs
Harbour

WARRUMBUNGLE
NATIONAL PARK

Mullaley

DORRIGO
NATIONAL
PARK

Tamworth

Coonabarabran

Walcha

GREAT DIVIDING RANGE

Gilgandra

Kempsey

Coolah

Dubbo

Scone

Gloucester

Port
Macquarie

TO LORD →
HOWE
ISLAND

Mudgee

Hunter River

HUNTER
VALLEY

Singleton

Bulahdelah

Parkes

Pokolbin

Maitland

Wollombi

Bathurst

Cessnock

Newcastle

BLUE MOUNTAINS

Cowra

Katoomba

Gosford

Springwood

Jenolan

Sydney

BLUE MOUNTAINS
NATIONAL PARK

Seacliff Bridge

Yass

Bowral

Mittagong

ROYAL NAT'L PARK

Berrima

Wollongong

Tasman
Sea

SOUTHERN HIGHLANDS

Goulburn

Kiama

Sutton Forest

Moss Vale

Bundanoon

Kangaroo
Valley

Nowra

Canberra

MORTON
NATIONAL
PARK

Queanbeyan

Pebbly Beach

Batemans
Bay

Cooma

Narooma

Bega

KEY

Rail Lines

New
South
Wales

Delegate

Eden

0   150 miles

0   225 km

Mallacoota

GREAT ITINERARIES

It's wise to decide in advance whether you'd like to cover a lot of ground quickly or choose one or two places to linger a while. If you have four days or fewer, stick close to Sydney. The most compelling choice would be the Blue Mountains, followed by the Hunter Valley or Southern Highlands. In a very busy week you could visit the Blue and Snowy mountains, plus either the Hunter Valley or Southern Highlands. Two weeks would allow a Blue Mountains–North Coast–Lord Howe circuit, or brief stops in most of the six regions.

IF YOU HAVE 4 DAYS

Start with a visit to the **Blue Mountains.** You could arrange a round-trip itinerary from Sydney in a fairly hectic day or, preferably, spend a night in **Katoomba, Blackheath,** or **Leura** and make it a two-day excursion. Return to Sydney, and then head north to the **Hunter Valley.** A two-day/one-night driving visit here would allow you enough time to see the main sights and spend time touring the wineries before traveling

back to Sydney on the last day. An alternative would be a quick visit to the Blue Mountains, then a tour of the **Southern Highlands.Lord Howe Island** is a unique experience, best explored over a four-day trip.

IF YOU HAVE 7 DAYS

Head to the Blue Mountains and Hunter Valley as described above, then continue to the North Coast. In three days of driving you wouldn't get much farther than **Coffs Harbour** (with overnights there and in **Port Macquarie**), and this would be rushing it, but it's possible to fly back to Sydney from Coffs. If the North Coast holds special appeal, head straight there from Sydney and give yourself a chance to take in more of it. You could also spend two days in the Southern Highlands, then continue south to the Snowy Mountains for some alpine air, trout fishing, and bushwalking in Australia's highest alpine region. Alternatively, you can spend two nights in the Blue Mountains or the Hunter Valley, then return to Sydney.

ABOUT THE HOTELS

Accommodations include everything from run-of-the-mill motels to wilderness lodges, and from historic, cliff-perched properties to large, glossy seaside resorts. Rates are often much lower on weekdays, particularly in the Blue Mountains, Hunter Valley, and Southern Highlands. In the Snowy Mountains prices are highest during the winter ski season, and some hotels close during the off-season (October through May). Although chains aren't typical, an upscale group of small Peppers resorts is scattered across the state and tends to have particularly lovely settings.

WHAT IT COSTS IN AUSTRALIAN DOLLARS				
	$$$$	$$$	$$	$	¢
FOR TWO PEOPLE	over A$300	A$201–A$300	A$151–A$200	A$100–A$150	under A$100

Prices are for two people in a standard double room in high season, including tax and service, based on the European Plan (with no meals) unless otherwise noted.

WHEN TO VISIT

For many visitors the Australian summer (approximately December–February), which complements the northern-hemisphere winter, has great pull. The Blue Mountains can be very hot in summer, but the Southern Highlands' unpredictable weather can often provide relief from Sydney's sometimes stifling humidity, and it's the ideal season for bushwalking in the cool Snowy Mountains. The best times to visit the Hunter Valley are during the February–March grape harvest season and the September Hunter Food and Wine Festival.

The North Coast resort region is often booked solid between Christmas and the first half of January, but autumn (March–May) and spring (September–November) are good times to visit. Lord Howe Island is driest and hottest in February, while August is the windiest month. Many of the island's hotels and restaurants close between June and August.

There are some wonderful options if you are in New South Wales in winter. The Snowy Mountains ski season runs from early June to early October. And the "Yulefest" season from June through August is a popular time to visit the Blue Mountains, with blazing log fires and Christmas-style celebration packages. Another big celebration in the mountains is the Winter Solstice, marking the shortest day of the year. Parades and food stalls fill the main street of Katoomba on the Saturday nearest to June 22.

THE BLUE MOUNTAINS

Sydneysiders have been doubly blessed by nature. Not only do they have a magnificent coastline right at their front door, but a 90-minute drive west puts them in the midst of one of the most spectacular wilderness areas in Australia—World Heritage Blue Mountains National Park. Standing 3,500-plus feet high, these "mountains" were once the bed of an ancient sea. Gradually the sedimentary rock was uplifted until it formed a high plateau, which was etched by eons of wind and water into the wonderland of cliffs, caves, and canyons that exists today.

Now the richly forested hills, crisp mountain air, cool-climate gardens, vast sandstone chasms, and little towns of timber and stone are supreme examples of Australia's diversity. The mountains' distinctive blue coloring is caused by the evaporation of oil from the dense eucalyptus forests. This disperses light in the blue colors of the spectrum, a phenomenon known as Rayleigh Scattering.

When a railway line from Sydney was completed at the end of the

ARTIST HAVEN

The Blue Mountains harbor a wealth of talent. You'll find artists, writers, composers, and performers living in this vibrant cultural community. Check out the galleries, browse in the bookshops, or pop into a café or pub to catch some good music. The **Blue Mountains Music Festival** (⊕ www.bmff.org.au), held every March in Katoomba, showcases folk, blues, and roots music.

19th century, the mountains suddenly became fashionable, and guesthouses and hotels flourished. Combined with the dramatic natural beauty of the region, the history and charm of local villages make the Blue Mountains one of the highlights of any tour of Australia. If your schedule allows just one trip out of Sydney, make the Blue Mountains your top priority.

Numbers in the margin correspond to points of interest on the Blue Mountains map.

SPRINGWOOD & THE LOWER BLUE MOUNTAINS

79 km (49 mi) northwest of Sydney.

❶ The National Trust–listed **Norman Lindsay Gallery and Museum,** dedicated
★ to the Australian artist and writer, is one of the cultural highlights of the Blue Mountains. Lindsay is best known for his paintings, etchings, and drawings (featured in the movie *Sirens,* starring other famous Australians Elle MacPherson and Portia di Rossi), but he also built model boats, sculpted, and wrote poetry and children's books, among which *The Magic Pudding* has become an Australian classic. Lindsay lived in this house during the latter part of his life until he died in 1969. The delightful landscaped gardens contain several of Lindsay's sculptures, and you can also take a short but scenic bushwalk beyond the garden. ⊠ *14 Norman Lindsay Crescent, Faulconbridge* ☎ *02/4751–1067* ⊕ *www.hermes.net.au/nlg* ⊠ *A$9* ⊙ *Daily 10–4.*

WENTWORTH FALLS

26 km (16 mi) west of Springwood.

This attractive township has numerous crafts and antiques shops, a lake, and a popular golf course. Wentworth Falls straddles the highway, but most points of interest and views of the Jamison Valley and Blue Mountains National Park are south of the road.

❷ From a lookout in **Falls Reserve,** south of the town of Wentworth Falls,
★ you can take in magnificent views both out across the Jamison Valley to the Kings Tableland and of the 935-foot-high **Wentworth Falls** themselves. To find the best view of the falls, follow the trail that crosses the stream and zigzags down the sheer cliff face, signposted NATIONAL PASS. If you continue, the trail cuts back across the base of the falls and along a narrow ledge to the delightful Valley of the Waters, where it ascends to the top of the cliffs, emerging at the Conservation Hut. The complete circuit takes at least three hours and is a moderately difficult walk. ⊠ *End of Falls Rd.*

WHERE TO STAY & EAT

$–$$ ✕ **Conservation Hut.** From its prime spot in Blue Mountains National Park, on a cliff overlooking the Jamison Valley, this spacious, mudbrick bistro serves simple, savory fare such as hearty soups, beef pies, and perch fillets with baked fennel and sorrel sauce, as well as lovely dessert cakes. An open balcony is a delight on warm days, and a fire

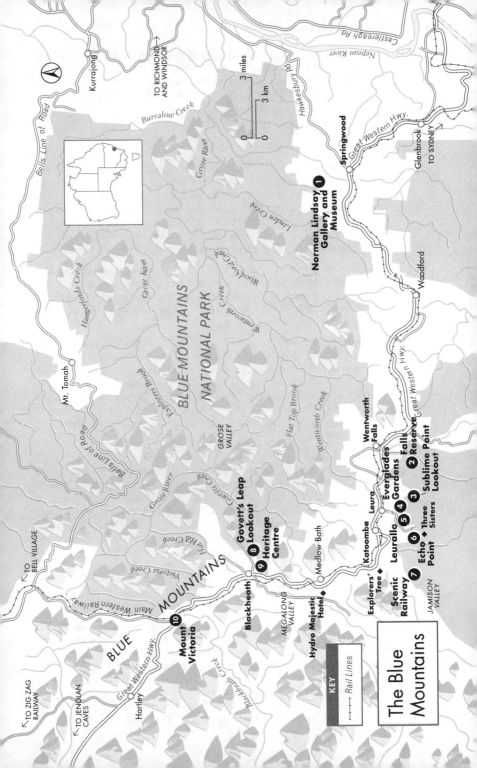

The Blue Mountains

KEY

├─┼─┤ Rail Lines

TO SYDNEY

Glenbrook

Great Western Hwy.

Springwood

❶ Norman Lindsay Gallery and Museum

Woodford

Hawkesbury Rd.

Nepean River

Castlereagh Rd.

TO RICHMOND AND WINDSOR

Kurrajong

Bells Line of Road

Burralow Creek

Grose River

Linden Creek

Woodford Creek

BLUE MOUNTAINS NATIONAL PARK

Grose River

Hungerfords Creek

Mt. Tomah

Wentworth Creek

Flat Top Brook

Wentworth Creek

Bells Line of Road

Explorers Brook

Grose River

GROSE VALLEY

Govett's Leap

Govett's Creek

Wentworth Falls

Everglades Gardens

Reserve ❷

Sublime Point Lookout

Leura

Falls ❸

❹

Three Sisters

❻ Echo Point

Katoomba

❽ Govett's Leap Lookout

❾ Heritage Centre

Medlow Bath

Govetts Creek

Rat Hill Creek

Blackheath

Victoria Creek

MEGALONG VALLEY

Hydro Majestic Hotel ◆

Explorers' Tree ◆

Scenic Railway ◆

Leuralla

❼

JAMISON VALLEY

Main Western Railway

BLUE

MOUNTAINS

Great Western Hwy.

Blackheath Creek

❿ Mount Victoria

Hartley

TO ZIG ZAG RAILWAY

TO JENOLAN CAVES

TO BELL VILLAGE

3 miles

3 km

blazes in the cooler months. A hiking trail from the bistro leads down into the Valley of the Waters, one of the splendors of the mountains. It's a wonderful pre- or post-meal walk. ⊠*Fletcher St.* ☎*02/4757–3827* ▭*AE, MC, V* ⌷❢*BYOB* ⊘*No dinner Sat. from mid-Sept.–May.*

LEURA

5 km (3 mi) west of Wentworth Falls.

Leura, the prettiest of the mountain towns, is lined with excellent cafés, restaurants, and gift shops, and has a strip of lovely trees dividing the main street. From the south end of the main street (The Mall), the road continues past superb local gardens as it winds down to the massive cliffs overlooking the Jamison Valley. The dazzling 19-km (12-mi) journey along Cliff Drive skirts the rim of the valley—often only yards from the cliff edge—providing truly spectacular Blue Mountains views.

❸ **Sublime Point Lookout,** just outside Leura, lives up to its name with a
★ great view of the Jamison Valley and the generally spectacular Blue Mountains scenery. It's a quiet vantage point that provides a different perspective from that of the famous **Three Sisters** lookout at nearby Katoomba. ⊠*Sublime Point Rd.*

❹ **Everglades Gardens,** a National Trust–listed, cool-climate arboretum and nature reserve established in the 1930s, is one of the best public gardens in the Blue Mountains region. Paths cut through settings of native bushland and exotic flora, a rhododendron garden, an alpine plant area, and formal European-style terraces. The views of the Jamison Valley are magnificent. ⊠*37 Everglades Ave.* ☎*02/4784–1938* ⊕*www. evergladesgardens.info* ⊠*A$7* ⊘*Oct.–Mar., daily 10–5; Apr.–Sept. daily 10–4.*

❺ **Leuralla,** a 1911 mansion, still belongs to the family of Dr. H. V. ("Doc") Evatt (1894–1965), the first president of the General Assembly of the United Nations and later the leader of the Australian Labor Party. A 19th-century Australian art collection and a small museum dedicated to Dr. Evatt are inside the home. Also on the grounds, the **New South Wales Toy and Railway Museum** has an extensive collection of railway memorabilia, including a toy display with tin-plate automobiles, ships, and planes, and antique dolls and bears. Directly across the street are the Leuralla Public Gardens, with spectacular views of the Jamison Valley. ⊠*36 Olympian Parade* ☎*02/4784–1169* ⊠*A$12, A$8 for gardens only* ⊘*Daily 10–5.*

WHERE TO STAY & EAT
$$ ✕**Cafe Bon Ton.** This smart bistro is a casual breakfast and lunch spot with indoor and courtyard dining. At night the white tablecloths and fine cutlery come out and an elegant restaurant emerges. Brunch and lunch fare include smoked trout hash, a variety of pasta dishes, and what the chef calls his "killer" club sandwich (that's Australian for excellent). The seasonal evening menu includes entrées such as braised pork cheeks and other French-influenced dishes. In winter a log fire burns in the grate. Book ahead on weekends. ⊠*192 The Mall* ☎*02/4782–4377*

⊟*AE, MC, V* ◐*No dinner Wed. and Thurs. in winter or Mon.–Wed. in summer.*

$$ ⨯ **Silks Brasserie.** Thanks to its Sydney-standard food, wine, and service, Silks rates as one of the finest Blue Mountains restaurants. The menu here changes seasonally, but might include pan-roasted Atlantic salmon with a honey–mustard-seed dressing on potato cake, or oven-baked lamb loin with mixed-herb mousseline and tomato compote. The locals' favorite dessert is the caramelized warm banana tart with coconut ice cream. In colder

Fodor's Choice
★

months a log fire warms the century-old shop's simple but elegant interior, where yellow ocher walls reach from a black-and-white checkerboard floor to high ceilings. ⊠ *128 The Mall, Leura, 2780* ☎ *02/4784–2534* ⌦ *Reservations essential* ⊟ *AE, DC, MC, V.*

$$$$ 🏨 **Peppers Fairmont Resort.** Perched spectacularly on the edge of cliffs overlooking the Jamison Valley, this is the colossus of accommodations in the region, and is a popular choice with conference groups. Although it can't hope to match the cozy warmth that's the hallmark of more traditional mountain guesthouses, it's a good choice if you want a hotel with all the trimmings, like tennis courts, spa services, and a game room for the kids. The best views are on the valley side. The Leura Golf Course, the area's finest, is next door. There is a two-night minimum stay on weekends. ⊠ *1 Sublime Point Rd., 2780* ☎ *02/4784–4144* ⊕ *www.peppers.com.au* ⇝ *193 rooms, 17 suites* ⌂ *In-room: kitchen (some), refrigerator (some), dial-up. In-hotel: 2 restaurants, room service, bar, tennis courts, pools, gym, spa, bicycles, laundry service, public Internet, no-smoking rooms* ⊟ *AE, DC, MC, V.*

$$–$$$$ 🏨 **Bygone Beautys Cottages.** These eight country cottages, scattered around Wentworth Falls and in nearby villages, provide self-contained accommodations for couples, families, and small groups. Some of these are set among leafy gardens; all have wood-burning fireplaces. Fresh flowers, fruit, chocolates, and all the ingredients for a country-size breakfast are included in each unit. There's a two-night minimum stay. ⊠ *Main office: Grose and Megalong Sts., 2780* ☎ *02/4784–3117* ⊕ *www.bygonebeautys.com.au* ⇝ *8 cottages* ⌂ *In-room: no a/c, kitchen, refrigerator, DVD (some), VCR. In-hotel: laundry facilities* ⊟ *AE, MC, V.*

KATOOMBA

2 km (1 mi) west of Leura.

The largest town in the Blue Mountains, Katoomba, developed in the early 1840s as a coal-mining settlement, turning its attention to tourism later in the 19th century. The town center on Katoomba Street has shops, restaurants, and cafés, but most travelers are keen to see the marvels at the lower end of town and don't linger here.

❻ **Echo Point,** which overlooks the densely forested Jamison Valley and three soaring sandstone pillars, has the best views around Katoomba. The formations—called the **Three Sisters**—take their name from an Aboriginal legend that relates how a trio of siblings was turned to stone by their witch-doctor father to save them from the clutches of a mythical monster. The area was once a seabed that rose over a long period and subsequently eroded, leaving behind tall formations of sedimentary rock. From Echo Point—where the visitor center is located—you can clearly see the horizontal sandstone bedding in the landscape. There is a wide viewing area as well as the start of walks that take you closer to the Sisters. At night the Sisters are illuminated by floodlights. ⊠ *Follow Katoomba St. south out of Katoomba to Echo Point Rd., or take Cliff Dr. from Leura.*

❼ Far below Echo Point, the **Scenic Railway** was built into the cliff face during the 1880s to haul coal and shale from the mines in the valley. After the supply of shale was exhausted, the railway was abandoned until the 1930s, when the Katoomba Colliery began using the open carts to give tourists the ride of their lives on the steep incline. Today the carriages are far more comfortable, but the ride down to the foot of the cliffs is no less exciting. From the bottom of the railway a 1½-km (1-mi) boardwalk loops through ancient rain forest littered with mining relics to the base of the world's steepest cable car, the **Cableway.** This enclosed gondola car glides between the forested valley floor and the rim of the cliff 1,700 feet above. If you do not want to walk the entire route, there are shortcuts on the boardwalk. Your return ticket allows you to ride the railway down and the cable car up. Just a few steps from the top stations of both the Scenic Railway and Flyway is the **Scenic Skyway,** a cable car that carries passengers for a short ride across the gorge, with a 1,000-foot drop below. If you're going to pick one, the railway is more spectacular. All three rides are part of **Scenic World.** ⊠ *Cliff Dr. at Violet St.* ☎ *02/4782–2699* ⊕ *www.scenicworld.com.au* ⊠ *Round-trip Railway, Cableway, or Skyway A$16 each* ☉ *Daily 9–5.*

The screen at the **Edge Maxvision Cinema** is the height of a six-story building. Specially filmed for this giant format, *The Edge,* shown six times daily starting at 10:20 (the last show is at 5:30), is an exciting 40-minute movie on the region's valleys, gorges, cliffs, waterfalls, dramatic scenery, and the mysterious Wollemi Pine (thought to be extinct until it was discovered in the region in the early 1990s). The complex includes a café and gift shop, and regular feature films screen three times a day, usually at 3, 6, and 8 or 9 PM. ⊠*225–237 Great Western Hwy.* ☎*02/4782–8928* ▭*A$14.50.*

WHERE TO STAY & EAT

$–$$ ✕**Paragon Restaurant.** With its chandeliers, gleaming cappuccino machine, and bas-relief figures above the booths, this wood-paneled 1916 restaurant recalls the Blue Mountains in their heyday. These days it's more of a tourist eatery, best known for its cakes and 52 varieties of homemade chocolates. ⊠*65 Katoomba St.* ☎*02/4782–2928* ▭*MC, V* ⊗*No dinner.*

$$$$ ✕▣**Echoes Boutique Hotel & Restaurant.** Perched on the edge of the

BLOOMIN' BEAUTIFUL

When Spring is in the air in the mountains, one of the most beautiful places to be is Leura. Dozens of cherry blossoms line the main street, and private gardens are open for viewing. Make a date for the weeklong **Leura Garden Festival** (☎*02/4757–2359* ⊕*www.leuragardensfestival.com.au*), held from late September to early October. The gardens are adorned with the work of local artists keen to win the annual art prize. A village fair caps off the celebrations.

Jamison Valley, this stylish boutique hotel has some of the best views in the Blue Mountains. A multimillion-dollar refurbishment in late 2005 transformed the space into an elegant retreat with Italian ambience. The marble lobby is impressive, and the glass-enclosed terrace is a great place to take advantage of the spectacular views. A day spa with plenty of indulgent treatments is also on the premises. Rooms are stylish and include the latest TVs, as well as wireless Internet access. The Mod-Oz–Asian fusion menu in the excellent restaurant (also named Echoes) includes dishes such as salt-crusted kingfish fillet spiced with chili and kaffir lime leaves. The hotel is an easy walk from the Three Sisters lookout. ⊠*3 Lilianfels Ave., 2780* ☎*02/4782–1966* ⊕*www.echoeshotel.com.au* ⊅*14 suites* ⚅*In-room: refrigerator, Wi-Fi. In-hotel: restaurant, bar, spa, public Internet, public Wi-Fi, no-smoking rooms* ▭*AE, DC, MC, V* ⋉*BP.*

$$$$ ✕▣**Lilianfels Blue Mountains Resort & Spa.** Teetering close to the brink of
★   Echo Point, this glamorous boutique hotel adds a keen sense of style to the traditional Blue Mountains guesthouse experience. This hotel has a lush European feel and all the luxury you'd expect of a member of the prestigious Orient Express hotel group. Rooms are spacious and luxuriously furnished, with lush fabrics, silk curtains, and elegant marble bathrooms with deep baths. The upscale Darley's restaurant, in the Heritage-listed original 1889 homestead, serves a cutting-edge menu; a highlight is the roasted duck breast with red lentils and figs. The first-class spa is the ultimate place to relax after exploring the Jamison Valley. There is a two-night minimum stay on weekends, and good packages are available midweek. ⊠*Lilianfels Ave. at Panorama Dr., 2780* ☎*02/4780–1200* ⊕*www.lilianfels.com.au* ⚲*Reservations essential* ⊅*81 rooms, 4 suites* ⚅*In-room: safe, refrigerator, VCR, ethernet. In-hotel: 2 restaurants, room service, bar, tennis court, pools, gym, spa, bicycles, concierge, laundry service, public Internet, no-smoking rooms, minibar* ▭*AE, DC, MC, V* ⋉*BP.*

$$$–$$$$ ✕▣**The Carrington.** Established in 1880, this is one of the grand dames
Fodor'sChoice   of the Blue Mountains, a Victorian-era treasure that, in its heyday, was
★

considered one of the four great hotels of the British Empire (along with Lake Louise Canada, Savoy London, and Raffles Singapore). Its lovely public areas are a reminder of its glorious past—the bar contains a mezzanine balcony where the Duke and Duchess of York (later King George VI and Queen Elizabeth, the Queen Mother)—watched a performance in 1927. Room 31 has an elaborate chrome shower system, built for the then Duchess. A permanent conservation order stipulates that 10 of the 59 rooms be kept in their original 1880 style, so they do not have private bathrooms, but at A$119 a night they're a good deal. The other rooms (added in 1927) are a mix of colonial-style rooms with bay-window seats and stained-glass features. The deluxe rooms have access to the terrific balcony on the first floor where you can take in the great valley views. Not all rooms have valley views; some overlook Katoomba township. The enormous, chandelier-lighted dining room serves modern Australian and traditional dishes. Snacks are available at the bar, and afternoon tea and drinks are a treat on the lovely veranda with views overlooking the garden. The day spa is one of the largest in the mountains. ⊠*15–47 Katoomba St., 2780* ☎*02/4782–1111* ⊕*www.thecarrington.com.au* ⟲*59 rooms, 49 with bath; 6 suites; 1 apartment* ⚷*In-room: no a/c (some), kitchen (some), refrigerator, Wi-Fi. In-hotel: 2 restaurants, bars, laundry service, public Wi-Fi, no-smoking rooms* ⊟*AE, DC, MC, V* ⧖|*BP.*

$$$ ⬚ **Melba House.** The Blaxland, Wentworth, and Lawson suites in this
★   19th-century house are named after the explorers who toiled across the Blue Mountains in 1813 and opened up the western plains to settlers—and they offer a welcome retreat to visitors today. Two of the suites have king-size beds, hot tubs, and marble-framed wood fireplaces; all have decorative plaster ceilings and windows looking out at a garden full of birds. You'll find a bowl of fruit and port in your room, and afternoon tea is served when you arrive. In the morning, you can awake to a sumptuous breakfast brought to your room. There's a two-night minimum stay on weekends during the winter. ⊠*98 Waratah St., 2780* ☎*02/4782–4141* ⊕*www.melbahouse.com* ⟲*3 suites* ⚷*In-room: refrigerator, DVD, Wi-Fi. In-hotel: room service, no elevator, no-smoking rooms* ⊟*AE, DC, MC, V* ⧖|*BP.*

$$–$$$ ⬚ **Mountain Heritage Hotel & Spa.** This hotel overlooking the Jamison Valley is steeped in history: it served as a "coffee palace" during the temperance movement, a rest-and-relaxation establishment for the British navy during World War II, and a religious retreat in the 1970s. Check out the collection of rare photographs depicting the Blue Mountains and Sydney in the 1880s. Spacious rooms here are filled with welcoming country-house furnishings; several have hot tubs. If you're looking to splurge, try the round Tower Suite, or one of the two Valley View suites—each has its own veranda, kitchen, living room with fireplace, and hot tub. ⊠*Apex and Lovel Sts., 2780* ☎*02/4782–2155* ⊕*www.mountainheritage.com.au* ⟲*37 rooms, 4 suites* ⚷*In-room: kitchen (some), refrigerator, VCR, dial-up. In-hotel: restaurant, bar, pool, gym, spa, laundry facilities, laundry service, no elevator, no-smoking rooms* ⊟*AE, DC, MC, V.*

¢ ⊡ **Blue Mountains YHA.** This sleek, popular hostel—don't let the name fool you, YHAs are open to all ages—is a 10-minute walk from Echo Point and the Three Sisters, while Katoomba township is just up the hill. In a fully renovated 1930s art deco guesthouse, this charming property includes a dance floor. The huge lounge room and attached dining area is abuzz with happy campers, and a lovely outdoor terrace is a great place to relax in the fresh mountain air. There are dorms, double rooms, and family rooms with in-room bathrooms. Bookings are essential on weekends, in summer, and during Christmas in July. ⊠207 *Katoomba St., 2780* ☎*02/4782–1416* ⊕*www.yha.com.au* ⮑*24 dorms; 26 doubles, 18 with bath; 4 family rooms* ⛋*In-room: kitchen. In-hotel: bar, no elevator, public Wi-Fi, parking (no fee)* ▤*MC, V.*

MEDLOW BATH

7 km (4 mi) west of Katoomba.

You could blink and miss this village (with a population of approximately 500 people) if it weren't for the magnificent Hydro Majestic Hotel on the highway, opposite the railway station. There are also a few tourist cottages and bed-and-breakfasts scattered about the bushland. At 3,445 feet above sea level, Medlow Bath has sensational views of beautiful Megalong Valley.

WHERE TO STAY & EAT

$$–$$$$
Fodor's Choice
★

✕⊡ **Hydro Majestic.** This iconic and much-loved hotel has the best views in the Blue Mountains. Built in 1904 by Sydney businessman and former department store owner Mark Foy, the property was Australia's first health retreat. No expense was spared on the retreat, and Foy filled the hotel with artwork from around the world. The dome of the hotel's Casino Ballroom was made in Chicago and shipped to Australia. The Hydro (as it was later affectionately known) was a favorite with honeymooners from the 1930s to the 1950s; however, in 1942 it was taken over by the U.S. Defense Department and turned into a hospital for American casualties from the war in the Pacific. By the late 1970s, signs of wear and tear were showing, and the building fell into disrepair for more than a decade. In the late 1990s it was bought by Angeline Mah, who invested A\$19 million restoring it to its former glory. The grand dining room with vaulted ceiling and open fireplaces serves breakfast, lunch, and dinner, and high tea takes place each day. There are private guest lounges, all with wonderful views, and the walls are adorned with pictures of the hotel's heyday. ⊠*Great Western Hwy., 2780* ☎*02/4688–1002* ⊕*www.hydromajestic.com.au* ⮑*81 rooms, 3 suites* ⛋*In-room: refrigerator, dial-up. In-hotel: 2 restaurants, bar, tennis courts, pool, gym, bicycles, no elevator, parking (no fee)* ▤*AE, DC, MC, V.*

BLACKHEATH

12 km (7½ mi) north of Katoomba.

Magnificent easterly views over the Grose Valley—which has outstanding hiking trails—and delightful gardens and antiques shops head the list of reasons to visit Blackheath, at the 3,495-foot summit of the Blue Mountains. The town was named by Governor Lachlan Macquarie, who visited in 1815 after a rough road had been constructed through here to the town of Bathurst, beyond the mountains.

❽ Blackheath's most famous view is from the **Govett's Leap Lookout,** with
★ its striking panorama of the Grose Valley and Bridal Veil Falls. Govett was a surveyor who mapped this region extensively in the 1830s. He calculated that the perpendicular drop near the falls is 528 feet. ⊠*End of Govett's Leap Rd.*

❾ The **Heritage Centre,** operated by the National Parks and Wildlife Service, provides useful information on Aboriginal and European historic sites, as well as helpful suggestions for camping, guided walks, and hiking in Blue Mountains National Park. The center, which is a two-minute stroll from Govett's Leap Lookout, also has videos, interactive educational displays, exhibitions, and a nature-oriented gift shop. ⊠*End of Govett's Leap Rd.* ☎*02/4787–8877* ⊕*www.nationalparks. nsw.gov.au* ⊠*Free* ☉*Daily 9–4:30.*

☾ The **Megalong Australian Heritage Centre,** in a deep mountain valley off the Great Western Highway, is the place to saddle up and explore a country property. Both adults and children can go horseback riding around the farm's 2,000 acres, and bigger adults might get to ride a Clydesdale. If you'd like to go farther afield, you can join an overnight muster ride from A$225. There's a farm with a baby-animal nursery where children can get close to chickens, ducks, and pigs. ⊠*Megalong Rd., Megalong Valley* ✛*15 km (9 mi) south of Blackheath* ☎*02/4787–8188* ⊕*www. bluemts.com.au/megalong* ⊠*A$8* ☉*Daily 9–5.*

WHERE TO STAY & EAT

$$
Fodor'sChoice
★ ✗**Vulcan's.** Make sure you book ahead at this popular café that revolutionized dining in rural New South Wales. Operated by Phillip Searle (formerly one of the leading lights of Sydney's dining scene) and Barry Ross, Vulcan's specializes in slow-roasted dishes, cooked in a century-old baker's oven and flavored with Asian or Middle Eastern spices. The restaurant's checkerboard ice cream—with star anise, pineapple, licorice, and vanilla flavors—is a favorite that looks as good as it tastes. Dinner is served at two sittings, so diners at the 6 PM sitting have little time to linger before they must vacate their tables for the 8 PM sitting. ⊠*33 Govetts Leap Rd., Blackheath, 2785* ☎*02/4787–6899* ⊟*AE, DC, MC, V* ⚙*BYO* ☉*Closed Mon.–Thurs. and Feb.*

$$–$$$
★ ▦**Jemby Rinjah Eco Lodge.** Designed for urbanites seeking a wilderness experience, these rustic, self-contained wooden cabins and lodges are set deep in the bush. All have natural wood furnishings and picture windows opening onto a small deck. One- and two-bedroom cabins have kitchenettes and lounge and dining areas, while the four-bedroom

The sandstone mounds at Purnululu (Bungle Bungle) National Park, Western Australia.

(top left) The perfect vineyard geometry of Coldstream Hills, located in Coldstream, Victoria. (top right) Taking in the meticulously restored splendor of the Queen Victoria building in Sydney. (bottom) Beach bungalows in Melbourne, Victoria.

(top) Sydney Opera House, designed to look like sails in port. (bottom) Aboriginal man playing the didgeridoo, a traditional instrument of Australia.

(top left) Palm Cove, Queensland, at dusk. (top right) Two red kangaroos duke it out. (bottom) A tourist in Tasmania surveys the scene at Cradle Mountain National Park.

The Remarkable Rocks, balanced precariously on the promontory of Kirkpatrick Point in Flinders Chase National Park, Kangaroo Island, South Australia.

(top left) Frozen water in a stream in the Mossman Gorge rain forest, Queensland. (top right) A traditional Aboriginal painted design. (bottom) The monorail at Darling Harbour, Sydney.

(top) Devil's Marbles, Northern Territory. (bottom) Australia's national icon, the koala bear.

(top) Lawn bowlers in Darwin. (bottom) A school of yellowfin goatfish, Great Barrier Reef.

2

lodges can sleep up to 20 people. (Lodges don't have kitchens, but breakfast can be arranged.) Dinner is available in the restaurant for A$36 for two courses and A$45 for three courses. Activities include self-guided walks of the Grose Valley, feeding wild parrots, and spotlighting possums at night. The stunning Evans Lookout is 500 yards away. ⊠ *336 Evans Lookout Rd., 2785* ☎ *02/4787-7622* ⊕ *www. jembyrinjahlodge.com.au* ⟿ *11 cabins, 3 lodges* ᴕ *In-room: no a/c, no phone, kitchen (some), refrigerator. In-hotel: restaurant, no elevator, laundry facilities, no-smoking rooms* ⊟ *AE, DC, MC, V.*

MOUNT VICTORIA

🔟 *7 km (4½ mi) northwest of Blackheath.*

The settlement of Mount Victoria has a Rip Van Winkle air about it—drowsy and only just awake in an unfamiliar world. A walk around the village reveals many atmospheric houses, stores, and a couple of stately old hotels with the patina of time spelled out in their fading paint. The pink circa-1888 **Hotel Imperial** (⊠ *1 Station St.* ☎ *02/4787–1878* ⊕ *www.hotelimperial.com.au*) was one of several historic Blue Mountains inns built a few years after the railway line was opened from Sydney. Antique toys can be found at **Trains, Planes and Automobiles** (⊠ *88 Great Western Hwy.* ☎ *02/4787–1590*), but like many shops in the area, it is only open for half the week (Thursday–Monday 10:30–4:30).

Mount Victoria is at the far side of the mountains at the western limit of this region, and the village serves as a good jumping-off point for a couple of out-of-the-way attractions.

Stalactites, stalagmites, columns, and lacelike rock on multiple levels fill **Jenolan Caves,** a labyrinth of vast limestone caverns sculpted by underground rivers. There are as many as 320 caves in the Jenolan area.

Three caves near the surface can be explored on your own, but a guide is required to reach the most intriguing formations. Standard tours lead through the most popular caves—many say that Orient Cave is the most spectacular—while more rigorous adventure tours last up to seven hours. The one- to two-hour walks depart every 15 to 30 minutes, on weekends less frequently. Prices range from A$22 for standard tours to $A58 for adventure tours. To get here, follow the Great Western Highway north out of Mount Victoria, then after Hartley turn southwest toward Hampton. There are also caves in Abercrombie and Wombeyan, to the west and south of Jenolan. ⊠ *59 km (37 mi) from Mount Victoria, Jenolan* ☎ *02/6359–3311* ⊕ *www.jenolancaves.org. au* ☉ *Daily 9:30–5:30.*

Fodor'sChoice
★
ᘓ

You'll be wiping the soot from your face after a ride on the huff-and-puff vintage steam engine, but that's part of the fun of this cliff-hugging 16-km (10-mi) round-trip experience on the **Zig Zag Railway.** Built in 1869, this was the main line across the Blue Mountains until 1910. The track is laid on the cliffs in a giant "Z," and the train climbs the steep incline by chugging back and forth along switchback sections of the track—hence its name. The steam engine operates on weekends, public holidays, and Wednesday, and weekdays during school holidays. A vintage self-propelled diesel-powered railcar is used at other times. ⊠ *Bells Line of Rd., 19 km (12 mi) northwest of Mount Victoria, Clarence* ☎ *02/6355–2955* ⊕ *www.zigzagrailway.com.au* ☜ *A$22* ⊙ *Departures from Clarence Station daily at 11, 1, and 3.*

BLUE MOUNTAINS ESSENTIALS

BUS TRAVEL

Public buses operate between the Blue Mountains settlements. However, to see the best that the Blue Mountains have to offer, take a guided tour or rent a car and drive from Sydney.

CAR RENTAL

Since the most scenic Blue Mountains routes and attractions are outside the towns, it's best to rent a car. If you're not driving from Sydney, you can reserve a vehicle from RediCAR in Valley Heights, near Springwood.

Contact RediCAR (⊠ *42 Great Western Hwy., Valley Heights, 2777* ☎ *02/ 4751–8920*).

CAR TRAVEL

The 110-km (68-mi) journey to Katoomba takes between 90 minutes and two hours. Leave Sydney via Parramatta Road and the M4 Motorway, which leads to Lapstone at the base of the Blue Mountains. From there, continue on the Great Western Highway and follow the signs to Katoomba.

EMERGENCIES

In an emergency, dial **000** to reach an ambulance, the police, or the fire department.

Hospital Blue Mountains District Anzac Memorial Hospital (⊠ *Great Western Hwy., 1 km [½ mi] east of town center, Katoomba* ☎ *02/4784–6500*).

TOURS

Since the Blue Mountains are one of Sydney's most popular escapes, you can take a day trip from there with a bus touring company or make your own way to the mountains and then link up with a guided tour. The region is also great for outdoor adventure and horseback-riding trips.

Blue Mountains Adventure Company runs rappelling, rock-climbing, canyoning, bushwalking, and mountain-biking trips. Most outings (from about A$135) last one day, and include equipment, lunch, and transportation from Katoomba.

High n Wild conducts rappelling, canyoning, rock-climbing, and mountain-biking tours. One-day rappelling trips cost A$140; combination rappelling and canyoning tours cost A$170.

2

Contacts Blue Mountains Adventure Company (⊠ *84A Bathurst Rd., Katoomba, 2780* ☏ *02/4782–1271* ⊕ *www.bmac.com.au*). **High n Wild** (⊠ *3/5 Katoomba St., Katoomba, 2780* ☏ *02/4782–6224* ⊕ *www.high-n-wild.com.au*).

Fantastic Aussie Tours arranges trips ranging from bus tours to four-wheel-drive expeditions. They also operate the double-decker Blue Mountains Explorer Bus (A$29), which connects with trains from Sydney at the Katoomba Railway Station. Running hourly from 9:30 to 4:30 every day, it makes 30 stops at major attractions around Katoomba and Leura, and you're free to hop off and on as you please. If you're overnighting in the mountains, you can use the pass for the duration of your stay.

Contact Fantastic Aussie Tours (⊠ *283 Main St., Katoomba* ☏ *02/4782–1866 or 1300/300915* ⊕ *www.fantastic-aussie-tours.com.au*).

Tread Lightly Eco Tours operates small-group tours of the Blue Mountains National Park and guided day and night walks. Four-wheel-drive vehicles take you to lookouts, caves, and waterfalls. A full-day Wilderness Experience for two costs from A$185 to A$265, depending on destination and food (gourmet picnic or restaurant).

Information Tread Lightly Eco Tours (⊠ *100 Great Western Hwy., Medlow Bath, 2780* ☏ *02/4788–1229 or 0414/976752* ⊕ *www.treadlightly.com.au*).

At the foot of the Blue Mountains, 10 km (6 mi) south of Blackheath, Werriberri Trail Rides conducts reasonably priced hour (A$48) to full-day (A$180) horseback rides through the beautiful Megalong Valley, as well as three-, four-, and five-day rides. These guided rides are appropriate for both adults and children, and hard hats and chaps are supplied.

Information Werriberri Trail Rides (⊠ *Megalong Rd., Megalong Valley* ☏ *02/4787–9171* ⊕ *www.australianbluehorserides.com.au*).

Auswalk operates five- and seven-day guided and self-guided walking holidays in Blue Mountains National Park. You carry a daypack on spectacular day walks while your luggage is transferred from guesthouse to guesthouse. The seven-day self-guided walk (A$1,350) requires a minimum of two people and can be booked for any day of the year except July. Seven-day guided walking holidays (from A$2,050) depart Sunday on demand.

Information Auswalk (✎ *42 Mount Zero Rd., Halls Gap, 3381* ☏ *03/5356–4971* ⊕ *www.auswalk.com.au*).

TRAIN TRAVEL

Train services from Sydney stop at most stations along the line to Mount Victoria. The Blue Mountains are served by Sydney's Cityrail commuter trains, with frequent services to and from the city between 5 AM and 11 PM. On weekdays it's A$11.60 one-way between Sydney's Central Station and Katoomba, the main station in the Blue Mountains. If you travel on weekends or begin travel after 9 on weekdays, it's A$16.20 round-trip.

Information Cityrail (☏ *13–1500* ⊕ *www.cityrail.info*).

VISITOR INFORMATION

Blue Mountains Visitor Information Centre offices are at Echo Point in Katoomba and at the foot of the mountains on the Great Western Highway at Glenbrook. The Echo Point office and Glenbrook are open daily 9–5. Sydney Visitor Centre, open daily 9:30–5:30, has information on Blue Mountains hotels, tours, and sights.

Information **Blue Mountains Visitor Information Centre** (⊠ *Echo Point Rd., Echo Point* ☎ *1300/653408* ⊕ *www.visitbluemountains.com.au* ⊠ *Great Western Hwy., Glenbrook* ☎ *1300/653408*). **Sydney Visitor Centre** (⊠ *The Rocks Centre, Argyle and Playfair Sts., The Rocks, Sydney, 2000* ☎ *02/9240–8788 or 1800/067676* ⊕ *www.sydneyvisitorcentre.com*).

THE HUNTER VALLEY

To almost everyone in Sydney, the Hunter Valley conjures up visions not of coal mines or cows—the area's earliest industries—but of wine. The Hunter is the largest grape-growing area in the state, with more than 120 wineries producing excellent wines. It is divided into seven sub-regions, each with its own unique character. The hub is the Pokolbin/Rothbury region, where many of the large operations are found, along with several boutique wineries. Many wines have found a market overseas, and visiting wine lovers might recognize the Hunter Valley labels of Rosemount, Tyrrell's, or Lindemans.

The Hunter Valley covers an area of almost 25,103 square km (9,692 square mi), stretching from the town of Gosford north of Sydney to 177 km (110 mi) farther north along the coast, and almost 300 km (186 mi) inland. The meandering waterway that gives this valley its name is also one of the most extensive river systems in the state. From its source on the rugged slopes of the Mt. Royal Range, the Hunter River flows through rich grazing country and past the horse stud farms around Scone in the upper part of the valley, home of some of Australia's wealthiest farming families. In the Lower Hunter region, the river crosses the vast coal deposits of the Greta Seam.

The Hunter Valley has become known for its long list of annual events. Wineries are attracting music lovers as rock, jazz, blues, and opera performances are regular summer events. Celebrities who have sung in the vines include Elvis Costello, John Fogarty, and k. d. lang. Foodies flock to the annual Lovedale Long Lunch, an all-day wine and food fair that takes place during the third weekend in May. Golfing holidays have boomed in the Hunter Valley, and several new resorts with championship golf courses have opened in the past few years.

OFF THE BEATEN PATH

Wollombi. Nothing seems to have changed in the atmospheric town of Wollombi, 24 km (15 mi) southwest of Cessnock, since the days when the Cobb & Co. stagecoaches rumbled through town. Founded in 1820, Wollombi was the overnight stop for the coaches on the second day of the journey from Sydney along the convict-built Great Northern Road—at that time the only route north. The town is full of delightful old sandstone buildings and

CLOSE UP

The Southern Highlands & South Coast

2

Sitting atop the Great Dividing Range at an altitude of around 2,300 feet are the **Southern Highlands,** a fertile semirural region southwest of Sydney. The region is dotted with villages and three main towns—Mittagong, Bowral, and Moss Vale. The Highlands were settled by farmers in the 1820s and many of the existing buildings, particularly old inns, date back to the 1840s. Some villages have only 300 to 500 inhabitants, and the area exudes an English quaintness with its grand old homes set in parkland.

From **Mittagong,** the gateway to the Southern Highlands (103 km [64 mi] southwest of Sydney), take the Hume Highway 14 km (9 mi) southwest to **Berrima** and explore this early Georgian colonial town—with a population of 320—preserved in almost original condition. You'll find convict-built sandstone and brick buildings, including the National Trust–listed Harpers Mansion and the Holy Trinity Church. The circa-1839 **Berrima Gaol** is still in use, and the **Surveyor General Inn** is one of Australia's oldest continuously licensed hotels (built in 1834). **Berrima Courthouse,** built in 1838, is the town's architectural highlight.

About 10 km (6 mi) northeast is **Bowral,** an English-style town with opulent country dwellings and refined tastes, considered the center of the Southern Highlands. For six weeks during September and October it holds the colorful **Tulip Time Festival.** Bowral's other famous attraction is the **Bradman Museum,** a shrine to legendary cricketer Sir Donald "The Don" Bradman, who captained the Australian team 1928–48.

From Bowral you can take a leisurely drive south (via Moss Vale) and mean-der through several tranquil villages. **Sutton Forest,** 13 km (8 mi) south of Bowral, was once the country seat of the governors of New South Wales.

The **South Coast** is a never-ending stretch of glorious beaches, beginning near **Kiama,** 119 km (74 mi) south of Sydney, and continuing another 357 km (223 mi) to **Eden,** the last major town before the Victorian border. With 20 national parks and no grand-scale developments, the coast is a favorite with vacationers.

Exploring the South Coast from Kiama to Eden is one of this region's greatest pleasures. About 39 km (24 mi) past Ulladulla, take the side road 8 km (5 mi) to **Pebbly Beach** where you'll find hundreds of kangaroos on the shore.

Eden, on Twofold Bay, is the third-deepest natural harbor in the world. It's also home to one of the state's largest fishing fleets and some of the best whale watching on the East Coast. An interesting place to spend the night is the beautifully restored B&B the **Crown and Anchor** (☏ *02/6496–1017*). Built in 1840, it is Eden's oldest building.

—Caroline Gladstone

antiques shops, and there's also a museum in the old courthouse with 19th-century clothing and bushranger memorabilia. The local hotel, the **Wollombi Tavern** (☎ *02/4998-3261* ⊕ *www.wollombitavern.com.au*), serves its own exotic brew, which goes by the name of Dr. Jurd's Jungle Juice. The pub also scores high marks for its friendliness and local color. The century-old **Avoca House** (☎ *02/4998-3233* ⊕ *www.avocahouse.com.au*) is the perfect place to chill out.

POKOLBIN

10 km (6 mi) northwest of Cessnock.

The Lower Hunter wine-growing region is centered around the village of Pokolbin, where there are antiques shops, good cafés, and dozens of wineries.

Any tour of the area's vineyards should begin at Pokolbin's **Hunter Valley Wine Country Visitors Information Centre,** which has free maps of the vineyards, brochures, and a handy visitor's guide. ✉ *455 Wine Country Dr.* ☎ *02/4990-0900* ⊕ *www.winecountry.com.au* ⊗ *Mon.–Thurs. 9–5, Fri. and Sat. 9–6, Sun. 9–4.*

Drop into **Binnorie Dairy** (at Tuscany Wine Estate) to try and buy—few can resist—Simon Gough's handcrafted soft cow and goat cheeses. You'd be hard-pressed to find a tastier marinated feta outside Greece— or even in it. ✉ *Hermitage Rd. at Mistletoe La.* ☎ *02/4998–6660* ⊗ *Tues.–Sat. 10–5, Sun. 10–4.*

In a delightful rural corner of the Mount View region, **Briar Ridge Vineyard** is one of the Hunter Valley's outstanding small wineries. It produces a limited selection of sought-after reds, whites, and sparkling wines. The semillon, chardonnay, shiraz, and intense cabernet sauvignon are highly recommended. The vineyard is on the southern periphery of the Lower Hunter vineyards, about a five-minute drive from Pokolbin. ✉ *593 Mt. View Rd., Mount View* ☎ *02/4990–3670* ⊕ *www.briarridge.com.au* ⊗ *Daily 10–5.*

★ The **Lindemans Hunter River Winery** has been one of the largest and most prestigious winemakers in the country since the early 1900s. In addition to its Hunter Valley vineyards, the company owns property in South Australia and Victoria, and numerous outstanding wines from these vineyards can be sampled in the tasting room. Try the burgundy, semillon, or chardonnay. The winery has its own museum, displaying vintage winemaking equipment, as well as two picnic areas, one near the parking lot and the other next to the willow trees around the dam. ✉ *McDonalds Rd. just south of DeBeyers Rd.* ☎ *02/4998–7684* ⊕ *www.lindemans.com.au* ⊗ *Daily 10–5.*

★ At **McWilliams Mount Pleasant Estate,** part of Australia's biggest family-owned wine company, chief winemaker Phil Ryan, the third since the winery was founded in 1921, continues the tradition of producing classic Hunter wines. Flagship Maurice O'Shea shiraz and chardonnay, and celebrated Elizabeth semillon, are among the wines that can be sampled in the huge cellar door. You can also sit down on the terrace to a tasting plate in Elizabeth's Café; this matches three vintages of Elizabeth semillon and one of premium Lovedale Semillon with four different foods. Guided winery tours run daily at 11 AM. ⊠*Marrowbone Rd.* ☎*02/4998–7505* ⊕*www.mcwilliams.com.au* ⊠*Tours A$3.30* ☉*Daily 10–4:30.*

A leading light in the new wave of Hunter winemakers, **Margan Family Winegrowers** produces some of the valley's best small-volume wines. Try their full-bodied verdelho, rosé-style Saignée shiraz, and House of Certain Views cabernet sauvignon. A riper-than-most semillon is the flagship, and the 2004 Decanter World Wine Awards rated Margan's botrytis semillon the world's best sweet wine under A$10—it's delicious. You can enjoy a glass of your pick with Mediterranean-inspired alfresco fare in the adjoining Beltree@Margan café. In 2007, a tasting room and restaurant opened in the nearby town of Broke. ⊠*266 Hermitage Rd.* ☎☎*02/6574–7004; 02/6574–7216 café* ⊕*www.margan. com.au* ☉*Daily 10–5.*

Founded in 1858, **Tyrrell's Wines** is the Hunter Valley's oldest family-owned vineyard. This venerable establishment crafts a wide selection of wines and was the first to produce chardonnay commercially in Australia. Its famous Vat 47 Chardonnay is still a winner. Enjoy the experience of sampling fine wines in the rustic tasting room, or take a picnic lunch to a site overlooking the valley. Free guided tours are given Monday to Saturday at 1:30. ⊠*Broke Rd., 2½ km (1½ mi) west of McDonalds Rd.* ☎*02/4993–7000* ⊕*www.tyrrells.com.au* ☉ *Weekdays 8:30–5, Sat. 8:30–4:30.*

The low stone-and-timber buildings of the **Hunter Valley Gardens** are the heart of the Pokolbin wine-growing district. This large complex includes a hotel and convention center, gift shops, restaurants, a pub, the underground **Hunter Cellars,** and 12 stunning gardens covering 50 acres. Here you'll find a classic European formal garden, rose garden, Chinese Moongate garden, and the delightful children's storybook garden featuring characters such as the Mad Hatter and Jack and Jill. There are wonderful chocolate and fudge to be had in the center's confectionery shop. ⊠*Broke and McDonalds Rds.* ☎*02/4998–7600* ⊕*www.hvg.com.au* ☉*Daily 9–5* ⊠*A$19.50.*

Adjoining the gardens is the cellar-door complex of **McGuigan Wines.** Here you can taste wines and the **Hunter Valley Cheese Company's** superb cheeses—look out for the washed-rind Hunter Valley Gold and the marinated soft, cows'-milk cheese—before you buy. You can also see the cheeses being made by hand. There is a cheese talk daily at 11, and winery tours are given on weekdays at noon, weekends at 11 and noon. ⊠*Broke and McDonalds Rds.* ☎*02/4998–7402* ⊕*www. mcguiganwines.com.au.*

You can't miss the ultra-modern **Tempus Two** in the heart of Pokolbin. This futuristic winery is a joint venture between two leading Hunter Valley families: the Roches (owners of Hunter Valley Gardens) and the

McGuigans, who have made wine for four generations. The winery is best known for its pinot gris; however, you can sample a wide variety including semillon, sauvignon blanc, chardonnay, and shiraz in the stylish tasting room. Jeff's Grill, serving Mod-Oz cuisine, and Oishii, a Japanese-Thai restaurant, are fine-dining options, while a Moroccan-theme café is more casual. The winery's amphitheatre is a venue for local and international acts, which included INXS and Simple Minds on a double bill in 2007. ⊠*Broke and McDonalds Rds.* ☎*02/4993–3999* ⊕*www.tempustwo.com.au* ⊙ *Daily 9–5.*

> ## FOR BEER LOVERS
>
> Here's the dilemma: one of you likes wine, while the other prefers beer. Pop into **Bluetongue Brewery** ⊠*Hermitage Rd., Pokolbin* ☎*02/4998-7777* ⊕*www.hunter-valley.com.au,* Hunter Valley's only brewery. Named after a lizard with a bright blue tongue, the brewery makes premium lager, pilsner, and ginger beer. You can watch it all happening, and sample the goods, too.

WHERE TO STAY & EAT

$$$
Fodor's Choice
★
✕**Robert's Restaurant.** Incorporating the 1876 Pepper Tree Cottage and encircled by grapevines, this charming restaurant matches its old-world surroundings with creative fare by chef Robert Molines. The modern Australian menu draws inspiration from the recipes of regional France and Italy, applied to local game, seafood, beef, and lamb. In the airy, country-style dining room—with antique furniture, bare timber floors, and a big stone fireplace—you might try grilled quail as a first course, and then follow it with basil-and-pine-nut-crusted John Dory fillet with trellis tomatoes and roast tomato sauce. The cozy fireside lounge is perfect for enjoying after-dinner liqueurs. ⊠*Halls Rd., Pokolbin, 2321* ☎*02/4998–7330* ☐*AE, DC, MC, V.*

$$
✕**Il Cacciatore.** Serving up a vast selection of northern Italian specialties, the outdoor terrace at Il Cacciatore is the perfect place for a leisurely weekend lunch. The exterior is classic Australian, with a bullnose veranda. Once you step inside, your senses will be overwhelmed by the wonderful aromas wafting from the kitchen. Italian favorites crowd this menu: try the grilled lamb fillets with oven-roasted tomato polenta and rosemary pesto, or the pork loin stuffed with spinach, almonds, and figs. Make sure you leave plenty of room for the long list of *dolci* (desserts), too. An extensive list of local and imported wines complements the menu. ⊠*McDonald and Gillard Rds.* ☎*02/4998-7639* ☐*AE, MC, V* ⊙*No lunch weekdays.*

$$$$
✕⊡**Casuarina Restaurant & Country Inn.** Lapped by a sea of grapevines, this luxurious country resort has a powerful sense of fantasy about it. Each of the palatial guest suites is furnished according to a particular theme, such as the French Bordello Suite, with its four-poster canopy bed; Romeo's Retreat, with mirrors everywhere and a hot tub in the lounge room; Susie Wong's Suite, with its original opium couch for a bed; and the movie-inspired Moulin Rouge Suite. The on-site Casuarina Restaurant ($$–$$$), open for dinner only, specializes in flambéed dishes theatrically prepared at your table. There's a minimum two-night stay on weekends. ⊠*Hermitage Rd. between Broke*

and Deasys Rds., 2320 ☎02/4998–7888 🌐www.casuarinainn.com.au ⇨9 suites, 2 cottages In-room: kitchen (some), DVD (some), dial-up. In-hotel: restaurant, pool, public Internet, no elevator, no-smoking rooms ▭AE, DC, MC, V.

$$$$ Fodor'sChoice ★ **Peppers Convent.** This former convent, the most romantic property in the Hunter Valley, was transported 605 km (375 mi) from its original home in western New South Wales. Rooms, decorated in a "shabby chic" style with cream and brown tones, have French doors that open onto a wide veranda. All rooms have LCD televisions with movies. The latest addition is the Endota Spa, which has a huge menu of treatments from body wraps to massage and facials. The house is surrounded by Pepper Tree Winery's vines and is adjacent to the renowned Robert's Restaurant. Rates include a full country breakfast plus afternoon drinks and canapés. There's a minimum two-night stay on weekends. *✉Halls Rd., 2320 ☎02/4998–8999 🌐www.peppers.com.au ⇨17 rooms In-room: refrigerator, dial-up. In-hotel: tennis court, pool, spa, bicycles, no elevator, no-smoking rooms, public Wi-Fi ▭AE, DC, MC, V BP.*

$$$–$$$$ ★ **Cedars Mount View.** This property, nestled in the hills above the valley, might tempt you to forget about wine tasting for a few days. The peaceful sounds of birds and wind in the eucalyptus leaves are that soothing. Each of the four wooden cottages here is different: the Ridge—a honeymoon cottage—has an open plan with a king-size bed and leather sofas; there's a two-person daybed beneath a picture window in the Gums; the Creek has a mezzanine main bedroom; the Terrace is the most private. All are comfortably luxurious, with fine bed linens, in-room hot tubs, stereos, and magazines to read beside the wood-burning fireplaces. You can pick up your helicopter flight (to whisk you to a nearby winery for lunch) near the front door. A generous breakfast hamper with free-range eggs, bacon, orange juice, breads, and a selection of teas and coffees is provided on arrival. *✉60 Mitchells Rd., Mount View, 2325 ☎0414/533070 or 02/4959–3072 🌐www.cedars.com.au ⇨4 cottages In-room: kitchen, refrigerator, DVD. In-hotel: no elevator, no smoking rooms ▭AE, MC, V BP.*

$$–$$$ **Carriages Country House.** On 36 acres at the end of a quiet country lane, this rustic-looking but winsome guesthouse is all about privacy. Each of the suites has antique country pine furniture and a large sitting area with cushy sofas, and many have open fireplaces. The two more expensive suites in the Gatehouse also have hot tubs and share a lounge with full kitchen facilities. A Continental breakfast is delivered each morning to your door. There's a two-night minimum stay on weekends. *✉Halls Rd., 2321 ☎02/4998–7591 🌐www.thecarriages.com.au ⇨10 suites In-room: kitchen, DVD (some), dial-up (some). In-hotel: tennis court, pool, no elevator, laundry service, public Internet, no kids ▭AE, MC, V CP.*

$$–$$$ **Glen Ayr Cottages.** Tucked away in the Pokolbin bushland, yet close to the heart of the wine region, these colonial-style wooden cottages are ideal for families, sleeping six to eight people. Built on a ridge, each has two to four bedrooms, with views of vineyards on one side and eucalyptus forest on the other. Furnishings are comfortable but simple:

no televisions are allowed to compete with the songs of birds. ✉776 *DeBeyers Rd., 2320* ☎*02/4998–7784* ⊕*www.glenayrcottages.com.au* ⇝*6 cottages* ☾ *In-room: no a/c (some), no phone, kitchen, refrigerator, no TV. In hotel: no elevator* ⊟*MC, V.*

$$ ⊡**Vineyard Hill.** Smart and modern, these one- and two-bedroom apart-
★ ments are a good value, offering attractive packages both during the week and on weekends. The apartments are close together, but they are set on 32 acres of bushland with views of Brokenback Range. Each pastel-color suite has its own high-ceilinged lounge area, a private deck, and a kitchenette. Full cooked breakfasts are available. There's a minimum stay of two nights on weekends. ✉*Lovedale and Lodge Rds., Lovedale, 2320* ☎*02/4990–4166* ⊕*www.vineyardhill.com.au* ⇝*8 apartments* ☾ *In-room: kitchen, refrigerator, VCR, DVDs. In-hotel: pool, no elevator, laundry service, public Internet, no-smoking rooms* ⊟*AE, MC, V.*

HUNTER VALLEY ESSENTIALS

BUS TRAVEL

Rover Coaches' Wine Country Xpress departs at 8:30 AM for the 2½-hour journey to Cessnock from Sydney's Central Coach Terminal on Eddy Avenue (near Central Station). The fare is A$40 one-way, A$70 round-trip.

To avoid driving after sampling too many wines, hop aboard one of the Cessnock-based Wine Rover buses. Minibuses travel between area hotels, restaurants, and about a dozen wineries and allow you to hop on and off during the day. A day pass with unlimited stops is A$30 during the week and A$40 on weekends; when combined with the Wine Country Xpress from Sydney the entire package is only A$90.

Locally based Shadows Hunter Wine Country Tours operates a local transfer service between wineries, restaurants, and your accommodation.

Contacts Rover Coaches (☎*02/4990–1699*). **Shadows Hunter Wine Country Tours** (☎*02/4990–7002*).

CAR TRAVEL

A car is a necessity for exploring the area. Other than taking a guided tour on arrival, this is the most convenient way to visit the wineries and off-the-beaten-path attractions, such as Wollombi.

To reach the area, leave Sydney by the Harbour Bridge or Harbour Tunnel and follow the signs for Newcastle. Just before Hornsby this road joins the Sydney–Newcastle Freeway. Take the exit from the freeway signposted HUNTER VALLEY VINEYARDS VIA CESSNOCK. From Cessnock, the route to the vineyards is clearly marked. Allow 2½ hours for the 151-km (94-mi) journey from Sydney.

EMERGENCIES

In an emergency, dial **000** to reach an ambulance, the police, or the fire department.

Contact Cessnock District Hospital (⊠ *View St., Cessnock* ☎ *02/4991–0555*).

TOURS

From Sydney, AAT Kings operates a daylong wine-tasting bus tour of the Hunter Valley and another to Hunter Valley Gardens. Buses collect passengers from city hotels, then make a final pickup from the Star City (Sydney Casino) bus terminal, departing at 8:30 AM. The tour returns to the casino at 7 PM. Tours cost from A$135, including lunch and wine tasting.

Drifting above the valley while the vines are still wet with dew is an unforgettable way to see the Hunter Valley. Balloon Aloft Hunter Valley runs hour-long flights for A$295.

Hunter Valley Wine and Dine Carriages, based at the Tuscany Wine Estate in Pokolbin, conducts half-day (from A$50) and full-day (from A$75) horse-drawn carriage tours of the wineries.

Contacts AAT Kings (☎ *02/9518–6095*). **Balloon Aloft Hunter Valley** (☎ *02/4938–1955 or 1800/028568*). **Hunter Valley Wine and Dine Carriages** (☎ *0410/515358*).

VISITOR INFORMATION

Hunter River Country Visitor Information Centre is open daily 9–5. Sydney Visitor Centre, open daily 9:30–5:30, has information on Hunter Valley accommodations, tours, and sights. Hunter Valley Wine Country Visitors Information Centre is open Monday–Thursday 9–5, Friday and Saturday 9–6, Sunday 9–4.

Contacts Hunter River Country Visitor Information Centre (⊠ *New England Hwy. at High St., Maitland* ☎ *02/4931–2800* ⊕ *www.hunterrivercountry.com.au*). **Hunter Valley Wine Country Visitors Information Centre** (⊠ *455 Wine Country Dr., Pokolbin, 2325* ☎ *02/4990–0900* ⊕ *www.winecountry.com.au*). **Sydney Visitor Centre** (⊠ *The Rocks Centre, Argyle and Playfair Sts., The Rocks, Sydney, 2000* ☎ *02/9240–8788* ⊕ *www.sydneyvisitorcentre.com*).

THE NORTH COAST

The North Coast is one of the most glorious and seductive stretches of terrain in Australia. An almost continuous line of beaches defines the coast, with the Great Dividing Range rising to the west. These natural borders frame a succession of rolling green pasturelands, mossy rain forests, towns dotted by red-roof houses, and waterfalls that tumble in glistening arcs from the escarpment.

A journey along the coast leads through several rich agricultural districts, beginning with grazing country in the south and moving into plantations of bananas, sugarcane, mangoes, avocados, and macadamia nuts. Dorrigo National Park, outside Bellingen, and Muttonbird Island, in Coffs Harbour, are two parks good for getting your feet on some native soil and for seeing unusual birdlife.

The tie that binds the North Coast is the Pacific Highway, but despite its name, this highway rarely affords glimpses of the Pacific Ocean. You can drive the entire length of the North Coast in a single day, but allow at least three—or, better still, a week—to properly sample some of its attractions.

Numbers in the margin correspond to points of interest on the North Coast map.

PORT MACQUARIE

⓫ *390 km (243 mi) northeast of Sydney.*

Port Macquarie was founded as a convict settlement in 1821, and is the third-oldest settlement in Australia. Set at the mouth of the Hastings River, the town was chosen for its isolation to serve as an open jail for prisoners convicted of second offenses in New South Wales. By the 1830s the pace of settlement was so brisk that the town was no longer isolated, and its usefulness as a jail had ended. Today's Port Macquarie has few reminders of its convict past and is flourishing as a vacation and retirement area. With its pristine rivers and lakes and 13 regional beaches, including beautiful Town Beach and Shelley Beach, which both have sheltered swimming, it's a great place to get into water sports, catch a fish for dinner, and watch migrating humpback whales in season, usually May to July and September to November.

☾ Operated by the Koala Preservation Society of New South Wales, the
★ town's **Koala Hospital** is both a worthy cause and a popular attraction. The Port Macquarie region supports many of these extremely appealing but endangered marsupials, and the hospital cares for 150 to 250 sick and injured koalas each year. The staff is passionate about their furry patients and will happily tell you about the care the animals receive. You can walk around the grounds to view the recuperating animals. Try to visit during feeding times—8 in the morning or 3 in the afternoon. There are guided tours daily at 3. ⊠ *Macquarie Nature Reserve, Lord St.* ☎ *02/6584–1522* ⊕ *www.koalahospital.org.au* ✉ *Donation requested* ⊘ *Daily 8–4:30.*

Fodor'sChoice   The **Sea Acres Rainforest Centre** comprises 178 acres of coastal rain for-
★ est on the southern side of Port Macquarie. There are more than 170 plant species here, including 300-year-old cabbage tree palms, as well as native mammals, reptiles, and prolific birdlife. An elevated board-walk allows you to stroll through the lush environment without disturbing the vegetation. The center has informative guided tours, as well as a gift shop and a pleasant rain-forest café. ⊠ *Pacific Dr. near Shelley Beach Rd.* ☎ *02/6582–3355* ✉ *A$7* ⊘ *Daily 9–4:30.*

Housed in a two-story shop dating from 1836, the eclectic **Port Macquarie Historical Museum** displays period costumes, memorabilia from World Wars I and II, farm implements, antique clocks and watches, and relics from the town's convict days. ⊠ *22 Clarence St.* ☎ *02/6583–1108* ✉ *A$5* ⊘ *Mon.–Sat. 9:30–4:30; Sun. 1–4:30.*

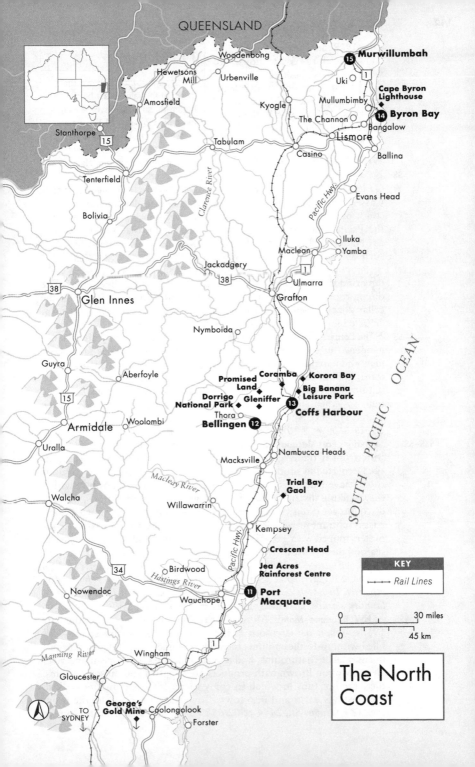

The 1828 **St. Thomas Church**, the country's third-oldest house of worship, was built by convicts using local cedar and stone blocks cemented together with powdered seashells. ⊠*Hay and William Sts.* ☎*02/6584–1033* ⊙*Weekdays 9:30–noon and 2–4.*

> ### THAR SHE BLOWS!
>
> Whales travel up and down the New South Wales coast by the hundreds, so book a whale-watching cruise to catch all the action at close range. Southern Right Whales and Humpbacks travel up from Antarctica from May to August and down again from September to November. Dolphins can be seen almost any time of the year—you never know when an agile pair will shoot through a wave or bob up near your boat.

WHERE TO STAY & EAT

$$ ✕**Ça Marche.** This terrific Mod-Oz lunch spot is part of the lovely
★ Cassegrain Winery, 20 minutes south of Port Macquarie, just off the Pacific Highway (also known as National Route 1). Entrées such as honey-crusted beef fillet, or tempura of Tasmanian salmon with sesame noodles, sweet chili-tamarind dressing, and toffeed lime complement the fine wines. The dining room has views of the vineyards and formal gardens, and the cellar door is open 9–5 for daily tastings. ⊠*764 Fernbank Creek Rd.* ☎*02/6582–8320* ▤*MC, V* ⊙*No dinner Sat.–Thurs.*

$–$$ ✕**The Corner.** This stylish café has been packed with happy diners since it opened in early 2007. The reason is clear, as it serves fabulously tasty and inexpensive meals. Try the Spanish omelette with arugula and tomato confit for breakfast, then return for dinner to sample the prosciutto-wrapped port cutlet with pea puree, tomato chutney, and sage butter. As the name suggests, it sits on a corner, part of the Macquarie Waters Hotel & Apartments complex. It's open seven days. ⊠*Clarence & Munster Sts.* ☎*02/6583–3300* ▤*AE, MC, V.*

$$$–$$$$ ⌕**Rydges Port Macquarie.** This imposing international-style hotel on the waterfront is the largest accommodation in laid-back Port Macquarie. Decorated in soothing chocolate-and-cream tones, all the spacious rooms have balconies; the best views are over the river. You're within easy walking distance of Port Macquarie's many attractions, and big discounts are often available outside school holidays. The hotel's Compass restaurant serves Mod-Oz food; you might start with Sydney rock oysters topped with garlic cream sauce and Brie, and move on to grilled seafood dusted with Moroccan spices on saffron risotto. ⊠*1 Hay St., 2444* ☎*02/6589–2888* ⊕*www.rydges.com/portmacquarie* ⤶*98 rooms, 25 apartments* ⴵ*In-room: safe, kitchen (some), refrigerator, ethernet. In-hotel: restaurant, room service, bar, pool, gym, concierge, laundry service, no-smoking rooms* ▤*AE, DC, MC, V.*

$–$$$ ⌕**HW Boutique Motel.** Although the building dates from the late 1960s—when its sawtooth shape was considered very stylish—it's filled with up-to-the-minute amenities: designer furnishings, luxurious linens, marble bathrooms, and private balconies with ocean and river views. Molton Brown bath products are supplied and, in some rooms, there are hot tubs in which to enjoy them. It's a five-minute walk to the Hastings River and into town. Town Beach is opposite the property. ⊠*1 Stewart St., 2444* ☎*02/6583–1200* ⊕*www.hwmotel.com.au*

⊋45 rooms ⅋ In-room: kitchen, refrigerator, ethernet. In-hotel: room service, pool, laundry facilities, public Internet, no-smoking rooms, minibar ☱AE, DC, MC, V.

EN ROUTE

Trial Bay Gaol, a jail dating from the 1870s, occupies a dramatic position on the cliffs overlooking the seaside village of South West Rocks, 100 km (62 mi) north of Port Macquarie. The building, now partly in ruins, was used to teach useful skills to the prisoners who constructed it, but the project proved too expensive and was abandoned in 1903. During World War I the building served as an internment camp for some 500 Germans. The A$5 admission includes entry to a small museum. A moonlight tour (A$12) takes place on the first Saturday of every month at 6 PM. Make sure you climb the tower for a stunning view of the coast. To get there, travel north through Kempsey and turn off to South West Rocks and follow the signs. ☎02/6566–6168.

2

BELLINGEN

⑫ *210 km (130 mi) north of Port Macquarie.*

In a river valley a few miles off the Pacific Highway, Bellingen is one of the prettiest towns along the coast. Many of Bellingen's buildings have been classified by the National Trust, and the museum, cafés, galleries, and crafts outlets are favorite hangouts for artists, craft workers, and writers. You'll find food, entertainment, and 250 stalls at the community markets that take place on the third Sunday of every month.

From Bellingen a meandering and spectacular road leads inland to Dorrigo before reaching the Pacific Highway, close to Coffs Harbour. This circular scenic route, beginning along the Bellinger River, climbs more than 1,000 feet up the heavily wooded escarpment to
★ the **Dorrigo Plateau.** At the top of the plateau is **Dorrigo National Park** (☎02/6657–2309), a small but outstanding subtropical rain forest that is included on the World Heritage list. Signposts along the main road indicate walking trails. The Satinbird Stroll is a short rain-forest walk, and the 6-km (4-mi) Cedar Falls Walk leads to the most spectacular of the park's many waterfalls. The excellent **Dorrigo Rainforest Centre,** open daily 9–5, has information, educational displays, and a shop, and from here you can walk out high over the forest canopy along the Skywalk boardwalk. The national park is approximately 31 km (19 mi) from Bellingen.

WHERE TO STAY

$ 🏨**Koompartoo Retreat.** These self-contained cottages on a hillside overlooking Bellingen are superb examples of local craftsmanship, particularly in their use of timbers from surrounding forests. Each has a complete kitchen, a family room, and a shower (no tub). Breakfast is available by arrangement. ☒*Rawson and Dudley Sts., 2454* ☎02/6655–2326 ⊕*www.koompartoo.com.au* ⊋4 cottages ⅋In-

room: no phone, kitchen, VCR. In-hotel: laundry facilities, no elevator, no-smoking rooms ☐*MC, V.*

EN
ROUTE

Beyond Dorrigo township, a gravel road completes the loop to the towns of Coramba and Moleton, the latter of which is the location for **George's Gold Mine** (✉*Bushmans Range Rd., Moleton* ☎*02/6654–5355* ⊕*www.meadowsweet.com.au*). Perched on a ridge high above the Orara Valley, this 250-acre cattle property still uses the slab huts and mustering yards built in the region's pioneering days. Owner George Robb is one of the legendary old-timers of the area, and his tour of his gold mine is a vivid account of the personalities and events from the days when "gold fever" gripped these hills. Admission, which includes a tour, is A$12.50. It's open Wednesday to Friday and Sunday, and daily during Christmas and Easter school holidays, with the last tour at 2:30.

COFFS HARBOUR

⓭ *35 km (22 mi) northeast of Bellingen via the Pacific Hwy., 103 km (64 mi) from Bellingen via the inland scenic route along the Dorrigo Plateau.*

The area surrounding Coffs Harbour is the state's "banana belt," where long, neat rows of banana palms cover the hillsides. Set at the foot of steep green hills, the town has great beaches and a mild climate. This idyllic combination has made it one of the most popular vacation spots along the coast. Coffs is also a convenient halfway point in the 1,000-km (620-mi) journey between Sydney and Brisbane.

The town has a lively and attractive harbor in the shelter of **Muttonbird Island,** and a stroll out to this nature reserve is delightful in the evening. To get here follow the signs to the Coffs Harbour Jetty, then park near the marina. A wide path leads out along the breakwater and up the slope of the island. The trail is steep, but the views from the top are worth the effort. The island is named after the muttonbirds (also known as shearwaters) that nest here between September and April. Between June and September Muttonbird Island is also a good spot to view migrating humpback whales.

Near the port in Coffs Harbour, the **Pet Porpoise Pool** aquarium includes sharks, colorful reef fish, turtles, seals, and dolphins. A 90-minute interactive sea-circus show takes place daily at 10 and 1. Children may help feed and shake "hands" with dolphins, as well as interact with kisses from seals. ✉*Orlando St. beside Coffs Creek* ☎*02/6652–2164* ☐*A$26* ⊙*Daily 9–4.*

Just north of the city, impossible to miss, is the Big Banana—the symbol of Coffs Harbour. This monumental piece of kitsch has stood at the site since 1964. It welcomes visitors to the **Big Banana Leisure Park** complex, which takes a fascinating look at the past, present, and future of horticulture. There's a multimedia display called "World of Bananas" and a walkway that meanders through the banana plantations. A lookout high on the plantation hill provides great views to the coast, and is a good whale-watching vantage point July–November. The park also includes toboggan rides, a ski run, and an ice-skating rink. There's a café on the premises, as well as the Banana Barn, which sells the park's own jams, pickles, and fresh tropical fruit. ⊠ *351 Pacific Hwy.* ☏*02/6652–4355* ⊕*www.bigbanana.com* ⊡*A$15* ⊙*Daily 9–4:30.*

WHERE TO STAY & EAT

$–$$ ✕**Shearwater Restaurant.** This waterfront restaurant with views of Coffs Creek (which is spotlighted at night—look for stingrays swimming by) leaves no culinary stone unturned in its search for novel flavors. The menu in the open-air dining room includes dishes such as wild barramundi fillet with potato rosti. The room is relaxed, and the service is friendly and attentive. ⊠ *321 Harbour Dr.* ☏*02/6651–6053* ▤*AE, MC, V.*

$$–$$$$ 🏨**BreakFree Aanuka Beach Resort.** Teak furniture and antiques collected
★ from Indonesia and the South Pacific fill the one-bedroom suites at this resort, which sits amid palms, frangipani, and hibiscus. Each suite has a kitchenette, lounge, laundry, and glass-ceiling bathroom with a two-person whirlpool tub. There are also hotel-room studios and two-bedroom suites and three- and four-bedroom split-level villas. Outside, the landscaping is highly imaginative; the pool is immersed in a miniature rain forest with a waterfall and hot tub. The resort borders a secluded white-sand beach on the blue waters of the Pacific. There is a three-night minimum stay during the high season (December 23–January 20, and during Easter). ⊠ *11 Firman Dr., 2450* ☏*02/6652–7555* ⊕*www. stellaresorts.com.au* ⥱*32 studio rooms, 38 suites* ♿*In-room: kitchen (some), refrigerator, DVD (some). In-hotel: 2 restaurants, room service, bar, tennis courts, pools, gym, spa, no elevator, laundry facilities, children's programs (ages 2–12), public Internet, no-smoking rooms* ▤*AE, DC, MC, V* ⊙*BP.*

$$–$$$$ 🏨**Novotel Pacific Bay Resort.** This large property—where the Australian Rugby Union team, the Wallabies, train— has direct beach access to Charlesworth Bay. Accommodations are grouped in two separate wings and include hotel rooms with balconies; one- and two-bedroom apartments with full kitchens and laundry areas; two-story, three-bedroom apartments; and penthouse suites (each with a private rooftop grill and a hot tub). Active travelers will love the 9-hole golf course, lighted tennis courts, volleyball area, and walking track. The day spa is equipped with 10 treatment rooms. ⊠ *Corner of Pacific Hwy. and Bay Dr., 2450* ☏*02/6659–7000* ⊕*www.pacificbayresort.com.au* ⥱*180 rooms* ♿*In-room: kitchen (some), refrigerator. In-hotel: restaurant, bars, golf course, tennis courts, pools, gym, spa, water sports, children's programs (ages 2–15), no-smoking rooms.*

SPORTS & THE OUTDOORS

The warm seas around Coffs Harbour make this particular part of the coast, with its moray eels, manta rays, turtles, and gray nurse sharks, a scuba diver's favorite. Best are the Solitary Islands, 7 km–21 km (4½ mi–13 mi) offshore. **Jetty Dive Centre** (☏*02/6651–1611* ⊕*www. jettydive.com.au*) also rents gear, schedules scuba and snorkeling trips, and hosts certification classes.

The highly regarded **Wildwater Adventures** (✉*754 Pacific Hwy., Boambee* ☎*02/6653–2067* ⊕*www.coffscentral.com/wildwater*) conducts one-, two-, and four-day rafting trips down the Nymboida River. Trips begin from Bonville, 14 km (9 mi) south of Coffs Harbour on the Pacific Highway, but pickups from the Coffs Harbour and Bellingen region can be arranged. One-day trips start at A$153, including meals.

EN ROUTE

An hour or so north of Coffs Harbour is the gracious town of Grafton, set on the banks of the Clarence River. The town is famous for the **Jacaranda Festival,** which has taken place the last week of October since 1935. A parade is held in the streets—lined with the beautiful purple flowering trees—and a new Jacaranda Queen is crowned each year. Between Grafton and the far North Coast, the Pacific Highway enters sugarcane country, where tiny sugarcane trains and thick, drifting smoke from burning cane fields are ever-present. The highway passes the fishing and resort town of **Ballina,** where beaches are the prime feature.

BYRON BAY

⑭ *176 km (109 mi) north of Grafton; 247 km (154 mi) north of Coffs Harbour.*

Byron Bay is the easternmost point on the Australian mainland and perhaps earns Australia its nickname, the "Lucky Country." Fabulous beaches, storms that spin rainbows across the mountains behind the town, and a sunny, relaxed style cast a spell over practically everyone who visits. For many years Byron Bay lured surfers with abundant sunshine, perfect waves on Watego's Beach, and tolerant locals who allowed them to sleep on the sand. These days a more-upscale crowd frequents Byron Bay.

Byron Bay is also one of the must-sees on the backpacker circuit, and the town has a youthful energy that fuels late-night partying. There are many art galleries and crafts shops, a great food scene, and numerous adventure tours. The town is at its liveliest on the first Sunday of each month, when Butler Street becomes a bustling market.

The East Coast Blues and Roots Festival takes place every Easter, with big-name international and local acts. Jackson Browne and Sir Bob Geldoff appeared in recent years. Byron Bay has a strong alternative bent, and you can find any number of crystal shops and plenty of places to get a holistic massage.

Cape Byron Lighthouse, the most powerful beacon on the Australian coastline, dominates the southern end of the beach at Byron Bay. You can tour the lighthouse (no children under five) on Tuesday and Thursday year-round, and weekends during New South Wales summer and term school holidays. Whale watching is popular between June and September, when migrating humpback whales come close to shore. Dolphins swim in these waters year-round, and you can often see pods of them from the cape. You can stay overnight in the lighthouse, but you must make a reservation at least six months in advance. ✉*Lighthouse*

Rd. ☎*02/6685–8565, 02/6685–6552 overnight reservations* 📧*Free, lighthouse tours A$8* ☉*Lighthouse grounds daily 8–5:30. Lighthouse tours Tues. and Thurs. at 11, 12:30, and 2; weekends at 10, 11, 12:30, 2, and 3:30 during school holidays.*

Cape Byron Walking Track circumnavigates a 150-acre reserve and passes through grasslands and rain forest. The headland is the highlight of the route. From several vantage points along the track you may spot dolphins in the waters below.

Byron Bay Hinterland. Inland from Byron Bay is some of the most picturesque country in Australia. Undulating green hills that once boasted a thriving dairy industry are dotted with villages with a New Age vibe. There are small organic farms growing avocados, coffee, fruits, and macadamia nuts. The best way to discover this gorgeous part of the world—nicknamed the Rainbow Region—is to grab a map and drive. From Byron, take the road towards the regional town of Lismore for about 15 km (9 mi) to the pretty village of **Bangalow**. Walk along the lovely main street lined with 19th-century storefronts and native Bangalow palms. Carefully follow your map and wind your way northwest for about 20 km (13 mi) to **Federal** for lunch at **Pogel's Wood Café** (☎*02/6688–4121*). Meander, via the cute towns of **Rosebank** and **Dunoon**, to **The Channon**, where on the second Sunday of every month you'll find a wonderful market with dozens of stalls and entertainment. You may want to relax for a few days at the town's **Eternity Springs Art Farm** (✉*483 Tuntable Creek Rd.* ☎*02/6688–6385* ⊕*www.eternitysprings.com*), a groovy B&B that also offers art classes and yoga.

OFF THE
BEATEN
PATH ★

2

BEACHES

Several superb beaches lie in the vicinity of Byron Bay. In front of the town, Main Beach provides safe swimming, and Clarks Beach, closer to the cape, has better surf. The most famous surfing beach, however, is Watego's, the only entirely north-facing beach in the state. To the south of the lighthouse Tallow Beach extends for 6 km (4 mi) to a rocky stretch of coastline around Broken Head, which has a number of small sandy coves. Beyond Broken Head is lonely Seven Mile Beach. Topless sunbathing is popular on many Byron Bay beaches.

WHERE TO STAY & EAT

$$ ★ ✕**Fig Tree Country Restaurant.** In this century-old farmhouse with distant views of Byron Bay, the draw is creative Mod-Oz cuisine blending Asian and Mediterranean flavors. Produce fresh from the owners' farm is featured on the menu. There are always salads served with homemade bread, and lots of seafood dishes. Desserts include a delicious homemade ice cream, and a coconut-and-rum panna cotta with mango sauce. Ask for a table on the veranda, amid the extravagant foliage. The restaurant is 5 km (3 mi) inland from Byron Bay. ✉*4 Sunrise La., Ewingsdale* ☎*02/6684–7273* ▤*MC, V* 🍷*BYO* ☉*Closed Mon.–Wed. No dinner Sun.*

$ ✕**Beach Café.** A Byron Bay legend, this open-air café is a perfect place to sit in the morning sun and watch the waves. Breakfast runs the gamut from wholesome (muesli with yogurt) to total calorific decadence (monstrous omelets with bacon, mushrooms, and more). For lunch you might try grilled fish with roast vegetables. The fresh juices and tropical fruits alone are worth the 15-minute stroll along the beach from town. ⊠ *Clarks Beach off parking lot at end of Lawson St.* ☎*02/6685–7598* ☐*MC, V* ⊘*No dinner.*

$$$$
Fodor'sChoice
★

×⛳ **Rae's on Watego's.** If a high-design boutique hotel is your cup of tea, you'd be hard-pressed to do better than this luxurious Mediterranean-style villa sur-

HIPPY DAYS

You'll think you've traveled back in time when you arrive in Nimbin, northwest of Byron Bay. There are psychedelic store fronts, a hemp museum, and stores such as Hippy High Herbs and Nimbin Apothecary. The annual "Mardi Grass" Fiesta, which advocates the legalization of cannabis, is held on the first weekend of May, and is a sight to behold.

rounded by a tropical garden. Each suite is individually decorated with an exotic collection of antiques, Indonesian art, Moroccan tables, and fine furnishings. The secluded rooms have gorgeous four-poster beds, tile floors, huge windows, in-room fireplaces, and private terraces; the service is top-notch, and the alfresco in-house restaurant ($$$) serves creative Australian-Thai dishes. There's a minimum two-night stay on weekends. ⊠ *Watego's Beach, 8 Marina Parade, 2481* ☎*02/6685–5366* ⊕*www.raes.com.au* ⪢*7 suites* ⬧*In-room: no a/c (some), refrigerator, VCR, Wi-Fi. In-hotel: restaurant, room service, pool, spa, no elevator, public Internet, no kids under 13* ☐*AE, DC, MC, V.*

$$
⛳ **Julian's Apartments.** These studio apartments opposite Clarks Beach are neat, spacious, and well equipped. All have a kitchen, a laundry, and either a balcony or a courtyard with rooms opening onto a generous private patio. Furnishings are simple, done in refreshing blond timbers, blue fabrics, and white walls. The beach is so close that the sound of the waves can rock you to sleep. ⊠*124 Lighthouse Rd., 2481* ☎*02/6680–9697* ⊕*www.juliansbyronbay.com* ⪢*11 apartments* ⬧*In-room: kitchen, DVD. In-hotel: laundry facilities, no elevator, no-smoking rooms* ☐*AE, DC, MC, V.*

¢
⛳ **Arts Factory Lodge.** This funky backpacker hostel, seven minutes from the beach, is a Byron Bay institution. Set on 15 acres of land, it is next door to the Arts Factory Village, one of *the* places to hang out in Byron. Accommodations are a mix of interesting dorms—there's a surf shack for 12 people, a women-only 6-bed cottage, and a tepee that sleeps 10. Accommodations for couples—called cubes and islands—are also available, though the Love Shack is the only room with an in-room bathroom. Many of the rooms are set along the pool or in secluded bushland. There's a communal kitchen, café at the lodge, and a restaurant and bar with nightly entertainment (which often includes fire twirling). ⊠*Arts Factory Village, Skinners Shoot Rd.* ☎*02/6685–7709* ⊕*www.artsfactory.com.au* ⪢*6 dorms* ⬧*In-room: refrigerator (some). In-hotel: restaurant, pool, spa, no elevator* ☐*MC, V.*

NIGHTLIFE

For a small town, Byron rocks by night. Fire dancing—where bare-chested men dance with flaming torches—is a local specialty. Bars and clubs are generally open until about 2 AM on weekends and midnight on weekdays.

Head to the **Arts Factory** (⊠ *Skinners Shoot Rd.* ☎ *02/6685–7709*) (also known as the Piggery) to catch a movie, grab a bite, or see a band. The **Beach Hotel** (⊠ *Bay and Jonson Sts.* ☎ *02/6685–6402*) often hosts live bands. Bar-restaurant-night-club **Cocomangas** (⊠ *32 Jonson St.* ☎ *02/6685–8493*) is a favorite of backpackers. Bands perform most evenings in the **Great Northern Hotel** (⊠ *Jonson and Byron Sts.* ☎ *02/6685–6454*). Live music rocks the **Railway Friendly Bar** (⊠ *Jonson St. Railway Station* ☎ *02/6685–7662*) most nights.

NO BULL

If there's one place that has milked its name for all its worth, then that's Mooball, a blink-and-you-miss it village about 20 minutes north of Byron Bay. Follow the black-and-white cow prints painted on telegraph poles to the Moo Moo Café, which serves Moo Moo Burgers, Moo Moo shakes, and lots of kitschy souvenirs. If you find cow puns udderly annoying, then it's best to graze in other pastures.

SPORTS & THE OUTDOORS

Dolphin Kayaking (☎ *02/6685–8044* ⊕ *www.dolphinkayaking.com.au*) has half-day trips twice daily (weather permitting) that take paddlers out to meet the local dolphins and surf the waves.

Byron Bay Kiteboarding (☎ *0402/008–926 or 0400/103–003* ⊕ *www. byronbaykiteboarding.com*) is an International Kiteboarding Organization–accredited school with beginner lessons and clinics. Two-day, two-student courses take place on a choice of local waterways.

The best local diving is at Julian Rocks Marine Reserve, some 3 km (2 mi) offshore, where the confluence of warm and cold currents supports a profusion of marine life. **Byron Bay Dive Centre** (⊠ *9 Marvel St.* ☎ *02/6685–8333 or 1800/243483* ⊕ *www.byronbaydivecentre. com.au*) has snorkeling and scuba-diving trips for all levels of experience, plus gear rental and instruction. **Sundive** (⊠ *8 Middleton St.* ☎ *02/6685–7755 or 1800/008755* ⊕ *www.sundive.com.au*) is a PADI dive center with courses for all levels of divers, as well as boat dives and snorkel trips.

SHOPPING

Byron Bay is one of the state's arts-and-crafts centers, with many innovative and high-quality articles for sale, such as leather goods, offbeat designer clothing, essential oils, natural cosmetics, and ironware. The community market, held on the first Sunday of every month, fills the Butler Street reserve with more than 300 stalls selling art, craft, and local produce.

Cape Gallery (⊠ *2 Lawson St.* ☎ *02/6685–7659*) sells glasswork, sculptures, ceramics, and paintings by local craft workers. Hours are weekdays 9–5 and weekends 10–4. **Colin Heaney Hot Glass Studio** (✉6 *Acacia St., Industrial Estate* ☏*02/6685–7044*) sells exquisite hand-blown glass goblets, wineglasses, paperweights, and sculpture. Glass-blowers work here on weekdays. The shop is open weekdays 9–5 and weekends 10–4. **In Depth Creations** (✉*3/2 Tasman Way, Byron Bay Arts & Industrial Estate* ☏*02/6628–8333*) sells custom-made surf-boards decorated with hand-painted art. It's open sporadic hours, so call ahead before visiting.

Postmarked BYRON (✉*Shop 3 Bay House, 11 Jonson St.* ☏*02/6658–8722*) sells home wares, collectibles and mementos, and lovely small gifts ideal for taking home in a suitcase. You'll also find a selection of jewelry and children's gifts. **Byron Fine Art Gallery** (✉*Byron Arcade, 13 Lawson St.* ☏*02/6680–8433*) has a large collection of Australian paintings, many by local artists. The **Byron Bay Hat Co.** (✉*4 Jonson St.* ☏*02/6685–8357*) is an institution with great hats and bags perfect for the beach.

MURWILLUMBAH

🔟 *53 km (33 mi) northwest of Byron Bay.*

★ Towering, conical **Mt. Warning,** the 3,800-foot central magma cham-ber of a now extinct volcano, dominates pleasant, rambling Mur-willumbah, which rests amid sugarcane plantations on the banks of the Tweed River. Its radical shape can be seen from miles away, including the beaches at Byron Bay. Apart from the seaside resort of Tweed Heads, Murwillumbah is the last town of any size before the Queensland border.

A well-marked **walking track** winds up Mt. Warning, which is a World Heritage national park, from the Breakfast Creek parking area at its base. The 4½-km (2½-mi) track climbs steadily through fern forest and buttressed trees where you can often see native brush turkeys and pademelons (small wallaby-like marsupials). The last 650 feet of the ascent is a strenuous scramble up a steep rock face using chain-link handrails. The local Aboriginal name for the mountain is Wollumbin, which means "cloud catcher," and the metal walkways on the summit are sometimes shrouded in clouds. On a clear day, however, there are fabulous 360-degree views of the massive caldera, one of the largest in the world: national parks crown the southern, western, and northern rims, and the Tweed River flows seaward through the eroded eastern wall. Many people undertake the Mt. Warning ascent before dawn, so they can catch the first rays of light falling on mainland Australia.

For information about the walk and Mt. Warning National Park, visit the **World Heritage Rainforest Visitors Information Centre** (✉*Corner of Tweed Valley Way and Alma St.* ☏*02/6672–1340* ⊕*www.tweed coolangatta.com.au*) in town. From here it is a 16½-km (10-mi) drive to the start of the walking track. Fill your water bottles in Murwil-lumbah; there is no drinking water in the park or on the mountain.

Allow at least four hours up and back, and don't start the walk after 2 PM in winter.

WHERE TO STAY

$$$$ ★ ⛰Crystal Creek Rainforest Retreat. High in the forested hinterland behind Murwillumbah, handsome timber bungalows dot a former banana plantation. Each spacious unit has a king-size bed, a kitchen, and a big deck that extends out into the rain forest. All have sunken whirlpool baths, where you can relax with only glass between you and the trees. The backdrop is Border Ranges National Park, a steep chunk of mossy rain forest furnished with huge trees and gushing creeks. You can breakfast on your veranda and listen to whipbirds calling from the depths of the forest. Dinners are also available, and served in your bungalow. There is a two-night minimum stay on weekends. ⛫ *Box 69, 2484* ☎*02/6679–1591* ⊕*www.crystalcreekrainforestretreat.com.au* ⛺*7 bungalows* ⛄*In-room: no phone, kitchen, refrigerator, DVD, VCR. In-hotel: bicycles, no-smoking rooms, no kids* ▤*AE, DC, MC, V.*

NORTH COAST ESSENTIALS

AIR TRAVEL

From Sydney, REX (Regional Express) Airlines services Ballina and Lismore (both about ½ hour from Byron Bay). Qantas Airways flies into Port Macquarie and Coffs Harbour. Virgin Blue flies into Ballina and Coffs Harbour.

Information Qantas Airways (☎*13–1313* ⊕*www.qantas.com.au*). **REX Airlines** (☎*13–1713* ⊕*www.regionalexpress.com.au*). **Virgin Blue** (☎*13–6789* ⊕*www. virginblue.com.au*).

BUS TRAVEL

Greyhound Australia and Premier Motor Service frequently run between Sydney and Brisbane, with stops at all major North Coast towns. Sydney to Coffs Harbour is a 9-hour ride; Sydney to Byron Bay takes 12 hours.

Information Greyhound Australia (☎*13–1499* ⊕*www.greyhound.com.au*). **Premier Motor Service** (☎*13–3410* ⊕*www.premierms.com.au*).

CAR TRAVEL

From Sydney, head north via the Harbour Bridge or Harbour Tunnel and follow the signs to Hornsby and Newcastle. Join the Sydney–Newcastle Freeway, then continue up the Pacific Highway (Highway 1). Port Macquarie is 390 km (243 mi) northeast of Sydney.

EMERGENCIES

In an emergency, dial **000** to reach an ambulance, the police, or the fire department.

Contacts Byron Bay District Hospital (✉*Shirley St., Byron Bay* ☎*02/6685–6200*). **Coffs Harbour Base Hospital** (✉*345 Pacific Hwy., Coffs Harbour* ☎*02/6656–7000*). **Murwillumbah District Hospital** (✉*Ewing St., Murwillumbah* ☎*02/6672–1822*).

TOURS

Mountain Trails Four-Wheel-Drive Tours conducts half- and full-day tours of the rain forests and waterfalls of the Great Dividing Range to the west of Coffs Harbour in style—a 7-seat Toyota Safari or a 14-seat, Australian-designed four-wheel-drive vehicle. The half-day tour costs A$65 and the full-day tour is A$95, including lunch and snacks.

Information Mountain Trails (☎ 02/6658-3333).

TRAIN TRAVEL

Trains stop at Kempsey, Coffs Harbour, Grafton, and Casino. Buses connect with the train at Casino to take passengers to Ballina, Byron Bay, and Murwillumbah. As most of the Sydney–Brisbane railway line runs inland, the service is not particularly useful for seeing the North Coast. Call Countrylink, the New South Wales rail operator, for fare and service details.

Information Countrylink (☎ 13-2232).

VISITOR INFORMATION

Byron Visitor Centre and Coffs Coast Visitors Information Centre are open daily 9–5. The World Heritage Rainforest Centre (in Murwillumbah) is open Monday–Saturday 9–4:30 and Sunday 9:30–4. Greater Port Macquarie Visitor Information Centre is open weekdays 8:30–5 and weekends 9–4. Sydney Visitor Centre, open daily 9:30–5:30, has information on North Coast accommodations, tours, and sights.

Information Byron Visitor Centre (⊠ 80 Jonson St., Byron Bay ☎ 02/6680-8558 ⊕ www.visitbyronbay.com). **Coffs Coast Visitors Information Centre** (⊠ Pacific Hwy. at McLean St., Coffs Harbour ☎ 02/6652-1522 or 1300/369070 ⊕ www. coffscoast.com.au). **Greater Port Macquarie Visitor Information Centre** (⊠ Gordon and Gore Sts., Port Macquarie ☎ 1300/303155 ⊕ www.portmacquarieinfo.com. au). **Sydney Visitor Centre** (⊠ The Rocks Centre, Argyle and Playfair Sts., The Rocks, Sydney, 2000 ☎ 02/9240-8788 🖶 02/9241-5010 ⊕ www.sydneyvisitorcentre. com). **World Heritage Rainforest Centre** (⊠ Tweed Valley Way and Alma St., Murwillumbah ☎ 02/6672-1340 ⊕ www.tweedcoolangatta.com.au).

LORD HOWE ISLAND

A tiny crescent of land 700 km (437 mi) northeast of Sydney, Lord Howe Island is the most remote and arguably the most beautiful part of New South Wales. With the sheer peaks of Mt. Gower (2,870 feet) and Mt. Lidgbird (2,548 feet) richly clad in palms, ferns, and grasses; golden sandy beaches; and the clear turquoise waters of the lagoon, this is a remarkably lovely place. Apart from the barren spire of Ball's Pyramid, a stark volcanic outcrop 16 km (10 mi) across the water to the southeast, the Lord Howe Island Group stands alone in the South Pacific. The island has been placed on UNESCO's World Heritage list as a "natural area of universal value and outstanding beauty."

Not only is the island beautiful, but its history is fascinating. The first recorded sighting was not until 1788, by a passing ship en route to the penal settlement on Norfolk Island, which lies to the east. And evidence, or lack of it, suggests that Lord Howe was uninhabited by humans until three Europeans and their Maori wives and children settled it in the 1830s. English and American whaling boats then began calling in for supplies, and by the 1870s the small population included a curious mixture of people from America (including whalers and former slaves), England, Ireland, Australia, South Africa, and the Gilbert Islands. Many of the descendants of these early settlers still live on Lord Howe. In the 1870s, when the importance of whale oil declined, islanders set up an export industry of the seeds of the endemic Kentia (*Howea forsteriana*), the world's most popular indoor palm. It's still a substantial business, but rather than seeds, seedlings are now sold.

Lord Howe is a remarkably safe and relaxed place, where cyclists and walkers far outnumber the few cars. No one locks their doors, the speed limit is a mere 25 kph (15 mph), and there's no cell phone service. There are plenty of walking trails, both flat and rather precipitous, and fine beaches. Among the many bird species is the endangered Lord Howe wood hen (*Tricholimnas sylvestris*). In the sea below the island's fringing reef is the world's southernmost coral reef, with more than 50 species of hard corals and more than 500 fish species. For its size, the island has enough to keep you alternately occupied and unoccupied for at least five days. Even the dining scene is of an unexpectedly high quality.

Fewer than 320 people live here, and visitor numbers are limited to 400 at any given time, though at present hotel beds can only accommodate 393 tourists. The allocation of those remaining seven tourists is the subject of local controversy.

EXPLORING LORD HOWE ISLAND

The first view of Lord Howe Island rising sheer out of the South Pacific is spectacular. The sense of wonder only grows as you set out to explore the island, which, at a total area of 3,220 acres (about 3 km by 11 km (2 mi by 7 mi), is manageable. You don't have to allow much time to see the town. Most of the community is scattered along the low-lying saddle between the hills that dominate the island's extremities. There are a few shops, a hospital, a school, and three churches. Everything else is either a home or lodge.

As one of the very few impediments to winds sweeping across the South Pacific, the mountains of Lord Howe Island create their own weather. Visually, this can be amazing as you stand in sunshine on the coast while clouds gather around the high peaks. The average annual rainfall of about 62 inches mostly comes down in winter. Note that, except during the period of Australia's summer daylight savings time (when Lord Howe and Sydney are on the same time), island time is curiously a half hour ahead of Sydney. Additionally, many of the lodges, restaurants, and tour operators close in winter—generally from June through August—and accommodation prices in the open establishments are reduced considerably during that period. Five- or seven-night flight-and-accommodation packages are the most economic way to visit Lord Howe.

WHAT TO SEE

Lord Howe Museum makes a good first stop in town. Inside there's an interesting display of historical memorabilia. The island's naturalist Ian Hutton and environmentalist Chris Murray conduct audiovisual presentations at 5 PM on weekdays (except Wednesday) on the area's flora, fauna, and marine life. ⊠ *Lagoon and Middle Beach Rds.* ☎ *02/6563–2111* ✑ *Donation requested* ☉ *Sun.–Fri. 9–4, Sat. 9–12:30; talks at 5 PM.*

The ultimate challenge on Lord Howe is the climb up the southernmost peak of **Mt. Gower,** which rises straight out of the ocean to an astonishing 2,870 feet above sea level. The hike is rated medium to hard, and national park regulations require that you use a guide. Fifth-generation islander **Jack Shick** (☎ *02/6563–2218*) is a highly recommended guide who makes the climb twice weekly, usually Monday and Thursday (call him to check). The cost is A$40 and reservations are essential. Meet at Little Island Gate at 7:30 AM sharp; bring lunch and drinks, and wear a jacket and sturdy walking shoes. The views, the lush vegetation, and the sense of achievement all make the hike worthwhile.

A very enjoyable way of filling a sunny day is to take a picnic down to **Ned's Beach,** on the eastern side of the island, where green lawns slope down to a sandy beach and clear blue waters. This is a fantastic place for swimming and snorkeling, and Ned's has been awarded Australia's Cleanest Beach title twice. Fish swim close to the shore and are fed every day at 4 PM. The coral is just a few yards out. From Ned's Beach at dusk during shearwater (muttonbird) season, you can watch thousands of these birds returning to their burrows in the sand.

Several walks take you around the island. Easy strolls are to forested Stevens Reserve; surf-pounded Blinky Beach; great Clear Place and Middle Beach; and a snorkeling spot beneath Mt. Gower, by Little Island. The climbs up Mt. Eliza and Malabar Hill at the island's northern end are more strenuous, although much less so than Mt. Gower or Mt. Lidgbird (the other peak that dominates the southern end of the island). They afford tremendous views of the island, including its hulking, mountainous southern end and the waters and islets all around. There are 17 accommodation houses on the island, including motel units, apartments, cottages, and resorts. Several of the resort restaurants are open to nonguests.

WHERE TO STAY & EAT

$$$ ✕ **Beachcomber Lodge.** The Beachcomber serves the island's popular fish-fry buffet on Sunday and Wednesday nights (there is an à la carte menu on Saturday nights). Locally caught fish is cooked in beer batter and accompanied by chips and salads. Desserts, a cheese platter, and coffee follow the main courses. The restaurant is open to nonguests. ⊠ *Anderson Rd.* ☎ *02/6563–2032* ⊕ *www.beachcomberlhi.com.au* ▭ *AE, DC, MC, V.*

2

$$$$ ✕🏨**Arajilla.** This intimate retreat is tucked away at the north end of the island amid banyan trees and Kentia palms. Spacious suites and two-bedroom apartments have well-equipped kitchens, separate lounge areas, and private decks. Snorkeling equipment and fishing tackle are provided; you can also rent mountain bikes. The overnight price includes breakfast, a light lunch, and a three-course dinner. The excellent on-site restaurant ($$) serves fine Australian wine and modern cuisine with Asian and European influences. You might try grilled local fish with a Mediterranean vegetable stack, or veal and herb sausages with potato mash and caramelized onion. Leave room, though, for desserts like chilled berry soup with raspberry mascarpone gelato. ⊠ *Old Settlement Beach, Lagoon Rd., 2898* ☎*02/6563–2002* ⊕*www.arajilla. com.au* 🛏*10 suites, 2 apartments* ♿*In-room: no a/c, kitchen, refrigerator, VCR. In-hotel: restaurant, bar, water sports, bicycles, no elevator, public Internet* ▤*AE, MC, V* ⏹*BP.*

$$$$ ✕🏨**Capella Lodge.** Lord Howe's most luxurious accommodation is a bit out of the way, but the reward is a truly dramatic panorama. The lodge's veranda overlooks beaches, the ocean, and the lofty peaks of Mt. Lidgbird and Mt. Gower. The nine high-ceiling guest suites are decked out in contemporary furnishings in soft sand and sea hues, and have shuttered doors that let light in while maintaining privacy. Four loft rooms have separate living areas and the one family suite has two bedrooms. The best accommodation is the Lidgbird Suite with a wraparound veranda and an outdoor plunge pool. The lodge has also added a day spa with treatments including mud wraps and sacred stone therapy. The equally stylish Capella Restaurant ($$$$) showcases local seafood. Nonguests are welcome to dine in the glass-walled dining room, but should call ahead for reservations. Your accommodation rate includes breakfast, afternoon drinks, and a three-course dinner with wine. ⊠*Lagoon Rd., 2898* ☎*02/6563–2008, 02/9544–2273 restaurant reservations, 02/9544–2387 Sydney booking office* ⊕*www.lordhowe.com* 🛏*9 suites* ♿*In-room: no a/c, DVD. In-hotel: restaurant, bar, pool, water sports, bicycles, no elevator, laundry service, public Internet, airport shuttle, no-smoking rooms* ▤*AE, DC, MC, V* ⏹*MAP.*

$$$$ ✕🏨**Pinetrees.** Descendants of the island's first settlers run the largest resort on the island, one of the few that stays open year-round. The original 1884 homestead forms part of this central resort, but most accommodations are in undistinguished motel-style units, which have verandas leading into pleasant gardens. Five garden cottages and two luxury suites are a cut above the other rooms. At the in-house restaurant, a limited, changing menu might include seared local kingfish with jasmine rice, bok choy, and red curry sauce, or satay-marinated Lord Howe trevally. Rates include all meals, and credit cards

---

WINGING IT

Masked boobies, brown noddies, providence petrels, red-tailed topic birds, and sooty terns will be more than just the cute names of feathered friends after a few days on Lord Howe Island. The skies are full of birds gliding and swooping on the warm currents, while at ground level Lord Howe wood hens will be picking at your feet. It's a birdlovers' paradise.

are accepted for advance reservations only. Good deals are available for stays of five nights or more. ✉*Lagoon Rd., halfway between airport and Middle Beach Rd., 2898* ☎*02/9262–6585, 02/6563–2177 for restaurant* ⊕*www.pinetrees.com.au* ☞*31 rooms, 2 suites, 5 cottages* ♿*In-room: no a/c, no phone, kitchen (some), refrigerator, no TV. In-hotel: restaurant, bar, tennis court, beachfront, water sports, bicycles, no elevator, laundry facilities, no-smoking rooms* ☐*AE, DC, MC, V* ⎐*FAP.*

$$$$ ☷ **Earl's Anchorage.** This accommodation on Lord Howe opened in mid-2005, and it's the only one on the island with reverse-cycle air-conditioning. The complex is set inland, not far from Ned's Beach. There are six bungalows (four one-bedroom and two two-bedrooms). Each bungalow is named after one of the yachts once owned by the late yachtsman Jack Earl, who co-founded the famous Sydney-to-Hobart yacht race. Bungalows have fully-equipped kitchens, handcrafted timber fittings, and modern beach-house decor. One bungalow is equipped for people with disabilities. ☎*02/6563–2019* ☞*6 apartments* ♿*In-room: kitchen. In-hotel: no elevator, laundry facilities* ☐*AE, MC, V.*

SPORTS & THE OUTDOORS

FISHING

Fishing is a major activity on Lord Howe. Several well-equipped boats regularly go out for kingfish, yellowfin tuna, marlin, and wahoo. A half-day trip with **Oblivienne Sports Fishing Charters** (☎*02/6563–2185*) includes tackle and bait, for around A$85. It's best to arrange an excursion as soon as you arrive on the island.

GOLF

Nonmembers are welcome at the spectacularly located—between the ocean on one side and two mountains on the other—9-hole, par-36 **Lord Howe Island Golf Club** (☎☎*02/6563–2179*), and you can rent clubs. Nonmembers can participate in the Friday Chicken Run, a 9-hole game beginning at 3 PM, and the 18-hole Sunday competition. The greens fee is A$20 for 9 or 18 holes.

SCUBA DIVING & SNORKELING

Lord Howe Island's reefs provide a unique opportunity for diving in coral far from the equator. And, unlike many of the Queensland islands, superb diving and snorkeling is literally just offshore, rather than a long boat trip away. Even though the water is warm enough for coral, most divers wear a wet suit. Dive courses are not available in June and July. If you're heading to Lord Howe specifically for diving, contact **Pro Dive Travel** (☎*02/9281–5066 or 1800/820820* ☎*02/9281–0660* ⊕*www.prodive.com.au*) in Sydney, which has packages that include accommodations, airfares, and diving. On the island they are located at the **Pro Dive Hut Lagoon** (☎*02/6563–2253*).

The best snorkeling spots are on the reef that fringes the lagoon, at Ned's Beach and North Bay, and around the Sylph Hole off Old Settlement Beach—a spot that turtles frequent. **Lord Howe Island Environmental**

Tours (☎ *02/6563–2214*) runs two-hour glass-bottom boat cruises that include snorkeling gear in the A$25 charge.

LORD HOWE ISLAND ESSENTIALS

2

AIR TRAVEL

Unless you have your own boat, the most practical way of getting to Lord Howe Island is by QantasLink from Brisbane or Sydney. Weekly summer flights between Port Macquarie and Lord Howe Island began in 2007. The flying time is about two hours. Your hosts on Lord Howe Island will pick you up from the airport. Note that the baggage allowance is only 14 kilograms (31 pounds) per person. Special discounts on airfares to the island are often available if you're coming from overseas and you purchase tickets outside Australia.

Contact **QantasLink** (☎ *13–1313* ⊕ *www.qantas.com.au*).

BIKE TRAVEL

Despite the island's hills and high peaks, much of the terrain is fairly flat, and bicycles, usually available at your lodge, are the ideal form of transportation. Helmets, which are supplied with the bikes, must be worn by law. If your hotel doesn't have free bikes, **Wilson's Hire Service** (⊠ *Lagoon Rd.* ☎ *02/6563–2045*) rents them from A$7 a day.

CAR RENTAL

There are just six rental cars on the island, and only 24 km (15 mi) of roads, with a maximum speed of 25 kph (15 mph). Your lodge can arrange a car (if available) for about A$55 per day.

EMERGENCIES

In an emergency, dial **000** to reach an ambulance, the police, or the fire department.

Emergency Contacts **Doctor** (☎ *02/6563–2000 Dr. Frank Reed*). **Hospital** (⊠ *Lagoon Rd. at Bowker Ave.* ☎ *02/6563–2000*).

MONEY MATTERS

Although most major credit cards are accepted, there are no ATMs on the island. Be sure to carry adequate cash for small purchases.

TOURS

Islander Cruises conducts several tours around the island, including cruises to North Bay for snorkeling, a two-hour sunset cocktail cruise on the lagoon, and a morning and evening cappuccino cruise around the lagoon. Prices run from A$30 to A$45.

Ron's Ramble is a scenic and highly informative three-hour stroll (A$15) around a small section of the island with knowledgeable guide Ron Matthews explaining much about Lord Howe's geology, history, and plant and animal life. The rambles take place on Monday, Wednesday, and Friday afternoons starting at 2 in front of the hospital.

Whitfield's Island Tours runs a three-hour air-conditioned bus tour (A\$28) that provides a good overview of the island's history and present-day life. The tours include morning or afternoon tea at the Whitfield home where you are also likely to encounter a family of wood hens.

Ian Hutton, a naturalist and author of four books on Lord Howe Island, conducts Lord Howe Nature tours. The half- and full-day tours venture into the rain forest, including seabird colonies.

Contacts Islander Cruises (☎ *02/6563–2021*). **Lord Howe Nature Tours** (☎ *02/6563–2447*). **Ron's Ramble** (☎ *02/6563–2010*). **Whitfield's Island Tours** (☎ *02/6563–2115*).

VISITOR INFORMATION

Contact the Lord Howe Island Board for advance information on the island. The Lord Howe Visitor Centre is open weekdays 9–12:30 for information, fishing charters, and tour bookings. The Sydney Visitor Centre, open daily 9:30–5:30, also has information on Lord Howe Island.

Contacts Lord Howe Island Board (✉ *Middle Beach Rd.* ☎ *02/6563–2066* 🖶 *02/6563–2127*). **Lord Howe Visitor Centre** (✉ *Middle Beach and Lagoon Rds.* ☎ *02/6563–2114 or 1800/240937* ⊕ *www.lordhoweisland.info*). **Sydney Visitor Centre** (✉ *The Rocks Centre, Argyle and Playfair Sts., The Rocks, Sydney* ☎ *02/9240–8788* 🖶 *02/9241–5010* ⊕ *www.sydneyvisitorcentre.com*).

THE SNOWY MOUNTAINS

Down by Kosciuszko, where the pine-clad ridges raise
Their torn and rugged battlements on high,
Where the air is clear as crystal, and the white stars fairly blaze,
At midnight in the cold and frosty sky…

Banjo Paterson's 1890 poem "The Man from Snowy River" tells of life in the Snowy Mountains—a hard life, to be sure, but one with its own beauty and rewards. It's still possible to experience the world that Paterson described by visiting any of the 100 or so old settlers' huts scattered throughout the Snowys. Hike the mountains and valleys with camera in hand, and breathe deeply the crystal-clear air.

Reaching north from the border with Victoria, this section of the Great Dividing Range is an alpine wonderland. The entire region is part of Kosciuszko (Australians say "kozeeosko") National Park, the largest alpine area in Australia, which occupies a 6,764-square-km (2,612-square-mi) chunk of New South Wales. The national park also contains Australia's highest point, 7,314-foot Mt. Kosciuszko. Mountain peaks and streams, high meadows, forests, caves, glacial lakes, and wildflowers provide for a wealth of outdoor activities.

This wilderness area lends itself to cross-country skiing in winter and, in other seasons, walking and adventure activities. The many self-guided walking trails are excellent, especially the popular Mt. Kosciuszko summit walk. Adventure tour operators arrange hiking, climbing, mountain biking, white-water rafting, and horseback-riding tours and excursions.

A number of lakes—Jindabyne, Eucumbene, Tooma, and Tumut Pond reservoirs—and the Murray River provide excellent trout fishing. Khancoban's lake is another favorite for anglers. Tackle can be rented in a few towns, and a local operator conducts excursions and instruction. The trout-fishing season extends from the beginning of October to early June.

Although the downhill skiing isn't what Americans and Europeans are used to, the gentle slopes and relatively light snowfalls are perfect for cross-country skiing. Trails from Cabramurra, Kiandra, Perisher Valley, Charlotte Pass, and Thredbo are very good; don't hesitate to ask locals about their favorites. The ski season officially runs from the June holiday weekend (second weekend of the month) to the October holiday weekend (first weekend of the month).

Après-ski action in the Snowys is focused on the hotels in Thredbo, the large Perisher Blue resort, and the subalpine town of Jindabyne. Most hotel bars host live music in the evenings during the ski season, ranging from solo piano to jazz to rock bands. Thredbo tends toward the cosmopolitan end of the scale, and Jindabyne makes up with energy what it lacks in sophistication. Note, however, that many of the hotels close from October through May (room rates are considerably cheaper these months in hotels that stay open), and nightlife is much quieter outside the ski season.

Numbers in the margin correspond to points of interest on the Snowy Mountains map.

JINDABYNE

⑯ *474 km (296 mi) southwest of Sydney, 170 km (106 mi) southwest of Canberra.*

This mountain resort area was built in the 1960s on the shores of Lake Jindabyne, which was created when the dam built by the Snowy Mountains Hydroelectric Scheme flooded the original town. (One of the world's modern engineering wonders, the Snowy Mountains Scheme comprises kilometers of pipes, tunnels, and three power stations, and generates almost 4 million kilowatts of electricity distributed to Victoria, South Australia, New South Wales, and the Australian Capital Territory.) In winter Jindabyne becomes a major base for budget skiers, with plenty of chalets and apartments at lower prices than on-snow lodges. In summer outdoor activities center on the lake, and you can rent hiking, boating, and fishing equipment.

The **Snowy Region Visitor Centre** (⊠ *Kosciuszko Rd.* ☎ *02/6450–5600*), open daily 8:30–5, has information on hikes, flora and fauna, and all that Kosciuszko National Park has to offer.

EN ROUTE

Wildbrumby Schnapps. Sipping on traditional schnapps or flavored varieties, such as peach, pear, and butterscotch, is a great way to warm up

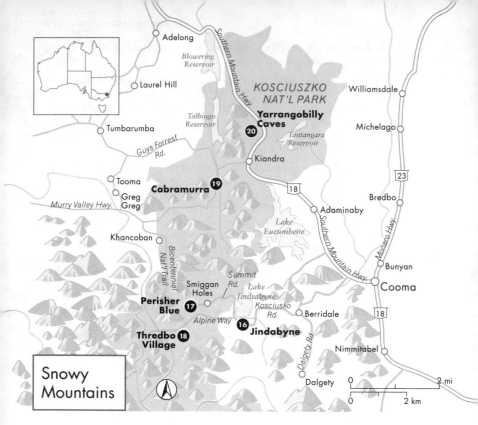

in winter. A gleaming brass distillery dominates this rustic tasting room and bar on the Alpine Way, the road linking Jindabyne to Thredbo Village. ⊠ *Thredbo Valley Distillery, Alpine Way, Thredbo Valley, Sydney* ☎ *02/6457–147* ⊕ *www.wildbrumby.com* ☒ *Free* ⊘ *Mid-June–early Oct., daily 11–4; early Oct.–early June, Thurs.–Mon. 11–6.*

WHERE TO STAY & EAT

$-$$ ✕ **Brumby Bar and Bistro.** Only the lighting is subdued at this hopping bistro where the food is as popular as the varied live music. The menu includes grilled steaks, pan-fried trout and other seafood, and schnitzels. You can help yourself to the salad-and-vegetable bar. ⊠ *Alpine Gables Motel, Kalkite St. at Kosciuszko Rd.* ☎ *02/6456–2526* ▭ *MC, V* ⊘ *No lunch.*

$$$$ ✕▥ **Crackenback Cottage.** This stone-and-timber bistro on the road
★ between Thredbo and Jindabyne glows with rustic warmth. Expect generous servings of traditional favorites—soup, roasts, and mountain trout—as well as wood-fired pizzas with innovative toppings such as local smoked trout or goat cheese. Hearty Monaro lamb pie is a popular choice. The restaurant ($$) also serves scones and afternoon tea, but it's famous for its *Glühwein* (mulled wine) and Australia's largest selection of schnapps. Call ahead, as the summer schedule varies. The Cottage is on Crackenback Farm, which also has guesthouse accom-

modation with seven rooms, a day spa, a pool, and a wedding chapel. ✉*Alpine Way, 18 km (11 mi) west of Jindabyne, Thredbo Valley* ☎*02/6456–2198* ⊕*www.crackenback.com* ⌁*7 rooms* ☐*AE, DC, MC, V* ⊙*Closed Tues. June–Aug.; No lunch Fri.–Sun. Sept.–May.*

$$$$ 🏨**Andrea's White House.** As its name suggests, this boutique B&B is all white. Tucked away in bushland and surrounded by a forest of snow gums, it is only 10 minutes by car from the center of Jindabyne. Each of the four rooms, as with the rest of the house, has under-floor heating. There's a huge doubled-sided fireplace in the guest lounge, and a separate TV room with DVD player and a good selection of movies. Two-course (A$33) and three-course (A$44) dinners can be arranged. ✉*Alpine Way, 2627* ☎*02/6456–1690* ⊕*www.andreaswhitehouse. com* ⌁*4 rooms* ⌂*In-room: no TV. In-hotel: restaurant, bar, no elevator* ☐*AE, MC, V.*

$$$–$$$$ 🏨**Quality Resort Horizons.** All apartments in this large lakeside resort have balconies with views of the lake or mountains. Part of the Quality chain, this modern complex is popular with fishermen and water-skiers in summer, and skiers in winter. Accommodations are comprised of studio, deluxe, and two-bedroom executive apartments that sleep three, four, or six people. All apartments have fully equipped kitchens and laundry areas, and executive apartments have hot tubs. The resort is a short walk from the Jindabyne shopping center with its many eateries and bars. ✉*Kosciuszko Rd., 2627* ☎*02/6456–2562* 🖷*02/6456–2488* ⊕*www.horizonsresort.com.au* ⌁*120 apartments* ⌂*In-room: kitchen, refrigerator. In-hotel: 2 restaurants, bar, tennis court, pool, no elevator, laundry facilities, public Internet* ☐*AE, DC, MC, V.*

$$$ 🏨**Eagles Range.** The cedar lodge on this 300-acre cattle ranch rates as
★   one of the region's outstanding finds. The five-bedroom lodge sleeps up to 18, but there's ample space for quiet reflection. Each bed is covered with a lovely handmade quilt made by Carol Pasfield, who owns and runs the lodge with her husband Greg. The lodge is modern but rustic in character, with exposed wood rafters, country-style furniture, an open fireplace, and spectacular 180-degree views of the surrounding ranges, which you can also enjoy from the outdoor Jacuzzi. A full cooked breakfast is included. The property is about 12 km (7½ mi) from Jindabyne. ✉*Box 922, Dalgety Rd., 2627* ☎*02/6456–2728* ⌁*5-bedroom lodge* ⌂*In-room: no a/c, no phone, VCR. In-hotel: no elevator, laundry facilities, no-smoking rooms, no kids under 14* ☐*MC, V* ⌐*BP.*

■ **OFF THE BEATEN PATH**
★

Reynella. In undulating country near the highest point in Australia, this 2,000-acre, all-inclusive sheep and cattle station lets you saddle up and head off into "The Man from Snowy River" country. Basic but comfortable lodge-style accommodations—no phones, no air-conditioning, no televisions—share bathrooms and all-you-can-eat roast lamb and Snowy Mountains trout in the dining room. It's a good winter base for downhill and cross-country skiing. The resort is renowned for its multiday horseback trips into Kosciuszko National Park. It's 72 km (45 mi) northeast of Jindabyne on the spectacular Snowy Mountains Highway. Three-day/four-night rides with all meals and tent accommodation cost about A$1,060 per person. ⊠*Kingston Rd., 2630* ☎*02/6454–2386 or 1800/029909* ⊕*www.reynellarides.com.au.*

EN ROUTE

From Jindabyne, divergent roads lead to two major destinations for walking, skiing, and generally exploring magnificent Kosciuszko National Park.

Kosciuszko Road heads north to Sawpit Creek, from which point you need snow chains between June 1 and October 10. (You can rent chains from gas stations in Jindabyne). This road continues to the vast Perisher Blue ski region (including the resorts of Smiggin Holes, Perisher Valley, Mt. Blue Cow, and Guthega), as well as the less-commercial skiing area around Charlotte Pass, which is at the very end of the road but accessible by over-snow transportation in winter. There are several excellent walks from Charlotte Pass, including a particularly scenic 10-km (6-mi) round-trip walk to Blue Lake, part of a 21-km (13-mi) loop that connects a number of peaks and a couple of other glacial lakes, and a more-strenuous 18-km (11-mi) round-trip walk to the summit of Mt. Kosciuszko. From Jindabyne take the **Alpine Way** southwest for 21 km (13 mi) to Thredbo Village. The 8-km (5-mi) **Skitube** (☎*02/6456–2010*) is an underground/over-ground shuttle train that transports skiers to the terminals at Perisher (10 minutes) and Mt. Blue Cow (19 minutes). The service operates 24 hours daily in winter (June to early October) and is closed in summer.

PERISHER BLUE

⑰ *30 km (19 mi) west of Jindabyne.*

The four adjoining skiing areas of Smiggin Holes, Perisher Valley, Mt. Blue Cow, and Guthega have merged to become the megaresort of **Perisher Blue** (☎*1300/655822* ⊕*www.perisherblue.com.au*). This is the largest snowfield in Australia, with 50 lifts and T-bars that serve all standards of slopes, as well as more than 100 km (62 mi) of cross-country trails. Because it is a snowfield area—at 5,575 feet above sea level—Perisher Blue virtually closes down between October and May. Some lodges and cafés do stay open, especially around the Christmas holidays.

Mt. Blue Cow in particular has terrain to suit most skill levels, and in fine weather it has the best ski conditions at the resort. There are fast, challenging runs off the Ridge chair and in the traverse through the trees to Guthega. Smiggins is also for beginners. Guthega is a starting point for backcountry skiing, although chairlift access is less developed than in other parts of Perisher Blue.

WHERE TO STAY & EAT

$$$$ ✕⊡ **Perisher Valley Hotel.** This ski-in, ski-out hotel is part of Perisher Centre, the retail and entertainment hub of the Perisher Valley ski fields. Luxurious suites with king-size beds accommodate up to six people. The common areas include a cocktail bar with blazing fireplace, a billiard room, and a spa with sauna and massage available. The room rate includes over-snow transportation to the hotel, as well as breakfast and

dinner at the in-house Snow Gums Restaurant, which has stunning views of the ski slopes. The hotel is open only during the ski season. ⊠*Kosciuszko Rd., Perisher Valley, 2624* ☎*02/6459–4455* ➸*31 suites* ⚲*In-room: refrigerator. In-hotel: 2 restaurants, bars, spa, no elevator, laundry service, no-smoking rooms* ⊟*AE, DC, MC, V* ⊘*Closed Oct.–May* ❢⦿❢*MAP.*

$$$$ ⏣**Perisher Manor.** Accommodations at this hotel on the slopes vary from pocket-size basic rooms with tea and shower-only bathrooms to stylish deluxe rooms with views and tubs. The hotel has 24-hour reception, a lobby lounge with an open fireplace, drying rooms, and ski lockers. It's open only in ski season, and there is a two-night minimum booking. Rates include a buffet breakfast and a three-course dinner. ⊠*Kosciuszko Rd., Perisher Valley, 2624* ☎*02/6457–5291* ⊕*www. perishermanor.com.au* ➸*49 rooms* ⚲*In-room: no a/c, no phone (some), refrigerator (some), no TV (some). In-hotel: restaurant, bar, no elevator* ⊟*AE, DC, MC, V* ⊘*Closed Oct.–May* ❢⦿❢*MAP.*

NIGHTLIFE

Bazil's Bar (☎*02/6459–4430*) in Perisher Centre, at the heart of the resort, is known for its Tuesday party nights and live entertainment. **Jax Nightclub** (☎*02/6459–4437*) (also in Perisher Centre) has live entertainment most nights in winter. You can have a drink and hear live music some evenings at the **Man From Snowy River Hotel** (☎*02/6457–5234*).

SKIING

Lift tickets for use at any of the ski areas at **Perisher Blue** (☎*02/6459–4495*) are A$95 per day, A$418 for five days. From the Bullocks Flat Skitube Terminal, combined Skitube and lift tickets are A$119 per day. From here skiers can schuss down the mountain to a choice of four high-speed quad chairlifts and a double chair. Blue Cow has a good choice of beginner- and intermediate-level runs, but no accommodations are available. Perisher, Smiggins, Guthega, and Bullocks Flat all have ski-hire facilities for children as well as adults. Skis, boots, and poles cost around A$66 per day, with discounted rates for multiday rentals.

THREDBO VILLAGE

⑱ *32 km (20 mi) southwest of Jindabyne.*

In a valley at the foot of the Crackenback Ridge, this resort has a European feel that is unique on the Australian snowfields. In addition to some of the best skiing in the country, this all-seasons resort has bushwalking, fly-fishing, canoeing, white-water rafting, tennis courts, mountain-bike trails, a 9-hole golf course, and a 2,300-foot alpine slide. In mid-January people in the village groove to the Thredbo Blues Festival, the annual weekend event that brings together international and Australian performers. Keep in mind that the altitude at Thredbo Village is 5,000 feet above sea level.

The pollution-free, high-country environment is home to the **Australian Institute of Sport's Thredbo Leisure Centre** (⊠ *Friday Dr. at Chimneys Way* ☎ *02/6459–4138*), which was primarily designed for elite athletes but is now open to the public. Facilities include an Olympic-size, heated, indoor swimming pool; a running track; an indoor, traverse climbing wall; squash, basketball, badminton, volleyball, and net ball courts; and a well-equipped gymnasium. It's open daily 7–7 in summer, 10 AM–8 PM in winter. A one-day pool/gym pass is A$15.50.

The **Kosciuszko Express** chairlift provides easy access to Mt. Kosciuszko, Australia's tallest peak, with great views of the Aussie Alps. From the upper chairlift terminal at 6,447 feet the journey to the 7,314-foot summit is a relatively easy 13-km (8-mi) round-trip hike in beautiful alpine country. You can also take a mile walk to a lookout. Be prepared for unpredictable and sometimes severe weather. The chairlift costs A$26 per person.

OFF THE BEATEN PATH

Beyond Thredbo the Alpine Way heads south, west, and then north as it skirts the flanks of Mt. Kosciuszko. A 195-km (122-mi) drive through heavily forested terrain with occasionally spectacular views brings you to Cabramurra—at 4,890 feet the highest town in Australia. The scenic **19** Goldseekers Track is a pleasant 3-km (2-mi) return walk that starts at Three Mile Dam, approximately 8 km (5 mi) beyond Cabramurra on the Kiandra road (known as the KNP5).

20 **Yarrangobilly Caves.** Twenty-one kilometers (13 mi) north of Kiandra up the Snowy Mountains Highway is this network of limestone grottoes, considered among the most beautiful in Australia. South Glory Cave has a self-guided tour, while two other caves—Jersey Cave is most visitors' favorite—must be toured with a guide. You can also bathe in a 27°C (80°F) thermal pool, an enjoyable complement to the 12°C (53°F) chill inside the passages. The caves are within Kosciuszko National Park, and the area contains pristine wilderness, including the spectacular Yarrangobilly Gorge. The caves are open daily from 9 to 5 (subject to winter road conditions); self-guided tours cost A$10.50, guided tours are A$13. ☎ *02/6454–9597*.

WHERE TO STAY & EAT

$$$$ ✕☎ **Bernti's Mountain Inn.** The boutique-style accommodations here come with friendly service and superb food, all within walking distance of the chairlifts. Most rooms have delightful mountain views and king-sized beds, and the lounge welcomes you with a fire, bar, and pool table. The popular terrace café ($) serves snacks and drinks during the day and innovative dishes alongside a comprehensive wine list at night. The inn is open year-round, and rates are considerably cheaper out of ski season. There's a two-night minimum in winter. ⊠ *Mowamba Pl. at Robuck La., 2625* ☎ *02/6457–6332* ⊕ *www. berntis.com.au* ➮ *27 rooms* ⚠ *In-room: refrigerator. In-hotel: res-*

CLOSE UP

Outback: New South Wales

The Outback is a vast region covering much of the Western Plains of New South Wales. The main city of **Broken Hill,** a former rich mining town nicknamed the "Silver City," is far from urban centers (1,150 km [720 mi] west of Sydney, 295 km (183 mi) north of Mildura, and 508 km (316 mi) northeast of Adelaide). Even with its remote location, Broken Hill (population 20,000) is a surprisingly sophisticated town with several art galleries. The **Pro Hart Gallery** (✉ *108 Wyman St.* ☎ *08/8087–2441*) is well worth a visit to see works of the late artist Kevin "Pro" Hart. The Outback has some stunning landscapes and quirky locations with a cast of colorful characters. There's self-titled "Mad Jock," who lives in the opal mining town of **White Cliffs,** 297 km (185 mi) northeast of Broken Hill, who will take you on a tour of his underground home and museum, **Jock's Place.** In **Silverton,** a mere 25 km (15 mi) away, is a ghost town much loved by film directors.

It's hard to beat the landscape of **Mungo National Park,** 321 km (200 mi) south of Broken Hill, the first national park to be World Heritage listed in Australia. Named after the 40,000-year-old skull of an Aboriginal man (Mungo Man) discovered in the park, it is a dry lake bed surrounded by a windswept landscape known as the Walls of China.

Aboriginal rock art, up to 30,000 years old, can be found in the **Mutawintji National Park,** 69 km (43 mi) north of Broken Hill, an area of rugged beauty with several colorful gorges and rock pools. Another amazing sight are the **Menindee Lakes,** 112 km (70 mi) south of Broken Hill, which hold three-and-a-half times more water than Sydney Harbour. Dry sand dunes surround the lakes, and the area is an important breeding habitat for 170 bird species. The Outback's impressive sights are best explored on one of the many four-wheel-drive tours that set off from Broken Hill. **Broken Hill's Outback Tours** (☎ *1800/670120* ⊕ *www.outbacktours.net*) has everything from one- to 10-day adventures. The best way to travel to Broken Hill is by air with REX Airlines (☎ 13–1717), which operates a two-hour flight from Sydney. You can also take the *Indian Pacific* train (☎ 13–2145) or the **Countrylink** (☎ 13–2232) rail and coach combined journey. Be warned: it's a 16-hour trip.

Fans of the 1994 camp Australian classic *The Adventures of Priscilla, Queen of the Desert* shouldn't leave Broken Hill without visiting ⬚ **Mario's Palace Hotel** (✉ *227 Argent St., 2880* ☎ *08/8088–1699*). This grand, old-style hotel's famous foyer is a colorful collection of mind-blowing murals—one of which is a copy of Botticelli's *Birth of Venus*—painted by longtime owner Mario Celotto. Your stay here will be more about character than comfort—a motto that best sums up the Outback.

–Caroline Gladstone

2

taurant, bar, pool, no elevator, laundry service, no-smoking rooms ⊟AE, DC, MC, V ⵔⵔⵔMAP.

$$$$ 🖬 **Novotel Lake Crackenback Resort.** Perched on the shore of a lake that mirrors the peaks of the Crackenback Range, these all-season apartments make great family accommodations. Luxurious one-, two-, and three-bedroom units are available. Each has a large balcony overlooking the lake, modern kitchen, laundry area, under-floor heating, fireplace, and lockable outdoor ski racks. In summer the resort runs Kosciuszko Alpine Guided Walks, which range from one-hour resort walks to two-day treks (with overnight stays in luxury tents). All meals are provided and backpack and waterproof clothing are supplied. ⊠*Alpine Way, 21 km (13 mi) southwest of Jindabyne, 2627* ☎*02/6456–2960 or 1800/020524* 🖶*02/6456–1008* ⊕*www.novotellakecrackenback. au* ⤳*46 apartments* ⚒*In-room: no a/c, kitchen. In-hotel: restaurant, room service, bar, golf course, tennis courts, pool, gym, bicycles, no elevator, laundry facilities, public Internet, parking (no fee), no-smoking rooms* ⊟*AE, DC, MC, V* ⵔⵔⵔ*BP.*

$$$$ 🖬 **Thredbo Alpine Hotel.** Warm autumn colors and contemporary wood-and-glass furnishings fill the rooms at this spacious and comfortable hotel within easy reach of the ski lifts at Thredbo. You can also rent private apartments in the nearby village. From January to September the hotel has entertainment on selected weekends, and the bars are favorite after-ski hangouts. ⊠*Friday Dr. near Thyne Reid Dr., 2625* ☎*02/6459–4200 or 1800/026333* ⊕*www.thredbo.com.au* ⤳*65 rooms* ⚒*In-room: no a/c, VCR. In-hotel: 2 restaurants, bars, tennis court, pool, no elevator, public Internet* ⊟*MC, V* ⵔⵔⵔ*BP.*

SKIING

Among downhill resorts of the area, **Thredbo** (☎*02/6459–4100 or 1800/020589* ⊕*www.thredbo.com.au*) has the most challenging runs—with the only Australian giant-slalom course approved for World Cup events—and the most extensive snowmaking in the country. Lift tickets are A$94 per day, A$351 for five days.

Thredbo Sports (⊠*Ski-lift terminal* ☎*02/6459–4100*) rents downhill and cross-country skis and snowboards.

SNOWY MOUNTAINS ESSENTIALS

AIR TRAVEL

REX (Regional Express) Airlines operates daily flights between Sydney and Cooma Airport (also known as Snowy Mountains Airport). From Cooma Airport it is a half-hour drive to Jindabyne and another half hour to Thredbo. Jindabyne to Perisher Blue is also about a half-hour drive.

Contact REX Airlines (☎*13–1713* ⊕*www.rex.com.au*).

BUS TRAVEL

During the ski season Greyhound Australia makes twice daily runs between Sydney and the Snowy Mountains via Canberra. The bus stops at Jindabyne, the Skitube at Bullocks Flat, and Thredbo. It's a seven-hour ride to Thredbo from Sydney, three hours from Canberra.

In winter, shuttle buses connect the regional towns with the ski fields. At other times of the year the only practical way to explore the area is by rental car or on a guided tour.

The Snowy Mountains Airport Shuttle runs year-round transfers from Cooma Airport and Jindabyne to Thredbo Village; and to Perisher Blue Ski Resort in winter.

The Transborder Alpinexpress bus makes a year-round trip from Canberra to Jindabyne, Bullocks Flat, and Thredbo. Sydney passengers can fly to Canberra or take a Countrylink Xplorer Train.

Information Greyhound Australia (☎ 13-1499 ⊕ www.greyhound.com.au). **Snowy Mountains Airport Shuttle** (☎ 02/6452-4455 or 1800/679754). **Transborder Alpinexpress** (☎ 02/6241-0033 ⊕ www.transborder.com.au).

CAR TRAVEL

From Sydney head for the airport and follow the signs to the M5 Motorway toll road (A$3.30). The M5 connects with the Hume Highway, southwest of Sydney. Follow the highway to just south of Goulburn and then turn onto the Federal Highway to Canberra. The Monaro Highway runs south from Canberra to Cooma, where you turn onto the Barry Highway to Jindabyne. The 474-km (296-mi) journey takes at least five hours.

To visit anything beyond the main ski resort areas, a car is a necessity. Be aware, however, that driving these often steep and winding mountain roads in winter can be hazardous, and you must carry snow chains from June through October.

TRAIN TRAVEL

The Skitube shuttle train—running from Bullocks Flat on the Alpine Way to the Perisher Blue area—operates in the ski season and is a fast way to get to Perisher Blue ski fields. Bullocks Flat station is between Jindabyne and Thredbo. The Skitube runs 24 hours a day, seven days a week, at 20-minute intervals during peak season. The ride to Perisher takes 10 minutes; it's an additional 7 minutes to Blue Cow. You can access the parking lot at Bullocks Flat without chains for your vehicle. The Skitube costs A$41 for a round-trip ticket.

Information Skitube (☎ 02/6456-2010).

EMERGENCIES

In an emergency, dial **000** to reach an ambulance, the police, or the fire department.

Information Cooma Hospital (✉ Bent St., Cooma, 2630 ☎ 02/6455-3222).

TOURS

Jindabyne's Mountain Adventure Centre arranges bushwalking, mountain biking, white-water rafting and canoeing, and horseback riding.

Outstanding cross-country ski programs are also available, from introductory weekends to snow-camping trips.

Murrays Australia operates both skiing-accommodation packages and a transportation service (during the ski season only) to the Snowy Mountains from Canberra. These depart from Canberra's Jolimont Tourist Centre at Alinga Street and Northbourne Avenue.

Oz Snow Adventures runs weekend and three- and six-day coach trips with overnight accommodations in Jindabyne, Thredbo, or Perisher Blue. The company also offers discounted lift tickets and ski-lesson packages.

Information **Mountain Adventure Centre** (⊠ *Kosciuszko Rd., Thredbo turnoff, Jindabyne, 2627* ☏ *02/6456–2922 or 1800/623459* ⊕ *www.mountainadventure centre.com.au).* **Murrays Australia** (☏ *13–2251* ⊕ *www.murrayscoaches.com.au).* **Oz Snow Adventures** (☏ *1800/851101* ⊕ *www.ozsnowadventures.com.au).*

VISITOR INFORMATION

Snowy Region Visitor Centre is open daily 8:30–5. Sydney Visitor Centre is open daily 9:30–5:30.

Information **Snowy Region Visitor Centre** (⊠ *Kosciuszko Rd., Jindabyne* ☏ *02/6450–5600* ⊕ *www.snowymountains.com.au).* **Sydney Visitor Centre** (⊠ *The Rocks Centre, Argyle and Playfair Sts., The Rocks, Sydney, 2000* ☏ *02/9240–8788* 🖶 *02/9241–5010* ⊕ *www.sydneyvisitorcentre.com).*

Canberra
& the A.C.T.

WORD OF MOUTH

"Hikes in Namadgi National Park—Stop at the visitor center for maps. Hike around the remains of the Honeysuckle Tracking Station used to track the Apollo astronauts. My favorite hike is the Yankee Hat Hike. It's an easy 6-km RT hike where you will see LOTS of kangaroos. At the turnaround point is a rock with Aboriginal drawings. A great walk in the bush!"

—longhorn55

Updated by
Roger Allnutt

AS THE NATION'S CAPITAL, CAN-BERRA is often maligned by outsiders, who associate the city with poor decisions made by greedy politicians. The reality is vastly different, however. Canberra is Australian through and through, and those who live here will tell you that to know Canberra is to love it.

From the very beginning this was to be a totally planned city. Walter Burley Griffin, a Chicago architect and associate of Frank Lloyd Wright, won an international design competition. Griffin arrived in Canberra in 1913 to supervise construction, but progress was slowed by two world wars and the Great Depression. By 1947 Canberra, with only 15,000 inhabitants, was little more than a country town.

Development increased during the 1950s, and the current population of more than 320,000 makes Canberra by far the largest inland city in Australia. The wide, tree-lined avenues and spacious parklands of present-day Canberra have largely fulfilled Griffin's original plan. The major public buildings are arranged on low knolls on either side of Lake Burley Griffin, the focus of the city. Satellite communities—using the same radial design of crescents and cul-de-sacs employed in Canberra—house the city's growing population.

Canberra gives an overall impression of spaciousness, serenity, and almost unnatural order. There are no advertising billboards, no strident colors, and very few buildings more than a dozen stories high. Framing the city are the separate areas of wooded hills and dry grasslands comprising Canberra Nature Park, which fills in much of the terrain just outside the suburban areas.

EXPLORING CANBERRA

Canberra's most important public buildings stand within the Parliamentary Triangle. Lake Burley Griffin wraps around its northeast edge, while Commonwealth and Kings avenues radiate from Capital Hill, the city's political and geographical epicenter, to form the west and south boundaries. The triangle can be explored comfortably on foot, but a vehicle is required to see the rest of this area. The monuments and other attractions within the Parliamentary Triangle and around Lake Burley Griffin are not identified by street numbers but all are clearly signposted.

Numbers in the text correspond to numbers in the margin and on the Canberra map.

WHEN TO VISIT
February to April, when autumn leaves paint the city parks with amber hues, is a particularly good time to visit. This season also coincides with the February Canberra National Multicultural Festival, just one

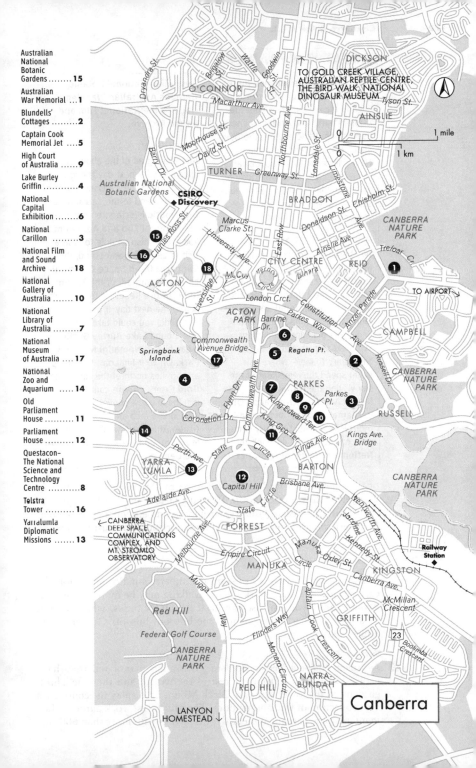

Canberra

GREAT ITINERARIES

Most of Canberra's galleries, museums, and public buildings can be seen in a couple of days—but the capital's parks and gardens, as well as Namadgi National Park, the Deep Space complex, and Tidbinbilla Nature Reserve, to the south, can easily delay you for another day or so. Several lesser-known attractions, such as Lanyon Homestead, also warrant a visit.

IF YOU HAVE 2 DAYS

Two busy days will cover most of the main city attractions. You could start Day 1 with the spectacular view from the **Telstra Tower,** and then visit the **National Capital Exhibition** for a good look into Canberra's planning and history. Your next stop should be the Parliamentary Triangle, where you might spend the remainder of the day visiting the **National Gallery of Australia,Questacon,Old Parliament House,** and **Parliament House.** Fill in the city-center gaps on the second day with the **National Museum of Australia,** **Australian National Botanic Gardens,Australian War Memorial,** and the **National Film and Sound Archive.**

IF YOU HAVE 5 DAYS

After seeing all of the above, try spending your next day taking a drive through the pleasant suburb of Yarralumla and to the **Yarralumla Diplomatic Missions** en route to the **National Zoo and Aquarium.** You should also be able to fit in a visit to **Lanyon Homestead,** the **Canberra Deep Space Communications Complex,** or the **Tidbinbilla Nature Reserve,** to the city's south. The next day, if you're feeling energetic, you could take a bike ride around **Lake Burley Griffin,** or a day hike in **Namadgi National Park.** On your final day, take a trip a few miles north of the city to the **Gold Creek Village** complex and indulge in some souvenir hunting. Also in this area are **Cockington Green,** the **National Dinosaur Museum,** and the **Australian Reptile Centre.**

of the celebrations leading up to Canberra Day festivities in March. The spring flower celebration, Floriade, lasts from mid-September to mid-October. In early January car enthusiasts gather for the popular Summernats, featuring street machines, hot rods, and custom cars.

CENTRAL CANBERRA

You can visit virtually all of central Canberra's major attractions by car, but in some places parking and walking may be more convenient. Around town you can use the local ACTION buses, which stop at most of the other sights, or join the hop-on, hop-off Canberra Day Tours bus.

WHAT TO SEE

15 **Australian National Botanic Gardens.** Australian plants and trees have evolved in isolation from the rest of the world, and these delightful gardens on the lower slopes of Black Mountain display the continent's best collection of this unique flora. The rain forest, rock gardens, Tasmanian alpine garden, and eucalyptus lawn—with more than 600 species of eucalyptus—number among the 125-acre site's highlights. Two self-guided nature trails start from the rain-forest gully, and free guided tours depart from the visitor center daily at 11 and 2. From December to February there is also a tour at 9:30 AM. Parking is A$1.40 per hour or A$4.80 per day. ⊠ *Clunies Ross St., Black Mountain* ☏ *02/6250–9540* ⊕ *www.anbg.gov.au* ☒ *Free* ⊘ *Gardens Jan., daily 8:30–8; Feb.–Dec., daily 8:30–5. Visitor center daily 9–4:30.*

❶ **Australian War Memorial.** Both as a memorial to Australians who served
Fodor$Choice their country in wartime and as a military museum, this is a shrine
★ of great national importance and the most popular attraction in the capital. The museum, built roughly in the shape of a Byzantine church, explores Australian military involvement from the Sudan campaign of the late 19th century through the 1970s and the Vietnam War. Displays include a Lancaster bomber, a Spitfire, tanks, landing barges, the giant German Amiens gun, and sections of two of the Japanese midget submarines that infiltrated Sydney Harbour during World War II. Each April 25 the memorial is the focus of Canberra's powerful Anzac Day ceremony, which honors fallen members of Australia's armed forces. Free guided tours take place daily at 10, 10:30, 11, 1:30, and 2.

You can best appreciate the impressive facade of the War Memorial from the broad avenue of **Anzac Parade.** Anzac is an acronym for the Australian and New Zealand Army Corps, formed during World War I. The avenue is flanked by several memorials commemorating the army, navy, air force, and nursing corps, as well as some of the campaigns in which Australian troops have fought, including the Vietnam War. The red gravel used on Anzac Parade symbolizes the blood of Australians spilled in war. ⊠ *Anzac Parade at Limestone Ave., Campbell* ☏ *02/6243–4211* ⊕ *www.awm.gov.au* ☒ *Free* ⊘ *Daily 10–5.*

❷ **Blundells' Cottage.** The 1858 cottage, once home to three families of
☼ farmers, is a testimony to the pioneer spirit of the early European settlers in the Canberra region. Furnished to represent the lifestyle of a farming community in the late 1800s, the home now provides a hands-on experience for visitors and school groups. ⊠ *Wendouree Dr., Kings Park, Parkes* ☏ *02/6273–2667 or 02/6257–1068* ⊕ *www.nationalcapital.gov.au* ☒ *A$4* ⊘ *Daily 11–4.*

❺ **Captain Cook Memorial Jet.** This water fountain in Lake Burley Griffin commemorates James Cook's discovery of Australia's east coast in 1770. On windless days the jet spurts a 6-ton plume of water 490 feet into the sky—making this one of the world's highest fountains.

❾ **High Court of Australia.** As its name implies, this gleaming concrete-and-glass structure is the ultimate court of law in the nation's judicial system. The court of seven justices convenes only to determine constitutional matters or major principles of law. Inside the main entrance, the public hall contains a number of murals depicting constitutional and geographic themes. Each of the three courtrooms over which the justices preside has a public gallery, and you can observe the proceedings when the court is in session. ⊠ *Parkes Pl. off King Edward Terr., Parkes* ☏ *02/6270–6811 or 02/6270–6850* ☒ *Free* ⊘ *Daily 9:45–4:30.*

④ Lake Burley Griffin. Stretching through the very heart of the city, Lake Burley Griffin is one of Canberra's most captivating features. The parks that surround the lake are ideal for walking and cycling, and you can rent bikes and boats from Acton Park on the northern shore.

⑥ National Capital Exhibition. Photographs, plans, audiovisual displays, and a laser model inside this lakeside pavilion illustrate the past, present, and future development of the national capital. Exhibits cover the time of the early settlers, Walter Burley Griffin's winning design for Canberra, and city plans for the coming decades. From the pavilion's terrace there are sweeping views of the Parliamentary Triangle across the lake: the National Library on the right and the National Gallery on the left form the base of the Parliamentary Triangle, which rises toward its apex at Parliament House on Capital Hill. The restaurant and kiosk on the terrace serve full meals and light snacks. ⊠*Regatta Point, Barrine Dr., Commonwealth Park* ☎*02/6257–1068* ⊕*www.nationalcapital.gov.au* ⊡*Free* ⊙*Daily 9–5.*

> ### LAKE BURLEY GRIFFIN
>
> Many of the main sights of Canberra are located on the edge of Lake Burley Griffin. The Central Basin between Commonwealth and Kings Avenue bridges is a great place to begin a stroll, as it's close to such attractions as the National Library, the National Gallery of Australia, and the National Capital Exhibition. A bike ride or a boat cruise are other great ways to see the lake.

③ National Carillon. The elegant, 53-bell tower, a gift from the British government to mark Canberra's 50th anniversary in 1963, rises up from Aspen Island in Lake Burley Griffin. Free 45-minute recitals, which include everything from hymns to contemporary music, are played Monday, Wednesday, Friday, and Sunday at 12:30. Although you can only visit the inside of the tower by taking a A$8 tour on Tuesday and Thursday at 12:30, lots of people are happy sitting outside and just listening while the bells play. ⊠*Aspen Island, off Wendouree Dr., Parkes* ☎*02/6257–1068.*

⑱ National Film and Sound Archive. Australia's movie industry was booming during the early 20th century, but it ultimately couldn't compete with the sophistication and volume of imported films. Concern that film stock and sound recordings of national importance would be lost prompted the construction of this edifice to preserve Australia's movie and musical heritage. The archive contains an impressive display of Australian moviemaking skills, including a short film that was shot on Melbourne Cup Day in 1896—the oldest film in the collection. Special exhibitions focus on aspects of the industry ranging from rock music to historic newsreels. ⊠*McCoy Circuit, Acton* ☎*02/6248–2000* ⊕*www.nfsa.afc.gov.au* ⊡*Free* ⊙ *Weekdays 9–5, weekends 10–5.*

⑩ National Gallery of Australia. The most comprehensive collection of Australian art in the country is on exhibit in the nation's premier art gallery, including superlative works of Aboriginal art and paintings by such famous native sons as Arthur Streeton, Sir Sidney Nolan, Tom

Roberts, and Arthur Boyd. The gallery also contains a sprinkling of works by European and American masters, including Rodin, Picasso, Pollock, and Warhol. Free guided tours commence from the foyer at 11 and 2 each day. Although admission is free, there's usually a fee for special exhibits, which often display artwork from around the world. ✉ *Parkes Pl., Parkes* 🕾 *02/6240–6502* ⊕ *www.nga.gov.au* ✉ *Free* ⏲ *Daily 10–5.*

NEED A BREAK?

A good spot to catch your breath amid the Parliamentary Triangle's mix of history, culture, and science is **Bookplate** (✉ *Parkes Pl., Parkes* 🕾 *02/6262– 1154*), in the foyer of the National Library; it extends out onto a patio overlooking the lake. Sandwiches, salads, cakes, and tea and coffee are served weekdays 8:30–6 and weekends 11–3.

7 **National Library of Australia.** The library, constructed loosely on the design of the Parthenon in Athens, houses more than 5 million books and 500,000 aerial photographs, maps, drawings, and recordings of oral history. Changing exhibitions of old Australian photos, manuscripts, and art are displayed in the ground-floor gallery. One-hour behind-the-scenes tours take place Tuesday at 12:30. ✉ *Parkes Pl., Parkes* 🕾 *02/6262–1111* ⊕ *www.nla.gov.au* ✉ *Free* ⏲ *Mon.–Thurs. 9–9, Fri.–Sun. 9–5.*

17 **National Museum of Australia.** This comprehensive museum is spectacu-
Fodor's Choice larly set on Acton Peninsula, thrust out over the calm waters of Lake
★ Burley Griffin. The museum highlights the stories of Australia and Australians by exploring the key people, events, and issues that shaped and influenced the nation. The numerous exhibitions focus on rare and unique objects that illustrate the continent's complex origins. Memorabilia include the carcass of the extinct Tasmanian tiger, the old Bentley beloved by former Prime Minister Robert Menzies, and the black baby garments worn by dingo victim Azaria Chamberlain (whose story was made famous in the Meryl Streep film *A Cry in the Dark*). ✉ *Lennox Crossing, Acton Peninsula* 🕾 *02/6208–5000 or 1800/026132* ⊕ *www. nma.gov.au* ✉ *Free* ⏲ *Daily 9–5.*

14 **National Zoo and Aquarium.** Display tanks alive with coral, sharks, rays,
and exotic sea creatures let you take a fish-eye view of the underwater world. The adjoining 15-acre wildlife sanctuary is a bushland park that provides a habitat for the more-remarkable species of Australia's fauna: emus, koalas, penguins, dingoes, kangaroos, and Tasmanian devils. Other exotic animals include cougars, pumas, snow leopards, tigers, and cheetahs. ✉ *Lady Denman Dr., Scrivener Dam, Yarralumla* 🕾 *02/6287–8400* ⊕ *www.zooquarium.com.au* ✉ *A$23.50* ⏲ *Daily 9–5.*

11 **Old Parliament House.** Built in 1927, this long white building was meant to serve only as a temporary seat of government, but it was more than 60 years before its much larger successor was finally completed on the hill behind it. Now that the politicians have moved out, the renovated building is open for public inspection. Guided tours, departing from Kings Hall on the half hour, take you through the legislative chambers, party rooms, and suites that once belonged to the prime minister and the president of the Senate. Old Parliament House also contains the expanding **National Portrait Gallery,** which displays likenesses of important Australians past and present. While you're in the area, take a stroll through the delightful

Rose Gardens on both sides of the Old Parliament House building. Across the road from the entrance visit the controversial **Aboriginal Tent Embassy,** established in 1972 to proclaim the Aboriginals as Australia's "first people" and to promote recognition of their fight for land rights. ⊠*King George Terr., Parkes* ☎*02/6270–8222* ⊕*www. oph.gov.au* ⊠*A$2* ⊙*Daily 9–5.*

⑫ **Parliament House.** Much of this vast futuristic structure is submerged,
Fodor'sChoice covered by a domed glass roof that follows the contours of Capital
★ Hill. You approach the building across a vast courtyard with a central mosaic entitled *Meeting Place,* designed by Aboriginal artist Nelson Tjakamarra. Native timber has been used almost exclusively throughout the building, and the work of some of Australia's finest contemporary artists hangs on the walls.

Parliament generally sits Monday to Thursday mid-February to late June and mid-August to mid-December. Both chambers have public galleries, but the debates in the House of Representatives, where the prime minister sits, are livelier and more newsworthy than those in the Senate. The best time to observe the House of Representatives is during **Question Time** (☎*02/6277–4889 sergeant-at-arms' office*), starting at 2, when the government and the opposition are most likely to be at each other's throats. To secure a ticket for Question Time, contact the sergeant-at-arms' office. Book a week in advance, if possible. Guided tours take place every half hour from 9 to 4. ⊠*Capital Hill* ☎*02/6277–5399* ⊕*www.aph.gov.au* ⊠*Free* ⊙*Daily 9–5, later when Parliament is sitting.*

⑧ **Questacon—The National Science and Technology Centre.** This interactive
Ⓒ science facility is the city's most entertaining museum. About 200 hands-on exhibits use high-tech computer gadgetry and anything from pendulums to feathers to illustrate principles of mathematics, physics, and human perception. Staff members explain the scientific principles behind the exhibits, and science shows take place regularly. ⊠*Enid Lyons St. off King Edward Terr., Parkes* ☎*02/6270–2800* ⊕*www. questacon.edu.au* ⊠*A$15.50* ⊙*Daily 9–5.*

⑯ **Telstra Tower.** The city's tallest landmark, this 600-foot structure on the top of Black Mountain is one of the best places to begin any tour of the national capital. Three observation platforms afford breathtaking views of the entire city as well as the mountain ranges to the south. The tower houses an exhibition on the history of telecommunications in Australia and a revolving restaurant with a spectacular nighttime panorama. The structure provides a communications link between Canberra and the rest of the country and serves as a broadcasting station for radio and television networks. ⊠ *Black Mountain Dr., Acton* ☎ *02/6219–6111 or 1800/806718* ⌷ *A$6* ⊙ *Daily 9* AM*–10* PM.

⑬ Yarralumla Diplomatic Missions. The expensive, leafy suburb of Yarralumla, west and north of Parliament House, contains many of the city's 70 or so diplomatic missions. Some of these were established when Canberra was little more than a small country town, and it was only with great reluctance that many ambassadors and their staffs were persuaded to transfer from the temporary capital in Melbourne. Today it's an attractive area where each building reflects the home country's architectural characteristics.

AROUND CANBERRA & THE A.C.T.

Canberra's suburbs and the rural regions of the A.C.T. are home to a variety of attractions. These include two national parks, a historic homestead, many wineries, a nature reserve with native animals, the Australian Institute of Sport, and Canberra's important contribution to the space race. A car is required to reach these sights.

WHAT TO SEE

Australian Institute of Sport (AIS). Established to improve the performance of Australia's elite athletes, this 150-acre site north of the city comprises athletic fields, a swimming center, an indoor sports stadium, and a sports-medicine center. Daily 1½-hour tours, some guided by AIS athletes, explore the facilities, where you may be able to watch some of the institute's Olympic-caliber squads in training for archery, gymnastics, swimming, soccer, and other sports. The latter half of the tour takes you through the **Sports Visitors Centre,** where displays, hands-on exhibits, and a video wall show the achievements of Australian sporting stars. Afterward, you can use the tennis courts and other facilities for a fee. ⊠ *Leverrier Crescent, Bruce* ☎ *02/6214–1010* ⊕ *www.ais. org.au* ⌷ *Guided tour A$13* ⊙ *Weekdays 8:30–4:45, weekends 9:45– 4:15. Tours daily at 10, 11:30, 1, and 2:30.*

Australian Reptile Centre. Australia has a remarkable diversity of snakes, lizards, and other reptilian creatures, and you can meet them face-to-face at this compact park. Those headed for the desert and bushland might want to spend some time becoming familiar with the collection of deadly snakes and other sorts. You can even meet (and be cuddled by) a python. ⊠ *O'Hanlon Pl., Gold Creek Village, Nicholls* ☎ *02/6253– 8533* ⊕ *www.contact.com.au/reptile* ⌷ *A$8* ⊙ *Daily 10–5.*

Canberra Deep Space Communication Complex. Managed and operated by the Commonwealth Scientific and Industrial Research Organization (CSIRO), this complex 40 km (25 mi) southwest of Canberra is one of just three tracking stations in the world linked to the Deep Space control center, the long-distance arms of the U.S. National Aeronautics and Space Administration (NASA). The function of the four giant antennae at the site is to relay commands and data between NASA and space vehicles or orbiting satellites. The first pictures of men walking on the moon were transmitted to this tracking station. The visitor information center houses models, audiovisual displays, and memorabilia from space missions. ⊠ *Discovery Dr. off Paddy's River Rd., Tidbinbilla* ☎ *02/6201–7838* ⊕ *www.cdscc.nasa.gov* ⊠ *Free* ⊙ *Apr.–Oct., daily 9–5; Nov.–Mar., daily 9–6.*

Cockington Green. Set in lovely gardens, a delightful collection of miniature thatch-roof houses, castles, and canals creates a small-scale slice of England. The international section, which was constructed with the support of many of Canberra's embassies, highlights such world-renowned sights as the Bojnice Castle in Slovakia and Machu Picchu in Peru. ⊠ *11 Gold Creek Rd., Nicholls* ☎ *02/6230–2273* ⊕ *www. cockingtongreen.com.au* ⊠ *A$13.50* ⊙ *Daily 9:30–5.*

Lanyon Homestead. When it was built in 1859 on the plain beside the Murrumbidgee River, this classic homestead from pioneering days was the centerpiece of a self-contained community. Many of the outbuildings and workshops have been magnificently restored and preserved. The adjacent **Nolan Gallery** (☎ *02/6235–5688*) displays a selection of the well-known Ned Kelly paintings by the famous Australian painter Sir Sidney Nolan. ⊠ *Tharwa Dr., Tharwa* ✚ *30 km (19 mi) south of Canberra off Monaro Hwy.* ☎ *02/6235–5677* ⊠ *Homestead A$7, gallery A$3* ⊙ *Tues.–Sun. 10–4.*

Mount Stromlo Observatory. Although terrible bushfires in January 2003 devastated the observatory, the facility is gradually being rebuilt. There are several rebuilt and brand-new telescopes, and stargazing evenings are held on Saturday nights. ⊠ *Cotter Rd., Weston Creek* ☎ *02/6125– 0232* ⊕ *www.mso.anu.edu.au* ⊠ *Donation requested for Sat.-night stargazing* ⊙ *Visitor center Wed.–Sun. 10–5; Sat.-night stargazing by booking only.*

Namadgi National Park. Covering almost half the total area of the Australian Capital Territory's southwest, this national park has a well-maintained network of walking trails across mountain ranges, trout streams, and some of the most accessible subalpine forests in the country. Some parts of the park were severely burned in the January 2003 bushfires, but the recovery powers of the native bush have been truly remarkable. The park's boundaries are within 35 km (22 mi) of Canberra, and its former pastures, now empty of sheep and cattle, are grazed by hundreds of eastern gray kangaroos in the early morning and late afternoon. Snow covers the higher altitudes June–September. ⊠ *Visitor center: Naas–Boboyan Rd., 3 km (2 mi) south of Tharwa* ☎ *02/6207–2900* ⊕ *www.environment.act.gov.au* ⊠ *Free* ⊙ *Park daily 24 hrs; visitor center weekdays 9–4, weekends 9–4:30.*

↻ **National Dinosaur Museum.** Dinosaur-lovers will be dazzled by the display of full-size dinosaur skeletons here, many of which were found in Australia. An impressive collection of 700-million-year-old fossils is also on display, including the hardened remnants of plants, bugs, sea creatures, birds, and mammals. ⊠ *Gold Creek Rd. at Barton Hwy.,*

Nicholls ☎*02/6230–2655* ⊕*www.nationaldinosaurmuseum.com.au* ☒*A$9.50* ⊙*Daily 10–5.*

Tidbinbilla Nature Reserve. The walking trails, wetlands, and animal exhibits within this reserve, many of which were badly damaged in the bushfires of 2003, have recovered beautifully since then. Check with the park office for latest details on opening hours; the park is 40 km (25 mi) southwest of Canberra. ⊠*Paddy's River Rd., Tidbinbilla* ☎*02/6205–1233* ⊕*www.environment.act.gov.au* ☒*Free.*

3

WHERE TO EAT

Canberra has more restaurants per person than any other city in Australia, and their variety reflects the city's cosmopolitan nature. In addition to eclectic Australian and fusion restaurants are authentic French, Italian, Turkish, Vietnamese, and Chinese dining options, among many others. Overall, Canberra dining spots hold their own against the restaurants of Sydney and Melbourne, although the feeling is generally more casual.

WHAT IT COSTS IN AUSTRALIAN DOLLARS				
$$$$	**$$$**	**$$**	**$**	**¢**
AT DINNER over A$50	A$36–A$50	A$21–A$35	A$10–A$20	under A$10

Prices are per person for a main course at dinner.

CENTRAL CANBERRA & NORTHERN SUBURBS

ITALIAN
$$
✗**Mezzalira on London.** Sleek and glossy, this city-center Italian restaurant is the fashionable gathering place for Canberra's smart set. The menu varies from robust pasta dishes and pizzas to char-grilled salmon with arugula and balsamic vinegar, grilled Italian sausages with truffle-oil mashed potato, and grilled vegetables in a red-wine sauce. Pizzas from the wood-fired oven make for good casual dining at a modest price. The espresso enjoys a reputation as Canberra's finest. ⊠*Melbourne Bldg., West Row and London Circuit, Canberra City* ☎*02/6230–0025* ▤*AE, DC, MC, V* ⊙*Closed Sun. No lunch Sat.*

$–$$
✗**Tosolini's.** A long-standing favorite with Canberra's café society, this Italian-accented brasserie offers a choice of indoor or sidewalk tables. Coffee not your cup of tea? Sit back and sip a fresh fruit juice or shake. A few heartier dishes like pasta, risotto, focaccia, and pizza are also available—but plan around the lunch crush. You can bring your own bottle of wine to dinner if you like. ⊠*East Row at London Circuit, Canberra City* ☎*02/6247–4317* ▤*AE, DC, MC, V* ⓧ*BYOB.*

MODERN
AUSTRALIAN
$$–$$$
✗**Boat House by the Lake.** There's something restful about looking out over the water of Lake Burley Griffin as you dine on the superb food of this modern, airy restaurant. High ceilings give the restaurant a spacious, open feel, and tall windows provide lovely views of the lake. Unusual and innovative choices include roasted kangaroo fillet served with lemon-balm salad and a spicy garlic sauce. Several excellent Australian wines are on hand to complement your meal. Leave

Wine Touring Around Canberra

Wineries began popping up everywhere around Canberra in the late 1990s, once it was discovered that the cool climate was optimal for producing chardonnays, Rieslings, cabernets, shirazes, merlots, and pinots. There are now about 140 vineyards set in the peaceful rural countryside surrounding the city—mostly small operations, where visiting the "cellar door" usually involves sampling the wines in the tasting room. There is no charge for tastings, although the vintners hope you'll be impressed enough with the wine to make some purchases.

Most are a maximum of 30 minutes from the city and are concentrated in the villages of Hall and Murrumbateman, and in the Lake George area and Bungendore. Many are open to visits on weekends only. If you want to explore the wineries on your own, pick up a copy of *The Canberra District Wineries Guide* from the Canberra and Region Visitor Centre, or from the **Kamberra Wine Centre** (✉ *Flemington Rd. at Northbourne Ave., Lyneham* ☎ *02/6262–2333* ⊕ *www.hardywines. com.au*) at the northern entrance to Canberra overlooking the Canberra Racecourse. If you don't want to combine driving with wine tasting, consider a wine tour. **Brindabella Wine Tours** (☎ *02/6231–6997* ⊕ *www. actwine.com.au*) provides escorted half- and full-day tours of the entire Canberra wine district. **Wine Wisdom Winery Tours** (☎ *02/6260–7773* ⊕ *www.winewisdom.com.au*) specializes in personally tailored wine-tour itineraries.

WINERIES ALONG THE BARTON HIGHWAY

From Canberra take the Barton Highway in the direction of Yass. After 20 km (12 mi) you'll reach a trio of wineries: **Brindabella Hills Winery, Pankhurst Wines,** and **Surveyors Hill Winery** around the village of Hall. A few minutes farther along Barton Highway, a right turn onto Nanima Road will bring you to the **Wily Trout Winery.** This winery shares its property with **Poachers Pantry,** which sells picnic-style smoked meats, poultry, and vegetables, and the **Smokehouse Cafe,** where you can have a decadent countryside dining experience.

WINERIES ALONG THE FEDERAL HIGHWAY

From Canberra take the Federal Highway for about 30 km (19 mi) north toward Sydney until you reach the Lake George area. Here you'll find **Lark Hill Winery, Gidgee Estate Wines, Lambert Vineyards,** and **Lerida Estate Wines.** At **Madew Wines** you can stop by **grapefoodwine** restaurant, for modern Australian, seasonally inspired cuisine and great views over Lake George.

On the banks of the Molonglo River, close to the airport, is one other winery that's well worth visiting: **Pialligo Estate Wines and Cafe,** which is surrounded by beautiful rose gardens. Here you can enjoy a wine tasting, lunch, or an antipasto platter as the sun sets behind Parliament House.

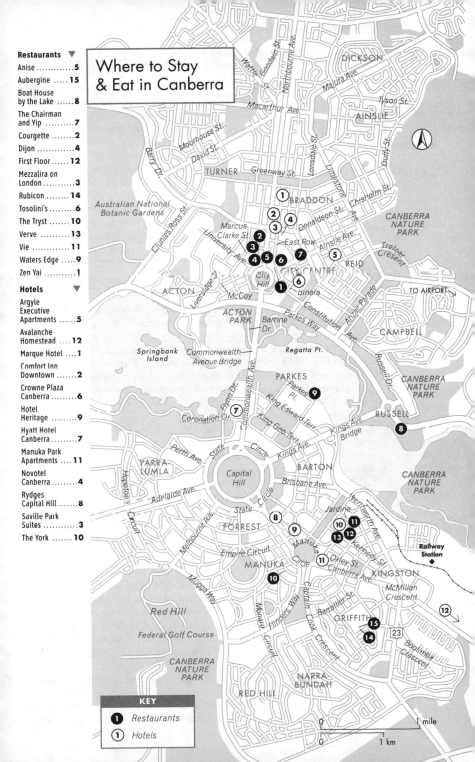

Where to Stay & Eat in Canberra

KEY

❶ Restaurants

① Hotels

room for scrumptious desserts like Black Forest brûlée with kirsch cream. ⊠ *Menindie Dr., Grevillea Park, Barton* ☎ *02/6273–5500* ▭ *AE, DC, MC, V* ☉ *Closed Sun. No lunch Sat.*

$$ ✕**Anise.** This calm, relaxing haven
Fodor'sChoice sits amid Canberra's West Row din-
★ ing strip. Have a drink at the quiet bar before being seated at one of the well-spaced, damask-covered tables. Filling selections include the roast veal rump with baby arti-chokes, peas, pancetta, and roasted garlic. The banana-and-frangipani tart, served with rum ice cream, is a superb way to finish a meal.

> **RESTAURANT ROW**
>
> The main restaurant precincts are around the city center and in the trendy suburbs of Manuka and Kingston. However, many fine eateries are tucked away in such suburban centers as Griffith, Ainslie, Belconnen, and Woden. In Dickson, Canberra's Chinatown, a line of inexpensive, casual eater-ies along Woolley Street includes many little spots serving Vietnam-ese, Malaysian, Chinese, Turkish, and Italian cuisine.

⊠ *20 West Row, Canberra City, 2600* ☎ *02/6257–0700* ▭ *DC, MC, V* ☉ *Closed Sun. and Mon. No lunch Sat.*

$$ ✕**Courgette.** Creative food served in spacious, stylish surroundings is the specialty of this popular Canberra restaurant on the city's outer edge. The seasonal menu has such dreamy dishes as prawn-crusted salmon served with a mushroom velouté and poached oysters. Leave room for the decadent chocolate-and-almond fondant with bitter cara-mel ice cream. The wine cellar here is impressive, and you can sample vintages of Australian and overseas wines by the bottle or glass. ⊠ *54 Marcus Clarke St., Canberra City* ☎ *02/6247–4042* ▭ *AE, DC, MC, V* ☉ *Closed Sun. No lunch Sat.*

$$ ✕**Dijon.** A cozy space, white tablecloths, and touches of elegance pro-vide the setting for an intimate dinner. The Mod-Oz menu is sprinkled with Asian flavorings, but includes classics like lamb saddle served with Lyonnaise potatoes, spinach, and shallots. Rich desserts include raspberry ragout and chocolate espresso mousse on vanilla shortbread. The extensive wine list includes local and overseas vintages, some avail-able by the glass. You can also dine outside in warm weather. ⊠ *24 West Row, Canberra City* ☎ *02/6230–6009* ▭ *AE, DC, MC, V* ☉ *No lunch Sat.–Tues.*

PAN-ASIAN ✕**Chairman and Yip.** The menu garners universal praise for its innova-
$$ tive mix of Asian and Western flavors against a backdrop of artifacts
Fodor'sChoice from Maoist China. Menu standouts include the duck pancakes, and
★ the steamed barramundi with kumquats, ginger, and shallots. Finish with a delicious dessert, such as cinnamon-and-star-anise crème brûlée. The service and wine list are outstanding, and you can bring your own bottle of wine, if you like. ⊠ *108 Bunda St., Canberra City, 2600* ☎ *02/6248–7109* ⌖ *Reservations essential* ▭ *AE, DC, MC, V* ☖ *BYO* ☉ *Closed Sun. No lunch Sat.*

$ ✕**Zen Yai.** From the deliciously light, tangy stir-fried noodles with king
★ prawns in tamarind sauce to the roast duck in red curry with lychees, the menu of this modern Thai restaurant is an inventive blend of traditional and contemporary flavors. The spacious dining room makes a relaxing

space to share new tastes, and the dedicated staff is on hand to help you choose dishes that suit your spice tolerance. ✉ *111–117 London Circuit, Canberra City* ☎ *02/6262–7594* ⊟ *AE, DC, MC, V* ⊗ *No lunch Sun.*

SOUTHERN SUBURBS

ECLECTIC
$$–$$$

✕**Rubicon.** Everything about this cozy restaurant speaks of attention to detail. For instance, savor the melded flavors of pan-roasted lamb rump served with crisp parsnip, grilled pears, brandied kumquats, and mint jus. Later you can linger over such delicious desserts as ginger- and lime-infused crème brûlée. For a lighter meal, sample the cheese board and a few choice picks from the extensive collection of wines. ✉ *6A Barker St., Griffith* ☎ *02/6295–9919* ⊟ *DC, MC, V* ⊗ *Closed Sun. and Mon.*

$$–$$$

✕**Waters Edge.** At this swanky spot, tables are set with fine linens and crystal, and huge windows look out over the sparkling waters of Lake Burley Griffin. The menu cleverly blends French and Mod-Oz influences with dishes such as roast venison loin with roasted beets and garlic potato purée, or a luscious dessert of bitter-chocolate fondant with star-anise and white-chocolate ice cream. For a special night out try the tasting menu. An impressive wine list has many by-the-glass vintages. ✉ *Commonwealth Pl. off Parkes Pl., Parkes* ☎ *02/6273–5066* ⊟ *AE, DC, MC, V* ⊗ *Closed Mon. No lunch Sat.*

$–$$
★

✕**The Tryst.** Set before the lush greenery of the Lawns at Manuka, this popular restaurant offers two very different settings. Inside, a serene dining room envelops you in sophistication, while outside tables place you right in the midst of the Bougainville Street shopping crowds. Cuisines are on hand to suit all moods and tastes, including spicy Moroccan lamb, prepared with a hint of balsamic oil and served with couscous. Afterward, a stroll through the surrounding shops will work off at least a few calories from the rich desserts like panna cotta with blueberry jus and brandy schnapps. ✉ *The Lawns, Bougainville St., Manuka* ☎ *02/6239–4422* ⊟ *AE, DC, MC, V* ⊗ *No dinner Sun.*

$–$$

✕**Verve.** Tables spill out onto the sidewalk of this hip, casual café. If you prefer, you can view the passing parade through the dining room's open front windows. Pasta, curries, and meat dishes form the bulk of the menu. Try the spaghetti *pescatore* (with seafood), served with garlic, parsley, basil, and olive oil. Weekends are busy with locals during breakfast and brunch, when the special menu lists a selection of old favorites: eggs, pancakes, waffles, and meats. ✉ *Franklin St. at Flinders Way, Manuka* ☎ *02/6239–4666* ⊟ *MC, V.*

MODERN
AUSTRALIAN
$$
Fodor'sChoice
★

✕**Aubergine.** The large, plate-glass windows of this cozy restaurant look out onto relaxing parkland. A seasonal menu combines fresh produce, subtle spices, and pungent sauces into such delicacies as pan-seared salmon with crusted prawn mousse, served with tomato and avocado salsa. Calorie-rich desserts include date pudding drizzled with Bailey's ice cream and caramel fudge sauce. The wine list includes some rare vintages from Australian vineyards. ✉ *18 Barker St., Griffith, 2603* ☎ *02/6260–8666* ⊟ *AE, DC, MC, V* ⊗ *No lunch weekends.*

$–$$

✕**First Floor.** A spacious dining room and modern decor add verve to this restaurant overlooking peaceful Kingston's Green Square. Here, above the gardens, Asian flavorings shake up the Mod-Oz menu in such dishes as garlic-and-chili squid sautéed in olive oil with parsley and onions, or fried fish fillet with watercress and red-pepper salsa. Milder seasonings are used for the baked chicken breast, marinated in Indian spices and served with dal. There's an extensive list of wines by the glass. ⊠ *Green Sq. at Jardine St., Kingston* ☎ *02/6260–6311* ▤ *AE, DC, MC, V* ⊘ *Closed Sun. No lunch Sat. or Mon.*

$–$$ ✕ **Vie.** Huge windows look out onto a sun-drenched patio at this relaxing restaurant. Asian-spiced lunches include delicacies like marinated rosemary chicken breast on roasted peppers and tomatoes, while evenings bring Balinese coconut-fish curry with tropical fruit chutney and jasmine rice. The excellent wine list includes many local and international varieties, some available by the glass. Warm weather draws diners out to the patio tables. ⊠ *15 Tench St., Kingston* ☎ *02/6234–8080* ▤ *AE, DC, MC, V* ⊘ *No dinner Sun.*

WHERE TO STAY

Canberra and its surrounding neighborhoods have comfortable, modern accommodations with basic room facilities and on-site activities. Most rooms have color TVs, coffee- and tea-making equipment, and refrigerators, and you can usually request hair dryers, irons, and other implements for personal grooming. Larger hotels have laundry and dry-cleaning services; hotels without these services usually have laundry facilities. Most hotels also have no-smoking rooms or floors, which you should be sure to reserve ahead of time.

	WHAT IT COSTS IN AUSTRALIAN DOLLARS				
	$$$$	$$$	$$	$	¢
FOR TWO PEOPLE	over A$300	A$201–A$300	A$151–A$200	A$100–A$150	under A$100

Prices are for two people in a standard double room in high season, including tax and service, based on the European Plan (with no meals) unless otherwise noted.

CENTRAL CANBERRA & NORTHERN SUBURBS

$$ 🏨 **Crowne Plaza Canberra.** In a prime location between the city center and the National Convention Centre, this atrium-style hotel has a touch of luxury. Decorated in cream and honey tones, guest rooms are large, comfortable, and well equipped. Public areas have a cool, contemporary style, with plenty of chrome and glass, giant potted plants, and fresh flowers. ⊠ *1 Binara St., Canberra City, 2601* ☎ *02/6247–8999 or 1300/662218* ⊕ *www.crowneplaza.com.au* ⌕ *287 rooms, 6 suites* ♿ *In-room: refrigerator, ethernet. In-hotel: 2 restaurants, bars, pool, gym, concierge, laundry service, public Wi-Fi, parking (no fee)* ▤ *AE, DC, MC, V.*

$$ 🏨 **Saville Park Suites.** Most of the accommodations at this hotel a block
Fodor's Choice   away from the city center are self-contained one- and two-bedroom
★   suites with spacious living and dining areas, full kitchens, and private balconies. Standard rooms are available for a lower price. Head down to the Zipp Restaurant and Wine Bar for delicious Mod-Oz fare—

or enjoy it in the comfort of your room. ⊠ *84 Northbourne Ave., Canberra City, 2612* ☎ *02/6243–2500 or 1800/630588* ⊕ *www.savillesuites.com.au* ↩ *52 rooms, 123 suites* ⌂ *In-room: refrigerator, ethernet. In-hotel: restaurant, bar, pool, gym, laundry facilities, parking (no fee)* ☐ *AE, DC, MC, V.*

> **DON'T WAIT**
>
> Book your room well ahead if you're visiting during major events like Floriade. Hotels fill quickly, so don't assume accommodations will be available at the last minute.

3

$–$$
★   🏨 **Argyle Executive Apartments.** Families enjoy the good value of these smart, comfy, fully self-contained two- and three-bedroom apartments barely a five-minute walk from the city center. Each unit has a large living and dining area, and a separate kitchen with a microwave and dishwasher. Set amid gardens, units have either a balcony or a private courtyard. There are also free laundry facilities and a secure garage. Rates are available with and without maid service. ⊠ *Currong and Boolee Sts., Reid, 2612* ☎ *02/6275–0800* ⊕ *www.argyleapartments.com.au* ↩ *30 apartments* ⌂ *In-room: kitchen, refrigerator, ethernet, VCR. In-hotel: laundry facilities, parking (no fee)* ☐ *AE, DC, MC, V.*

$–$$ 🏨 **Comfort Inn Downtown.** Travelers on a budget appreciate this motel close to the city center. Some rooms have kitchenettes, which make them good for families. The place is kept absolutely spotless. ⊠ *82 Northbourne Ave., Braddon, 2601* ☎ *02/6249–1388 or 1800/026150* ⊕ *www.comfortinn.com.au* ↩ *61 rooms, 4 suites* ⌂ *In-room: kitchen (some). In-hotel: restaurant, gym, laundry facilities, parking (no fee)* ☐ *AE, DC, MC, V.*

$–$$ 🏨 **Novotel Canberra.** A central location at the Jolimont Tourist Centre complex, a heated indoor pool, and crisply decorated rooms make this an appealing choice. Rooms have desks and broadband connections, making them practical for business travelers. A large cluster of good restaurants is within easy walking distance. ⊠ *65 Northbourne Ave., Canberra City, 2000* ☎ *02/6245–5000* ⊕ *www.novotel.com.au* ↩ *159 rooms, 38 suites* ⌂ *In-room: refrigerator, ethernet. In-hotel: room service, pool, gym, public Internet, parking (fee)* ☐ *AE, DC, MC, V.*

SOUTHERN SUBURBS

$$$–$$$$
Fodor's Choice
★   🏨 **Hyatt Hotel Canberra.** Occupying a National Heritage building dating from 1924, this elegant hotel has been restored to its original art-deco splendor. Warm peach and earth tones decorate the large, luxurious rooms and spacious suites. Enormous marble bathrooms will appeal to anyone who enjoys a good soak in the tub. The hotel has extensive gardens and is within easy walking distance of the Parliamentary Triangle. Afternoon tea, served daily between 2:30 and 5 in the gracious Tea Lounge, is one of Canberra's most popular traditions. ⊠ *Commonwealth Ave., Yarralumla, 2600* ☎ *13–1234 or 02/6270–1234* ⊕ *www.canberra.hyatt.com* ↩ *231 rooms, 18 suites* ⌂ *In-room: safe, refrigerator, ethernet. In-hotel: 2 restaurants, room service, bars, tennis court, pool, gym, spa, concierge, laundry service, public Wi-Fi, parking (no fee)* ☐ *AE, DC, MC, V.*

$$–$$$
Fodor'sChoice
★
🏨 **Rydges Capital Hill.** With its atrium ceiling composed of immense fabric sails, this is one of Canberra's most luxurious hotels and a magnet for a largely business-focused clientele. Spacious, airy, and comfortable rooms are filled with contemporary furnishings; sumptuous decor highlights the 40 suites. Close to Parliament House, the hotel and its bar have an ever-present flow of political gossip from parliamentary staff and members of the press, who drop in regularly. ⊠*Canberra Ave. at National Circle, Forrest, 2603* ☎*02/6295–3144 or 1800/020011* ⊕*www.rydges.com.au* ↻*146 rooms, 40 suites* ⚭*In-room: refrigerator, ethernet. In-hotel: restaurant, room service, bar, pool, gym, concierge, laundry service, parking (no fee)* ▤*AE, DC, MC, V.*

$$–$$$
★
🏨 **The York.** This family-owned boutique hotel in the heart of the trendy Kingston café area provides a blend of comfort and convenience. Choose from roomy one- and two-bedroom suites or attractive studios with fully-equipped kitchens and separate dining and living areas. All have balconies, some overlooking a quiet garden courtyard. The chic Artespresso restaurant is also an art gallery presenting quality contemporary exhibitions. ⊠*Giles and Tench Sts., Kingston, 2603* ☎*02/6295–2333* ⊕*www.yorkcanberra.com.au* ↻*9 studios, 16 suites* ⚭*In-room: kitchen, ethernet. In-hotel: restaurant, laundry service, parking (no fee)* ▤*AE, DC, MC, V.*

$–$$
🏨 **Manuka Park Apartments.** The comfortable one- and two-bedroom apartments and suites in this low-rise building all have kitchens, living rooms, and laundry areas. The open floor plans give them a clean, contemporary feel. In a leafy suburb, the units are within easy walking distance of the restaurants, boutiques, and antiques stores of the Manuka shopping district. Landscaped gardens surround the apartments, all of which have a private balcony or courtyard. ⊠*Manuka Circle at Oxley St., Manuka, 2603* ☎*02/6239–0000 or 1800/688227* ⊕*www.manukapark.com.au* ↻*40 apartments* ⚭*In-room: kitchen, refrigerator, Wi-Fi. In-hotel: pool, parking (no fee)* ▤*AE, DC, MC, V.*

¢–$
🏨 **Hotel Heritage.** Although it's in a quiet residential area, this budget hotel is only minutes from many of Canberra's attractions. Huddled around a large courtyard and pool, the Plain-Jane rooms are done in neutrals and have patios or balconies. With varying sizes and configurations, they can accommodate couples and family groups. The adjacent Capital Golf Course is open to guests. ⊠*203 Goyder St., Narrabundah, 2604* ☎*02/6295–2944 or 1800/026346* ⊕*www.hotelheritage.com.au* ↻*208 rooms* ⚭*In-room: refrigerator, ethernet. In-hotel: restaurant, room service, bar, pool, laundry facilities, parking (no fee)* ▤*AE, DC, MC, V.*

OUTSIDE CANBERRA

$$$$
🏨 **Avalanche Homestead.** Perched on a hillside in the Tinderry Mountains, this large, modern homestead offers a taste of the "real" Australia. The inviting lounge, where guests tend to gather, is warmed by an open fire. Rooms are spacious and comfortable. Dinners are splendid banquets served in a vast baronial hall. Daily activities include horseback riding, cattle mustering, sheep shearing, trout fishing, and bushwalking. The property is 45 km (28 mi) south of Canberra and adjoins an 80,000-acre nature reserve that abounds with kangaroos, wallabies,

wombats, and colorful birds. Rates include all meals and activities, although you can opt for just a bed-and-breakfast option. ☏ *Box 544, Burra Creek, Queanbeyan, 2620* ☎*02/6236–3245* ⊕*www.avalanche homestead.com.au* ⇄*3 rooms* ☖*In-hotel: pool, no elevator, laundry service, ethernet, parking (no fee)* ⊟*AE, DC, MC, V* ☉*AI.*

NIGHTLIFE & THE ARTS

Canberra after dark has a reputation for being dull. Actually, the city isn't quite as boring as the rest of Australia thinks, nor as lively as the citizens of Canberra would like to believe. Most venues are clustered in the city center and the fashionable southern suburbs of Manuka and Kingston. Except on weekends, few places showcase live music.

The Thursday edition of the *Canberra Times* has a "What's On" section (in the Times Out supplement) listing performances around the city. The Saturday edition's Arts pages also list weekend happenings.

THE ARTS

The **Canberra Theatre Centre** (⊠*Civic Sq., Canberra City*) is the city's main live performance space. The center has two different theaters, which host productions by the Australian Ballet Company, touring theater companies, and overseas artists. The theater's ticketing agency, **Canberra Ticketing** (⊠*Civic Sq., Canberra City* ☎*02/6275–2700 or 1800/802025* ⊕*www.canberraticketing.com.au*), is in the space joining the two theaters.

Smaller stage and musical companies perform at neighborhood venues like the **Erindale Theatre** (⊠*McBryde Crescent, Wanniassa* ☎*02/6207–2703*). The Australian National University's School of Music has classical recitals and modern-style concerts on-campus at **Llewellyn Hall** (⊠*Childers St., Acton* ☎*02/6125–4993*).

The **Street Theatre** (⊠*Childers St. at University Ave., Canberra City* ☎*02/6247–1223*), near the Australian National University campus, showcases the best in local talent with excellent productions ranging from musicals to avant-garde plays.

ART GALLERIES
Apart from the major galleries already listed above in the Exploring section, Canberra has a wealth of smaller private art galleries showcasing and selling the works of Australian artists. You can find paintings, sculpture, woodworks, glassware, and jewelry at these spots. Entry to most galleries is free, and most are open daily during regular business hours (9 or 10 AM to 5 PM).

Beaver Galleries (⊠*81 Denison St., Deakin* ☎*02/6282–5294*) has four exhibition galleries and a sculpture garden, where works by contemporary Australian artists are showcased. There is also a café.

Bungendore Wood Works Gallery (⊠*Kings Hwy., Bungendore* ☎*02/6238–1682*) exhibits the work of Australian wood artists, whose sculpture and contemporary furniture are made from the finest native timbers.

Chapman Gallery (⊠*1/11 Murray Crescent, Manuka* ☎*02/6295–2550*) has rotating exhibits by leading Australian artists, with a special emphasis on Aboriginal art.

Solander Gallery (⊠*10 Schlich St., Yarralumla* ☎*02/6285–2218*) displays a range of paintings and sculpture by leading Australian artists.

NIGHTLIFE

Nightspots in the city center offer everything from laser light shows and noisy bands to dance and comedy clubs. Many waive cover charges except for special events.

Academy and Candy Bar. Canberra's hottest nightspot draws the hip crowd to its stylish, glitzy premises. The main room, which hosts DJs and live bands, attracts a young crowd. Upstairs, Candy Bar serves innovative cocktails in a chic lounge setting. ⊠*Centre Cinema Bldg., Bunda St., Canberra City* ☎*02/6257–3355* 💳*A$5–A$20* ⊙*Academy Thurs.–Sat. 10 PM–late; Candy Bar Wed.–Mon. 5 PM–late.*

Casino Canberra. The European-style gaming room forgoes slot machines in favor of more sociable games like roulette, blackjack, poker, and keno. There are 40 gaming tables here, and the complex includes a restaurant and two bars. ⊠*21 Binara St., Canberra City* ☎*02/6257–7074* 💳*Free* ⊙*Daily noon–6 AM.*

FMs. This modern club attracts a twentysomething crowd for hip DJ-spun music on weekends. ⊠*40–42 Franklin St., Manuka* ☎*02/6295–1845* 💳*No cover* ⊙*Thurs.–Sun. 8 PM–late.*

Holy Grail. With locations in the city center and in Kingston, Holy Grail not only serves fabulous food, but also hosts great rhythm-and-blues bands. Grab a table and meet friends over a glass of wine. ⊠*Bunda St. near Akuna St., Canberra City* ☎*02/6257–9717* 💳*Green Sq., Kingston* ☎*02/6295–6071* 💳*A$5 cover* ⊙*Bar daily 10 PM–late, music Thurs.–Sat. at 10 PM.*

ICBM and Insomnia. Professionals and students in their twenties and thirties dance to Top 40 hits at this loud, modern bar. Wednesday is Comedy Night, and a DJ spins tunes on Saturday. ⊠*50 Northbourne Ave., Canberra City* ☎*02/6248–0102* 💳*Comedy Night show A$5, Sat. DJ dance A$5* ⊙*Wed.–Sat. 9 PM–2 AM.*

Minque. This relaxing bar is a great place to sit back and groove to the nightly music, which might be rock or rhythm and blues. ⊠*17 Franklin St., Manuka* ☎*02/6295–8866* 💳*No cover* ⊙*Tues.–Sun. 3–midnight.*

Tilley's Devine Café Gallery. This 1940s-style club was once just for women, but now anyone can sit at the wooden booths and enjoy a relaxing meeting with friends or a meal at the café. ⊠*Wattle and*

Brigalow Sts., Lyneham ☎*02/6249–1543* 🚪*No cover* ⊗*Mon.–Sat. noon–late, Sun. noon–6.*

SPORTS & THE OUTDOORS

BICYCLING

Canberra has almost 160 km (100 mi) of cycle paths, and the city's relatively flat terrain and dry, mild climate make it a perfect place to explore on two wheels. One of the most popular cycle paths is the 40-km (25-mi) circuit around Lake Burley Griffin.

Mr. Spokes Bike Hire rents several different kinds of bikes as well as tandems and baby seats. Bikes cost A$12 for the first hour, including helmet rental, A$30 for a half day, and A$40 for a full day. ⊠*Acton Ferry Terminal, Barrine Dr., Acton Park* ☎*02/6257–1188* ⊗*Closed Mon. and Tues. except during school holidays.*

> ### TAKE A HIKE
>
> Canberra has excellent walking paths around the three major lakes: Lake Burley Griffin, Lake Tuggeranong in the Tuggeranong Valley, and Lake Ginninderra in Belconnen. Many parts of the Canberra Nature Park have well-marked trails, such as Black Mountain, Mt. Ainslie, and Red Hill. Ask for trail maps at the **Canberra Visitor Information Centre** (⊠ *330 Northbourne Ave., Dickson* ☎*02/6205–0044).*

BOATING

You can rent paddleboats, kayaks, and canoes daily (except May–August) for use on Lake Burley Griffin from **Burley Griffin Boat Hire.** Rates start at A$15 for a half hour. ⊠*Acton Ferry Terminal, Barrine Dr., Acton Park* ☎*02/6249–6861.*

Southern Cross Cruises has daily one-hour sailings (A$15) around Lake Burley Griffin on the MV *Southern Cross* at 10 and 3. ⊠*Lotus Bay, Mariner Pl. off Alexandrina Dr., Acton Park* ☎*02/6273–1784.*

HOT-AIR BALLOONING

Balloon Aloft (☎*02/6285–1540* ⊕*www.balloonaloft.com*) provides spectacular sunrise views over Canberra from around A$190. **Dawn Drifters** (☎*02/6285–4450* ⊕*www.dawndrifters.com.au*) offers sunrise panoramas over Lake Burley Griffin, Parliament House, and other local sights from around A$195.

SHOPPING

Canberra is not known for its shopping, but there are a number of high-quality arts-and-crafts outlets where you are likely to come across some unusual gifts and souvenirs. The city's markets are excellent, and the galleries and museums sell interesting and often innovative items designed and made in Australia. In addition to the following suggestions, there are several malls and shopping centers in Canberra City (the main one is the Canberra Centre mall) and the major suburbs of Woden, Belconnen, and Tuggeranong.

Cuppacumbalong Craft Centre. A former pioneer homestead near the Murrumbidgee River, this is now a crafts gallery for potters, weavers, painters, and woodworkers, many of whom have their studios in the outbuildings. The quality of the work is universally high, and you can often meet and talk with the artisans. The center is about 34 km (21 mi) south of Canberra, off the Monaro Highway. ⊠ *Naas Rd., Tharwa* ☎ *02/6237–5116* ⊙ *Wed.–Sun. 11–5.*

Gold Creek Village. The charming streets of this shopping complex on the city's northern outskirts are lined with all sorts of fun little places to explore. Peek into art galleries and pottery shops, browse through clothing boutiques and gift stores, and nosh at several eateries. ⊠ *O'Hanlon Pl., Nicholls* ☎ *02/6230–2273* ⊙ *Daily 10–5.*

Old Bus Depot Markets. South of Lake Burley Griffin, a lively Sunday market is in the former Kingston bus depot. Handmade crafts are the staples here, and buskers and exotic inexpensive food enliven the shopping experience. ⊠ *Wentworth Ave., Kingston Foreshore, Kingston* ☎ *02/6292–8391* ⊙ *Jan.–Nov., Sun. 10–4; Dec., weekends 10–4.*

CANBERRA ESSENTIALS

TRANSPORTATION

BY AIR

Several domestic airlines connect Canberra with the rest of Australia, including Qantas and its subsidiary Airlink, and Virgin Blue. There are regular (about hourly) flights to Sydney and Melbourne, as well as frequent service to Brisbane. Some direct connections to Adelaide, the Gold Coast, and Perth are available, but most flights to these destinations are still via either Sydney or Melbourne.

Canberra International Airport is the only airport in the area, and is used by large commercial aircraft, small private planes, and the air force alike. Flights are about one-half hour to Sydney, an hour to Melbourne, and two hours to Brisbane. Early flights may be fogged in, especially during winter months, so plan for delays. The airport is 7 km (4½ mi) east of the city center.

Airlines Qantas Airways (☎ *13–1313*). **Virgin Blue** (☎ *13–6789*).

Airport Canberra International Airport (☎ *02/6275–2236*).

TRANSFERS Taxis are available from the line at the front of the terminal. The fare between the airport and the city is about A$18. A shuttle bus operated by Deane's Buslines runs every half hour between the airport and the city. In the city the bus stops in East Row at the Civic Bus Interchange. The fare is A$7 per person.

Taxis & Shuttles Deane's Buslines (☎ *02/6299–3722* ⊕ *www.deanesbuslines. com.au*).

BY BUS

The main terminal for intercity buses is the Jolimont Tourist Centre. Canberra is served by two major bus lines, Greyhound Australia and Murrays Australia, both of which have at least five daily buses to and from Sydney. One-way fares to Sydney start from A$25.

Contacts Greyhound Australia (☎ 13–1499). **Jolimont Tourist Centre** (✉ 61 Northbourne Ave., Canberra City ☎ No phone). **Murrays Australia** (☎ 13–2251).

BUS TRAVEL WITHIN CANBERRA Canberra's public transportation system is the ACTION bus network, which covers the entire city. Buses operate weekdays 6:30 AM–11:30 PM, Saturday 7 AM–11:30 PM, and Sunday 8–7. There's a flat fare of A$3 per ride. If you plan to travel extensively on buses, purchase a one-day ticket for A$6.60, which allows unlimited travel on the entire network. If you're traveling only between 9:30 and 4:30, your best bet is an off-peak daily ticket, which costs A$4.10. Tickets, maps, and timetables are available from the Canberra and Region Visitor Centre and the Bus Information Centre.

Contact Bus Information Centre (✉ East Row, near London Circuit, Canberra City ☎ 13–1710 ⊕ www.action.act.gov.au).

BY CAR

International car-rental operators with agencies in Canberra include Avis, Budget, Europcar, Hertz, and Thrifty. Rumbles Rent A Car is a local operator that offers discount car rentals. The major companies have pickup points at the airport.

Although locals maintain otherwise, Canberra can be difficult to negotiate by car, given its radial roads, erratic signage, and often large distances between suburbs. Still, because sights are scattered about and not easily connected on foot or by public transportation, a car is a good way to see the city itself, as well as the sights in the Australian Capital Territory. You can buy maps with clearly marked scenic drives at the Canberra and Region Visitor Centre.

Contacts Avis (✉ 17 Lonsdale St., Braddon ☎ 02/6249–6088 or 13–6333). **Budget** (✉ Rydges Lakeside Hotel, London Circuit, Canberra City ☎ 02/6257–2200 or 13–2727). **Europcar** (✉ 74 Northbourne Ave., Braddon ☎ 02/6284–5170 or 13–1390). **Hertz** (✉ 32 Mort St., Braddon ☎ 02/6257–4877 or 13–3039). **Rumbles Rent A Car** (✉ 11 Paragon Mall, Gladstone St., Fyshwick ☎ 02/6280–7444). **Thrifty** (✉ 29 Lonsdale St., Braddon ☎ 02/6247–7422 or 1300/367227).

BY TAXI

You can phone for a taxi, hire one from a stand, or flag one down in the street. Taxis in Canberra have meters, and fees are set based on the mileage. There's an extra fee for reservations by phone. You can bargain an hourly rate for a day tour of the area. Tipping isn't customary, but drivers appreciate it when you give them the change.

Contact Canberra Cabs (☎ 13–2227). **Elite Taxis** (☎ 02/6239–3666).

BY TRAIN

The Canberra Railway Station is on Wentworth Avenue, Kingston, about 6 km (4 mi) southeast of the city center. Xplorer trains, operated by Countrylink, make the four-hour trip between Canberra and Sydney twice daily. A daily bus-rail service by Countrylink makes the 10-hour run between Canberra and Melbourne, but first requires a bus to Cootamundra.

Countrylink has reservation and information offices at the Canberra Railway Station.

Contacts **Canberra Railway Station** (☎ *02/6295-1198*). **Countrylink** (☎ *13-2232* ⊕ *www.countrylink.nsw.gov.au*).

CONTACTS & RESOURCES

EMBASSIES

The British High Commission is open weekdays 8:45–5 for visa and passport problems. The counter at the Consular Office is open weekdays 9–3; you can phone between 9 and 5. The Canadian High Commission is open weekdays 8:30–12:30 and 1:30–4:30, and the U.S. Embassy is open weekdays 8:30–12:30.

Canada **Canadian High Commission** (⊠ *Commonwealth Ave. near Coronation Dr., Yarralumla* ☎ *02/6270-4000*).

United Kingdom **British High Commission** (⊠ *Commonwealth Ave. near Coronation Dr., Yarralumla* ☎ *02/6270-6666*). **Consular Office** (⊠ *39 Brindabella Circuit, Brindabella Business Park, Canberra Airport* ☎ *1902/941555*).

United States **U.S. Embassy** (⊠ *Moonah Pl. off State Circle, Yarralumla* ☎ *02/6214-5600*).

EMERGENCIES

In an emergency, dial **000** to reach an ambulance, the police, or the fire department. Canberra Hospital has a 24-hour emergency department.

If medical or dental treatment is required, seek advice from your hotel reception desk. There are doctors and dentists on duty throughout the city, but their office hours vary.

Pharmacies are in shopping areas throughout the city, and your hotel desk or concierge can help you find the closest one. Major chains include Capital Chemists and Amcal Chemists. Two convenient pharmacies with extended hours are Canberra Day and Night Chemist, open daily 9 AM–11 PM, and Manuka Amcal Pharmacy, open daily 9–9.

Hospitals **Calvary Hospital** (⊠ *Belconnen Way at Haydon Dr., Bruce* ☎ *02/6201-6111*). **Canberra Hospital** (⊠ *Yamba Dr., Garran* ☎ *02/6244-2222*).

Pharmacies **Canberra Day and Night Chemist (Capital Chemist)** (⊠ *O'Connor Shopping Centre, Sargood St., O'Connor* ☎ *02/6248-7050*). **Manuka Australian Pharmacy** (⊠ *Shop 8, Manuka Arcade, Franklin St., Manuka* ☎ *02/6295-0059*).

TOURS

A convenient (and fun!) way to see the major sights of Canberra is on the Red Bus, operated by Canberra Day Tours, which makes a regular circuit around the major attractions. Tickets are A$35, and you can hop on and off all day. Go Bush Tours runs half- and full-day tours of Canberra and the surrounding countryside.

Contacts Canberra Day Tours (☎ *0418/455099* ⊕ *www.canberradaytours.com. au*). **Go Bush Tours** (☎ *02/6231–3023* ⊕ *www.gobushtours.com.au*).

VISITOR INFORMATION

The Canberra and Region Visitor Centre, open weekdays 9–5:30 and weekends 9–4, is a convenient stop for those entering Canberra by road from Sydney or the north. The staff makes accommodation bookings for Canberra and the Snowy Mountains.

Information booths are found at the airport, Canberra Centre shopping mall, and Jolimont Tourist Centre. They're open during business hours on weekdays. Most hotels also have displays of brochures highlighting the city's attractions.

Contacts Canberra and Region Visitor Centre (✉ *330 Northbourne Ave., Dickson* ☎ *02/6205–0044* ⊕ *www.visitcanberra.com.au*). **Jolimont Tourist Centre** (✉ *61 Northbourne Ave., Canberra City* ☎ *No phone*).

Melbourne

WORD OF MOUTH

"St. Kilda is fun, particularly on a sunny day. There are lots of opportunities to people-watch. If you walk a bit farther along the Esplanade, you will end up at Acland [Street], which has the most fantastic cake shops. Take the tram down St. Kilda Road, which will take you past some of the city gardens and the Shrine of Remembrance."

—marg

Updated
by Caroline
Gladstone

MELBOURNE (SAY *MEL*-BUN) IS
THE cultivated sister of brassy Sydney. To the extent that culture is
synonymous with sophistication—
except when it comes to watching
Australian Rules Football or the
Melbourne Cup—some call this
city the cultural capital of the continent. Melbourne is also known
for its rich migrant influences, particularly those expressed through
food: the espresso cafés on Lygon
Street, Melbourne's "little Italy,"
Brunswick's Middle Eastern/Indian/Turkish enclave, Richmond's "little
Vietnam," or the Chinatown district of the city center.

> ### WORD OF MOUTH
>
> "We were in Sydney and Mel-
> bourne in early to mid-August
> (from North Carolina) and found
> the weather great. Some sprinkles
> and definitely sweater and wind-
> breaker weather, but perfectly
> pleasant to walk around."
>
> —rmp

4

If Victoria, like its dowager namesake, is a little stuffy and old-fashioned, then the state capital of Melbourne still holds onto some old-
world attitudes. Melbourne society displays an almost European
obsession with class. The city is the site of some of the nation's most
prestigious schools and universities, and a status is still attached to
attending the right one. Yet there is another, more progressive side to
the city: cutting-edge restaurants and groovy bars, hip boutiques lining
back streets, and a thriving art scene. There is also a friendliness that
permeates Melbourne.

Whatever appearances they maintain, Melburnians do love their
sports, as evidenced by their successful bid to host the 2006 Commonwealth Games. The city is sports mad—especially when it comes
to the glorious, freewheeling Melbourne Cup horse race that brings
the entire nation to a grinding halt on the first Tuesday in November.
The city also comes alive during the Australian Tennis Open, one of
the four tennis Grand Slam events, which is held every January at
Melbourne Park.

For years Melbourne's city center was seen as an inferior tourist attraction compared with Sydney's sparkling harbor. But a large-scale building development along the Yarra River in the early '90s transformed
what was once an eyesore into a vibrant entertainment district known
as Southbank. Located behind Flinders Street Station on the south side
of the river, Southbank is a stylish myriad of bars, shops, and restaurants. An assortment of unusual water displays farther along mark the
entrance to Southbank's brash Crown Casino, where gasoline-fueled
towers shoot bursts of flames on the hour after dark. Many changes
have also taken place in the heart of the city, where Federation Square,
a large civic landmark built in 2002, now houses a second branch of
the National Gallery of Victoria, the Centre for the Moving Image,
the Australian Racing Museum, the Melbourne Visitor Center, and an
assortment of shops and restaurants.

EXPLORING MELBOURNE

Consistently rated among the "world's most livable cities" in quality-of-life surveys, Melbourne is built on a coastal plain at the top of the giant horseshoe of Port Phillip Bay. The city center is an orderly grid of streets where the state parliament, banks, multinational corporations, and splendid Victorian buildings that sprang up in the wake of the gold rush now stand. This is Melbourne's heart, which you can explore at a leisurely pace in a couple of days.

In Southbank, one of the new precincts south of the city center, the Southgate development of bars, restaurants, and shops has refocused Melbourne's vision on the Yarra River. Once a blighted stretch of factories and run-down warehouses, the southern bank of the river is now a vibrant, exciting part of the city, and the river itself is finally taking its rightful place in Melbourne's psyche. Just a hop away, Federation Square—and its host of galleries—has become a civic landmark for Melburnians. Stroll along the Esplanade in the suburb of St. Kilda, amble past the elegant houses of East Melbourne, enjoy the shops and cafés in Fitzroy or Carlton, rub shoulders with locals at the Victoria Market, nip into the Windsor for afternoon tea, or rent a canoe at Studley Park to paddle along one of the prettiest stretches of the Yarra—and you may discover Melbourne's soul as well as its heart.

WHEN TO VISIT

Melbourne is at its most beautiful in fall, March to May. Days are crisp, sunny, and clear, and the foliage in parks and gardens is glorious. Melbourne winters can be gloomy, but by September the weather clears up, the football finals are on, and spirits begin to soar. Book early if you want to spend time in Melbourne in late October or early November when the Spring Racing Carnival and the Melbourne International Festival are in full swing. The same advice goes for early March when the city hosts a Formula 1 car-racing grand prix and in mid-January during the Australian Tennis Open.

CITY CENTER

Melbourne's center is framed by the Yarra River to the south and a string of parks to the east. On the river's southern bank, the Southgate development, the arts district around the National Gallery of Victoria, and the King's Domain–Royal Botanic Gardens areas also merit attention.

GREAT ITINERARIES

IF YOU HAVE 1 DAY

If you're short on time, the free **City Circle Tram** and the **Yarra River Shuttle Service** (A$9) are both hop-on and hop-off ways to see many of the city's sights without exhausting yourself. The Parliament House tram stop gives access to the Princess Theatre, the grand Windsor Hotel, **Parliament House,** the Paris End of Collins Street, and St. Patrick's Cathedral. Get off at Flinders Street, take a peek in **Young and Jackson's** pub at the infamous *Chloe* painting, and then walk over the **Princes Bridge.** There you can stroll along the bank of the Yarra looking back at Federation Square and the city skyline, and then wander along Southbank while checking out the restaurants and shops at **Southgate** and the **Crown Casino.** A trip to the **Melbourne Observation Deck** will put the city into perspective and you can decide whether or not you want to head northeast to Fitzroy for a meander along groovy **Brunswick Street,** or north towards **Carlton** to immerse yourself in Little Italy.

IF YOU HAVE 3 DAYS

You might squeeze in a bit more exploring on Day 1 with a stroll through Treasury Gardens and over to Fitzroy Gardens for a look at Captain Cook's Cottage, or see the sharks at the **Melbourne Aquarium** opposite Southbank. On your second day, stroll through the **Royal Botanic Gardens** and see the **Shrine of Remembrance.** Then take a tram on St. Kilda Road to the hip **Acland Street area,** in the suburb of **St. Kilda,** for dinner. On Day 3, take a tour of Chapel Street's shops, restaurants, and bars; it's Melbourne's hippest district.

IF YOU HAVE 5 DAYS

Take in one or more sights outside the city. Head east to the Yarra Valley on an organized winery tour, or head to the Dandenong Ranges for a ride on the Puffing Billy steam railway from Belgrave through the fern gullies and forests of the Dandenong ranges. On the way back, stop at a teahouse in Belgrave or Olinda and browse the curio stores. Or, take an evening excursion to Phillip Island for the endearing sunset **Penguin Parade.** A trip to the **Mornington Peninsula** wineries and **Arthurs Seat,** just 90 minutes south of Melbourne, is another great day trip. There you can rest and recuperate with a soak in the **Peninsula Hot Springs.** *For these and other nearby activities and destinations, see the Victoria chapter.*

4

WHAT TO SEE

20 **Athenaeum Theatre and Library.** The first talking picture show in Australia was screened at this 1896 theater. Today the building also houses a library, and is used mainly for live theatrical performances. ⊠ *188 Collins St., City Center* ☎ *03/9650–3504* ⊗ *Weekdays 8:30–5, Sat. 9–3.*

8 **Block Arcade.** Melbourne's most elegant 19th-century shopping arcade dates from the 1880s, when "Marvelous Melbourne" was flush with the prosperity of the gold rushes. A century later, renovations scraped back the grime to reveal a magnificent mosaic floor. Tours operate on Tuesday and Thursdays and conclude with afternoon tea in the lovely Hopetoun Tea Rooms. ⊠ *282 Collins St., City Center* ☎ *03/9654–5244.*

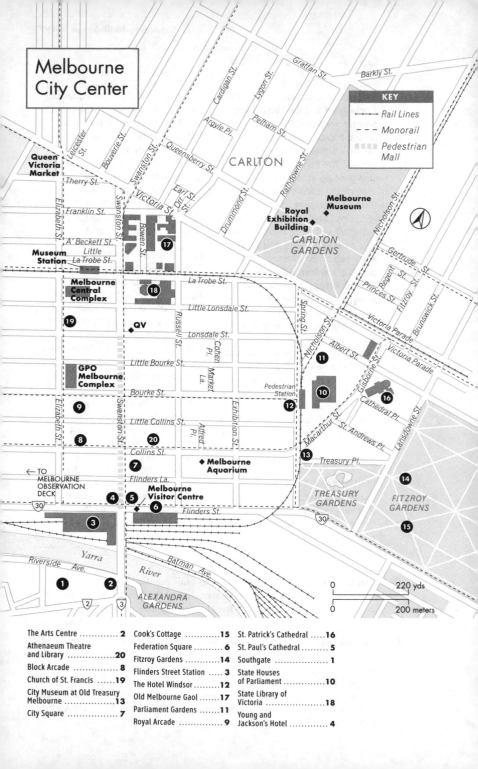

Melbourne City Center

Carlton Gardens. Forty acres of tree-lined paths, artificial lakes, and flower beds in this English-style 19th-century park form a backdrop for the outstanding Museum of Victoria, as well as the World Heritage–listed Royal Exhibition Building, erected in 1880. ⊠ *Victoria Parade at Nicholson, Carlton, and Rathdowne Sts., City Center* 🕾 *No phone.*

⑲ **Church of St. Francis.** This 1841 Roman Catholic church was constructed when the city was barely a decade old. The simple, frugal design starkly contrasts with the Gothic exuberance of St. Paul's, built 40 years later. The difference illustrates just what the gold rush did for Melbourne. ⊠ *Elizabeth and Lonsdale Sts., City Center* 🕾 *03/9663–2496.*

EXPLORING THE THEATERS

Melburnians love their theater and major shows often open in Melbourne first. If you want to take in Broadway or West End–style theater in grand surroundings, check out what's playing at the Regent and the Princess. Both are owned by Marriner Theatres, which lovingly restored the Regent for its re-opening in the mid-1990s. You can tread the boards (i.e., act on stage) with a theater-loving tour guide on the Historic Rambles tour. Contact Wilma Farrow (🕾 003/9820–0239) for the details. For performances check out ⊕ *www.marrinertheatres.com.au.*

⑬ **City Museum at Old Treasury Melbourne.** The neoclassical bluestone-and-sandstone building, designed by 19-year-old architect J. J. Clark, was built in 1862 to hold the gold that was pouring into Melbourne from mines in Ballarat and Bendigo. Subsequently, underground vaults were protected by iron bars and foot-thick walls. Not to be missed is the Built on Gold show staged in the vaults. ⊠ *Treasury Pl. at Spring St., City Center* 🕾 *03/9651–2233* ⊕ *www.citymuseummelbourne.org.au* 🕾 *A$8.50* ☉ *Weekdays 9–5, weekends 10–4.*

⑦ **City Square.** Here you'll find the statue of explorers Robert Burke and William Wills, whose ill-fated 1860–61 expedition was the first to cross Australia from south to north. Grab a seat at a stylish café on the square and people-watch. ⊠ *Swanston St. between Collins St. and Flinders La., City Center.*

NEED A BREAK?

Journal (⊠ *253 Flinders La., City Center* 🕾 *03/9650–4399*) has leather couches, bookcases filled with magazines and newspapers, and communal tables where you can enjoy tapas, salads, antipasto platters, and selections from an excellent wine list.

At the **Transport Hotel** (⊠ *Federation Sq., City Center* 🕾 *03/9654–8808*) the steel-and-glass dining room with views across the Yarra River is a sophisticated place to enjoy a glass of wine and organic munchies.

⑮ **Cook's Cottage.** Once the property of the Pacific navigator Captain James Cook, the modest home, built in 1755, was transported stone by stone from Great Ayton in Yorkshire and rebuilt in the lush Fitzroy Gardens in 1934. It's believed that Cook lived in the cottage between voyages. The interior is simple and sparsely furnished, a suitable domestic realm for a man who spent much of his life in cramped quarters aboard sailing ships. ✉ *Fitzroy Gardens near Lansdowne St. and Wellington Parade, East Melbourne* ☎ *03/9419–4677* 🎟 *A$4* ⏲ *Daily 9–5.*

6 ★ **Federation Square.** Encompassing a whole city block, the bold, abstract-style landmark was designed to house the second branch of the National Gallery of Victoria, which exhibits only Australian art. The square also incorporates the Centre for the Moving Image; the BMW Edge amphitheater, a contemporary music and theater performance venue; the Victorian Wine Precinct, showcasing the best of local wine; Champions: Australian Racing Museum; the Melbourne Visitor Centre; and restaurants, bars, and gift shops. ✉ *Flinders St. between Swanston and Russell Sts., City Center* ☎ *03/9655–1900* 🌐 *www.fedsq.com* 🎟 *Free* ⏲ *Mon.–Thurs. 10–5, Fri. 10–9, weekends 10–6.*

14 **Fitzroy Gardens.** This 65-acre expanse of European trees, manicured lawns, garden beds, statuary, and sweeping walks is Melbourne's most popular central park. Among its highlights is the **Avenue of Elms,** a majestic stand of 130-year-old trees that is one of the few in the world that has not been devastated by Dutch elm disease. ✉ *Lansdowne St. at Wellington Parade, East Melbourne* 🎟 *Free* ⏲ *Daily sunrise–sunset.*

3 **Flinders Street Station.** Melburnians use the clocks on the front of this grand Edwardian hub of Melbourne's suburban rail network as a favorite meeting place. When it was proposed to replace them with television screens, an uproar ensued. Today there are both clocks and screens. ✉ *Flinders St. at St. Kilda Rd., City Center.*

King's Domain Gardens. This expansive stretch of parkland includes Queen Victoria Gardens, Alexandra Gardens, the Shrine of Remembrance, Pioneer Women's Garden, the Sidney Myer Music Bowl, and the Royal Botanic Gardens. The temple-style **Shrine of Remembrance** is designed so that a beam of sunlight passes over the Stone of Remembrance in the Inner Shrine at 11 AM on Remembrance Day—the 11th day of the 11th month, when in 1918 the armistice marking the end of World War I was declared. ✉ *Between St. Kilda and Domain Rds., Anderson St., and Yarra River, City Center.*

Melbourne Aquarium. Become part of the action as you stroll through transparent tunnels surrounded by water and the denizens of the deep at play. Or take a ride on an electronic simulator. The aquamarine building illuminates a previously dismal section of the Yarra bank, opposite Crown Casino. If you're feeling brave, check out the shark dives—they're held daily, include scuba equipment, and are led by an instructor. ✉ *Flinders and King Sts., City Center* ☎ *03/9620–0999* 🌐 *www.melbourneaquarium.com.au* 🎟 *A$24, shark dives from A$124* ⏲ *Feb.–Dec., daily 9:30–6; Jan., daily 9:30–9.*

Melbourne Observation Deck. If you want a 360-degree panorama of Melbourne, there's no better (or more popular) place than from the 55th floor of the city's tallest building. Admission includes a 20-minute film and use of high-power binoculars. ⊠ *Level 55, 525 Collins St., at King St., City Center* ☎ *03/9629–8222* ☜ *Observation deck A$14.50* ☉ *Sun.–Thurs. 10–10, Fri. and Sat. 10–11.*

⑰ Old Melbourne Gaol. A museum run by the Victorian branch of the National Trust is housed in the city's first jail. The building—rumored to be haunted—has three tiers of cells with catwalks around the upper levels. Its most famous inmate was the notorious bushranger Ned Kelly, who was hanged here in 1880. The Hangman's night tours (reservations essential) are a popular, if macabre, facet of Melbourne nightlife. ⊠ *Russell and Mackenzie Sts., City Center* ☎ *03/9663–7228 or 13/2849* ⊕ *www.nattrust.com.au* ☜ *Self-guided day tours A$12.50, guided tours A$25* ☉ *Daily 9:30–5. Tours Sept.–May, Mon., Wed., Fri., and Sun. 8:30; June–Aug., Mon., Wed., Fri., and Sun. 7:30.*

> ## WHERE THE WILD THINGS ARE
>
> For most visitors, Melbourne is a genteel, highly cultivated experience. However, you can get a taste of the wilds on a Slumber Safari at Werribee Open Range Zoo. Kick off the night with a gourmet BBQ while watching African animals roam freely, then bunker down under canvas with the wild night sounds of Africa only a few hundred yards away. Great fun for city slickers! ⊕ *www.zoo.org.au*

⑪ Parliament Gardens. Stop here for a breath of cool green air in the center of the city. The gardens have a modern fountain and an excellent view of the handsome yellow Princess Theatre across Spring Street. ⊠ *Parliament, Spring, and Nicholson Sts., East Melbourne* ☉ *Daily dawn–dusk.*

⑨ Royal Arcade. Opened in 1870, this is the country's oldest shopping arcade, and despite alterations it retains an airy, graceful elegance. Walk about 30 feet into the arcade to see the statues of Gog and Magog, the mythical monsters that toll the hour on either side of **Gaunt's Clock.** ⊠ *355 Bourke St., City Center* ☎ *No phone.*

⑯ St. Patrick's Cathedral. Ireland supplied Australia with many of its early immigrants, especially during the Irish potato famine in the middle of the 19th century. A statue of the Irish patriot Daniel O'Connell stands in the courtyard. Construction of the Gothic Revival building began in 1858 and took 82 years to finish. ⊠ *Cathedral Pl., East Melbourne* ☎ *03/9662–2233* ☉ *Weekdays 6:30–5, weekends 7:15–7.*

⑤ St. Paul's Cathedral. This 1892 headquarters of Melbourne's Anglican faith is one of the most important works of William Butterfield, a leader of the Gothic Revival style in England. In 2006 the cathedral underwent a massive renovation and was restored to its former glory. Outside is the statue of Matthew Flinders, the first seaman to circumnavigate the Australian coastline, between 1801 and 1803. ⊠ *Flinders and Swanston Sts., City Center* ☎ *03/9653–4333* ☉ *Sun.–Fri. 8–6, Sat. 9–5.*

4

1 ★ Southgate. On the river's edge next to the Victorian Arts Center, the development is a prime spot for lingering—designer shops, classy restaurants, bars, and casual eating places help locals and visitors while away the hours. The promenade links with the forecourt of Crown Casino. ⊠ *Maffra St. at City Rd., Southbank* ☎ *03/9699–4311* ⊕ *www.southgate-melbourne.com.au.*

10 State Houses of Parliament. Dating from 1856, this building was used as the National Parliament from the time of federation in 1900 until 1927, when the first Parliament House was completed in Canberra. Parliament usually sits Tuesday to Thursday from March through July and again from August through November. ⊠ *Spring and Nicholson Sts., East Melbourne* ☎ *03/9651–8911* ☜ *Free* ☽ *Weekdays 9–4; guided tour at 10, 11, 2, 3, and 3:45 when parliament is not in session.*

18 State Library of Victoria. On a rise behind lawns and heroic statuary, this handsome 1853 building was constructed during the gold-rush boom. Today more than 1.5 million volumes are housed here as well as bushranger Ned Kelly's famous armor. Large reading areas make this a comfortable place for browsing, and three galleries display works from the library's Pictures Collection. ⊠ *328 Swanston St., City Center* ☎ *03/8664–7000* ⊕ *www.statelibrary.vic.gov.au* ☜ *Free* ☽ *Mon.– Thurs. 10–9, Fri.–Sun. 10–6.*

2 Victorian Arts Centre. Melbourne's most important cultural landmark is the venue for performances by the Australian Ballet, Australian Opera, and Melbourne Symphony Orchestra. It also encompasses Hamer Hall (formerly the Melbourne Concert Hall), the Arts Complex, the original National Gallery of Victoria, and the outdoor Sidney Myer Music Bowl. One-hour tours begin from the information desk at noon and 2:30, Monday through Saturday. On Sunday a 90-minute backstage tour (no children) begins at 12:15. At night look for the center's spire, which creates a magical spectacle with brilliant fiber-optic cables. ⊠ *100 St. Kilda Rd., Southbank* ☎ *03/9281–8000* ⊕ *www.theartscentre.net.au* ☜ *Tour A$11, backstage tour A$13.50* ☽ *Mon.–Sat. 9 AM– 11 PM, Sun. 10–5.*

12 The Hotel Windsor. Not just a grand hotel, the Windsor is home to one of Melbourne's proudest institutions—the ritual of afternoon tea (from A$35), served daily 3:30–5:30. Ask about theme buffet teas served on weekends, such as the Chocolate Indulgence, available June–October (from A$55), with a vast selection of chocolates and chocolate cakes and desserts. Although the Grand Dining Room—a belle-epoque extravaganza with a gilded ceiling and seven glass cupolas—is open only to private functions, try to steal a look anyway. ⊠ *111 Spring St., City Center* ☎ *03/9633–6000* ⊕ *www.thewindsor.com.au.*

4 Young and Jackson's Hotel. Pubs are not generally known for their artwork, but climb the steps to the bar here to see *Chloe,* a painting that has scandalized and titillated Melburnians for many decades. The larger-than-life nude, painted by George Lefebvre in Paris in 1875, has hung on the walls of Young and Jackson's Hotel (now owned by Fosters Brewery) for most of the last century. ⊠*1 Swanston St. (opposite Flinders Street Station), City Center* ☎*03/9650–3884.*

RICHMOND

Home of Victoria Street—Melbourne's "little Vietnam"—and the lively shopping stretch of Bridge Road, Richmond is 2 km (1 mi) east of the city center. If you're looking for a new wardrobe, a Vietnamese soup kitchen, a Korean barbecue, a Laotian banquet, or a Thai hole-in-the-wall, this is the place to come.

Victoria Street. Fast becoming one of Melbourne's most popular "eat streets," this 2-km (1-mi) stretch has restaurants ranging from simple canteens (eat until you drop for A$10) to dressy, tablecloth-and-candlelight dining spots. The street also features Vietnamese grocers, kitchenware stores, several art galleries, and several chichi drinking spots. Once a year in late September the street comes to life with a Moon Lantern Festival, during which children wander the streets carrying handmade paper lanterns. ⊠*Victoria St., Richmond.*

Bridge Road. Once a run-down area of Richmond, this street is now a bargain shopper's paradise. It's chockablock with clothing shops, cafés, and factory outlets selling leather goods, shoes, and gourmet foods. Take Tram 48 or 75 from the city. ⊠*Bridge Rd., Richmond.*

EAST MELBOURNE

The harmonious streetscapes in this historic enclave of Victorian houses, which date from the boom following the gold rushes of the 1850s, are a great excuse for a stroll. Start at the southeast corner of Fitzroy Gardens and head north on Clarendon to George Street; a right turn will lead you past a procession of superb terrace houses and mature European trees. Two blocks ahead, turn left on Simpson, then again on wide, gracious Hotham Street. On either side of the grassy median that divides the roadway, the mix of terrace houses and freestanding mansions includes some of the suburb's finest architecture. Back at Clarendon, turn north. Bishopscourt, the bluestone residence of the Anglican Archbishop of Melbourne, occupies the next block. Wind right again down Gipps Street and make your way to Darling Square. For different scenery on the way back, take Simpson Street south and turn right on Wellington Parade.

WALTZING MATILDA

Shopping mixes with history and a touch of patriotism at Melbourne Central shopping center. The main attraction, apart from the stores, is the historic brick shot tower, rising 50 meters (165 feet) above the center and encased in a glass cone. Built in 1890, the shot tower was used to make "shot" or bullets. Also suspended from the roof is a hot-air balloon and a huge fob-watch that entertains shoppers on the hour with a musical rendition of Australia's unofficial national anthem, "Waltzing Matilda." You'll find this huge shopping center on the corner of La Trobe and Swanston streets.

㉑ Melbourne Cricket Ground (MCG). A tour of this complex is essential for an understanding of Melbourne's sporting obsession. Outstanding museums here include the Australian Gallery of Sport and Olympic Museum, and the MCG Museum and Library. The site is a pleasant 10-minute walk from the city center or a tram ride to Jolimont Station. ✉ *Jolimont Terr., Jolimont* ☎ *03/9657–8864* ⊕ *www.mcg.org.au* 🎟 *A$10* ⊙ *Tours daily every half-hr 10–3, except on event days.*

ST. KILDA

It often seems that every Melburnian heads to St. Kilda on a Saturday night. The dozens of alfresco restaurants overflow into the streets and the cafés and bars are buzzing with the young fashionistas. The holiday atmosphere continues on Sunday with open air markets and people enjoying the beach. The seaside suburb still has a Victorian-era atmosphere—the tree-lined promenade and the classic pier extending out into Port Phillip Bay are perfect for strolling and people watching. While no one wanted to live there in the 1970s and '80s, it is now a very smart address and many visitors choose to stay in St. Kilda and then hop on the tram for a short and scenic ride into the city.

㉙ Luna Park is a five-minute stroll southeast of the pier. A Melbourne icon, the park's gates take the shape of an enormous mouth, swallowing visitors whole and delivering them into a world of ghost trains, pirate ships, and carousels. Built in 1912, the **Scenic Railway** is the park's most popular ride. It's said to be the oldest continually operating roller coaster in the world and was renovated in 2006. The railway is less roller coaster and more relaxed loop-the-loop, offering stunning views of Port Phillip Bay between each dip and turn. Numerous music festivals, including Push Over (held each March) are held within the park's grounds each year. ✉ *Lower Esplanade, St. Kilda* ☎ *03/9525–5033 or 1300/888272* ⊕ *www. lunapark.com.au* 🎟 *Free entry, A$7 per ride, A$35.95 for unlimited rides* ⊙ *Victorian school holiday: early to mid-Apr., July, Sept., and late Dec.–Jan., daily 11 AM–6 PM. Rest of the year: mid-Apr.–June, Aug., Oct.–late Dec., Feb., and Mar., Fri. 7 PM–11 PM, Sat. 11 AM–11 PM, Sun. 11–6.*

㉚ Acland Street. An alphabet soup of Chinese, French, Italian, and Lebanese eateries—along with a fantastic array of cake shops—lines the sidewalk of St. Kilda's ultrahip restaurant row. The street faces Luna Park. ✉ *Acland St. between Barkly St. and Shakespeare Grove, St. Kilda.*

㉘ St. Kilda to Williamstown Bay Ferry. A leisurely way to experience the area is to hop on this ferry service in the morning and head over to Williamstown for lunch at a seafood restaurant or café. Grab a cone (the town has famously good ice-cream shops) before heading back to St. Kilda Pier as the sun goes down. Views of Melbourne from the waters of Port Phillip Bay are breathtaking. Ferries depart from St. Kilda Pier

Melbourne
Suburbs

each Saturday and Sunday and on public holidays return from Gem Pier, Williamstown. ⊠*St. Kilda Pier, Lower Esplanade, St. Kilda, Williamstown* ☎*03/9506–4144* ⊕*www.williamstownferries.com.au* ⛴*A$8 one-way, A$15 round-trip, all-day pass A$35* ⊙*Departures from St. Kilda Pier weekends at 11:30, 12:30, 1:30, 2:30, 3:30, 4.30; departures from Gem Pier weekends at 11, noon, 1, 2, 3, 4.*

FITZROY

Melbourne's bohemian quarter is 2 km (1 mi) northeast of the city center. If you're looking for an Afghan camel bag or a secondhand paperback, or yearn for a café where you can sit over a plate of tapas and watch Melbourne go by, Fitzroy is the place. Take Tram No. 11 or 86 from the city.

㉒ Brunswick Street. Along with Lygon Street in nearby Carlton, Brunswick Street is one of Melbourne's favorite places to dine. You might want to step into a simple lunchtime café serving tasty pizza for less than A$10, or opt for dinner at one of the stylish, highly regarded bar-restaurants. The street also has many galleries, bookstores, and arts-and-crafts shops. ⊠*Brunswick St. between Alexandra and Victoria Parades, Fitzroy.*

BRUNSWICK

Just 2 km (1 mi) north of the city center, Brunswick is Melbourne's multicultural heart. Here Middle Eastern spice shops sit next to avant-garde galleries, Egyptian supermarkets, Turkish tile shops, Japanese yakitori eateries, Lebanese bakeries, Indian haberdasheries, and secondhand bookstores. Take Tram 19 from the city.

㉕ Sydney Road. There's nowhere in Melbourne quite like Sydney Road. Cultures collide as Arabic mingles with French, Hindi does battle with Bengali, and the muezzin's call to prayer argues with Lebanese pop music. Scents intoxicate and colors beguile. Cafés serving everything from pastries to *tagines* (Moroccan stews) to Turkish delights huddle by the roadside, as do quirky record shops, antiques auction houses, and Bollywood video stores. ⊠*Sydney Rd. between Brunswick Rd. and Bell St., Brunswick.*

A DAY AT THE RACES

The usually serene atmosphere of Albert Park is turned into motor-head heaven every March when Melbourne stages the Australian Grand Prix. It's the opening event of the Formula One season with four full-throttle days of excitement on and off the track. Drivers scream around Albert Park Lake to the delight of fans, and horror of some nearby residents. Albert Park is 3 km (2 mi) south of the city center. ⊕*www. grandprix.com.au*

CARLTON

To see the best of Carlton's Victorian-era architecture walk along Drummond Street, with its rows of gracious terrace houses, and Canning Street, which has a mix of workers' cottages and grander properties. Take Tram 1 or 22 from the city.

24 **Lygon Street.** Known as Melbourne's Little Italy, Lygon Street is a perfect ★ example of the city's multiculturalism: where once you'd have seen only Italian restaurants, there are now Thai, Malay, Caribbean, and Greek eateries. The city's famous café culture was also born here, with the arrival of Melbourne's first espresso machine at one of the street's Italian-owned cafés in the 1950s. The street has great color, particularly at night when the sidewalks are thronged with diners, strollers, and a procession of high-revving muscle cars rumbling along the strip. The Italian-inspired **Lygon Street Festival** in October gathers the neighborhood in music and merriment. ⊠ *Lygon St. between Victoria and Alexandra Parades, Carlton.*

23 **Melbourne Museum.** A spectacular, postmodern building surrounds displays of the varied cultures around Australia and the Pacific Islands. The Bunjilaka exhibit covers the traditions of the country's Aboriginal groups, while the Australia Gallery focuses on Victoria's heritage (and includes the preserved body of Australia's greatest racing horse, Phar Lap). There's plenty for kids, too, with the wooded Forest Gallery, Children's Museum, Mind and Body Gallery, and Science and Life Gallery. ⊠ *Carlton Gardens, 11 Nicholson St., Carlton* ☎ *13–1102 or 03/8341–7777* ⊕ *melbourne.museum.vic.gov.au* ⊠ *A$6* ⊙ *Daily 10–5.*

SOUTH YARRA–PRAHRAN

One of the coolest spots to be on any given night is in South Yarra and Prahran. If you're feeling alternative, head for Greville Street, which runs off Chapel near the former Prahran Town Hall and has more bars and eateries, groovy clothes, and music shops. Take Trams 6, 8, 72, and 78 from the city.

27 **Chapel Street.** The heart of the trendy South Yarra–Prahran area, this Fodor'sChoice long road is packed with pubs, bars, notable restaurants, and upscale ★ boutiques—more than 1,000 shops can be found within the precinct. The Toorak Road end of the street (nearest to the city) is the fashion-conscious, upscale section where Australian designers showcase their original designs. Walk south along Chapel Street to Greville Street, a small lane of hip bars, clothing boutiques, and record stores. Past Greville Street, the south end of Chapel Street is grungier, with pawnshops and kitschy collectibles stores. ⊠ *Chapel St. between Toorak and Dandenong Rds., South Yarra–Prahran* ☎ *03/9529–6331* ⊕ *www.chapelstreet.com.au.*

㉖ **Royal Botanic Gardens.** The present design and layout were the brain-
☺ child of W.R. Guilfoyle, curator and director of the gardens from
★ 1873 to 1910. Within its 100 acres are 12,000 species of native and
imported plants and trees, sweeping lawns, and ornamental lakes
populated with ducks and swans that love to be fed. Guided walks
leave from the visitor center, including the Aboriginal Heritage Walk,
led by an Aboriginal cultural interpreter. The Children's Garden is a
fun and interactive place for kids to explore. Summer brings alfresco
performances of classic plays, usually Shakespeare, children's classics
like *Wind in the Willows,* and the popular Moonlight Cinema series.
✉*Anderson St., between Alexandra and Birdwood Aves., South Yarra*
☎*03/9252–2300* ⊕*www.rbg.vic.gov.au* ✐*Free* ☉*Nov.–Mar., daily
7:30 AM–8:30 PM; Apr.–Oct., daily 7:30 AM–5:30 PM. Children's Garden
Wed.–Sun. 10–4.*

OUTSIDE MELBOURNE

☺ **Melbourne Zoological Gardens.** Flourishing gardens and open-environ-
ment animal enclosures are hallmarks of this world-renowned zoo,
which sits 4 km (2½ mi) north of the city center. A lion park, reptile house, and butterfly pavilion where more than 1,000 butterflies
flutter through the rain-forest setting are also on-site, as is a simulated African rain forest where a group of Western Lowland goril-
las resides. The spectacular Trail of the Elephants, home of Asiatic
elephants Mek Kapah and Bong Su, has a village, gardens, and a
swimming pool. A new orangutan sanctuary opened in 2007 with
viewing from tree-high boardwalks.Twilight jazz bands serenade
visitors on summer evenings. ✉*Elliott Ave., Parkville* ☎*03/9285–
9300* ⊕*www.zoo.org.au* ✐*A$22* ☉*Daily 9–5, twilight evenings
to 9 or 9:30.*

WHERE TO EAT

Melbourne teems with top-quality restaurants, particularly in St. Kilda,
South Yarra, the Docklands, and the Waterfront City precinct. Lygon
Street is still a favorite with those who love great coffee and bakeries.
The city center also has many back-alley coffee shops for first-class java
and pastries. Reservations are generally advised, and although most
places are licensed to sell alcohol, the few that aren't usually allow you
to bring your own. Lunch is served noon–2:30, and dinner is usually
7–10:30. A 10% tip is customary for exemplary service, and there may
be a corkage fee in BYO restaurants.

WHAT IT COSTS IN AUSTRALIAN DOLLARS				
$$$$	**$$$**	**$$**	**$**	**¢**
AT DINNER	over A$50	A$36–A$50	A$21–A$35	A$10–A$20	under A$10

Prices are per person for a main course at dinner.

CITY CENTER

CAFÉS

$$ ✗ **Brunetti.** This Romanesque bakery is still just as heavenly as when
★ it opened nearly 30 years ago; it's still filled with perfect biscotti
and mouthwatering cakes. More substantial pastas and risottos have
recently been added to the menu, and you can finish off your lunch
with a tremendous espresso and *cornetto con crema* (custard-filled
croissant). Dinner is served in the attached, stylish restaurant every
night except Sunday. City workers can now enjoy all these sweet
delights with the opening of a branch in Flinders Lane. ✉ *198–204
Faraday St., Carlton* ☎ *03/9347–2801* ✉ *214 Flinders La., at Swan-
ston St.* ☎ *03/9663—8085* ▤ *AE, DC, MC, V* ⊘ *No dinner Sun.*

¢–$ ✗ **Babka.** Food-lovers in the know are often found loitering at this mod-
est café. Try the excellent pastries, fresh-baked breads, or more sub-
stantial offerings like the omelet spiced with *dukkah* (an Egyptian-style
spice and sesame blend). ✉ *358 Brunswick St., Fitzroy* ☎ *03/9416–
0091* ⌦ *Reservations not accepted* ▤ *No credit cards* ⊘ *Closed Mon.
No dinner.*

¢ ✗ **Bimbo Deluxe.** This eclectic bar, with deep comfy sofas and the feel
of a local hangout, has the cheapest and possibly the most delicious
pizzas in town. On weekdays between noon and 4 PM you can order
a dinner-plate-size pizza (from 19 choices) for a mere A$4. If you
miss the special, fear not: the same great pizzas are only A$6–A$8
at other times. Try the Agnello (tomato, mozzarella, spiced lamb,
arugula, pine nuts, and sultanas). If you're hankering for a sugar
rush, there are also sweet pizzas such as chocolate with mascar-
pone. A range of chilled infused vodkas—including watermelon and
lychee—are available, and the bar's signature "blonde bimbo" beer
is a popular choice. The space is decorated with weird and wonderful
bric-a-brac, including Kewpie dolls. A second branch with the title of
Lucky Coq opened in the suburb of Windsor, which borders Prahran.
✉ *376 Brunswick St.* ☎ *03/9419–8600* ✉ *179 Chapel St., Windsor*
☎ *03/9525–1288* ▤ *MC, V.*

CHINESE

$$–$$$ ✗ **Flower Drum.** Superb Cantonese cuisine is the hallmark of one of Aus-
★ tralia's truly great Chinese restaurants, which is still receiving awards
after 32 years in business. The restrained elegance of the decor, deft-
ness of the service, and intelligence of the wine list puts most other
restaurants to shame. Simply ask your waiter for the day's special and
prepare yourself for a feast: perhaps crisp-skin Cantonese roast duck
served with plum gravy, succulent dumplings of prawn and flying-fish
roe, a perfectly steamed Murray cod, or huge Pacific oysters with black
bean sauce. ✉ *17 Market La., City Center* ☎ *03/9662–3655* ⌦ *Reser-
vations essential* ▤ *AE, DC, MC, V* ⊘ *No lunch Sun.*

ECLECTIC

$$–$$$ ✗ **Taxi.** Housed in an innovatively designed steel-and-glass dining room
★ above Federation Square, Taxi boasts both extraordinary food and
spectacular views over Melbourne. East meets West on a menu that

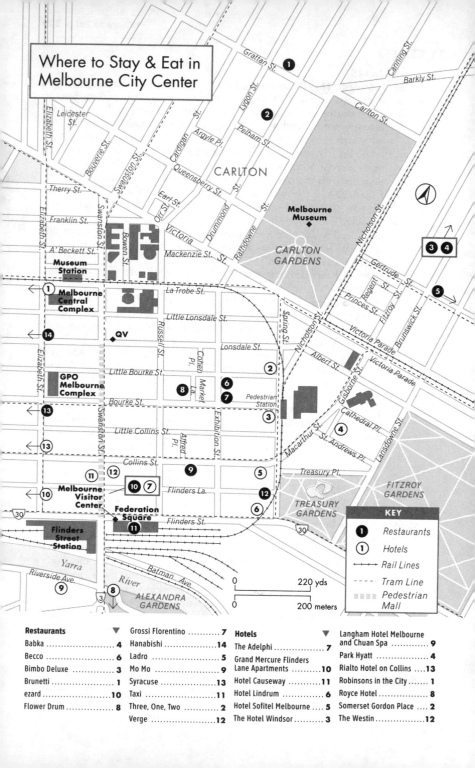

Where to Stay & Eat in Melbourne City Center

KEY

1 Restaurants
(1) Hotels
Rail Lines
Tram Line
Pedestrian Mall

combines Japanese flavors—tuna tataki chased by udon noodles in a mushroom hot pot—with such traditional European fare as pork cutlets with red cabbage and date sauce. Kingfish with shredded ginger, roasted duck, and an impressive wine list complete the mix. ✉*Level 1, Transport Hotel, Federation Sq., Flinders St. at St. Kilda Rd., City Center* ☎*03/9654–8808* ⌖*Reservations essential* ▭*AE, DC, MC, V* ⊘*Closed Sun.*

ITALIAN

$$$–$$$$ ✗**Grossi Florentino.** Since 1900, dining at Florentino has meant experiencing the height of Melbourne hospitality. After taking a seat in the famous mural room, with its wooden panels, Florentine murals, and hushed conversations, you can sample dishes like braised rabbit with muscatel and *farro* (a speltlike Italian grain), or tender veal shank with basil broth and black cabbage. Downstairs, the Grill Room has more businesslike fare, while the cellar bar is perfect for a glass of wine and pasta of the day. ✉*80 Bourke St., City Center* ☎*03/9662–1811* ⌖*Reservations essential* ▭*AE, DC, MC, V* ⊘*Closed Sun. No lunch Sat.*

$$$ ✗**Becco.** Every city center needs a place like this, with a drop-in bar, lively dining room, and groovy upstairs nightclub. At lunchtime, no-time-to-dawdle business types tuck into whitebait fritters, tagliolini with fresh tuna, and ricotta cake. Things get a little moodier at night, when a Campari and soda at the bar is an almost compulsory precursor to dinner. ✉*11–25 Crossley St., City Center* ☎*03/9663–3000* ⌖*Reservations essential* ▭*AE, DC, MC, V* ⊘*Closed Sun.*

$–$$ ✗**Ladro.** Rita Macalli's stellar Italian bistro emphasizes flavor over
★ starchy linen or stuffy attitude. Here eggplant is molded into gentle round *polpettes* (meatball-like mounds), lamb rump is scented with garlic and parsley and slow-roasted to impossible tenderness, and the service is as upbeat as the wine list. Delicious wood-fired pizzas are yet another reason to visit this suburban gem (thankfully, it's within walking distance from the city). ✉*224 Gertrude St., Fitzroy* ☎*03/9415–7575* ⌖*Reservations essential* ▭*MC, V* ⊘*Closed Mon. and Tues. No lunch.*

JAPANESE

$$ ✗**Hanabishi.** Touted as the city's best Japanese restaurant, Hanabi-
★ shi sits in slightly seedy King Street, an area known for its bars, club venues, and occasionally unsavory clientele. Featuring wooden floors, blue walls, and traditional ceramic serving trays, Hanabishi is the playground of Osakan chef Akio Soga, whose menu includes such gems as *hagi kimo* (salty steamed fish liver served with miso). The long list of hot and chilled sake, as well as the expansive wine list, ranges from reasonable to pricey. The former inexpensive bento boxes now contain the sought after wagu beef, but at A$28 each they are still considered a bargain and attract a lunchtime crowd. ✉*187 King St., City Center* ☎*03/9670–1167* ⌖*Reservations essential* ▭*AE, DC, MC, V* ⊘*Closed weekends.*

MEDITERRANEAN

$-$$ ✗ **Syracuse.** Some call this restaurant a wine lounge with good food due to the number of wines you can enjoy by the glass. Set in a 19th-century building in Melbourne's legal precinct, dining is best at lunchtime (dinner consists of a series of tasting dishes to enjoy with wine). A busy legal-eagle crowd gathers in the space decked out with red velvet curtains, mismatched antiques, and Greek columns. Try the house version of salade niçoise with kingfish instead of tuna, or the papardelle with rabbit. Save room for the stellar panna cotta for dessert. ✉ *23 Bank Pl., near Little Collins St.* ☎ *03/9670–1777* ☐ *AE, DC, MC, V.*

MIDDLE EASTERN

$$-$$$ ✗ **Mo Mo.** This exotic, pillow-laden basement restaurant re-opened in mid-2007 in the newly developed Grand Hyatt Hotel retail plaza, so it is virtually next door to its old digs. With more room to move, chef Greg Malouf has taken his pungent mix of spicy Middle Eastern dishes to a wider audience by adding a casual dining area and bar to accompany his more upscale restaurant. Favorites such as *bastourma* (cured beef) salad with wild arugula and goat cheese, and tagine (Moroccan stew) remain on the menu. ✉ *123 Collins St., City Center* ☎ *03/9650–0660* ☐ *AE, DC, MC, V* ⊘ *Closed Sun. No lunch Sat.*

MODERN AUSTRALIAN

$$$-$$$$ ✗ **ezard.** Chef Teage Ezard's adventurous take on fusion pushes the boundaries between Eastern and Western flavors. Some combinations may appear unusual, even reckless—crème brûlée flavored with roasted Jerusalem artichoke and truffle oil, for example—but everything works deliciously at this spot in the Adelphi hotel. ✉ *187 Flinders La., City Center* ☎ *03/9639–6811* ⟆ *Reservations essential* ☐ *AE, DC, MC, V* ⊘ *Closed Sun. No lunch Sat.*

$$-$$$ ✗ **Three, One, Two.** Taking the name from its street address, this new restaurant (on the site of the former, very popular, Mrs. Jones) has shot to fame in a very short time. It was not only named New Restaurant of the Year in the prestigious Age Newspaper Good Food Guide 2007, but chef Andrew McConnell was named Chef of the Year as well. The menu is a mixture of degustation (tasting menus) and à la carte dinners (with just four choices for appetizer, entrée, and dessert). There is also a light lunch and Sunday brunch. You might want to start dinner with the poached and fried five spice quail, celery, coriander, and cashew salad before moving on to the aromatic seafood braise of snapper, scampi, scallop, and clam, and finishing off with fresh white peach and champagne granita (a frozen dessert) with raspberries and almond milk. ✉ *312 Drummond St., Carlton, 3053* ☎ *03/9347–3312* ⟆ *Reservations essential* ☐ *AE, DC, MC, V* ⊘ *Closed Mon.*

$$ ✗ **Verge.** A favorite of the local arty set, and also of office workers dropping in for after-work drinks and dinner, this eatery serves up modern
★   French bistro food with a Japanese twist. Don't miss the Wagu beef tartare, and *gyoza* (Japanese dumpling) filled with scallops, soybeans, smoked tofu, and ginger, topped with a truffle dressing. The bar, which stays open later, serves coffee from 10 AM and has a range of light

meals. ⊠*1 Flinders La., City Center* ☎*03/9639–9500* ▤*AE, DC, MC, V* ☾*Closed Sun.*

MELBOURNE SUBURBS

CAFÉS

$–$$ ✗**Richmond Hill Café and Larder.** This bright and buzzy café–cum–produce store is popular for those seeking a late breakfast and brunch that extends well into the day. The bistro fare brims with wonderful flavors, from the chicken and mushroom pie to the crab risotto and avocado almond pagrattato. Desserts are mouth-wateringly simple and impossible to resist. After you've eaten, pick up some marvelous cheese and country-style bread from the adjoining cheese room and grocery. ⊠*48–50 Bridge Rd., Richmond* ☎*03/9421–2808* ▤*AE, DC, MC, V* ☾*No dinner.*

ITALIAN

$$–$$$ ✗**Café di Stasio.** This upscale bistro treads a very fine line between mannered elegance and decadence. A sleek marble bar and modishly ravaged walls contribute to the sense that you've stepped into a scene from *La Dolce Vita*. Happily, the restaurant is as serious about its food as its sense of style. Crisply roasted duck is now a local legend, chargrilled baby squid is a sheer delight, and the pasta is always al dente. If the amazingly delicate lobster omelet is on the menu, do yourself a favor and order it. ⊠*31 Fitzroy St., St. Kilda, 3182* ☎*03/9525–3999* ⌖*Reservations essential* ▤*AE, DC, MC, V.*

Fodor'sChoice
★

$$ ✗**Caffe e Cucina.** It's easy to imagine you're in Italy when dining at this always-packed restaurant/café. If you're looking for a quintessential Italian dining experience, this is it. Fashionable, look-at-me types flock here for coffee and pastry downstairs, or for more leisurely meals upstairs in the warm, woody dining room. Try the melt-in-your-mouth gnocchi, or calamari San Andrea (lightly floured and deep fried), but save room for dessert—the tiramisu is even better looking than the crowd. Reservations are essential upstairs, but not accepted downstairs. ⊠*581 Chapel St., South Yarra* ☎*03/9827–4139* ▤*AE, DC, MC, V.*

$–$$ ✗**Melbourne Wine Room Restaurant.** Although the Wine Room itself buzzes day and night with young, black-clad types, the adjoining restaurant is far less frenetic. Elegantly whitewashed, it casts a moody glow that turns dinner for two into a romantic tête-à-tête. Located in the George Hotel, a grand old building, the restaurant has a gloriously down-at-the-heels sense of glamour. The Italianate fare, at once confident and determinedly single-minded, runs from powerful risottos to forceful pastas and grills that make you sit up and take notice. ⊠*125 Fitzroy St., St. Kilda* ☎*03/9525–5599* ⌖*Reservations essential* ▤*AE, DC, MC, V* ☾*No lunch Mon.–Thurs.*
★

$ ✗**Café a Taglio.** Rarely has Roman-style pizza been this delicious, or this groovy. Although there's a blackboard menu of pastas and other Italian dishes, regulars prefer to cruise the counter, choosing from the giant squares of pizza on display. Toppings include ricotta, eggplant, and marinated mushrooms with truffle oil. Following popular

4

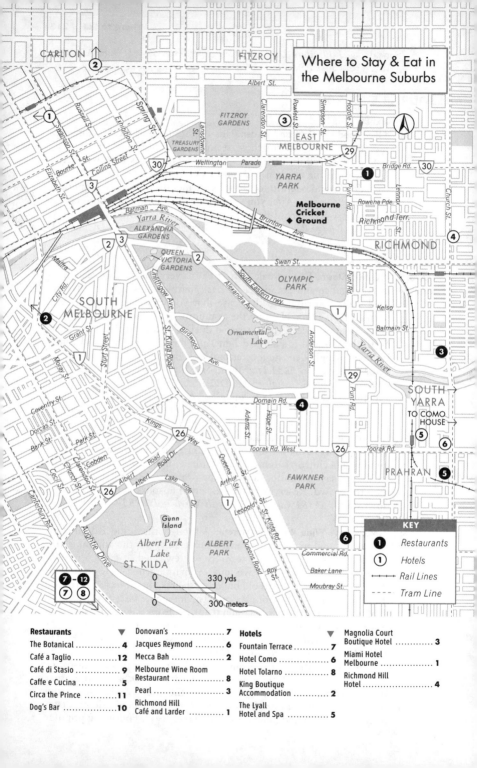

Where to Stay & Eat in the Melbourne Suburbs

CARLTON

FITZROY

FITZROY GARDENS

Albert St.

TREASURY GARDENS

EAST MELBOURNE

Spring St.

Exhibition St.

Russell St.

Swanston St.

Elizabeth St.

Bourke St.

Collins Street

Lansdowne St.

Clarendon St.

Powlett St.

Simpson St.

Hoddle St.

Wellington Parade

Bridge Rd.

YARRA PARK

Melbourne Cricket Ground ◆

Rowena Pde.

Richmond Terr.

Lennox St.

Church St.

Batman Ave.

Yarra River

ALEXANDRA GARDENS

Brunton Ave.

RICHMOND

QUEEN VICTORIA GARDENS

Swan St.

OLYMPIC PARK

Punt Rd.

Kelso

Balmain St.

City Rd.

Malifra

SOUTH MELBOURNE

Grant St.

Sturt Street

Moray St.

St. Kilda Road

Linlithgow Ave.

Birdwood Ave.

Alexandra Ave.

South Eastern Hwy.

Ornamental Lake

Anderson St.

Yarra River

SOUTH YARRA

TO COMO HOUSE

Coventry St.

Dorcas St.

Bank St.

Park St.

Clarendon St.

Cecil St.

Church St.

Cobden

Kings Way

Albert Road

Albert Road Dr.

Lakeside Dr.

Queens St.

Arthur St.

Domain Rd.

Hope St.

Adams St.

Toorak Rd. West

Toorak Rd.

PRAHRAN

FAWKNER PARK

Leopold St.

St. Kilda Rd.

Canterbury Rd.

Aughtie Drive

Gunn Island

Albert Park Lake

ST. KILDA

ALBERT PARK

Queens Road

Roy St.

Commercial Rd.

Baker Lane

Moubray St.

0   330 yds
0   300 meters

KEY

- ❶ Restaurants
- ① Hotels
- ┼┼┼┼ Rail Lines
- ╌╌╌ Tram Line

Restaurants ▼

The Botanical 4
Café a Taglio 12
Café di Stasio 9
Caffe e Cucina 5
Circa the Prince 11
Dog's Bar 10
Donovan's 7
Jacques Reymond 6
Mecca Bah 2
Melbourne Wine Room Restaurant 8
Pearl 3
Richmond Hill Café and Larder 1

Hotels ▼

Fountain Terrace 7
Hotel Como 6
Hotel Tolarno 8
King Boutique Accommodation 2
The Lyall Hotel and Spa 5
Magnolia Court Boutique Hotel 3
Miami Hotel Melbourne 1
Richmond Hill Hotel 4

demand it is now open for breakfast on weekends. ⊠*157 Fitzroy St., St. Kilda* ☎*03/9534–1344* ♤*Reservations not accepted* ▤*AE, MC, V.*

MEDITERRANEAN

$–$$ ✕**Dog's Bar.** With its blazing fires, artfully smoky walls, and striking wrought-iron chandeliers, this restaurant has a lived-in, neighborly look. The regulars at the bar look as if they grew up there, while the young, artistic-looking groups who mooch around the front courtyard seem so satisfied you can practically hear them purr. Wine is taken very seriously here, and you can find some particularly fine local pinot noir and sauvignon blanc at prices that won't break the bank. The specials— a great value at A$16—include a glass of wine. Night owls will love the tasty (but limited) supper menu from 11 PM each night. ⊠*54 Acland St., St. Kilda* ☎*03/9525–3599* ♤*Reservations not accepted* ▤*AE, DC, MC, V.*

MIDDLE EASTERN

$ ✕**Mecca Bah.** Chef Cath Claringbold serves up delicious chicken and green-olive tagine, lemony grills, and sumac-dusted salads at this harbor-front eatery. It's the sort of good, honest food that mum would've served…if she were from Lebanon. In the evening you can enjoy splendid sunset views of the city skyline and the bay, or watch the hundreds of Melburnians who flock to Docklands every weekend. ⊠*55A New Quay Promenade, Docklands* ☎*03/9642–1300* ♤*Reservations not accepted* ▤*AE, DC, MC, V.*

MODERN AUSTRALIAN

$$$$ ✕**Jacques Reymond.** French and Asian flavors blend delightfully at this
Fodor's Choice glamorous, century-old Victorian mansion-turned-eatery, which has
★ picked up some prestigious awards in recent years. The wine list is the stuff an oenophile dreams of, and the Burgundian-born chef uses the finest Australian produce to create such classics as seared venison and tamarind sauce, and crispy ravioli of blue swimmer crab. There are two-, three-, and four-course menus (ranging from A$75 to A$125) and seven-course degustation menus (A$140) which can be teamed with wonderful wines (A$215). There is also a vegetarian seven-course degustation option. ⊠*78 Williams Rd., Prahran* ☎*03/9525–2178* ♤*Reservations essential* ▤*AE, DC, MC, V* ☉*Closed Sun. and Mon. No lunch Sat.*

$$$ ✕**Donovan's.** Grab a window table at this bay-side hot spot (housed in the former 1920s bathing pavillion), and enjoy wide-open views of St. Kilda beach and its passing parade of rollerbladers, skateboarders, dog walkers, and ice-cream lickers. Chef Robert Castellani serves wonderful pasta and risotto, a thoroughly delicious fish soup, and a memorable hot chocolate soufflé with espresso. Owners Kevin and Gail Donovan are such natural hosts you may feel like bunking down on the plush pillows near the cozy fireplace. ⊠*40 Jacka Blvd., St. Kilda* ☎*03/9534–8221* ♤*Reservations essential* ▤*AE, DC, MC, V.*

$$$ ✕**Pearl.** Geoff Lindsay's restaurant, with its white and shimmery interior, is a favorite hangout for Melbourne's beautiful people. But it's also

home to some truly innovative dishes, such as watermelon-and-feta salad with satiny tomato jelly, and a sour yellow curry of Queensland scallops. ☒ *631–633 Church St., Richmond* ☏ *03/9421–4599* ▤ *AE, DC, MC, V* ⊘ *No lunch Sat.*

$$–$$$ ✕ **The Botanical.** From one side it looks like a bottle shop—and it is.
★ From the other it looks like a modern bistro, serving chateaubriand in an opened-out hotel space—and that it is, too. Here, Chef Paul Wilson redefines the art of eating out with a casual Aussie ambience and loads of flavor. Retro touches mix effortlessly with 21st-century choices; note the menu changes daily but may feature sticky pork salad with Vietnamese herbs, green papaya, and chilli caramel. ☒ *169 Domain Rd., South Yarra* ☏ *03/9820–7888* ⚁ *Reservations essential* ▤ *AE, DC, MC, V.*

$$–$$$ ✕ **Circa the Prince.** Egyptian tea lights, white leather lounges, and walls draped with organza and silk contribute to this restaurant's Arabian Nights feel. Here chef Andrew McConnell serves Mod-Oz dishes with a European flair such as slow-cooked duck wrapped in Tunisian brik pastry, alongside an exhaustive and tempting wine list. ☒ *2 Acland St., St. Kilda* ☏ *03/9536–1122* ⚁ *Reservations essential* ▤ *AE, DC, MC, V.*

WHERE TO STAY

WHAT IT COSTS IN AUSTRALIAN DOLLARS				
$$$$	$$$	$$	$	¢
FOR TWO PEOPLE	over A$300	A$201–A$300	A$151–A$200	A$100–A$150	under A$100

Prices are for two people in a standard double room in high season, including tax and service, based on the European Plan (with no meals) unless otherwise noted.

CITY CENTER

$$$$ ⌷ **The Adelphi.** This chic, design-conscious boutique hotel is decorated with minimalist-style furnishings of brushed-steel, maple, and glass. The best rooms are those at the front (with room numbers ending in 01). The pièce de résistance is the top-floor, 80-foot lap pool, which has a glass bottom jutting out from the edge of the building: bathers literally swim into space. Top-floor bar views, framed by the Gothic spires of St. Paul's, are heavenly. The restaurant ezard serves daring Mod-Oz fusion fare. ☒ *187 Flinders La., City Center, 3000* ☏ *03/9650–7555* ✎ info@adelphi.com.au ⊕ *www.adelphi.com.au* ⥲ *26 rooms* ⚭ *In-room: broadband, Wi-Fi. In-hotel: restaurant, bars, pool, gym, laundry service, no-smoking rooms, parking (fee)* ▤ *AE, DC, MC, V* ⏀ *CP.*

$$$$ ⌷ **Hotel Lindrum.** Housed in the Heritage-listed Lindrum family bil-
★ liards center, a short walk from Federation Square, this is one of Melbourne's savviest boutique properties. Rooms are spacious, with high ceilings and timber floors. A smart restaurant, cozy cigar bar, and lounge with an open fire are the perfect settings for sipping local wines. Flinders Lane, lined with chic bars and eateries, is a short

stroll away. ✉ *26 Flinders St., City Center, 3000* ☎ *03/9668–1111* ✐ reservations@hotellindrum.com.au ⊕ *www.hotellindrum.com.au* ⤴ *59 rooms* ♿ *In-room: safe, refrigerator, ethernet. In-hotel: restaurant, bar, laundry service, parking (no fee), no-smoking rooms* ▭ *AE, DC, MC, V.*

$$$$ ▣ **Hotel Sofitel Melbourne.** Designed by world-famous architect I. M. Pei, this half of the twin-towered, 50-story Collins Place complex combines glamour and excellent facilities with a prime location. Rooms, which begin on the 35th floor, are built around a mirrored central atrium and have exceptional views. The 35th-floor Atrium bar and Café La restaurant are great places to enjoy the scenery that stretches for miles. The hotel's rooms and views are among the best in town. ✉ *25 Collins St., City Center, 3000* ☎ *03/9653–0000 or 1300/656565* ⊕ *www. sofitelmelbourne.com.au* ⤴ *311 rooms, 52 suites* ♿ *In-room: safe, dial-up. In-hotel: 2 restaurants, bars, gym, laundry service, no-smoking rooms* ▭ *AE, DC, MC, V.*

$$$$ ▣ **The Hotel Windsor.** This century-old aristocrat of Melbourne hotels
★ combines Victorian-era character with modern comforts. Plush rooms have Laura Ashley–style wall coverings and rosewood furnishings, although the marble bathrooms are modest in size. Standard rooms are also small; if you need space, book one of the vast Victorian suites, or a two-room executive suite. The 111 Spring Street Restaurant serves Continental-style dishes in a formal setting. The hotel commands a position opposite the State Houses of Parliament close to theaters, parks, and fine shops. ✉ *103 Spring St., City Center, 3000* ☎ *03/9633–6000* ✐ reservations@thewindsor.com.au ⊕ *www. thewindsor.com.au* ⤴ *180 rooms, 20 suites* ♿ *In-room: ethernet. In-hotel: restaurant, bars, gym, laundry service, parking (no fee), no-smoking rooms* ▭ *AE, DC, MC, V.*

$$$$ ▣ **Langham Hotel Melbourne and Chuan Spa.** In the bustling Southgate
★ river district, the Langham (formerly Sheraton Hotel Southbank) has a terrific vantage point—the Melba Brasserie—from which to view passing pedestrian and Yarra River traffic. Autumn tones decorate the rooms, as do marble bathrooms, and a cascading fountain bubbles in the hotel's elegant foyer. This hotel is popular with business travelers. ✉ *1 Southgate Ave., Southbank, 3006* ☎ *03/8696–8888* ✐ mel. resv@langhamhotels.com ⊕ *www.langhamhotels.com* ⤴ *387 rooms, 11 suites* ♿ *In-room: safe, dial-up. In-hotel: restaurant, bar, pool, gym, spa, laundry service, no-smoking rooms* ▭ *AE, DC, MC, V.*

$$$$ ▣ **Park Hyatt.** Set right next to Fitzroy Gardens and opposite St. Pat-
Fodor's Choice rick's Cathedral, this elegant hotel overlooks some of the city's most
★ beautiful historic buildings. Warm colors, rich wood paneling, and art deco–style furnishings adorn the rooms—all of which have walk-in wardrobes, king-size beds, Italian marble bathrooms, and roomy, modern work spaces. Suites are even more luxurious, some with fireplaces, terraces, and hot tubs. The seven-level radii restaurant and bar is artsy and chic; and contemporary artworks by international talents are on exhibit throughout the hotel (some are for sale). ✉ *1 Parliament Sq., City Center, 3000* ☎ *03/9224–1234* ✐ Melbourne@hyatt. com.au ⊕ *www.Hyatt.com* ⤴ *216 rooms, 24 suites* ♿ *In-room: safe,*

broadband, hot tubs (some). In-hotel: restaurant, room service, bar, pool, gym, spa, concierge, laundry service, public Internet, parking (fee) ⊟*AE, DC, MC, V.*

$$$$ 🏨 **The Westin.** Overlooking Regent Place and City Square, the Westin sits in the heart of the city, a stone's throw from Federation Square, Southbank, and the boutique-lined alleys of Flinders Lane and Little Collins Street. Sophisticated and contemporary, the hotel features a spectacular lobby, an impressive collection of avant-garde Australian artwork, stunning rooms with Juliet balconies overlooking the city, a martini bar, a wellness center (with lap pool, gym, hot tub, and sauna), and the Allegro restaurant. ⊠*Regent Pl., 205 Collins St., City Center, 3000* ☎*03/9635–2222 or 1800/656535* ⊕*www.westin.com.au* ⬩*262 rooms* ⚐*In-room: safe, broadband, hot tubs (some). In-hotel: restaurant, bar, laundry service, no-smoking rooms, Wi-Fi, pool, spa, steam, gym, sauna* ⊟*AE, DC, MC, V.*

$$$–$$$$ 🏨 **Royce Hotel.** Built in a former Rolls-Royce showroom, the rooms in this elegant, 1920s-style hotel are suffused with natural light. A multi-million dollar upgrade in 2006 added two extra floors of accommodation. Luxurious touches, such as Italian marble bathrooms and 42-inch plasma TVs, have been added to many of the existing rooms and every room now has broadband. Choose from one-bedroom suites, suites with hot tubs, two-story mezzanine rooms, and others with balconies. All of the really good rooms have views of the Melbourne skyline and the Royal Botanic Gardens. The refurbished internal courtyard is now an even more pleasant spot to relax with a coffee and the newspaper. The amberroom bar schedules live jazz on weekends, and the dish restaurant is on-site. ⊠*379 St. Kilda Rd., City Center, 3004* ☎*03/9677–9900 or 1800/820909* ✐reservations@roycehotels.com.au ⊕*www.royce hotels.com.au* ⬩*71 rooms* ⚐*In-room: kitchen, refrigerator, hot tubs (some), Wi-Fi (some), broadband. In-hotel: restaurant, bar, laundry service, parking (no fee), no-smoking rooms, Wi-Fi in lobby and restaurant* ⊟*AE, DC, MC, V.*

$$–$$$$ 🏨 **Rialto Hotel on Collins.** Within walking distance of the Crown Casino and Southgate, this 19th-century, European-style hotel has a dramatic lobby and six-story historic atrium. The suites here are spacious and decorated in soothing beige and citrus tones; some have Juliet balconies, and all have extras like hair dryers, tea- and coffee-making supplies, and fluffy bathrobes. For the ultimate luxury, try booking the Courtyard Suite, with its dramatic turreted bedroom. Guests who want a real bird's-eye view of the city need only walk next door to access the Melbourne Observation Deck. ⊠*495 Collins St., City Center, 3000* ☎*03/9620–9111* ⊕*www.rialtohotel.com.au* ⬩*244 suites* ⚐*In-room: safe. In-hotel: restaurant, bars, pool, sauna, Jacuzzi, laundry facilities, laundry service, public Internet (broadband)* ⊟*AE, DC, MC, V.*

$$$ 🏨 **Grand Mercure Flinders Lane Apartments.** The smallest of the city's upscale hotels, the Grand Mercure has a central location and a mix of lovely one- and two-bedroom suites, which sleep four to eight people. Rooms are beautifully furnished and decorated in apricot, burgundy,

and pale-green tones. All have kitchenettes with microwaves and refrigerators. Guests have use of a small private terrace on the sixth floor, inspired by the Renaissance gardens of Italy. ⊠*321 Flinders La., City Center, 3000* ☎*03/9629–4088* ✐grandmercurehotelmel@bigpond. com ⊕*www.mercure.com* ↩*57 suites* ♿*In-room: kitchen, refrigerator, some broadband, some Wi-Fi. In-hotel: gym, laundry service, parking (fee), no-smoking rooms, Wi-Fi* ▤*AE, DC, MC, V.*

$$$ ⊞**Hotel Causeway.** Set among fashion boutiques, restaurants, and a host of hip cafés in the alleyways off Little Collins Street is this small, stylish hotel. The property is a two-minute walk from the upscale department store David Jones, and the lovely Block Arcade. Rooms have cream-color walls, deep-walnut furnishings, and wine-color upholstery. Three split-level duplexes, which sleep four, are perfect for families. For a breath of fresh air, you can relax on the roof-top terrace. ⊠*275 Little Collins St., City Center, 3000* ☎*03/9660–8888* ⊕*www.causeway.com.au* ↩*42 rooms, 3 duplexes* ♿*In-room: dial-up. In-hotel: restaurant, bar, gym, laundry facilities, no-smoking rooms* ▤*AE, DC, MC, V* ⦿*CP.*

$$–$$$ ⊞**Robinsons in the City.** Melbourne's tiniest and possibly quaintest hotel occupies a converted 1850s bakery. The six beautifully furnished rooms have private bathrooms and are decorated with artworks from around the world. New owners have brightened up the rooms with fresh coats of paint, new air conditioners, and the latest digital TVs. Guests without computers can check their e-mail using the office laptop. Homemade breakfasts—including fruit, smoked trout, sausage, bacon, eggs, and toast—are a real highlight. ⊠*405 Spencer St., at Batman St., City Center, 3000* ☎*03/9329–2552* ⊕*www.robinsonsinthecity.com.au* ↩*6 rooms* ♿*In-room: Wi-Fi. In-hotel: bar, laundry facilities, parking (no fee), no elevator* ▤*AE, DC, MC, V* ⦿*BP.*

$–$$ ⊞**Somerset Gordon Place.** This historic 1883 structure is one of the most
★ interesting and comfortable apartment hotels in the city. It's just steps from the Parliament building and is surrounded by excellent restaurants and theaters. The modern, comfortable accommodations contain washing machines, dryers, and dishwashers. The studios and one- and two-bedroom apartments face a courtyard with a 60-foot pool and a century-old palm tree. ⊠*24 Little Bourke St., City Center, 3000* ☎*03/9663–2888* ⊕*www.somersetgordonplace.com* ↩*64 apartments* ♿*In-room: kitchen, broadband, Wi-Fi. In-hotel: pool, gym, laundry facilities, laundry service, no-smoking rooms* ▤*AE, DC, MC, V.*

THE FRINGES OF THE CITY

$$$$ ⊞**Hotel Como.** With its opulence and funky modern furnishings, this lux-
★ ury hotel is as popular with business travelers as it is with visiting artists and musicians. Gray marble and chrome are prominent throughout the pop art–meets–art deco interior. Suites have king-size beds and bathrobes; several even have Jacuzzis. Some of the third-floor suites have access to private Japanese gardens, while others have fully equipped kitchenettes. Outstanding services (including free limousine rides into the city each day) and a swank clientele make this one of the best picks on the city's fringe. Good restaurants are only a short walk away. ⊠*630 Chapel St., South Yarra, 3141* ☎*03/9825–2222* ✐reservations@como.mirvac.

com.au ⊕*www.mirvachotels.com. au* ⌖*107 suites* ⌕*In-room: safe, kitchen (some), dial-up. In-hotel: room service, bar, pool, gym, laundry service, no-smoking rooms* ⊟*AE, DC, MC, V.*

$$$$ ▣ **The Lyall Hotel and Spa.** The spacious one- and two-bedroom suites at this exclusive hotel come

with all the luxuries: CD and DVD players, velour bathrobes and slippers, gourmet minibars, and a pillow "menu." The in-house spa offers a full range of massages, facials, and body treatments (try the lime-and-ginger salt glow); the champagne bar is the perfect place to relax after a day of sightseeing. Mini art galleries adorn each floor of the hotel. ⊠*14 Murphy St., South Yarra, 3141* ☎*03/9868–8222* ✉reservations@thelyall.com ⊕*www.thelyall.com* ⌖*40 suites* ⌕*In-room: hot tubs (some), dial-up, Wi-Fi (free). In-hotel: restaurant, bar, gym, spa, bicycles, laundry facilities, laundry service, parking (fee), no-smoking rooms, Wi-Fi (free)* ⊟*AE, DC, MC, V.*

$$–$$$ ▣ **Fountain Terrace.** Set on a tree-lined street in one of Melbourne's picturesque bay-side areas, this 1880 property has seven guest suites, all of them immaculate and furnished with opulent antiques. Each suite is named after a prominent Australian figure; the Henry Lawson, for example (named for a famous Aussie poet), is decorated in blue-and-gold brocade and has a hot tub. The Dame Nellie Melba suite is the most spacious and has French doors opening onto a private balcony. Guests have complimentary access to the nearby St. Kilda Salt Water Sea Baths, a complex with a large pool, hydrotherapy spa, and steam room. ⊠*28 Mary St., St. Kilda West, 3182* ☎*03/9593–8123* ⊕*www. fountainterrace.com.au* ⌖*7 suites* ⌕*In-room: no phone. In-hotel: public Internet* ⊟*AE, DC, MC, V* ⧖*BP.*

$$–$$$ ▣ **Magnolia Court Boutique Hotel.** Although its name might imply modernity, the rooms and furnishings are slightly Victorian (and spotless) at this small inn. Standard rooms are modest in size, but the suites have more space and comfort at just a moderately higher rate. A family suite with a kitchen and space for six is also available. The hotel is separated from the city center by Fitzroy Gardens and is about a 12-minute walk from Spring Street. ⊠*101 Powlett St., East Melbourne, 3002* ☎*03/9419–4222* ⊕*www.magnolia-court.com.au* ⌖*26 rooms, 4 suites, 1 cottage* ⌕*In-room: safe, kitchen (some), dial-up. In-hotel: laundry service* ⊟*AE, DC, MC, V.*

$–$$ ▣ **Hotel Tolarno.** Set in the heart of St. Kilda's café, bar, and club precinct, Hotel Tolarno was once owned by artists who ran a gallery out of the space. Even today the place has an artistic bent; many of the rooms and common spaces are decorated with paintings by students of the Victorian College of the Arts (VCA) and Royal Melbourne Institute of TAFE (RMIT). The color schemes here are a bit garish (red, purple, and orange dominate), and the furnishings are basic, but this is a friendly, funky place to stay (or to have a bite in Tolarno's new Mirka restaurant). ✉ *42 Fitzroy St., St. Kilda, 3182* ☎ *03/9537–0200* ✍ mail@hoteltolarno.com. au ⊕ *www.hoteltolarno.com.au* ⇨ *35 rooms* ♿ *In-room: kitchen, Wi-Fi (some). In-hotel: restaurant, laundry facilities, laundry service* ▭ *AE, DC, MC, V.*

$–$$ ★ ⛱ **King Boutique Accommodation.** Overlooking the Carlton Gardens, this regal Italianate mansion con-

> ## TRASHY FILMS
>
> There's no such thing as a bad movie when it's screened at the Junkyard Cinema in Melbourne's hip and quirky Fitzroy neighborhood. This outdoor cinema screens "cult" classics every Sunday night during summer. Even if one person's cult classic is another's worst celluloid nightmare, one thing's certain—you won't see any glossy new releases here. ⊕ *www. junkyardcinema.com.au*

tains three meticulously decorated bedrooms, each featuring chic modern furniture and gorgeous picture windows. The two first-floor rooms have marble bathrooms. The common lounge has TV, telephone, and a library with books and magazines. A sumptuous breakfast is served every morning in the dining room. ✉ *122 Nicholson St., Fitzroy, 3065* ☎ *03/9417–1113* ⊕ *www. kingaccomm.com.au* ⇨ *3 rooms* ♿ *In-room: no phone, no TV. In-hotel: parking (free street parking permit), no-smoking rooms* ▭ *AE, DC, MC, V* ⊘ *BP.*

$ ⛱ **Richmond Hill Hotel.** Just a short ride from the city center (on the No. 79 tram), this boutique hotel occupies a regal, garden skirted mansion. Lodgings here include single and double rooms with shared bathrooms, doubles with in-room bathrooms, and two- and three-bedroom apartments. The basic dorm rooms are used primarily for school groups. There are an Internet room, garden terrace, bar, and guest lounge with newspapers and complimentary tea and coffee. ✉ *353 Church St., Richmond, 3121* ☎ *03/9428–6501* ⊕ *www.richmondhillhotel.com.au* ⇨ *60 rooms* ♿ *In-room: Wi-Fi. In-hotel: bar, laundry facilities* ▭ *AE, DC, MC, V* ⊘ *CP.*

¢–$ ⛱ **Miami Hotel Melbourne.** Like a Motel 6, only fancier, Miami Hotel is an excellent value for the budget- and style-conscious. Accommodations range from budget rooms with shared bathrooms to newer rooms with air-conditioning and TVs suitable for doubles, triples, and families. There are three TV lounges with cable movies and breakfast can be provided on request. This efficiently run hotel and its friendly staff have picked up top accolades, and has been short-listed by the Victorian Tourism Awards. ✉ *13 Hawke St., at King St., West Melbourne, 3003* ☎ *03/9321–2444 or 1800/132333* ⊕ *www.themiami.com.au* ⇨ *81 rooms, 41 with bath* ♿ *In-room: no a/c (some), no TV (some), dial-up. In-hotel: laundry facilities, public Internet* ▭ *MC, V.*

NIGHTLIFE & THE ARTS

THE ARTS

Melbourne Events, available from tourist outlets, is a comprehensive monthly guide to what's happening in town. For a complete listing of performing arts events, galleries, and film, consult the "EG" (Entertainment Guide) supplement in the Friday edition of the *Age* newspaper. The *Age's* daily "Metro" section has a comprehensive listing of city events such as gallery openings, theater performances, public talks, bands, workshops, and festivals in its "If You Do One Thing Today" pages. Tourism Victoria hosts a fantastic Web site (⊕ www.visitmelbourne.com), detailing all of Melbourne's upcoming and current events. The free local music magazine *Beat* is available at cafés, stores, markets, and bars. *Brother Sister* is the local gay paper.

DANCE

In the 2,000-seat State Theatre at the Arts Centre, the **Australian Ballet** (⊠ *Victorian Arts Centre, 100 St. Kilda Rd., Southbank* ☎ *03/9669–2700 Ballet, 13–6100 Ticketmaster7*) stages five programs annually and presents visiting celebrity dancers from around the world.

MUSIC

The **Hamer Hall** (⊠ *The Arts Centre, 100 St. Kilda Rd., Southbank* ☎ *03/9281–8000*) stages classy concerts. Big-name, crowd-drawing contemporary artists perform at **Melbourne Park** (⊠ *Batman Ave., City Center* ☎ *03/9286–1600*).

The **Melbourne Symphony Orchestra** (⊠ *Victorian Arts Centre, 100 St. Kilda Rd., Southbank* ☎ *13–6100 Ticketmaster7*) performs year-round in the 2,600-seat Hamer Hall.

Open-air concerts take place December through March at the **Sidney Myer Music Bowl** (⊠ *King's Domain near Swan St. Bridge, South Melbourne* ☎ *13–6100 Ticketmaster7*).

Summer Fun in the Parks (⊕ *www.visitmelbourne.com*), which is open January–March on Friday, Saturday, and Sunday evenings, brings green spaces around the city alive with the sound of world music, jazz, blues, soul, and hip-hop. Venues include Birrarung Marr, Fitzroy Gardens, Royal Botanic Gardens, Treasury Gardens, Carlton Gardens, and Federation Square. Stalls sell food and drinks; most concerts are free.

OPERA

The **Opera Australia** (⊠ *The Arts Centre, 100 St. Kilda Rd., Southbank* ☎ *03/9686–7477*) has regular seasons, often with performances by world-renowned stars. The length and time of seasons vary, but all performances take place in the Melbourne Concert Hall.

THEATER

The **Half-Tix** (⊠ *Melbourne Town Hall, Swanston and Collins Sts., City Center* ☎ *03/9650–9420*) ticket booth in the Melbourne Town Hall sells tickets to theater attractions at half price on performance days. It's open Monday and Saturday 10–2, Tuesday–Thursday 11–6, and Friday 11–6:30. Sales are cash only.

The **Melbourne Theatre Company** (✉ *129 Ferrars St., Southbank* ☎ *03/9684–4500* ⊕ *www.mtc.com.au*) is the city's first and most successful theater company. The two annual seasons host classical, international, and Australian performances at the **Russell Street Theatre** (✉ *129 Ferrars St., Southbank* ☎ *1300/136166*). The city's second-largest company, the **Playbox at the CUB Malthouse Company** (✉ *113 Sturt St., Southbank*

WORD OF MOUTH

"Melbourne is quite safe in the central business district but keep away from Swanston Street near the Railway Station after about 7 PM. The city is well lit and heaps of people are around at night. Lots of trams take you up and down the main and across the streets of Melbourne. Its really pretty at night. Its also safe to walk along South gate up to the Casino. It's a lovely walk along the Yarra."

–RosieR

☎ *03/9685–5111*), stages about 10 new or contemporary productions a year. The CUB Malthouse theater is a flexible space designed for drama, dance, and circus companies.

Revues and plays are staged at the **Comedy Theatre**, which along with the Princess, Regent, and Forum theaters, is owned by the Marriner's Theatre company and often uses the same telephone number. (✉ *240 Exhibition St., City Center* ☎ *03/9299–9800 or 03/9299–9500*). **Her Majesty's Theatre** (✉ *219 Exhibition St., City Center* ☎ *03/8643–3300, Box Office 1300/795012*), which opened in 1886, hosts international musicals like *Fiddler on the Roof, Chicago,* and the occasional opera. **La Mama** (✉ *205 Faraday St., Carlton* ☎ *03/9347–6142*) puts on innovative and contemporary productions in a bohemian theater. The **Princess Theatre** (✉ *163 Spring St., City Center* ☎ *03/9299–9800 or 03/9299–9500*), an ornate, 1886 wedding cake–style edifice refurbished for the late-1980s hit *Phantom of the Opera,* is the home of Broadway-style blockbusters. The **Regent Theatre** (✉ *191 Collins St., City Center* ☎ *03/9299–9800 or 03/9299–9500*) presents mainstream productions. **Theatreworks** (✉ *14 Acland St., St. Kilda* ☎ *03/9534–3388*) concentrates on contemporary Australian plays.

NIGHTLIFE

BARS & COCKTAIL LOUNGES

Crown Casino, Melbourne's first gambling center, has blackjack, roulette, and poker machines. There are also dozens of restaurants, retail shops, bars, and two nightclubs open until late. Look for the impressive water and lighting displays on the first floor. The casino is on the south bank of the Yarra. ✉ *Riverside Ave., Southbank* ☎ *03/9292–8888* ⊕ *www.crowncasino.com.au* ☽ *Daily 24 hrs.*

Angelucci's (✉ *500 Chapel St., South Yarra* ☎ *03/9826–3086*) is a sophisticated lounge bar, with an A-list clientele to match. **The Atrium**

(⊠25 Collins St., City Center ☎03/9653–0000), a cocktail bar on the 35th floor of the Hotel Sofitel, has spectacular views. **Cookie** (⊠252 Swanston St., City Center ☎03/9663–7660), in a huge warehouse-style space with a balcony, focuses on imported beer and great Thai food. Find classic charm in the heart of the Windsor Hotel at the **Cricketer's Bar** (⊠103 Spring St., City Center ☎03/9633–6000).

In addition to being a hallowed live music venue, the **Esplanade Hotel** (⊠11 Upper Esplanade, St. Kilda ☎03/9534–0211) is a historic pub—built in 1878—listed with the National Trust. The **George Hotel Bar** (⊠Fitzroy and Grey Sts., St. Kilda ☎03/9525–5599) is in a superb 19th-century building. Reminiscent of Hollywood opulence, **Gin Palace** (⊠190 Little Collins St., City Center ☎03/9654–0533) has more than enough types of martinis to satisfy any taste. Enter from Russell Street. The **Hairy Canary** (⊠212 Little Collins St., City Center ☎03/9654–2471) is one of the grooviest places in the city, but it's standing room only unless you get here early. Nosh includes tapas and pizzas.

Lexington Bar (⊠Level 2, GPO Melbourne, between Elizabeth, Bourke, and Little Bourke Sts., City Center ☎03/9662–2909) is the definitive big-city bar housed in the stunning heritage GPO Building. The artsy, laid-back patrons of **Loop Bar** (⊠23 Meyers Pl., South Yarra ☎03/9654–0500) watch avant-garde documentaries as they drink. Antique leather sofas and cigars characterize the classy milieu at the **Melbourne Supper Club** (⊠161 Spring St., City Center ☎03/9654–6300).

The **Money Order Office (M.O.O.)** (⊠Basement, Drivers La. behind 318 Little Bourke St., City Center ☎03/9639–3020) is a sophisticated spot. Stop by the **Polly** (⊠401 Brunswick St., Fitzroy ☎03/9417–0880), which combines antique red-velvet lounges, art deco mirrors, one of Melbourne's best wine lists, and colorful and quirky clientele with a magnificent fish tank, for which it is famous. **Revolver Upstairs** (⊠229 Chapel St., Prahran ☎03/9521–4644) caters to the young. The **Undertaker** (⊠329 Burwood Rd., Hawthorn ☎03/9818–3944) is the site of what was once an actual undertaker's parlor. Today the building contains a very live bar and restaurant. The **Xchange** (⊠119 Commercial Rd., South Yarra ☎03/9867–5144) is a popular gay bar in the busy gay district of Prahran.

A FUNNY NIGHT OUT

Melburnians love a laugh and the annual comedy festival is the funniest place to be to catch top Australian and international performers. The month-long event takes place in the Town Hall and venues across town, and there are free events in open spaces. The festival also seeks out new talent and culminates with the Raw Comedy awards for the best new Australian stand-up performer. If you're in town in April, you won't be laughing if you miss it. ⊕www.comedyfestival.com.au

COMEDY CLUBS

Comedy Club Melbourne (✉*380 Lygon St., Carlton* ☎*03/9650–1977*) is a popular place to see top-class Australian and international acts. Another good place for a laugh is the **Comic's Lounge** (✉*26 Errol St., North Melbourne* ☎*03/9348–9488*).

DANCE CLUBS

Most of the central city's dance clubs are along the King Street strip or nestled in Little Collins Street. Clubs usually open at 9 or 10 weekends and some weeknights, and stay open until the early-morning hours. Expect to pay a small cover at most clubs—between A$10 and A$15.

The action ranges from fast to furious at the multilevel, high-tech **Metro** (✉*20–30 Bourke St., City Center* ☎*03/9663–4288*), which has eight bars, a glass-enclosed café, and three dance floors. This nightclub is one of the hottest clubs in town for Melbourne's twenty-somethings. **The Saint** (✉*54 Fitzroy St., St. Kilda* ☎*03/9593–8333*) is a glamorous hangout for the young and upwardly mobile. The city's enduring nightspot **Seven** (✉*52 Albert Rd., South Melbourne* ☎*03/9690–7877*) is a spot for chic young hipsters with fancy tastes in both fashion and cocktails.

JAZZ CLUBS

Bennetts Lane (✉*25 Bennetts La., City Center* ☎*03/9663–2856*) is one of the city center's jazz mainstays. Cutting-edge cabaret acts are featured at **45 Downstairs** (✉*45 Flinders La., City Center* ☎*03/9662–9966*). **Manchester Lane** (✉*36 Manchester La., City Center* ☎*03/9663–0630*) has late-night jazz and blues. The **Night Cat** (✉*141 Johnston St., Fitzroy* ☎*03/9417–0090*) hosts jazzy evening shows most nights of the week.

POPULAR LIVE MUSIC CLUBS

The **Corner Hotel** (✉*57 Swan St., Richmond* ☎*03/9427–7300*) has alternative, reggae, rock, blues, and jazz acts with an emphasis on homegrown bands. At the **Crown Casino** (✉*Level 3, Crown Entertainment Complex, Riverside Ave., Southbank* ☎*03/9292–8888* ⊕*www.crowncasino.com.au*), the Showroom and the Mercury Lounge attract big international and Australian headliners. You can catch rock headline acts at the **Ding Dong Lounge** (✉*Level 1, 18 Market La., City Center* ☎*03/9662–1020*).

The **Hi-Fi Bar** (✉*125 Swanston St., City Center* ☎*03/9654–0992*) is a popular venue for live local and less-known international rock bands. The **Palais Entertainment Complex** (✉*Lower Esplanade, St. Kilda* ☎*03/9534–0655*) features alternative and hard-rock headline acts, such as Nick Cave and Queens of the Stone Age and U2. A diverse range of Australian and international acts, including rap, rock, reggae, and hip-hop, plays at **Pony** (✉*68 Little Collins St., City Center* ☎*03/9662–1026*). For rock and roll, punk, and grunge, head to the **Prince of Wales** (✉*29 Fitzroy St., St. Kilda* ☎*03/9536–1166*), which attracts a straight and gay crowd.

CLOSE UP

Australian Rules Football

Despite its name, novice observers frequently ask the question: "What rules?" This fast, vigorous game, played between teams of 18, is one of four kinds of football Down Under. Aussies also play Rugby League, Rugby Union, and soccer, but Australian Rules, widely known as "footy," is the one to which Victoria, South Australia, the Top End, and Western Australia subscribe. It's the country's most popular spectator sport.

Because it is gaining an international television audience, the intricacies of Aussie-rules football are no longer the complete mystery they once were to the uninitiated: the ball can be kicked or punched in any direction, but never thrown. Players make spec-

tacular leaps vying to catch a kicked ball before it touches the ground, for which they earn a free kick. The game is said to be at its finest in Melbourne, and any defeat of a Melbourne team—particularly in a Grand Final—is widely interpreted as a sign of moral lassitude in the state of Victoria.

If you miss out on seeing a match, a good way to learn about the game and it's hold on the city is to visit the **AFL Hall of Fame & Sensation** (⊠ *292 Swanston St., City Center* ☎ *03/8660–5555* ⊕ *www.aflhalloffame.com.au*). The museum's interactive exhibition recounts the history of the sport and lets you have a go at kicking a goal and commentating on a game.

SPORTS & THE OUTDOORS

AUSTRALIAN RULES FOOTBALL

Tickets for Australian Rules Football are available through **Ticketmaster7** (☎ *13–6100* ⊕ *ticketmaster.com.au*) or at the playing fields. The **Melbourne Cricket Ground** (⊠ *Brunton Ave., Yarra Park* ☎ *03/9657–8867*) is the prime venue for AFL games.

The multimillion-dollar residential and commercial Docklands, along the docks and former factory sites at the city's western edge, surrounds the high-tech, indoor **Telstra Dome** (⊠ *Bourke St. W, Docklands* ☎ *03/8625–7700*). It's home to a number of Australian Rules Football clubs. You can reach the district on foot from the Southern Cross Station (formerly Spencer Street Station).

BICYCLING

Melbourne and its environs contain more than 100 km (62 mi) of bike paths, including scenic routes along the Yarra River and Port Phillip Bay. Bikes can be rented for about A$25 per day from trailers alongside the bike paths.

Bicycle Victoria (⊠ *Level 10, 446 Collins St., City Center* ☎ *03/8636–8888* ⊕ *www.bv.com.au*) can provide information about area bike paths. Its excellent Web site has trail maps and descriptions as well as directions.

Melbourne City-Bike Company (☎ *0433/174077* ✎ chris@citybike.com. au) has a fleet of pedal-electric bicycles (emission-free) made out of recycled materials. It's a healthy way—for you and the environment—to see some of the city's best sights. One-hour tours cost A$50 and operate daily between 10 AM and 4 PM.

BOATING

Studley Park Boathouse (⊠ *Boathouse Rd., Kew* ☎ *03/9853–1828*) rents canoes, kayaks, and rowboats for journeys on a peaceful stretch of the lower Yarra River, about 7 km (4½ mi) east of the city center. Rentals are A$24 per hour for a two-person kayak or rowboat and A$28 per hour for a four-person rowboat. The boathouse is open daily from 9 until sunset.

CAR RACING

Australian Formula 1 Grand Prix (⊠ *220 Albert Rd., South Melbourne* ☎ *03/9258–7100* ⊕ *www.grandprix.com.au*) is a popular fixture on Melbourne's calendar of annual events. It's held every March in the suburb of Albert Park, a small neighborhood 4 km (2½ mi) south of the city, which encompasses the area surrounding Albert Park Lake.

CRICKET

All big international and interstate cricket matches in Victoria are played at the **Melbourne Cricket Ground** (⊠ *Brunton Ave., Yarra Park* ☎ *03/9657–8867 stadium, 13–6100 Ticketmaster7*) from October to March. The stadium has lights for night games and can accommodate 100,000 people. Tickets are available at the gate or through Ticketmaster7.

GOLF

Melbourne has the largest number of championship golf courses in Australia. Four kilometers (2½ mi) south of the city, **Albert Park Golf Course** (⊠ *Queens Rd., South Melbourne* ☎ *03/9510–5588*) is an 18-hole, par-72 course that traverses Albert Park Lake, near where the Formula 1 Grand Prix is held in March. Greens fees are A$18 (9 holes), A$23.50–A$25 (18 holes). The 18-hole, par-67 **Brighton Public Golf Course** (⊠ *232 Dendy St., Brighton* ☎ *03/9592–1388*) has excellent scenery but is quite busy on weekends and midweek mornings. Club rental is available. Greens fees are A$16 (9 holes), A$24 (18 holes). **Ivanhoe Public Golf Course** (⊠ *Vasey St., East Ivanhoe* ☎ *03/9499–7001*), an 18-hole, par-68 course, is well suited to the average golfer and is open to the public every day except holidays. Greens fees are A$16 (9 holes), A$23 (18 holes). Five minutes from the beach, **Sandringham Golf Links** (⊠ *Cheltenham Rd., Sandringham* ☎ *03/9598–3590*) is one of the better public courses. The area is known as the Golf Links because there are several excellent courses in the vicinity. Sandringham is an 18-hole, par-72 course. Greens fees are A$23 (18 holes).

HORSE RACING

Melbourne is the only city in the world to declare a public holiday for a horse race—the Melbourne Cup—held on the first Tuesday in November since 1861. The Cup is also a fashion parade, and most of Melbourne society turns out in full regalia. The rest of the country comes to a standstill, with schools, shops, offices, and factories tuning in to the action.

The city has four top-class racetracks. **Caulfield Race Course** (⊠*Station St., Caulfield* ☎*03/9257–7200*), 10 km (6 mi) from the city, runs the Blue Diamond in February and the Caulfield Cup in October. **Flemington Race Course** (⊠*Epsom Rd., Flemington* ☎*03/9371–7171*), 3 km (2 mi) outside the city, is Australia's premier racecourse and home of the Melbourne Cup. **Moonee Valley Race Course** (⊠*McPherson St., Moonee Ponds* ☎*03/9373–2222*) is 6 km (4 mi) from town and holds the Cox Plate race in October. **Sandown Race Course** (⊠*Racecourse Dr., Springvale* ☎*03/9518–1300*), 25 km (16 mi) from the city, hosts the Sandown Cup in November. **Champions–Australian Racing Museum and Hall of Fame** (⊠*Flinders St., City Center* ☎*1300/139407*) is chock-full of horse-racing information.

SOCCER
Pickup or local-league soccer games are played in all seasons but summer in **Olympic Park** (⊠*Ovals 1 and 2, Swan St., Richmond* ☎*03/9286–1600*).

TENNIS
The **Australian Open** (☎*03/9286–1175* ⊕*www.australianopen.com.au*), held in January at the **Melbourne & Olympic Parks** (⊠*Batman Ave., City Center* ☎*03/9286–1244*), is one of the world's four Grand Slam events. You can buy tickets at the event.

Brought your racket? **Melbourne Park Tennis Centre** (⊠*Batman Ave., City Center* ☎*03/9286–1244*) has 22 outdoor and 4 hard indoor Rebound Ace courts. Play is canceled during the Australian Open in January. **East Melbourne Tennis Centre** (⊠*Powlett Reserve, Albert St., East Melbourne* ☎*03/9417–6511*) has five synthetic-grass outdoor courts. **Fawkner Park Tennis Center** (⊠*Fawkner Park, Toorak Rd. W, South Yarra* ☎*03/9820–0611*) has six synthetic-grass outdoor courts.

SHOPPING

Melbourne has firmly established itself as the nation's fashion capital. Australian designer labels are available on High Street in Armadale, on Toorak Road and Chapel Street in South Yarra, and on Bridge Road in Richmond. High-quality vintage clothing abounds on Greville Street in Prahran. Most shops are open Monday–Thursday 9–5:30, Friday until 9, and Saturday until 5. Major city stores are open Sunday until 5.

DEPARTMENT STORES

Bourke Street Mall. Once the busiest east–west thoroughfare in the city, Bourke is now a pedestrian zone (but watch out for those trams!). Two of the city's biggest department stores are here, **Myer** (⊠*314 Bourke St., City Center* ☎*03/9661–1111*) and **David Jones** (⊠*310 Bourke St., City Center* ☎*03/9643–2222*). An essential part of growing up in Melbourne is being taken to Myer at Christmas to see the window displays. ⊠*Bourke St. between Elizabeth and Swanston Sts., City Center.*

MARKETS

Camberwell Market (⊠ *Station St., Camberwell* ☎*1300/367712*), open Sunday only, is a popular haunt for memorabilia seekers. More than 300 stalls display antiques, knickknacks, and food.
Chapel Street Bazaar (⊠*217–223 Chapel St., Prahran* ☎*03/9529–1727*), open daily 10–6, has wooden stalls selling everything from stylish secondhand clothes to memorabilia and knickknacks.
Prahran Market (⊠ *177 Commercial Rd., Prahran* ☎*03/8290–8220* ⊕*www.prahranmarket.com.au*) sells nothing but food—a fantastic, mouthwatering array imported from all over the world. Committed foodies seek out everything from star fruit and lemongrass to emu eggs and homemade relishes. It's open Tuesday and Saturday dawn–5 PM, Thursday and Friday dawn–6 PM, and Sunday 10–3.
Queen Victoria Market (⊠*Elizabeth and Victoria Sts., City Center* ☎*03/9320–5822* ⊕*www.qvm.com.au*) is the oldest market in the southern hemisphere. With more than 1,000 stalls, this sprawling, spirited bazaar is the city's prime produce outlet—most of Melbourne comes here to buy its strawberries, fresh flowers, and imported cheeses. On Sunday you can find deals on jeans, T-shirts, and every manner of bric-a-brac and secondhand stuff. It's open Tuesday–Thursday 6 AM–2 PM, Friday 6 AM–6 PM, Saturday 6 AM–3 PM, and Sunday 9–4. Later, it becomes the Suzuki Gaslight Night Market, open nightly from 5:30 to 10 from December to mid-February, and Wednesday nights the rest of the year, has wandering entertainment and simple food stalls. Market tours take you deep inside the labyrinth and cooking classes are conducted by well known chefs.
St. Kilda Esplanade Art and Craft Market (⊠*Upper Esplanade, St. Kilda* ☎*03/9209–6777*) has more than 200 stalls selling paintings, crafts, pottery, jewelry, and homemade gifts. It's open Sunday 10–5.
South Melbourne Market (⊠*Cecil and Coventry Sts., South Melbourne* ☎*03/9209–6295*), established in 1867, is Melbourne's second-oldest market. You'll find a huge selection of fresh produce and foodstuffs. It's open Wednesday and weekends 8–4 and Friday 8–6.

CHEAP TRICKS!

There's nothing quite like playing a trick on someone, no matter how old you are! And maybe putting a whoopee cushion under your friend's seat is your idea of fun. This little shop of horrors stocks everything you need for satisfying your inner trickster. Think card tricks, fake doggie poo, and cat's vomit to drop on your neighbor's carpet, and all the ingredients to cast a really good spell. If you loved the Addams Family and yearn for a set of blood-drenched Dracula fangs, look no farther than **Bernard's Magic Shop.** ⊠*211 Elizabeth St.* ☎*03/9670—9270.*

SHOPPING CENTERS, MALLS & ARCADES

Australia on Collins (⊠*260 Collins St., City Center* ☎*03/9650–4355*) offers fashion, housewares, beauty products, and lots of food. Labels include Gazman, Made in Japan, Country Road, and Sirocco Leather.

Block Arcade (⊠282 *Collins St., City Center* ☎03/9654–5244), an elegant 19th-century shopping plaza, contains the venerable Hopetoun Tea Rooms, the French Jewel Box, Orrefors Kosta Boda, Dasel Dolls and Bears, and Australian By Design.

Bridge Road, in Richmond at the end of Flinders Street, east of the city, is a popular shopping strip for women's retail fashion that caters to all budgets. Take Tram 48 or 75 from Flinders Street Station.

★ **Brunswick Street,** northeast of the city in Fitzroy, has hip and grungy restaurants, coffee shops, gift stores, and clothing outlets selling the latest look.

Chapel Street, in South Yarra between Toorak and Dandenong roads, is where you can find some of the ritziest boutiques in Melbourne, as well as cafés, art galleries, bars, and restaurants.

Crown Entertainment Complex (⊠*Riverside Ave., Southbank* ☎03/9292–8888), the mall adjacent to the casino, sells Versace, Donna Karan, Gucci, Armani, and Prada, among others.

Dotted with chic boutiques, many of them selling merchandise by up-and-coming Australian designers, **Flinders Lane** will make fashionistas happy. Between Swanston and Elizabeth streets, look for shops like Christine and Alice Euphemia, which stock eclectic, sometimes whimsical, clothing designs by young designers.

Most Melburnians express a love-hate relationship with **GPO Melbourne** (⊠*Between Elizabeth, Little Bourke, and Bourke Sts. and Postal La., City Center* ☎03/9663–0066), but whether you like or loathe this landmark–post office–turned–shopping mall, you'll find it hard not to browse through its big-name designer-label shops. Built in 1859, the neo-Renaissance-style building is now Heritage listed.

High Street, between the suburbs of Prahran and Armadale, to the east of Chapel Street, has the best collection of antiques shops in Australia.

The **Jam Factory** (⊠*500 Chapel St., South Yarra* ☎03/9829–2641) is a group of historic bluestone buildings that house cinemas, fashion, food, and gift shops, as well as a branch of the giant Borders book-and-music store.

★ **Little Collins Street,** a precinct of stores frequented by shoppers with perhaps more money than sense, is still worth a visit. In between frock shops, you'll find musty stores selling classic film posters, antique and estate jewelry, and Australian opals. At the eastern end of **Collins Street,** beyond the cream-and-red, Romanesque facade of St. Michael's Uniting Church, is **Paris End,** a name coined by Melburnians to identify the elegance of its fashionable shops as well as its general hauteur. The venerable **Le Louvre** salon (No. 74) is favored by Melbourne's high society.

Melbourne Central (⊠*300 Lonsdale St., City Center* ☎03/9922–1100) is a dizzying complex huge enough to enclose a 100-year-old shot tower (used to make bullets) in its atrium.

QV (⊠*Swanston and Lonsdale Sts., City Center* ☎03/9658–0100) encompasses a site that was formerly occupied by the Victoria Women's Hospital. The shops here lie along six open-air lanes, and range from posh clothing boutiques like Christensen Copenhagen to chocolate shops and sushi restaurants. There are events most weekends—fashion parades, live music concerts, cooking classes, skateboard demonstrations—in the lanes.

Royal Arcade (⊠ *355 Bourke St., City Center* ☎*No phone*), built in 1846, is Melbourne's oldest shopping plaza. It remains a lovely place to browse, and it's home to the splendid Gaunt's Clock, which tolls away the hours.

★ **Southgate** (⊠*4 Southbank Promenade, Southbank* ☎*03/9699–4311*) has a spectacular riverside location. The shops and eateries here are a short walk both from the city center across Princes Bridge and from the Victorian Arts Center. There's outdoor seating next to the Southbank promenade.

SPECIALTY STORES

BOOKS

Borders (⊠*Jam Factory, Chapel St., South Yarra* ☎*03/9824–2299*) is a gigantic book-and-music emporium.

Brunswick Street Bookstore (⊠*305 Brunswick St., Fitzroy* ☎*03/9416–1030*) sells modern Australian literature and art- and design-oriented books.

Hill of Content (⊠*86 Bourke St., City Center* ☎*03/9662–9472*), with a knowledgeable staff and an excellent selection of titles, is a Melbourne favorite.

Kay Craddock (⊠*156 Collins St., City Center* ☎*03/9654–8506*) is an antiquarian bookseller selling a large range of rare books. Collectors love this shop, located in the National Trust neo-Gothic building known as the Assembly Hall.

Readings (⊠*309 Lygon St., Carlton* ☎*03/9347–6633*), with an exceptional range of books, magazines, and CDs, is a Melbourne institution.

CLOTHING

Andrea Gold (⊠*104 Bridge Rd., Richmond* ☎*03/9428–1226*) stocks a wide selection of women's skirts, dresses, evening coats, jackets, and blouses. There's also a range of hip jewelry, belts, and handbags.

Anthea Crawford (⊠*205 Bridge Rd., Richmond* ☎*03/9428–1670*) is an exclusive Australian women's clothing designer known for her stylish suits. This clearance store often discounts pieces 30%–70%.

Aquila Shoes (⊠*147 Bourke St., City Center* ☎*03/9650–4483*) sells the latest quality footwear for men and women. There are more than 20 branch stores in Australia.

Collette Dinnigan (⊠*553 Chapel St., South Yarra* ☎*03/9822–9433*) is a household name in Australia, having dressed celebrities such as Nicole Kidman and Cate Blanchett. This is a great place to shop for feminine dresses.

Cose Plus (⊠*3/286 Toorak Rd., South Yarra* ☎*03/9826–5788*) has a range of ultracool designs for men and women, with high price tags to match.

Jean Pascal (⊠*144A Cotham Rd., Kew* ☎*03/9817–3671*) specializes in made-to-order classic and elegant women's clothing, with a focus on suits.

Kookai (⊠*110 Greville St., Prahran* ☎*03/9529–8599*) has a chain of stores across Melbourne. Check out the range of funky women's knit-wear in a multitude of colors and patterns.

Sam Bear (⊠*225 Russell St., City Center* ☎*03/9663–2191*), a Mel-bourne institution, sells everything from Aussie outerwear and foot-wear to Swiss Army knives.

GIFTS

The **Aboriginal Gallery of Dreamings** (⊠*73–77 Bourke St., City Center* ☎*03/9650–3277*) sells arts and crafts created by Aborigines.

Aboriginal Handcrafts (⊠*Mezzanine, 130 Little Collins St., City Center* ☎*03/9650–4717*) stocks handcrafts created by Aborigines, including paintings, drawings, cooking implements, and more.

Alison Kelly (⊠*543A High St., Prahran* ☎*03/9533–8444* ⊠*10 Wood-side Crescent, Toorak* ☎*03/9824–2583*) sells arts and crafts created by Aborigines from regional collectives.

Arts of Asia (⊠*1136 High St., Armadale* ☎*03/9576–0917*), in a popu-lar shopping strip, sells paintings, drawings, prints, and antiques from Southeast Asia.

Gallery Gabrielle Pizzi (⊠*73–77 Flinders La., City Center* ☎*03/9654–2944*) represents the work of Aboriginal artists from the communities of Balgo Hills, Papunya, Utopia, Maningrida, Haasts Bluff, and the Tiwi Islands.

Kimberley Art (⊠*76 Flinders La., City Center* ☎*03/9654–5890*) sells Aboriginal arts and crafts from Arnhem Land, the Kimberley, and the Western Desert.

JEWELRY

Altmann and Cherny (⊠*128 Exhibition St., City Center* ☎*03/9650–9685*) sells opals at tax-free prices to overseas tourists.

Dressed up to look like a Victorian-era bedroom, complete with a dress-ing table draped in jewelry, plush armchairs, and old-fashioned wall hangings, **gina & bron** (⊠*119 Hardware La., City Center* ☎*03/9602–4455*), specializes in handmade resin jewelry and housewares, and also conducts jewelry-making workshops.

Craft Victoria (⊠*31 Flinders La., City Center* ☎*03/9650–7775*) fosters creativity with seminars and exhibits, and has a top-notch selection of international and local pottery and jewelry.

Dinosaur Designs (⊠*562 Chapel St., South Yarra* ☎*03/9827–2600*) sells a range of luminous bowls and vases, and funky resin and silver jewelry.

Exhibiting work from more than 80 Australian and New Zealand designers, **eg.etal** (⊠*185 Collins St., City Center* ☎*03/9663–4334*) offers spectacular handmade one-off jewelry pieces.

A haunt of the incredibly affluent, **Kozminsky** (⊠*421 Bourke St., City Center* ☎*03/9670–1277*) has been a Melbourne institution since its opening in 1851. It's crowded with antiques, estate jewelry, and gilt-edged objects from days gone by.

Makers Mark Gallery (⊠*88 Collins St., City Center* ☎*03/9650–3444*) showcases the work of some of the country's finest jewelers and designers.

MUSIC

CD Discounts (⊠*Shop 4, AMP Sq., 121 William St., City Center* ☎*03/9629–1662*) sells CDs, records, DVDs, and tapes.

Discurio (⊠*113 Hardware St., City Center* ☎*03/9600–1488*) carries a cross section of pop, rock, and contemporary music by international artists.

Gaslight (⊠*85 Bourke St., City Center* ☎*03/9650–9009*) carries a range of pop, rock, and contemporary music by Australian and international artists, along with DVDs, T-shirts, and event tickets.

Greville Records (⊠*152 Greville St., Prahran* ☎*03/9510–3012*) is a Melbourne music institution. It carries rare releases in rock, alternative, and vinyl.

Gloomy, small, and always crowded, **Record Collector's Corner** (⊠*240 Swanston St., City Center* ☎*03/9663–3442*) stocks an impressive range of CDs, vinyl, and (believe it or not) cassettes, from a wide cross section of genres. Secondhand CDs and hard-to-find import CD singles are the specialties of the house.

The **Basement Discs** (⊠*24 Block Pl., City Center* ☎*03/9654–1110*) has a strong collection of country, blues, roots, jazz, folk, and world music. Midweek, lunchtime performances feature local and international acts. Call ahead for show information.

MELBOURNE ESSENTIALS

TRANSPORTATION

BY AIR

Melbourne is most easily reached by plane, as it—like many places in Australia—is hours by car from even the nearest town. International airlines flying into Melbourne include Air New Zealand, British Airways, United, Singapore Airlines, Emirates, Japan Airlines, Thai Airways, and Malaysia Airlines.

Domestic carriers serving Melbourne are Qantas, Virgin Blue, O'Connor Airlines, Jetstar, and Regional Express. Qantas and Virgin Blue fly daily to Sydney, Adelaide, Perth, Brisbane, Hobart, and the Gold Coast, while smaller carriers like O'Connor Airlines and Regional Express fly to outer towns like Wagga Wagga, Mount Gambier, and Mildura. Jetstar flies to Sydney, Adelaide, the Gold Coast, Townsville, and Cairns. It also has flights from Avalon Airport (near Geelong), about 70 km (44 mi) southwest of Melbourne.

Melbourne Airport is 22 km (14 mi) northwest of the central business district and can be reached easily from the city on the Tullamarine Freeway. The international terminal is in the center of the airport complex. Domestic terminals are on either side.

Contact Melbourne Airport (☎*03/9297–1600* ⊕*www.melbourne-airport. com.au*).

Airlines Air New Zealand (☎*13–2476*). **British Airways** (☎*03/9656–8133*). **Emirates** (☎*1300/303777*). **Japan Airlines** (☎*03/8662–8333*). **Jetstar**

Airways (☎ *13–1538*). **Malaysia Airlines** (☎ *03/9279–9999*). **O'Connor Airlines** (☎ *08/8723–0666*). **Qantas Airways** (☎ *13–1313*). **Regional Express** (☎ *13–1713*). **Singapore Airlines** (☎ *13–1011*). **Thai Airways** (☎ *1300/651960*). **United** (☎ *13–1777*). **Virgin Blue** (☎ *13–6789*).

TRANSFERS Skybus, a public transportation bus service, runs between the airport and city center, making a loop through Melbourne before terminating at Southern Cross Station (formerly Spencer Street Station). The A$15 shuttle departs every 15 minutes from 7 am to 7 pm, then every half hour until 12:30 am, and hourly until 4:30 am. The journey takes 20 minutes from the city center.

For three or more people traveling together, a taxi is a better value for airport connections. You can catch a taxi in front of the building. The cost into town is A$40. Limousines to the city cost about A$160. Astra is one of the larger companies.

Contacts Astra Chauffeured Limousines Of Australia (☎ *1800/819797*). **Skybus** (☎ *03/9600–1711* ⊕ *www.skybus.com.au*).

BY BUS

TO & FROM MELBOURNE Greyhound Australia links the city with all Australian capital cities and with major towns and cities throughout Victoria. The terminal is on the corner of Swanston and Franklin streets. From Melbourne, it's about 10 hours to Adelaide, about 12 hours to Sydney, about 50 hours to Perth (consider flying), and about 8 hours to Canberra.

Contact Greyhound Australia (☎ *13–1499* ⊕ *www.greyhound.com.au*).

WITHIN MELBOURNE The city's public transportation system is operated by Metropolitan Transit, which divides Melbourne into three zones. Zone 1 is the urban core, where most tourists spend their time. The basic ticket (called a Metcard) is the one-zone ticket, which can be purchased on board the bus or tram (or purchased at a 7-11 store) for A$3.20. It's valid for travel within a specific zone on any tram, bus, or train for two hours after purchase. For travelers, the most useful ticket is probably the Zone 1 day ticket, which costs A$6.10 and is available on board any tram. A free route map is available from the Melbourne Visitor Centre at Federation Square.

Trams run until midnight and can be hailed wherever you see a green-and-gold tram-stop sign. A free City Circle tram run by Metropolitan Transit operates every 10 minutes daily 10–6 on the fringe of the Central Business District, with stops in Flinders, Spencer, La Trobe, Victoria, and Spring streets. Look for the burgundy-and-cream trams.

Contacts Melbourne Visitor Centre (☎ *03/9658–9658* ⊕ *www.visitmelbourne. com*). **Metropolitan Transit** (☎ *13–1638* ⊕ *www.metlinkmelbourne.com.au*).

BY CAR

The major route into Melbourne is Hume Highway, which runs northeast to Canberra, a distance of 646 km (400 mi), and Sydney, 868 km (538 mi). Princes Highway follows the coast to Sydney in one direction and to Adelaide, 728 km (451 mi) northwest of Melbourne, in the other. The Western Highway runs northwest 111 km (69 mi) to Ballarat, and the Calder Highway travels north to Bendigo, a journey of 149 km (92 mi). From Melbourne it takes 10–12 hours to reach Sydney, about 9 hours to Adelaide, and about 1½ hours to Bendigo and Ballarat. The Royal Automobile Club of Victoria (RACV) is the major source of information on all aspects of road travel in Victoria. You can also check the Route Planner on the Visit Victoria Web site ⊕ *www.visitvictoria.com.au.*

Melbourne's regimented layout makes it easy to negotiate by car, but two unusual rules apply because of the tram traffic on the city's major roads. Trams should be passed on the *left,* and when a tram stops to allow passengers to disembark, the cars behind it also must stop unless there is a railed safety zone for tram passengers.

At some intersections within the city, drivers wishing to turn *right* must stay in the *left* lane as they enter the intersection, then wait for the traffic signals to change before proceeding with the turn. This is known as a "hook turn". The rule is intended to prevent traffic from impeding tram service. For complete directions, look for the black-and-white traffic signs suspended overhead as you enter each intersection where this rule applies. All other right-hand turns are made from the center. It's far easier to understand this rule by seeing it in action rather than reading about it.

Motorists using various tollways—roadways you pay to use—including the Citylink from the airport to downtown Melbourne, have 72 hours to pay the toll after using the highway. To pay by credit card, call 13–2629. Alternatively, you can buy passes at the airport before using the tollways. A weekend pass is around A$10.

Avis, Budget, and Hertz have branches at Melbourne Airport as well as downtown. If you rent from a major company, expect to pay about A$60 per day for a compact standard model. If you don't mind an older model and can return the car to the pick-up point, consider a smaller local rental agency, such as Rent-a-Bomb.

Contacts Citylink (☎ *13–2629* ⊕ *www.citylink.com.au*). **Royal Automobile Club of Victoria** (*RACV* ☎ *13–1955* ⊕ *www.racv.com.au*).

Rentals Airport Rent A Car (☎ *1800/331220*). **Avis** (☎ *13–6333*). **Budget** (☎ *13–2727*). **Hertz** (☎ *13–3039*). **Rent-a-Bomb** (☎ *13–1553*).

BY TAXI

Melbourne's taxis are gradually adopting a yellow color scheme, and drivers are required to wear uniforms. Taxis are metered, and can be hailed on the street and at taxi stands or ordered by phone. Major taxi companies include Yellow Cabs, North Suburban, and Silver Top.

Information North Suburban (☎ *13–1119*). **Silver Top** (☎ *13–1008*). **Yellow Cabs** (☎ *13–2227*).

BY TRAIN

Connex, a private company, runs trains throughout metropolitan Melbourne from 4:30 AM until around 1 AM. The zone structure is similar to that of the city's buses and trams. Prepurchase a Metcard at the station or from a 7-11 store. One-zone, two-hour tickets are A$3.20; all-day tickets are A$6.10. The main terminal for metropolitan trains is Flinders Street Station, at the corner of Flinders and Swanston streets.

Southern Cross Railway Station is at Spencer and Little Collins streets. From here the countrywide V-Line has 11-hour trips to Sydney, as well as service to many regional centers in Victoria. Public transportation is available, but if you have cumbersome luggage, you'd do better to head for the taxi stand outside the station.

Information Connex (☎ *13–1638* ⊕ *www.connexmelbourne.com.au*). **Metlink** (☎ *13–1638* ⊕ *www.metlinkmelbourne.com.au*). **V-Line** (☎ *13–6196* ⊕ *www. vlinepassenger.com.au*).

CONTACTS & RESOURCES

CONSULATES

Most embassies are in Canberra, but many countries also have consulates or honorary consuls in Melbourne. Others are usually listed in the telephone directory under the specific country.

Contacts American Consulate-General (✉ *553 St. Kilda Rd., St. Kilda* ☎ *03/9526–5900*). **British Consulate-General** (✉ *90 Collins St., City Center* ☎ *03/9652–1600*). **New Zealand Consulate-General** (✉ *Level 3, 350 Collins St., City Center* ☎ *03/9642–1279*).

EMERGENCIES

In an emergency, dial **000** to reach an ambulance, the police, or the fire department. The Collins Place Pharmacy is open daily 9–6.

Doctors & Dentists Medical Center (✉ *115–125 Victoria Rd., Northcote* ☎ *03/9482–2866*). **Royal Dental Hospital** (✉ *Elizabeth St. at Flemington Rd., Parkville* ☎ *03/9341–0222*). **Swanston Street Medical Centre** (✉ *393 Swanston St., City Center* ☎ *03/9654–2722*).

Hospitals Alfred Hospital (✉ *Commercial Rd. at Hoddle St., Prahran* ☎ *03/9276–2000*). **Royal Women's Hospital** (✉ *132 Grattan St., Carlton* ☎ *03/9344–2000*). **St. Vincent's Hospital** (✉ *Nicholson St. at Victoria Parade, Fitzroy* ☎ *03/9288–2211*).

Pharmacy Collins Place Pharmacy (✉ *45 Collins St., City Center* ☎ *03/ 9650–9034*).

SIGHTSEEING TOURS

BOAT TOURS One of the best ways to see Melbourne is to board the Parks Victoria Yarra River Shuttle Service, which takes in Federation Square and Docklands, with stops at Southbank, the aquarium, the casino, and Victoria Harbour. Ferries depart every 30 minutes, every day. Daily pass tickets, which allow passengers to jump on and off en route, are available daily and cost A$14. The ferry operates on weekends and public holidays from 1 AM to 8 PM.

The modern, glass-enclosed boats of the Melbourne River Cruises fleet take 1- and 2½-hour Yarra River cruises daily (A$19.80 and A$33.80, respectively), traversing either west through the commercial heart of the city or east through the parks and gardens, or a combination of the two. Daily tours run every half hour from 10 to 4.

Melbourne Water Taxis pick passengers up at all piers and landings along the Yarra River from Victoria Street, Richmond, to Williamstown. The company operates daily year-round.

Gray Line also has boat tours.

Information **Gray Line** (⊠ *180 Swanston St., City Center* ☎ *1300/858687* ⊕ *www.grayline.com.au*). **Melbourne River Cruises** (⊠ *Vault 18, Banana Alley and Queensbridge St., City Center* ☎ *03/8610–2600* ⊕ *www.melbcruises.com. au*). **Melbourne Water Taxis** (⊠ *Melbourne Maritime Museum, South Wharf Rd., Southbank* ☎ *03/9686–0914*). **Parks Victoria** (⊠ *535 Bourke St., City Center* ☎ *13–1963*).

BUS TOURS   Gray Line has guided tours of Melbourne and its surroundings by bus and boat. The Melbourne Experience tour visits the city center's main attractions and some of the surrounding parks. The three-hour, A$55 tour departs daily at 8:45 from the company's headquarters.

AAT Kings, Australian Pacific Tours, and Melbourne Sightseeing all have similar general-interest trips and prices.

Information **AAT Kings** (⊠ *33 Palmerston Crescent, South Melbourne* ☎ *1300/556100*). **Australian Pacific Touring (APT)** (⊠ *475 Hampton St., Hampton* ☎ *03/9277–8555 or 1300/675222*). **Melbourne Experience** (⊠ *Melbourne Town Hall, Swanston St., City Center* ☎ *03/9650–7000*). **Melbourne Sightseeing** (⊠ *184 Swanston Walk, City Center* ☎ *03/9663–3377* ⊕ *www. ozhorizons.com.au*).

FOOD TOURS   Foodies Dream Tours (A$25) and cooking classes (2½ hours, A$70–A$75) are available at the Victorian Arts Centre. The center is open Tuesday and Thursday 6–2, Friday 6–6, and Saturday 6–3.

Chocoholic Tours offers several different Saturday touring options for chocolate lovers: the Chocoholic Brunch Walk (10–noon), the Chocoholic Indulgence Tour (12:15–2:15), and the Chocolate and Other Desserts Walk (2:15–4:30). Each offers a different combination of chocolate-fueled tastings and activities, and each costs A$28.

Vietnam on a Plate runs a guided walking tour of the Asian precincts, visiting traditional Chinese herbalists, food stalls, spice and herb specialists, and the "Little Saigon" shopping district of Footscray. The tour includes lunch, numerous food tastings—from the weird (chili, pork blood, and pickled pig's lung) to the wonderful (fresh ginger and lemongrass tea). Be sure and call ahead; tours are usually held Saturday 9:30–12:30, and cost A$50. Reservations required.

Information Chocoholic Tours (✉14 Rae St., Hawthorn ☎03/9815–1228 ⊕ www.chocoholictours.com.au). **Foodies Dream Tours** (✉Queen and Victoria Sts., City Center ☎03/9320–5822 ⊕ www.qvm.com.au). **Vietnam on a Plate** (✉Footscray Market, Footscray ☎03/9689–1186).

TOWN HALL TOUR
Yours truly can learn about the history and architectural significance of Melbourne's beautiful Town Hall with these tours. Among the sights you'll see are the Council Chambers and the 30-foot-high Town Hall Organ, which was built in 1929 and has more than 10,000 pipes. Tours are available weekdays at 11 AM and 1 PM; although they're free, reservations are essential.

Information Melbourne Town Hall (✉Swanston and Little Collins Sts., City Center ☎03/9658–9658).

WALKING TOURS
The Melbourne Greeters service, a Melbourne Information Centre program, provides free half-hour personalized tours by pairing you with a local volunteer who shares your interests. Melbourne's Golden Mile Heritage Trail runs guided walking tours of the city's architectural and historic sites. Tours, which cost A$20 and take 2½–3½ hours, depart daily at 1 from Federation Square and finish at the Melbourne Museum.

Information Golden Mile Heritage Trail (☎03/9650–3663 or 1300/130152 ⊕ www.visitvictoria.com). **Melbourne Greeters** (✉Federation Sq., Flinders and Swanston Sts., City Center ☎03/9658–9524 🖷03/9654–1054 ✉greeter@ melbourne.vic.gov.au).

VISITOR INFORMATION

The Melbourne Visitor Centre at Federation Square provides touring details in six languages. Large-screen videos and touch screens add to the experience, and permanent displays follow the city's history. Daily newspapers are available, and there's access to the Melbourne Web site (⊕www.visitmelbourne.com). The center is open daily 9–6. The Best of Victoria Booking Service here can help if you're looking for accommodations. It also has cheap Internet access.

City Ambassadors—easily spotted by the red uniforms—paid by the City of Melbourne, rove the central retail area providing directions and information for anyone who needs their assistance (Monday–Saturday 10–5).

Information Best of Victoria Booking Service (☎03/9642–1055 or 1300/780045). **City of Melbourne Ambassadors Program** (☎03/9658–9658). **Melbourne Visitor Centre** (✉Federation Sq., Flinders and Swanston Sts., City Center ☎03/9658–9658 ⊕www.melbourne.vic.gov.au).

Victoria

WORD OF MOUTH

"In Melbourne, we rented a car and drove on the Great Ocean Road to Port Campbell to see the Twelve Apostles. LOOOONG DRIVE...but STUNNING DRIVE!!! One moment you are clinging to a cliff, the next you are driving through lush forests. Wow!!!"

–highness67

Updated by Caroline Gladstone

SEPARATED FROM NEW SOUTH WALES by the mighty Murray River and fronted by a beautiful coastline, Victoria's terrain is as varied as any in the country. Sweeping landscapes are quilted together in this compact state. On the West Coast, cliff-lined seascapes alternate with thick forests and charming resort towns; inland are historic goldfield communities, villages along the Murray, and esteemed vineyards. The region contains striking national parks, including the weathered offshore rock formations of Port Campbell; the rocky outcrops, waterfalls, and fauna of the Grampians; and the high-country solitude of Alpine National Park.

> **PRECIOUS RESOURCE**
>
> You won't be able to escape the "save water" signs as you travel around Victoria. Like much of Australia, parts of Victoria are in the grip of the worst drought in more than a century. Some hotels ask guests to participate in water-saving practices and may even provide buckets to catch the excess (non-soapy) shower water and use it on the garden. It's a lot of fun to get involved and help feed those thirsty plants.

Many of Victoria's best sights are within a day's drive of Melbourne. Without venturing too far from the city limits, you can indulge in all sorts of pastimes—exploring the spectacular western coastline to the stunning Twelve Apostles; toasting the sunrise over the Yarra Valley vineyards from the basket of a hot-air balloon; or taking in a Murray River sunset from the deck of a paddle steamer.

EXPLORING VICTORIA

The best way to explore Victoria is by car. The state's road system is excellent, with clearly marked highways linking the Great Ocean Road to Wilson's Promontory, the Yarra Valley, the Murray River region, and the Mornington Peninsula. Distances are not as extreme as in other states. Many of the most scenic places (Bendigo, Ballarat, Beechworth, and Echuca, for instance) are less than three hours from Melbourne; the vineyards of the Yarra Valley and the Mornington Peninsula are an easy 90-minute drive. Buses and trains, which cost less but take more time, also run between most regional centers.

ABOUT THE RESTAURANTS

Chefs in Victoria take pride in their trendsetting preparations of fresh local produce. International flavors are found in both casual and upscale spots—and since prices are lower here than in Sydney, you can have your fill without breaking the bank. On Sunday be sure to join in the Victorian tradition of an all-day "brekky."

WHAT IT COSTS IN AUSTRALIAN DOLLARS				
$$$$	$$$	$$	$	¢
AT DINNER over A$50	A$36–A$50	A$21–A$35	A$10–A$20	under A$10

Prices are per person for a main course at dinner.

ABOUT THE HOTELS

Accommodations in Victoria include grand country hotels, simple roadside motels, secluded bushland or seaside cabins, friendly bed-and-breakfasts, and backpacker hostels. Although you won't find many sprawling resorts in this state, most of the grand old mansions and country homes have air-conditioning, home-cooked meals, and free parking. Rates are usually reduced after school and national holidays. Melbourne Visitor Centre (⊕ *www.visitvictoria.com*) has a list of the state's accommodations to help you plan.

WHAT IT COSTS IN AUSTRALIAN DOLLARS					
	$$$$	$$$	$$	$	¢
FOR TWO PEOPLE	over A$300	A$201–A$300	A$151–A$200	A$100–A$150	under A$100

Prices are for two people in a standard double room in high season, including tax and service, based on the European Plan (with no meals) unless otherwise noted.

WHEN TO VISIT

Victoria is at its most beautiful in fall, March through May, when days are crisp, sunny, and clear and the foliage in parks and gardens is glorious. Winter, with its wild seas and leaden skies, stretches May through August in this region, providing a suitable backdrop for the dramatic coastal scenery. It's dry and sunny in the northeast, however, thanks to the cloud-blocking bulk of the Great Dividing Range. Northeast summers, November through February, are extremely hot, so it's best to travel here and through Gold Country in spring and fall.

AROUND MELBOURNE

YARRA VALLEY & THE DANDENONGS

Melburnians come to the beautiful Dandenong Ranges for a breath of fresh air, especially in autumn when the deciduous trees turn golden, and in spring when the gardens explode into color with tulip, daffodil, azalea, and rhododendron blooms. At Mt. Dandenong, the highest point (2,077 feet), a scenic lookout affords spectacular views over Melbourne and the bay beyond. Dandenong Ranges National Park, which encompasses five smaller parks, including Sherbrooke Forest and Ferntree Gully National Park, has dozens of walking trails, while the quaint townships of Olinda, Sassafras, and Kallista have clusters of antiques, Devonshire tea, and bric-a-brac shops. A little farther north, the vine-carpeted Yarra Valley—home of more than 70 wineries—is a favorite at all times of the year, although its superb pinot noirs always taste better by a crackling open fire in autumn or winter.

HEALESVILLE

60 km (37 mi) northeast of Melbourne.

The township of Healesville began its days in the 1860s as a coach stop along the road to the Gippsland and Yarra Valley goldfields. Two decades later, when the region's gold mining declined, Healesville

NEW SOUTH WALES

Lake Victoria

Murray R.

Sturt Hwy. 20

Merbein
Mildura
Red Cliffs 79

MALLEE CLIFFS NATIONAL PARK

MURRAY-KULKYNE PARK

Murrumbidgee R.

Balranald 20 20 Hay

Cobb Hwy. 75

HATTAH-KULKYNE NATIONAL PARK

Hattah
Murray *Valley* *Hwy.* 16

PINK LAKES STATE PARK

Calder Hwy.

Ouyen

Ouyen Hwy. 12 Underbool

Swan Hill

WYPERFELD NATIONAL PARK

BIG DESERT WILDERNESS AREA

Lake Albacutya

Birchip 79

Kerang

Cohuna
Gunbower 16

Echuca

Numurkah

Lake Hindmarsh

Western Hwy. 8 Nhill

Charlton

Shepparton
Midland Hwy.

Dimboola

Borung Hwy. Warracknabeal

Wedderburn 79

Eaglehawk

Northern Hwy.

Mitchellstown

Hume Hwy.

LITTLE DESERT NAT'L PARK

Horsham

Wimmera Hwy.

Bendigo
Maldon
Castlemaine

Seymour

Goulburn R.

Wartook

Maryborough

8

Halls Gap
Zumstein

Stawell Avoca

Pyrenees Hwy.

Hepburn Springs

Daylesford 75 39

Edenhope

Glenelg R.

GRAMPIANS NATIONAL PARK

GARDIWERD

Ararat 8

Western Hwy.

Calder Hwy. 79

Casterton

Glenelg Hwy.

Ballarat

Western Hwy.

31

Yarra Valley

Hamilton

OTWAY RANGES

Melbourne

Werribee

Yarra Maroondah Hwy.

1

Nelson

LOWER GLENELG NATIONAL PARK

Macarthur

Mortlake
Hamilton Hwy.

Darlington

Woolsthorpe

Camperdown

Geelong

Dandenong
Port Phillip Bay

Mornington

Queenscliff

Portland

Port Fairy

Princes Hwy.

Warrnambool

Colac

Torquay

Portsea

Bellarine Peninsula

French I.

San Remo

Peterborough
Port Campbell

Lorne

MORNINGTON PENINSULA

PHILLIP I.

PORT CAMPBELL NAT'L PARK

Princetown

Apollo Bay

OTWAY NAT'L PARK

Bass Strait

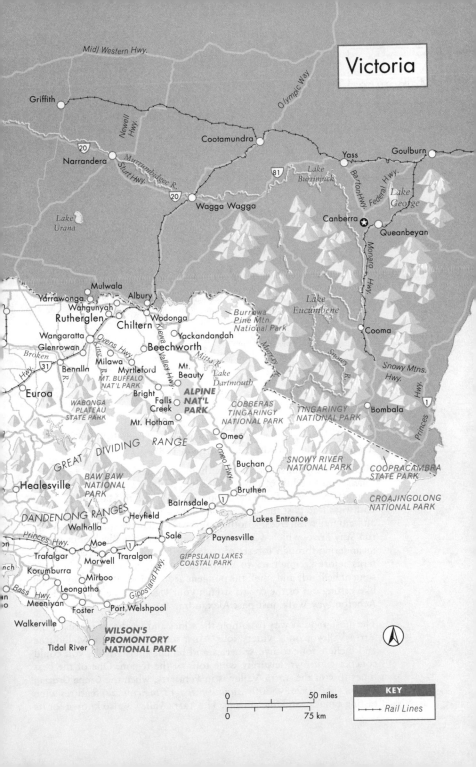

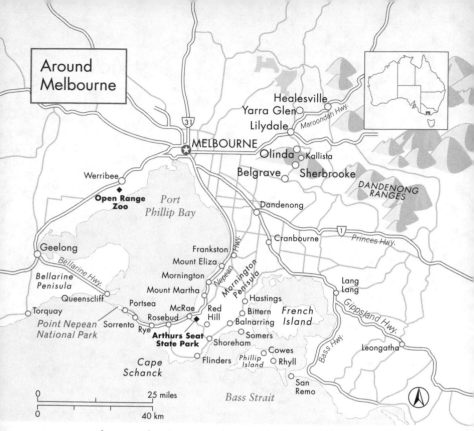

became a logging center that grew by leaps and bounds, especially after it was linked by rail with Melbourne in 1889.

★ Healesville's main street, lined with antiques dealers, two old art deco hotels, and a huddle of shops, makes for a pleasant wander after lunch at a nearby winery. From here you can travel east to Marysville, where pathways lead past the Steavensons Falls and through forests of beech and mountain ash trees. Another option is to take the spectacular **Acheron Way** drive, which winds over the summit of the Black Spur range, meandering through forests of towering mountain ash trees and tree ferns before circling back to Warburton. Along the way you'll hear the song of bellbirds and smell the pungent aroma of eucalyptus. If you feel like getting out of the car to stretch your legs, find the 4-km (2½-mi) Acheron Way Walk, just past Alexandra.

The most popular way to sample the wines and see the vineyards of the Yarra Valley is on a winery tour. Most tours depart from Melbourne and include four to five wineries and lunch; alternatively, you could concoct your own leisurely wine tour of the region. One of the best times to visit the Yarra Valley is in February, when the **Grape Grazing Festival** (☎ *03/5962–6600* ⊕ *www.grapegrazing.com.au*) features wine tastings, music, and fine cuisine. The Yarra Valley is also known for its

GREAT ITINERARIES

Victoria's relatively compact size makes the state's principal attractions appealingly easy to reach. Another region, another taste of this richly endowed state, is never too far away. Head off to the Melbourne suburbs for antiquing and nightlife, drive along the Great Ocean Road, explore Phillip Island, take a wine-tasting tour, hike through the forested mountains, or settle back into the Hepburn Springs spas. The longer you stay, the more you'll find to keep you in this fascinating state of myriad outdoor settings.

IF YOU HAVE 3 DAYS

On the first morning that you leave Melbourne, head for the town of Belgrave. Here you can ride the **Puffing Billy** through the fern gullies and forests of the **Dandenongs**. In the afternoon, travel to **Phillip Island** for the endearing sunset penguin parade. Stay the night, and on the third morning meander along the coastal roads of the **Mornington Peninsula** through such stately towns as Sorrento and Portsea. Stop at a beach, or pick a Melbourne neighborhood or two to explore in the afternoon.

IF YOU HAVE 5 DAYS

Make your way west from Melbourne stopping at Werribee Mansion and Zoo and travel down to the Great Ocean Road. This is one of the world's finest scenic drives, offering stops at some irresistible beaches. Overnight in **Lorne,** beneath the Otway Ranges, then drive west to **Port Campbell National Park** on Day 2. Here you can view the Twelve Apostles rock formations, take a walk to the beach, and continue to **Port Fairy** for the night making sure you check out the wonderful Bay of Islands and Bay of Martyrs rock stacks (in the sea) along the way. On Day 4 wander along the banks of Port Ferry's Moyne River and amble around Griffiths Island. You can then drive northeast to the goldfields center of **Ballarat**. That evening you can explore the town's 19th-century streetscapes, then catch the sound-and-light show at Sovereign Hill. Spend the night here, and in the morning, head to the wineries and spas around Daylesford before returning to Melbourne.

wonderful produce—fruit, vegetables, herbs, bread, and cheeses—on sale at the monthly regional farmers' market.

★ Take one of the daily tours at **De Bortoli** (✉ *Pinnacle La., Dixon's Creek* ☎ *03/5965–2271* ⊕ *www.debortoli.com.au*) to follow the wine-making process from the vineyards to the barrel sheds. Chardonnays and Rieslings are specialties, and you'll have ample opportunity to sample a few. The restaurant, which has stunning views of the surrounding vines, landscaped gardens, and mountains, serves delectable dishes using Yarra Valley produce. Sunday lunch is known as the Italian Family Feast, a leisurely five-course meal for A\$65 a head.

★ **Domaine Chandon** (✉ *Maroondah Hwy. between Coldstream and Healesville, Green Point* ☎ *03/9738–9200* ⊕ *www.greenpointwines. com.au*) schedules free tours that take visitors through the step-by-step production of sparkling wine, including visits to the vines and the bottling area. You'll find out why the winery's parent, the renowned French champagne producer Moët and Chandon, chose the Yarra Valley. Tastings are in the beautiful Green Point Room, where huge glass windows overlook the vines.

☺ Taking a walk through the tranquil bush exhibits at the **Healesville Sanctuary,** you can come face-to-face with wedge-tailed eagles, grumpy wombats, nimble sugar gliders, and shy platypuses. You can also book a behind-the-scenes tour of the animal hospital. ⊠*Badger Creek Rd.* ☎*03/5957–2800* ⊕*www.zoo.org.au* ⊠*A$22* ☉*Daily 9–5.*

> ### WINE AND SONG
>
> Catch a little jazz at lunch or spend the whole day watching great performances from local and international headline acts; Victoria's wineries can provide an array of entertainment for music connoisseurs. Vineyards come alive with the summer, so check out the events with local tourist offices. Make sure you book early for the popular "Day on the Green" concert series held in the Yarra Valley and Rutherglen wine regions.

Several pungent reds and whites—including notable pinot noir, shiraz, cabernet, merlot, and chardonnay—are ready for sampling at **Kellybrook Winery** (⊠*Fulford Rd., Wonga Park* ☎*03/9722–1304* ⊕*www.kellybrookwinery.com.au*), where visitors can attend tastings and then wander through the vineyards. The restaurant serves such delicacies as Yarra Valley homemade ravioli with smoked trout and goat's cheese filling, and porterhouse steak served with Kellybrook Shiraz jus.

Rochford Wines (⊠*Maroondah Hwy. at Hill Rd., Coldstream* ☎*03/5962–2119* ⊕*www.rochfordwines.com*) inhabits a striking-looking property; an architect-designed building crafted almost entirely of glass looks over the vineyards and rolling green paddocks. There are a wine-tasting bar and a restaurant, and live music entertains the crowds from December to March. Tastings are daily 10–5.

Skirted by acres of sprawling vineyards, **St. Huberts** (⊠*St. Huberts Rd., Coldstream* ☎*03/9739–1118* ⊕*www.sthuberts.com.au*) produces a wide selection of highly regarded wines, including cabernet sauvignon, pinot noir, chardonnay, merlot, and roussanne. There's a picnic area with barbecue facilities, as well as jazz and blues performances on most summer Sundays.

WHERE TO STAY & EAT

$$$$
Fodor's Choice
★

✕⊞**Chateau Yering.** Stockmen William, Donald, and James Ryrie built this homestead in the 1860s, and it was later one of the Yarra Valley's first vineyards. It's now a luxury hotel with opulent suites, beautiful gardens, and the upscale Eleonore's Restaurant ($$$). This is a favorite base for sunrise balloon flights over the Yarra Valley, followed by a champagne breakfast at the on-site Sweetwater Café ($$). Balloon packages range from A$1,040 to A$1,345 for two including dinner, breakfast, and lodging. ⊠*42 Melba Hwy., Yering, 3770* ☎*03/9237–3333 or 1800/237333* ⊕*www.chateauyering.*

com.au ☞*32 suites* ⚠*In-hotel: restaurants, room service, tennis court, pool* ▤*AE, DC, MC, V* ⦿*MAP.*

¢–$$$$ ✕⌷ **Healesville Hotel.** Housed in a restored 1910 pub, this famous local
★ lodge has bright, modern upstairs rooms with high ceilings, tall windows, and genteel touches such as handmade soaps. Bathrooms are shared, so be sure to pack a suitably funky robe to wear for the short walk along the hallway. Downstairs you can dine beneath pressed-metal ceilings in a stylish restaurant that's won many awards for its fine cuisine; try fresh local catches such as salmon or oil-drizzled yabbies (small crustaceans resembling lobsters). The hotel's front bar has been transformed into a bistro for casual evening meals, while the adjoining Harvest Café is the place for breakfast and a light lunch. You can also pick up fresh produce and gourmet foods at the hotel's Kitchen and Butcher Shop. Those who want total serenity can book into either of the two rustic (but luxurious) cottages at Harvest Farm, located on 18 acres of bushland and gardens just a few minutes out of town. Cottages can take up to four people and breakfast is provided. ⌂*256 Maroondah Hwy., 3777* ☎*03/5962–4002* ⊕*www.healesvillehotel. com.au* ☞*7 rooms, 2 cottages* ⚠*In-hotel: 3 restaurants, bar, no elevator* ▤*AE, DC, MC, V* ⦿*BP.*

$$$–$$$$ ⌷ **Woolrich Cottage.** The most upmarket of three cottages in the Candelight Cottages collection, Woolrich is ideal for one couple wanting total privacy or two couples seeking a small party atmosphere. Built in 1920 and retaining many original features such as art deco stained glass windows and doors, Woolrich is set in 5 acres of gardens that also adjoins the Cloudhill display gardens and teahouse. There are two bedrooms, each with their own dressing room, and two bathrooms with oval-shaped hot tubs. There is also a separate room with a four-person Jacuzzi that looks out over the gardens. Everything needed for a cozy weekend away is provided including DVD player and a selection of movies, CD player and CDs, espresso coffee machine, books, magazines, and a wood-burning open fire. A hearty array of breakfast ingredients are supplied—free range eggs, bacon and sausages from the local butcher, quality teas and coffee—and meals can be taken on the deck overlooking the gardens or on the lovely antique dining setting under a bay window. There is also a selection of gourmet frozen meals in the freezer (made by a local caterer), which cost extra and can be heated up for a quick meal. There's a two-night minimum stay for bookings that include Saturday but they toss in a complimentary bottle of champagne. Candelight Cottages head office is in Olinda and the cottage is about one mile or a five-minute drive away. ✉*7–9 Monash Ave., 3788* ☎*03/9751– 2464 or 1300/553011* 📠*02/9751–0552* ⊕*www.candlelightcottages. com.au* ☞*1 cottage with two bedrooms* ⚠*In-hotel: kitchen, room service, hot tubs, Jacuzzi, no children under 11, except infants* ▤*AE, DC, MC, V* ⦿*BP.*

$$$ ⌷ **Kangaroo Ridge.** These two cozy, mud-brick cabins are perched on a
★ hillside with balconies overlooking the Yarra Valley. Inside you'll find polished jarrah-wood floors, Persian rugs, and well-designed kitchens. Breakfast is included, and you can buy barbecue dinner hampers.

5

Although it's a little isolated—20 km (12 mi) from Healesville along a couple of dirt tracks—it is not too far from three wineries, the closest being Long Gully Estate on nearby Long Gully Road. There's a minimum two-night stay on weekends. ⊠*38 Turners La., 3777* ☎*03/5962–1122* ⊕*www. kangarooridge.com.au* ⌨*2 cabins* ⌂*In-room: kitchen, hot tubs, DVD* ☰*AE, DC, MC, V* ⍾*BP.*

> ## PERFECT PICNICS
>
> The Dandenongs are heaven for fresh-air freaks and foodies. Pick up some goodies at Olinda's Saturday morning market and work up an appetite taking the 1½-mi-loop walk to Sherbrooke Falls from Donohue Picnic Grounds. Ask the tourist office about other great walks and picnic spots.

OLINDA
48 km (30 mi) east of Melbourne, 40 km (25mi) south-west of Healesville.

The **National Rhododendron Gardens** are a sight to behold in October, when acres of white, mauve, and pink blooms make for spectacular countryside vistas. A small train provides transportation throughout the garden. For a perfect afternoon, combine your visit with tea and scones in one of the many little cafés dotting this part of the Dandenongs. ⊠*Georgian Rd. off Olinda-Monbulk Rd.* ☎*13–1963* ⌨*A$8* ⏱*Daily 10–5.*

WHERE TO EAT

$$ ✕**Woods Sherbrooke.** Formerly a post office, this light-filled space is where chef Jason Dousset now whips up delicate, tantalizing fare. Menu choices may include Yarra Valley game duck and shiitake pie, or lobster-tail risotto served with sesame-ginger dressing. Meat lovers will want to sample the venison sausage and prosciutto. Sherbrooke is 10 km (6 mi) from Olinda via a picturesque route of twisting lanes. Should you want to stay the night, there's a cottage that rents for A$165–A$195 per night. ⊠*21 Sherbrooke Rd., Sherbrooke* ☎*03/9755–2131* ☰*MC, V* ⏱*Closed Mon.–Thurs. No dinner Sun.*

$–$$ ✕**Wild Oak Restaurant and Bar.** At one of the oak tree–shaded outdoor tables here you can nibble on such delicate dishes as crab and paw-paw salad, accompanied by a glass of crisp chardonnay. Local musicians perform on the last Friday night of the month and every Sunday afternoon. ⊠*232 Ridge Rd.* ☎*03/9751–2033* ☰*AE, DC, MC, V* ⏱*Closed Mon. and Tues.*

MORNINGTON PENINSULA

The Mornington Peninsula circles the southeastern half of Port Phillip Bay. Along the coast a string of seaside villages stretches from the larger towns of Frankston and Mornington to the summer holiday towns of Mount Martha, Rosebud, Rye, Sorrento, and Portsea. On the Western Port Bay side, the smaller settlements of Flinders, Somers, and Hastings have prettier, and quieter, beaches without the crowds.

Set aside at least a day for a drive down the peninsula, planning time for lunch and wine tasting, an afternoon cliff-top walk along the bluffs, or even a game of golf at Cape Schanck, one of 30 golf courses in the region. In summer pack a swimsuit and sunscreen for impromptu ocean dips as you make your way around the peninsula's string of attractive beaches.

RED HILL
121 km (75 mi) southeast of Melbourne.

Together with Main Ridge and Merricks, Red Hill is one of the state's premium producers of cool-climate wines, particularly pinot noir and shiraz. For an afternoon of fine wine, excellent seafood, and spectacular coastal views, plan a route that winds between vineyards. Red Hill has a busy produce and crafts market on the first Saturday morning of each month.

Crittenden Wines (⊠*25 Harrisons Rd., Dromana* ☎*03/5987–3800 winery, 03/5981–9555 restaurant* ⊕*www.crittendenwines.com.au*) is one of the area's most beautiful wineries. Run by Garry Crittenden, it produces chardonnay, pinot noir, and pinot grigio under four labels: Crittenden, Schinus, Pinocchio, and Geppetto. The cellar door is open for tastings daily in summer and during public holidays, and on weekends at other times. The restaurant, Stillwater at Crittenden, is open daily for lunch and weekends for dinner. Look out for the braised pork belly with seared scallops—it's one of chef Zac Poulier's best dishes.

Red Hill Estate (⊠*53 Shoreham Rd., Red Hill South* ☎*03/5989–2838* ⊕*www.redhillestate.com.au*) has picked up numerous medals for its chardonnay, pinot noir, and shiraz. Max's Restaurant (☎*03/5931–0177*) is equally as famous for its food and sweeping views over the 30-acre vineyards to Western Port Bay and Phillip Island. Dishes include prime Gippsland eye fillet of beef atop truffled kipfler potatoes with Red Hill Estate shiraz jus. For dessert, don't miss the summer pudding with double cream. It's open for lunch daily and dinner on weekends.

Established in 1977, **Stonier Winery** (⊠*Corner of Frankston–Flinders Rd. and Thompsons La., Merricks* ☎*03/5989–8300* ⊕*www.stoniers. com.au*) is one of the peninsula's oldest vineyards. Notable wines here include chardonnay, pinot noir, and cabernet. Although there's no restaurant, cheeses and hors d'oeuvres accompany the daily tastings, and winemaking tours are available.

★ **T'Gallant Winemakers** (⊠*Corner of Mornington–Flinders Rd. and Shand Rd., Main Ridge* ☎*03/5989–6565* ⊕*www.tgallant.com.au*) produces such wines as the Imogen pinot gris, pinot noir, chardonnay, and muscat à petits grains. La Baracca Trattoria is always buzzing—the food is exceptional, with dishes made from local ingredients (some from the house herb garden). Try the wild Italian herb-ricotta gnocchi with braised duck and wilted spinach for a taste-bud delight.

WHERE TO EAT

$$$ ✗ **Bittern Cottage.** Influenced by their adventures in northern Italy and southern France, chef-owners Jenny and Noel Burrows show off their provincial-style cooking skills using regional Australian produce. The set menu for Saturday night dinner and Sunday lunch may include Provençale lamb and panna cotta with cherries and chocolate or wine-simmered duck breast. Tucked away in the bush, the restaurant that been drawing patrons for 28 years and is just 1½ km (1 mi) north of tiny Bittern village. ⊠ *2385 Frankston–Flinders Rd., Bittern* ☎ *03/5983–9506* ⊟ *MC, V* ☻ *Fri.–Sat. dinner and Sun. lunch.*

> ### BE AMAZED
>
> Victorians do love their mazes, and you'll find these quaint English-garden features dotted around the Mornington Peninsula. Not content with a collection of hedges to get lost in, these maze complexes have topiary and sculptured creations, mystery lawn puzzles, and big garden chess sets. Wander through **Arthurs Seat Maze** (⊠ *55 Purves Rd.* ☎ *03/5981–8449*) which also has an "amazing" candy shop, or check out the world's first circular rose maze at **Aschombe Maze & Water Gardens** (⊠ *15 Shoreham Rd., Shoreham* ☎ *03/5989–8387*).

$$ ✗ **Salix at Willow Creek.** Although views of the vineyard through the restaurant's glass walls are spectacular year-round, Willow Creek's gardens break into a flurry of roses come autumn. The menu, which changes seasonally, always showcases local produce; if you're lucky, choices might include duck, venison, or zucchini flower fritters. There's also a light tapas menu. ⊠ *166 Balnarring Rd., Merricks North* ☎ *03/5989–7640* ⊟ *AE, DC, MC, V* ☻ *No dinner Sun.–Thurs.*

$–$$ ✗ **Montalto Vineyard & Olive Grove.** Overlooking an established vineyard Fodor'sChoice with vistas of rolling green hills, this place serves French-inspired cuisine made with the freshest local ingredients. Chef Barry Davis prepares ★ such creative dishes as Red Hill goat cheese soufflé with walnut and goat's cheese dressing, and garden nettle risotto with Flinders mussels and Montalto lemon–infused olive oil. The wine list borrows from the best of the estate's vintages, as well as classic wines from other regions. If it's a nice day you can picnic on the grounds from hampers prepared by the restaurant. ⊠ *33 Shoreham Rd., Red Hill South* ☎ *03/5989–8412* ⊟ *AE, DC, MC, V* ☻ *No dinner Sun.–Thurs. (No dinner Sun. only in Jan.).*

ARTHURS SEAT

76 km (47 mi) south of Melbourne, 10 km (6 mi) north of Red Hill.

Ⓒ Sweeping views of the surrounding countryside, Port Phillip Bay, Port Phillip Heads, and—on a clear day—the city skyline, the You Yangs, and Mt. Macedon are the attractions at **Arthurs Seat State Park.** Walking tracks meander through stands of eucalyptus and a marked scenic drive snakes its way up the mountainside. Seawinds, a public garden established by a local gardener in the 1940s, also forms part of the park and is a 10-minute walk or about 500 yards away. The mountain, which gives the park its name, is the highest point on the Mornington Peninsula; it was named after Arthurs Seat in Edinburgh. The road from Mornington is open at all times, so you can enjoy the spectacular mountaintop view even when the park is closed. ⊠ *Arthurs Seat Rd. at Mornington Peninsula Hwy., Arthurs Seat* ☏ *03/5987–2565* ⬚ *Free* ⊗ *Nov.–Mar., daily 8–8; Apr.–Oct., daily 8–5.*

PHILLIP ISLAND

★ *125 km (78 mi) south of Melbourne.*

A nightly waddling parade of miniature fairy penguins, known as Little Penguins, from the sea to their burrows in nearby dunes is this island's main draw, attracting throngs of onlookers on summer weekends and holidays. But Phillip Island, a pleasant 1½-hour drive from Melbourne, has plenty of other attractions. At low tide you can walk across a basalt causeway to the **Nobbies**. A boardwalk takes you around the windswept coastline to a blowhole. Thousands of shearwaters (also known as mutton birds) nest here from September to April, when they return north to the Bering Strait in the Arctic. Farther out, **Seal Rocks** host Australia's largest colony of fur seals; more than 5,000 creatures bask on the rocky platforms and caper about here in midsummer.

It only takes about 20 minutes to travel from one side of Phillip Island to the other by car, but within its small area are a handful of villages clinging to an unusually beautiful coast and wildlife parks with koalas and kangaroos and enough good dining and lodging choices that you may be tempted to stay longer than a day.

The seaside town of **Cowes** is the hub of Phillip Island; the pier is where you can board sightseeing cruises and the passenger ferry that travels across Western Port Bay to Stony Point on the Mornington Peninsula. It has a lively café scene and several quality gift shops interspersed with the traditionally cheaper tourist fare. Restaurant and hotel bookings are essential in the busy summer months.

Quieter than Cowes, **Rhyll** is a charming fishing village on the eastern side of the island. You can rent a boat from the dock or take a sightseeing cruise from the pier. A mangrove boardwalk leads to Conservation Hill and the Koala Conservation Centre.

The **Phillip Island Grand Prix Circuit** continues the island's long involvement with motor sports, dating back to 1928 when the Australian Grand Prix was run on local unpaved roads. The circuit was completely redeveloped in the 1980s, and in 1989 hosted the first Australian Motorcycle Grand Prix. The circuit holds regular races as well as big-ticket events, such as the Grand Prix in October. Speed freaks can travel on the actual circuit on a go-kart (A\$25 per lap) during December and January, or a high-performance sports car (A\$199 for three laps) driven by a professional. There are guided tours of the track every day at 11 and 2, and a museum tracing the history of motor sports. ⊠ *Back Beach Rd., Phillip Island* ☎ *03/5952-9400* 🔲 *A$18* ⊙ *Daily 9-7.*

Phillip Island's famous Little Penguins (the smallest in the world) are the main draw for international visitors. Every night at the **Penguin Parade** dozens of the little guys come ashore and waddle to their sand-dune burrows. It's memorable to see fluffy young penguin chicks standing outside their burrows, waiting for their parents to return with their dinner. Watching the parade is hardly a back-to-nature experience, however. Often there are thousands of spectators watching as the penguins emerge from the surf onto a floodlighted beach, while a commentator in a tower describes their progress over a public-address system.

There are several ways to view the penguins: general admission where viewing is from concrete bleachers; a viewing platform that is closer to the action; and an elevated tower where five adults join the ranger who is narrating the action. The Ultimate Penguin Tour, for private groups, includes headphones and night-vision equipment and a spot on the beach. The spectacle begins at around 8 PM each night; booking ahead is essential in summer and during public holidays. Bring warm clothing—even in summer—and rain protection gear. ⊠ *Summerland Beach* ☎ *03/5951-2800* ⊕ *www.penguins.org.au* 🔲 *General admission A$17.40; viewing platform A$29; skybox A$40; Ultimate Penguin Tour A$60* ⊙ *Daily.*

At the **Koala Conservation Centre** you can stroll along treetop-high board-walks and view koalas in their natural habitats. At the visitor center you can learn some fascinating facts about the cute furry creatures—such as the fact that they sleep 21 hours a day. Daily ranger-guided tours take you behind the scenes to learn more about research being conducted at the facility. It is located just a short drive from the tourist information center at Newhaven; follow the signs along Phillip Island Tourist Road. ⊠ *Phillip Island Tourist Rd.* ☎ *02/5951-2800* ⊕ *www.penguins.org.au* 🔲 *A$9.20* ⊙ *Daily 10-5.*

WHERE TO STAY & EAT

$-$$$ ✕ **Foreshore Bay and Restaurant.** This modern bar and restaurant over-looks the peaceful bay at Rhyll. There's a lovely covered terrace that's perfect for summer dining. The menus changes seasonally, but freshly shucked oysters are always popular—try them with raspberry and chive vinaigrette. Pan-roasted kangaroo with fennel, and baby barramundi with lemon and arugula risotto are popular options. The extensive Australian wine list includes Phillip Island labels. Reservations are essential in summer. ⊠ *11 Beach Rd., Rhyll* ☎ *03/5956-9520* 🔲 *AE, DC, MC, V.*

$-$$ ✕ **Harry's on the Esplanade.** Spilling onto an upstairs terrace above Cowes's main beach, Harry's is something of a Phillip Island institution. Its menu, which changes regularly, draws heavily on seafood bought fresh from the trawlers, and locally raised beef, lamb, and pork. Don't pass up the crayfish if it's on the menu. The wine list has an Australian emphasis and includes local wines. The bread is made on the premises, as are the pastries and ice cream. ✉*Upper level, 17 The Esplanade, Cowes* ☎*03/5952–6226* ▭*AE, DC, MC, V.*

¢–$ ✕**Café Lugano.** At the top of Thompson Avenue, Café Lugano is one of the island's best coffee houses. It's a small affair, with tables on the street and in a pocket-handkerchief courtyard. There's local art on the walls, and a funky vibe pervades. The Swiss-Italian coffee is good, but the specialty here is the freshly squeezed juice (try the "Revitalise," a blend of apple, carrot, celery, beetroot, and ginger). There are light meals and an all-day breakfast menu. It's open every day for lunch, and Saturday night for dinner. ✉*71 Thompson Ave., Cowes* ☎*03/5952–5636* ▭*No credit cards.*

$$$–$$$$ 🛏**Glen Isla House.** This luxurious B&B has six individually themed rooms in one lodge. There's also a separate suite as well as a modern two-story cottage that sleeps up to four. Hosts Ian and Madeleine Baker live in an adjoining historic residence that was transported from the United States in the late 1800s and served as one of the island's original homesteads. The property has extensive terraces, lush gardens, and a delightful summerhouse; the beach is right at the doorstep. A table d'hôte dinner is available by prior arrangement on Saturday for A$80 per person. The gourmet breakfasts include Ian's homemade fruit compote. There is a minimum two-night stay. ✉*230–232 Church St., Cowes, 3922* ☎*03/5952–1882* 🖷*03/5952–5028* ⊕*www.glenisla.com* 🛏*1 king suite, 6 house rooms, 1 two-story gate cottage* ⚴*In-room: no TV, Wi-Fi. In-hotel: restaurant, airport shuttle, no elevator, parking (no fee)* ▭*AE, DC, MC, V* ⧖*BP.*

OFF THE BEATEN PATH

Wilson's Promontory National Park. Once connected to Tasmania, this park is the southernmost point of mainland Australia. A granite peninsula of more than 123,000 acres, it is a haven for birdlife and native animals, with many kangaroos, koalas, and wombats spotted around Tidal River. Mountains, beaches, wetlands, lakes, and plains make it a hiker's paradise, and many set off on the famous 19-km (12-mi) trek inland to the windswept lighthouse. Adventurous types might want to stay in one of the three lighthouse cottages that are available on Friday and Saturday nights (☎*03/5680–9500* ⊕*www.parkweb.vic.gov.au*); would-be guests should bear in mind that the walk is 19 km (12 mi), one-way, from Telegraph Saddle car park, or 23 km (14 mi) from Tidal River. There are more than 30 self-guided walks that can take an hour to a day to explore. To get to Wilson's Promontory National Park, take the Princes Highway to Dandenong, and then the South Gippsland Highway to Meeniyan or Foster. Tidal River is another 70 km (43 mi). There's no public transportation to the park.

AROUND MELBOURNE ESSENTIALS

TRANSPORTATION

BY CAR

Renting a car in Melbourne and driving south is the most practical way of seeing the Mornington Peninsula, although there are daily V-Line buses from Melbourne to much of regional Victoria. To reach Phillip Island, you can drive from Melbourne along the B420, or catch a ferry from Stony Point on the Mornington Peninsula to Cowes.

CONTACTS & RESOURCES

EMERGENCIES

In an emergency, dial **000** to reach an ambulance, the police, or the fire department.

The Phillip Island Medical Group has offices in Cowes and San Remo; both are open weekdays 9 AM–5:30 PM and Saturday 9–11:30 AM. There's also a pharmacy right next to the offices in Cowes.

Contact **Phillip Island Medical Group** (⊠ *14 Warley St., Cowes* ☎ *03/5952–2072* ⊠ *123 Marine Parade, San Remo* ☎ *03/5678–5402*).

TOURS

Day trips from Melbourne are run by local tour operators, including Australian Pacific Tours and Gray Line. Tours of the Dandenongs cost A\$58 (half day) to A\$109 (full day), while those to Phillip Island's Penguin Parade cost A\$95 (penguins only) to A\$115 (with an island tour).

Contacts **Australian Pacific Tours** (⊠ *180 Swanston St., City Center, Melbourne* ☎ *1300/655965* ⊕ *www.aptouring.com.au*). **Gray Line** (⊠ *180 Swanston St., City Center, Melbourne* ☎ *1300/858687* ⊕ *www.grayline.com*).

VISITOR INFORMATION

Contacts **Dandenong Ranges & Knox Visitor Information Centre** (⊠ *1211 Burwood Hwy., Upper Ferntree Gully* ☎ *03/9758–7522* 🖷 *03/9758–7533* ⊕ *www. dandenongrangestourism.com.au*). **Melbourne Visitor Centre** (⊠ *Federation Sq., Flinders St. at St. Kilda Rd., Melbourne* ☎ *03/9658–9658* 🖷 *03/9650–6168* ⊕ *www.visitmelbourne.com*). **Mornington Peninsula Visitor Centre** (⊠ *359B Point Nepean Rd., Dromana* ☎ *03/5987–3078 or 1800/804009* 🖷 *03/5987–3726* ⊕ *www.visitmorningtonpeninsula.org*). **Phillip Island Information Centre** (⊠ *Tourist Rd., Newhaven* ☎ *03/5956–7447 or 1300/366422* 🖷 *03/5956–7905* ⊕ *www.visitphillipisland.com*). **Yarra Valley Visitor Information Centre** (⊠ *Old Courthouse, Harker St., Healesville* ☎ *03/5962–2600* 🖷 *03/5962–2040* ⊕ *www. visityarravalley.com.au*).

WEST COAST REGION

Victoria's Great Ocean Road, which heads west from Melbourne along rugged, windswept beaches, is arguably the country's most spectacular coastal drive. The road, built during the Great Depression atop majestic cliffs, occasionally dips down to sea level. Here in championship surfing country some of the world's finest waves pound mile after mile of uninhabited, golden, sandy beaches. As you explore the coastline, be sure to check out Bell's Beach, site of the annual Easter Surfing Classic, one of the premier events of the surfing world. But you'll want to think twice before bringing your own board here; the fierce undertow all along this coast can be deadly.

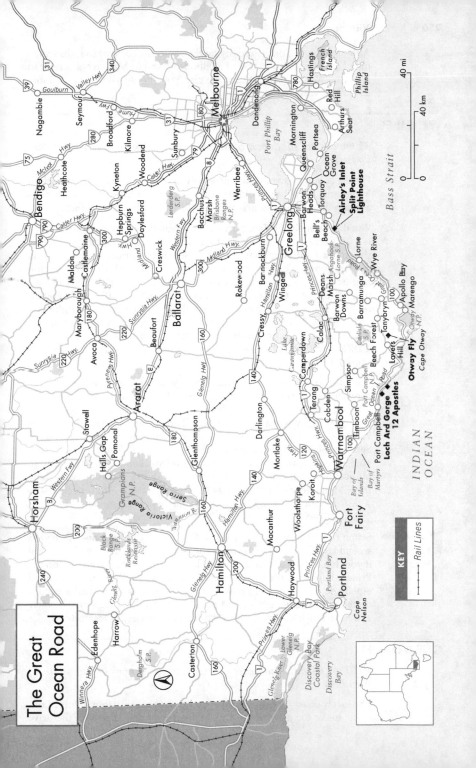

Although this region is actually on the southeast coast of the Australian mainland, it lies to the west of Melbourne, and so Melburnians refer to it as the "West Coast." From the city, you should allow two or more days for a West Coast sojourn.

WERRIBEE

32 km (20 mi) southwest of Melbourne, 157 km (97 mi) west of Phillip Island.

Once a country town, now a generally undistinguished outer suburb of Melbourne, Werribee is notable for the glorious Werribee Park Mansion—a luxury hotel and a safari-style zoo all within the one complex.

☺ **Victoria's Open Range Zoo,** part of the original Werribee Park property,
★ is a 200-acre safari-style zoo of the highest caliber. Safari buses travel through a landscape that replicates southern Africa, passing among giraffes, lions, rhinos, zebras, and hippos. A walk-through section houses cheetahs, apes, meerkats, and other African animals in natural conditions. Overnight slumber safaris (A$2,050), held September through April, let you watch wildlife at feeding time, partake in a "Rhythm of Africa" musical performance, and get close up and personal with a rhino or giraffe. Australian animals also live in the park. ⊠*K Rd.* ☎*03/9731–9600* ⊕*www.zoo.org.au* ⊠*A$21* ☉*Daily 9–5, tours 10–3:40.*

★ The 60-room Italianate **Werribee Park Mansion,** dating from 1877, is furnished with period antiques. More than 25 acres of formal gardens surround the mansion. This was one of the grandest homes in the colony, built by wealthy pastoralists Thomas and Andrew Chirnside. Part of the mansion is now a luxurious hotel, the Sofitel Mansion & Spa. The Shadowfax Winery is a short walk away. You can take a self-guided tour of the property; or come on weekends for wine tasting, musical performances, and other events. A shuttle bus runs twice daily from Melbourne's Victoria Arts Centre; the cost is A$20 per person. ⊠*K Rd.* ☎*03/9741–2444* ⊠*Mansion entry A$12, guided tour A$15* ☉*Daily 10–5.*

EN ROUTE Set on the western shores of Corio Bay, the city of **Geelong**—Victoria's second largest—has a waterfront route that's worth driving along, even if you don't plan to stop. About 40 km (25 mi) west of Werribee on the Princes Highway, turn left into Bell Parade and follow the palm-lined esplanade as it meanders past gracious homes, gardens, and a harbor dotted with yachts. It's a good place to stretch your legs by the water and have lunch as you head down toward the Great Ocean Road.

QUEENSCLIFF

103 km (64 mi) southwest of Melbourne, 71 km (44 mi) south of Werribee.

The lovely coastal village of Queenscliff, and nearby sibling Point Lonsdale, make for a worthy—and well-signposted—detour on the drive between Werribee and Lorne. (You can also travel to Queenscliff by ferry from Sorrento on the other side of Port Phillip Bay on the Mornington Peninsula.) In the late 19th century Queenscliff was a favorite weekend destination for well-to-do Melburnians, who traveled on paddle steamers or by train to stay at the area's grand hotels. Some, like the Vue Grand and the Queenscliff Hotel, welcome tourists to this day. Be sure to check out Fort Queenscliff, another landmark from bygone days.

Good restaurants and quiet charm are also traits of Queenscliff. The best beach is at Lonsdale Bay, where a long stretch of golden sand and gentle surf makes a great place to wade, walk, or swim in summer. The playground of families during the day and dog walkers come dusk, Queenscliff is a restful alternative to the resort towns of Sorrento and Portsea on the other side of the bay. Point Lonsdale, once a sleepy little village known primarily for its lighthouse, is now a busy summer resort. On the last weekend in November the annual Queenscliff Music Festival draws hundreds of visitors to town.

> **LIGHT UP YOUR TRIP**
>
> If you're into lighthouses, then this coast is a must-see. Here you can find seven historic lighthouses of varying shapes and sizes—from Point Lonsdale in the east to Portland in the west. Don't miss the tall white back and red cap of beautiful **Split Point lighthouse** at Aireys Inlet, while **Cape Otway lighthouse** is the oldest on mainland Australia and marks the point where the Southern Ocean and Bass Strait collides. Farther west at Portland is majestic **Cape Nelson lighthouse**, high above ferocious seas. Guided tours are available.

WHERE TO STAY & EAT

$$$$ ✗🏠 **Athelstane House.** This charming, welcoming old home has been a guesthouse since 1860. Although the historic exterior is unchanged, inside you will find the latest furnishings. Eight of the nine rooms have bathrooms with corner hot tubs; three have balconies. A private cottage is also available. The restaurant ($$) is famed for its Mod-Oz cuisine, and dishes may include Cajun-spiced kangaroo loin with green-pea puree and caramelized onion jus. Wines from the local Bellarine vineyards accompany lunch and dinner meals; at breakfast you can sit outside in one of the expansive courtyards. There is a minimum two-night stay on weekends. ✉4 Hobson St., 3225 ☎03/5258–1024 ⊕www.athelstane.com.au ⇆9 rooms, 1 cottage ♿In-room: hot tubs, VCR. In-hotel: restaurant, room service, parking (no fee) ▭AE, DC, MC, V ⌾BP.

$$$–$$$$ ✗🏠 **Vue Grand Hotel.** Built by George Admans in 1881, the Vue Grand blends old-world elegance with modern trimmings (you'll realize this as you laze in the heated indoor swimming pool while listening to classical music). Billiard tables, a gymnasium, and a conservatory also beckon, although the hotel's prime focus is its grand dining room. Filled with flowers and with live piano music every Saturday night, it is one of the finest places on the peninsula to wine and dine ($–$$). All guest rooms have full bathrooms (quite rare for a historic

hotel) and feature high ceilings, antique furniture, period fittings, and, in a nod to contemporary comforts, CD players. Snapshots depicting the hotel's history adorn walls in the foyer and bar-lounge. Guests with children should notify the hotel in advance so special arrangements can be made. ⊠*46 Hesse St., 3225* ☎*03/5258–1544* 🖷*03/5258–3471* ⊕*www.vuegrand.com.au* ⮱*27 rooms, 5 suites* ♿*In-hotel: restaurant, bar, pool, gym, parking (no fee), minibar* ▱*AE, DC, MC, V* ❢◎❢*BP.*

$$$
Fodor's Choice
★

✕🖳 **Queenscliff Hotel.** Gloriously restored, this 19th-century beauty has soaring, pressed-metal ceilings, stained-glass windows, antique furnishings, and opulent sitting rooms graced with open fires and enormous armchairs. If you're after period charm rather than spacious modernity, this is the place for you. Dining ($–$$) is offered in the small formal room, a leafy conservatory, or an outdoor courtyard with an ornate fountain; the international cuisine might include braised rabbit leg with parsnips. The hotel's location—across from a park and with views to the ocean—is enviable. ⊠*16 Gellibrand St., 3225* ☎*03/5258–1066* ⊕*www.queenscliffhotel.com.au* ⮱*18 rooms* ♿*In-room: no a/c, no phone, no TV. In-hotel: 2 restaurants, bar, laundry facilities* ▱*AE, DC, MC, V* ❢◎❢*BP.*

EN ROUTE

From Queenscliff, follow signs toward the Great Ocean Road for 45 km (28 mi) to **Torquay**, Australia's premier surfing and windsurfing resort, and Bell's Beach, famous for its Easter surfing contests and its October international windsurfing competitions. Great Ocean Road, a positively magnificent coastal drive, officially begins at Eastern View, 10 km (6 mi) east of Lorne. The seaside towns of Anglesea, Aireys Inlet, and Fairhaven also make good warm-weather swimming stops.

LORNE

140 km (87 mi) southwest of Melbourne, 95 km (59 mi) southwest of Queenscliff, 50 km (31 mi) southwest of Torquay.

A popular holiday town between sweeping Loutit Bay and the Otway Mountain Range, Lorne is the site of both a wild celebration every New Year's Eve and the popular Pier-to-Pub Swim held on the first weekend in January. Some people make their reservations a year or more in advance. It's also the home of the Great Otway Classic, a footrace held annually on the second weekend in June. The town has a lively café and pub scene, as well as several upscale restaurants, trendy boutiques, and a day spa.

WHERE TO STAY & EAT

$–$$
★

✕ **Marks.** Fresh seafood—from fried calamari to grilled flathead—is the draw at this Lorne institution. The decor is "funky seaside" with bright walls, blue chairs, and a smattering of local art and sculpture for sale. Pan-fried barramundi, grilled Atlantic salmon, and local baby snapper are popular choices. It's located on the main road across from the beach. ⊠*124 Mountjoy Parade* ☎*03/5289–2787* ▱*AE, MC, V.*

$-$$
★
✕**Reifs.** You could easily while away most of the day at this casual eatery across from the beach. Lunch might include salt-and-chili squid, soft-shell crab, or saffron seafood linguine with chunks of fish, prawns, mussels, and squid. You might fancy an early alfresco dinner before taking in a movie at the quaint cinema right next door. ⊠ *84 Mountjoy Parade* ☎ *03/5289–2366* ⊟*AE, MC, V.*

$$$-$$$$
🏨**Mantra Erskine Beach Resort.** This huge complex, set on 12 acres near the water's edge, reopened in early 2006 following a A$20 million upgrade. All rooms and apartments, including those in the 1868 guesthouse, have been given a facelift and now have nice touches like hot tubs. A stylish new restaurant, a funky café, and a chic cocktail lounge were also added, along with that must-have resort experience, the day spa. ⊠ *Mountjoy Parade, 3232* ☎ *03/5289–1209* ⊕ *www.stellaresorts.com.au* ⇄*157 rooms, 130 apartments* ♿*In-room: kitchen (some), DVD, dial-up, Wi-Fi. In-hotel: 2 restaurants, bar, tennis courts, pool, gym, spa, beachfront, laundry facilities, parking (no fee)* ⊟*AE, DC, MC, V* ⍥*BP.*

$$$
🏨**Stanmorr Bed and Breakfast.** Built in the 1920s, this gracious homestead sits a stone's throw from the water, just beyond Lorne's main huddle of shops. Rooms are spacious and private, with picture windows and private balconies offering water views and opportunities to meet colorful locals—including king parrots, rosellas, and kookaburras. Hot tubs, open fireplaces, and hearty home-cooked breakfasts add to the appeal. ⊠ *64 Otway St., 3232* ☎ *03/5289–1530* ⊕ *www.stanmorr.com* ⇄*1 studio, 1 suite, 3 rooms in a cottage* ♿*In-hotel: restaurant, bar, Internet room* ⊟*AE, DC, MC, V* ⍥*BP.*

EN ROUTE
About an hour's drive and 70 km (43 mi) from Lorne (follow the Great Ocean Road until it joins Skenes Creek Road, then take Forrest Apollo Bay Road to Beech Forest Road, then Colac Lavers Hill Road until you reach the signed turnoff to Phillips Track) you'll find the entrance to the **Otway Fly** (☎ *03/5235–9200 or 1800/300477* ⊕ *www.otwayfly.com*). The Fly is a 1,969-foot-long elevated treetop walk, where you can meander on a steel walkway structure (one section is springboard-cantilevered, and gently bounces as you pass over Young's Creek) above the rain-forest canopy. You'll see the tops of giant myrtle beech, blackwood, and mountain ash trees, as well as spectacular views of the surrounding region. It's open daily 9–5; tickets are A$17.

APOLLO BAY

★
186 km (116 mi) southwest of Melbourne, 44 km (28 mi) southwest of Lorne.

The locals call Apollo Bay "paradise by the sea," and its lovely setting at the base of forested hills facing a crescent-shape beach makes it easy to see why. This is more working fishing village than party town—the main catch here is crayfish and abalone—but there are many natural attractions to entice you to stay a day or two. The beach is long and great for swimming and surfing; fishing is excellent. The rain forest, waterfalls, and a glowworm colony are nearby.

The Great Ocean Walk begins at Marengo, just west of Apollo Bay. The walk stretches 91 km (57 mi) to Glenample Homestead, adjacent to the Twelve Apostles, passing through national parks and rugged coastline.

WHERE TO STAY & EAT

$$$–$$$$ ✕🏠 **Chris's Beacon Point Restaurant**
FodorśChoice **and Villas.** Set high in the Otway
★ Ranges with stunning views over the ocean, this is a wonderful place to dine or bed down for the night. The accommodations have uninterrupted views from the floor-to-ceiling windows and timber balconies. The studios can accommodate four people. The restaurant ($$–$$$), opened in 1978 by owner Chris Talihmanidis, draws people from all over the region for Greek-inspired dishes such as souvlaki (lamb cubes marinated in rosemary and honey). To get here, take the Skenes Creek Road turnoff about 3 km (2 mi) from Apollo Bay and wind up a hill to Beacon Point. ⊠*280 Skenes Creek Rd., 3233* ☎*03/5237–6411* ⊕*www.visitvictoria.com/ christos* ⏰*6 villas, 2 studios* ⚂*In-room: no phone, kitchen (some), DVD. In-hotel: restaurant, room service, parking (no fee), no elevator* ☰*AE, DC, MC, V.*

¢ 🏠 **Apollo Bay Eco Beach YHA.** More like a hip beach house than a youth
★ hostel, this friendly two-story lodge has earned its name with a low-impact architectural design, solar hot water, and recycling systems. There are dorm rooms as well as single, twin, double, and family rooms, many with balconies with great bay views. Public areas—two lounges with quiet reading nooks, a separate TV room, and an Internet room—have comfy sofas and beanbags. There's plenty of room to create culinary feasts in the two shared kitchens. The hostel is part of the YHA chain and offers discounts for members. ⊠*5 Pascoe St., 3233* ☎*03/5237–7899* ⊕*www.yha.com.au* ⏰*30 rooms, 6 dorm rooms (4 beds in each)* ⚂*In-hotel: bar, bicycles, public Internet, no elevator* ☰*MC, V.*

> ## STACKS OF ROCKS
>
> The Twelve Apostles need no introduction since these sandstone structures adorn every tourist brochure. But few visitors know about the wonderful Bay of Islands and Bay of Martyrs just west of the town of Peterborough. Here dozens of "rock stacks" litter the ocean forming a colossal natural sculpture park. You can even view them from the comfort of your car in one of the seaside car parks. For those who want to take in the fresh air, there are sign-posted walking tracks leading to the site of famous shipwrecks.

PORT CAMPBELL NATIONAL PARK

FodorśChoice *225 km (140 mi) southwest of Melbourne, 56 km (35 mi) west of*
★ *Lorne.*

Stretching some 30 km (19 mi) along the southern Victoria coastline, Port Campbell National Park is the site of some of the most famously beautiful geological formations in Australia. Along this coast the ferocious Southern Ocean has gnawed at the limestone cliffs for aeons, creating a sort of badlands-by-the-sea, where strangely shaped formations stand offshore amid the surf. The most famous of these formations is the Twelve Apostles, as much a symbol for Victoria as the Sydney Opera House is for New South Wales. (The name has always been a misnomer, as there were only nine of these stone columns. Then, in 2005, one of them collapsed into the sea, leaving behind just eight.) If you happen to be visiting the Twelve Apostles just after sunset, you're likely to see bands of Little Penguins returning to their burrows on the beach. There's a population of around 3,000 of the cute creatures in the area.

Loch Ard Gorge, named after the iron-hulled clipper that wrecked on the shores of nearby Mutton Bird Island in 1878, is another spectacular place to walk. Four of the *Loch Ard*'s victims are buried in a nearby cemetery, while a sign by the gorge tells the story of the ship and its crew. This stretch of coast is often called the Shipwreck Coast for the hundreds of vessels that have met an untimely end in the treacherous waters. The Historic Shipwreck Trail, with landmarks describing 25 of the disasters, stretches from Moonlight Head to Port Fairy.

The best time to visit the park is late September to April, when you can also witness the boisterous birdlife on nearby Mutton Bird Island. Toward nightfall, hundreds of hawks and kites circle the island in search of baby mutton birds emerging from their protective burrows. The hawks and kites beat a hasty retreat at the sight of thousands of adult shearwaters approaching with food for their chicks as the last light fades from the sky.

The **Port Campbell Visitors Centre** (⊠*26 Morris St., Port Campbell* ☎*03/5598–6089*) is open daily 9 to 5. A self-guided, 1½-hour Discovery Walk begins near Port Campbell Beach, where it's safe to swim. The pounding surf and undertow are treacherous at other nearby beaches. ⊠*Parks office: Tregea St., Port Campbell* ☎*13–1963.*

WHERE TO STAY & EAT

$$ ✗ **Waves.** You won't see any waves from this relaxed, main-street eatery even though it's only yards from the water. You will find enormous breakfasts and fireside seafood dinners, a spacious sundeck, and a friendly staff. The menu may feature such diverse dishes as Asian spiced Flinders Island wallaby (a dish rarely, if ever, seen on a menu) and sizzling steaks. ⊠*29 Lord St., Port Campbell* ☎*03/5598–6111* ⊟*AE, MC, V.*

$$$ ▦ **Southern Ocean Villas.** Ideally situated on the edge of Port Campbell National Park, within short walking distance of the town center and beach, these villas are stylishly furnished, and fitted with polished wood floors, picture windows, and high ceilings. Each unit has two bedrooms and an upstairs loft. One villa accommodates six. ⊠*2 McCue St., Port Campbell, 3269* ☎*03/5598–4200* ⊕*www.southernoceanvillas.com* ➥*18 villas* ⚫*In-room: kitchen, DVD. In-hotel: laundry facilities, no elevator* ⊟*AE, DC, MC, V.*

$–$$ ▦ **Daysy Hill Country Cottages.** Five sandstone-and-cedar cottages, set alongside manicured gardens, have views over the Newfield Valley.

Inside, the spacious rooms have comfortable couches, wooden furnishings, open fireplaces, TVs with cable movies, VCRs, and CD players. Breakfast provisions can be provided for around $A10 per person. Luxury suites with hot tubs and deluxe self-contained cabins are also available. ⊠*7353 Timboon/Port Campbell Rd., Port Campbell, 3269* ☎*03/5598–6226* ⊕*www.greatoceanroad.nu/daysyhill* ⬢*5 cottages, 4 suites, 3 cabins* ⚭*In-room: kitchen. In-hotel: laundry facilities, no elevator* ⊟*AE, DC, MC, V.*

PORT FAIRY

291 km (180 mi) southwest of Melbourne, 29 km (18 mi) west of Warrnambool.

Port Fairy is widely considered to be the state's prettiest village. The second-oldest town in Victoria, it was originally known as Belfast, and there are indeed echoes of Ireland in the landscape and architecture. More than 50 of the cottages and sturdy bluestone buildings that line the banks of the River Moyne have been classified as landmarks by the National Trust, and few towns repay a leisurely stroll so richly. The town still thrives as the base for a fishing fleet, and as host to the Port Fairy Folk Festival, one of Australia's most famous musical events, held every March.

The town has a large colony of short-tailed shearwaters that nest on Griffiths Island. Amazingly, these birds travel here from the Aleutian Islands near Alaska, always arriving within three days of September 22. You can take a 45-minute walk around the island on marked trails to the historic lighthouse.

Founded during the whaling heyday in the 19th century, Port Fairy was once a whaling station with one of the largest ports in Victoria. The **Historical Society Museum** contains relics from whaling days and from the many ships that have foundered along this coast. ⊠*Old Courthouse, Gipps St.* ☎*03/5568–2492* ⬢*A$3* ☉ *Wed. and weekends 2–5.*

Mott's Cottage is a restored limestone-and-timber cottage built by Sam Mott, a member of the 1830s whaling crew from the cutter *Fairy* who founded the town. ⊠*5 Sackville St.* ☎*03/5568–2682* ⬢*A$2* ☉ *Wed. and weekends 2–4, or by appointment.*

The **Port Fairy Maritime & Shipwreck Heritage Walk** is a 2-km (1-mi) trail that passes the sites of several shipwrecks: the bark *Socrates,* which was battered by huge seas in 1843; the bark *Lydia,* which wrecked off the coast in 1847; the schooner *Thistle,* which went down in 1837; and the brigantine *Essington,* which sank while moored at Port Fairy in 1852. Other historic attractions en route include the town port, the lifeboat station, riverside warehouses, and Griffiths Island Lighthouse. The walk is well marked.

WHERE TO STAY & EAT

¢–$ ✕🏨 **Dublin House Inn.** This solid stone building with a striking pink color scheme dates from 1855. The four suites, however, are contemporary in design and fitted with modern conveniences. The 32-seat restaurant ($–$$), open for dinner daily, is where chef Nick Strapp whips up traditional Mediterranean dishes. His duet of ocean fish (using the two catches of the day) is a local favorite. ✉*57 Bank St., 3284* ☎*03/5568–2022* ⊕*www.myportfairy.com/dublinhouse* ➪*3 suites, 1 cottage* ⚷*In-room: no phone, kitchen (some). In-hotel: restaurant, laundry facilities, laundry service, parking (no fee), no elevator* ⊟*AE, MC, V* ⦿*BP.*

$$$ 🏨 **Oscars Waterfront Boutique Hotel.** Overlooking the waterfront and a
★ marina of yachts, Oscar's takes French provincial style and gives it an Australian edge. Each room is individually decorated—some in stripes, others in florals—and various communal lounges have open fireplaces, plush armchairs, and regional artwork. Gourmet breakfasts, for which Oscars is renowned, include banana hotcakes and tomato bruschetta with basil butter. If the weather allows, breakfast is served on the lovely veranda overlooking the river. ✉*41B Gipps St., 3284* ☎*03/5568–3022* ⊕*www.oscarswaterfront.com* ➪*6 rooms, 1 suite* ⚷*In-room: refrigerator. In-hotel: bar, no elevator* ⊟*AE, MC, V* ⦿*BP.*

$$–$$$ 🏨 **Goble's Mill House.** An imaginative refurbishment of an 1865 flour mill on the bank of the Moyne River transformed it into six guest rooms with private bathrooms and spacious sitting areas, all furnished with antiques. The upper-story loft bedroom is especially appealing, with a balcony overlooking the ever-active river. The open fire makes the sitting room cozy, and a separate guest pantry is stocked with juices and freshly baked shortbreads. You can also enjoy fishing off the Mill House's private jetty. ✉*75 Gipps St., 3284* ☎*03/5568–1118* ⊕*www.goblesmill.myportfairy.com* ➪*6 rooms* ⚷*In-room: no a/c, no phone, no TV. In-hotel: parking (no fee), no elevator* ⊟*MC, V* ⦿*BP.*

$–$$$ 🏨 **Merrijig Inn.** Overlooking the riverbank from King George Square, this beautifully restored 1841 Georgian-style building is Victoria's oldest inn. In late 2006 the inn was bought by local chef Ryan Sessions and partner Kirstyn White, who re-opened the restaurant for dinner. One of Ryan's signature dishes is sea scallops with truffle butter sauce. Accommodation is a mix of cozy attic bedrooms with storybook atmospheres, and ground-floor suites with snug sitting rooms. The roaring fireplaces are perfect for whiling away the hours with a good book. Breakfast is served in the light-filled conservatory with views of the charming cottage garden. ✉*Campbell and Gipps Sts., 3284* ☎*03/5568–2324* ⊕*www.merrijiginn.com* ➪*4 rooms, 4 suites* ⚷*In-room: No TV in attic rooms, no phone. In-hotel: restaurant, bar, no elevator* ⊟*AE, MC, V* ⦿*BP.*

WEST COAST REGION ESSENTIALS

TRANSPORTATION

BY BOAT

The Queenscliff–Sorrento Ferry departs on the hour (in both directions) from 7 AM to 6 PM. The journey takes 40 minutes and costs A$9 for pedestrians, A$47 for cars, and A$6 for each car passenger in the high season.

Contact **Queenscliff–Sorrento Ferry** (☎ *03/5258-3244* ⊕ *www.searoad. com.au*).

BY CAR

Driving is the most convenient way to see the region, and the only way to really enjoy the Great Ocean Road. Distances are considerable, and the going may be slow on the most scenic routes, especially during the summer holiday period.

Start out by taking the Princes Highway west from Melbourne to Geelong. From there, follow signs to Queenscliff and Torquay, where you'll connect with the Great Ocean Road. For an alternative inland route to Warrnambool (much quicker, but vastly less interesting), take the Princes Highway.

BY TRAIN

V-Line operates daily services between Melbourne and Warrnambool, with some trains stopping at Geelong along the way. Although the trains provide a restful means of getting to the South West region, they run inland and don't provide the extraordinary views you can see by car. However, V-Line buses connect with the trains to provide transport to coastal towns; take the train to Marshall (one stop beyond Geelong) to connect with a bus to Lorne, Apollo Bay, and Port Campbell, or travel by train to Warrnambool and take a bus to Port Fairy.

Contact **V-Line** (☎ *13-6196* ⊕ *www.vline.com.au*).

CONTACTS & RESOURCES

EMERGENCIES

In an emergency, dial **000** to reach an ambulance, the police, or the fire department.

Contacts **Geelong Private Hospital** (✉ *Ryrie and Bellarrine Sts., Geelong* ☎ *03/5226-1600*). **Medical Centre Pharmacy** (✉ *262 Shannon Ave., Geelong West* ☎ *03/5229-7727*).

TOURS

AAT Kings has a day tour of the Great Ocean Road from Melbourne for A$160. Passengers can stay overnight in a selection of accommodations before returning to Melbourne on a bus the next day.

The Wayward Bus is a minibus that takes 3½ days to meander from Melbourne to Adelaide via the Great Ocean Road, Mt. Gambier, and the Coorong, with overnight stops at Apollo Bay and Port Fairy.

Passengers can leave the bus at either overnight stop and catch the following bus. Tours depart from Melbourne on Tuesday, Thursday, and Saturday October–April. It's A$355 per person (with hostel accommodation) or A$460 (twin-share room), including three nights' accommodation and breakfasts.

Great Ocean Road Helicopters has 10-, 15-, and 25-minute flights that take in the Twelve Apostles and Loch Ard Gorge on the shorter trips, adding London Bridge, the Bay of Martyrs, and the Bay of Islands on longer runs. Prices range from A$90 to A$195 per person.

> ## BRUSH STROKES
>
> The riches of Victoria's goldfields are reflected in beautiful Victorian buildings, and in the treasures of the art galleries of Ballarat, Bendigo, and Castlemaine. Among Australia's top five regional galleries, they show the works of famous artists such as Arthur Boyd and Sidney Nolan. Take advantage of the opportunity to view the masterpieces away from the big-city crowds.

Contacts AAT Kings (⊠ *180 Swanson St., City Center, Melbourne* ☎ *03/9663–3377 or 1300/556100* ⊕ *www.aatkings.com.ae*).

VISITOR INFORMATION
The Geelong Great Ocean Road Visitor Information Centre, Port Fairy Tourist Information Centre, and Warrnambool Visitor Information Centre are open daily weekdays 9–5. Contact Parks Victoria for more information on area parks.

Contacts Geelong Great Ocean Road Visitor Information Centre (⊠ *Stead Park at corner of Princes Hwy. and St. Georges Rd., Corio, Geelong* ☎ *03/5275–5797 or 1800/620888* ⊕ *www.visitgeelong.org*). **Parks Victoria** (☎ *13–1963* ⊕ *www. parkweb.vic.gov.au*). **Port Fairy Tourist Information Centre** (⊠ *Bank St., Port Fairy* ☎ *03/5568–2682* ⊕ *www.port-fairy.com*). **Warrnambool Visitor Information Centre** (⊠ *Flagstaff Hill, Merri St., Warrnambool* ☎ *03/5559–4620 or 1800/637725* ⊕ *www.warrnamboolinfo.com.au*).

THE GOLD COUNTRY & THE GRAMPIANS

Victoria was changed forever in the early 1850s by the discovery of gold in the center of the state. Fantastic news of gold deposits caused immigrants from every corner of the world to pour into Victoria to seek their fortunes as "diggers"—a name that has become synonymous with Australians ever since. Few miners became wealthy from their searches, however. The real money was made by those supplying goods and services to the thousands who had succumbed to gold fever.

Gold towns like Ballarat, Castlemaine, Maldon, and Bendigo sprang up like mushrooms to accommodate these fortune seekers, and prospered until the gold rush receded. Afterward, they became ghost towns or turned to agriculture to survive. Today Victoria's gold is again being mined in limited quantities, while these historic old towns remain interesting relics of Australia's past.

About 120 km (79 mi) west of the Gold Country are the Grampians, sometimes referred to by their Aboriginal name Gariwerd. This 415,000-acre region combines stunning mountain scenery, abundant native wildlife, and invigorating outdoor activities. The sharp sandstone peaks here were long ago forced up from an ancient seabed, and sculpted by aeons of wind and rain. Today the park has more than 160 km (106 mi) of walking trails, as well as some 900 wildflower species, 200 species of birds, and 35 species of native mammals. The best time to visit is October–December, when wildflowers carpet the landscape, the weather is mild, and summer crowds have yet to arrive.

GOLD COUNTRY

Although Victoria was not the first Australian state to experience a gold rush, when gold was discovered here in 1851 it became a veritable El Dorado. During the boom years of the 19th century, 90% of the gold mined in Australia came from the state. The biggest finds were at Ballarat and then Bendigo, and the Ballarat diggings proved to be among the richest alluvial goldfields in the world.

This region of Victoria is now considered a center for modern-day rejuvenation. Between Ballarat and other historic gold towns to the north are the twin hot spots of Daylesford and Hepburn Springs—which together constitute the spa capital of Australia.

BALLARAT
106 km (66 mi) northwest of Melbourne, 146 km (91 mi) east of Halls Gap.

In the local Aboriginal language, the name Ballarat means "resting place." In pre-gold-rush days, nearby Lake Wendouree provided the area with a plentiful supply of food. Once the boom hit, however, the town became much less restful; in 1854 Ballarat was the scene of the battle of the Eureka Stockade, a skirmish that took place between miners and authorities over gold license fees that miners were forced to pay. More than 20 men died in the battle. Today their flag—the Southern Cross—is a symbol of Australia's egalitarian spirit.

Despite the harsh times, fortunes made from the mines (and from the miners) resulted in the grand Victorian architecture on Sturt and Lydiard streets—note the post office, the town hall, Craig's Royal Hotel, and Her Majesty's Theater. The Old Colonists' Hall and the Mining Exchange (at 20 and 26 Lydiard St., respectively) now house shops and cafés. The visitor center has a self-guided heritage walk.

☾ All sorts of native animals, including saltwater crocodiles, snakes, lizards, wombats, echidnas, and kangaroos, can be found at **Ballarat Wildlife Park.** Daily tours of the park are led at 11, with a koala show at 2, a wombat show at 2:30, and a crocodile feeding at 3. The park also has a café, and barbecue and picnic areas. ⊠ *Fussel and York Sts., East Ballarat* ☎ *03/5333–5933* ⊕ *www.wildlifepark.com.au* 🖾 *A$20* ⊙ *Daily 9–5:30.*

Ballarat Fine Art Gallery has a large collection of contemporary Australian art. It also has some impressive historical exhibits, like the tattered remains of the Southern Cross flag that was flown defiantly by the rebels at the Eureka Stockade. ⊠ *40 Lydiard St.* ☎ *03/53201–5858* ⊕ *www.balgal.com* 🖾 *A$5* ⊙ *Daily 10:30–5.*

On the shores of Lake Wendouree, Ballarat's **Botanic Gardens** are identifiable by the brilliant blooms and classical statuary. At the rear of the gardens, the Conservatory is the focus of events during the town's Begonia Festival, held each March. ⊠ *Wendouree Parade* ☎ *No phone* 🖾 *Free* ⊙ *Daily sunrise–sunset.*

At **Eureka Centre,** an enormous flag flutters from a towering mast outside this futuristic museum that depicts the battle at the Eureka Stockade. There is also a stone monument erected by miners in the 1880s and memorial gardens. ⊠ *Eureka and Rodier Sts.* ☎ *02/5333–1852* ⊕ *www.eurekaballarat.com* 🖾 *A$8* ⊙ *Daily 9–4:30.*

⟳ **Sovereign Hill,** built on the site of the Sovereign Hill Quartz Mining Company's mines, provides an authentic look at life, work, and play in this area during the gold rush. The main street features a hotel, blacksmith's shop, bakery, and post office—all perfectly preserved relics of their time. You can have your photo taken in period costumes, take a mineshaft tour, pan for gold, ride in a stagecoach, or head to the "lolly shop" to sample old-fashioned candy. You can also watch "Blood on the Southern Cross," a 90-minute sound-and-light spectacular that focuses on the Eureka uprising. Your ticket also gets you into the **Gold Museum,** across Bradshaw Street. It displays an extensive collection of nuggets from the Ballarat diggings. ⊠ *Bradshaw St.* ☎ *03/5337–1100* 🖾 *A$32.50, multimedia show A$39, combination ticket A$67* ⊙ *Daily 10–5.*

About 20 km (12 mi) southeast of Ballarat, **Yuulong Lavender Estate** is a lovely estate which features a retail nursery, a craft and tea-room complex, and a large garden fronting contoured fields of lavender. Music and farming festivals are scheduled throughout the summer months, and many culinary, craft, and skin-care products made from lavender are produced here. ⊠ *Yendon Rd., Mt. Egerton* ☎ *03/5368–9453* 🖾 *A$4.40* ⊙ *Oct.–Apr., Wed.–Sun. 10–4:30* ⊙ *May–Sept.*

WHERE TO STAY & EAT

$$–$$$ ✗ **Cincotta's.** Asian, Middle Eastern, and European dishes are paired
★ here with wonderful wines. This restaurant, casual and relaxed by day, with tablecloths and candlelight in the evening, is the perfect place for a leisurely brunch, afternoon tea, or a romantic dinner. The calamari in Parmesan batter, walnut-stuffed spatchcock, and Thai beef salad are ideally matched with local wines. ⊠ *102 Sturt St.* ☎ *03/5331–1402* ⊟ *AE, DC, MC, V.*

$–$$ ✗**Europa Cafe.** The all-day break-
fast at this hip yet relaxed dining
spot is legendary, but the lunches
and dinner are also worth a trip.
Lunch includes such savory treats
as smoked-salmon bruschetta. For
dinner, go for the lamb and prune
tajine or the duck breast on sweet-
potato pancake and dark cherry
sauce. ✉*411 Sturt St.* ☎*03/5331–
2486* ▭*AE, DC, MC, V* ☾*No
dinner Mon.–Wed.*

$ ✗**L'espresso.** Meals at this local
★   institution taste like they're from
your grandmother's kitchen. It's
open for breakfast and lunch, with
specials like salmon fillet with
lemon aioli or bruschetta with mas-
carpone and figs. This was a popular record shop back in the 1970s,
and you can still buy good blues,
jazz, and interesting contemporary
music CDs here. ✉*417 Sturt St.* ☎*03/5333–1789* ▭*No credit cards*
☾*No dinner.*

$–$$ ✗▦**The Ansonia.** Built in the 1870s as professional offices—and res-
★   cued by new owners, who refurbished it completely—the Ansonia is
now an excellent boutique hotel and dining spot. You enter through
impressive wrought-iron gates under a grand portico to a light-filled
atrium. There are several different styles of accommodation, from
studios to two-bedroom apartments. The restaurant, Tozers at the
Ansonia ($$), serves Mod-Oz cuisine. ✉*32 Lydiard St. S, 3350*
☎*03/5332–4678* ⊕*www.Ansonia.com.au* ⮐*20 rooms* ♿*In-room:
Wi-Fi. In-hotel: restaurant, laundry service, public Internet, parking
(no fee)* ▭*AE, DC, MC, V.*

$–$$$ ▦**Ballarat Heritage Homestays.** This group manages a number of his-
toric properties in and around Ballarat, including Ravenswood, Wil-
ton House, Glen Eira, Kingsley Place, Quamby on Errard, and Tait's
Cottage. These range from self-contained cottages to traditional B&B
properties. Tucked behind a garden brimming with peach trees, pussy
willows, fuchsias, and climbing roses, Ravenswood is a three-bedroom
timber cottage ideal for families or small groups. The house, a bit less
than 1½ km (1 mi) from the center of Ballarat, has contemporary decor
and a full kitchen. Breakfast supplies are provided. ✉*185 Victoria St.,
3354* ☎*03/5332–8296* ⊕*www.heritagehomestay.com* ⮐*6 properties*
▭*AE, DC, MC, V* ⦿*CP.*

DAYLESFORD & HEPBURN SPRINGS

109 km (68 mi) northwest of Melbourne, 45 km (28 mi) northeast of Ballarat.

Nestled in the slopes of the Great Dividing Range, Daylesford and its nearby twin, Hepburn Springs, are a spa lover's paradise. The water table here is naturally aerated with carbon dioxide and rich in soluble mineral salts, making it ideal for indulging in mineral baths and other rejuvenating treatments. The natural springs were first noted during the gold rush, and Swiss-Italian immigrants established a spa at Hepburn Springs in 1875. There are now about 70 natural springs in the area. The best time to visit the area is autumn, when the deciduous trees turn bronze and you can finish up a relaxing day next to an open fire with a glass of local red.

Perched on a hillside overlooking Daylesford, the **Convent Gallery** is a former nunnery that has been restored to its lovely Victorian state. At the front of the gallery is Bad Habits, a sunny café that serves light lunches and snacks. Altar Bar is a hip place for a drink. ⊠ *Daly St., Daylesford* ☎ *03/5348–3211* 🖼 *A$4.50* ⊙ *Daily 10–5.*

Fodor's Choice
★

Mineral baths and treatments are available at the bright, modern **Hepburn Spa Mineral Springs Wellness Retreat,** where the facilities include communal and private hot-spring baths, flotation tanks, and saunas. Established in 1895, it is still the only spa in town with public pools utilizing the natural underground springs, whose water is rich in minerals including calcium, silica, magnesium, bicarbonate, and iron. Massages, facials, and an extensive menu of body treatments are available. The resort is set in a leafy valley, and skirted by herb gardens. ⊠ *1 Mineral Springs Reserve, Hepburn Springs* ☎ *03/5348–8888* ⊕ *www. hepburnspa.com.au* 🖼 *Weekdays A$30, weekends A$45* ⊙ *Sun.–Fri. 10–6, Sat. 9–7.*

Above the Hepburn Springs Spa Mineral Springs Wellness Retreat, a path winds through a series of mineral springs at the **Mineral Springs Reserve.** Each spring has a slightly different chemical composition—and a significantly different taste. You can bring empty bottles, if you like; they can be filled with the mineral water of your choice, for free.

WHERE TO STAY & EAT

$$$$
Fodor's Choice
★

✕🖼 **Lake House & Restaurant.** Consistently rated one of central Victoria's best restaurants, this rambling lakeside pavilion brings glamour to spa country. The seasonal menu ($–$$), which utilizes fresh Australian produce, lists such delicacies as hot gravlax of Atlantic salmon, as well as a selection of imaginative Asian-accented and vegetarian dishes. Choose the elegant dining room or the deck overlooking the beautiful lake. The accommodations, set in 6 acres of gardens, are standard rooms in the original homestead and waterfront rooms and suites. All have balconies; the suites have private lounges. A day spa offers "treatments with a twist" such as the "aromatherapy sugar shock," along with the more-traditional pampering. ⊠ *King St., Daylesford, 3460* ☎ *03/5348–3329* 🖶 *03/5448–3995* ⊕ *www.lakehouse.com.au* 🛏 *33 rooms and suites* ⚡ *In-room: no a/c (some). In-hotel: restaurant, bar,* *tennis court, pool, bicycles, laundry service, parking (no fee), no elevator* ⊟*AE, DC, MC, V* ⏀|*BP.*

$$$ ⊡**Holcombe Country Retreat.** This luxurious lodge is an exclusive retreat for couples or groups of friends. This beautifully designed split-level stone structure has two bedrooms and two bathrooms, each with a hot tub. You can fish for trout, wander the landscaped property, or spot kangaroos and kookaburras in between trips to the spa that's 10 minutes away in Hepburn Springs. The new owners Grant and Rozzie Stuart provide guests with a breakfast basket of goodies. There's a minimum two-night stay on weekends. ⊠*Holcombe Rd., Glenlyon, 3461* ✛*12 km (8 mi) northeast of Daylesford* ☎*03/5348–7514* ⊕*www.holcombe.com.au* ⟿*1 lodge* ఉ*In-room: no a/c (some), kitchen, dial-up. In-hotel: tennis court, bicycles, laundry service, parking (no fee), no kids, no elevator* ⊟*AE, DC, MC, V* ⏀|*BP.*

BENDIGO

150 km (93 mi) northwest of Melbourne, 36 km (22 mi) northeast of Maldon, 92 km (57 mi) south of Echuca.

Gold was discovered in the Bendigo district in 1851, and the boom lasted well into the 1880s. The city's magnificent public buildings bear witness to the richness of its mines. Today Bendigo is a bustling, enterprising small city, with distinguished buildings lining both sides of Pall Mall in the city center. These include the **Shamrock Hotel, General Post Office,** and **Law Courts,** all majestic examples of late-Victorian architecture. Although these glorious relics of a golden age dominate the landscape, the city is far from a time warp. You'll also find a lively café and restaurant scene, 30 boutique wineries, and one of the best regional art galleries in Australia.

Fodor'sChoice   The beautifully refurbished **Bendigo Art Gallery** houses a notable collec-
★   tion of contemporary Australian paintings, including the work of Jeffrey Smart, Lloyd Rees, and Clifton Pugh. (Pugh once owned a remote Outback pub infamous for its walls daubed with his own pornographic cartoons.) The gallery also has some significant 19th-century French realist and impressionist works, bequeathed by a local surgeon. ⊠*42 View St.* ☎*03/5443–4991* ⊠*Free* ⊙*Daily 10–5.*

Bendigo Pottery, Australia's oldest working pottery shop, turns out the distinctive brown-and-cream style that many Australians have in their kitchens. First established in 1858, the historic workshop offers demonstrations. You can even get your hands dirty with your own clay creation. It's located 6½ km (4 mi) northeast of Bendigo on the way to Echuca. ⊠*146 Midland Hwy., Epsom* ☎*03/5448–4404* ⊕*www. bendigopottery.com.au* ⊠*Free, museum A$7* ⊙*Daily 9–5.*

Central Deborah Gold Mine, with a 1,665-foot mine shaft, yielded almost a ton of gold before it closed in 1954. To experience life underground, take a guided tour of the mine. An elevator descends 200 feet below ground level. ⊠*76 Violet St.* ☎*03/5443–8322* ⊠*A$19* ⊙*Daily 9:30–5; last tour at 4:05.*

The superb **Golden Dragon Museum** evokes the Chinese community's role in Bendigo life, past and present. Its centerpieces are the century-old Loong imperial ceremonial dragon and the Sun Loong dragon, which, at more than 106 yards in length, is said to be the world's longest. When carried in procession, it requires 52 carriers and 52 relievers; the head alone weighs 64 pounds. Also on display are other ceremonial objects, costumes, and historic artifacts. ✉ *5–11 Bridge St.* ☎ *03/5441–5044* 🎫 *A$8* 🕙 *Daily 9:30–5.*

SPOIL YOURSELF

If your muscles are stiff from bush walking, or too much driving has taken its toll, a visit to **Blaze Rock Spa** may be just what you need. The spa serves up tantalizing choice of pampering treatments that use natural plant ingredients and techniques inspired by traditional Aboriginal methods. Craig, who owns the business with wife Sharon, delivers a massage that will cure your aches and pains. ☎ *03/5356–6171* ⊕ *www.blazerock.com.au.*

A good introduction to Bendigo is a tour aboard the **Vintage Talking Tram,** which includes a taped commentary on the town's history. The hourly tram runs on its 8-km (5-mi) circuit between the Central Deborah Gold Mine and the Tram Museum making five stops at historic sites. ☎ *03/5443–8322 or 03/5442–2821* 🎫 *A$13* 🕙 *Daily 10–4:20.*

WHERE TO STAY & EAT

$$ ✗**Whirrakee.** This family-run restaurant and wine bar in one of Bendigo's grand old buildings serves Mediterranean- and Asian-inspired dishes. The twice-cooked lamb shank on roasted pumpkin mash is a great winter choice that literally melts in your mouth. The wine list showcases local wineries. ✉ *17 View Point* ☎ *03/5441–5557* ▤ *AE, DC, MC, V.*

$–$$ ✗**Bazzani.** This restaurant fuses a Mod-Oz menu with Asian influences under the capable stewardship of chef Brendan Tuddenham. Try the slow-cooked rabbit with pappardelle pasta and sage-asparagus cream, or the tiger prawn spaghettini. A two-course weekday lunch special with a glass of wine and coffee is A$27.50. A good selection of local and Pyrenees wines is very well priced. ✉ *2–4 Howard Pl.* ☎ *03/5441–3777* ▤ *AE, DC, MC, V.*

$$ 🏨**Langley Hall.** Housed in a circa-1903 Edwardian mansion, Lang-
★ ley Hall was originally built as a residence for the Anglican Archbishop of Bendigo. After incarnations as a convalescent home and an orphanage, it was beautifully restored by Allan and Anne Broadhead. Features include a parlor, billiard room, and drawing room—all filled with period details from the town's heyday. Breakfast is served in a grand dining room; you can enjoy drinks from an honor bar in the billiard room. The house is 4 km (2½ mi) from the center of town. ✉ *484 Napier St., 3550* ☎ *03/5443–3693* ⊕ *www.innhouse.com.au/langleyhall* 🛏 *6 rooms* 🚫 *No elevator* ▤ *AE, DC, MC, V* ⏚ *CP.*

$–$$ 🏨**Comfort Inn Shamrock.** The lodgings at this landmark Victorian hotel in the city center range from traditional guest rooms to spacious suites. If you're looking for reasonably priced luxury, ask for the

Amy Castles or the Dame Nellie Melba suites. Named after famous 19th-century Australian singers, they have hot tubs and overlook beautiful Rosalind Gardens. The hotel's location, its grand public areas, and its beautiful wrought-iron balcony are the big draws. ⊠*Pall Mall at Williamson St., 3550* ☎*03/5443–0333* ⚲*24 rooms, 4 suites* ⚙*In-hotel: restaurant, bars, laundry facilities, parking (no fee)* ⊟*AE, DC, MC, V.*

THE GRAMPIANS NATIONAL PARK

FodorsChoice *260 km (162 mi) west of Melbourne, 100 km (62 mi) north of*
★ *Hamilton.*

Comprising four mountain ranges—Mt. Difficult, Mt. William, Serra, and Victoria—the Grampians National Park spills over 412,000 acres. Its rugged peaks, towering trees, web of waterfalls and creeks, and plethora of wildlife make it a haven for bushwalkers, rock climbers, and nature lovers. In spring the region wears a carpet of spectacular wildflowers, while a number of significant Aboriginal rock-art sites make it an ideal place to learn about Victoria's indigenous history. Dawn balloon flights over the park offer visitors the chance to see the park's hidden charms without working up a sweat. The township of Halls Creek (population 300) is in the national park and with its 10,000 tourist beds becomes quite a busy place in the summer and at Easter. If you're staying in a self-catering accommodation it is very wise to stock up on groceries and wine in the big towns of Ballarat, Arafat, Hamilton, or Horsham, since prices at the Halls Gap general store are inflated. One of the most picturesque drives in the park is the 60-km (37-km) stretch from Halls Gap to Dunkeld.

★ Owned and operated by Aboriginal people, the **Brambuk Cultural Centre** provides a unique living history of Aboriginal culture in this part of Victoria. Displays of artwork, weapons, clothes, and tools here give a glimpse into the life of indigenous Koori people (Aboriginal people of southeastern Australia). In the Dreaming Theatre, dancing, music, and educational programs are presented daily. ⊠*Dunkeld Rd., Halls Gap* ☎*03/5356–4452* ▦*Free, Dreaming Theatre performances A$5* ⊙*Daily 9–5, show hourly 10–4.*

WHERE TO STAY & EAT

$–$$ ✕**Kookaburra.** This place is one of the best dining options you'll find in the park area. Venison is popular here; you can try it prepared as steak, sausage, or pie. You can also choose duckling or pork fillet smoked over cherrywood embers, and finish with a traditional bread-and-butter pudding. The restaurant is often closed in winter from late July to early August. ⊠*125 Grampian Rd., Halls Gap* ☎*03/5356–4222* ⊟*AE, DC, MC, V.*

$$$$ ▦**Boroka Downs.** Set among 300 acres of bush, scrub, and grassland,
FodorsChoice Boroka's five villas are nothing short of spectacular. Studios have soar-
★ ing ceilings, roof-to-floor windows—which frame the bush-clad ridges of the Grampians—fireplaces, and enormous in-room hot tubs. You can wake to the sound of kookaburras laughing and sunset finds groups of

kangaroos, emus, and wallabies grazing in the paddocks that skirt the villa. Owners Julian and Barbara Carr are committed environmentalists. They've planted more than 15,500 trees, use solar and wind energy, and re-cycle just about everything. There's a two-night minimum stay in high season (long weekends, Easter, Christmas–New Year); however, during non-peak times guests get one free night when they book a two-night package. ⊠ *Birdswing Rd., Halls Gap, 3381* ☎ *03/5356–6243* ⊕ *www.borokadowns.com.au* ⊅ *5 villas* ⌂ *In-room: kitchen, DVD with movies, laundry facilities, VCR. In-hotel: parking (no fee), no kids* ⊟ *AE, DC, MC, V* ⧌⃝ *BP.*

$$$ 🏠 **Glenisla Homestead.** This 1870 heritage-classified B&B, built from local Grampians sandstone, nestles in a valley between the Victoria and Black ranges. It's part of a 2,000-acre working sheep station that produces superfine merino wool, and guests are welcome to participate in farm activities. The property also borders Grampians National Park, so you'll see kangaroos, emus, and other animals. ⊠ *Off Hamilton-Horsham Rd. (follow signs), Cavendish, 3314* ☎ *03/5380–1532* ⊅ *2 suites* ⌂ *In-room: no a/c, no phone, no TV. In-hotel: restaurant, laundry service, parking (no fee), no kids* ⊟ *AE, MC, V* ⧌⃝ *BP.*

¢ 🏠 **Grampians YHA Eco Hostel.** This stylish hostel is one of the new brand of eco-friendly properties in the Youth Hostel Australia (YHA) network. It uses solar energy and water-conservation devices, is open to people of all ages, and has accommodation to suit everyone (dorm rooms, double rooms, and family rooms can sleep four). The two modern adjoining kitchens are fully equipped and the three lounges (including an Internet room with two computers) are ideal for socializing. There is an outdoor BBQ and eating area with spectacular mountain views. All bathrooms are shared facilities. ⊠ *Corner Grampians and Buckler Rds., Halls Gap, 3381* ☎ *03/5356–4544* ⊟ *03/5356–4543* ⊕ *www.yha.com.au* ⊅ *8 dorms, 5 double rooms, 5 family rooms* ⊟ *AE, MC, V.*

THE GOLD COUNTRY & THE GRAMPIANS ESSENTIALS

TRANSPORTATION

CAR TRAVEL

For leisurely exploration of the Gold Country, a car is essential. Although public transportation adequately serves the main centers, access to smaller towns is less assured, and even in the bigger towns attractions tend to be widely dispersed.

To reach Bendigo, take the Calder Highway northwest from Melbourne; for Ballarat, take the Western Highway. The mineral springs region and Maldon lie neatly between the two main cities.

Halls Gap (the base town for the Grampians National Park) is reached via Ballarat and Ararat on the Western Highway (Highway 8). The town is 260 km (162 mi) northwest of Melbourne, 97 km (60 mi) northeast of Hamilton, 146 km (91 mi) west of Ballarat.

5

TRAIN TRAVEL

V-Line operates trains to Ballarat or Bendigo from Melbourne. V-Line buses connect with the trains to take passengers to Daylesford and Halls Gap. For timetables and fares contact V-Line.

CONTACTS & RESOURCES

EMERGENCIES

Dial **000** to reach an ambulance, the police, or the fire department.

Contacts Ballarat Hospital (⊠ *Drummond St., Ballarat* ☎ *03/5321–4000).* **Bendigo Public Hospital** (⊠ *Lucan and Arnold Sts.* ☎ *03/5454–6000).* **East Grampians Health Service** (⊠ *Girdlestone St., Ararat* ☎ *03/5352–9300).* **Stawell Medical Centre** (⊠ *26 Wimmera St., Stawell* ☎ *03/5358–1410).*

TELEPHONES

In the town of Halls Gap there are several public phones. There is limited cell reception in this area.

TOURS

Gray Line, Australian Pacific Tours, and AAT Kings cover the Gold Country; all three depart from 180 Swanston Street in Melbourne. Gray Line also operates a one-day tour of the Grampians (A$130) that departs from Melbourne on Monday and Saturday.

Contacts AAT Kings (☎ *03/9663–3377 or 1300/556100* ⊕ *www.aatkings.com.au).* **Australian Pacific Tours** (☎ *03/9663–1611* ⊕ *www.aptouring.com.au).* **Gray Line** (☎ *1300/858686* ⊕ *www.grayline.com.au).*

Contact V-line (☎ *13–6196* ⊕ *www.vline.com.au).*

VISITOR INFORMATION

The visitor center in Ballarat is open weekdays 9–5 and weekends 10–4, the center in Bendigo is open daily 9–5, and the one in Daylesford is open daily 10–4. Visitor centers in Halls Gap and Stawell and the Grampians are open 9–5 daily.

Contacts Ballarat Tourist Information Centre (⊠ *Eureka Centre, Rodier and Eureka Sts., Ballarat* ☎ *03/5320–5741* ⊕ *www.visitballarat.com.au).* **Bendigo Tourist Information Centre** (⊠ *Old Post Office, 51–67 Pall Mall, Bendigo* ☎ *03/5444–4445 or 1800/813153* ⊕ *www.bendigotourism.com.au).* **Daylesford Regional Visitor Information Centre** (⊠ *98 Vincent St., Daylesford* ☎ *03/5321–6123* 🖶 *03/5321–6193* ⊕ *www.visitdaylesford.com).* **Halls Gap Visitor Information Centre** (⊠ *Grampians Rd., Halls Gap* ☎ *03/5356–4616 or 1800/065599* ⊕ *www.visithallsgap.com.au).* **Stawell and Grampians Visitor Information Centre** (⊠ *50–52 Western Hwy., Stawell* ☎ *03/5358–2314 or 1800/330080* ⊕ *www.visitgrampians.com.au).*

MURRAY RIVER REGION

From its birthplace on the slopes of the Great Dividing Range in southern New South Wales, the Mighty Murray winds 2,574 km (1,596 mi) on a northwesterly course before it empties into Lake Alexandrina, south of Adelaide. On the driest inhabited continent on Earth, such a river, the country's largest, assumes great importance. Irrigation schemes that tap the river water have transformed its thirsty surroundings into a garden of grapevines and citrus fruits.

Once prone to flooding and droughts, the river has been laddered with dams that control the floodwaters and form reservoirs for irrigation. The lakes created in the process have become sanctuaries for native birds. In the pre-railroad age of canals, the Murray was an artery for inland cargoes of wool and wheat, and old wharves in such ports as Echuca bear witness to the bustling and colorful riverboat era.

Victoria, Tasmania, New South Wales, and Western Australia were planted with grapevines in the 1830s, fixing roots for an industry that has earned international praise. One of the earliest sponsors of Victorian viticulture was Charles LaTrobe, the first Victorian governor. LaTrobe had lived at Neuchâtel in Switzerland and married the daughter of the Swiss Counsellor of State. As a result of his contacts, Swiss winemakers emigrated to Australia and developed some of the earliest Victorian vineyards in the Yarra Valley, east of Melbourne.

Digging for gold was a thirst-producing business, and the gold rushes stimulated the birth of an industry. By 1890 well over half the total Australian production of wine came from Victoria. But then, in the mid-1800s, a strain of tiny plant lice, phylloxera, arrived from Europe and wreaked havoc in Victoria (it had similarly devastated the vineyards of France). In the absence of wine, Australians turned to beer, and not until the 1960s did the wineries here start to regain their footing. Today Victoria exports more than A$100 million worth of wine annually. High-quality muscat and port are still made in many parts of the Murray River region. The Rutherglen area, in particular, produces the finest fortified wine in the country, and anyone who enjoys the after-dinner "stickies" (dessert wines) is in for a treat when touring here.

EASTERN MURRAY RIVER VALLEY AND HIGH COUNTRY

Steeped in history and natural beauty, this region has become a gourmet food lovers' heaven known for its fruit, olives, honey, and cheeses. It's also a renowned wine region. This region is a genteel holiday enclave, and the lovely town of Beechworth is an ideal place to stop off on the drive between Sydney and Melbourne.

BEECHWORTH
271 km (168 mi) northeast of Melbourne, 96 km (60 mi) northwest of Alpine National Park.

One of the prettiest towns in Victoria, Beechworth flourished during the gold rush. When gold ran out the town of 30,000 was left with all the trappings of prosperity—fine banks, imposing public buildings, breweries, parks, and hotels wrapped in wrought iron—but with scarcely two nuggets to rub together. However, poverty preserved the town from such modern improvements as aluminum window frames,

Ned Kelly

The English have Robin Hood, the Americans Jesse James. Australians have Ned Kelly, a working-class youth whose struggles against police injustice and governmental indifference captured the country's heart. The best way to learn about the local legend is to visit the town of Beechworth, where a Ned Kelly Walking Tour departs from the visitor information center every day at 10:30 AM. You'll see the courthouse where he was tried and the jail where he was imprisoned during his many scrapes with the law. The Burke Museum dis-

plays his death mask, made shortly after he was hanged at Melbourne Gaol. If you long to hear more, visit Glenrowan, (40 km [25 mi] southwest of Beechworth), the scene of his famous "last stand." It was here that Kelly, dressed in his legendary iron armor, walked alone down the main street fending off police bullets. He was shot in the leg and arrested. A huge statue, and a sound and light show, commemorate Australia's most infamous outlaw.

–Caroline Gladstone

and many historic treasures that might have been destroyed in the name of progress have been brought back to life.

A stroll along **Ford Street** is the best way to absorb the character of the town. Among the distinguished buildings are **Tanswell's Commercial Hotel,** the **Town Hall,** and the **Courthouse.** It was in the latter that the committal hearing for the famous bushranger Ned Kelly took place in August 1880. His feisty mother, Ellen Kelly, was also sentenced to three years in jail at this court. A$12.50 pass gives admission to all the historic buildings and the Burke Museum.

Beechworth Cemetery. Established in 1856, this cemetery contains the graves of many of Beechworth's pioneers. Two distinctive red ceremonial burning towers mark the section with the graves of 2,000 Chinese laborers who perished while seeking their fortunes in the goldfields. A brochure outlining a walking tour can be picked up inside the cemetery gates. ⊠ *Cemetery and Balaclava Rds.* ☎ *03/5728–1556* 🎟 *Free* 🕙 *Daily.*

The **Burke Museum** takes its name from Robert O'Hara Burke, who, with William Wills, became one of the first white explorers to cross Australia from south to north in 1861. Burke served as superintendent of police in Beechworth from 1856 to 1859. Not surprisingly, the small area and few mementos dedicated to Burke are overshadowed by the Ned Kelly exhibits, including letters, photographs, and memorabilia that give genuine insight into the man and his misdeeds. The museum also displays a reconstructed streetscape of Beechworth in the 1880s. ⊠ *Loch St.* ☎ *03/5728–8067* 🎟 *A$5.50* 🕙 *Daily 9–5.*

Murray Breweries Historic Brewery Museum brewed beer in the 1860s, but now concentrates on nonalcoholic cordials produced using old-time recipes. You'll find a display of antique brewing equipment, worldwide beer labels, and rare bottles. Also here is the Carriage Museum, which has a collection of 20 horse-drawn vehicles and Australian Light Horse Infantry memorabilia from World War I. ⊠ *29 Last St.* A$2 ⊙ *Daily 10–4.*

WHERE TO STAY & EAT

$$ ✕⌷**Bank Restaurant and Mews.** This restaurant's refined, dignified setting befits its status as a former Bank of Australasia. Built in the 1850s, this building near the historic precinct has high ceilings, antique furnishings, and the bank's original gold vault (which now holds a treasure of wines). The food, based on local produce and high-country beef, duck, and venison, is delicious and presented with style. Four character-filled garden suites, built overlooking manicured gardens and private courtyards, occupy what was originally the carriage house and stables. Rates include breakfast. ⊠ *86 Ford St., 3747* 03/5728–2223 03/5728–2883 *4 suites* *In-hotel: restaurant, laundry facilities, parking (no fee), no-smoking rooms, minibar, no elevator* AE, DC, MC, V ⎪ *BP.*

$$ ✕⌷**Kinross.** Chintz fabrics and dark-wood antiques fill the rooms of ★ this former manse just a two-minute walk from the center of Beechworth. Each room has its own fireplace—a plus on chilly evenings. The Burke Room (after the ill-fated explorer and local police superintendent) has a lovely 1870s French carved-oak bed, while the Kelly room is a favorite with North American guests. Hosts Gail and Terry Walsh provide scrumptious breakfasts and will arrange dinner for three or more couples. Terry, who also works at the Visitor Information Centre and runs winery tours of the area, is a wealth of local information. ⊠ *34 Loch St., 3747* 03/5728–2351 *www.innhouse.com.au/ kinross.html* *5 rooms* *In-room: some a/c, no phone. In-hotel: restaurant, laundry facilities, public Internet, parking (no fee), no elevator* AE, MC, V ⎪ *BP.*

$$–$$$$ ⌷**Country Charm Swiss Cottages.** Landscaped gardens overlooking the Beechworth Gorge surround these charming pine and cedar cottages. Each unit has nice little touches, like fireplaces, whirlpool tubs, and fully-equipped kitchens. This was the site of the original Beechworth vineyard, established in the 1800s; a 130-year-old drystone wall is all that remains. While walking the grounds, note the views across the Woolshed Valley to Mt. Pilot. There is a two-night minimum stay on weekends. ⊠ *22 Malakoff Rd., 3747* 03/5728–2435 *5 cottages* *In-room: kitchen, refrigerator, VCR, no elevator* MC, V.

EN ROUTE The cute town of **Yackandandah,** 23 km (14 mi) northeast of Beechworth, shot to fame after the release of the lighthearted comedy *Strange Bedfellows,* starring Paul Hogan. The town's historic buildings (including the two pubs, the post office, and the bank) were used as settings, and many of the town's 700 residents were movie extras. The *Crocodile Dundee* star is now a local hero.

RUTHERGLEN

274 km (170 mi) northeast of Melbourne, 40 km (25 mi) northwest of Beechworth.

The surrounding red-loam soil signifies the beginning of the Rutherglen wine district, the source of Australia's finest fortified wines. If the term conjures up visions of cloying ports, you're in for a surprise. In his authoritative *Australian Wine Compendium*, James Halliday says, "Like Narcissus drowning in his own reflection, one can lose oneself in the aroma of a great old muscat."

The main event in the region is Tastes of Rutherglen, held over two consecutive weekends in March. The festival is a celebration of food, wine, and music—in particular jazz, folk, and country. Events are held in town and at all surrounding wineries. Another popular day in the vineyards is the Rutherglen Winery Walkabout held in June, where wine, food, and music are again on the menu.

For more information on these events, contact the **Rutherglen Wine Experience and Visitor Information Centre** (⊠ *57 Main St.* ☎ *02/6033–6300 or 1800/622871* ⊕ *www.rutherglenvic.com*).

★ **All Saints Vineyards & Cellars** has been in business since 1864. It's owned and operated by the children of the late Peter Brown, one of the first to produce wine in the region. The long driveway, flanked by an impressive avenue of towering elm trees, leads to a castle built in 1878 that was modeled on one in Scotland. Products include the Museum Muscat and Museum Tokay, both made from 50-year-old grapes. The Terrace restaurant is on-site. ⊠ *All Saints Rd., Wahgunyah* ✛ *9 km (5½ mi) southeast of Rutherglen* ☎ *02/6035–2222* ⊕ *www.allsaintswine.com. au* ⊠ *Free* ⊗ *Mon.–Sat. 9–5:30, Sun. 10–5:30.*

Another long-established winery, **Buller's Calliope Vineyard,** has many vintage stocks of muscat and fine sherry distributed through its cellar outlet. Also on the winery's grounds is **Buller Bird Park**, an aviary of rare parrots and native Australian birds. ⊠ *Three Chain Rd. at Murray Valley Hwy.* ☎ *02/6032–9660* ⊕ *www.buller.com.au* ⊠ *Free* ⊗ *Mon.–Sat. 9–5, Sun. 10–5.*

Campbell's Rutherglen Winery is a family business that dates back more than 130 years. Famed for their award-winning Bobbie Burns Shiraz and Merchant Prince Muscat, the property spills over a picturesque 160 acres. You can wander freely through the winery on a self-guided tour. Campbell Family Vintage Reserve is available only at the cellar door. ⊠ *Murray Valley Hwy.* ☎ *02/6032–9458* ⊕ *www.campbells wines.com.au* ⊠ *Free* ⊗ *Mon.–Sat. 9–5, Sun. 10–5.*

Chambers Rosewood Winery was established in the 1850s and is one of the heavyweight producers of fortified wines. Bill Chambers's muscats are legendary, with blending stocks that go back more than a century. Don't miss the chance to sample the vast tasting selection. ⊠ *Barkly St. off Corowa Rd.* ☎ *02/6032–8641* ⊠ *Free* ⊗ *Mon.–Sat. 9–5, Sun. 10–5.*

Along with exceptional fortified wine, **Pfeiffer Wines** has fine varietal wine, including chardonnay. It also has one of the few Australian plantings of gamay, the classic French grape used to make Beaujolais. At this small rustic winery you can order a picnic basket stuffed with crusty bread, pâté, cheese, fresh fruit, wine, and smoked salmon, but be sure to reserve in advance. Winemaker Christopher Pfeiffer sets up tables on the old wooden bridge that spans Sunday Creek, where you can take your picnic provisions. Phone ahead to book a table. ☒ *Distillery Rd., Wahgunyah* ⊕ *9 km (5½ mi) southeast of Rutherglen* ☎ *02/6033–2805* ⊕ *www.pfeifferwines.com.au* ☒ *Free* ⊙ *Mon.–Sat. 9–5, Sun. 10–4.*

WHERE TO STAY & EAT

$$ ✕ **Beaumont's Cafe.** Red-gum smoked rack of lamb with polenta and roasted-vegetable ratatouille is a highlight at this century-old storefront dining room with exposed brick and distressed walls. On warm nights the rear courtyard with its scented herb garden is the best place to indulge in desserts like hazelnut and sherry cake with raisin ice cream and chocolate sauce. Boutique regional labels dot the wine list. ☒ *84 Main St.* ☎ *02/6032–7428* ☒ *AE, DC, MC, V* ⊙ *Closed Sun. and Mon.*

$$ ✕ **The Terrace.** Part of the All Saints Estate, this restaurant is a welcome spot for relaxing after a day of wine tastings. The brick floor and wide wooden tables add rustic charm to the dining room, which sits conveniently next to the cellar door. The menu changes daily, but might include starters like prawn-filled zucchini flowers and such entrées as pan-roasted Lake Hume trout filled with ciabatta, tomato, basil, and lemon. Desserts are excellent, especially when combined with a formidable northeast fortified wine. A degustation menu featuring seven dishes is A$70 per person, or A$90 with paired wines. ☒ *All Saints Rd., Wahgunyah* ☎ *02/6033–1922* ☒ *AE, DC, MC, V* ⊙ *No dinner.*

$$ ▒ **Tuileries.** Incorporating a vineyard, olive groves, and a renowned
★ restaurant, Tuileries offers lodging with the feel of an exclusive retreat. Individually decorated suites are spacious and appointed with nice touches like hot tubs. There's a hammock draped across the veranda, with a lovely view of the estate's orchard. Next door is the Rutherglen's Estate Winery and a boutique brewery. ☒ *13–35 Drummond St., 3685* ☎ *02/6032–9033* ⊕ *www.tuileriesrutherglen.com.au* ⟿ *4 rooms, 5 suites* ⟐ *In-hotel: restaurant, room service, tennis courts, pool, parking (no fee), no-smoking rooms, minibar, no elevator* ☒ *AE, DC, MC, V* ⊙|*BP.*

EN ROUTE **Mt. Buffalo National Park** is a perfect day trip from Beechworth or the towns of Myrtleford and Porepunkah. Its highest points—Anderson Peak and the Horn—both top 5,000 feet. The park is full of fascinating granite formations, waterfalls, and animal and plant life. There are many more miles of walking tracks than you're likely to cover. The gorge walk is particularly scenic. Lake Cantani has swimming and a camping area. ☒ *The park is 50 km (31 mi) south of Beechworth and 10 km (6 mi) west of Bright* ▒ ▒ *$9.60.*

5

ALPINE NATIONAL PARK
323 km (200 mi) northeast of Melbourne, 40–50 km (25–31 mi) south to southeast of Mt. Buffalo.

The name Alpine National Park actually applies to three loosely connected areas in eastern Victoria that follow the peaks of the Great Dividing Range. One of these areas, formerly called Bogong National Park, contains some of the highest mountains on the continent. As such, it is a wintertime destination for skiers who flock to the resorts at Falls Creek, Mt. Buller, and Mt. Hotham.

The land around here is rich in history. *Bogong* is an Aboriginal word for "big moth," and it was to Mt. Bogong that Aborigines came each year after the winter thaw in search of bogong moths, considered a delicacy. Aborigines were eventually displaced by cattle ranchers who brought their cattle here to graze.

For information on walks and parks in the area, contact the **Parks Victoria Information Centre** (☎*13–1963* ⊕*www.parkweb.vic.gov.au*).

WHERE TO STAY & EAT

$–$$ ✕ **Sasha's of Bright.** Crispy-skinned duck is the highlight of Czech-born chef Sasha Cinatl's menu. Hungarian goulash, smoked pork, and spatchcock in a rich port sauce are also dishes to look for. For dessert you have to try the apple strudel crepes with fresh local berries and cream. The well-priced wine list focuses on northeast Victorian vintages. ⊠*2D Anderson St., Bright* ☎*03/5750–1711* ▭*AE, DC, MC, V.*

¢–$ ✕ **Food, Wine, Friends.** This fine food emporium has a small café offering homemade muesli for breakfast and sandwiches on freshly baked breads for lunch, as well as great coffee and wines by the glass. But it's the amazing array of preserves, conserves, mustards, pestos, and chutneys that is the star attraction. How does chocolate-muscat butter sound? Or blackberry-merlot conserve? The shop sells individual items for as little as A$4.95; the staff is happy to put together delicious picnic hampers. ⊠*Shop 2, 6 Ireland St., Bright* ☎*03/5750–1312* ▭*MC, V.*

$$$ ✕▦ **Villa Gusto.** Colin McLaren is an Australian, but one with a passion for all things Italian. Everything in his Tuscan-inspired lodging has been imported from Italy: cast-iron fountains, marble fittings, 17th-century antiques, and exquisite tapestries—even the retro movie posters above the bar. Each suite is individually designed and has an Italian name: perhaps cioccolato, rosso, or limone will suit your mood. Four-course set meals ($$$$) include dishes that showcase regional ingredients, especially Milawa poultry and cheeses and Ovens Valley veal and lamb. Desserts may include the delicious blue-cheese panna cotta with pear puree and walnut praline. From Bright drive towards Porepunkah and then take Buckland Valley Road turnoff for another 6 km (4 mi). ⊠*630 Buckland Valley Rd., Buckland, 3741* ☎*03/5756–2000* ⊕*www.villagusto.com.au* ↻*12 suites* ♨*In-hotel: restaurant, bar, no kids under 10, no elevator* ▭*AE, DC, MC, V* ⊙*Restaurant closed Mon. and Tues. nights. No lunch* ❙❙*BP.*

Fodor's Choice
★

SPORTS & THE OUTDOORS The Australian ski season is brief and unpredictable, but if you're keen to try one of the mountains in the alpine area, it's best to check conditions and prices online first: ⊕*www.fallscreek.com.au*, ⊕*www.mtbuller.com. au*, ⊕*www.mtbuffalochalet.com.au*, and ⊕*www.mthotham.com.au*

CENTRAL AND WESTERN MURRAY RIVER

The mighty Murray River is a summertime playground. Victorians fish for the elusive Murray cod, swim in the refreshing waters, and cruise on historic riverboats. There are plenty of other outdoor activities, such as teeing off at one of the region's fine golf courses.

ECHUCA

206 km (128 mi) north of Melbourne, 194 km (120 mi) west of Rutherglen, 92 km (57 mi) north of Bendigo.

The name Echuca comes from a local Aboriginal word meaning "meeting of the waters," a reference to the town's location at the confluence of the Murray, Campaspe, and Goulburn rivers. In the second half of the 19th century Echuca was Australia's largest inland port. Many reminders of Echuca's colorful heyday remain in the restored paddle steamers, barges, and historic hotels, and in the Red Gum Works, the town's sawmill, now a working museum.

A tour of the **Historic River Precinct** begins at the Port of Echuca office on Murray Esplanade, where you can purchase a ticket that gets you into some of the historic buildings. The **Bridge Hotel** was built by Henry Hopwood, ex-convict father of Echuca, who had the foresight to establish a punt, and then to build a bridge at this commercially strategic point on the river. The **Star Hotel**, built in the 1860s, has an underground bar and escape tunnel, which was used by after-hours drinkers in the 19th century to evade the police. The **Historic Wharf** displays the heavy-duty side of the river-trade business, including a warehouse, old railroad tracks, and riverboats. Among the vessels docked at the wharf is the *Adelaide*, Australia's oldest operating paddle steamer.

You can hop aboard the historic *Pevensey*, the *Canberra*, and the *Emmylou* for one-hour river excursions, a refreshing treat at the end of a hot summer's day. The paddle wheelers depart regularly from 10 AM to 4 PM; tickets, available from the port office or Bond Store on Murray Esplanade, cost from A$17.50 to A$18.50 for a one-hour cruise.

WHERE TO STAY & EAT

$$ ✕**Oscar W's Wharfside.** Named after the last paddle steamer ever built in
Fodor'sChoice Echuca, Oscar W's is one of the port's finest restaurants. With a beauti-
★ ful, tree-fringed view of the Murray River, it's a comfortable, relaxed establishment with a casual Deck Bar and upscale Redgum Grill, the latter serving such treats as crispy skin roasted Murray Cod with warm salad of fennel and artichokes. ⊠*Murray Esplanade* ☎*03/5482–5133* ▭*AE, DC, MC, V.*

$$$ ⚏ **PS** *Emmylou.* Departing from Echuca around sunset, this paddle steamer shuffles downriver during a three-course dinner, a night in a cabin, and breakfast the following morning. The boat can accommodate 18 guests in eight bunk rooms and one double-bed cabin, all with shared bathrooms. Sunrise over the river, as the boat churns past mist-cloaked gum trees and laughing kookaburras, is a truly memorable experience. Two- and three-night cruises are also available. ⊠ *57 Murray Esplanade, 3564* ☎ *03/5480–2237* ⊕ *www.emmylou.com.au* ⮐ *9 rooms without bath* ⌂ *In-room: no a/c, no phone, no TV. In-hotel: restaurant, bar, no-smoking rooms, no elevator* ⊟ *MC, V* ⦿ *MAP.*

$$–$$$ ⚏ **River Gallery Inn.** This hotel occupies a 19th-century building just a stone's throw from the port. Each of the rooms is furnished in a different theme, such as frilly French provincial, opulent Victorian, and rustic early Australian. There's even a Tuscan room with sunken bath and private courtyard. Four rooms overlook the street but are still quiet. Six rooms have whirlpool tubs and all of the rooms, bar one, have open fireplaces. Rates include breakfast. ⊠ *578 High St., 3564* ☎ *03/5480–6902* ⮐ *6 rooms, 2 suites* ⌂ *In-room: no phone. In-hotel: restaurant, parking (no fee), minibar, no kids, no elevator* ⊟ *AE, MC, V* ⦿ *EP.*

MURRAY RIVER REGION ESSENTIALS

TRANSPORTATION

BY BUS

Bus services to Alpine National Park operate from Albury on the New South Wales border in the north. In ski season, Pyles Coaches depart from Mt. Beauty for Falls Creek and Mt. Hotham, and depart from Melbourne for Falls Creek.

Contact Pyles Coaches (☎ *03/5754–4024* ⊕ *www.pyles.com.au*).

BY CAR

The wide-open spaces of the region surrounding the Murray River make driving the most sensible and feasible means of exploration. There's enough scenic interest along the way to make the long drives bearable, especially if you trace the river route. The direct run from Melbourne to Mildura is quite daunting (557 km [345 mi]).

Beechworth and Rutherglen are on opposite sides of the Hume Freeway, the main Sydney–Melbourne artery. Allow four hours for the journey from Melbourne, twice that from Sydney. Echuca is a three-hour drive from Melbourne, reached most directly by the Northern Highway (Highway 75).

BY TRAIN

V-Line trains run to most of the major towns in the region, including Echuca, Rutherglen, Swan Hill, and Mildura—but not Beechworth. This reasonable access is most useful if you do not have a car or want to avoid the long-distance drives. As with most country Victorian areas, direct train access from Melbourne to the main centers is reasonable, but getting between towns isn't as easy. The train to Mildura may be an appealing option for those utterly discouraged by the long drive.

Contact **V-Line** (☎ *13–6196* ⊕ *www.vline.com.au*).

CONTACTS & RESOURCES

EMERGENCIES

In an emergency, dial **000** to reach an ambulance, the police, or the fire department.

Contacts **Amcal Pharmacy** (⊠ *192 Hare St., Echuca* ☎ *03/5482–6666*). **Echuca and District Hospital** (⊠ *Francis St., Echuca* ☎ *03/5482–2800*).

TOURS

Gray Line operates one-day bus tours of Echuca. It departs from Melbourne on Friday and Sunday at 8:45 AM. The cost is A$124.

Contact **Gray Line** (⊠ *180 Swanson St., City Center, Melbourne* ☎ *03/9663–4455* ⊕ *www.grayline.com.au*).

VISITOR INFORMATION

The information centers in Beechworth and Rutherglen are open daily 9–5:30; the center in Echuca is open daily 9–5; and the Mildura center is open weekdays 9–4 and weekends 10–4, but they close for lunch weekdays 12:30–1.

The ranger station for the Alpine National Park is on Mt. Beauty, where there are various ranger-led programs.

Contacts **Beechworth Tourist Information Centre** (⊠ *Old Town Hall, Ford St., Beechworth* ☎ *03/5728–3233 or 1300/366321*). **Bright Visitor Centre** (⊠ *119 Gavan St., Bright* ☎ *03/5755–2275 or 1800/500117*). **Echuca Tourist Information Centre** (⊠ *2 Heygarth St., Echuca* ☎ *1800/804446* ⊕ *www.echucamoama. com*). **Mildura Visitor Information & Booking Centre** (⊠ *Alfred Deakin Centre, 180–190 Deakin Ave., Mildura* ☎ *1300/550858 or freecall 1800/039043* ⊕ *www. visitmildura.com.au*). **Parks Victoria** (☎ *13–1963* ⊕ *www.parkweb.vic.gov.au*). **Rutherglen Wine Experience and Visitor Information Centre** (⊠ *57 Main St., Rutherglen* ☎ *02/6033–6300 or 1800/622871* ⊕ *www.rutherglenvic.com*).

Tasmania

WORD OF MOUTH

"TAS is not a place you want to rush through—loads to see and do—great hikes, wildlife, good food and very friendly locals. Three days isn't nearly enough."

—tropo

Updated by
Roger Allnutt

ABOUT THE SIZE OF WEST Virginia, and with a population of less than a half million, Tasmania is an unspoiled reminder of a simpler, slower lifestyle. It has been called the England of the south, as it, too, is richly cloaked in mists and rain, glows with russet and gold shades in fall, and has the chance of an evening chill year-round. Where the English tradition of a Christmas roast may strike you as strange in a steamy Sydney summer, such rites appear natural amid Tasmania's lush quilt of lowland farms and villages. Many towns retain an English look, with their profusion of Georgian cottages and commercial buildings, the preservation of which attests to Tasmanians' attachment to their past.

Aborigines, who crossed a temporary land bridge from Australia, first settled the island some 45,000 years ago. Europeans discovered it in 1642, when Dutch explorer Abel Tasman arrived at its southwest coast. It was first called Van Diemen's Land, after the Governor of the Dutch East Indies. Tasmania's violent history since the arrival of Europeans has episodes that many residents may wish to forget. The entire population of full-blooded Aborigines was wiped out or exiled to the Bass Strait islands by English troops and settlers. The establishment in 1830 of a penal settlement at Port Arthur for the colony's worst offenders ushered in a new age of cruelty.

Today, walking through the lovely grounds in Port Arthur or the unhurried streets of Hobart, it's difficult to picture Tasmania as a land of turmoil and tragedy. But in many ways Tasmania is still untamed. Twenty-eight percent of the land is preserved in national parks, where impenetrable rain forests and deep river gorges cut through the massive mountain valleys. The coastlines are scalloped with endless desolate beaches—some pristine white, fronting serene turquoise bays, and some rugged and rocky, facing churning, wind-whipped seas. The island's extreme southern position also results in a wild climate that's often hammered by Antarctic winds, so be prepared for sudden, severe weather changes. A snowstorm in summer isn't unusual.

EXPLORING TASMANIA

Tasmania is compact—the drive from southern Hobart to northern Launceston takes little more than two hours. The easiest way to see the state is by car, as you can plan a somewhat circular route around the island. Begin in Hobart or Launceston, where car rentals are available from the airport city agencies, or in Devonport if you arrive on the ferry from Melbourne. Although distances seem small, allow plenty of time for stops along the way. Bring a sturdy pair of shoes for impromptu mountain and seaside walks; you'll most often have huge patches of forest and long expanses of white beaches all to yourself.

In some cases the street addresses for attractions may not include building numbers (in other words, only the name of the street will be given). Don't worry—this just means either that the street is short and the attractions are clearly visible, or that signposts will clearly lead you there.

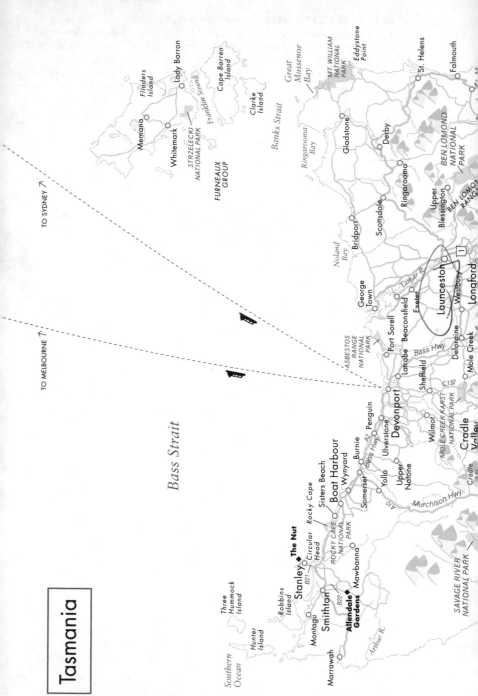

Tasmania

ABOUT THE RESTAURANTS

Although there are elegant dining options in the larger towns—especially Hobart—most eateries here serve filling meals in a casual setting. Local seafood, steaks, hearty meat pies, produce, and wines are usually menu highlights; ask your waiter, or even the restaurant owner, for recommendations.

WHAT IT COSTS IN AUSTRALIAN DOLLARS				
$$$$	$$$	$$	$	¢
AT DINNER	over A$50	A$36–A$50	A$21–A$35	A$10–A$20	under A$10

Prices are per person for a main course at dinner.

ABOUT THE HOTELS

In Tasmania, hotels of all levels usually include tea- and coffee-making facilities, room refrigerators, TVs, heating, electric blankets, irons, and hair dryers on request, and laundry facilities. Most hotels also have air-conditioning, but bed-and-breakfast lodgings often do not. Apart from a few hotels right in the main city center, most Hobart accommodations have free parking. In many smaller places, especially the colonial-style cottages, no smoking is allowed inside. For a comprehensive list of B&B establishments around Tasmania, look at ⊕ *www.tasmanianbedandbreakfast.com.*

WHAT IT COSTS IN AUSTRALIAN DOLLARS				
$$$$	$$$	$$	$	¢
FOR TWO PEOPLE	over A$300	A$201–A$300	A$151–A$200	A$100–A$150	under A$100

Prices are for two people in a standard double room in high season, including tax and service, based on the European Plan (with no meals) unless otherwise noted.

WHEN TO VISIT

Tasmanian winters can draw freezing blasts from the Antarctic, so this is not the season to explore the highlands or wilderness areas. It's better in the colder months to enjoy the cozy interiors of colonial cottages and the open fireplaces of welcoming pubs. Summer can be surprisingly hot—bushfires are common—but temperatures are generally lower than on the Australian mainland. Early autumn is beautiful, with deciduous trees in full color. Spring, with its splashes of pastel wildflowers, is the season for rainbows.

Tasmania is a relaxing island with few crowds, except during the mid-December to mid-February school holiday period and at the end of the annual Sydney-to-Hobart yacht race just after Christmas. Most attractions and sights, including the national parks, are open year-round.

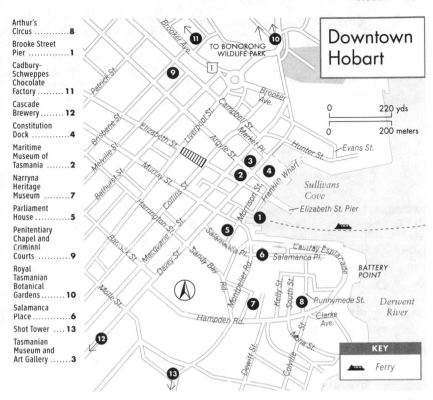

Downtown Hobart

TO BONORONG
WILDLIFE PARK

0 ——— 220 yds
0 ——— 200 meters

Brooker Ave.

Brooker Ave.

Patrick St.

Brisbane St.

Elizabeth St.

Campbell St.

Liverpool St.

Ardyle St.

Market Pl.

Hunter St.

Evans St.

Melville St.

Murray St.

Collins St.

Morrison St.

Franklin Wharf

Sullivans
Cove

Elizabeth St. Pier

Bathurst St.

Harrington St.

Barrack St.

Macquarie St.

Salamanca Pl.

Salamanca Pl.

Castray Esplanade

BATTERY
POINT

Davey St.

Sandy Bay Rd.

Montpelier Rd.

Kelly St.

South St.

Runnymede St.

Derwent
River

Molle St.

Hampden Rd.

Clarke
Ave.

Mona St.

Dewitt St.

Colville St.

KEY

🚢 Ferry

6

HOBART

Straddling the Derwent River at the foot of Mt. Wellington's forested slopes, Hobart was founded as a penal settlement in 1803. It's the second-oldest city in the country after Sydney, and it certainly rivals its mainland counterpart as Australia's most beautiful state capital. Close-set colonial brick-and-sandstone shops and homes line the narrow, quiet streets, creating a genteel setting for this historic city of 200,000. Life revolves around the broad Derwent River port, one of the deepest harbors in the world. Here warehouses that once stored Hobart's major exports of fruit, wool, and corn, and products from the city's former whaling fleet still stand alongside the wharf today.

Hobart sparkles between Christmas and New Year's—summer Down Under—during the annual Sydney-to-Hobart yacht race. The event dominates conversations among Hobart's citizens, who descend on Constitution Dock to welcome the yachts and join in the boisterous festivities of the crews. The new year also coincides with the Tastes of Tasmania Festival, when the dockside area comes alive with the best of Tasmanian food and wine on offer in numerous cafés, bars, and waterfront stalls. Otherwise, Hobart is a placid city whose nightlife

is largely confined to excellent restaurants, jazz clubs, and the action
at the Wrest Point Casino in Sandy
Bay.

WHAT TO SEE

8 Arthur's Circus. Hobart's best-preserved street is an enchanting collection of tiny houses and cottages
in a circle around a village green
on Runnymede Street, in the heart
of historic Battery Point. Most of
these houses, which were built in the 1840s and 1850s, have been
nicely restored.

**OFF THE
BEATEN
PATH**

Bonorong Wildlife Park. Situated 25 km (16 mi) north of Hobart on the
highway to Launceston, the park has a wide selection of Australian
species, including koalas, wombats, quolls (indigenous cats), and the
notorious Tasmanian devil. ⊠*Briggs Rd., Brighton* ☎*03/6268–1184*
🖰 ⌨*A$14* ⊙*Daily 9–5.*

1 Brooke Street Pier. The busy waterfront at Brooke Street Pier is the
departure point for harbor cruises. Nearby **Elizabeth Street Pier** has
trendy restaurants and bars. ⊠*Franklin Wharf, Hobart City.*

11 Cadbury-Schweppes Chocolate Factory. Very few children (or adults!) can
🖰 resist a trip to the best chocolate and cocoa factory in Australia. Visits
are by 1½-hour guided tour only; book through the visitor information center. Of course, the best part of the tour is getting to sample
some of the scrumptious products. ⊠*Cadbury Estate, Cadbury Rd.,
Claremont ⊹12 km (7½ mi) north of Hobart* ☎*03/6249–0333 or
1800/627367* ⊕*www.cadbury.com.au* ⌨*A$12.50* ⊙*Tours weekdays
at 9, 9:30, 10:30, and 1.*

12 Cascade Brewery. This is Australia's oldest brewery, producing fine beers
since 1824. You can see its inner workings only on the two-hour tours,
which require lots of walking and climbing, but you're rewarded with
a free drink at the end. Note that appropriate attire—no shorts, no
sandals—is required, and tour reservations are essential. ⊠*140 Cascade Rd., South Hobart* ☎*03/6224–1117* ⌨*A$18* ⊕*www.cascade-
brewery.com.au* ⊙*Tours weekdays at 9:30 and 1.*

4 Constitution Dock. Yachts competing in the annual Sydney-to-Hobart race
moor at this colorful marina dock from the end of December through
the first week of January. Buildings fronting the dock are century-
old reminders of Hobart's trading history. ⊠*Argyle and Davey Sts.,
Hobart City* ☎*No phone* ⌨*Free* ⊙*Daily 24 hrs.*

2 Maritime Museum of Tasmania. The old state library building houses one
of the best maritime collections in Australia, including figureheads,
whaling implements, models, and photographs dating from as far
back as 1804. ⊠*Argyle and Davey Sts., Hobart City* ☎*03/6234–
1427* ⊕*www.maritimetas.org* ⌨*A$7* ⊙*Daily 10–4:30.*

7 **Narryna Heritage Museum.** Exhibits in this gracious old town house depict the life of Tasmania's upper-class pioneers. Of particular interest are the collections of colonial furniture, clothes, paintings, and photos. ⊠*103 Hampden Rd., Battery Point* ☎*03/6234–2791* ⊠*A$6* ☉*Aug.–June, weekdays 10:30–5, weekends 2–5.*

5 **Parliament House.** Built by convicts in 1840 as a customs house, this building did not acquire its present function until 1856. Although it's closed to the general public, tours run on weekdays. Contact the Clerk of the House if you'd also like to watch a session of parliament from the viewing gallery. The grounds are maintained by the Royal Botanic Gardens. ⊠*Morrison St. between Murray St. and Salamanca Pl., Hobart City* ☎*03/6233–2374* ⊠*Free* ☉*Guided tours weekdays 10–2.*

9 **Penitentiary Chapel and Criminal Courts.** Built and used during the early convict days, these buildings vividly portray Tasmania's penal, judicial, and religious heritage in their courtrooms, old cells, and underground tunnels. If you want to get spooked, come for the nighttime ghost tour (reservations recommended). ⊠*Brisbane and Campbell Sts., Hobart City* ☎*03/6231–0911* ⊠*A$8, ghost tour A$9* ☉*Tour weekdays 10–3, ghost tour daily 7:45* PM.

NEED A BREAK?

Drop into Sugo (⊠*Shop 9, Salamanca Pl., Hobart City* ☎*03/6224–5690*) if you get hungry while strolling the shops of Salamanca Place. This funky café serves great breakfasts, as well as tasty pizzas, pastas, and coffee. You're welcome to bring your own bottle of wine. It's open Tuesday–Friday 8–5 and weekends 9–5.

10 **Royal Tasmanian Botanical Gardens.** The largest area of open land in Hobart, these well-tended gardens are rarely crowded and provide a welcome relief from the city. Plants from all over the world are here—more than 6,000 exotic and native species in all. (The collection of Tasmania's unique native flora is especially impressive.) One section has been specially designed for wheelchairs. The Japanese Garden is dominated by a miniature Mt. Fuji. ⊠*Lower Domain Rd., Queen's Domain* ☎*03/6236–3076* ⊕*www.rtbg.tas.gov.au* ⊠*Free* ☉*Daily 8–4:45, education center noon–4.*

FodorsChoice ★

6 **Salamanca Place.** Old whaling ships used to dock at Salamanca Place. Today many of the warehouses that were once used by whalers along this street have been converted into crafts shops, art galleries, and restaurants. At the boisterous Saturday market, dealers in Tasmanian arts and crafts, antiques, old records, and books—and a fair bit of appalling junk—display their wares between 8 and 3. Keep an eye open for items made from beautiful Tasmanian timber, particularly Huon pine.

13 **Shot Tower.** Built in the 1860s, this 160-foot structure adjacent to the road in the town of Taroona is now the only remaining circular sandstone tower in the world. Lead bullets were once manufactured here for use in the firearms of the day. Climb the internal, 259-step

6

staircase for breathtaking views of
the Derwent estuary, then reward
yourself at the ground-level café
with delicious scones, homemade
jam, and fresh cream. ⊠ *Channel
Hwy., Taroona* ☎ *03/6227–8885*
⌨ *A$5.50* ◷ *Daily 9–5.*

❸ **Tasmanian Museum and Art Gallery.**
This building overlooking Constitution Dock houses many exhibits
on Tasmania's history. It's the best

> **BELLERIVE VILLAGE**
>
> Take the ferry across the River
> Derwent to Bellerive, a lovely little
> village-like suburb that will make
> you feel as if you've stepped back
> in history. There are great restau-
> rants and the view back to the
> city with Mt. Wellington looming
> in the background.

place in Hobart to learn about the island's Aborigines (the last native
Aboriginal inhabitants here died in the late 1800s), and unique wildlife.
⊠ *40 Macquarie St., Hobart City* ☎ *03/6211–4177* ⊕ *www.tmag.tas.
gov.au* ⌨ *Free* ◷ *Daily 10–5.*

WHERE TO EAT

Constitution Dock is the perfect place for yacht-watching, as well as for
gobbling fresh fish-and-chips from one of the punts (floating fish-and-
chips shops) moored on the water. Ask for the daily specials, such as
local blue grenadier or trevally, which cost A$6–A$8. The city's main
restaurant areas include the docks and around Salamanca Place.

$$–$$$ ✕ **Henry's Harbourside.** Part of the Henry Jones Art Hotel, this restau-
Fodor's Choice rant is renowned for its use of the freshest local fruits and vegetables.
★ Seafood, beef, lamb, game, and seasonal produce are featured in dishes
like sashimi-style ocean trout with wasabi mayonnaise, or spice-roasted
loin of fallow deer with butternut squash and beet jus. The wine list
features selections from only the finest Tasmanian, mainland Australia,
and overseas wineries. ⊠ *25 Hunter St., Hobart City* ☎ *03/6210–7706*
⊟ *AE, DC, MC, V.*

$$ ✕ **Kelleys.** Some of Hobart's best seafood is served up in this 200-
Fodor's Choice year-old sailmaker's cottage, where an open fireplace glows on chilly
★ nights. Feast on lightly spiced sea trout fillets, panfried and served
with shaved Parmesan; blue-eye trevally topped with basil pesto, and
wrapped in parchment with fresh spring vegetables; or the fabulous
seafood platter—a smorgasbord of shellfish, prawns, fish, and squid,
served with an array of dipping sauces. ⊠ *5 Knopwood St., Bat-
tery Point* ☎ *03/6224–7225* ⌨ *Reservations essential* ⊟ *AE, MC, V*
◷ *No lunch weekends.*

$$ ✕ **Marque IV.** Views of the docks and river provide a perfect backdrop
for enjoying the exquisite dishes served here. We love the Spring Bay
scallops with smoked salmon and wasabi sauce. In addition to an
excellent cheese and wine selection, they also have special vegetarian
and gluten-free menus. ⊠ *Elizabeth St. Pier, Hobart* ☎ *03/6224–4428*
⊟ *AE, DC, MC, V* ◷ *No lunch Sat.*

$$ ✕ **Restaurant 373.** For those who enjoy a little culinary creativeness,
don't miss this casual little bistro. It's very popular and you often
have to wait for a table, but well worth it. The slow cooked lamb

with mash and balsamic braised onions is delicious, but be sure to leave room for the truly inspired desserts. ✉ *373 Elizabeth St., North Hobart* ☎ *03/6231–9031* ▭ *AE, DC, MC, V* ⊗ *Closed Mon. No lunch.*

$-$$ ✕ **Ball and Chain Grill.** Set in an old sandstone warehouse, this eatery is the place to go if you like your meat, game, and seafood cooked over a real charcoal fire. The huge, succulent hunks of meat here will leave even the biggest eater satisfied; there's also a self-serve salad bar. ✉ *87 Salamanca Pl., Battery Point* ☎ *03/6223–2655* ▭ *AE, DC, MC, V* ⊗ *No lunch weekends.*

$-$$ ✕ **Mures Fish House Complex.** On the top floor of this complex on the
★   wharf, Mures Upper Deck Restaurant has superb indoor and alfresco views of the harbor. Try the flathead—a house version of the local fish, trevally, panfried with smoked trout pâté and Brie. Downstairs, Mures Lower Deck is a less-expensive, cash-only alternative: you order, take a number, pick up your food, and eat it at tables outside. Also in the complex, Orizuru has Hobart's best and freshest sushi and sashimi. ✉ *Victoria Dock, Hobart City* ☎ *03/6231–1999 Upper Deck, 03/6231–2121 Lower Deck, 03/6231–1790 Orizuru* ▭ *AE, DC, MC, V.*

$ ✕ **Annapurna.** In the bustling restaurant strip of North Hobart, this local favorite has maintained an enviable reputation for many years. Tandoori, curries (take care, they can be searingly hot), and a wide selection of other Indian delicacies keep people coming back. Inexpensive lunch boxes available. ✉ *305 Elizabeth St, North Hobart* ☎ *03/6236–9500* ▭ *AE, DC, MC, V.*

$ ✕ **Maldini.** Reminiscent of an Italian café in a charming country village, this popular spot lets you watch the parade of Salamanca Place shoppers as you dine on appetizers like antipasto or char-grilled sardines. Heartier fare includes pastas, osso buco, and free-range-chicken breast with potato gnocchi and creamy Gorgonzola. Although Australian wines dominate the list, there are a few Italian labels to match the setting. ✉ *47 Salamanca Pl., Hobart City* ☎ *03/6223–4460* ▭ *AE, DC, MC, V.*

¢–$ ✕ **Jackman and McRoss.** A perfect place to refuel when you're exploring Battery Point and Salamanca Place, this lively café serves up fantastic breads, pies, cakes, and pastries accompanied by a selection of coffees. The hearty, slow-cooked beef pie is a Tasmanian classic. For a sandwich with an unusual twist, try the pastrami and spiced pear with mustard on sunflower rye bread. ✉ *57–59 Hampden Rd., Battery Point* ☎ *03/6223–3186* ▭ *No credit cards* ⊗ *No dinner.*

WHERE TO STAY

Area accommodations include hotels, guesthouses, B&Bs, and self-catering cottages. Although there are several new hotels in Hobart, as well as many chain accommodations, the greatest attractions are the lodgings in old, historic houses and cottages, most of which have been beautifully restored.

6

$$$$
Fodor'sChoice
★ ⊞ **Islington Hotel.** Built in 1847, this elegant Regency mansion was converted to a five-star luxury boutique hotel, and is now considered to be one of the finest in Australia. Set in an acre of landscaped gardens (complete with a Heritage-listed willow tree over 100 years old) and breathtaking views over Mt. Wellington, the property incorporates six garden suites and the main house. The common areas include a dramatic marble conservatory and a library with elegant bookshelves and flickering fireplaces. All guest suites have been completely refurbished with a blend of antique and modern style, and an eclectic collection of art. Full breakfasts and evening cocktails are included in your room rate, and a Rolls-Royce is available to drive you to a local restaurant or for sightseeing. ⊠*321 Davey St., South Hobart, 7000* ☎*03/6220–2123* ⊕*www.islingtonhotel.com* ☞*11 suites* ⌂*In-room: dial-up, Wi-Fi (some). In-hotel: laundry service, parking (no fee)* ⊟*AE, DC, MC, V* ⋈*BP.*

$$$–$$$$
Fodor'sChoice
★ ✕⊞ **Henry Jones Art Hotel.** Right on the Hobart waterfront, this row of historic warehouses and former jam factory have been transformed into a sensational, art-theme hotel, where the work of Tasmania's finest visual and performing artists is displayed. The spacious guest suites, also artistically decorated, reflect the influences of a rich colonial trading history with India and China: all suites have natural wood furnishings and king-size beds with exotic silk covers. Bathrooms are supermodern, with stainless-steel and translucent-glass fittings. Some suites have harbor views; others overlook the stunning glassed-in courtyard atrium. ⊠*25 Hunter St., Hobart, 7000* ☎*03/6210–7700 or 1300/665581* ⊕*www.thehenryjones.com* ☞*50 suites* ⌂*In-room: dial-up, Wi-Fi (some). In-hotel: Wi-Fi, restaurant, room service, bar, concierge, laundry service, parking (no fee), no-smoking rooms* ⊟*AE, DC, MC, V.*

$$$–$$$$
★ ⊞ **Hotel Grand Chancellor.** Across the street from the old wharves and steps from some of the best restaurants in Hobart, this imposing glass-and-stone building seems a bit out of place amid Hobart's colonialism. What it lacks in period charm, however, it more than makes up for in luxury. All rooms have large wooden desks and thick, white guest bathrobes. Some rooms overlook the harbor. ⊠*1 Davey St., Hobart City, 7001* ☎*03/6235–4535 or 1800/753379* ⊕*www.ghihotels.com* ☞*212 rooms, 12 suites* ⌂*In-room: dial-up, Wi-Fi (some). In-hotel: 2 restaurants, bar, pool, gym, laundry service, airport shuttle, parking (no fee)* ⊟*AE, DC, MC, V.*

$$$–$$$$
⊞ **Moorilla Vineyard Chalets.** Built in 1958, these stylish cottages occupy a lush private peninsula along the Derwent River. Four spacious, light-filled, self-contained chalets—two with two bedrooms and two with one bedroom—have views of the Derwent River and the estate's small but impressive vineyard, known for its chardonnay and pinot noir. Don't miss the Moo Brew beers or lunch at the excellent Source restaurant. Moorilla is 13 km (8 mi) north of Hobart. ⊠*655 Main Rd., Berridale, 7011* ☎*03/6277–9900* ⊕*www.moorilla.com.au* ☞*4 chalets* ⌂*In-room: kitchen, dial-up. In-hotel: restaurant, parking (no fee)* ⊟*AE, DC, MC, V.*

$$$ ⚀**Somerset on the Pier.** Located on one of Hobart's historic piers, this
★ all-suites complex is just a five-minute walk from the city, Salamanca
Place, and many popular restaurants and nightspots. Spacious, modern-
furnished units have loft-style bedrooms, stereos, DVD players, and
full kitchens with dishes and cutlery; many have balconies with harbor
views. The adjacent conference facility makes this a favorite of busi-
ness travelers. ✉*Elizabeth St. Pier, Hobart City, 7000* ☎*03/6220–*
6600 or 1800/620462 ⊕*www.somersetonthepier.com* ☞*56 suites*
⚐*In-room: kitchen, refrigerator, dial-up. In-hotel: restaurant, room*
service, bar, gym, some Wi-Fi, laundry facilities, parking (no fee)
☐*AE, DC, MC, V.*

$$–$$$ ⚀**Old Woolstore.** Formerly an early-20th-century wool store, this
★ intriguing complex now houses a combination of lodgings. Hotel-style
rooms are bright and airy, while all the studio, one- and two-bedroom,
and executive apartments have kitchens and laundry facilities. Equip-
ment and old photos of the original wool store are displayed through-
out the buildings, the Bau Bau, and Stockmans Restaurant. The central
setting near the waterfront makes this an ideal base for exploring the
city on foot. ✉*1 Macquarie St., Hobart City, 7000* ☎*03/6235–5355*
or 1800/814676 ⊕*www.oldwoolstore.com.au* ☞*59 rooms, 183 apart-*
ments ⚐*In-room: kitchen (some), dial-up, Wi-Fi (some). In-hotel: res-*
taurant, bar, laundry facilities (some), parking (no fee), minibar ☐*AE,*
DC, MC, V.

$$–$$$ ⚀**Salamanca Inn.** These elegant, self-contained apartments blend in
well with the surrounding historic district. Queen-size beds, modern
kitchens, and free laundry facilities make the accommodations per-
fect for families. Ask for a room on the sunny western side, but don't
expect great views from a three-story building. ✉*10 Gladstone St.,*
Battery Point, 7000 ☎*03/6223–3300 or 1800/030944* ⊕*www.sala-*
mancainn.com.au ☞*65 rooms* ⚐*In-room: kitchen, dial-up, Wi-Fi*
(some). In-hotel: restaurant, pool, laundry facilities, parking (no fee)
☐*AE, DC, MC, V.*

$$ ⚀**Corinda's Cottages.** This charming residence was built in the 1880s
★ for Alfred Crisp, a wealthy timber merchant who later became Lord
Mayor of Hobart. Three historic outbuildings—including a gardener's residence, servants' quarters, and coach house—have been lovingly converted into delightful self-contained cottages filled with
period antiques. The B&B is close to the woodland, yet it's only
a few minutes from the city center. ✉*17 Glebe St., Glebe, 7000*
☎*03/6234–1590* ⊕*www.corindascottages.com.au* ☞*3 cottages*
⚐*In-room: kitchen. In-hotel: laundry service, parking (no fee)*
☐*AE, MC, V* ⦿*BP.*

$–$$ ⚀**Lodge on Elizabeth.** This opulent grand manor, convict-built in 1829,
and home over the years to many Hobart notables, is within walking distance of the city center, but far enough removed to feel like a
sanctuary. The courtyard garden is a fine place to relax, as is the fireside common room, where you can sip a glass of wine before retreat-
ing upstairs to your room with private hot tub. ✉*249 Elizabeth St.,*
Hobart City, 7000 ☎*03/6231–3830* ⊕*www.thelodge.com.au* ☞*14*

6

rooms ☾*In-room: refrigerator, dial-up. In-hotel: restaurant, laundry facilities, parking (no fee)* ▤*MC, V* ⏃❘*CP.*

$ 🎦**Bluff Lodge.** Built in 1889 as a "gentleman's residence," this lodge on the eastern shore of the Derwent River has been lovingly restored with antique Tasmanian furnishings. The rooms all have either queen- or king-size beds, and the guest lounge is the perfect place to enjoy a glass of port before the open fire. The full breakfast will set you up for a day's sightseeing. ⊠*40 King St., Bellerive, 7018* ☎*0407/445500* ⊕*www.blufflodge.com.au* ⏎*3 rooms* ☾*In-room: no phone. In-hotel: bar, parking (no fee)* ▤*AE, DC, MC, V* ⏃❘*BP.*

NIGHTLIFE & THE ARTS

Although Hobart has the only true nightlife scene in Tasmania, it's extremely tame compared to what's in Melbourne and Sydney. There are few dance clubs, and most bars have live music only on Friday and Saturday. Consult the Friday or Saturday editions of the *Mercury* newspaper before heading out. *This Week in Tasmania,* available at most hotels, is a comprehensive guide to current stage performances and contemporary music concerts.

BARS & DANCE CLUBS

The waterfront area is lined with bars that cater to the local, very thirsty after work crowds. If you have a chance, be sure to stop by **T42** (⊠*Elizabeth St. Pier, Hobart City* ☎*03/6224–7742*), a cleverly named waterfront spot, popular for both dining and drinking. The food is good, but the main draw is the lively bar.

Quarry (⊠*27 Salamanca Place* ☎*03/6223–6552*) is a busy bar and café with tables spilling out on to the pavement, which is great for people watching.

Grape (⊠*55 Salamanca Place* ☎*03/6224–0611*) is a lovely little wine bar that has a wonderful shop where you can pick up great Tasmanian wines and a cheese platter for an impromptu little picnic.

Bar Celona (⊠*24 Salamanca Sq., Hobart City* ☎*03/6224–7557*) is another nice wine bar with a good selection of local vintages by the glass or bottle.

The **Grand Chancellor** (⊠*1 Davey St., Hobart City* ☎*03/6235–4535*) has a relaxing piano bar that is popular with professionals. The cool kids go for the raucous, art deco **Republic Bar and Cafe** (⊠*299 Elizabeth St., North Hobart* ☎*03/6234–6954*) **Soak** (⊠*237 Elizabeth St., North Hobart* ☎*03/6231–5699*) operates as a café called Kaos during the day. At night they attract a largely gay clientele.

Round Midnight (⊠*39 Salamanca Pl., Battery Point* ☎*03/6223–2491*) has a mix of youngish live bands and DJs. **Syrup** (⊠*39 Salamanca Pl., Battery Point* ☎*03/6224–8249*), in the same building as Round Midnight, also spins music, features live bands, and is popular with the under-thirty somethings.

CASINO

The **Wrest Point Casino** (⊠*410 Sandy Bay Rd., Sandy Bay* ☎*03/6225–0112*) in the Wrest Point Hotel has blackjack, American roulette, mini-baccarat, keno, minidice, craps, federal wheel, federal poker and stud poker, and Two-up. It's open Monday–Thursday 1 PM–3 AM, Friday and Saturday 1 PM–4 AM, and Sunday noon–3 AM.

LIVE MUSIC

Federation Concert Hall (✉ *1 Davey St., Hobart City* ☎*03/6235–4535*) is the permanent home of the world-acclaimed Tasmanian Symphony Orchestra. Adjacent to the Hotel Grand Chancellor, the 1,100-seat auditorium also often welcomes touring musicians and speakers.

THEATER

Playhouse Theatre (✉*106 Bathurst St., Hobart City* ☎*03/6234–1536*) stages a mix of traditional, locally cast plays and cutting-edge works. **Theatre Royal** (✉*29 Campbell St., Hobart City* ☎*03/6233–2299*), an 1834 architectural gem with portraits of composers painted on its magnificent dome, stages classic and contemporary plays by Australian and international playwrights.

SPORTS & THE OUTDOORS

Walking is excellent around Mt. Wellington, which has a number of well-marked trails. The best hiking is a bit farther away, in South West National Park or in Mt. Field National Park.

BICYCLING

Although most of Hobart and its surrounding areas are too hilly to make for easy cycling, some old railway lines along the western bank of the Derwent River (which are quite flat) have been transformed into bicycle paths. These offer a relaxing way to explore parts of the city. Bikes can be rented from **Derwent Bike Hire** (✉*Regatta Grounds, Queens Domain* ☎*03/6234–2910*). **Island Cycle Tours** (☎*1300/880334*) also rents bikes.

BUSHWALKING

The Tasmanian Travel and Information Centre has details on local hiking trails; many are within easy reach of Hobart. Although shops around town stock outdoor equipment, you should bring your own gear if you're planning any serious bushwalking. Sneakers are adequate for walking around Mt. Wellington and along beaches. A car is necessary to access several of the trails around Mt. Wellington.

FISHING

Tasmania's well-stocked lakes and streams are among the world's best for trout fishing. The season runs from August through May, and licensed trips can be arranged through the Tasmanian Travel and Information Centre.

Several professional fishing guides are based on the island. For information on these guides, as well as related tours, accommodations, and sea charters, check out **www.troutguidestasmania.com.au** or inquire at the Tasmanian Travel and Information Centers for a professional guide in the area you are visiting.

SHOPPING

Tasmanian artisans and craftspeople work with diverse materials to fashion unusual pottery, metalwork, and wool garments. Items made from regional timber, including myrtle, sassafras, and Huon pine, are very popular. The wonderful scenery around the island is an inspiration for numerous artists.

Along the Hobart waterfront at Salamanca Place are a large number of shops that sell arts and crafts. On Saturday the area turns into a giant market, where still more local artists join produce growers, bric-a-brac sellers, and itinerant musicians to sell their wares.

Aspect Design (⊠*79 Salamanca Pl., Battery Point* ☎*03/6223–2642*) stocks blown glass, wooden products, pottery, and jewelry. **Handmark Gallery** (⊠*77 Salamanca Pl., Battery Point* ☎*03/6223–7895*) sells Hobart's best wooden jewelry boxes as well as art deco jewelry, pottery, painting, and sculpture. **Tasmania Shop and Gallery** (⊠*65 Salamanca Pl., Battery Point* ☎*03/6223–5022*) specializes in products made in Tasmania, including wood, paintings, and jewelry. The **Wilderness Society Shop** (⊠*33 Salamanca Pl., Battery Point* ☎*03/6234–9370*) sells prints, cards, books, and T-shirts, all made in Australia.

SIDE TRIPS FROM HOBART

Hobart is a perfect base for short trips to some of Tasmania's most historic and scenic places. Although you can visit them in a day, it's best to stay a night or two and experience their delights at a leisurely pace.

THE HUON VALLEY

★ *40 km (25 mi) south of Hobart.*

En route to the vast wilderness of South West National Park is the tranquil Huon Valley. Sheltered coasts and sandy beaches are pocketed with thick forests and small farms. William Bligh planted the first apple tree here, founding one of the region's major industries. Salmon and trout caught fresh from churning blue rivers are also delicious regional delicacies.

The valley is also famous for the Huon pine, much of which has been logged over the decades. The trees that remain are strictly protected, so other local timbers are used by the region's craftspeople.

The **Forest and Heritage Centre** has fascinating displays on the history of forestry in the area, as well as some beautiful tables, vases, and cabinetry that have been crafted from the timber. ⊠*Church St., Geeveston* ☎*03/6297–1836* ⊡*A$5* ☉*Daily 9–5.*

En route to Huonville, the **Huon Valley Apple Museum** is in a former apple-packing shed. Some 500 varieties of apples are grown in the valley, and the museum displays farming artifacts, picking and processing equipment, and early-settler memorabilia from the area's orchards.

⊠*Main Rd., Grove* ☎*03/6266–4345* ✆*A$5.50* ☉*Sept.–May, daily 9–5; June–Aug., daily 10–4.*

Beyond Geeveston, the cantilevered, 1,880-foot-long **Tahune Forest Airwalk** rises to 150 feet above the forest floor, providing a stunning panorama of the Huon and Picton rivers and the Hartz Mountains. The best views are from the platform at the end of the walkway. ⊠*Arve Rd.* ☎*03/6297–0068* ✆*A$17* ☉*Daily 9–5.*

Spectacular cave formations and thermal pools amid a fern glade await at the **Hastings Caves and Thermal Springs.** The caves are about 110 km (70 mi) from Hobart, past Huonville and Dover. You can take a tour of the chambers, or just relax at the well-equipped picnic areas. The route to the site is well marked from the town of Dover on. ☎*03/6298–3209* ✆*A$19.50* ☉*Daily 9–5.*

WHERE TO STAY & EAT

$–$$ ✕ **Home Hill Restaurant.** Large plate-glass windows here open to the Home Hill winery's endless hillside vineyards. The seasonal menu includes such delicacies as oven-baked salmon smothered in black olives, tomatoes, and served on homemade noodles—perfect for pairing with the Home Hill chardonnay. The crisp sylvaner (a light, Alsace-style white wine) goes beautifully with the quail salad. After dinner, you can head down to the cellar to sample more of the winery's excellent cool-climate labels. ⊠*38 Nairn St., Ranelagh* ☎*03/6264–1200* ⊕*www.homehill wines.com.au* ⊟*DC, MC, V* ☉*No dinner Sun.–Thurs.*

$–$$ 🏠 **Matilda's of Ranelagh.** The official greeters at this delightful, 1850
Fodor'sChoice Heritage-listed B&B are five golden retrievers. Elegant Victorian and
★ Edwardian furnishings provide the ultimate in refinement and comfort—and two of the rooms even have hot tubs. Outside, it's a pleasure to stroll through the 5-acre English-style gardens, which are filled with trees, shrubs, and thousands of flowers that bloom seasonally. A hearty breakfast is served each morning in the pretty blue-and-white dining room. ⊠*44 Louisa St., Ranelagh, 7109* ☎*03/6264–3493* 🖷*03/6264–3491* ⊕*www.matildasofranelagh.com.au* 🛏*5 rooms* ◊*In-hotel: restaurant, laundry facilities, parking (no fee), no-smoking rooms, no kids under 15, no elevator* ⊟*MC, V* ⍊*BP.*

$ 🏠 **Heron's Rise Vineyard.** Mornings in either of the vineyard's two self-contained cottages are bucolic and gorgeous; you'll wake to glorious water views out over the flower gardens, where you might see rabbits nibbling. Both cottages have queen-size beds and wood-burning fireplaces. Dinner is available in your cottage by prior arrangement. ⊠*Saddle Rd., Kettering, 7155* ☎*03/6267–4339* 🖷*03/6267–4245* ⊕*www.heronsrise.com.au* 🛏*2 cottages* ◊*In-room: kitchen. In-*

hotel: laundry facilities, parking (no fee), no-smoking rooms ⊟*DC, MC, V* ⦿|*CP.*

BRUNY ISLAND

★ From the village of Kettering 25 km (16 mi) south of Hobart, a ferry crosses the narrow D'Entrecasteaux Channel to reach Bruny Island, a little-publicized, gemlike satellite of Tasmania. Names here reflect the influence of the French explorers who sailed through this region in the 1770s and '80s. At Bruny's southern tip are a convict-built lighthouse and magnificent coastal scenery.

To fully appreciate the dramatic panorama, take the three-hour, 50-km (31-mi) ecology-focused cruise run by **Bruny Island Charters.** You'll sail past towering cliffs and hidden caves, and likely see dolphins, seals, and penguins gliding all around the boat. Eagles, albatrosses, and shore-birds also dart and dive overhead, and can often be seen nesting amid the craggy outcrops. Cruise reservations are required in winter. ⊠*915 Adventure Bay Rd., Adventure Bay, Bruny Island* ☏*03/6293–1465* ⦿*Cruises daily yr-round.*

RICHMOND

★ *24 km (15 mi) northeast of Hobart.*

Twenty minutes' drive from Hobart and a century behind the big city, this colonial village in the Coal River valley is a major tourist magnet. Visitors stroll and browse through the craft shops, antiques stores, and cafés along the main street. Richmond is also home to a number of vineyards, all of which produce excellent cool-climate wines.

Richmond Bridge, Australia's oldest bridge, a scenic counterpoint to the village's church-spire skyline, is a convict-built stone structure dating from 1823. It's at the eastern end of the main street.

The well-preserved **Richmond Jail,** built in 1825, has eerie displays of chain manacles, domestic utensils, and instruments of torture. ⊠*37 Bathurst St.* ☏*03/6260–2127* ⊜*A$5.50* ⦿*Daily 10–5.*

WHERE TO STAY & EAT

$–$$ ✕**Coal Valley Vineyard.** This winery restaurant, accessible via the road from Cambridge, is set amid scenic vineyards with views over a golf course to the waters of Barilla Bay. It's open daily for lunch from 10 to 4. Try the roasted free-range-chicken breast filled with King Island double Brie and baby spinach, and served with Coal Valley chardonnay sauce. ⊠*257 Richmond Rd., Cambridge* ☏*03/6248–5367* ⊟*AE, DC, MC, V* ⦿*No lunch Thurs.–Mon. No dinner Fri.*

$–$$ ✕**Meadowbank.** Wine tasting and an art gallery complement this restaurant with its views over the vineyards of Meadowbank Estate and the waters of Barilla Bay. Local oysters make a fine starter; main courses include duck breast with savoy cabbage and rabbit braised in cider. Save room for the warm, caramel-soaked sponge pudding served with vanilla crème anglaise and Tasmanian blackberries. ⊠*699 Richmond Rd., Cambridge* ☎*03/6248–4484* ▭*DC, MC, V* ⊗*No dinner.*

$ 🖼**Mrs. Currie's House B&B.** This gracious Georgian house, built between
★ 1820 and 1860, is set in a peaceful garden with lovely views over the village of Richmond and the surrounding countryside. Oriental rugs and wood-burning fireplaces give a cozy feel to both the lounge and the breakfast room (where a cooked meal is served every morning). The guest rooms are furnished with antiques and wrought-iron bedsteads; some have graceful canopy-style nets overhead. ⊠*4 Franklin St., 7025* ☎*03/6260–2766* ⊕*www.mrscurrieshouse.com.au* ⇨*4 rooms* ⚴*In-hotel: laundry service, parking (no fee), no elevator* ▭*DC, MC, V* ◉*BP.*

MT. FIELD NATIONAL PARK

70 km (43 mi) northwest of Hobart.

This popular park contains easily navigable trails, picnic areas, and well-maintained campsites that are ideal for family outings. Especially notable is the 1-km (½-mi) **Russell Falls Nature Walk,** which winds up a hill to the gorgeous Horseshoe Falls, then to the fascinating Tall Trees Walk, then another 20 minutes to Lady Barron Falls. Animals, including wallabies and possums, are often out and about around dusk.

SOUTH WEST NATIONAL PARK

Maydena is 98 km (61 mi) northwest of Hobart, Geeveston is 60 km (37 mi) southwest of Hobart.

The South West National Park encompasses the entire southwestern portion of the state, creating an extraordinary World Heritage wilderness area. This is one of the few virgin land tracts in Australia, whose mountain ranges and lakes were virtually unknown to all but the most avid bushwalkers until the 1970s. Although the park holds the greatest appeal for the hardy and adventurous, within its boundaries are some pleasant but quite underpublicized easy-access locales.

Roads in the park are few, and those that exist skirt only the edges of the wilderness area. The two main ways to access the park are through the town of Maydena, north of Hobart, and the town of Geeveston in the Huon Valley.

Maydena is a few miles west of the entrance to Mt. Field National Park. From there the Gordon River Road takes you through to Strathgordon, close to where Lake Pedder was dammed in 1972 for hydroelectricity production. The scenery is magnificent, with lakes surrounded by mountains in pristine wilderness. Take care if you are tempted to walk away from the road, however; the terrain is rugged and weather conditions can change rapidly, even in summer.

Beyond Geeveston and the Tahune Forest Airwalk, the Arve River Road takes you to a number of parking areas from where you can walk on trails on the edge of the Hartz Mountain part of the South West National Park.

For more information on exploring the park, contact the **main park office** (⊠ *Park Rd., Maydena* ☎*03/6288–1283*), or the **Southern District Office** (⊠*22 Main St., Huonville* ☎*03/6264–8473*).

PORT ARTHUR & THE TASMAN PENINSULA

102 km (63 mi) southeast of Hobart.

When Governor George Arthur, Lieutenant-Governor of Van Diemen's Land (now Tasmania) was looking for a site to dump his worst convict offenders in 1830, the Tasman Peninsula was a natural choice. Joined to the rest of Tasmania only by the narrow Eaglehawk Neck, the spit was easy to isolate and guard. Between 1830 and 1877 more than 12,000 convicts served sentences at Port Arthur in Britain's equivalent of Devil's Island. Dogs patrolled the narrow causeway, and guards spread rumors that sharks infested the waters. Reminders of those dark days remain in some of the area names—Dauntless Point, Stinking Point, Isle of the Dead.

> **WORD OF MOUTH**
>
> "Port Authur is fascinating. I did it as a day trip via the bus/boat from Hobart. It was a full day but manageable, and you can certainly tour the grounds at your own pace or limit yourself to the museum portions."
>
> —kazoo

EXPLORING PORT ARTHUR

Fodor's Choice **Port Arthur Historic Site.** This property, formerly the grounds of the Port
★   Arthur Penal Settlement, is now a lovely—and quite large—historical park. Be prepared to do some walking between widely scattered sites. Begin at the excellent visitor center, which introduces you to the experience by "sentencing, transporting, and assigning" you before you ever set foot in the colony. Most of the original buildings were damaged by bushfires in 1895 and 1897, shortly after the settlement was abandoned, but you can still see the beautiful church, round guardhouse, commandant's residence, model prison, hospital, and government cottages.

The old **lunatic asylum** is now an excellent museum with a scale model of the Port Arthur settlement, a video history, and a collection of tools, leg irons, and chains. Along with a walking tour of the grounds and entrance to the museum, admission includes a harbor cruise, of which there are eight scheduled daily in summer. There's a separate twice-daily cruise to and tour of the **Isle of the Dead,** which sits in the middle of the bay. It's estimated that 1,769 convicts and 180 others are buried here, mostly in communal pits. Ghost tours (reservations are essential) leave the visitor center at dusk and last about 90 minutes. ⊠*Arthur Hwy.* ☎*03/6251–2310 or 1800/659101* ☜*2-day entry ticket A$25,*

Tasmania's Convict Past

They came in chains to this hostile island, where the seasons were all the wrong way around and the sights and smells unfamiliar. They were the men and women whom Great Britain wanted to forget, the desperately poor refuse of an overcrowded penal system that considered seven years of transportation an appropriate penalty for stealing a loaf of bread that might have meant the difference between survival and starvation. They were mostly young, usually uneducated, and often—from 1830 onward—they were Irish.

In the 50 years following the establishment of the first settlement in Tasmania (Van Diemen's Land) in 1803, a total of 57,909 male and 13,392 female prisoners were sent to the island. From 1830 on, many ended up at the newly built penal settlement at Port Arthur. Contrary to today's legend, Port Arthur was never the most ghastly hellhole of the convict gulag; that dubious honor was shared by Sarah Island on Tasmania's west coast and Norfolk Island in the South Pacific—both extremely remote, and with terribly primitive conditions.

The location of the settlement on the Tasman Peninsula was ideal; joined to the "mainland" of Tasmania by a narrow neck of land with steep cliffs

pounded by surging surf, it was easy to isolate and guard. As the number of prisoners increased more buildings went up, and a semaphore system advising of escapes linked Port Arthur with Hobart via numerous hilltop stations. The penal colony became a self-sufficient industrial center where prisoners sawed timber, built ships, laid bricks, cut stone, and made tiles, shoes, iron castings, and clothing.

Convict banishment to Van Diemen's Land ceased in 1853. Most of the Port Arthur inmates were given tickets of leave or were sent to the countryside as agricultural laborers. Insane convicts (and there were many who had gone quite mad here) were incarcerated in the old wooden barracks until a special asylum was finished in 1868.

The settlement closed in 1877 after some 12,000 sentences had been served. For a while the authorities tried to expunge all memories of the peninsula's shame. They even changed the name for a time to Carnarvon. This halfhearted cover-up failed. Today, memories of Tasmania's convict past burn brighter than ever, as society once again wrestles with the same dilemmas of good and evil, crime and punishment.

—Steve Robertson

6

Isle of the Dead tour A$10, ghost tour A$15 ⊕www.portarthur.org. au ⊗Daily 8:30–dusk.

Tasmanian Devil Park. This is probably the best place in the state to see Tasmanian devils (burrowing carnivorous marsupials about the size of a dog), as well as quolls, boobooks (small, spotted brown owls), masked owls, eagles, and other native fauna. Watch the live "Kings of the Wind" show, which stars birds of prey and other species in free flight. ⊠*Arthur Hwy., Taranna ✛11 km (7 mi) north of Port Arthur* ☎*03/6250–3230* ☒*A$19* ⊗*Daily 9–5.*

WHERE TO STAY & EAT

$–$$ ✕**Felons.** This restaurant at the Port Arthur Historic Site serves fresh Tasmanian seafood and game. The ever-succulent local fish of the day is served New Orleans style (with a spicy Cajun coating), oven-baked with lemon butter, or deep-fried tempura-style in a light batter. If it's teatime, pop in for one of the exceedingly rich desserts. ⊠*Port Arthur Historic Site, Port Arthur* ☎*03/6251–2314 or 1800/659101* ▤*AE, DC, MC, V.*

> ### THE CONVICT TRAIL
>
> Apart from the main penal colony, a number of outstations were established at strategic locations around the Tasman Peninsula. The "Convict Trail," which you can follow by car, takes in seven such sites, including the remains of a coal mine. (Local tourism offices have maps of the trail.) This once-foreboding peninsula has become Tasmania's major tourist attraction, filled with beautiful scenery and historic sites that recapture Australia's difficult beginnings.

$–$$$ ▥**Cascades Colonial Accommodation.** Part of a onetime convict outstation that dates to 1841, the original buildings here have been transformed into luxury accommodations. Each has kitchen facilities with breakfast provisions included. A small museum related to the property is also on-site and there are some lovely bushwalks on the property. ⊠*531 Main Rd., Koonya, 7187* ✥*20 km (12 mi) north of Port Arthur* ☎*03/6250–3873* ⊕*www.cascadescolonial.com.au* ➷*5 cottages* ⚏*In-room: kitchen. In-hotel: laundry facilities, parking (no fee), no elevator* ▤*No credit cards* ❙◎❙*CP.*

$ ▥**Comfort Inn Port Arthur.** On a ridge behind an old church, this motel overlooks the entire historic penal settlement site. There's a range of lodging options here, from interconnecting "Guards' Rooms," which are great for families, to more-standard hotel rooms. As well as providing excellent food, the Commandant's Table Restaurant and Bistro has arguably the best view over the historic site. ⊠*29 Safety Cove Rd., 7182* ☎*03/6250–2101 or 1800/030747* ⊕*www.comfortinn.com* ➷*35 rooms* ⚏*In-hotel: restaurant, bar, laundry facilities, parking (no fee)* ▤*AE, DC, MC, V.*

FREYCINET NATIONAL PARK & EAST-COAST RESORTS

The east coast of Tasmania has a mild climate, beautiful swimming and surfing beaches, and excellent fishing spots. The stretches of white sand here are often so deserted you can pretend you're Robinson Crusoe. The towns in this region are quiet but historically interesting; in Louisville, for example, you can catch a ferry to the Maria Island National Park, which was a whaling station and penal settlement in the mid-19th century. Farther north, the town of Swansea has numerous stone colonial buildings that have been restored as hotels and restaurants, as well as the unusual Spiky Bridge (so named because of its vertically placed sandstone "spikes") and the convict-built Three Arch Bridge, both of which date from 1845.

One of the jewels of the eastern coast is Freycinet National Park, renowned among adventure seekers and those who appreciate stunning scenery. The spectacular granite peaks of the Hazards and the idyllic protected beach at Wineglass Bay have been dazzling visitors to this peninsula since it became a park in 1916.

EAST-COAST RESORTS

★ From Hobart the east-coast Tasman Highway travels cross-country to Orford, then passes through beautiful coastal scenery with spectacular white-sand beaches, usually completely deserted, before reaching Swansea. Bicheno, just north of Freycinet National Park, and St. Helens, which is farther north, are both fishing and holiday towns with quiet, sheltered harbors. Taking the four-day **Bay of Fires Walk** along the coast north of St. Helens is a wonderful way to enjoy the rugged beauty and tranquillity of the coast. The walk, which is about 32 km (20 mi) long, winds along the edge of Mt. William National Park, and allows you to visit stunning beaches, dunes, heathlands, Aboriginal sites, and peppermint forests, where a profusion of plant and animal life flourish. During part of the walk, you'll stay at a comfortable campsite, with canvas-room lodgings and kitchen facilities, but for the rest of the time you'll get to stay at the dramatic, remote, and ecologically sustainable **Bay of Fires Lodge**. All meals are provided. For details and prices, check out ⊕www.bayoffires.com.au or call Cradle Huts Pty., Ltd. at ☎03/6391–9339.

WHERE TO STAY

$–$$$ ⊞ **Diamond Island Ocean View Apartments.** Located 2½ km (1½ mi) north of Bicheno's town center, this property overlooks the Tasman Sea and has direct beach access. Twelve duplex units, each with two bedrooms, are nestled within 7 acres of landscaped gardens; there are also three smaller, one-bedroom units. All have private bathrooms. The resort hosts group tours to see wild fairy penguins, who come ashore each night after a day of fishing; be sure to reserve a spot when you book your room. ⊠69 Tasman Hwy., Bicheno, 7215 ☎03/6375–0100 or 1800/030299 ⊕www.diamondisland.com.au ➪15 rooms ♿In-hotel: restaurant, tennis courts, pool, laundry facilities, parking (no fee) ☰DC, MC, V.

$$ ⊞ **Kabuki by the Sea.** You can look out over Schouten Island and the Hazards from the terraces of this cliff-top inn for some of the most stunning coastal views in the state—then watch the moon rise over Great Oyster Bay while dining at the on-site Japanese restaurant. Cottages have all the comforts of a true Japanese *ryokan* (a traditional Japanese inn), including private sitting and dining rooms, and kitchen facilities. ⊠Tasman Hwy., 7190 ✛8 km (5 mi) south of Swansea ☎03/6257–8588 ⊕www.kabukibythesea.com.au ➪5 cottages ♿In-room: kitchen. In-hotel: restaurant, laundry service, parking (no fee) ☰AE, MC, V.

$$ ⊞ **Meredith House.** Exquisite red-cedar furnishings and antiques decorate this 1853 refurbished residence in the center of Swansea. Comfortable rooms overlook the tranquil waters of Great Oyster Bay.

You can request morning and evening meals in the dining room or choose from the many cafés and restaurants in town. ⊠*15 Noyes St., Swansea, 7190* ☎*03/6257–8119* ⊕*www.meredith-house. com.au* ⇆*11 rooms* ⌂*In-hotel: restaurant, parking (no fee)* ▭*AE, MC, V* ⦿|*BP.*

$$ ⊞ **Wagners Cottages.** These four charming stone cottages, two of which date from the 1850s, sit amid rambling gardens. Each is decorated with country antique-style furniture, and has its own fireplace and hot tub. There are also two guest rooms in the main house, each with a private bathroom. A full breakfast is served in the sunny atrium overlooking the rose garden. ⊠*Tasman Hwy. near Francis St., 3 km (2 mi) south of town, Swansea, 7190* ☎*03/6257–8494* ⊕*www. wagnerscottages.com.au* ⇆*4 cottages, 2 rooms* ⌂*In-room: kitchen (some). In-hotel: laundry facilities, parking (no fee), no elevator* ▭*AE, DC, MC, V* ⦿|*BP.*

$ ⊞ **Eastcoaster Resort.** This seaside complex in the town of Louisville is a great jumping-off point for exploring Maria Island National Park; the resort's catamaran, the *Eastcoaster Express*, makes three or four trips a day to the island. There are motel-type rooms here with kitchenettes, and also detached cabins (four of which have hot tubs). The on-site Marlin restaurant specializes in local seafood and Tasmanian wines. ⊠*Louisville Point Rd., Louisville, 7190* ☎*03/6257–1172* ⊕*www. eastcoaster.com.au* ⇆*48 rooms, 8 cabins* ⌂*In-room: kitchen (some). In-hotel: restaurant, tennis court, pools* ▭*DC, MC, V.*

FREYCINET NATIONAL PARK

Fodor'sChoice ★ *238 km (149 mi) north of Port Arthur, 214 km (133 mi) southwest of Launceston, 206 km (128 mi) northeast of Hobart.*

The road onto the Freycinet Peninsula ends just past the township of Coles Bay; from that point the Freycinet National Park begins and covers 24,700 acres.

Highlights of the dramatic scenery here include the mountain-size granite rock formations known as **the Hazards.** On the ocean side of the peninsula there are also sheer cliffs that drop into the deep-blue ocean; views from the lighthouse at Cape Tourville (reached by a narrow dirt road) are unforgettable. A series of tiny coves called the Honeymoon Bays provide a quieter perspective on the Great Oyster Bay side. **Wineglass Bay,** a perfect crescent of dazzling white sand, is best viewed from the lookout platform, about a 30-minute walk from the parking lot; if you're feeling energetic, though, the view from the top of Mt. Amos, one of the Hazards, is worth the effort. A round-trip walk from the parking lot to Wineglass Bay takes about 2½ hours. The park's many trails are well signposted.

Daily entry to the park costs A$10.

WHERE TO STAY & EAT

$$$–$$$$
Fodor'sChoice
★

✕⌂ **Freycinet Lodge.** These 60 plush cabins are scattered among the densely wooded forest above Great Oyster Bay. They range from relatively simple one-bedroom units to "Premier Wineglass cabins," which have double hot tubs, CD players, and fluffy bathrobes. All have private balconies, and are outfitted with Tasmanian wood furnishings. The on-site Bay Restaurant ($$–$$$) has breathtaking sunset views, as well as an extensive wine list; the more-casual Richardson's is the place for light lunches and coffee, while Hazards Bar and Lounge is a relaxing place to swap stories or curl up with a book by the open fire. ⊠*Freycinet National Park, Coles Bay, 7215* ☎*03/6257–0101* ⊕*www.freycinetlodge.com.au* ⇆*60 cabins* ⌂*In-room: no phone, no TV. In-hotel: 2 restaurants, bar, tennis court, laundry facilities, parking (no fee), no elevator* ⊟*AE, DC, MC, V.*

$$–$$$
✕⌂ **Edge of the Bay.** The views from these modern, minimalist-style beachfront suites and cottages stretch across Great Oyster Bay to the Hazards. All have private decks and kitchenettes. The Edge restaurant ($$) uses Tasmanian produce and serves local wines. Activities like tennis, as well as bicycles and rowboats for exploring, are all free. There's a minimum stay of two nights. ⊠*2308 Main Rd., Coles Bay, 7215* ☎*03/6257–0102* ⊕*www.edgeofthebay.com.au* ⇆*8 suites, 15 cottages* ⌂*In-room: kitchen. In-hotel: restaurant, bar, tennis court, beachfront, laundry facilities, parking (no fee)* ⊟*AE, MC, V.*

LAUNCESTON

200 km (124 mi) north of Hobart.

Nestled in a fertile agricultural basin where the South Esk and North Esk rivers join to form the Tamar, the city of Launceston (pronounced *Lon*-sess-tun) is the commercial center of Tasmania's northern region. Its abundance of unusual markets and shops is concentrated downtown (unlike Hobart, which has most of its stores in the historic center, set apart from the commercial district).

Launceston is far from bustling, and has a notable number of pleasant parks, late-19th-century homes, historic mansions, and private gardens. However, refurbished restaurants, shops, and art galleries along the banks of the Tamar and North Esk rivers (the Seaport Dock) have turned run-down railway yards into a glitzy new social scene. Another appeal of this city is the sumptuous countryside surrounding it: rolling farmland and the rich loam of English-looking landscapes are set off by the South Esk River meandering through towering gorges.

6

The Midlands

You can speed between Hobart and Launceston on the 200-km (124-mi) Highway 1 (Midlands Highway; locals sometimes call it Heritage Highway) in less than 2½ hours. Doing so, however, would mean bypassing one of Tasmania's most charmingly lovely pastoral regions.

Heading north from Hobart, the first community you'll encounter (it's about 85 km [53 mi] outside the city) is the Georgian town of **Oatlands,** set on the shore of Lake Dulverton. Built in the 1820s as a garrison for the local farming community, the town still retains many original buildings that were built from the glorious golden sandstone of the region. There are also some fine old churches, and a wind-powered mill.

The quaint village of **Ross,** about 55 km (34 mi) northeast of Oatlands, also has some wonderful historic buildings dating from the mid-19th century. The town's most iconic landmark, though, is the 1836 **Ross Bridge,** whose graceful sandstone arches are adorned with decorative carving.

A short detour from the Midlands Highway will bring you to **Longford** (it's 72 km [45 mi] northwest of Ross). Settled in 1813, Longford was one of northern Tasmania's first towns, and

is now a National Trust historic site. Of particular early historic interest here is **Christ Church,** built in 1839. Although it's only open on Sunday, the church has a beautiful west window which is regarded as one of the country's finest.

There are a number of other **historic villages** in the vicinity of Longford that are worth a visit. Hadspen, Carrick, Hagley, Perth, and Evandale are all within a short 25-km (16-mi) radius of the town, and all have their own unique charms. Near Evandale on the road toward Nile, **Clarendon House** is one of the great Georgian houses of Australia, restored by the National Trust.

Spending the night in one of the towns along the Midlands Highway will let you more fully indulge in the historic-charm experience; many of the lodgings in the region occupy beautiful old buildings. Perhaps most impressive of all is **Brickendon** (☎03/6391–1383 or 03/6391–1251 ⊕ www.brickendon.com.au) in Longford, whose restored cottages have antique tubs, fireplaces, and private gardens. The compound is a true colonial village, with a chapel, a trout lake, and more than 20 National Trust–classified buildings.

EXPLORING LAUNCESTON

The **Queen Victoria Museum and Art Gallery,** opened in 1891, combines items of Tasmanian historical interest with natural history. The museum has a large collection of stuffed birds and animals (including the now-extinct thylacine, or Tasmanian, tiger), as well as a joss house (a Chinese shrine) and a display of coins. ⊠ *Wellington and Paterson Sts.* ☎ *03/6323–3777* ⊡ *Free* ⊗ *Mon.–Sat. 10–5, Sun. 2–5.*

Queen Victoria Museum Inveresk site (⊠ *2 Invermay Rd., Launceston* ☎ *03/6323–3777* ⊡ *Free*), a major arts and cultural project, comprises the transformed old Launceston railway workshops. Early colonial paintings and traditional Tasmanian Aboriginal shell necklaces come to life again amidst the sights and sounds of the old workshops.

Almost in the heart of the city, the South Esk River flows through **Cataract Gorge** on its way toward the Tamar River. A 1½-km (1-mi) path leads along the face of the precipices to the **Cliff Gardens Reserve**, where there are picnic tables, a pool, and a restaurant. Take the chairlift in the first basin for a thrilling aerial view of the gorge—at just over 900 feet, it's the longest single chairlift span in the world. Self-guided nature trails wind through the park. ✉ *Paterson St. at Kings Bridge* ☎ *03/6331–5915* ✉ *Gorge free, chairlift A$7* ☉ *Daily 9–4:40.*

★ Along both sides of the Tamar River north from Launceston the soil is perfect for grape cultivation. A brochure on the **Wine Route of the Tamar Valley and Pipers Brook Regions,** available from Tasmanian Travel and Information Centre, can help you to plan a visit to St. Matthias, Ninth Island, Delamere, Rosevears, Jansz, Velo, and Pipers Brook wineries. Many establishments serve food during the day so you can combine your tasting with a relaxing meal.

Franklin House. Built in 1838, this fine Georgian house was a private boarding school before being purchased in 1960 by the National Trust. The building is notable for its beautiful cedar architecture, and its collection of period English furniture, clocks, and fine china. Morning and afternoon teas are served in the tearoom. ✉ *413 Hobart Rd., Franklin Village* ☎ *03/6344–6233* ✉ *A$8* ☉ *Aug.–June, daily 9–4.*

J. Boag & Son Brewery. Since 1881, J. Boag & Son has been brewing quality Tasmanian beer in this imposing brick building. Tours of the brewery, which are available on weekdays, show you the entire process, from brew house to packaging, and end with a beer tasting. Advance bookings are essential. ✉ *39 William St.* ☎ *03/6332–6300* ✉ *Tour A$18* ☉ *Weekdays 8:45–4:30.*

Waverly Woollen Mills. Opened in 1874, these mills on the North Esk River are still powered by a waterwheel. The store sells wool yarn and products made on-site from fine Tasmanian wool, such as sweaters, rugs, and blankets. ✉ *Tasman Hwy. at Waverly Rd.* ☎ *03/6339–1106* ✉ *A$4* ☉ *Weekdays 9–5.*

WHERE TO EAT

$$-$$$ ✕ **Fee and Me.** One of Tasmania's top dining venues, this popular restaurant has won more culinary accolades than you could poke a mixing spoon at. ("Fee" refers to the talented chef, Fiona Hoskin.) You might begin your meal here with Tasmanian Pacific oysters or chicken dumplings in a fragrant broth, then choose from entrées like roasted quail with honeyed chili sauce, and roasted loin of Tasmanian venison. Wine from Australia's top vineyards is also served here. ✉ *190 Charles*

FodorsChoice ★

St. 🕾03/6331–3195 🖎*Reservations essential* Jacket required ⊟*AE, MC, V* 🕙*Closed Sun. and Mon.*

$$–$$$ ✕**Lucks.** This refurbished old butcher shop is now a classic French bistro. The seasonal menu is filled with culinary gems like organic Kurobuta pork loin with aromatic chili chickpea and spinach, and wild mushroom, spinach, and Heidi Raclette calzone with blistered tomato and peas. A terrific range of appetizers gets the juices flowing, but don't leave without tasting vanilla bean crème brûlée. Their excellent wine list will keep you busy, especially since any bottle up to A$60 is also available by the glass—it's possible to taste 130 different kinds of wine. ⊠*70 George St.* 🕾*03/6334–8596* ⊟*AE, DC, MC, V.*

$$ ✕**Navaro's.** Classic Italian food served with style. Try the Tasmanian green lip abalone with white truffle oil. An extensive range of wines includes Australian and Italian. ⊠*28 Brisbane St.* 🕾*03/6334–5589* ⊟*AE, MC, V* 🕙*Dinner only Mon.–Sat.*

$$ ✕**Stillwater.** Part of Ritchie's Mill (a beautifully restored 1830s flour
★ mill beside the Tamar River) this restaurant serves casual fare during the day. The dinner menu, however, includes some wonderfully creative seafood dishes, such as shaved baby Tasmanian abalone with ginger-and-miso panna cotta, and lime-grilled trevally with wilted Asian greens, saffron sabayon, and wasabi crisps. There's also a great selection of Tasmanian wines. The produce shop and art gallery are part of the same complex. ⊠*2 Paterson St.* 🕾*03/6331–4153* ⊟*AE, MC, V.*

$$ ✕**Synergy.** This popular, stylish restaurant serves modern Australian sea-
★ sonally based cuisine and provides impeccable service. Tingle your taste buds with the unusual wallaby fillet, served with preserved lemon and roast-pepper couscous, or, alternatively, the Japanese tea-smoked trout. Tasmanian wines are featured on the excellent wine list. ⊠*135 George St.* 🕾*03/6331–0110* ⊟*AE, DC, MC, V* 🕙*Closed Sun. No lunch.*

$–$$ ✕**Hallams Waterfront.** The menu at this restaurant overlooking the Tamar River highlights local fresh seafood. You can try such dishes as scallops baked in a white wine, dill, and Freycinet cheddar Mornay sauce, or seafood (it might be prawns, scallops, mussels, clams, or fish) curry of the day with jasmine rice. There's always a friendly, exuberant crowd to make you feel part of the waterfront scene. ⊠*13 Park St.* 🕾*03/6334–0554* ⊟*AE, MC, V.*

$–$$ ✕**Jailhouse Grill.** If you have to go to jail, this is the place to do it; you can have a delectable steak as soon as you get there. Surrounded by chains and bars, you can feast on prime beef (or fish and chicken), vegetable dishes, and a salad bar. The wine list—all Tasmanian—is comprehensive. ⊠*32 Wellington St.* 🕾*03/6331–0466* ⊟*AE, DC, MC, V* 🕙*No lunch Thurs.–Sun.*

WHERE TO STAY

$$$ 🏨**Hatherley House.** This magnificent 1830s mansion, set among lav-
Fodor'sChoice ish English gardens, has been transformed into a hip, intimate hotel.
★ The guest suites here, which are all individually decorated according

to theme (you can choose, for example, from the Ballroom Suite, with its high ceilings and French doors, or the Oriental Suite, furnished with Asian antiques and art). All suites have ultramodern bathrooms with hot tubs, king-size beds, and flat-screen TVs with DVD players. Afternoon tea and cappuccino are served daily in the library and salon, which looks over the gardens. ✉*43 High St., 7250* ☎*03/6334-7727* ⊕*www.hatherleyhouse.com.au* 🛏*9 suites* ⚷*In-room: dial-up. In-hotel: laundry facilities, parking (no fee), minibar* ▤*AE, DC, MC, V.*

$$$ ★ 🏨**Peppers Seaport Hotel.** Superbly located on the Tamar River riverfront, this hotel is part of the new Seaport Dock area. Designed in the shape of a ship, its steep pitched gable roofs are reminiscent of old warehouses seen on the docks; the interior also reflects its nautical heritage. The interiors reflect the nautical history of the site and use local Tasmanian materials; there's lots of open space and light-color wood. The Mud Bar and Restaurant serves up an eclectic menu and a good selection of Tasmanian wines. ✉*28 Seaport Blvd., 7250* ☎*03/6345-3333* ⊕*www.peppers.com.au* 🛏*24 rooms, 36 suites* ⚷*In-room: dial-up, Wi-Fi (some). In-hotel: restaurant, laundry service, parking (no fee)* ▤*AE, DC, MC, V* ⏺*BP.*

$$-$$$ 🏨**Alice's Cottages.** Constructed from the remains of three 1840s buildings, this delightful B&B is full of whimsical touches. Antique furniture drawers might contain old-fashioned eyeglasses or books; an old turtle shell and a deer's head hang on the wall; and a Victrola and a four-poster canopy bed lend colonial charm. ✉*129 Balfour St., 7250* ☎*03/6334-2231* 🛏*9 rooms* ⚷*In-hotel: laundry facilities, parking (no fee), minibar* ▤*AE, MC, V* ⏺*BP.*

$$-$$$ 🏨**Country Club Tasmania.** At this luxury property on the outskirts of Launceston you can choose between resort rooms and villas, some of which have fully-equipped kitchens. The Terrace Restaurant serves specialties such as smoked duck breast and local scallops. The curved driveway to the club is lined with flowers and manicured gardens, and the championship golf course is one of the best in Australia. ✉*Country Club Ave., Prospect Vale, 7250* ☎*1800/030211* ⊕*www.countryclubtasmania.com.au* 🛏*88 rooms, 16 suites* ⚷*In-room: kitchen (some), dial-up. In-hotel: restaurant, room service, golf course, tennis court, pool, parking (no fee)* ▤*AE, DC, MC, V.*

$$-$$$ 🏨**Hotel Grand Chancellor.** This modern, six-story building in the city center has big rooms that blend classic furnishings with modern conveniences. Its convention center and function rooms make it a favorite with business travelers, but pleasure seekers will appreciate that it's just a short walk from the shops and restaurants of downtown. After a day of meetings or sightseeing, you can dine at the Avenue Restaurant, or join the crowds at Jackson's Tavern and the Lobby Bar. ✉*29 Cameron St., 7250* ☎*03/6334-3434 or 1800/753379* ⊕*www.ghihotels.com* 🛏*162 rooms, 7 suites* ⚷*In-room: dial-up. In-hotel: 3 restaurants, room service, bars, laundry service, parking (no fee)* ▤*AE, DC, MC, V.*

$$-$$$ ★ 🏨**Waratah on York.** Built in 1862, this grand Italianate mansion has been superbly restored. Spacious modern rooms are tastefully deco-

6

rated to reflect the era in which the building was constructed; six rooms have hot tubs. Many rooms have panoramic views over the Tamar, and the property is just a quick walk away from the city center. Continental breakfast is served in the elegant dining room. ⊠ *12 York St., 7250* ☎ *03/6331–2081* ⊕ *www.waratahonyork.com.au* ⇆ *9 rooms* ⌂ *In-hotel: restaurant, laundry service, parking (no fee), no-smoking rooms* ⊟ *AE, MC, V* ⊺ *CP.*

$$ ▦ **TwoFourTwo.** Three contemporary apartments built within a historic Launceston property, have all mod cons and feature the wonderful timber design work of Alan Livermore, one of the owners. The city center is but a short stroll away. A small shop on the same site offers an interesting choice of art, souvenirs, and local wines. ⊠ *242 Charles St., Launceston, 7250* ☎ *03/6331–9242* ⊟ *03/6334–6169* ⊕ *www. twofourtwo.com.au* ⌂ *In-hotel: kitchen, breakfast provisions, laundry, DVDs, parking (no fee)* ⊟ *AE, DC, MC, V.*

$ ▦ **Old Bakery Inn.** You can choose from three areas at this colonial complex: a converted stable, the former baker's cottage, or the old bakery. A loft above the stables is also available. All rooms reflect colonial style, with antique furniture and lace curtains. One room in the old bakery was actually the oven. ⊠ *York and Margaret Sts., 7250* ☎ *03/6331–7900 or 1800/641264* ⇆ *23 rooms* ⌂ *In-hotel: restaurant, parking (no fee)* ⊟ *AE, MC, V.*

NIGHTLIFE & THE ARTS

The local *Examiner* is the best source of information on local nightlife and entertainment. The **Country Club Casino** (⊠ *Country Club Ave., Prospect Vale* ☎ *03/6335–5777*) has blackjack, American roulette, minibaccarat, keno, minidice, federal and stud poker, federal wheel, and Two-up.

Live bands and jazz are a feature of the entertainment at the **Royal on George** (⊠ *90 George St.* ☎ *03/6331–2526*), a refurbished 1852 pub. The **Lounge Bar** (⊠ *63 St. John St.* ☎ *03/6334–6622*), in a 1907 former bank, has bands upstairs and a vodka bar in the old vault.

Ursul'a on Brisbane (⊠ *63 Brisbane St.* ☎ *03/6334–7033*) has a great range of tapas, while **Star Bar** (⊠ *113 Charles St.* ☎ *03/6331–6111*) is popular for after-work drinks with tables spilling out on to the pavement.

The curtain at the **Princess Theatre** (⊠ *57 Brisbane St.* ☎ *03/6323–3666*) rises for local and imported stage productions. The **Silverdome** (⊠ *55 Oakden Rd.* ☎ *03/6344–9988*) holds regular music concerts—everything from classical to heavy metal.

SHOPPING

Launceston is a convenient place for a little shopping, with most stores central on George Street and in nearby Yorktown Mall. The **Design Centre of Tasmania** (⊠ *Brisbane and Tamar Sts.* ☎ *03/6331–5506*) carries wonderful items made from Tasmanian wood, including custom-designed furniture. Other choice products are the high-quality woolen wear, pottery, and glass. One of the best arts-and-crafts stores in town is the **Old Umbrella Shop** (✉ *60 George St.* ☎ *03/6331–9248*), which sells umbrellas and gifts such as tea towels and toiletries. The **Sheep's Back** (✉ *53 George St.* ☎ *03/6331–2539*) sells woolen products such as sweaters, blankets, and rugs.

THE NORTHWEST & CRADLE MOUNTAIN–LAKE ST. CLAIR NATIONAL PARK

THE NORTHWEST

Tasmania's northwestern region is one of the most exciting and least known areas of the state. Most of the local inhabitants are farmers, fisherfolk, or lumberjacks. The rugged coastline here has long been the solitary haunt of abalone hunters, and from the area's lush grazing land comes some of Australia's best beef and cheese. Tasmanian farmers are the only legal growers of opium poppies (for medicinal use) in the Southern Hemisphere, and fields in the northwest are blanketed with their striking white and purple flowers.

Inland from the coast the mountain ranges rear up in dramatic fashion and these regions, especially in the Cradle Mountain National Park, are a major draw for hikers and sightseers. The western side of the northwest tip of Tasmania bears the full force of the Roaring '40s winds coming across the Indian Ocean, and this part of Tasmania contains some of the island's most dramatic scenery. Mining was a major industry a century ago, and although some mines still operate, the townships have a rather forlorn look.

It should be noted that the northern part of the Cradle Mountain–Lake St. Clair National Park (that is, Cradle Mountain itself) is accessed by roads inland from Devonport and the nearby town of Sheffield. The southerly Lake St. Clair end of the park, though, is reached by the Lyell Highway between Hobart and Queenstown at Derwent Bridge.

DEVONPORT & ENVIRONS

89 km (55 mi) northwest of Launceston, 289 km (179 mi) northwest of Hobart.

In the middle of the north coast, Devonport is the Tasmanian port where the ferries from Melbourne and Sydney dock. Visitors often dash off to other parts of Tasmania without realizing that the town and its surroundings have many interesting attractions.

The **Maritime Museum** contains a fascinating collection of local and maritime history artifacts, including examples of rope work, ironwork, and whaling equipment. It's the collection of boat models, though—ranging from Aboriginal canoes to modern passenger ferries—that will really interest nautical buffs. ⊠ *6 Gloucester Ave.* ☏ *03/6424–7100* ⊑ *A$3* ☉ *Tues.–Sun. 10–4.*

At the **Tiagarra Aboriginal Cultural and Art Centre,** remnants of Tasmania's Aboriginal past are housed in a series of reproduced Aboriginal huts. Among the exhibits are many beautiful Aboriginal rock engravings, which were discovered on the nearby Mersey Bluff headland in 1929 and subsequently collected here for protection. ⊠ *Mersey Bluff* ☏ *03/6424–8250* ⊑ *A$3.80* ☉ *Daily 9–5.*

The **Don River Railway** re-creates an early-20th-century passenger railway with working steam and diesel engines. The hour-long journey along the banks of the Don River, which leads through native vegetation and has lovely water views, is well worth the price. The train departs from the restored railway station, where there's a large collection of vintage engines, carriages, and wagons. ⊠ *4th Main Rd.* ☏ *03/6424–6335* ⊑ *A$10* ☉ *Daily 10–5.*

South from Devonport along the Bass Highway toward Launceston, the **House of Anvers** specializes in making exquisite chocolates—and you can watch the confectionery staff as they mold and dip different truffles, pralines, and fudges. (If your mouth starts to water, hit the on-site café for a yummy chocolate dessert or hot cocoa.) ⊠ *9025 Bass Hwy., Latrobe* ☏ *03/6426–2958* ☉ *Daily 7–5.*

The **Ashgrove Farm Cheese Factory** makes delicious English-style cheeses like cheddar, Lancashire, and Cheshire. Stop in to sample some of the varieties, and also to browse through other locally produced goods, like jams, olive oils, and honey. The café serves great snacks. ⊠ *6173 Bass Hwy., Elizabeth Town* ☏ *03/6368–1105* ⊑ *Free* ☉ *Daily 9–5.*

In the small village of **Sheffield,** 32 km (20 mi) south of Devonport, more than 30 murals painted on the exterior walls of local buildings depict scenes of local history. Similar to murals found at Chemainus, British Columbia, they were painted in the late 1980s and depict industries (farming, cement manufacture) that had been carried out over the previous century but were then in decline.

WHERE TO STAY & EAT

$$ ✕ **The Deck Café and Restaurant.** This restaurant overlooks the Mersey River and has views of the nearby port. Executive chef and owner Troy Baggett offers up creative renditions of modern Tasmainian cuisine. A casual café-style lunch gives way to a set two- or three-course dinner menu, with culinary creations such as quince-basted chicken breast in prosciutto and Brie and served on a leek risotto cake. Be sure to try their selection of local wines and beers. ⊠ *188 Tarleton St., East Devonport* ☏ *03/6427–7188* ⊟ *AE, MC, V.*

$ ✕ **Pedro's.** Seaside bounty is caught fresh and cooked up daily in this kitchen on the edge of the Leven River. You can relax above the flowing water while sampling local crayfish, calamari, Tasmanian scallops, flounder, or trevally. The take-out fish-and-chips window lets you make a picnic of your feast in a nearby park. ⊠ *Wharf Rd.,*

Ulverstone ☎*03/6425–6663 restaurant, 03/6425–5181 take-out counter* ▤*MC, V.*

$–$$ ▦**Killynaught Spa Cottages.** Five cozy, decorative one- and two-bedroom cottages comprise this property 15 km (9 mi) west of the town of Wynyard. Each has a hot tub, a fireplace, a fully equipped kitchen, laundry facilities, and an antique queen-size brass or iron bed. The adjacent renovated 1890s main homestead also has a two-bedroom apartment and a one-bedroom suite. ⊠*17266 Bass Hwy., Boat Harbour, 7321* ☎*03/6445–1041* ⊕*www.killynaught.com.au* ⬐*1 apartment, 1 suite, 5 cottages* ♿*In-room: kitchen. In-hotel: restaurant, laundry facilities, parking (no fee), no-smoking rooms, no elevator* ▤*DC, MC, V.*

$ ▦**Birchmore.** This elegant B&B is housed in a beautifully restored mansion in the heart of Devonport. Rooms are luxuriously appointed, and have writing desks and faxes (on request) for business travelers. ⊠*10 Oldaker St., Devonport, 7310* ☎*03/6423–1336* ⬐*6 rooms* ♿*In-room: dial-up. In-hotel: laundry service, parking (no fee)* ▤*DC, MC, V.*

$ ▦**Westella House.** This charming 1885 period homestead has stunning sea views. Wood-burning fireplaces in each room, handcrafted banisters and mantels, and antique furnishings draw you into the cozy setting. A hearty, home-cooked breakfast starts the day. ⊠*68 Westella Dr., Ulverstone, 7315* ☎*03/6425–6222* ⊕*www.westella.com* ⬐*3 rooms* ♿*In-hotel: restaurant, laundry facilities, parking (no fee), no elevator* ▤*MC, V* ⏏*BP.*

STANLEY
140 km (87 mi) northwest of Devonport, 430 km (267 mi) northwest of Hobart.

Stanley is one of the prettiest villages in Tasmania, and a must for anyone traveling in the northwest. A gathering of historic cottages at the foot of the Nut, Tasmania's version of Uluru (Ayers Rock), it's filled with friendly tearooms, interesting shops, and old country inns.

At the **Highfield Historic Site,** you can explore the town's history at the fully restored house and grounds where Van Diemen's Land Company once stood. ⊠*Just outside Stanley* ☎*03/6458–1100* 🎫*A$7* ⏰*Sept.–May, daily 9–5; June–Aug., daily 10–4.*

★ **The Nut,** a sheer volcanic plug some 12.5 million years old, rears up right behind the village. It's almost totally surrounded by the sea. You can ride a chairlift to the top of the 500-foot-high headland, where the views are breathtaking; or, you can make the 20-minute trek on a footpath leading to the summit, where walking trails lead in all directions. ☎*03/6458–1286 Nut chairlifts* 🎫*1-way chairlift A$6, round-trip A$9* ⏰*Chairlift runs 9–5 daily.*

WHERE TO STAY & EAT

$$ ✕**Stanley's on the Bay.** Set on the waterfront in the fully restored old
★ Bond Store, this restaurant specializes in fine steaks and seafood. Try the eye fillet of beef—Australian terminology for the top-quality beef

cut—topped with prawns, scallops, and fish fillets, served in a creamy white-wine sauce. ✉15 Wharf Rd. ☎03/6458–1404 ▭DC, MC, V ⊘Closed Sun. No lunch, July–Aug.

$–$$　✕**Julie and Patrick's.** Some say this restaurant serves the best fish-and-chips in Tasmania. Formal diners stay upstairs, while snackers head to the casual downstairs café, and those on the run grab meals from the take-out counter. Whatever's fresh, from crayfish and king crabs to local salmon and flathead, you'll find it swimming live in the huge water tanks—the choice is yours. ✉2 Alexander Terr. ☎03/6458–1103 ▭MC, V.

$$–$$$　🏨 **Beachside Retreat West Inlet.** These modern-lined, environmentally ★ friendly cabins are set on waterfront sand dunes overlooking the sea. The 180-plus-acre farmland property is also adjacent to protected wetlands, which are perfect for bird-watching (keep an eye out for white-breasted sea eagles) and other wildlife-spotting. Many of the furnishings in the cabins are made by the owners and other local artisans from hand-turned Tasmanian wood. You can relax on your private deck after a morning on the beach and shuck your own oysters for lunch. ✉253 Stanley Hwy., 7331 ☎03/6458–1350 🖶03/6458–1350 ⊕www.beachsideretreat.com ➬4 cabins ⚘In-room: kitchen. In-hotel: laundry facilities, parking (no fee), no elevator ▭DC, MC, V ⏐◯⏐CP.

$$　🏨 **Touchwood Cottage.** Built in 1840 right near the Nut, this is one of Stanley's oldest homes, and it's furnished with plenty of period pieces. The cottage is known for its doorways of different sizes and its oddly shaped living room. Rooms are cozy, with open fires that add romance. Afternoon tea is served on arrival. The popular Touchwood crafts shop, where guests receive a discount, is part of the cottage complex. ✉31 Church St., 7331 ☎03/6458–1348 ➬3 rooms without bath ⚘In-hotel: restaurant, parking (no fee) ▭MC, V ⏐◯⏐BP.

SMITHTON

140 km (87 mi) northwest of Devonport, 510 km (316 mi) northwest of Hobart.

The gateway to the rugged northwest coast, the Smithton area boasts two rain forest–clad nature reserves—Julius River and Milkshakes Hills—which give lots of opportunities to spot wildlife, particularly Tasmanian devils. About 65 km (40 mi) west of Smithton, the Bass Highway reaches the wild west coast at Marrawah and continues on to Arthur River and down the west coast.

Around each corner of the private **Allendale Gardens** is a surprise: a cluster of native Tasmanian ferns or a thicket of shrubs and flowers. Self-guided forest walks of 10–25 minutes take you past trees more than 500 years old. The gardens shelter many birds; you may see pheasants, peacocks, guinea fowl, and pigeons wandering freely. ✉Allendale La., Edith Creek ✛14 km (9 mi) from Smithton ☎03/6456–4216 ▭A$7.50 ⊘Oct.–Apr., daily 10–4.

WHERE TO STAY & EAT

$-$$ ✕🏨 **Tall Timbers.** This lodge is one of the finest establishments in the northwest. Rooms, in a building away from the main house, are simply yet elegantly decorated. A bistro and a cozy bar are found in the main lodge, which was built with Tasmanian wood. The more formal Grey's Fine Dining restaurant, also in the main house, serves such specialties as rock crayfish, chicken breast, rabbit hot pot, Atlantic salmon, and crêpes suzette for dessert. ⊠*Scotchtown Rd.* ☎*03/6452–2755 or 1800/628476* ⊕*www.talltimbershotel.com.au* ⤴*75 rooms* ⌂*In-hotel: 2 restaurants, bar, tennis court, laundry service, parking (no fee)* ▭*AE, DC, MC, V.*

LEISURELY STROLLS

Several of Cradle Mountain's most alluring natural attractions can be enjoyed on short (20-minute to three-hour) walks. The best include the Enchanted Walk, Wombat Pool, Lake Lilla, Dove Lake Loop, and Marion's Lookout. These walks take you along the edge of Lake Dove, up ridges with panoramic views to the mountains or to secluded small pools of water surrounded by dense forest. In late April you can make your way up the Truganini Track to see the native fagus bushes turn the hillsides a dazzling yellow and orange. It's the closest thing Australia has to Vermont in autumn.

CRADLE MOUNTAIN–LAKE ST. CLAIR NATIONAL PARK

173 km (107 mi) northwest of Hobart to Lake St. Clair at the southern end of the park, 85 km (53 mi) southwest of Devonport, 181 km (113 mi) from Launceston, 155 km (97 mi) from Strahan to Cradle Mountain at the northern end of the park.

Cradle Mountain–Lake St. Clair National Park contains some of the most spectacular alpine scenery and mountain trails in Australia. Popular with hikers of all abilities, the park has several high peaks, including Mt. Ossa, the highest in Tasmania (more than 5,300 feet). The Cradle Mountain section of the park lies in the north. The southern section of the park, centered on Lake St. Clair, is popular for boat trips and hiking. Many walking trails lead from the settlement at the southern end of the lake, which is surrounded by low hills and dense forest.

One of the most famous trails in Australia, the **Overland Track** traverses 85 km (53 mi) between the park's northern and southern boundaries. The walk usually takes four or five days, depending on the weather, and on clear days the mountain scenery seems to stretch forever. Tasmania's Parks and Wildlife Service has provided several basic sleeping huts that are available on a first-come, first-served basis. Because space in the huts is limited, hikers are advised to bring their own tents. If you prefer to do the walk in comfort, you can use well-equipped, heated private structures managed by Cradle Mountain Huts (☎03/6391–9339 ⊕www.cradlehuts.com.au).

6

WHERE TO STAY

$$$-$$$$ **Cradle Mountain Lodge.** This wilderness lodge with its collection of cabins is the most comfortable place to stay at Cradle Mountain. The high-ceilinged guest rooms, two per cabin, are cheerfully decorated and homey. A couple of walking trails begin at the lodge door. Breakfast is included in your room rate ⊠*60 km (37 mi) from Sheffield* ⊡*Box 153, Sheffield, 7306* ☏*03/6492–1303* ⊕*www.cradlemountainlodge. com.au* ↗*96 rooms* ⌂*In-hotel: restaurant* ☰*MC, V* ⏧*BP.*

$$$-$$$$ **Lemonthyme Lodge.** Perhaps the largest log cabin in the Southern
★ Hemisphere, this huge lodge lies about 12 km (7½ mi) east of the park, near the tiny village of Moina. With its large stone fireplace and soaring ceiling, this hotel has a grander look than Cradle Mountain Lodge but is not as close to the park. Guided walks let you view the towering trees and native wildlife. ⊡*Locked Bag 158, Devonport, 7310* ☏*03/6492–1112* ⊕*www.lemonthyme.com.au* ↗*31 rooms* ⌂*In-room: kitchen (some). In-hotel: restaurant, laundry service, parking (no fee)* ☰*AE, MC, V.*

¢-$ **Cosy Cabins Cradle Mountain.** Near the forest at the northern edge of the park, Cosy Cabins has campgrounds, RV sites, four-bed bunkhouses with cooking facilities, and self-contained cabins with kitchens. Fees for tent and RV sites and bunkhouse rooms are per person, per night, and advance booking is essential for all accommodations. The tour desk can help you plan trips around the area. ⊠*3832 Cradle Mountain Rd., Cradle Mountain, 7306* ☏*03/6492–1395* ⊟*03/6492–1438* ↗*38 unpowered sites, 10 powered sites, 75 bunkhouse beds, 36 cabins* ⌂*Flush toilets, partial hookups, guest laundry, showers, grills, picnic tables* ☰*MC, V.*

THE WEST COAST

Much of this rugged area lies in protected zones or conservation areas, and there are lingering tensions among conservationists, loggers, and local, state, and federal government agencies. Strahan is the major center for tourism, and the departure point for cruises along the pristine Gordon River and Macquarie Harbour. The area's rich mining history is kept alive in smaller towns such as Queenstown and Zeehan.

The remoteness of the region, however, is what makes the area a major tourist draw. Pristine, untouched ocean beaches are readily accessible from Strahan; and cruises on Macquarie Harbour and to the lower reaches of the Gordon River reveal spectacular scenery, including majestic Huon pine trees growing right down to the water's edge.

A former rack-and-pinion train line carrying ore is now the restored **West Coast Wilderness Railway** (⊠*Esplanade, Strahan* ☏*1800/628288* ⊕*www.puretasmania.com.au* ⊠*Driffield St., Queenstown*), which makes the 35-km (22-mi) journey between Queenstown and Strahan. The line passes through one of the world's last pristine wilderness areas, as well as through historic settlements and abandoned camps, across 40 bridges and wild rivers, and up and down steep gradients. Tickets are from A\$99 one-way, A\$114 round-trip (one way by train, return by bus). Lunch is included.

The **West Coast Pioneers' Museum,** housed in the old Zeehan School of Mines and Metallurgy (established in 1894), displays a remarkable selection of minerals, historical items, and personal records of the region. Some exhibits are in a re-created underground mine. ⊠ *Main St., Zeehan, 7469* 🕾 *03/6471–6225* 🖾 *A\$10* ⏲ *Daily 9–5.*

STRAHAN

265 km (164 mi) south of Smithton, 305 km (189 mi) northwest of Hobart.

This lovely, lazy fishing port, once a major stop for mining companies, has one of the deepest harbors in the world. The brown color that sometimes appears on the shoreline isn't pollution, but naturally occurring tannin from the surrounding vegetation. The town, which has a population of fewer than 750, sits on the edge of Macquarie Harbour and mixes a still-active fishing industry with tourism. The foreshore walking track gives an excellent view of the Strahan area. Don't overlook the short easy trail from the foreshore through the rain forest to Hogarth Falls.

Fodor'sChoice **Franklin-Gordon Wild Rivers National Park** is the main reason to visit Strahan. This is the best-known section of the Tasmanian Wilderness World ★ Heritage Area, with its mountain peaks, untouched rain forest, and deep gorges and valleys that wind through the wilderness. In the late 1970s and early '80s this area was the focus of one of Australia's most bitter conservation battles, when a hydroelectric power scheme was proposed that called for damming the Franklin River and flooding the river valley. Conservationists eventually defeated the proposal, but tensions remained high in the community for years.

About 50 km (31 mi) of the Lyell Highway, which stretches from Hobart to Queenstown, winds through the heart of the park to the west of Derwent Bridge. Making this drive is a great way to appreciate the area's natural beauty; there are several well-signposted walks along the way that let you do some easy exploring. The **Franklin River Nature Trail** is a 1-km (½-mi) wheelchair-accessible route through the rain forest; the **Nelson Falls Nature Trail** is a pleasant 20-minute stroll which takes you to the waterfall of the same name. The more-challenging **Donaghys Hill Wilderness Lookout Walk** (40-minute round trip) is one you should bring your camera for; it brings you to a beautiful panoramic lookout dominated by the peak called Frenchman's Cap.

The park is also accessible by boat from the town of Strahan; cruises from there take you across Macquarie Harbour and into the early reaches of the Gordon River, where you can stop for a short walk in the rain forest. Some cruises include a stop at **Sarah Island,** once one of the harshest penal settlements in Tasmania, and venture out through the narrow entrance to Macquarie Harbour for a glimpse of the tempestuous ocean beyond. Half- and full-day cruises run daily; some include a smorgasbord lunch and other refreshments.

Other worthwhile destinations around Strahan include the towering Henty Dunes north of town, the lush forest along the walk to Teepookana Falls, and—for the adventurous—a true rain-forest trek along the Bird River Track to some eerie overgrown ruins on the shores of Macquarie Harbour.

The **Strahan Visitor Centre** is also a museum that concentrates on local subjects and isn't afraid to tackle such controversial issues as past conservation battles over the area's rivers and the fate of Tasmania's Aborigines. Don't miss performances of the play *The Ship That Never Was,* based on a true story of convict escape and a loophole in British justice. ⊠*Esplanade at Harold St.* ☎*03/6471–7622* ⊠*A\$15* ⊘*Daily 10–6.*

WHERE TO STAY & EAT

$ ✕**Hamers Hotel.** This basic, bar-style restaurant specializes in seafood and steak, and the food is better than most pub counter meals for about the same price. Dessert includes a choice of fresh cakes. ⊠*Esplanade at Harold St.* ☎*03/6471–7191* ⊟*MC, V.*

$$$ ⛲**Ormiston House.** Utterly luxurious, this mansion has been faithfully
★ restored to ultimate elegance. Four-poster beds, spacious rooms, and cozy fireplaces make this the best romantic hideaway on the west coast. You can still keep in touch with the modern world, though, as the hotel provides fax and e-mail services. ⊠*Esplanade at Bay St., 7468* ☎*03/6471–7077 or 1800/625745* ⊕*www.ormistonhouse.com.au* ⤒*5 rooms* ⛺*In-hotel: bar, parking (no fee)* ⊟*AE, DC, MC, V.*

$$–$$$ ⛲**Franklin Manor.** Located on a hillside overlooking the harbor, this century-old mansion is surrounded by landscaped gardens that skirt the edge of the forest wilderness. Charmingly decorated rooms, some with fireplaces and hot tubs, are in the main house, while the separate, self-contained, open-plan Stables cottages each sleep five. The restaurant serves lobster, oysters, pot-roasted quail, and sea trout. ⊠*Esplanade at Vivian St., 7468* ☎*03/6471–7311* ⊕*www.franklinmanor.com.au* ⤒*14 rooms, 4 cottages* ⛺*In-room: kitchen (some). In-hotel: restaurant, room service, bar, parking (no fee), no-smoking rooms, no elevator* ⊟*AE, DC, MC, V* �Ⓞ*BP.*

$$ ⛲**Risby Cove.** Art is a main theme at this elegant waterfront property—a gallery of contemporary paintings, sculpture, and weaving graces the main building. The room furnishings are bright and modern, made of native woods. Whirlpool tubs add to the comfort. The restaurant, with a menu that lists Tasmanian wines and such seafood delicacies as ocean trout risotto, overlooks the marina. Dinghies are available for rent. ⊠*Esplanade at Trafford St., 7468* ☎*03/6471–7572* ⊕*www. risbycove.com.au* ⤒*8 rooms* ⛺*In-hotel: restaurant, bicycles, parking (no fee)* ⊟*AE, MC, V.*

TASMANIA ESSENTIALS

TRANSPORTATION

BY AIR

Hobart International Airport is 22 km (14 mi) east of Hobart, one hour by air from Melbourne or two hours from Sydney. Although most interstate flights connect through Melbourne, Qantas, Jetstar, and Virgin Blue also run direct flights to Sydney and Brisbane. On the island, Tasair can get you to the northwest, and to bucolic King Island. Tickets can be booked through the airlines or through Tasmanian Travel and Information Centres.

It's 20 minutes between the airport and Hobart along the Eastern Outlet Road. Tasmanian Redline Coaches has airport shuttle service for A$11 per person between the airport and its downtown depot. Metered taxis are available at the stand in front of the terminal. The fare to downtown Hobart is approximately A$30.

Airlines Jetstar (☎ 13–1538 ⊕ www.jetstar.com.au). **Qantas** (☎ 13–1313 ⊕ www.qantas.com.au). **Tasair** (☎ 1800/062900 ⊕ www.tasair.com.au). **Virgin Blue** (☎ 13–6789 ⊕ www.virginblue.com.au).

Airport Hobart International Airport (✉ Holyman Ave., Cambridge ☎ 03/6216–1600)

Airport Transfers Tasmanian Redline Coaches (✉ 199 Collins St., Hobart City ☎ 03/6231–3233 or 1300/360000 ⊕ www.tasredline.com.au).

Launceston airport is located at Western Junction, 16 km (10 mi) south of central Launceston. It's served by Jetstar and Virgin Blue. Airlines of Tasmania has services to Flinders Island.

Airlines Airlines of Tasmania (☎ 1800/144460 ⊕ www.airtasmania.com.au).

Airport Launceston Airport (☎ 03/6391–8699).

Jetstar connects Devonport with the Australian mainland, while Tasair connects Devonport to King Island. The airport is on the eastern side of the Mersey River in East Devonport, about 10 km (6 mi) from the city center.

Airport Devonport Airport (☎ 03/6424–7088).

BY BOAT

Spirit of Tasmania I and *II* ferries operate in reverse directions between Melbourne and Devonport across Bass Strait, making the 10-hour, overnight crossing daily. In peak periods, extra daylight sailings are added to meet the demand. Each ferry carries a maximum of 1,400 passengers and up to 600 vehicles. A standard-size car is free except during the December and January summer school holiday period; *however, most rental-car companies do not allow their vehicles on the ferries.* Accommodations are in airlines-type seats or cabins, and facilities include children's playrooms, a games arcade, gift shops, and several restaurants and bars. Advance bookings are essential.

Contacts *Spirit of Tasmania* (✉ *Station Pier, Port Melbourne* ☎ *13–2010 or 1800/634906* ⊕ *www.spiritoftasmania.com.au* ✉ *Berth 1, Esplanade, Devonport* ☎ *13–2010 or 1800/634906*).

BY BUS

Tasmanian Redline Coaches run daily to towns and cities across the state. Buses also meet the ferries arriving in northern Devonport from Melbourne and Sydney.

TassieLink also has daily services around the state, including daily buses to Geeveston via Huonville for easy access to South West National Park. The TassieLink Explorer Pass is a one-week ticket (to be used within 10 days) for unlimited travel around Tasmania (A$172). A two-week pass (to be used in 20 days) costs A$237, and other passes are also available.

The "Metro," operated by Metropolitan Tasmania, runs a bus system from downtown Hobart to the surrounding suburbs daily from 6 AM to midnight. Special "Day Rover" tickets for A$4.40 permit unlimited use of buses for a day from 9 AM onward.

Contacts Metro (✉ *GPO Bldg., 9 Elizabeth St., Hobart City* ☎ *13–2201*). **Tasmanian Redline Coaches** (✉ *199 Collins St., Hobart City* ☎ *03/6231–3233 or 1300/360000* ⊕ *www.tasredline.com.au*). **TassieLink** (✉ *Hobart Transit Ctr., 199 Collins St., Hobart City* ☎ *1300/300520* ⊕ *www.tassielink.com.au*).

BY CAR

If you're arriving in Devonport on the *Spirit of Tasmania* ferry from Melbourne or Sydney, Hobart is about four hours south by car. Most places in Tasmania are within easy driving distance, rarely more than three or four hours in a stretch, although some of the narrow, winding secondary roads are unsuitable for camper vans and motor homes. If you drive in Hobart, be wary of the one-way street system.

Cars, campers, caravans, and minibuses are available for rent in Hobart. The largest rental-car companies are Autorent Hertz, Avis, Budget, Curnow's, and Thrifty, all of which have airport locations. One lower-price rental company is Lo-Cost Auto Rent. Companies with motor-home and camper-van rental include Cruisin' Tasmania, Tasmanian Campervan Hire, and Trailmaster Campervan.

Contacts Autorent Hertz (☎ *03/6237–1111 or 1800/030222*). **Avis** (☎ *03/6234–4222 or 13–6333*). **Budget** (☎ *03/6234–5222 or 13–2727*). **Cruisin' Tasmania** (☎ *1300/664485*). **Curnow's** (☎ *03/6236–9611*). **Lo-Cost Auto Rent** (☎ *03/6231–0550*). **Rent-a-Bug** (☎ *03/6231–0300*). **Tasmanian Campervan Hire** (☎ *1800/807119*). **Thrifty** (☎ *03/6234–1341 or 1300/367227*). **Trailmaster Campervan** (☎ *1800/651202*).

The Tasman Highway is a paved road, and though it's narrow in places it's easy to drive. Picnic and rest spots are frequent and there are some wonderful coastal views along the way, especially across to the Freycinet Peninsula from around Swansea. Gas stations can be found in all the towns.

Cars, campers, caravans, and minibuses are available for rent from the airport and several locations in Launceston. The main companies for car rental are Autorent Hertz, Avis, Budget, and Thrifty.

Contacts Autorent Hertz (✉ *58 Paterson St.* ☎ *03/6335–1111*). **Avis** (✉ *29 Cameron St.* ☎ *03/6334–7722*). **Budget** (✉ *Launceston Airport* ☎ *03/6391–8566*). **Thrifty** (✉ *151 St. John St.* ☎ *03/6333–0911*).

Many of the northwest roads are twisty and even unpaved in the more remote areas. A few may require four-wheel-drive vehicles. However, two-wheel drive is sufficient for most touring. Be prepared for sudden weather changes. This is one of the colder parts of Tasmania, and snow in the summertime is not uncommon in the highest areas.

Lake St. Clair is 173 km (107 mi) northwest of Hobart and can be reached via the Lyell Highway, or from Launceston via Deloraine or Poatina. Cradle Mountain is 85 km (53 mi) south of Devonport and can be reached by car via Claude Road from Sheffield or via Wilmot. Both lead 30 km (19 mi) along Route C132 to Cradle Valley. The last 10 km (6 mi) are unpaved, but the road is in very good condition.

Cars, campers, and minibuses are available for rent in Devonport.

Contacts Autorent Hertz (✉ *26 Oldaker St., Devonport* ☎ *03/6424–1013*). **Avis** (✉ *Devonport Airport, Devonport* ☎ *03/6427–9797*). **Budget** (✉ *Airport Rd., Devonport* ☎ *03/6427–0650 or 13–2727*). **Thrifty** (✉ *10 Esplanade, Devonport* ☎ *03/6427–9119*).

Port Arthur is an easy 90-minute drive from Hobart via the Arthur Highway. Sights along the route include the Tessellated Pavement, a checkered-pattern geological formation; the Blowhole, spectacular in wild weather; and Tasman Arch, a naturally formed archway at Eaglehawk Neck. At the peninsula's far northwest corner is the fascinating Coal Mines Historic Site where convicts mined Australia's first coal in dreadful conditions.

A private vehicle is essential if you want to explore parts of the Tasman Peninsula beyond the historic settlement.

A vehicle is absolutely essential on the west coast. The road from Hobart travels through the Derwent Valley and past lovely historic towns such as Hamilton before rising to the plateau of central Tasmania, famous for its lake and stream fishing. Craggy mountain peaks and dense forests are scenic highlights along the road to Queenstown; the denuded hillsides resemble a moonscape.

The north highway snakes down from Burnie (a link road joins Cradle Mountain with the highway) to the mining towns of Rosebery and Zeehan. From here a newer link road to Strahan passes the Henty Dunes and Ocean Beach (often battered by the storms of the Roaring '40s). The adventurous can head north from Zeehan, cross the Pieman River (by barge), and then track through pristine forest and plains to rejoin the coast at the Arthur River.

BY TAXI

You can hail metered taxis on the street or find them at designated stands and major hotels. Cabs for hire have lighted signs on their roofs. Contact City Cabs or Taxi Combined.

Contacts City Cabs (☎13–1008). **Taxi Combined** (☎13–2227).

CONTACTS & RESOURCES

DISCOUNTS & DEALS

If you're planning to explore all of the island, the See Tasmania Smartvisit Card provides unbeatable convenience and value. Three-, 7-, and 10-day cards give you free (or greatly reduced) admission at more than 60 of Tasmania's most popular attractions. A 3-day card costs A$149; a 7-day card costs A$209; and a 10-day card costs A$279.

Contact See Tasmania Smartvisit Card (☎1300/661771 ⊕www.seetasmania card.com).

EMERGENCIES

In an emergency, dial **000** to reach an ambulance, the police, or the fire department.

Hospitals Calvary Hospital (✉49 Augusta Rd., Lenah Valley ☎03/6278–5333). **Royal Hobart Hospital** (✉48 Liverpool St., Hobart City ☎03/6222–8308). **St. Helen's Private Hospital** (✉186 Macquarie St., Hobart City ☎03/6221–6444). **Launceston General Hospital** (✉Charles St. ☎03/6348–7111). **St. Luke's Hospital** (✉24 Lyttleton St. ☎03/6335–3333). **St. Vincent's Hospital** (✉5 Frederick St. ☎03/6331–4999).

Pharmacies Macquarie Pharmacy (✉180 Macquarie St., Hobart City ☎03/6223–2339) open until 10 PM daily.**Healthwise Pharmacy** (✉84 Brisbane St. ☎03/6331–7777), open to 9 PM daily.

Mersey Community Hospital (✉Bass Hwy., Latrobe ☎03/6426–5111). **North West Regional Hospital** (✉Brickport Rd., Burnie ☎03/6430–6666).**West Coast District Hospital** (✉53 McNamara St., Queenstown ☎03/6471–3300).

TOURS

AIRPLANE TOURS Par Avion Tours and Tasair have some of the most exciting ways to see Hobart and its surroundings. One flight by Par Avion goes to Melaleuca Inlet on the remote southwest coast and includes lunch, tea, and a boat trip and bushwalking around Bathurst Harbour (A$275). Shorter, less-expensive flights by both Par Avion Tours and Tasair cover just as much territory but don't include meals or time for exploring. Other flights from Hobart include the Tasman Peninsula, the Derwent River estuary, the Freycinet Peninsula, and Maria Island.

Tasmanian Seaplanes has three scenic flights over Port Arthur and the massive sea cliffs of the Tasman Peninsula and its national park. Costs start at A$80 for a 20-minute flight.

On the west coast, Wilderness Air flies seaplanes from Strahan Wharf over Frenchman's Cap, the Franklin and Gordon rivers, Lake Pedder, and Hells Gates, with a landing at Sir John Falls. It's a great way to see the area's peaks, lakes, coast, and rivers. Seair Adventure Charters has similar tours by helicopter and small plane.

Contacts Par Avion Tours (☎ *03/6248–5390* ⊕ *www.paravion.com.au*). **Seair Adventure Charters** (☎ *03/6471–7718*). **Tasair** (☎ *03/6248–5088* ⊕ *www. tasair.com.au*). **Tasmanian Seaplanes** (☎ *03/6227–8808*). **Wilderness Air** (☎ *03/6471–7280*).

BIKE TOURS Island Cycle Tours has many trips around Tasmania, including three-, four-, six-, and seven-day coastal tours. Prices include equipment, accommodations, meals, guides, van service, and entry to nearby attractions and activities. The exhilarating descent from the top of Mt. Wellington into Hobart is a must.

Contact Island Cycle Tours (✉ *Box 2014, Lower Sandy Bay, 7005* ☎ *1300/880334* ⊕ *www.islandcycletours.com*).

BOAT TOURS The Hobart Cruises catamaran zips through the majestic waterways of the Derwent River and the D'Entrecasteaux Channel to Peppermint Bay at Woodbridge. Wildlife is abundant, from sea eagles and falcons soaring above the weathered cliffs to pods of dolphins swimming alongside the boat. Underwater cameras explore kelp forests and salmon in the floating fish farms. Dine on local produce at Peppermint Bay.

A number of companies offer cruises on the River Derwent, boating around the city docks, up the river to the Cadbury Chocolate Factory, or to Moorilla Winery. Some include factory tours or lunch and prices vary depending on the type of tour you chose.

In Launceston, Tamar River Cruises conducts relaxing trips on the Tamar, past many wineries and into Cataract Gorge.

On the west coast, Gordon River Cruises has half- and full-day tours on Macquarie Harbour and the Gordon River; the full day tour includes a smorgasbord lunch. An informative commentary accompanies the trip to historic Sarah Island, and you can disembark at Heritage Landing and take a half-hour walk through the vegetation to a 2,000-year-old Huon pine tree. Reservations are essential.

Also on the west coast, World Heritage Cruises has half- and full-day cruises, which sail daily from Strahan Wharf. Meals and drinks are available on board. The leisurely journey pauses at Sarah Island, Heritage Landing, and the Saphia Ocean Trout Farm on Macquarie Harbour. From November through April they also operate the luxury three-day and two-night Wilderness Escape Cruise on the MV *Discovery*; limited to 24 passengers, this is the ultimate way to experience the Gordon River.

West Coast Yacht Charters has daily Macquarie Harbour twilight cruises aboard the 60-foot ketch *Stormbreaker*; a crayfish dinner is included. A two-day and two-night sailing excursion, a morning fishing trip, and overnight cruises on the Gordon River are also available.

Offices of all west-coast tour operators are on Strahan Wharf. Prices of tours vary depending on length and inclusions (some have options for meals as part of the package); but costs for cruises generally start at around A$70, and flights at around A$150.

Contacts **Captain Fell's Historic Ferries** (✉ *Franklin Wharf Pier, Hobart Waterfront* ☎ *03/6223-5893* ⊕ *www.captainfellshistoricferries.com.au*). **Gordon River Cruises** (☎ *03/6471-4300* ⊕ *www.strahanvillage.com.au*). **Hobart Cruises** (✉ *Brooke St. Pier, Hobart Waterfront* ☎ *1300/137919* ⊕ *www.hobartcruises.com*). **Navigators** (✉ *Franklin Wharf Ferry Pier, Hobart Waterfront* ☎ *03/6223-1914* ⊕ *www.navigators. net.au*). **Tamar River Cruises** (☎ *03/6334-9900* ⊕ *www.tamarrivercruises.com. au*). **West Coast Yacht Charters** (☎ *03/6471-7422*). **World Heritage Cruises** (☎ *03/6471-7174* 🖷 *03/6471-7431* ⊕ *www.worldheritagecruises.com.au*).

BUS TOURS Hobart City Explorer operates a hop-on, hop-off tram bus between the main sights.

From Hobart, Tigerline Coaches and Gray Line run half- and full-day tours to Salamanca Place, Mt. Wellington, the Huon Valley, Bruny Island, Bonorong Wildlife Center, Port Arthur, and Richmond.

You can book a city sights tour of Launceston by replica tram through the Coach Tram Tour Company. Tours run November through April twice daily.

From Launceston, Tiger Wilderness Tours, and Treasure Island Coaches all run tours to Launceston city highlights, Tamar River and wineries, and Cradle Mountain.

Contacts **Coach Tram Tour Company** (☎ *03/6336-3133*). **Gray Line** (✉ *Brooke St. Pier, Hobart Waterfront* ☎ *03/6234-3336*). **Hobart City Explorer** (*Tasmanian Travel and Information Centre* ✉ *20 Davey St., at Elizabeth St., Hobart City* ☎ *03/6230-8233*). **Tiger Wilderness Tours** (☎ *03/6394-3212* ⊕ *www. tigerwilderness.com.au*). **Treasure Island Coaches** (☎ *03/6343-2056* ⊕ *www. treasureislandcoaches.com.au*).

NATIONAL PARK TOURS At Freycinet National Park, Freycinet Adventures has sports tours, including sea kayaking, rappelling, and rock climbing, that range from a half day to five days in length. Other ways to experience the wonders of the Freycinet Peninsula include cruises on the MV *Kahala* with Freycinet Sea Charters. At Bicheno the nightly tour to see the penguins emerge from the water and clamber up to their nesting area is popular.

At Cradle Mountain–Lake St. Clair National Park, Seair Adventure Charters conducts scenic flights that depart from Cradle Valley Airstrip and take you over sights in the area. Doors on the planes are removable for photography. Flights are also available from Wynyard Airport.

Arthur River Cruises runs boat trips on the serene Arthur River 14 km (9 mi) south of Marrawah. Glide through pristine rain forest unchanged for centuries.

An evening of spotting Tasmanian devils in their natural habitat is the highlight of Joe King's Kings Run Tours.

Contacts Arthur River Cruises (✉ *Arthur River* ☎ *03/6457–1158* ⊕ *www. arthurrivercruises.com*). **Bicheno Penguin Tour** (☎ *03/6375–1333*). **Freycinet Adventures** (☎ *03/6257–0500* 🖷 *03/6257–0447* ⊕ *www.freycinetadventures. com.au*). **Freycinet Air** (☎ *03/6375–1694* ⊕ *www.freycinetair.com.au*). **Freycinet Sea Charters** (☎ *03/6257–0355* ⊕ *www.freycinetseacharters.com*). **Kings Run Tours** (✉ *Marrawah* ☎ *03/6457–1191*). **Seair Adventure Charters** (✉ *Cradle Valley Airstrip, Cradle Valley* ☎ *03/6492–1132* ✉ *Wynyard Airport, Wynyard* ☎ *03/6442–1220*).

WALKING
TOURS

In Hobart, walks led by the National Trust provide an excellent overview of Battery Point, including visits to mansions and 19th-century houses. Tours, which depart Saturday at 9:30 from the wishing well (near the Franklin Square post office), include morning tea. The National Trust also conducts daily tours (hourly 10–2) of the courthouse, Campbell Street chapel, and the old penitentiary (there's also a spooky night tour).

Hobart Historic Tours offers guided walks through old Hobart, around the waterfront and maritime precinct, and a historic pub tour.

In Launceston, Launceston Historic Walks conducts a leisurely stroll through the historic heart of the city. Walks leave from the Tasmanian Travel and Information Centre weekdays at 9:45 AM.

Contacts Hobart Historic Tours (✉ *27 Carr St., North Hobart* ☎ *03/6278–3338*). **Launceston Historic Walks** (☎ *03/6331–3679*). **National Trust** (✉ *6 Brisbane St., Hobart City* ☎ *03/6223–5200*).

VISITOR INFORMATION

The Hobart Tasmanian Travel and Information Centre hours are weekdays 9–5 and Saturday 9–noon, often longer in summer.

Contact Tasmanian Travel and Information Centre (✉ *20 Davey St., at Elizabeth St., Hobart City, 7000* ☎ *03/6230–8233* ⊕ *http://www.tasmaniasouth.com/tassouth/ visitors.html*).

Contact Freycinet National Park directly for information about hiking, camping, and wildlife. The office is open daily from 9 to 5.

Contact Freycinet National Park (✉ *Park Office* ☎ *03/6256–7000*).

The Launceston Tasmanian Travel and Information Centre is open weekdays 9–5 and Saturday 9–noon.

Contact Tasmanian Travel and Information Centre (✉ *St. John and Paterson Sts.* ☎ *03/6336–3133*).

Tasmanian Travel and Information Centre has offices in Devonport and Burnie. Hours are usually weekdays 9–5 and Saturday 9–noon, and often longer in summer.

Contacts Cradle Mountain Visitor Center (☎ *03/6492–1110*). **Lake St. Clair Visitor Center** (☎ *03/6289–1172*). **Tasmanian National Parks** (✉ *134 Macquarie St., Hobart City, Hobart* ☎ *03/6233–6191* ⊕ *www.parks.tas.gov.au*). **Tasmanian Travel and Information Centre** (✉ *92 Formby Rd., Devonport* ☎ *03/6424–4466* ✉ *48 Civic Sq., off Little Alexander St., Burnie* ☎ *03/6434–6111*).

Queensland

"We travelled by car from Brisbane up to Port Douglas and found it to be our absolute favorite part of our trip! The sea is incredibly warm and the shopping is really good."

—traveljunkie28

Updated by
Merran White

A FUSION OF FLORIDA, Las Vegas, and the Caribbean, Queensland attracts crowd lovers and escapists alike. Whether you want to soak in the Coral Sea, stroll from cabana to casino with your favorite cocktail, or cruise rivers and rain forests with crocs and other intriguing creatures of the tropics—it's here.

At 1,727,999 square km (667,180 square mi) and more than four times the size of California, Queensland has enormous geographic variety. Its eastern seaboard stretches 5,200 km (3,224 mi)—about the distance from Rome to Cairo—from the subtropical Gold Coast to the wild and steamy rain forests of the far north. Up until the 1980s, the northern tip and the Cape York Peninsula had not yet been fully explored, and even today crocodiles still claim a human victim once in a while. Away from the coastal sugar and banana plantations, west of the Great Dividing Range, Queensland looks as arid and dust-blown as any other part of Australia's interior. Few paved roads cross this semidesert and, as in the Red Centre, communication with remote farms is mostly by radio and air. Not surprisingly, most of the state's 4 million inhabitants reside on the coast.

Local license plates deem Queensland the "Sunshine State," a sort of Australian Florida—a laid-back stretch of beaches and sun where many Australians head for their vacations. The state has actively promoted tourism, and such areas as the Gold Coast in the south and Cairns in the north have exploded, with high-rise buildings, casinos, and beachfront amusements popping up on every block. The major attraction for Australians and foreign tourists alike is the Great Barrier Reef, the 1,900-km (1,178-mi) ecological masterpiece that supports thousands of animal species. *For more information on the reef, an integral part of any trip to the state, see Chapter 8.*

7

EXPLORING QUEENSLAND

The Great Barrier Reef parallels most of the state's edge, all the way south to Hervey Bay. A coastal road makes for easy travel between the major cities and little towns that are jumping-off points to Fraser Island, the Whitsundays, and Magnetic Island, but vast distances make flying the best option between mainland cities and the offshore resorts. If you have more time, taking the train is a relaxing option.

The southern end of the state bordering New South Wales is known as the Gold Coast, where sprawling beach towns mimic Miami Beach and Waikiki. North of Brisbane is the quieter Sunshine Coast, where you can kick back on nearly deserted beaches or take four-wheel-drive expeditions into beautiful rain forests. North of Cairns, the Cape York Peninsula is all tropical terrain, where you can hike and camp in the jungle. In the western hinterlands, mountains stretch into the central deserts that border the country's Northern Territory and South Australia.

Queensland

PAPUA NEW GUINEA

PACIFIC OCEAN

Coral Sea

GREAT BARRIER REEF MARINE PARK

GREAT BARRIER REEF

Magnetic Island

Bamaga

Cape Grenville

Iron Range

Cape Direction

Weipa

ARCHER BEND NATIONAL PARK

Coen

CAPE YORK PENINSULA

Kowanyama

Cape Melville

LAKEFIELD NATIONAL PARK

Laura

Palmerville

Cooktown

CAPE TRIBULATION NAT'L PARK

DAINTREE NAT'L PARK

Daintree

Mossman

Port Douglas

Kuranda

Mareeba

Cairns

Gordonvale

Babinda

Innisfail

WOOROONOORAN NATIONAL PARK

Mungana

Mount Surprise

Hinchinbrook Island

Cardwell

Ingham

Charters Towers

Townsville

Ayr

STAATEN RIVER NATIONAL PARK

Normanton

Croydon

Georgetown

Forsayth

1

Cattle Corridor Byway

Gulf of Carpentaria

Mornington Island

Bentinck Island

Karumba

Flinder's River

Gateway to the Gulf Byway

83

The Matilda Hwy

Burketown

LAWN HILL NATIONAL PARK

Camooweal

Kajabbi

66

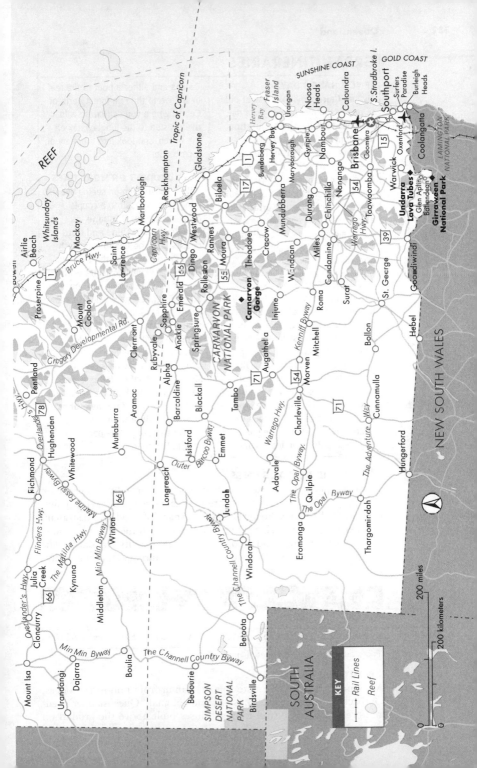

GREAT ITINERARIES

IF YOU HAVE 3 DAYS

Fly into **Cairns** and take a boat out to one of the reef islands for a day, then head up to **Cape Tribulation** for the next two days to take in the sights and sounds of the rain forest. If you'd rather have a Miami Beach–style trip, fly into **Brisbane** and head straight for the glitzy **Gold Coast**, overnighting in **Surfers Paradise.** You could end the spree with a final night and day in **Lamington National Park** for its subtropical wilderness and birdlife.

IF YOU HAVE 5 DAYS

Spend three days on shore and two days on the reef. Stay the first night in **Brisbane,** then head up the **Sunshine Coast** for a hike up one of the **Glass House Mountains** on the way to **Noosa Heads.** Apart from beach and surf time, take in the Sunshine Coast's monument to kitsch, the **Big Pineapple,** and indulge in one of their famous ice-cream sundaes. Then make your way back to Brisbane for a flight to

Cairns and either a boat to the reef or a drive to the rain forest north of Cairns, where you can cruise wild rivers, listen to the jungle, relax on the beach, and look into the maw of a crocodile.

IF YOU HAVE 7 OR MORE DAYS

Unless you're keen on seeing everything, limit yourself to a couple of areas, such as **Brisbane,** its surrounding **Sunshine and Gold coasts,** and the rain forests north from Cairns, and take three to four days in each—Queensland's warm climate is conducive to slowing down. Extended stays will also allow you to take a four-wheel-drive trip all the way to the top of **Cape York Peninsula** from **Cairns,** go for bushwalking expeditions in national parks, spend a few days on a liveaboard dive boat exploring islands and reefs north of Cairns, trek inland to the ancient **Undara lava tubes,** take the **Matilda Highway** through the Outback, or just lie back and bask in the heat.

ABOUT THE RESTAURANTS

The concept of specialized rural cuisines is virtually unknown in Queensland. Steak and seafood predominate once you leave city limits behind. Brisbane, however, has its share of modern Australian, Mediterranean- and Asian-influenced menus, and the cuisine at many of Queensland's high-end resorts now rivals big-city standards. The coastal towns are full of casual, open-air restaurants that take advantage of the tropical climate.

WHAT IT COSTS IN AUSTRALIAN DOLLARS				
$$$$	$$$	$$	$⁻	¢
AT DINNER	over A$50	A$36–A$50	A$21–A$35	A$10–A$20	under A$10

Prices are for a main course at dinner.

ABOUT THE HOTELS

Accommodations in this state run the gamut from rain-forest lodges, Outback pubs, backpacker hostels, and colonial "Queenslander" bed-and-breakfasts—beautiful timber houses built above the ground on stilts, with big wraparound verandas—to deluxe beachside resorts and big-city hotels. The luxury resorts are clustered around the major tourist areas of Cairns, the islands, and the Gold and Sunshine coasts. In the smaller coastal towns, accommodation is mostly in motels, apartments, and B&Bs.

WHAT IT COSTS IN AUSTRALIAN DOLLARS					
	$$$$	$$$	$$	$	¢
FOR 2 PEOPLE	over A$300	A$201–A$300	A$151–A$200	A$100–A$150	under A$100

Prices are for two people in a standard double room in high season, including tax and service, based on the European Plan (with no meals) unless otherwise noted.

WHEN TO VISIT

North of Cairns, the best time for visiting is between May and September, when the daily maximum temperature averages around 27°C (80°F) and the water is comfortably warm. From about December through March, expect monsoon conditions. The tropical coast is besieged from October through May by deadly box jellyfish and the tiny transparent Irukandji jellyfish, which make ocean swimming impossible. Because of school holidays, sea- and reef-side Queensland tends to fill up around Christmas, and can be heavily booked around Easter. When making travel plans, remember that there's no daylight saving time in the state.

7

BRISBANE

Founded in 1823 on the banks of the wide, meandering Brisbane River, the former penal colony of Brisbane was for many years thought of as just a big country town. Many beautiful timber Queenslander homes, built in the 1800s, still dot the riverbanks and suburbs, and the city's numerous parks erupt in a riot of colorful jacaranda, flame tree, and bougainvillea blossoms in spring. Today, the Queensland capital is one of Australia's up-and-coming cities, where glittering high-rises mark the polished business center and numerous outdoor attractions beckon. In summer, temperatures here are broilingly hot, a reminder that this city is part of a subtropical region.

The inner suburbs, just a 5- to 10-minute drive or a 15- to 20-minute walk from the city center, have a mix of intriguing eateries and quiet accommodations. Fortitude Valley combines Chinatown with a cosmopolitan influx of clubs, cafés, and boutiques. Spring Hill has several high-quality hotels, and Paddington, New Farm, and the West End in South Brisbane are full of restaurants and bars. Brisbane is also a convenient base for trips to the Sunshine and Gold coasts, the mountainous hinterlands, and the Moreton Bay islands.

EXPLORING BRISBANE

CITY CENTER

Brisbane's inner-city landmarks—a combination of Victorian, Edwardian, and slick high-tech architecture—are best explored on foot. Most of them lie within the triangle formed by Ann Street and the bends of the Brisbane River. Hint: the streets running toward the river are named after female (British) royalty; those running parallel to the river are named after male royalty.

WHAT TO SEE

5 **Anzac Square and the Shrine of Remembrance.** Walking paths stretch across green lawns toward the Doric Greek Revival shrine constructed of Queensland sandstone. An eternal flame burns here for Australian soldiers who died in World War I. Equally spine-tingling is the **Shrine of Remembrance,** where a subsurface crypt stores soil samples collected from battlefields on which Australian soldiers perished. On April 25, Anzac Day, a moving dawn service is held here in remembrance of Australia's fallen soldiers. ✉ *Adelaide St. between Edward and Creek Sts., City Center* 💲*Free* ⊗ *Shrine weekdays 11–3.*

7 **Brisbane City Hall.** Opened in 1930, this substantial Italianate structure was once referred to as the "million-pound town hall" because of the massive funds poured into its construction. Today it's a major symbol of Brisbane's civic pride, where visitors and locals "ooh" and "aah" at the grand pipe organ and circular concert hall. Groups of 10 or more can take a tour of City Hall on weekdays, but it's essential to book first. This is also the home of the **Museum of Brisbane.** The ground-floor museum portrays the social history of the city; its changing art and social history exhibitions have included entries in the Lord Mayor's photographic awards (an annual photographic competition that has a different, distinctly Brisbane theme each year). Other attractions include a ground-floor art gallery, a tower housing one of Australia's largest civic clocks, and an observation platform with superb city views. ✉ *King George Sq. at Adelaide St., City Center* 🕾 *07/3403–4048 City Hall, 07/3403–8888 museum* 💲 *City Hall entry, museum, and clock tower free; City Hall tours A$4.90* ⊗ *Clock tower weekdays 10–3, Sat. 10–2:30; City Hall weekdays 8–5; museum daily 10–5.*

14 **Brisbane Convention and Exhibition Centre.** This 4½-acre building is equipped with four exhibition halls, a 4,000-seat Great Hall, and a Grand Ballroom. Apart from conferences and trade expos, it is the venue for large concerts. In 2005, '60s legends The Moody Blues and Jethro Tull played here; in 2006, British stars Simple Minds and James Blunt staged concerts, and Jane Fonda hosted a literary luncheon; 2007 saw Ronan Keating and Kanye West perform. ✉ *Glenelg and Merivale Sts., South Brisbane* 🕾 *07/3308–3000* ⊕ *www.bcec.com.au.*

8 **Conrad Treasury Brisbane.** This massive Edwardian baroque edifice overlooking the river stands on the site of the officers' quarters and military barracks from the original penal settlement. Bronze figurative statuary surrounds the structure. Constructed between 1885 and 1889, the former treasury reopened as the **Conrad Treasury Hotel & Casino Brisbane.**

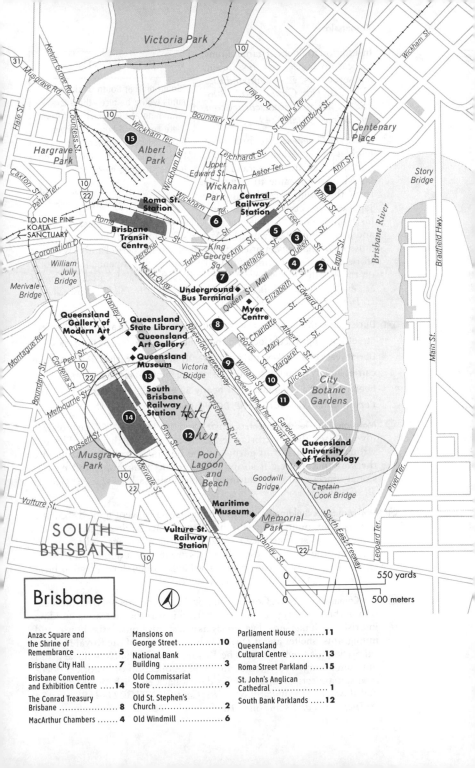

Brisbane

In addition to floors of game rooms, the casino houses five restaurants and seven bars. ⊠ *William and Elizabeth Sts., City Center* ☎*07/3306–8888* ⊕*www.conradtreasury.com.au* ☐*Free* ⊙*Daily 24 hrs.*

❹ MacArthur Chambers. As commander-in-chief of the Allied Forces fighting in the Pacific, General Douglas MacArthur came to Australia from the Philippines, leaving the Japanese in control there with

> **WORD OF MOUTH**
>
> "Some time at South Bank Parklands would be nice—there is swimming at the 'beach' and from there you could hop on a city cat ferry and get a different perspective of Brisbane from the river. The ferries are quite inexpensive."
>
> –stormbird

his famous vow, "I shall return." This present-day bookstore, mall, and apartment block was MacArthur's World War II headquarters. A museum displaying countless photographs of the period and newspaper stories, with a smattering of military memorabilia, opened in late 2004 on the eighth floor, where MacArthur's office was located. ⊠*Queen St., entrance at 201 Edward St., City Center* ☎*07/3211–7052* ☐*A$5* ⊙*Tues., Thurs., and Sun. 10–3.*

NEED A BREAK? Duck around the corner from MacArthur Chambers, taking a right on Elizabeth Street, and stop in at the locally owned American Bookstore. In the back, **Caffè Libri** serves coffee, cakes, and extravagantly filled sandwiches. The bookstore carries literary fiction, academic, design, and foreign-language titles, and has been run by the same family for nearly 50 years. ⊠*197 Elizabeth St., City Center* ☎*07/3229-4677* ☐*AE, DC, MC, V.*

❿ Mansions on George Street. Constructed in 1890 as six fashionable town houses, these Victorian terrace homes are worth a visit. Elegant, wrought-iron lace trim garnishes the buildings' exterior; inside are the National Trust gift shop, a restaurant, bookshops, and professional offices—all open during regular business hours. ⊠*40 George St., City Center.*

❸ National Bank Building. Brisbane's National Bank went up in 1885, and is one of the country's finest Italian Renaissance–style structures. Aside from the majestic entrance hall with its ornate ceilings and eye-catching dome, the most interesting features are the front doors, which were crafted from a single cedar trunk. The bank is open during regular business hours. ⊠*308 Queen St., City Center.*

❾ Old Commissariat Store. Convict-built in 1829, and erected over the location of the city's original timber wharf, this was the first stone building in Brisbane. It has served variously as a customs house, storehouse, and immigrants' shelter and is currently headquarters of the Royal Historical Society of Queensland. The Royal Historical Society library and museum are open to visitors, and hold a collection of historical documents, manuscripts, and artifacts dating back to Brisbane's early colonial days. ⊠*115 William St., City Center* ☎*07/3221–4198* ☐*A$4* ⊙*Tues.–Fri., and some Sun. 10–4.*

② **Old St. Stephen's Church.** The tiny 1850 church that adjoins St. Stephen's Catholic Cathedral is Brisbane's oldest house of worship, and a particularly fine example of Gothic Revival architecture. The church is believed to have been designed by Augustus Pugin, a noted English architect who designed much of London's Houses of Parliament. The church is not open to the public. ⊠*Elizabeth St. near Creek St., City Center.*

⑥ **Old Windmill.** This 1828 construction is the oldest remaining convict-built structure in Brisbane. Because it never worked very well, it was dubbed the "Tower of Torture" by the convicts who were forced to power a treadmill to crush grain for the colony's bread whenever the wind died down. When fire erupted across the city in 1864, scorching almost everything in its path, the windmill survived with only minimal damage. Stripped of its blades, the tower now looks much like a lighthouse. Currently, it's closed to the public, but a revamp to make the site safe for visitors is underway. ⊠*Wickham Park, Wickham Terr., City Center.*

⑪ **Parliament House.** Opened in 1868, this splendid, stone-clad, French Renaissance building with a Mount Isa copper roof earned its colonial designer a meager 200-guinea (A$440) salary. A legislative annex was added in the late 1970s. The interior is fitted with polished timber, brass, and frosted and engraved glass. There are free half-hour tours weekdays on demand, when staff are available and Parliament is not in session. The adjacent kid-friendly **City Botanic Gardens** have native and exotic plants and themed areas, including the Bamboo Grove and Weeping Fig Avenue, along with sculptures and ponds. ⊠*George and Alice Sts., City Center* ☎*07/3406–7562* ⊠*Free* ☉*Parliament House weekdays 9–5, weekends 10–2, gardens daily 5 AM–9 PM.*

⑬ **Queensland Cultural Centre.** The Queensland Museum, State Library of Queensland, and Performing Arts Centre (QPAC) are all here, as well as the Queensland Art Gallery and a short stroll away, the Queensland Gallery of Contemporary Art. There's also a host of restaurants, cafés, and shops. The State Library shop sells books and cards, and is an agent for ticketing the outlet Qtix. On Fridays from 11:30 (arrive 11:15), there are hour-long tours of the Performing Arts Centre for A$7.50. Backstage peeks at the 2,000-seat concert hall and Cremorne Theatre are often included. ⊠*Melbourne and Grey Sts., South Brisbane* ☎*07/3840–7303 art gallery, 07/3842–9555 modern art gallery, 07/3840–7555 museum, 07/3840–7666 library, 07/3840–7576 library shop, 07/3840–7444 or 13–6246 performing arts center* ⊕*www.qag. qld.gov.au (galleries), www.southbank.qm.qld.gov.au (museum), www. slq.qld.gov.au (library), www.qtix.com.au (ticket outlet), www.qpac. com.au (performing arts center)* ⊠*Free* ☉*Galleries weekdays 10–5, weekends 9–5; museum daily 9:30–5; library daily 10–5; library shop Mon.–Thurs. 10–8, Fri.–Sun. 10–5.*

⑮ **Roma Street Parkland.** The world's largest subtropical garden within a city is a gentle mix of forest paths and structured plantings surrounding a lake. Look for unique artwork on display along the walkways.

7

Highlights include the Lilly Pilly Garden, which displays native evergreen rain-forest plants; and interesting children's play areas. Pack a picnic, take advantage of the free grills, or stop for lunch at one of two on-site cafés. Hop aboard the park's train for a 15-minute ride with commentary (A$5.50). Free guided garden tours begin daily at 10 and 2 and last around an hour; brochures for self-guided walks are available. ⊠ *1 Parkland Blvd., City Center* ☎*07/3006–4545* ⊕*www. romastreetparkland.com* ✉*Free* ⊗*Daily 24 hrs.*

❶ **St. John's Anglican Cathedral.** Under construction for more than a century (its spires are due to be completed in 2009), this cathedral begun in 1901 is a fine example of Gothic Revival architecture. Free guided tours are available Monday through Saturday and most Sundays. Inside the cathedral grounds is the **Deanery** (the residence of the ecclesiastical dean) which predates the construction of the cathedral by almost 50 years. Unfortunately, it's not open to the public. The shop, open Monday–Saturday 9:30–2:30 and Sunday after morning services, sells souvenirs. ⊠*373 Ann St., City Center* ☎*07/3835–2222* ⊗*Tours Mon.–Sat. at 10 and 2, most Sun. at 2.*

⓬ **South Bank Parklands.** One of the most appealing urban parks in Australia and the site of Brisbane's World Expo '88, this massive complex includes parklands, shops, a maritime museum, foot- and cycling paths, a sprawling man-made beach (complete with lifeguards), a Nepalese-style carved-wood pagoda, and excellent views of the city. The Friday-night Market by Moonlight and weekend South Bank Lifestyle Market bristle with handmade goods, live entertainers, and New Age pundits. South Bank Visitor Information on the Stanley Street Plaza provides free visitor information and sells tickets for cultural events. The park stretches along the riverbank, south of the Queensland Cultural Centre as far as the Goodwill Bridge. ⊠*Grey St. south of Melbourne St., South Bank* ☎*07/3867–2051 parklands, 07/3844–5361 museum* ⊕*www.visitsouthbank.com.au* ✉*Parklands free, maritime museum A$7* ⊗*Parklands daily 5 AM–midnight, information center daily 9–5, museum daily 9:30–4:30 (last entry 3:30), markets Fri. 5 PM–10 PM, Sat. 11–5, Sun. 9–5.*

AROUND BRISBANE

Lone Pine Koala Sanctuary. Queensland's most famous fauna park, founded in 1927, is recognized by the *Guinness Book of World Records* as the world's first and largest koala sanctuary. The attraction for most people are the koalas (more than 130 in all), although

Fodor'sChoice
★

emus, wombats, crocs, bats, and lorikeets also reside here. You can hand-feed baby kangaroos in the free-range 'roo and wallaby enclosure, have a snake wrapped around you, or cuddle a koala (and have your photo taken with one for A$15, until 4:30). There's also a thrice-daily sheepdog show; and a new birds of prey flight show. The **MV** *Mirimar* (☎07/3221–0300 or 1300/749732), a historic 1930s ferry, travels daily to Lone Pine Koala Sanctuary from the Queensland Cultural Centre pontoon opposite Victoria Bridge, departing at 10 sharp (board from 9:30), departing Lone Pine at 1:30 and returning to the city at 2:50 (A$48 round-trip, including entrance to the sanctuary). Bus 430 from Stop 116A on George Street, and Bus 445 from Stop 11 on Ann Street also stop at the sanctuary. Taxis cost about A$35 from the city center (distance from the CBD is around 11 km [6.5 mi]). ⊠*Jesmond Rd., Fig Tree Pocket* ☎07/3378–1366, 07/3221–0300 for ferry ⊕*www.koala.net* ⊠A$20 ⊙*Daily 8:30–5.*

WHERE TO EAT

AUSTRALIAN

$$ ✕**Tukka Restaurant.** Dreamy music and earth-tone walls lined with Aboriginal artworks are a fitting backdrop for chef Stephane Bremont's imaginative, beautifully presented "gourmet Australian" cuisine. This restaurant in Brisbane's colorful West End specializes in authentic Aussie dishes: seared wallaby, emu fillet, croc tail, or mud crab. Leave room for dessert: perhaps the native spiced poached pear, with pear blini and finger lime cream, or a chocolate assiette with strawberry-eucalypt tart. The wine list showcases top vintages from boutique wineries around Australia. You can buy jams, spices, sauces, and chutneys to take home, too. ⊠*145 Boundary St., West End* ☎07/3846–6333 ⊕*www.tukka restaurant.com.au* ⊟*AE, DC, MC, V* ⊙*No dinner Sun.*

ECLECTIC

$$–$$$ ✕**Oxley's on the River.** By day the dining room at Brisbane's only floating restaurant is sunny and has a bird's-eye view of boat traffic. By night, light from the city and the moon dimple the water and lend an intimate, romantic feel. This purpose-built restaurant with floor-to-ceiling windows on three sides is permanently moored to the wharf at the inner-city suburb of Milton, a five-minute taxi ride from the city center. Queensland saltwater barramundi, steamed Moreton Bay bugs (lobsterlike crustaceans), and the restaurant's signature chilled seafood platter for two, as well as "surf 'n' turf" and vegetarian dishes, are on the à la carte menu, while the three-course set menu—at A$43.95 per head—is very popular. There's a large, all-Australian wine list. ⊠*330 Coronation Dr., Milton* ☎07/3368–1866 ⊕*www.oxleys.com. au* ⊟*AE, DC, MC, V.*

MODERN AUSTRALIAN

$$$ ✕**e'cco.** Consistently rated as the best restaurant in town, this petite eatery serves innovative food to a loyal following. The white-columned entry leads into a maroon-and-eggplant dining room, where an open kitchen and bar await. The menu lists a wide selection of seasonally

Fodor'sChoice
★

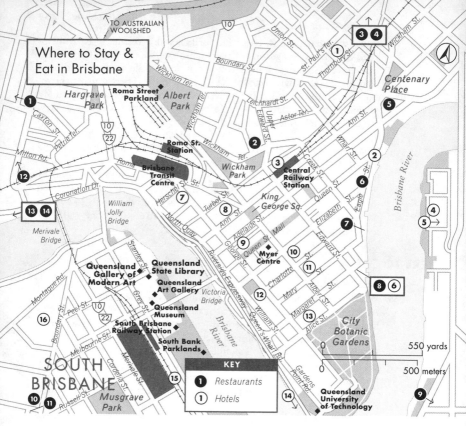

Where to Stay & Eat in Brisbane

changing, Mediterranean- and Asian-inspired dishes, which use local produce and are beautifully presented. Superb choices include field mushrooms on olive toast with arugula, truffle oil, and lemon; salmon poached in tomato, chili, and lemongrass broth; crab ravioli; and mussels. For dessert, the buttermilk panna cotta with passion-fruit syrup is wonderful. Pay attention to the waiter's suggestions for accompanying wines. ⊠*100 Boundary St., City Center, 4003* ☎*07/3831–8344* ⊕*www.eccobistro.com* ⌖*Reservations essential* ▤*AE, DC, MC, V* ☾*Closed Sun. and Mon. No lunch Sat.*

$$$ ✕**Siggi's at the Port Office.** Socialites rub shoulders with visiting celebrities at this charming restaurant and bar in the Stamford Plaza Brisbane hotel. Service is impeccable, and decor makes full use of the 19th-century Port of Brisbane Office architecture. Monthly five-course degustation menus showcase the finest local seafood and seasonal produce, and might feature barramundi, duck, or truffles (A$89 per person, A$140 with matched wines). These offerings are supplemented by ever-changing Continental dishes, which could include Petuna ocean trout with pickled wild mushrooms or pancetta-wrapped aged beef fillet. Desserts, such as pistachio soufflé, chocolate truffle tart, or Siggi's signature crepes suzette à deux, prepared at the table, are just as worthy. There's a tapas menu for balcony and bar patrons, and an extensive wine list. ⊠*Edward and Margaret Sts., City Center* ☎*07/3221–1999* ⊕*www.stamford.com.au* ⌖*Reservations essential* ▤*AE, DC, MC, V* ☾*Closed Sun. and Mon. No lunch.*

$$–$$$ ✕**Summit Restaurant.** Perched beside the lookout on the slope of Mt. Coot-tha, this restaurant affords unbeatable views of the city, especially at night. Since the view is a bigger attraction than the food, diners tend to be from out of town. The original building dates from 1925 and has been patronized by such lights and dignitaries as Katharine Hepburn and Britain's Princess Alexandra. From a diverse menu that features contemporary cuisine with Asian influences, treat yourself to the Summit's signature crisp Atlantic salmon on potato mash and wilted English spinach with tomato and chili jam, or choose something healthy from the vegetarian or gluten-free menus. For dessert, there's strawberry Vacherin: a meringue nest filled with fresh cream and sweet berries and drizzled in chocolate sauce. Taxi fare to the Summit from the city center, 10 minutes' drive away, is about A$20. ⊠*Sir Samuel Griffith Dr., Mt. Coot-tha* ☎*07/3369–9922* ⊕*www.brisbanelookout. com* ▤*AE, DC, MC, V.*

$$ ✕**Seasalt at Armstrong's.** Well-known local chef Russell Armstrong works seafood magic at this popular, 45-seat restaurant. Choices include "freelance fish"—the day's freshest catch, generally pan-seared and served with an asparagus-and-champagne cream sauce or seafood pilaf; or the popular roast duck breast over tart tartine with fire-roasted Spanish onion and beetroot relish. Perennial favorites include a tender grilled lamb loin and braised shank with spiced couscous. ⊠*73 Wickham Terr., City Center* ☎*07/3832–4566* ⊕*www.armstrongsrestaurant.com.au* ▤*AE, DC, MC, V* ☾*Closed Sun. No lunch Sat.*

7

$–$$ ✕ The Gunshop Café. Named for its previous business, this West End café is the place to go for breakfast on weekends (the potato-and-feta hash cakes are locally famous). The unfinished brick walls, where guns used to hang, lend a rustic ambience. Vases of lilies fill arches separating the open kitchen from the wooden tables; you can also dine outside on the sidewalk. An eclectic Mod-Oz menu incorporates Mediterranean and Asian flavors in dishes featuring local lamb, beef, goat, and seafood, along with vegetarian dishes and exciting salads. Australian foodies flock here for lunch and dinner, or for coffee and memorable cheesecakes—white chocolate and blueberry, Rocky Road, or berry-smothered Top Deck. ⊠ *53 Mollison St., West End* ☎ *07/3844–2241* ▭ *AE, DC, MC, V* ☉ *Closed Sun. and Mon.*

$–$$ ✕ Luxe. This casual restaurant-cum-bar serves delicious tapas-style starters and seasonally changing dishes with a Euro-Mediterranean edge. Sample the popular smoked trout spaghettini, confit duck, or fillet of beef with endive and goat cheese tartlet. Dessert could be a delectable crème brûlée: honey-cinnamon, vanilla-lychee, or wicked soft chocolate with berries. The wine and seasonal cocktail lists are impressive. In nice weather, try for a table on the sidewalk. ⊠ *39 James St., Fortitude Valley* ☎ *07/3854–0671* ✑ luxe@tpg.com.au ▭ *AE, MC, V.*

$ ✕ Freestyle Tout. Tucked away in an inner-city suburb, this art-gallery ★ café is famous for the 20 beautiful desserts that grace its menu. Savvy owner Martin Duncan focuses on healthful dishes, so you can indulge in wonderful sweets (such as artfully designed sundaes, served in vases) without guilt. The lunch menu is full of freshly made, interesting salads, burgers, quesadillas, and dishes such as stuffed red peppers. An extensive assortment of teas, coffees, and wines is available. The flamboyant flowers and modern Australian artwork are for sale. A second Freestyle Tout offers similarly health-conscious Mod-Oz cuisine, taken up a notch. It's open for dinner, with pricier à la carte dishes but the same dessert list as the original Tout. ⊠ *21 Nash St., Rosalie* ☎ *07/3876–2288* ⊠ *1000 Ann St., Fortitude Valley* ☎ *07/3252–0214* ⊕ *www.freestyletout.com.au* ▭ *AE, DC, MC, V* ☉ *No dinner.*

SEAFOOD

$$$ ✕ Michael's Riverside Restaurant. Of Michael Platsis's two very different restaurants in the Riverside Centre, this silver-service establishment is the jewel. Enjoy sweeping views of the Brisbane River and the Story Bridge here, as well as a menu that changes seasonally and focuses on fine fresh Queensland produce, with seafood a specialty. A popular dish is the Moreton Bay bug ravioli with scallops in coriander, coconut, and pineapple juice. Michael's has what just might be the best wine cellar in town. ⊠ *123 Eagle St., City Center* ☎ *07/3832–5522* ⊕ *www.michaelsrestaurant.com.au* ⌁ *Reservations essential* ▭ *AE, DC, MC, V* ☉ *No lunch weekends, closed Sun.*

$$$ ✕ Pier Nine Oyster Bar & Seafood Grill. The city's most stylish seafood ☾ restaurant has fantastic views of the Brisbane River and the Story ★ Bridge. The kitchen prepares everything from fish-and-chips to seasonal steamed crabs. Only the freshest catches appear here, such as oysters delivered daily and shucked to order. Try the local prawns or Moreton Bay bugs, as well as barramundi and mud crabs, in season. A full vegetarian menu is also available. ⊠*Eagle Street Pier, 1 Eagle St., City Center* ☎*07/3226–2100* ⊕*www.piernine.com.au* ▤*AE, DC, MC, V* ⊘*No lunch Sat.*

STEAK

$-$$ ✕**Breakfast Creek Hotel.** A Brisbane institution, this enormous hotel is perched right on the wharf at Breakfast Creek. Pristine National Heritage–listed interiors and a lush tropical beer garden are almost as much of a drawing card as its superb trademark steaks. Just choose your cut, how you'd like it cooked, and a sauce to go with it. Vegetarians also have plenty of options. Big Sunday breakfasts, served 8–10:30, are popular. Look around as you dig in; many Australian sports and entertainment notables dine here. ⊠*2 Kingsford Smith Dr., Albion* ☎*07/3262–5988* ⊕*www.breakfastcreekhotel.com* ▤*AE, DC, MC, V.*

THAI

¢-$ ✕**Caxton Thai.** This pale-grey-walled Thai restaurant, where you dine surrounded by traditional art and sculptures, is popular with both locals and tourists. The most requested dish is the pork chop with basil, and in this otherwise traditional Thai restaurant, you can find a warm Thai salad: a mixture of chicken, prawns, glass noodles, and vegetables. There's a generous vegetarian menu. ⊠*47B Caxton St., Petrie Terrace* ☎*07/3367–0300* ⊕*www.caxtonthai.com.au* ▤*AE, DC, MC, V* ⊘*No lunch.*

VIETNAMESE

$$-$$$ ✕**Green Papaya.** The small selection of simple dishes here is beautifully prepared from 90% local ingredients (including certified organic meat, poultry, and rice) in what former owner Lien Yeomans refers to as "Modern Classic Vietnamese" style (the new owners have, thankfully, retained the old chef). Among the most popular choices are grilled lemon-myrtle prawns, Hanoi-style bouillabaisse, and Emperor pork. Lunches are available on Friday; best to book ahead. ⊠*898 Stanley St., East Brisbane* ☎*07/3217–3599* ⊕*www.greenpapaya.com.au* ▤*AE, DC, MC, V* ⊘*Closed Sun. and Mon. No lunch Sat.–Thurs.*

WHERE TO STAY

$$$$ ▥**Brisbane Marriott Hotel.** This slender, 28-story tower is easy to recognize by its distinctive bronze dome. The top floor houses the fantastic dome retreat day spa, which offers just about every treatment imaginable, from body scrubs and wraps to foot baths and a lap pool. The rooms are decorated in elegant cream tones and tasteful wood furnishings, and have marble bathrooms. Fitness facilities include a Grecian-style indoor-outdoor swimming pool with a sundeck overlooking the river. The hotel is a short walk from the CityCat high-speed ferry wharf, and several restaurants and bars in the Riverside Centre. ⊠*515 Queen St., City Centre, 4000* ☎*07/3303–8000 or 1800/899899* ✑brisbane.reservations@marriotthotels.com ⊕*www.*

7

marriott.com.au ↻*263 rooms, 4 suites* ⚲*In-room: safe, refrigerator, dial-up (some), ethernet (some). In-hotel: restaurant, room service, bar, pool, gym, spa, concierge, laundry facilities, laundry service, executive floor, public Internet, public Wi-Fi, airport shuttle, parking (fee), some pets allowed, no-smoking rooms, minibar* ▭*AE, MC, V.*

$$$$ 🖥**The Conrad Treasury Brisbane.** Like the Conrad Treasury Casino one
★ block to the north, this National Heritage–listed hotel represents a beautiful sandstone example of Edwardian baroque architecture. Rooms have 18-foot-high ceilings, colonial furniture, and large, luxurious bathrooms as well as flat-screen TVs with pay movies, Internet, and Sony PlayStation games. Deluxe suites have mosaic fireplaces, separate lounge areas, and private balconies. The hotel has five very different restaurants to suit all tastes and budgets, bars for all occasions and 24-7 action. ✉*130 William St., City Center, 4000* ☎*07/3306– 8888* 📠*07/3306–8880* ✐hotelres@conradtreasury.com.au ⊕*www. conradtreasury.com.au* ↻*115 rooms, 15 suites* ⚲*In-room: safe, refrigerator, DVD (some), ethernet. In-hotel: 5 restaurants, room service, bars, gym, laundry service, concierge, public Internet, public Wi-Fi, parking (no fee), no-smoking rooms, disabled-access room* ▭*AE, DC, MC, V.*

$$$$ 🖥**Quay West Suites Brisbane.** This modern hotel, perfectly positioned opposite the City Botanic Gardens and overlooking the Brisbane River and Kangaroo Cliffs, has sophisticated pressed-metal ceilings, sandstone columns, hammered-iron decorations, white-louvered windows, and a furnished balcony. The sleek 1-, 2-, and 3-bedroom suites are fitted with plantation teak furniture and include separate lounge and dining areas, two TVs, stereo/CD players, and fully-equipped kitchens and laundry facilities. The pool on the first floor has a feature waterfall and is surrounded by a tropically landscaped area, where intricately carved early-19th-century teak columns from South Africa support a poolside pergola. ✉*132 Alice St., City Center, 4000* ☎*07/3853–6000 or 1800/672726* ✐reservations@qwsb.mirvachotels.com ⊕*www. mirvachotels.com.au* ↻*63 suites (44 1-bedroom, 17 2-bedroom, 2 3-bedroom)* ⚲*In-room: safe, kitchen, refrigerator, pay movies, DVD, ethernet, Wi-Fi (some). In-hotel: restaurant, room service, bar, pool, gym, hot tub, sauna, concierge, laundry facilities, laundry service, public Internet, public Wi-Fi, parking (fee), no-smoking rooms, minibar* ▭*AE, DC, MC, V.*

$$$$ 🖥**Rydges South Bank.** Sandwiched between the Brisbane Convention and Exhibition Centre and South Bank Parklands, within walking distance of numerous cultural and culinary attractions, this hotel is an excellent choice for both business and leisure travelers. There are seven styles of accommodation, from guest rooms to family suites. Rooms, given a soft refurbishment in 2007, have modern furnishings and computer workstations with fast Internet access; suites have separate lounge areas. Although there's no pool, the artificial beach at South Bank Parklands is within easy walking distance. ✉*9 Glenelg St., at Grey St., South Brisbane, 4101* ☎*07/3364–0800* ⊕*www.rydges.com/ southbank* ↻*130 rooms, 64 suites* ⚲*In-room: kitchen (some), refrig-*

erator/minibar, ethernet, Wi-Fi (some). In-hotel: 2 restaurants, room service, bars, gym, spa, concierge, laundry facilities, laundry service, public Internet, public Wi-Fi, parking (fee), no-smoking rooms, disabled-access suite ☰AE, MC, V.

$$$$ ⊞**The Sebel & Citigate, King George Square.** The largest hotel in Brisbane, rebranded in 2007 as a Mirvac property, is ideally situated opposite City Hall and close to the center of town. A central lobby elegantly furnished with French-style sofas and carpets is flanked by the deluxe rooms and suites of The Sebel on one side, and the elegant contemporary rooms of Citigate on the other. Rooms and suites in both towers have been given a full soft refurbishment, plus chic new appointments such as high-speed Internet access and flat-screen TVs. The heated rooftop pool lets you soak up the sun in summer. Picasso's restaurant, on ground level, serves Mediterranean cuisine. ☒*Ann and Roma Sts., City Center, 4000* ☎*07/3229–9111* ✐reservations@tskgsb.mirvac.com.au (Sebel) or reservations@ckgsb.mirvac.com.au ⊕*www.mirvachotels.com.au* ➱*203 rooms, 7 suites (Sebel); 228 rooms (Citigate)* ⌂*In-room: safe, refrigerator/minibar, ethernet. In-hotel: 2 restaurants, room service, bars, pool, gym, concierge, laundry facilities, laundry service, concierge, executive floor, parking (fee), no-smoking rooms* ☰*AE, DC, MC, V.*

$$$$ ⊞**The Sebel Suites Brisbane.** Minimalist furnishings create an elegant, uncluttered look in the studio and one-bedroom suites here, decorated in navy, cream, and red. Spacious one-bedroom suites have fully-equipped kitchenettes, laundry centers, lounge areas, CD players, and dual TVs; all suites have high-speed Internet connections and balconies. Palettes Brasserie and Bar is popular with the after-work crowd. ☒*Albert and Charlotte Sts., City Center, 4000* ☎*07/3224–3500, 1800/888298 or 13–1515 (central reservations)* ✐reservations@tssb.mirvac.com.au ⊕*www.mirvachotels.com.au* ➱*150 suites* ⌂*In-room: kitchen (some), laundry facilities (some), refrigerator/minibar, pay movies, cable TV, ethernet. In-hotel: restaurant, room service, bar, pool, gym, sauna, concierge, laundry facilities, laundry service, executive floor, parking (fee), no-smoking rooms* ☰*AE, DC, MC, V.*

$$$–$$$$ ⊞**Royal Albert Hotel.** This Heritage-listed building is right in the heart of Brisbane and offers more than you might expect from a standard hotel. Each larger-than-average room has a self-contained kitchen and laundry. The reproduction antique furniture and cream-and-plum plush carpets add elegant finishing touches. All rooms have free Foxtel cable TV access, including movie channels. Staff members are friendly and personable. There is a licensed brasserie on the ground floor. ☒*167 Albert St., at Elizabeth St., City Center, 4000* ☎*07/3291–8888 or 1800/655054* ✐stay@royalalbert.com.au ⊕*www.royalalbert.com.au* ➱*28 rooms, 28 suites* ⌂*In-room: kitchen, refrigerator/minibar, ethernet, Wi-Fi. In-hotel: restaurant, room service, concierge, laundry facilities, laundry service, airport shuttle, parking (fee), no-smoking rooms, minibar* ☰*AE, DC, MC, V.*

$$$–$$$$ ⛄ **Sofitel Brisbane.** Despite its position above the city's main rail station, this hotel is a quiet and pleasant place to stay. Completely refurbished in 2005, with a restaurant renovation and a new day spa in 2007, it has a new look, beginning with the wood-paneled lobby. The spacious rooms and suites have marble bathrooms (suites have separate baths and showers), and what are advertised as "the world's most comfortable beds." Floors 26 through 29 are the pricier executive floors, where the rate includes breakfast, hors d'oeuvres, and cocktails in a club lounge. The 30th floor—with sweeping views across the city—is an ultrahip lounge with sleek decor, attracting a corresponding clientele. A day spa was added in 2007. ⊠*249 Turbot St., City Center, 4006* ☎*07/3835–3535* ⊕*www.sofitelbrisbane.com.au* ⇲*387 rooms, 26 suites* ⌂*In-room: safe, kitchen (some), refrigerator/minibar, DVD (on request), ethernet, Wi-Fi (some). In-hotel: 2 restaurants, room service, 2 bars, pool, gym, spa, concierge, laundry service, executive floor, public Internet, public Wi-Fi, airport shuttle (by arrangement), parking (fee), no-smoking rooms, disabled-friendly room* ▤*AE, DC, MC, V.*

$$$–$$$$ ⛄ **Stamford Plaza Brisbane.** This refined riverfront hotel next to the City
★   Botanic Gardens is a quiet retreat from the bustling city. The soaring lobby, full of artwork, flower arrangements, a sweeping timber staircase, and expanses of glass, is warm and inviting and looks out onto a leafy courtyard. Guest rooms, decorated in neoclassical style in muted yellow and beige, enjoy clear views over the river and have flat-screen TVs. Four dining spots include the hotel's signature restaurant, Siggi's, and the lively Kabuki, considered the best teppanyaki restaurant in the city. Probably the most famous of the many celebrities and performers who have stayed here is Queen Elizabeth II, who visited in 2002. ⊠*Edward and Margaret Sts., City Center, 4000* ☎*07/3221–1999 or 1800/773700* ⊕*www.stamford.com.au/spb* ⇲*232 rooms, 20 suites* ⌂*In-room: safe, kitchen (some), refrigerator/minibar, DVD, ethernet. In-hotel: 4 restaurants, room service, bars, pool, gym, spa, bicycles, laundry service, concierge, executive floor, public Internet, public Wi-Fi, parking (fee), no-smoking rooms* ▤*AE, DC, MC, V.*

$$–$$$ ⛄ **The Point Brisbane.** Across the Brisbane River from the central business district, this modern hotel on picturesque Kangaroo Point has great views of the city skyline from each balcony. Accommodations include studios, two-bedroom apartments, and executive suites (including customized "women's suites"), most with high-speed broadband access, fully-equipped kitchens, and laundries. The gym, refurbished in late 2006, has state-of-the-art equipment. The hotel provides a courtesy shuttle bus to the city, and the Inner City Ferry (dockside ferry stop) is 100 yards from the front door. ⊠*21 Lambert St., Kangaroo Point, 4169* ☎*07/3240–0888 or 1800/088388* ☎*07/3392–1155* ✉reservations@thepointbrisbane.com.au ⊕*www.thepointbrisbane.com.au* ⇲*106 rooms* ⌂*In-room: safe (some), kitchen (some), ethernet, Wi-Fi. In-hotel: restaurant, room service, bar, tennis court, pool, gym, laundry service, public Internet, public Wi-Fi, parking (no fee), no-smoking rooms* ▤*AE, DC, MC, V.*

$$ 🖼**Annerley B&B: Ridge Haven.** This late-19th-century B&B is for those who would rather stay outside the hubbub of central Brisbane. With high ceilings, ornate cornices, and reproduction antiques, the rooms exude both comfort and old-fashioned romance—but each has its own TV. Breakfast is served in the dining room or on a patio with a view of the suburbs. Proprietors Peter and Morna Cook are happy to let guests use the kitchen or barbecue grill for lunch or dinner. Complimentary homemade aromatherapy toiletries are a classy touch. For stays of two nights or more, you get a reduced rate. ✉ *374 Annerley Rd., Annerley, 4103* ☎ *07/3391–7702* ✐ *stay@annerleybnb.com.au* ⊕ *www.annerleybnb.com.au* ➲ *3 rooms* ⚷ *In-room: no a/c (one room), no phone, refrigerator/mini-bar, kitchen, ethernet (free), Wi-Fi (free). In-hotel: bar, laundry facilities, laundry service, no-smoking rooms, no elevator* ⊟ *D, MC, V* ⊓◯ *BP.*

$–$$ 🖼**Hotel George Williams.** This modern hotel is right in the heart of the city, 150 yards from the Brisbane Transit Center. Rooms are decorated in sandstone and green or blue color schemes; some have outdoor terraces, and all have fast Internet access. Cerellos Bar and Café serves contemporary Australian cuisine. ✉ *317–325 George St., City Center, 4005* ☎ *07/3308–0700 or 1800/064858* ⊕ *www.hgw.com.au* ➲ *81 rooms* ⚷ *In-room: refrigerator, Wi-Fi. In-hotel: restaurant, room service, bar, gym, laundry facilities, laundry service, public Internet, public Wi-Fi, airport shuttle (on request), parking (fee), no-smoking rooms* ⊟ *AE, DC, MC, V* ⊓◯ *BP.*

¢ 🖼**La Torretta Bed & Breakfast.** A 10-minute walk from the South Bank Parklands takes you to this West End Queenslander dating from the early 20th century. The sprawling timber house has two simple, comfortable ground-floor guest rooms, and a large guest lounge that looks out onto a tropical garden. The price includes a self-service breakfast of homemade muesli, bread and jam, juice, cereal, yogurt, and brewed coffee. Guests can use the kitchen to make their own lunch and dinner. The lounge has a TV with cable channels, as well as DVD and CD players, and you can request a TV for your room. Groups taking both rooms have the option of self-catering. The owners, Charles and Dorothy Colman, speak Italian, French, and German. There's a minimum stay of seven nights. ✉ *8 Brereton St., South Brisbane, 4101* ☎ *07/3846–0846* ⊕ *www.latorretta.com.au* ➲ *2 rooms* ⚷ *In-room: no phone, safe, Wi-Fi. In-hotel: restaurant, public Internet, public Wi-Fi, parking (no fee), no-smoking rooms* ⊟ *MC, V* ⊓◯ *CP.*

NIGHTLIFE & THE ARTS

THE ARTS

The Saturday edition of the *Courier–Mail* newspaper lists concerts, ballet, opera, theater, jazz, and other events. Thursday's paper includes a free *What's On* magazine, which is Brisbane's most comprehensive entertainment guide.

The Heritage-listed **Brisbane Powerhouse** (✉ *119 Lamington St., New Farm* ☎ *07/3358–8600* ⊕ *www.brisbanepowerhouse.com*), built in a former power plant, hosts live performances in flexible 200- and 400-seat theaters and art exhibits. Cafés, restaurants, bikeways, boardwalks, and picnic areas complement the funky art space. An early-2007 renovation added a new eatery and enlarged theater spaces.

The **Queensland Performing Arts Centre** (⊠*Melbourne and Grey Sts., South Brisbane* ☎*07/3840–7444 or 13–6246* ⊕*www.qpac.com.au*), the city's cultural heart, hosts both international and Australian entertainers. Artists in recent years have included songstress Norah Jones, folk-rocker Jackson Browne, the Soweto Gospel Choir, and Australia's hit folk group from the 1960s, the Seekers.

NIGHTLIFE

Conrad Treasury Casino (⊠*Queen and George Sts., City Center* ☎*07/3306–8888*)—with a "neat and tidy" dress code geared toward securing an upscale clientele—is a European-style casino. Open 24 hours, the facility has three levels of gaming, with more than 100 gaming tables and more than 1,000 machines, plus five restaurants and seven bars.

Cru Bar + Cellar (⊠*James Street Market, 22 James St., Fortitude Valley* ☎*07/3252–2400* ⊕*www.crubar.com*) is one of Brisbane's places to see and be seen. The decor is sleek and sophisticated, with leather ottomans, a long onyx bar, and a circa-1800 French chandelier. The staff here describes the clientele as "people who love good wine." Cru's huge cellar houses hundreds of top Australian boutique vintages, available for sale, or to drink on-site. There's a Modern Australian bistro-restaurant open for lunch and dinner, and low-key jazz to listen to as you sip long into the night.

Empire Hotel (⊠*339 Brunswick St., at Ann St., Fortitude Valley* ☎*07/3852–1216* ⊕*www.empirehotel.com.au*) packs in four bars under one roof. Relax with a cocktail and cool jazz at the adjacent Press Club, fitted with ultrahip leather sofas, retro fans, and pendant lamps; have a casual drink at Corner Bar; or mix with the cool crowd on levels two and three. Fans of electro-house music flock to "Middle" Bar, which has a cocktail lounge and balcony on one side, a large dance floor on the other. Mingle upstairs in the Moonbar, with its vast dance floor and balcony. Friday nights feature edgier dance styles, electro house, and breaks; Saturday's "Fresh N Funky" is Brisbane's longest-running breaks night, with funk, hip hop, and disco in Middle Bar. Corner Bar is open daily from 10 AM until late, Levels 2 and 3, Friday–Sunday 9 PM–5 AM, no re-entry after 3 AM.

Family (⊠*8 McLachlan St., Fortitude Valley* ☎*07/3852–5000* ⊕*www. thefamily.com.au and www.fluffy.com.au*) bills itself as "Brisbane's superclub," and with good reason. You can find Brisbane's hip crowd getting a groove on to a rotating line-up of DJs from near and far who spin various brands of house and funk on Friday and Saturday nights, and host a gay-friendly hospitality night, Fluffy, on Sundays (cover charge varies from A$10 to A$15). Four floors, including two dance floors, a mezzanine for people-watching, and a "VIP" chillout area lined with flock wallpaper and cozy couches, accommodate most moods. Family's strictly applied dress code is "urban streetwear"—no flip-flops, shorts, suits, fancy dress, or uncool outfits! Proximity to the Empire Hotel's multitude of bars means those wanting a quieter drink only have to go next door. **The Monastery** (✉ *621 Ann St., at Marshall St., Fortitude Valley* ☎ *07/3257–7081*), with its long curved bar illuminated by tall stained-glass window panels and chandeliers, and staffed by cocktail-shaker-wielding "flair-tenders", has a Euro-club feel. Despite the name, it's anything but an ascetic retreat for quiet contemplation, with electro-house and dance music ripping through the airwaves. The dark interior echoes the techno atmosphere, and the dance floor is rarely less than full. It is open Thursday–Saturday 9 PM–5 AM.

> ### EARTH'S FASTEST MOVING ISLAND
>
> **Moreton Island is** the fastest-moving island on earth, shifting one metre (3¼ feet) a year towards the Queensland coast. You can hand-feed wild dolphins at **Tangalooma Wild Dolphin Resort** (☎ *07/3268–6333* ⊕ *www.tangalooma.com*). Camping on Moreton is possible (A$4.50 permit; info available at ⊕ *www. qld.gov.au/camping*). Catch a ferry from Scarborough Harbour, north of Brisbane, to Bulwer (daily except Tuesday), or Tangalooma's thrice-daily launch ⊕ *www. moreton-island.com.*

Union Jack's (✉ *127 Charlotte St., Brisbane* ☎ *07/3210-1172* ⊕ *www. unionjacks.com.au*). is a British-themed bar (English, Irish, Scottish, and Welsh) has dartboards, and live music on Fridays from 5:30. It's popular with locals and British visitors. Open Monday to Friday 11:30 AM–5 AM, Saturday 3 PM–5 AM.

SPORTS & THE OUTDOORS

BIKING

An extensive network of bicycle paths crisscrosses Brisbane. A highlight is to follow the Bicentennial Bikeway southeast along the Brisbane River, across the Goodwill Bridge, and then along to South Bank Park lands or the Kangaroo Point cliffs.

The *Brisbane Bikeways Experience* CD, detailing more than 400 km (250 mi) of cycling paths, is available for A$16.50, along with maps and info, from the **Brisbane City Council** (✉ *266 George St. [enter Queen St.], City Center* ☎ *07/3403–8888* ⊕ *www.brisbane.qld.gov.au*). The Council's Web site includes maps and lets you search for bikeways. **Brisbane Bicycle Sales and Hire** (✉ *87 Albert St., City Center* ☎ *07/3229– 2433* ⊕ *www.brizbike.com*) rents out bikes from the heart of the city for A$20 per day. They're open weekdays 8:30–5:30, weekends 10–3. **Valet Cycle Hire and Tours** (☎ *0408–003198* ⊕ *www.valetcyclehire.com*), on Alice Street, near the Albert Street gate to the City Botanic Gardens, hires out bicycles for A$15 for an hour or A$35 a day. For a fee of A$10, they'll deliver a rental bike right to your hotel. They also do special longer-term deals.

7

GOLF

St. Lucia Golf Links (✉*Indooroopilly Rd. at Carawa St., St. Lucia* ☎*07/3870–7084*) is an 18-hole, par-71 course open to visitors; greens fee, A$26–A$31. You can dine at one of two stylish options: the Clubhouse or the 100 Acre Bar (☎07/3870–3433) overlooking the 18th green.

TENNIS

Contact **Tennis Queensland** (✉*83 Castlemaine St., Milton* ☎*07/3871–8555* ⊕*www.tennis.com.au*) for information about playing at Brisbane's municipal or private courts and details on upcoming tournaments.

SHOPPING

DEPARTMENT STORES

The renowned **David Jones** (✉*Queens Plaza, 149 Adelaide St., City Center* ☎*07/3243–9000* ⊕*www.davidjones.com.au*), downtown in the Queen Street Mall, is open Monday–Thursday 9:30–6, Friday 9:30–9, Saturday 9–5:30, and Sunday 10–6.

Myer (✉*91 Queen St., City Center* ☎*07/3232–0121* ⊕*www.myer.com.au*), also in Queen Street Mall, is open Monday–Thursday 9–5:30, Friday 9–9, Saturday 9–5:30, and Sunday 10–5:30.

MALLS & ARCADES

The historic and aesthetically pleasing **Brisbane Arcade** (✉*160 Queen Street Mall, City Center* ☎*07/3831–2711*) joins Queen Street Mall and Adelaide Street and has elegant designer boutiques and jewelry shops.

Myer Centre (✉*Queen, Elizabeth, and Albert Sts., City Center* ☎*No phone*) houses the national department store of the same name, as well as boutiques, specialty shops, delis, restaurants, and cinemas.

The **Pavilion** (✉*Queen and Albert Sts., City Center*) has two levels of exclusive shops. **Queen Street Mall** (✉*City Center* ☎*07/3229–5918* ⊕*www.ourbrisbane.com.au*) is considered the best downtown shopping area, with numerous buskers and a generally festive crowd.

The nearest rival to Queen Street Mall's crown is the city's bustling new shopping center, **QueensPlaza** (✉*City Center* ☎*07/3234–3900*). Another new mall, **Brisbane Place,** is located opposite the Conrad Treasury Casino. **Rowes Arcade** (✉*235 Edward St., City Center* ☎*No phone*) is a rebuilt 1920s ballroom and banquet hall with boutique clothing stores.

Tattersalls Arcade (✉*Queen and Edward Sts., City Center* ☎*No phone*) caters to discerning shoppers with a taste for upscale designer labels.

Wintergarden Complex (✉*Queen Street Mall, City Center* ☎*07/3229–9755*) houses boutiques and specialty shops, as well as a food court.

MARKETS

The **Brisbane Powerhouse** (✉ *119 Lamington St., New Farm* ☎ *07/3358–8600* ⊕ *www.brisbanepowerhouse.com*) hosts a farmers' market (all produce) from 6 AM to noon on the second and fourth Saturdays of the month. Afterwards, stroll through glorious New Farm Park, nearby.

The **Riverside Markets** (✉ *Riverside Centre, 123 Eagle St., City Center* ☎ *07/3870–2807*), an upscale arts-and-crafts bazaar, sells everything from pressed flowers to hand-painted didgeridoos. It's open Sunday 8–3.

South Bank Parklands (✉ *Grey St. between Melbourne St. and the Goodwill Bridge, City Center* ☎ *07/3844–2440* ⊕ *www.southbankmarket.com.au*) hosts a Friday-night Market by Moonlight from 5 to 10, and the South Bank Lifestyle Market, with good-quality homemade clothing, art, crafts, and other items Saturday 10–5 and Sunday 9–5.

SPECIALTY STORES

ANTIQUES **Brisbane Antiques** (✉ *23 Crosby Rd., Albion* ☎ *07/3262–1444* ⊕ *www.brisbaneantiques.com.au*), near the airport, is a large store selling mostly 19th-century (Georgian, Edwardian, and Victorian) antiques, collectibles, metalware, and fine Banbury Cross jewelry.

Paddington Antique Centre (✉ *167 Latrobe Terr., Paddington* ☎ *07/3369–8088*) is a converted theater filled with antiques and bric-a-brac. Around 50 dealers operate within the center.

AUSTRALIAN **Australia The Gift** (✉ *150 Queen Street Mall, City Center* ☎ *07/3210–*
PRODUCTS *6198* ⊕ *www.australiathegift.com.au*) sells quality Australian-made handicrafts, including authentic Aboriginal artifacts, as well as postcards, books, and novelty items. It's open Monday–Saturday 8:30 AM–9 PM, Sunday 8:30–8. The on-site gallery, open daily 10–6, shows and sells work by Australian photographer Nick Rains.

Greg Grant Saddlery (✉ *683 Ipswich Rd., Annerley* ☎ *07/3892–2144* ⊕ *www.greggrantsaddlery.com.au*) specializes in the legendary Driza-Bone oilskin coats, Akubra and leather hats, whips, R. M. Williams boots, and moleskins.

SIDE TRIP TO SOUTHERN DOWNS

If the cityscapes of Brisbane have given you a thirst for pastoral rolling hills—and fabulous wine—the two-hour drive west on the Cunningham Highway to the Southern Downs is a must. This area, which ranges from Cunninghams Gap in the east to Goondiwindi in the west, to Allora in the north and Wallangarra in the south, is one of Queensland's premier wine-producing areas.

Spring brings the scent of peach and apple blossoms to the air here; in autumn the 40-odd vineyards are ripe for harvest. Winter brings wine-country excursions.

More than half a dozen companies run tours of wineries in the area, but most require groups of at least six people. Family-run **Cork 'n Fork Win-**

ery Tours (☎ *07/5543–6584 or 0407/144396* ⊕ *www.corknfork.com. au*) is an exception, running daily tours for couples and small groups. Their popular full-day tour includes hotel pickups, lunch, and five winery visits with guided tastings.

In the tiny, blink-and-you'll-miss-it town of Glen Aplin, 235 km (146 mi) southwest of Brisbane, is **Felsberg Winery.** Known for both its red and white wines (including award-winning merlot) and honey mead, this winery has a tasting room inside a German-inspired château, with hilltop views over the Severn River valley and the Granite Belt area. Guided tours are available on request. ⊠ *116 Townsends Rd., Glen Aplin* ☎ *07/4683–4332* ⊠ *Free* ⊙ *Daily 9:30–4:30.*

Just south of Glen Aplin is the town of Ballandean, home to the award-winning **Ballandean Estate Wines.** This property includes the oldest family-owned and -operated vineyard and winery in Queensland; the first grapes were grown on the site in 1931. There are tours of the facility at 11, 1, and 3. The tasting room is the original brick shed built in 1950, and the Barrel Room Cafe behind it—complete with massive 125-year-old wooden barrels lining one wall—serves light lunches and coffee. ⊠ *354 Sundown Rd., Ballandean* ☎ *07/4684–1226* ✑ enquiries@ballandeanestate.com ⊕ *www.ballandeanestate.com* ⊠ *Free* ⊙ *Daily 9–5.*

ⓒ **Girraween National Park,** one of the most popular parks in southeast Queensland, sits at the end of the New England Tableland, a stepped plateau area with elevations ranging from 1,968 feet to 4,921 feet. The 17 km (11 mi) of walking tracks, most starting near the information center and picnic area, wind past granite outcrops, precariously balanced rocks, eucalyptus forests, and wildflowers in spring. Along the way you might encounter kangaroos, echidnas, brush-tailed possums, turquoise parrots, and blue wrens. If you want to camp, you'll need an A$4.50 permit from the Queensland Parks and Wildlife Service. ⊠ *Ballandean, 4382* ✣ *11 km (7 mi) north of Wallangarra or 26 km (16 mi) south of Stanthorpe on the New England Hwy.* ☎ *07/4684–5157 (park info) or 13–1304 (permits)* ⊕ *www.qld.gov.au.*

WHERE TO STAY & EAT

$$–$$$
Fodor's Choice
★

✕⊡ **Vineyard Cottages and Café.** Built around a turn-of-the-20th-century church that is now the Vineyard Café, this property has four cottages and a row of two-story houses (known as terraces) set amid 2 acres of beautiful gardens, hedgerows, and arbors, two blocks from Ballandean village. The charming lodgings, built in the 1990s in a style that complements the rustic church, are furnished with comfortable sofas, colonial antique furniture, and vases brimming with roses from the gardens. The one-bedroom cottages (which have in-room hot tubs big enough for two) and terraces can sleep four people; the two-story, two-bedroom cottage accommodates up to seven. The guests' lounge has an open fireplace, bar, library, and games. Chef Janine Cumming, who co-owns the property with husband Peter, varies her menus seasonally to take advantage of fresh produce from local farms, and does a great gourmet hamper on request. ⊠ *New England Hwy., near Bents*

Rd.,Ballandean, 4382 ☎*07/4684–1270* 🖷*07/4684–1324* 🖉info@
vineyardcottages.com.au ⊕*www.vineyardcottages.com.au* 💬*4 cottages, 3 terraces* ♿*In-room: no a/c (some), fans (some), no phone,
kitchen (some), refrigerator/minibar, DVD, VCR (some), hot tub
(some). In-hotel: restaurant, room service, bar, massage, no-smoking
rooms, disabled access (one King Terrace)* 🗖AE, MC, V.

BRISBANE ESSENTIALS

TRANSPORTATION

AIR TRAVEL

Flight time from Brisbane to Bundaberg is 45 minutes; to Cairns, 2
hours; to Coolangatta, 30 minutes; to Emerald, 1 hour 40 minutes;
to Gladstone, 1 hour 15 minutes; to Hamilton Island, 1 hour 45 minutes; to Hervey Bay, 55 minutes; to Mackay, 1 hour 35 minutes; to
Maroochydore, 25 minutes; to Maryborough, 45 minutes; to Rockhampton, 1 hour 10 minutes; to Townsville, 1 hour 50 minutes, and to
Sydney 1 hour 30 minutes.

AIRLINES Brisbane is Queensland's major travel crossing point. Many international airlines have head offices in the city center as well as information
booths at the airport. Qantas and Virgin Blue Airlines fly to all Australian capital cities and most cities within Queensland. Jetstar links
Brisbane with Cairns, Hamilton Island, Mackay, Proserpine, and Rockhampton, as well as the Gold and Sunshine coasts.

Many international carriers fly to and from Brisbane. Air Nauru, Air
Vanuatu, and Solomon Airlines link Brisbane with islands in the South
Pacific. Air New Zealand, Air Pacific, Cathay Pacific, EVA Airways,
Garuda Indonesia, Malaysian Airlines, Royal Brunei Airlines, Singapore
Airlines, and Thai Airways fly between Brisbane and points throughout
Asia, with connections to Europe and the U.S. West Coast.

Contacts Air Nauru (✉*Level 4, 97 Creek St., City Center* ☎*07/3229–6455
or 1300/369044).* **Air New Zealand** (✉*Level 7, 360 Queen St., City Center*
☎*13–2476).* **Air Pacific** (✉*Level 2, 410 Queen St., City Center* ☎*1800/230150).*
Air Vanuatu (✉*Level 5, 293 Queen St., City Center* ☎*1300/780737).* **Cathay
Pacific Airways** (✉*Level 1, Brisbane International Airport, Airport Dr., Eagle Farm*
☎*13–1747).* **EVA Air** (✉*127 Creek St., City Center* ☎*07/3229–8000).* **Garuda
Indonesia** (✉*340 Adelaide St., City Center* ☎*1300/365330).* **Jetstar** (✉*Brisbane
International Airport, Eagle Farm, Brisbane* ☎*13–1538* ⊕*www.jetstar.com.au).*
Qantas (✉*247 Adelaide St., City Center* ☎*07/3238–2700 or 13–1313* ⊕*www.
qantas.com.au).* **Singapore Airlines** (✉*Level 19, 344 Queen St., City Center*
☎*13–1011).* **Thai Airways** (✉*410 Queen St., City Center* ☎*07/3215–4700).* **Virgin Blue** (✉*Level 7, Centenary Sq., 100 Wickham St., Fortitude Valley* ☎*13–6789*
⊕*www.virginblue.com.au).*

AIRPORT Brisbane International Airport is 9 km (5½ mi) from the city center.
&TRANSFERS Coachtrans provides a daily bus service to and from Roma Street Station and Brisbane city and Gold Coast hotels every 30 minutes between
5 AM and 9 PM. From the airport, the first shuttle goes at 6 AM and the

last at midnight. The one-way fare is A$9–A$11 per person; the round-trip fare is A$15–A$18.

Airtrain has train services to Central Station and other stations throughout Brisbane and the Gold Coast. The one-way fare is A$12 per person, or A$22 round-trip. Trains depart up to four times an hour and it takes 20 minutes to reach the city center.

Taxis to downtown Brisbane cost A$40 to A$50, depending on time of day.

Contacts Airtrain (☎07/3216–3308 ⊕ www.airtrain.com.au). **Brisbane International Airport** (✉ Airport Dr., Eagle Farm ☎07/3406–3191). **Coachtrans** (☎07/3358–9700 ⊕ www.coachtrans.com.au).

BOAT & FERRY TRAVEL
Speedy CityCat ferries, operated byTranslink, dock at 14 points along the Brisbane River, from Bretts Wharf to the University of Queensland. They run daily about every half hour between 6 AM and 10:30 PM. The CityCat ferries are terrific for taking a leisurely look at Brisbane river life. From the city skyline to the homes of the well-heeled, there's always something of interest to see.

Contact CityCat ferries (☎13–1230 ⊕ www.translink.com.au).

BUS TRAVEL
Greyhound Australia, the country's only nationwide bus line, travels to more than 1,000 destinations all over Australia. Bus stops are well signposted, and vehicles almost always run on schedule. It's 1,716 km (1,064 mi) and 30-plus hours between Brisbane and Cairns. Greyhound Australia's Roma Street office is open daily from 6 AM to 6:45 PM; you can also book by phone or online. Purchase point-to-point tickets, or flexible passes, such as the prepaid Aussie Explorer or Aussie Kilometre Pass, that allow multiple stops.

Crisps Coaches operates a regular daily service to the Southern Downs area from Brisbane, as well as towns to the south and west.

Trans Info's help line and Web site can help you find bus lines that run to your destination.

Contacts Crisps Coaches (✉ Warwick Transit Centre ☎07/3236–5266). **Greyhound Australia** (✉ Brisbane Transit Centre, Roma St., City Center ☎07/3236–2020 or 13–1499 ⊕ www.greyhound.com.au). **Trans Info** (☎13–1230 ⊕ www.transinfo.qld.gov.au).

CAR RENTAL
Most major car-rental companies have offices in Brisbane, including Avis, Thrifty, and Budget. Four-wheel-drive vehicles, motor homes, and camper vans (which sleep two to six people) are available from Britz Campervan Rentals, Maui Rentals, and Kea Campers. If you're heading north along the coast or northwest into the bush, you can rent in Brisbane and drop off in Cairns or other towns. One-way rental fees usually apply.

Contacts **Britz Campervan Rentals** (✉ *647 Kingsford Smith Dr., Eagle Farm* ☎ *07/3630–1151* ⊕ *www.britz.com.au*). **Kea Campers** (✉ *348 Nudgee Rd., Hendra* ☎ *1800/252555 or 07/3868–4500* ⊕ *www.keacampers.com*). **Maui Rentals** (✉ *647 Kingsford Smith Dr., Eagle Farm* ☎ *1300/363800 or 07/3630–1153* ⊕ *www.maui-rentals.com*).

CAR TRAVEL
Brisbane is 1,002 km (621 mi) from Sydney, a 12-hour drive along the Pacific Highway (Highway 1). Another route follows Highway 1 to Newcastle, then heads inland on the New England Highway (Highway 15). Either drive can be made in a long day, although two days or more are recommended for ample time to sightsee.

TAXIS
Taxis are metered and relatively inexpensive. They are available at designated taxi stands outside hotels, downtown, and at the railway station, although it is often best to phone for one.

Contacts **Black and White Cabs** (✉ *11 Dryandra Rd., Eagle Farm* ☎ *13–1008* ✉ *Brisbane International Airport* ☎ *07/3860–1800* ⊕ *www.blackandwhitecabs.com.au*). **Yellow Cabs** (✉ *116 Logan Rd., Woolloongabba* ☎ *13–1924* ⊕ *www.yellowcab.com.au*).

TRAIN TRAVEL

CountryLink trains make the 15-hour journey between Sydney and Brisbane. Service from Brisbane to the Gold Coast runs regularly from 5:30 AM until midnight. The *Sunlander* runs up Queensland's coast from Brisbane four times weekly. Cairns-bound trains, departing on Sunday and Thursday (returning Tuesday and Saturday) include luxurious *Queenslander* class carriages with comfortable twin-berth sleeping cabins, fine food and wine, and maître d's commentary. The trip takes around 32 hours. Tuesday and Saturday Sunlander services, minus *Queenslander* class, terminate at Townsville (returning Wednesday and Sunday) and take around 24 hours.

The speedy, state-of-the-art *Tilt Train* runs between Brisbane and Rockhampton daily except Saturday; from Brisbane to Bundaberg Monday–Thursday; and from Brisbane to Cairns (a comparatively quick 25-hour trip) on Tuesdays and Saturdays, stopping at towns including Mackay (13.5 hrs), Proserpine (15 hrs), and Townsville (20 hrs), and returning the following day.

Other long-distance passenger trains from Brisbane include the *Westlander*, to Charleville (twice weekly, from Brisbane Tuesday and Thursday, returning from Charlesville Wednesday and Friday); and the *Spirit of the Outback*, to Longreach, via Rockhampton (twice weekly, departing Brisbane Tuesday and Saturday, Longreach Monday and Thursday). Trains depart from the Roma Street Station. For details contact Queensland Rail Travel Centre.

Contact **Queensland Rail Travel Centre Traveltrain Holidays** (✉ *Central Station, Roma St., City Center* ☎ *07/3235–1323 or 1300/131722* ⊕ *www.qr.com.au*).

CONTACTS & RESOURCES

EMERGENCIES

Dial **000** for an ambulance, the police, or the fire department.

The Travel Clinic is a medical center specializing in travel-related medicines, vaccinations, etc. Consultations cost A$55. The staff can also recommend dentists and pharmacies. It's open Monday–Thursday 7:30 AM–7 PM, Friday 8–6, Saturday 8:30–5, and Sunday 9:30–5. Two pharmacies with extended hours are Delahunty's and Queen Street Mall.

Doctors & Hospitals Royal Brisbane Hospital (⊠ *Herston Rd., Herston* ☎ *07/3636–8111*). **The Travel Clinic** (⊠ *Level 1, 245 Albert St., City Center* ☎ *07/3211–3611 or 0412/452400 after hrs* ⊕ *www.cbdmedical.com.au*).

Pharmacies Delahunty's Costless Pharmacy (⊠ *245 Albert St., City Center* ☎ *07/3221–8155*).**Queen Street Mall Day & Night Pharmacy** (⊠ *141 Queen St., City Center* ☎ *07/3221–4585*).

TOURS

Australian Day Tours conducts half- and full-day tours of Brisbane, as well as trips to the Gold Coast, Noosa Heads, and the Sunshine Coast, from A$48 to A$189, and a three-day Fraser Island tour for A$669 per person.

City Sights, run by the Brisbane City Council, operates air-conditioned buses that make circuits of city landmarks and other points of interest, including South Bank and Chinatown. They leave from Post Office Square every 45 minutes, starting at 9 AM, with the last departure at 3:45 PM. You can buy tickets on the bus and get on or off at any of the 19 stops for A$22.

Kookaburra River Queens is a paddle wheeler that runs lunch and dinner cruises on the Brisbane River. The lunch cruises include scenic and historic commentary; live entertainment and dancing are highlights of the dinner cruise. The weekend seafood buffet dinner cruise is especially popular. Tours run A$30–A$95 per person.

Brisbane City Walks and the *Brisbane CBD Walking Guide* are informative brochures put out by the Brisbane City Council and Our Brisbane, available from tourist information offices and many hotels.

Contacts Australian Day Tours (⊠ *Level 3, Brisbane Transit Centre, Roma St., City Center* ☎ *07/3489–6444 or 1300/363436* ⊕ *www.daytours.com.au*). **City Sights and walking guides** (⊠ *Brisbane City Council, 69 Ann St., City Center* ☎ *13–1230* ⊕ *www.brisbane.qld.gov.au*). **Kookaburra River Queens** (⊠ *Eagle Street Pier, 1 Eagle St., City Center* ☎ *07/3221–1300* ⊕ *www.kookaburrariverqueens.com*).

VISITOR INFORMATION

The Brisbane Marketing Visitor Information Centre is open Monday–Thursday 9–5:30, Friday 9–7, Saturday 9–5, and Sunday 9:30–4:30. The Southern Downs Tourist Association runs a tourist information center at Warwick, open 8:30–5 daily.

Contacts Brisbane Marketing Visitor Information Centre (⊠ *George St., Box 12260, 4003* ⊠ *Queen Street Mall, City Center* ☎ *07/3006–6200* ⊕ *www.bris-*

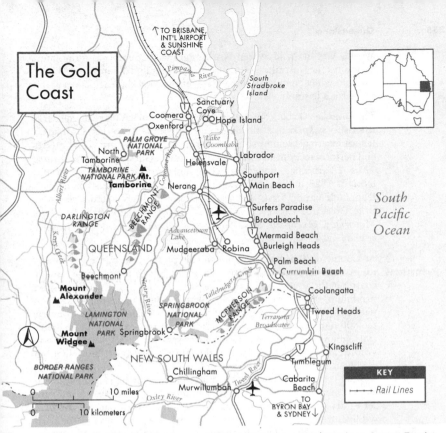

The Gold Coast

TO BRISBANE, INT'L AIRPORT & SUNSHINE COAST

South Pacific Ocean

QUEENSLAND

NEW SOUTH WALES

KEY

↦ Rail Lines

0 ━━━━ 10 miles
0 ━━━━ 10 kilometers

banemarketing.com.au and www.ourbrisbane.com.au).**Southern Downs Tourist Association** (✉ 49 Albion St., Warwick ☎ 07/4661-3122 ⊕ www.southern-downsholidays.info).

THE GOLD COAST

Three hundred days of sunshine a year and an average temperature of 24°C (75°F) ensure the popularity of the Gold Coast, the most developed tourist destination in Australia, with plenty of amusement complexes and resorts. December through the last week of January, and Easter weekend are peak seasons. An hour south of Brisbane, the Gold Coast stretches some 70 km (43 mi) from Labrador in the north to Coolangatta–Tweed Heads in the south, and has now sprawled as far inland as Nerang. It has 35 patrolled beaches and 446 km (277 mi) of canals and tidal rivers, nine times the length of the canals of Venice.

COOMERA & OXENFORD

48–51 km (30–32 mi) south of Brisbane.

The biggest draw of these two northern Gold Coast suburbs are the family-oriented theme parks—Dreamworld, Warner Bros. Movie

World, Wet 'n' Wild Water World, Paradise Country, and the latest additions, the Australian Outback Spectacular and WhiteWater World. The sprawling complexes have many attractions and each takes about a day for a leisurely visit.

☺ The **Australian Outback Spectacular,** the latest Warner Village theme park, lets visitors experience "the heart and soul of the Australian Outback." It's an exciting evening show featuring state-of-the-art visual effects and performances from top local stunt riders. Guests get a three-course "Aussie barbecue" dinner and complimentary drinks during the 90-minute, A$23 million extravaganza, plus a souvenir stockman's hat. Doors open at 6:15 PM, and showtime is at 7:30 PM. Return transfers from Gold Coast hotels cost A$15; on-site parking is free. ⊠*Pacific Motorway, Oxenford* ☎*07/5573–8289* ⊕*www.outbackspectacular. com.au* ☜*A$95.*

☺ **Fodor'sChoice ★** At Coomera's **Dreamworld,** you can ride on the fastest, highest ride in the world, the Tower of Terror; the tallest high-speed gravity roller coaster in the Southern Hemisphere, the Cyclone; or the world's largest pendulum, the Claw. You can also watch Bengal tigers play and swim with their handlers on Tiger Island, cuddle a koala in Koala Country, see 800 native animals at the Wildlife Sanctuary, cool off in an artificial lagoon, or cruise the park's waterways on a paddle wheeler. Bring swimwear and you can also try the latest boardsport: Flowrider, an amalgam of surfing and skateboarding. The *Big Brother* house, used for the Australian version of the hit reality TV show, is here, and you can go inside when the show isn't filming. A guided, two-hour Sunset Safari (A$15) promises close-up encounters with tigers and native wildlife, from 4:45 PM in season. The park is 45 minutes outside Brisbane and 25–30 minutes from Surfers Paradise along the M1 Pacific Motorway: take exit 54 at Coomera. ⊠*Dreamworld Pkwy., Coomera* ☎*07/5588–1111 or 1800/073300* ⊕*www.dreamworld.com.au* ☜*A$64 park entry; A$5 per half-hour FlowRider session with Dreamworld entry, or A$20 an hour, NightRider pass; A$99 2-Day World Pass (2 entries each to Dreamworld & Whitewater World; second visits within 14 days)* ⊙*Daily 10–5; Flowrider 10–4:30; NightRider Thurs. and Fri. 5–10.*

☺ **Fodor'sChoice ★** Next door to Dreamworld, and under the same management, is the Gold Coast's latest thrill-seeking theme park, **WhiteWater World.** Here, you'll find state-of-the-art water rides including the Blue Ringed Octopus (BRO), a convoluted 8-lane racer slide; The Rip—Australia's biggest corkscrew-cored whirlpool; an inner-tube "aquacoaster" ride packed with serpentine curves, drops, slides, and 360° turns known as the Temple of Huey; and The Green Room, a 20-meter-high "tube" simulating the inside of a monster wave. Anklebiters will enjoy Nickelodeon's Pipeline Plunge, with 100-plus watery activities. Toddlers can play safely at Wiggle Bay, with its pint-size water slides, water cannons, shade, and supervision. The park is 48 km [25 mi], or around 45 minutes' drive, from Brisbane, 17 km [10.5 mi] or 25–30 minutes' drive from Surfers Paradise along the M1 (exit 54 at Coomera). ⊠*Dreamworld Pkwy., Coomera* ☎*07/5588–1111 or 1800/073300*

⊕ *www.dreamworld.com.au* 🎟️ *A$42 park entry; A$99 2-Day World Pass* 🕐 *Daily 10:30–4:30.*

🔄 **Paradise Country.** Billed as "an authentic Australian farm experience," the park appeals to families with three half-day farm tours beginning at 9:30 AM, 11:45 AM, and 1 PM. You'll see displays of horsemanship, sheep-shearing, boomerang-throwing, and whip-cracking. Kids will enjoy koala cuddling and kangaroo feeding. An optional barbecue lunch is accompanied by bush dancing and Aussie-theme live entertainment. The park is directly behind Warner Bros. Movie World. ✉️ *Pacific Motorway, Oxenford* ☎️ *07/5573–8270 or 07/5588–2412* ⊕ *www.paradisecountry.com.au* 🎟️ *A$27 (farm tour only), A$43 (tour and lunch)* 🕐 *Daily 9:30–4:15.*

🔄 **Warner Bros. Movie World,** one of the few movie theme parks outside the United States, lets you share virtual space with an animated ogre in the eye-popping *Shrek* 4D Adventure, play airborne super-hero on the Batwing Spaceshot, or travel 96 km (60 mi) an hour in just two seconds on the awesome new Superman Escape ride. You can also check out the props, sets, and costumes of the *Matrix* films, shot in Sydney, laugh at the antics of the *Police Academy* stunt show, and rocket through the spine-tingling Scooby-Doo Spooky Coaster. Little kids will want to see the daily Main Street Star Parade and visit Bugs Bunny and friends at Looney Tunes Village. Take center stage in (then buy) your own music video at the Hi-5 Be A Star studio, or indulge yourself at numerous outlets selling Warner Bros. souvenirs. ✉️ *Pacific Motorway, Oxenford* ☎️ *07/5573–8495* ⊕ *www.movieworld.com.au* 🎟️ *A$64* 🕐 *Daily 10–5.*

🔄 Oxenford's **Wet 'n' Wild Water Park** has magnificent waterslides, including the aptly named Mammoth Falls, Terror Canyon II, and Super-8 Aqua Racer; a giant whirlpool; a wave pool with 3-foot-high surf; and a new Extreme H20 zone, in which you can plunge down pitch-black spirals of water in the Black Hole, hang on through the churning Tornado, or survive the scary Mach 5. Enough aquatic thrills? Take it easy on Calypso Beach, a "tropical island" fringed with white-sand beaches and a slow-moving river in which you can laze about in brightly colored tubes; or chill out at a Dive'n'Movie. Keep kids entertained at Buccaneer Bay, a state-of-the-art aquatic playground with multiple levels. The park is ½ km (¼ mi) down the Pacific Highway from Warner Bros. Movie World. ✉️ *Pacific Hwy., Oxenford* ☎️ *07/5556–1660* ✉️ *info@wetnwild.com.au* ⊕ *www.wetnwild.com.au* 🎟️ *A$42* 🕐 *Daily 10–5.*

WHERE TO STAY

$$$$ 🏨 **Ruffles Lodge.** The architect-designed, immaculate luxury lodge is 5 km (3 mi) from Dreamworld, but its tranquil location makes it seem worlds away. Set high on a hill, surrounded by forest and manicured gardens, five private villas, three tree houses, and an executive lodge suite with an expansive separate living room have views to the Gold Coast beaches and high-rises as well as the surrounding bushland. The tree-house villas have their own plunge pools, while the spacious spa

villas and elegant executive lodge suite have wood-burning fireplaces, hot tubs, plasma TVs, and high-speed Internet connections. Owners John and Jan Nicholls create a comfortable environment, with a choice of dinner-party-style or private meals in the main lodge's view-rich, sleekly refurbished dining room. Predinner drinks, hors d'oeuvres, and a three-course set dinner cost A$60 per person. Between meals, get pampered at Ruffles' tranquil day spa. ⊠ *423 Ruffles Rd., Willow Vale, 4209* ☎ *07/5546–7411* ⊕ *www.ruffleslodge.com.au* ⊘ *jj@ ruffleslodge.com.au* ⤳ *5 villas, 3 tree houses, 1 suite* ⚘ *In-room: no TV, safe (some), refrigerator (minibar), DVD, dial-up, Wi-Fi (some). In-hotel: restaurant, room service, bar, pool, spa, public Internet, public Wi-Fi, airport shuttle, parking (no fee), no-smoking rooms, no kids under 14, no smoking, no elevator* ⊟ *AE, DC, MC, V* ⧍ *BP.*

HOPE ISLAND

6 km (4 mi) east of Oxenford.

This isn't your average island with swaying palm trees and white-sand beaches. Like several Gold Coast islands, it is actually a mile or two inland, and is circled by the Coomera River and a series of canals. The resort has a marina full of luxury launches and yachts, two golf courses, a swanky hotel, beautiful condos, and upscale restaurants, nightclubs, and shops. Beyond the gates of Sanctuary Cove there are also a handful of other hotels and a shopping center.

Hope Island is accessed via bridges from both the west side (the towns of Oxenford and Coomera) and the eastern, coastal side (from Paradise Point, Hollywell, and Runaway Bay). Route 4, also known as the Oxenford–Southport Road, begins in Oxenford at Pacific Highway's Exit 57 and travels through Hope Island on its way to the coast.

WHERE TO STAY

$$$–$$$$ ⌗ **Hyatt Regency Sanctuary Cove.** Landscaped tropical gardens surround
☾ this opulent low-rise hotel, which resembles a monumental Australian
★ colonial mansion. Each luxuriously appointed room has parquet flooring, plantation shutters, and colonial-style furnishings, including one king-size or two double sleigh beds, plus a large, furnished balcony. Guests in club rooms and suites have free access to a private lounge that serves light breakfasts and pre-dinner cocktails and hors d'oevres. Spa Chakra delivers restorative massages and treatments. The sandy beach lagoon next to the hotel's main harbor is fed with filtered saltwater, and a walkway from the hotel leads directly to the main resort village. ⊠ *Casey's Rd., Sanctuary Cove, 4212* ☎ *07/5530–1234* ⊘ *sanctuary@hyatt.com.au* ⊕ *www.sanctuarycove.hyatt.com* ⤳ *223 rooms, 24 suites* ⚘ *In-room: kitchen (some), refrigerator/minibar, hot tub (some), DVD/VCR (some), ethernet, Wi-Fi (some). In-hotel: 5 restaurants, room service, bars, golf course, pools, spa, beachfront, concierge, safe, children's programs (ages 4–12), laundry service, public Internet, public Wi-Fi, business center, parking (no fee), some pets allowed, no-smoking rooms, no elevator* ⊟ *AE, DC, MC, V.*

SOUTH STRADBROKE ISLAND

1 km (½ mi) east of the Gold Coast.

White-sand beaches, diverse flora and fauna, and a peaceful interior draw visitors to South Stradbroke Island, which is just 22 km (12 mi) long and 2 km (1 mi) wide. The island and its northern neighbor (North Stradbroke Island) were once connected, but in 1896 a fierce storm separated them at a narrow neck called Jumpinpin. Unlike its northern namesake, South "Straddie" is less populated and does not have a public ferry service. It's a good spot for fishing and boating.

You can get to the island by taking one of the boat services operated by the three island resorts. Couran Cove Island Resort (☎1800/268726) operates multiple return trips a day leaving Hope Harbour terminal at 10:30, 2, 4, and 6, and returning at 9, noon, 3, 5, and 7, with extra services on weekends.

WHERE TO STAY

$$$$ ▣ **Couran Cove Island Resort.** Just 35 minutes by boat from the glitz of the Gold Coast, this ecotourism resort is a haven of peace and harmony. The vision of Olympic athlete Ron Clarke, a long-distance runner, the property has an exceptionally wide selection of sports opportunities: biking, swimming, tennis, rock climbing, baseball, basketball, various water sports, and more. There's also an Aboriginal culture center, a gallery and art studio, a tour desk and a general store, as well as music, games, and Internet rooms. The marine resort area includes deluxe rooms, suites, and two- and four-bedroom lodges (all with kitchenettes and cooking facilities). Some are built over the water so you can fish right off the balcony. The resort's nature cabins were refurbished in 2007. ⊠*Hope Harbour Marina, John Lund Ave., Hope Harbour, South Stradbroke Island,4212* ☎*07/5509–3000 or 1800/268726* ⊕*www.couran.com* ⇄*95 rooms, 92 suites, 22 lodges, 16 villas* ⟁*In-room: safe, kitchen (some), refrigerator, ethernet (some), dial-up (some). In-hotel: 4 restaurants, room service (some), bars, tennis courts, pool, gym, spa, beachfront, water sports, bicycles, children's programs (ages 3–14), laundry facilities, laundry service, concierge, business center, public Internet, airport shuttle (fee), parking (fee), no-smoking rooms, disabled access (no elevator)* ▭*AE, DC, MC, V.*

SOUTHPORT & MAIN BEACH

16 km (10 mi) southeast of Oxenford.

South of Southport, look for the turnoff to the **Spit,** a natural peninsula that stretches 4 km (2½ mi) north, almost to the tip of South Stradbroke Island. Sea World Drive runs the full length of the Spit, from Mariner's Cove (a popular covered area with affordable restaurants and fast-food outlets) to a nature reserve. This narrow peninsula is bordered by the Pacific Ocean to the east and the calm waters of the Broadwater (a long lagoon) to the west. Two of the Gold Coast's best hotels face each other across Sea World Drive and are connected to

Marina Mirage, arguably the most elegant shopping precinct on the Gold Coast. Farther up the road is Sea World itself.

🐾 **Sea World,** Australia's largest marine theme park, has four daily shows that highlight the resident dolphins and sea lions, as well as three resident polar bears in a state-of-the-art home, an endangered dugong exhibit, and various other marine creatures. Don't miss Shark Bay, the world's largest artificial lagoon system for sharks, an innovative dual enclosure with dangerous tiger sharks in one section and harmless reef sharks, rays, and fish in another. Patrons can snorkel in the latter, then get close-up views of the predators through the massive windows that separate the lagoons. Rides include a monorail, a corkscrew roller coaster, waterslides, and Sea World Eye, a 60-metre (195-foot) high observation wheel offering bird's-eye views of the action. ⊠ *Seaworld Dr. (at end of this long street), The Spit, Main Beach* ☎ *07/5588–2222* ⊕ *www.seaworld.com.au* ⊠ *A$64* ⊙ *Daily 10–5.*

WHERE TO STAY & EAT

$–$$$ ✕**Omeros Bros. Seafood Restaurant.** The Omeros brothers, who arrived from Greece in 1953, have operated seafood restaurants in eastern Australia for more than 30 years. This one on the waterfront at the lovely Marina Mirage center provides an entire menu of seafood—from bouillabaisse, barbecued prawns, mussels, and barramundi to classic surf-and-turf, lobsters, and mud crabs. There are also meat, vegetarian, and pasta dishes. ⊠ *Marina Mirage, Seaworld Dr.* ☎ *07/5591–7222* ⊕ *www.omerosbros.com* ⊟ *AE, DC, MC, V.*

$–$$$ ✕**Saks.** Perched on the edge of the Broadwater and just a short boardwalk away from Palazzo Versace is this hip restaurant and bar, with both indoor and outdoor areas. Relax on faux-suede lounge seats and ottomans while nibbling tapas, or nab a waterside table. Savor one of the steak or seafood dishes, or go for broke with the Saks Sensation: Moreton Bay bugs, king prawns, scallops, and eye fillet, for A$49. Live music on Friday, Saturday, and Sunday nights attracts a crowd. ⊠ *Marina Mirage, 74 Seaworld Dr., Main Beach* ☎ *07/5591–2755* ⊕ *www.saksrestaurantandbar.com* ⊟ *AE, DC, MC, V.*

$$$$
Fodor's Choice
★
🏨**Palazzo Versace.** Sink into one of the sofas, armchairs, or circular banquettes in the sensational lobby, refurbished in 2006 but still very Versace, and watch the beautiful people walk by. The Italian fashion house lent its flair to this stunning hotel, the first of its kind in the world. The original marble-and-mosaic tiled floor and gigantic chandelier remain, but the ornate marbled columns have been reborn as sleek, cream, black-topped pillars and are offset by tropical foliage and opulent soft furnishings in turquoise and fuschia. Rooms in low-rise wings surround a lagoon pool edged with palm trees and a sandy artificial beach. Some have balconies with views over the Broadwater; others look out at the pool. Condos have full kitchens and laundries; some come with private plunge pools, barbecues, and marina berths. The signature restaurant, Vanitas, serves fine French-Mediterranean cuisine; Vie's contemporary Australian menu is a relaxed alternative. ⊠ *94 Seaworld Dr., adjoining Marina Mirage, Main Beach, 4217* ☎ *07/5509–8000* ⊕ *www.palaz-*

zoversace.com 🛏*151 rooms, 54 suites* ♿*In-room: safe, refrigerator, dial-up, hot tub, DVD, CD, ethernet. In-hotel: 3 restaurants, room service, bars, pool, gym, spa, concierge, laundry service, public Internet, public Wi-Fi, airport shuttle, parking (no fee), no-smoking rooms* 🖃*AE, DC, MC, V* 🍽*BP.*

$$$$ 🖵 **Sheraton Mirage Resort & Spa.** A
Fodor'sChoice cascading waterfall, floor-to-ceil-
★ ing glass walls, and creamy marble
floors create a Zen atmosphere in the light-filled lobby of this low-rise resort. Tasteful rooms have either terraces or views of 35 acres of gardens, the surf, or the lagoon on which glide the resort's signature white swans. A secluded gate leads from the sprawling grounds to a long, often-deserted strip of beach. The health club is a branch of the renowned Golden Door Spa, which has holistic treatments. An aerial bridge links the hotel with the elegant Marina Mirage shopping center. ⊠*Seaworld Dr., Main Beach, 4217* ☎*07/5591–1488* ⊕*www.sheraton.com/goldcoast* 🛏*251 rooms, 11 suites, 35 villas* ♿*In-room: safe, kitchen (some), refrigerator/minibar, hot tub (some), DVD (some), VCR (some), ethernet. In-hotel: 2 restaurants, room service, 3 bars, tennis courts, pool, gym, spa, beachfront, concierge, laundry service, public Internet, public Wi-Fi, no-smoking rooms* 🖃*AE, DC, MC, V.*

SHOPPING

Marina Mirage Gold Coast (⊠*74 Seaworld Dr., Main Beach* ☎*07/5555–6400 or 07/5528–2328* ⊕*www.marinamirage.com.au*) is perhaps the most beautiful place on the Gold Coast for retail and food therapy. Among the 80-plus stores are designer boutiques including Nautica, Louis Vuitton, La Perla, Hermès, and Versace, along with famous Australian stores, many fine waterfront restaurants, and marina facilities. On the first, third, and fifth Saturday of each month, pick up fresh gourmet produce between 7 and noon at the Marina Mirage Farmers Markets.

SURFERS PARADISE

5 km (3 mi) south of Southport, 72 km (45 mi) south of Brisbane.

Before the Gold Coast existed as a tourism entity, there was Surfers Paradise, a long, 3-km (2-mi) stretch of beach and great surf. Now overrun with a glut of high-rises all jammed into a few square miles, it's still a vibrant beachside town that draws a good mix of overseas travelers, students, and families.

The heart of Surfers is bordered by Elkhorn and Cavill avenues, the beachfront Esplanade, and Surfers Paradise Boulevard. Here you'll find souvenir shops, restaurants, and bars. Office workers and visitors lunch along Cavill Avenue; at night the young and the boisterous fill the bars and parlors.

☾ If the attractions and crowds haven't satisfied your need for visual stimulation in Surfers Paradise, the displays at **Ripley's Believe It or Not! Museum** may give you that extra thrill. Here you'll find models of the world's tallest man and the world's largest man, and a pair of African fertility statues that bring good luck to women who rub them—according to Ripley's, they have been responsible for well over 50 confirmed pregnancies. ⊠*Raptis Plaza, Cavill Ave.* ☎*07/5592–0040* ⊕*www. ripleys.com.au* ⊒*A$15* ☉*Daily 9* AM*–11* PM.

Surfers Paradise hosts the annual **Lexmark Indy 300** (☎*07/5588–6800* ⊕*www.indy.com.au*) for four days in late October. It's the biggest event on the local calendar, with streets blocked off to create a challenging course for the world's top speed demons. The track follows a loop around the streets of Surfers Paradise, Main Beach, and MacIntosh Island. The race (and dozens of off-track events) brings revelers from around the globe.

☾ On Wednesday and Friday nights the beachfront promenade spills over with crafts and gifts at the **Surfers Paradise Beachfront Markets,** held throughout the year. The market's theme is "make it, bake it, grow it," and finds include exotic home wares, ceramics, jewelry, cosmetics, children's toys and games, leather goods, and oils and potions. ⊠*Esplanade beachfront promenade between Hanlan St. and Elkhorn Ave.* ☎*No phone* ⊕*www.surfersparadise.com* ⊒*Free* ☉*Wed. and Fri. 5–10.*

WHERE TO STAY & EAT

\$\$–\$\$\$ ✕**Grumpy's Wharf Restaurant.** Towering coconut palms shade this quiet restaurant on the bank of the Nerang River, but it's still just a short walk to all the action of Surfers Paradise. Eat on the terrace before fine river views, or take an exquisitely prepared meal in the elegant Sante Fe dining room. The Adobe Bar has comfortable lounges, while the candle-filled Courtyard is frequented by couples. Seafood platters, fish cooked to order, mud crabs, and super-fresh lobsters (choose them from a tank) are the main fare. There are also steak, pasta, and vegetarian dishes. ⊠*Tiki Village, Cavill Ave., river end* ☎*07/5531–6177* ⊒*AE, DC, MC, V.*

\$–\$\$ ✕**Sayas Restaurant Café Bar.** A magnificent Inca-style bungalow lends an exotic feel to this eatery on the grounds of the Outrigger Sun City Resort. The Modern Australian cuisine blends Asian, Mediterranean, and Moroccan flavors, with the menu changing seasonally. ⊠*Ocean Ave. at Gold Coast Hwy.* ☎*07/5584–6060* ⊒*AE, DC, MC, V* ☉*No lunch.*

\$\$\$\$ 🏨**Gold Coast International Hotel.** In the heart of Surfers Paradise, this hotel is a block from the beach, with views of the Pacific Ocean or the Gold Coast hinterland from almost every one of the luxurious rooms, all refurbished in 2006–2007. If the beach seems too far, there's a heated pool with a swim-up bar. Wander down from your relaxed, beachy quarters to the stylish lobby bar or the Yamagen Japanese Restaurant, where the entertaining chefs perform culinary magic at teppanyaki tables. ⊠ *7 Staghorn Ave. at Gold Coast Hwy., 4217* ☎ *07/5584–1200* ✐ res@gci.com.au ⊕ *www.gci.com.au* ↝ *296 rooms, 21 suites* ⚹ *In-room: safe, refrigerator, hot tub (some), ethernet, Wi-Fi (some). In-hotel: 3 restaurants, room service, bars, tennis courts, pool, gym, spa, concierge, beachfront, diving, water sports, laundry facilities, laundry service, business center, public Internet, public Wi-Fi, parking (fee), no-smoking rooms, disabled access* ▭ *AE, DC, MC, V.*

$$$$ 🏨 **Moroccan Resort Apartments.** Opposite a lifeguard-patrolled section of ☾ the beach, these white Mediterranean-style apartments contrast strikingly with the blue of the sky and water. The pick of the three towers is the Esplanade, which faces the beach. The one- and two-bedroom apartments are spacious and well-appointed; the oceanfront premium suites have panoramic Pacific views and hot tubs. All are well equipped with kitchen and laundry facilities, separate lounge areas, and dining settings. There's a minimum stay of seven days in high season. ⊠ *14 View Ave., 4217* ☎ *07/5526–9400 or 1800/501880 (bookings)* ✐ info@moroccan.com.au ⊕ *www.moroccan.com.au* ↝ *80 apartments* ⚹ *In-room: no a/c (some), fans (some), kitchen, refrigerator, laundry facilities, dial-up. In-hotel: 2 pools, hot tubs, parking (no fee)* ▭ *AE, DC, MC, V.*

$$$–$$$$ 🏨 **Surfers Paradise Marriott Resort & Spa.** The lobby's giant columns ☾ and grand circular staircase, cooled by a colorful Indian *punkah* (a **Fodor's**Choice decorative, rope-operated fan), typify this hotel's opulent style. The ★ large guest rooms, decorated in gentle hues of beige, light plum, and moss green, have walk-in closets, marble bathrooms, balconies, and ocean and river views. The fish-filled lagoon swimming pool has a sandy beach and a cave grotto with a waterfall and is deep enough for scuba lessons or snorkeling. There's also a meandering freshwater pool. You can rent windsurfing equipment, water-skis, and catamarans to take on the river. ⊠ *158 Ferny Ave., 4217* ☎ *07/5592–9800* ⊕ *www.marriott.com/sdsp* ↝ *300 rooms, 30 suites* ⚹ *In-room: safe, refrigerator/minibar, Wi-Fi. In-hotel: 2 restaurants, room service, bar, tennis courts, pool, gym, spa, diving, water sports, laundry service, concierge, public Wi-Fi, parking (fee), no-smoking rooms* ꙮ *BP (some)* ▭ *AE, DC, MC, V.*

$$$–$$$$ 🏨 **Vibe Hotel Gold Coast.** One of the fresher mid-range options on the ☾ Gold Coast, this avocado-hued high-rise has an excellent location and a **Fodor's**Choice hip, relaxed vibe. Rooms and suites have simple but chic contemporary ★ decor and user-friendly add-ons such as Sony PlayStations. King-sized beds are jazzed up with burnt-orange pillows; suites have sofas and dining settings. All rooms have breezy balconies with ocean or Nerang River views. The second-floor restaurant, Curve, serves daily buffet breakfasts, and overlooks the river and hinterland. There's a decent-size pool with a large deck, sun lounges, and a hot tub. ⊠ *42 Ferny Ave., 4127* ☎ *07/5539–0444 or 13–8423* ⊕ *www.vibehotels.com.au* ↝ *199 rooms, 32 suites* ⚹ *In-room: safe, refrigerator, kitchen (some), pay TV, Wi-Fi. In-hotel: restaurant, room service, bar, pool, gym, laun-*

7

dry facilities, laundry service, public Wi-Fi, airport shuttle, parking (no fee), no-smoking rooms ▭AE, DC, MC, V.

$$–$$$ ⚃**Chateau Beachside Resort.** If you hanker after a view of Surfers Paradise beach and want to stay within walking distance of all the action, this comfortable, budget-style hotel across the road from the famous beach is for you. Each room, studio, or one-bedroom apartment is done in bright blues and whites, accented by a tropical bedspread and cane tables and chairs. Apartments have their own cooking facilities. All have views of the surf. The all-you-can-eat buffet breakfast is legendary. ✉*52 The Esplanade at Elkhorn Ave., 4217* ☎*07/5538–1022 or 1800/807336* ✑info@chateaubeachside.com.au ⊕*www.chateaubeachside.com.au* ⮱*100 rooms (including studios and apartments)* ⌂*In-room: no a/c (some), kitchen (some), refrigerator, DVD, VCR, dial-up. In-hotel: restaurant, bar, tennis court, pool, gym, hot tub, sauna, watersports, bicycles, laundry facilities, laundry service, public Internet, parking (no fee)* ▭AE, DC, MC, V.

NIGHTLIFE

Surfers Paradise is the entertainment hub of the Gold Coast, full of bars, clubs, restaurants, and live-entertainment venues. But it's unmistakably the domain of the young party animals. Miniskirted young women and the guys looking to meet them seem to make up the bulk of the Surfers crowd on a typical Saturday night. Most nightclubs can be found on Orchid, Elkhorn, and Cavill avenues, though there are some scattered elsewhere in Surfers and in the more-upscale enclave of Chevron Island. Most clubs are free during the week, but may have a cover charge of A$10–A$15 on Friday and Saturday nights. You'll also pay to play pool and other games.

The Drink (✉*4 Orchid Ave.* ☎*07/5526–9222* ⊕*www.thedrinknightclub.com.au*) claims to be "the sexiest club on the coast." Popular with the rich and famous—especially during the Lexmark Indy 300 festival in October—the club plays commercial dance music, although it is best known for its popular R&B night every Wednesday.

Melba's on the Park (✉*46 Cavill Ave.* ☎*07/5538–7411* ⊕*www.melbas.com.au*), one of Surfers Paradise's oldest clubs, has been in business for more than two decades. It attracts an upscale crowd and plays the latest dance and pop music. A Melba's Tickle (butterscotch schnapps, Baileys, and milk) is just one of the cocktails on a long list. There's a restaurant serving Modern Australian food if you're feeling hungry, and a new gaming area has its own bar.

Another trendy spot is **mybar** (✉*Lower level, Mark Complex, Orchid Ave.* ☎*07/5592–4111* ⊕*www.mybar.net.au*), which has a "selective" door policy; a plush, luxe-Bohemian fitout; and a quality wine and cocktail list. The sophisticated dress code ensures that it's the fabulous and beautiful who groove to the funky house music spun by DJs well into the early hours.

Minus 5 Ice Lounge (✉*3084–3214, Shop 39, Circle on Cavill, Cavill Ave.* ☎*07/5527–5571* ⊕*www.minus5experience.com*) has an interior sculpted entirely from ice, along with the world's first "ice aquarium", koala, 'roo, and surfboard ice sculptures, and Absolut vodka-based cocktails and mocktails (all A$10). The A$30 door charge affords you 30 minutes to chill out in the minus-8.3-degrees-Celsius lounge, plus snow gear and a complimentary signature cocktail. Kids, accompanied by an adult, get in for A$10. It's open Sunday–Thursday 3 PM–1 AM; Friday and Saturday noon–3 AM.

BROADBEACH

8 km (5 mi) south of Southport.

With clean beaches, great cafés, and trendy nightspots, Broadbeach is one of the most popular areas on the Gold Coast, especially with the locals. It's home to Pacific Fair, one of Australia's leading shopping centers, and is also a good base for visiting the wildlife parks south of town.

David Fleay Wildlife Park, located in the town of Burleigh Heads and named for an Australian wildlife naturalist, takes you along a boardwalk trail through pristine wetlands and rain forests. Koalas, kangaroos, dingoes, platypuses, and crocodiles, grouped together in separate zones according to their natural habitat, are just some of the creatures you might see. Daily presentations are free. There's a café and a gift shop. ⊠ *7 km (4½ mi) south of Broadbeach, Tallebudgera Creek Rd. near W. Burleigh Rd., Burleigh Heads* ☎ *07/5576–2411* ⊕ *www.epa. qld.gov.au* ⊠ *A$15.40* ☉ *Daily 9–5.*

A Gold Coast institution, the **Currumbin Wildlife Sanctuary** is a 60-year-old, 70-acre National Trust Reserve that shelters Australian species such as crocodiles, snakes, wombats, dingoes, Tasmanian devils, and kangaroos. There are daily animal shows, informative talks, Aboriginal dancers, baby kangaroo feedings, and koala cuddling. Come between 8 and 9:30 or 4 and 5:30 when the lorikeets are fed and you'll find yourself surrounded by the colorful birds. Or take the guided Wild Night Adventure tour, A$49, from 7:15 nightly (bookings essential). Return transfers to and from Gold Coast cost $A13. ⊠ *28 Tomewin St., off Gold Coast Hwy., 14 km (8½ mi) south of Broadbeach, Currumbin* ☎ *07/5534–1266* ⊕ *www.cws.org.au* ⊠ *A$29.50* ☉ *Daily 8–5, grounds close 5:30.*

WHERE TO STAY & EAT

$$–$$$ ✗**Sopranos.** The wooden tables here spill out onto the terra-cotta-tile sidewalk of Surf Parade, Broadbeach's restaurant strip. With a well-stocked bar, a frequently changing menu that takes advantage of the local seafood, and a generous display of desserts, the restaurant is rarely empty. The dishes combine Mediterranean and pan-Asian flavors and include barramundi with spicy green curry sauce and a grilled seafood platter with prawns, mussels, and oysters. ⊠ *Shop 11, Surf Parade* ☎ *07/5526–2011* ⊕ *www.sopranosrestaurant.com.au* ▤ *AE, DC, MC, V.*

7

$$$$ ✕⊞ **Hotel Conrad and Jupiters Casino.** This massive resort is always bustling. Executive and Superior rooms, the latter refurbished in 2007, have rich, earth-toned furnishings with emerald accents, high-speed Internet access, and slim line TVs with cable channels and pay movies; most rooms have either a balcony or a sunny terrace. Front-facing rooms lack balconies, but have great views of the Gold Coast; other rooms look out across the hinterland. Luxury suites are fully self-contained. Restaurants include Andiamo, with a Mod-Oz-meets-Mediterranean menu, and Charters Towers, which specializes in contemporary Queensland cuisine and offers fresh mud crab, lobster, local seafood, and premium steaks. ⊠*Broadbeach Island, off Gold Coast Hwy., Broadbeach, 4218* ☎*07/5592–8100 or 1800/074344* ⊕*www. conradjupiters.com.au* ↪*459 superior, 32 corner, and 74 executive rooms, 29 suites, 2 penthouses* ⑂*In-room: safe, refrigerator/minibar, DVD (some), dial-up, ethernet. In-hotel: 7 restaurants, room service, 8 bars, tennis court, pool, gym, spa, concierge, laundry service, public Internet, public Wi-Fi, airport shuttle, parking (fee), executive floor, business center, no-smoking rooms* ⊟*AE, DC, MC, V* ⎮⊙⎮*BP.*

$$ ⊞ **Antigua Beach Resort.** Less than a minute's walk from the beach and around the corner from shopping centers and restaurants, this three-story, Caribbean-style hotel has balconies or patios on all sides. Self-contained one- and two-bedroom apartments are decorated in bright tropical colors. The pool and terrace are ringed by landscaped gardens with a barbecue. There's a minimum seven-night stay around Christmas Day. ⊠*6 Queensland Ave., 4218* ☎*07/5526–2288* ⊕*www.antiguaresort.com.au* ↪*23 apartments* ⑂*In-room: no a/c (some), no phone (some), kitchen, refrigerator, dial-up. In-hotel: pool, laundry service, no smoking* ⊟*MC, V.*

NIGHTLIFE

Jupiters Casino (⊠*Gold Coast Hwy.* ☎*07/5592–1133* ⊕*www.conradjupiters.com.au*) provides flamboyant round-the-clock entertainment. There are two levels of blackjack, baccarat, craps, sic bo, and keno tables and more than 1,200 round-the-clock slot machines. Since the casino's A$53 million expansion in 2006, there are more dining, drinking, and entertainment options, including seven restaurants and eight bars. The 950-seat showroom hosts glitzy Las Vegas–style productions.

Howl at the Moon (⊠*Neicon Plaza, Victoria Mall* ☎*07/5538–9911* ⊕*www.howlatthemoon.com.au*) is a fun place to go, especially if you like a good sing-along and know the words of popular '80s, '90s, and current songs. Every night it's a case of dueling pianos as three (often very different) pianists with great voices belt out a medley of tunes (some requested by patrons) to an appreciative crowd of thirty- to fortysomethings. Even the staff join the fun with an energetic piano-top show. Grab a Cosmopolitan and hit the always-jumping—even midweek—dance floor.

SHOPPING

The Oasis Shopping Centre (✉*Victoria Ave. near Burleigh Rd.* ☎*07/5592–3900* ⊕*www.oasisshopping.com*) is the retail heart of beachside Broadbeach, with more than 120 shops and an attractive mall where open-air coffee shops stand umbrella-to-umbrella. A monorail runs from the center to Jupiters Casino.

Fodor's Choice ★ **Pacific Fair** (✉*Hooker Blvd. at Gold Coast Hwy., opposite Jupiters Casino* ☎*07/5581–5100* ⊕*www.pacificfair.com.au*), a sprawling outdoor shopping center, is Queensland's largest. Its major retailers and more than 250 specialty stores should be enough to satisfy even diehard shoppers. Myer (one of Australia's two leading department stores) is the main anchor. There are also landscaped grounds with three small lakes, a children's park, and a village green. It's open Monday, Tuesday, Friday, and Saturday 9–5:30; Thursday 9–9; and Sunday 9–5.

SIDE TRIP TO THE GOLD COAST HINTERLAND

A visit to the Gold Coast wouldn't be complete without a short journey to the nearby **Gold Coast Hinterland.** Be forewarned, however, that this may induce culture shock: the natural grandeur of the area contrasts dramatically with the human-made excesses of the coastal strip. The area's national parks have magnificent waterfalls, cool rock pools, mountain lookouts with expansive views of the coast, and walking trails traversing dense rain forest with ancient trees. Among the parks lie a handful of wineries and quaint villages where high-rise is anything over one story. The parks form part of a geological region known as the Scenic Rim, a chain of mountains running parallel to the coast along southeast Queensland and northern New South Wales.

Because it rises to 3,000 feet above sea level, some parts of the hinterland are 4°C–6°C (7°F–11°F) cooler than the coast. The main areas—Tamborine Mountain, Lamington National Park, and Springbrook—can be reached from the Pacific Highway or via Beaudesert from Brisbane, and are 30–40 minutes from the Gold Coast.

More than 20 million years ago, volcanic eruptions created rugged landscapes of exceptional beauty, while fertile volcanic soils produced the luxuriant patches of rain forest that make up make up **Tamborine National Park.** This is the most developed region of the Gold Coast Hinterland, and it's worth spending a day or two here. Apart from the natural environment, there are wineries, lodges, restaurants, and the famed Gallery Walk, a 1-km-long (½-mi-long) street full of art galleries. Within the park there are numerous easy trails: most take under two hours to traverse. Some of the simplest and best are the Cedar Creek Falls track with waterfall views; the Palm Grove Rainforest Circuit; and Macdonald Rainforest Circuit, a quieter walk popular with birdwatchers. Start your visit with a stop at the Tamborine Mountain Visitor Information Centre, open 10 AM to 3 PM daily. ✉*Doughty Park, Geissman Dr., cnr. Main Western Rd., North Tamborine.*

7

☾ Several fragmented parks make up Tamborine National Park. Queensland's first national park, **Witches Falls,** has excellent picnic facilities and a 3-km (2-mi) walk that snakes downhill through open rain forest and past lagoons. To the east of Witches Falls is **Joalah National Park,** where a 1½ km (1 mi) circuit takes you to a rocky pool at the base of Curtis Falls. **MacDonald National Park** has a flat, easy 1½-km (1-mi) walk. To reach Tamborine, around 80 km (50 mi) south of Brisbane and 36 km (24 mi) from Southport take Exit 57 off the Pacific Motorway to Oxenford–Tamborine Road; or take Exit 71 off the Pacific Motorway and proceed along the Nerang–Beaudesert Road to Canungra. From Canungra, follow the signs to Tamborine, 4 km (2.5 mi) along Tamborine Mountain Road. ☎07/5576–0271 ⊕*www. epa.qld.gov.au* ✉*Free* ☉*Daily dawn–dusk.*

The peaks of **Springbrook National Park** rise to around 3,000 feet, dominating the skyline west of the Gold Coast. The park has three separate regions—Springbrook, Natural Bridge, and Mt. Cougal. Thanks to steep, winding roads and longish distances between sections, it takes at least a full day to explore. It's about 30 km (19 mi) from the tiny hamlet of Springbrook to Natural Bridge—a lovely waterfall that cascades through the roof of a cave into an icy pool. This cave is home to Australia's largest glowworm colony, which at night lights the cavern to stunning effect. Several waterfalls, including the area's largest, Purling Brook Falls, can be reached via a 4-km (2½-mi) path. The path includes stairs and uphill walking; for sedentary souls, there's a lookout near the parking lot with waterfall views. Camping isn't permitted, except in designated private campgrounds.

To reach Springbrook from the south, take Exit 80 off the Pacific Motorway (from the north, take Exit 79), then follow the Gold Coast—Springbrook Road through Mudgeeraba. Springbrook Plateau is 29 km (18 mi) on. Or take Exit 69 (Nerang) off the Pacific Motorway, then the Nerang-Murwillumbah Road for 42 km (25 mi) to Pine Creek Road (Springbrook turn-off), or for 30 km (18 mi) to reach Natural Bridge. Both roads, though paved, are steep and narrow. The park is about 100 km (60 mi) south of Brisbane. ☎07/5533–5147 ⊕*www.epa.qld.gov. au* ✉*Free* ☉*Daily dawn–dusk.*

Lamington National Park is a subtropical-temperate ecological border zone with a complex abundance of plant and animal life. Its 50,600-acre expanse comprises two sections: Binna Burra and Green Mountains. Lamington National Park is listed as a World Heritage Area, which protects its extensive and varied rain forest. In many places you can see ancient Antarctic beech trees dating back 3,000 years. Lamington has 160 km (100 mi) of bushwalking tracks, waterfalls, mountain pools, exceptional views, and some 120 native bird species. All camping areas within Lamington National Park require a camping permit (A$4.50), obtained in advance.

To reach the park, take Exit 71 (Nerang) off the Pacific Motorway, then the Nerang–Beaudesert Road toward Canungra. For Green Mountains, proceed to Canungra, then follow the signs to Lamington. Past

Canungra, it's 36 km (22 mi) of winding, often narrow road—allow 50-plus minutes for this section. From Broadbeach, drive 38 km (24 mi) to Beechmont, via Nerang (65–70 minutes). From the north, take exit 34 (Beenleigh) off the Pacific Motorway, then route 92 to Tamborine, and route 90 to Canungra. It's then a narrow, 18-km (11-mi) road to Beechmont. ⊠*Binna Burra Rd.* ☎*07/5544–0634 or 13–1304 (permits)* ⊕*www.epa.qld.gov.au* ✐*Free* ⊗*Park daily, 24 hrs; Green Mountains park office opens weekdays 9–11 and 1–3:30 (Tues. & Fri. 1–3:30); Binna Burra park office is open weekdays, 1–3:30.*

WHERE TO STAY

$$$–$$$$ ⛺ **O'Reilly's Rainforest Retreat.** Since 1926, the O'Reilly family has welcomed travelers into their forested world. Accommodations range from original 1930s guesthouse rooms with shared facilities to luxurious lodgings with handcrafted wood furniture, four-poster beds, entertainment systems, fireplaces, whirlpool baths, and spectacular mountain views and, from September 2008, chic architect-designed villas with vast private decks and hot tubs. For a little extra, you can join expert guides on outdoorsy activities, such as bird, rain-forest and glow-worm walks, flying fox and giant swing sessions, wine-tasting tours, and four-wheel-drive bus expeditions. The treetop suspension bridge is a must-do. Or just relax in the retreat's heated pool, hot tub, or sauna (or, from late 2008, a dedicated day spa). O'Reilly's room rate includes country-style morning and afternoon teas and daily audiovisual presentations. You can also get all-meals and dinner-breakfast packages. There's a minimum stay at Christmas/New Year. In 2008, there will be renovation in progress, but they'll be open for business as usual. ⊠*Lamington National Park Rd., via Canungra, 4275* ☎*07/5502–4900 or 1800/688722* ✐*reservations@oreillys.com.au* ⊕*www.oreillys.com.au* ⇆*67 rooms, 5 suites, 48 villas (from Sept. 2008)* ⌂*In-room: no a/c (some), no phone, refrigerator, no TV, CD (some), ethernet (some), hot tub (some). In-hotel: 3 restaurants, bar, pool, spa (opening Sept. 2008), laundry facilities, public Internet, airport shuttle, no-smoking rooms* ▭*AE, DC, MC, V.*

$$$–$$$$ ⛺ **Pethers Rainforest Retreat.** In 12 acres of privately owned rain forest, this couples-only resort comprises 10 spacious tree houses with timber floors, French doors opening onto verandas, fireplaces, hot tubs, and open-plan interiors furnished with Asian antiques. Undercover walkways link each house with the main lodge, a stunning building with 16-foot-high glass walls affording rain-forest views. You can while away the hours in the library or hike on the trails, where you might be lucky enough to spot wallabies and koalas. Restaurants are nearby, but there's a A$48, three-course dinner available for guests. ⊠*28B Geissmann St., North Tamborine, 4272* ☎*07/5545–4577* ⊕*www. pethers.com.au* ✐*retreat@pethers.com.au* ⇆*10 tree houses* ⌂*In-room: no a/c, no phone, refrigerator/minibar, DVD. In-hotel: restaurant, bar, gym, parking (no fee), no-smoking rooms, no kids* ▭*AE, DC, MC, V* ⊚*BP.*

$–$$$ ⛺ **Binna Burra Mountain Lodge & Campsite.** Founded in 1933, this group of hilltop cabins has sweeping views across the hinterland to the Gold

Coast. Rustic lodge rooms and log cabins are cozy, secluded, and simply furnished, with a deliberate absence of TVs, radios, telephones, and clocks; some have shared bathrooms. There are two new luxury suites, built in 2007. Rates vary—good-value packages include breakfasts, or all meals, guided nature walks, and other activities, plus evening entertainment. Budget travelers can camp on-site, in tents, powered vans, or furnished safari-style tents with verandas. The main guest lounge has log fires in winter, while the Cliff-Top Dining Room has panoramic views over the Coomera Valley. Rejoove Health Spa (⊘Daily 10–8) has a doctor, chiropractor, and naturopath, along with beauty, massage, and Gestalt therapists. Multi-night minimum stays are required in holiday periods. The Binna Burra shuttle bus (☎1800/074260) makes a daily round-trip between the property, Gold Coast Airport, and Nerang Station (book 24 hours ahead, A$30–$40). ⊠*Binna Burra Rd., Lamington National Park, via Beechmont, 4211* ☎*07/5533–3622 or 1800/074260* ⊘*info@binnaburralodge.com.au* ⊕*www.binnaburralodge.com.au* ⇨*35 cabins (9 with shared bath), 2 suites* ♿*In-room: no a/c, no phone, no TV, hot tub (some). In-hotel: 2 restaurants, bar, spa, children's programs (ages 5–16), laundry facilities, public Internet, airport shuttle, parking (no fee), no-smoking rooms, no elevator* ▤*MC, V* ◖❙*AI, BP.*

GOLD COAST ESSENTIALS

TRANSPORTATION

AIR TRAVEL

Gold Coast Airport, also known as Coolangatta Airport, is the region's main transit point. From the Gold Coast it's 30 minutes to Brisbane, 2 hours 10 minutes to Melbourne, and 1 hour 25 minutes to Sydney. Qantas, Virgin Blue, and Jetstar operate domestic flights from the Gold Coast to all capital cities and some regional centers.

Airport Gold Coast Airport (*Coolangatta Airport* ⊠*Gold Coast Hwy., Bilinga* ☎*07/5589–1100*).

Airlines Jetstar (☎*13–1538* ⊕*www.jetstar.com.au*). **Qantas** (☎*13–1313* ⊕*www.qantas.com.au*). **Virgin Blue** (☎*13–6789* ⊕*www.virginblue.com.au*).

BUS TRAVEL

Long-distance buses traveling between Sydney and Brisbane stop at Coolangatta and Surfers Paradise.

Allstate Scenic Tours leaves the Brisbane Transit Centre for O'Reilly's Rainforest Retreat in the Gold Coast Hinterland (A$69 round-trip) daily at 8:30. The cost is for a full-day tour, but Retreat guests can use it for transfers.

Greyhound Australia runs an express coach from the Gold Coast to Brisbane International and Gold Coast airports, as well as day trips that cover southeast Queensland with daily connections to Sydney and Melbourne.

From the Gold Coast, Mountain Coach Company buses pick passengers up from the major bus depots, most of the major hotels, and from Coolangatta Airport for O'Reilly's Rainforest Retreat in the Gold Coast Hinterland (A$53 round-trip day tour; A$38 one-way transfer).

Surfside Buslines' Gold Coast Tourist Shuttle runs around the clock between Gold Coast attractions, theme parks, and the airport, along the strip between Tweed Heads and Southport. Services run at 5-minute intervals during the day and at least half-hourly after dark. Buy single tickets or a 3-, 5-, 7-, or 14-day Freedom Pass—A$65 gives you 3 days' unlimited Shuttle travel.

Contacts Allstate Scenic Tours (⌧ *Brisbane Transit Centre, Roma St.* ☎ *07/3003-0700).*

Greyhound Australia (⌧ *Surfers Paradise Bus Station, 6 Beach Rd., Surfers Paradise* ☎ *13-1499* ⊕ *www.greyhound.com.au).* **Mountain Coach Company** (☎ *07/5524-4249* ⊕ *www.mountaincoach.com.au).* **Surfside Buslines** (⌧ *1-10 Mercantile Ct., Ernest* ☎ *07/5571-6555 or 13-1230 (bookings)* ⊕ *www.surfside.com.au or www.translink.com.au).*

CAR RENTAL
Most major car-rental agencies have offices in Brisbane, Surfers Paradise, and at Gold Coast Airport. Companies operating on the Gold Coast include Avis, Budget, and Thrifty. Four-wheel-drive vehicles are available.

Contacts Avis (⌧ *Ferny and Cypress Aves., Surfers Paradise* ☎ *07/5539-9388 or 13-6333 (bookings)* ⊕ *www.avis.com.au).* **Budget** (⌧ *Gold Coast Airport, Gold Coast Hwy., Bilinga* ☎ *07/5536-5377 or 1300/362848 (international bookings)* ⊕ *www.budget.com.au).* **Thrifty** (⌧ *3006 Gold Coast Hwy., Surfers Paradise* ☎ *07/5570-9999 or 1800/367227 (bookings)* ⊕ *www.thrifty.com.au).*

CAR TRAVEL
The Gold Coast begins 65 km (40 mi) south of Brisbane. The Pacific Highway, or M1, bypasses the Gold Coast towns, but well-marked signs guide you to your destination. If you're coming from Brisbane International Airport, take the toll road over Gateway Bridge to avoid traversing Brisbane, then follow signs to the Gold Coast. Driving distances and times from the Gold Coast via the Pacific Highway are 859 km (533 mi) and 12–13 hours to Sydney, 105 km (65 mi) and just over 1 hour to Brisbane, and 1,815 km (1,125 mi) and 22 hours to Cairns.

TRAIN TRAVEL
Queensland Rail service from 5:30 AM until midnight connects Brisbane and the Helensvale, Nerang, and Robina stations on the Gold Coast.

Contact Queensland Rail (☎ *1300/131722 or 13-1617* ⊕ *www.qr.com.au).*

CONTACTS & RESOURCES

EMERGENCIES
Dial **000** for an ambulance, the police, or the fire department.

Hospital Gold Coast Hospital (⌧ *108 Nerang St., Southport* ☎ *07/5519-8211).*

Pharmacies Broadbeach Pharmacy (✉ *2717 Main Pl., Broadbeach* ☎ *07/5539–8751*). **Chevron Renaissance Chemmart Pharmacy** (✉ *Elkhorn Ave., Surfers Paradise* ☎ *07/5561–0850*).

VISITOR INFORMATION

Contacts Gold Coast Tourism Information & Booking Centres (✉ *Surfers Paradise Blvd. at Cavill Ave., Surfers Paradise, 4217* ☎ *07/5536–7765* ✉ *Shop 22, Showcase on the Beach, Coolangatta, 4225* ☎ *07/5538–4419* ⊕ *www.verygc. com*). **Tweed Heads Visitor Information Centre** (✉ *Wharf and Bay Sts., Tweed Heads 4285* ☎ *1800/674414*).

THE SUNSHINE COAST & AIRLIE BEACH

One hour's drive from Brisbane to its southernmost point, the Sunshine Coast is a 60-km (37-mi) stretch of white-sand beaches, inlets, lakes, and mountains. It begins at the Glass House Mountains and extends to Rainbow Beach in the north. Kenilworth is its inland extent, 40 km (25 mi) from the ocean. For the most part, the Sunshine Coast avoided the high-rise glitz of its southern cousin, the Gold Coast. Although there are plenty of stylish restaurants and luxurious hotels, this coast is best loved for its national parks, secluded coves, and charming mountain villages.

More than 970 km (600 mi) to the north, Airlie Beach shares many of the characteristics of its southerly coastal neighbors. Like Noosa, Maroochydore, and other Sunshine Coast towns, Airlie enjoys great weather throughout the year. Since it's popular with the adventurous set, who use it as a jumping-off point for trips to the Whitsunday Islands and the Great Barrier Reef, its main street is packed with cafés, bars, travel agencies, and hotels.

Numbers in the margin correspond to points of interest on the Sunshine Coast map.

GLASS HOUSE MOUNTAINS AREA

⑯ *65 km (40 mi) north of Brisbane.*

More than 20 million years old, the Glass House Mountains consist of nine dramatic, conical outcrops. These eroded remnants of volcanoes are a spectacular sight, seeming to appear out of the ground from nowhere. They lie along the old main road about a half hour outside Brisbane, to the west of the Bruce Highway.

One of the best places to view the mountains is from the Glass House Mountains Lookout. It's accessed via the Glass House Mountains Tourist Route, which begins in the quaint Glass House Mountains Village off the Bruce Highway. From the lookout, you can take a 25-minute walk. Several longer walks begin from other lookouts and summits, such as Mt. Beerburrum and Wild Horse Mountain Lookout, that are all about 6 km (4 mi) from Glass House Mountains Lookout.

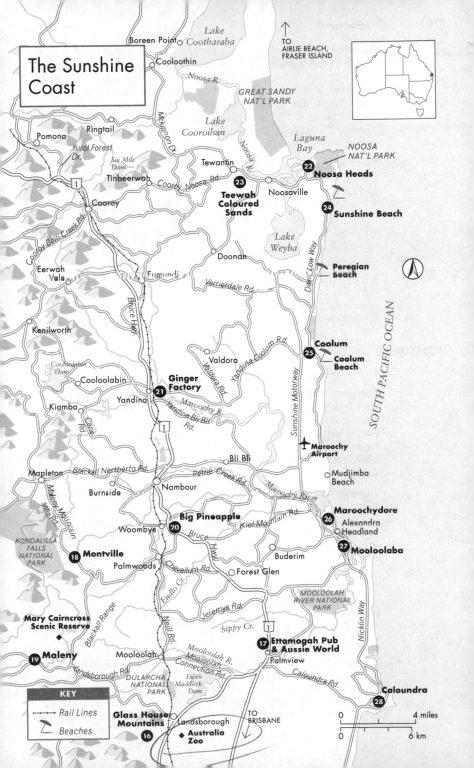

Australia Zoo, made famous by the late Steve Irwin, has all manner of Australian animals: pythons, taipans, adders, koalas, kangaroos, wallabies, eagles—and, naturally, crocodiles. There are also otters, elephants, and a giant rain forest aviary. Daily shows feature crocs, birds of prey, and koalas. A courtesy bus shuttles visitors to and from Beerwah station. ⊠ *Glass House Mountains Tourist Rte., 5 km (3 mi) north of Glass House Mountains, Beerwah* ☎ *07/5494–1134* ⊕ *www. australiazoo.com.au* ⊠ *A$49* ⊙ *Daily 9–4:30.*

17 The **Ettamogah Pub** (☎ *07/5494–5444*), whose name and design are based on the famous pub featured for decades in the work of Australian cartoonist Ken Maynard, is on the left side of the Bruce Highway a few kilometers north of Palmview (21 km [13 mi] north of Glass House Mountains). It has an upstairs bistro, a beer garden, and a bar, and is open daily 9 AM–8 PM. Nearby, the **Ettamogah Bakery** sells excellent pies.

☉ The **Aussie World** amusement area, adjacent to the Ettamogah Pub, has a large shed with pool tables, and a fairground with 30-plus rides, including Dodgems, a rollercoaster, and minigolf. ⊠ *Bruce Hwy. at Frizzo Rd.* ☎ *07/5494–5444* ⊕ *www.aussieworld.com.au* ⊠ *A$25* ⊙ *Daily 9–5.*

MONTVILLE

18 *16 km (10 mi) northwest of Forest Glen.*

This charming mountain village, settled in 1887, is known as the creative heart of the Sunshine Coast, as many artists live here. There are panoramic views of the coast from the main street, which was built with a blend of Tudor, Irish, and English cottages of log or stone; Bavarian and Swiss houses; and old "Queenslander" homes. Shops are a browser's delight, full of curiosities and locally made crafts; galleries showcase more-serious pieces by local artists.

☉ **Kondalilla National Park** (⊠ *Kondalilla Falls Rd. off Montville–Mapleton Rd., near Flaxton* ☎ *07/5494–3983 or 07/5459–6110* ⊕ *www.epa.qld. gov.au*), with its swimming hole, waterfall, picnic grounds, and walking trails, is a popular local attraction. Three different bushwalks begin near the large grassy picnic area: the Picnic Creek circuit, the Rock Pools walk, and the Kondalilla Falls circuit. They're all rated easy to moderate and range from 2 km (1 mi) to 5 km (3 mi) in length. The **Great Sunshine Coast Great Hinterland Walk** (58 km [34 mi]), for more serious hikers, is accessible from the Falls Loop track, and links with parks farther north. Download maps from the Environmental Protection Agency Web site.

WHERE TO STAY & EAT

¢–$$ ✕**Poets Café.** Pictures of famous poets adorn the walls, which gives you the feeling of being immersed in high culture. French doors open out on to a balcony where you can dine surrounded by tall rain-forest trees. The eclectic menu includes "gourmet" open sandwiches, seafood risotto, barramundi, eye fillet steak, and pasta dishes. Save room for the caramel macadamia tart. On Friday it's also open for dinner. ✉*167 Main St.* ☎*07/5478–5479* ▭*AE, DC, MC, V* ☽*No dinner Sat.–Thurs.*

$$$ 🏠**The Falls Rainforest Cottages.** Adjacent to the forest of Kondalilla Falls National Park and built in the style of traditional Queensland houses, these secluded cottages make for a romantic getaway. Hardwood floors and balconies, country furnishings, and wood-burning fireplaces fill the spacious cottages, which also have whirlpool tubs and cooking facilities. A daily country-style breakfast basket is included in the price; for an additional A$40 you get a pre-packed BBQ picnic hamper. The management can also organize local tours and in-room massages. There's a A$25 surcharge for single night stays. ✉*20 Kondalilla Falls Rd., 4560* ☎*07/5445–7000* ⊕*www.thefallscottages. com.au* ✉info@thefallscottages.com.au ⬗*6 cottages* ♿*In-room: no phone, kitchen, VCR. In-hotel: no-smoking rooms, no kids under 16, parking, no elevator* ▭*AE, DC, MC, V* �🍴*CP.*

$$–$$$ 🏠**The Spotted Chook Ferme & Amelies.** A French provincial touch infuses ☙ this newly built Queenslander home. Four rooms and a self-contained cottage are brightly painted and furnished with a combination of antique and modern furniture; some rooms have fireplaces. Each has sweeping views of the property's 100 acres of rain forest and the distant Obi Gorge. The garden and its gazebo provide a tranquil haven. A three-course dinner (at A$65 per person) is available and may include such delights as crayfish risotto. If you have kids, call ahead to book the Snowpea Suite, which has an adjoining children's room. The cottage is wheelchair-friendly, with access to public areas via wheelchair walkways. There's a two-night minimum stay on weekends. ✉*176 Western Ave., 4560* ☎*07/5442–9242* ⊕*www.spottedchook.com* ⬗*4 rooms, 4 suites, 1 cottage* ♿*In-room: no phone, refrigerator (some), kitchen (cottage only), DVD (some), VCR (some). In-hotel: restaurant, room service, no-smoking rooms, laundry service, public Internet, no kids under 6, no smoking, disabled access* ▭*AE, DC, MC, V* �🍴*BP* ☽*Closed Christmas Day, Boxing Day.*

SHOPPING

Enigmas Montville (✉*Shop 4, 192 Main St.* ☎*07/5442–9355*) has a good selection of local art, including paintings, handicrafts, and pottery. **Verde** (✉*174 Main St.* ☎*07/5478–5855*) stocks a wide selection of locally made skin-care products, jewelry, and quilts.

MALENY

⑲ *14 km (8½ mi) west of Montville.*

The hinterland village of Maleny is a lively mix of rural life, the arts, wineries, cafés, and cooperative ventures. First settled around 1880, Maleny is now a working dairy town and popular tourist resort with a strong community spirit. A number of arts-and-crafts festivals take place here from September to November.

Mary Cairncross Scenic Reserve (☎07/5499–9907), one of the area's most popular picnic spots, is 5 km (3 mi) southeast of Maleny at the intersection of the Landsborough–Maleny and Mountainview roads. The 130 acres of rain forest shelter an array of wildlife that includes bandicoots, goannas, echidnas, wallabies—and even pythons. There's an excellent information center and two easy walks. Eat in the café or at picnic tables for magnificent views of the Glass House Mountains. It's open daily from dawn to dusk, info center 9–5.

WHERE TO STAY & EAT

$ ✕**Maple 3 Café.** A covered veranda and courtyard surround this local favorite, now licensed. The menu changes daily, but there are always salads, focaccias, salmon steaks, and many dessert options. Come in for brunch, grab a sandwich and a huge slice of home-made cake, and head down to Lake Baroon for a picnic, or just sit out front on the deck and watch the eclectic mix of Maleny townsfolk go about their day. ✉3 Maple St. ☎07/5499–9177 ⊟AE, DC, MC, V.

$$–$$$ ▦**Maleny Tropical Retreat.** At the end of a steep, winding driveway is a dense, misty rain-forest valley; in its midst is this B&B. Tropical gardens surround the two-story house furnished with Balinese touches—right down to the incense and piped-in music. Each room has a balcony with dual hammocks or elevated deck overlooking the rain forest, a fireplace, a CD player, and a glass-wall spa bath, both of which provide fabulous views of Lake Baroon and Obi Obi Creek. There's also a well-appointed cabin. Hiking trails from the house lead to the creek. There's a two-night minimum stay on weekends. ✉540 Maleny–Montville Rd., 4552 ☎07/5435–2113 ⊕www.malenytropicalretreat.com ✉unwind@malenytropicalretreat.com.au ⇋3 rooms, 1 cabin ⬥In-room: fan (some), no phone, refrigerator/minibar, DVD/VCR, hot tub. In-hotel: no-smoking rooms, no kids under 16, no elevator ⊟AE, DC, MC, V ❍IBP.

NAMBOUR

20 9 km (5½ mi) northwest of Forest Glen, 101 km (63 mi) north of
☾ Brisbane.

★ Sunshine Plantation is home to the impossible-to-miss **Big Pineapple.** The 50-foot fiberglass monster towers over the highway. Climb inside to learn how pineapples are grown. You can also see how macadamia nuts and other tropical fruits are cultivated. The plantation has a shop selling souvenirs, leisurewear, jewelry, art, and crafts. There are also flume rides, train excursions, an animal nursery, and a nocturnal wildlife walkthrough. The culinary focus of the on-site café is, of course, pineapples. ✉Nambour Connection Rd., 6 km (4 mi) south of Nambour ☎07/5442–1333 ✉Free, rides extra ☾Daily 9–5.

YANDINA

㉑ *9 km (5½ mi) north of Nambour.*

The **Ginger Factory**, a legendary Queensland establishment, goes far beyond its original factory-door sale of ginger. However, you can still take a 40-minute guided tour of the facility for A$10.95. A restaurant and large shop sell ginger in all forms—from crystallized ginger to ginger incorporated into jams, chocolates, ice cream, wine, and herbal products. There is also a train excursion (A$5.50) and a boat ride, both with animated puppetry en route (A$9.50). ⊠ *50 Pioneer Rd., 1 km (½ mi) east of Bruce Hwy.* ☎ *07/5446–7100* ⊕ *www.gingerfactory. au* ⊡ *Free* ⊙ *Daily 9–5.*

Fodor's Choice
★
The big attraction to this area is the Wednesday and Saturday **Eumundi Market** (☎ *07/5442–7106 or 0419/733468* ⊕ *www.eumundimarkets. com.au*)—the best street market on the Sunshine Coast—when 300-plus stall holders gather along Memorial Drive in the picturesque town of Eumundi to sell arts, crafts, clothing, accessories, and fresh and gourmet produce, from 6:30 AM to 2 PM on Saturday and 8 AM to 1:30 PM on Wednesday. Buses run to Eumundi from Noosa on market days, when the town swells to near-cosmopolitan proportions.

WHERE TO EAT

$$
Fodor's Choice
★
✕ **Spirit House.** Mention you are going to eat in Yandina, and locals and even Brisbane foodies say "Spirit House" with an envious grin. Owners Peter and Helen Brierty, who lived in Thailand for five years, have done a remarkable job re-creating contemporary Asian cuisine on Queensland soil. The menu changes seasonally, but worthy signature dishes are the whole crispy fish with tamarind, chili, and garlic sauce and the sticky pork and scallop salad. Save room for desserts such as crème brûlée, Asian-inspired panna cotta, caramelized lime tart, or fruit sorbet. The lush garden setting has a lagoon and Buddhist shrines. A hydroponic farm and cooking school are on-site. ⊠ *20 Ninderry Rd., 4561* ☎ *07/5446–8977* ⊕ *www.spirithouse.com.au* ⊛ *Reservations essential* ⊟ *AE, DC, MC, V* ⊙ *No dinner Sun.–Tues.*

7

NOOSA HEADS

22 *39 km (24 mi) northeast of Nambour, 17 km (11 mi) north of Coolum, 140 km (87 mi) north of Brisbane.*

Set along the calm waters of Laguna Bay at the northern tip of the Sunshine Coast, Noosa Heads is one of Australia's most stylish resort areas. The town consisted of little more than a few shacks until the mid-1980s, then surfers discovered the spectacular waves that curl around the sheltering headland of Noosa National Park. Today, Noosa Heads is a charming mix of surf, sand, and sophistication, with a serious reputation for unique and evolving cuisine. Views along the trail from Laguna Lookout to the top of the headland take in miles of magnificent beaches, ocean, and dense vegetation.

23 About 3 km (2 mi) east of Noosa Heads you'll find **Teewah Coloured Sands,** an area of multicolor sand dunes that were created by natural chemicals in the soil. Dating from the Ice Age, some of the 72 different hues of sand form cliffs rising to 600 feet and stretch inland from the beach to a distance of about 17 km (11 mi). A four-wheel-drive vehicle is essential for exploring both this area and interesting sites to the north, such as Great Sandy National Park, the wreck of the *Cherry Venture* near the beachside hamlet of Freshwater, and Rainbow Beach. Access is by ferry across the Noosa River at the town of Tewantin.

Tour operators run day trips that take in these sights, and some include an overnight or longer visit to Fraser Island, north of Rainbow Beach. **Beyond Noosa's Great Escapes** (☎97/5448–9177 *or 1800/657666* ⊕*www.beyondnoosa.com.au*) runs cruises along the Noosa River and the Everglades, and a combined cruise and four-wheel-drive tour to the Coloured Sands and Rainbow Beach area. From A\$69 for the four-hour afternoon tea cruise.

WHERE TO STAY & EAT

\$\$–\$\$\$ ✕**Cato's Restaurant and Bar.** This split-level restaurant attached to the Sheraton Noosa Resort & Spa has a bar downstairs next to bustling Hastings Street, and a relaxed dining section above. Seafood dominates the menu at both; among the favorites are Caesar salad with seared scallops and prosciutto, and spiced tuna steak with baby beets. A fantastic seafood buffet is available every evening, and there's an extensive wine list with many wines available by the glass. ⊠*16 Hastings St.* ☎*07/5449–4754* ▭*AE, DC, MC, V.*

\$\$ ✕**Aromas.** This coffee shop was at the forefront of Noosa's famous café culture, and it's still one of the best sipping spots in town. The loyal clientele comes for the film-noir setting and great people-watching. There's a Mod-Oz slant to the menu, which also lists an impressive selection of homemade cakes, biscuits, and coffees. ⊠*32 Hastings St.* ☎*07/5474–9788* ▭*AE, DC, MC, V.*

$-$$ ✗**Berardo's on the Beach.** Expatriate New Yorker Jim Berardo came to Noosa to retire, but he ended up with two restaurants. Berardo's on the Beach, the more-casual one, has a prime location open to the Noosa shores, and attracts a constant stream of customers. Quirky fish sculptures line the walls, and handblown chartreuse carafes are on every table. The weekly menu lists fresh juices, cocktails, extravagant open sandwiches, and light meals such as steamed mussels with *gremolata* (Italian seasonings), oregano, tomato, and toasted sourdough. There's also a gourmet deli bar with takeout options. ✉*49 Hastings St., on the beach* ☎*07/5448–0888* ⊕*www.berardos.com.au* ▭*AE, MC, V.*

$$ ✗**Bistro C.** Spectacular views of the bay from the open dining area make a stunning backdrop for this restaurant's Mod-Oz cuisine. The menu highlights seafood, though landlubbers can partake of several vegetarian and meat dishes. Try the signature fresh medley of local seafoods, served in the pan, the coconut-poached tiger prawns, or the justly famous egg-fried calamari. Book ahead for Thursday night's "seafood platter" for $A65; you get cold, then hot platters for two, brimming with Moreton Bay bugs, prawns, squid, mussels, barramundi, and more. ✉*On the Beach Complex, Hastings St.* ☎*07/5447–2855* ⊕*www.bistroc.com.au* ▭*AE, DC, MC, V.*

¢ **Halse Lodge.** This National Heritage–listed guesthouse with colonial-style furnishings sits in 2 acres of gardens on the edge of Noosa National Park. Vintage photographs of Noosa decorate the large functional rooms. Standard rooms and bunk rooms that sleep four or six people all have shared bathrooms (A$29 per person, per night in high season). The restaurant serves daily breakfasts and dinners, and there's a bar on-site. Reservations are essential at this popular backpacker hangout. ✉*2 Halse La., at Noosa Dr., near Lions Park, 4567* ☎*07/5447–3377 or 1800/242567* ⊕*www.halselodge.com.au* ✍backpackers@halselodge.com.au *26 rooms without bath* △*In-room: no a/c, no phone, safe, refrigerator, no TV. In-hotel: restaurant, bar, guest kitchen, DVD, VCR, beachfront, diving, bicycles, laundry facilities, public Internet (ethernet and Wi-Fi), airport shuttle (fee), parking (no fee), some pets allowed, no-smoking rooms* ▭*MC, V.*

$$$ **La Mer Beachfront Apartments.** This two-story hotel near Noosa Heads in Sunshine Beach has apartment-style suites with free satellite TV, video and CD players, and balconies facing the ocean. Large rooms have cane furniture, tile floors, and gorgeous sunrise views. A short bush trail leads to the Esplanade. You can walk to the shopping village and restaurants, and book a range of area tours in the lobby. There's a two-night minimum stay in high season. ✉*5 Belmore Terr., Sunshine Beach, 4567* ☎*07/5447–2111* ⊕*www.lamersunshine.com. au* *20 suites* △*In-room: no a/c (some), fans, kitchen, refrigerator, DVD, VCR, ethernet (some), dial-up (some). In-hotel: pool, beachfront, laundry facilities, airport shuttle, parking (no fee), no-smoking rooms* ▭*MC, V.*

$$$$ **Netanya Noosa.** Most of the airy one-, two-, and three-bedroom
FodorsChoice suites in this low-rise beachfront complex look directly over the main
★

7

beach; a few are in a garden wing. All suites come with entertainment systems and soft bathrobes; most have hot tubs and large verandas. The lavishly appointed penthouse, Presidential, and rock-star-style Starlight suites have large lounge areas, five-star facilities, and private terraces with outdoor Jacuzzis, BBQs, and ocean views. ⊠*75 Hastings St., 4567* ☎*07/5447–4722 or 1800/072072* ⊕*www.netanya noosa.com* ↩*47 suites* ⌂*In-room: safe, kitchen, refrigerator, VCR, DVD, dial-up. In-hotel: restaurant, room service, pool, spa, beachfront, laundry service, executive floor, parking (no fee), no-smoking rooms* ⊟*AE, MC, V.*

$$ ✕**Ricky's River Bar + Restaurant.** A dining room overlooking the Noosa River makes this restaurant perfect for a relaxed lunch or a romantic dinner. The menu features "modern Noosa cuisine," which means Mediterranean flavors mingle with Australian ingredients. Sip a mojito or a mango daiquiri and dig into a plate of tapas before moving on to a main course of fresh reef fish. ⊠*Noosa Wharf, Quamby Pl.* ☎*07/5447–2455* ⊕*www.rickys.com* ⊟*AE, DC, MC, V.*

$$ ✕**Sails.** "Super fresh and super simple" could be the motto at Sails, which serves Mod-Oz cuisine with an emphasis on seasonal local produce. Try the signature grilled Moreton Bay bugs (at market price— A\$65-plus). The open dining pavilion backs straight onto Noosa's famous beach. ⊠*Park Rd. at Hastings St.* ☎*07/5447–4235* ⊕*www. sailsrestaurantnoosa.com* ⊟*AE, DC, MC, V.*

$$$$ ⊞**Sheraton Noosa Resort & Spa.** You can't miss this stepped, six-story,
★ horseshoe-shaped complex as you drive into Noosa Heads. It faces fashionable Hastings Street on one side and the river on the other, and is playfully painted apricot with lavender and sea-green trim. The foyer area is equally colorful, though the adjoining River Lounge is stylish and subdued. It's hard to find fault with the spacious rooms: each has a kitchenette (with coffeemaker), balcony, and hot tub, and a terrace or balcony with river or pool views. The luxurious spa studios are filled with natural products to soothe body and soul. All rooms have private balconies with outdoor hot tubs. Spa studio packages include free use of selected spa facilities. ⊠*14–16 Hastings St., 4567* ☎*07/5449–4888* ⊕*www.sheraton.com/noosa* ↩*140 rooms, 29 suites, 7 spa studios* ⌂*In-room: safe, kitchen, refrigerator, minibar, DVD (some), ethernet, pay movies. In-hotel: restaurant, room service, bars, pool, gym, spa, bicycles, concierge, laundry facilities, laundry service, public Internet, public Wi-Fi, airport shuttle, parking (some free), no smoking, minibar* ⊟*AE, DC, MC, V.*

SUNSHINE BEACH

24 *4 km (2½ mi) south of Noosa Heads.*

Ten minutes away from the bustle and crowds of Hastings Street and Noosa Beach, south of the headland and Noosa National Park, is the serene suburb of Sunshine Beach. It's home to a number of good restaurants, a small shopping village, and, as the name suggests, 16 km (10 mi) of beachfront that stretches north to the national park.

COOLUM

25 *17 km (11 mi) south of Noosa Heads, 25 km (16 mi) northeast of Nambour.*

At the center of the Sunshine Coast, Coolum makes an ideal base for exploring the countryside. It has what is probably the finest beach along the Sunshine Coast, and a growing reputation for good food and quality accommodation.

WHERE TO STAY & EAT

$$$–$$$$
★
✕🏨**Hyatt Regency Coolum.** Spread out at the foot of Mt. Coolum, this is one of the best health resorts in Australia. Accommodations, grouped in low-rise clusters throughout the sprawling complex, include studio suites, two-bedroom villas, and luxurious three-bedroom residences. Villas and residences have kitchens and laundry facilities; residences also have rooftop terraces and hot tubs. The Sun Spa, given a facelift in 2007, has pools, aerobics/yoga/Pilates area, a supervised gym with state-of-the-art equipment, hot tubs, a hair and beauty salon, and dozens of pampering treatments. There's also a tennis center and a golf pro shop. McKenzie Grill serves a juicy steak; Bruschetta, open all day, serves Mediterranean-inspired dishes. A shuttle will transport you around the 370-acre property. ✉*1 Warran Rd., 4573* ☎*07/5446–1234* ⊕*www.coolum.regency.hyatt.com* ➳*156 suites, 168 villas, 5 residences* ♿*In-room: safe, kitchen (some), refrigerator/minibar, DVD, ethernet, hot tub (some). In-hotel: 6 restaurants, room service, bars, golf course, tennis courts, pools, gym, spa, beachfront, water sports, bicycles, concierge, children's programs (ages 6 wks–12 yrs), laundry service, public Internet, public Wi-Fi, airport shuttle, parking (no fee), no-smoking rooms, no elevator, disabled access* ▤*AE, DC, MC, V* ⦿*CP.*

$$$–$$$$
🏨**Coolum Seaside.** These spacious, sunny, one- to four-bedroom apartments and studios, sleekly refurbished in 2007, have excellent views of the coast and are around the corner from Coolum's main restaurant strip, shops, and beach. Each unit has a kitchen, lounge area, entertainment facilities, and a large balcony; the ritziest ones have private rooftop terraces with BBQs and outdoor kitchen areas. The penthouse's view-laden rooftop comes complete with private Jacuzzi, but must be booked for a four-night minimum stay. There's also one fully compliant disabled-friendly apartment, plus swimming and lap pools, a well-equipped gym, and an Internet café. ✉*23 Beach Rd., 4573* ☎*07/5255–7200 or 1800/809062* 🖷*07/5455–7288* ⊕*www.*

7

coolumseaside.com ✑*info@coolumseaside.com* ⇥*44 apartments*
⚬*In-room: safe, kitchen, refrigerator, cable TV, DVD, VCR, ethernet.
In-hotel: tennis court, pools, gym, beachfront, bicycles, laundry facilities, public Internet, no-smoking rooms* ▤*AE, MC, V.*

MAROOCHYDORE

㉖ *18 km (11 mi) south of Coolum, 18 km (11 mi) east of Nambour.*

Maroochydore, at the mouth of the Maroochy River, has been a popular beach resort for years, and has its fair share of high-rise towers. Its draw is excellent surfing and swimming beaches.

WHERE TO STAY & EAT

$$–$$$ ✗**ebb Waterfront.**Faux-suede sofas and ottomans in varying shades of cool blue set the mood at this riverside seafood restaurant specializing in top-quality regional produce. Floor-to-ceiling windows line one side of the long dining room. Start with one of five oyster dishes, the exquisite champagne lobster, or king prawns, before moving on to a beef, venison, or panfried ocean trout dish. Finish with something from the cheese or chocolate menu. ⊠*Duporth Riverside, Duporth Ave.* ☏*07/5452–7771* ⊕*www.ebbwaterfront.com* ▤*AE, MC, V.*

$–$$ ✗**Flags Restaurant at the Maroochy Surf Club.** After a day in the sun, head to this beachside restaurant. Hearty surf-and-turf dishes—grilled rib fillet with garlic prawns—dominate the menu, but grilled swordfish and barramundi are also excellent. Although you can lounge in beachwear by day, smart-casual dress is the rule in the evenings, and live bands play on weekends. A courtesy bus shuttles patrons to and from local hotels. ⊠*34–36 Alexandra Parade* ☏*07/5443–1298* ⊕*www.maroochysurfclub.com.au* ▤*AE, DC, MC, V.*

$$–$$$$ ✗▣**Novotel Twin Waters Resort.** About 9 km (5½ mi) north of Maroochydore, this hotel was built around a 15-acre saltwater lagoon bordering Maroochy River and Mudjimba Beach. The family-friendly resort lies adjacent to one of Queensland's finest golf courses, where golfers share the greens with kangaroos. There are resident golf, surfing, circus and tennis pros, and catamaran sailing, windsurfing, and canoeing on the lagoon is free for guests. Choose from three accommodation styles: twin Resort rooms; King Spa suites, each with a kitchenette, lounge area, and hot tub; and lavish over-water Lagoon Spa suites, popular with couples. All rooms have high-speed Internet, pay movies, and Sony PlayStations, and were given fresh soft furnishings in 2007. Lagoons day spa, perched over the water, incorporates a hair salon and art gallery. The resort's fine-dining restaurant, Lily's-on-the-Lagoon, sits over the water. ⊠*Ocean Dr., Twin Waters, 4564* ☏*07/5448–8000* ⊕*www.twinwatersresort.com.au* ⇥*235 rooms, 129 suites* ⚬*In-room: kitchen (some), refrigerator, minibar (some), ethernet, Wi-Fi. In-hotel: 4 restaurants, room service, 3 bars, golf course, tennis courts, pool, gym, spa, beachfront, water sports, bicycles, children's programs (ages 2–12), laundry facilities, laundry service, public Internet, public Wi-Fi, airport*

shuttle, parking (no fee), no-smoking rooms, no elevator ▤AE, DC, MC, V ⦿BP.

$$$$ ▦**The Sebel Maroochydore.** Each one- or two-bedroom apartment in this stylish hotel has a curved feature wall and a kitchen bristling with European appliances. Most have separate media rooms with all the latest entertainment wizardry. All apartments have stylish blond-wood furniture, cream-colored sofas in sitting areas and bedrooms, and two bathrooms, one with a hot tub. Glass doors lead to spacious, furnished balconies with views over Maroochy River, the beach, or Mount Coolum and the hinterland. The rooftop barbecue area is the perfect place to unwind. A clutch of cafés and restaurants is a short walk away, as is the beach. ⊠*20 Aerodrome Rd., Maroochydore, 4558* ☎*07/5479–8000 or 1800/137106* ⊕*www.mirvachotels.com* ⤷*70 apartments, 6 penthouses* ♿*In-room: safe, kitchen, refrigerator, laundry facilities, DVD, dial-up (some), ethernet (some). In-hotel: room service, pool, hot tub, laundry service, public Internet, parking (no fee), no-smoking rooms* ▤*AE, DC, MC, V.*

MOOLOOLABA

㉗ *5 km (3 mi) south of Maroochydore.*

Mooloolaba stretches along a lovely beach and riverbank, both an easy walk from town. The Esplanade has many casual cafés, upscale restaurants, and fashionable shops. Head to the town outskirts for picnic spots and prime coastal views.

♻ **Underwater World** has round-the-clock marine presentations including stingray feedings, guided shark tours, seal shows, and croc feedings, all accompanied by informative talks. A clear underwater tunnel lets you get face-to-face with creatures from the deep. You can also swim with seals, and scuba dive with resident sharks: the cost, including training, gear, and 30 minutes underwater, is A$165 for beginners, A$99 for certified divers. There are a souvenir shop and a café on-site, as well as an educational dinosaur exhibit. The aquarium is part of Mooloolaba's Wharf Complex, which also has a marina, restaurants, and a tavern. ⊠*Parkyn Parade, The Wharf* ☎*07/5444–8488* ⊕*www.underwaterworld.com.au* ⊠*A$25.50 (includes entry to Dinosaur World)* ⊙*Daily 9–5.*

WHERE TO STAY & EAT

$$–$$$ ✕**Bella Venezia Italian Restaurant & Bar.** A large wall mural of Venice,
★   simple wooden tables, and terra-cotta floor tiles decorate this popular restaurant at the back of an arcade, near the Esplanade. You can eat in or take out traditional and modern Italian cuisine, such as the *penne pollo,* with chicken, avocado, and sun-dried tomatoes, infused in a lime and lemon sauce. There's an extensive wine and cocktail list. On alternate Wednesday nights, stick around for live music in the lounge. ⊠*Pacific Beach Resort, 95 The Esplanade* ☎*07/5444–5844* ⊕*www.bellav.com.au* ▤*AE, DC, MC, V.*

¢–$$ ⌐⌐Sirocco Resort Apartments. The futuristic curves of this apartment complex stand out on Mooloolaba's main drag, just across the road from the beach. Choose from two-, three-, and five-bedroom plans, each with sleek modern furnishings, hot tubs, balconies, and magnificent beach views. A minimum five-night stay is required during high season, from late December through January. Several smart restaurants are just outside the resort's front doors. ⊠ *59–75 The Esplanade, 4557* ☎*07/5444–1400 or 1300/553800 (bookings)* ⊕*www.sirocco-apartments.com.au* ⪡*41 apartments* ⌂ *In-room: kitchen, refrigerator, laundry facilities, DVD (some), VCR (some), dial-up. In-hotel: pool, gym, laundry facilities, laundry service, parking (no fee), no-smoking rooms* ⊟*AE, DC, MC, V.*

CALOUNDRA

28 *29 km (18 mi) south of Maroochydore, 63 km (39 mi) south of Noosa Heads, 91 km (56 mi) north of Brisbane.*

This unassuming southern seaside town has nine beaches of its own, which include everything from placid wading beaches (King's Beach and Bulcock Beach are best for families) to bays with thundering surf, such as Dicky, Buddina, and Wurtulla beaches.

WHERE TO STAY & EAT

$$–$$$ ✕Alfie's mooo char + bar. Owned by legendary (and now retired) Queensland Rugby League footballer Allan "Alfie" Langer, this restaurant has an ideal setting right on Bulcock Beach. It overlooks the sheltered inlet known as Pumicestone Passage. The decor and design are light and bright, and there's both indoor and outdoor dining. Try the restaurant's most popular steak, the Australian rib on the bone; or oysters, done one of half a dozen ways. At lunchtime, there are also burgers and salads. ⊠*The Esplanade at Oranto St.* ☎*07/5492–8155* ⊕*www.alfies.net.au* ⊟*AE, DC, MC, V.*

$$$ ⌐⌐Rolling Surf Resort. The white sands of King's Beach front this resort enveloped in tropical gardens. Wooden blinds, cane furniture, and beach prints fill well-equipped, one- to three-bedroom beachfront and poolside apartments. All rooms have hot tubs; many also have large, curved balconies overlooking the beach. There's a well-equipped gymnasium, a sauna and steam room, and a 60-meter (80-yard) heated pool that can be directly accessed from some ground-floor units, or viewed via underwater portholes from the gym and lobby. The resort's own excellent café-restaurant, Tanja's, does big buffet breakfasts, light and à la carte meals, with white linen service after dark and Indian feasts on alternate Fridays. The Sun Air Bus Service or A1 Airport Transfers will deliver you to the front door from Brisbane Airport. ⊠*Levuka Ave., King's Beach, 4551* ☎*07/5491–9777* ⊕*www.rollingsurfresort. com* ⪡info@RollingSurfResort.com ⪡*74 apartments* ⌂*In-hotel: restaurant, pool, gym, beachfront, laundry facilities, public Internet, parking (no fee)* ⊟*MC, V.*

¢–$ 🏨 **Caloundra City Backpackers.** This purpose-built modern hostel prides itself on being the best value in town. There are twin rooms (without bathrooms), doubles with en suites, and one triple, plus two eight-bed dorms (from A$22 per person, per night). All rooms are

simple but tasteful, outfitted in blue and white. Guests share two fully-equipped kitchens and, when they're not out surfing or sightseeing, can watch DVDs or get online in the hostel's sociable common areas. It's a five-minute walk to the beach, two minutes into town. ⊠ *84 Omrah Ave., 4551* ☎ *07/5499–7655* ⊕ *www.caloundracitybackpackers.com. au* ✐ *wirz@westnet.com.au* ⇆ *14 rooms with shared bath, 5 with bath; 2 dorms* ♿ *In-room: no a/c, no phone, no TV. In-hotel: guest kitchen, refrigerator, safes, DVD, VCR, laundry facilities, public Internet, parking (no fee), no-smoking rooms, disabled access* ⊟ *MC, V.*

AIRLIE BEACH

1,130 km (702 mi) north of Brisbane, 635 km (395 mi) south of Cairns.

Although it's not part of the Sunshine Coast, Airlie Beach has a similar feel to many of the Pacific beach towns far to the south. The waterfront Esplanade, with its boardwalk, landscaped gardens, and Saturday-morning crafts markets, is a lively gathering place. So is the main street, which is chockablock with hotels, restaurants, bars, and shops—many catering to the backpacker crowd.

Beachfront **Airlie Lagoon** is a popular spot for locals and tourists, and provides a stinger-free swimming enclosure open all day, seven days a week. It is patrolled by lifeguards from 9 to 5 daily and has two adjoining children's pools.

Shute Harbour, 11 km (7 mi) southeast from Airlie Beach, is the main ferry terminal and gateway to the islands and the reef. The large sheltered inlet is sprinkled with boats and flanked by steep wooded banks. Shute Harbour is such a hive of marine activity that it's ranked as the second-busiest commuter port in Australia after Sydney's Circular Quay. Though some accommodation is available, the harbor is geared toward transferring visitors to the islands or used as the departure point for yachters or commercial launches to the reef. For a great view over the harbor and Whitsunday Passage, take a drive to the top of Coral Point.

Conway National Park, a 10-minute drive southeast from Airlie Beach, is a 54,000-acre expanse that hugs the coast from Shute Harbour south. It has diverse vegetation, including mangroves, canopies, and tropical lowlands. If you're very lucky, you'll see the endangered Proserpine rock wallaby. Two of the country's mound-building birds—the Australian brush-turkey and the orange-footed scrubfowl—also make their homes here. Walking trails range in length from 1 km (½ mi) to 16 km (10 mi); most start at the park's picnic area on Shute Harbour Road, 4 km (2½ mi) from the information center. Mount Rooper Walking Track meanders through bushland and up to a lookout with breathtaking views of the Whitsunday Islands. The Swamp Bay track follows the creek at the mountain's base to a coral-strewn beach with a bush camping area. Campers need permits (A$4.50 per night), as well as food, water, and all other supplies. Play it safe and avoid swimming at beaches north of Rockhampton October to May, the box-jellyfish season. ⊠*Shute Harbour Rd. at Mandalay Rd.* ☎*07/4945–3711 or 13–1304 (permits)* ⊕*www.epa.qld.gov.au or www.qld.gov.au/camping.*

WHERE TO STAY & EAT

$$–$$$ ✕**Capers at the Beach Bar and Grill.** Tables spill out across bleached terracotta tiles at this busy, beachside restaurant in the Airlie Beach Hotel. The cuisine is Mod-Oz, with nods to Asian and Mediterranean flavors. Seafood and steak dishes highlight a well-rounded menu. Lots of alfresco tables mean you can sit outside on balmy nights, even if you haven't booked ahead. ⊠*The Esplanade at Coconut Grove* ☎*07/4964–1777* ⊕*www.airliebeachhotel.com.au* ▤*AE, DC, MC, V.*

$ ✕**Airlie Thai.** Overlooking the water from the second floor of a beachfront building, this authentic Thai restaurant is a very popular spot for dinner. The local favorite dish is the Thai fish cakes (lightly fried patties of minced fish and spices). The jungle curry spiced with *kachai* (a sweet, aromatic spice in the ginger family) lime leaves, red curry paste, and fresh chilies is another great dish. There are also plenty of vegetarian options such as the hot-and-sour coconut soup. The sweet sticky rice wrapped in banana leaf is the only dessert, but it's perfect. ⊠*Beach Plaza, The Esplanade* ☎*07/4946–4683* ▤*AE, DC, MC, V.*

$$$–$$$$ ▦**Airlie Beach Hotel.** With the beach right at its doorstep and the main street directly behind, this hotel is arguably the most convenient base from which to explore the region. Spacious rooms are decorated with photographs of the reef, ocean, and islands; most open onto balconies overlooking the palm-lined beachfront. ⊠*16 The Esplanade, at Coconut Grove, 4802* ☎*07/4964–1999 or 1800/466233* ⊕*www.airliebeachhotel.com.au* ⤢*56 rooms, 4 suites* ⟁*In-room: refrigerator (some), dial-up, Wi-Fi (some). In-hotel: 3 restaurants, 3 bars, pool, beachfront, laundry facilities, public Wi-Fi, parking (no fee), no-smoking rooms* ▤*AE, DC, MC, V.*

$$
Fodor's Choice
★
▦**Whitsunday Moorings B&B.** Overlooking Abel Point Marina, the two spacious, self-contained guest suites both have panoramic views from their patios. The house is surrounded by mango and frangipani trees filled with frolicking lorikeets. Although host Peter Brooks is extraordinarily helpful with regard to local activities, the lure of his poolside hammock can sidetrack even energetic guests. Rooms are tiled in terra-cotta, with bamboo-mat ceilings and cedar blinds. The rate includes breakfast—a five-star affair: complete with white linen, heavy silverware, beautifully presented tropical fruits and flowers, homemade jams, freshly squeezed juice, and a wide choice of dishes. ⊠*37 Air-*

lie Crescent, 4802 ☎07/4946–4692 ✐info@whitsundaymooringsbb. com.au ⊕*www.whitsundaymooringsbb.com.au* ⌑2 rooms ⌂*In-room: refrigerator, kitchen. In-hotel: pool, laundry facilities, parking (no fee), no smoking, no elevator* ▤*AE, DC, MC, V* ¶❙*BP.*

¢ ▣**Beaches Backpackers.** With the liveliest bar and bistro in Airlie Beach on the premises, this hostel in the center of town attracts a party crowd, which makes things noisy (but keeps dorms near-empty) until around midnight. Stay in an eight-bed dorm or opt for a more private double or twin room; each is air-conditioned, serviced daily, and has an en suite bathroom, small TV, fridge, and balcony; some dorms are sex-segregated. There's a small, palm-shaded on-site pool, and an Internet and games room. Friendly reception staff will store your bags and valuables, and book tours. Beaches Bistro, downstairs, serves reasonably priced lunches, snacks, and nightly dinners. A free shuttle bus service runs between the bus terminal and the hostel. ✉*356 Shute Harbour Rd., 4802* ☎*07/4946–6244 or 1800/636630* ⊕*www.beaches.com.au* ⌑*7 rooms, 24 dorms* ⌂*In-room: refrigerator. In-hotel: restaurant, bar, pool, beachfront, laundry facilities, public Internet, parking (no fee), no elevator* ▤*MC, V.*

NIGHTLIFE

Shute Harbour Road is where it all happens in Airlie Beach. Bars and nightspots offer the backpacker crowd all kinds of undergraduate entertainment, from Jell O wrestling to pole-dancing competitions. Some clubs have live music on weekends.

The crowd's friendly at **Beaches Bar & Bistro** (✉*362 Shute Harbour Rd.* ☎*072/4946–6244* ⊕*www.beaches.com.au*), part of the backpackers' hostel of the same name. Catch one of the nightly live bands or watch sports games on TV.

Head to **Magnums** (✉*366 Shute Harbour Rd.* ☎*07/4946–7929 or 1800/624634* ⊕*www.magnums.com.au*) to join the party. The club is split into two venues: one has wilder activities, like toad racing, bull riding, wet T-shirt contests, and foam parties. The other has live music and happy-hour drink specials.

THE SUNSHINE COAST & AIRLIE BEACH ESSENTIALS

TRANSPORTATION

AIR TRAVEL

Sunshine Coast Airport (also known as Maroochy airport) is the main airport for the Sunshine Coast area, servicing nine domestic flights a day by Jetstar and Virgin Blue from capital cities around Australia. By air from Maroochydore, it's 2 hours 25 minutes to Melbourne, 2 hours to Adelaide, and 1 hour 35 minutes to Sydney.

The Whitsunday Coast Airport in Proserpine, 25 km (16 mi) southeast from Airlie Beach, has daily flights from Sydney and Brisbane with Jetstar and flights to all capital cities with Virgin Blue.

Airports Maroochydore Airport (*Sunshine Coast Airport* ✉*Friendship Ave. off David Low Way, Marcoola* ☎*07/5453–1500*). **Whitsunday Coast Airport** (✉*Air Whitsunday Dr. off Shute Harbour Rd., Proserpine* ☎*07/4945–3352*).

Airlines Jetstar (☎*13–1538* ⊕*www.jetstar.com.au*).**Virgin Blue** (☎*13–6789* ⊕*www.virginblue.com.au*).

BUS TRAVEL

SunCoast Pacific offers daily bus service from Brisbane Airport and the Roma Street Transit Centre in Brisbane to all main Sunshine Coast townships. Distances are short, usually between 10 and 30 minutes between towns. Sun Air Bus Service has daily links from Brisbane and Maroochy airports to Sunshine Coast towns. Henry's Transport Group meets all flights, and runs services from Maroochy Airport to the northern Sunshine Coast (airport to Noosa is A$20) and, on market days, to Eumundi (A$15).

Greyhound Australia and Oz Experience offer about 12 services daily into Airlie Beach from Sydney, Brisbane, and many towns between, as well as from Cairns.

Contacts Greyhound Australia (☎*13–1499* ⊕*www.greyhound.com.au*). **Henry's Transport Group** (☎*07/5474–0199* ⊕*www.henrys.com.au*). **Oz Experience** (☎*1300/300028* ⊕*www.ozexperience.com.au*). **Sun Air Bus Service** (☎*07/5478–2811*). **SunCoast Pacific Coaches** (☎*07/5443–1011 or 07/5449–9966 [lost property]* ⊕*http://www.suncoastpacific.com.au/*).

CAR TRAVEL

A car is a virtual necessity on the Sunshine Coast. The traditional route to the coast from Brisbane is along the Bruce Highway (Highway 1) to the Glass House Mountains, with a turnoff at Cooroy. This makes for a two-hour drive to Noosa, the heart of the area. However, the motorway may be faster. Turn off the Bruce Highway at Tanawha (toward Mooloolaba) and follow the signs. The most scenic route is to turn off the Bruce Highway to Caloundra and follow the coast to Noosa Heads.

TRAIN TRAVEL

Trains leave regularly from Roma Street Transit Centre in Brisbane en route to Nambour, the business hub of the Sunshine Coast. They continue on to Yandina and Eumundi and other noncoastal towns. Once in Nambour, however, a car is a necessity, so it may make more sense to drive from Brisbane.

Queensland Rail operates approximately six northbound and six southbound trains weekly into the Proserpine Railway Station, about 27 km (17 mi) from Airlie Beach. The Whitsunday Transit shuttle bus (☎ *07/4946–1800*) meets all trains, traveling to Airlie Beach and Shute Harbour (about 30 minutes' drive).

Contacts Proserpine Railway Station (✉*Hinschen St., Proserpine* ☎*07/4945–1013 or 13–1617*).**Queensland Rail** (☎*13–1617 or 1800/627655* ⊕*www.qr.com.au*).

CONTACTS & RESOURCES

EMERGENCIES

Dial **000** to reach an ambulance, the police, or the fire department.

Hospitals Nambour General Hospital (⊠ *Hospital Rd., Nambour* ☎ *07/5470–6600*). **Whitsunday Doctors' Service** (⊠ *257 Shute Harbour Rd., Airlie Beach* ☎ *07/4946–6241*).

Pharmacies Noosa Heads Day and Night Pharmacy (⊠ *1 Laguna Ct., Hastings St., Noosa Heads* ☎ *07/5447–3298*).

TOURS

Southern Cross Motorcycle Tours provides one of the best ways to get a feel for the Sunshine Coast: by riding a Harley-Davidson motorcycle from the beach to the Blackall Range. The company's team of experienced guides know the area and will take you on an hour-long, half- or full-day's excursion on the back of a bike. The company arranges door-to-door pickups anywhere on the Sunshine Coast. From A$95 for an hour-long tour including helmet and jacket.

Koala Adventures, part of a chain of backpacker hostels along the Queensland coast, runs three-day sailing trips around the Whitsunday Islands from A$329 (2 days, 3 nights) to A$429 (3 days, 3 nights). The cost includes all meals, bedding, and snorkeling equipment. There's an additional marine tax of A$33 per person.

Oz Adventure Sailing runs overnight sailing and snorkeling trips around the islands on any of its 23 vessels from A$339 (plus A$33 marine tax) for a two-day excursion with all meals, bedding, and snorkeling gear (stinger suits extra).

Contacts Koala Adventures (⊠ *Koala Beach Resort, Shute Harbour Rd., Airlie Beach* ☎ *07/4946–6001 or 1800/466444* ⊕ *www.koala-backpackers.com*). **Oz Adventure Sailing** (⊠ *293 Shute Harbour Rd., Airlie Beach* ☎ *1300/653100* ⊕ *www.ozsailing.com.au*). **Southern Cross Motorcycle Tours** (⊡ *Box 7175, Sippy Downs, 4556* ☎ *0408/884057* ⊕ *www.motorcycle-tours.com.au*).

VISITOR INFORMATION

Contacts Maroochy Tourism (⊠ *Sunshine Coast airport, Friendship Ave., Mudjimba,* ☎ *1800/882032 or 07/5479–1566* ⊕ *www.maroochytourism.com*) has branches at the airport, Maroochydore, Mooloolaba, Coolum, and Montville.

Tourism Noosa (⊠ *Hastings St. at the roundabout, Noosa Heads* ⊠ *Noosa Marina, 2 Parkyn Ct., Tewantin* ☎ *1300/066672* ⊕ *www.tourismnoosa.com.au*).

Whitsundays Information Centre (⊠ *Bruce Hwy., Proserpine* ☎ *1800/801252* ⊕ *www.tourismwhitsundays.com.au*).

FRASER ISLAND

Some 200 km (124 mi) north of Brisbane, Fraser Island, at 1,014 square km (630 square mi), is both the largest of Queensland's islands and the most unusual. Originally known as K'gari to the local Butchulla Aboriginal people, the island was later named after Eliza Fraser, who in 1836 was shipwrecked here and lived with local Aborigines for several weeks. It's the world's largest sand island—instead of coral reefs and coconut palms, it has wildflower-dotted meadows, freshwater lakes, a teeming bird population, dense stands of rain forest, towering sand dunes, and sculpted, multicolor sand cliffs along its east coast. That lineup has won the

island a place on UNESCO's World Heritage list. The surf fishing is legendary, and humpback whales and their calves can be seen wintering in Hervey Bay between May and September. The island also has interesting Aboriginal sites dating back more than a millennium.

Hervey Bay is the name given to the expanse of water between Fraser Island and the Queensland coast. It's also the generic name given to a conglomeration of four nearby coastal towns—Urangan, Pialba, Scarness, and Torquay—that have grown into a single settlement. This township, along with Rainbow Beach, are the main jumping-off points for most excursions. (Note that maps and road signs usually refer to individual town names, not Hervey Bay.)

You can pitch a tent anywhere you don't see a NO CAMPING sign; there are three main public campgrounds—Central Station, Dundubara, and Waddy Point—that require you to book in advance. These campgrounds have fenced sites, toilet blocks, drinking water, hot showers (some campgrounds have coin-operated showers, taking A$1 coins), gas grills, phones, and other amenities. There are also smaller designated camping areas along Fraser Island's Great Walk, and a number of established beach campsites, all run by Queensland Parks and Wildlife Service. They have toilet blocks, picnic tables, and walking trails. Most lack drinking water, so be sure to bring plenty with you. Because the entire island is a World Heritage site, permits for camping (A$4.50 per person, per night) are required and there's a maximum stay of 22 nights.

Fraser's east coast marks the intersection of two serious Australian passions: an addiction to the beach and a love affair with the motor vehicle. Unrestricted access has made this coast a giant sandbox for four-wheel-drive vehicles during busy school-holiday periods. All vehicles entering the island by car barge from the mainland must have a one-month Vehicle Access Permit (A$32.60). There are a number of places in southeast Queensland including Maryborough, Urangan, and Rainbow Beach, where you can obtain these and camping permits for the island. (If you prefer your wilderness *sans* dune-buggying, head for the unspoiled interior of the island.)

For the closest permit center, contact the **Environmental Protection Agency (EPA) Customer Service Centre** (✉*160 Ann St., Brisbane, 4000* ☎*1300/130372 or 07/3227–8185 (info), or 13–1304 (permits)* ⊕*www. epa.qld.gov.au or www.qld.gov.au/camping*).

EXPLORING FRASER ISLAND

Note that swimming in the ocean off the east coast is not recommended because of the rough conditions and sharks that hunt close to shore.

Highlights of a drive along the east coast, which is known as Seventy-Five Mile Beach for its sheer distance, include **Eli Creek,** a great freshwater swimming hole. North of this popular spot lies the rusting hulk of the *Maheno,* half buried in the sand, a roost for seagulls and a prime hunting ground for anglers when the tailor are running. Once a luxury passenger steamship that operated between Australia and New Zealand (and served as a hospital ship during World War I), it was wrecked during a cyclone in 1935 as it was being towed to Japan to be sold for scrap metal. North of the wreck are the **Pinnacles**—dramatic, deep-red cliff formations. About 20 km (12 mi) south of Eli Creek, and surrounded by massive sand-blow (or dune), is **Lake Wabby,** the deepest of the island's lakes.

Great Sandy National Park (☎07/5449–7792 ⊕*www.epa.qld.gov.au*) covers the top third of the island. Beaches around Indian Head are known for their shell middens—shell heaps that were left behind after Aboriginal feasting. The head's name is another kind of relic: Captain James Cook saw Aborigines standing on the headland as he sailed past, and he therefore named the area after inhabitants he believed to be "Indians." Farther north, past Waddy Point, is one of Fraser Island's most magnificent variations on sand: wind and time have created enormous dunes. Nearby at Orchid Beach are a series of bubbling craters known as Champagne Pools.

The center of the island is a quiet, natural garden of paperbark swamps, giant satinay and brush box forests, wildflower heaths, and 40 freshwater lakes. The spectacularly clear **Lake McKenzie,** ringed by a beach of incandescent whiteness, is the perfect place for a refreshing swim.

The island's excellent network of walking trails converges at **Central Station,** a former logging camp at the center of the island. Services here are limited to a map board, parking lot, and campground. It's a promising place for spotting dingoes, however. Comparative isolation has meant that Fraser Island's dingoes are the most purebred in Australia. They're also wild animals, so remember: don't feed them, watch from a distance, and keep a close eye on children, especially between late afternoon and early morning. Dingo alerts are in force around Eurong and Happy Valley. Most of the island's well-marked trails are sandy tracks that take anywhere from 15 minutes to 10 hours to traverse. Guides advise wearing sturdy shoes and carrying first-aid supplies and drinking water on all walks.

A boardwalk heads south from Central Station to **Wanggoolba Creek,** a favorite spot for photographers. The little stream snakes through a

7

green palm forest, trickling over a bed of white sand between clumps of rare angiopteris fern. The 1-km (½-mi) circuit takes 30 minutes to an hour.

One trail from Central Station leads through rain forest—growing, incredibly enough, straight out of the sand—to **Pile Valley,** which has a stand of giant satinay trees. Allow two hours to walk this 4½-km (2¼-mi) circuit.

WHERE TO STAY & EAT

The island's only official private campground, **Frasers at Cathedral Beach** (☎07/4127–9177 or 1800/444234 ⊕*http://www.fraserislandco.com. au/*), costs A$22 to A$42 per night. Cabins with two and three bed-rooms are A$130–A$205 per night and A$680–A$1155 per week, depending on the season. Booking well in advance is essential. The University of Sunshine Coast runs **Dilli Village Campground** (☎07/4127–9130), just south of Eurong on the east coast. The Queensland Parks and Wildlife Service manages the island and maintains ranger bases at Dundubara, Eurong, and Waddy Point.

$$$ ✕▦ **Kingfisher Bay Resort and Village.** This stylish, high-tech marriage
Ⓒ of glass, stainless steel, dark timber, and corrugated iron nestles in the
Fodor'sChoice tree-covered dunes of the island's west coast. The impressive lobby,
★ with its cathedral ceiling and polished floorboards, leads out to wrap-around decks with outdoor dining areas and one of the resort's four pools. Lodgings include elegantly furnished standard rooms with bal-conies, lovely villas, and wilderness lodges for groups. Rangers conduct informative four-wheel-drive eco tours; free nature walks; spotlight-ing tours; and whale-, dugong-, and dolphin-watch cruises in season. Children can join junior ranger or kids' club activities. Free fishing classes and boat rentals are available: the chefs here will even cook your catch! You can hire canoes, catamarans, and snorkeling gear; or get pampered at the spa/salon. There are medical facilities and an ATM on-site. Seabelle's excellent menu incorporates native ingredients and local seafood, with vegetarian options. Maheno restaurant has nightly themed buffet dinners; the Wilderness Bar nightclub is a short shuttle bus-ride from reception. Accommodation-meal packages are avail-able. ⊠*North White Cliffs, 75 Mile Beach* ⌖*PMB 1, Urangan, 4655* ☎*07/4120–3333 or 1800/072555* ✆reservations@kingfisherbay. com ⊕*www.kingfisherbay.com* ⇥*152 rooms, 109 villas, 184 beds in lodges (for 18-35s)* ⓓ*In-room: kitchen (some), refrigerator, DVD (some), VCR (some), dial-up. In-hotel: safe, 4 restaurants, 6 bars, 4 tennis courts, 4 pools, spa, beachfront, water sports, children's pro-grams (ages 1–14), laundry facilities, laundry service, public Internet, airport shuttle, 4WD rental, no-smoking rooms, no elevator (but dis-abled access)* ▤*AE, DC, MC, V.*

$–$$$ ▦ **Eurong Beach Resort.** This east-coast resort has the best of Fraser Island at its doorstep. Lake McKenzie and Central Station are 20 min-utes away, and the famous Seventy-Five Mile Beach, Eli Creek, and other coastal attractions are within an easy drive. Lodgings range from four-person dorms (mainly for groups) to standard rooms and two-bedroom apartments. Some units overlook the ocean, others the resort and pool area. Fully inclusive, two-day Fraser Explorer tour packages (from A$255 quad-share, with room upgrades available) include all meals. Buffet dinners are available for A$25 per person, and there's a bakery for snacks. The resort store sells everything from food to fuel and fishing gear. ⊠ *75 Mile Beach* ⊡ *Box 7332, Hervey Bay, 4655* ☎ *07/4120–1600* ✉ *eurong@fraser-is.com* ⊕ *www.eurong.com* ↪ *24 rooms, 16 apartments* ♿ *In-room: no a/c (some), fans, kitchen (some), refrigerator, DVD (some). In-hotel: 2 restaurants, 2 bars, tennis court, 2 pools, beachfront, laundry facilities, public Internet, parking, no elevator* ⊟ *MC, V.*

$$ 🏠 **The Fraser Island Company (Fraser Island Wilderness Retreat).** This cluster of wooden beachside cottages—some small, some large enough for families—is nestled in landscaped gardens on the Happy Valley hillsides, halfway down the island's eastern coast. Each cottage is self-contained but serviced daily. There's a bar and bistro that serves three meals daily. It's centrally located, a 15-minute drive from Eli Creek and 20 minutes from the *Maheno* shipwreck and the Pinnacles. ⊠ *Happy Valley,* ⊡ *Box 5224, Torquay, 4655* ☎ *07/4127–9144 or 1800/446655* ⊕ *www.fraserislandco.com.au* ↪ *9 cottages* ♿ *In-room: no a/c, no phone, kitchen, refrigerator, DVD. In-hotel: restaurant, bar, pool, beachfront, laundry facilities, airport shuttle* ⊟ *AE, MC, V.*

7

FRASER ISLAND ESSENTIALS

TRANSPORTATION

AIR TRAVEL

The Fraser Coast (Hervey Bay) airport now has direct Jetstar services to and from Sydney on Monday, Wednesday, Friday, and Sunday, and Virgin Blue has daily flights to and from Sydney. Two shuttlebuses link the airport to mainland and coastal towns, meeting all flights.

Airport Fraser Coast (Hervey Bay) Airport (⊠ *Don Adams Dr., Urangan* ☎ *07/4194–8100).*

Airlines Jetstar (☎ *13–1538* ⊕ *www.jetstar.com).* **Virgin Blue** (☎ *13–6789* ⊕ *www.virginblue.com.au).* **Airport Shuttle Hervey Bay** (☎ *07/4194–0953* ⊕ *www.airportshuttleherveybay.com.au).*

BOAT & FERRY TRAVEL

A number of car ferry services connect the mainland with Fraser Island. The Rainbow Venture and Fraser Explorer ferries run continuously 6 AM–5:30 PM between Inskip Point near Rainbow Beach on the mainland (between Brisbane and Hervey Bay via the Bruce Highway) and Hook Point at the southern end of the island. The round-trip fare is A$90 per vehicle, including driver and passengers. No advance reservations are required.

The Fraser Dawn ferry departs from Urangan Boat Harbour (on the mainland) for the one-hour journey to Fraser Island's Moon Point twice a day (8:30 AM, returning 9:30; and 4 PM, departing Moon Point for the return trip at 5). Round-trip fare is A$140 for a vehicle, driver, and up to three passengers. The Kingfisher vehicle barge connects River Heads (on the mainland) with Kingfisher Bay Resort in 45 minutes. Trips run three times daily, and round-trip fare is A$140 for a vehicle, driver, and up to three passengers. You'll need to book ahead for these services. Kingfisher Bay also runs two passenger ferries, K1 and K2, from Urangan marina to Kingfisher Bay Resort on Fraser Island six times daily (A$50 return, passenger only). The trip takes 30–45 minutes.

Manta Ray has two distinctive green-and-yellow barges that go between Inskip Point and Hook Point, making up to 40 round-trips daily from 6:30 AM to 5:30 PM, depending on demand. The trip takes around 15 minutes, so if you miss one barge, the next will be along soon. The round-trip cost per vehicle is A$75 (A$50 one-way); it's $A115 for a four-wheel-drive vehicle and trailer. Buy tickets as you board or online.

Contacts Fraser Island Barges (Fraser Dawn) (☎ 07/4194–9222). **Kingfisher Bay Ferry & vehicle barge** (☎ 1800/072555 ⊕ www.kingfisherbay.com). **Rainbow Venture and Fraser Explorer** (☎ 07/5486–3227 or 0400/707–791). **Manta Ray** (☎ 0418/872–599 or 07/5486–8888 ⊕ www.fraserislandbarge.com.au).

BUS TRAVEL

Greyhound Australia operates daily services from Brisbane to Hervey Bay and Maryborough, a township just south of Hervey Bay; Greyhound and Suncoast Pacific have daily coaches from Brisbane to the Sunshine Coast.

Contacts Greyhound Australia (✉ Bay Central Coach Terminal, 1st Ave., Pialba ☎ 13–1499 ⊕ www.greyhound.com.au).

Suncoast Pacific Coaches (✉ Maroochydore Terminal, 1st Ave., Maroochydore ☎ 07/5443–1011 or 07/5443–4180 ⊕ www.suncoastpacific.com.au).

CAR RENTAL

You can rent four-wheel-drive vehicles at Kingfisher Bay Resort and Village and Fraser Island Wilderness Retreat for around A$250 a day, or from Budget car rentals at Urangan on the mainland for considerably less.

Contacts Fraser Island Wilderness Co. Tour Desk (☎ 1800/063933). **Budget Car Rental** (☎ 07/4125–3633 ⊕ www.budget.com.au). **Kingfisher Bay Resort and Village** (☎ 07/4120–3333 or 1800/072555 ⊕ www.kingfisherbay.com).

CAR TRAVEL

The southernmost tip of Fraser Island is 200 km (124 mi) north of Brisbane. The best access is via vehicle ferry from Rainbow Beach, or from the Hervey Bay area, another 90 km (56 mi) away. For Rainbow Beach, take the Bruce Highway toward Gympie, then follow the signs to Rainbow Beach. For Hervey Bay, head north to Maryborough, then follow signs to Urangan.

Four-wheel-drive rentals may be cheaper on the mainland, but factoring in the ferry ticket makes it less expensive to get your rental on-island. Most commodities, including gas, are pricier on the island than the mainland.

Wet weather and sandy surfaces can make island driving hazardous. Mechanical assistance for basic repairs is available from Eurong, and there are tow-truck services at Eurong. Orchid Beach has emergency towing only. If you can't get the mechanical assistance you need, phone Eurong Police.

Contacts Mechanical assistance (✉ *Eurong* ☎ *07/4127–9449 or 0428/353–164* ✉ *Orchid Beach* ☎ *07/4127–9220).* **Fraser Island Eastern Beaches/Eurong Police** (✉ *Eurong* ☎ *07/4127–9268*).

CONTACTS & RESOURCES

EMERGENCIES

Dial **000** to reach an ambulance, the police, or the fire department.

Fraser Island does not have a resident doctor. Emergency medical assistance can be obtained at the ranger stations in Eurong, Waddy Point, and Dundubara, but these have variable hours—if no answer, phone the base station at Nambour on the mainland. Kingfisher Bay Resort has first-aid facilities and resident nursing staff.

Contacts Dundubara Ranger Station (☎ *07/4127–9138*). **Eurong Ranger Station** (☎ *07/4127–9128*). **Nambour Base Station** (☎ *07/4041–1333*). **Waddy Point Ranger Station** (☎ *07/4127–9190*).

TOURS

Air Fraser Island operates whale-watching flights of 45 minutes or more across Hervey Bay between July and October for A$85, and scenic flights and day trips to the island year-round. Fly/dive day-tour packages include flights to and from the island, plus four-wheel-drive vehicle rental, for A$125 per person. Book through Oz Horizons.

For day-trippers, Kingfisher Bay Resort runs a Day Away package (A$55) that includes catamaran transfers between Urangan and Kingfisher Bay Resort, lunch, and a ranger-led walking tour. The resort also conducts various ranger-led island tours in air-conditioned coaches, departing daily from Rainbow Beach (A$135), Hervey Bay (A$145), and Noosa (A$135), as well as an overnight Fraser Explorer tour. From August to October, the resort runs daily whale-watching excursions from Kingfisher Bay (A$100).

Contacts Air Fraser Island/Oz Horizons (☎ *07/4125–3600 or 1800/252668* ⊕ *www.ozhorizons.com.au*).**Kingfisher Bay Resort and Village** (☎ *1800/072555* ⊕ *www.kingfisherbay.com*).

VISITOR INFORMATION

Fraser Coast Booking Office, on the mainland, is a good source of information, maps, and brochures. The center will also help you with tour and accommodations bookings. Another useful pit stop is Hervey Bay Visitor & Tourist Information.

The Outback

Queensland's Outback region is a vast and exciting place, filled with people used to relying on each other in isolated townships. If you choose to tour this vast, rugged region, there are two popular routes.

THE CAPRICORN HIGHWAY ROUTE

Heading inland from Rockhampton along Route 66 means you can stop at the **gem fields** near the towns of Rubyvale, Sapphire, Anakie, and the Willows. These towns have a Wild West, frontier feel, and the 25,000-acre area around them comprises one of the world's richest source of sapphires. You can fossick for your own gems; if you make a find you can visit one of the 100-plus gem cutters in the area to have your jewel cut and polished. At **Gemfest** (☎07/4985-4375 ⊕www.gemfest.com.au), held the second week of August, miners, merchants, and traders converge to swap information, showcase local gems, and sell or barter their wares. Before continuing to Longreach, 400 km (320 mi) to the west, swing southward and spend a night or two at **Carnarvon Gorge.** This amazing series of towering sandstone cliffs is the most visited site in Carnarvon National Park. Walking trails here lead to the Gallery and Cathedral Cave, painted with ancient Aboriginal rock art (in the rainy season, these can be washed away—phone for condition reports). There are a campsite and other accommodations; for details, contact the **Queensland Parks and Wildlife Service** (☎07/4984-4505 or 07/4622-4266 ⊕www.epa.qld.gov. au). Carnarvon National Park is 230 km (144 mi) south of Emerald via the Gregory and Dawson highways.

At Longreach, you'll find one of the highlights of the Queensland Outback, the **Australian Stockman's Hall of Fame & Outback Heritage Centre.** Exhibits on everything from Aboriginal history to droving (moving cattle from town to market over vast areas of land), mustering (rounding up cattle), and bush crafts pay tribute to the pioneers who sought to tame the Australian Outback. In winter months, a twice-daily stockman show provides bargain-priced thrills (A$5). There's a café, large souvenir and gift outlet, and an RM Williams bush-gear store on-site. ⊠ Off Landsborough (aka Matilda) Hwy., Longreach ☎07/4658-2166 ⊕www.outbackheritage.com.au ☎A$22.50 ☉Daily 9–5.

If you continue northwest of Longreach for another 186 km (115 mi), you'll come to the town of Winton, home of the interactive **Waltzing Matilda Centre.** An art gallery, history museum, restaurant, and sound-and-light show are all here, as is the Qantilda Museum, a diverse collection of Outback pioneering memorabilia. ⊠Elderslie St., Winton ☎07/4657-1466 ⊕www.experiencewinton.com. au ☎A$19 ☉Apr.–Oct., daily 8:30–5; Nov.–May, daily 9–4.

A bit farther north, just outside the little town of Kyuna, you can stop to dip your toes in **Combo Waterhole,** where A. B. "Banjo" Paterson wrote the lyrics for "Waltzing Matilda," Australia's unofficial national anthem.

THE OVERLANDER'S HIGHWAY ROUTE

Heading west from Townsville on the Flinders Highway (aka the Overlander's Way) will give you the chance to stop at **Charters Towers,**, which has more than 60 buildings of historical significance. Farther west is Hughenden, known for the many ancient fossils found in the region. "Hughie," a Muttaburrasaurus skeleton, is on display at the **Flinders Discovery Centre** (⊠ *37 Gray St., Hughenden* ☎ *07/4741–1021* ⊕ *www.hughenden. com* ⊗ *Daily 9–5* ▧ *A$3.50*), along with natural history, gem and fossil exhibits, and a gift shop.

From Hughenden, continue via Cloncurry to Mount Isa, a city of 22,000 people from 50 different nations, where you'll find the sprawling Mount Isa Mine, Australia's deepest underground mine and one of the world's largest producers of copper, silver, lead, and zinc. The southern hemisphere's biggest rodeo takes place here each July or August (☎ *1800/763361* or *07/4743–2706* ⊕ *www.isarodeo.com.au*). Mount Isa is also a good jumping-off point for exploring the spring-fed rivers and gorges of **Boodjamulla (Lawn Hill) National Park** (☎ *07/4722–5224* *(weekdays 10–4)* or *13–1304 (permits)* ⊕ *www.epa.qld.gov.au*), where you can canoe amid freshwater crocodiles and camp in the wilderness for A$4.50 per person, per night (BYO tents, gear and water). Mount Isa is also home to the **Outback at Isa**, an interpretive center in the heart of Mount Isa, which has fossil exhibits from the Riversleigh Fossil site, some 300 km (186 mi) away. Here, you can participate in the Hard Times Underground Mine Experience, where you'll dress in a miner's outfit—hard hat, white suit, and headlamp—and tour a "mock-up" mine shaft 49½ feet below the surface. ⊠ *19 Marion St., Mount Isa* ☎ *1300/659660* or *07/4749–1555* ⊕ *www.outbackatisa.com.au* ▧ *Mine and all museums A$55, mine only A$45* ⊗ *Daily 8:30–5.*

If you're a fan of the movie *Crocodile Dundee,* you might want to head south from Cloncurry via Route 66 to the tiny dusty town of McKinlay. This little hamlet's claim to fame is the low-framed, rustic **Walkabout Creek Hotel** (⊠ *Middleton St., McKinlay* ☎ *07/4746–8424*), featured in the movie.

When traveling any of these routes by car, take the necessary precautions. Use a four-wheel-drive vehicle—some roads are unpaved and become slippery after it rains. Always carry spare water, a first-aid kit, a good local map, and sufficient fuel to get to the next town (which may mean carrying spare gas cans). If you're traveling into remote areas, advise local police or another responsible person of your travel plans and report back to them when you return. If you have an on-road emergency, call **000** from the nearest phone to reach an ambulance or the police.

If you prefer to let someone else do the driving, you can travel through the Outback by bus or train. **Greyhound Australia** (☎ *13–1499* ⊕ *www.greyhound.com.au*) services all towns on the Flinders Highway between Townsville and Mount Isa, with connections to the Northern Territory. It also travels between Brisbane and Cloncurry, via Charleville, Longreach, and Winton, and from Rockhampton to Longreach via the gemstone towns. **Queensland Rail**'s *Spirit of the Outback* travels from Brisbane, via Rockhampton to Longreach (connecting with the bus to Winton) twice weekly, departing Tuesdays and Saturdays. *The Westlander* links Brisbane with Charleville on Tuesdays and Thursdays; *The Inlander* travels from Townsville to Mount Isa every Thursday and Sunday. Phone Traveltrain at ☎ *1300/131722* or contact ⊕ *www.qr.com.au*

7

Contacts **Fraser Coast Tour Booking Office** (✉ *Buccaneer Ave., Urangan* ☎ *07/4128–9800*).**Hervey Bay Tourist & Visitor Information** (✉ *401 The Esplanade, Hervey Bay, 4655* ☎ *07/4124–4050* 🖷 *07/4124–5557* ⊕ *www.her-veybaytouristinfo.com.au*).

TOWNSVILLE & MAGNETIC ISLAND

Townsville—and its adjacent twin city of Thuringowa—make up Australia's largest tropical city, with a combined population of around 160,000. It's the commercial capital of the north, and a major center for education, scientific research, and defense. Spread along the banks of Ross Creek and around the pink granite outcrop of Castle Hill, Townsville is a pleasant city of palm-fringed malls, historic colonial buildings, and lots of parkland and gardens. It's also the stepping-off point for Magnetic Island, one of the state's largest islands and a haven for wildlife.

TOWNSVILLE

The summit of **Castle Hill,** 1 km (½ mi) from the city center, provides great views of the city as well as Magnetic Island. While you're perched on top, think about the proud local resident who, along with several scout troops, spent years in the 1970s piling rubble onto the peak to try to add the 23 feet that would officially make it Castle Mountain. (Technically speaking, a rise has to exceed 1,000 feet to be called a mountain, and this one tops out at just 977 feet.) Most people walk to the top, along a steep walking track that doubles as one of Queensland's most scenic jogging routes.

☺ **Reef HQ Aquarium,** on the waterfront, only a few minutes' walk from the city center, has the world's largest live coral reef aquarium—a living slice of the Great Barrier Reef. There are more than 100 species of hard coral, 30 soft corals, and hundreds of fish. Also here are an enclosed underwater walkway, theater, café, and shop. ✉ *2–68 Flinders St. E* ☎ *07/4750–0800* ⊕ *www.reefhq.com.au* 🖭 *A$22.50* ⊙ *Daily 9:30–5.*

☺ The **Museum of Tropical Queensland** displays relics of the HMS *Pandora,* which sank in 1791 while carrying 14 crew members of the infamous ship *Bounty.* The Troppo! gallery is a fun introduction to North Queensland's culture and lifestyle. Also on display are tropical wildlife, dinosaur fossils, local corals, deep-sea creatures, and a new shipwreck exhibit. ✉ *70–102 Flinders St. E* ☎ *07/4726–0600* ⊕ *www.mtq. qm.qld.gov.au* 🖭 *A$13* ⊙ *Daily 9:30–5.*

A stroll along **Flinders Street** will show you some of Townsville's turn-of-the-20th-century colonial architecture. **Magnetic House** and other buildings have been beautifully restored. The old **Queens Hotel** is built in Classical Revival style, as is the 1885 **Perc Tucker Regional Gallery,** originally a bank. The former post office, now the Brewery, had an impressive **masonry clock tower** (✉ *Flinders and Denham Sts.*) when it was erected in 1889. The tower was dismantled in 1942 so it wouldn't be a target during World War II air raids, but was put up again in 1964. The Exchange, Townsville's oldest pub, was built in 1869, burnt down in 1881, and rebuilt the following year.

The Strand, a 2½-km (1½-mi) beachfront boulevard, is lined with restaurants, cafés, bars, barbecue grills, swimming enclosures, water-sports facilities, and a water playground for children. The avenue runs along Cleveland Bay, with views to Magnetic Island.

Townsville Common Environmental Park nature preserve is home to spoonbills, jabiru storks, pied geese, herons, and ibis, and occasional wallabies, goannas, echidnas, and dingoes. Most birds leave the swamp in dry season, May through August, but they're back by October. The Common is open daily 6:30 AM–6:30 PM; entrance is free. Take Cape Pallarenda Road north to Pallarenda, 7 km (4½ mi) from Townsville.

Queen's Gardens is a lovely place to spend a cool couple of hours. The compact (10 acre) park is bordered with frangipani and towering Moreton Bay fig trees, whose unique hanging roots veil the entry to the grounds. ✉ *Gregory St. near Warburton St. (enter off Paxton St.)* ☎ *No phone* 🖼 *Free* 🕐 *Daily dawn–dusk.*

OFF THE BEATEN PATH

Billabong Sanctuary. This 22-acre nature park 17 km (11 mi) south of Townsville shelters crocodiles, koalas, wombats, dingoes, wallabies, and birds—including cassowaries, kookaburras, and red-tailed black cockatoos. Educational shows throughout the day give you the chance to learn more about these native animals. There are a café and a swimming pool on-site. The sanctuary, a 20-minute drive south of Townsville, is well signposted. ✉ *Bruce Hwy., Nome, 4816* ☎ *07/4778–8344* 🌐 *www.billabongsanctuary.com.au* 💲 *A$28* 🕐 *Daily 8–5.*

Wallaman Falls. Wallaman Falls is the highest sheer-drop waterfall in Australia. In the surrounding Girringun National Park, ancient rain forests shelter rare plants and animals that include the endangered southern cassowary, platypus, and musky rat-kangaroo. You might also spot eastern water dragons, saw-shelled turtles, and the odd crocodile. The park is the start of the Wet Tropics Great Walk, suitable for experienced hikers. For day-trippers there are two spectacular lookouts and some scenic short walks, such as the 45-minute Banggurru circuit along Stony Creek's bank, or the steeper, two-hour walk to the base of the falls. ☎ *07/4722–5224* 🌐 *www.epa.qld.gov.au* 🖼 *Free* 🕐 *Daily dawn–dusk.*

WHERE TO STAY & EAT

$–$$ ✕ **The Australian Hotel.** This restored 1888 building, with its beautiful bull-nose veranda and original iron lacework, is a classic example of Townsville colonial architecture. Rumor has it that back when it was a hotel actor Errol Flynn once stayed here and paid for his keep by selling autographs. Today the building contains a restaurant serving everything from gourmet pizzas to "reef and beef" specialties with an upmarket spin. ✉ *11 Palmer St.* ☎ *07/4722–6999* 🌐 *www.australian-hotel.com.au* 💳 *AE, DC, MC, V.*

$–$$ ✕**Yotz Watergrill + Bar.** Right on the seafront, this restaurant has great views across Cleveland Bay. The clientele and atmosphere are casual chic, and if you're looking to "see and be seen," this is the perfect spot. Seafood is the specialty, and a changing menu might include fresh barramundi and chips, Moreton Bay bugs, or a tender, double-roasted ribeye fillet. There are plenty of vegetarian options, and a varied "grazing menu." At the bar, quaff Australian wines, boutique beers, or tropical-tinged cocktails: try the mango-coconut martini. ⊠ *Gregory St. Headland, the Strand* ☎ *07/4724–5488* ⊕ *www.yotz.com.au* ☉ *Sun. dinner* ⌕ *Reservations essential* ▤ *AE, DC, MC, V.*

$$$–$$$$ ✕▥ **Jupiters Townsville Hotel & Casino.** Dominating Townsville's waterfront area, this hotel complex is the city's entertainment center. Rooms, which have terrific views across the bay to Magnetic Island from all 11 floors, are large, bright, and colorful—and surprisingly quiet, given their proximity to North Queensland's first casino. The health club and tennis courts have ocean views. At Essence, a Mediterranean-flavor menu features premium local produce, while at Aqua, the "tropical cuisine" includes all-you-can-eat buffet dinners for A$25 Sunday through Thursday, and a great seafood buffet on weekends for A$37. Daily buffet breakfasts are A$22.50–A$25. ⊠ *Sir Leslie Thiess Dr., Box 1223, 4810* ☎ *07/4722–2333 or 1800/079210* ⊕ *www.jupiterstownsville.com.au* ⊲ *178 rooms, 16 suites* ⌕ *In-room: kitchen (some), refrigerator/minibar, ethernet. In-hotel: 3 restaurants, room service, 5 bars, tennis courts, pool, gym, spa, concierge, laundry service, public Internet, airport shuttle, parking (no fee), no-smoking rooms* ▤ *AE, DC, MC, V.*

$–$$ ▥ **Seagulls Resort.** Three acres of palm tree–studded tropical gardens form the backdrop for this appealing two-story brick complex. Cane furniture and tropical color schemes brighten the spacious hotel rooms; comparatively stylish corporate rooms have extras such as flat-screen TVs, high-speed Internet access, and bathrobes. Self-contained apartments and suites have kitchenettes or full kitchens, and some have hot tubs. Seagulls restaurant serves generous portions of local seafood. The resort is 2½ km (1½ mi) from the city center (with free shuttle service) and about a 10-minute walk from the beach. ⊠ *74 The Esplanade, 4810* ☎ *07/4721–3111* ⊕ *www.seagulls.com.au* ⊲ *42 rooms, 27 suites* ⌕ *In-room: kitchen (some), refrigerator, DVD (some), dial-up, Wi-Fi (some). In-hotel: restaurant, room service, bars, tennis court, pools, laundry facilities, laundry service, public Internet, public Wi-Fi, parking (no fee), no-smoking rooms, no elevator* ▤ *AE, DC, MC, V.*

¢–$ ▥ **Historic Yongala Lodge.** This late-19th-century lodge was originally the home of building magnate Matthew Rooney, whose family was shipwrecked off the Townsville coast on the SS *Yongala* in 1911. Public areas retain much of their 1880s and 1920s decor, including original wrought-iron ceiling fittings, complemented by antiques and old photographs. There are also motel-style rooms, some with Heritage decor, and modern one- and two-bedroom apartments. The dining room serves steaks, seafood, and pasta dishes. You can also dine or drink cocktails outside on the wide, colonial-style veranda. The hotel is a stroll from numerous attractions and the city's main beach. ⊠*11 Fryer St., 4810* ☏*07/4772–4633* 🖷*07/4721–1074* ✐*info@historicyongala.com.au* ⊕*www.historicyongala.com.au* 🛏*10 rooms, 10 apartments* ⟁*In-room: kitchen (some), refrigerator, VCR, dial-up. In-hotel: restaurant, room service, bar, (saltwater) pool, beachfront, laundry facilities, parking (no fee), no elevator (some level-access rooms)* 🗏*AE, DC, MC, V.*

NIGHTLIFE

The **Bank Lounge Bar** (⊠*Flinders St. E* ☏*07/4771–6148*) dates from 1888, but now sees a lot of modern dancing. **The Brewery** (⊠*252 Flinders St.* ☏*07/4724–2999*), once the Townsville Post Office, now houses a bar serving light meals and an award-winning microbrewery. The owners have done a fine job combining ultramodern finishes with the original design, incorporating old post office fittings, such as the bar—once the stamp counter.

For a rollicking Irish-style night on the town, hit **Molly Malone's Irish Pub** (⊠*Flinders St. E at Wickham St.* ☏*07/4771–3428* ⊕*www.mollymalones.com*), which occupies Townsville's historic Tattersall Hotel. Built in 1865, it has wide verandas with iron lacework. Here, you can listen to live bands, Tuesday to Saturday, as you down pints of Guinness, or groove to DJ-spun tunes at the adjoining nightclub, Fuse. Molly's also does pub-style lunches and dinners from A$7.50; try their famous crumbed steak for A$22.

SPORTS & THE OUTDOORS

BEACHES Townsville is blessed with a golden, 2-km (1-mi) beach that stretches along its northern edge. Four man-made headlands jut into the sea, and a long pier is just the spot for fishing. There is no surf, as the beach is sheltered by the reef and Magnetic Island. The permanent swimming enclosure, known as the Rockpool, is fitted with temporary nets during box-jellyfish season. The surrounding area has picnic facilities, barbecues, toilets, formal gardens, and gazebos. ⊕*www.townsville.qld.gov.au/parks*

BOATING **Magnetic Island Sea Kayaks** (⊠*Horseshoe Bay Rd., Horseshoe Bay* ☏*07/4778–5424* ⊕*www.seakayak.com.au*) organizes kayak trips to the quieter bays of Magnetic Island. The 4½-hour morning tour includes a tropical breakfast and costs A$69 per person; the 2½-hour, seasonal sunset tour is A$45 per person.

SCUBA DIVING Surrounded by tropical islands and warm waters, Townsville is a top-notch diving center. Diving courses and excursions tend to be less crowded than those in the hot spots of Cairns or the Whitsunday Islands.

The wreck of the *Yongala*, a steamship that sank just south of Townsville in 1911, lies in 99 feet of water about 16 km (10 mi) offshore, 60 km (37 mi) from Townsville. Now the home of teeming marine life, it's one of Australia's best dive sites and can be approached as either a one- or two-day trip. All local dive operators conduct trips to the wreck.

Adrenalin Dive (✉9 *Wickham St.* ☎*07/4724–0600* ⊕*www.adrenalin dive.com.au*) has day trips to a number of popular sites in the region, including the wreck of the *Yongala*. From A$199 for a day trip with two dives, plus A$35 for gear.

Pro-Dive Townsville (✉*12 Plume St.* ☎*07/4721–1760* ⊕*www.pro-divetownsville.com.au*) arranges PADI-certified dive courses and live-aboard dive trips. Sites include the *Yongala* and the outer Barrier Reef. From A$775 per diver for a 3-day, 3-night all inclusive trip with around 10 dives.

> ### WORD OF MOUTH
>
> "If you have time, you must take in Magnetic Island, its not the reef as its only about a 25-min ferry trip from Townsville. But many beaches, hiking, scenery and wildlife galore including large colony of koalas, rock wallabies on beaches—diversity of bird life there is astounding."
>
> – pat_woolford

MAGNETIC ISLAND

More than half of Magnetic Island's 52 square km (20 square mi) is national parkland, laced with miles of walking trails and rising to a height of 1,640 feet on Mt. Cook. The terrain is punctuated with huge granite boulders and softened by tall hoop pines, eucalyptus forest, and rain-forest gullies. A haven for wildlife, the island shelters rock wallabies, koalas, echidnas, frogs, fruit bats, and nonvenomous green tree snakes. Its beaches, mangroves, and sea-grass beds support turtle nesting, fish hatching, and a significant dugong population. You can escape to 23 beaches and dive nine offshore shipwrecks.

The 2,500-plus residents, who fondly call their island "Maggie," mostly live on the eastern shore at Picnic Bay, Arcadia, Nelly Bay, and Horseshoe Bay. Many locals are artists and craftspeople, and there are numerous studios and galleries around the island.

The island has 24 km (15 mi) of hiking trails, most of which are relatively easy. The popular Forts walk leads to World War II gun emplacements overlooking Horseshoe and Florence bays. At a leisurely pace it takes 45 minutes each way from the Horseshoe–Radical Bay Road. (Look up en route, and you may spot a sleepy koala.) The best views are on the 5-km (3-mi) Nelly Bay to Arcadia walk, which is rewarding if you take the higher ground. Look out for shell middens created over thousands of years by the island's Aboriginal owners, the Wulgurukaba, or "Canoe People." Also look for interpretative signs detailing the island's fascinating heritage and maritime history. Wear sturdy footwear and a hat, and carry plenty of water, sunscreen, and insect repellent.

Swimming and snorkeling are other popular activities, but from November to May stingers are a hazard: swim at Picnic and Horseshoe bays, which have stinger nets. At other times, Alma Bay and Nelly Bay, as well as Picnic, Florence, Radical, Horseshoe, and Balding bays, are all suitable swimming spots. Horseshoe has daily lifeguards, although Alma and Picnic bays are patrolled over weekends and school holidays from September to May. Geoffrey Bay has a well-marked snorkel trail, and free, self-guiding trail cards identifying local corals and sea life are available at the information center adjacent to the Picnic Bay Jetty. Other good snorkeling spots include Nelly Bay, and the northern ends of Florence and Arthur bays. Near the northeastern corner of the island, Radical Bay has a small, idyllic beach surrounded by tree-covered rock outcrops. Horseshoe Bay has the largest beach, with boat rentals and a campground.

One way to get an overview of Magnetic Island is to ride the **Magnetic Island Bus Service.** Your A$11 ticket allows one day of unlimited travel to different points on the island, enabling you to return to the places you like most. A three-hour guided tour, including morning or afternoon tea, is A$38. Reservations are essential, and tours depart daily at 9 and 1. ⊠*44 Mandalay Ave., Nelly Bay* ☎*07/4778–5130* ⊕*www. magneticurnes.com.*

WHERE TO STAY & EAT
Magnetic Island began "life" as a holiday-home getaway for Townsville residents, and never attracted the kind of large-scale development that other tropical islands near the Barrier Reef have. As a result, accommodations here are a mix of functional but not very attractive 1970s properties; small budget lodges; and upmarket, but relatively small, apartment complexes and resorts. Luxurious Peppers Blue Resort, opened in 2007, is the exception to the rule.

$$$$ ✕▣ **Peppers Blue On Blue Resort.** This five-star waterfront resort is adjacent to Nelly Bay ferry terminal and overlooks the island's private marina. Opened in mid-2007, it has state-of-the-art facilities and luxury appointments. Ultra-modern dual-key guest rooms and two- and three-bedroom suites have balconies with water views and high-speed broadband Internet access. The Boardwalk Restaurant & Bar has full-frontal bay views. Tropical landscaping, a free-form lagoon pool, and the marina-front boardwalk encourage guests to get outside. There's a diving center next to the resort. ⊠*Magnetic Island Marina, Magnetic Island, 4819* ☎*02/9302–4333* ⊕*www.peppers.com.au/Blue-On-Blue* ➾*60 dual-key (twin) rooms, 127 suites* ♿*In-room: kitchen, refrigerator, mini-bar, broadband Internet, pay TV. In-hotel: restaurant, bar, pool, spa, gym, beachfront, marina, laundry service, conference facilities, business services, meeting rooms, parking (fee), no-smoking, no elevator* ▤*AE, DC, MC, V.*

$–$$ ✕▣ **Magnetic International Resort.** This comfortable resort nestles amid 11 acres of lush gardens 2 km (1 mi) from the beach. At the terrace restaurant, MacArthur's ($$), beef, chicken, and fresh seafood and tropical fruits are featured; try Cajun-style barramundi. Hiking trails into the national parkland are nearby, there are eight beaches to explore, and the energetic can take advantage of flood-lighted tennis courts in the cool evenings. There are also a children's playground and a games room. Courtesy bus transfers from Picnic Bay to the resort are available. ✉*Mandalay Ave., Nelly Bay, 4819* ☎*07/4778–5200* ✐*reservations@magneticresort.com* ⊕*www.magneticresort.com* ⇝*80 rooms, 16 suites* ⚘*In-room: kitchen, refrigerator, dial-up, ethernet (some). In-hotel: restaurant, bar, 2 tennis courts, pool, bicycles, laundry facilities, executive floor, public Internet, public Wi-Fi, parking (no fee), no-smoking rooms* ▭*AE, DC, MC, V.*

$$–$$$ 🏨**Sails on Horseshoe.** As the name suggests, this modern complex is located at Horseshoe Bay, the biggest of Magnetic Island's 23 beaches. It's also the farthest from the ferry terminal—but on Maggie, that's still not very far. The fully-equipped one-bedroom beachside studio apartments and two-bedroom villas (one disabled-friendly) and town houses are decorated in pastels or tropical designs and have fully-equipped kitchens and laundries. The low-rise units are set around a palm-shaded pool with a hot tub and barbecue area. ✉*13–15 Pacific Dr., Horseshoe Bay, 4819* ☎*07/4778–5117* ⊕*www.sailsonhorseshoe. com.au* ⇝*2 studios, 2 villas, 10 town house (2-story) apartments* ⚘*In-room: kitchen, DVD/CD/VCR, dial-up, Wi-Fi. In-hotel: pool, beachfront, laundry facilities, parking (no fee), no-smoking rooms, no elevator* ▭*AE, DC, MC, V.*

SPORTS & THE OUTDOORS

HORSEBACK RIDING   ★   With **Bluey's Horseshoe Ranch,** you can take a two-hour bush-and-beach ride with the chance to take the horses swimming (A$85). Half-day rides are also offered (A$115). ✉*38 Gifford St., Horseshoe Bay* ☎*07/4778–5109* ⊕*www.blueyshorseranch.com.*

SNORKELING & SCUBA DIVING   **Pleasure Divers** (✉*10 Marine Parade, Arcadia* ☎*07/4778–5788* ⊕*www. pleasuredivers.com.au*) rents snorkeling and diving gear (including stinger-proof suits for protection against jellyfish), and runs trips to sites including the coral gardens and canyons off Alma Bay (A$60 per person, including gear, stinger suit, and guide). You can also do short live-aboard trips to the Outer Great Barrier Reef and the wreck of the SS *Yongala* (from A$599, all meals, guides, and gear included).

TOAD RACES   One of the more-unusual evening activities on Magnetic Island is the weekly toad racing at **Magnum's on Magnetic Backpacker Resort** (✉*7 Marine Parade, Arcadia* ☎*07/4778–5177*). Held at 8 PM every Wednesday night for more than two decades, the event raises funds for local charities. The crowd is generally a mix of tourists and locals. After the race, the winner kisses his or her toad and collects the proceeds.

WATER SPORTS   **Adrenalin Jet Ski Tours** (✉*46 Gifford St.* ☎*07/4778–5533 or 0407/785–538*) provides three-hour guided, self-drive tours around Magnetic Island on jet skis, as well as an hour-long "Top End" jet-ski tour, with up to two people on each ski.

TOWNSVILLE & MAGNETIC ISLAND ESSENTIALS

TRANSPORTATION

AIR TRAVEL

Qantas flies frequently from Townsville Airport to Brisbane, Cairns, Hervey Bay, and several overseas destinations. Jetstar has services to Brisbane and Sydney; Virgin Blue connects Townsville with Brisbane and Rockhampton. There are no air connections to Magnetic Island; you need to take a ferry from Townsville.

Townsville Taxis are available at the airport. The average cost of the ride to a city hotel is A$15.

Airport Townsville Airport (☎ *07/4727–3211*).

Airlines Qantas (☎ *13–1313* ⊕ *www.qantas.com.au*).**Jetstar** (☎ *13–1538* ⊕ *www.jetstar.com*).**Virgin Blue** (☎ *13–6789* ⊕ *www.virginblue.com.au*).

BOAT & FERRY TRAVEL

The 40-minute Fantasea Cruising Magnetic (formerly known as the Magnetic Island Passenger and Car Ferry) runs several departures daily from the mainland to Nelly Bay on the island, 10 km (6 mi) offshore. Round-trip fares are A$144 for a car with up to three people, or A$22 per person, return trip, for those without a car.

Sunferries has 25-minute catamaran service daily from Townsville to Nelly Bay on Magnetic Island. Bus and island transfers meet the ferry during daylight hours. There are up to 15 departures daily; a round-trip ticket costs A$27.

Contacts Fantasea Cruising Magnetic (☎ *07/4772–5422* ⊕ *www.magneticislandferry.com.au*).**Sunferries** (☎ *07/4771–3855* ⊕ *www.sunferries.com.au*).

BUS TRAVEL

Greyhound Australia coaches travel regularly to Cairns, Brisbane, and other destinations throughout Australia from the Sunferries Terminal on the Breakwater in Townsville.

Magnetic Island Bus Service meets each boat at Nelly Bay and transports passengers to Picnic Bay in the south and Horseshoe Bay in the north. An unlimited day pass costs A$11; single tickets are A$2–A$3.

Contacts Greyhound Australia (✉ *The Breakwater, Sir Leslie Thiess Dr., Townsville* ☎ *07/4772–5100 or 13–1499* ⊕ *www.greyhound.com.au*).**Magnetic Island Bus Service** (☎ *07/4778–5130* ⊕ *www.magvac.com.au/bus.html*).

CAR RENTAL

The tiny Mini Moke, a soft-top convertible version of the Minor Mini car, provides an ideal means of exploring Magnetic Island. Moke Magnetic, opposite the Magnetic Island ferry terminal, rents Mini Mokes for A$68 a day, including fuel (60 free kilometers' [35 miles'] worth); driver's license required.

Motorbikes or scooters are a cheap and easy way to get around Magnetic Island. Road Runner Scooter Hire rents trail bikes for A$50 per day, and scooters from A\$30 (9 AM–5 PM) or A\$40 (24 hours). The cost includes helmets and unlimited mileage; you top up the gas yourself.

Information Moke Magnetic (✉*112 Sooning St., Nelly Bay* ☎*07/4778-5377* ⊕*www.mokemagnetic.com*).

Road Runner Scooter Hire (✉*3/64 Kelly St., Nelly Bay* ☎*07/4778-5222*).

CAR TRAVEL

Townsville is 1,400 km (868 mi) by road from Brisbane—a colossal, flat and, for longish sections, dull drive. The 370-km (230-mi) journey from Townsville to Cairns, with occasional Hinchinbrook Island views, is more scenic.

TAXIS

You can flag Townsville Taxis on the street or find one at stands or hotels. Magnetic Island Taxi has a stand at the island's ferry terminal.

Contacts Magnetic Island Taxi (☎*07/4778-9566 or 13-1008*).**Townsville Taxis** (☎*07/4778-9500 or 13-1008*).

TRAIN TRAVEL

Traveling to and from Townsville via rail is a low-stress, scenic alternative to driving. The *Sunlander* travels along the coast between Brisbane and Townsville four times weekly, taking approximately 24 hours. On the *Sunlander*'s twice-weekly Queenslander service (departing Brisbane Thursday and Sunday, returning from Cairns Friday and Monday), you have the choice of first and economy class seats, and twin sleeper berths, as well as chef-cooked meals, premium Australian wines, and informative commentary from the maître d'. On the smooth, state-of-of-the-art *Tilt Train* (departing Brisbane for Cairns, Tuesday and Friday, returning Wednesday and Saturday), business-class passengers can watch individual TV screens, or plug laptops into seat-side sockets during less scenic segments of the journey. The *Inlander* connects Townsville with Mount Isa twice weekly, departing Sunday and Thursday from Townsville, returning Monday and Friday from Mt. Isa. Trains are operated by Queensland Rail.

INFORMATION

Contact Queensland Rail (☎*1300/131722* ⊕*www.qr.com.au*).

CONTACTS & RESOURCES

EMERGENCIES

Dial **000** to reach an ambulance, the police, or the fire department.

Hospitals Aitkenvale Family Health (✉*295 Ross River Rd., Aitkenvale, Townsville* ☎*07/4725-6060*).**Townsville Hospital** (✉*100 Angus Smith Dr., Douglas, Townsville* ☎*07/4796-1111*).

TOURS

Coral Princess Cruises has regular three- to seven-night cruises that leave from Townsville and Cairns. The comfortable, 54-passenger ship stops for snorkeling, diving, and rain-forest hikes. The crew includes marine biologists who give lectures and accompany you on excursions.

Divers can rent equipment from the company. Lessons are also available. Prices start at A$1,375 for a three-night, four-plus-dive live-aboard trip, twin share.

The Tropicana Guided Adventure Company runs island expeditions to normally inaccessible bays and beaches in a converted, extra-long jeep. Bush-tucker adventures let you taste native foods, and other trips let you meet and feed island wildlife. Daytrips start from A$66 per person for a three-hour eco-orientation tour, with free pick-up from Townsville accommodations. Coral Sea Skydivers offer tandem sky dives on the beach and preparatory training from A$315.

Contacts Coral Princess Cruises (⊠ c/o Sunferries Terminal, Townsville ☎ 07/4040–9999 ⊕ www.coralprincess. com.au).**Coral Sea Skydivers** (⊠ 181 Flinders St., South Townsville, Townsville ☎ 07/4772–4889 ⊕ www.coralseaskydivers.com.au).**Tropicana Guided Adventure Company** (☎ 07/4758–1800 ⊕ www.tropicanatours.com.au).

> ### GREAT DIVES
>
> Just off Townsville lies one of the world's best wreck-dive sites, the SS *Yongala*. A luxury passenger ship, the SS *Yongala* sank in a 1911 cyclone. The wreck, discovered in 1958, was later declared a national historic site. Turn-of-the-century artifacts, colorful corals, and a lot of marine life make diving the SS *Yongala* an extraordinary experience. It's no place for novices, though: you'll need deep-diving certification to fully explore the 109-meter-long boat, 14 to 28 meters underwater. Numerous operators, including Yongala Dive, Adrenaline Dive, and Pleasure Divers, visit the site from Townsville and Magnetic Island.

VISITOR INFORMATION

The Queensland Parks and Wildlife Service has an office on Magnetic Island, but Townsville Enterprise's Flinders Mall and Museum of Tropical Queensland (MTQ) information kiosks, on the mainland, are the best source of tourist information about the island. Both kiosks are open 9–5 weekdays, 9–1 weekends. Townsville Enterprise has a wide selection of material and information on all local attractions and is open weekdays 8:30–5.

Contacts Queensland Parks and Wildlife Service, Magnetic Island (⊠ 22 Hurst St., Picnic Bay ☎ 07/4778–5378 ⊕ www.epa.qld.gov.au).**Townsville Enterprise Visitor Information Centres** (⊠ Flinders Mall between Stokes and Stanley Sts., Townsville, 4810 ☎ 07/4721–3660 or 1800/801902 ⊠ Museum of Tropical Queensland Marine Centre, Reef HQ Building, 2–68 Flinders St. E ☎ 07/4721–1116 ⊕ www.townsvilleonline.com.au).

CAIRNS

Tourism is the lifeblood of Cairns (pronounced *Caans*). The city makes a perfect base for exploring the wild top half of Queensland, and tens of thousands of international travelers use it as a jumping-off point for activities like scuba diving and snorkeling trips to the Barrier Reef, as well as boating, parasailing, and rain-forest treks.

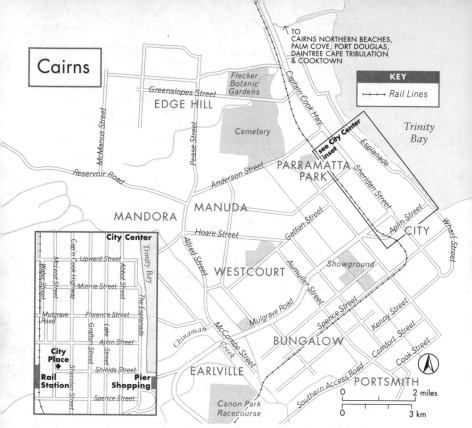

It's a tough environment, with intense heat and fierce wildlife. Along with the cuddly koalas and hop-happy kangaroos of the south, you'll find stealthy saltwater crocodiles, poisonous snakes, and jellyfish so deadly they keep the stunning beaches virtually unswimmable for half the year. Yet despite the formidable setting, Cairns and Tropical North Queensland are far from intimidating. The people here are warm and friendly, the sights spectacular, and the beachside lounging world class—at the right time of year.

Fodor's Choice A beautiful drive is along what locals call the **Great Green Way,** the
★ main road connecting Townsville to Cairns. The road travels through sugarcane, papaya, and banana plantations, passing dense rain forest, white beaches, and bright blue water dotted with tropical islands. The 345-km (215-mi) drive along the Bruce Highway takes around four hours—longer if you get caught behind a tractor or if the sugarcane rail is running—plus stops to explore towns, parks, waterfalls, and rain-forest tracts along the way.

Babinda Boulders is a popular swimming hole, as well as a sacred Aboriginal site. It's located 6 km (4½ mi) inland from Babinda, which is accessible via the Bruce Highway. Stop in at the volunteer-run information center for more information and to check weather advisories; the swimming hole sometimes floods in the wet season. If you'd rather hike than drive to the boulders, take the 19-km (12-mi) **Goldfield Track,** which starts in Goldsborough Valley, a 90-minute drive southwest of Cairns. ⊠*Babinda Information Centre, Munro St., Babinda, 4861* ☎*07/4067–1008, 07/4067–6304 park ranger weather conditions* ⊕*www.ttnq.com.au* ☽*Information center daily 9* AM*–4* PM.

Paronella Park. A sprawling Spanish-style castle and accompanying gardens grace this eco-certified National Trust site, set in the lush Mena Creek Falls rain forest. It's an unusual place in that it lets you explore both horticulture and Aboriginal culture. After a self-guided botanical walk or bush-tucker tour with members of the area's indigenous Baddagun people, enjoy traditional Devonshire tea on the café's deck or buy local art and craft at the gift shop. Cool off under a 48-foot waterfall on the property (BYO swimming gear). On the torch-lighted evening tours, you might spot eels, water dragons, fireflies, glowworms, and the odd snake. Allow three hours to fully explore the grounds and buildings. It's about 1½ hours south of Cairns, via the Bruce Highway. ⊠*Japoonvale Rd., Box 88, Mena Creek, 1871* ☎*07/1065 3225* ⊕*www.paronellapark.com.au* ☎*A\$28* ☽*Daily 9* AM*–7:30* PM.

Tully Gorge. Located in the wettest zone of the Wet Tropics World Heritage area, the mighty Tully River is a magnet for white-water rafters. Access the gorge via Tully township, about 100 km (62 mi) south of Cairns, then drive 40 minutes to Kareeya Hydroelectric Station, where there's a parking lot and viewing platform. Other excellent vantage points are the Flip Wilson and Frank Roberts lookouts. In butterfly season (September–February), the short (20-minute) Rainforest Butterfly walk is filled with fluttering creatures. Parts of the forest can be waterlogged in the wet season, especially January through April; rocks can be slippery; and Tully River water levels can change rapidly. ☎*07/4068–2288 (Tully Information Centre)* ⊕*www.epa.qld.gov.au.*

Wooroonooran National Park, which extends from just south of Gordonvale and stretches to the Palmerston Highway between Innisfail and Milla Milla, is one of the most densely vegetated areas in Australia. Rain forest dominates Wooroonooran—from lowland tropical rain forest to the stunted growth on Mt. Bartle Frere—at 5,287 feet, the highest point in Queensland and Australia's largest remaining area of upland rain forest. Tracks include the Tchupala Falls circuit (30 mins), Tchupala Falls to Goolagan's picnic area (1–2 hrs); Goolagan's to Henrietta Creek (30 mins); the Nadroya Falls Circuit (3–4 hrs); and the steep, challenging Mt. Bartle Frere trail, accessed from Josephine Falls (2 days). Bush camping is allowed, with ranger permission, throughout the park, except at Josephine Falls. At Henrietta Creek rain-forest campground, sites, toilets, and picnic facilities are provided, but you'll need drinking water and a cooking stove. The creek is home to platypus and freshwater turtles; possums can be spotted after dark. Daily permits cost A\$4.50 per person. To reach the park, look for signs about 50 km (31 mi) south of Cairns on the Bruce Highway—the trip takes about 2½ hours. ⊠*Box 93, Miriwinni, 4871* ☎*07/4067–6304 (Josephine Falls), 07/4046–6600 (Palmerston), 13–1304 (camping permits).* ⊕*www.epa.qld.gov.au or www.qld.gov.au/camping.*

EXPLORING CAIRNS

The **Esplanade,** which fronts Cairns Harbour between Minnie and Spence streets, is the focal point of life in Cairns. A lagoon-style swimming pool—common throughout Queensland, where the temperatures are hot and the beaches often inhospitable—is open well after sunset, and is always buzzing with activity. As well as being a free and convenient place to cool off from the sticky air, it's well situated for viewing the boats around Marlin Jetty. Some of the town's best shops, hotels, and restaurants are found on the Esplanade, many of the backpackers who throng to Cairns gather here, giving it a lively feel.

Trinity Bay is a shallow stretch of hundreds of yards of mangrove flats, uncovered at low tide, that attract birds such as herons, cranes, sea eagles, and egrets. In the late 1980s, some of the waterfront was filled in, and **Pier Shopping,** a retail complex, was constructed.

Cairns can trace its beginnings to the point where the Esplanade turns into **Wharf Street.** In 1876, this small area was a port for the gold and tin mined inland. Chinese and Malaysian workers, as well as immigrants from other countries, settled in the area during that period to participate in the gold trade, and Cairns eventually grew into one of the most multicultural cities in Australia. As the gold rush receded and the sugarcane industry around the Atherton Tableland grew, Cairns turned its attention to fishing. It is still a thriving port.

Charter fishing boats moor at **Marlin Marina.** Big-game fishing is a major industry, and fish weighing more than 1,000 pounds have been caught in the waters off the reef. Docks for the dive boats and catamarans that conduct Great Barrier Reef tours are found here and at nearby Trinity Wharf.

The actual center of Cairns is **City Place,** a pedestrian mall at the corner of Lake and Shields streets. Some of the town's few authentic pubs, as well as the major shopping area, are around this square.

The **Cairns Museum,** next to City Place, houses a collection of Aboriginal artifacts, including musical instruments and paintings, as well as old tools, memorabilia, and photographs documenting the city's history. A gift shop sells books on local and Aboriginal history and culture. ⊠*Lake and Shields Sts., CBD* ☏*07/4051–5582* ⊕*www.cairnsmuseum.org.au* ⊠*A$5* ☉*Mon.–Sat. 10–4.*

★ The largest regional gallery in Queensland, the **Cairns Regional Gallery,** is housed in the former Public Office building at City Place. Built in the early 1930s, the magnificent, two-story edifice has high ceilings and maple-paneled rooms with native wood floors. A diverse collection of artwork by local, national, international, and indigenous artists is on display, with a particular emphasis on photography from around Australia. One-hour guided tours are on Wednesday and Friday: be sure to book ahead. Workshops are often held in conjunction with exhibits. ⊠*Shields and Abbott Sts., CBD* ☏*07/4046–4800* ⊕*www.cairnsregionalgallery.com.au* ⊠*A$6* ☉*Mon.–Sat. 10–5, Sun. 1–5.*

At **Reef Teach,** certified marine biologists present a unique, informative, and entertaining lecture series on the Great Barrier Reef six nights a week to a packed house (maximum 100 people). They use slides and samples of coral to inform prospective divers and general sightseers about the reef's evolution and the unique inhabitants of this delicate marine ecosystem. Be sure to sign up for a seat at the lecture by midday. ⊠ *Bolands Centre, 14 Spence St., CBD* ☎ *07/4031-7794* ⊕ *www. reefteach.com.au* ✉ *A$15* ⊙ *Shows Mon.–Sat. 6:30–8:30.*

AROUND CAIRNS

The **Kuranda Scenic Railway** makes a 100-minute ascent past a rain forest and through 15 hand-hewn tunnels before arriving in tiny, tropical Kuranda, the gateway to the Atherton Tablelands. This elevated area of rich volcanic soil that produces some of Australia's finest beef, dairy, and produce was also home to several strategic sites during World War II. Excerpts from that point in history, as well as a narration of the railway's construction, are broadcast on the historic railway car by a high-tech audiovisual presentation system. Several tours are available, from full-day rain-forest safaris to simple round-trip train and bus rides combining railway and cable-car trips, Cairns–Kuranda transfers, and visits to local Aboriginal centers and wildlife parks. Many visitors take the train out to Kuranda and return via the Skyrail Rainforest Cableway. ⊠ *Cairns Railway Station, Bunda St. behind Cairns Central Shopping Centre, CBD* ☎ *07/4036-9333* ⊕ *www.ksr.com.au* ✉ *1-way ticket A$39, round-trip A$56* ⊙ *Train departs from Cairns daily 8:30 AM and 9:30 AM, returning at 2 and 3:30.*

From the remarkable **Skyrail Rainforest Cableway,** six-person cable cars carry you on a 7½-km (5-mi) journey across the top of the rain-forest canopy to the tiny highland village of Kuranda, where you can visit some local attractions or shop for Aboriginal art. There are two stations along the way, Barron Falls and Red Peak, allowing you to explore and learn more about the rain forest from the forest floor (ticket price includes a short ranger-guided tour at Red Peak, and there's an info center and lookout at Barron Falls). The base station for the cableway is 15 km (9 mi) north of Cairns. Many visitors take the Kuranda Scenic Railway out to Kuranda and the cableway on the return trip. ⊠ *Captain Cook Hwy., at Cairns Western Arterial Rd., Smithfield* ☎ *07/4038-1555* ✍ *info@skyrail.com.au* ⊕ *www.skyrail. com.au* ✉ *1-way ticket A$39, round-trip A$56* ⊙ *Daily 8:15–5:15, last round-trip boards at 2:45; last 1-way trip boards at 3:30.*

Tiny, tropical Kuranda offers several nature-oriented attractions, including the Australian Butterfly Sanctuary, Birdworld Kuranda, and Kuranda Koala Gardens. You can visit these sites individually, or buy a Kuranda Wildlife Experience pass (A$36), which lets you visit them as part of a package with both the Scenic Railway and the Skyrail; or a Bird & Butterfly pass (A$23). More information on packages and passes is available at ⊕ *www.skyrail.com.au.*

The **Australian Butterfly Sanctuary,** an aviary where thousands of tropical butterflies—including the glorious electric-blue Ulysses—flutter within a rain-forest environment. It is home to the largest butterfly in Australia, the Cairns, also known as the birdwing. ⊠*Kuranda Heritage Market, Kuranda* ☎*07/4093-7575* ⊕*www.australianbutterflies.com* 🎟*A$15* 🕙*Daily 9:45-4.*

You'll get one of your best chances to see the cassowary, a prehistoric bird resembling the emu, at **Birdworld Kuranda,** also home to 78 avian species, around 500 birds—all flying freely in a giant rain-forest aviary. ⊠*Kuranda Heritage Market, Kuranda* ☎*07/4093-9188* ⊕*www.birdworldkuranda.com.au* 🎟*A$14* 🕙*Daily 9-4.*

☺ All kinds of Australian wildlife make their homes at **Kuranda Koala Gardens,** but the namesake marsupials are the starring attractions. It's a compact park, ideal for time-strapped visitors, where a relaxing 20-minute walk brings you face to face with koalas, wombats, wallabies, freshwater crocs, and lizards, as well as snakes in a walk-through enclosure (where no glass separates you from them). There's an additional A$15 fee to have your photo taken with a "teddy," as koalas are known locally. ⊠*Kuranda Heritage Market, Kuranda* ☎*07/4093-9953* ⊕*www.koalagardens.com* 🎟*A$15* 🕙*Daily 9-4.*

☺ **Tjapukai Aboriginal Cultural Park,** a unique Aboriginal cultural center
★ located at the base of the Skyrail Rainforest Cableway, provides many opportunities to learn about the history and lifestyle of the indigenous Djabugay people. Not only is this one of the most unusual and informative cultural attractions in the country, it's also one of few that returns its profits back to the community. Watch a dance performance, learn traditional songs, throw a spear, chuck a boomerang, or play a didgeridoo; you also can learn about bush foods and medicines. The staff is friendly and knowledgeable. Aboriginal artworks are for sale. Ticket options include a lunch package, or the Tjapukai by Night buffet dinner and performance (A$87 per person, A$103 with Cairns or Northern beaches transfers). ⊠*Kamerunga Rd., Smithfield* ⊹*15 km (9 mi) north of Cairns* ☎*07/4042-9999* ⊕*www.tjapukai.com.au* 🎟*A$31* 🕙*Daily 9-5.*

**OFF THE
BEATEN
PATH**

Undara Volcanic National Park. The lava tubes here are a fascinating geological oddity in the Outback, attracting an ever-increasing number of visitors. A volcanic outpouring 190,000 years ago created the hollow basalt tubelike tunnels, many of which you can wander through on a tour led by a trained guide. The tunnels are 35 km (22 mi) long in total—some are 62 feet high and half a mile long, covering a total of 19,700 acres. Undara is the Aboriginal word for "long way." ☎*07/4097-1485* 🎟*Free* 🕙*Daily dawn-dusk.*

Vintage railway cars have been converted into comfortable (if compact) motel rooms (A$75-A$85) at the **Undara Experience** (⊠*Mt. Surprise* ☎*07/4097-1411* ⊕*www.undara.com.au*). You can also camp, with powered and unpowered sites avail-

WORD OF MOUTH

"I spent 9 days in the Cairns region and did a lot—the wildlife was fantastic! I highly recommend going out to Undara—quite an experience! "

– pb_and_j

able (A$8–A$12 per night). The lodge, 275 km (171 mi) from Cairns, has 10 three-person dorm rooms (A$25 per person) and is set amid savanna and woodlands. It supplies the complete Outback experience: bush breakfasts, campfires, lava tube tours, and guided evening wildlife walks. Lava tube tours cost A$38–A$110. One-day (A$150) and two- and three-night Outback Experience packages incorporate tours, transfers, and accommodation—from A$454, or A$278, self-drive, for the two-day package.

WHERE TO EAT

$–$$$$ ✕**Villa Romana Trattoria.** This classic Italian chain doesn't feel like one—in fact, its Tuscan-style, terra-cotta decor seems unique among the Esplanade's Mod-Oz restaurants. Serving authentic cuisine like pizza and home-style pasta with a focus on fresh seafood, Villa Romana also prepares specialty dishes like crispy-skin quail, saltimbucca, and bistecca (steak of the day). The hot-and-cold seafood platter for two (A$130) and tropical or chili mud crab (market price) are popular choices. Open until 2 AM, the restaurant becomes more like an Italian wine bar and less like a restaurant as the night draws on. ⊠*The Esplanade at Aplin St., CBD* ☎*07/4051–9000* ⊕*www.villaromana. com.au* ☐*AE, DC, MC, V.*

$$–$$$ ✕**Breezes Brasserie.** The floor-to-ceiling windows overlooking Trinity
★ Inlet at this Hilton Cairns restaurant make you feel like you're dining right in the middle of the water. The decor is bright, with tropical greenery. A sumptuous seafood and Mediterranean buffet is available nightly, and a table d'hôte menu featuring North Queensland's specialties changes regularly. ⊠*Hilton Cairns, 34 The Esplanade, CBD* ☎*07/4052–6786* ☐*AE, DC, MC, V* ☽*No lunch.*

$$–$$$ ✕**Mangostin's.** Combining traditional Mediterranean and Asian flavors with fresh Australian ingredients, Mangostin's seafood offerings are among the most creative in town. Try the herb-crusted wild barramundi, or the popular hot and cold seafood platter for two (A$99). They also do a decent breakfast. The chic Lagoon lounge is a great spot for light meals, cocktails, and people-watching. ⊠*65 The Esplanade, CBD* ☎*07/4031–9888* ⊕*www.mangostins.com* ☐*AE, DC, MC, V.*

$$ ✕**Barnacle Bill's Seafood Inn.** Complete with netting and mounted, shellacked fish on the walls, Barnacle Bill's serves fresh, delicious seafood, such as mud crabs, crayfish, prawns, oysters, and coral trout, cooked various ways. The kitchen also dabbles in Aussie specialties. Try the Taste of Australia plate, with grilled barramundi, kangaroo, and crocodile. The wine list favors quality mid-range Australian vintages. Early diners get a 20% discount. ⊠*103 The Esplanade, near Aplin St., CBD* ☎*07/4051–2241* ⊕*www.barnaclebills.com.au* ☐*AE, DC, MC, V* ☽*No lunch.*

$$ ✕**Red Ochre Grill.** Local seafood and native ingredients have top billing
Fodor'sChoice at this elegant spot that specializes in bush dining. Try the Australian
★ antipasto platter of emu pâté, crocodile wontons, and smoked salmon for starters, followed by kangaroo sirloin with quandong-chili glaze. Some dishes have a Pacific Rim flavor, like the tea-smoked duck with

mango or the twice-cooked pork. Red Ochre's signature dessert, wattleseed pavlova with Davidson plum sorbet, makes a fine finish; or you can linger and sip a glass of Australian wine while nestled into a violet velvet booth. ⊠*43 Shields St., CBD, 4870* ☎*07/4051–0100* ⊕*www. redochregrill.com.au* ⊟*AE, DC, MC, V* ⊘*No lunch weekends.*

$-$$ ✕**Bayleaf Balinese Restaurant.** Dining alfresco under the glow of tiki
Fodor'sChoice torches, you can enjoy some of the most delicious, innovative cuisine in
★ North Queensland. The expansive menu combines traditional Balinese spices with native Australian ingredients—this may be the only place where you'll have the opportunity to try crocodile satay. The pork in sweet soy sauce sounds simple, but is mouthwatering. The classic rijsttafel course for two—rice with lots of curry and pickle dishes—is the best way to sample the Bali-trained chefs' masterly cooking. ⊠*Lake and Gatton Sts., CBD, 4870* ☎*07/4047–7955* ⊕*www.bayvillage. com.au* ⊟*AE, DC, MC, V* ⊘*No lunch weekends.*

$-$$ ✕**Perrotta's at the Gallery.** This outdoor café with galvanized steel tables and chairs at the Cairns Regional Gallery also has a wine bar. Sumptuous breakfasts are served here from 7:30 AM, including French toast with star anise–scented pineapple and lime mascarpone. Lunch fare includes warm chicken salads and a variety of sandwiches. Tuck into Modern Italian mains and desserts, such as vanilla-bean panna cotta with seasonal fruits. ⊠*Gallery Deck, Cairns Regional Gallery, Abbott and Shields Sts., CBD* ☎*07/4031–5899* ⊕*www.cairnsregionalgallery. com* ⊟*AE, DC, MC, V.*

¢-$ ✕**Night Markets Food Court.** The food court in the night owl–friendly Night Markets offers something for every palate, from spicy Malaysian *laksa* (coconut-milk soup) to meaty kebabs to fried chicken. It's officially open daily with the markets, from 5 to 11 PM, but some outlets, such as the Coffee Club, open as early as 6:30 AM, and most start serving food from 11 AM. ⊠*71–75 The Esplanade, between Shield and Spence Sts., CBD* ☎*07/4051–7666* ⊕*www.nightmarkets.com.au* ⊟*No credit cards.*

WHERE TO STAY

$$$$ ▥**Shangri-La Hotel, The Marina.** With an ultraminimalist lobby featur-
Fodor'sChoice ing golden-orb chandeliers and suede chaise longues, this resort is
★ Cairns's hippest place to stay. Everything about the property exudes elegance: outside, there are extensive wooden decking and swimming pools shaded by palms; inside, rooms are decorated in muted colors, and have flat-screen TVs and flow-through views of the pool, gardens, city, and the surrounding mountains, bay, or marina. Upmarket Sirocco Restaurant offers "Tropical North Queensland" cuisine with views of Trinity Inlet and Marlin Marina on the side. Cocktails and snacks are available at the Poolside Cafe. Should you decide to tear yourself away from the on-site facilities, the savvy concierge and tour desk can arrange your entertainment, such as a reef excursion from the adjacent marina. ⊠*Pierpoint Rd., CBD, 4870* ☎*07/4031–1411* ⊕slmc'shangri-la.com ⊕*www.shangri-la.com* ⇲*230 rooms, 25 suites* ⚇*In-room: fans*

(some), safe, kitchen (some), refrigerator/minibar, DVD (some), VCR (some), ethernet, Wi-Fi (some), cable TV. In-hotel: restaurant, café, room service, bar, room service, pools, gym, spa, concierge, drycleaning, laundry service, executive floor, airport shuttle, parking (no fee), no-smoking rooms ⊟AE, DC, MC, V.

$$$$
★ **Sofitel Reef Casino Cairns.** Part of an entertainment complex in the heart of Cairns, this hotel has rooms and suites—as well as gambling tables, several bars, and a nightclub. This is the place to stay if having a big room is a priority. Accommodations have tropical-style ceiling fans, louver doors, floor-to-ceiling windows, and garden balconies. Pacific Flavours Brasserie gives a fresh, flavorsome spin to International cuisine, while Tamarind serves Asian-inspired cuisine. Flinders Bar & Grill is a suprisingly inexpensive and tasty dining option for such an upscale hotel. ☒ *35–41 Wharf St., CBD, 4870* ☎ *07/4030–8888 or 1800/808883* 🖷 *07/4030–8777* ✐ *sales@reefcasino.com.au* ⊕ *www. reefcasino.com.au* ⇔ *120 rooms, 28 suites* ⌂ *In-room: safe, refrigerator/minibar, DVD (some), ethernet, Wi-Fi (some). In-hotel: 4 restaurants, room service, bars, pool, gym, spa, concierge, laundry service, public Internet, public Wi-Fi, parking (no fee), no-smoking rooms ⊟AE, DC, MC, V.*

$$–$$$
★ **The Hotel Cairns.** One of the region's best examples of the Queenslander heritage style, the family-run Hotel Cairns retains a genteel ambience despite extensive remodeling and refurbishment. Spacious rooms and suites, most with large balconies (and balcony furniture), have white plantation shutters, flat-screen TVs with 50-plus complimentary cable channels, DVD and CD players, luxurious linen, Molton Brown toiletries, and bathrobes. Smart but restful rooms are given an elegant spin with soft green cushions and contemporary wood-and-cane furniture. There's a well-equipped gym and a spacious indoor-outdoor restaurant, The Plantation Bar & Grill, serving bistro-style dinners and big buffet breakfasts. It's an easy block from the Esplanade. ☒ *Abbott St. at Florence St., CBD, 4870* ☎ *07/4051–6188* 🖷 *07/4051–1806* ✐ *reservations@thehotelcairns.com* ⊕ *www.thehotelcairns.com.au* ⇔ *89 rooms, 3 suites* ⌂ *In-room: fans, Wi-Fi. In-hotel: restaurant, room service, snack bar, pool, outdoor hot tub, gym, bicycles, laundry facilities, public Wi-Fi, Internet, business facilities, meeting rooms, parking (no fee), tour desk, no-smoking rooms ⊟AE, DC, MC, V.*

$$–$$$
Pacific International Hotel. A soaring three-story lobby makes an impressive entrance to this hotel facing the waterfront and marina. Cane-and-rattan chairs, soft pastel colors, plants, and Gauguin-style prints give the guest rooms a South Pacific feel, which extends to the private balconies and pool, which has a large fish painted on the bottom. Within the hotel are two restaurants and high-speed Internet access. ☒ *43 The Esplanade, at Spence St., CBD, 4870* ☎ *07/4051–7888 or 1800/079001* ✐ *reservations@pacifichotelcairns.com* ⊕ *www. pacifichotelcairns.com* ⇔ *176 rooms* ⌂ *In-room: safe, refrigerator, dial-up. In-hotel: 2 restaurants, room service, pool, concierge, laundry facilities, laundry service, public Internet, public Wi-Fi, parking (no fee), no-smoking rooms ⊟AE, DC, MC, V.*

7

$$ ⊞**Cairns Colonial Club Resort.** Though it's just a few minutes outside the city center, this resort's 11 acres of tropical gardens make you feel a world away from the hubbub of Cairns. The colonial-style compound is built around three lagoonlike swimming pools, including a toddler pool, and a poolside café. A children's playground and babysitting services make it a great spot for families. Rooms, given fresh soft furnishings and carpets in 2007, have simple appointments, ceiling fans, and DVD players; studios also have cooking facilities. There's no dedicated spa on-site, but spa-style treatments are available. A free shuttle makes the run to the city center hourly, and courtesy airport transfers are provided. ⊠*18–26 Cannon St., Cairns, 4870* ☎*07/4053–5111* ✐info@ cairnscolonialclub.com.au ⊕*www.cairnscolonialclub.com.au* ⚲*342 rooms, 3 suites* ⚖*In-room: safe (some), kitchen (some), refrigerator, dial-up (some), ethernet (some), Wi-Fi (some). In-hotel: 3 restaurants, 4 bars, tennis court, pools, gym, bicycles, concierge, laundry facilities, laundry service, concierge, executive floor, public Internet, public Wi-Fi, airport shuttle, parking (no fee), no-smoking rooms, no elevator* ⊟*AE, DC, MC, V.*

$$ ⊞**Il Palazzo Boutique Apartments Hotel.** Cairns might be a long way from
★ Europe, but you can easily imagine yourself at the Italian Rivera at this Continental boutique hotel. A 6½-foot Italian marble replica of Michelangelo's *David* greets you in the foyer, and other intriguing objets d'art appear throughout. Spacious suites have a soft-green-and-coral color scheme, forged-iron and glass tables, and cane furniture plus fully-equipped kitchens and laundry facilities. There's a Mediterranean-style heated pool and a gazebo. ⊠*62 Abbott St., CBD, 4870* ☎*07/4041–2155 or 1800/813222* ✐info@ilpalazzo.com.au ⊕*www. ilpalazzo.com.au* ⚲*38 suites* ⚖*In-room: safe, kitchen, refrigerator, DVD, VCR, Wi-Fi. In-hotel: pool, laundry facilities, laundry service, parking (no fee), no-smoking rooms* ⊟*AE, DC, MC, V.*

$ ⊞**Bay Village Tropical Retreat & Apartments.** Resident managers Klaus and Lyn Ullrich have taken their expertise in hospitality, culled from years working at Sydney's poshest hotels and restaurants, to create this family-friendly hotel. Rooms, ranging from studios to three-bedroom apartments, are clean and comfortable, with tiled floors, tropical colour schemes, some more restful than others, and rattan-wood furniture. The Bayleaf Balinese Restaurant should be on anyone's itinerary: its imaginative dishes leave a stronger impression than the somewhat characterless rooms. There's a large lagoon pool and the staff here is accommodating and helpful; they'll even pick you up from the airport between 7 AM and 7 PM. There are two rooms for people with disabilities and all public areas are wheelchair-accessible. ⊠*Lake and Gatton Sts., CBD, 4870* ☎*07/4051–4622* ✐reservations@bayvillage.com. au ⊕*www.bayvillage.com.au* ⚲*62 suites, 28 apartments* ⚖*In-room: safe (some), kitchen (some), refrigerator, dial-up (some). In-hotel: restaurant, room service, bar, pool, laundry facilities, laundry service, concierge, public Internet, airport shuttle, parking (no fee), no smoking* ⊟*AE, DC, MC, V.*

¢–$ **⊡ Gilligan's Backpacker Hotel & Resort.** If you're headed to Cairns for
Fodor's Choice   action, not relaxation, this upscale budget property is the perfect place.
★   Offering clean, modern hostel-type four- and six-bed dorms and private
rooms, all with user-friendly en suite facilities, Gilligan's is a cheap
and cheerful way to travel without feeling like you've compromised.
"Deluxe" twin and double rooms (A$130 per night) have fridges, TVs,
and lounges; some have balconies. Modern public facilities include a
TV lounge, an Internet café-pizzeria, a licensed gaming room, a water-
fall-fed lagoon pool, and an on-site nightclub, Pure (open Friday–Sunday from 10 PM until late). It's hugely popular with younger travelers,
but tourists who wheel their luggage are welcome, too—though they
might find the gigantic beer hall and deck, complete with sportscasts
on Cairns's largest outdoor screen and loud, live entertainment (including big-name bands) Tuesday and Thursday–Sunday, a bit intense.
⊠ 57–89 Grafton St., CBD, 4870 ☎ 07/4041–6566 ◇ reservations@
gilligansbackpackers.com.au ⊕ www.gilligansbackpackers.com.au ↘
120 rooms ⌂ In-room: no phone, refrigerator (some), no TV (some).
In-hotel: guest kitchen, restaurant, bar, nightclub, pool, gym, massage,
hot tub, beachfront, volleyball, laundry facilities, public Internet, airport shuttle, tour desk, lobby shop, parking (no fee) ▤ MC, V.

¢–$ **⊡ Hides Hotel.** This 1880s building with breeze-buffeted verandas is a
superb example of colonial Outback architecture, and has 30 heritage
style rooms with shared bathrooms. The adjoining motel has modern
rooms, all with tropical decor and en suites. Rates include Continental breakfast and a light evening meal from PJ O'Brien's pub, which
can get rowdy on weekends. The hotel is in the center of the Cairns
Mall. ⊠ 87 Lake St., at Shields St., CBD, 4870 ☎ 07/4051–1266 or
1800/079266 ☎ 07/4031–2276 ⊕ www.oceanhotels.com.au ↘ 102
rooms, 72 with en suites (baths) ⌂ In-room: safe, refrigerator. In-hotel:
restaurant, pool, laundry facilities, drycleaning, laundry service, public
Internet, no-smoking rooms, no elevator ▤ AE, MC, V ⦿ CP.

¢–$ **⊡ Lilybank Bed & Breakfast.** In the early 1900s this two-story Queenslander
was the home of the mayor of Cairns, as well as the homestead of
North Queensland's first tropical-fruit plantation. A wooden veranda
surrounds the entire building, and each pristine, high ceilinged room
has a private balcony area and en suite bathroom. There's also a guest
kitchen and a lounge with books and TV. The saltwater pool, surrounded by a brick patio and lush trees, is particularly pleasant on hot
afternoons. Hosts Pat and Mike Woolford are happy to book tours, and
to share their extensive local knowledge, and the affections of their pet
poodles and galah. They also do a great cooked breakfast, with local
specialties such as kangaroo sausage. ⊠ 75 Kamerunga Rd., Stratford,
4870 ☎ 07/4055–1123 ◇ lilybank@bigpond.net.au ⊕ www.lilybank.
com.au ↘ 5 suites ⌂ In-room: no phone, refrigerator (some), no TV,
ethernet. In-hotel: pool, laundry facilities, parking (no fee), public
Internet, no-smoking rooms, no elevator ⦿ BP ▤ AE, MC, V.

7

NIGHTLIFE

The entire Esplanade comes alive at night, with most restaurants serving until late, and wine a staple with the evening meal. Several rowdy pubs catering to backpackers and younger travelers line the center of City Place, while a few hotel venues manage to be upscale while remaining true to the easygoing spirit of Cairns. Unless noted, bars are open every night and there's no cover charge.

If you're looking for a fiesta, **Casa de Meze** (⊠ *Level 1, Aplin St. at the Esplanade, CBD* ☎ *07/4051–5550* ⊕ *www.casademeze.com.au*), with its tapas bar and Latin music, is the place. On Thursday and Sunday nights, there's karaoke from 8:30. It's open daily until midnight, till 2 AM on weekends.

Velvet Rope (⊠ *Hotel Sofitel Reef Casino, 35–41 Wharf St., CBD* ☎ *07/4031–3373 or 07/4030–8888*) is an art-deco space inspired by 1930s Manhattan. It has cabaret-style shows, Tuesday–Saturday, and a dance floor pumping R&B on Thursdays, and commercial dance music from big-name DJs on weekends.

PJ O'Brien's (⊠ *87 Lake St., CBD* ☎ *07/4031–5333*), a traditional Irish pub chain, is always buzzing with backpackers swapping travel tales over pints, and generally enjoying the *craic* (Gaelic for "good time"). It's open nightly until around 1 AM.

Verdi's (⊠ *Sheridan and Shields Sts., CBD* ☎ *07/4052–1010* ⊕ *www. verdis.com.au*), an Italian eatery, is a local favorite for casual (but not shabby) drinks. It is lively until around midnight during the week, later on weekends.

SPORTS & THE OUTDOORS

ADVENTURE TRIPS

Cairns is chockablock full of adventure-tour companies and activities, and there's no shortage of tourist offices, booking agents, and tour desks around the Esplanade to help you choose what to do and who to do it with.

Raging Thunder (⊠ *52–54 Fearnley St., CBD* ☎ *07/4030–7990* ⊕ *www. ragingthunder.com.au*) has a variety of adventure packages: dive and snorkel on the Barrier Reef; glide over the scenic Atherton Tablelands in one of the world's largest hot-air balloons; or white-water raft through the hinterland's rugged gorges. Some tours can be combined with a visit to Tjapukai Aboriginal Cultural Park. From A$155 for a day's sea kayaking around Fitzroy Island.

R 'n' R Rafting (⊠ *278 Hartley St., CBD* ☎ *07/4041–9444* ⊕ *www.raft. com.au*) runs white-water expeditions on the North Johnstone River and Tully River for adults of all skill levels. From A$98 for a half-day's river rafting tour.

BEACHES

Since Cairns has no city beaches, most people head right out to the reef to swim and snorkel. North of the airport, the neighborhood beach communities of **Machans Beach, Holloways Beach, Yorkey's Knob, Trinity Beach,** and **Clifton Beach** are prime for swimming from June through September. It's crucial to avoid the water at other times, however, when deadly box jellyfish (marine stingers) and invisible-to-the-eye Irukandji jellyfish float in the water along the coast.

DIVING

Be sure to ask at a tour desk or tourist office before you book a diving tour. Tours vary in size and some specifically cater to certain people; if you're an experienced diver, for example, you won't want to be stuck on a daylong introductory dive trip with aquaphobic tourists. If you're a relatively new diver, on the other hand, you'll need to make sure to visit a dive site that doesn't require advanced skills, and where plenty of qualified, certified staff will be on hand to assist you if necessary.

Deep Sea Divers Den (⊠ *319 Draper St., CBD* ☎ *1800/612223* ⊕ *www. diversden.com.au*) has a roaming permit that allows guides to go to any part of the reef, including 17 private moorings. The company organizes day trips on one of two boats that include two or three dives, gear, and lunch; and multi-day live-aboard trips. From A$90 for a two-dive day trip.

Fodor's Choice
★
American **Mike Ball Dive Expeditions** (⊠ *143 Lake St., CBD* ☎ *07/4031– 5484 or 1800/643216* ⊕ *www.mikeball.com*) has been diving the Great Barrier Reef since 1969 and is credited with many underwater "firsts." Ball runs multi-day, multi-dive trips along the Queensland coastline on which experienced divers get to set their own bottom times and dive their own plans—or be expertly guided. Custom-built, twin-hulled live-aboard boats bristling with top-end gear, serious divers, and qualified chefs depart Mondays and Thursdays—prices are all-inclusive. From A$1,300 for a three-night, 12-dive trip.

Pro Dive Cairns (⊠ *116 Spence St., CBD* ☎ *07/4031–5255* ⊕ *www.pro-divecairns.com.au*) conducts two-night trips to the Great Barrier Reef as well as night dives for all skill levels.

★ **Quicksilver** (⊠ *Great Adventures office, Marlin Marinathe Esplanade, CBD* ☎ *07/4031–4299*) is the best one-stop shop for getting out to the reef, especially if you're a beginner. Excellent, personable staff run sightseeing, snorkeling, and diving tours on sleek high-speed catamarans to activity platforms at Agincourt Reef on the outer Great Barrier Reef for A$186 per person, with optional Sea Walker helmeted seabed walks (A$134) and scuba diving (A$99–A$134). The underwater observatory here lets you get a close-up view of the fish. Quicksilver also takes small-group sailing tours to the Low Isles coral cay with a marine biologist (A$132) and scenic helicopter flights (from A$125). A$5 reef tax

7

is levied on all passengers. Tours depart daily from Cairns, Palm Cove, and Port Douglas.

Fodor's Choice
★ **Tusa Dive** (⊠*Shield St. at The Esplanade, CBD* ☎*07/4047–9100* ⊕*www.tusadive.com*) is renowned as being the best day-dive boat. Boats take up to 28 divers, but underwater groups are limited to about 6 (for an extra A$25, get your own underwater guide). The fast, well-equipped boats have roving permits to visit 21 different dive and snorkel sites—generally two per trip. Between dives, watch underwater videos, refuel, and relax on deck. A staff photographer snaps everyone underwater: purchase pics of yourself bonding with that turtle 10 minutes after you surface. A full day trip, including two dives, gear,

> **GAME FISHING**
>
> Some of the world's top-rated deep-sea sites are on the outer Barrier Reef. Several operators take novice and experienced anglers out to the reef's edge to trawl for large pelagic fish including giant black (and occasional) blue marlin, Spanish mackerel, tuna, sailfish, and wahoo. Closer in, sea perch, sweet lip, red emperor, and coral trout are there for the taking. Trolling, jig, popper, bottom, and live-bait fishing are all options. If you're lucky, you'll see passing whales and dolphins while you are waiting for that monster fish to bite. Catch mud crabs and barramundi in the estuaries. One of the best game-fishing boats is long-

buffet lunch, and snacks is A$205 (plus a reef tax of A$15). Tusa's *Spirit of Freedom* luxury live-aboard runs three-, fou-, and seven-day dive trips to Cod Hole and Ribbon reefs or Osprey reef in the Coral Sea (from A$1,190 per person).

SHOPPING

MALLS

Cairns Central (⊠*McLeod and Spence Sts., CBD* ☎*07/4041–4111*), adjacent to the Cairns railway station, houses 180 specialty stores, a Myer department store, an international food court, and cinemas.

Pier Shopping (⊠*Pierpoint Rd., CBD* ☎*07/4051-7244* ⊕*www.piershopping.com.au*) houses the shops of local and international designers. Many of the bars and restaurants open onto verandas on the waterside and the newly expanded boardwalk along the marina.

Trinity Wharf (⊠*Wharf St., CBD* ☎*No phone*) has everything from designer boutiques and souvenirs shops to restaurants and a bus terminal.

MARKETS

If you're looking for inexpensive beachwear, local art and craft, or souvenirs, the **Cairns Night Markets** (⊠*The Esplanade at Aplin St., CBD* ☎*No phone* ⊕*www.nightmarkets.com.au*) are the place to go. Bring cash—many of the 70-plus merchants charge additional fees for credit cards.

The best street market in Cairns is **Rusty's** (✉*Spence and Sheridan Sts., CBD* ☎*07/4051–5100* ⊕*www.rustysmarkets.com.au*), with home-grown produce, art and crafts, jewelry, clothing, and food (burgers, Thai, Vietnamese, and sushi) on sale Friday 6 AM–6 PM, Saturday 6–3, and Sunday 6–2.

SPECIALTY STORES

Jungara Gallery (✉*99 The Esplanade, CBD* ☎*07/4051–5355* ⊕*www. jungaraaboriginalart.com.au*) sells authentic Aboriginal arts and artifacts from all over Australia, plus some pieces from Torres Strait Island.

23 Karat Goldsmiths + Reef and Rainforest Gallery (✉*Cairns Central Shopping, CBD* ☎*07/4031–9666*) sells paintings, prints, and sculpture by local artists, and handmade jewelry incorporating local gold nuggets and gems.

CAIRNS ESSENTIALS

TRANSPORTATION

AIR TRAVEL

Cairns Airport is a major international gateway and a connection point for flights to other parts of Queensland, including Townsville, Mackay, Rockhampton, Hamilton Island, and the Northern Territory, as well as all Australian capital cities. Airport Connections runs coaches from the airport and town—an 8-km (5-mi) trip that takes about 10 minutes and costs A$11–A$15. The company also services Cairns's Northern beaches, Palm Cove, and Silky Oaks Lodge, past Daintree (A$17–A$42). Express Chauffeured Coaches & Limousines provides bus services from the airport to Palm Cove and Port Douglas, north of Cairns (A$18–A$30 by coach, A$100–A$210 in a stretch limo). Private taxis make these trips as well (A$15–A$20 to Cairns).

Airlines based at Cairns Airport include Air New Zealand, Cathay Pacific, Continental, Qantas, Jetstar, and Virgin Blue.

Airport & Transfers Cairns Airport (✉*Airport Rd.* ☎*07/4052–9703*).**Airport Connections** (☎*07/4099–5950* ⊕*www.tnqshuttle.com*). **Express Chauffeured Coaches & Limousines** (☎*07/4098–5473* ⊕*www.eccportdouglas.com*).

Airlines Air New Zealand (☎*1300/365525*). **Cathay Pacific** (☎*07/4035–9800*). **Continental** (☎*1300/737640 or 07/4034–9122*). **Jetstar** (☎*13–1538* ⊕*www. jetstar.com.au*). **Qantas** (☎*13–1313* ⊕*www.qantas.com.au*). **Virgin Blue** (☎*13–6789* ⊕*www.virginblue.com.au*).

BUS TRAVEL

Greyhound Australia operates daily express buses from major southern cities to Cairns. By bus, Cairns to Brisbane takes 30-plus hours, to Sydney it's around 45 hours, and to Melbourne it's a gargantuan trip of nearly 60 hours, best broken into bearable segments.

Contact Greyhound Australia (✉*Reef Fleet Terminal, 7 Spence St., CBD* ☎*07/4051–5899 or 13–1499* ⊕*www.greyhound.com.au*).

CAR RENTAL

Avis, Budget, Hertz, and Thrifty all have rental cars and four-wheel-drive vehicles available in downtown Cairns and at Cairns International Airport. An economical, reliable alternative is Leisure Wheels, just off Captain Cook Highway. Leisure Wheels operates daily 7 AM–8:30 PM and offers free delivery and pickup.

CAR TRAVEL

The 1,712-km (1,061-mi) route from Brisbane to Cairns runs along the Bruce Highway (Highway 1), which later becomes the Captain Cook Highway. Throughout its length, the often monotonous road rarely touches the coast. Unless you're planning to stop off en route, it's best to fly or take the fast Tilt Train to Cairns, and rent a car there.

TRAIN TRAVEL

Trains arrive at the Cairns Railway Station on Bunda Street. The *Sunlander,* with its luxury *Queenslander*-class sleeping and fine-dining carriages, makes the 32-hour journey between Brisbane and Cairns twice weekly (departing Brisbane Thursday and Sunday, returning from Cairns Friday and Monday). The fast, modern *Tilt Train* plies the coast from Brisbane to Cairns, Tuesday and Friday, leaving Cairns for Brisbane on Wednesday and Saturday. Business-class passengers have six channels of entertainment on individual TV screens, or watch DVDs in the bar-car. The *Savannahlander* service on Wednesdays links Cairns and Forsyth, traveling through rain-forest, savannah land, and outback en route. Trains are operated by Queensland Rail.

Contacts Cairns Railway Station (⊠ *Bunda St., CBD* ☎ *07/4036–9330 or 07/4036–9333* ⊕ *www.qr.com.au).***Queensland Rail** (☎ *1300/131722* ⊕ *www.qr.com.au).*

CONTACTS & RESOURCES

EMERGENCIES

Dial **000** to reach an ambulance, the police, or the fire department.

Hospital Cairns Base Hospital (⊠ *The Esplanade at Florence St., CBD* ☎ *07/4050–6333).*

Pharmacy Esplanade Day & Night Pharmacy (⊠ *Shop 10, 85 The Esplanade, CBD* ☎ *07/4041–4545).*

TOURS

BOAT TOURS Coral Princess Cruises has three-, four-, and seven-night trips from Cairns and Townsville on a comfortable 54-passenger expedition-style ship. There are plenty of stops for snorkeling, guided coral-viewing, rain-forest hikes, fishing, and beach barbecues. Onboard marine biologists give lectures and lead excursions. Divers can rent equipment on board; lessons are also available.

Great Adventures Reef and Green Island Cruises, which caters primarily to Asian tourist groups, runs three trips daily out of Cairns on fast catamarans to Green Island and the outer Barrier Reef, where diving, snorkeling (with the option of using zippy Scuba-scooters), and helicopter overflights are available. Some trips include a buffet lunch and coral viewing from an underwater observatory and a semisubmersible. On Green Island trips, non-divers can take a guided ocean-floor "Sea Walker" tour, wearing a special helmet. Costs range from A$69 for a half-day Green Island Eco Tour to A$194 for the full-day Green Island and Barrier Reef Adventure.

Ocean Spirit Cruises conducts four-hour and full-day tours aboard the *Ocean Spirit I*, a large catamaran, and the smaller *Ocean Spirit II and III*, from A$110–A$179 per person, snorkeling gear included. Daily trips include four hours at the Great Barrier Reef, coral viewing from a semisubmersible or glass-bottom boat at Upolo Cay, swimming, snorkeling, and a fresh seafood lunch. Introductory diving lessons (A$95–A$150), and certified dives (A$55–A$110) are available. *Ocean Spirit IV* takes a maximum of 100 guests on a nightly, four-course dinner cruise along Trinity Inlet from 6:45 to 9:30 (A$79). Boats depart Marlin Jetty, Cairns and Palm Cove Jetty. Transfers from Cairns, Northern Beaches, Palm Cove, and Port Douglas are available (free A$39).

Contacts Coral Princess Cruises (⊠ *24 Redden St., CBD* ☎ *07/4040–9999 or 1800/079545* ⊕ *www.coralprincess.com.au*).**Great Adventures Reef and Green Island Cruises** (⊠ *1 Spence St., Reef Fleet Terminal* ☎ *07/4044–9944 or 1800/079080* ⊕ *www.greatadventures.com.au*).

Fodor's Choice
★ **Ocean Spirit Cruises** (⊠ *140 Mulgrave Rd., CBD* ☎ *07/4031–2920 or 1800/644227* ⊕ *www.oceanspirit.com.au*).

HORSEBACK-RIDING TOURS Blazing Saddles organizes half-day horse rides (A$107) through bushland around Kuranda. You can also rent all-terrain vehicles for A$127 for a half day; A$217 for a full day, insurance included.

Contact Blazing Saddles (⊠ *2326 Kennedy Hwy., Kuranda* ☎ *07/4093–9100* ⊕ *www.blazingsaddles.com.au*).

NATURE TOURS Daintree Rainforest River Trains organizes full-day coach tours through mangrove swamps and rain forest to see native orchids, birds, and crocodiles. You can also arrange self-drive tours. From A$145 for a full-day guided tour out of Cairns, including entrance fees and lunch.

Wilderness Challenge runs trips to the top of the Cape York Peninsula from May through November, including off-the-tourist-track "advanced" safaris, and a 3 Day Rock Art & Rainforest Safari. Most tours visit the world-renowned Quinkan Aboriginal rock art site near Laura, and stay in bush cabins or safari tents at **Jowlbinna rock art safari camp** (☎ *07/4035–4488* ⊕ *www.jowalbinna.com.au*). Down Under Tours makes day trips and four-wheel-drive excursions to Kuranda, Cape Tribulation, the Daintree, and the southern tablelands (A$65 per person). The company's luxury arm, Down Under By Appointment, takes small groups on customized journeys, with expert guide-driver on hand.

Contacts Daintree Rainforest River Trains (☎ *01/4090–7676 or 1800/808309* ⊕ *www.daintreerivertrain.com*).**Down Under Tours** (⊠ *26 Redden St., CBD, Cairns, 4870* ☎ *07/4035–5566* ⊕ *www.downundertours.com*).**Wilderness Challenge**

7

(✉ *Box 254, Cairns, 4870* ☎ *07/4035–4488* ⊕ *www.wilderness-challenge. com.au*).

VISITOR INFORMATION

Tourism Tropical North Queensland, open daily 8:30–6:30, offers information and recommends accommodations and tours. Its two Web sites give information and advice on touring the region.

Contact Tourism Tropical North Queensland (✉ *51 The Esplanade, between Spence and Shield Sts., CBD* ☎ *07/4051–3588* ⊕ *www.tropicalaustralia.com.au and www.safetraveltnq.com.au*).

NORTH FROM CAIRNS

The Captain Cook Highway runs from Cairns to Mossman, a relatively civilized stretch known mostly for the resort town of Port Douglas. Past the Daintree River, wildlife parks and sunny coastal villages fade into one of the most sensationally wild corners of the continent. If you came to Australia in search of high-octane sun, pristine coral cays, steamy jungles filled with exotic bird noises and riotous vegetation, and a languid beachcomber lifestyle, then head straight for the coast between Daintree and Cooktown.

The southern half of this coastline lies within Cape Tribulation, Daintree National Park, part of the Greater Daintree Wilderness Area, a region named to UNESCO's World Heritage list because of its unique ecology. If you want to get a peek at the natural splendor of the area, there's no need to go past Cape Tribulation. However, the Bloomfield Track does continue on to Cooktown, a destination that will tack two days onto your itinerary. This wild, rugged country breeds some notoriously maverick personalities and can add a whole other dimension to the far North Queensland experience.

Prime time for visiting the area is from May through September, when the daily maximum temperature averages around 27°C (80°F) and the water is comfortably warm. During the wet season, which lasts from about December through March, expect rain, humidity, and lots of bugs. Highly poisonous box and transparent Irukandji jellyfish make the coastline unsafe for swimming from October through May, but the jellies hardly ever drift out as far as the reefs, so you'll be safe there.

Numbers in the margin correspond to points of interest on the North from Cairns map.

PALM COVE

26 *23 km (14 mi) north of Cairns.*

Fodor's Choice
★

A mere 20-minute drive north of Cairns, Palm Cove is one of the jewels of Queensland and an idyllic, though expensive, base for exploring the far north. It's a quiet place that those in the know seek out for its magnificent trees, calm waters, and excellent restaurants. The loudest noises you're likely to hear in this place are the singing of birds and the lapping of the Pacific Ocean against the shore.

At the **Outback Opal Mine** you can glimpse huge specimens of this unique Australian gemstone and opalized seashells and fossils. A documentary film shows you how an opal is formed, cut, and polished; the walk-through simulated mine has natural opals embedded in its walls. The on-site jewelry showcases opals, naturally (A$6 to more than A$1,000). The mine is adjacent to the Tropical Zoo. ⌧*Captain Cook Hwy.* ☎*07/4055–3492* ⊕*www.outbackopalmine.com.au* ⌧*Free* ☼*Daily 8–6.*

☺ The 10-acre **Cairns Tropical Zoo** is home to many species of Australian wildlife, including kangaroos, huge saltwater crocodiles and other reptiles, pelicans, and cassowaries. Most distinguished among its residents is Sarge, a 17-foot, 1,540-pound croc that the park claims is more than 100 years old. The park also has snake, crocodile, and free-flight bird shows, during which resident white cockatoo Rumpole collects money for the zoo's wildlife fund. You can hand-feed and handle koalas and tame kangaroos. The daily Breakfast at the Zoo (A$39) includes a wildlife presentation on the deck. The zoo incorporates Cairns Night Zoo, where a maximum of 100 guests are treated to close-up glimpses of Australia's fascinating nocturnal creatures. The Night Zoo experience costs from A$89 per person, including barbecue dinner, a wildlife-spotting tour, and campfire sing-along (bookings essential). ⌧*Captain Cook Hwy.* ☎*07/4055–3669* ⊕*www.cairnstropicalzoo.com* ⌧*A$29* ☼*Daily 8:30–5; Night Zoo Mon.–Thurs. and Sat. 6:50–10.*

WHERE TO STAY & EAT

$$–$$$$ ✕**Nunu.** The sexy suede lounges and intimate banquettes, combined with the unspoiled view of Palm Cove beach, make lingering easy at this spot adjacent to the Outrigger Beach Club. (The spicy-sweet vanilla-ginger mojitos help, too.) The chef, decamped from Melbourne, prides himself on an ever-changing menu featuring Aussie seafood creations with a cutting-edge, flavorful twist, such as blue swimmer crab tortellini or poached yellow fin tuna with crispy southern octopus, plus duck, lamb, and beef dishes, and interesting vegetarian options: try the "Millionaires" salad of shaved palm hearts, baby herbs, and chili. Nunu's big breakfasts feature organic produce with home-made breads and pastries (daily 8–noon). ⌧*123 Williams Esplanade* ☎*07/4059–1880* ⊕*www.nunu.com.au* ⊟*AE, MC, V.*

$$–$$$ ✕**Casmar.** The ocean's bounty is the focus at this innovative waterfront restaurant. The grilled Moreton Bay bugs with mango and fresh coconut are just the right combination of smoky and buttery; a delectable Asian-style "fruits of the sea" includes scallops, prawns, barramundi, and reef fish. Confit of duck, roasted lamb rack, and beef tenderloin on horseradish mash are other crowd-pleasers. The food is a pleasure

7

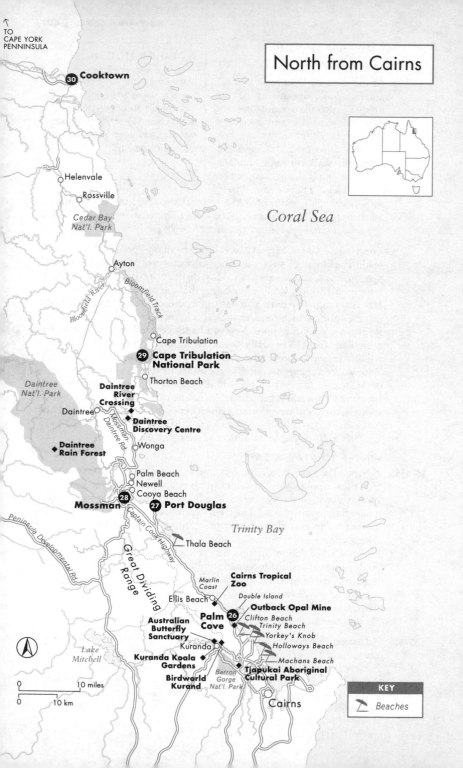

to linger over, and creative cocktails make dinner here more magical still. For A$150, you can get a chilled seafood feast, including Moreton Bay bugs, mud crab, salad, and tropical fruit, to eat in or take away: perfect for beach picnics. ⊠*Harpa St. at Williams Esplanade* ☎*07/4059–0013* ⊟*AE, DC, MC, V* ⊗*No lunch.*

$$$$ ⌗**Angsana Resort & Spa.** Fine landscaping, pools, barbecues, and plenty of sunny areas in which to relax enhance this classy colonial-style complex of vacation apartments, which opens directly onto a large, white-sand beach. Each vast apartment has a large private veranda, a comfortable sitting and dining area, and one, two, or three bedrooms with king-size beds. The furnishings, custom-designed and completely modern, are more luxurious still since their 2007 refurb; kitchens have granite-top counters, and there are laundry facilities in every apartment. The spa has open-air pavilions and is staffed by gentle Thai therapists, most trained at Banyan Tree Phuket. Far Horizons restaurant fronts Palm Cove Beach and serves excellent modern International cuisine. There's a helpful tour desk and guest library. ⊠*1 Veivers Rd., 4879* ☎*07/4055–3000 or 1800/672236* ✐*reservations@angsana.com* ⊕*www.angsana.com/gbr* ⤳*67 apartments* ⟁*In-room: safe, kitchen, refrigerator/minibar, laundry facilities, DVD, dial-up, Wi-Fi. In-hotel: restaurant, room service, bar, pools, spa, beachfront, laundry service, concierge, public Internet, public Wi-Fi, airport shuttle, parking (no fee), no-smoking rooms, no elevator* ⊟*AE, DC, MC, V.*

$$$$ ⌗**The Sebel Reef House Palm Cove.** Set amid lovely gardens, this charm-
★ ing hotel seems more like a private club. The lobby, along with its mural of the Queensland rain forest, is decorated with a superb collection of New Guinea Sepik River handicrafts. The main building dates from 1885, and the comfortable rooms have a turn-of-the-20th-century decor characterized by whitewashed walls and pastel furnishings. Waterfalls spill into one of three swimming pools. At the award-winning spa, you can unwind with the Mala-Mayi, a 90-minute treatment that includes exfoliation, a mud bath, a scalp massage, and rain therapy. ⊠*99 Williams Esplanade, 4879* ☎*07/4055–3633* ✐*info@reefhouse.com.au* ⊕*www.mirvachotels.com* ⤳*63 rooms, 6 suites* ⟁*In-room: safe, kitchen (some), refrigerator/minibar, DVD, dial-up (some), Wi-Fi (some), laundry facilities (some). In-hotel: 3 restaurants, room service, bar, pools, spa, beachfront, concierge, laundry service, executive floor, public Internet, public Wi-Fi, airport shuttle, parking (no fee), no-smoking rooms* ⊟*AE, DC, MC, V.*

$$$$ ⌗**Peppers Beach Club & Spa.** The open-air reception area of this gor-
⟳ geous tropical resort flows seamlessly into the first of three pools, where
★ a cascade of water immediately soothes the spirit. The swim-up, thatch-roof bar is a great place to have a cocktail. Sparkling white buildings here house spacious, sophisticated rooms and suites with cool contemporary furnishings, flatscreen TVs, CD players, whirlpool hot tubs, and lagoon or ocean views. But with landscaped grounds and dazzling Palm Cove beach a few steps away, you won't want to stay inside for long. Do make time for a treatment at the on-site Sanctum Spa. The resort's signature restaurant, Tamara's at the Beach, serves Modern Australian

7

cuisine and tropical buffet breakfasts (open 6:30 AM till late). ✉*123 Williams Esplanade, 4879* ☎*07/4059–9200 or 1800/134444* ⊕*www. peppers.com.au* ⇌*220 rooms, 83 suites* ⌂*In-room: safe, fans, kitchen (some), refrigerator, hot tub, CD/DVD, cable and pay TV, dial-up, room service. In-hotel: 5 restaurants, bar, babysitting, pools, children's playground, gym, spa, salon, drycleaning, laundry facilities, laundry service, meeting rooms, business center, airport shuttle, parking (no fee), no elevator* ▭*AE, DC, MC, V.*

EN ROUTE ★ North of Palm Cove, where the Captain Cook Highway swoops toward the sea, a sign announces the beginning of the **Marlin Coast**, and for the next 30 km (19 mi) the road plays hide-and-seek with a glorious stretch of shoreline, ducking inland through tunnels of coconut palm and curving back to the surf.

Hartley's Crocodile Adventures, 40 km (25 mi) north of Cairns, houses crocodiles farmed for meat and skin, as well as koalas, wallabies, snakes, lizards, colorful cassowaries, and other tropical birds in natural environs, accessible via boardwalks and boats. Lagoon boat cruises and crocodile-farm tours guarantee you close-up views of crocs, and there are daily cassowary and koala feedings, croc and snake shows, and more. Lilies Restaurant showcases local delicacies including crocodile and 'roo. The education center has useful info on how to avoid croc attacks. Down Under Tours (☎07/4035–5566) and Wildlife Discovery Tours (☎07/4099–6612) both include Hartley's on their day-tour itineraries. ✉*Cook Hwy.* ☎*07/4055–3576* ⊕*www.crocodileadventures. com* ✇*A$29* ⊙*Daily 8:30–5.*

PORT DOUGLAS

㉗ *61 km (38 mi) northwest of Cairns.*

Known simply as "Port" to locals, Port Douglas offers a similarly wide range of outdoor adventures as Cairns, but in a smaller, more laidback tropical setting. As a burgeoning tourist town, there's a palpable buzz, despite the sleep-inducing tropical haze and humidity. Travelers from around the world flock here to be close to the north's wild rain forests and the Great Barrier Reef, and to take advantage of the varied lodgings, restaurants, and bars on and around the main strip, Macrossan Street.

Like most of North Queensland, Port Douglas was settled on the promise of, and the search for, gold. When the gold rush receded in the 1880s, Port Douglas became a sugar town, and it remained the port for sugar milled in nearby Mossman until the 1950s. The many colonial "Queenslander" buildings give it the feel of a humble seaside settlement, despite its modern resorts and, some might say, overbuilt landscape. The rain forests and beaches—such as Four Mile Beach—surrounding the town are, for the most part, World Heritage sites, so fortunately, Port's growing popularity won't encroach on the bounteous natural beauty of the region.

You'll have many chances to dine with animals around Australia, but the "Breakfast with the Birds" experience at the **Rainforest Habitat Wildlife Sanctuary**—where exceptionally tame avian creatures surround you, even perching on your shoulders as you dine—is among the best. The park houses more than 180 species of tropical native wildlife, including cassowaries, parrots, wetland waders, koalas, kangaroos, and crocodiles in world-class "immersion" woodland, wetland, rain forest, and grassland environs. The sumptuous buffet breakfast, daily from 8 to 11, is A$39, including sanctuary admission and a guided tour. You can also Lunch with the Lorikeets for A$39, every day between 12 and 2. Get insider information via expertly guided tours and croc, snake, and koala shows, or take a self-guided stroll along the boardwalks. ⊠ *Port Douglas Rd. at Agincourt St.* ☎ *07/4099-3235* ⊕ *www. rainforesthabitat.com.au* ⊞ *A$29* ☉ *Daily 8–5.*

> **THE WETLANDS**
>
> An hour northwest of Port Douglas, giant termite mounds dot savannah scrub, and vast reclaimed wetlands serve as a bird refuge. The **Mareeba Tropical Savanna & Wetlands Reserve** (☎ *07/4093-2514* ⊕ *www.mareebawetlands.com*) runs a great-value 2½-hour Twilight Safari that combines a cruise; a savannah drive; and a stop for "billy" tea, and wine and cheese. Luxury safari-tent accommodation comes with BBQ and breakfast baskets, and wildlife-spotting and birdwatching walks. All proceeds feed back into the Wetlands' environmental work.

WHERE TO STAY & EAT

$$-$$$ ✕ **Il Pescatore.** This modern restaurant in the Sheraton Mirage is one of the classier dining spots in Port Douglas. Eat indoors in air-conditioned comfort or outdoors surrounded by swimming lagoons. Mediterranean-style dishes are prepared with fresh seafood and local produce and artfully presented. Try the signature oven-roasted whole baby barramundi in a Malaysian paste with a tropically flavored risotto, or the seasonal Mossman prawns, and don't miss the soufflé of the day. ⊠ *Davidson St.* ☎ *07/4099-5888* ⊟ *AE, DC, MC, V* ☉ *Closed Wed. and Thurs. No lunch.*

$$-$$$ ✕ **Nautilus Restaurant.** Tables with high-backed cane chairs stand under a canopy of magnificent coconut palms at this family-owned, but not completely family-friendly, restaurant (no children under age eight are allowed). The contemporary Australian dishes are fresh, original, and beautifully presented. The focus is on local seafood: try the justifiably famous chili mud crab. Superb desserts include a delicious mango soufflé. ⊠ *17 Murphy St.* ☎ *07/4099-5330* ⊕ *www.nautilus-restaurant. com.au* ⊰ *Reservations essential* ⊟ *AE, DC, MC, V* ☉ *No lunch.*

$-$$ ✕ **Salsa Bar & Grill.** This lively seaside restaurant is a Port Douglas institution. The louver-windowed interior is bright and beachy, and the huge wooden deck overlooking Dickson Inlet becomes an intimate dining area once the sun sets. Seafood, steaks, salads, and light snacks all grace the lunch menu, and an extensive Tropical Modern Australian dinner menu includes local delicacies such as soft shell mud crab, ocean trout, yellow fin tuna, and wild boar. Happy hour comes daily between 3 and 5: down a tropical daiquiri or two. ⊠*26 Wharf St., 4922* ☎*07/4099–4922* ⊕*www.salsaportdouglas.com.au* ⊟*AE, DC, MC, V.*

¢–$$ ✕**Ironbar.** Built like a ramshackle, corrugated-iron shack, this restaurant has a menu scattered with Aussie colloquialisms. But don't be fooled into thinking the food is as slaphappy as the surroundings; here you can "dip your lid" to taste the prime rib-eye fillet served with your choice of sauce, or kangaroo steak with a Moroccan-style salad and minted yogurt. If you time it right, you might catch a cane-toad race in the back-room bar. Kick on after dinner, with live music most nights. ⊠*5 Macrossan St.* ☎*07/4099–4776* ⊟*AE, DC, MC, V.*

$$$$ ▥**Sheraton Mirage Port Douglas.** Elegant guest rooms at this deluxe
ⓒ resort have cool, modern furnishings and wood-shuttered, openable windows overlooking manicured gardens, the golf course, or 5 acres of swimmable saltwater lagoons. On-call valets will assist you with everything from replenishing ice buckets to arranging in-room candlelight dinners. There are vast public areas and three distinctive dining spots: *Zai* does divine Japanese; *Il Pescatore* has Mediterranean-style fare; and light-filled *Lagoons* serves International cuisine with changing culinary themes, and big buffet breakfasts. You're free to use the gym and tennis courts at the neighboring Mirage Country Club. ⊠*Davidson St., 4871* ☎*07/4099–5888* ✎portdouglas.switch370@sheraton.com ⊕*www.starwoodhotels.com/sheraton* ⇆*291 rooms, 3 suites, 100 villas* ⚿*In-room: fans, safe, refrigerator, kitchen (some), ethernet, dial-up, CD, cable TV and pay movies, hot tub (some). In-hotel: 3 restaurants, room service, bars, golf course, tennis courts, pools, gym, massage, sauna, salon, beachfront, marina, water sports, horseriding, babysitting, children's program, concierge, laundry facilities, laundry service, drycleaning, businesss center with Wi-Fi (fee), meeting rooms, heliport, airport shuttle, car rental, shops, tour desk, no-smoking rooms, minibar, disabled-access rooms* ⊟*AE, DC, MC, V.*

$$$–$$$$ ▥**Mantra Treetops Resort & Spa Port Douglas.** The first resort on your way
ⓒ into Port Douglas off the Captain Cook Highway, this is also one of the coolest, thanks to the lush, tall rain-forest gardens that envelop the resort. Guest wings overlook dense vegetation, and linked lagoon pools contribute to a laidback, tropical ambience, as do the friendly staff. The bar often has live evening entertainment, and can get lively. The on-site day spa is a wood-lined oasis. A plus: it's opposite the delightful Rainforest Habitat Sanctuary. ⊠*315 Port Douglas Rd., 4877* ☎*07/4030–4333* ⊕*www.mantratreetops.com.au* ⇆*297 rooms* ⚿*In-room: safe, refrigerator, ethernet (some), dial-up. In-hotel: 2 restaurants, room service, bars, pools, gym, spa, concierge, laundry facilities, laundry service, public Internet, public Wi-Fi, airport shuttle, no-smoking rooms* ⊟*AE, DC, MC, V* ⍟*BP (some).*

$$–$$$ ▥**Hibiscus Gardens Spa Resort.** Four Mile Beach is just a short walk from
★ this bustling, Balinese-inspired resort and spa. Terra-cotta tiled floors contrast nicely with warm teak furnishings, cedar bifold doors, and

Balinese-style fabrics in each spacious apartment (choose from studio, 1- or 2-bedroom, some with hot tubs and dual bathrooms). Most have daybeds, and private, lockable balconies affording views of the lush gardens, Mossman Gorge, and the mountains beyond. You can hire VCRs and DVD players from reception. If you haven't already gotten your fill of rain and mud, try the Li'Tya day spa's relaxing local-ochre wraps and rain therapy treatments, which incorporate native ingredients and indigenous healing techniques. An excellent tropical breakfast with à la carte options is served by the resort's second pool; at other times, you can order drinks from the resort's bottle-shop menu. Friendly, knowledgeable staff mean service here is comparable to that at the region's luxury resorts. ⊠ *22 Owen St., at Mowbray St., 4871* ☎ *07/4099–5315 or 1800/995995* ⊕ *www.hibiscusportdouglas.com. au* ⇥ *62 apartments* ☐ *In-room: safe, kitchen, refrigerator, DVD, CD, dial-up, ethernet (some), hot tub (some). In-hotel: room service (bar beverages only), 2 pools, spa, diving, water sports, laundry facilities, airport shuttle, parking (no fee), no smoking (except on balconies), no elevator (one disabled-friendly apartment)* ☐ AE, DC, MC, V.

SHOPPING

The **Marina Mirage** (⊠ *Wharf St.* ☎ *07/4099–5775* ⊕ *www.marinamiragepd.com.au*) houses 40 fashion and specialty shops for souvenirs, jewelry, accessories, resort wear, and designer clothing, along with three restaurants and, at Shop 54, Port Douglas's only nightclub, **Fluid** (☎ *07/4099–5200*).

SPORTS & THE OUTDOORS

Several tour companies conduct day trips to the rain forest in four-wheel-drive buses and vans, and have river cruises for crocodile-spotting. The oldest and most established is **BTS Tours** (⊠ *49 Macrossan St.* ☎ *07/4099–5665* ⊕ *www.btstours.com.au*). It runs various trips out of both Cairns and Port Douglas. The popular full-day Kuranda tour includes the train, cable car, and two hours exploring the township (A$106). Day tours to Cape Tribulation cost A$139 per person; the shorter Daintree River and Mossman Gorge tour is A$50—or do the Daintree (A$40) or Mossman Gorge (A$16) part separately. Lunch isn't included in BTS's tour prices, but there are scheduled food stops en route. **Poseidon Diving** (⊠ *Grant and Macrossan Sts., 4877* ☎ *1800/085674 or 07/4099–4772* ⊕ *www.poseidon-cruises.com.au*) conducts daily snorkeling and diving trips to Agincourt Ribbon Reef, and longer cruises to Outer Barrier Reef sites. A marine naturalist will explain the biology and history of the reef before you dive down to see it yourself. A day's snorkeling cruise is A$155; introductory diving, including tuition, cruise, all gear, and up to three underwater forays, is A$205 with one dive; subsequent dives are A$40 each. For certified divers, a full day in the water, including two or three dives and a buffet lunch, is A$195–A$210. You can hire wetsuits onboard for A$5; dive gear is an extra A$20; and everyone pays a small fuel surcharge and reef tax.

Quicksilver (⊠ *Marina Mirage* ☎ *07/4087–2100* ⊕ *www.quicksilvercruises.com*) runs fast, modern catamarans to a large activity platform on the Outer Barrier Reef, where there's a semisubmersible underwater observatory (A$186). Pay extra for guided snorkeling tours (A$59); an introductory dive with tuition (A$134); one or two certified dives (A$92–A$134); or a Sea Walker helmeted ocean-bed walk (A$134). A sailing excursion to a Low Isles coral cay includes a marine biologist guide and a glass-bottom boat trip (A$132) with optional introductory dive (extra A$112). Also available are 10-minute scenic helicopter flights over the spectacular reef, starting at A$125. You'll also pay a reef tax of A$5. The staff is patient, efficient, and knowledgeable. All tours depart daily from Cairns, Palm Cove, and Port Douglas.

MOSSMAN

❷❽ *14 km (8½ mi) northwest of Port Douglas, 75 km (47 mi) north of Cairns.*

Mossman, a sugar town 20 minutes' drive from Port Douglas, has a population of less than 2,000.

Fodor's Choice
★

Its appeal lies not in the village itself but 5 km (3 mi) out of town where you find the beautiful waterfalls and river at **Mossman Gorge.** Ice-cold water flows here year-round, and there are several boulder-studded swimming holes where you can take a cool, crocodile-free dip. (Swimming in the river is not recommended, due to swift currents, slippery rocks, and flash flooding.) There's a suspension bridge across the Mossman River and a 2½-km (1½-mi) rain-forest walking track. Keep your eyes peeled for indigenous creatures including tree kangaroos, musky rat-kangaroos, Boyd's water dragons, and bright butterflies. Avoid touching stinging vines—those plants with heart-shaped leaves found at rain-forest edges. ⊠ *End of Johnston Rd.* ☎ *07/4098–2188* ⊕ *www. epa.qld.gov.au.*

WHERE TO STAY

$$$$
Fodor's Choice
★

🏨 **Daintree Eco Lodge & Spa.** A flotilla of stars have taken time out at this 30-acre boutique eco-resort in the ancient Daintree rain forest. Elevated boardwalks link the spa, heated pool, restaurant-bar-lounge, and 15 self-contained tree houses, each with a king-size canopy bed, balcony hot tub, handcrafted wood furnishings, and satellite TV. Julaymba restaurant's menu incorporates local "bush tucker" ingredients. The spa has an alfresco couples treatment area. The Malone family and their Aboriginal staff run a terrific activities program that includes bush tucker walks, wildlife-spotting, art workshops, cultural shows, river cruises, and multi-day expeditions. ⊠ *20 Daintree Rd., (3 km [2 mi] past Daintree village—110 km [68 mi] north of Cairns), Daintree, 4873* ☎ *1800/808010 or 07/4098–6100* ✑ *info@daintree-ecolodge.com.au* ⊕ *www.daintree-ecolodge.com.au* ⤴ *15 rooms* ⚒ *In-room: refrigerator, hot tub, cable TV, DVD, Wi-Fi. In-hotel: restaurant, room service, bar, pool, spa, laundry service, airport shuttle, parking (no fee), no kids under 6, no-smoking rooms, no elevator* ☰ *AE, DC, MC, V* ⦿❘ *BP.*

$$$–$$$$
Fodor'sChoice
★

⚏**Voyages Silky Oaks Lodge.** On a hillside surrounded by national parkland, this hotel is reminiscent of the best African safari lodges. Air-conditioned, tropically inspired tree-house villas on stilts overlook either the rain forest and river or a natural-rock swimming pool, and have warm timber floors and furnishings, hot tubs, day beds, and verandas slung with hammocks. The lodge is the starting point for four-wheel-drive, cycling, and canoeing trips into otherwise inaccessible national park rain forest. You can recharge at the Healing Waters Spa, where the treatments use all-natural Australian products. Delightful public areas, including the open-sided Tree House restaurant and bar, overlook the Daintree River and rain forest. Guests can borrow board games from reception. Fabulous gourmet breakfasts are included in the price, and the restaurant serves à la carte lunches and dinners ⊠ *Finlayvale Rd., Mossman Gorge, 4871* ☎ *1300/134044 or 07/4098–1666* ✆ reservations@ poresorts.com ⊕ *www.voyages.com.au/silky* ⪢ *37 rooms, 13 suites* ⚭ *In-room: refrigerator, CD, hot tub, dial-up. In-hotel: safe, restaurant, bar, tennis court, pool, gym, spa, diving, water sports, bicycles, laundry facilities, laundry service, public Internet, concierge, parking (no fee), no kids under 13, no-smoking rooms, disabled-access rooms* ⊟ *AE, DC, MC, V* ⦿ *BP.*

▌EN
ROUTE

New species of fauna and flora are still being discovered in the **Daintree Rain Forest,** the world's oldest living tropical rain forest, where tropical vegetation is as impressive as anything found in the Amazon Basin. Collect information and maps for exploring beforehand, since the best areas for walking are off the main road. You can also arrange guided four-wheel-drive tours, which include walking within the rain forest and/or a ride on a riverboat. The national park is 35 km (22 mi) northwest of Mossman off the Mossman–Daintree Road; get information from rangers on-site, or at the **Queensland Parks and Wildlife Service** (⊠ *Level 1, Centenary Bldg., 1 Front St.* ☎ *07/4098–2188* ⊕ *www. epa.qld.gov.au*) office in Mossman. **Daintree Discovery Centre,** a World Heritage–accredited organization, provides detailed information on the rain forest and its ecosystem. There are four audio-guided trails, including a "bush tucker" walk and a cassowary circuit. You also can take an aerial walkway across part of the bush, and climb the 75-foot-high Canopy Tower. The shop sells books, cards, souvenirs, and clothing. ⊠ *Tulip Oak Rd., off Cape Tribulation Rd., 10 km (6 mi) north of Daintree River ferry station* ☎ *07/4098–9171* ⊕ *www.daintree-rec. com.au* ⊟ *A$25* ⦿ *Daily 8:30–5.*

The intrepid can follow the Mossman–Daintree Road as it winds through sugarcane plantations and towering green hills to the **Daintree River.** The Daintree is a relatively short river, yet it's fed by heavy monsoonal rains that make it wide, glossy, and brown—and a favorite inland haunt for saltwater crocodiles. On the other side of the river, a sign announces the beginning of Cape Tribulation National Park. There's only one ferry, so although the crossing itself is only five minutes and the new boat takes 27 cars, the wait can be 15 minutes, especially between 11 AM and 1 PM and in peak holiday periods ☎ *07/4098–7536*

7

📨 *A$18 per car (return), A$2 per walk-on passenger* ⊙ *Ferry crossings daily 6 AM–midnight.*

CAPE TRIBULATION

34 km (21 mi) north of the Daintree River crossing, 139 km (86 mi) north of Cairns.

Set dramatically at the base of Mt. Sorrow, Cape Tribulation was named by Captain James Cook after a nearby reef snagged the HMS *Endeavour*, forcing him to seek refuge at the site of present-day Cooktown. Today, the tiny settlement, which has little more than a general store and a few lodges, is the activities and accommodations base for the surrounding national park. A bunch of regional tours—including rain-forest walks, reef trips, horseback riding, and fishing—can be booked through **Cape Tribulation Store & Mason's Tours** (⊠ *CMA 4, Cape Tribulation Rd.* ☎ *07/4098–0070* ⊕ *www.masonstours.com.au*), or at PK's Jungle Village backpackers' lodge (☎ *07/4098–0040*). Both places are the last stops for food, supplies, and fuel as you head north. Note that though most outlets in the region accept credit cards, Daintree is the last town before Cooktown with ATM facilities. There's public Internet access and an ATM at the Daintree Palms Resort shop, Wonga Beach (between Mossman and Daintree River crossing). You can refuel, stock up, and get cash out at the BP or Caltex Wonga service stations. ⊕ *www.daintreevillage.asn.au*

㉙
Fodor'sChoice
★

Cape Tribulation, Daintree National Park is an ecological wonderland, a remnant of the forests in which flowering plants first appeared on Earth. Here experts can identify species of angiosperms, the most primitive flowering plant, many of which are found nowhere else on the planet. The park is approximately 22,000 acres, although the entire Wet Tropics region (which stretches from Townsville to Cooktown, and is 12,000 square km [4,633 square mi]) was declared a World Heritage site in 1998.

The park stretches along the coast and west into the jungle from Cow Bay to Aytor. The beach is usually empty, except for the tiny soldier crabs that move about by the hundreds and scatter when approached. If you hike among the mangroves, you're likely to see an incredible assortment of small creatures that depend on the trees for survival. Most evident are mudskippers and mangrove crabs, but keen observers may spot green-backed herons among mangrove roots.

The prime hiking season is May through September, and the best method is by walking along dry creek beds. Bring plenty of insect repellent.

WHERE TO EAT

$$–$$$ ✕ **Cape Restaurant & Bar.** Set in a soaring A-frame wooden building with 30-foot ceilings, this restaurant at Voyages Coconut Beach Rainforest Lodge has floor-to-ceiling windows and a pool surrounded by rain forest. Polished wood and wicker tables and chairs surround a giant palm growing up through a hole in the floor—a classic tropical environment in which to sample creative cuisine. Dishes combine quintessentially Australian ingredients with Asian culinary methods—think croc and chicken pie with a lemon myrtle–mustard sauce or local barramundi. The wine list is heavy on Australian vintages. The Cape also serves full buffet breakfasts and light lunches. ☒*Lot 10, Cape Tribulation Rd.* ☎*07/4098–0033* ⊟*AE, DC, MC, V.*

$–$$ ✕**Dragonfly Gallery Café.** Constructed by local craftspeople from native timber and stone, this gallery sits among rain-forest gardens and overlooks natural barramundi pools. The café is open all day for coffee, sweets, and lunch, as well as for dinner. Try a grilled barramundi fillet or the café's signature prawn salad. A book and gift store and an Internet café are also on-site. The gallery showcases local art and craft. ☒*9 Camelot Close* ☎*07/4098–0121* ⊟*MC, V.*

WHERE TO STAY

Camping at unpowered sites is permitted at **Noah's Beach** (☎*07/4098–2188 ranger, 13–1304 permits* ⊕*www.epa.qld.gov.au*), in the national park, about 8 km (5 mi) south of Cape Tribulation, for A$4.50 per person, per night. BYO tents and drinking water; there are toilets on-site. Buy your permits in advance from Queensland Parks and Wildlife Service. Privately run campgrounds and small resorts can be found along the Daintree Road at Myall Creek and Cape Tribulation.

$$$$ ⊞**Coconut Beach Resort.** The most splendid accommodations at Cape
Fodor'sChoice Tribulation sit in a jungle of fan palms, staghorn ferns, giant mela-
★ leucas, and strangler figs about 2 km (1 mi) south of the cape itself. Daintree Retreats have high-tech touches like CD players, day beds, and aromatherapy oil burners, while Rainforest Retreats focus on the serenity of the natural setting and are fan-cooled. All have modern wood furnishings, polished wooden floors, and balconies. The beach is a two-minute walk away, albeit across the main road, and there's an elevated walkway set into the nearby rain-forest canopy. The resort offers nightly guided rain-forest walks, day hikes, four-wheel-drive tours, sea kayaking, and trips out to the reef. A new day spa is due to open in 2008. ☒*Lot 10, Cape Tribulation Rd., 4873* ☎*07/4098–0033* ✎*reservations@coconutbeachoceanhotels.com.au* ⊕*www.coconutbeachresort.com.au* ➥*66 suites* ☾*In-room: no a/c (some), refrigerator, dial-up (some), no TV. In-hotel: restaurant, bar, room service, 2 pools, spa, beachfront, diving, water sports, bicycles, laundry facilities, concierge, airport shuttle, parking (no fee), no-smoking rooms, no elevator* ⊟*AE, DC, MC, V* ⍟*BP.*

¢–$$ ⊞**Cape Trib Beach House.** These cabins set on the border of the rain forest are simple and airy, with verandas that lead right down to the beach. The beachfront St. Crispin cabins, which have air-conditioning and private balconies, are the most luxurious; the Escape Cabins, with their multiple bed configurations, are best for families; and there are five-bed dorms for budget travelers (A$25 per bed). Much of the hotel, including the bistro, is set outdoors—partially under a man-made canopy and partially under the rain forest's own ceiling of fan palms. The restaurant serves tropical Australian cuisine. ☒*7 Rykers*

7

Rd., 4873 ☎*07/4098–0030* ✉*reservations@capetribbeach.com.au*
⊕*www.capetribbeach.com.au* ⇌*120 cabins, 18 with shared bath, 21
suites* ♿*In-room: no a/c (some), no phone, kitchen (some), refrigerator, dial-up (some), no TV. In-hotel: restaurant, bar, pool, beachfront,
water sports, laundry facilities, public Internet, parking (no fee), no-
smoking rooms, disabled access* ☰*AE, DC, MC, V.*

SPORTS & THE OUTDOORS

Cape Trib Beach Horse Rides (☎*1800/111124* ⊕*www.capetribbeach.
com.au*) has two daily rides. The A$94 cost includes a four-hour ride,
tea, insurance, and transportation from Cape Tribulation hotels. Rides
leave at 8 and, in the dry season, also at 1:30, meandering through rain
forest, along Myall Beach, and across open paddocks, with opportunities to swim in the rain forest.

Daintree Rainforest River Trains (✉*Daintree River Ferry Crossing*
☎*07/4090–7676 or 1800/808309* ⊕*www.daintreerivertrain.com*) has
what's billed as the world's only floating river train, the *Spirit of Daintree,* which cruises down the Daintree River. On the daylong coach and
river train tour (A$145), there are stops for strolls along the rain forest
and mangrove boardwalk, tropical-fruit tasting, and lunch, including
tropical barramundi salad, at Daintree Village. Keep an eye out for
saltwater crocodiles. Choose from a variety of River Train–centered
options, including the full-day tour and twice-daily cruises. Self-driv-
ers can take an hour-long River Train cruise for just A$20 (or A$26
for 90 mins).

COOKTOWN

㉚ *96 km (60 mi) north of Cape Tribulation, 235 km (146 mi) north of
Cairns.*

The last major settlement on the east coast of the continent, Cooktown
is a frontier town on the edge of a difficult wilderness. Its wide main
street consists mainly of two-story pubs with four-wheel-drives parked
out front. Despite the frontier air, Cooktown has a long and impressive
history. It was here in 1770 that Captain James Cook beached HMS
Endeavour to repair her hull. Any tour of Cooktown should begin at
the waterfront, where a statue of Captain Cook gazes out to sea, overlooking the spot where he landed.

Cooktown is now just a sleepy shadow of those dangerous days—when
64 pubs once lined the 3-km-long (2-mi-long) main street—but a significant slice of history has been preserved at the **James Cook Historical Museum,** formerly a convent of the Sisters of Mercy. The museum
houses relics of the gold-mining era and Chinese settlement, as well
as Aboriginal artifacts, canoes, and a notable collection of seashells.
The museum also contains mementos of Cook's voyage, including the
anchor and one of the cannons that were jettisoned when the HMS
Endeavour ran aground. The shop sells books and souvenirs. ✉*Helen
and Furneaux Sts.* ☎*07/4069–5386* ⊕*www.nationaltrust.qld.org*
🖂*A$7.50* ⊙*Daily 9:30–4.*

WHERE TO STAY & EAT

$$ ✕⚏**Sovereign Resort Hotel.** This attractive, colonial-style hotel in the heart of town is the best bet in Cooktown. With verandas across the front, terra-cotta tiles, and soft colors, the two-story timber-and-brick affair has the air of a plantation house. Air-conditioned guest rooms and apartments, outfitted with rustic wooden doors, tiled floors, and balconies, overlook tropical gardens or the Endeavour River. The Balcony restaurant is the most upscale dining spot around these parts, serving classic Aussie dishes with Asian flavors—try the salt-and-pepper prawn and crocodile. The Turkish doughnuts with lime syrup and honey ice cream make an excellent dessert. It's open Monday–Saturday for breakfast but also serves lunch and dinner in the dry season, April to November. The Café bar has Internet access, and serves light lunches, coffee, and local beers. ✉*128 Charlotte St. at Green St., 4895* ☎*07/4069–5400* ⊕*www.sovereign-resort.com.au* ⤶*31 rooms, 7 apartments* ♿*In-room: kitchen (some), refrigerator, dial-up, laundry facilities (some). In-hotel: 2 restaurants, room service, bar, pool, laundry service, public Internet, airport shuttle, parking (no fee), no-smoking rooms, no elevator* ▤*AE, DC, MC, V* ☉*Restaurant and café closed Sun.*

NORTH FROM CAIRNS ESSENTIALS

TRANSPORTATION

BUS TRAVEL

Coral Reef Coaches runs a daily bus service from Cairns to Port Douglas (1½ hours, A$50 return), Mossman and Cape Tribulation (4 hours, A$90 return). Coral Reef Coaches also has a bus that makes the 1½-hour run between the Daintree Ferry crossing and Cape Tribulation once a day, stopping at Daintree Village on request.

Contact Coral Reef Coaches (☎*07/4098–2800* ⊕*www.coralreefcoaches. com.au*).

CAR RENTAL

This is tough driving territory. Many of the roads near the Top End are unpaved; major thruways around Daintree are occasionally closed in the wet season due to flooding. The road is now paved north of the river as far as Cape Tribulation, but four-wheel-drive vehicles still come in handy, especially if you're exploring in wet season.

Avis has four-wheel-drive Toyota Land Cruisers for rent from Cairns. The cost varies daily depending on availability of vehicles. Cooktown Car Hire rents four-wheel-drive Suzuki jeeps and Land Cruisers, with big discounts for guests of **Milkwood Lodge Rainforest Retreat** (☎*07/4069–5007* ⊕*www.milkwoodlodge.com*).

Contacts Avis (✉*Lake and Aplin Sts., Cairns* ☎*07/4051–5911* ⊕*www.avis. com.au*).**Cooktown Car Hire** (✉*Annan Rd., Cooktown* ☎*07/4069–5007* ⊕*www. cooktown-car-hire.com*).

CAR TRAVEL

To head north by car from Cairns, take Florence Street from the Esplanade for four blocks and then turn right onto Sheridan Street, which is the beginning of northbound Highway 1. Highway 1 leads past the airport and forks 12 km (7½ mi) north of Cairns. Take the right fork for Cook Highway, which goes as far as Mossman. From Mossman, the turnoff for the Daintree River crossing is 29 km (18 mi) north on the Daintree–Mossman Road. The road north of the river winds its way to Cape Tribulation, burrowing through dense rain forest and onto open stretches high above the coast, with spectacular views of the mountains and coastline. Stock up on everything—food, cash, fuel, and water—before you cross the Daintree. Limited services are available north of the river, and you'll pay more for them.

CONTACTS &RESOURCES

EMERGENCIES

Be advised that doctors, ambulances, firefighters, and police are scarce to nonexistent between the Daintree River and Cooktown.

Contacts Cooktown Hospital (⊠ *Hope St., Cooktown* ☎ *07/4069–5433).***Mossman District Hospital** (⊠ *Hospital St., Mossman* ☎ *07/4084–1200).***Mossman Police** (☎ *07/4098–1200).***Port Douglas Police** (☎ *07/4099–5220).*

TOURS

ABORIGINAL TOURS Daintree Eco Lodge & Spa runs a raft of Aboriginal-guided activities. The hour-long Aboriginal Rainforest Culture Walk gives insights into the Kuku Yalanji culture, indigenous "bush tucker" and medicinal plants, and local wildlife, and takes in a waterfall important for women's healing. Three-day, two-night Aboriginal-led expeditions travel along the Bloomfield Track to Cooktown, taking in significant rock art sites, rain forest, and beaches. A hands-on, sociable Aboriginal art workshop takes place most afternoons on the bar/restaurant's airy deck. You can also dine on cuisine showcasing indigenous local ingredients at the Lodge's restaurant, and enjoy traditional, all-natural treatments at the on-site spa (daily 10–6).

Contact Daintree Eco Lodge & Spa (⊠ *20 Daintree Rd. (3 km [2 mi] past Daintree village), Daintree, 4873* ☎ *07/98–6100* ⊕ *www.daintree-ecolodge.com.au).*

BOAT TOURS *Crocodile Express,* a flat-bottom boat run by experienced operators who've been plying this waterway since 1979, cruises the Daintree River on crocodile-spotting excursions. Sixty-minute cruises depart from the Daintree River crossing, hourly from 9 AM to 4 PM (A$20 per person). Ninety-minute trips depart from Daintree Village at regular intervals from 10 to 4 (A$26).

Contact Crocodile Express (⊠ *End of Mossman–Daintree Rd, Daintree, 4873* ☎ *07/4098–6120* ⊕ *www.daintreevillage.asn.au).*

FOUR-WHEEL-DRIVE TOURS Australian Wilderness Experience has a one-day Daintree and Cape Tribulation Safari aboard air-conditioned vehicles. All tours depart ★ from Port Douglas or Mossman, are led by naturalists, and include a Daintree River Cruise, barbecue lunch at Mason's Creek, and afternoon tea. Groups are limited to 11 people. This A$185 rain-forest tour is one of the longest established and one of the best.

Deluxe Safaris conducts three daylong safaris in top-of-the-range four-wheel-drive vehicles or their 14-seat, custom-built 4-wheel-drive truck—complete with dual guides and luxurious leather seats. You can visit Mossman Gorge and Cape Tribulation (A$155), rough it on the rugged track to the magnificent Bloomfield River Falls (A$165), or spot kangaroos and other wildlife in the Outback region of Cape York on a day-long private charter (A$800). Lunch and refreshments, included in the price, keep your strength up for these energetic journeys.

Contacts Australian Wilderness Experience (☎ *07/4098–1666* ⊕ *www. voyages.com.au*).**Deluxe Safaris** (✉ *Port Douglas* ☎ *07/4099–6406* ⊕ *www. deluxesafaris.com.au*).

SIGHTSEEING
TOURS
Reef and Rainforest Connections organizes excursions out of Port Douglas. One day trips include visits to Kuranda Scenic Railway, Skyrail Rainforest Cableway, and Tjapukai Aboriginal Cultural Park. You can also journey to Cape Tribulation and Bloomfield Falls, the Daintree River, and Mossman Gorge. Tours start from A$95 per person.

Contact Reef and Rainforest Connections (✉ *40 Macrossan St., Port Douglas* ☎ *07/4099-5777* ⊕ *www.reefandrainforest.com.au*).

VISITOR INFORMATION
Contacts Daintree Village Tourist Association (☎ *No phone* ⊕ *www.daintree village.asn.au*).**Cape Tribulation Tourist Information Centre** (✉ *Cape Tribulation Rd., Cape Tribulation* ☎ *07/4098-0070*).**Cooktown Travel Centre** (✉ *Charlotte St., Cooktown* ☎ *07/4069-5446*).

MAIL, SHIPPING & THE INTERNET
The main post office in Port Douglas is open weekdays 8:30–5:30, Saturday 9–2. You can retrieve e-mail and check the Internet at a number of locations, including backpackers' and youth hostels.

Port Douglas's Cyberworld Internet Café is open weekdays 9–5. Uptown Internet Café is open daily 9–10.

Internet Cafés Cyberworld Internet Café (✉ *38A Macrossan St., Port Douglas* ☎ *07/4099-5661*). **Uptown Internet Café** (✉ *48 Macrossan St., Port Douglas* ☎ *07/4099-6900*).

Mail Service Port Douglas Post Office (✉ *5 Owen St., near Macrossan St.* ☎ *07/4099-5210*).

MONEY MATTERS
ANZ Bank can change money and cash traveler's checks. National Australia Bank accepts most overseas cards. Westpac is one of Australia's largest banks.

Contacts ANZ Bank (✉ *Macrossan St., Port Douglas* ☎ *13-1314*). **National Australia Bank** (✉ *Port Douglas Shopping Center, Macrossan St., Port Douglas* ☎ *13-2265*). **Westpac** (✉ *Charlotte St., Cooktown* ☎ *13-2032*).

The Great Barrier Reef

Updated by
Merran White

A MAZE OF 3,000 INDIVIDUAL reefs and 900 islands stretching for 2,600 km (1,616 mi), the Great Barrier Reef is one of the world's most spectacular natural attractions, and one of which Australia is extremely proud. Known as Australia's "Blue Outback," the reef was established as a marine park in 1975, and is a collective haven for thousands of species of sea life, as well as turtles and birds. In 1981 the United Nations designated the Great Barrier Reef a World Heritage Site. In 2004 strict legislation was enacted prohibiting fishing along most of the reef—a further attempt to protect the underwater treasures of this vast, yet delicate ecosystem. Any visitor over the age of four must pay an A$4.50 reef tax to help support the preservation of the reef.

The reef system began to form approximately 6,000–7,000 years ago, according to scientists. It's comprised of individual reefs and islands, which lie to the east of the Coral Sea and extend south into the Pacific Ocean. Most of the reef is about 65 km (40 mi) off the Queensland coast, although some parts extend as far as 300 km (186 mi) offshore. Altogether it covers an area bigger than Great Britain, forming the largest living feature on Earth and the only one visible from space.

Most visitors explore this section of Australia from one of the two dozen or so resorts along the islands in the southern half of the marine park. Although most are closer to the mainland than to the more spectacular outer reef, all offer chartered boats to outer-reef sites. Live-aboard dive boats ply the more-remote sections of the northern reef and Coral Sea atolls, exploring large cartographic blank spots on maritime charts that simply read, in bold purple lettering, "Area unsurveyed."

8

EXPLORING THE GREAT BARRIER REEF

This chapter is arranged in three geographical sections covering islands off the mid-Queensland coast from south to north. The sections group together islands that share a common port or jumping-off point. Addresses for resorts often include the word "via" to indicate which port town to use to reach the island.

If you had the time, money, and patience, you could string together a long holiday that would take you to all the major island resorts. The map linking these coastal ports and offshore resorts would look like a lace-up boot 1,600 km (1,000 mi) long—but it would also take most of a month, even if you only spent one night in each place. From Lady Elliot Island as far north as Lizard Island, you'd only see half the reef, which continues north along the roadless wilderness of Cape York to the shores of Papua New Guinea.

Although most travelers are aware of the reef's expanse, they still tend to say they're visiting the reef, rather than naming a particular destination. But the island from which you choose to base your travels is actually very important. Each island—and each accommodation option—has its own distinctive charms.

It's worth noting that if you'd like to visit the reef briefly, as just one stop on a packed Australia itinerary, it's easiest and most economical to

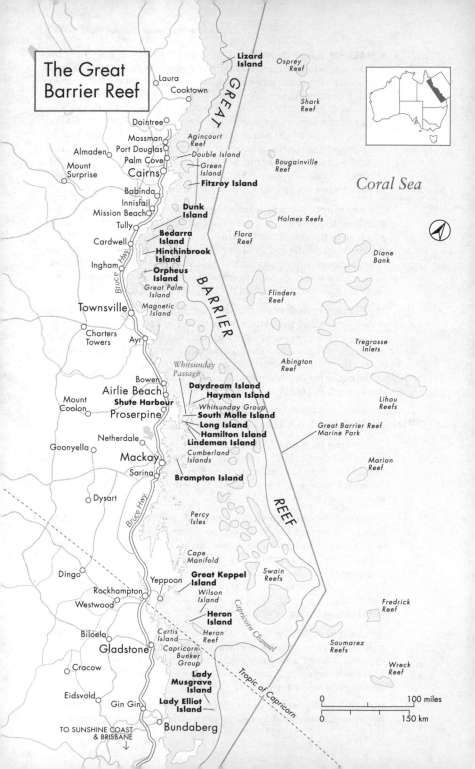

The Great Barrier Reef

Laura
Cooktown
Daintree
Mossman
Port Douglas
Almaden
Palm Cove
Mount
Surprise
Cairns
Babinda
Innisfail
Mission Beach
Tully
Cardwell
Ingham
Townsville
Charters
Towers
Ayr
Bowen
Airlie Beach
Shute Harbour
Proserpine
Netherdale
Goonyella
Mackay
Sarina
Dysart
Dingo
Rockhampton
Westwood
Yeppoon
Biloela
Gladstone
Cracow
Eidsvold
Gin Gin
Bundaberg

TO SUNSHINE COAST
& BRISBANE

Lizard Island
Osprey Reef
Shark Reef
Agincourt Reef
Double Island
Green Island
Fitzroy Island
Bougainville Reef

Coral Sea

Dunk Island
Bedarra Island
Hinchinbrook Island
Orpheus Island
Great Palm Island
Magnetic Island

Holmes Reefs
Flora Reef
Diane Bank
Flinders Reef
Tregrosse Inlets
Abington Reef

Whitsunday Passage
Daydream Island
Hayman Island
Whitsunday Group
South Molle Island
Long Island
Hamilton Island
Lindeman Island
Cumberland Islands
Brampton Island

Lihou Reefs

Great Barrier Marine Park

Marion Reef

Percy Isles

Cape Manifold
Great Keppel Island
Wilson Island
Heron Island
Swain Reefs

Fredrick Reef

Curtis Island
Heron Reef
Capricorn-Bunker Group

Capricorn Channel

Saumarez Reefs

Lady Musgrave Island
Lady Elliot Island

Tropic of Capricorn

Wreck Reef

GREAT BARRIER REEF

Bruce Hwy

0 — 100 miles
0 — 150 km

day-trip from the mainland. Some reef-island resorts are accessible by boat, but many others can be reached only by plane, and both airfare and lodging rates can be expensive. Day trips to the reef depart several times each day from major coastal cities like Cairns, Port Douglas, Townsville, and Airlie Beach. These tours let you dive, snorkel, sail, or beachcomb on the reef—some of the island resorts let you visit and use their facilities for the day—then return you to the mainland at day's end to continue your traveling.

ABOUT THE RESTAURANTS
Most restaurants are part of each island's main resort, so many resorts' rates include all meals. Some resorts have a range of restaurants, with formal dining rooms, outdoor barbecues, and seafood buffets; some have a premium dining option for which you pay extra.

WHAT IT COSTS IN AUSTRALIAN DOLLARS				
$$$$	$$$	$$	$	¢
AT DINNER over A$65	A$46–A$65	A$36–A$45	A$25–A$35	under A$25

Prices are per person for a main course at dinner.

ABOUT THE HOTELS
You can't pick and choose hotels on the Great Barrier Reef islands—most of the islands have just one main resort, usually offering a range of lodging types and prices. Choose your destination based on your budget, and on the kind of vacation you want—active, relaxed, or a mix of both. Resorts on Bedarra, Lizard, and Hayman islands offer white-glove service to a discerning international clientele, who take their leisure, and their privacy, very seriously. Eco-focused island resorts such as Heron, Wilson, Lady Elliott, South Long Island Nature Lodge, and Hinchinbrook are great for getting back to nature (without really roughing it). A vacation at South Molle, Lindeman, Daydream, or Great Keppel Island is almost like a trip to sleepaway camp: activities are scheduled from early morning until late at night and include dozens of water sports, nature walks, and beachy activities; outdoor movies; live entertainment; and theme nights. Daydream Island, with its focus on family-friendly entertainment, can seem more like it belongs in Orlando, Florida, than in the Australian tropics.

Dress in general is island casual. Some upscale restaurants, however—like those on Hayman Island—require men to wear jackets for dinner, and frown on flip-flop sandals. All but the most rustic resorts have air-conditioning, telephones, televisions, refrigerators, and Internet access.

WHEN TO VISIT
The majority of Barrier Reef islands lie north of the tropic of Capricorn and have a distinctly monsoonal climate. In Australian summer (roughly December–February), expect tropical downpours that can limit outdoor activities and mar underwater visibility for days. The islands are warm even in winter; it's hot during summer months—and the farther north you go, the hotter it gets. The water temperature is

mild to cool, varying only by a few degrees between winter and summer. Regardless of water tempeture, tour operators will often recommend that you wear at least a "shortie" wet suit to help keep you buoyant, a Lycra suit to protect you against unexpected stings from coral while you're exploring, and in some cases, a full-body stinger suit for protection against box jellyfish tentacles. The warm days, clear skies, and balmy nights of the "dry" season, especially winter (June–August) are ideal for traveling around and above Cairns. If you choose an island on the southern end of the chain, keep in mind that some winter days may be too cool for swimming.

WHAT IT COSTS IN AUSTRALIAN DOLLARS				
$$$$	$$$	$$	$	¢
FOR TWO PEOPLE over A$450	A$301–A$450	A$201–A$300	A$150–A$200	under A$150

Prices are for two people in a standard double room in high season, including tax and service, based on the European Plan (with no meals) unless otherwise noted.

MACKAY–CAPRICORN ISLANDS

Despite its name, this group of islands is closer to the southern half of Queensland—between Bundaberg and Rockhampton—than they are to the Queensland city of Mackay. These islands comprise the section of the reef known as Capricorn Marine Park, which stretches for 140 km (87 mi) and cuts through the Tropic of Capricorn (Heron Island being the closest point). This is a great area for wildlife: turtles use several of the islands as breeding grounds, and seabirds nest here as well. Humpback whales also pass through while migrating to Antarctica each spring (generally between July and October).

LADY ELLIOT ISLAND

Fodor'sChoice ★ Lady Elliot Island is a 104-acre coral cay on the southern tip of the Great Barrier Reef, positioned 85 km (50 mi) off the Queensland coast, within easy reach of Bundaberg. One of just six island resorts actually on the Reef, it's a high-level Marine National Park Zone. Wildlife here easily outnumbers the guests (a maximum of 105 can visit at any one time)—and that reality is underscored by the ammoniacal odor of thousands of nesting seabirds and, in season, the sounds and sights of them courting, mating, and nesting. Ornithophobes might want to holiday elsewhere.

Divers will enjoy the easy access to the reef and the variety of diving sites around Lady Elliot. Fringed on all sides by the reef and blessed with a stunning white-sand, coral-strewn shore, this oval isle seems to have been made for diving—there's a busy dive shop and a reef education center complete with saltwater-fish, turtle, shell, and other marine-themed exhibits (plus an educational video library—great for rainy days). The land is often battered by waves, which can sometimes

GREAT ITINERARIES

Most visits to the Great Barrier Reef combine time on an island with time in Queensland's mainland towns and parks. With a week or more, you could stay at two very different resorts, perhaps at a southern coral cay and a mountainous northern island, allowing a day or two to travel between them. For the good life, try Orpheus, Hayman, Bedarra, or Lizard Island. If you want to resort-hop, pick the closely arranged Whitsundays, or Orpheus, Hinchinbrook, and Bedarra islands, all relatively close to one another.

To fully experience the Great Barrier Reef, divers should jump on one of the many live-aboards that run from Port Douglas to Lizard Island and back, or those that explore the uncharted reefs of the far north and the Coral Sea. Live-aboard trips, which can be surprisingly affordable, run from 2 to 10 days. For land-based diving, consider such islands as Heron, Lady Elliot, or Lizard, which have fringing reefs.

IF YOU HAVE 1 DAY

Take a boat from Cairns or Port Douglas to a pontoon on the outer reef for a day on the water. A heli-copter flight back will provide an astounding view of the reef and islands from above. Or catch an early boat from Cairns to **Fitzroy Island,** or from Shute Harbour to **Daydream Island.** Spend a couple of hours snorkeling, take a walk around the island, then settle on a quiet beach for an idyllic afternoon.

IF YOU HAVE 3 DAYS

Pick one island with a variety of aquatic and land-based activities and attractions—flora and fauna, beaches and dive sites, sports and relaxation facilities, resort-style nightlife—and give yourself a taste of everything.

IF YOU HAVE 7 OR MORE DAYS

Planning a full week on an island probably means that you're a serious diver, a serious lounger, or both. Divers should hop on one of the Lizard Island–Port Douglas live-aboards for several days, then recuperate on an island that has fringing coral, such as **Lady Elliot, Heron,** or **Lizard.** Beachlovers might prefer to skip the live-aboard and concentrate on exploring one or two of the islands with outstanding beaches and hiking terrain, such as **Hinchinbrook, Orpheus, Lizard,** or **Hayman.**

8

cancel dives and wash out underwater visibility. When the waters are calm, you'll see turtles, morays, sharks, rays, and millions of tropical fish. Many divers visit Lady Elliot specifically to encounter the large resident population of manta rays that feed off the coral.

From October to April, Lady Elliot becomes a busy breeding ground for crested and bridled terns, silver gulls, lesser frigate birds, and the rare red-tailed tropic bird. Between November and March, green and log-gerhead turtles emerge from the water to lay their eggs; hatching takes place after January. During the hatchling season, staff biologists host guided turtle-watching night hikes. From about July through October, pods of humpback whales are visible from the beachfront restaurant.

Lady Elliot is one of the few islands in the area where camping—albeit modified—is part of the resort, and a back-to-basics theme pervades the accommodations.

WHERE TO STAY & EAT

$$ ✕⛌ **Lady Elliot Island Eco Resort.** Here, you're more like a marine biologist at an island field camp than a tourist enjoying a luxury resort. Linens are changed every third day, and rooms lack televisions and mod cons (though there are some air-conditioned rooms on the beachfront). Clearly, the eco-resort's focus is on simplicity, functionality, and conservation, rather than luxurious amenities or aesthetics. There are four types of rooms: beachfront island suites; reef units with multiple bed configurations and private facilities; shearwater rooms with bunk beds, great for groups of friends; and permanent, powered safari-style tents. There's a free children's "reef ranger" program during school holiday periods. Dinner and breakfast are served buffet-style in the airy dining room and on the adjoining covered veranda. It's hearty fare, with the emphasis on seafood, grilled dishes, and salads, a good selection of desserts, and limitless tea and coffee. Upbeat staff encourage guests to mingle with activities such as coconut bowling, pool games, and dress-up theme nights in the bar, along with daily guided walks and snorkeling trips, and video/information nights. *Box 5206, Torquay, QLD, 4655* *07/4194–6700 or 1800/072200* *www.ladyelliot.com.au* *reservations@ladyelliot.com.au* *21 rooms, 12 rooms with shared bath, 5 suites, 11 tents* *In-room: no a/c (some), no phone, refrigerator (some), no TV. In-hotel: restaurant, bar, pool, beachfront, diving, water sports, bicycles, children's programs (ages 3–12), video/DVD lounge, laundry facilities, public Internet, Wi-Fi (from reception), no-smoking rooms* *AE, DC, MC, V* *MAP.*

SPORTS & THE OUTDOORS

You can arrange dive courses and rent equipment at the resort dive shop to various excellent sites including Lighthouse Bommie, home to a 40-strong manta ray colony, and the Blow Hole and Hiro's cave. Refresher pool dives, a shore snorkeling trip, and guided reef, nature, and historical walks are free for resort guests. Off-boat snorkeling and glass-bottom boat rides are A$20. Two-tank boat dives start at A$50; night dives are A$65. Open-water certification courses cost A$525; "Discover Scuba Diving" short courses are A$150, and referral courses, available to those who've completed the classroom and pool portions of a certification course prior to arrival, are A$400. Diving here is weather-dependent, so plan accordingly if you're pursuing an advanced course over multiple days. Four-night packages including nine dives, flights from the Fraser coast, guest activities, meals, reef tax, and accommodation start at A$1,159, while all-inclusive seven-night packages, with 15 dives, start at A$1,754. There is a onetime A$15 environmental management charge for all non-package guests.

ARRIVING & DEPARTING

BY PLANE Lady Elliot is the only coral cay with its own airstrip. Small aircraft make the flight from Hervey Bay (40 minutes), Bundaberg (30 minutes), and Gladstone (40 minutes), though pickups can be arranged from as far south in Queensland as the Gold Coast (1 hour, 50 minutes). For day tourists, flights to Lady Elliot on **Seair Pacific** (☎07/5599–4509 ⊕*www.seairpacific.com.au*) cost A$275–A$294 round-trip from Whitsunday coastal towns and A$699 from Brisbane or the Gold or Sunshine Coast. Round-trip fares for island guests are A$219 from Hervey Bay or Bundaberg, A$599 from farther south. Strict luggage limits for both hand and checked baggage allow 10 kilograms (22 pounds) per person. If you exceed this limit, you can repack at the ticket-counter scale or wave good-bye to the plane.

DAY TRIPS

You can day-trip to Lady Elliot with **Seair Pacific.** The cost—including scenic flight, buffet lunch, reef walking, glass-bottom boat ride, snorkeling, and island tour—is A$699 per person from Brisbane, the Gold Coast, or the Sunshine Coast; A$499 from Gladstone, subject to availability; and A$275 (off-peak)–$294 (peak) from Bundaberg or Hervey Bay. Tours require a minimum of two passengers, and use planes that can carry an average of 12 passengers.

LADY MUSGRAVE ISLAND

★ Lady Musgrave Island sits at the southern end of the Great Barrier Reef Marine Park, about 40 km (25 mi) north of Lady Elliot. Five kilometers (3 mi) of coral reef and a massive yet calm 3,000-acre lagoon surround the island, a true coral cay of 35 acres, 500 yards wide. When daytrippers, yachties, divers, and campers converge, traffic gets heavy, but the island has some of the best diving and snorkeling in Queensland. In quiet times, campers have a chance to view the myriad sea life surrounding this tiny speck of land in the Pacific.

In summer (December through February) the island is a bird and turtle rookery with white-capped noddies, wedge-tailed shearwaters, and green and loggerhead turtles. There's also an abundance of flora, including casuarina and pisonia trees.

CAMPING

The island, part of the Capricornia Cays National Park, is uninhabited and has only basic facilities (one toilet block and emergency radio equipment) for campers. Commercial tour operators from the interestingly named Town of 1770 on the mainland have all camping equipment and necessary provisions available for rent. More information can be obtained from the Gladstone office of the **Queensland Parks and Wildlife Service** (☎07/4971–6500). The **Environmental Protection Agency** (☎1300/130372 ⊕*www.epa.qld.gov.au*) is a good source of information on camping in Capricornia Cays National Park. Contact the EPA Hotline (☎13–1304) for camping permits (A$4.50 per person per night, or a maximum of A$18 per family). Reservations can be made 11 months in advance. Book early, as school breaks and holidays fill up fast. No more than 40 campers may visit the island at any one time.

Camping here can be rugged and isolated: take first-aid supplies and, if possible, an emergency radio (available for rent from Marine Rescue

8

Dangers of the Reef

It's true: there are creatures in the water here that can kill you, or at least inflict some serious pain. The most ubiquitous offenders near the tropical mainland are jellyfish; the sting of the tiny, transparent Irukandji, no bigger than a thumbnail, can cause severe pain, vomiting, and soaring blood pressure, which may be life-threatening to people with already high blood pressure or diabetes. Even more dangerous, however, are the deadly Chironex jellyfish—commonly known as sea wasps or box jellyfish. These transparent, cube-shaped creatures are the most venomous sea creatures on Earth; their stings, which cause the lungs and heart to stop functioning, are fatal unless they are treated within three minutes. Jellyfish season unfortunately coincides with the tourist season and prime beach weather; many of the most popular beaches in North Queensland have stinger nets, which will keep box jellyfish out of the swimming areas.

The good news is that on the outer reef and islands jellyfish aren't a problem. Here, though, another danger you need to be careful of is the coral. Millepora, or stinging coral, ranges in form from large upright sheets and blades to branching, antlerlike stalks with a yellow-brown color. If this coral inadvertently scrapes or tears your skin, you'll get painful, burning welts. Try to swim with your arms and legs close to your body, and of course notify someone if you think you have rubbed up against anything.

Sharks are present in the waters of the inner and outer reef but, unlike jellyfish, aren't likely to come near you. The small sharks off the shores of North Queensland and around the inner reef islands only eat fish. Tiger sharks and hammerheads, which hunt in deeper waters, tend to swim away from people. You are unlikely to see a great white shark while on the reef; they prefer the colder waters of the southern Pacific. But even if you do see one, remember that these mythically fearsome creatures aren't hard-wired to make a meal out of you. There are plenty of convenient nonhuman feeding options available on the reef. They're only likely to pursue a human if provoked, or if the irresistible smell of blood is flowing in the water.

There are other more exotic but equally dangerous creatures lurking around the reef, such as stonefish and sea snakes. But your worst enemy in this part of Australia—whether you're in or out of the water—is the sun. The ozone layer in Australia is almost nonexistent, and one in three Australians eventually develops some form of skin cancer. Many a snorkeler has had a day on the water ruined by a nasty sunburn on the back of his or her legs. Be sure to coat yourself in sunblock consistently the whole time you're visiting the reef.

volunteers at Gladstone ☎07/4972–3333). Be aware of local hazards, including year-round marine stingers (wear stinger suits), large centipedes, and bird ticks. Hurricanes may necessitate emergency evacuation in wet season. The island is generally closed from January 27 until Good Friday (March or early April), during the turtle nesting season.

SPORTS & THE OUTDOORS

1770 Great Barrier Reef Cruises (☎ *07/4974–9077* ⊕ *www.1770reef cruises.com* or *www.spiritof1770.com.au*) now operates a pontoon in the deep-water coral lagoon off Lady Musgrave Island, with an underwater observatory, snorkeling deck, changing rooms, and sheltered seating. Their Lady Musgrave day cruises get you out to the reef in 90 minutes, giving you six hours to snorkel or dive. For an extra A$10, you can spend 90 minutes fishing on the Great Barrier Reef; A$30 (certified divers) or A$65 (beginners) buys you one dive (with gear). There's a per-person reef tax of A$5. Day trips depart daily from the town of 1770 on the mainland, and cost A$145, tropical buffet lunch, morning and afternoon tea, and all gear included.

ARRIVING & DEPARTING

BY BOAT **1770 Great Barrier Reef Cruises** (☎ *07/4974–9077* ⊕ *www.1770 reef-cruises.com* or *www.spiritof1770.com.au*) is the only carrier servicing Lady Musgrave Island. Boats depart daily at 8 AM from Gladstone marina, arriving around 2½ hours later. Baggage is limited to 1½ cubic feet per person, as space on board is tight. You'll have to use wheelbarrows to haul all your gear to the campground from the island drop-off point. The return journey departs between 10:30 and 11 AM. You get a buffet lunch and a 90-minute stopover on the Outer Reef, where you can snorkel or do a spot of reef fishing before the cruise boat heads back to the mainland. The round-trip journey, including all extras, is A$290 per person. If you're carrying a dinghy for getting around the island, it costs an extra A$120. Campers must have a permit at time of boarding.

You can also charter a boat to the island, but this is an expensive option unless you're with a group.

8

HERON ISLAND

FodorsChoice
★
Most resort islands lie well inside the shelter of the distant reef, but Heron Island, some 70 km (43 mi) northwest of the mainland port of Gladstone, is actually part of the reef. The waters off this 41-acre island are spectacular, teeming with fish and coral, and ideal for snorkeling and scuba diving. The water is clearest in June and July and cloudiest during the rainy season, January and February.

Heron Island operates on "island time"—an hour ahead of Eastern Standard Time—and at its own leisurely pace. You won't find much in the way of nightlife, as the island's single accommodation accepts a cozy maximum of 250 people—and there are no day-trippers. But these might be reasons why you decide to come here.

Only guests of the Heron Island Resort can visit uninhabited **Wilson Island** (☎ *1300/134044* ⊕ *www.voyages.com.au/Wilson*), a coral cay 10 km (6 mi) north, a 40-minute day trip from Heron Island. In January and February, Wilson Island becomes the breeding ground for roseate terns and green and loggerhead turtles. The island also has its own exclusive, six-suite, luxury tented resort, catering to a maximum of 12 guests (and no children under 16), with all meals included in the rate—A$495 per person, per night in high season. Combination packages are available, allowing for two nights at Heron Island and three nights at Wilson Island, including meals. The island closes in February, however, to protect nesting birds.

WHERE TO STAY & EAT

$$–$$$$ ╳▦**Voyages Heron Island.** Set among palm trees and connected by sand
☾   paths, this secluded, eco-certified resort offers six accommodation types that range from the deluxe Beach House with private outdoor shower and beach boardwalk to the compact, garden-level Turtle Rooms. The large, elegantly modern suites, which include amenities such as CD players and well-stocked minibars, separate lounge areas and private, furnished decks or terraces, merit the extra expense. All snorkeling and diving excursions cost extra, as does the kids' program, open during Australian school holidays. Room rates include breakfast; some packages also include buffet lunches and three-course set dinners. There's a Saturday seafood smorgasbord and a mid-week Aussie BBQ. Complimentary activities include guided reef and nature walks, stargazing, snorkeling lessons, trivia nights, and outdoor movie screenings. The delightfully zen Aqua Soul Spa offers treatments with marine-based and natural botanical products, and a spa menu. There's a well-stocked resort shop. ⌂ *Voyages, GPO 3859, Sydney, NSW, 2001* ☎*02/8296–8010 or 1800/134044* ✉bookings@voyages.com.au ⊕*www.voyages. com.au/heron* ☞*32 rooms, 76 suites, 1 house* ⌂*In-room: no a/c (some), no TV, refrigerator/minibar (some), dial-up (some). In-hotel: 3 restaurants, bar, tennis court, pools, spa, beachfront, diving, water sports, children's programs (ages 7–12), laundry facilities, laundry service, public Internet, no-smoking rooms* ▭*AE, DC, MC, V* ◎*BP, FAP (some).*

SPORTS & THE OUTDOORS

You can book snorkeling, scuba diving, and fishing excursions through the **Heron Island Marine Centre & Dive Shop** (☎*07/4978–1399* ⊕*www. marine.uq.edu.au/hirs* ✉dive@heron.voyages.com.au). Snorkeling lessons and refresher dive courses are free. Snorkeling boat trips are A$27.50; children under 8 aren't permitted, and those under 14 must be accompanied by an adult. A resort diving course, with one guided dive, is A$155 (subsequent dive A$105). For certified divers, it's A$55 per dive (A$35 per dive for upwards of four dives). Referral diving courses cost A$410; booking ahead is essential. A full-day excursion with a tour of neighboring islands and dives among pristine reefs is A$320, including lunch and drinks.

Nondivers who want to explore the reef's underwater world can take a half-day, guided reef snorkeling tour of Heron, Wistari, and Bloomfield reefs for A$115; or a semisubmersible tour with a naturalist guide for A$30. Guided reef walks, interpretive nature walks, turtle-watching tours, and visits to the island's Marine Research Station are free.

Heron Island Marine Centre also conducts three-hour fishing trips for A$70 per person, hour-long sunset wine and cheese cruises for A$50, and dive charters.

ARRIVING & DEPARTING

BY BOAT All transfers are booked with your accommodations through the resort. The high-speed launch makes the 2¼ hour run to Heron Island from Gladstone, on the Queensland coast, for A$200 round-trip, departing at 11 AM daily and arriving in time for a late lunch. The return boat departs Heron Island for the mainland at 2:30 island time (1:30 EST). This is a rough journey by any standards, so take some anti-nausea medicine ½ hour before the boat departs. A courtesy shuttle bus transfers guests from Gladstone airport, leaving at 10 AM daily, and meets all afternoon boats. (Fly to Gladstone from most capital cities daily, with Virgin or Jetstar.) You can also arrange transfers to and from Gladstone Station (get here on Queensland Rail's fast Tilt Train or Sunlander from north or south). ⊕ *www.qr.com.au.*

BY HELICOPTER **Australian Helicopters** (☎ *07/4978–1177* ⊕ *www.austheli.com*) makes the 25-minute helicopter flight to Heron Island from Gladstone for A$555.45 round-trip. The baggage restriction is 15 kilograms (33 pounds) per person. Lockup facilities for excess baggage are free.

GREAT KEPPEL ISLAND

The Contiki Great Keppel Island Resort used to have a reputation similar to that of Fort Lauderdale at spring break. Only people ages 18–35 were allowed in, and the focus was on raucous parties, adventure sports, and showing off tanned bodies on the beach and on the dance floor. Now under new management, after being bought and sold by the Accor Mercure hotel group, Great Keppel Island Resort was open for family-friendly business as usual at the time this guide went to print. Do ask whether there are renovations in progress when booking, however, as planned (but as yet unscheduled) upgrades may cause a certain amount of disruption.

Although Great Keppel is large, at 8 km (5 mi) by 11 km (7 mi), it lies 40 km (25 mi) from the Great Barrier Reef, which makes for a long trip from the mainland. There's lots to do, though, with walking trails, 17 stunning safe swimming beaches, dozens of water and beach sports activities, and excellent coral growth in many sheltered coves. An underwater observatory at nearby Middle Island allows you to watch marine life without getting wet. A confiscated Taiwanese fishing boat has been sunk alongside the observatory to provide shelter for tropical fish.

WHERE TO STAY

¢–$$ ⌂ **Great Keppel Island Holiday Village.** Tucked in among the welcome shade of gum trees is this modest, quiet alternative for couples and older travelers looking to get back to basics without a party scene. The village centers around a large reception hall where you can buy island maps, arrange tours, pick up snorkeling gear, and meet other guests. Varied accommodation includes two solar-powered, self-contained family houses, two cabins that suit couples or close four-somes, twin and double rooms in the main lodge; four- and six-bed dorms, and tents with wood floors, twin or double beds, lights, and chairs. There's a well-equipped communal kitchen, and barbecues for cooking out. You can hike, take a canoe or kayak tour of the island for A$35–A$40, or flop on one of the island's 17 beaches. ⊠ *Community Mailbag, Great Keppel Island, QLD, 4700* ☎ *07/4939–8655* ⊕ *www. gkiholidayvillage.com.au* ⌐ *15 suites, 2 with baths; 2 houses; 2 cabins* ⚲ *In-room: no a/c, fans, no phone, refrigerator (some), kitchen (some), DVD (some), no TV (some). In-hotel: beachfront, water sports, laundry facilities, no-smoking rooms* ⊟ *AE, DC, MC, V.*

¢–$$ ▦ **Great Keppel Island Resort.** The resort was once a Generation X party haven, but now the tone is more *Rugrats* than *Friends.* The villas and garden rooms stand among lush foliage, and extend up the island's hills. Hillside villas have wonderful rooms and air-conditioning, but are 100 meters or more from the beach. Buffet breakfasts and à la carte dinners are served at the resort's restaurant; or dine on wood-fired pizzas. Dozens of activities are available to guests—everything from basketball to bocce, giant Twister to touch football. You can also get an hour-long in-house massage for A$65. ⌁ *PMB 8001, North Rockhampton, QLD, 4701* ☎ *07/4939–5044 or 1800/245658 (toll-free within Australia)* ✎ *gkeppel@gkeppel.com.au* ⊕ *www.greatkeppelresort.com.au* ⌐ *121 rooms, 60 villas* ⚲ *In-room: no a/c (some), refrigerator, dial-up, no TV. In-hotel: restaurant, 3 bars, golf course, tennis courts, pools, gym, beachfront, diving, water sports, bicycles, children's programs, 12:30–4 PM, 5–9 PM (ages 3–12), laundry facilities, public Internet, no-smoking rooms, no elevator* ⊟ *AE, DC, MC, V.*

SPORTS & THE OUTDOORS

Great Keppel Island is great for beachcombers and water lovers, with 17 beaches and excellent snorkeling and diving sites. Great Keppel Island Resort offers dozens of free activities, from tennis to windsurfing, as well as pre-booked paid activities including half-hour camel treks (A$40), and hour-long glass-bottom-boat tours (A$25), boom-netting cruises (A$30), or jet-ski tours (A$140). A full day's sailing aboard the Resort's 40-foot yacht, *Grace,* is A$125 per person. Book all activities through the resort.

ARRIVING & DEPARTING

BY BOAT **Great Keppel Island Resort** transfers guests to the island from Rockhampton Airport to Rosslyn Bay Marina, near Yeppoon, where a high-speed launch takes a half-hour to reach the island. A coach and launch service from the airport costs A$79.50 round-trip; the launch alone costs A$37 round-trip. **Keppel Bay Marina** (☎ *07/4933–6244* ⊕ *www. keppelbaymarina.com.au*) operates daily island launch services, for A$41 round-trip, from Rosslyn Bay, aboard the catamaran *Freedom Fast Cat.* Departures from Rosslyn Bay are at 9, 11:30, and 3:30. Return trips are at 10, 2:15, and 4:15. The marina also runs a day cruise, departing daily at 9, that includes snorkeling, boom-netting, coral viewing, a glass-bottom boat trip, and lunch.

BY PLANE **Great Keppel Island Resort** (☎ *1800/245658*) can arrange the scenic 20-minute flight to the island, which has its own airstrip, from Rockhampton, timed to coincide with domestic flights: generally three scheduled flights per day (A$65 per person, each way). Two or more people can charter a flight for A$120 each at other times. There's a 20-kg (44-pound) baggage limit per person. Low-cost carrier **Jetstar** (☎ *13–1538* ⊕ *www.jetstar.com*) has daily flights to Rockhampton from Brisbane, connecting to other capital cities. **Virgin Blue** (☎ *13–6789* ⊕ *www. virginblue.com.au*) flies to Rockhampton from Brisbane and Sydney, with connections to all major Australian cities. **Qantas** (☎ *13–1313* ⊕ *www.qantas.com.au*) has direct flights to Rockhampton from Brisbane, Townsville, and Mackay, connecting to other capitals.

THE WHITSUNDAY ISLANDS

The Whitsundays are a group of 74 islands situated within 161 km (100 mi) of each other, just 50 km (31 mi) from Shute Harbour, the mainland departure point. Discovered in 1770 by Captain James Cook of the HMS *Endeavour* (though not actually discovered on Whitsunday, due to a time-zone change oversight on his part), the Whitsundays are a favorite sailing destination, as well as an easy-access base point for exploring the reef. Some of the islands' beaches, particularly famous Whitehaven Beach, are picture-postcard gorgeous, though the islands themselves look more scrubby than tropical. The entire region is actually subtropical, making for very moderate air and water temperatures year-round. Almost all of the Whitsunday islands are national parks; although animals aren't very plentiful on them, birds are—more than 150 species make their homes here. Only seven islands have resorts on them; others are destinations for day trips, beach, and bushwalks, or simply serve as backdrop at scenic mooring spots.

8

BRAMPTON ISLAND

Twelve coral-and-white sandy beaches encircle Brampton Island, and kangaroos, colorful rainbow lorikeets, and butterflies populate the hilly interior's rain forests. Located at the southern entrance to the Whitsunday Passage, this 195-acre island, 40 km (25 mi) offshore from Mackay, is one of the prettiest in the area. Most of the island is a designated national park, with seven of the island's beaches accessible via walking trails. Just offshore lie a diverse array of fringing hard and soft coral reefs sheltering a myriad of marine creatures. Though the resort area is lively after dark, with live music, theme nights, beach parties, alfresco movies, and plenty of poolside drinking, the biggest attractions are on and under the water—especially snorkeling over the reef between Brampton and the adjoining Carlisle islands. The resort has Internet and phone access but no mobile phone reception (though you may get a signal from the opposite end of the island).

WHERE TO STAY & EAT

¢–$$$ ✕ **Voyages Brampton Island.** As if in recognition that its greatest assets are outside, this resort has rooms that are airy, modern, and functional, but nothing to write home about. The beachfront ocean-view rooms are the most lavish, with CD players, aromatherapy oil burners, private hammocks, turn-down service, and waffle-weave bathrobes. The Bluewater Restaurant serves a buffet breakfast, smorgasbord lunch, and a three-course or themed buffet dinner, including a lavish weekly seafood buffet. You can also order balcony dinners, beach picnics, and six-course candlelight dinners on the sand, or take a private sunset-and-starlight dinner cruise. A packed activities schedule is divided into Eco, Energize, Entertain, and Enjoy programs. Breakfasts are included in all lodging rates; other packages include dinner and/or lunch. There's a five-night minimum stay. *Voyages, GPO 3589, Sydney, NSW, 2000* ☎ *1300/134044 or 02/8296–8010* travel@voyages.com.au *www.voyages.com.au/brampton* *108 suites* *In-room: refrigerator, DVD, dial-up. In-hotel: safe, restaurant, bar, tennis courts, pools, gym, spa, beachfront, diving, water sports, laundry facilities, laundry service, concierge, public Internet, ATM, no kids under 13, no-smoking rooms* *AE, DC, MC, V* *BP, FAP available.*

> **ISLAND INTERIORS**
>
> Most folk are so busy getting on or under the water that they don't bother to explore their land-based environs. Overcast days are perfect for exploring island trails. Many Barrier Reef islands include significant tracts of national parkland, and trails often lead to or past truly spectacular views. Careful walkers may spot possums, goannas (iguanas), blue-tongued lizards, various birds, the odd wallaby, as well as nesting green and loggerhead turtles on beaches in season. Carry a good map, snacks, and plenty of water; wear a hat and sunscreen regardless of weather, and don't forget your camera.

SPORTS & THE OUTDOORS

Brampton Island's resort has extensive facilities and activities included in the rate—from aqua aerobics and circuit classes to volleyball, golf and soccer, guided nature walks to beach massage demos, as well as free use of snorkeling gear, paddle skis, sailboards, and catamarans. For an extra charge, you can also take boom-netting cruises (where you get trailed behind a boat by a net); guided walks; Jet Ski and sea kayak island tours; fishing trips; flights over the Great Barrier Reef; day trips to Hamilton Island, Whitehaven Beach, and the Reefworld pontoon; island and sunset cruises; wakeboarding, kneeboarding, and waterskiing 'tube rides (where you ride in an inner tube pulled along behind the ski boat); scuba training; dive trips; and guided snorkeling safaris. Activities cost between A$20 for a 15-minute tube ride and A$400, for a private moonlight cruise.

ARRIVING & DEPARTING

BY BOAT *Heron II* (☎13–2469), a high-speed monohull, leaves Mackay Outer Harbour daily at 11:30, arriving at Brampton at 12:45. Fare is A$55 one-way; A$110 round-trip. Complimentary coach transfers from Mackay airport are at 11 AM. Return boats leave Brampton marina at 1:15, connecting with the coach at 2:30 for a 3 PM arrival at Mackay airport.

BY PLANE **Australasian Jet** (☎07/4953–3261 ⊕*www.ausjet.com.au*), flies to Brampton Island from Mackay and Hamilton Island airports, taking 15–20 minutes, a minimum of two passengers, and a maximum of 29 kg (64 pounds) of baggage each (including hand luggage). Fare is A$69 one-way; A$138 round-trip from Mackay; A$119 return or A$238 return from Hamilton Island. Complimentary coach transfers from Mackay airport are at 11 AM. Return boats leave Brampton marina at 1:15, connecting with the coach at 2:30 for a 3 PM arrival at Mackay airport.

LINDEMAN ISLAND

More than half of Lindeman Island—which at 2,000 acres, is one of the largest in the Whitsunday group—is national park, with 20 km (12 mi) of walking trails that wind through tropical growth and up hills for fantastic views. Bird-watching is excellent here, although the blue tiger butterflies that you can see in Butterfly Valley may be even more impressive than the birds. With its natural and sporting attractions, the island draws lots of families. The island lies 40 km (25 mi) northeast of Mackay near the southern entrance to the Whitsunday Passage.

WHERE TO STAY & EAT

$$$$ ✗⊞ **Club Med Lindeman Island.** This three-story, palm-tree-filled resort, Australia's only Club Med, sits on 1,750 acres on the southern end of the island. Rooms are sparsely furnished, as is the habit at Club Med: those that are poolside or have hot tubs cost more. All overlook the sea and have a balcony or patio, and all border the beach and pool. Six- to eight-night packages—the minimum available here—include accommodations, buffet-style dining, and what the resort bills as "all-day snacking and full bar service," along with evening entertainment and a broad range of outdoor activities. The on-site spa has a selection of pampering treatments. ⊠*La Pointe Aux Sables PMB 1, Mackay Mail Centre, QLD, 4741* ☎*07/4946–9333 or 1800/258263* ⊕*www. clubmed.com.au* ⊅*217 rooms, 1 suite rooms* ⟳*In-room: safe, refrigerator, ethernet. In-hotel: 2 restaurants, bars, golf course, tennis courts, pools, gym, spa, beachfront, diving, water sports, children's programs (ages 4–13), laundry facilities, public Internet, public Wi-Fi, airport shuttle, no-smoking rooms* ⊟*AE, DC, MC, V* ⊠*AI.*

SPORTS & THE OUTDOORS

Club Med's basic price includes most activities, including their trademark flying trapeze school, a 9-hole golf course, tennis, basketball, sailing, sea-kayaking, and swimming, although you have to pay for motorized water sports. You can also take refresher scuba-diving

8

courses, go deep-sea fishing, or enjoy offshore excursions to White-haven Beach and the Great Barrier Reef at additional cost. Dive excursions to the outer reef by air are 30 minutes each way; by boat, it's two hours each way.

ARRIVING & DEPARTING

BY BOAT   There are direct half-hour water-taxi transfers to Lindeman Island from **Hamilton Island Airport** (☎07/4946–9999).

BY PLANE   **Island Air Taxis** (☎07/4946–9933 ⊕www.avta.com.au ✎gldbookings@avta.com.au) fly to the Lindeman airstrip on demand. The one-way cost is A$60 from Airlie Beach (15 mins), or Hamilton Island (5 mins), and A$135 from Mackay (25 mins).

Air Whitsunday (☎07/4946–9111 ⊕www.airwhitsunday.com.au) offers seaplane connections from Airlie Beach to Lindeman Island for A$1,100 (up to 10 passengers); and to other island and mainland destinations on request. They also operate scenic Reef flights.

LONG ISLAND

This aptly named narrow island lies off the coast south of Shute Harbour, 12 km (7 mi) west of Hamilton Island. Although it's 9 km (5½ mi) long and no more than 1½ km (1 mi) wide—7,680 acres total—it has 20 km (12 mi) of walking trails through large areas of thick, undisturbed rain forest, 2,500 acres of which are protected as national parkland and are home to birds, butterflies, goannas, and wallabies. You can circumnavigate the island on foot, but it's a demanding nine-hour hike. Some of the beaches here are pretty and picturesque; others are rocky and windblown. Though waters may not be as clear as on the outer reef islands, there are some excellent snorkeling spots where you'll share the balmy water with turtles, soft and hard corals, tropical fish, and turtles. You may also see dolphins, and migrating humpback whales (July through September).

WHERE TO STAY & EAT

$$$$ ✕⌂ **Peppers Palm Bay.** This luxury chain has a great reputation—and
★   this elegant property, with its attentive service, gorgeous setting, and good food, lives up to the hype. The 21 stylishly outfitted cabins, *bures* (tropical-style bungalows with thatched roofs), and A-frame bungalows strung along the shore all have private balconies with hammocks overlooking the beach. Cabins, roughly equivalent to standard rooms, have dark wood furnishings and neutral hues; bures have lounges; bungalows are full suites with separate lounge areas. Guests can snorkel, fly over, or dive the reef and use the resort's canoes and paddle-skis. Those needing to relax can take advantage of the saltwater pool, outdoor Jacuzzi, Pandanus Bar's excellent tropical cocktails, or the endota spa's long list of treatments. After-dark entertainment is low-key and sophisticated: fine wine, fine dining, conversation, perhaps a hit of tennis on the floodlit court, or a film at the resort's mini-cinema. You can book just a room, or pay for a package that includes meals. ✉*Long Island, Whitsundays, 4802* ☎07/4946–9233 ✎palmbay@peppers.

com.au ⊕*www.peppers.com.au* ⇆*15 bungalows/bures, 6 cabins* ⌂*In-room: fans, no phone, refrigerator/minibar, no TV. In-hotel: restaurant, bar, tennis court, pool, spa, beachfront, water sports, laundry facilities, public Internet, no kids under 14, no-smoking rooms* ▤AE, DC, MC, V ⦿CP.

$$$$ ╳▥**South Long Island Nature Lodge.** Talk about secluded—this intimate, eco-conscious lodge on the isolated southern tip of Long Island is accessible only by helicopter. Each of the private bungalows fronting Paradise Bay beach has both a king-size and a single bed, and a super-private veranda with a double hammock—perfect for watching sunsets. They're crafted from solid Australian hardwood, with cathedral ceilings, polished wood floors, walls adorned with photos from around the island, and picture windows with 180-degree water views. Unlike some other exclusive resorts, this one welcomes solo travelers, imposing no surcharge for sole occupancy. There's a 10-percent discount for online bookings. With a maximum of 12 guests at a time, and a five-night minimum stay, it's easy to get the perfect balance of solitude and sociability—and as fellow guests are a worldly bunch, conversation is generally rewarding. The lodge owns and operates its own 34-foot sailing catamaran; daily excursions with a local skipper visit nearby islands, beaches, and coral gardens every day except Sunday. The tariff includes your room, excellent chef-prepared meals, helicopter transfers from Hamilton Island, free use of snorkeling gear and beach towels, sailing excursions, and sea kayaking. In addition to its complimentary activities, the Lodge offers half-day helicopter tours to the outer Great Barrier Reef for A$600 per person (minimum two). The tour includes a 40-minute scenic flight each way, snorkeling at Fantasea Reefworld pontoon—before the crowds arrive—and, for an extra A$80, one optional dive including gear and divemaster guide. Bring essential supplies and medicines, but leave power-guzzling appliances behind: the resort runs on limited solar-generated electricity. ⌂*Box 842, Airlie Beach, QLD, 4802* ☎07/4946–9777 ✉info@ southlongisland.com ⊕*www.southlongisland.com* ⇆*10 cabins* ⌂*In-room: no a/c, fans, refrigerator, no phone, no TV. In-hotel: restaurant, bar, beachfront, water sports, no public Internet, no kids under 12* ▤AE, MC, V ⦿AI.

$–$$$ ╳▥**Long Island Resort.** A short walk over the hill from Palm Bay, this family-focused resort might as well be on an entirely different island. This is not the place to commune quietly with nature, because the resort focuses on outdoor activities, particularly water sports, and group-oriented fun. Although the no-cost kids' club is meant to enable adults to enjoy their leisure time, the program is adjourned from noon to 5 PM, which means there are lots of little ones running around. At night, entertainment might be karaoke, live music, a beach party, a trivia night, casino, or "hyper" games. Guests in air-conditioned beachfront and garden-view rooms have extra mod cons, balconies, and three daily buffet-style meals included in their rate; guests in the fan-cooled budget lodges must fend for themselves. Order a picnic hamper from the licensed café and escape the crowd. The island and the resort are easily accessed via ferry, launch, and two airports, making it a great base for island-hopping. 🖃*Box 798, Airlie Beach, QLD, 4802* 🖀*07/4946–9400 or 1800/075125* 🖂longislandres@clubcroc.com.au ⊕*www.clubcroc.com.au* 🖃*161 rooms, 31 lodges without bath* ♿*In-room: no a/c (some), fans, safe (some), refrigerator (some), no TV (some), dial-up (some). In-hotel: 2 restaurants, bars, 2 tennis courts, pools, hot tub, sauna, beachfront, diving, water sports, children's programs (ages 4–14), no-smoking rooms* ▭*AE, DC, MC, V* ⑩*CP.*

ARRIVING & DEPARTING

You can reach Long Island (but not Peppers Palm Bay or South Long Island Nature Lodge) several times a day via **Fantasea Cruises** (🖀*07/4946–5111 or 1800/650851* ⊕*www.fantasea.com.au*) from either Shute Harbour or Hamilton Island. Fantasea's air-conditioned catamarans leave Shute Harbour for Long Island Resort daily; the 20-minute journey costs A$45 from Hamilton Airport (Fantasea reps meet all incoming planes) or A$34 from Shute Harbour. The transfer to Long Island Resort costs A$90 round-trip.

The private Peppers Palm Bay launch runs from Shute Harbour for A$70 round-trip.

Air Whitsunday (🖀*07/4946–9111* ⊕*www.airwhitsunday.com.au*) provides seaplane connections from Hamilton to Hayman for A$760 each way (up to 6 passengers). They'll also fly you from Airlie Beach to Hamilton for A$289 each way (up to 6); to Peppers Palm Bay on South Long Island for A$109 per person; to Lindeman Island for A$1100 (up to 10); and to other island and mainland destinations on request.

Guests of South Long Island Nature Lodge can take a helicopter from Hamilton Island airport to South Long Island (or back again), anytime between 7:30 AM and 5 PM; or fly from Airlie Beach on the mainland, a 15-minute trip, anytime between 9 and 5. The scenic flight is included in guests' tariffs. Baggage is limited to 15 kg (30 pounds) per person, and should be in soft-sided bags. Excess luggage can be stored at the airport. Virgin, Qantas, and Jetstar fly between Hamilton Island and Sydney, Brisbane, and Cairns daily.

HAMILTON ISLAND

Though it's the most heavily populated and developed island in the Whitsunday group, more than 70% of Hamilton Island has been carefully preserved in its natural state, which translates into beautiful beaches (such as the long, curving palm-dotted Catseye Beach), native bush trails, and spectacular lookouts. Yet for all its natural beauty the 1,482-acre island is more of a place to have an action-packed, sociable holiday than to get away from it all.

Only 30 minutes by ferry from Shute Harbour, Hamilton (called "Hamo" by locals) buzzes with activity. Guests of the resort, and its six types of accommodation, make up most of the population, but there are private residences here as well as throngs of day-trippers from the mainland, other islands, and cruising yachts, who wander the island's studio-back-lot-style marina and village each day.

Hamilton is set up as a small city, with its own school, post office, bank, supermarket, video store, shops, restaurants, bars, and nightclub that both guests and day-trippers are free to visit. But little on Hamilton is free. Because amenities are targeted to resort guests, prices can be steep. Even the ubiquitous golf carts that guests rent to zip around the island in are around A$15 an hour, or A$80 per day (☎ 07/4946–8263 or 07/4946–8095). Save a few bucks by using the free resort shuttle service that runs around the island at regular intervals between 7 AM and 11 PM.

Hamilton Island offers a range of dining options, from bare-bones take-out places to elegant sit-down restaurants. Although the island has tried to improve the quality of its eateries, it still tends to be on the lower end of the scale, especially when compared with some of the more private, exclusive islands. For a family-friendly, one-stop reef experience in a beautiful setting, however, Hamo is a good bet.

WHERE TO EAT

Hamilton Island Resort has lots of great dining options, including several casual cafés and takeaway outlets, a pub serving counter meals, a dinner cruise boat, and restaurants.

$$–$$$ ✕ **Beach House.** This is Hamilton Island's signature dress-up restaurant, set right on Catseye Beach in a charming, airy beach shack overlooking the cerulean waters. Lunches, including an extravagant six-course option for A$55, and à la carte dinners focus on the freshest ingredients, with an emphasis on locally caught seafood; cuisine is contemporary tropical Australian with Asian influences. ⊠ *Main resort complex* ☎ 07/4946–8580 ⊟ *AE, DC, MC, V* ☾ *Closed Mon.*

¢–$$ ✕ **Romano's Italian Restaurant.** With polished wood floors and a balcony overlooking the marina, Romano's is the place to come for casual fine dining. The kitchen produces traditional Italian favorites such as pasta *amatriciana* (with tomato, bacon, onion, and chili), but the real focus is on fresh produce and local seafood—try the Spring Bay mussels with fresh tomato sauce, herbs, and chili. ⊠ *Marina Village, Harbourside* ☎ 07/4946–8212 ⊟ *AE, DC, MC, V* ☾ *Closed Tues. No lunch.*

¢–$ ✕ **Toucan Tango Café.** This is the island's relaxed all-day dining option, with bright, cheerful decor; it's perfect for casual poolside meals. The daily buffet breakfast by the beach is definitely worth climbing out of bed for. Lunch offerings include café-style wraps, burgers, sandwiches, seafood, and salads; a crowd-pleasing dinner menu balances seafood with beef, chicken, lamb, and pasta dishes. There are a kids' menu, a small children's play area, and an adjoining bar. ⊠ *Main resort complex* ☎ 07/4946–8562 ⊟ *AE, DC, MC, V.*

WHERE TO STAY

You can make reservations for all accommodations on Hamilton Island with the **Hamilton Island Resort** (⊠ *Hamilton Island, Whitsunday Islands, QLD, 4803* ☎ 02/9433–0444 or 13–7333 ✐ vacation@hamiltonisland.

com.au ⊕*www.hamiltonisland.com.au*). The resort also manages a range of self-catered apartments, including studio, split-level, and two-story designs. Each has a full kitchen, laundry area, combined living-dining area, and a private balcony with views.

$$$$ ★ **Hamilton Island Beach Club.** If you never leave the gorgeous infinity pool at the Beach Club, and take all your meals poolside and your cocktails in the Club Lounge and Bar, you might believe you're in the ultimate beach resort. The rooms, given a "designer beachside" make-over in 2005, have flat-screen TVs, entertainment systems with surround sound, hip furnishings, and shuttered doors leading to private balconies. There's a concierge service, useful for booking activities and making restaurant reservations at the resort's various island eateries— 10 in all, plus free use of golf carts to get you there. Also complimentary are tennis and squash court hire, and Internet access. The staff is efficient, but don't expect them to go that extra mile. If you stay four or more nights, however, daily buffet breakfasts are included. ⊠*Hamilton Island, Whitsunday Islands, QLD, 4803* ☎*07/4946–9999 or 13–7333* ✍vacation@hamiltonisland.com.au ⊕*www.hamiltonisland.com.au* ➥*57 rooms* ☖*In-room: safe, refrigerator/minibar, VCR/CD, ethernet, dial-up. In-hotel: restaurant, room service, bar, tennis courts, pool, gym, spa, diving, water sports, laundry service, concierge, executive floor, public Internet, public Wi-Fi, airport shuttle, no kids under 18, no-smoking rooms, minibar* ℣◎∣*BP (some)* ▤*AE, DC, MC, V.*

$$$–$$$$ **Hamilton Island Reef View Hotel.** This hotel only lives up to its name on the higher floors; rooms on the fifth floor and above have spectacular vistas of the Coral Sea, while those on the lower levels overlook a landscaped, tropical garden. All have private balconies. Rooms are spacious and comfortable, although decor in many looks dated. Suites on the 19th floor were refurbished in 2006: the new-look split-level accommodations have simple blond-wood dining settings, neutral-toned soft furnishings, flat-screen TVs, ocean views, and access to a private terrace and lap pool. Terrace Suites have their own outdoor hot tubs. Suite guests get complimentary hire of tennis and squash courts. Stay four or more nights, and you get daily buffet breakfasts for free. ⊠*Hamilton Island, Whitsunday Islands, QLD, 4803* ☎*07/4946–9999 or 13–7333* ✍vacation@hamiltonisland.com.au ⊕*www.hamiltonisland.com.au* ➥*363 rooms, 17 suites* ☖*In-room: safe (some), refrigerator/minibar, ethernet, dial-up. In-hotel: safe, restaurant, bar, room service, bar, tennis courts, pool, gym, spa, diving, water sports, children's program (infant–14 years, daily 8:30–5:30), laundry facilities, laundry service, concierge, public Internet, airport shuttle, no-smoking rooms* ℣◎∣*BP (some)* ▤*AE, DC, MC, V.*

$$$–$$$$ **Hamilton Island Whitsunday Holiday Apartments.** These twin 13-story towers, which overlook the Coral Sea toward Whitsunday Island, are self-contained one-bedroom apartments with pastel walls, comfortable wooden and cane furniture, large balconies, fully-equipped kitchens, Sony PlayStations, and dining and sitting areas. Those on the seventh floor and above have ocean views. If you stay four nights or longer, buffet breakfasts are free. ⊠*Hamilton Island, Whitsun-*

day Islands, QLD, 4803 ☎*07/4946–9999 or 13–7333* ✍*vacation@ hamiltonisland.com.au* ⊕*www.hamiltonisland.com.au* ⇄*165 apartments* ⌂*In-room: kitchen, refrigerator/minibar, DVD, dial-up. In-hotel: safe, restaurant, room service (6* AM*-midnight), bar, tennis courts, pool, gym, spa, diving, water sports, children's program (infant–14 years, daily 8:30–5:30), airport shuttle, no-smoking rooms* ⏐◯⏐*BP (some)* ▭*AE, DC, MC, V.*

$$$ ⊡ **Hamilton Island Palm Bungalows and Terraces.** The steep-roofed, free-standing bungalows resemble Polynesian huts, and each has a private furnished balcony, cool tile floors, a small bar, and a king-size bed. Terraces are budget-friendlier, contemporary hotel rooms with group-friendly configurations. All have furnished balconies or tropical garden outlooks. With four-night or longer stays, buffet breakfasts are included in the rate. ⊠*Hamilton Island, Whitsunday Islands, QLD, 4803* ☎*07/4946–9999 or 13–7333* ✍*vacation@hamiltonisland.com. au* ⊕*www.hamiltonisland.com.au* ⇄*49 bungalows, 60 rooms* ⌂*In-room: refrigerator/minibar, dial-up. In-hotel: safe, restaurant, room service (6* AM*–6* PM*), bar, tennis courts, pool, gym, spa, diving, water sports, children's program (infant–14 years, daily 8:30–5:30), laundry facilities, laundry service, airport shuttle, no-smoking rooms* ⏐◯⏐*BP (some)* ▭*AE, DC, MC, V.*

NIGHTLIFE

At **Boheme's Bar & Nightclub** (⊠*Main resort complex* ☎*07/4946–8268*) you can dance to live or DJ-spun music and shoot a round of pool. The bar is open Tuesday–Saturday 9 PM–late, and the nightclub is open 11 PM–late.

SPORTS & THE OUTDOORS

Hamilton Island Resort has the widest selection of activities in the Whitsundays. Activities include bushwalking, game fishing, scuba diving, waterskiing, parasailing, sea kayaking, and windsurfing. There are also go-carts, a golf driving range, a miniature golf course, a flying fox, squash courts, a health club, a target-shooting range, seven resort swimming pools, and floodlighted tennis courts, as well as food-and-wine focused classes and events. Reserve ahead through the **Tour Booking Desk** (☎*07/4946–8305* ⊕*www.hamiltonisland.com.au*).

Hamilton Island is so family-friendly it allows kids to stay free, provided they use existing beds in the rooms (no roll-away beds or cribs). Kids under age 14 also can eat free at four of the island's restaurants when accompanied by their parents. The **Clownfish Club** (☎*07/4946–8941* ⊕*www.clownfishclub.com.au*), for children ages 6 weeks to 14 years, has organized sand-castle making, snorkeling, water polo, beach sports, and more. Babysitting services cost A$50 for the first three hours; A$18 for every hour thereafter. (◷*Daily 8:30–5:30*).

FISHING The resort can arrange half- and full-day, share or private charter sport-fishing trips for anglers looking to catch coral trout, mackerel, and tuna. Private charters cost A$2,400 for a full day, A$1,350 for a half day; shared charters are A$300 for a full day and A$160 for a half day. Three-day big-game fishing charters for marlin, sailfish, wahoo,

8

giant trevally, Spanish mackerel, and yellow and blue-fin tuna are also available. All equipment is included. You can also hire dinghies here. Charters can be arranged through Hamilton Island's **Tour Booking Desk** (☎07/4946–8318 ⊕*www.renegadecharters.com.au*).

SCUBA DIVING Hamilton Island has a complimentary introductory scuba course including instruction, equipment, and a guided dive. If you're already qualified, you can rent your own equipment for trips out to the reef. A day trip including two dives with **H2O Sportz** (☎07/4946–8217 ⊕*www.h2osportz.com.au*), the island's dive shop, is A$265. Also available are glass-bottom boat tours of the reef that run A$40 during the day and A$50 at night.

WILDLIFE Hamilton Island's **Koala Gallery & Wildlife Sanctuary** houses koalas, kan-
PARK garoos, wallabies, crocodiles, wombats, and Tassie devils. There's a daily Breakfast with the Koalas, that features animal talks and feedings. You can also get koala happy snaps. (✉*A$15 [unlimited entry]*).

SHOPPING

Hamilton Island's Marina Village houses many shops selling resort wear, children's clothes, souvenirs, and gifts. An art gallery, art studio, florist, small supermarket, pharmacy, real-estate agent, bakery, bottle shop, medical center, video store, and hair salon are also on the island.

ARRIVING & DEPARTING

BY BOAT **Fantasea Cruises** (☎07/4946–5111 or 1800/650851 ⊕*www.fantasea.com.au*) makes the 30-minute journey from Shute Harbour to Hamilton Island eight times daily. The cost is A$68 round-trip.

BY PLANE **Jetstar** (☎13–1538) flies directly to Hamilton Island from Brisbane. **Qantaslink** (☎13–1313) has direct daily flights from Cairns and Brisbane. **Virgin Blue** (☎13–6789) operates daily flights from Melbourne, Sydney, and Brisbane.

Air Whitsunday (☎07/4946–9111 ⊕*www.airwhitsunday.com.au*) provides seaplane connections from Airlie Beach on the mainland to Hamilton Island for A$289 each way (up to 6 passengers); from Airlie to Whitehaven Beach for A$165; and to other island and mainland destinations on request. They also operate scenic flights over the Great Barrier Reef.

TOUR OPERATORS

Hamilton Island Aviation (☎07/4946–8249 ⊕*www.avta.com.au/Whitsundays.html*) has seaplane and helicopter flights over the Whitsunday Islands and the Great Barrier Reef. Transfers to the other islands are also available.

★ **Fantasea Cruises** (☎07/4946–5111 ⊕*www.fantasea.com.au*) runs reef trips daily from Hamilton Island and other islands, including Daydream Island and Long Island. From Hamilton it's a 55-km (34-mi) trip to magnificent **Hardy Reef Lagoon**, where you can swim, snorkel, ride in a semisubmersible, or simply relax. The cost is A$189, including a buffet lunch. You can take a dive lesson and introductory dive for A$95 or opt for a daylong diving package that costs A$265. It's also possible to overnight on the boat (A$395 per person in a shared, four-bunk dorm, or A$495 per double room). Fantasea also runs reef trips out of Shute Harbour on the mainland.

Fodor's Choice Fantasea also runs daily high-speed catamarans to **Whitehaven Beach,** ★ a justifiably famous and spectacular stretch of pure white silica sand as fine (and as messy) as talcum powder. Find a secluded spot on the 6½-km (4-mi) beach—slather yourself in sunblock, as the sand acts as a reflector for the sun—or swim in the crystal-clear water. The trips on the air-conditioned vessels cost A$94.

Sunsail Australia (⊠*Front St., Hamilton Island* ☎*07/4948–9510 or 1800/803988* ⊕*www.sunsail.com.au*) has more than two dozen boats available for bareboat charter, and runs luxury crewed catamaran cruises (from A$1,100 per person for a three-night, all-inclusive trip, with snorkeling gear, kayaks, and an onboard hostess).

SOUTH MOLLE ISLAND

South Molle, a 1,040-acre island close to Shute Harbour, was originally inhabited by Aborigines, who collected basalt here to use for their axes. Much later, it became the first of the Whitsundays to be used for grazing, hence its extensive grassy tracts. Now the island is a national park with a single, family-oriented resort settled on sheltered Bauer Bay in the north. Protected between two headlands, the bay often remains calm when wind rips through the rest of the Whitsundays.

WHERE TO STAY & EAT

$$$ ✗⊞ **South Molle Island Resort.** Known as an Aussie budget getaway, this resort is a good all-rounder, offering great value as well as easy reef access. Every room has a balcony, a whirlpool tub, and sea or garden views. Package deals include three daily buffet meals and numerous activities, from archery to windsurfing. This is one of the few islands on the reef that has a golf course (set in a national park, with beach and island views), and the family-oriented setting means first-timers never feel intimidated trying to jet ski. Every night brings free entertainment, which might be karaoke, live music, a movie on the big screen in the Discovery Bar, or a trivia night; on Friday evening, there's a Polynesian-themed seafood feast and show. ⊠*South Molle Island, via Shute Harbour, QLD, 4741* ☎*07/4946–9433 or 1800/075080* ⊕*www. southmolleisland.com.au* ⇆*200 rooms* ⌂*In-room: refrigerator/ minibar (some), hot tub. In-hotel: 2 restaurants, golf course, tennis courts, pool, gym, hot tub, beachfront, diving, water sports, children's programs (ages 4–14), laundry facilities, public Internet* ⊟*AE, DC, MC, V* ⍩*AI.*

ARRIVING & DEPARTING

BY BOAT **Cruise Whitsundays** (☎*07/4946–4662 or 1800/426403* ⊕*www.cruise whitsundays.com.au*) transports passengers from Abel Point Marina near Airlie Beach to South Molle Island for A$26 one-way, A$52 return (A$100 round-trip transfer from Proserpine railway station or airport).

The Reef

The Great Barrier Reef is a living animal. Early scientists, however, thought it was a plant, which is forgivable. Soft corals have a plantlike growth and a horny skeleton that runs along the inside of the stem. In contrast, the hard, calcareous skeletons of stony corals are the main building blocks of the reef. There are also two main classes of reefs: platform or patch reefs, which result from radial growth, and wall reefs, which result from elongated growth, often in areas of strong water currents. Fringing reefs occur where the growth is established on sub-tidal rock, either on the mainland or on continental islands.

It's hard to imagine that the reef, which covers an area about half the size of Texas, is so fragile that even human sweat can cause damage. However, despite its size, the reef is a finely balanced ecosystem sustaining zillions of tiny polyps, which have been building on top of each other for thousands of years. So industrious are these critters that the reef is more than 1,640 feet thick in some places. These polyps are also fussy about their living conditions and only survive in clear, salty water around 18°C (64°F) and less than 98 feet deep.

Closely related to anemones and jellyfish, marine polyps are primitive, sacklike animals with a mouth surrounded by tentacles. Coral can consist of one polyp (solitary) or many hundreds (colonial), which form a colony when joined together. These polyps create a hard surface by producing lime; as they die, their coral "skeletons" remain, which form the reef's white substructure. The living polyps give the coral its colorful appearance.

The Great Barrier Reef begins south of the Tropic of Capricorn around Gladstone and ends in the Torres Strait below Papua New Guinea, making it about 2,000 km (1,240 mi) long and 356,000 square km (137,452 square mi) in area. Declared a World Heritage Site in 1981, it is managed by the Great Barrier Reef Marine Park Authority, which was itself established in 1976. Consequently, detailed observations and measurements of coral reef environments only date back to around this time.

Dive sites are unlimited, set around approximately 3,000 individual reefs, 300 coral cays, 890 fringing reefs, and 2,600 islands (including 618 continental islands that were once part of the mainland). Despite the vast amount of water surrounding the islands, though, freshwater is nonexistent here and thus is a precious commodity; self-sufficiency is particularly important for explorers and campers. Removing or damaging any part of the reef is a crime, so divers are asked to take home only photographs and memories of one of the world's great natural wonders.

–Jane Carstens

Cruise Whitsundays' office at Hamilton Island airport transfers South Molle guests directly to the island on speedy, air-conditioned cruisers, taking just 10 minutes, for A$49. Or take a half-day or full-day trip to South Molle (and/or Daydream), lunching on either island, with discounted use of resort facilities, for A$65 or A$80. Individual and two-island cruises leave from Abel Point Marina near Airlie Beach at 9:35 and 11:05 daily, with multiple return trips in the afternoon.

DAYDREAM ISLAND

The resort on this small, 42-acre island is especially welcoming to day-trippers. Just 30 minutes' boat-ride from Shute Harbour, it's a perfect place to relax or pursue outdoor activities such as snorkeling and water sports—all of which are relatively affordable. The resort has lush gardens that blend into a small tract of rain forest, frequented by tame wallabies and mournful curlews. The island is surrounded by clear blue water and fringing coral reefs.

WHERE TO STAY & EAT

$$$–$$$$ ✕▦ **Daydream Island Resort & Spa.** Colorfully decorated, with whimsical touches like starfish-and-shell-embedded toilet seats, pewter mermaid statues perched on rocks, and outsized marine mobiles and murals, this family-friendly resort has a staff that's youthful and cheerful. Spacious condo-style garden- or ocean-view apartments have modern cane and blond-wood furniture, cool terra-cotta-tile floors, and beach-theme fabrics; suites have hot tubs. Resort activities vary from fish-feeding at the ocean-fed living reef that meanders through the resort, to snorkeling, windsurfing, or parasailing. A mere A$10 per player, the million-dollar, Australiana-themed 19-hole mini-golf course at the island's southern end is bargain-priced hilarity. Here, you can also catch new-release movies on a gigantic beachfront screen (deckchairs and blankets provided). Breakfast is included in most room packages. Child care is available at additional cost: drop the kids off and head out on a day cruise, or to the 16-room Daydream Rejuvenation Spa. ⊠ *Daydream Island, Whitsunday Islands, QLD, 4870* ✆ *Daydream Island, PMB 22, via Mackay, QLD, 4740* ☎ *07/4948–8488 or 1800/075040* ⊕ *www.daydreamisland.com* ⤢ *280 rooms, 9 suites* ⚅ *In-room: safe, refrigerator/minibar, dial-up. In-hotel: 3 restaurants, bars, 2 tennis courts, pools, gym, spa, beachfront, diving, water sports, children's program (3–13 years), laundry facilities, laundry service, concierge, airport shuttle, no-smoking rooms* ⊟ *AE, DC, MC, V* ⊚ *BP (some).*

SPORTS & THE OUTDOORS

At Daydream Island Resort some activities are included in room rates, while fishing, snorkeling, scuba diving, parasailing, waterskiing, jet skiing, and miniature golf are provided for an additional charge. The resort offers introductory dives through Daydream Dive (☎ 07/494–8782 ⊕ www.daydreamdive.com) for around A$100, as well as multi-dive excursions from A$165 and PADI-certified dive courses. Daylong excursions to the surrounding islands and the Great Barrier Reef are also available: a full-day sailing trip on fast purple catamaran *Camira,* stopping off on Whitehaven beach for walks, beach games, and snorkeling, with a big BBQ lunch, snacks, all beverages (including alcohol), and snorkeling gear, is bargain-priced at A$140 per person, but be prepared to share the boat with boisterous young travelers. Non-guests can also book activities through the resort.

8

ARRIVING & DEPARTING

BY BOAT **Cruise Whitsundays** (☎07/4946–4662 or 1800/426403 ⊕www.cruisewhitsundays.com.au) runs daily services between Daydream Island and Hamilton Island's Great Barrier Reef Airport for A$49 one-way, A$98 round-trip, and between the island and Abel Point Marina for A$26 one-way, A$52 round-trip. Transfers from Proserpine station or airport to the island are A$50 each way.

Fantasea Cruises (☎07/4946–5111 or 1800/650851 ⊕www.fantasea.com.au) runs several daily catamarans to Daydream Island from Shute Harbour (A$46 round-trip). For those flying into Great Barrier Reef Airport, the company also runs boats to Hamilton Island (A$90 round-trip).

> ### ONE WITH NATURE
>
> At Barrier Reef resorts, part of the fun is sharing your vacation with the local wildlife. On Hinchinbrook, lace monitor lizards up to 3 feet long frequently wander into the pool area and open-sided restaurant looking for food. Daydream Island resort has a resident mob of tame, very cute wallabies that lope downhill towards Sunlover's Cove each afternoon at dusk; and big-eyed, mournful curlews roam the grounds by night in many Whitsunday resorts. Unsuspecting Hayman guests may be subject to fly-by room raids from cheeky white cockatoos.

BY PLANE Although most people arrive by boat from Hamilton Airport, an alternative is to fly to Proserpine Airport on the mainland, catch a bus to Shute Harbour, and take a boat to the island.

Jetstar (☎13–1538 ⊕www.jetstar.com.au), **Qantas** (☎13–1313 ⊕www.qantas.com.au), and **Virgin Blue** (☎13–6789 ⊕www.virginblue.com.au), operate flights to and from Hamilton Island and Proserpine airports, and capital cities, as well as Townsville and Cairns. Check with each carrier for weight restrictions.

HAYMAN ISLAND

Fodor'sChoice ★ Hayman Island, in the northern Whitsunday Passage, is a 900-acre crescent with a series of hills along its spine. The closest of the Whitsundays to the Outer Barrier reef, Hayman's renowned resort is one of the oldest and most opulent in the region, and is consequently very popular with jet-setters who take their play and leisure seriously. The service here—understated yet completely attentive—truly merits the price you pay for it; staff members even traverse the resort via underground tunnels so they're not too much of a "presence." Reflecting pools, sandstone walkways, manicured tropical gardens, and sparkling waterfalls provide the feel of an exclusive club within the resort grounds, while beautiful walking trails crisscross the island around it. The main beach sits right in front of the hotel, but more secluded sands, as well as fringing coral, can be reached by boat.

WHERE TO EAT

All restaurants are in the resort. Reservations are recommended and can be booked through the resort's concierge.

$$-$$$ ✕**Azure.** Directly in front of the island's main beach, this casually ele-
★   gant restaurant affords glorious views. Dine indoors or alfresco: seating
extends onto the sand. There's a splendid buffet breakfast each morning, with à la carte options, freshly baked breads and pastries, tropical
fruits and juices, and brewed coffee. At night, a contemporary Australian menu showcasing seafood, and candlelit, white-linen dining, are
the drawcards. A lavish seafood buffet is available on selected evenings
for $A85 per person. There's also a kids' menu. ▭*AE, DC, MC, V.*

$$-$$$ ✕**La Fontaine.** With Waterford crystal chandeliers and Louis XVI fur-
★   nishings, this elegant restaurant, open at least twice a week for dinner,
is the resort's culinary showpiece. Its fine "modern European" cuisine
has a definite French accent. Live music generally accompanies dinner.
A private dining room, with the option of designing your own menu
in consultation with the resort's chef, is available. ▭*AE, DC, MC, V*
🕙*No lunch.*

$$-$$$ ✕**Oriental Restaurant.** This Asian establishment, a Hayman staff favor-
ite, overlooks a tranquil Japanese garden, complete with rock pools
and waterfalls, a teahouse, and dining platforms. Menu choices include
exotic and classic pan-Asian creations like *hoi man poo* (Thai-style
mussels in black-bean sauce) and shark-fin soup. ▭*AE, DC, MC, V*
🕙*No lunch.*

$-$$ ✕**La Trattoria.** With its red-and-white–checkered tablecloths and casual
furnishings, "Tratt's" is a classic provincial Italian restaurant. Seated
either inside or outdoors, you can choose from an extensive list of pastas and traditional Italian dishes, a spectacular antipasto buffet, and a
well-chosen wine list with some excellent reds. A live jazz band adds to
the sociable atmosphere. ▭*AE, DC, MC, V* 🕙*No lunch.*

WHERE TO STAY

$$$$ ⊞**Hayman.** This magnificently solid, hurricane-proof resort is the
grand dame of the Whitsundays, attracting high-flying guests seeking
precious down time. Lavish decor, including Asian and Australian artifacts, European tapestries, Persian rugs, and exquisite objets d'art set
a quietly elegant tone in the lobby, restaurants, walkways, and rooms.
Lagoon, pool, garden, penthouse, and beachfront suites are all beautifully appointed and overlook the areas of the resort they're named for.
For luxury, nothing tops the penthouse suites, decorated in distinct
themes, including French, English, Moroccan, Tropical Australian, Oriental, and Italian. There are a 24-hour indoor-outdoor gym; a tranquil
day spa; a flotilla of boats ready to whisk guests to secluded beaches,
islands, and the Reef; a screening room showing new-release films;
a genteel lounge bar and library with billiards room; and an arcade
of upmarket boutiques. Hayman's smoothly-run activities program
includes Pilates and yoga classes, art and kitchen tours, beach picnics,
scenic flights, and sailing trips. Children here are virtually invisible,
thanks to a crèche and organized kids' activities 9–12 and 2–5 daily.
Expect to pay handsomely for all this excellence—even small things like
drinks cost that little bit more. ✉*Hayman Island, Great Barrier Reef,
QLD, 4801* ☎*07/4940–1234 or 1800/075175* ✐reserve@hayman.

8

com.au ⊕*www.hayman.com.au* ⇨*198 rooms, 30 suites, 11 pent-houses, 1 villa* ⚠*In-room: fans, safe, refrigerator/minibar, DVD, ethernet, dial-up. In-hotel: 4 restaurants, room service, 2 bars, 5 tennis courts, pools, gym, spa, beachfront, diving, water sports, children's programs (ages infant–12), laundry service, concierge, public Internet, airport shuttle* ☰*AE, DC, MC, V.*

SPORTS & THE OUTDOORS

All nonmotorized water sports on Hayman Island are included in the room rates. The resort's water-sports center has a training tank for diving lessons, and a dive shop sells everything from snorkel gear to complete wet suits and sports clothing. The marina organizes parasailing, waterskiing, sailing, boating, fishing, windsurfing, and snorkeling, as well as dive trips. You can also arrange scenic flights to nearby beaches and over the reef. Contact the resort's **Recreation Information Centre** (☎*07/4940–1882*) for reservations and information.

ARRIVING & DEPARTING

BY PLANE Hayman doesn't have an airstrip of its own, but you can fly into Hamilton Island on **Jetstar** (☎*13–1538* ⊕*www.jetstar.com.au*), Qantas (☎*13–1313* ⊕*www.qantas.com.au*), or **Virgin Blue** (☎*13–6789* ⊕*www.virginblue.com.au*) , and transfer onto one of Hayman's luxury motor yachts. Australian sparkling wine is served during the 60-minute trip to the island. Upon your arrival at the wharf, a shuttle whisks you to the resort about ½ km (¼ mi) away. On the return journey, you'll get full bar service, food platters, and tea and coffee. Make sure you're ticketed all the way to Hayman Island, including the motor-yacht leg, as purchasing the round-trip yacht journey from Hamilton Island to Hayman separately costs upward of A$300.

Air Whitsunday (☎*07/4946–9111* ⊕*www.airwhitsunday.com.au*) provides seaplane connections from Hamilton to Hayman for A$760 each way (up to 6 passengers). They'll also fly you from Airlie Beach to Hamilton for A$289 each way (up to 6); to Peppers Palm Bay on South Long Island for A$109 per person; to Lindeman Island for A$1100 (up to 10); from Airlie to Whitehaven Beach for A$165; and to other island and mainland destinations on request. They also run scenic flights over the Reef.

TOUR OPERATORS

Hayman Island Guest Services (☎*07/4940–1234* ⊕*www.hayman.com.au*) provides information on all guided tours around the island. For example, you can take scenic flights over or to the Great Barrier Reef for A$290 per person in a seaplane or helicopter. At the reef, activities include snorkeling, coral viewing from a semisubmersible sub, and refreshments. Or take the three-hour Reef Adventure tour, with 90 minutes' snorkeling on the reef, for A$365.

A 90-minute coral-viewing trip aboard the *Reef Dancer* (A$70 per person) departs three times daily, at 9:30, 12:45, and 2:30. The coral is viewed from a semisubmersible sub. A Whitehaven Beach Picnic Cruise (A$275) departs Sundays at 10, returning at 3: the price includes lunch.

Cruise Whitsunday runs a daily snorkel and dive trip from Hayman to Knuckle Reef pontoon on the outer Reef from 9:15 to 4:30. The cost is A$215 for snorkelers, A$315 for introductory divers, and includes guides, all gear, lunch, and soft drinks.

NORTH COAST ISLANDS

ORPHEUS ISLAND

Volcanic in origin, this narrow island—11 km (7 mi) long and 1 km (½ mi) wide, 3,500 acres total—uncoils like a snake in the waters between Halifax Bay and the Barrier Reef. It's part of the Palm Island Group, which consists of 10 islands, 8 of which are Aboriginal reservations. Orpheus is a national park, occupied only by a marine research station and the island's fantastic resort. Although there are patches of rain forest in the island's deeper gullies and around the sheltered bays, Orpheus is a true Barrier Reef island, ringed by seven unspoiled sandy beaches and superb coral. Incredibly, 340 of the known 350 species of coral inhabit these waters, as well as more than 1,100 types of tropical fish, and the biggest giant clams in the southern hemisphere. The marine life is so easily accessed and so extraordinary here, it's no wonder the island is the sole domain of the maximum 42 guests allowed at the resort. You may occasionally see unfamiliar boats offshore, which is their right according to a marine park treaty, but you'll know everyone on Orpheus at any given time, maybe even by name.

WHERE TO STAY & EAT

$$$$
Fodor's Choice
★

✕⊞ **Orpheus Island Resort.** Nestled among palm trees and lush tropical gardens, this intimate island sanctuary offers two types of beachfront accommodation: Nautilus Suites and Orpheus Retreats. Retreats are immaculate, comfortable, and decorated with tasteful sophistication and an eye to intimacy: each has a hammock-slung private patio, kitchenette, lounge area, CD player, hot tub, aromatherapy oil burner, and bathrobes. Suites have similarly luxurious appointments but are considerably larger. You won't want to spend long inside, though—not when coral gardens under cerulean water and white-sand beaches are beckoning. With only 42 guests (and no clocks) on the island, activities, including snorkeling, beach picnics, diving the outer Reef, and exploring the island's coves by dinghy, can be scheduled any time you like. Extravagant seven-course degustation dinners showcasing exotic delicacies and local seafood are served nightly in the open-sided resort restaurant. Dining with the tides on the jetty and feeding local mullet by candlelight is an unforgettable experience. ✉ *Orpheus Island, Box 702, Brisbane, QLD, 4001* ☎ *07/4777–7377* ✎ *bookings@orpheus.com.au* ⊕ *www.orpheus.com.au* ➘ *17 rooms, 4 suites* ⚐ *In-room: no phone, fans, safe (some), kitchen, refrigerator/ minibar, no TV. In-hotel: restaurant, 2 bars, tennis court, pools, hot tub, gym, beachfront, diving, water sports, laundry service, public Internet, airport shuttle, no kids under 15, no-smoking rooms* ⊟ *AE, DC, MC, V* ❖ *AI* ⊗ *Closed Feb.*

8

SPORTS & THE OUTDOORS

The resort is surrounded by walking trails, and there's spectacular snorkeling and diving right off the beaches. The resort's purpose-built 32-foot Cougar catamaran, *Orpheus,* takes a maximum of 18 guests cruising around the Palm Isles, and up to 12 on dive-and-snorkel trips to the outer Reef (A$250 per person includes snorkeling, gear, and a picnic lunch; dives cost extra). Outer-reef fishing charters can be arranged for an additional fee. The resort no longer offers scuba diving certification, but dive operators on the island provide courses and various boat-diving options.

ARRIVING & DEPARTING

BY PLANE   Orpheus Island lies 24 km (15 mi) offshore of Ingham, about 80 km (50 mi) northeast of Townsville, and 190 km (118 mi) south of Cairns. The 25-minute flight from Townsville Airport to Orpheus aboard a **Nautilus Aviation** (☎ *07/4725–6056* ⊕ *www.orpheus.com*) seaplane costs A$450 per person round-trip. There are usually two flights daily at 11:30 and 2:15 (returning 12:15 and 3). Book flights when you make your reservation with Orpheus Island Resort. A maximum of 15 kilograms (33 pounds) of luggage is allowed per person, though you can arrange to ship excess baggage by barge.

TOUR OPERATORS

The coral around Orpheus is some of the best in the area, and cruises to the outer reef can be arranged through the resort. Whereas most of the islands are more than 50 km (31 mi) from the reef, Orpheus is just 15 km (9 mi) away.

HINCHINBROOK ISLAND

This 97,000-acre national park is the largest island on the Great Barrier Reef. It's a nature-lover's paradise, with dense tropical rain forests, mangroves, mountain peaks, and sandy beaches. When Captain Cook discovered it in 1770, he didn't realize it was an island, and mistakenly named it Mt. Hinchinbrook (likely imagining that 3,746-foot Mt. Bowen, Australia's third-highest mountain, was part of the mainland). Dolphins, dugongs, tiger sharks, and sea turtles inhabit the waters, as well as fish that you're permitted to catch (a rarity, given the strict protection of the reef's marine life), and there are also estuarine crocodiles, adders, numerous birds, goannas, and small mammals. The island is virtually untouched, save for a small resort on its northeast corner and some well-placed toilets and campsites. Experienced walkers can trek the famed but difficult Thorsborne Trail. Contact the **Rainforest and Reef Information Centre** (☎ *07/4066–8601 or 13–1304* ⊕ *www.epa.qld.gov.au*) for essential information and camping permits. Costing A$4.50 per night, mandatory camping permits need to be reserved up to eight weeks in advance of your visit.

WHERE TO STAY & EAT

$$–$$$ ✕🏠 **Hinchinbrook Wilderness Lodge.** Limited to 50 guests, this small resort specializes in quiet enjoyment and natural attractions. Set amid the beautiful bush on the northeast corner of the island, clean, modern,

elegantly appointed tree houses and functional self-contained cabins offer unspoiled sea views from private balconies. Experienced chefs cater to guests' specific requests, with a focus on modern Australian cuisine, though menu options are limited. Self-catering is an option for guests of the beach cabins; bring your own provisions or have the resort bring them over from the mainland with 24 hours' notice. Service here is responsive, but understated. Some packages include all meals. The resort is closed annually between early February and late March. ⊠ *Cape Richards, Hinchinbrook Island, 4849* ⌂ *Box 3, Cardwell, QLD, 4849* ☎ *07/4066–8270* ✎ *info@hinchinbrooklodge.com.au* ⊕ *www.hinchinbrooklodge.com.au* ⬌ *15 tree houses, 7 beach cabins* ⌂ *In-room: fans, no a/c, kitchen (some), refrigerator, no phone, no TV. In-hotel: restaurant, bar, pool, beachfront, water sports, laundry facilities, public Internet, airport shuttle, no-smoking rooms, no elevator* ⎟⊚⎜ *AI (packages available)* ⊟*MC, V* ⊘*Closed Feb. and Mar.*

SPORTS & THE OUTDOORS

The focus here is on the island's environment, not the one underwater. Snorkeling and swimming are both good here (do take the daily snorkeling trip), but nature walks through the varied and spectacular landscapes are the primary attraction. Conditions can be hot and, on some tracks, demanding: wear sturdy shoes and take drinking water, sunscreen, and a map of the island. The Lodge has morning and afternoon beach and island drop-offs/pickups (you walk one way). All bushwalking guests must sign in and out, ensuring their safe return.

ARRIVING & DEPARTING

BY BOAT   Hinchinbrook is a 50-minute ferry ride from the mainland town of Cardwell, which is 190 km (118 mi) south of Cairns and 161 km (100 mi) north of Townsville. Scheduled ferries depart from Cardwell at 9 AM and return at 4 PM. Round-trip fare is A$96. Nonscheduled departures can be arranged for A$120. Contact the Rainforest and Reef Information Centre for more information.

> ### THE NOT-SO-BEATEN TRACK
>
> The famed Thorsborne Trail runs the length of Hinchinbrook Island's east coast. The spectacular walk takes three to four days and includes some difficult sections, steep climbs, and river crossings. Carry plenty of water, gear, and supplies (as well as all your rubbish). It's not for the faint-hearted, especially after rain. It's best to be well prepared, join an experienced group if you can, and check weather conditions. Catch a ferry from Lucinda on the mainland to the island's southern end, then follow the marked trail for 32 km (20 mi). Book well in advance. ⊕ *www.epa.qld.com.au.*

DUNK ISLAND

A member of the Family Islands, this 2,397-acre island is divided by a hilly spine that runs its entire length. The eastern side consists mostly of national park, with dense rain forest and secluded beaches accessible only by boat. Beautiful paths have been created through the rain forest, where you might be lucky enough to glimpse a Ulysses butterfly—a beautiful blue variety with a wingspan that can reach 6 inches. Dunk is located 4½ km (2 mi) from Mission Beach on the mainland, making it a popular spot for day-trippers.

WHERE TO STAY & EAT

$–$$ ✕▣**Voyages Dunk Island.** Coconut palms, flowering hibiscus, and frangipani surround this elegantly informal, family-oriented resort on the island's west side. Spacious beach front suites and rooms have split-level designs (bedroom upstairs, living area downstairs) and glass doors leading onto big balconies, as well as luxurious appointments such as minibars and bathrobes; suites also have CD players. Airy garden rooms lack beach views but sit among tropical gardens, a short stroll from the main resort. Beachfront and garden rooms can be configured to suit families and groups. Beachcomber Restaurant, with its polished wood floors and killer views, serves tropical Australian cuisine, with lots of local seafood and two themed buffet dinners weekly. The Plantation Bar and Deck, overlooking the beachfront pool, serves modern brasserie-style food, gourmet sandwiches, salads, and Asian dishes, and has live music most nights. Get light lunches and fresh seafood at the rustic Jetty Café. Five-course dinners on the sand and picnic hampers can also be arranged. Although the resort touts itself as an activity-fueled holiday spot (a broad menu of activities includes social and water sports, fitness classes, and bushwalks), relaxation is easily found beachside, poolside, or at the resort's Spa of Peace and Plenty. Kids stay and eat for free. *⌂ Voyages, GPO 3859, Sydney, NSW2000* ☎*1300/134044 or 02/8296–8010* ✉*bookings@voyages. com.au* ⊕*www.voyages.com/dunk* ☎*160 rooms/suites* ♿*In-room: safe, refrigerator/minibar, dial-up. In-hotel: 5 restaurants, room service, 2 bars, golf course, tennis courts (indoor, outdoor), pools, gym, spa, beachfront, water sports, children's programs (ages 3–12, fee), laundry facilities, laundry service, concierge, public Internet, no-smoking rooms* ▭*AE, DC, MC, V* �|◎|*BP, MAP available.*

SPORTS & THE OUTDOORS

In addition to reef cruises and fishing charters, the resort has many choices of land and water sports. Rates include a dozen-plus sports; you'll pay extra for beach and rain-forest horseback rides, kayak and bike tours, golf and archery, as well as activities requiring fuel—skydiving, water skiing, tube rides, wake boarding. Prices range from A$35 to A$60. The resort also organizes fishing, snorkeling and scuba diving trips (from A$140, dives A$35–A$80), scenic flights, and beach drop-offs. Golf, tennis, snorkeling, and boomerang-throwing lessons are free. Half-hour pool scuba lessons are A$20; PADI-accredited dive courses cost from A$385. The resort provides a bushwalking map of the island's well-maintained trails. Kids will enjoy the island's farm, Coonanglebah; you can also visit the island's artists colony.

ARRIVING & DEPARTING

BY BOAT **Quick Cat Cruises** (☎07/4068–7289 ⊕*www.quickcatcruises.com.au*) runs fast, comfortable catamarans to Dunk Island Resort from Clump Point Jetty at Mission Beach four times daily. Departures are at 8:30, 10, 2, and 4, returning at 9:15, 1:30, 3:30, and 4:30. The round-trip fare is A$48; one way is A$24. Quick Cat also runs Barrier Reef cruises for A$155 from Mission Beach or Dunk Island. **Mission Beach-Dunk Island Connections** (☎07/4059–2709) runs coaches from Cairns, the northern beaches, and Cairns airport that connect with all Quickcat services.

Despite the very choppy ride, the **Mission Beach-Dunk Island Water Taxi** (☎07/4068–8310 ⊕*www.missionbeachwatertaxi.com*) is the best option for day-trippers. It departs from Mission Beach at 8:30, 9, 11, 12:30, 2:30, and 4, returning at 9, 10, noon, 2, 3:30, and 4:45. It's necessary to disembark in shallow waters, so take care to keep your luggage from getting wet (though help is available). The round-trip fare costs A$25 for day-trippers, A$30 for those not returning the same day.

BY PLANE Dunk Island has its own landing strip. **Hinterland Aviation** (☎1300/134044 or 02/8296–8010 ⊕*www.voyages.com.au*) serves the island up to three times daily from Cairns (flight time 45 minutes). Private transfers are also available. You can check up to 27 kilograms (60 pounds) of luggage and bring an additional 4 kilograms (9 pounds) on board as hand luggage. Secure baggage storage is available at Cairns Airport.

BEDARRA ISLAND

This tiny, 247-acre island 5 km (3 mi) off the coast of Mission Beach has natural springs, a dense rain forest, and eight separate beaches. Bedarra Island is a tranquil getaway popular with affluent executives and entertainment notables who want complete escape. It's the only Great Barrier Reef resort with an open bar (except for exclusive Double Island, off Palm Cove), and the liquor—especially champagne—flows freely. Bedarra accommodates a maximum of 30 people, and you stay in freestanding villas hidden amid thick vegetation but just steps from golden beaches.

WHERE TO STAY & EAT

$$$$ ✕🏠 **Voyages Bedarra Island.** Elevated on stilts, the open-plan, two-
Fodor'sChoice story or split-level, tropical-style villas at this super-exclusive resort
★ blend into the island's dense vegetation. Polished wood floors, exposed beams, and expansive use of glass make for sophisticated accommodations that bear little resemblance to standard hotel rooms. Each villa has a balcony with a double hammock, a view of the ocean, a king-size bed, an entertainment system, and a complimentary minibar. Secluded luxurious pavilions and split-level Points suites are a short walk from the main compound and have ultra-modern appointments and big private decks with daybeds and oceanfront plunge pools. All meals and drinks are included in the rate—and although there's

no room service, there's a 24-hour, fully stocked open bar. The restaurant's modern Australian cuisine showcases seafood and tropical fruit, and despite a daily-changing à la carte menu, you are urged to request dishes. No children under 15 are allowed, but this is no place for anyone not of legal drinking age. ⌖ *Voyages, Box 3589, Sydney, NSW, 2000* ☏ *02/8296–8010 or 1300/134044* ✐ *bookings@ voyages.com.au* ⊕ *www.voyages. com.au/bedarra* ⇄ *12 villas, 4 bungalows* ⌂ *In-room: refrigerator/ minibar, DVD, dial-up. In-hotel: safe, restaurant, bar, tennis court, pool, gym, spa, beachfront, diving, water sports, laundry facilities, laundry service, concierge, public Internet, airport shuttle, no kids under 15, no-smoking rooms* ☰ *AE, DC, MC, V* ⍔ *FAP.*

> ### PACKING TIPS
>
> Even if you plan on diving, pack light for your Barrier Reef vacation—especially if you're flying in on light aircraft. Most resort dive shops have newish, well-maintained gear, so at most, bring your favorite mask-snorkel set and dive computer. Do bring sunscreen, sturdy lightweight footwear for exploring island interiors, a wide-brimmed hat because the sun is fierce here, something smart for after dark, and a sweater/windbreaker for boat trips and the odd cool day. Throw in a compact camera for all those glorious photo ops, too.

SPORTS & THE OUTDOORS

Bedarra's geared for relaxation (think massages on the beach), but there's plenty to engage active guests. Snorkeling is possible around the island, although the water can get cloudy during summer rains. You can also windsurf, scuba dive, paddle-ski, sail catamarans, or fish. Other sporting activities, including transfers, can be organized on nearby Dunk Island, and fishing and diving charters can be arranged.

ARRIVING & DEPARTING

BY BOAT Bedarra Island lies a few minutes away by boat from Dunk Island. Boat transfers are included in the rate.

TOUR OPERATORS

To get to the Barrier Reef from Bedarra, you have to return to Dunk Island, from which all reef excursions depart.

FITZROY ISLAND

This ruggedly picturesque, heavily forested national park has vegetation ranging from rain forest to heath, and an extensive fringing reef for snorkeling and diving. Only 6 km (4 mi) from Cairns (less than an hour's cruise), the 988-acre island is popular with day-trippers. From June to August, manta rays and humpback whales swim around the island as part of their migratory route.

WHERE TO STAY & EAT

Fitzroy Island Resort, the island's only accommodation, was closed for redevelopment at the time this book went to press. It is expected to reopen early in 2008. In the meantime, day-trippers can get food and drinks at the bar and café now located at the Beach Bar at the southern end of the island, and can hire water sports gear from the adjacent Beach Hire Hut.

¢–$$ ✕🖼️**Fitzroy Island Resort.** The extensively redeveloped reef retreat, freshly reopened in early 2008, will have four dozen brand-new two-bedroom dual-key apartments with a luxurious Balinese feel; upgraded dorm rooms are complete with ensuites and air-conditioning. The new day-tripper and entertainment complex has an à la carte restaurant and bar, a day spa, a dive shop, and conference facilities. There's a boutique selling beach and resort wear, plus a kiosk, mini-mart, bakery, and ice-cream parlour. ⌂ *Fitzroy Island Resort, 52-54 Fearnley St., Cairns, QLD, 4870* ☎ *07/4051–9588* ⊕ *www.fitzroyisland.com. au* 🛏 *48 apartments, 32 bunk rooms* ⌂ *In-room: refrigerator, kitchen (some), dial-up (some). In-hotel: restaurants, bars, pool, spa, diving, water sports, laundry facilities, public Internet, no-smoking rooms* ▭ *AE, DC, MC, V.*

SPORTS & THE OUTDOORS

Day-trippers can rent catamarans, paddle-skis, fishing, diving and snorkeling gear, and stinger suits from the Beach Hire Hut at the southern end of Fitzroy Island. Here, you can also arrange sea-kayaking tours for A$113, introductory scuba dives for A$65, and guided certified dives for A$50. There are also daily glass-bottom boat tours. The new resort, opening in early 2008, has a dedicated dive shop.

ARRIVING & DEPARTING

BY BOAT   The **Fitzroy Ferries** (☎ *07/4030–7907*), which take 45 minutes to reach the island, depart daily at 8:30 AM from Marlin Marina in Cairns, returning at 5 PM. Between April and December there is an additional departure at 10:30 AM and an additional return at 3 PM. Round-trip fare is A$42. The company also operates a high-speed vessel that gets you there in less than 30 minutes, departing daily at 12:30 PM and costing A$52, round-trip.

LIZARD ISLAND

★   The small, upscale resort on secluded Lizard Island is the farthest north of any Barrier Reef hideaway. At 2,500 acres, it's larger than and quite different from other islands in the region. Composed mostly of granite, Lizard has a remarkable diversity of vegetation and terrain, where grassy hills give way to rocky slabs interspersed with valleys of rain forest.

Ringed by stretches of white-sand beaches, the island is actually a national park with some of the best examples of fringing coral of any of the resort areas. Excellent walking trails lead to key lookouts with spectacular views of the coast. The highest point, Cook's Look (1,180 feet), is the historic spot from which, in August 1770, Captain Cook finally spied a passage through the reef that had held him captive for a thousand miles. Large monitor lizards, for which the island is named, often bask in this area.

★ Diving and snorkeling in the crystal-clear waters off Lizard Island are a dream. **Cod Hole,** 20 km (12 mi) from Lizard Island, ranks as one of the best dive sites in the world. Massive potato cod swim right up to you like hungry puppies—an awesome experience, considering these fish weigh 300 pounds and are more than 6 feet long. In the latter part of the year, when black marlin are running, Lizard Island becomes the focal point for big-game anglers.

WHERE TO STAY & EAT

$$$$
Fodor's Choice
★

✕⊞ **Voyages Lizard Island.** One of Australia's premier resorts, this property has stylishly appointed beachside suites and sumptuous villas with sail-shaded decks and views of the turquoise bay, as well as an elegant pavilion on the point. The large, comfortable rooms, decorated in oceanic blues, sand, and white, have polished wood floors and blinds, ceiling fans, CD players, and private verandas. An on-site spa offers a range of health and beauty treatments, as well as relaxing massages. The Departure Lounge, overlooking the pool, incorporates Azure day spa, a compact gym, and a guest lounge with TV, video, and free broadband Internet access. Meals, included in the rate, change daily, and emphasize seafood and tropical fruits; dinner here might be coral trout with passionfruit sauce. An excellent wine list complements the menu. *Voyages, GPO 5389, Sydney, NSW, 2000* ☎*02/8296–8010 or 1300/134044* ✒bookings@voyages.com.au ⊕*www.voyages.com.au/ lizard* ⟿*39 villas, 1 pavilion* ⌂*In-room: safe, refrigerator/minibar, no TV, dial-up. In-hotel: safe, 2 restaurants, bar, tennis court, pool, gym, spa, beachfront, diving, water sports, laundry facilities, laundry service, public Internet, no kids under 15, no-smoking rooms* ▭*AE, DC, MC, V* ⦿*FAP.*

SPORTS & THE OUTDOORS

The lodge has catamarans, outboard dinghies, paddle skis, and fishing supplies. There is superb snorkeling around the island's fringing coral, or take a glass-bottom boat tour. Guided walks and nature slide shows get guests in touch with the local flora and fauna. Arrange a picnic hamper with the kitchen staff, and you can take a rowboat or sailboat out for an afternoon on your own private beach. All these activities are included in your room rate.

FISHING Lizard Island is one of the big-game-fishing centers in Australia, with several world records set here in the last decade. Fishing is best between August and December, and giant black marlin weighing more than 1,200 pounds are no rarity. The folks from Voyages Lizard Island run half- and full-day trips on the outer reef on its 51-foot cruiser, *Serranidae*; the cost, including tackle and light refreshments, is A$1,850 for a half-day trip and A$2,050 for a full-day trip with lunch, for up to four people. Inner reef trips are also available for A$1,350, half-day outer reef trips cost A$1,600, for up to four people. Marlin fishing trips are available in season (August to early January).

SCUBA DIVING The resort arranges supervised scuba-diving and snorkeling trips to the inner and outer reef, as well as local dives. An introductory one-dive course, including classroom and beach sessions, is A$175. Half- or full-day reef trips are A$130/A$180, plus you can hire gear. If you have a queasy stomach, take ginger or seasickness tablets before heading out to the reef, as crossings between dive sites in the exposed ocean can make for a bumpy ride.

ARRIVING & DEPARTING

BY PLANE Lizard Island has its own small airstrip served by **Hinterland Aviation** (☎ *1300/134044* ⊕*www.voyages.com.au*). The flights depart twice a day from Cairns, departing at 12:30 and 3:25, returning at 11 and 2; the flight takes 45–55 minutes and costs A$398 per person, round-trip. You can also arrange charter flights to the island through Hinterland Aviation.

TOUR OPERATORS

The reefs around Lizard Island have some of the best marine life and coral anywhere. There's a 16-km (10-mi), full-day snorkeling and diving trip to the outer reef, which takes you to the world-famous Cod Hole (A$180 for the boat trip, plus A$130 for two optional dives and A$30 for dive gear). There are also half-day inner reef trips (A$130, plus A$70 for one optional dive and A$20 for dive gear). Glass-bottom boat and snorkeling trips, guided walks, nature slide shows, and the use of catamarans, paddle skis, and motorized dinghies are included in guests' rates.

GREAT BARRIER REEF ESSENTIALS

TRANSPORTATION

8

BY AIR

Regular boat and air services are available to most of the Great Barrier Reef resorts, but because all of the destinations are islands, they require extra travel time. Generally, island launches and charter flights are timed to connect with domestic flights, but do double-check, and be sure to schedule other transport (flights, buses, trains) to coordinate with your resort's transfer schedule.

Smaller aircraft and helicopter pilots follow strict weight guidelines, often no more than 15 kg (33 pounds) per person, including hand baggage. Travel light, or separate excess baggage before check-in and store it in the secure airport facilities. If you're a diver, just bring a mask and snorkel, and rent other gear from resort dive shops. *For information about reaching the islands, see Arriving and Departing under individual island headings.*

BY BOAT

Several operators provide skipper-yourself charters to explore the Whitsundays. Most have a fleet of sailing yachts, catamarans, and motor cruisers; a five-day minimum charter period; and discounts for multi-day hire. Some also operate crewed charters.

Cumberland Charter Yachts, a well-established operator, has 28 well-maintained boats in 23 styles, permits for 74 islands, and 43 anchorages. Costs start at A$2,175 for five nights on a Beneteau 311 monohull, carrying up to six.

Queensland Yacht Charters have been in business more than 20 years and have cats and yachts for bareboat charter—from A$400 per night, you can skipper your own small yacht with up to three others.

Whitsunday Rent a Yacht has a fleet of 46 2- to 12-berth vessels. Charter a 2- to 4-person yacht for A$38 per night, or a 35-foot motor cruiser carrying eight people for A$465 per night, with a five-night minimum. The company also runs crewed charters with customized itineraries.

Whitsunday Private Yacht Charters has a minimum of five nights/six days for all charters, and 17 sailing craft including new sailing and motor cruisers for hire for A$430–$1,050 per night; and luxury, all-inclusive crewed charters from A$2,300 per night for two people (minimum three nights).

Sunsail Australia, a huge Asia-Pacific operator, has a fleet of 40 yachts and catamarans ranging from 32 to 50 feet, based on Hamilton Island. The company's large cruising area ranges from Bowen to Mackay. Self-skippered charters start from around A$100 per person, per night, depending on the vessel, numbers, and length of hire.

Contacts Cumberland Charter Yachts (⊠ *Abel Point Marina, Airlie Beach, QLD, 4802* ☎ *07/4946–7500 or 1800/075101* ⊕ *www.ccy.com.au*).

Queensland Yacht Charters (⊠ *Abel Point Marina, Airlie Beach, QLD, 4802* ☎ *07/4946–7400* ⊕ *www.yachtcharters.com.au*).

Sunsail Australia (⌂ *Box 65, Hamilton Island, QLD, 4803* ☎ *07/4948–9510 or 1800/803988* ⊕ *www.sunsail.com.au*).

Whitsunday Private Yacht Charters (⊠ *Abel Point Marina, Airlie Beach, QLD, 4802* ☎ *07/4946–6880 or 1800/075055* ⊕ *www.whitsunday-yacht.com.au*).

Whitsunday Rent a Yacht (⊠ *Shute Harbour, Airlie Beach, QLD, 4802* ☎ *07/4946–9232 or 1800/075111* ⊕ *www.rentayacht.com.au*).

CONTACTS & RESOURCES

BANKS & EXCHANGE SERVICES

Resorts on the following islands have money-changing facilities: Daydream, Fitzroy, Hamilton, Hayman, Lindeman, Lizard, Long, Orpheus, and South Molle. However, it's better to change money before arriving on the island, as rates are generally more favorable elsewhere. Hamilton Island has a National Australia Bank branch with an ATM. Bedarra, Brampton, Dunk, Hinchinbrook, Heron, and Lady Elliott islands have limited currency-exchange facilities and no ATMs.

Bank National Australia Bank (⊠ *Hamilton Island, Whitsunday Islands, QLD* ☎ *13–2265*).

CAMPING

Camping is popular on the myriad islands of the Whitsunday group. To pitch a tent on islands lying within national parks, you need a A$4.50 permit from the Queensland Parks and Wildlife Service. The Whitsunday Information Centre, on the Bruce Highway at Proserpine, is open Monday and Wednesday to Friday 8:30–5:30, Tuesday 9:30–5:30, and weekends 10–4.

Contacts Queensland Parks and Wildlife Service (✉ *160 Ann St., Brisbane, QLD, 4002* ☎ *07/3224–8816 or 1300/723684* ⊕ *www.epa.qld.gov.au).*

Whitsunday Information Centre (✉ *Box 83, Proserpine, QLD, 4802* ☎ *07/4945– 3711 or 1800/801252* ⊕ *www.tourismwhitsundays.com* ✉ info@tourismwhitsundays. com.au).*

EMERGENCIES

Emergencies are handled by the front desk of the resort on each island, which can summon aerial ambulances or doctors. Remote islands have what are known as flying doctor kits, which contain a range of medicines and medical equipment. Hamilton Island has its own doctor; some other island resorts have staff with nursing and/or medical training.

MAIL, SHIPPING & THE INTERNET

E-mail and Internet access is available everywhere, though connectivity may be limited and some resorts actively discourage getting online.

Australia Post has an official outlet on Hamilton Island. Other islands offer postal services from reception desks at each resort. You can also arrange special mail services, such as DHL and Federal Express, but overnight delivery isn't guaranteed.

Mail Services Australia Post (✉ *Hamilton Island, Whitsunday Islands, QLD* ☎ *07/4946–8238).*

TELEPHONES

International direct-dial telephones are available throughout the islands. You can use calling cards at any resort, and most islands listed in this chapter now have at least some cell-phone reception, though you'll have problems getting a signal from South Long Island Nature Lodge and parts of Hinchinbrook Island.

TOURS

BOAT CHARTERS FROM AIRLIE BEACH The Whitsundays are a boat-lover's haven, and there's an entire cottage industry of boating charters that will take you out to the reef for longer than a day trip. Barefoot Cruises operates three- and six-night cruises around the Whitsunday Islands on three distinctive vessels that vary with respect to comfort and price. The 115-foot *Reef Odyssey* is the largest, taking 39 passengers; the 72-foot luxury schooner *Windjammer* is the smallest, taking just 9; in between is the *Coral Trekker*, a 75-year-old, fully restored Norwegian-built sailing ship. From A$1,200–A$1,680 per person, twin-share, for a three-night, all-inclusive cruise.

Oz Adventure Sailing has skippered charters that provide a high level of service on a range of cruising vessels, including meticulously restored tall ships, comfortable catamarans, and superfast maxi racing yachts. Several vessels have onboard diving options, and sailing guests are given opportunities to handle the workings of classic, contemporary, and specialized yachts. For A$339, you can take a two-day, two-night sailing trip on a classic cruising vessel.

Southern Cross Sailing Adventures, the longest-running crewed sailing operator in Airlie Beach, runs two- to six-day sailing holidays on one of eight distinctive sailing vessels (including onetime World Cup racer *Ragamuffin II,* Whitbread Around the World racing maxi *British Defender,* and the 103-year-old tall ship *Solway Lass*). Costs start at A$299 per person for a one-night, two-day maxi-yacht charter.

Sunsail, the world's largest boating holiday company, is based on Hamilton Island but sails all round the Whitsundays. It has a fleet of 40 vessels, and runs charters over a vast cruising area. Most are self-skippered, but you can hire crew; itineraries are flexible. Prices start from A$390 per night for a four-person yacht. Sunsail also runs sailing lessons.

Contacts Barefoot Cruises (☎ *07/4946–1777* ⊕ *www.barefootcruises.com.au*).

Oz Adventure Sailing (☎ *1300/653100* ⊕ *www.ozsailing.com.au*).

Southern Cross Sailing Adventures (☎ *1800/675790* ⊕ *www.soxsail.com.au*).

Sunsail (☎ *07/4948–9150 or 1800/803988* ⊕ *www.sunsail.com.au*).

BOAT
CHARTERS
FROM CAIRNS

Divers can hop on Explorer Venture's 72-foot, 18-passenger *Nimrod Explorer,* which runs four- to eight-day trips to the Ribbon Reefs and Cod Hole and out to Osprey and Holmes Reef in the Coral Sea, skirting Cooktown and the far North Queensland coastline en route. Scenic low-level flights are included. Packages start from A$1,095 per person.

Coral Princess runs three-, four-, and seven-night cruises that leave from either Cairns or Townsville on a comfortable 54-passenger, expedition-style ship. There are stops for snorkeling, guided coral-viewing, and hikes through unspoiled rain forest. Marine biologists guide excursions and give lectures. Divers can rent equipment on board. Lessons are also available. Prices start at A$1,375 for a three-night, four-plus-dive live-aboard trip, twin share.

Great Adventures Reef and Green Island Cruises runs full- and half-day tours in fast catamarans from Cairns to Green Island and the Outer Barrier Reef. Trips may include barbecue lunches, snorkeling, scuba diving, parasailing, semisubmersible trips, glass-bottom boat trips, and helicopter tours; all include snorkeling. A Green Island eco-tour, including an interpretative walk and either snorkeling or a glass-bottom boat tour is A$60; a Green Island lunch cruise costs A$75; and a full day's cruise to the Outer Reef, including buffet lunch, is A$174.

Ocean Spirit Cruises conducts four-hour and full-day tours aboard the well-maintained, spacious *Ocean Spirit* and the smaller *Ocean Spirit II* and *III* for A$110–A$179 per person. A daily trip to Michaelmas Cay (a seabird nesting island located 43 km [27 mi] from Cairns) or Upolu Cay (a sand island 29 km [18 mi] from Cairns) includes four hours at the Great Barrier Reef, coral viewing in a semisubmersible (at Upolu Cay), snorkeling, and a big seafood lunch. Introductory diving lessons (A$95–A$150) and certified dives (A$55–A$110) are available. Ocean Spirit Cruises also runs a nightly three-hour, four-course dinner cruise along Trinity Inlet, with live entertainment and a seafood buffet, for A$79. Quicksilver Connections has well-run sightseeing, snorkeling, and diving tours on sleek, fast catamarans to coral cays and reef activity platforms on the outer Barrier Reef (A$186) and Low Isles (A$132). On the reef cruise, you can take an optional Sea Walker helmeted seabed walk for an additional A$134; or scuba dive for an extra A$99–A$134. Everyone pays A$5 reef tax. Trips depart daily from Cairns, Palm Cove, and Port Douglas.

Cruise Whitsundays runs a full-day dive-snorkel cruise to Knuckle Reef Lagoon on the Great Barrier Reef for A$215 per snorkeler, A$315 per introductory diver, including gear and lunch; and a day-long sailing cruise on super-fast purple catamaran *Camira,* with a stop at Whitehaven Beach, big BBQ lunch, snorkeling gear, and all drinks (including alcoholic ones) for A$135. There are free pick-ups from South Molle, Daydream, and Hayman islands, and from Airlie and Cannonvale on the mainland.

Contacts Coral Princess (07/4040–9999 or 1800/079545 ⊕ www.coralprincess. com.au).

Cruise Whitsundays (07/4946–4662 or 1800/426403 ⊕ www.cruisewhitsundays. com.au).

Explorer Ventures (07/4031–5566 ⊕ www.explorerventures.com).

Great Adventures Reef and Green Island Cruises (07/4044–9944 ⊕ www. greatadventures.com.au).

Ocean Spirit Cruises (07/4031–2920 ⊕ www.oceanspirit.com.au).

Quicksilver Connections (07/4087–2100 or 07/4031–4299 ⊕ www.quick-silvergroup.com.au).

VISITOR INFORMATION

Tourist Information **General tourist information** (⊕ www.queenslandholidays. com.au). **Queensland Parks and Wildlife Service Rainforest and Reef Information Centre** (✉ Box 74, Cardwell, QLD, 4849 07/4066–8601 ⊕ www.epa. qld.gov.au). **Queensland Parks and Wildlife Service Reef and National Parks Information Centre** (✉ Box 5391, Townsville, QLD, 4810 07/4722–5224 ⊕ www.epa.qld.gov.au).

Adelaide & South Australia

WORD OF MOUTH

"I would certainly recommend popping into Coober Pedy. I doubt you'll see anywhere else quite like it. Where else in the world can you 'noodle' for opals. There are noodling pits out front of a number of opal stores—my son (who was 9 at the time) couldn't pass one without having a good look and a noodle to see if he might not have some luck and find a good opal."

—stormbird

Updated by
Melanie Ball

RENOWNED FOR ITS CELEBRATIONS OF the arts, its multiple cultures, and its bountiful harvests from vines, land, and sea, South Australia is both diverse and divine. Here you can taste some of the country's finest wines, sample from its best restaurants, and admire some of the world's most valuable gems. Or, skip the state's sophisticated options and unwind on wildlife-rich Kangaroo Island, hike in the Flinders Ranges, or live underground like opal miners in the vast Outback.

Spread across a flat saucer of land between the Mt. Lofty ranges and the sea, the capital city of Adelaide is easy to explore. The wide streets of its 1½-square-km (½-square-mi) city center are organized in a simple grid that's ringed with parklands. The plan was laid out in 1836 by William Light, the colony's first surveyor-general, making Adelaide the only early-Australian capital not built by English convict labor. Today Light's plan is recognized as being far ahead of its time. This city of 1.1 million still moves at a leisurely pace, free of the typical urban menace of traffic jams and glass canyons.

Nearly 90% of South Australians live in the fertile south around Adelaide, because the region stands on the very doorstep of the harshest, driest land in the most arid of Earth's populated continents. Jagged hills and stony deserts fill the parched interior, which is virtually unchanged since the first settlers arrived. Desolate terrain and temperatures that top 48°C (118°F) have thwarted all but the most determined efforts to conquer the land. People who survive this region's challenges do so only through drastic measures, such as in the far-northern opal-mining town of Coober Pedy, where residents live underground.

Still, the deserts hold great surprises, and many clues to the country's history before European settlement. The ruggedly beautiful Flinders Ranges north of Adelaide hold Aboriginal cave paintings and fossil remains from when the area was an ancient seabed. Lake Eyre, a great salt lake, filled with water in the year 2000 for only the fourth time in its recorded history. The Nullarbor ("treeless") Plain stretches west across state lines in its tirelessly flat, ruthlessly arid march into Western Australia.

Yet South Australia is, perhaps ironically, gifted with the good life. It produces most of the nation's wine, and the sea ensures a plentiful supply of lobster and famed King George whiting. Cottages and guesthouses tucked away in the countryside around Adelaide are among the most charming and relaxing in Australia. Farther afield, unique experiences like watching seal pups cuddle with their mothers on Kangaroo Island would warm any heart. South Australia may not be grand in reputation, but its attractions are extraordinary, and after a visit you'll know you've indulged in one of Australia's best-kept secrets.

9

EXPLORING ADELAIDE & SOUTH AUSTRALIA

South Australia comprises the dry hot north and the greener, more-temperate south. The green belt includes Adelaide and its surrounding hills and orchards, the Barossa Region and Clare Valley vineyards, the beautiful Fleurieu Peninsula, and the cliffs and lagoons of the mighty Murray, Australia's longest river. Offshore, residents of Kangaroo Island live at a delightfully old-fashioned pace, savoring their domestic nature haven.

The best way to experience this diverse state is by road. In general, driving conditions are excellent, although minor lanes are unpaved. It's two hours from Adelaide to the wine regions, the southern coast, and most other major sights. The most direct route to the Flinders Ranges is via the Princes Highway and Port Augusta, but a more-interesting route takes you through the Clare Valley vineyards. Two classic train journeys also wind through this state: the *Ghan,* which runs north via Alice Springs to Darwin, and the *Indian Pacific,* which crosses the Nullarbor Plain to reach Perth.

ABOUT THE RESTAURANTS

Adelaide has more restaurants per capita than anywhere else in Australia, so travelers are spoiled for choice when dining in town. Restaurants in Adelaide and the surrounding regions favor Mod-Oz cuisine, with main dishes showcasing oysters, crayfish, and whiting prepared with Asian and Mediterranean flavors. Bush foods are also popular; look for *quandongs* (native plums), wattle seed, and kangaroo.

Many restaurants are closed Monday and Tuesday, and even Wednesday in more rural spots. Same-day reservations are recommended across the board as a courtesy to the restaurant. Some upscale institutions require booking well in advance, and tables are tight during major city festivals and holidays.

WHAT IT COSTS IN AUSTRALIAN DOLLARS					
	$$$$	$$$	$$	$	¢
AT DINNER	over A$50	A$36–A$50	A$21–A$35	A$10–A$20	under A$10

Prices are for a main course at dinner.

ABOUT THE HOTELS

South Australia abounds with delightful lodgings. Bed-and-breakfasts are tucked into contemporary studios, converted cottages and stables, restored homesteads, and grand mansions. Modern resorts sprawl along the coastal suburbs, the Barossa Valley, and other tourist centers, while intimate properties for 10 or fewer guests nestle in hidden corners of the land. Budget hotels have basic rooms with beds and coffee-making facilities.

WHAT IT COSTS IN AUSTRALIAN DOLLARS					
	$$$$	$$$	$$	$	¢
FOR TWO PEOPLE	over A$300	A$201–A$300	A$151–A$200	A$100–A$150	under A$100

Prices are for two people in a standard double room in high season, including tax and service, based on the European Plan (with no meals) unless otherwise noted.

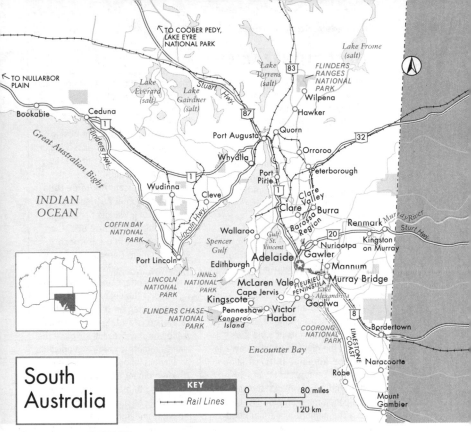

TO COOBER PEDY,
LAKE EYRE
NATIONAL PARK

TO NULLARBOR
PLAIN

South Australia

KEY
Rail Lines
0   80 miles
0   120 km

TIMING

Adelaide has the least rainfall of all Australian capital cities, and the midday summer heat is oppressive. The Outback in particular is too hot for comfortable touring during this time, but Outback winters are pleasantly warm. South Australia's national parks are open year-round, and the best times to visit are in spring and autumn. In summer extreme fire danger may close walking tracks, and in winter heavy rain can make some roads impassable. Boating on the Murray River and Lake Alexandrina is best from October to March, when the long evenings are bathed in soft light. The ocean is warmest from December to March.

ADELAIDE

Australians think of Adelaide as a city of churches, but Adelaide has outgrown its reputation as a sleepy country town dotted with cathedrals and spires. The Adelaide of this millennium is infinitely more complex, with a large, multiethnic population and thriving urban art and music scenes.

Bright and clean, leafy Adelaide is a breeze to explore, with a grid pattern of streets surrounded by parks. The heart of the greenbelt is

GREAT ITINERARIES

Many of the state's attractions are an easy drive or bus ride from Adelaide. However, for a taste of the real South Australia a trip to a national park or to the Outback is definitely worth the extra travel time. Short flights between destinations make any journey possible within a day or overnight, but the more time you leave yourself to explore the virtues of this underrated state, the better.

IF YOU HAVE 3 DAYS

Spend a leisurely day in **Adelaide** enjoying the museums and historic sights, as well as the bustling Central Market. Take a sunset stroll along the Torrens, then have dinner and drinks at one of the city's vibrant restaurants or wine bars. Spend the night, then take Day 2 to tour the **Adelaide Hills,** strolling the 19th-century streets of **Hahndorf** and other villages and taking in the panorama from atop **Mt. Lofty.** Stay the night in a charming bed-and-breakfast in one of the region's small towns, or come back down to North Adelaide and rest among the beautiful sandstone homes. Save Day 3 for wine tasting in the **Barossa Region.**

IF YOU HAVE 5 DAYS

After exploring Adelaide for a day, expand your horizons beyond the city and take a tram-car ride to the beach at Glenelg, where you can laze on the white sands and dine at tasty outposts. Spend the night here or at a B&B on the **Fleurieu Peninsula,** then take Day 3 to explore the vineyards and catch the ferry to **Kangaroo Island.** After a night here, use Day 4 to explore and appreciate the island's wildlife and untamed beauty. Return to Adelaide in the afternoon on Day

5 and drive up to the **Adelaide Hills** for sunset at **Mt. Lofty.**

IF YOU HAVE 7 DAYS

Spend Day 1 in **Adelaide** nosing through museums and picnicking in a park or on the banks of the River Torrens. After a night in the city, head into the leafy **Adelaide Hills** to meet nocturnal Australian wildlife at Warrawong Wildlife Sanctuary. Stay the night in a local B&B, then on Day 3 travel to the **Barossa Region,** where German and English influences are strong and the dozens of wineries offer tempting free tastings. Spend the evening at a country house, then on Day 4 cross to **Kangaroo Island.** Stay two nights, giving you Day 5 to fully explore the island's remote corners and unwind. On Day 6, plunge into the Outback at extraordinary **Coober Pedy** (consider flying to maximize your time). There you can eat, shop, and stay the night underground as the locals do and "noodle" (rummage) for opal gemstones. If you're a hiker, consider heading for **Flinders Ranges National Park** on Day 7 to explore one of the country's finest Outback parks.

divided by the meandering River Torrens, which passes the Festival Centre at its prettiest stretch.

WHAT TO SEE

⑪ **Adelaide Zoo.** The second-oldest in Australia, Adelaide's zoo still retains much of its original architecture. Enter through the 1883 cast-iron gates to see such animals as Sumatran tigers, Australian rain-forest birds, and chimpanzees, housed in modern, natural settings. The zoo is world renowned for its captive breeding and release programs, and rare species including the red panda and South Australia's own yellow-footed rock wallaby are among its successes. ⊠ *Frome Rd. near War Memorial Dr., City Center* ☎ *08/8267–3255* ⊕ *www.adelaidezoo.com.au* ⌼ *A$18* ⊗ *Daily 9:30–5.*

❼ **Art Gallery of South Australia.** Many famous Australian painters, including Charles Conder, Margaret Preston, Clifford Possum Tjapaltjarri, Russell Drysdale, and Sidney Nolan, are represented in this collection. Extensive Renaissance and British artworks are on display, and a separate room houses Aboriginal pieces. A café and bookshop are also on-site. ⊠ *North Terr. near Pulteney St., City Center* ☎ *08/8207–7000* ⊕ *www.artgallery.sa.gov.au* ⌼ *Free* ⊗ *Daily 10–5.*

❽ **Ayers House.** Between 1855 and 1897 this sprawling colonial structure was the home of Sir Henry Ayers, South Australia's premier and the man for whom Uluru was originally named Ayers Rock. Most rooms—including the unusual Summer Sitting Room, in the cool of the basement—have been restored with period furnishings, and the state's best examples of 19th-century costumes are displayed in changing exhibitions. Admission includes a one-hour tour. ⊠ *288 North Terr., City Center* ☎ *08/8223–1234* ⊕ *www.nationaltrustsa.org.au* ⌼ *A$8* ⊗ *Tues.–Fri. 10–4, weekends 1–4.*

❿ **Botanic Gardens.** These magnificent formal gardens include an international rose garden, giant water lilies, an avenue of Moreton Bay fig trees, acres of green lawns, and duck ponds. The Bicentennial Conservatory—the largest single-span glass house in the Southern Hemisphere—provides an environment for lowland rain-forest species such as the Cassowary Palm and Torch Ginger. Daily free guided tours leave from the trees at the restaurant at 10:30. ⊠ *North Terrace, City Center* ☎ *08/8222–9311* ⊕ *www.environment.sa.gov.au/botanicgardens* ⌼ *Gardens free, conservatory A$4.50* ⊗ *Weekdays 8–5, weekends 9–5; 7PM closing in summer.*

NEED A BREAK? Many locals insist that you haven't been to Adelaide unless you've stopped at a curbside **pie cart**, found on North Terrace outside the railway station after dark. The floater—a meat pie topped with tomato sauce (ketchup) and submerged in pea soup—is South Australia's original contribution to the culinary arts. More-traditional pie options, like beef, or chicken with veggies, are also available.

❺ **Migration Museum.** Chronicled in this converted 19th-century Destitute Asylum are the origins, hopes, and fates of some of the millions of

9

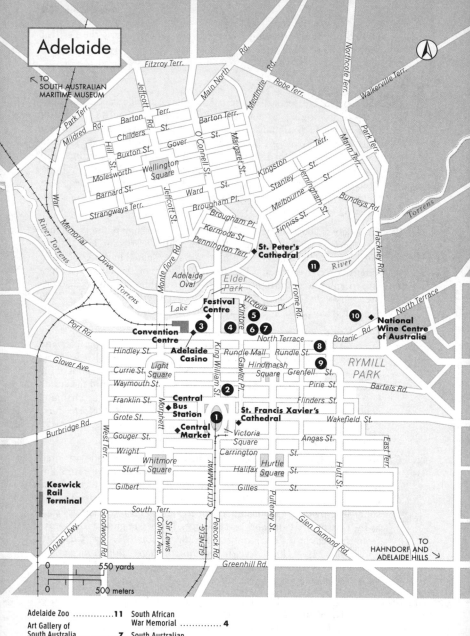

Adelaide

TO
SOUTH AUSTRALIAN
MARITIME MUSEUM

Fitzroy Terr.

Park Terr.

Jeffcott Rd.

Mildred St.

Barton Rd.

Childers St.

Buxton St.

Gover St.

Hill St.

Molesworth

Wellington
Square

Jeffcott St.

Ward

Barnard St.

Strangways Terr.

Main North Rd.

Medindie Rd.

Robe Terr.

Northcote Terr.

Walkerville Terr.

Barton Terr.

Margaret St.

O'Connell St.

Kingston Terr.

Stanley St.

Melbourne St.

Finniss St.

Jerningham St.

Mann Terr.

Bundeys Rd.

Brougham Pl.

Brougham Pl.

Kermode St.

Pennington Terr.

St. Peter's Cathedral

War Memorial Drive

River Torrens

Torrens

Port Rd.

Glover Ave.

Adelaide Oval

Lake

Montefiore Rd.

Festival Centre

Convention Centre

Adelaide Casino

Hindley St.

Currie St.

Waymouth St.

Franklin St.

Light Square

Grote St.

Central Bus Station

Central Market

Morphett St.

Gouger St.

Wright

Whitmore Square

Sturt

Gilbert

West Terr.

Burbridge Rd.

Keswick Rail Terminal

Anzac Hwy.

Goodwood Rd.

Sir Lewis Cohen Ave.

South Terr.

Elder Park

Victoria Dr.

Kintore Ave.

Gawler Pl.

King William St.

3

4

5

6 **7**

North Terrace

Rundle Mall

Rundle St.

8

Hindmarsh Square

9

Grenfell St.

Pirie St.

Flinders St.

2

1

St. Francis Xavier's Cathedral

Victoria Square

Carrington

Halifax

Hurtle Square

Gilles St.

St.

St.

Pulteney St.

CITY TRAMWAY

GLENELG

Peacock Rd.

Greenhill Rd.

11

River

Torrens

Hackney Rd.

North Terrace

10 **National Wine Centre of Australia**

Botanic Rd.

RYMILL PARK

Bartels Rd.

Wakefield St.

Angas St.

Hutt St.

East Terr.

Glen Osmond Rd.

TO
HAHNDORF AND
ADELAIDE HILLS

0   550 yards

0   500 meters

immigrants who settled in Australia during the past two centuries. The museum is starkly realistic, and the bleak welcome that awaited many migrants is graphically illustrated in the reconstructed quarters of a migrant hostel. ⊠ *82 Kintore Ave., City Center* ☎ *08/8207–7580* ⊕ *www.history.sa.gov.au* ⊠ *Free* ☉ *Weekdays 10–5, weekends 1–5.*

National Wine Centre of Australia. Timber, steel, and glass evoke the

WHAT YOU'LL SEE

As soon as you pull into Adelaide you'll be greeted with the sight of tiny stone cottages aglow in morning sunshine, or august sand-stone buildings gilded by night-time floodlights. These are visual cues to the relaxed but vibrant arts and culture that emanate from here.

ribs of a huge wine barrel, and a soaring, open-plan concourse make this a spectacular showcase for Australian wines. The Wine Discovery Journey takes you from neolithic pottery jars to a stainless-steel tank; you can even make your own virtual wine on a touch-screen computer. Some of the best vintages from more than 20 Australian wine-growing regions are also available for tasting at the Concourse Café. ⊠ *Hackney and Botanic Rds., City Center* ☎ *08/8303–3355* ⊕ *www.wineaustralia. com.au* ⊠ *Free* ☉ *9:30–5 weekdays, 10–5 weekends.*

❸ Parliament House. Ten Corinthian columns are the most striking features of this classical parliament building. It was completed in two stages 50 years apart: the west wing in 1889 and the east wing in 1939. Alongside is **Old Parliament House,** which dates from 1843. There's a free guided tour of both houses weekdays at 10 and 2 during nonsitting weeks, and on Friday only when parliament is in session. ⊠ *North Terr. at King William St., City Center* ☎ *08/8237–9467* ⊠ *Free* ☉ *Tours only.*

St. Francis Xavier's Cathedral. This church faced a bitter battle over construction after the 1848 decision to build a Catholic cathedral. It's now a prominent, decorative church with a soaring nave, stone arches through to side aisles with dark-wood ceilings, and beautiful stained-glass windows. ⊠ *Wakefield St. at Victoria Sq., City Center* ☎ *08/8231–3551* ⊠ *Free* ☉ *Mass weekdays 8 AM, 12:10, 5:45 PM, Sat. 8, 11:30 AM, and 6 PM, Sun. 7, 9, 11 AM, and 6 PM.*

St. Peter's Cathedral. The spires and towers of this cathedral dramati-cally contrast with the nearby city skyline. St. Peter's is the epitome of Anglican architecture in Australia, and an important example of grand Gothic Revival. Free 45-minute guided tours are available Wednesday at 11:30 and Sunday at 2:30. ⊠ *1–19 King William St., North Adelaide* ☎ *08/8267–4551* ⊠ *Free* ☉ *Services daily.*

❹ South African War Memorial. This statue was unveiled in 1904 to com-memorate the volunteers of the South Australian Bushmen's Corps who fought with the British in the Boer War. ⊠ *King William St. at North Terr., City Center* ☎ *No phone.*

❻ South Australian Museum. The Australian Aboriginal Cultures Gallery in this museum—the world's largest—houses 3,000 items, including cere-monial dress and paintings. Old black-and-white films show traditional

9

dancing, and touch screens convey desert life. Aboriginal guides lead tours and share personal insights. Also in the museum is an exhibition commemorating renowned Antarctic explorer Sir Douglas Mawson, after whom Australia's main Antarctic research station is named; a Fossil Gallery housing the opalized

> **CENTRAL MARKET**
>
> Don't leave Adelaide without plunging into the panoply of flavors, aromas, sounds, and colors at the Central Market, founded in 1869.

partial skeleton of a 19-foot-long plesiosaur; and a café. ☒*North Terr. near Gawler Pl., City Center* ☎*08/8207–7500* ⊕*www.samuseum. sa.gov.au* ☒*Free* ☉*Daily 10–5; tours weekdays at 11, weekends at 2 and 3; Aboriginal tours Thurs. and Fri. at 11:30.*

❾ **Tandanya Aboriginal Cultural Institute.** The first major Aboriginal cultural facility of its kind in Australia, Tandanya houses high-quality changing exhibitions of works by Aboriginal artists and a theater where you can watch didgeridoo performances (Tuesday to Friday at noon) and Torres Strait Islander dancing (weekends at noon). ☒*253 Grenfell St., City Center* ☎*08/8224–3200* ⊕*www.tandanya.com.au* ☒*A$5* ☉*Daily 10–5.*

❷ **Town Hall.** An imposing building constructed in 1863 in Renaissance style, the Town Hall was modeled after buildings in Genoa and Florence. Tours visit the Colonel Light Room, where objects used to map and plan Adelaide are exhibited. ☒*128 King William St., City Center* ☎*08/8203–7203* ☒*Free* ☉*Tours by appointment Mon. at 10.*

❶ **Victoria Square.** The fountain in the square, which is floodlighted at night, celebrates the three rivers that supply Adelaide's water: the Torrens, Onkaparinga, and Murray are each represented by a stylized man or woman paired with an Australian native bird. Shady trees and park benches attract lunching office workers, while shoppers and tourists come and go from the Glenelg Tram, which terminates here. ☒*King William, Grote, and Wakefield Sts., City Center* ☎*No phone.*

GREATER ADELAIDE

☾ **National Railway Museum.** Steam-train buffs will love this collection of locomotive engines and rolling stock in the former Port Adelaide railway yard. The finest of its kind in Australia, the collection includes enormous "mountain"-class engines and the "Tea and Sugar" train, once the lifeline for camps scattered across the deserts of South and Western Australia. ☒*Lipson St. near St. Vincent's St., Port Adelaide* ☎*08/8341–1690* ⊕*www.natrailmuseum.org.au* ☒*A$10* ☉*Daily 10–5.*

★ **Penfolds Magill Estate.** Founded in 1844 by immigrant English doctor Christopher Rawson Penfold, this working vineyard in east Adelaide is the birthplace of Australia's most famous wine, Penfolds Grange. Introduced in 1951, Grange is the flagship of a huge stable of wines priced from everyday to special-occasion selections (collectors pay thousands of dollars to complete sets of Grange). Hour-long winery tours (A$15) leave daily at 11 and 3. The Great Grange Tour is the ultimate Magill

Estate experience; over 2½ hours you visit the original Penfold family cottage, tour the winery, and enjoy a tasting of premium wines, including Grange. This tour departs at 1 PM on the first and third Sunday of each month and costs A$150 per person; reservations are essential. ✉ *78 Penfold Rd., Magill* ☎ *08/8301–5569* ⊕ *www.penfolds.com.au* ☞ *Free* ⊘ *Daily 10:30–4:30.*

♻ **South Australian Maritime Museum.** Inside a restored stone warehouse, this museum brings maritime history vividly to life with ships' figureheads, shipwreck relics, and intricate scale models. In the basement you can lie in a bunk bed aboard an 1840's immigrant ship and hear passengers telling of life and death on their journeys to South Australia. In addition to the warehouse displays, the museum includes a lighthouse and a restored steam tug at the nearby wharf. ✉ *126 Lipson St., Port Adelaide* ☎ *08/8207–6255* ⊕ *www.history.sa.gov.au/maritime/maritime. htm* ☞ *A$8.50 (lighthouse entry included); steam-tug tours from A$7 per person* ⊘ *Daily 10–5; lighthouse closed Sat.*

WHERE TO EAT

Melbourne, Gouger, O'Connell, and Rundle streets, along with the Norwood Parade and Glenelg neighborhoods, are the main eating strips. In any of these areas it's fun to stroll around until a restaurant or café takes your fancy.

CAFÉS

$–$$ ✕ **Paul's on Gouger.** Get hooked on King George whiting at this Gouger-street veteran of 60 years, which is hailed as one of Adelaide's best—and best-priced—seafood restaurants. The deep-fried baby prawns with sweet chili sauce are another local favorite. For a great view of the bustle in the open kitchen, request a table upstairs on the ship's-deck-like mezzanine floor. ✉ *79 Gouger St., City Center* ☎ *08/8231–9778* ⊟ *AE, DC, MC, V* ⊘ *No lunch weekends.*

$–$$ ✕ **The Store.** North Adelaide yuppies fuel up on aromatic coffee, fresh-squeezed juices, and simple, wholesome food here before trawling the adjacent delicatessen and upscale supermarket. Try the corn and spinach cakes, with ham, scrambled eggs, tomato, and pesto for brunch. More-substantial meals are available after 11 AM. Weekend crowds mean slow service, so grab a sidewalk table, kick back, and watch the comings and goings of couples, families, and dogs (there's a water bowl for thirsty pooches). ✉ *157 Melbourne St., North Adelaide* ☎ *08/8361–6999* ✐ info@thestore.com.au ⊟ *AE, DC, MC, V.*

$–$$ ✕ **Universal Wine Bar.** Adelaide's fashionable crowd loves this high-gloss, split-level bar-café with its giant mirrors and wine racks. Join their ranks for a coffee or organic tea, or settle in for a tasty lunch or dinner inside or at a sidewalk table. If you're lucky, the seasonal menu might include pan-seared local prawn in chili and lemon butter, or roasted free-range chicken on sweet potato and chive dumplings. South Australian oysters arrive soused with lime and a shot of Bloody Mary. Many

9

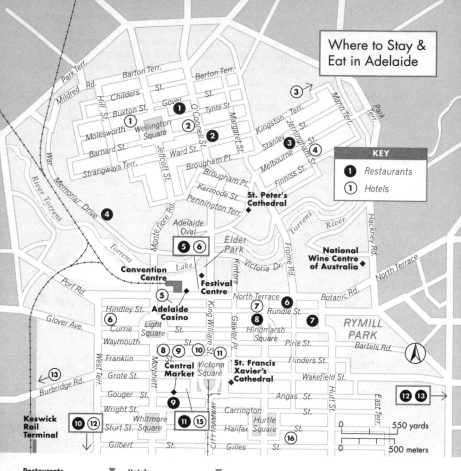

Where to Stay & Eat in Adelaide

KEY

1 *Restaurants*

1 *Hotels*

Restaurants ▼

Amalfi Pizzeria
Ristorante **6**

Blake's Restaurant
and Wine Bar **5**

The Grange **11**

Jasmin **8**

Kwik Stix **2**

Magill Estate **12**

The Manse **1**

Paul's on Gouger **9**

Red Ochre **4**

Sammy's on
the Marina **10**

The Store **3**

Universal Wine Bar **7**

Urban Bistro **13**

Hotels ▼

Adelaide Central YHA **8**

Adelaide Shores
Holiday Village **13**

Franklin Central
Apartments **9**

Levi Park **3**

Medina Grand
Adelaide Treasury **11**

North Adelaide
Heritage Group **1, 2, 4**

Oaks Plaza Pier **12**

Quest Mansions **7**

Rendezvous Allegra
Hotel Adelaide **10**

Saville City Suites **6**

The Sebel Playford **5**

Wisteria Terrace **14**

of the wines on the 300-plus list are sold by the glass. ✉*285 Rundle St., City Center* 🕾*08/8232–5000* 🖃*AE, DC, MC, V* ⊙*Closed Mon.*

ECLECTIC

$$$ ✕ **Magill Estate.** Do you inhale deeply from your wine glass before drinking? Do you know your back palate from your front? Then you're ready to join the wine buffs at this pavilion-style vineyard restaurant. The restaurant looks across vines to the city skyline and coast, and sunset is a spectacle that makes eating here a memorable experience. The menu might include such European-flavored Oz delights as prosciutto and mint-crusted lamb loin with eggplant caviar. You can enjoy the multicourse set menu, or dine à la carte. The wine list is a museum of Penfolds' finest. ✉*78 Penfold Rd., Magill* 🕾*08/8301–5551* ⌨*Reservations essential* 🖃*AE, MC, V* ⊙*Closed Sun. and Mon. No lunch Tues.–Thurs. and Sat.*

$$–$$$ ✕ **Blake's Restaurant & Wine Bar.** Rustic timber and small, cozy spaces
★ lighted by floating candles create a wine-cellar intimacy in this sophisticated spot. The innovative seasonal menu might include blue swimmer crab risotto, or Moroccan spiced lamb rump on orange couscous. The highly regarded wine list of more than 600 vintages includes some of the country's finest labels. ✉*Hyatt Regency Adelaide, North Terr., City Center* 🕾*08/8238–2381* ⌨*Reservations essential* 🖃*AE, DC, MC, V* ⊙*Closed Sun. and Tues. No lunch.*

FRENCH

$$ ✕ **The Manse.** Tailcoats were de rigueur dinner attire when this Victorian church manse was built in the heart of North Adelaide, but the dress code for the modern French gem it houses is thankfully more relaxed. Continental cuisine, such as fillet of leatherjacket with bone marrow, is prepared with flair, and special effort is made to add local ingredients to classic and contemporary dishes (try the steamed King George whiting with squid-ink linguine). Wood-burning fireplaces and an outdoor terrace make dining a pleasure any time of year. The wine list includes both cellar-aged and boutique vintage bottles. ✉*142 Tynte St., North Adelaide* 🕾*08/8267–4636* 🖃*AE, DC, MC, V* ⊙*No lunch Sat.–Thur.* ⌨*Reservations essential.*

INDIAN

$$ ✕ **Jasmin.** Wooden filigree screens, bejeweled Buddhas, and beaten-metal horses amid dark-wood tables bring India to life in this restaurant downstairs from busy Hindmarsh Square. Mostly Punjabi-style food, such as prawn sambal and tandoori barramundi, complemented by more than 100 wines from Australia's smaller vineyards and overseas, has attracted Adelaide regulars and touring international cricketers since 1980. Bats signed by teams who have dined here line the short corridor to the bathrooms. ✉*31 Hindmarsh Sq., City Center* 🕾*08/8223–7837* 🖃*AE, DC, MC, V* ⊙*Closed Sun. and Mon. No lunch Tues., Wed., and Sat.*

9

ITALIAN

$–$$ ✗**Amalfi Pizzeria Ristorante.** If not for the Australian accents here, you'd swear you were in a regional Italian eatery. The dining room is furnished with bare wooden tables, around which sit professionals and university students enthusiastically discussing life. The paper place-mat menu lists traditional pizza and pasta dishes in two sizes—appetizer and entrée—so you can sample from lots of different plates. There's also the classic *bistecca* (a thick loin steak on the bone). ⊠*29 Frome St., City Center* ☎*08/8223–1948* ▤*AE, DC, MC, V* ⊘*Closed Sun. No lunch Sat.*

MODERN AUSTRALIAN

$$$$ ✗**The Grange.** With a philosophy of pursuing "the flavor of things,"
Fodor'sChoice world-renowned chef Cheong Liew works nightly culinary magic.
★ Liew, who pioneered East-West fusion cuisine in Australia in the early 1970s, offers three- to eight-course tasting menus, most of which open with the famous "Four Dances of the Sea"—snook, raw calamari with black-ink noodles, octopus, and spiced prawn sushi. Each course can be paired with thrilling wines. Be prepared to splurge, though; this is one of South Australia's most expensive, as well as inventive, restaurants. ⊠*Hilton Hotel, 233 Victoria Sq., City Center* ✈*Box 1871, Adelaide, S.A. 5001* ☎*08/8237–0698* ✍*Reservations essential* ▤*AE, DC, MC, V* ⊘*Closed Jan. and July, and Sun.–Tues. No lunch.*

$$–$$$ ✗**Red Ochre.** A sweeping view of Adelaide is the backdrop for contemporary workings of traditional bush meats, herbs, and fruits at this riverfront restaurant. Looking across Lake Torrens to the city skyline, you can tuck into pepperleaf-spiced and crisp fried whole baby barramundi served with wild lime and paw paw salsa, or order a game platter for two and graze kangaroo, wallaby, and emu. Don't miss the wattle-seed pavlova, Red Ochre's version of Australia's famous meringue dessert. ⊠*War Memorial Dr., North Adelaide* ☎*08/8211–8555* ▤*AE, DC, MC, V* ⊘*Closed Sun. No lunch* ✍*Reservations essential.*

$$ ✗**Urban Bistro.** The interior of this restaurant is an almost clinical inter-
★ pretation of minimalism, with scalpel-blade-edge furnishings—yet the food is as imaginative as it gets. The quick-witted, friendly twenty-something staff serve up such pleasures as pecorino and hazelnut soufflé with baby celery leaves and shredded apple, and twice cooked crisp pork belly served with chili pineapple and caramel sauce. This place also has one of the best breakfasts in town; don't miss the roast Swiss brown mushrooms with thyme, olive toast, and truffle Parmesan. ⊠*160 Fullarton Rd., Rose Park, 5067* ☎*08/8331–2400* ▤*AE, DC, MC, V* ⊘*Closed Mon. No dinner Sun.* ✍*Reservations recommended.*

PAN ASIAN

$ ✗**Kwik Stix.** Delicious Asian food packs people around the dark-wood tables and into the black-upholstered booths at this O'Connell Street eatery. Food sizzles, woks clang, voices are loud, and service is borderline frantic when there's a crowd—which is often. You can walk past the open kitchen to order and pay at the high-gloss bar, then drink Australian or New Zealand wine while eating your way from Indonesia to

Japan; don't miss the spicy barramundi with crispy basil leaves. ✉42 *O'Connell St., North Adelaide* ☎*08/8239–2023* ✉*Main North and Kings Rds., Parafield* ☎*08/8258–3500* ✉*Main South Rd. at Flinders Ave., Bedford Park* ☎*08/8177–0035* ▤*AE, DC, MC, V.*

SEAFOOD

$$ ✕**Sammy's on the Marina.** Enormous fishbowl windows frame views of million-dollar yachts at this restaurant—one of Adelaide's top seafood eateries—in Glenelg's upscale Holdfast Marina. Watch the setting sun silhouette playing dolphins or a storm rolling across Gulf St. Vincent as you tuck into skewered scallops or crispy skin Atlantic salmon topped with olive tapenade. The menu here charts South Australia's ocean bounty, and the hot seafood platter (for two people) would feed a school of sharks. ✉*1–12 Holdfast Promenade, Glenelg* ☎*08/8376–8211* ⚓*Reservations essential* ▤*AE, DC, MC, V.*

WHERE TO STAY

At first glance, large international, business-style hotels seem to dominate Adelaide, but there's actually a wide choice of places to rest your head. Adelaide's accommodations are a mix of traditional mid-rise hotels, backpacker hostels, self-contained apartments, and charming bed-and-breakfasts, many in century-old sandstone buildings. With a car you'll be within easy reach of a Glenelg beach house or an Adelaide Hills B&B.

$$$$ 🏨**Rendezvous Allegra Hotel Adelaide.** Black-tile-and-timber columns
Fodor'sChoice frame the Hollywood-glamorous marble lobby of this ultrasleek,
★ upscale boutique hotel. Beveled-glass elevators with marble floors, designed to resemble the interior of a diamond, whisk you to snazzy, contemporary quarters of glass, marble, and wood. A picture window separates bathroom and bedroom. The first-floor Glasshouse restaurant can deliver treats day and night; you can work them off in the cerulean-blue tile pool, which has underwater portholes for watching the hotel entrance. ✉*55 Waymouth St., City Center, 5000* ☎*08/8115–8888* ⊕*www.rendezvoushotels.com/adelaide/* 🛏*166 rooms and 35 suites* ⚭*In-room: refrigerator, ethernet. In-hotel: restaurant, room service, bar, pool, gym, concierge, laundry service, public Wi-Fi, no-smoking rooms* ▤*AE, DC, MC, V.*

$$$$ 🏨**The Sebel Playford.** Showy chandeliers illuminate a movie-set-like
★ celebration of art nouveau in the lobby of this luxury hotel. Check your reflection in a huge gilt mirror before relaxing in a club lounge or around the grand piano in the bar, where the tables have statue bases and marble tops. Room decorations are a subtler nod to the art nouveau era. In the unusual loft suites, wrought-iron stairs climb to a king-sized bed on the mezzanine floor. The colonnaded indoor hotel pool feels like a Roman bathhouse. ✉*120 North Terr., City Center, 5000* ☎*08/8213–8888* ⊕*www.sebelplayford.com.au* 🛏*110 rooms, 72 suites* ⚭*In-room: safe (some), kitchen (some), refrigerator, ethernet. In-hotel: restaurant, room service, bar, pool, gym, concierge, laundry*

9

facilities, laundry service, public Internet, public Wi-Fi, parking (fee), no-smoking rooms ⊟*AE, DC, MC, V.*

$$$-$$$$
Fodor'sChoice
★

North Adelaide Heritage Group. Tucked into the city's leafy, oldest section, these 21 lodgings are stunningly unique. Antiques dealers Rodney and Regina Twiss have converted Heritage-listed mews houses, a meeting chapel, an Arts and Crafts manor house, and a fire station (complete with 1942 fire engine) into apartments and suites, and filled them with Australian antiques and contemporary furnishings. Each one- to four-bedroom unit has a bath or hot tub, sitting room, and kitchen, most complete with a milk-shake maker; all are charming. The Bishop's Garden apartment is the most luxurious and secluded spot in Adelaide, with a sophisticated kitchen and lounge opening into a private garden with a rock-adorned fish pool. American, lactose-free, kosher—any breakfast can be arranged. ⊠*Office: 109 Glen Osmond Rd., Eastwood, 5063* ☎☎*08/8272–1355* ⊕*www.adelaideheritage.com* ➷*10 cottages, 3 suites, 8 apartments* ⟡*In-room: kitchen (some), refrigerator, DVD (some), VCR (some), ethernet (some), dial-up (some). In-hotel: room service, no elevator, laundry facilities, laundry service, parking (no fee), no-smoking rooms* ⊟*AE, DC, MC, V.*

$$$

Saville City Suites. Step out your door at this three-story redbrick complex and you might think you're in the tropics; open-air walkways and palm trees suggest you're closer to the beach than the western-parkland end of Hindley Street. The compact apartments are decked out in pin-striped charcoal, chocolate, and cream. All have full kitchens, washing machines, and dryers. The open-plan one-bed studios feel roomier than the two-bedroom standard apartments. The complex is on the Adelaide FREE bus route. ⊠*255 Hindley St., City Center, 5000* ☎*08/8217–2500* ⊕*www.savillesuites.com* ➷*48 studios, 94 2-bedroom apartments* ⟡*In-room: kitchen, refrigerator, ethernet. In-hotel: restaurant, room service, bar, concierge, public internet, laundry facilities, laundry service, parking (fee), no-smoking rooms* ⊟*AE, DC, MC, V.*

$$$

Wisteria Terrace. Sweetcorn-yellow is the backdrop for ceiling roses and polished floorboards in this two-story 19th century bluestone terrace house on a quiet street near the southern parklands. The first-floor lounge has a wood-burning fireplace and the separate dining room opens onto a wisteria-draped courtyard. You can sleep in a king-size mahogany sleigh bed in the main bedroom, or climb the old timber staircase to three more bedrooms. It's a 15-minute walk to central Adelaide, or 5 minutes to the free Connector Bus. ⊠*26 Blackburn St., 5000* ☎*08/8364–5437* ⊕*www.adelaideoldterraces.com.au* ➷*1 house* ⟡*In-room: kitchen, refrigerator, DVD, VCR, dial-up. In-hotel: no elevator, laundry facilities, parking (no fee), no-smoking rooms* ⊟*AE, DC, MC, V* ⌾*CP.*

$$-$$$
★

Medina Grand Adelaide Treasury. Contemporary Italian furnishings in white, slate gray, and ocher are juxtaposed with 19th-century Adelaide architecture in this stylish Victoria Square hotel. Cast-iron columns, archways, and barrel-vaulted ceilings—original features of the former Treasury building—add texture to clean lines in the studio rooms and serviced apartments. The lobby lounge incorporates an 1839 sandstone wall, one of the oldest remaining colonial structures in South Australia. Great food is as close as the adjoining Treasury Restaurant. ⊠*2 Flinders St., City Center, 5000* ☎*08/8112–0000 or 1300/633462* ⊕*www.medina.com.au* ☞*20 studio rooms, 59 apartments* ⏚*In-room: safe, refrigerator (some), ethernet. In-hotel: restaurant, bar, pool, gym, laundry facilities, laundry service, public Wi-Fi, parking (fee), no-smoking rooms* ⊟*AE, DC, MC, V.*

$$–$$$ ▥**Oaks Plaza Pier.** Sea air wafts through open balcony doors in this all-apartment complex on Adelaide's favorite beach. Floor-to-ceiling windows frame either Glenelg and parkland views or white sand and turquoise sea. The spacious suites have fully-equipped kitchens and many high-tech gadgets, including Sony Playstations (fee). After a night spent exploring Glenelg's waterfront restaurants and bars, you can fall asleep in your huge, comfortable bed listening to waves washing ashore. ⊠*16 Holdfast Promenade, Glenelg, 5045* ☎*08/8350–6688 or 1300/551111* ⊕*www.theoaksgroup.com.au* ☞*121 1-bedroom apartments, 34 2-bedroom apartments, 1 3-bedroom apartment* ⏚*In-room: safe, kitchen, refrigerator, ethernet. In-hotel: restaurant, room service, bars, pool, gym, beachfront, concierge, laundry facilities, laundry service, parking (fee), no-smoking rooms* ⊟*AE, DC, MC, V.*

$–$$$ ▥**Franklin Central Apartments.** Check in here and you'll have room to move in one of Adelaide's most crowded quarters. Behind a historic facade within sniffing distance of the Central Market and Gouger Street eateries, the one-, two-, and three-bedroom apartments have everything you need for a short or long stay, including a pantry service; all are decked out in polished timbers and shades of blue. ⊠*36 Franklin St., City Center, 5000* ☎*08/8221–7050 or 1300/662288* ⊕*www.franklinapartments.com.au* ☞*62 apartments* ⏚*In-room: kitchen, refrigerator, ethernet. In-hotel: restaurant, laundry facilities, laundry service, public Wi-Fi, parking (fee), no-smoking rooms* ⊟*AE, DC, MC, V.*

$–$$ ▥**Adelaide Shores Holiday Village.** The breeze is salty, the lawns are green, and white sand is only a few lazy steps from this summery resort on the city's coastal fringe. The seldom-crowded beach beyond the dunes fronts a mix of raised two- and three-bedroom bungalows with private balconies (some have hot tubs), deluxe villas, standard holiday units, cabins, and budget vans. It's a 20-minute drive to the city, but the pools, many sports facilities, and barbecues are reasons enough to stay put. ⊠*Military Rd., West Beach, 5045* ☎*08/8355–7360* ⊕*www.adelaideshores.com.au/holidayvillage.htm* ☞*16 bungalows, 30 villas, 32 units, 16 cabins* ⏚*In-room: no phone, kitchen (some), refrigerator, DVD (some), VCR (some). In-hotel: tennis court, pools, beachfront, no elevator, laundry facilities, public Internet, parking (no fee), no-smoking rooms* ⊟*AE, DC, MC, V.*

$ ▥**Quest Mansions.** Self-catering studios and one-bedroom apartments are housed in this handsome, Heritage-listed building between North Terrace and Rundle Mall. All rooms are spacious and comfortable

9

and have complete kitchens. There are communal barbecues and a sauna on the rooftop terrace. The basement Mansions Tavern serves good counter grub, and you can charge meals back to your room at several local restaurants. ✉*21 Pulteney St., City Center, 5000* ☎*08/8232–0033* ⊕*www.questapartments.com.au* ➪*5 studios, 30 apartments* ♿*In-room: kitchen, refrigerator, Wi-Fi. In-hotel: restaurant, room service, bar, laundry facilities, parking (fee), no-smoking rooms* ▭*AE, DC, MC, V.*

¢ ▦**Adelaide Central YHA.** Mostly young people buzz around this purpose-built, city-center hostel like bees at a hive. Adelaide's only YHA far exceeds the standards of its affiliation. There's a community feel throughout the property, from the declaration of human rights on the front door, to the free big-screen movie nights and seven-day activity program, including quiz nights and Ping-Pong competitions. Bright, airy standard rooms, family rooms, and dorms (six beds maximum) have metal-frame beds and individual luggage lockers. There's a huge, modern communal kitchen, TV rooms, and a smoking lounge. Nightclubs, restaurants, and city attractions are within easy walking distance. Doors lock at 11 PM, but if you pick up the external phone, the night staff will let you in whatever the hour. ✉*135 Waymouth St., City Center, 5000* ☎*08/8414–3010* ⊕*www.yha.com.au* ➪*63 rooms* ♿*In-room: no phone, no TV, Wi-Fi. In-hotel: bicycles, laundry facilities, public Internet, public Wi-Fi, parking (fee), no-smoking rooms* ▭*AE, DC, MC, V.*

★ ⚠**Levi Park.** Port Lincoln parrots and black ducks are regulars at this caravan park overlooking the River Torrens, 5 km (3 mi) from central Adelaide. From here it's a scenic walk or cycle along a shared river path to the city, and buses pass the front gate. Grassy tent sites have river frontage, with en suite cabins and camper vans behind. A fully-equipped camp kitchen and separate children's and disabled-access bathrooms are bonuses. In the middle of the park is Adelaide's oldest surviving colonial residence. Built within five years of South Australia's settlement, Heritage-listed Vale House is now a six-suite luxury B&B. ♿*Flush toilets, partial hookups (electric and water), dump station, drinking water, guest laundry, showers, grills, picnic tables, electricity, public telephone, general store, play area* ➪*20 unpowered sites, 66 powered sites, 30 cabins* ✉*69 Lansdowne Terr., Walkerville, 5081* ☎*08/8344–2209 or 1800/442209* ⊕*www.levipark.com.au* ▭*MC, V.*

NIGHTLIFE & THE ARTS

THE ARTS

The three-week Adelaide Festival of Arts, Australia's oldest arts festival, takes place in February and March of even-numbered years. It's a cultural smorgasbord of outdoor opera, classical music, jazz, art exhibitions, comedy, and cabaret presented by some of the world's top artists. Recent highlights include Berlin's Schaubühne production of Nora and Cielo Che Danza (The Dancing Sky). Visit ⊕*www.adelaidefestival.*

com.au or contact the South Australian Visitor and Travel Centre for more information. The annual, three-day WOMADelaide Festival of world music, arts, and dance, which takes place in early March, makes noise and raises consciousness on stages in Botanic Park; see ⊕*www.womadelaide.com.au* for details.

For a listing of performances and exhibitions, look to the entertainment pages of the *Advertiser,* Adelaide's daily newspaper. The *Adelaide Review,* a free monthly arts paper, reviews exhibitions, galleries, and performances and lists forthcoming events. Tickets for most live performances can be purchased from **BASS Ticket Agency** (⊠*Adelaide Festival Centre, King William St., City Center* ☎*13–1246* ⊕*www.bass.net.au*).

The **Adelaide Festival Centre** (⊠*King William St. near North Terr., City Center* ☎*13–1246* ⊕*www.adelaidefestivalcentre.com.au*) is the city's major venue for the performing arts. The State Opera, the State Theatre Company of South Australia, and the Adelaide Symphony Orchestra perform here regularly. Performances are in the Playhouse, the Festival and Space theaters, the outdoor amphitheater, and Her Majesty's Theatre at 58 Grote Street. The box office is open Monday–Saturday 9–6.

NIGHTLIFE

BARS & CLUBS There's something going on every evening in Adelaide, although clubs are especially packed on weekends. Cover charges vary according to the night and time of entry. Nightlife for the coming week is listed in *Adelaide (Scene),* a pullout section of Thursday's edition of *The Advertiser. Rip It Up* is a free Thursday music-and-club publication aimed at the younger market. *Onion,* published fortnightly on Thursday, is Adelaide's top dance music magazine. *dB,* a twice-monthly free independent publication, covers music, arts, film, games, and dance.

9

Bars along Rundle Street and East Terrace are trendy, while Hindley and Waymouth streets are lined with traditional pubs. North Adelaide's O'Connell Street buzzes every night, and the popular Sunday-evening beer-and-banter sessions really pack in the crowds.

Austral Hotel (⊠*205 Rundle St., City Center* ☎*08/8223–4660*), the first bar in South Australia to put Coopers beer on tap, is a local favorite. You can down shooters or sip cocktails from a long list while listening to a band play or a DJ spin groovy tunes. It's open daily 11 AM–3 AM.

Botanic Bar (⊠*310 North Terr., City Center* ☎*08/8227–0799*), a cool city lounge, has cordovan banquettes encircling the U-shape, marble-top bar. Muddlers (crushed ice drinks) are the specialty, and they bring in mostly young professionals. It's open until the wee hours Tuesday to Sunday.

Cargo Club (⊠*213 Hindley St., City Center* ☎*08/8231–2327*) attracts a stylish clientele with disco and House DJs, live bands, and theme nights, such as Indian or Greek. It's open Wednesday, Friday, and Saturday 10 PM–5 AM; covers are A$5–A$10.

Earth (✉*27 Hindley St., City Center* ☎*08/8410–8838*) attracts a mixed crowd with banging club beats, DJs, commercial, house music, and flashback nights, all with lots of black lights. It's open Wednesday, Friday, and Saturday; admission is free–A$10.

★ **The Gov** (✉*59 Port Rd., Hindmarsh, 5007* ☎*08/8340–0744*) is the favorite venue of a mixed crowd. Young homeowners and long-term regulars come for Irish music sessions, all-weekend metal fests, and everything in between. Cabaret, comedy, Latin music—if you can name it, you can probably hear it here. There's good pub grub, too. It's open weekdays 11 AM to late and Saturday noon to late. It's closed Sunday unless there is a show.

Grace Emily (✉*232 Waymouth St., City Center* ☎*08/8231–5500*), a multilevel music-lover's pub, has bartenders spouting the mantra, "No pokies, no TAB, no food." (Pokies are the poker machines found in many pubs, and TAB, Australia's version of OTB, lets you place bets on horse races.) Instead, there's live music nightly, and a pool table. The beer garden is one of the city's best, with secluded spots for those wanting a quiet tipple and big round tables for groups to drink en masse and alfresco. It's open daily 4 PM–late.

The **Wellington Hotel** (✉*36 Wellington Sq., North Adelaide* ☎*08/8267–1322*), first licensed in 1851, is hops-lovers' heaven, with 32 Australian-brewed beers on tap. Line up six "pony" (sample) glasses on a taster tray, then enjoy a schooner (large glass) of your favorite.

CASINO   Head to **SkyCity** for big-time casino gaming, including the highly animated Australian Two-up, in which you bet against the house on the fall of two coins. Four bars and four restaurants are also within the complex. It's one of a handful of places in Adelaide that keep pumping until dawn. ✉*North Terr., City Center* ☎*08/8212–2811* ⏰*24 hrs.*

SPORTS & THE OUTDOORS

SPECTATOR SPORTS

Venue•Tix (✉*Shop 24, Da Costa Arcade, Grenfell St. at Gawler Pl., City Center* ☎*08/8225–8888* ⊕*www.venuetix.com.au*) sells tickets for domestic and international one-day and test (five-day) cricket matches, other major sporting events, and concerts.

CRICKET   The main venue for interstate and international competition is the Ade-
★ laide Oval. During cricket season October–March, the **Cricket Museum** (✉*Adelaide Oval, War Memorial Dr. and King William St., North Adelaide* ☎*08/8300–3800*) has two-hour tours (A$10) weekdays (except on match days).

FOOTBALL   Australian Rules Football is the most popular winter sport in South Australia. Games are played on weekends at **AAMI Stadium** (✉*Turner Dr., West Lakes* ☎*08/8268–2088*). Teams play in the national AFL competition on Friday, Saturday, or Sunday. The season runs March to August. Finals are in September.

SHOPPING

Shops in Adelaide City Center are generally open Monday–Thursday 9–5:30, Friday 9–9, Saturday 9–5:30, and Sunday 11–5. In the suburbs shops are often open until 9 PM on Thursday night instead of Friday. As the center of the world's opal industry, Adelaide has many opal shops, which are around King William Street. Other good buys are South Australian regional wines, crafts, and Aboriginal artwork.

MARKETS

★ One of the largest produce markets in the southern hemisphere, **Central Market** (✉ *Gouger St., City Center* ☎ *08/8203–7494*) is chock-full of stellar local foods, including glistening-fresh fish, meat, crusty Vietnamese and Continental breads, German baked goods, cheeses of every shape and color, and old-fashioned lollies (candy). You can also buy souvenir T-shirts, CDs, books, cut flowers, and a great cup of coffee. Hours are Tuesday 7–5:30, Thursday 9–5:30, Friday 7 AM–9 PM, and Saturday 7–3.

SPECIALTY STORES

ANTIQUES **Megaw and Hogg Antiques** (✉ *118 Grote St., City Center* ☎ *08/8231–0101*) sells antique furniture and decorative arts.

CHOCOLATE **Haigh's Chocolates** (✉ *2 Rundle Mall at King William St., City Center* ☎ *08/8231–2844* ✉ *Haigh's Visitors Centre, 154 Greenhill Rd.,*
★ *Parkside* ☎ *08/8372–7077*), Australia's oldest chocolate manufacturer, has tempted people with corner shop displays since 1915. The family-owned South Australian company produces exquisite truffles, pralines, and creams—as well as the chocolate Easter bilby (an endangered Australian marsupial), Haigh's answer to the Easter bunny. Shop hours are Monday–Thursday 8:30–6, Friday 8:30 AM–9 PM, Saturday 9–6, and Sunday 10:30–5:30. Free chocolate-making tours at the visitors center run Monday–Saturday at 11, 1, and 2; bookings are essential.

HOMEWARES The **Jam Factory** (✉ *19 Morphett St., City Center* ☎ *08/8231–0005*), a contemporary craft-and-design center, exhibits and sells unique Australian glassware, ceramics, wood, and metal designs. For quirky locally made jewelry, pottery, glass, and sculptures, visit **Urban Cow Studio** (✉ *11 Frome St., City Center* ☎ *08/8232–6126*).

SIDE TRIPS TO THE ADELAIDE HILLS

With their secluded green slopes and flowery gardens, the Adelaide Hills are a pastoral shelter in this desert state. The patchwork quilt of vast orchards, neat vineyards, and avenues of tall conifers resembles the Bavarian countryside, a likeness fashioned by the many German immigrants who settled here in the 19th century. During the summer months the Adelaide Hills are consistently cooler than the city, although the charming towns and wineries are pleasant to visit any time of year. To reach the region from Adelaide, head toward the M1 Princes Highway or drive down Pulteney Street, which becomes Unley Road and then Belair Road. From here signs point to Crafers and the freeway.

BIRDWOOD

44 km (27 mi) east of Adelaide.

Birdwood's historic flour mill, built in 1852, houses Australia's best motoring museum.

MT. LOFTY

16 km (10 mi) southeast of Adelaide.

There are splendid views of Adelaide from the lookout atop 2,300-foot Mt. Lofty. A 3½-km (2-mi) round-trip walk from the Waterfall Gully parking lot in Cleland Conservation Park (15 minutes' drive from Adelaide) takes you along Waterfall Creek before climbing steeply to the white surveying tower on the summit; the track is closed on Total Fire Ban days. By car from Adelaide, take the Crafers exit off the South Eastern Freeway and follow Summit Road.

NICE VIEWS
There is no better view of Adelaide—day or night—than the city-and-sea sweep from atop 2,300-foot Mt. Lofty. There's an appropriately-named glass-front restaurant here called Summit.

Mt. Lofty Botanic Gardens, with its rhododendrons, magnolias, ferns, and exotic trees, is glorious in fall and spring, when free guided walks leave the lower parking lot on Thursday at 10. ⊠ *Picadilly entrance off Lampert Rd.* ☎ *08/8370–8370* ⊕ *www.environment.sa.gov.au/botanicgardens* ⊡ *Free* ⊙ *Weekdays 8:30–4, weekends 10–5.*

☾ A short drive from Mt. Lofty Summit brings you to **Cleland Wildlife Park,** where many animals roam free in three different forest habitats. Walking trails crisscross the park and its surroundings, and you're guaranteed to see emus and kangaroos in the grasslands and pelicans around the swampy billabongs. There are also enclosures for wombats and other less sociable animals. Koala cuddling is a highlight of koala close-up sessions. Monthly two-hour night walks (A$21.50) let you wander among nocturnal species such as potoroos and brush-tailed bettongs. Private guided tours can be arranged for A$63 per hour (A$126 on Sunday). Reservations are essential for tours. The park is closed when there's a fire ban (usually between December and February). ⊠ *Summit Rd.* ☎ *08/8339–2444* ⊕ *www.environment.sa.gov.au/parks/cleland* ⊡ *A$13* ⊙ *Daily 9:30–5.*

MYLOR

10 km (6 mi) south of Mt. Lofty via the town of Crafers, the South Eastern Fwy., and Stirling; 25 km (16 mi) southeast of Adelaide via the South Eastern Fwy.

The attractive little village of Mylor draws in crowds for its wildlife.

☾
★ The 85-acre **Warrawong Wildlife Sanctuary,** a beautiful combination of rain forest, gurgling streams, and black-water ponds, is the place to spot kangaroos, wallabies, bandicoots, turtles, and platypuses. Because most of the animals are nocturnal, the guided dusk walk is more rewarding. It's essential to reserve for the evening walks, which are at 5 PM in winter and 7:30 PM in summer. You can meet and handle other sanctuary residents, such as lizards and snakes, at the daily Animal Shows (11 AM and 2 PM). In the Bilby Café you can watch

native marsupials forage outside the windows as you eat. ✉ *Stock Rd.* ☎ *08/8370–9197* ⊕ *www.warrawong.com* 🚶 *Self-guided walks A$8, guided evening walks A$20* ⊗ *9–9.*

BRIDGEWATER
6 km (4 mi) north of Mylor, 22 km (14 mi) southeast of Adelaide.

Bridgewater came into existence in 1841 as a refreshment stop for bullock teams fording Cock's Creek. More English than German, with its flowing creek and flower-filled gardens, this leafy, tranquil village was officially planned in 1859 by the builder of the first Bridgewater flour mill.

The handsome **stone flour mill,** built in 1860, stands at the western entrance to the town, where its waterwheel churns away. These days the mill houses the first-class Bridgewater Mill Restaurant and serves as the shop front for Petaluma Wines, one of Australia's finest labels; try the chardonnay and viognier. The prestigious Croser champagne is matured on the lower level of the building. ✉ *Bridgewater and Mt. Barker Rds.* ☎ *08/8339–9222* 💲 *Free* ⊗ *Daily 10–5.*

WHERE TO STAY & EAT

$$$$ ✗ **Bridgewater Mill Restaurant.** A stylish and celebrated restaurant in a
Fodor's Choice converted flour mill, this is one of the state's best dining spots. Using
★ mostly local produce, chef Le Tu Thai creates an imaginative contemporary Australian lunch menu; dishes might include oyster and leek pie, or roasted Kangaroo Island chicken dressed with scampi, coconut, and green mango salad. In summer book ahead to get a table on the deck beside the waterwheel. If you're feeling flush, ask to see the special wine list. ✉ *Bridgewater and Mt. Barker Rds.* ⏏ *Box 69, Bridgewater, 5155* ☎ *08/8339–9200* 🖃 *AE, DC, MC, V* ⊗ *Closed Tues. and Wed. No dinner.*

$–$$ ✗ **Aldgate Pump Bistro.** You get a leisurely glimpse of local culture at this friendly two-story country pub. There is an extensive, eclectic selection of hearty fare such as Cajun-style blackened salmon and grilled kangaroo with summer-berry glaze. Warmed by log fires in winter, the dining room overlooks a shaded beer garden. The place is 2 km (1 mi) from Bridgewater, in the delightful village of Aldgate. ✉ *Strathalbyn and Mt. Barker Rds., Aldgate* ☎ *08/8339–2015* 🖃 *AE, DC, MC, V.*

¢–$ ✗ **Organic Market and Café.** Pram-wheeling parents, hikers resting their walking poles, and friends catching up on gossip keep this red-and-blue café and adjoining organic supermarket buzzing all day. Reasons to linger include focaccias, soups, home-baked muffins and cakes, and all kinds of purportedly healthy and unquestionably delicious drinks. It's in Stirling (3 km [2 mi] from Bridgewater). ✉ *5 Druids Ave., Stirling* ☎ *08/8339–7131* 🖃 *MC, V* ⊗ *No dinner.*

$$$$ 🏨 **Thorngrove Manor.** This romantic Gothic folly of turrets and towers
★ is *Lifestyles of the Rich and Famous* written large. Opulent suites, set amid glorious gardens, have different decorative themes: a four-poster bed carved with heraldic lions is the centerpiece of the tapestry- and brocade-draped Queen's Chambers, and there are 1860 Scottish

9

stained-glass windows and a Hapsburg piano in the King's Chambers. All the suites have entrances that ensure total privacy. Valet Kenneth Lehmann makes your every wish his command. ⊠*2 Glenside La., Stirling, 5152* ☎*08/8339–6748* ⊕*www.slh.com/thorngrove* ⇖*6 suites* △*In-room: safe, refrigerator, DVD, dial-up. In-hotel: restaurant, room service, no elevator, laundry service, public Internet, airport shuttle, no-smoking rooms* ⊟*AE, DC, MC, V* ⦿|*BP.*

$$$ ⊡**The Orangerie.** Gardens filled with statuettes and fountains sur-
★   round the French Provincial one-bedroom suite in this delightful 1890s sandstone residence. Sunlight streams through walls of French doors and windows, gilding the elegant sitting room and adjoining country kitchen, which open onto a private terrace. There's an exqui-site Botticelli screen in the bedroom tucked behind. ⊠*4 Orley Ave., Stirling, 5152* ☎*08/8339–5458* ✆*orangeri@senet.com.au* ⊕*www. orangerie.com.au* ⇖*1 suite* △*In-room: kitchen, refrigerator, DVD, VCR, dial-up. In-hotel: tennis court, pool, no elevator, laundry facil-ities, laundry service, no kids under 16 years, no-smoking rooms* ⊟*AE, MC, V* ⦿|*BP.*

ADELAIDE ESSENTIALS

TRANSPORTATION

BY AIR

Adelaide Airport is 6 km (4 mi) west of the city center. The inter-national and domestic terminals share a modern building opened in December 2005.

Airlines serving Adelaide include Singapore Airlines, Malaysia Airlines, and Cathay Pacific. Qantas also connects Adelaide with many inter-national cities (usually via Melbourne or Sydney). Domestic airlines flying into Adelaide include Jetstar, O'Connor Airlines, REX/Regional Express, and Virgin Blue.

Airport Adelaide Airport (⊠*1 James Schofield Dr.* ☎*08/8308–9211*).

Airlines Cathay Pacific Airways (☎*13–1747*). **Jetstar** (☎*13–1538*). **Malaysia Airlines** (☎*13–2627*). **O'Connor Airlines** (☎*13–1313*). **Qantas Airways** (☎*13–1313*). **REX/Regional Express** (☎*13–1713*). **Singapore Airlines** (☎*13–1011*). **Virgin Blue** (☎*13–6789*).

BY BOAT

Pop-Eye Motor Launches connect Elder Park, in front of the Adelaide Festival Centre, with Adelaide Zoo's rear gate. Boats leave hourly on weekdays from 11 to 3, and every 20 minutes on weekends from 10:30 until 4:30. Tickets are A$6 one-way, A$9 round-trip.

Contact Pop-Eye Motor Launches (⊠*Elder Park* ☎*08/8295–4747*).

BY BUS

The Central Bus Station, open daily 6 AM–9:30 PM, is near the city center. From here Premier Stateliner operates buses throughout South

Australia, and Firefly Express and Greyhound Australia run interstate and some local services.

Bus Station **Central Bus Station** (✉ *111 Franklin St., City Center* ☎ *No phone*).

Bus Lines **Firefly Express** (☎ *1300/730740* ⊕ *www.fireflyexpress.com.au*). **Greyhound Australia** (☎ *13–1499* ⊕ *www.greyhound.com.au*). **Premier Stateliner** (☎ *08/8415–5555* ⊕ *www.premierstateliner.com.au*).

BUS TRAVEL WITHIN ADELAIDE Fares on the public transportation network are based on morning and afternoon peak and off-peak travel. A single-trip peak ticket is A$3.80, off-peak A$2.30. Tickets are available from most railway stations, newsstands, post offices, and the Adelaide Metro Info Centre. If you plan to travel frequently you can economize with a multitrip ticket (A$25.10), which allows 10 rides throughout the three bus zones. Off-peak multitrip tickets are A$13.80. Another economical way to travel is with the day-trip ticket, which allows unlimited bus, train, and tram travel throughout Adelaide and most of its surroundings from first until last service. It costs A$7.20.

No-cost Adelaide FREE buses make about 30 downtown stops. The BeeLine Bus runs around King William Street and North Terrace Monday–Thursday 7:40 AM–6:10 PM, Friday 7:40 AM–9:20 PM, Saturday 8:20 AM–5:35 PM, and Sunday 10 AM–5:30 PM. The City Loop Bus runs every 15 minutes in two central city directions, Monday–Thursday 8 AM–6:15 PM, Friday 8 AM–9:15 PM, Saturday 8:15 AM–5:45 PM, and Sunday 10 AM–5:15 PM. The free Adelaide Connector, which links North Adelaide and the city center, runs Monday–Thursday 8 AM–6 PM, Friday 8 AM–9:30 PM, and weekends 10 AM–5 PM. Buses have ramp access for wheelchairs and baby carriages, and they stop at most major attractions.

Wandering Star is a late-night bus service that operates on Friday and Saturday. From 12:30 AM to 5 AM you can travel from the city to your door (or as near as possible) in 11 suburban zones for A$6.

The Adelaide metropolitan network also serves the Adelaide Hills, but you need to catch two or more buses to more remote attractions, such as Bridgewater Mill.

Free guides to Adelaide's public bus lines are available from the Adelaide Metro Info Centre, open weekdays 8–6, Saturday 9–5, and Sunday 11–4.

Contact **Adelaide Metro Info Centre** (✉ *Currie and King William Sts., City Center* ☎ *08/8210–1000* ⊕ *www.adelaidemetro.com.au*).

BY CAR

A car gives you the freedom to discover the country lanes and villages in the hills region outside the city, and Adelaide also has excellent road connections with other states. Highway 1 links the city with Melbourne, 728 km (451 mi) southeast, and with Perth, 2,724 km (1,689 mi) to the west, via the vast and bleak Nullarbor Plain. The Stuart Highway provides access to the Red Centre. Alice Springs is 1,542 km

(956 mi) north of Adelaide. The Royal Automobile Association (RAA) offers emergency and roadside assistance to members, and allows you to join on the spot if you're in a jam.

Most of the major car-rental agencies have offices both at the airport and in downtown Adelaide.

Contacts Avis (✉ *136 North Terr., City Center* ☎ *08/8410–5727 or 13–6333*). **Budget** (✉ *274 North Terr., City Center* ☎ *08/8418–7300 or 13–2727*). **Thrifty** (✉ *23 Hindley St., City Center* ☎ *08/8211–8788 or 1300/367227*). **Royal Automobile Association** (✉ *55 Hindmarsh Sq., City Center* ☎ *08/8202–4600* ⊕ *www.raa.com.au*).

BY TAXI

Taxis can be hailed on the street, booked by phone, or boarded at a taxi stand, and most accept credit cards. Outside the CBD it's best to phone for a taxi. Expect a wait if you're heading into town on Friday and Saturday night.

Contacts Suburban Taxi Service (☎ *13–1008*). **Yellow Cabs** (☎ *13–2227*).

BY TRAIN

Four suburban train lines serve north- and south-coast suburbs, the northeast ranges, and the Adelaide Hills. Trains depart from Adelaide Station. The station for interstate and country trains is the Keswick Rail Terminal, west of the city center. The terminal has a small café, and taxis are available from the stand outside. The *Overland* connects Adelaide and Melbourne (11 hours) Thursday through Sunday. The *Ghan* makes the 19-hour journey to Alice Springs on Sunday and Friday, continuing north to Darwin on Monday and Saturday. The *Indian Pacific* links Adelaide with Perth (40 hours) and Sydney (24½ hours) twice a week.

Contact Keswick Rail Terminal (✉ *Keswick, 2 km (1 mi) west of city center* ☎ *13–2147* ⊕ *www.trainways.com.au*).

BY TRAM

The city's only surviving tram route runs between Victoria Square and beachside Glenelg. Ticketing is identical to that on city buses.

CONTACTS & RESOURCES
EMERGENCIES

In an emergency, dial **000** to reach an ambulance, the police, or the fire department.

Contact Royal Adelaide Hospital (✉ *North Terr. at Frome Rd., City Center* ☎ *08/8222–4000*).

TOURS

Mary Anne Kennedy, the owner of A Taste of South Australia, is one of the most knowledgeable regional food and wine guides. Her private tours (A$350 and up) are a taste treat. Adelaide's Top Food and Wine Tours showcases Adelaide's food-and-wine lifestyle—as in the behind-the-scenes guided tour of the Central Market (A$35), which lets you meet stall holders, share their knowledge, and taste the wares. Tours are scheduled Tuesday and Thursday–Saturday at 9:30 AM.

The Adelaide Explorer (a bus tricked up to look like a tram) makes city highlights tours, which can be combined with a trip to Glenelg. Passengers may leave the vehicle at any of the attractions along the way and join a following tour. Trams depart every 90 minutes and cost A$25 for just the city, A$30 for the city and Glenelg.

Adelaide Sightseeing operates a morning city sights tour for A$55. The company also runs a daily afternoon bus tour of the Adelaide Hills and the German village of Hahndorf for A$55. For A$49, Gray Line Adelaide provides morning city tours that take in all the highlights. They depart from 101 Franklin Street at 9:30 AM.

Tourabout Adelaide has private tours with tailored itineraries. Prices run from around A$30 for an Adelaide walking tour to A$150 for day-long excursions to the Barossa Valley. Jeff Easley, the owner and chief tour guide, can arrange almost anything.

Rundle Mall Information Centre hosts 45-minute free guided walks. The First Steps Tour points out the main attractions, facilities, and transportation in central Adelaide. Tours depart weekdays at 9:30 AM from outside the booth. Bookings are not required.

Food & Wine Tours Adelaide's Top Food and Wine Tours (☎ *08/8263–0265* ⊕ *www.topfoodandwinetours.com.au*). **A Taste of South Australia** (☎ *08/8271–7777 or 0419/861588* ⊕ *www.tastesa.com.au*).

Van Tours Adelaide Explorer (☎ *08/8293–2966* ⊕ *www.adelaideexplorer.com.au*). **Adelaide Sightseeing** (☎ *08/8413–6199* ⊕ *www.adelaidesightseeing.com.au*). **Gray Line Adelaide** (☎ *1300/858687* ⊕ *www.grayline.com*). **Tourabout Adelaide** (☎ *08/8333–1111* ⊕ *www.touraboutadelaide.com.au*).

Walking Tour Rundle Mall Information Centre (✉ *Rundle Mall at King William St., City Center* ☎ *08/8203–7611*).

TRAVEL AGENTS

Budget travel agents Flight Centre and STA Travel have offices throughout Adelaide and its suburbs. International firms Harvey World Travel and Bunnick Travel/American Express are reliable travel agents where you can arrange tour packages and book flights.

Contacts Bunnik Travel/American Express (✉ *122 Pirie St., City Center* ☎ *08/8359–2295*). **Flight Centre** (✉ *186 Rundle St., City Center* ☎ *08/8227–0404*). **Harvey World Travel** (✉ *Shop 3, 200 The Parade, Norwood* ☎ *08/8332–9933*). **STA Travel** (✉ *235 Rundle St., City Center* ☎ *08/8223–2426*).

VISITOR INFORMATION

The South Australian Visitor and Travel Centre, open weekdays 8:30–5 and weekends 9–2, has specialist publications and tourism brochures on South Australia and excellent hiking and cycling maps.

Sightseeing South Australia is a comprehensive monthly newspaper (there's also an extensive Web site) with feature articles on current events, destinations, and experiences throughout the whole state. It's free at most tourist outlets, hotels, and transportation centers.

City Guides, wearing signature green shirts and white hats, stroll around Rundle Mall, Victoria Square, and North Terrace. They can help with lots of tourist information and some brochures.

The Adelaide Hills Visitor Information Centre is open weekdays 9–5 and weekends 10–4.

Contacts Adelaide Hills Visitor Information Centre (⊠ *41 Main St., Hahndorf* ☎ *08/8388–1185 or 1800/353323* ⊕ *www.visitadelaidehills.com.au*). **BASS** (⊠ *Adelaide Festival Centre, King William St.* ☎ *13–1246* ⊕ *www.bass.net.au*). **Sightseeing South Australia** (☎ *08/8339–0000* ⊕ *www.sightseeing.com.au*). **South Australian Visitor and Travel Centre** (⊠ *18 King William St., City Center* ☎ *1300/655276* ⊕ *www.southaustralia.com*).

THE BAROSSA REGION

Some of Australia's most famous vineyards are in the Barossa Region, an hour's drive northeast of Adelaide. More than 70 wineries across the two wide, shallow valleys that make up the region produce numerous wines, including aromatic Rhine Riesling, Seppelt's unique, century-old Para Port—which brings more than A$1,000 a bottle—and Penfolds Grange, Australia's most celebrated wine.

Cultural roots set the Barossa apart. The area was settled by Silesian immigrants who left the German-Polish border region in the 1840s to escape religious persecution. These farmers brought traditions that you can't miss in the solid bluestone architecture, the tall slender spires of the Lutheran churches, and the *kuchen,* a cake as popular as the Devonshire tea introduced by British settlers. Together, these elements give the Barossa a charm that is unique among Australian wine-growing areas.

Most wineries in the Barossa operate sale rooms—called cellar doors— that usually have 6 to 12 varieties of wine available for tasting. You are not expected to sample the entire selection; to do so would overpower your taste buds. It's far better to give the tasting-room staff some idea of your personal preferences and let them suggest wine for you to sample.

Numbers in the margin correspond to points of interest on the Barossa Region map.

LYNDOCH

 58 km (36 mi) northeast of Adelaide.

This pleasant little town surrounded by vineyards was established in 1840 and is the Barossa's oldest settlement site. It owes the spelling of its name to a draftsman's error—it was meant to be named after the British soldier Lord Lynedoch.

Australian Wine

Prepare to be thoroughly taken aback, or at least a touch startled, at Australia's refreshing wine-and-food pairings. From the wineries of northeast Victoria, an area known for its full-bodied reds, come some truly remarkable fortified Tokays and muscats, all with a delicious, wild, untamed quality that is so rich and sticky you don't know whether to drink them or spread them. Among the more-notable varieties are the All Saints Classic Rutherglen Tokay, Campbell's Liquid Gold Tokay, and Bailey's Old Muscat. Believe it or not, these are perfect with Australia's distinctive farmhouse cheeses, such as Milawa Gold (northeast Victoria), Yarra Valley Dairy's Persian Feta, and Meredith Blue (from Victoria's Western District).

Practically unknown beyond these shores is what was once affectionately but euphemistically known as sparkling burgundy, an effervescent red made mainly from shiraz grapes using the traditional *méthode champenoise*. A dense yet lively wine with fresh, fruity tones, it's suited to game and turkey and is now an integral part of a festive Australian Christmas dinner. Look for labels such as Seppelt, Yalumba, and Peter Lehmann's Black Queen.

Then there are the classic Rieslings of South Australia's Barossa region and Clare Valley, first introduced by German and Silesian settlers. Today wines such as Heggies Riesling, Petaluma Riesling, and Wirra Wirra Hand Picked Riesling are as much at home with Middle Eastern merguez sausage and couscous as they are with knockwurst and sauerkraut.

Also very Australian in style are the big, oaky semillons of the Hunter Valley (try Tyrrell's Vat 1 Semillon and Lindeman's Hunter Valley Semillon) and the powerful steak-and-braised-meat–loving cabernets from the rich, red "terra rossa" soil of the Coonawarra district in South Australia. These wines, including Petaluma Coonawarra, Lindeman's Pyrus, and Hollick cabernet sauvignon, will knock first-timers' socks off.

As a breed, the Australian shiraz style has delicious pepper-berry characteristics and food-friendly companionability. A clutch of worthy labels includes Penfolds' Bins 128 and 389, Elderton Shiraz from the Barossa Region, Brokenwood Graveyard Vineyard from the Hunter Valley, and Seppelts Great Western Shiraz from the Grampians in Victoria.

Shiraz is very much at home with modern Australian cooking, working beautifully with Moroccan-inspired lamb, Mediterranean roasted goat, pasta, and yes, even kangaroo with beetroot. Also worth a mention are the elegant, berry-laden pinot noirs of Tasmania and Victoria's Mornington Peninsula (perfect with Peking duck); the fresh, bright-tasting unwooded chardonnays of South Australia (fabulous with fish); and the fragrant sauvignon blancs of Margaret River (excellent with Sydney Rock oysters).

So there you have it. If you are about to embark on your own personal discovery of Australian wine and food pairing, get ready to be amazed, astonished, and shocked—into having another glass.

–Terry Durack

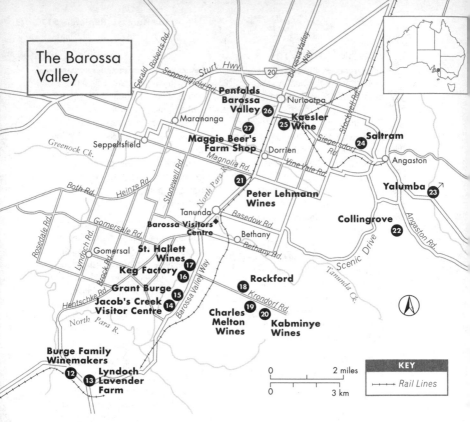

The Barossa Valley

KEY

↦ Rail Lines

Lyndoch Lavender Farm, a family-friendly tribute to the purple flower that adorns the hills, grows more than 80 varieties on 6 lush acres high above Lyndoch. Light café meals are available, and the farm shop sells essential oils, creams, and other products. ⊠ *Hoffnungsthal and Tweedies Gully Rds.* ☎☎ *08/8524–4538* ⊡ *A$2* ☉ *Sept.–Feb., daily 10–4:30; Mar.–Aug., weekends 10–4:30.*

❶❷ **Burge Family Winemakers.** You can drink in a leafy vineyard view while tasting among the wine barrels in this understated cellar door. Winemaker Rick Burge's best include the powerful yet elegant Draycott Shiraz and Olive Hill shiraz-grenache-mourvedre blend. There is also sometimes A Nice Red—read the label! ⊠ *Barossa Valley Way near Hermann Thumm Dr.* ☎ *08/8524–4644* ⊕ *www.burgefamily.com.au* ⊡ *Free* ☉ *Thurs.–Sat. and Mon. 10–5 (ring ahead).*

WHERE TO STAY

$$$$
Fodor'sChoice
★

🛏 **Abbotsford Country House.** Tranquillity reigns at this property on 50 acres of rolling beef farm with Barossa views. Silence and blissfully comfortable beds with superhigh thread-count Egyptian linens make drifting off easy. Collected

TAKE IT SLOW

Allow yourself only one day in the Barossa and you'll regret it. Slow down and savor the food and wine and warm hospitality.

antiques decorate the eight rooms, one of which has a jetted tub, another a deep, claw-foot enamel bathtub, and the rest double showers. All have complimentary port and chocolate. Relax in your room (TVs are available on request) or venture out to sit by the fireplace in the main house. The abundant, home-cooked breakfast, which uses farm-grown and local ingredients, will fuel you up for a day of exploring the valley. ⊠ *Yaldara Dr. at Fuss Rd., Lyndoch, 5351* ⌖ *Box 675, Lyndoch, SA, 5351* ☎ *08/8254–4662* ⊕ *www.abbotsfordhouse.com* ⇨ *8 rooms* ⚠ *In-room: no phone, refrigerator, no TV, Wi-Fi. In-hotel: restaurant, laundry service, public Wi-Fi, no-smoking rooms, no kids under 12* ☰ *MC, V* ⏁*BP.*

$–$$$ ⌂ **Belle Cottages.** Rose-filled gardens or sweeping rural acres surround these classic Australian accommodations. Wood-burning fireplaces in several invite you to relax with a bottle of red after a day in the Barossa region, and comfy beds tempt you to sleep late. In Christabelle Cottage, an 1849 Heritage-listed former chapel, a spiral staircase winds up to a mezzanine bedroom. The other cottages, houses, and suites have one, two, or three bedrooms and country kitchens. ⌖ *Box 481, 5351* ☎ *08/8524–4825* ⊕ *www.bellescapes.com* ⇨ *5 cottages, 3 suites* ⚠ *In-room: no phone (some), kitchen, refrigerator, VCR (some), DVD (some). In-hotel: no elevator, laundry facilities (some), no-smoking rooms, some pets allowed* ☰ *AE, MC, V* ⏁*BP.*

TANUNDA

13 km (8 mi) northeast of Lyndoch, 70 km (43 mi) northeast of Adelaide.

The cultural heart of the Barossa, Tanunda is its most German settlement. The four Lutheran churches in the town testify to its heritage, and dozens of shops selling German pastries, breads, and wursts (sausages)—not to mention wine—line the main street. Many of the valley's best wineries are close by.

⑲ At **Charles Melton Wines,** tasting is relaxing and casual at this brick-floor, timber-wall cellar door, which is warmed by a log fire in winter. After making sure the resident cats have vacated it first, settle into a director's chair at the long wooden table and let the staff pour. Nine Popes, a huge, decadent red blend, is the flagship wine, and the ruby-red Rose of Virginia is arguably Australia's best rosé. You can enjoy a glass of either with a cheese platter or game pie on the veranda. ⊠ *Krondorf Rd. near Nitschke Rd.* ☎ *08/8563–3606* ⊕ *www.charlesmeltonwines. com.au* ⌑*Free* ⊗ *Daily 11–5.*

⑮ **Grant Burge** is one of the most successful of the Barossa's young, independent wine labels. Wines include impressive chardonnays, crisp Rieslings, and powerful reds such as Meshach shiraz. Don't miss the Holy Trinity—a highly acclaimed Rhône blend of grenache, shiraz, and mourvedre. It's 5 km (3 mi) south of Tanunda. ⊠ *Barossa Valley Way near Koch Rd.* ☎ *08/8563–3700* ⊕ *www.grantburgewines.com.au* ⌑*Free* ⊗ *Daily 10–5.*

9

⑭ An impressive block of glass, steel, and recycled timber, **Jacob's Creek Visitor Centre** overlooks the creek whose name is familiar to wine drinkers around the world. Inside the building, plasma screens and pictorial displays tell the history of the label. Cabernet sauvignon, merlot, chardonnay, and the shiraz-rosé, served chilled, can be tasted at a 60-foot-long counter. There is a lunch-only restaurant with broad glass doors opening onto a grassy lawn edged with towering eucalyptus trees. ✉*Barossa Valley Way near Jacob's Creek* ☎*08/8521–3000* ⊕*www. jacobscreek.com* ✄*Free* ◷*Daily 10–5.*

⑳ Built from local mud brick and corrugated iron, with a winglike roof,
★ the light-filled cellar door at **Kabminye Wines** was a controversial addition to the valley—but there's no argument about the wines and the food. Each wine has its own unique and surprising taste, particularly the excellent Ilona rosé and the full-frontal flagship Hubert Shiraz. The café cooks up traditional Silesian fare such as pork chops with a dried fruit sauce on egg noodles. Changing art exhibitions are displayed in the upstairs gallery. ✉*Krondorf Rd. near Nitschke Rd.* ☎*08/8563–0889* ⊕*www.kabminye.com* ✄*Free* ◷*Daily 11–5.*

㉑ **Peter Lehmann Wines** is owned by a larger-than-life Barossa character whose wine consistently wins international awards. Art-hung stonework and a wood-burning fireplace make the tasting room one of the most pleasant in the valley. This is the only place to find Black Queen Sparkling Shiraz. Wooden tables on a treed lawn encourage picnicking on Barossa platters, served daily. ✉*Para Rd. off Stelzer Rd.* ☎*08/8563–2500* ⊕*www.peterlehmannwines.com.au* ✄*Free* ◷*Weekdays 9:30–5, weekends 10:30–4:30.*

⑱ Nestled in a cobbled stable yard, **Rockford** is a small winery with a tast-
★ ing room in an old stone barn. The specialties are heavy, rich wines made from some of the region's oldest vines. Several notable labels have appeared under the Rockford name—be sure to try the cabernet sauvignon and the Basket Press Shiraz (at cellar door from March until sold out), outstanding examples of these most traditional of Australian varieties. ✉*Krondorf Rd. near Nitschke Rd.* ☎*08/8563–2720* ⊕*www.rockfordwines.com.au* ✄*Free* ◷*Daily 11–5.*

⑰ "Stewy" the parrot chatters a welcome as you stroll from rose-studded
★ gardens into the tasting room at **St. Hallett Wines,** one of the region's best. The signature Old Block Shiraz, a classic and fantastic Australian red, is harvested from century-old vines. Poacher's Blend Semillon-Sauvignon Blanc is another good sampling choice. ✉*St. Halletts Rd.* ☎*08/8563–7000* ⊕*www.sthallett.com.au* ✄*Free* ◷*Daily 10–5.*

⑯ **Keg Factory** uses traditional methods to repair oak casks for winer-
☺ ies. You can watch coopers (barrel makers) working the American and French oak staves inside the iron hoops. Small, handmade port kegs make wonderful souvenirs of the Barossa. ✉*St. Halletts Rd.* ☎*08/8563–3012* ✄*Free* ◷*Daily 8–5.*

WHERE TO STAY & EAT

$$ ✕**1918 Bistro & Grill.** This rustic restaurant in a restored villa makes exemplary use of the Barossa's distinctive regional produce in a seasonal menu. Local olive oil, cold cut meats, venison, quail, and seasonal fruit and vegetables, some brought to the kitchen by producers, influence the dishes. Meals are served beside a two-sided fireplace in winter and alfresco in the garden in summer. The mostly Barossa wine list includes rare classics and newcomers. ✉*94 Murray St.* ☎*08/8563–0405* ▭*AE, DC, MC, V.*

¢–$ ✕**Die Barossa Wurst Haus & Bakery.** For a hearty German lunch at a reasonable price, no place beats this small, friendly café and shop. The wurst is fresh from local butchers, the sauerkraut is direct from Germany, and the potato salad is made on-site from a secret recipe. ✉*86A Murray St.* ☎*08/8563–3598* ▭*No credit cards* ◔*No dinner.*

$$–$$$ ⊞**Lawley Farm.** Amid 20 acres of grapes, in a courtyard shaded by
★ gnarled peppercorn trees, these delightful stone cottage-style suites were assembled from the remains of barns dating from the Barossa's pioneering days. A wood-burning stove warms the Krondorf Suite, in the original 1852 cottage, while in the Para Suite—former stables with ceiling beams from Adelaide shearing sheds—you can soak in a hot tub and then sleep late in a brass bed. Breakfast feasts of local German bacon or salmon, free-range farm eggs, and fresh-ground coffee are brought on a tray to your cottage each morning. The farm is within easy walking distance of six wineries. ✉*Krondorf and Grocke Rds., Box 103, 5352* ☎🖷*08/8563–2141* ⊕*www.lawleyfarm.com.au* 🛏*4 suites* ♿*In-room: no phone, refrigerator, dial-up (some). In-hotel: room service, no elevator, laundry service, public Internet, no-smoking rooms* ▭*AE, DC, MC, V* ¶⊙*BP.*

$–$$ ⊞**Blickinstal Barossa Valley Retreat.** Its name means "view into the valley," which understates the breathtaking panoramas from this lovely B&B. Amid vineyards in foothills five minutes from the Barossa's heart, the retreat is a tranquil base for exploring. Gardens surround the self-contained lodge apartments and studios, and breakfast is served on the homestead veranda. You can also indulge in afternoon tea. ✆*Box 17, Rifle Range Rd., 5352* ☎🖷*08/8563–2716* ✎*blickinstal@bigpond. com* ⊕*www.users.bigpond.com/blickinstal* 🛏*4 studios, 2 apartments* ♿*In-room: no phone, kitchen, refrigerator, DVD. In-hotel: no elevator, laundry facilities, public Internet, no-smoking rooms* ▭*AE, MC, V* ¶⊙*BP.*

9

ANGASTON

16 km (10) northeast of Tanunda via Menglers Hill Rd. Scenic Drive, 86 km (53 mi) northeast of Adelaide.

Named after George Fife Angas, the Englishman who founded the town and sponsored many of the German and British immigrants who came here, Angaston is full of jacaranda trees and its main street lined with stately stone buildings and tiny shops. Schulz Butchers has been making and selling wurst (German sausage) since 1939; 17 varieties hang above the counter. You can buy other delicious regional produce every Saturday morning at the Barossa Farmers Market, behind Vintners Bar & Grill.

㉒ **Collingrove** was the ancestral home of the Angas family, the descendants of George Fife Angas, one of South Australia's founders. At the height of its fortunes, the family controlled more than 14 million acres from this house. Today the property is administered by the National Trust, and you can inspect the Angas family portraits and memorabilia, including Dresden china, a hand-painted Louis XV cabinet, and Chippendale chairs, on guided tours. You can also stay overnight at Collingrove in evocative old-world B&B luxury. ⊠*Eden Valley Rd. near Collingrove Rd.* ☎*08/8564–2061* ⊕*www.collingrovehomestead. com.au* ⊡*A$10* ⊘*Tours weekdays 1:30, 2:30, and 3:30, weekends 12:30, 1:30, 2:30, and 3:30.*

㉔ Low-beamed ceilings and ivy-covered trellises give **Saltram** an urbanized sort of rustic charm. The vineyard's robust wine list includes the Pepperjack Barossa Grenache Rosé, a delightful vintage available only in summer. It's a delicious accompaniment to the Italian-influenced menu at the adjacent—and excellent—Salter's Kitchen restaurant. ⊠*Nuriootpa Rd., 1 km (½ mi) west of Angaston* ☎*08/8561–0200* ⊕*www. saltramwines.com.au* ⊡*Free* ⊘*Daily 10–5.*

㉓ Australia's oldest family-owned winery, **Yalumba** sits within a hugely impressive compound resembling an Italian monastery. The cellar door is decorated with mission-style furniture, antique wine-making materials, and mementos of the Hill Smith family, who first planted vines in the Barossa in 1849. The Octavius shirazes are superb, and the "Y Series" Viognier is thoroughly enjoyable. ⊠*Eden Valley Rd. just south of Valley Rd.* ☎*08/8561–3200* ⊕*www.yalumba.com* ⊡*Free* ⊘*Daily 10–5.*

WHERE TO EAT

$$ ✕**Vintners Bar & Grill.** The Barossa region is at its best in this sophisti-
★   cated spot, where vivid contemporary artworks adorn the walls and wide windows look out on rows of vineyards. The menu blends Australian, Mediterranean, and Asian flavors in such dishes as soft-shell crab tempura with mango and papaya salad, and roasted local rabbit with savoy cabbage roll. Scarlet and charcoal suede chairs and an upbeat jazz soundtrack make it easy to relax; top winemakers often come here to sample from the cellar's 160 wines. ⊠*Nuriootpa Rd. near Stockwell Rd.* ☎*08/8564–2488* ⊟*AE, DC, MC, V* ⊘*No dinner Sun.*

NURIOOTPA

8 km (5 mi) northwest of Angaston, 74 km (46 mi) northeast of Adelaide.

Long before it was the Barossa's commercial center, Nuriootpa was used as a bartering place by local Aboriginal tribes, hence its name: Nuriootpa means "meeting place."

㉕ Kaesler Wine is a charming boutique winery, whose fantastic "Old Bastard" shiraz is made from century-old vines; this and other wines are sold at a cellar door built to look like a 19th-century stone barn. There is also a restaurant serving lunch (daily) and dinner (Thursday to Saturday). Cottage accommodations go for A$160–A$180 per night. ⊠ *Barossa Valley Way near Kaiser Stuhl Ave.* ☎ *08/8562–4488 (cellar door), 08/8562–2711 (restaurant & cottages)* ⊕ *www.kaesler.com.au* ☞ *Free* ⊘ *Weekdays 10–5, weekends 11–4.*

㉗ ★ Renowned cook, restaurateur, and food writer Maggie Beer is an icon of Australian cuisine. Burned-fig jam, ice cream, *verjus* (a golden liquid made from unfermented grape juice and used for flavoring), and her signature Pheasant Farm Pâté are some of the delights you can taste and buy at **Maggie Beer's Farm Shop.** Treat-filled picnic baskets are available all day to take out or dip into on the deck overlooking a tree-fringed pond full of turtles. Don't miss the daily cooking demonstrations at 2 PM. ⊠ *End of Pheasant Farm Rd. off Samuel Rd.* ☎ *08/8562–4477* ⊕ *www.maggiebeer.com.au* ☞ *Free* ⊘ *Daily 10:30–5.*

㉖ Penfolds Barossa Valley. A very big brother to the 19th-century Magill Estate in Adelaide, this massive wine-making outfit in the center of Nuriootpa lets you taste shiraz, cabernet merlot, chardonnay, and Riesling blends—but not the celebrated Grange—at the cellar door. To savor the flagship wine and other premium vintages, book a Taste of Grange Tour (A$180 per person, minimum of 4). ⊠ *Barossa Valley Hwy. at Railway Terr.* ☎ *08/8568–9408* ⊕ *www.penfolds.com.au* ☞ *Free* ⊘ *Daily 10–5.*

9

Banrock Station Wine & Wetland Centre. The salt-scrub-patched Murray River floodplain 150 km (94 mi) east of Nuriootpa is an unlikely setting for a winery, but it is worth making the journey to this spot at Kingston-on-Murray. Within the stilted, mud-brick building perched above the vineyard and river lagoons here you can select a wine to accompany a grazing platter or light lunch on the outdoor deck—try the emu, sundried tomato, and saltbush pie. Afterward, you can take the 8-km (5-mi) Boardwalk Trail (A$5, bookings essential) to view the surrounding wetlands, and learn about the ongoing wildlife habitat restoration and conservation work

---

SHIPPING WINE

Wouldn't it be wonderful if international airlines showed some empathy for wine fanciers and stopped charging exorbitant excess baggage fees for cases of wine? In the meantime you can appeal to the better nature of the Barossa vignerons who have overseas stockists or can arrange shipping.

Fish Tales

With nearly 4,800 km (3,000 mi) of coastline and hundreds of miles of rivers, South Australia has almost as many opportunities for fishing as it has varieties of fish. You can join local anglers of all ages dangling hand lines from a jetty, casting into the surf from coastal rocks, hopping aboard charter boats, or spending a day sitting on a riverside log.

The Murray River is the place to head for callop (also called yellow belly or golden perch) and elusive Murray cod. In the river's backwaters you can also net a feed of yabbies, a type of freshwater crayfish, which make a wonderful appetizer before you tuck into the one that didn't get away. In the ocean King George whiting reigns supreme, but there is also excellent eating with mulloway, bream, snapper, snook, salmon, and sweep. The yellowtail kingfish, a great fighter usually found in deep water, prefers the shallower waters of Coffin Bay, off the Eyre Peninsula. **Baird Bay Charters & Ocean Eco Experience** (☎ *08/8626–5017* ⊕ *www.bairdbay. com*) runs fishing charters to Coffin Bay and other top spots. Another popular destination is the Yorke Peninsula. **S.A. Fishing Adventures** (☎ *08/8854–4098* ⊕ *www.safishing-adventures.com.au*) takes anglers to great spots around the Yorke Peninsula. Last, but certainly not least, is legendary Kangaroo Island. You can spend from a few hours to a few days aboard the *Cooinda* fishing the waters around Kangaroo Island with **KI Diving** (☎ *08/8553–1072* ⊕ *www. kidiving.com*).

–Melanie Ball

funded by Banrock Station wine sales. ⊠ *Holmes Rd. just off Sturt Hwy., Kingston-on-Murray* ☎ *08/8583–0299* ⊕ *www.banrockstation. com.au* ✉ *Free* ⊙ *Daily 10–5.*

BAROSSA REGION ESSENTIALS

TRANSPORTATION

BY CAR

The most direct route from Adelaide to the Barossa Region is via the town of Gawler. From Adelaide, drive north on King William Street. About 1 km (½ mi) past the Torrens River Bridge, take the right fork onto Main North Road. After 6 km (4 mi) this road forks to the right—follow signs to the Sturt Highway and the town of Gawler. At Gawler leave the highway and follow the signs to Lyndoch on the Barossa's southern border. The 50-km (31-mi) journey should take about an hour. A more attractive, if circuitous, route to Lyndoch takes you through the Adelaide Hills' Chain of Ponds and Williamstown.

Because the Barossa wineries are relatively far apart, a car is by far the best way to get around. But keep in mind that there are stiff penalties for driving under the influence of alcohol. Police in patrol cars can pull you over for a random breath test anywhere in the state, and roadside mobile breath-testing stations—locally known as "Booze Buses"—are particularly visible during special events, such as the Barossa Vintage Festival, held in March and April each year.

CONTACTS & RESOURCES
EMERGENCIES
In an emergency, dial **000** to reach an ambulance, the police, or the fire department.

TOURS
Gray Line Adelaide's full-day tour of the Barossa Region (A$107) leaves from Adelaide Central Bus Station. It includes lunch at a winery. Enjoy Adelaide runs a full-day (A$65) Barossa tour that visits four vineyards and includes lunch. Groovy Grape Getaways offers full-day (A$69) Barossa tours with a visit to the Adelaide Hills and a barbecue lunch.

Contacts Enjoy Adelaide (☎ *08/8332–1401* ⊕ *www.enjoyadelaide.com.au*). **Gray Line Adelaide** (☎ *1300/858687* ⊕ *www.grayline.com.au/adelaide*). **Groovy Grape Getaways** (☎ *08/8371–4000 or 1800/661177* ⊕ *www.groovygrape.com.au*).

VISITOR INFORMATION
The Barossa Visitors Centre has printed information and displays on the area's attractions, as well as an extensive display on the region's history. The center is open weekdays 9–5, weekends 10–4.

Contact Barossa Visitors Centre (✉ *66–68 Murray St., Tanunda* ☎ *08/8563–0600* ⊕ *www.barossa.com*).

THE CLARE VALLEY

Smaller and less well known than the Barossa, the Clare Valley nonetheless holds its own among Australia's wine-producing regions. Its robust reds and delicate whites are among the country's finest, and the Clare is generally regarded as the best area in Australia for fragrant, flavorsome Rieslings. On the fringe of the vast inland deserts, the Clare is a narrow sliver of fertile soil about 30 km (19 mi) long and 5 km (3 mi) wide, with a microclimate that makes it ideal for premium wine making.

The first vines were planted here as early as 1842, but it took a century and a half for the Clare Valley to take its deserved place on the national stage. The mix of small family wineries and large-scale producers, 150-year-old settlements and grand country houses, snug valleys and dense native forests has rare charm.

SEVENHILL
126 km (78 mi) north of Adelaide.

Sevenhill is the Clare Valley's geographic center, and the location of the region's first winery, established by Jesuit priests in 1851 to produce altar wine. The area had been settled three years earlier by Austrian Jesuits who named their seminary after the seven hills of Rome.

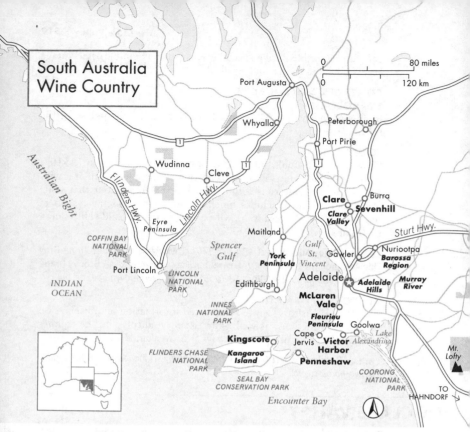

South Australia
Wine Country

The Riesling Trail, a walking and cycling track that follows an old Clare Valley railway line, runs through Sevenhill. The 25-km (16-mi) trail passes wineries and villages in gently rolling country between Auburn and Clare, and three loop trails take you to vineyards off the main track.

Bikes can be rented from **Clare Valley Cycle Hire** (⊠ *32 Victoria Rd., Clare* ☎ *08/8842–2782 or 0418/802077).*

Kilikanoon Wines. A rising star of the Clare Valley, Kilikanoon is already renowned for multilayered reds, such as the dense, richly colored Oracle Shiraz (occasionally available for tasting); Prodigal Grenache is another beauty. ⊠ *Penna La., Penwortham, 2 km (1 mi) off Main North Rd.* ☎ *08/8843–4377* ⊕ *www.kilikanoon.com.au* ⊠ *Free* ⊗ *Thurs.–Sun. 11–5.*

Fodor's Choice
★
The area's first winery, **Sevenhill Cellars** was created by the Jesuits, and they still run the show, with any profits going to education, mission work, and the needy within Australia. In the 1940s the winery branched out from sacramental wine into commercial production, and today 14 wine varieties, including Riesling (try the St Aloysius label), verdelho, grenache, and fortified wines, account for 75% of its business. Book a guided tour with the charming Brother John

May, Jesuit Winemaker Emeritus, who takes you to the cellars, the cemetery, and the church crypt where Jesuits have been interred since 1865. You can also rent bicycles here to explore the rolling hills and vineyards. ⊠*College Rd. just off Main North Rd.* ☎*08/8843–4222* ⊕*www.sevenhillcellars.com.au* 🎫*Free, tours A$5* ⊙*Weekdays 9–5, weekends 10–5; tours Tues. and Thurs. at 2.*

Skillogalee Winery is known for its excellent Riesling, Gewürztraminer, and shiraz, as well as its wonderful restaurant. Wine tasting takes place in a small room in the 1850s cottage (the restaurant occupies the others). Don't miss the sparkling Riesling. ⊠*Hughes Park Rd.* ☎*08/8843–4311* ⊕*www.skillogalee.com* 🎫*Free* ⊙*Daily 10–5.*

WHERE TO STAY & EAT

$–$$ ✗**Rising Sun.** People have watched the world go by from the veranda of this landmark hotel in Auburn, 16 km (10 mi) south of Sevenhill, since it was built in 1849. Pull up a chair overlooking the street and partake in the delicious modern Australian food, perhaps kangaroo fillet with sweet-potato mash and quandong (a native fruit), or butterfish in a batter of Coopers Pale Ale (Adelaide's own beer). The wine list shows off the Clare Valley's best. ⊠*Main North Rd., Auburn* ☎*08/8849–2015* 🗖*AE, MC, V.*

$–$$ ✗**Skillogalee Winery.** The dining area here spills from an 1850s cottage ★ onto a beautiful veranda overlooking a flower-filled garden and rows of grapevines. The menu changes seasonally, but you can't go wrong with the "vine pruner's lunch," chef Diana Palmer's spin on the British plowman's meal, a platter of rum-glazed local ham, cheddar cheese, chutney, and crusty bread. Entrées might include duck leg braised in coconut milk and lemongrass, or Northern Territory barramundi with Skordalia (Greek garlic sauce); rich whiskey chocolate cake with raspberry coulis is the long-term favorite dessert. Gourmet picnic baskets can be ordered and group dinners are available by prior arrangement. Skillogalee also has self-contained cottage accommodation. ⊠*Hughes Park Rd.* ☎*08/8843–4311* 🗖*AE, DC, MC, V* ⊙*No dinner.*

$$$$ 🏨**Thorn Park Country House.** Saved from ruin by owners David Hay
Fodor'sChoice and Michael Speers, this mid-19th-century sandstone is one of Australia's finest gourmet retreats. Wood-burning fireplaces warm the ★ antique-filled sitting room and small library on wintry days. Bay windows look out on hawthorns and heritage roses. Rooms are named for colors; the largest and most inviting is the Blue-and-White Room, which is adorned with works by women artists; the White Room has a second bedroom that makes it perfect for children. The Barn is a small French provincial suite in the old dairy. Hay's cooked breakfasts and dinners (reservations required) are scrumptious—sometimes sinfully so. Hay also offers cooking classes, and Speers teaches art. ⊠*College Rd.,1½ km (1 mi) off Main North Rd* 🖂*Box 63, Sevenhill via Clare, 5453* ☎*08/8843–4304* ✉*stay@thornpark.com.au* ⊕*www.thornpark.com.au* 🛏*4 rooms, 2 suites* ⚬*In-room: no phone, kitchen (some), refrigerator (some), VCR (some), no TV (some). In-*

9

hotel: restaurant, no elevator, laundry service, public Internet, no-smoking rooms ⊟*AE, MC, V* ⦿⎮*BP.*

CLARE

10 km (6 mi) north of Sevenhill, 136 km (84 mi) north of Adelaide.

The bustling town of Clare is the Clare Valley's commercial center. Unusual for ultra-English South Australia, many of its early settlers were Irish—hence the valley's name, after the Irish county Clare, and place-names such as Armagh and Donnybrook.

☺ The **Old Police Station Museum** has an interesting collection of memorabilia from Clare's early days, as well as Victorian furniture and clothing, horse-drawn vehicles, and agricultural machinery. The 1850 stone building was Clare's first courthouse and police station. ⊠*Neagles Rock Rd., 1 km (½ mi) west of Main North Rd.* ☎*08/8842–2376* ⊠*A$2* ⦿ *Weekends 10–noon and 2–4.*

On Clare's fringe is **Leasingham Wines,** among the biggest producers in the valley. The winery began operation in 1893, which also makes it one of the oldest. The tasting room is in an old, vine-covered two-story stone still house complete with copper still. Leasingham's reputation of late has been forged by its red wines, particularly the peppery shiraz; don't miss the sparkling shiraz. ⊠*7 Dominic St.* ☎*08/8842–2785* ⊕*www.leasingham-wines.com.au* ⊠*Free* ⦿ *Weekdays 8:30–5, weekends 10–4.*

★ The small, no-frills tasting room means there is nothing to distract you from discovering why **Tim Adams Wines** has a big reputation. The standout in an impressive collection of reds and whites, which includes a celebrated Riesling and delicious Pinot Gris, is the purple-red Aberfeldy Shiraz, made from hundred-year-old vines. ⊠*Warenda Rd. just off Main North Rd., 5 km (3 mi) south of Clare* ☎*08/8842–2429 or 1800/356326* ⊕*www.timadamswines.com.au* ⊠*Free* ⦿ *Weekdays 10:30–5, weekends 11–5.*

WHERE TO STAY

$$$$ 🏠 **North Bundaleer.** The spoils of wealthy pastoral life await you at this
Fodor'sChoice   century-old sandstone homestead 61 km (38 mi) north of Clare, on the
★   scenic route to the Flinders Ranges. Beyond the jewel-box hall lined with hand-painted wallpaper is a ballroom where you can play the grand piano, and a peppermint-pink drawing room that's perfect for reading. After dining with hosts Marianne and Malcolm Booth at a Georgian table, you can slip into the canopy bed in the Red Room Suite, the most luxurious of six bedrooms. Rural isolation is a great excuse for taking a dinner/bed-and-breakfast package here. ⊠*Spalding–Jamestown Rd., Jamestown* ⊞*Box 255, Jamestown, 5491* ☎*08/8665–4024* ⊕*www.northbundaleer.com.au* ⇆*5 rooms, 1 suite* ⚬*In-room: no a/c (some), no phone, no TV. In-hotel: restaurant, bar, pool, no elevator, public Wi-Fi, no-smoking rooms* ⊟*AE, DC, MC, V* ⦿⎮*BP, MAP.*

$-$$ 🏨 **Clare Country Club.** Bordering the 11th fairway of Clare Golf Course, this country club is ideal for travelers keen on sports facilities. Several types of accommodation are available, from standard rooms to spacious two-room suites with kitchenettes. All have high-quality furnishings and whirlpool tubs. ⊠ *White Hutt Rd., 5453* ☎*08/8842–1060 or 1800/685337* ✎clare@countryclubs.com.au ⊕*www.countryclubs. com.au/clare-country-club/* 🛏*44 rooms, 3 suites* ⚫*In-room: kitchen (some), refrigerator, dial-up, Ethernet (some), Wi-Fi (some). In-hotel: restaurant, room service, bar, tennis court, pool, gym, no elevator, laundry facilities, no elevators, laundry service, no-smoking rooms* ▭*AE, DC, MC, V.*

CLARE VALLEY ESSENTIALS

TRANSPORTATION

BY CAR

The Clare Valley is about a 90-minute drive from Adelaide via Main North Road. From the center of Adelaide, head north on King William Street through the heart of North Adelaide. King William becomes O'Connell Street. After crossing Barton Terrace, look for Main North Road signs on the right. The road passes through the satellite town of Elizabeth, bypasses the center of Gawler, and then runs due north to Auburn, the first town of the Clare Valley when approaching from the capital. Main North Road continues down the middle of the valley to Clare.

As with the Barossa, a car is essential for exploring the Clare Valley in any depth. Taste wine in moderation if you're driving; as well as keeping yourself and others safe, you'll avoid paying the extremely high penalties for driving while intoxicated.

VISITOR INFORMATION

The Clare Valley Visitor Centre is open Monday–Friday 9–5, Saturday 10–4, and Sunday 11–4. It's 6 km (4 mi) south of Clare.

Contact Clare Valley Visitor Centre (⊠*Main North and Spring Gully Rds,* ☎*1800/242131 or 08/8842-2131* ⊕*www.clarevalley.com.au*).

FLEURIEU PENINSULA

The Fleurieu has traditionally been seen as Adelaide's backyard. Generations of Adelaide families have vacationed in the string of beachside resorts between Victor Harbor and Goolwa, near the mouth of the Murray River. McLaren Vale wineries attract connoisseurs, and the beaches and bays bring in surfers, swimmers, and sunseekers. The countryside, with its rolling hills and dramatic cliff scenery, is a joy to drive through.

Although the region is within easy reach of Adelaide, you should consider spending the night if you want to enjoy all it has to offer. You can also easily combine a visit here with one or more nights on Kangaroo Island. The ferry from Cape Jervis, at the end of the peninsula, takes less than an hour to reach Penneshaw on the island, and there are coach connections from Victor Harbor and Goolwa.

MCLAREN VALE

39 km (24 mi) south of Adelaide.

This region has a distinctly modern, upscale look, even though many of the more than 80 wineries in and around town are as old as their Barossa peers. The first vines were planted in 1838 at northern Reynella by Englishman John Reynell, who had collected them en route from the Cape of Good Hope. The McLaren Vale region has always been known for its big—and softer—reds, including shiraz, as well as a few white varietals.

The stone cellar door at **Coriole Vineyards** sits among nasturtiums and hollyhocks on a hill with St. Vincent Gulf views. From the surrounding vines, winemakers Grant Harrison and Mark Lloyd make some of Australia's best Italian varietal wines, such as Sangiovese and Nebbiolo, and a fine chenin blanc that tastes of guava. Coriole grows olives, too, and you can taste olive oils as well as wine. Enjoy a platter of estate-grown and local produce—cheese, smoked kangaroo, roasted vegetables, and chutney—in the flagstone courtyard (Friday to Monday). ⊠*Chaffeys Rd. near Kays Rd.* ☎*08/8238–0000* ⊕*www.coriole. com* ⊡*Free* ⊘ *Weekdays 10–5, weekends 11–5.*

A fine restaurant complements excellent wine at **d'Arenberg Wines,** family-run since 1912. Winemaker Chester d'Arenberg Osborn is known for his quality whites, including the luscious Noble Riesling dessert wine, as well as powerful reds and fortified wines with equally compelling names. Reservations are recommended for d'Arry's Verandah restaurant, which overlooks the vineyards, the valley, and the sea. The tempting seasonal menu uses local produce for pan-national dishes. Lunch is served daily. ⊠*Osborn Rd.* ☎*08/8329–4822 or 1800/882335* ⊕*www.darenberg.com.au* ⊡*Free* ⊘ *Daily 10–5.*

★ On a clear day you can indeed see forever from the cellar door at **Hugh Hamilton Wines.** Floor-to-ceiling windows in the geometric building offer 360-degree views down to the sea and up to the Mt. Lofty ranges. One of a dozen wines with fun names, the crisp white "Trickster" verdelho is as refreshing as the don't-miss scenery. Another must is "The Mongrel" Sangiovese blend. The first Sunday of the month from May to November is Oyster Day, when the winery throws a party in the name of everyone's favorite mollusk. ⊠*McMurtrie Rd. just east of McLaren Vale-to-Willunga cycling/walking track* ☎*08/8323–8689* ⊕*www.hamiltonwines.com.au* ⊡*Free* ⊘ *Weekdays 10–5:30, weekends 11–5:30.*

On a quiet, unpaved backroad, boutique winery **Pertaringa** (meaning "belonging to the hills") makes limited quantities of mouth-filling reds, and several whites. At the cellar-door, facing the vines, you can sip Two Gentlemen's Grenache and Scarecrow Sauvignon Blanc. It is worth buying some of the premium Over the Top Shiraz even without tasting—you won't be disappointed. ✉*Hunt and Rifle Range Rd.* ☎*08/8323–8125* ⊕*www.pertaringa.com.au* ☎*Free* ⊙*Weekdays 10–5, weekends 11–5.*

WHERE TO STAY & EAT

$$ ✗**Star of Greece.** More for the linen-slacks-and-deck-shoes set than the
★ board-shorts-and-sunscreen crowd, this extended weatherboard kiosk on the cliffs at Port Willunga, 10 km (6 mi) southwest of McLaren Vale, is beach-ball bright. Wooden chairs painted in mandarin, lime, and sky-blue stripes sit at paper-draped tables, and windows frame the aqua sea. (The offshore buoy marks where the three-masted *Star of Greece* foundered in 1888.) Reading the menu nets mostly seafood. You could order seared scallops wrapped in octopus bacon, or crispy skinned ocean trout on prawn salsa, but every white-plated dish the hip staff carries past may make you question your choice. ✉*The Esplanade, Port Willunga, 5173* ☎*08/8557–7420* ▭*AE, DC, MC, V* ⊙*No dinner Mon.–Thurs. (phone to check Apr.–Oct.).*

$–$$ ✗**Market 190.** With its worn floorboards and pressed-metal ceilings,
★ this café feels like a country corner store. Bottled olive oil and local jams line the shelves, and an assortment of cakes and other baked goods fills the glass-front counter. Come early for a cup of coffee and the best breakfast outside Adelaide. The menu shows off Fleurieu Peninsula produce: for a taste of McLaren Vale, order a regional platter, and for something spicier, tuck into aromatic duck curry. To finish, try the slow-baked lemon-and-lime tart. Book ahead for weekends. ✉*190 Main Rd.* ☎*08/8323–8558* ▭*AE, DC, MC, V* ⊙*No dinner.*

$ ✗**Blessed Cheese.** It's hard to disappoint when cheese and chocolate are your specialties, particularly when they're adeptly paired with local wines. Cheese maker and co-owner Mark Potter uses his PhD in biochemistry to mix up flavorful combinations of small-vineyard wines and cheese, available in A$15-per-head platters. He also runs daylong home cheese-making courses. The organic coffee is the best in the vale, and the baked cherry cheesecake is its perfect match. Blessed Cheese is the home and start point for the McLaren Vale Cheese & Wine Trail, a progressive picnic trail through the region. ✉*150 Main Rd.* ☎*08/8323–7958* ▭*AE, DC, MC, V* ⊙*No dinner.*

$$$ ▦**Wine and Roses B&B.** It may look like a regular residential house from the outside, but this luxury B&B has an interior that's far from ordinary. Liqueur-filled chocolates and port await you in your suite, where you can set the mood for romance with music or a movie, and relax in the double jetted tub or wrapped in a plush bathrobe beside the wood-burning fire. Choose from the pillow menu for bedtime. The house is five minutes from the main McLaren Vale road. ✉*39 Caffrey St., 5171* ☎*08/8323–7654* ⊕*www.wineandroses.com.au* ↩*3 suites* ♿*In-room: safe, kitchen (some), refrigerator, VCR (some), DVD (some), Wi-Fi. In-hotel: restaurant, no elevator, laundry service, no-smoking rooms, no kids under 16* ▭*AE, MC, V* ⊙*BP.*

$$–$$$ ▦**Willunga House B&B.** Parquet floors, pressed-metal ceilings, and marble fireplaces are among the original features in this inviting

1850s Georgian-style residence. Once the town's post office and general store, the house now has five double guest rooms with antique brass-and-iron beds. In winter a log fire blazes in the communal sitting room, which opens onto the first-floor balcony. The hearty complimentary breakfast includes produce fresh from the organic garden. Willunga is 7 km (4½ mi) south of McLaren Vale. ✉*1 St. Peter's Terr., Willunga, 5172* ☎*08/8556–2467* ✉*info@ willungahouse.com.au* ⊕*www. willungahouse.com.au* ❧*5 rooms* ⚘*In-room: no a/c (some), no phone. In-hotel: restaurant, pool, no elevator, laundry service, public Internet, no-smoking rooms, no kids under 16* ⊟*MC, V* ❍*BP.*

> **LIFE'S A PICNIC**
>
> Created by local winemakers after an afternoon of wine appreciation, the McLaren Vale Cheese & Wine Trail is the most civilized way to sample the region's best. Pick up a picnic hamper of four artisan cheeses, crackers, olives, and dried muscatel grapes at Blessed Cheese, and spend the next few hours following the trail map from cellar door to cellar door, tasting recommended wines with each cheese course.

VICTOR HARBOR

18 km (11 mi) west of Goolwa, 83 km (51 mi) south of Adelaide.

As famous for its natural beauty and wildlife as for its resorts, Victor Harbor is South Australia's seaside getaway town. In 1802 English and French explorers Matthew Flinders and Nicolas Baudin met here at Encounter Bay, and by 1830 the harbor was a major whaling center. Pods of southern right whales came here to breed in winter, and they made for a profitable trade through the mid-1800s. By 1878 the whales were hunted nearly to extinction, but the return of these majestic creatures to Victor Harbor in recent decades has established the city as a premiere source of information on whales and whaling history.

☾ The **South Australian Whale Centre** tells the often graphic story of the
★ whaling industry along South Australia's coast, particularly in Encounter Bay. Excellent interpretive displays spread over three floors focus on dolphins, seals, penguins, and whales—all of which can be seen in these waters. In whale-watching season the center has a 24-hour information hotline on sightings. There's a Discovery Trail and craft area for children. ✉*2 Railway Terr.* ☎*08/8552–5644, 1900/931223 whale information* ⊕*www.sawhalecentre.com* ✉*A$6* ❍*Daily 11–4:30.*

The **Bluff,** 7 km (4½ mi) west of Victor Harbor, is where whalers once stood lookout for their prey. Today the granite outcrop, also known as Rosetta Head, serves the same purpose in very different circumstances. It's a steep, 1,400-foot climb to the top, on a formed trail, to enjoy the Bluff views.

For cycling enthusiasts, there's also **Encounter Bikeway,** a paved track that runs 30 km (19 mi) from the Bluff along a scenic coastal route to

Laffin Point (east of Goolwa). Almost flat, the bikeway is suitable for riders of most ages and experience levels.

C **Granite Island** is linked to the mainland by a 650-yard causeway, along which Clydesdales pull a double-decker tram. Within Granite Island Nature Park a self-guided walk leads to the island's summit, and a penguin interpretive center runs guided walking tours to view the colony of about 1,500 fairy penguins. There is also an excellent seafood bistro (lunch only) with deck dining overlooking the harbor entrance (look out for seals in the shallows). ⊠ *Granite Island* ☎ *08/8552–7555* ⊕ *www.graniteisland.com.au* ✉ *Round-trip tram A$7, penguin tours A$12.50* ⊙ *Daily; penguin tours at dusk.*

C The **Cockle Train** travels the route of South Australia's first railway line. Originally laid between Goolwa and Port Elliot, and extended to Victor Harbor in 1864, the line traces the lovely Southern Ocean beaches on its 16-km (10-mi), half-hour journey. The train runs by steam power daily during summer school holidays (late December to late January), on Easter weekend, and on the third Sunday of each month from June to November. A diesel locomotive pulls the heritage passenger cars (or a diesel railcar operates) on other Sundays and public holidays, and days of Total Fire Ban. ⊠ *Railway Terr. near Coral St.* ☎ *08/8552–2782 (day of train journey), or 1300/655991* ⊕ *www.steamranger.org.au* ✉ *Round-trip A$26.*

WHERE TO STAY

$-$$ ▦ **Whalers Inn Resort.** The vibe is more tropical than maritime at Victor Harbor's upscale resort complex, with palm trees and spectacular surf as the backdrop for spacious, well-equipped rooms of varying configurations. Suites, all decorated in hazy seaside hues, can be joined together to make family quarters. Cook meals in your modern kitchen or head down to the Waterside restaurant and bar for fresh seafood and shoreline views. ⊠ *121 Franklin Parade, 5211* ☎ *08/8552–4400* ⊕ *www.whalersinnresort.com.au* ➫ *47 rooms, 12 apartments, 14 studios, 14 suites, 4 pool studios, 1 cottage* ⬥ *In-room: kitchen (some), refrigerator (some), VCR (some), dial-up. In-hotel: restaurant, bar, tennis court, pool, bicycles, no elevator, laundry facilities, laundry service, public Internet* ⊟ *AE, MC, V.*

  ⬣ **Port Elliot Caravan & Tourist Park.** Six kilometers (4 mi) east of Victor Harbor, this grassy park fronts beautiful tree-lined Horseshoe Bay, one of South Australia's best swimming beaches. Choose from campsites and self-contained cabins, villas, and spacious cottages (basic linens are provided). The park is within a regional reserve and close to cycling tracks and coastal walking paths. In whale-watching season (usually June to October) you can sometimes see southern right whales from the park. ⬥ *Flush toilets, partial hookups (electric and water), dump station, drinking water, guest laundry, showers, picnic tables, electricity, public telephone, general store, play area, swimming* ➫ *7 unpowered and 250 powered campsites, 9 villas, 3 cottages, 4 units, 4 cabins* ⊠ *Off Goolwa Rd. near Hussey St., Port Elliot, 5212* ☎ *08/8554–2134* 🖷 *08/8554–3454* ⊕ *www.portelliotcaravanpark.com.au* ⊟ *MC, V.*

9

FLEURIEU PENINSULA ESSENTIALS

TRANSPORTATION

BY CAR

Renting a car in Adelaide and driving south is the best way to visit the Fleurieu Peninsula, especially if you wish to tour the wineries, which aren't served by public transportation.

The Fleurieu is an easy drive south from Adelaide. McLaren Vale itself is less than an hour away. Leave central Adelaide along South Terrace or West Terrace, linking with the Anzac Highway, which heads toward Glenelg. At the intersection with Main South Road, turn left. This road takes you almost to McLaren Vale. After a detour to visit the wineries, watch for signs for Victor Harbor Road. About 20 km (12 mi) south the highway splits. One road heads for Victor Harbor, the other for Goolwa. Those two places are connected by a major road that follows the coastline. Drivers heading to Cape Jervis and the Kangaroo Island ferries should stay on Main South Road.

CONTACTS & RESOURCES
VISITOR INFORMATION

Inside the Victor Harbor Visitor Information Centre, open daily 9–5, try the Top Choice Travel desk for planning tours and accommodations. The large, open-plan McLaren Vale and Fleurieu Visitor Centre in the heart of the vineyards resembles a winery. In addition to tourist information, it has a café and wine bar. The center is open daily 10–5.

Contacts **McLaren Vale and Fleurieu Visitor Centre** (⊠ *Main St., McLaren Vale* ☎ *08/8323-9944* ⊕ *www.mclarenvale.info/visitorcentre*). **Top Choice Travel** (⊠ *The Causeway, Victor Harbor* ☎ *08/8552-7000*). **Victor Harbor Visitor Information Centre** (⊠ *The Causeway, Victor Harbor* ☎ *08/8552-5738* ⊕ *www. tourismvictorharbor.com.au*).

KANGAROO ISLAND

Kangaroo Island, Australia's third largest (after Tasmania and Melville), is barely 16 km (10 mi) from the Australian mainland. Yet the island belongs to another age—a folksy, friendly, less-sophisticated time when you'd leave your car unlocked and knew everyone by name.

The island is most beautiful along the coastline, where the land is sculpted into a series of bays and inlets teeming with bird and marine life. The stark interior has its own charm, however, with pockets of red earth between stretches of bush and farmland. Wildlife is probably the island's greatest attraction; in a single day you can stroll along a beach crowded with sea lions and watch kangaroos, koalas, pelicans, and fairy penguins in their native environments.

Its towns and most of its accommodations are on the island's eastern third. The standout sights are on the southern coast, so if you've only one day—you could easily spend a week—it's best to tour the island in a clockwise direction, leaving the north-coast beaches for the afternoon. Before heading out, fill your gas tank and pack a picnic lunch. Shops are few and far between outside the towns, general stores being the main outlets for food and gas.

The Kangaroo Island Tour Pass (A$45, A$121 families) is available from any National Parks and Wildlife site, or from the **National Parks and Wildlife SA Office** (✉ *37 Dauncey St., Kingscote* ☎ *08/8553–2381* ⊕ *www.parks. sa.gov.au/parks/visitors/pass/ki_pass*). The pass covers a selection of guided tours and park entry fees and is valid for a year.

> **HOW REMARKABLE**
>
> Balanced precariously on the promontory of Kirkpatrick Point in Flinders Chase National Park, the Remarkable Rocks are aptly named. Sitting with your back against one of these fantastically shaped boulders is the best way to view sunset or sunrise on Kangaroo Island.

KINGSCOTE

121 km (75 mi) southwest of Adelaide.

Kangaroo Island's largest town, Kingscote is a good base for exploring. Reeves Point, at the town's northern end, is where South Australia's colonial history began. Settlers landed here in 1836 and established the first official town in the new colony. Little remains of the original settlement except Hope Cottage, now a small museum; several graves; and a huge, twisted mulberry tree that grew from a cutting the settlers brought from England—locals still use the fruit to make jam. Today American River, about halfway between Kingscote and Penneshaw, the island's second-largest town, is another accommodation and restaurant hub.

Make sure you catch the **Pelican Feeding** "show" at 5 PM daily on the rock wall beside Kingscote Jetty. A guide in fishing waders gives an informative and entertaining talk as he feeds handfuls of seafood to a comic mob of noisy pelicans. This is great fun. ✉ *Kingscote Jetty* ☎ *08/8553–3112 Kangaroo Island Marine Centre* 🖼 *A$2* ⏲ *Daily 5 PM.*

WHERE TO STAY & EAT

$$ ✗**Restaurant Bella.** This contemporary Italian restaurant serves dishes prepared with the freshest local ingredients. Starters such as basil-topped vegetable ragout on tomato risotto evoke the Mediterranean, while Asian flavors spice up some of the main courses. Look out for the king-prawn-and-squid salad with vermicelli noodles, Asian greens, and tamarind sauce. You can also order gourmet pizza, cooked in the adjoining café. A simplified café menu is available at lunchtime under the sidewalk awning. ✉ *54 Dauncey St.* ☎ *08/8553–0400* ⊟ *AE, DC, MC, V.*

$–$$$ 🖼**Ozone Seafront Hotel.** The Victorian facade on this two-story 1920s hotel hides surprisingly modern and spacious rooms that overlook Nepean Bay. The choicest accommodations, however, are in the adjoining wing built in 2006. Lots of windows, flat-screen TVs, vibrant mod-

9

ern artworks, and some in-room whirlpool tubs make the new Ozone Suites and Penthouse Apartments among the island's best. The huge bistro menu stars local seafood, and the wine list runs to 100 vintages, many of them local. There are daily wine tastings in the bar. The airport is a 15-minute drive away. ⊠*Chapman Terr. at Commercial St., 5223* ☎*08/8553–2011 or 1800/083133* ✎info@ozoneseafront. com ⊕*www.ozonehotel.com* ⇖*85 rooms, 4 apartments* ⌂*In-room: safe (some), refrigerator, DVD (some). In-hotel: restaurant, bars, pool, gym, beachfront, no elevator, laundry facilities, public Internet, public Wi-Fi, no-smoking rooms* ⊟*AE, DC, MC, V.*

$$ 🏨**Wanderers Rest.** Delightful local artworks dot the walls in this country inn's stylish units. The elevated veranda and à la carte restaurant, where breakfast is served, have splendid views across American River to the mainland. ⊠*Bayview Rd., Box 34, American River, 5221* ☎*08/8553–7140* ✎wanderers@kin.net.au ⊕*www.wanderersrest.com.au* ⇖*9 rooms* ⌂*In-room: no phone, refrigerator. In-hotel: restaurant, bar, pool, no elevator, public Internet, no kids under 10, no-smoking rooms* ⊟*AE, DC, MC, V* ⏚*BP.*

PENNESHAW

62 km (39 mi) east of Kingscote.

This tiny ferry port has a huge population of penguins, which are visible on nocturnal tours. Gorgeous shoreline, views of spectacularly blue water, and rolling green hills are a few lovely surprises here.

☉ **Penneshaw Penguin Centre** offers two ways to view the delightful fairy penguins indigenous to Kangaroo Island. From the indoor interpretive center, where you can read about bird activity—including mating, nesting, and feeding—a boardwalk leads to a viewing platform above rocks and sand riddled with burrows. Because the penguins spend most of the day fishing at sea or inside their burrows, the best viewing is after sunset. You can take a self-guided walk or an informative guided tour, which starts with a talk and video at the center. You might see penguins waddling ashore, chicks emerging from their burrows to feed, or scruffy adults molting. ⊠*Middle and Bay Terrs.* ☎☎*08/8553–1103 or 08/8553–1016* ✉*Interpretive center free, guided tours A$9, self-guided tours A$6* ☉*Tours at 7:30 and 8:30 PM in winter, 8:30 and 9:30 PM in summer.*

WHERE TO STAY & EAT

¢–$$ ✕**Fish.** Belly up to the counter in this tiny shop for cheap local seafood
★ to take out or enjoy with a glass of wine in the seating area next door. Choose your fish—whiting, John Dory, garfish—from the blackboard menu and have it beer-battered, crumbed, or grilled. Or you might prefer a paper-wrapped parcel of scallops, prawns, lobster, and oysters (in season) shucked to order. The team behind the shop also runs 2 Birds & A Squid, which prepares seafood packs and cooked meals for pickup or delivery to your accommodation anywhere on the island.

✉ *43 North Terr.* ☎ *08/8553–1177 (Fish), 08/8553–7406 (2 Birds & A Squid)* ⊕ *www.2birds1squid.com* ▭ *No credit cards* ⊘ *Closed June–Sept. No lunch.*

$ ✕ **Isolo.** Piping-hot pizza in all sizes and flavors is a great way to fuel up for an evening of penguin-spotting. Take your meal to the adjacent park on the water, or dine in and enjoy the traditional pizzeria setting. The lasagna is great, too. ✉ *North Terr. near Nat Thomas St.* ☎ *08/8553–1227* ▭ *MC, V* ⊘ *No lunch.*

$ 🏠 **Beach House on the Bay.** Apple-green, hot-pink, and crimson cushions
★ on white cane couches make this tiny sky-blue weatherboard a seaside treasure. Opening off the glass-fronted sitting room are two bedrooms, and there are more stainless-steel utensils in the compact adjoining kitchen than even a holidaying chef could find a use for. Feel the polished floorboards underfoot as you read a book or listen to a CD; then stroll across the road and get white sand between your toes on Hog Bay beach. ✉ *Frenchman's Terr. near Choops St., 5222* ☎ *08/8339–3103 or 0428/339310* ⇆ *2 bedrooms, 1 bungalow* ⌂ *In-room: no phone, kitchen, refrigerator, DVD. In-hotel: beachfront, no elevator, laundry facilities, no-smoking rooms* ▭ *No credit cards.*

SEAL BAY CONSERVATION PARK

⟳ *60 km (37 mi) southwest of Kingscote via South Coast Rd.*

Fodor'sChoice
★ This top Kangaroo Island attraction gives you the chance to visit one of the state's largest Australian sea-lion colonies. About 300 animals usually lounge on the beach, except on stormy days, when they shelter in the dunes. You can only visit the beach, and get surprisingly close to females, pups, and bulls, on a tour with an interpretive officer; otherwise, you can follow the self-guided boardwalk to a lookout over the sand. Two-hour sunset tours depart on varied days in December and January; a minimum of four people is required, as is 24-hour advance booking. The park visitor center has fun and educational displays, and a touch table covered in sea lion skins and bones. There is also a shop. ✉ *End of Seal Bay Rd., Seal Bay* ☎ *08/8559–4207* 🌐 *Group tour A$13 per person, sunset tour A$31, boardwalk A$9.50* ⊘ *Tours Dec. and Jan., daily 9–5:15, every 15–45 mins; Feb.–Nov., daily 9–4:15, every 45 mins.*

FLINDERS CHASE NATIONAL PARK

★ *102 km (64 mi) west of Kingscote.*

Some of the most beautiful coastal scenery in Australia is in Flinders Chase National Park on Kangaroo Island's western end. Much of the island has been widely cultivated and grazed, but the park has protected a huge area of original vegetation since it was declared a national treasure in 1919.

The seas crashing onto Australia's southern coast are merciless, and their effects are visible in the oddly shaped rocks off Kangaroo Island's shores. A limestone promontory was carved from underneath at Cape du Couedic on the island's southwestern coast, producing what is known as **Admiral's Arch.** From the boardwalk you can see the New Zealand fur seals that have colonized the area around the rock formation. About 4 km (2½ mi) farther east are the aptly named **Remarkable Rocks,** huge fantastically shaped boulders balanced precariously on the promontory of Kirkpatrick Point. This is a great place to watch the sun set or rise.

Flinders Chase has several 1½-km- to 9-km- (1-mi- to 5½-mi-) loop walking trails, which take one to three hours to complete. The trails meander along the rivers to the coast, passing mallee scrub and sugar gum forests, and explore the rugged shoreline. The 4-km (2½-mi) Snake Lagoon Hike follows Rocky River over and through a series of broad rocky terraces to the remote sandy beach where it meets the sea. The sign warning of freak waves is not just for show.

The park is on the island's western end, bounded by the Playford and West End highways. The state-of-the-art visitor center, open daily 9–5, is the largest National Parks and Wildlife office. Displays and touch screens explore the park's history and the different habitats and wildlife in Flinders Chase. The center provides park entry tickets and camping permits, and books stays at the Heritage cabins. A shop sells souvenirs and provisions and there is also a café.

WHERE TO STAY & EAT

Accommodations within the national park (and in Cape Willoughby Conservation Park at the other end of the island) are controlled by the **Flinders Chase National Park Office** (☎08/8559–7235 ⊕*www.parks. sa.gov.au/flinderschase*). Rustic sofas, chairs, and tables furnish huts, cottages, homesteads, and lighthouse lodgings at Cape Willoughby (at the island's southeastern point), Cape du Couedic (southwest), and Cape Borda (northwest). All accommodations have kitchens or cooking facilities; blankets and pillows are supplied and you can rent bed linens and towels. Camping is allowed only at designated sites at Rocky River and in bush campgrounds and permits are essential.

$–$$$$ ✕🏠**Kangaroo Island Wilderness Retreat.** With wallabies and possums treating the grounds as their own domain, this eco-friendly retreat is everything a wildlife-loving traveler could want. Rooms in the low-slung log courtyard buildings have recycled Oregon pine furniture; private rear decks in the two corner suites open onto thick banksia scrub. Family-friendly one-bed apartments and motel-style rooms share the barnlike Lodge. Rain is the only water source and showers are solar heated. The dining room serves Mod-Oz fare that uses many island products; the kitchen also prepares picnic lunches. The gas pump here is the last one for 35 km (21 mi). ⊠*1 South Coast Rd., Flinders Chase, 5223* ☎*08/8559–7275* ✐stay@kiwr.com ⊕*www.kiwr.com* 🛏*18 courtyard rooms, 2 suites, 4 apartments, 7 lodge rooms* △*In-room: no phone (some), kitchen (some), refrigerator (some), DVD (some),* *no TV (some), ethernet (some), Wi-Fi (some). In-hotel: restaurant, bar, no elevator, laundry service, public Internet, public Wi-Fi, no-smoking rooms* ⊟*AE, DC, MC, V.*

⚠**Rocky River Campground.** Birds sing rousing morning choruses and wallabies and possums are everywhere—so keep everything shut and zipped—in this campground a few hundred yards behind the Flinders Chase visitor center. There are tent and camper-van sites (but no electricity), a covered communal eating area, and a rainwater tank. The camp abuts a beautiful grassy swamp, and you can follow walking trails from here to platypus-viewing platforms on Rocky River; look for koalas in the trees along the way. ⚍*Flush toilets, drinking water, showers, picnic tables, public telephone, general store, ranger station* ⤴*21 campsites, group camping area* ⊠*Just off Cape Couedic Rd., 5223* ☎*08/8559–7235* ⊕*www.parks.sa.gov.au/flinderschase* ⊟*MC, V.*

KANGAROO ISLAND ESSENTIALS

TRANSPORTATION

BY AIR

REX/Regional Express flies twice daily between Adelaide and Kingscote, the island's main airport. Ask about 14-day advance-purchase fares and holiday packages in conjunction with SeaLink. Flights to the island take about 30 minutes.

Airlines REX/Regional Express (☎*13–1713* ⊕ *www.rex.com.au*).

BY BOAT

SeaLink ferries allow access for cars through Penneshaw from Cape Jervis, at the tip of the Fleurieu Peninsula, a 90-minute drive from Adelaide.

SeaLink operates the vehicular passenger ferry *Sea Lion 2000* and *Spirit of Kangaroo Island,* a designated freight boat with passenger facilities. These ferries make 45-minute crossings between Cape Jervis and Penneshaw. There are three daily sailings each way, with up to eight crossings at peak times. Ferries are the favored means of transportation between the island and the mainland, and reservations are advisable during the holidays.

Adelaide Sightseeing operates coaches in conjunction with the SeaLink ferry services from Cape Jervis and Penneshaw, linking Adelaide, Victor Harbor, and Goolwa with Cape Jervis.

Contacts Adelaide Sightseeing (⊠*101 Franklin St., City Center, Adelaide* ☎*08/8413–6199* ⊕ *www.adelaidesightseeing.com.au*). **SeaLink** (☎*13–1301* ⊕ *www.sealink.com.au*).

BY CAR

Kangaroo Island's main attractions are widely scattered; you can see them best on a guided tour or by car. The main roads form a paved loop, which branches off to such major sites as Seal Bay, and Admirals Arch and Remarkable Rocks in Flinders Chase National Park. Stretches of unpaved road lead to lighthouses at Cape Borda and Cape Willoughby, South Australia's oldest. Roads to the island's northern beaches, bays, and camping areas are also unpaved. These become very rutted in summer, but they can be driven carefully in a conventional vehicle. Be alert for wildlife, especially at dawn, dusk, and after dark. Slow down and dip your lights so you don't blind the animals you see.

Contacts Budget (⊠ *51A Dauncey St., Kingscote, 5223* ☎ *08/8553–3133*). **Hertz Kangaroo Island** (⊠ *Franklin St. at Telegraph Rd., Kingscote* ☎ *08/8553–2390*).

CONTACTS & RESOURCES

In Kingscote there is a health clinic and a hospital with an emergency department. General practitioners make visits at least twice a month to health centers in Penneshaw, American River, and Parndana.

Contacts American River Health Service (⊠ *Tangara Dr., American River, 5221* ☎ *08/8553–7110*). **Kangaroo Island Health Service & Hospital** (⊠ *The Esplanade, Kingscote, 5223* ☎ *08/8553–4200*). **Kangaroo Island Medical Clinic** (⊠ *64 Murray St., Kingscote, 5223* ☎ *08/8553–2037*). **Penneshaw Community Health Centre** (⊠ *Howard Dr., Penneshaw, 5222* ☎ *08/8553–1101*).

TOURS

Exceptional Kangaroo Island has quality four-wheel-drive and bush-walking tours from A$340 per person per day. Tailor-made itineraries, including bird-watching and photography, and flight-accommodation packages can also be arranged. Kangaroo Island Odysseys operates luxury four-wheel-drive nature tours from one to three days priced from A$315 per person. Kangaroo Island Wilderness Tours has four personalized four-wheel-drive wilderness tours with full accommodations ranging from one to four days and starting at A$365 per person.

Adventure Tours Exceptional Kangaroo Island (☎ *08/8553–9119* 🖷 *08/8553–9122* ⊕ *www.adventurecharters.com.au*). **Kangaroo Island Odysseys** (☎ *08/8553–0386* 🖷 *08/8553–0387* ⊕ *www.kiodysseys.com.au*). **Kangaroo Island Wilderness Tours** (☎ *08/8559–5033* 🖷 *08/8559–5088* ⊕ *www.wildernesstours.com.au*).

VISITOR INFORMATION

The Gateway Visitor Information Centre in Penneshaw (🕑 weekdays 9–5, weekends 10–4) is a model for tourist-information offices. Ask for the *Fast Fact Finder* to get an overview of where to shop, bank, surf the Web, and fuel up your car on the island.

Contact Gateway Visitor Information Centre (⊠ *Howard Dr., Penneshaw* ☎ *08/8553–1185* 🖷 *08/8553–1255* ⊕ *www.tourkangarooisland.com.au*).

THE OUTBACK

South Australia is the country's driest state, and its Outback is an expanse of desert vegetation. But this land of scrubby salt bush and hardy eucalyptus trees is brightened after rain by wildflowers—including the state's floral emblem, the blood-red Sturt's desert pea, with its black, olivelike heart. The terrain is marked by geological uplifts, abrupt transitions between plateaus broken at the edges of ancient, long-inactive fault lines. Few roads track through this desert wilderness—the main highway is the Stuart, which runs all the way to Alice Springs in the Northern Territory.

The people of the Outback are as hardy as their surroundings. They are also often eccentric, colorful characters who happily bend your ear over a drink in the local pub. Remote, isolated communities attract loners, adventurers, fortune-seekers, and people simply on the run. In this unyielding country, you must be tough to survive.

PONY EXPRESS

The Coober Pedy–Oodnadatta Mail Run Tour is the most unusual experience you'll have anywhere. Former miner–turned–entrepreneur Peter Rowe and his brother Derek Rowe, a renowned horseman, run the tour, delivering mail and supplies to remote cattle stations and Outback towns. You also get a good look at the Dog Fence, and at the dingoes it was built to keep away.

COOBER PEDY

850 km (527 mi) northwest of Adelaide.

Known as much for the way most of its 3,500 inhabitants live—underground in dugouts gouged into the hills—as for its opal riches, Coober Pedy is arguably Australia's most singular place. The town is ringed by mullock heaps, pyramids of rock and sand left over after mine shafts are dug.

Opals are Coober Pedy's reason for existence. Australia has 95% of the world's opal deposits, and Coober Pedy has the bulk of that wealth; this is the world's richest opal field.

Opal was discovered here in 1915, and soldiers returning from World War I excavated the first dugout homes when the searing heat forced them underground. In midsummer temperatures can reach 48°C (118°F), but inside the dugouts the air remains a constant 22°C–24°C (72°F–75°F).

Coober Pedy is a brick and corrugated-iron settlement propped unceremoniously on a scarred desert landscape. It's a town built for efficiency, not beauty. However, its ugliness has a kind of bizarre appeal. There's a feeling that you're in the last lawless outpost in the modern world, helped in no small part by the local film lore—*Priscilla Queen of the Desert, Pitch Black, Kangaroo Jack,* and *Mad Max 3* were filmed here. Once you go off the main street you get an immediate sense of the apocalyptic.

EXPLORING COOBER PEDY

Fossicking for opal gemstones—locally called noodling—requires no permit at the Jewellers Shop mining area at the edge of town. Take care in unmarked areas and always watch your step, as the area is littered with abandoned opal mines down which you might fall. (Working mines are off-limits to visitors.)

Although most of Coober Pedy's devotions are decidedly material in nature, the town does have its share of spiritual houses of worship. In keeping with the town's layout, they, too, are underground. **St. Peter and St. Paul's Catholic Church** is a National Heritage–listed building, and the Anglican **Catacomb Church** is notable for its altar fashioned from a windlass (a winch) and lectern made from a log of mulga wood. The **Serbian Orthodox Church** is striking, with its scalloped ceiling, rock-carved icons, and brilliant stained-glass windows. The **Revival Fellowship Underground Church** has lively gospel services.

★ The **Old Timers Mine** is a genuine opal mine turned into a museum. Two underground houses, furnished in 1920s and 1980s styles, are part of the complex, where mining memorabilia is exhibited in an extensive network of hand-dug tunnels and shafts. You can also watch demonstrations of opal mining machines. Tours are self-guided. ⊠ *Crowders Gully Rd. near Umoona Rd.* ☎ *08/8672–5555* ⊕ *www.oldtimersmine.com* ⊡ *A$10* ⊙ *Daily 9–7.*

Umoona Opal Mine & Museum is an enormous underground complex with an original mine, a noteworthy video on the history of opal mining, an Aboriginal Interpretive Centre, and clean, underground bunk camping and cooking facilities. Guided tours of the mine are available. ⊠ *14 Hutchison St.* ☎ *08/8672–5288* ⊕ *www.umoonaopalmine.com. au* ⊡ *Tour A$10* ⊙ *Daily 8–7; tours at 10, 2, and 4.*

AROUND TOWN

Breakaways, a striking series of buttes and jagged hills centered on the Moon Plain, is reminiscent of the American West. There are fossils and patches of petrified forest in this strange landscape, which has appealed to makers of apocalyptic films. *Mad Max 3—Beyond Thunderdome* was filmed here, as was *Ground Zero.* The scenery is especially evocative early in the morning. The Breakaways area is 30 km (19 mi) northeast of Coober Pedy.

Fodor'sChoice The Coober Pedy–Oodnadatta **Mail Run Tour** (⊠ *Post Office Hill Rd.*
★   ☎ *08/8672–5226 or 1800/069911* ⊕ *www.mailruntour.com*), a 12-hour, 600-km (372-mi) tour through the Outback (A$165), is one of the most unusual experiences anywhere. Tours depart at 8:45 AM from Underground Books on Post Office Hill Road.

Radeka's Night Sky Presentation (☎ *08/8672–5223* ⊕ *www.radekadownunder.com.au*) is a one-hour introduction to the southern sky, including the famous Southern Cross constellation depicted on the Australian flag. Ideal for beginners and suitable for all ages, the show takes place at the Moon Plain Desert, about 6 km (4 mi) outside Coober Pedy. The guide will pick you up at your hotel immediately after dark. Trips are A$25.

WHERE TO STAY & EAT

$$ ✕ **Umberto's.** Perched atop the monolithic Desert Cave Hotel, this eatery named after the hotel's founding developer is Coober Pedy's most urbane restaurant. The Mod-Oz menu takes you from the Outback

(oven-baked kangaroo loin with grilled figs) to the sea (lemon sole). ⊠*Hutchison St.* ☎*08/8672–5688* ▭*AE, DC, MC, V* ☺*No lunch.*

$$ 🖪**Desert Cave Hotel.** What may be the world's only underground hotel presents a contemporary, blocky face to the desert town. In the 19 spacious, subsurface rooms, luxurious furnishings in desert hues complement and contrast the red-striated rock walls that protect sleepers from sound and heat. Aboveground rooms are also available. The hotel offers daily tours of the town and surrounding sights. ⊠*Hutchison St. at Post Office Hill Rd., 5723* ☎*08/8672–5688 or 1800/088521* ⊕*www.desertcave.com.au* ⤳*50 rooms* ⚘*In-room: no a/c (some), refrigerator, dial-up, Wi-Fi (some). In-hotel: 2 restaurants, room service, bar, pool, gym, no elevator, laundry facilities, public Internet, no-smoking rooms, minibar* ▭*AE, DC, MC, V.*

$ 🖪**Mud Hut Motel.** Mud brick is the building material used here, and desert hues in the guest rooms continue the earthy theme. Two-bedroom apartments have cooking facilities. One unit is available for travelers with disabilities. The à la carte restaurant has outside dining and serves international fare. ⊠*Lot 102 St. Nicholas St., 5723* ☎*08/8672–3003, 1800/646962 South Australia and Northern Territory only* ⊕*www. mudhutmotel.com.au* ⤳*24 rooms, 4 apartments* ⚘*In-room: kitchen (some), refrigerator, DVD, dial-up. In-hotel: restaurant, room service, bar, no elevator, laundry facilities, public Internet, airport shuttle, no-smoking rooms* ▭*AE, DC, MC, V.*

¢–$ 🖪**Opal Inn.** Owned by the same folks who run the Desert Cave, this lodging is the place to meet Coober Pedy characters and opal buyers. You can chat with them over a drink in the bistro (a favorite local gathering spot) or play a game of pool on one of two tables. The accommodations include everything from budget rooms with shared bathrooms to family-size suites. You can also pitch a tent or bring your camper. ⊠*Hutchison and Wright Sts., 5723* ☎*08/8672–5054 or 1800/088523* ⊕*www.opalinn.com.au* ⤳*77 rooms, 2 suites* ⚘*In-room: no phone (some), kitchen (some), refrigerator, dial-up (some). In-hotel: restaurant, bars, no elevator, laundry facilities, public Internet, some pets allowed, no-smoking rooms* ▭*AE, DC, MC, V.*

THE OUTBACK ESSENTIALS

TRANSPORTATION

BY AIR

REX/Regional Express Airlines flies direct to Coober Pedy from Adelaide Sunday–Friday. Because it's the only public carrier flying to Coober Pedy, prices are sometimes steep. However, anyone holding a valid ISIC, YHA, or VIP card is eligible for unlimited air travel throughout Australia on the Backpackers pass for a flat rate of A$499 for one month, or A$949 for two months.

The airport is open only when a flight is arriving or departing. At other times, contact the Desert Cave Hotel.

Airport Coober Pedy Airport (⊠ *Stuart Hwy., 2 km (1 mi) north of town, Coober Pedy* ☎ *08/8672–5688*).

Airline REX/Regional Express (☎ *13–1713* ⊕ *www.rex.com.au*).

BY BUS
Greyhound Australia buses leave Adelaide's Central Bus Terminal for Coober Pedy daily. Tickets for the 12-hour ride cost A$156 each way.

Contacts Greyhound Australia (☎ *1300/473946863* ⊕ *www.greyhound.com.au*).

BY CAR
The main road to Coober Pedy is the Stuart Highway from Adelaide, 850 km (527 mi) to the south. Alice Springs is 700 km (434 mi) north of Coober Pedy. The drive from Adelaide to Coober Pedy takes about nine hours. From Alice Springs it's about seven hours.

Contact Budget (☎ *08/8672–5333 or 1300/362848*).

CONTACTS & RESOURCES
EMERGENCIES
There are hospitals with accident and emergency departments in Coober Pedy and in Hawker, the nearest town to Wilpena Pound.

Hospitals Coober Pedy Hospital (⊠ *Hospital Rd., Coober Pedy* ☎ *08/8672–5009*). **Hawker Memorial Hospital** (⊠ *Craddock St., Hawker* ☎ *08/8648–4007*).

VISITOR INFORMATION
The Coober Pedy Visitor Information Centre is open weekdays 8:30–5. More information about national parks can be obtained through the Department for Environment and Heritage, or from the Wilpena Pound Visitor Centre.

Contacts Coober Pedy Visitor Information Centre (⊠ *Coober Pedy District Council Bldg., Hutchison St., Coober Pedy* ☎ *08/8672–5298 or 1800/637076* ⊕ *www.opalcapitaloftheworld.com.au*). **Department for Environment and Heritage** (⊠ *Level 1, 100 Pirie St., City Center, Adelaide* ☎ *08/8204–1910* ⊕ *www. environment.sa.gov.au/parks/outback.html*). **Wilpena Pound Visitor Centre** (⊠ *Wilpena Rd., Wilpena Pound* ☎ *08/8648–0048*).

The Red Centre

WORD OF MOUTH

"I think that Uluru is a magical place that is worth visiting. Instead of a tour, I would fly to Alice Springs, rent a campervan, and do my own tour, which would include Uluru, Kata Tjuta, Kings Canyon, and the McDonnel Range. To be sure, there is quite a bit of driving here (over 1,000 km), but you will get a much better appreciation for the varied terrain and vastness of the Red Centre!"

—ALF

"You cannot tell from the one picture of Uluru (Ayers Rock) how stunning and varied the features of the rock are. There are no images of these because they are sacred to the Aboriginal people, who ask that photos not be taken."

—kerikeri

Updated by
Emily Burg

THE LUMINESCENT LIGHT IN THE Red Centre—named for the deep color of its desert soils—has a purity and vitality that photographs only begin to approach. For tens of thousands of years, this vast desert territory has been home to Australia's indigenous Aboriginal people. Uluṟu, also known as Ayers Rock, is a great symbol in Aboriginal traditions, as are many sacred sites among the Centre's mountain ranges, gorges, dry riverbeds, and spinifex plains. At the center of all this is Alice Springs, Australia's only desert city.

The essence of this ancient land is epitomized in the paintings of the renowned Aboriginal landscape artist Albert Namatjira and his followers. Viewed away from the desert, their images of the MacDonnell Ranges may appear at first to be garish and unreal in their depiction of purple-and-red mountain ranges and stark-white ghost gum trees. Seeing the real thing makes it difficult to imagine executing the paintings in any other way.

Uluṟu (pronounced *oo*-loo-*roo*), that magnificent stone monolith rising from the plains, is but one focus in the Red Centre. The rounded forms of Kata Tjuṯa (*ka*-ta *tchoo*-ta), also known as the Olgas, are another. Watarrka National Park and Kings Canyon, Mt. Conner, and the cliffs, gorges, and mountain chains of the MacDonnell Ranges are other worlds to explore.

EXPLORING THE RED CENTRE

The primary areas of interest are Alice Springs, which is flanked by the intriguing eastern and western MacDonnell Ranges; Kings Canyon; and Uluṟu–Kata Tjuṯa National Park, with neighboring Ayers Rock Resort. Unless you have more than three days, focus on only one of these areas.

To reach the Red Centre, you can fly from most large Australian cities into either Alice Springs or direct to Ayers Rock Resort. You can also fly the 440 km (273 mi) between the two centers. By rail, you can take one of the world's classic train journeys from Adelaide to Alice Springs (16 hours) or Darwin (23 hours) on the *Ghan,* named after the Afghan camel-train drivers who once traveled the Adelaide–Alice Springs route.

ABOUT THE RESTAURANTS

Restaurants in Alice Springs and at Ayers Rock Resort cater primarily to tourists, and accordingly specialize in native Australian meats, such as crocodile, kangaroo, and camel. Meals are often served with local fruits, berries, and plants. Definitely try this "bush tucker," perhaps within the pioneer setting of a saloon or steak house.

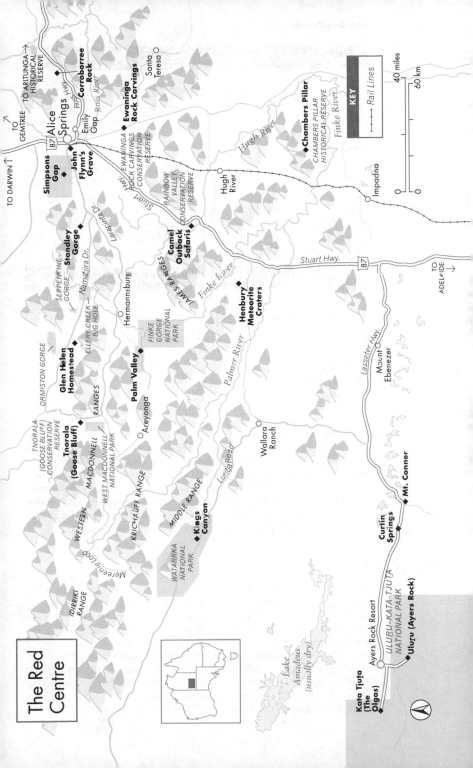

WHAT IT COSTS IN AUSTRALIAN DOLLARS				
$$$$	$$$	$$	$	¢
AT DINNER	over A$50	A$36–A$50	A$21–A$35	A$10–A$20	under A$10

Prices are for a main course at dinner.

ABOUT THE HOTELS

Alice Springs has all kinds of accommodation choices: youth hostels and motels, a casino-hotel, and top-quality resorts. Caravan and camping parks are also popular, and have numerous facilities and even entertainment. Ayers Rock Resort—which is the only place to stay in the vicinity of Uluru–Kata Tjuta National Park—is actually a group of seven different accommodations with different price ranges, all of which are managed by Voyages Hotels & Resorts.

WHAT IT COSTS IN AUSTRALIAN DOLLARS				
$$$$	$$$	$$	$	¢
FOR TWO PEOPLE	over A$300	A$201–A$300	A$151–A$200	A$100–A$150	under A$100

Prices are for two people in a standard double room in high season, including tax and service, based on the European Plan (with no meals) unless otherwise noted.

WHEN TO VISIT

May through September (Australian winter) are the best months to visit, as nights are crisp and cold and days are pleasantly warm. Summer temperatures—which can rise above 43°C (110°F)—are oppressive. Every August or September, Alice Springs comes alive with the

★ **Henley-on-Todd Regatta,** a colorful event in the dry Todd riverbed that runs through the middle of town, where the racers scamper along inside

★ bottomless boats. At the **Alice Springs Camel Cup,** held on the second Saturday in July, jockeys race camels around a sand track. The Bangtail Muster cattle and float parade wanders along Alice's main street on May Day. National parks are open daily year-round, but the heat during the summer months limits tourists' options in the region. Many spots in Alice Springs also close down for the summer months.

ALICE SPRINGS

Once a ramshackle collection of dusty streets and buildings, Alice Springs—known colloquially as "the Alice" or just "Alice"—is today an incongruously suburban tourist center with a population of more than 28,000 in the middle of the desert. Visited by more than 300,000 tourists annually, the town's ancient sites, a focus for the Arrernte Aboriginal people's ceremonial activities, lie cheek by jowl with air-conditioned shops and hotels. Alice derives most of its income from tourism. The MacDonnell Ranges dominate Alice Springs, changing color according to the time of day from brick red to purple. Another striking feature of the town is the Todd River. Water rarely runs in the desert, and the Todd's deep sandy beds, fringed by majestic ghost gum trees, suggest a timelessness far different from the bustle of the nearby town.

Until the 1970s the Alice was a frontier town servicing the region's pastoral industry, and life was tough. During World War II it was one of the few (barely) inhabited stops on the 3,024-km (1,875-mi) supply lines between Adelaide and the front line at Darwin. First established at the Old Telegraph Station as the town of Stuart, it was moved and renamed Alice Springs—after the wife of the telegraph boss Charles Todd—in 1933. Alice still is a hub for Aborigines. If you're looking for Aboriginal art, galleries abound along Todd Mall (the main shopping street in town); they're filled with canvas and bark paintings, as well as handcrafted didgeridoos and other artifacts. You can also buy art directly from Aborigines on weekends outside Flynn Memorial Church in the mall.

It's worth noting, however, that many Aborigines living in or around Alice Springs have been asked to leave their native villages by tribal elders because of their problems with alcohol. Crime and violence stemming from alcohol abuse can make Alice unsafe at night, especially for women travelers. Sections of the dry Todd riverbed function as makeshift campsites for some Aborigines, so caution is advised when traversing the Todd, especially after dark.

EXPLORING ALICE SPRINGS

Anzac Hill, the highest point in Alice Springs, is the ideal place to start exploring. After taking in the views south to the MacDonnell Ranges, walk down the path on the town side of the hill. From the base, head east along Wills Terrace to the Todd River. On Leichardt Terrace, walk south among the wonderfully colored and textured ghost gums along the river. At Parsons Street, turn right (west), then left at the shade awnings into Todd Mall, Alice Springs' main shopping precinct. Through the Mall, explore the area south of the Mall before returning north to Parsons Street via Hartley. Expect to spend about five hours in this area.

10

WHAT TO SEE: CITY CENTER

❸ Aboriginal Australia Arts & Culture Centre. You can learn all about Arrernte Aboriginal culture and music in this gallery of western desert art and artifacts. Try playing the didgeridoo at the music school, or wandering through the Living History Museum. An outstanding place to purchase Aboriginal art, the center also runs half-day cultural tours of the Alice Springs region which allow for a deeper understanding of the art and the stories it represents. ✉ *125 Todd St.* ☎ *08/8952–3408* ⊕ *aboriginalart.com.au* ✉ *Free* ⊙ *Daily 9–5.*

❷ Adelaide House Museum. This was the first hospital in Alice Springs, designed by the Reverend John Flynn and run by the Australian Inland Mission (which Flynn founded) from 1926 to 1939. An ingenious system of air tunnels and wet burlap bags once cooled the hospital rooms

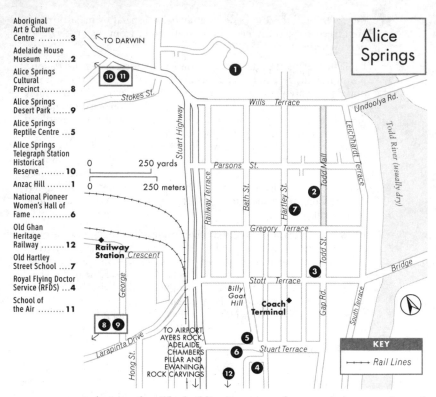

in hot weather. The building is now a volunteer-run museum devoted to the mission and pioneering days in Alice Springs. The stone hut at the rear was the site of the first field radio transmission in 1926, which made viable Flynn's concept of a flying doctor. The Royal Flying Doctor Service continues to maintain its "mantle of safety" over all Australia's remote settlements. ⊠*Todd Mall* ☎*08/9952–1856* ⊠*A$5* ⊗*Mon.–Sat. 10–4.*

❺ Alice Springs Reptile Centre. Thorny devils, frill-neck lizards, and some of the world's deadliest snakes inhabit this park in the heart of town, opposite the Royal Flying Doctor Service. May to August (winter) the viewing's best from 11 to 3, when the reptiles are most active. You can even feed the snakes by hand and pick up the pythons. There's also a fossil cave. Free talks are conducted daily at 11, 1, and 3:30. ⊠*9 Stuart Terr.* ☎*08/9952–8900* ⊕*www.reptilecentre.com.au* ⊠*A$12* ⊗*Daily 9:30–5.*

❶ Anzac Hill. North of downtown, Anzac Hill has an excellent view of Alice Springs and the surrounding area, including the MacDonnell Ranges; it's a great spot for watching sunrise and sunset. From atop the hill you can see that Todd Mall, the heart of Alice Springs, is just one block west of the Todd River, which at best flows only every few years. To reach the top, head up Lions Walk, which starts opposite the Catholic church on Wills Terrace downtown.

⑥ National Pioneer Women's Hall of Fame. Founded in 1993 by outback character Molly Clark, owner of Old Andado cattle station 200 km (124 mi) southeast of Alice Springs, this museum is dedicated to Australia's pioneering women. The first female university graduate (1880s) is among the 100 women honoured in the "First in their Field" display, one of several permanent and changing exhibitions of photographs and memorabilia. The Hall is housed in the old Alice Springs jail (1938–96) and you can wander around the prison grounds. ⊠*2 Stuart Terr.* ☎*08/8952–9006* ⊕*www.pioneerwomen.com.au* ⊠*A$6.50* ⊙*Daily 10–5 Feb.–mid-Dec.*

⑦ Old Hartley Street School. Alas, little remains here that recalls the blackboards and lift-top desks in use in 1930, when Miss Pearl Burton was the school's first teacher, but it's worth a peek anyway. The school is also the headquarters of the Alice Springs National Trust branch, and brochures on local sights are available. ⊠*Hartley St. between Parsons St. and Gregory Terr.* ☎*08/8952–4516* ⊠*A$2* ⊙*Mar.–Nov., 10:30–2:30.*

④ Royal Flying Doctor Service (RFDS). Directed from this RFDS radio base, doctors use aircraft to make house calls on settlements and homes hundreds of miles apart. Like the School of the Air, the RFDS is a vital part of Outback life. The visitor center has historical displays and an audiovisual show. Tours run every half hour throughout the year. The cakes served at the in-house café are to die for! ⊠*8–10 Stuart Terr.* ☎*08/8952–1129* ⊕*www.flyingdoctor.net* ⊠*A$6.50* ⊙*Mon.–Sat. 9–4, Sun. 1–4.*

Todd Mall. Cafés, galleries, banks, and tourist shops line this pedestrian area, the heart of Alice Springs. ⊠*Todd St. between Wills and Gregory Terraces.*

AROUND ALICE SPRINGS

⑧ Alice Springs Cultural Precinct. The most distinctive building in this com-
★ plex is the Museum of Central Australia, which charts the evolution of the land and its inhabitants—human and animal—around Central Australia. Exhibits include include a skeleton of the 10½-foot-tall duck relative *Dromornis stirtoni*, the largest bird to walk on earth, which was found northeast of Alice. Also in the precinct are the Aviation Museum, Territory Craft, and the Araluen Centre, home to the Araluen Art Galleries and the Namatjira Gallery, a collection of renowned Aboriginal landscapes. The precinct is 2 km (1 mi) southwest of town and is on the Alice Wanderer tourist bus itinerary. ⊠*61 Larapinta Dr.* ☎*08/8951–1120* ⊠*A$9* ⊙*Weekdays 10–4, weekends 11–4.*

⑨ Alice Springs Desert Park. Focusing on the desert, which makes up 70% of
☽ the Australian landmass, this 75-acre site presents 320 types of plants
★ and 120 animal species in several Australian ecosystems—including the largest nocturnal-animal house in the Southern Hemisphere. Local Aboriginal guides are on hand to share their native stories about the

10

wildlife and the land. You should allow about four hours to explore the park; it's 6½ km (4 mi) west of Alice Springs and is on the Alice Wanderer bus itinerary. ⊠ *Larapinta Dr.* ☎ *08/8951–8788* ⊕ *www. alicespringsdesertpark.com.au* ⬗ *A$20* ⊙ *Daily 7:30–6.*

⑩ Alice Springs Telegraph Station Historical Reserve. The first white settlement in the area was at this reserve 3 km (2 mi) north of Alice Springs, beside the original freshwater spring named after the wife of Charles Todd. As the South Australian Superintendent of Telegraphs, Todd planned and supervised construction of 12 repeater stations—including this one—along the telegraph line to Darwin, completed in 1872. The restored telegraph-station buildings evoke the Red Centre as it was at the turn of the 20th century. Within the buildings, exhibits of station life and a display of early photographs chronicle its history. A scenic walking and cycling path runs along the Todd River between Alice Springs and the reserve; the picnic grounds are open daily from 8 AM to 9 PM. ⊠ *Stuart Hwy.* ☎ *08/8952–3993* ⊕ *www.nt.gov.au/nreta/parks/find/ astelegraphstation.html* ⬗ *A$7.20* ⊙ *Daily 8–5.*

⑫ Old Ghan Heritage Railway. Set on an original section of rail line 10 km (6 mi) south of Alice Springs, adjoining the Transport Hall of Fame, this is the resting place of the restored *Old Ghan,* a train named for the Afghans who led camel trains on the route from Adelaide. The train began passenger service to Alice Springs on August 6, 1929, and over the next 51 years it provided a vital, if erratic, link with the south. In times of flood it could take up to three months to complete the journey. Today the *Ghan* uses modern trains to connect Adelaide and Darwin.

The site comprises a museum, in the old stone station building, chock-full of *Ghan* memorabilia, and original rolling stock. You can climb aboard steam and diesel locomotives, and on Sunday ride a train several kilometers down the line. The Alice Wanderer bus stops here. ⊠ *Stuart Hwy.* ☎ *08/8955–5047* ⬗ *A$8, train rides A$25* ⊙ *Mar.–late Dec. 9–5, late Dec.–Feb. weekdays 9–1.*

⑪ School of the Air. Operating in many remote areas of the country, and unique to Australia, the School of the Air teaches faraway students in an ingenious way: children take their classes by correspondence course, supplemented by lessons over the Royal Flying Doctor radio network. Observing the teacher-student relationship by way of radio is fascinating. The school is 3 km (2 mi) northwest of town, on the Alice Wanderer route. ⊠ *80 Head St.* ☎ *08/8951–6834* ⊕ *www.assoa.nt.edu.au* ⬗ *A$6.50* ⊙ *Mon.–Sat. 8:30–4:30, Sun. 1:30–4:30.*

WHERE TO EAT

$$–$$$ ✕ **Barra on Todd.** Northern Territory barramundi prepared three
★   ways—char-grilled, grilled, and battered—is the highlight at this classy restaurant and bar, at Voyages Alice Springs Resort. It's popular with locals, too. Other delicious seafood dishes on offer include South Australian oysters and prawns flambéed in Malibu. Like any good Aussie restaurant, though, it still caters to carnivores with art-

ful beef, chicken, and lamb dishes, which you can eat under thatch-roof ceilings, overlooking the happening pool. ⊠ *34 Stott Terr.* ☎ *08/8952–3523* ⊟ *AE, DC, MC, V.*

$–$$ ✕**Bluegrass Restaurant.** This exposed-brick and red-walled restaurant feels more urban than other Alice eateries, and prides itself on being the only Red Centre restaurant with a bistro-style blackboard menu, which changes daily. Seafood is always featured; you might get to try seared tuna or whole grilled flounder. There's also usually a kangaroo dish—such as steak with coriander, bok choy, and red wine sauce. Ask your waitperson to recommend a bottle from the extensive, pan-Australian wine list. ⊠ *Stott Terr. at Todd St.* ☎ *08/8955–5188* ⊟ *AE, DC, MC, V* ⊗ *Closed Tues.*

$–$$ ✕**Bojangles Saloon and Restaurant.** Cowhide seats, tables made from old *Ghan* railway benches, and a life-size replica of bushranger Ned Kelly give this lively restaurant true Outback flavor. Food is classic Northern Territory tucker: barramundi, kangaroo, camel, emu, thick slabs of ribs, and huge steaks—and the peanuts are free! Jangles and Jungle, two 8-foot pythons, live with a skeleton and a rusty motorbike in a glass case left of the bar. ⊠ *80 Todd St.* ☎ *08/8952–2873* ⊟ *AE, DC, MC, V.*

$–$$ ✕**DJs Bistro@Todd Tavern.** The only traditional Australian pub in Alice Springs serves cheap, hearty meals all day. Theme-dinner nights, which cost from A$9.95, include schnitzel on Thursday, and a traditional Sunday roast dinner. Dinner-and-a-movie deals, which include a ticket for the cinema next door, are available on Monday nights for A$18. Pick your wine from the on-site bottle shop (liquor store), or stick around the pub bar for an after-dinner drink. ⊠ *1 Todd Mall* ☎ *08/8952–1255* ⊟ *AE, DC, MC, V.*

$–$$
Fodor'sChoice
★ ✕**Hanuman Thai.** Known primarily as a Thai restaurant, this comfortably plush, plum-wall spot also has a tandoori menu, making it the only spot in the desert to offer a range of big-city-quality Southeast Asian food. The grilled Hanuman oysters—seasoned with lemongrass and sweet basil—are the big draw; reportedly they've converted even avowed seafood-haters. The wild barramundi with a sticky passionfruit and ginger sauce is also popular. Desserts include black-rice brûlée, and banana spring rolls with dates. ⊠ *Crown Plaza Alice Springs, 82 Barrett Dr.* ☎ *Box 1634, 0871* ☎ *08/8953–7188* ⚑ *Reservations recommended* ⊟ *AE, DC, MC, V* ⊗ *No lunch.*

$–$$ ✕**Oriental Gourmet.** This plain but historic weatherboard government building—1939 is old for Alice Springs—has been serving the best Chinese food in the Red Centre for 20 years. There are no surprises on the menu—honey prawns, beef with black bean sauce, duck with lemon sauce—but all the dishes are fresh, simple, and well prepared. Step inside to dine or sit in the garden waiting area until your take-out order is ready. ⊠ *80 Hartley St.* ☎ *08/8953–0888* ⊟ *AE, DC, MC, V* ⊗ *No lunch.*

10

WHERE TO STAY

$$$ ⬚ **Lasseters Hotel Casino.** The lip-synching drag queens of the movie *The Adventures of Priscilla, Queen of the Desert* put on their show in this spot; it's also the real-life hub of Alice nightlife. Limerick's Irish Bar is a haven for karaoke mavens, and you can enjoy the Mod-Oz cuisine of Samphire Restaurant on-site or as a take-out picnic pack. Rooms are spacious and modern, with brightly colored upholstery that echoes the casino's neon lights. You can escape the ringing of the slot machines by lounging around the pool, or by borrowing a bike and riding around the expansive property. ⬚ *93 Barrett Dr., 0870* ☎ *08/8950–7777* ⬚ *www.lhc.com.au* ⬚ *127 rooms, 13 suites* ⬚ *In-room: safe, refrigerator, VCR (some), ethernet, dial-up. In-hotel: restaurant, room service, bar, tennis court, pool, gym, bicycles, laundry facilities, laundry service, public Internet, public Wi-Fi, parking (no fee), no-smoking rooms* ⬚ *AE, DC, MC, V.*

$$ ⬚ **Crowne Plaza Resort Alice Springs.** Landscaped lawns with elegant
★ eucalyptus and palm trees greet you at this upscale, international chain about a mile outside town. Inside, the rooms are decorated in light, tropical colors, inviting thoughts of seaside resorts, and have balcony views of either the garden and pool or of the Alice Springs Golf Club and the low, barren mountains behind. The on-site Hanuman Thai restaurant is a local favorite; you can also ask about room rates that include breakfast at the more-casual Balloons restaurant. ⬚ *82 Barrett Dr., 0870* ☎ *08/8950–8000* ⬚ *www.crowneplaza.com.au* ⬚ *236 rooms, 7 suites* ⬚ *In-room: safe, refrigerator, ethernet. In-hotel: 2 restaurants, room service, bars, tennis courts, pool, gym, laundry facilities, laundry service, public Internet, public Wi-Fi, parking (no fee), no-smoking rooms* ⬚ *AE, DC, MC, V* ⬚ *BP, EP.*

$ ⬚ **Alice on Todd Apartments.** On the Todd riverbank about a mile south
★ of Todd Mall, these self-contained accommodations are great value, especially for families. Studios sleep two, one-bedrooms sleep four, and two-bedrooms sleep six. Light streaming through a patio or balcony fills each earth-toned apartment, all of which have cooking and laundry facilities. You can make friends at the barbecue area, then hop across the dry riverbed to try your luck at Lasseters Hotel Casino. ⬚ *South Terr. at Strehlow St., 0870* ☎ *08/8953–8033* ⬚ *www.aliceontodd. com* ⬚ *15 studios, 4 1-bedroom and 15 2-bedroom apartments* ⬚ *In-room: kitchen, refrigerator, DVD (some), dial-up. In-hotel: pool, no elevator, laundry facilities, public Internet, parking (no fee), no-smoking rooms* ⬚ *MC, V.*

$ ⬚ **Nthaba Cottage B&B.** Whether staying in the antiques-filled cottage,
★ which sleeps two, or the bedroom inside the main house, a night at this lovely bed-and-breakfast feels like a visit with old friends. The accommodations in the large terrace house are done up in Laura Ashley–esque floral prints, and the dining room has a similar English-country feel. Bird lovers will feel right at home here; owners Will and Anne Cormack are experts on the 50 varieties of winged creatures that flutter around the property's gardens. ⬚ *83 Cromwell Dr., 0870* ☎ *08/8952–9003*

⊕*www.nthabacottage.com.au* ↜*1 room, 1 cottage* ♧*In-room: no phone, refrigerator (some), DVD (some), VCR (some). In-hotel: restaurant, bar, no elevator, laundry facilities* ▤*MC, V* ○|*BP.*

¢–$ 🗔**Heavitree Gap Outback Lodge.** Wild, black-footed rock wallabies are fed nightly in this resort at the base of the MacDonnell Ranges, a few hundred yards south of the break in the ranges known as Heavitree Gap. All rooms here are functional rather than stylish, with lodge and kitchenette rooms and four-bed dorm accommodations offering cooking facilities. There are 90 powered campsites and 3 acres of unpowered campsites available for travelers with caravans. Nightly entertainment from April to September, including a bush balladeer and a hands-on reptile show, contribute to the theme-park atmosphere. A free shuttle runs from the resort to Alice Springs, which is five minutes away. ⊠*Palm Circuit off Stuart Hwy., 0870* ☏*08/8950–4444* ⊕*www.auroraresorts.com.au* ↜*60 rooms, 18 dormitories, 90 powered campsites* ♧*In-room: no phone (some), kitchen (some), refrigerator, dial-up (some). In-hotel: restaurant, pool, no elevator, laundry facilities, laundry service, public Internet, parking (no fee), no-smoking rooms* ▤*AE, DC, MC, V.*

¢ 🗔**Alice Springs YHA.** This corrugated iron–clad hostel used to be Alice's open-air cinema, and a wonderful old projector in the communal lounge-cum-kitchen is a reminder of the property's colorful history (as are regular outdoor movie nights). Today international travelers swap tales around a small, grassy pool area adjacent to the two-story main accommodation block, where doors open into bright, spotless four-, six-, and eight-bed dorms, all with shared bath. The older 16-bed dorm is behind the main building. There are two double rooms, two twin rooms, and two family rooms for travelers who prefer fewer bunk mates. ⊠*Leichhardt Terr. at Parsons St., 0870* ☏*08/8952–8855* ⊕*www.yha.com.au* ↜*21 rooms without bath* ♧*In-room: no phone, no TV. In-hotel: pool, bicycles, no elevator, laundry facilities, concierge, public Internet, no kids under 7, no-smoking rooms* ▤*MC, V.*

★ ⌂**MacDonnell Ranges Holiday Park.** Hidden behind the ranges 5 km (3 mi) south of town, this extensive, well-planned park has many trees, good children's facilities, Internet access, entertainment five nights a week from April to September and a free pancake breakfast on Sunday. The accommodation options include villas and cabins for those less oriented to the great outdoors, plus a host of campsites, most of which are powered. Facilities for people with disabilities are also provided. ⊠*Palm Pl. off Palm Circuit, Box 9025, 0871* ☏*08/8952–6111 or 1800/808373* ⊕*www.macrange.com.au* ↜*432 sites, 14 villas, 24 cabins* ♧*Restaurant, pools, flush toilets, full hookups, drinking water, showers, picnic tables, electricity, public telephone, general store, play area, service station* ▤*AE, MC, V.*

10

NIGHTLIFE & THE ARTS

Sounds of Starlight (⊠ *40 Todd Mall* ☎*08/8953–0826*) is the place to enjoy Outback theater performances and didgeridoo music accompanied by a slide show of Red Centre images. Concerts (A$30) are held at 8 PM Tuesday, Friday, and Saturday April–November; call ahead to check schedule. A pretheater-dinner and show package (with dinner at the Red Ochre Grill across the street on the mall) costs A$73.

Maxim's Bar (⊠ *1 Todd Mall* ☎*08/8952–1255*), in Todd Tavern, the only traditional Australian pub in town, has something going on every night. In addition to the bar, the property includes a restaurant, bottle shop (liquor store), and gambling facilities. You can bet on horse races across the country with TAB (the Australian equivalent of OTB)—but keep some change aside for the slot machines.

SPORTS & THE OUTDOORS

CAMEL RIDING

☾ You can ride a camel to dinner or breakfast, or just ramble along the dry Todd riverbed, astride a "ship of the desert" with **Frontier Camel Tours** (⊠ *Ross Hwy., 4 km [2½ mi] southeast of Alice Springs* ☎*08/8950–3030* ⊕ *cameltours.ananguwaai.com.au*). Short rides, river rambles, and breakfast rides begin at 6:30 AM daily; 4 PM dinner rides (5 PM October–April) include a three-course meal, wine, and beer. Prices run from A$45 for a short ride to A$110 for a dinner date with a camel. Transfers from Alice Springs hotels are included with the breakfast and dinner tours.

HIKING/BUSHWALKING

The MacDonnell Ranges, the craggy desert mountains that frame Alice Springs, are rich with desert landscapes and Aboriginal significance. The **Emily and Jessie Gaps Nature Park**, located in the East MacDonnells, just 10 km (6 mi) east of Alice Springs along the Ross Highway, contains registered sacred Aboriginal sites, including rock paintings depicting the caterpillar story of the Dreamtime—the Aboriginal stories of the world's creation.

The **Larapinta Trail** is a 223-km-long (145-mi-long) walking track that runs west from Alice Springs into the West MacDonnell Ranges. It's a spectacular, though challenging, track that takes hikers through classically rugged and dry central Australian landscape. Hikers are encouraged to participate in the voluntary Overnight Walker Registration Scheme, designed to insure that all trekkers on the trail can be tracked and accounted for in case of emergency. Contact the **Northern Territory Parks & Wildlife Service** (☎08/8951–8250) for more information. The **Central Australian Tourism** office in Alice Springs (☎08/8952–5800) can also advise you if you're interested in planning bushwalking itineraries.

HOT-AIR BALLOONING

At dawn on most mornings, hot-air balloons float in the sky around Alice Springs. **Outback Ballooning** (⊠*Box 2702, 0871* ☎*1800/809790* ⊕*www.outbackballooning.com.au*) makes hotel pickups about an hour before dawn and returns between 9 AM and 10 AM. The A$255 fee covers 30 minutes of flying time, insurance, and a champagne breakfast. A 60-minute flight costs A$385 including insurance.

QUAD-BIKE RIDING

Hop aboard a motorbike with four huge wheels and explore the Northern Territory's oldest working cattle station with **Outback Quad Adventures** (⊠*Undoolya Station, Undoolya Rd.* ☎*08/8953–0697*). The company collects you from Alice Springs and takes you to the station, 17 km (10 mi) out of town on the edge of the MacDonnell Ranges. No special license is needed and all tours are escorted by guides with two-way radios. Rides of 2½ hours (A$115) and 3½ hours (A$189), and overnight tours—which include barbecue dinner with wine, sleeping bags, and breakfast (A$329)—operate year-round.

SIDE TRIPS FROM ALICE SPRINGS

EAST MACDONNELL RANGES

Spectacular scenery and Aboriginal rock art in the MacDonnell Ranges east of the Alice are well worth a day or more of exploration. Emily Gap (a sacred Aboriginal site), Jessie Gap, and Corroboree Rock, once a setting for important men-only Aboriginal ceremonies, are within the first 44 km (27 mi) east of Alice Springs. Beyond these are Trephina Gorge, John Hayes Rockhole, and N'Dhala Gorge Nature Park (with numerous Aboriginal rock carvings).

Arltunga Historical Reserve, 110 km (69 mi) northeast of Alice, contains the ruins of a former 19th-century gold-rush site. If you fancy fossicking (prospecting) for your own semiprecious stones, you can take your pick—and shovel—at Gemtree in the Harts Ranges, 140 km (87 mi) northeast of Alice.

WHERE TO STAY

⚠ **Gemtree.** You can fossick for gems by day and sleep under the stars at night at this bush-style caravan park. Powered sites are A$24, campsites are A$20 for two adults (you can hire a tent for A$15 plus site fee), and two-person cabins cost A$70 per night. It's A$70 to join a tag-along gem-fossicking tour, including equipment. Although it's rustic, and 140 km (87 mi) northeast of Alice Springs, the park has its own golf course. ⊠*Plenty Hwy., approximately 70 km (43 mi) from Stuart Hwy. junction.* ☎*08/8956–9855* ⊕*www.gemtree.com.au* ⇆*50 powered sites, 50 campsites, 2 cabins* ♿*Flush toilets, partial hookups,* *drinking water, guest laundry, showers, fire pits, grills, picnic tables, electricity, public telephone, general store, service station* ▤*MC, V.*

WEST MACDONNELL RANGES

The MacDonnell Ranges west of Alice Springs are, like the eastern ranges, broken by a series of chasms and gorges. To reach the sights, most within the West MacDonnell National Park, drive out of town on Larapinta Drive, the western continuation of Stott Terrace.

John Flynn's Grave memorializes the Royal Flying Doctor Service founder. It's on a rise with the stark ranges behind, in a memorable setting 6 km (4 mi) west of Alice Springs. ⊠*Larapinta Dr.* ☎*No phone* ▨*Free* ☉*Daily 24 hrs.*

Simpsons Gap isn't dramatic, but it's the closest gorge to town. Stark-white ghost gums, red rocks, and the purple-haze mountains will give you a taste of the scenery to be seen farther into the ranges. The gap itself can be crowded in the morning and late afternoon, since these are the best times to see rock wallabies, but unlike Standley Chasm, it's only a short walk from the parking lot. ⊠*Larapinta Dr., 18 km (11 mi) west of Alice Springs, then 6 km (4 mi) on side road* ☎*08/8951–8250* ▨*Free* ☉*Daily 5–8.*

★ **Standley Chasm** is one of the most impressive canyons in the MacDonnell Ranges. At midday, when the sun is directly overhead, the 10-yard-wide canyon glows red from the reflected light—this lasts for just 15 minutes. The walk from the parking lot takes about 20 minutes and is rocky toward the end. There's a kiosk selling snacks and drinks at the park entrance. ⊠*Larapinta Dr., 40 km (25 mi) west of Alice Springs, then 9 km (5½ mi) on Standley Chasm Rd.* ☎*08/8956–7440* ▨*A$8* ☉*Daily 8–5.*

ULURU & KATA TJUTA

It's easy to see why the Aborigines attach spiritual significance to Uluru (Ayers Rock). It's an awe-inspiring sight, rising above the plain and dramatically changing color throughout the day. The Anangu people are the traditional owners of the land around Uluru and Kata Tjuta. They believe they are direct descendants of the beings—which include a python, an emu, a blue-tongue lizard, and a poisonous snake—who formed the land and its physical features during the Tjukurpa (the "Dreamtime," or creation period). Tjukurpa also refers to the Anangu religion, law, and moral system, a knowledge of past and present handed down from memory through stories and other oral traditions.

Rising more than 1,100 feet from the surrounding plain, Uluru is one of the world's largest monoliths, though such a clinical classification belies the otherworldly, spiritual energy surrounding it. Much of that may stem from its historical use as a sacred site to the Aborigines, and from that a great controversy has arisen over whether it's appropriate to climb the rock. The Anangu people have politely requested that

The Heartland

For most Australians the Red Centre is the mystical and legendary core of the continent, and Uluru is its beautiful focal point. Whether they have been there or not, locals believe its image symbolizes a steady pulse that radiates deep through the red earth, through the heartland, and all the way to the coasts.

Little more than a thumbprint within the vast Australian continent, the Red Centre is harsh and isolated. Its hard, relentless topography and lack of the conveniences found in most areas of civilization make this one of the most difficult areas of the country in which to survive, much less explore. But the early pioneers—some foolish, some hardy—managed to set up bases that thrived. They created cattle stations, introduced electricity, and implemented telegraph services, enabling them to maintain a lifestyle that, if not luxurious, was at least reasonably comfortable.

The people who now sparsely populate the Red Centre are a breed of their own. Many were born and grew up here, but many others were "blow-ins," immigrants from far-flung countries and folk from other Australian states who took up the challenge to make a life in the desert and stayed on as they succeeded. Either way, folks out here have at least a few common characteristics. They're laconic and down-to-earth, canny and astute, and very likely to try to pull your leg when you least expect it.

No one could survive the isolation without a good sense of humor: where else in the world would you hold a bottomless-boat race in a dry riverbed? The Henley-on-Todd, as it is known, is a sight to behold, with dozens of would-be skippers bumbling along within the bottomless-boat frames.

As the small towns grew and businesses quietly prospered in the mid-1800s, a rail link between Alice Springs and Adelaide was planned. However, the undercurrent of challenge and humor that touches all life here ran through this project as well. Construction began in 1877, but things went wrong from the start. No one had seen rain for ages, and no one expected it; hence, the track was laid right across a floodplain. It wasn't long before locals realized their mistake, when intermittent, heavy floods regularly washed the tracks away. The railway is still in operation today and all works well, but its history is one of many local jokes here.

For some, the Red Centre is the real Australia, a special place where you will meet people whose generous and sincere hospitality may move you. The land and all its riches offer some of the most spectacular and unique sights on the planet, along with a sense of timelessness that will slow you down and fill your spirit. Take a moment to shade your eyes from the sun and pick up on the subtleties that nature has carefully protected and camouflaged here, and you will soon discover that the Red Centre is not the dead center.

–Bev Malzard

10

visitors not scale Uluṟu, but the fact that thousands of tourists wish to do so every year means that if you want to make the climb, there is a well-marked path that will help you do it.

Kata Tjuṯa (the Olgas), 53 km (33 mi) west, is a series of 36 gigantic rock domes hiding a maze of fascinating gorges and crevasses. The names Ayers Rock and the Olgas are used out of familiarity alone; at the sites themselves, the Aboriginal Uluṟu and Kata Tjuṯa are the respective names of preference. The entire area region is called Yulara, though the airport is still known as Ayers Rock.

Uluṟu and Kata Tjuṯa have very different compositions. Monolithic Uluṟu is a type of sandstone called arkose, while the rock domes at Kata Tjuṯa are composed of conglomerate. It was once thought that they rested upon the sandy terrain like pebbles; however, both formations are the tips of tilted rock strata that extend thousands of yards into the earth. The rock strata tilted during a period of intense geological activity more than 300 million years ago—the arkose by nearly 90 degrees and the conglomerate only about 15 degrees. The surrounding rock fractured and quickly eroded about 40 million years ago, leaving the present structures standing as separate entities. But this is just one, albeit scientific, interpretation—an Aboriginal guide can relate the ancient creation stories of the rock, which are just as interesting.

Both of these intriguing sights lie within Uluṟu–Kata Tjuṯa National Park, which is protected as a World Heritage Site. As such, it's one of just a few parks in the world recognized in this way for both its landscape and cultural values. The whole experience is a bit like seeing the Grand Canyon turned inside out, and a visit here will be remembered for a lifetime.

ON THE WAY TO ULUṞU

The 440-km (273-mi) drive to Uluṟu from Alice Springs along the Stuart and Lasseter highways takes about five hours or longer if you veer off the track a bit to see some other impressive geological sites.

Rainbow Valley Conservation Reserve. Amazing formations in the sandstone cliffs of the James Range take on rainbow colors in the early-morning and late-afternoon light. The colors were caused by water dissolving the red iron in the sandstone, and further erosion created dramatic rock faces and squared towers. To reach the reserve, turn left off the Stuart Highway 75 km (46 mi) south of Alice. The next 22 km (13 mi) are on a dirt track, requiring a four-wheel-drive vehicle. ✉ *Stuart Hwy.* ☎ *08/8951–8250* ⊕ *www.nt.gov.au/nreta/parks/find/ rainbowvalley.html* ✆ *Free.*

Neil and Jayne Waters, owners of **Camels Australia,** offer everything from quick jaunts to multi-day safaris. Phone beforehand for all rides; 72 hours' notice for day and longer treks. It's A$40 for a one-hour ride, and A$150 for a day trek with lunch; safaris, including camping gear and meals, cost A$450 for three days and A$750 for five days, and depart three times each month in fall and winter (check the dates). ✉ *Stuarts*

Well, Stuart Hwy., 90 km (56 mi) south of Alice Springs ☎*08/8956–0925* 🖷*08/8956–0909* ⊕*www.camels-australia.com.au.*

The **Henbury Meteorite Craters,** 12 depressions between 6 feet and 600 feet across, are believed to have been formed by a meteorite shower about 5,000 years ago. One is 60 feet deep. To get here, you must travel off the highway on an unpaved road. ⊠*Ernest Giles Rd., 114 km (71 mi) south of Alice Springs and 13 km (8 mi) west of Stuart Hwy.* ☎*08/8951–8250.*

TELEPHONES

The area code for Ayers Rock Resort (and all the Northern Territory, Western Australia, and South Australia) is 08. Mobile phones work within a 10-km (6-mi) radius of Ayers Rock Resort, but not within Uluru–Kata Tjuta National Park; you can call friends back at the resort from public phones at the Cultural Centre inside the park. There are banks of public pay phones in the Ayers Rock Resort Shopping Centre and at all hotels.

An important navigational landmark for 19th-century pioneers—you can still see their signatures in its base—is Chamber's Pillar, a solitary sandstone column rising 170 feet above the red plains of the northwest Simpson Desert. Over millions of years, oxidation and minerals created the pillar's red-and-gold hues, which are most dramatic in the late-afternoon sunlight. To reach **Chamber's Pillar Historical Reserve,** drive 119 km (74 mi) south of Alice Springs on Old South Road (mostly unpaved), then turn west at Maryvale Station homestead. The next 41 km (25 mi) are suitable only for high-clearance, four-wheel-drive vehicles. ⊠*Chamber's Pillar Track* ☎*08/8951–8250* ◻*Free.*

On the road to Chamber's Pillar, 39 km (24 mi) south of Alice, more than 3,000 ancient Aboriginal rock engravings (petroglyphs) are etched into sandstone outcrops in the **Ewaninga Rock Carvings Conservation Reserve.** Early-morning and late-afternoon light are best for photographing the lines, circles, and animal tracks. A 2-km (1-mi) trail leads to several art sites. The reserve is open all day, year-round, and is accessible by ordinary (rather than just four-wheel-drive) cars. ⊠*Old South Rd., 39 km (24 mi) south of Alice Springs* ☎*08/8951–8250* ◻*Free.*

A drive through **Watarrka National Park** takes you past desert foliage and wildflowers to **Kings Canyon.** The park is accessible by car on the Mereenie Loop road from Glen Helen Gorge, or from the Lasseter Highway via Luritja Road. An Aboriginal Land Entry Permit is required to drive the Mereenie Loop around the West MacDonnell Ranges. It's A\$2.20 from the **Central Australian Tourism Industry Association** (☎*08/8952–5800 or 1800/645199)* in Alice Springs. ⊠*Luritja Rd., 167 km (104 mi) from the turnoff on Lasseter Hwy.*

Fodor's Choice ★ **Kings Canyon,** in **Watarrka National Park,** is one of the most spectacular sights in central Australia. You may recognize it from a scene near the end of *Priscilla, Queen of the Desert,* when the actors in full drag costume ascend the main path. Sprawling in scope, the canyon's sheer cliff walls shelter a world of ferns and woodlands, permanent springs and rock pools. The main path is the 6-km (4-mi) Canyon Walk, which starts with a short but steep climb to the top of the escarpment; the view 886 feet down to the base of the canyon is amazing. The trail then leads through a colony of beehive sandstone domes, known as the Lost City, to a refreshing water hole in the so-called Garden of Eden halfway through the four-hour walk. All this is visible during the half-hour scenic helicopter flight over the canyon and range from Kings Canyon Resort (A$220 or A$115 for 15 minutes). ⊠ *Luritja Rd., 167 km (104 mi) from turnoff on Lasseter Hwy.*

South of Kings Canyon, on the Lasseter Highway heading toward Uluṟu, you can see **Mt. Conner** from the side of the road. Set on Curtin Springs Cattle Station, and often mistaken for Uluṟu from a distance, it's actually a huge mesa. Nearby on the highway is Curtin Springs Roadhouse, a good stopover for refreshments; you can also arrange guided tours (minimum 2 people) of Mt. Conner, the 1,028,960-acre cattle station, and Lake Amadeus, as well as scenic flights. The roadhouse has cabins with private facilities, caravan sites, and free camping. ⊠ *Lasseter Hwy., 41 km (25 mi) west of the Luritja Rd. junction* 🕾 *08/8956–2906.*

WHERE TO STAY & EAT

$–$$$$ ✕🎬 **Kings Canyon Resort.** The only place to stay within Watarrka National Park, this resort is 7 km (4½ mi) from the canyon. If you've come directly from the truly upscale Ayers Rock Resort (also operated by Voyages) this property may disappoint. Accommodations include two- and four-bed lodge rooms in desert hues, but even the deluxe rooms are sparse and functional. Whirlpool baths surrounded by wraparound windows are a nice touch—however, you can't actually see any of the park or the canyon from them. The local water supply is treated with sulfur, so there's also an unpleasant smell around the entire compound. The staff is very helpful, doing the best it can with the resort's limited resources. The lively pub is a good distraction from the accommodations, and there are also a large gas station and grocery, casual and upscale dining options, and two pools. Its most unique feature is the six-course, couples-only Sounds of Firelight (A$139), where you dine in style around a desert campfire under the stars (though not during the summer months). ⌂ *Box 136, Alice Springs, NT, 0871* 🕾 *08/8956–7442* ⊕ *www.kingscanyonresort.com.au* ⇩ *124 deluxe rooms, 36 budget rooms, 50 powered caravan sites, unlimited tent sites* ⌂ *In-room: no phone (some), refrigerator, dial-up (some). In-hotel: restaurant, bars, tennis court, pools, no elevator, laundry facilities, public Internet, parking (no fee), no-smoking rooms* ⊟ *AE, DC, MC, V.*

¢–$ 🎬 **Kings Creek Station.** Just down the road from Watarrka National Park, this well-equipped, 500,000-acre cattle station offers every possible means by which to enjoy the area, from camel rides to helicopter tours. Accommodation is in 25 permanent tents with shared facilities, and includes the bushman's-style breakfast of greasy bacon, eggs, and toast. There are also cooking facilities to prepare your own meals, and plenty of campsites. ⌂ *PMB via Alice Springs, NT, 0872* 🕾 *08/8956–7474* ⊕ *www.kingscreekstation.com.au* ⇩ *25 safari cabins, unlimited* *campsites* ♿*In-hotel: restaurant, pool, no elevator, laundry facilities, public Internet, parking (no fee), some pets allowed, no-smoking rooms* ▭*MC, V.*

ULURU

An inevitable sensation of excitement builds as you approach the great monolith. If you drive toward it in a rental car, you may find yourself gasping at the first glimpse of it through the windshield; if you're on a tour bus, you'll likely want to grab the person sitting next to you and point out the window as it looms larger and larger. Rising like an enormous red mountain in the middle of an otherwise completely flat desert, Uluru really is a marvel to behold.

The **Uluru–Kata Tjuta Cultural Centre** (✉*Off Lasseter Hwy.* ☎*08/8956–1128*) is the first thing you'll see after entering the park through a tollgate. The two buildings are built in a serpentine style, reflecting the Kuniya and Liru stories about two ancestral snakes who fought a long-ago battle on the southern side of Uluru. Inside, you can learn about Aboriginal history, and the return of the park to Aboriginal ownership in 1983. There's also an excellent park's ranger station where you can get maps and hiking guides, as well as an art shop, and a pottery store with lovely collectibles. As you work your way around Uluru, your perspective of the great rock changes significantly. You should allow four hours to walk the 10 km (6 mi) around the rock and explore the several deep crevices along the way; you can also drive around it on the paved road. Be aware that some places are Aboriginal sacred sites and cannot be entered, nor can they be photographed. These are clearly signposted. Aboriginal art can be found in caves at the rock's base. If you're looking for an easy walk that takes you just partway around the base, the **Mala Walk** is 2 km (1 mi) in length and almost all on flat land. The walk goes to the Kanju Gorge from the base of the climbing trail; park rangers provide free tours daily at 8 AM from October to April and at 10 AM from May to September.

There's only one trail that leads to the top of the rock. Though many people visit Uluru with the explicit intention of climbing it, there are a few things you should bear in mind before attempting this. First, Aboriginal people consider climbing the rock to be sacrilege—so if you believe in preserving the sanctity of sacred native sites, you may have to be content with admiring it from below. Your entry pass into the park even says, "It is requested that you respect the wishes of the Anangu by not climbing Uluru." Second, if you do decide to make the climb, be aware that it's a very strenuous hike, and not suitable for those who aren't physically fit. The ascent is about 1½ km (1 mi), and the round-trip climb takes about three hours. Sturdy hiking boots, a hat, sunscreen, and drinking water are absolute necessities (no food or water available at the summit). The climb is closed when temperatures rise above 36°C (97°F)—which means after 9 AM most mornings in the summertime. Tour buses that bring groups to climb the rock often arrive at the site as early as 4:30 AM for this reason. Remember that

10

regardless of the season, travelers are advised to drink a quart of water for every hour that they are walking around the national park.

Another popular way to experience Uluru is far less taxing but no less intense: watching the natural light reflect on it from one of the two sunset-viewing areas. As the last rays of daylight strike, the rock positively glows, as if lighted from within. Just as quickly, the light is extinguished and the color changes to a somber mauve and finally to black.

SHOPPING

The **Cultural Centre** (☎08/8956–1128) not only has information about the Anangu people and their culture, but houses the **Ininti Store** (☎08/8956–2214), which carries souvenirs. The adjoining **Maruku Arts** (☎08/8956–2558) is owned by Aborigines and sells Aboriginal painting and handicrafts. There's also a display of traditional huts and shelters. The Cultural Centre is open daily 7–6; Ininti Store is open daily 7–5:15; Maruku Arts is open daily 8:30–5:30.

KATA TJUTA

Fodor's Choice Many visitors feel that Kata Tjuta is more satisfying to explore than
★ Uluru. Whereas Uluru is one immense block, so you feel as if you're always on the outside looking in, Kata Tjuta, as its Aboriginal name ("many heads") suggests, is a collection of huge rocks, hiding numerous gorges and chasms that you can enter and explore. There are three main walks, the first from the parking lot into **Olga Gorge,** the deepest valley between the rocks. This is a 2-km (1-mi) walk, and the round-trip journey takes about one hour. More rewarding but also more difficult is a walk that continues through the major cleft between the Olgas, known as the Valley of the Winds. Experienced walkers can complete this 8-km (5-mi) walk in about four hours. The Valley of the Winds walk is closed when temperatures rise above 36°C (97°F), which is after 11 AM most days in summer. The **Kata Tjuta Viewing Area,** 25 km (16 mi) along the Kata Tjuta Road, offers a magnificent vista and is a relaxing place for a break. Interpretive panels give you an understanding of the natural life around you.

AYERS ROCK RESORT

This complex of lodgings, restaurants, and facilities, which officially is known as the township of Yulara, is base camp for exploring Uluru and Kata Tjuta. The accommodations and services here are the only ones in the vicinity of the national park. Uluru is about a 20-minute drive from the resort area (there's a sunset-viewing area on the way); driving to Kata Tjuta will take another 30 minutes. The park entrance fee of A$25 is valid for three days.

The properties at the resort, which range from luxury hotels to a campground, are all run by Voyages Hotels & Resorts and share many of the same facilities. The resort "village" includes a bank, newsstand, supermarket, several souvenir shops, Aboriginal art gallery, hair salon, and child-care center.

WHERE TO EAT

Indoor dining is limited to each hotel's restaurants and the less-expensive Geckos Cafe, all of which can be charged back to your room. All reservations can be made through Voyages Hotel & Resorts on-site, or their central reservations service in Sydney. **Central reservations service** (☎02/8296–8010 or 1300/134044 ⊕*www.voyages.com.au*).

★ The most memorable group-dining experience in the region is the unique, but expensive (A$149) **Sounds of Silence,** an elegant (although heavily attended) outdoor dinner served on a june (dune) that provides sunset views of either Uluru or Kata Tjuta (though you can request to attend a dinner being held at the site that allows you to view both). Champagne and Northern Territory specialty dishes—including bush salads and Australian game—are served on tables covered with crisp white linens, right in the desert. An astronomer takes you on a star-gazing tour of the southern sky while you dine. In winter, hot mulled wine is served around a campfire. Dinners can be reserved through the resort's central service.

$–$$ ✗**Geckos Cafe.** This mess hall–like eatery in the resort's main shopping center is the most casual dining option on-site, but is by no means cheap. The all-day dining options include inexpensive appetizers, yellowfin tuna kebabs, and several pastas and pizzas. There's a big focus on deserts, with signs out front boasting each day's cake or pastry special, including a dessert pizza. ⊠*Town Sq., Yulara Centre, Yulara* ☎08/8957–7722 ⊟*AE, DC, MC, V.*

WHERE TO STAY

$$$$ ★ 🏨**Lost Camel Hotel.** Blocks and splashes of lime, purple, and orange in contemporary, boxy white rooms make this the funkiest hotel for a thousand miles. The resort's boutique-hotel style property is built around a blue-tile, rivet-and-glass-paneled, reverse infinity pool. Central to each room is the bed, which backs onto an open hand-basin area. The only windows are in the divided bathroom—which is an enclosed balcony with separate rooms for the toilet and shower—so remember to draw the curtains. Grouped around courtyard gardens, the rooms have sound systems and CDs, as well as irons, ironing boards, and tea- and coffee-making equipment. A café, wine bar, and plasma-screen TV with cable channels encourage socializing in the lobby lounge. ⊠*Yulara Dr., Yulara, 0872* ☎08/8957–5650 ⊕*www. ayersrockresort.com.au* 🛏*99 rooms* ⚄*In-room: safe, refrigerator, no TV. In-hotel: restaurant, room service, bar, pool, airport shuttle, parking (no fee)* ⊟*AE, DC, MC, V.*

$$–$$$$ ★ 🏨**Outback Pioneer Hotel & Lodge.** The most affordable hotel option at the resort is also the most popular. The theme here is the 1860s Outback, complete with corrugated iron, timber beams, and camel saddles, but you won't be roughing it here—not with a pool and two restaurants. Guests at the adjoining lodge, a budget accommodation with large and small dorms, and a communal kitchen, share the hotel's facilities. The Bough House serves a set-price dinner buffet of traditional roasts and bush specialties like kangaroo, and the Pioneer

10

Ayers Rock Resort

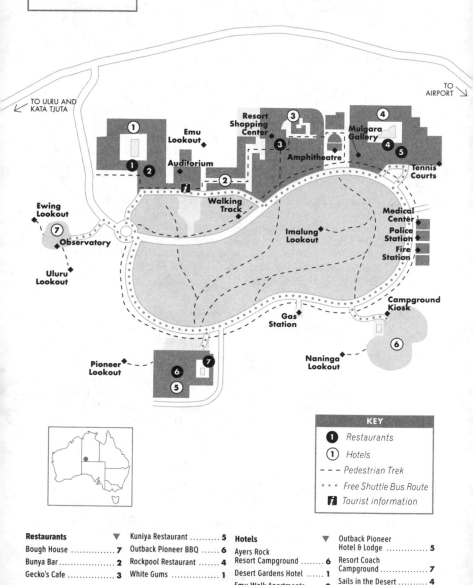

TO ULRU AND KATA TJUTA

TO AIRPORT

Emu Lookout

Resort Shopping Center

Mulgara Gallery

Auditorium

Amphitheatre

Tennis Courts

Walking Track

Ewing Lookout

Imalung Lookout

Medical Center

Police Station

Observatory

Fire Station

Uluru Lookout

Campground Kiosk

Gas Station

Pioneer Lookout

Naninga Lookout

KEY

- ❶ *Restaurants*
- ① *Hotels*
- – – *Pedestrian Trek*
- • • • *Free Shuttle Bus Route*
- 🛈 *Tourist information*

Restaurants ▼	Kuniya Restaurant 5	**Hotels** ▼	Outback Pioneer Hotel & Lodge 5
Bough House 7	Outback Pioneer BBQ 6	Ayers Rock Resort Campground 6	Resort Coach Campground 7
Bunya Bar 2	Rockpool Restaurant 4	Desert Gardens Hotel 1	Sails in the Desert 4
Gecko's Cafe 3	White Gums 1	Emu Walk Apartments 2	
		Lost Camel Hotel 3	

BBQ self-cook restaurant opens at 6:30 PM. A shuttle bus connects the lodge to the other properties every 15 minutes. ✉ *Yulara Dr., Yulara, 0872* ☎ *08/8957-7606* ⊕ *www.ayersrockresort.com.au* ⇆ *125 hotel rooms, 42 budget rooms; 168 lodge bunk beds* ⌂ *In-room: no phone (some), kitchen (some), refrigerator (some), no TV (some). In-hotel: 2 restaurants, bar, pool, no elevator, laundry facilities, public Internet, public Wi-Fi, airport shuttle, parking (no fee), no-smoking rooms* ▭ *AE, DC, MC, V.*

⚠ **Ayers Rock Resort Campground.** Sand goannas wander around this large campground amid the red dunes, where 220 tent sites are scattered around 29 green lawns. Powered sites, permanent tents (with linen), and air-conditioned cabins are also available; cabins come with linens, full kitchens, and TVs—but no bathrooms. It's a 50-yard walk to the nearest amenities block. There's also a well-equipped camper's kitchen, a grocery, an Outback-style shelter with free gas barbecues, and bicycle rentals. Leashed dogs are allowed. ✉ *Yulara Dr., Ayers Rock Resort, Yulara, 0872* ☎ *08/8957-7001* ⊕ *www.ayersrockresort. com.au* ⇆ *418 sites, 15 permanent tents, 14 cabins (all without bath)* ⌂ *Pool, flush toilets, partial hookups, drinking water, guest laundry, showers, fire grates, grills, picnic tables, electricity, public telephone, general store, play area* ▭ *AE, DC, MC, V.*

LONGITUDE 131°

$$$$

Fodor's Choice

★

⛺ **Longitude 131°.** Set on its own in the desert 3 km (2 mi) from Ayers Rock Resort and accessible only by four-wheel-drive vehicle, this is the be-all and end-all of Outback luxury. Fifteen "tents" that pop out of the desert like a colony of perfect white mushroom caps make up this unique resort, which caters to a maximum of 30 guests at any one time. Each tent is named after a prominent regional explorer, and has a balcony with floor-to-ceiling sliding-glass doors for a panoramic view of the rock from the king-size bed. The excellent, discreet staff provides a customized turndown service, stocking your minibar according to your specifications. Gourmet meals are served in the Dune House, which also contains a formal lounge with an extensive library, and an honor bar of top-shelf liquors. Set just 49 feet outside of Uluru–Kata Tjuta National Park, it's the closest accommodation to the main sites; the tour program is exclusive to the resort. You can park free at Desert Gardens Hotel and hop a complementary transfer bus here. ✎ *Yulara Dr., Yulara, 0872* ☎ *08/8957-7131* ⊕ *www.longitude131. com.au* ⇆ *15 tents* ⌂ *In-room: safe, refrigerator, no TV, dial-up. In-hotel: restaurant, bar, pool, no elevator, laundry service, public Internet, parking (no fee), airport shuttle, no children under 16* ▭ *AE, DC, MC, V* ⦿ *FAP.*

10

THE RED CENTRE ESSENTIALS

TRANSPORTATION

BY AIR

Alice Springs Airport, with its bright, cool passenger terminal, is 15 km (9 mi) southeast of town. Qantas is the only airline that flies in and out of Alice Springs, offering daily direct flights from Sydney, Melbourne, Adelaide, Perth, Darwin, and Cairns, as well as Ayers Rock itself. It's three hours flying time from Sydney, Melbourne, and Brisbane; two hours from Adelaide and Darwin; and about 40 minutes from Ayers Rock. Flights run less frequently in the summer months.

Qantas also operates daily direct flights from Sydney, Perth, and Cairns (and twice weekly flights from Melbourne) to Ayers Rock Airport, which is 5 km (3 mi) north of the resort complex. Passengers from other capital cities fly to Alice Springs to connect with flights to Ayers Rock Airport.

All other air services are charter flights. AAT Kings runs a complimentary shuttle bus between the airport and Yulara, which meets every flight. If you have reservations at the resort, there's no need to call ahead to reserve a spot on one of these shuttles; you'll find resort representatives waiting outside the baggage-claim area of the airport to whisk you and other guests away on the 10-minute drive.

Airports Alice Springs Airport (☎ 08/8951–1211 ⊕ www.ntapl.com.au/ASIndex. htm). **Ayers Rock Airport** (☎ 08/8956–2020

Airlines Qantas (☎ 13–1313 ⊕ www.qantas.com). **AAT Kings** (☎ 08/8952–1700 or 1800/334009).

AIRPORT TRANSFERS Alice Springs Airport Shuttle Service meets every flight. The ride to all hotels and residential addresses in town costs A$12 each way. On request, the bus will also pick you up at your hotel and take you back to the airport. Alice Springs Taxis maintains a stand at the airport. The fare to most parts of town is about A$25.

Contacts Alice Springs Airport Shuttle Service (✉ Shop 6, Capricornia Centre, Gregory Terr., Alice Springs ☎ 08/8953–0310). **Alice Springs Taxis** (☎ 08/8952–1877).

BY BUS

Greyhound-operated interstate buses arrive and depart from 3/313 Todd Street, in Alice Springs. AAT Kings coaches, which run day and extended tours, have a separate terminal. Both make daily departures to Ayers Rock.

Bus Lines AAT Kings (☎ 08/8952–1700 or 1800/334009 ⊕ www.aatkings.com). **Greyhound Australia** (☎ 08/8952–7888 ⊕ www.greyhound.com.au).

BY CAR

DRIVING TO AND AROUND ALICE SPRINGS The Stuart Highway, commonly called the Track, is the only road into Alice Springs. The town center lies east of the highway. The 1,693-km (1,000-mi) drive from Adelaide takes about 24 hours. The drive from

Darwin is about 160 km (100 mi) shorter than the drive from Adelaide, and takes about 21 hours.

A speed limit of 130 km per hour (80 mph) applies on the Stuart Highway and 110 km per hour (70 mph) on most other regional roads.

There is almost no cell phone reception along the entire Stuart Highway in this area, but it is a well-traveled road, so in case of emergency put on your hazard lights and stay by your car—someone will be along soon. If you break down, contact the Automobile Association of the N.T. for emergency road assistance. And whatever happens, don't leave your vehicle.

DRIVING TO AND AROUND AYERS ROCK RESORT The five-hour-plus 440-km (273-mi) trip from Alice Springs to Ayers Rock Resort is a very long haul, and somewhat of an adventure. The road is paved, but lacks a shoulder, and is one lane in each direction for the duration. The un-scenic route often induces fatigue, and signs along the road encourage drivers to stop and rest.

From the resort it's 19 km (12 mi) to Uluru or 53 km (33 mi) to Kata Tjuta. The road to Kata Tjuta is paved. Routes between hotels and sights are clearly marked, and since car-rental costs are competitive with bus tours, renting a car may be best for larger parties.

Contacts Automobile Association of N.T. (☎ *08/8981–3837, emergency road assistance 13–1111* ⊕ *www.aant.com.au*). **N.T. Road Report** (☎ *1800/246199* ⊕ *www.roadreport.nt.gov.au*).

CAR RENTAL Avis, Budget, Hertz, and Thrifty have offices in Alice Springs. All rent conventional cars as well as the four-wheel-drive vehicles needed to drive some of the wilder, unpaved Territory roads. Britz and Maui rent motor homes, which are another popular way to explore the Red Centre.

Rental Agencies Avis (✉ *Shop 21B, Coles Complex, Bath St. at Gregory Terr., Alice Springs* ☎ *08/8953–5533 or 13–6333* ⊕ *www.avis.com.au*). **Britz** (✉ *Stuart Hwy. at Power St., Alice Springs* ☎ *08/8952–8814 or 1800/331454* ⊕ *www.britz.com*). **Budget** (✉ *Shop 6, Capricorn Centre, Gregory Terr., Alice Springs* ☎ *08/8952–8899 or 13 2727* ⊕ *www.budget.com.au*). **Hertz** (✉ *76 Hartley St., Alice Springs* ☎ *08/8952–2644 or 13–3039* ⊕ *www.hertznt.com*). **Maui** (✉ *Stuart Hwy. at Power St., Alice Springs* ☎ *08/8952–8049 or 1300/363800* ⊕ *www.maui-rentals.com*). **Thrifty** (✉ *Stott Terr. at Hartley St., Alice Springs* ☎ *08/8952–9999 or 1300/367227* ⊕ *www.rentacar.com.au*).

BY TAXI

Uluru Express minibuses can whisk you from the lodgings at Ayers Rock Resort to the sights for much less than the cost of a guided bus tour—plus, you can go at your own convenience.

Contacts Uluru Express (☎ *08/8956–2152* ⊕ *www.uluruexpress.com.au*).

BY TRAIN

The *Ghan* train leaves Adelaide at 12:20 PM Sunday and Wednesday, arriving in Alice Springs at 1:45 PM Monday and Thursday. Return

10

trains leave Alice Springs at 12:45 PM Thursday and 3:15 PM Sunday, arriving in Adelaide at 1:10 PM on Friday and Monday. On Monday and Thursday at 6 PM the *Ghan* continues to Darwin via Katherine, arriving at 5:30 PM Tuesday and 6:30 PM Friday. Trains from Darwin depart Wednesday at 10 AM and Saturday at 9 AM. Trains from Sydney and Melbourne to Adelaide also connect with the *Ghan*. You can transport your car by train for an extra charge. The Alice Springs railway station is 2½ km (1½ mi) west of Todd Mall.

Contact *Ghan* (*Great Southern Railway* ☎ *13–2147 bookings, 1300/132147 holiday packages* ⊕ *www.gsr.com.au*).

CONTACTS & RESOURCES
EMERGENCIES
The medical centre at the Royal Flying Doctor Base at Ayers Rock Resort in Yulara is open weekdays 9–noon and 2–5 and (for emergencies only) weekends 10–11 AM.

Contacts Police (☎ *08/8956–2166*).

Doctors & Dentists Central Clinic (✉ *76 Todd St., Alice Springs* ☎ *08/8952–1088*). **Community Dental Centre** (✉ *Flynn Dr. off Memorial Dr., Alice Springs* ☎ *08/8951–6713*). **Royal Flying Doctor Service Ayers Rock Medical Centre** (✉ *Royal Flying Doctor Base, Yulara Dr. near police station, Ayers Rock Resort* ☎ *08/8956–2286* ⊕ *www.flyingdoctor.net/central/yulara.htm*).

Hospital Alice Springs Hospital (✉ *Gap Rd. between Traeger Ave. and Stuart Terr., Alice Springs* ☎ *08/8951–7777*).

TOURS
ABORIGINAL TOURS   Owned and operated by local Aboriginal people, Anangu Tours organizes several trips through the Uluru and Kata Tjuta region. Tours, which leave from the Ayers Rock Resort, include the Aboriginal Uluru Tour (A$119 with breakfast), led by an Aboriginal guide; the Kuniya Sunset Tour (A$99); and the Anangu Culture Pass, which combines the first two tours over one or two days (A$189). You can drive to the trailhead of the Liru Walk (A$58). Guides are Aborigines who work with interpreters. Aboriginal art aficionados can attend Dot Painting workshops (A$79).

Contact Anangu Tours (☎ *08/8950–3030* ⊕ *www.ananguwaai.com.au/anangu_tours/*).

AIR TOURS   The best views of Uluru and Kata Tjuta are from the air. Lightplane tours, with courtesy hotel pickup from Ayers Rock Resort hotels, include 40-minute flights over Ayers Rock and the Olgas, and day tours to Kings Canyon. Prices run from A$165 to A$665 per person; for options, contact Ayers Rock Scenic Flights. Helicopter flights are A$105 per person for 15 minutes over Ayers Rock, or A$210 for 30 minutes over the Olgas and the rock.

Contacts Ayers Rock Helicopters (☎ *08/8956–2077* 🖷 *08/8956–2060* ⊕ *www.helicoptergroup.com*). **Ayers Rock Scenic Flights** (☎ *08/8956–2345* 🖷 *08/8956–2472* ⊕ *www.ayersrockflights.com.au*).

ALICE SPRINGS TOURS
The *Alice Wanderer* bus completes a 70-minute circuit (with narration) of 15 tourist attractions in and around Alice Springs, 9–5 daily. You can leave and rejoin the bus whenever you like over two days for a flat rate of A$40. Entry into attractions is extra. It is part of Alice Wanderer Centre Sightseeing, a company that also runs half-day tours of Alice. AAT Kings and Tailormade Tours operate three-hour trips and all companies include visits to the Royal Flying Doctor Service Base, School of the Air, Telegraph Station, and Anzac Hill scenic lookout.

Contacts **AAT Kings** (✉ *74 Todd St., Alice Springs* ☎ *08/8952–1700 or 1300/556100* ⊕ *www.aatkings.com*). **Alice Wanderer** (☎ *08/8952–2111 or 1800/722111* ⊕ *www.alicewanderer.com.au*). **Tailormade Tours** (☎ *08/8952–1731 or 1800/806641* ⊕ *www.tailormadetours.com.au*).

CAMEL TOURS
A great way to get out in the open and see the sights is from the back of one of the desert's creatures. Uluru Camel Tours, a subsidiary of Anangu Tours, has sunrise and sunset tours that last for 2½ hours for A$95; tours leave from the Ayers Rock Resort.

Contact **Uluru Camel Tours** (☎ *08/8950–3030* 📠 *08/8950–3034* ⊕ *ulurucamel-tours.ananguwaai.com.au*).

WALKING TOURS
The free Mala Walk at Uluru is led by Aboriginal rangers who show you the land from their perspective. The walk starts from the base of the Uluru climbing trail at 8 AM daily from October to April and at 10 AM the rest of the year. Discovery Ecotours specializes in small group tours with guides who have extensive local knowledge. The Uluru Walk, a 10-km (6-mi) hike around the base, gives fascinating insight into the area's significance to the Aboriginal people. It departs daily, includes breakfast and hotel transfers, and costs A$115. Book at least a day in advance.

Contacts **Discovery Ecotours** (☎ *08/8956–2563* ⊕ *www.ecotours.com.au*). **Mala Walk** (☎ *08/8956–1128*).

VISITOR INFORMATION

In Alice Springs the Central Australian Tourism Industry Association (weekdays 8:30–5:30, weekends 9–4) dispenses information, advice, and maps and will book tours and cars.

The Uluru–Kata Tjuta Cultural Centre is on the park road just before you reach the rock. It also contains the park's ranger station. The Cultural Centre is open daily 7–6. The Ayers Rock Visitor Centre next to the Desert Gardens Hotel on Yulara Drive is open daily 9–5:30.

Contacts **Ayers Rock Visitor Centre** (☎ *08/8957–7377*). **Central Australian Tourism Industry Association** (✉ *60 Gregory Terr., Alice Springs, 0870* ☎ *08/8952–5800 or 1800/645199* ⊕ *www.centralaustraliantourism.com*). **Uluru–Kata Tjuta Cultural Centre** (☎ *08/8956–3138*).

10

11

Darwin, the Top End & the Kimberley

WORD OF MOUTH

"Darwin is great for seeing the Top End, Aboriginal art sites, and the wetlands animals—especially crocodiles."

—SnRSeattle

Updated
by Graham
Hodgson

THE TOP END IS A geographic description—but it's also a state of mind. Isolated from the rest of Australia by thousands of miles of desert and lonely scrubland, Top Enders are different and proud of it. From the remote wetlands and stone country of Arnhem Land—home to thousands of Aborigines—to the lush tropical city of Darwin, the Top End is a gateway to a region where people from 50 different national and cultural backgrounds live in what they regard as the real Australia. It's an isolation that contributes to strong feelings of independence from the rest of the country—Southerners are regarded with a mixture of pity and ridicule.

For thousands of years this area of northern Australia has been home to Aboriginal communities. Stunning examples of ancient Aboriginal rock art remain—on cliffs, in hidden valleys, and in Darwin art galleries. Today, however, the region is a melting pot of cultures and traditions. Darwin and Broome—closer geographically to the cities of Southeast Asia than to any Australian counterparts—host the nation's most racially diverse populations: Aborigines, Anglos, and Asians sharing a tropical lifestyle.

The starkness of the isolation of the Top End and Western Australia's Kimberley is reflected in its tiny population. Although the Northern Territory occupies one-sixth of Australia's landmass, its population of 200,000 makes up just more than 1% of the continent's citizenry—an average density of around one person per 8 square km (.3 square mi). In many areas kangaroos and cattle vastly outnumber the locals. The Kimberley, an area larger than the state of Kansas, is home to only 30,000 people. Traveling by road from Darwin to Broome is the best way to see the Kimberley, but you pass through only nine communities in 2,016 km (1,250 mi).

The Kimberley offers some of the most dramatic landscapes in Australia. A land of rugged ranges, tropical wetlands, and desert, of vast cattle stations and wonderful national parks, including the bizarre, beautiful, red-and-black-striped sandstone domes and towers of Purnululu National Park, the Kimberley is still the frontier. Like Top Enders, the people of the Kimberley region see themselves as living in a land apart from the rest of the nation, and it's easy to see why: landscape and distance combine to make the Kimberley one of the world's few uniquely open spaces.

See Chapter 13 for more information on four-wheel-driving in the Top End and the Kimberley's great outdoors.

EXPLORING DARWIN, THE TOP END & THE KIMBERLEY

The telltale recurring phrase "tyranny of distance" was first used to describe Australia's relationship to the rest of the world. In many ways it still describes the Top End and the Kimberley, with vast distances setting this region apart from the rest of the nation.

Here the year is divided into two seasons: the Wet (December–April) and the Dry (May–November). The Dry is a period of idyllic weather

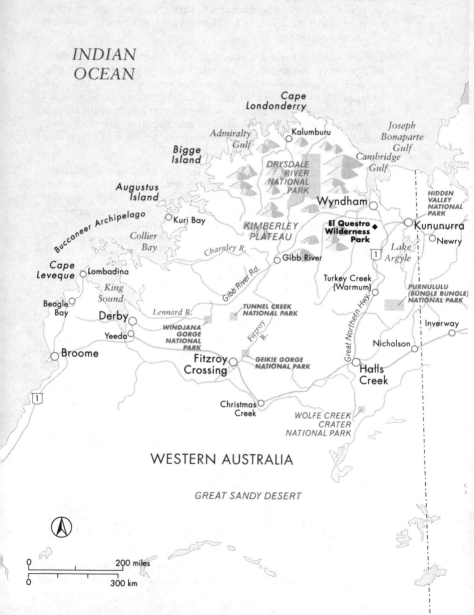

The Top End & the Kimberley

Timor Sea

INDIAN OCEAN

Cape Londonderry

Kalumburu

Admiralty Gulf

Joseph Bonaparte Gulf

Bigge Island

Cambridge Gulf

DRYSDALE RIVER NATIONAL PARK

Augustus Island

Wyndham

HIDDEN VALLEY NATIONAL PARK

Buccaneer Archipelago

Kuri Bay

KIMBERLEY PLATEAU

El Questro Wilderness Park

Kununurra

Newry

Collier Bay

Charnley R.

Gibb River

Lake Argyle

Cape Leveque

Lombadina

Gibb River Rd.

Turkey Creek (Warmum)

PURNULULU (BUNGLE BUNGLE) NATIONAL PARK

King Sound

Beagle Bay

Lennard R.

TUNNEL CREEK NATIONAL PARK

Inverway

Derby

WINDJANA GORGE NATIONAL PARK

Fitzroy R.

Nicholson

Yeeda

Broome

Fitzroy Crossing

GEIKIE GORGE NATIONAL PARK

Halls Creek

Christmas Creek

WOLFE CREEK CRATER NATIONAL PARK

WESTERN AUSTRALIA

GREAT SANDY DESERT

0 — 200 miles
0 — 300 km

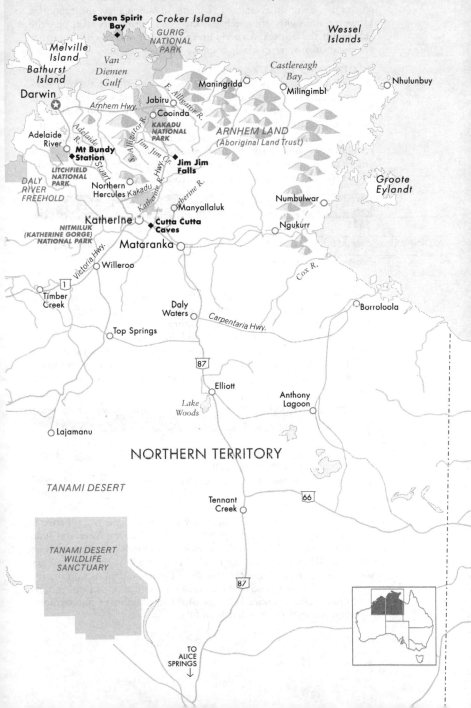

Arafura Sea

Seven Spirit Bay
Croker Island
GURIG NATIONAL PARK
Wessel Islands

Melville Island
Van Diemen Gulf
Castlereagh Bay
Nhulunbuy

Bathurst Island
Maningrida
Milingimbi

Darwin
Arnhem Hwy.
Jabiru
E. Alligator R.

Adelaide River
Cooinda
ARNHEM LAND
(Aboriginal Land Trust)
Groote Eylandt

Mt Bundy Station
KAKADU NATIONAL PARK

LITCHFIELD NATIONAL PARK

DALY RIVER FREEHOLD
Northern Hercules
Jim Jim Falls

Numbulwar

Katherine
Manyallaluk
Ngukurr

NITMILUK (KATHERINE GORGE) NATIONAL PARK
Cutta Cutta Caves

Mataranka
Cox R.

Willeroo
Borroloola

Timber Creek
1
Daly Waters
Carpentaria Hwy.

Top Springs

87

Elliott
Anthony Lagoon

Lake Woods

Lajamanu

NORTHERN TERRITORY

TANAMI DESERT

Tennant Creek
66

TANAMI DESERT WILDLIFE SANCTUARY

87

TO ALICE SPRINGS
↓

with warm days and cool nights, while the Wet brings monsoonal storms that dump an average of 52 inches of rain in a few short months. However, the sights are much less crowded during the Wet, plus the rain paints the landscape a vivid green. You can also catch spectacular electrical storms, particularly over the ocean.

ABOUT THE RESTAURANTS

As well as restaurants and cafés serving up local seafood and Aussie tucker (including buffalo, crocodile, and kangaroo), Darwin and Broome have establishments specializing in European and Asian fare. Reservations are advisable at all but the most casual of places, and tipping is welcomed but not expected. On the road, wayside inns and roadhouses supply basic burgers, steaks, pies, and refreshments. If you're driving long distances, it's a good idea to stock up on snacks and drinks in Darwin, Katherine, or Broome.

WHAT IT COSTS IN AUSTRALIAN DOLLARS				
$$$$	$$$	$$	$	¢
AT DINNER	over A$50	A$36–A$50	A$21–A$35	A$10–A$20	under A$10

Prices are for a main course at dinner.

ABOUT THE HOTELS

Apart from Darwin hotels and Top End resorts, accommodations fall into the more basic category. Roadhouse accommodations can be anything from rudimentary rooms in prefabricated huts with sagging mattresses, wheezing air conditioners, and doors without locks to clean, comfortable, no-frills lodgings. Places without air-conditioning are rare. Homestays and working cattle stations provide a true bush experience that often includes trail rides, fishing, and participation in station activities.

WHAT IT COSTS IN AUSTRALIAN DOLLARS				
$$$$	$$$	$$	$	¢
FOR TWO PEOPLE	over A$300	A$201–A$300	A$151–A$200	A$100–A$150	under A$100

Prices are for two people in a standard double room in high season, including tax and service, based on the European Plan (with no meals) unless otherwise noted.

WHEN TO VISIT

Unless you're used to heat and humidity, the best time to tour is between May and August, during the peak months of the Dry. May and June are when the waterfalls of Kakadu and the Kimberley are at their most dramatic. When you're on the road, early starts beat the heat and get you to swimming holes in the middle of the day—the crucial time for cooling off. Morning and evening cruises are best to avoid the heat, to see animals, and to take advantage of the ideal light for photography (by noon the light is often harsh and flat).

GREAT ITINERARIES

IF YOU HAVE 3 DAYS

Start from **Darwin** just after dawn and head east on the Arnhem Highway to Fogg Dam to view the birdlife. Continue into **Kakadu National Park,** and picnic at the rock-art site at Ubirr. Take a scenic flight in the afternoon, then a trip to the Bowali Visitors Centre, and you can overnight in **Jabiru.** On the second day, head to Nourlangie Rock; then continue to the Yellow Water cruise at **Cooinda** and stay there for the night. The next day, drive to **Litchfield National Park** and visit Florence, Tjaynera, or Wangi Falls.

IF YOU HAVE 5 DAYS

From **Darwin,** drive to **Litchfield National Park,** entering through Batchelor. A swim at the Florence Falls plunge pool and a picnic in the rain forest will help you sleep well here. After an early start on the second day, head toward **Kakadu National Park** via the Arnhem Highway. Pause en route at the Bark Hut Inn for morning tea. You should reach the rock-art site and magnificent floodplain vistas at Ubirr in time for a late lunch. In the afternoon visit the Warradjan Aboriginal Cultural Centre at Cooinda, then take the evening Yellow Water cruise. On the third day head down to the southern half of Kakadu National Park. After lunch continue to Edith

Falls to camp in **Nitmiluk (Katherine Gorge) National Park** or head into **Katherine** for the night. Next morning cruise up Katherine Gorge in Nitmiluk National Park. After lunch head south to **Cutta Cutta Caves** and the thermal pools. On Day 5 meander back toward Darwin, exploring the sights around the townships of Pine Creek and Adelaide River along the way.

IF YOU HAVE 10 DAYS

Take the five-day tour above, then head back through **Katherine** and take the Victoria Highway, passing through mesa formations and Timber Creek to **Kununurra** for the night. On the sixth day, take in the spectacular landscapes of **Purnululu National Park** by four-wheel-drive or with a guided tour, and spend the night in **Halls Creek.** It'll be a long haul west the seventh day on the Great Northern Highway, but you can make it to **Geikie Gorge National Park** for an afternoon boat tour, a welcome and interesting respite before heading off to camp the night at **Windjana Gorge National Park.** Another early start on Day 8 will get you to **Broome,** the fascinating old pearling town. Spend the night, then take a fishing charter the ninth day or just amble around this attractive and historic town for a while.

DARWIN

There's no other city in Australia that defines its history by a single cataclysmic event. For the people of Darwin—including the vast majority who weren't here at the time—everything is dated as before or after 1974's Cyclone Tracy, which hit on Christmas Eve. It wasn't just the death toll (65 people) that left a lasting scar in the area; it was the immensity of the destruction wrought by Tracy. More than 70% of Darwin's homes were destroyed or suffered severe structural damage; all services—communications, power, and water—were cut off.

The resulting food shortage, lack of water, and concerns about disease moved government officials to evacuate the city; some 25,600 were airlifted out and another 7,200 left by road.

It's a tribute to those who stayed and to those who have come to live here after Tracy that the rebuilt city now thrives as an administrative and commercial center for northern Australia. Old Darwin has been replaced by something of an edifice complex—such buildings as Parliament House and the Supreme Court all seem a bit too grand for such a small city, especially one that prides itself on its relaxed, multicultural openness.

The seductiveness of contemporary Darwin lifestyles belies a Top End history of failed attempts by Europeans dating back to 1824 to establish an enclave in a harsh, unyielding climate. The original 1869 settlement, called Palmerston, was built on a parcel of mangrove wetlands and scrub forest that had changed little in 15 million years. It was not until 1911, after it had already weathered the disastrous cyclones of 1878, 1882, and 1897, that the town was named after the scientist who had visited Australia's shores aboard the *Beagle* in 1839.

Today Darwin is the best place from which to explore the beauty and diversity of Australia's Top End, as well as the wonders of Kakadu, Nitmiluk (Katherine Gorge), and the mighty Kimberley region.

WHAT TO SEE: CITY CENTER

⓫ **Australian Pearling Exhibition.** Since the early 19th century, fortune seekers have hunted for pearls in Australia's northern waters. Exhibits at this museum cover everything from pearl farming to pearl jewelry settings. ✉ *Kitchener Dr., Wharf Precinct* ☎ *08/8999–6573* 💲 *A$6.60* 🕙 *Daily 10–5.*

⓭ **Brown's Mart Community Arts Theatre.** This 1885 building has seen duty as an emporium, a mining exchange, and currently as a theater. ✉ *Smith St. at Harry Chan Ave., City Center* ☎ *08/8981–5522* 💲 *Free admission, fee for performances* 🕙 *Open during performances.*

❹ **Cenotaph/War Memorial.** The site of World War II memorial services on February 19 and Anzac Day on April 25, this monument is dedicated to members of the Australian armed forces, rescue services, and civilians who lost their lives in times of war. The monument is opposite Herbert Street. ✉ *Bicentennial Park, Esplanade, Bicentennial Park.*

NEED A BREAK?

⓮ The balcony of the **Victoria Hotel** (✉ *27 Smith St. Mall, City Center* ☎ *08/8981–4011*), overlooking the passing parade on Smith Street Mall, is a good place for a cool drink. A Darwin institution since its construction in 1894, the Vic has been hit by every cyclone and rebuilt afterward.

❻ **Government House.** The oldest building in Darwin, Government House has been the home of the administrator for the area since 1870. Despite being bombed by Japanese aircraft in 1942 and damaged by the cyclones of 1897, 1937, and 1974, the building looks much as it did in 1879 when it was first completed. The house, which is not open

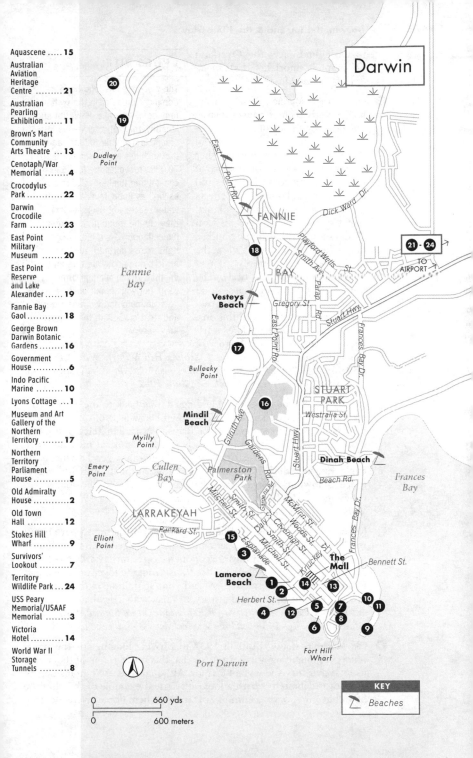

Darwin

Dudley Point

FANNIE

BAY

Fannie Bay

Vesteys Beach

Bullocky Point

Mindil Beach

Myilly Point

Emery Point

Cullen Bay

Palmerston Park

LARRAKEYAH

Elliott Point

Packard St.

Lameroo Beach

Herbert St.

Port Darwin

STUART PARK

Westralia St.

Dinah Beach

Frances Bay

Beach Rd.

The Mall

Bennett St.

Fort Hill Wharf

East Point Rd.

Dick Ward Dr.

Playford St.

Wells St.

Smith Ave.

Parap Rd.

Gregory St.

Stuart Hwy.

Frances Bay Dr.

Gilruth Ave.

Gardens Rd.

Stuart Hwy.

McMinn St.

Woods St.

Smith St.

Cavenagh St.

Mitchell St.

Esplanade

Knuckey St.

Frances Bay Dr.

TO AIRPORT

21 - 24

KEY

Beaches

0   660 yds

0   600 meters

to the public, faces the Overland Telegraph Memorial. ⊠ *Esplanade S, East Esplanade.*

⑩ **Indo Pacific Marine.** This marine
★ interpretive center houses a large open tank with one of the few self-contained coral-reef ecosystems in the Southern Hemisphere. Other exhibits include a static display of rare, deepwater coral skeletons and an exhibit explaining the effects of global warming on the planet. Night tours, which begin at 7 on Wednesday, Friday, and Sunday, take you by flashlight to view the biodiversity of the fluorescing reef and live venomous animals. The tours include a four-course seafood dinner, followed by a nocturnal coral reef tour of the exhibitions. Bookings are essential. The pearling exhibition tracks the history of

> ### CROCS BITE!
>
> The crocodile has long been a dominant predator in the wetland regions of Australia. Powerful and stealthy, the saltwater (estuarine) crocodile has little to fear—and that includes humans. More than 70,000 crocodiles are found in the coastal and tidal areas of rivers, as well as floodplains and fresh-water reaches of rivers. In fact, they can be found in the larger rivers, lagoons, and billabongs right across northern Australia. Attacks on people are rare and deaths few (an average of one a year), but you should observe all no swimming and warning signs, and treat crocs with the respect they deserve.

this important local industry. ⊠ *Stokes Hill Wharf, Wharf Precinct* ☎ *08/8981–1294* ⊠ *A$16, night tours A$84* ⊗ *Apr.–Oct., daily 10–5; Nov.–Mar., Mon.–Fri. 9–1, Sat. and Sun. 10–2.*

❶ **Lyons Cottage.** One of several buildings dating back to the early settlement of northern Australia in downtown Darwin, Lyons Cottage was built in 1925 for executives of the British-Australian Telegraph Company (B.A.T.). The stone building is now a historical museum with exhibits on the town's history, Chinese immigrants, pearl diving, early explorers, and the Macassans, who came by boat from Indonesia, touched down in Australia, and had contact with the Aborigines centuries ago. ⊠ *74 The Esplanade, Bicentennial Park* ☎ *08/8981–1750* ⊠ *Free* ⊗ *Daily 10–4:30.*

❺ **Northern Territory Parliament House.** Australia's northernmost parliament resides in a gleaming home set on cliffs at the edge of the sea. Ninety-minute tours of the building are conducted on Saturday at 9 and 11 AM and Wednesday (May–Sept.) at 10.30 AM from the foyer of Parliament House (reservations essential). Spend your spare time in the extensive library brushing up on local history, or relax with a drink at the Speaker's Corner Café. ⊠ *Smith St. at Esplanade, State Square, East Esplanade* ☎ *08/8946–1434* ⊠ *Free* ⊗ *Weekdays 8–6, weekends 9–6.*

❷ **Old Admiralty House.** Built in 1937 to provide lodging for the naval officer commanding northern Australia, this house is one of the few of its kind that survived Cyclone Tracy. Although you can't go inside, the exterior is definitely worth a look; it's a great example of the old style of architecture, once common in Darwin, where homes were elevated on columns to beat the heat. ⊠*Knuckey St. at The Esplanade, Bicentennial Park.*

12 Old Town Hall. Built of stone in 1883 during the first mining boom, the building was a naval administration center during World War II; later it was a library and art gallery. It was destroyed by Cyclone Tracy in 1974. The ruins are now used for outdoor theater performances and concerts during the Dry. ⊠*Smith St. opposite Brown's Mart, City Center* ☎*No phone* ⊠*Free.*

9 Stokes Hill Wharf. The best views of Darwin Harbour are from this working pier, which receives cargo ships, trawlers, defense vessels, and, occasionally, huge cruise liners. It's also a favorite spot for Darwinites to fish, and when the mackerel are running you can join scores of locals over a few beers. The cluster of cafés and restaurants gets busy on weekends and when cruise ships arrive. ⊠*McMinn St., Darwin Harbour* ☎*08/8981–4268.*

7 Survivors' Lookout. On the site of World War II's first Japanese bombing raid on Australia, this memorial commemorates those who died, including sailors of the USS *Peary.* The shaded viewing platform holds a panoramic illustrated map describing the events of that fateful day. The lookout is also the gateway, via stairs down the cliff face, to the wharf precinct. ⊠*Esplanade S, East Esplanade.*

3 USS *Peary* Memorial/USAAF Memorial. Although this ship was sunk in Darwin Harbour by Japanese bombers on February 19, 1942, a 4-inch gun salvaged from its deck is now the centerpiece of a memorial to the officers and crew who lost their lives. Also overlooking the harbor is a memorial to USAAF fighter pilot Lieutenant Robert Buel, who was shot down in a P-40 Kittyhawk on February 15, 1942, while defending an Allied convoy in the Timor Sea. His was one of only two serviceable fighters in the Top End at the time. ⊠*Bicentennial Park, Esplanade, opposite Holiday Inn, Bicentennial Park.*

8 World War II Storage Tunnels. Darwin's storage tunnels were built during World War II to protect fuel from Japanese bombing raids on the city. Carved into solid rock, the main tunnel is 22 feet high and 210 feet deep. There is a self-guided tour of the atmospheric tunnels, which now house photographic records of the war period. The entrance is at the bottom of the stairs below Survivors' Lookout. ⊠*Esplanade S, Darwin Harbour* ☎*08/8985–6333* ⊠*A$5* ☉*May–Sept., daily 9–4; Oct.–Apr., Tues.–Fri. 9–4.*

A TROPICAL SUMMER

Darwin's wet season—when the humidity rises and monsoonal rains dump around 52 inches—runs from December to April. The days offer a predictable mix of sunshine and afternoon showers, along with some spectacular thunder and lightning storms. There are fewer visitors at this time of the year, and Darwin slows to an even more relaxed pace. Across the Top End, waterfalls increase in size, floodplains rejuvenate to a lush green, and flowers bloom. Despite the rains, Darwinites still prefer the outdoors—eating, drinking, and shopping at the markets.

AROUND DARWIN

⑮ Aquascene. You can hand-feed hundreds of fish at this beach on the northwestern end of the Esplanade. At high tide people wade into the water with buckets of bread to feed the schools of batfish, bream, catfish, milkfish, and mullet that come inshore in a feeding frenzy. ✉*28 Doctor's Gully Rd., Doctor's Gully* ☎*08/8981–7837* ⊕*www.aquascene.com.au* ✑*A$8* ⊙*Daily at high tide; check local publications or hotels for feeding times.*

㉑ Australian Aviation Heritage Centre. Due to its isolation and sparse population, the Northern Territory played an important role in the expansion of aviation in Australia, and this impressive museum traces the history of flight Down Under. Planes on exhibition include a massive B-52 bomber on permanent loan from the United States—one of very few not on U.S. soil—as well as a Japanese Zero shot down on the first day of bombing raids in 1942. ✉*557 Stuart Hwy., 8 km (5 mi) northeast of city center, Winnellie* ☎*08/8947–2145* ⊕*www.darwinairwar. com.au* ✑*A$11* ⊙*Daily 9–5.*

㉒ Crocodylus Park. This world-renowned research facility has an excellent air-conditioned crocodile museum and education center. The saurian section of the zoo includes the croc-infested Bellairs Lagoon and pens for breeding and raising. The park also has enclosures with lions, tigers, cassowaries, primates, and turtles. Tours and feedings are at 10, noon, and 2. ✉*815 McMillans Rd. opposite Berrimah Police Centre, Berrimah* ☎*08/8922–4500* ⊕*www.wmi.com.au/crocpark* ✑*A$25* ⊙*Daily 9–5.*

㉓ Darwin Crocodile Farm. With more than 36,000 fresh- and saltwater crocodiles, this farm supplies much of the meat on menus around the Northern Territory. Guided tours are offered at noon. Since the crocs are fed at 2 PM, this is also an ideal time to visit. The café serves crocodile delicacies such as Croc Burger and Crocodile Drumsticks. ✉*Stuart Hwy. past Arnhem Hwy. turnoff, 40 km (25 mi) south of Darwin, Berry Springs* ☎*08/8988–1491* ⊕*www.crocfarm.com.au* ✑*A$10* ⊙*Daily 9–4.*

㉒ East Point Military Museum. This hub of local military history is attractively framed by tropical gardens at the edge of Fannie Bay. Exhibits detail the city's role as a major military base in World War II and include some of the actual weapons and vehicles, observation towers, and bunkers used to defend the city against frequent Japanese air attacks. ✉*E. Point Rd., Fannie Bay* ☎*08/8981–9702* ✑*A$10* ⊙*Daily 9:30–5.*

⑲ East Point Reserve and Lake Alexander. East Point Road leads past the beaches of Fannie Bay onto the headland occupied by the reserve. This is a pleasant expanse of small beaches, cliffs, lawns, and forest, where wallabies can be seen grazing at dawn and dusk. There's also a saltwater lake safe for swimming, a children's playground, and barbecue facilities. ✉*E. Point Rd., Fannie Bay* ✑*Free* ⊙*Daily 5 AM–11 PM.*

18 Fannie Bay Gaol. If the sordid stuff of prison life stirs your blood, take a trip out to the gaol (pronounced "jail"), which served as a prison from 1883 to 1979. When it was hit during Japanese raids in World War II, all prisoners were pardoned and released. The grounds, which are now a museum, include even the gallows where the last executions in the Northern Territory took place in 1952. The gaol also houses a Cyclone Tracy display with an excellent photographic collection and a 30-minute video of the devastation. ⊠ *E. Point Rd., Fannie Bay* ☎ *08/8999–8264* 🖾 *Free* ☉ *Daily 10–4:30.*

16 George Brown Darwin Botanic Gardens. First planted in 1886 and largely destroyed by Cyclone Tracy, the 92-acre site today displays rain-forest, coastal fore dunes, mangroves, and open woodland environments. There are more than 450 species of palms growing in the gardens. A popular walk takes visitors on a self-guided tour of plants Aborigines used for medicinal purposes. There's also a waterfall and a children's playground. The greenhouse displays ferns and orchids. ⊠ *Gardens Rd. at Geranium St., Mindil Beach* ☎ *08/8981–1958* 🖾 *Free* ☉ *Geranium St. gates daily 7 AM–7 PM, Gardens Rd. gates daily 7 AM–7 PM, information center Mon.–Fri. 8 AM–4 PM; weekends and public holidays 8:30–4.*

17 Museum and Art Gallery of the Northern Territory. Collections at this premier cultural institution encompass Aboriginal and South-East Asian art and material culture, visual arts, crafts, maritime archaeology, Northern Territory history, and natural sciences. One gallery is devoted to Cyclone Tracy, and you can also see "Sweetheart," a 16-foot 10-inch stuffed saltwater crocodile that attacked fishing boats on the Finniss River in the 1970s. The Cornucopia Museum Café overlooks tropical gardens and the Darwin Harbour and is open all day for meals. ⊠ *19 Conacher St., Bullocky Point, Fannie Bay* ☎ *08/8999–8264* 🖾 *Free* ☉ *Weekdays 9–5, weekends and public holidays 10–5.*

24 Territory Wildlife Park. In 1,000 acres of natural bushland, this impressive park is dedicated to the Northern Territory's native fauna and flora. In addition to saltwater crocodiles, water buffalo, dingoes, and waterbirds, it also has an underwater viewing area from which to observe freshwater fish and a nocturnal house kept dark for viewing animals. The treetop-level walkway through the huge aviary provides an opportunity to watch native birds from the swamps and forests at close range. ⊠ *Cox Peninsula Rd., 47 km (29 mi) south of Darwin, Berry Springs* ☎ *08/8988–7200* ⊕ *www.territorywildlifepark.com.au* 🖾 *A$20* ☉ *Daily 8:30–4; exit open until 6.*

OFF THE BEATEN PATH

Litchfield National Park. This beautiful, relatively new park lies just 122 km (76 mi) south of Darwin off the Stuart Highway. The 1,340 square km (515 square mi) here are covered by an untouched wilderness of monsoonal rain forests, rivers, and striking rock formations. The highlights are four separate, spectacular waterfalls—**Florence, Tjaynera, Wangi, and Tolmer Falls**—all of which have secluded plunge pools (there are crocs here, so be sure to observe the NO SWIMMING signs). There is also a dramatic group of large, freestanding sandstone pillars known as the **Lost City;** and the **Magnetic Termite Mounds,** which have an eerie resemblance to eroded grave markers, dot the black-soiled plains of the park's northern area. You'll need to camp if you want to stay in the park; campgrounds and RV sites are located near several of the major sights (call the Parks and Wildlife Service of the Northern Territory at ☎08/8976–0282 for information). There are also a few restaurants and a modest hotel (the Batchelor Resort, which has RV and camping facilities available in the nearby town of Batchelor ☎08/8976–0123).

WHERE TO EAT

$$–$$$$ ✕**Crustaceans on the Wharf.** In a corrugated-iron storage shed at the end of a commercial pier, this large restaurant is dominated by a traditional Macassan fishing prau. Open to sea breezes, it's an ideal place to escape the city's summer heat. Seafood takes center stage here; stand-out choices include the Moreton Bay bugs (which are like small lobsters), calamari, and chili mud crabs, a specialty of the house. ⊠*Stokes Hill Wharf, Wharf Precinct* ☎*08/8981–8658* ⊕*www.crustys.com.au* ▤*AE, DC, MC, V* ⊘*Closed Sun. Oct.–Apr. No lunch.*

$$–$$$ ✕**Pee Wee's at the Point.** Uninterrupted views of Darwin Harbour at
★   East Point Reserve make this restaurant a favorite with locals and visitors. Dine inside with views of the harbor through large glass doors, or out on the tiered timber decks beneath the stars. The cooking is modern Australian with a touch of creole spice, and the carefully considered wine list has good values. Highlights include locally caught crisp-skin saltwater barramundi fillet on wokcharred choy sum; eye fillet steak wrapped in prosciutto and sage, stacked on smashed roast garlic chats with char-grilled zucchini; and seared Atlantic salmon stacked with coconut, sautéed bok choy and black beans and grilled half shell scallops. ⊠*Alec Fong Ling Dr., East Point Reserve, Fannie Bay* ☎*08/8981–6868* ⊕*www.peewees.com.au* ◿*Reservations essential* ▤*AE, DC, MC, V* ⊘*No lunch.*

$–$$ ✕**Buzz Café.** This is just one of many thriving waterfront eateries on the finger peninsula northwest of downtown, where Darwinites come to socialize. You can mingle at the bar with neighborhood millionaires, visiting boaties, and locals relaxing by the water, then dine on fresh seafood presented in a contemporary Australian style. There's air-conditioned comfort in the glass-walled dining room, or you can head out to the umbrella-shaded decks overlooking yachts and cruisers moored in the marina. One of the more curious panoramas is from the men's glass-sheeted urinal, which has one-way views over the restaurant. ⊠*The Slipway, 48 Marina Blvd., Cullen Bay* ☎*08/8941–1141* ▤*AE, DC, MC, V* ⊘*Closed Sun. and Christmas Eve–New Year's Day.*

$–$$ ✕**Hanuman Thai and Nonya Restaurant.** Dark furniture and warm colors
Fodor'sChoice   make the perfect backdrop for fine food and a wine list that includes
★   the best from every grape-growing region in Australia. By drawing on Thai, Nonya (Malaysian), and Indian tandoori culinary traditions, Hanuman's chefs turn local herbs, vegetables, and seafood into sump-

Aboriginal Art & Music   **11**

Aborigines can lay claim to one of the oldest art and music traditions in the world. Traditionally a hunter-gatherer society with an oral lore, Aborigines used these modes to impart knowledge and express beliefs.

The underlying sacred and ritual themes were based primarily upon the Dreaming (an oral history that established the pattern of life for each clan). Pictures were drawn in sand, painted on trees or implements, and carved or painted onto rock surfaces. Similarly, songs and music were used to portray events such as sacred rituals, bushfires, or successful hunts.

There are several different and easily recognizable types of Aboriginal art. X-ray art reveals the exterior of creatures, as well as their internal organs and skeleton. Mimi art is myriad small matchlike figures of men, women, and animals engaged in some obvious activity, such as a hunt. Another type is stenciling, especially of the hands, which are sprayed with an outline of paint to leave an impression on a particular surface or object. Symbolic art uses diagonal, parallel, or concentric lines painted or carved onto surfaces of the body art.

The oldest form of Aboriginal art is painting or engraving on rocks. Archaeologists have evidence that the marks made in Koonalda cave, beneath the Nullarbor Plain in South Australia, are up to 20,000 years old.

Rock art is predominately magical-cum-religious expression in ghostly red or white figures.

Like visual art, music also had a purpose and followed regional or song lines. For example, a clan might sing about the bushfire in different ways according to their song line—how and where the fire started, how it spread, and how it eventually died down. Music was also used to recount stories of travels made by animal or human ancestors, often in minute detail describing each place and event, to define tribal lands and boundaries.

The didgeridoo, made from tree trunks hollowed out by termites, is possibly the world's oldest musical instrument. Originally found in northern Australia, it's played by sealing your mouth at one end and vibrating your lips so the tube acts as an amplifier to produce a haunting, hollow sound.

Today there is not only a resurgence of Aboriginal art and music, but also an acceptance of it in contemporary mainstream Australian art. At the Tjapukai Aboriginal Cultural Park near Cairns, local Aborigines have resurrected their tribal language and culture, presenting it to the public through music and art. They can also exhibit contemporary artworks that are connected with their Dreaming, and keep their ancestral connection alive to pass on to future generations.

---

tuous and innovative dishes. Of special note are Hanuman oysters, lightly cooked in a spicy coriander-and-lemongrass sauce; barramundi baked with ginger flower; and any of the curries. ⊠ *28 Mitchell St., City Center, Darwin, 0800* ☎*08/8941–3500* ⊟*AE, DC, MC, V* ⊘*No lunch weekends.*

WHERE TO STAY

$$$ ⊞**Novotel Atrium.** Vying for the
★   title of Darwin's prettiest hotel, the Atrium has five floors served by glass elevators opening onto a central, vine-hung atrium. The bar and restaurant are set around a tiny artificial stream amid tropical plants. Guest rooms are attractive and airy, decorated in off-white with touches of deep blue and gold. ⊠ *100 Esplanade, 0800* ☎ *08/8941–0755* ⊕ *www.noveldarwin.com.au* ↻ *140 rooms, 18 suites* ⌂ *In-room: ethernet, Wi-Fi (some). In-hotel: restaurant, bar, pool, laundry service, parking (no fee), no-smoking rooms, minibar* ☐ *AE, DC, MC, V.*

¢–$$$ ⊞**Mount Bundy Station.** This farm near Adelaide River, 115 km (72 mi) south of Darwin, provides myriad outdoor activities amid country hospitality. It's handy for visiting Litchfield National Park, then continuing on to Kakadu National Park. There's a choice of accommodation from budget rooms, with shared shower and toilets (A$60), to the Homestead where rooms have king-size beds and private baths; some have a balcony. Older children are given their own room. A silver-service cooked breakfast, afternoon tea, and sunset drinks are included for all Homestead guests. Other meals are also available with prior booking, or from nearby Adelaide River. You can bring your own barbecue supplies and beverages. A self-contained, self-catering cottage is an economical option for families (A$150 for four people). There are a communal kitchen, a camp kitchen, and a TV lounge. Buffalo are bred on the property, and there are extensive wildlife (including wallabies and kangaroos) and native birds. You can even fish (bring your own tackle) during the Wet. ⊠ *Haynes Rd., Adelaide River, 0846* ☎ *08/8976–7009* ⊕ *www.mtbundy.com.au* ↻ *5 rooms* ⌂ *In-room: no phone, no TV. In-hotel: pool, laundry facilities, no-smoking rooms* ☐ *AE, DC, MC, V* ⦿*BP.*

$ ⊞**Holiday Inn Esplanade Darwin.** With its colorful, round exterior, this five-story hotel is one of the city's most architecturally striking. Rooms, arranged around a central foyer, are decorated in subtle earthy hues and accented by natural wood. Most have city or harbor views. ⊠ *The Esplanade, 0800* ☎ *08/8980–0800 or 1300/666747* ⊕ *www.holiday-inn.com/hidarwin* ↻ *197 rooms, 33 suites* ⌂ *In-room: safe, dial-up. In-hotel: restaurant, bars, pool, gym, laundry service, parking (fee), no-smoking rooms, minibar* ☐ *AE, DC, MC, V.*

¢   ⊞**Chilli's Backpackers.** In the center of the tourist precinct, this popular budget choice has a great location and lots of on-site perks. Drop your bags in a dorm, twin, or double room, then head up to the rooftop deck, barbecue area, and hot tubs. There are also a large, modern communal kitchen, a TV room, lockers, and a travel desk. Continental breakfast is included. ⊠ *69A Mitchell St., City Center, 0800* ☎ *08/8941–9722 or 1800/351313* ⊕ *www.chillis.com.au* ↻ *162 beds in 6 twins, 6 dou-*

bles, and 48 dorms ⚑ In-room: no phone, no TV. In-hotel: restaurant, laundry facilities, public Internet, no elevator ⊟ MC, V ⑩ CP.

¢ 🏠**Frogshollow Backpackers.** Opposite the Frogs Hollow parklands, this traditionally Territorian establishment sits in peaceful, shady surroundings. Dormitories sleep 3, 6, 8, 10, or 12 people, and some of the private rooms have bathrooms. There are a plunge pool and two hot tubs, plus a common room with TV, a communal kitchen, and an open-air dining and common area. A Continental breakfast is included in the rates. ✉ 27 Lindsay St., City Center, 0800 ☎ 08/8941–2600 ⊕ www.frogs-hollow. com.au ⇄ 12 dorms, 14 rooms, some with bath ⚑ In-room: no phone, no TV (some). In-hotel: kitchen, pool, laundry facilities, parking (no fee), no-smoking rooms, no elevator ⊟ MC, V ⑩ CP.

GOING FISHING

Joining a local tour guide is the best way to hook a big one. They know the best spots and techniques, and their local knowledge can make an enjoyable experience even better. In the estuaries you can catch threadfin and blue salmon, cod, queenfish, golden snapper, and the Top End's most famous fighting fish, the barramundi—barra in the local parlance. You don't have to go far to fish—Darwin's harbor teems with fish.

GURIG NATIONAL PARK

$$$$ 🏠**Seven Spirit Bay Wilderness Lodge.** This remote resort on the pristine
Fodor's Choice Cobourg Peninsula in Arnhem Land is accessible only by a 45-minute
★ flight from Darwin. Hexagonal huts with private outdoor bathrooms are linked by winding paths to the main complex, lagoon-style pool, and ocean beyond. Guided nature walks and four-wheel-drive safaris are available to the wildlife sanctuary, where dingoes, wallabies, crocodiles, buffalo, and Timorese ponies make their home. Meals, which are included, emphasize light, Mod-Oz cuisine using local seafood, meats, and produce. ✉ PMB 261, Winnellie, NT, 0822 ☎ 08/8979–0281 ⊕ www.sevenspiritbay.com ⇄ 23 huts ⚑ In-room: no a/c, no TV. In-hotel: restaurant, bar, pool, laundry service, no kids under 12, minibar ⊟ AE, MC, V ⑩ FAP.

NIGHTLIFE & THE ARTS

BARS & LOUNGES

The atmospheric **Blue Heeler Bar** (✉ Mitchell and Herbert Sts., City Center ☎ 08/8941–7945) is a typically laid-back watering hole with good dancing and Australian Outback decor. Irish flavor and pub food are available at **Kitty O'Shea's** (✉ Mitchell and Herbert Sts., City Center ☎ 08/8941–7947). **Rorke's Drift** (✉ 46 Mitchell St., City Center ☎ 08/8941–7171) resembles an English pub and has 10 beers on tap. There's a large menu available until 10 PM with kids' meals and premium steaks. **Shenannigans Irish Pub** (✉ 69 Mitchell St., City Center ☎ 08/8981–2100) has Guinness on tap, along with those other two famous Irish beers, Kilkenny and Harp. Traditional Irish pub food is also available, with meat roasts on Sunday. **Throb** (✉ 64 Smith St., City

Center ☎08/8942–3435), a wild and wicked nightclub renowned for its floor shows and drag acts, is Darwin's premier gay nightclub. Open Friday and Saturdays only, the fun starts around 11 PM and doesn't end until 4 AM. Cover charge is A$10. The young and hip frequent **Time Nightclub** (✉3 Edmunds St., City Center ☎08/8981–9761), next door to Squire's tavern, where you can dance the night away to techno and funk. For a beer and live contemporary music, visit the **Top End Hotel** (✉Daly and Mitchell Sts., Bicentennial Park ☎08/8981–6511), a Darwin landmark, which has the city's biggest beer garden, a sports bar, a nightclub, and a band room.

CASINO

MGM Grand Hotel Casino, SkyCity Darwin (✉Gilruth Ave., Mindil Beach ☎08/8943–8888 🖷08/8946–9777 ⊕www.skycitydarwin.com.au) is one of Darwin's most popular evening entertainment spots. The 460 gaming machines are open 24 hours, while gaming tables are open Friday and Saturday 10 AM–6 AM, Sunday–Thursday 10 AM–4 AM.

THEATERS & CONCERTS

The **Darwin Entertainment Centre** (✉93 Mitchell St., City Center ☎08/8980–3333 ⊕www.darwinentertainment.com.au), behind the Carlton Hotel, has a large theater that regularly stages concerts, dance, and drama. It also doubles as booking office for other touring concerts in town—especially those at the Amphitheatre, Australia's best outdoor concert venue (entrance next to Botanic Gardens on Gardens Road). Check their Web site or the *Northern Territory News* or the *Sunday Territorian* for current shows.

SPORTS & THE OUTDOORS

BICYCLING

Darwin is fairly flat and has a good network of bike paths, so cycling is a good way to get around—although you might need something waterproof during the Wet. Rentals are available at some hotels.

BOATING

The mangrove-fringed arms of Darwin Harbour have a tidal rise and fall of up to 24 feet. Although there have been no crocodile-related fatalities in Darwin Harbour in recent decades, it's worth noting that up to 180 crocs are removed from the harbor and its immediate surroundings each year. Due to the seasonal influx of deadly box jellyfish, these waters are unsafe for swimming between October and May. Sailing races on the harbor are conducted year-round. Dry-season competition is conducted by **Darwin Sailing Club** (✉Aitkins Dr., Fannie Bay ☎08/8981–1700 ⊕www.dwnsail.com.au). Wet-season races are run by the **Dinah Beach Cruising Yacht Association** (✉Frances Bay Dr., Tipperary Waters ☎08/8981–7816 ⊕www.dinahbeachcya.com.au).

Canoes can be rented at Nitmiluk (Katherine Gorge) and on the upper reaches of the Roper River at Mataranka.

FISHING

Barramundi, the best-known fish of the Top End, can weigh up to 110 pounds and are excellent fighting fish that taste great on the barbecue afterward. The **Northern Territory Fisheries Division's Recreational Fishing Office** (✉ *Berrimah Research Farm, Makagon Rd., Berrimah* ☎ *08/8999–2372* ⊕ *www.fishingthe territory.com*) has information on licenses and catch limits.

Equinox Fishing Charters has day and extended fishing trips on the *Equinox*, a 33-foot aluminum vessel, and the 38-foot *Tsar*. Both are licensed to carry 12 passengers and two crew. *Equinox II* can carry 23 people on full-day fishing trips. Full-day fishing charters with all meals and tackle provided are A$220 per person. ✉ *Shop 8, 56 Marina Blvd., Cullen Bay* ☎ *08/8942–2199* ✐ equinoxcharters@arafura.net.au ⊕ *www.equinoxcharters.com.au.*

SCUBA DIVING

Coral Divers (✉ *Unit 13 Makagon Rd., Berrimah* ☎ *08/8947–4525* ⊕ *www.coraldivers.com.au*) conducts day and night dives on reefs and wrecks in Darwin Harbour on neap tides (low tides at the first and third moon quarters), as well as freshwater dives at sites as far south as Mataranka.

Darwin Dive Centre (✉ *66 Marina Blvd., Cullen Bay* ☎ *08/8981–3049* ⊕ *www.darwindivecentre.com.au*) runs reef trips and dives on wrecks from World War II and Cyclone Tracy, as well as scuttled Vietnamese fishing vessels. Training and classes are available, including PADI and technical diving certification courses. Prices are from A$120 to A$220 for half-day dives.

SHOPPING

MARKETS

The **Mindil Beach Sunset Market** (✉ *Beach Rd., Mindil Beach* ☎ *08/8981–3454* ⊕ *www.mindil.com.au*) is an extravaganza that takes place April–October, Thursday 5 PM–10 PM, as well as May–October, Sunday 4–9. Come in the late afternoon to snack at a choice of 60 stalls offering food from more than 25 different countries, shop at more than 200 artisans' booths, and watch singers, dancers, and musicians. Or join the other Darwinites with a bottle of wine to watch the sun plunge into the harbor.

The **Darwin Night Markets** (✉ *52 Mitchell St., City Center* ☎ *0418/600830*) are open daily 5–11 and include arts, crafts, souvenirs, and Aboriginal

---

THE INDIGENOUS ARTS SCENE

Start at the Museum and Art Gallery of the Northern Territory for a comprehensive understanding of Indigenous art and artifacts. Then head to one of many art and craft outlets in and around Darwin to purchase an authentic and unique piece of art. In many Indigenous communities throughout the tropical outback—including Maningrida, Oenpelli, Tiwi islands, and Yirrikala—you can buy direct from the artist, a truly unique experience.

artifacts. **Nightcliff Market** (✉ *Progress Dr., Nightcliff* ☎ *0414/368773*) takes place Sunday 8 AM–2 PM in Nightcliff Village, with craft and food stalls and entertainers. North of downtown, the **Parap Markets** (✉ *Parap Sq., Parap* ☎ *0438/882373*) are open Saturday 7:30 AM–1:30 PM and have a great selection of ethnic Asian food. The **Rapid Creek Markets** (✉ *Rapid Creek Shopping Centre, Trower Rd., Rapid Creek* ☎ *08/8930–0441*), open Sunday 7 AM–1 PM, is a trash-and-treasure-style flea market.

DARWIN ESSENTIALS

TRANSPORTATION

BY AIR

Darwin's International Airport is serviced from overseas by Qantas, Garuda, Royal Brunei, Jetstar, Tiger Airways, and Air North. Qantas and Garuda fly from Darwin to Bali several times a week, Tiger Airways and Jetstar connect Darwin with Singapore, and Air North flies to East Timor.

Qantas, Air North, Virgin Blue Airlines, and Jetstar fly into Darwin regularly from other parts of Australia and also operate regional flights within the Top End. Air North flies west to Kununurra and Broome, and east to Gove. Check the Qantas Web site for last-minute regional air specials.

The airport is 15 km (9 mi) northeast of the city by car. After leaving the terminal, turn left onto McMillans Road and left again onto Bagot Road. Continue until you cross the overpass that merges onto the Stuart Highway, which later becomes Daly Street. Turn left onto Smith Street to reach the Smith Street Mall in the heart of the city.

The Darwin Airport Shuttle has regular service between the airport and the city's hotels. The cost is A$9.50 one-way, A$15 round-trip; be sure to book a day in advance. Taxis are available from the taxi rank at the airport. The journey downtown costs about A$15.

Airlines Air North (☎ *08/8920–4000 or 1800/627474* ⊕ *www.airnorth.com. au*). **Garuda Indonesia** (☎ *1300/365330* ⊕ *www.garuda-indonesia.com*). **Jetstar** (☎ *13–1538* ⊕ *www.jetstar.com.au*). **Qantas** (☎ *13–1313* ⊕ *www.qantas. com*). **Royal Brunei** (☎ *08/8941–0966* ⊕ *www.bruneiair.com*). **Tiger Airways** (⊕ *www.tigerairways.com.au*). **Virgin Blue Airlines** (☎ *13–6789* ⊕ *www. virginblue.com.au*).

Airport & Shuttle Darwin International Airport (☎ *08/8920–1811* ⊕ *www. darwinairport.com.au*). **Darwin Airport Shuttle** (☎ *08/8981–5066*).

BY BUS

Greyhound Australia operates from the Darwin Transit Centre in the Mitchell Street tourist precinct. There are daily services to and from Alice Springs, Tennant Creek (connections to Queensland), Katherine, Broome, and Perth.

Bus Station Darwin Transit Centre (✉ *67–69 Mitchell St., City Center*).

Bus Line Greyhound Australia (☎ 08/8981–8700, 1300/4739–46863 central reservations ⊕ www.greyhound.com.au).

BUS TRAVEL WITHIN DARWIN The bus network in Darwin links the city with its far-flung suburbs, and a choice of minibus operators, including the 24-hour Arafura minibuses, run all over town for fixed prices starting at A$4. The main bus terminal (Darwin Bus) is on Harry Chan Avenue, near the Bennett Street end of Smith Street Mall. A minibus stand is also located at the front of Darwin's airport terminal.

Contacts Arafura Shuttle (☎ 08/8981–3300). **Darwin Bus** (☎ 08/8924–7666).

BY CAR

The best way to get around Darwin is by car. The Stuart Highway is Darwin's land connection with the rest of Australia, and anyone arriving by car will enter the city on this road. By road Darwin is 15 hours from Alice Springs (1,491 km [926 mi]), 2½ days from Broome via the Great Northern Highway (1,875 km [1,165 mi]), 4–5 days from Brisbane (3,387 km [2,105 mi]), and 5–6 days from Perth (3,981 km [2,474 mi]). Driving times include rest breaks and are approximations only.

For drivers headed outside the Northern Territory, one-way drop-off fees can be prohibitive, often twice as much as a weekly rental. Also, very few travelers, even Australians, drive the highways after dark, due to the dangers presented by buffalo, cattle, horses, donkeys, wallabies, and potoroos on the road.

Contacts Advance Car Rental (✉ 86 Mitchell St., City Center ☎ 1800/002227 ⊕ www.advancecar.com.au). **Avis** (✉ Airport ✉ 89 Smith St., City Center ☎ 08/8981–9922 ⊕ www.avis.com.au). **Britz-Rentals** (✉ 17 Bombing Rd., Winnellie ☎ 08/8981–2081 ⊕ www.britz.com). **Budget** (✉ Airport ✉ Daly Rd., at Doctors Gully Rd., City Center ☎ 08/8981–9800 ⊕ www.budget.com). **Europcar** (✉ Airport ✉ 77 Cavenagh St., City Center ☎ 08/8941–0300 ⊕ www.europcar. com). **Hertz** (✉ Airport ✉ Smith and Daly Sts., City Center ☎ 08/8941–0895 ⊕ www.hertz.com.au). **Thrifty** (✉ 64 Stuart Hwy., Stuart Park ☎ 08/8924–0000 ⊕ www.thrifty.com.au).

BY TAXI

In town look for Yellow Cab Co. and Darwin Radio Taxis for local transport; City Radio Taxis and Tropical Taxis also provide service. A taxi stand is also located at the front of the airport terminal.

Contacts City Radio Taxis (☎ 08/8981–3777). **Darwin Radio Taxis** (☎ 13–1008). **Tropical Taxis** (☎ 08/8947–3333). **Yellow Cab Co.** (☎ 13–1924).

BY TRAIN

The *Ghan* train connects Darwin with Adelaide via Alice Springs. The two-night 2,979-km (1,861-mi) journey departs from Adelaide for Alice Springs on Sunday and Friday at 5:15 PM, and from Alice for Darwin on Monday at 4:10 PM. Heading south, the *Ghan* departs from Darwin on Mondays at 9:45 AM and from Alice Springs at 12:40 PM on Tuesdays. On Wednesdays the train departs Darwin at 10 AM and from Alice at 12:45 PM Thursday. The transcontinental trip costs A$1,920 for Gold Kangaroo Service, including all meals; A\$1,490 for a sleeper; and A\$555 for a reclining seat. Book two Gold Kangaroo seats and you can take your car on the Motorail vehicle carrier for just A\$99.

Contact The Ghan (☎13–2147 *bookings, 1300/132147 holiday packages* ⊕ *www.gsr.com.au*).

CONTACTS & RESOURCES

BANKS & EXCHANGE SERVICES

The main banks with tourist services are Westpac and Commonwealth, both on the intersection of Smith and Bennet streets. Banking hours are Monday–Thursday 9:30–4 and Friday 9:30–5. Currency exchange facilities are available on Smith Street Mall and Mitchell Street.

EMERGENCIES

Doctors & Dentists Night & Day Medical & Dental Surgery (⊠ *Shop 31, Casuarina Shopping Centre, Trower Rd., Casuarina* ☎ *08/8927–1899*).

Hospital Royal Darwin Hospital (⊠ *Rocklands Dr. at Floreyr Ave., Tiwi* ☎ *08/8922–8888*).

VISITOR INFORMATION

Darwin City Council operates a tourist information booth toward the Bennett Street end of Smith Street Mall. The most extensive selection of information and tour bookings can be found at Top End Tourism. Tours can also be booked through hostel travel desks and hotels.

Contact Darwin City Council (⊠ *Civic Centre, Harry Chan Ave., City Center* ☎ *08/8930–0300* ⊕ *www.darcity.nt.gov.au*). **Top End Tourism** (⊠ *Beagle House, Mitchell and Knuckey Sts., City Center* ☎ *08/8936–2499* ⊕ *www.tourismtopend. com.au*).

KAKADU NATIONAL PARK

Fodor'sChoice
★

Begins 166 km (104 mi) east of Darwin.

Kakadu National Park is a jewel among the many Top End parks, and many come to the region just to experience this tropical wilderness. Beginning east of Darwin, and covering some 19,800 square km (7,645 square mi), the park protects a large system of unspoiled rivers and creeks, as well as a rich Aboriginal heritage that extends back to the earliest days of humankind.

The superb gathering of Aboriginal rock art is one of Kakadu's major highlights. Two main types of Aboriginal artwork can be seen here. The Mimi style, which is the oldest, is believed to be up to 20,000 years old. Aborigines believe that Mimi spirits created the red-ocher stick figures to depict hunting scenes and other pictures of life at the time. The more recent artwork, known as X-ray painting, dates back fewer than 9,000 years and depicts freshwater animals—especially fish, turtles, and geese—living in floodplains created after the last ice age.

Most of the region is virtually inaccessible during the Wet. As the dry season progresses, billabongs (water holes) become increasingly important to the more than 280 species of birds that inhabit the park. Huge flocks often gather at Yellow Water, South Alligator River, and Magela Creek. Scenic flights over the wetlands and Arnhem Land escarpment provide unforgettable moments in any season.

Bowali Visitors Centre has state-of-the-art audiovisual displays and traditional exhibits that give an introduction to the park's ecosystems and its bird population, the world's most diverse. ✉ *Arnhem and Kakadu Hwys.* ☎ *08/8938–1121* 🎫 *Free* ◷ *Daily 8–5.* **Warradjan Aboriginal Cultural Centre,** named after the pig-nose turtle unique to the Top End, provides an excellent experience of local Bininj (pronounced *bin*-ing) tribal culture. Displays take you through the Aboriginal Creation period, following the path of the creation ancestor Rainbow Serpent through the ancient landscape of Kakadu. ✉ *5 km (3 mi) off Kakadu Hwy. on road to Gagudju Lodge, Cooinda* ☎ *08/8979–0051* 🎫 *Free* ◷ *Daily 9–5.*

> ## LOCAL LANGUAGE
>
> The name Kakadu comes from an Aboriginal floodplain language called Gagudju, which was one of the languages spoken in the north of the park at the beginning of the 20th century. Although languages such as Gagudju and Limilngan are no longer regularly spoken, descendants of these language groups are still living in Kakadu.

EXPLORING KAKADU NATIONAL PARK

Like the main Kakadu escarpment, **Nourlangie Rock** is a remnant of an ancient plateau that is slowly eroding, leaving sheer cliffs rising high above the floodplains. The main attraction is the **Anbangbang Gallery,** an excellent frieze of Aboriginal rock paintings. ✉ *19 km (12 mi) from park headquarters on Kakadu Hwy.; turn left toward Nourlangie Rock, then follow paved road, accessible yr-round, 11 km (7 mi) to parking area* 🎫 *Free* ◷ *Daily 7 AM–sunset.*

Ubirr has an impressive display of Aboriginal paintings scattered through six shelters in the rock. The main gallery contains a 49-foot frieze of X-ray paintings depicting animals, birds, and fish. A 1-km (½-mi) path around the rock leads to all the galleries. It's just a short clamber to the top for wonderful views over the surrounding wetlands, particularly at sunset. ✉ *43 km (27 mi) north of park headquarters along paved Rd.* 🎫 *Free* ◷ *Apr.–Nov., daily 8:30–sunset; Dec.–Mar., daily 2–sunset.*

The best way to gain a true appreciation of the natural beauty of Kakadu is to visit the waterfalls running off the escarpment. Some 39 km (24 mi) south of the park headquarters along the Kakadu Highway, a track leads off to the left toward **Jim Jim Falls,** 60 km (37 mi) away (about a two-hour drive). The track is unpaved, and you'll need a four-wheel-drive vehicle to navigate it. From the parking lot you have to walk 1 km (½ mi) over boulders to reach the falls and the plunge pools they have created at the base of the escarpment. After May, the water flow over the falls may cease, and the unpaved road is closed in the Wet.

As you approach the **Twin Falls,** the ravine opens up dramatically to reveal a beautiful sandy beach scattered with palm trees, as well as the crystal waters of the falls spilling onto the end of the beach. This spot is a bit difficult to reach, but the trip is rewarding. Take the Jim Jim Falls Road, turn off just before the parking lot, and travel 10 km (6 mi) farther to the Twin Falls parking lot. A regular boat shuttle (A$12.50) operates a return service up the Twin Falls gorge and then you need to walk over boulders, sand, and a boardwalk to the falls. Saltwater crocodiles may be in the water in the gorge, so visitors are urged not to enter the water. The round trip, including the boat shuttle, takes around two hours.

WHERE TO STAY

There are several lodges in the park, and campgrounds at Merl, Muirella Park, Mardugal, and Gunlom have toilets, showers, and water. Sites are A$5 per night. Alcohol is not available in Jabiru, so stock up in Darwin.

$$$ ⊡ **Gagudju Crocodile Holiday Inn.** Shaped like a crocodile, this unusual hotel with spacious rooms is the best of the area's accommodation options. The reception area, a de facto art gallery, is through the mouth, and the swimming pool is in the open courtyard in the belly. ⊠ *1 Flinders St., Jabiru, 0886* ☎ *08/8979–9000 or 1300/666747* ↩ *110 rooms* ⚅ *In-hotel: restaurant, bar, pool, parking (no fee), no elevator.* ▤ *AE, DC, MC, V.*

¢–$ ⊡ **Aurora Kakadu.** This comfortable hotel has doubles, dorms that sleep four, and family rooms. Spread through lush tropical gardens, the rooms, bare cabins, and campgrounds are clean and provide good value for the money. Rates are significantly lower during the Wet. Gas and diesel fuel are available. ⊠ *On Arnhem Hwy., 2½ km (1½ mi) before the highway crosses the S. Alligator River* ⊡ *Box 221, Winnellie, 0822* ☎ *08/8979–0166 or 1800/818845* ⊕ *www.auroraresorts.com.au* ↩ *138 rooms, 20 powered sites, 250 tent sites* ⚅ *In-hotel: restaurant, tennis court, pool, laundry facilities, parking (no fee)* ▤ *AE, DC, MC, V.*

¢ ⊡ **Kakadu Lodge.** Lush grounds surround this privately operated campground with budget accommodation, cabins, power-equipped sites for motor homes, and basic tent sites. Lodge rooms have queen-size beds or bunks, and the cabins come in studio and one- and two-bedroom sizes. The caravan park is within walking distance of trailheads, the Jabiru recreational lake, and shops. A camp kitchen, bar-cum-bistro, and lagoon-style pool are also on the property. ⊠ *Jabiru Dr., Jabiru, 0886* ☎ *08/8979–2422 or 1800/811154* ⊕ *www.auroraresorts.com.au* ↩ *100 tent sites, 186*

> ## ANCIENT ART AND NATURE
>
> Almost the size of West Virginia, Kakadu National Park is an ancient landform, with wetlands, gorges and waterfalls, and rugged escarpments. It also has one of the highest concentrations of accessible Aboriginal rock art sites in the world. Take a tour with an Aboriginal guide from one of the cultural centers near Jabiru or Cooinda. The art sites date back 20,000 years.

powered RV sites, 15 cabins, 32 lodge rooms ⌂ *Pool, flush toilets, full hookups, drinking water, showers, general store* ▤ *AE, DC, MC, V.*

¢ ⛺ **Gagudju Lodge Cooinda Campground.** Campsites are in the tropical forest near the resort. Some are supplied with power for motor homes, but basic, bare-bones tent sites with shared bath facilities are also available. ✉ *Kakadu Hwy., Cooinda, 0886* ☎ *08/8979–0145 or 1800/500401* ⊕ *www.gagudjulodgecooinda.com.au* ⛺ *80 powered sites, 300 unpowered sites* ⌂ *Pit toilets, full hookups, showers, fire pits* ▤ *No credit cards.*

KAKADU NATIONAL PARK ESSENTIALS

TRANSPORTATION

BY AIR

Light aircraft charters from Darwin to Kakadu can be arranged through local operators like Air North and Vincent Aviation.

Contacts Air North (☎ *08/8920–4000* ⊕ *www.airnorth.com.au*). **Vincent Aviation** (☎ *08/8928–1366* ⊕ *www.vincentair.com.au*).

BY CAR

From Darwin take the Arnhem Highway east to Jabiru. Although four-wheel-drive vehicles are not necessary to travel to the park, they are required for many of the unpaved roads within, including the track to Jim Jim Falls. Entry is free.

CONTACTS & RESOURCES

TOURS

During the Dry, park rangers conduct free walks and tours at several popular locations. You can pick up a program at the entry station or at either of the visitor centers.

Kakadu Air makes scenic hour and half-hour flights out of Jabiru. In the Dry, the flight encompasses the northern region, including floodplains, East Alligator River, and Jabiru Township. During the Wet only, a one-hour flight takes in Jim Jim and Twin Falls.

The Gagudju Lodge Cooinda arranges boat tours of Yellow Water, the major water hole where innumerable birds and crocodiles gather. There are six tours throughout the day; the first (6:45 AM) is the coolest. Tours, which run most of the year, cost A$43 for 90 minutes and A$50 for two hours.

Billy Can Tours provides camping and accommodation tours in Kakadu of between two and seven days. Far Out Adventures runs customized tours of Kakadu, as well as other regions of the Top End, for small groups. Odyssey Tours and Safaris offers two- to seven-day deluxe four-wheel-drive safaris into Kakadu, Litchfield, and Nitmiluk national parks, as well as a two-day Arnhem Land Aboriginal Tour to Nipbamjen.

Air Tours Albatross Helicopters (☎ *08/8988–5081* 🖷 *08/8988–5083* ✉ albatross helicopters@bigpond.com ⊕ *www.albatrosshelicopters.com.au*). **Kakadu Air** (☎ *1800/089113 or 08/8979–2411* ⊕ *www.kakaduair.com.au*).

Boat Tours Gagudju Lodge Cooinda (☏ *08/8979–0145* ⊕ *www.yellowwater-cruises.com*).

Vehicle Tours Billy Can Tours (✉ *Box 1206, Darwin, 0801* ☏ *08/8947–1877 or 1800/813484* 🖷 *08/8984–2926* ⊕ *www.billycan.com.au*). **Far Out Adventures** (✉ *Box 54, Katherine, 0850* ☏ *04/2715–2288* 🖷 *02/6557–6076* ⊕ *www.farout. com.au*). **Odyssey Tours & Safaris** (✉ *Box 3012, Darwin, 0801* ☏ *08/8984–3540 or 1800/891190* 🖷 *08/8948–0646* ⊕ *www.awtours.com.au/odysaf*).

VISITOR INFORMATION
You can contact the Kakadu National Park directly for information, or Tourism Top End.

Contacts Kakadu National Park (✉ *Box 71, Jabiru, 0886* ☏ *08/8938–1100* ⊕ *www.deh.gov.au/parks/kakadu*). **Tourism Top End** (✉ *Beagle House, Mitchell and Knuckey Sts., Darwin, 0800* ☏ *08/8936–2499* ⊕ *www.tourismtopend.com.au*).

THE KIMBERLEY

Perched on the northwestern hump of the loneliest Australian state, only half as far from Indonesia as it is from Sydney, the Kimberley remains a frontier of sorts. The first European explorers, dubbed by one of their descendants as "cattle kings in grass castles," ventured into the heart of the region in 1879 to establish cattle stations. They subsequently became embroiled in one of the country's longest-lasting conflicts between white settlers and Aborigines, who were led by Jandamarra of the Bunuba people.

The Kimberley remains sparsely populated, with only 30,000 people living in an area of 351,200 square km (135,600 square mi). That's 12 square km (4½ square mi) per person. The region is dotted with cattle stations and raked with desert ranges, rivers, tropical forests, and towering cliffs. Several of the country's most spectacular national parks are here, including Purnululu (Bungle Bungle) National Park, a vast area of bizarrely shaped and colored rock formations that became widely known to white Australians only in 1983. Facilities in this remote region are few, but if you're looking for a genuine bush experience, the Kimberley represents the opportunity of a lifetime.

This section begins in Kununurra, just over the northwestern border of the Northern Territory, in Western Australia.

KUNUNURRA

516 km (322 mi) west of Katherine, 840 km (525 mi) southwest of Darwin.

Kununurra is the eastern gateway to the Kimberley. With a population of 6,000, it's a modern, planned town developed in the 1960s for the nearby Lake Argyle and Ord River irrigation scheme. It's a convenient base from which to explore local attractions such as Mirima National

Katherine: Crossroads of the Top End

To get a taste of the Red Centre without heading too far inland, head south to the Katherine River (317 km [196 mi] southeast of Darwin). The river is the last permanently flowing water you'll find until you reach Adelaide, 2,741 km (1,700 mi) to the south! This makes the town of Katherine not only a crossroads but something of an oasis, as well. It's the second-largest town in the Top End, and makes a great base for exploring some of the spectacular scenery around the region. For visitor information, **Katherine Visitors Information Centre** (☎1800/653142 ⊕ www.krta.com.au) is open weekdays 8:30–5, weekends and holidays 10–3.

Nitmiluk, 31 km (19 mi) north of Katherine, is one of the Northern Territory's most famous national parks. **Katherine Gorge,** the park's European name, is derived from the Katherine River, which connects a series of deep gorges separated by rapids. You can take a flat-bottom boat tour on two-hour to full-day safaris through the gorges, a trip that requires hiking to circumnavigate each rapid. During the Wet, jet boats provide access into the flooded gorges. In general, the best time to visit is May through early November.

For adventurous travelers, the park has more than 100 km (62 mi) of the best bushwalking trails in the Top End. Ten well-marked walking tracks (ranging from one hour to five days) lead hikers on trails parallel to the Katherine River and north toward **Edith Falls,** at the edge of the park. Some of the longer overnight walks lead past Aboriginal paintings and through swamps, heath, cascades, waterfalls, and rain forest. The best is the four-day, 66-km (41-mi) **Jatbula Trail,**

which passes a number of Edenesque pools and spectacular waterfalls on its route from Katherine Gorge to Edith Falls. Before departure, be sure to register with the **Nitmiluk Visitor Centre** (☎08/8972–1886 ⊕ www.nt.gov.au/nreta/parks/find/nitmiluk.html) near the mouth of the gorge.

Cutta Cutta Caves, 29 km (18 mi) south of Katherine, is a 3,704-acre nature park with a series of limestone caverns 45 feet underground (where rare bats congregate). Daily 45-minute, ranger-led tours (A$12.50) into the system take place at 9, 10, 11, 1, 2, and 3, weather permitting. For more information call ☎1800/653142; or sign on to ⊕ www.nt.gov.au/nreta/parks/find/cuttacuttacaves.html.

For overnight stays in Katherine, **St. Andrews Serviced Apartments** (☎08/8971–2288 or 1800/686106 ⊕ www.standrewsapts.com.au) offers clean and spacious two-bedroom units overlooking a swimming pool and barbecue area. **Knotts Crossing Resort** (☎08/8972–2511 ⊕ www.knottscrossing.com.au), on the bank of the Katherine River, has well-designed motel rooms and low-slung cabins, two pools, and an outside bar.

If you'd like to take a guided tour of the area's highlights, **Billy Can Tours** (☎08/8981–9813 or 1800/813484) combines excursions to Nitmiluk with Litchfield and Kakadu national parks. **Nitmiluk Tours** (☎08/8972–1253 ⊕ www.nitmiluktours.com.au) has boat cruises on Katherine Gorge, including two-hour lunch cruises, as well as powerboat rides when the river height is over 6 feet, usually between January and March. You can also hire canoes.

—Graham Hodgson

Park (a mini–Bungle Bungle on the edge of town), Lake Argyle, and the River Ord. The town is also the starting point for adventure tours of the Kimberley.

WHERE TO STAY & EAT

$–$$ ✗**Chopsticks Chinese Restaurant.** As its name suggests, this restaurant in the Country Club Hotel serves fresh and tasty Aussie-style Chinese cuisine. The dining room is simple but stylish, and brightly lighted by the floor-to-ceiling windows looking out to the veranda and tropical gardens. The menu features local dishes like barramundi, and Szechuan specialties like honey-chili king prawns. ⊠47 Coolibah Dr. ☎08/9168–1024 ▤AE, DC, MC, V.

> ### DROUGHT DOWN SOUTH
>
> The Top End's wet season drenches the region with more than 50 inches of rain. Just a tiny fraction is captured in Lake Argyle at Kununurra (with nine times the water volume of Sydney Harbour) and later used to irrigate crops. Meanwhile, in Australia's more densely populated and heavily farmed southern states, a severe drought and declining annual rainfall—some say caused by global climate change—has sparked a major debate: How to bring the Top End's water south, or how to convince people to move north.

¢–$ ✗**George Room in Gulliver's Tavern.** Lots of dark jarrah timber gives this restaurant an Old English atmosphere. Although the tavern alongside it has simple counter meals, the George aims higher with steaks and seafood. ⊠196 Cottontree Ave. ☎08/9168–1666 ⌖Reservations essential ▤AE, DC, MC, V ⊗Closed Sun. No lunch.

$$ ⌸**All Seasons Kununurra.** Set in tropical gardens, the brightly furnished rooms here provide a comfortable base from which to explore the eastern Kimberley. The hotel is at the edge of town, just 4 km (2½ mi) from the airport; its swimming pool, which is surrounded by shady palm trees, is the place to be on a hot day. ⊠Victoria Hwy. and Messmate Way, 6743 ☎08/9168–1455 or 1800/656565 ⌖h1899-re01@accor.com ⊛www.accor.com.au ⌖60 rooms ⌂In-room: dial-up. In-hotel: restaurant, bar, pool, laundry facilities, parking (no fee) ▤AE, DC, MC, V.

GIBB RIVER ROAD, EL QUESTRO & BEYOND

Gibb River Road is the cattle-carrying route through the heart of the Kimberley. It also provides an alternative—albeit a rough one—to the Great Northern Highway between Kununurra–Wyndham and the coastal town of Derby.

Fodor'sChoice
★ With 1 million acres, **El Questro Wilderness Park** is a working ranch in some of the most rugged country in Australia. Besides providing an opportunity to see Outback station life, award-winning El Questro has a full complement of such recreational activities as fishing and swimming, and horse, camel, and helicopter rides. Individually tailored walking and four-wheel-drive tours let you bird-watch or examine

ancient spirit figures depicted in the unique *wandjina* style of Kimberley Aboriginal rock painting—one of the world's most striking forms of spiritual art. At **Zebedee Springs,** a short walk off the graded road leads you through dense Livingstonia palms to a series of thermal pools for soaking and relaxing.

✉ *Turnoff for El Questro 27 km (17 mi) west of Kununurra on Gibb River Rd.* ☎ *08/9169–1777* ⊕ *www. elquestro.com.au* ✉ *El Questro Wilderness Park permit (required) A$15 for 1- to 7-day pass with access to gorge walks, thermal springs, fishing holes, rivers, and use of the Emma Gorge Resort swimming pool* ⊙ *Daily Apr.–Oct. Entry to Zebedee Springs closes at noon.*

Branching off toward the coast from Gibb River Road, 241 km (149 mi) from where it begins in the east, is the route to the extraordinary **Mitchell Plateau and Falls.** The natural attraction is a slow-going 162 km (100 mi) trek north on Kalumburu Road.

Adcock Gorge, 380 km (236 mi) from Kununurra on Gibb River Road, conjures up images of Eden with its large swimming hole, lush vegetation, and flocks of tropical parrots.

Bell Gorge, 433 km (268 mi) from Kununurra, is a series of small falls that are framed by ancient rock and drop into a deep pool. The gorge is reached by a 29-km (18-mi) four-wheel-drive track from the Gibb River Road. There are campsites at nearby Silent Grove and Bell Creek.

Lennard Gorge, 456 km (283 mi) from Kununurra, is a half-hour drive down a rough four-wheel-drive track. But the discomfort is worth it: Lennard is one of the Kimberley's most spectacular gorges. Here a thin section of the Lennard River is surrounded by high cliffs that bubble with several breathtaking waterfalls.

WHERE TO STAY

Just off Kalumburu Road there are campsites at Mitchell Plateau (at King Edward River on the early part of the Mitchell Plateau Track) and at Mitchell Falls Car Park; the latter grounds have toilets. The atmospheric Silent Grove campsite (close to Bell Gorge) has showers, toilets, firewood, and secluded sites (with no facilities) beside Bell Creek. Access is restricted from December to April. Camping information can be obtained from the **Department of Environment and Conservation** (✉ *Box 942, Kununurra, WA, 6743* ✉ *Messmate Wy., Kununurra* ☎ *08/9168–4200* ⊕ *www.calm.wa.gov.au*).

$$$$
Fodor'sChoice
★

Bush Camp at Faraway Bay. Far away both in name and in nature, this idyllic hideaway is perched upon a cliff along the remote Kimberley coast 280 km (173 mi) northwest of Kununurra. Accessible only by light aircraft from Kununurra and catering to a maximum of 12 guests, the camp epitomizes tranquillity. You can explore the nearby untouched coastline by boat and on foot, or simply sit back and enjoy the scenery. Accommodations are simple, bush-style cabins overlooking the bay; and sea breezes float through on even the hottest days. The room rate includes all meals, beverages, transfers, and activities. *Box 901, Kununurra, 6743 ☎08/9169–1214 ⊕www.farawaybay.com.au ⇨8 cabins ⚲In-room: no a/c, no phone, no TV. In-hotel: restaurant, bar, pool, laundry service ▤AE, MC, V ⑩AI.*

¢–$$$$ ⚏ **El Questro.** The location of this
★   property, at the top of a cliff face above the Chamberlain River, is one of the most spectacular in

> ## A FANTASY LANDSCAPE
>
> For millions of years nature has savaged the rocks of Purnululu National Park with water and wind, creating one of the most unique landscapes in the world. Traveling into the area is a remarkable experience—the timelessness of the ancient rocks draws you back across the millennia. All around, the conically weathered formations cluster together like a meeting of some metamorphic executives.

Australia. Developed in 1991, the property includes a working cattle station with a herd of approximately 5,000 Brahman and Shorthorn cattle. Five independent accommodation facilities are on-site, each different in style and budget: the luxury Homestead; the safari-style tented cabins at Emma Gorge Resort; air-conditioned Riverside Bungalows and Riverside Campgrounds at the Station Township; and Mt. Cockburn Lodge, which runs two-day adventure safaris around Cockburn Range. Each has a restaurant, and rates at the Homestead include drinks and food, laundry, activities, and round-trip transportation from Kununurra. If you want to get away from telephones and television, this is the place. *⊠100 km (60 mi) west of Kununurra, via Great Northern Hwy.; take Gibb River Rd. for 42 km (14 mi) from the highway exit *Box 909, Kununurra, 6743 ☎08/9169–1777, 08/9161–4388 Emma Gorge Resort ⊕www.voyages.com.au ⇨6 suites, 60 tented cabins, 12 bungalows, 31 campsites, 6 lodge cabins ⚲In-room: no a/c (some), no phone, no TV. In-hotel: 4 restaurants, bars, tennis court, pools, laundry facilities, parking (no fee) ▤AE, DC, MC, V ☉Closed Nov.–Mar.*

PURNULULU (BUNGLE BUNGLE) NATIONAL PARK

252 km (156 mi) southwest of Wyndham and Kununurra.

Fodor'sChoice   Purnululu (Bungle Bungle) National Park covers nearly 3,120 square
★   km (1,200 square mi) in the southeast corner of the Kimberley. Australians of European descent first "discovered" its great beehive-shaped domes—their English name is the Bungle Bungle—in 1983, proving how much about this vast continent remains outside of "white" experience. The local Kidja Aboriginal tribe, who knew about these scenic wonders long ago, called the area Purnululu.

The striking, black-and-orange-stripe mounds seem to bubble up from the landscape. Climbing on them is not permitted because the sandstone layer beneath their thin crust of lichen and silica is fragile, and would quickly erode without protection. Walking tracks follow rocky, dry creek beds. One popular walk leads hikers along the **Piccaninny Creek** to **Piccaninny Gorge,** passing through gorges with towering 328-foot cliffs to which slender fan palms cling.

Although there are two designated campsites in the area, neither has facilities. Both the Bellburn Creek and Walardi campgrounds have simple chemical toilets; fresh drinking water is available at both campgrounds. **Kununurra Visitor Centre** (☎08/9168–1177) has information about the campsites. The nearest accommodations are in Kununurra. Tour operators often fly clients in from Kununurra, Broome, and Halls Creek and drive them around in four-wheel-drive vehicles. April through December, the most popular tours include a night of camping. The mounds are closed from January through March.

GEIKIE GORGE NATIONAL PARK

16 km (10 mi) northeast of Fitzroy crossing, 400 km (250 mi) east of Broome.

Geikie Gorge is part of a 350-million-year-old reef system formed from fossilized layers of algae—evolutionary precursors of coral reefs—when this area was still part of the Indian Ocean. The limestone walls you see today were cut and shaped by the mighty Fitzroy River; during the Wet, the normally placid waters roar through the region. The walls of the gorge are stained red from iron oxide, except where they have been leached of the mineral and turned white by the floods, which have washed as high as 52 feet from the bottom of the gorge.

When the Indian Ocean receded, it stranded a number of sea creatures, which managed to adapt to their altered conditions. Geikie is one of the few places in the world where freshwater barramundi, mussels, stingrays, and prawns swim. The park is also home to the freshwater archerfish, which can spit water as far as a yard to knock insects out of the air. Aborigines call this place Kangu, meaning "big fishing hole."

Although there's a 5-km (3-mi) walking trail along the west side of the gorge, the opposite side is off-limits because it's a wildlife sanctuary.

The best way to see the gorge is aboard one of the several daily 90-minute boat tours led by a ranger from the **National Park Ranger Station** (⌂Box 37, Fitzroy Crossing, WA, 6765 ☎08/9191–5121 or 08/9191–5112 ⊕www.calm.wa.gov.au). The rangers are extremely knowledgeable and helpful in pointing out the vegetation, strange limestone formations, and the many freshwater crocodiles along the way. You may also see part of the noisy fruit-bat colony that inhabits the region. The park is open for day visits daily from 6:30 AM to 6:30 PM between April and November. Entry is restricted during the Wet, from December to March when the Fitzroy River floods. The closest accommodations to the park are in the nearby town of Fitzroy Crossing, which is 16 km (10 mi) southwest on the Great Northern Highway. There are a few basic restaurants and hotels here, including the **Crossing Inn** (✉Skulthorpe Rd. ☎08/9191–5080), established in 1897 and the oldest hotel in the Kimberley region, where some of the Kimberley's more colorful characters gather on weekend afternoons, and **Fitzroy River Lodge** (⊠ *Great Northern Hwy.* ☎ *08/9191–5141*), with campsites, safari-style lodges, and motel rooms.

OFF THE BEATEN PATH

Tunnel Creek & Windjana Gorge National Parks. North of Fitzroy Crossing are these two geological oddities. **Tunnel Creek** (111 km [69 mi] north of Fitzroy Crossing) was created when a stream cut an underground course through a fault line in a formation of limestone. You can follow the tunnel's path on foot for almost 1 km (½ mi); the only natural light comes from those areas where the tunnel roof has collapsed. Bring a flashlight and you'll spot flying foxes and other types of bats that inhabit the tunnel. Be prepared to get wet and possibly cold. About 100 years ago a band of outlaws and their Aboriginal leader Jandamarra—nicknamed "Pigeon"—used the caves as a hideout, and Aboriginal paintings can be seen in and around the tunnel. **Windjana Gorge** (145 km [90 mi] northwest of Fitzroy Crossing) has cliffs nearly 325 feet high, which were carved out by the flooding of the Lennard River. During the Wet the Lennard is a roaring torrent, but it dwindles to just a few still pools in the Dry. This is one of the best places in Australia to see freshwater crocodiles (up close!) in their natural environment. Camping is available for A$10.

BROOME

1,032 km (640 mi) southwest of Kununurra via Halls Creek, 1,544 km (957 mi) southwest of Katherine, 1,859 km (1,152 mi) southwest of Darwin.

Broome is the holiday capital of the Kimberley. It's the only town in the region with sandy beaches, and is the base from which most strike out to see more of the region. In some ways, with its wooden sidewalks and charming Chinatown it still retains the air of its past as a boisterous shantytown. However, with tourism increasing every year it is becoming more upscale all the time.

Long ago Broome depended on pearling for its livelihood, and by the early 20th century 300 to 400 sailing boats employing 3,000 men provided most of the world's mother-of-pearl shell. Many of the pearlers were Japanese, Malay, and Filipino, and the town is still a wonderful multicultural center today. Each August during the famous Shinju Matsuri (Festival of the Pearl), Broome commemorates its early pearling years and heritage. The 10-day festival features many traditional Japanese ceremonies. Because of the popularity of the festival, advance bookings for accommodations are highly recommended. Several tour operators have multiday cruises out of Broome along the magnificent Kimberley coast. The myriad deserted islands and beaches, with 35-foot tides that create horizontal waterfalls and whirlpools, make it an adventurer's delight.

Broome marks the end of the Kimberley. From here it's another 2,250 km (1,395 mi) south to Perth, or 1,859 km (1,152 mi) back to Darwin.

Broome By Camelback

Though not native to Australia, camels played a big part in exploring and opening up the country's big, dry, and empty interior. In the 1800s around 20,000 camels were imported from the Middle East to use for cross-country travel—along with handlers (many from Afghanistan) who cared for them.

When railways and roads became the prime methods of transport in the early 20th century, many camels were simply set free in the desert. A steady population of wild camels—some 400,000 of them—now roams across the Australian Outback.

Broome has for many years been a place where people enjoy camel rides—especially along the broad, desertlike sands of Cable Beach. Two tour companies in town now offer camel "adventures" on a daily basis; they're a great way to see the coast and get a taste of history.

Red Sun Camels (☎ 08/9193-7423 or 0419-954996 🖷 08/9193-7423 ⊕ www.redsuncamels.com.au) runs both morning and sunset rides every day on Cable Beach. The morning rides last for 40 minutes and cost A$30; the sunset rides take an hour and cost A$50.

Broome Camel Safaris (☎ 0419-916101 🖷 08/9192-3617 ⊕ www.broomecamelsafaris.com.au) operates Monday–Saturday, and offers 30-minute afternoon rides (A$30) and one-hour sunset rides (A$45).

CITY CENTER

The life-size bronze statues of the **Cultured Pearling Monument** are near Chinatown. The monument depicts three pioneers of the cultured pearling industry that is so intertwined with the city's development and history. ⊠ *Carnarvon St.*

More than 900 pearl divers are buried in the **Japanese Cemetery,** on the road out to Broome's deepwater port. The graves are a testimony to the contribution of the Japanese to the development of the industry in Broome, as well as to the perils of gathering pearls in the industry's early days. ⊠ *Port Dr.*

★ The **Pearl Luggers** historical display sheds light on the difficulties and immense skill involved in pearl harvesting. It has two restored luggers along with other such pearling equipment as diving suits. Informative videos run all day. Pearl divers, who spent years living aboard pearling luggers and diving for pearl shells, also offer tours (allow 1½ hours). Tours run at 9 AM, 11 AM, 2 PM, and 4 PM weekdays from April to October; 11 AM and 2 PM weekdays from November to March; and weekends at 11 AM only. This is a must-see for those interested in Broome's history. ⊠ *31 Dampier Terr.* ☎ *08/9192-2059* 🖭 *A$18.50* ☉ *May–Dec., daily 9:30–5; Jan.–Apr., weekdays 10–4, weekends 10–1.*

Opened in 1916, **Sun Pictures** is the world's oldest operating outdoor movie theater. Here silent movies—accompanied by a pianist—were once shown to the public. These days current releases are shown in the undeniably pleasant outdoors. Historical tours of the theater are also available weekdays for A$5 per person. ⊠ *8 Carnarvon St.*

☎*08/08/9192–1077* ⊕*www.sunpictures.com.au* ✉*A$14.50* ⊙*Daily 6:30* PM*–11* PM.

AROUND BROOME

The **Broome Bird Observatory,** a nonprofit research and education facility, provides the perfect opportunity to see many of the Kimberley's 310 bird species, some of which migrate annually from Siberia. On the shores of Roebuck Bay, 25 km (15 mi) east of Broome, the observatory has a prolific number of migratory waders. ✉*Crab Creek Rd., 15 km (9 mi) from Broome Hwy.* ☎*08/9193–5600* ✉*A$5 for day visitors* ⊙*By appointment.*

You can watch demonstrations of the cultured pearling process, including the seeding of a live oyster, at **Willie Creek Pearl Farm,** 38 km (23½ mi) north of Broome. Drive out to the farm yourself (you must make reservations first), or join a tour bus leaving from town. ✉*Drive 9 km (5½ mi) east from Broome on Broome Hwy., turn left onto Cape Leveque Rd., for 15 km (9 mi), turn left onto Manari Rd. for 5 km (3 mi), turn left and follow signs for 2½ km (1½ mi). Allow about 1 hr* ☎*08/9193–6000* ⊕*www.williecreekpearls.com.au* ✉*Self-drive A$32.50, coach tour A$65* ⊙*Guided tours daily 9* AM *and 2* PM.

WHERE TO STAY & EAT

$–$$ ✕**Matso's Café, Art Gallery, and Broome Brewery.** There's a bit of every-
★   thing at this convivial eatery: excellent food, beer brewed on-site, and Kimberley artwork adorning the walls. For dinner try their Beer Battered Barra or lamb shanks braised in Smokey Bishop Lager with coriander mash and balsamic jus. From Thursday to Tuesday nights there's Indian curry available from 6 PM to 9 PM. Matso's is also a great place to meet locals. The café and brewery are both open for breakfast and until late at night. ✉*60 Hammersley St.* ☎*08/9193–5811* ▤*AE, DC, MC, V.*

$$$–$$$$ ▥**Cable Beach Club Resort Broome.** Just a few minutes out of town oppo-
★   site the broad, beautiful Cable Beach, this resort is the area's most luxurious accommodation. Single and double bungalows are spread through tropical gardens; studio rooms and suites are also available. The decor is colonial with a hint of Asian influence. Some rooms and facilities are closed during the Wet. ✉*Cable Beach Rd., 6725* ☎*08/9192–0400 or 1800/199099* ⊕*www.cablebeachclub.com* ⇆*263 rooms, 34 bunga-lows, 2 villas, 3 suites* ⚘*In-room: kitchen (some). In-hotel: restaurant, bars, tennis courts, pools, gym, spa, beachfront, concierge, laundry service, parking (no fee), minibar* ▤*AE, DC, MC, V.*

$$$ ▥**Moonlight Bay Suites.** Rooms with bay views and a five-minute stroll
★   from Chinatown add luxury and convenience to this complex of posh, self-contained apartments. It's a great place to recuperate by the pool after a rugged Kimberley tour. ✉*51 Carnarvon St., 6725* ⌂*Box 198, Broome, 6725* ☎*08/9193–7888 or 1800/818878* ⊕*www.broome accommodation.com.au* ⇆*52 apartments* ⚘*In-room: dial-up, kitchen. In-hotel: restaurant, pool, gym, spa, laundry facilities, parking (no fee)* ▤*AE, DC, MC, V.*

$$–$$$ Mangrove Hotel. Overlooking Roebuck Bay, this highly regarded hotel has one of the best locations of any accommodation in Broome. All the spacious rooms have private balconies or patios, many with bay views, and several dining and drinking spots are on-site. Plus, it's a five-minute walk to Chinatown. ⊠*47 Carnarvon St., 6725* ☎*08/9192–1303 or 1800/094818* ⊕*www.mangrovehotel.com.au* 🛏*68 rooms* ⚹*In-room: refrigerator. In-hotel: 2 restaurants, bars, pools, laundry facilities, parking (no fee)* ⊟*AE, DC, MC, V.*

¢–$ Ocean Lodge. Rates plummet during the Wet at this budget-price motel, which sits amid shady gardens between Chinatown and Cable Beach. Lodgings are in self-contained double and twin motel-style rooms and two-room family suites. Children can splash in the wading pool. The Broome Recreation & Aquatic Centre and Café is across the road. The center is open year-round and has swimming pools, tennis courts, net-ball and basketball courts, and a skate park. ⊠*1 Cable Beach Rd., 6725* ☎*08/9193–7700 or 1800/600603* ⊕*www.oceanlodge.com.au* 🛏*44 rooms, 14 suites* ⚹*In-room: dial-up (some), kitchen. In-hotel: pool, laundry facilities, parking (no fee)* ⊟*AE, DC, MC, V.*

THE KIMBERLEY ESSENTIALS

TRANSPORTATION

BY AIR

Distances in this part of the continent are colossal. Flying is the fastest and easiest way to get to the Kimberley.

Qantas and its subsidiaries fly to Broome from Brisbane, Sydney, Melbourne, and Adelaide via Perth. On Saturday there are faster flights from Sydney and Melbourne via Alice Springs (with connections from Brisbane and Adelaide). Air North has an extensive air network throughout the Top End, linking Broome and Kununurra with Darwin, Alice Springs, and Perth. Virgin Blue also services Broome from Perth and Adelaide. Skywest flies to Broome from Perth. Broome's airport is right next to the center of town, on the northern side. Though it's called Broome International Airport, there are no scheduled overseas flights, but charter flights and private flights arrive there. Approvals are in place for international flights in the future.

Airlines Air North (☎*08/8920–4000 or 1800/627474* ⊕*www.airnorth.com.au*). **Qantas** (☎*13–1313* ⊕*www.qantas.com*). **Skywest** (☎*1300/660088* ⊕*www. skywest.com.au*). **Virgin Blue** (☎*13–6789* ⊕*www.virginblue.com.au*).

Airports Broome International Airport (☎*08/9193–5455* ⊕*www.broomeair. com.au*). **Darwin International Airport** (☎*08/8920–1811* ⊕*www.darwinairport. com.au*).

BY BUS

Greyhound Australia traverses the 1,859 km (1,152 mi) between Darwin and Broome in just under 24 hours. Greyhound also operates the 32-hour regular route and a 27-hour express daily between Perth and

Broome. The Broome bus station is handily next door to the visitor center, at the corner of Broome Highway and Bagot Road.

Contact Greyhound Australia (☎ *13–1499* ⊕ *www.greyhound.com.au*).

BY CAR

The unpaved, 700-km (434-mi) Gibb River Road runs through a remote area between Derby and Kununurra. If you like views, it's considered best to start the drive at Kununurra, and the trip should be done only with a great deal of caution. The road is passable by conventional vehicles only after it has been recently graded (smoothed). At other times you need a four-wheel-drive vehicle, and in the Wet it's mostly impassable.

The Bungle Bungle are 252 km (156 mi) south of Kununurra along the Great Northern Highway. A very rough, 55-km (34-mi) unpaved road, negotiable only in a four-wheel-drive vehicle, is the last stretch of road leading to the park from the turnoff near the Turkey Creek–Warmum Community. That part of the drive takes about 2½ hours.

From Broome to Geikie Gorge National Park, follow the Great Northern Highway east 391 km (242 mi) to Fitzroy Crossing, then 16 km (10 mi) north on a paved side road to the park. Camping is not permitted at the gorge, so you must stay in Fitzroy Crossing.

From Darwin to Kununurra and the eastern extent of the Kimberley it's 827 km (513 mi). From Darwin to Broome on the far side of the Kimberley it's 1,859 km (1,152 mi), a long two-day drive. The route runs from Darwin to Katherine along the Stuart Highway, and then along the Victoria Highway to Kununurra. The entire road is paved but quite narrow in parts—especially so, it may seem, when a road train (an extremely long truck convoy) is coming the other way. Drive with care. Fuel and supplies can be bought at small settlements along the way, but you should always keep supplies in abundance.

The West Australian Main Roads Information Service provides information on road conditions, including the Gibb River Road.

Contact West Australian Main Roads Information Service (☎ *1800/013314*).

CONTACTS & RESOURCES

EMERGENCIES

In an emergency dial **000** to reach an ambulance, the police, or the fire department.

Doctors Royal Flying Doctor Service (☎ *1800/625800*).

Hospitals Broome District Hospital (⊠ *Robinson St., Broome* ☎ *08/9194–2222*). **Derby Regional Hospital** (⊠ *Clarendon St., Derby* ☎ *08/9193–3333*). **Kununurra District Hospital** (⊠ *96 Coolibah Dr., Kununurra* ☎ *08/9166–4222*).

TOURS

Kimberley Wilderness Adventures conducts tours from Broome and Kununurra, which include excursions along Gibb River Road and into Purnululu National Park. The "Best of Bungle Bungle" day-tour costs A$775, and includes a four-wheel-drive tour, lunch, and scenic flights over the national park. East Kimberley Tours run multiday adventures along Gibb River Road, and fly-drive packages into Purnululu from A$550.

Broome Day Tours conducts several tours via air-conditioned coach with informative commentary in the western Kimberley region—including a four-hour Broome Explorer tour of the town's major sights for A$90, and day trips farther afield to Windjana Gorge and Geikie Gorge for A$210. Another company that tours the Kimberley is Flak Track Tours. Their nine-day Broome-to-Kununurra tour is A$2,520. A 14-day, round-trip Broome tour (covering the Gibb River Road, Mitchell Falls, Kununurra, the Ord River, and Purnulu) is A$3,920.

Alligator Airways operates both fixed-wing floatplanes from Lake Kununurra and land-based flights from Kununurra Airport. A 35-minute scenic flight costs $145. Slingair conducts both fixed wing and helicopter flights from Kununurra and Purnululu National Park.

A 30-minute helicopter flight costs A$265 from their helipad in the Purnululu National Park. An alternative 2½-hour fixed wing flight over the Bungle Bungle and Lake Argyle is A$250.

Lake Argyle Cruises operates excellent trips on Australia's largest expanse of freshwater, the man-made Lake Argyle. Tours run daily March to October, and it's A$60 for the two-hour morning cruise, A$140 for the six-hour cruise, and A$80 for the sunset cruise (which starts around 2:45).

Pearl Sea Coastal Cruises has multiday Kimberley adventures along the region's magnificent coastline in their luxury *Kimberley Quest* cruiser. All meals and excursions (including fishing trips) are included in the cost of A$7,585 for 7 days to A$10,955 for 14 days. Cruising season runs from March to December.

Astro Tours organizes entertaining, informative night-sky tours of the Broome area. Two-hour shows (offered four nights a week) cost A$65, including transfers from your hotel, folding-stool seating, hot beverages, and cookies. The company also offers four-wheel-drive Outback stargazing adventures farther afield. Discover the Kimberley Tours operates four-wheel-drive adventures into the Bungle Bungle massif.

Adventure Tours Broome Day Tours (☎ *1800/801068* 🖷 *08/9193-5575* ✆ Brmcoach@wn.com.au). **East Kimberley Tours** (☎ *08/9168–2213* ✆ bookings@ekt. com.au ⊕ *www.eastkimberleytours.com.au*). **Flak Track Tours** (☎ *08/8894–2228* 🖷 *08/9192–1275* ✆ sales@flaktrak.com ⊕ *www.flaktrak.com*). **Kimberley Wilderness Adventures** (☎ *03/9277–8444 or 1800/675222* ✆ info@kimberleywilderness. com.au ⊕ *www.kimberleywilderness.com.au*).

Air Tours Alligator Airways (☎ *08/9168–1333 or 1800/632533* ⊕ *www.alligator airways.com.au*). **Slingair Heliwork** (☎ *08/9168–1811* ⊕ *www.slingair.com.au*).

Boat Tours Lake Argyle Cruises (✉ *Box 710, Kununurra, 6743* ☎ *08/9168–7687* 🖷 *08/9168–7461* ✆ info@lakeargylecruises.com ⊕ *www.lakeargylecruises.com*). **Pearl Sea Coastal Cruises** (✉ *Box 2838, Broome, 6725* ☎ *08/9193–6131*

🖩 *08/9193–6303* ✉ cruises@kimberleyquest.com.au ⊕ *www.kimberleyquest. com.au).*

Four-Wheel-Drive Tours Astro Tours (✑ *Box 2537, Broome6725* ☎ *08/9193–5362* 🖩 *08/9193–5362* ⊕ *www.astrotours.net).* **Discover the Kimberley Tours** (✑ *Box 2615, Broome, 6725* ☎ *08/9193–7267 or 1800/636802* ✉ distours@tpgi. com.au ⊕ *www.bunglebungle.com.au).*

VISITOR INFORMATION

Contacts Broome Visitor Centre (✉ *Broome Rd. at Short St., Broome* ☎ *08/9192–2222* 🖩 *08/9192–2063* ✉ enquiries@broomevisitorcentre.com.au ⊕ *www.broome visitorcentre.com.au).* **Kununurra Visitor Centre** (✉ *75 Coolibah Dr., Kununurra* ☎ *08/9168–1177* 🖩 *08/9168–2598* ⊕ *www.kununurratourism.com).* **Western Australian Tourism Commission S**(✉ *Wellington St. at Forrest Pl., Perth* ☎ *08/9483–1111 or 1300/361351* 🖩 *08/9481–0190* ⊕ *www.westernaustralia.com).*

Perth & Western Australia

12

WORD OF MOUTH

"We love Western Australia wine country and all the national parks (we enjoy hiking). We spent most of our time in Albany, Pemberton and Margaret River."

–Melnq8

Updated
by Graham
Hodgson

WESTERN AUSTRALIA IS ENORMOUS. TWICE the size of Texas, it sprawls across more than 1 million square mi. It's also a stunningly diverse place, with rugged interior deserts, a tropical coast of white-sand beaches, and a temperate, forested south. A growing number of excellent wineries, restaurants, seaside parks, and hiking trails means that Australia's "undiscovered state" likely won't stay undiscovered for much longer.

Although the existence of a southern continent—*terra australis*—was known long before Dutch seafarer Dirk Hartog first landed on the coast of "New Holland" in 1616 in today's Shark Bay, the landscape he encountered was so bleak he didn't even bother to plant his flag and claim it for the Dutch crown. It took an intrepid English seaman, William Dampier, to see past the daunting prospect of endless sands, rugged cliffs, heat, flies, and sparse, scrubby plains to claim the land for Britain, 20,000 km (12,400 mi) away.

Such isolation would ordinarily doom a community to life as a backwater, but the discovery of natural resources here eventually helped the region become vibrant. A gold rush around Kalgoorlie and Coolgardie in the 1890s brought people and wealth, especially to the fledgling city of Perth; much later, in the 1970s, the discovery of massive mineral deposits throughout the state attracted international interest and began an economic upswing that still continues.

Today Western Australia produces much of Australia's mineral, energy, and agricultural wealth. Perth, the capital city and home to nearly 75% of the state's 2.1 million residents, is a modern, pleasant metropolis with an easygoing, welcoming attitude. However, at 3,200 km (2,000 mi) from any other major city in the world, it has fondly been dubbed "the most isolated city on earth." In fact, since it is closer to Indonesia than to its overland Australian cousins, many West Australians choose to take their vacations in Bali rather than in, say, Sydney or Melbourne.

The remoteness, though, is part of what makes Western Australia so awe-inspiring. The scenery here is magnificent; whether you travel through the rugged gorges and rock formations of the north; the green pastures, vineyards, and hardwood forests of the south; or the coastline's vast, pristine beaches, you'll be struck by how much space there is here. If the crowds and crush of big-city life aren't your thing, this is the part of Australia you may never want to leave.

The Kimberley region in Western Australia's tropical north is closer geographically and in character to the Northern Territory city of Darwin than it is to Perth. *For this reason, information about Broome and the Kimberley is included in Chapter 11.*

EXPLORING PERTH & WESTERN AUSTRALIA

Most trips to Western Australia begin in Perth. Apart from its own points of interest, there are a few great day trips to take from the city: to Rottnest Island, for example, or north to the coastal Nam-

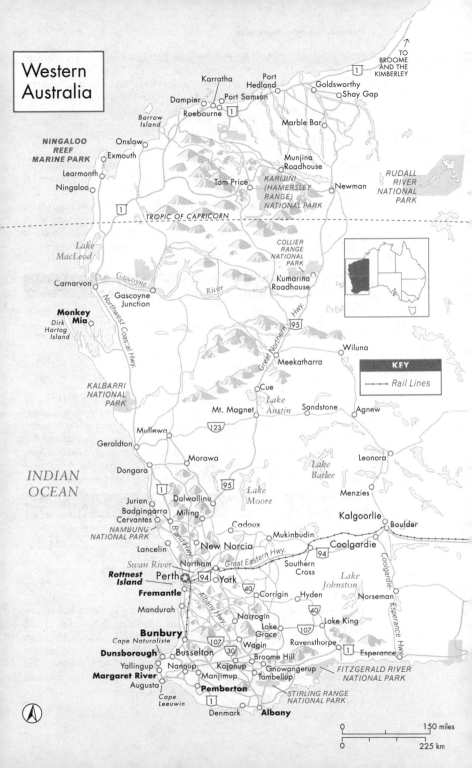

bung National Park. The port city of Fremantle is a good place to unwind, and, if you have the time, a tour of the South West—with its seashore, parks, hardwood forests, wildflowers, and first-rate wineries and restaurants—is highly recommended. The old goldfield towns east of Perth are a slice of the dust-blown Australia of yore.

ABOUT THE RESTAURANTS

Perth's restaurants and cafés reflect Western Australia's energetic outdoor lifestyle, with menus strongly influenced by the state's continual influx of European, Asian, and African immigrants. First-class food is matched by wines and beers from some of Australia's most innovative vineyards and breweries. A jacket and tie are rarely needed, and most places are either licensed (able to serve wine and beers with food) or BYO (bring your own wine or beer). Tips aren't expected, but leaving 10% extra for exceptional service is welcome.

WHAT IT COSTS IN AUSTRALIAN DOLLARS				
$$$$	$$$	$$	$	¢
AT DINNER	over A$50	A$36–A$50	A$21–A$35	A$10–A$20	under A$10

Prices are for a main course at dinner.

ABOUT THE HOTELS

Most first-class properties and international names are in Perth's city center, and all have many modern facilities. Apartment-style accommodations have two or three bedrooms, a kitchen, and a larger living space, although these lack the hotel advantages of room service and 24-hour restaurants. Outside the city, bed-and-breakfasts provide comfort, charm, and a glimpse of local life. In farther-flung parts of the state—and there are plenty of these—much of the lodging is motel style.

WHAT IT COSTS IN AUSTRALIAN DOLLARS				
$$$$	$$$	$$	$	¢
FOR TWO PEOPLE	over A$300	A$201–A$300	A$151–A$200	A$100–A$150	under A$100

Prices are for two people in a standard double room in high season, including tax and service, based on the European Plan (with no meals) unless otherwise noted.

WHEN TO VISIT

There's no wrong time to visit Western Australia. In Perth and south, you can view wildflowers in spring (September through November) and watch whales along the coast in fall (February through May). Although winter (May through August) is the wettest season, it's also when the orchards and forests are lush and green. North of Perth, winter is the dry season, and it can get chilly inland throughout the state. Summer (December through February) is *hot,* when temperatures can rise to 40°C (100°F) and higher.

GREAT ITINERARIES

Planning your time out west requires focus on a couple of areas. It's unlikely you'll cover the whole state, even if you decide to permanently relocate. To narrow down your choices, consider whether you have a few days to spend in and around Perth and Fremantle. Does the thought of cooler air and the coastal scenery of the South West appeal to you, or would you rather get in a car and drive to far reaches east or north? Or, do you want to trek north along the coast to Monkey Mia or Ningaloo Reef Marine Park to frolic in and under the waves with amazing sea creatures?

IF YOU HAVE 3 DAYS

Spend most of the first day knocking around **Perth**'s city center. Take the train to pleasantly restored **Fremantle** and stroll through the streets, stopping for breaks at sidewalk cafés. In the evening in either city, have dinner overlooking the water. Over the next two days, take a ferry to **Rottnest Island** and cycle around, walk on the beach, fish, or try to spot the small local marsupials called quokkas. For a longer excursion, take a coach tour to **Nambung National Park** Pinnacles, the captivating coastal rock formations, or south to the Treetop Walk.

IF YOU HAVE 5 DAYS

Now you can take on some of the larger distances in Western Australia. Fly north to **Monkey Mia** to learn

about and interact with dolphins, or to **Ningaloo Reef Marine Park** to dive with whale sharks and watch the annual coral spawning. Or drive a couple of hours to the **South West** coastal area to see spring wildflowers, wineries, orchards, forests, grazing dairy and beef herds, and national parks, and to generally enjoy the good life. You'll have enough time for a day or two around **Perth** before flying to the old goldfields towns of **Kalgoorlie** and **Coolgardie**. They may remind you of America's Wild West—except that camel teams rather than stagecoaches used to pull into town—but this is pure Oz all the way.

IF YOU HAVE 7 DAYS OR MORE

With seven days you can consider all options, mixing parts of the three- and five-day itineraries. Of course, you could opt to spend the entire week leisurely making your way along the coast of the **South West**, tasting the top-quality regional wines and locally grown foods. Or, you could head for the caves and rough shorelines that define **Leeuwin–Naturaliste National Park**. **Stirling Range National Park** is a great place for hiking, especially in spring amid the vast wildflowers. If you plan to go north to view **Karijini National Park** and its stunning gorges and rockscapes, taking a plane will give you more time to explore.

PERTH

Buoyed by mineral wealth and foreign investment, high-rise buildings dot the skyline of Perth, and an influx of immigrants gives the city a healthy diversity. Some of Australia's finest sandy beaches, sailing, and fishing are on the city's doorstep, and seaside villages and great beaches lie just north of Fremantle. The main business thoroughfare is St. George's Terrace, an elegant street with a number of the city's most appealing sights. Perth's literal highlight is King's Park, 1,000 acres of greenery atop Mt. Eliza, which affords panoramic views of the city.

EXPLORING PERTH

Because of its relative colonial youth, Perth has an advantage over most other capital cities in that it was laid out with foresight and elegance. Streets were planned so that pedestrian traffic could flow smoothly from one avenue to the next, and this compact city remains easy to negotiate on foot. Most of the points of interest are in the downtown area close to the banks of the Swan River, while shopping arcades and pedestrian malls are a short stroll away.

The city center (or Central Business District), a pleasant blend of old and new, runs along Perth's major business thoroughfare, St. George's Terrace, as well as on parallel Hay and Murray streets.

THE SWAN RIVER

By the water's edge Perth sits astride the Swan River. Though not a great river by global standards, it is the focus of many of the city's festivities, from weekend sailing and boating to annual blockbuster fireworks spectaculars. For the visitor, it's best to start exploring the riverside at the cluster of boatsheds, cafés, jetties, and ticket offices at the bottom of Barrack Street. From here, you can take trips up or downriver.

WHAT TO SEE

8 Art Gallery of Western Australia. More than 1,000 treasures from the state's art collection are on display, including one of the best exhibits of Aboriginal art in Australia. Other works include Australian and international paintings, sculpture, prints, crafts, and decorative arts. Free guided tours run at 11 AM and 1 PM Tuesday, Wednesday, Thursday, and Sunday and at 1 PM on Saturday. The 12:30 PM Friday's Focus tour examines one particular painting, and guest speakers are scheduled at 2 PM the first Sunday of every month. ⊠ *Perth Cultural Centre, 47 James St. Mall, at corner of Beaufort and Roe Sts., CBD* ☎ *08/9492–6600* ⊕ *www.artgallery.wa.gov.au* ⊠ *Free* ☉ *Daily 10–5.*

3 Barracks Arch. Perth's oddest architectural curiosity, this freestanding brick arch in the middle of the city center stands more or less in front of the seat of government—the highway actually comes between them. All that remains of the former headquarters of the Pensioner Forces (demolished in 1966) is this Tudor-style edifice, built in the 1860s with Flemish bond brickwork, a memorial to the earliest settlers. ⊠ *St. George's Terr. at Malcolm St., CBD.*

6 General Post Office. A handsome, colonnaded sandstone building, the post office forms an impressive backdrop to the city's major public square, Forrest Place. ⊠ *Forrest Pl. between Murray and Wellington Sts., CBD.*

4 His Majesty's Theatre. Restoration has transformed this Edwardian 1904 building, one of Perth's most gracious, into a handsome home for the Western Australian opera and ballet companies. The busiest month for

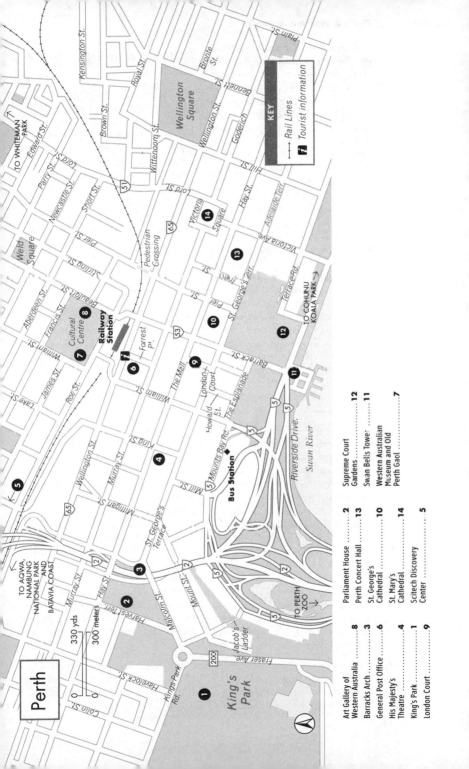

Perth

KEY

→ Rail Lines
i Tourist information

performances is February, during the Perth International Arts Festival. Auditorium and backstage tours, which run weekdays 10–4, must be booked in advance. The Grand Historical Tour (two hours) takes you on a gossipy and anecdotal wander through nine decades of colorful show-business history. You will view theater foyers, the auditorium, dressing rooms, backstage, and the Museum of Performing Arts. Available weekdays 10:30–4 for groups of 10–30; the cost is A$22 per person. The Behind the Scenes Tour (one hour) commences in the Stalls foyer and includes a view of the auditorium and backstage areas of the theater as well as a visit to the Museum of Performing Arts. It's conducted Thursday mornings 10:30–noon; the cost is A$15. Visitors may then choose to attend the weekly Lunchtime Concert in the Dress Circle Bar, from 12:30 to 1:10 PM (A$8). Both tours can include refreshments for an extra charge. Downstairs, the **Museum of Performing Arts** has rotating exhibitions of costumes and memorabilia. ✉ *825 Hay St., CBD* 🕾 *08/9494–1133* ⊕ *www.hismajestystheatre.com.au* 🎫 *Theater tours free, backstage tours A$15, Grand Historical Tour A$22, museum donations suggested* ⊗ *Box office weekdays 9–5:30, museum weekdays 10–4.*

> ### THE VIEW FROM KING'S PARK
>
> The best view in town King's Park is a must-see for most visitors to Perth. The best spot is the manicured eastern edge of the park, overlooking Perth's Central Business District and the Swan River. There are picture-perfect lookout points with the city in the background, as well as many of the city's most-treasured memorials, including the most-recent to local victims of the 2002 terrorist bombing in Bali.

❶ ★ ♨ King's Park. Once a gathering place for Aboriginal people and established as a public space in 1890, this 1,000-acre park overlooking downtown Perth is one of the city's most visited attractions. Both tourists and locals enjoy picnics, parties, and weddings in the gardens, as well as regular musical and theater presentations and the summer Moonlight Cinema. In spring the gardens blaze with orchids, kangaroo paw, banksias, and other wildflowers, making it ideal for a walk in the bushland. The steel-and-timber **Lotterywest Federation Walkway** takes you into the treetops and the 17-acre botanic garden of Australian flora. The **Synergy Parkland** details Western Australia's fossil and energy history. The **Lotterywest Family Area** has a playground for youngsters. Free walking tours take place daily at 10 AM and 2 PM, and details on seasonal and themed tours are available from the information kiosk near Fraser's Restaurant. ✉ *Fraser Ave. at King's Park Rd., West Perth* 🕾 *08/9480–3600* ⊕ *www.bgpa.wa.gov.au/kingspark* 🎫 *Free* ⊗ *Daily 24 hrs.*

❾ London Court. Gold-mining entrepreneur Claude de Bernales built this outdoor shopping arcade in 1937. Today it's a magnet for buskers (street performers) and anyone with a camera. Along its length are statues of Sir Walter Raleigh and Dick Whittington, the legendary lord mayor of London. Above the arcade, costumed mechanical knights joust with one another when the clock strikes the quarter hour. ⊠ *Between St. George's Terr. and Hay St., CBD.*

12

2 Parliament House. From its position on the hill at the top of St. George's Terrace, this building dominates Perth's skyline and serves as a respectable backdrop for the Barracks Arch. Shady old Moreton Bay fig trees and landscaped gardens make the hub of Western Australian government one of the most pleasant spots in the city. Drop in for a free one-hour tour Monday or Thursday at 10:30; groups are accommodated by appointment. You can visit the Public Galleries whenever Parliament is sitting. On days when Parliament is not sitting, a 45-minute tour takes participants to the Legislative Council public gallery and onto the floor of the Legislative Assembly. All tours cover the special features and symbols of the Parliament of Western Australia. ⊠ *Harvest Terr., West Perth* ☎ *08/9222–7259* ⊕ *www.parliament.wa.gov.au* ⊠ *Free* ☉ *Tours Mon. and Thurs. 10:30.*

13 Perth Concert Hall. When it was built, this small rectangular 1960s concert hall was considered both elegant and impressive. Although its architectural merit may now seem questionable to some, its acoustics are still clean and clear. The hall serves as the city's main music performance venue. ⊠ *5 St. George's Terr., CBD* ☎ *08/9231–9900* ⊕ *www.perth concerthall.com.au* ⊠ *Ticket prices vary* ☉ *During performances.*

10 St. George's Cathedral. The church and its **Deanery** are the city's most distinctive European-style complexes. Built in the late 1850s as a home for the first dean of Perth, the Deanery is one of the few remaining houses in Western Australia from this period. The Deanery is now used as offices for the Anglican Church and is not open to the public. ⊠ *Pier St. at St. George's Terr., CBD* ☎ *08/9325–5766* ⊕ *www.perthcathedral.org* ⊠ *Free* ☉ *Weekdays 7:45–5, Sun. services at 8, 10, and 5.*

14 St. Mary's Cathedral. Victoria Square is the home of the Gothic Revival St. Mary's. Its environs house the headquarters for the Roman Catholic Church. ⊠ *Victoria Sq., CBD* ☎ *08/9223–1350* ⊠ *Free* ☉ *Mass weekdays 7 AM and 12:10 PM, Sat. 7 AM and 6:30 PM, Sun. 7:30, 9, 10, 11:30, and 5.*

5 Scitech Discovery Centre. The interactive displays of science and technology here educate and entertain children of all ages. There are more than 100 hands-on exhibits, including a stand where you can freeze your own shadow, and another that examines the science and technology used in movies and television. Visitors can star in their own minimovie, scaling an ice mountain, or jumping from a 14-story building. Scitech was inducted into the Western Australian Tourism Commission's Hall of Fame as an outstanding Major Tourist Attraction. ⊠ *City West Railway Parade, Sutherland St., West Perth* ☎ *08/9481–6295* ⊕ *www.scitech.org.au* ⊠ *A$14* ☉ *Sat., Sun., school holidays and public holidays 10–5; weekdays 9:30–4.*

⑫ Supreme Court Gardens. Opened in 1845 as botanical gardens, the Supreme Court Gardens is a favorite lunch spot for office workers and is also home to some of the finest Moreton Bay fig trees in the state. A band shell in the rear of the gardens hosts summer concerts, such as Opera in the Park, which take place in the evenings December through February and twice weekly as part of the Perth International Arts Festival. ⊠ *Barrack St. at Adelaide Terr., CBD* ☎ *08/9461–3333* ⊠ *Free; some concerts require prepaid tickets* ⊙ *Daily 9–5.*

⑪ Swan Bells Tower. Comprising one of the world's largest musical instruments, the 12 ancient bells installed in the tower are originally from St. Martin-in-the-Fields Church of London, England. The same bells rang to celebrate the destruction of the Spanish Armada in 1588, the homecoming of Captain James Cook in 1771, and the coronation of every British monarch. The tower contains fascinating displays on the history of the bells and bell ringing, and provides stunning views of the Perth skyline. ⊠ *Barrack Sq., Barrack St. at Riverside Dr., CBD* ☎ *08/9218–8183* ⊕ *www. swanbells.com.au* ⊠ *A$10* ⊙ *Daily 10–4:30; bell-handling demonstrations (single bell) Wed. and Fri. 11:30 AM–12:30 PM; full bell ringing Sat.–Tues. and Thurs. noon–1 PM. Flat, closed shoes must be worn for access to the observation deck; strollers, large bags, backpacks, and bulky items are not permitted in the tower.*

CITY-DWELLING WATERBIRDS

When a series of lakes was created with construction of the freeways and the Narrows Bridge across the Swan River in 1959, city planners probably didn't realize that these bodies of water would become an oasis for waterbirds. It's a pleasant stroll or bike ride along the riverside, west from the Barrack Street jetties. Laze on the grassy banks, or relax under a tree and check out the different species of waterbirds, including the famous black swan, egret, and red-necked stint, migrating from as far afield as Siberia.

⑦ Western Australian Museum and Old Perth Gaol. The state's largest and most comprehensive museum includes some of Perth's oldest structures, such as the Old Perth Gaol. Built of stone in 1856, this was Perth's first and only prison until 1888. Today, it has been reconstructed in the museum courtyard, and you can go inside the cells for a taste of life in Perth's criminal past. Exhibitions include Diamonds to Dinosaurs, which uses fossils, rocks, and gemstones to take you back 3.5 billion years; and Katta Djinoong: First Peoples of Western Australia, which has a fascinating collection of primitive tools and lifestyle items used thousands of years ago by Australia's Aborigines. ⊠ *Perth Cultural Centre, James and Beaufort Sts., CBD* ☎ *08/9212–3700* ⊕ *www. museum.wa.gov.au* ⊠ *Free* ⊙ *Daily 9:30–5.*

AROUND PERTH

AQWA: Aquarium of Western Australia. Huge tanks filled with some 400 different species of local sea creatures let you view what's beneath the waves. Sharks, stingrays, octopus, cuttlefish, lobsters, turtles, and thou-

12

sands of fish swim overhead as you take the moving walkway beneath a clear acrylic tunnel. You can even snorkel or scuba dive with the sharks at 1 PM and 3 PM daily. Mammals like Australian sea lions and New Zealand fur seals are also part of the show. ⊠ *Hillarys Boat Harbour, 91 Southside Dr., Hillarys* ☎ *08/9447–7500* ⊕ *www.aqwa.com.au* ☑ *A$25; shark experience A$125, plus A$20 snorkel or A$40 scuba equipment rental* ☉ *Daily 10–5.*

Ⓒ **Cohunu Koala Park.** The 40-acre Cohunu (pronounced co-*hu*-na) lets you cuddle with a koala. But the other native animals, such as emus and wombats in their natural surroundings, are worth visiting, too. The walk-through aviary is the largest in the Southern Hemisphere, and there's also a kid-friendly miniature railway and a revolving restaurant that overlooks the city. ⊠ *Mills Rd. E, Gosnells* ☎ *08/9390–6090* 🖷 *08/9495–1341* ✑ *koalas@cohunu.com.au* ⊕ *www.cohunu. com.au* ☑ *A$22* ☉ *Daily 10–5, koala cuddle with photo souvenir daily 10–4.*

Ⓒ **Perth Zoo.** Some 1,300 creatures—from 230 different species—are housed in this gathering of spacious natural habitats. Popular attractions include the Australian Walkabout, the Penguin Plunge, and the Australian Bushwalk. You can also wander down a dry riverbed in the African Savannah, or delve through the thick foliage in the Asian Rainforest. To reach the zoo, catch the number 30 or 31 bus or take a ferry ride across the Swan River from the bottom of Barrack Street and then a 10-minute walk following the signs. ⊠ *20 Labouchere Rd., South Perth* ☎ *08/9474–0444 or 08/9474–3551* ⊕ *www.perthzoo.wa.gov.au* ☑ *A$17* ☉ *Daily 9–5.*

Ⓒ **Whiteman Park.** Barbecue facilities, picnic spots, bike trails, vintage trains and electric trams, and historic wagons and tractors fill this enormous recreation area linked by more than 30 km (19 mi) of bushwalking trails and bike paths. You can watch potters, blacksmiths, leather workers, toy makers, printers, and stained-glass artists at work here in their shops. Naturally, the wildlife includes free-ranging (or, more
Ⓒ accurately, free-lazing) kangaroos. **Caversham Wildlife Park** (☎ *08/9248– 1984* ⊕ *www.cavershamwildlife.com.au*), in Whiteman Park, has more than 200 wildlife species. Visitors can greet birds, feed animals, cuddle koalas and wombats, and ride camels. Admission is A$16. ⊠ *Lord St. at Gnangara Rd., West Swan* ☎ *08/9209–6000* ⊕ *www.whitemanpark. com.au* ☑ *Free* ☉ *Daily 8:30–6; 9–7 during summer months.*

OFF THE BEATEN PATH

Nambung National Park. Set on the Swan coastal plain 245 km (152 mi) north of Perth, Nambung National Park surrounds its most famous attraction: the **Pinnacles Desert.** Over the years, wind and drifting sand have sculpted eerie limestone forms that loom as high as 15 feet. These "pinnacles" are actually the fossilized roots of ancient coastal plants fused with sand, and you can walk among them along a 1,650-foot-long trail that starts at the parking area. There's also a 3-km (2-mi), one-way Pinnacles Desert Loop scenic drive (not suitable for large RVs or buses). August through October the heath blazes with wildflowers. Entrance fees are A$9 per car or A$3.40 per bus passenger. Call ☎08/9652–7043 for more information.

BEACHES

★

★

★

Perth's beaches and waterways are among the city's greatest attractions. Traveling north from Fremantle, the first beach you come to is **Leighton,** where windsurfers and astonishing wave-jumpers ride boards against the surf and hurl themselves airborne. **Cottesloe** and **North Cottesloe** attract families. **Trigg,** a top surf site and arguably Perth's best beach, overlooks an emerald-green bay. **Scarborough** is favored by teenagers and young adults. **Swanbourne** (between North Cottesloe and City Beach) is a "clothing-optional" beach.

WHERE TO EAT

Northbridge, northwest of the railway station, is *the* dining and nightclubbing center of Perth, and reasonably priced restaurants are everywhere. Elsewhere around Perth are seafood and international restaurants, many with stunning views over the Swan River or city, and cantilevered windows that make for a seamless transition between indoor and alfresco dining.

For those on a budget, the noisy fun of a dim sum lunch at one of Perth's many traditional Asian teahouses (especially in Northbridge) is cheap and delicious. Along with a refreshing cup of green tea, you can enjoy steamed pork buns, fried chicken feet, and egg tarts served at your table from the trolley. Food halls in Perth, Northbridge, and Fremantle are other budget options. These one-stop eateries cater to diverse tastes; not all are the same, but you can usually take your pick from stalls selling vegetarian items, roast meats, fresh fruits and juices, Aussie burgers, and fried chicken. Some also serve Southeast Asian, Indian, Japanese, Korean, and Thai cuisine, usually for less than A$10.

CHINESE

$–$$$$ ✕**Yu.** Some of the best Chinese food in the city is served at this elegant casino restaurant. Cantonese flavors predominate under the guidance of chef de cuisine, Pat Cheong, with signature dishes including Peking duck, fillet steak with Szechuan or Cantonese sauce, Portuguese crab, and sea salt prawns. ⊠*InterContinental Perth Burswood, Great Eastern Hwy. at Bolton Ave., Burswood* ☎*08/9362–7551* ☱*AE, DC, MC, V* ⊗*No lunch Sat.*

$$–$$$ ✕**Shun Fung on the River.** Right on the waterfront next to the Swan Bells Tower, this Chinese restaurant has rapidly gained accolades as one of Perth's classiest. There's a huge selection of fresh seafood here, including abalone in oyster sauce, steamed Sydney rock oysters with black bean sauce, and crispy king prawns with spiced salt and chili. Banquet menus (8–10 courses) are a specialty, and an extensive collection of rare vintage wines complements the menu. ⊠*Barrack Sq. Jetty, CBD* ☎*08/9221–1868* ⊕*www.shunfung.com.au* ☱*AE, DC, MC, V.*

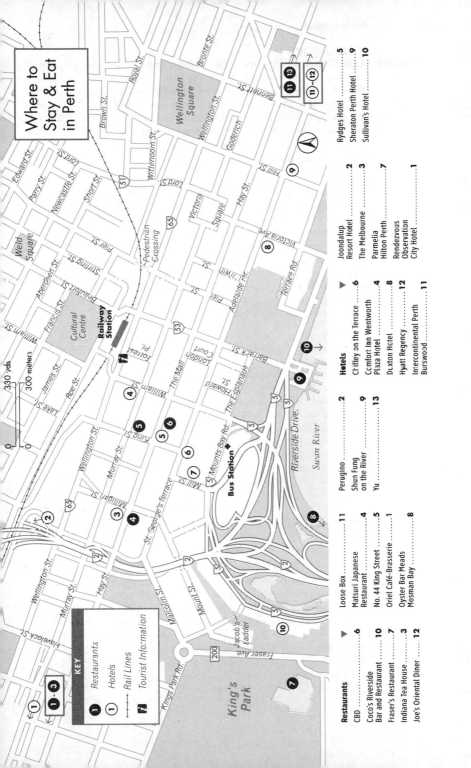

Where to Stay & Eat in Perth

KEY
- **1** Restaurants
- **①** Hotels
- —†— Rail Lines
- **†** Tourist Information

Restaurants ▸

CBD	**6**
Coco's Riverside Bar and Restaurant	**10**
Fraser's Restaurant	**7**
Indiana Tea House	**3**
Joe's Oriental Diner	**12**
Loose Box	**11**
Matsuri Japanese Restaurant	**4**
No. 44 King Street	**5**
Oriel Café-Brasserie	**1**
Oyster Bar Meads	**8**
Mosman Bay	**8**
Perugino	**2**
Shun Fung on the River	**9**
Yu	**13**

Hotels ▸

Critley on the Terrace	**6**
Comfort Inn Wentworth Plaza Hotel	**4**
Duxton Hotel	**8**
Hyatt Regency	**12**
Intercontinental Perth Burswood	**11**
Joondalup Resort Hotel	**2**
The Melbourne	**3**
Parmelia Hilton Perth	**7**
Rendezvous Observation City Hotel	**1**
Rydges Hotel	**5**
Sheraton Perth Hotel	**9**
Sullivan's Hotel	**10**

CONTEMPORARY

$$–$$$ ✕**CBD.** The trendiest place in Perth's West End, this spot has an unusual leaf-shaped bar where both diners and drinkers congregate. The steamed chicken breast, marinated in red bean curd and served with coriander pesto, is one of the most popular dishes, and 24 varieties of table wine and "stickies" (dessert wines) are available by the glass. Late hours bring in the nightcap crowd after shows at the adjacent His Majesty's Theatre. ✉*Hay and King Sts., CBD* ☎*08/9263–1859* ⊕*www.rydges.com/perth* ⊟*AE, DC, MC, V.*

ECLECTIC

$–$$ ✕**Oriel Café-Brasserie.** At this quintessential 24-hour Perth brasserie just outside the city center, both the dimly lighted interior and the outdoor areas are packed with tables, people, and noise. Crowds come for the breakfasts of pancakes with fresh strawberries and clotted cream and maple syrup, eggs Benedict with shaved leg ham, or Bircher muesli with pistachio yogurt and poached vanilla apples. The lunch and dinner menus—which include pea and thyme risotto, pork sausage, garlic mash and balsamic onions, and chicken tikka with coconut rice and pappadums—are equally popular. ✉*483 Hay St., Subiaco* ☎*08/9382–1886* ⚞*Reservations not accepted* ⊟*AE, DC, MC, V.*

FRENCH

$$$$ ✕**Loose Box.** Perth's finest French restaurant is run by owner-chef Alain
Fodor'sChoice Fabregues, who has received France's highest culinary honor, the Meil-
★ leur Ouvrier de France, as well as a French knighthood—Chevalier Dans L'Ordre National du Merite—for his contribution to French culture and cuisine. His degustation menu applies classical French culinary principles to Australia's best seasonal bounty: there's La Couronne d'Escargots Façon Loose Box—a crown made of profiteroles, filled with mushrooms and snails braised in Pernod; and Le Canard à l'Orange—a small breast of duck marinated in orange zest and Cointreau, slow-cooked until tender and served with orange sauce. Each of the rooms here (the restaurant used to be a house) is cozy, intimate, and warm. Accommodations are also available, if you just can't bring yourself to leave. ✉*6825 Great Eastern Hwy., Mundaring, Western Australia, 6073* ☎*08/9295–1787* ⊕*www.loosebox.com.au* ⚞*Reservations essential* ⊟*AE, DC, MC, V* ⊗*Closed Mon., Tues., and last 2 wks July. No lunch Mon.–Sat.*

ITALIAN

$$–$$$ ✕**Perugino.** Chef Giuseppe Pagliaricci takes an imaginative yet simple
★ approach to the cuisine of his native Umbria here. Only the freshest produce is used for such creations as *saltimbocca alla Romana* (scallops of veal topped with Parma ham, panfried with sage and white wine); or *congilio in salmi* (rabbit stew with capers, white wine, and lemon juice). The five-course degustation menu highlights the best of the house. ✉*77 Outram St., West Perth* ☎*08/9321–5420* ⊕*www.perugino.com.au* ⚞*Reservations essential* ⊟*AE, DC, MC, V* ⊗*Closed Sun., Mon. No lunch Sat.*

12

JAPANESE

$–$$ ✕**Matsuri Japanese Restaurant.** Discerning diners fill every table most nights at this contemporary glass-and-steel restaurant. Set at the base of an office tower, Perth's most popular casual Japanese dining spot is famous for its fresh, flavorful, and authentic cuisine. Served with steamed rice, miso soup, salad, and green tea, the sushi and sashimi sets start at A$12 and are an excellent value. House specialties include delicately light tempura vegetables and *una don* (grilled eel in teriyaki sauce). ⊠*Lower level 1, QV1 Bldg., 250 St. George's Terr., CBD* ☎*08/9322–7737* ⊕*www.matsuri.com.au* ▤*AE, DC, MC, V* ⊗*No lunch weekends.*

MODERN AUSTRALIAN

$$–$$$$ ✕**Fraser's Restaurant.** In fair weather the large outdoor area at this King's Park restaurant fills with people enjoying food and views of the city and Swan River. The ever-changing menu highlights daily seafood specials, depending on what's at the local markets, and the wine list is 100% Australian. Look for crispy fried soft-shell crabs with turmeric and pumpkin curry; whitebait fritters with spiced tamarind dipping sauce; chargrilled local rock lobster with lemon butter; or roasted kangaroo loin with potato cake and mushroom lentils. Fraser's has also opened the adjacent **Botanical Cafe** (☎*08/9482–0122*), providing breakfast, lunch, and dinner daily, with mains from A$11 to A$26. ⊠*Fraser Ave., King's Park, West Perth* ☎*08/9481–7100* ⊕*www.frasersrestaurant. com.au* ⌖*Reservations essential* ▤*AE, DC, MC, V.*

$$–$$$$ ✕**Indiana Tea House.** Overlooking the beach at Cottesloe, this opulent restaurant serves food that's as spectacular as the ocean views. The menu emphasizes seafood, but there are choices for landlubbers, too. Highlights are panfried reef fish fillets with tiger prawns in phanang curry, with eggplant and basil; soft shell crab with choy sum and pickled vegetable; duck confit with sautéed potato, baby beetroot, and cabernet sauce; and braised beef cheek in Guinness, with pearl barley and porcini risotto. ⊠*99 Marine Parade, Cottesloe* ☎*08/9385–5005* ⌖*Reservations essential* ▤*AE, DC, MC, V.*

$$–$$$ ✕**Coco's Riverside Bar and Restaurant.** Overlooking the Swan River in South Perth, this restaurant has a menu that changes daily depending on fresh produce. Most items are available in both appetizer and main-course portions. Try the Rottnest calamari with butternut pumpkin, shallots, and almonds; the double-roasted muscovy duckling with caramelized figs; or the home-made pasta with chicken, sun-dried tomatoes, and arugula leaves in a creamy basil sauce. The wine list is extensive and includes many of the best from the Margaret River region. ⊠*Southshore Centre, 85 Esplanade, South Perth* ☎*08/9474–3030* ⊕*www.cocosperth.com* ⌖*Reservations essential* ▤*AE, DC, MC, V.*

$–$$ ✕**No. 44 King Street.** Noted for its cutting-edge modern Australian cuisine served from an open-view kitchen, this restaurant is popular with a see-and-be-seen lunchtime business crowd. The seasonal menu changes weekly. Winter brings savory soups, while the summer menu highlights seafood salads. The coffee, cakes, and wines (70 are available by the glass) are all excellent, and the service is superefficient. ✉ *44 King St., CBD* ☎ *08/9321–4476* ⊟ *AE, DC, MC, V.*

PAN-ASIAN

$–$$ ✗ **Joe's Oriental Diner.** On the street level of the Hyatt Regency Hotel on Adelaide Terrace, Joe's features a wide range of dishes from Indonesia, Thailand, Malaysia, and Singapore. The rattan-and-bamboo decor is reminiscent of the many noodle houses one finds throughout Southeast Asia, and you can watch as meals are prepared in the spectacular open kitchen. Hearty soups and delicious noodle dishes, like *laksa* (rice noodles in a spicy coconut-milk broth with chicken, bean curd, and prawns), are the standouts here. Each dish carries a chili coding indicating its relative spiciness—so you won't breathe fire unless you want to. ✉ *Hyatt Regency, 99 Adelaide Terr., CBD* ☎ *08/9225–1268* ⊟ *AE, DC, MC, V* ☺ *Closed Sun. No lunch Sat.*

SEAFOOD

$$–$$$
Fodor's Choice
★

✗ **Oyster Bar Meads Mosman Bay.** Visitors to this spot can never seem to decide what's more spectacular: the delicious seafood or the gorgeous setting on the Swan River, overlooking yachts and mansions. The hip bar and oyster bar are popular, but the reliably excellent daily menu is the real draw here. While gazing at a squadron of pelicans lazily gliding over the river, you can feast on Abrolhos Island scallops and tiger prawns with chili coriander butter; grilled Rottnest crayfish with garlic prawns and lemon sauce; or boneless sand whiting fillets, lightly fried in a crisp beer batter. Reservations are essential. The restaurant is a 15-minute cab ride from town. ✉ *15 Johnson Parade, Mosman Park, 6012* ☎ *08/9383–4424* ⊕ *www.meads.com.au* ⊟ *AE, DC, MC, V.*

> ## EATING OUT
>
> While there are plenty of top-notch restaurants in and around Perth, it's also possible to eat on the cheap. Northbridge has a plethora of competitively priced restaurants, especially along James Street, and especially at lunchtime. A dim sum lunch at a traditional Asian teahouse is inexpensive and delicious. Food halls in Perth, Northbridge, and Fremantle are another budget option. These one-stop eateries cater to diverse tastes; not all are the same, but you can usually take your pick from stalls selling all sorts of delicious food, usually for less than A$10.

WHERE TO STAY

$$$
★

🛏 **Hyatt Regency.** Within walking distance of Perth's central business district, this hotel on the Swan River is both comfortable and convenient. Standard rooms are spacious, while the higher-priced Regency Club rooms and suites (on the top two floors) have stunning views, complimentary Continental breakfast, and evening drinks and canapés. The Conservatory, a sitting area with tasteful cane furniture and a fountain under a large domed atrium, is a civilized spot for relaxing. ✉ *99 Adelaide Terr., CBD, 6000* ☎ *08/9225–1234* ✉ *hyatt@hrp.com.au* ⊕ *www.perth.hyatt.com* ⇄ *367 rooms, 32 suites* ⚫ *In-*

room: safe, ethernet. In-hotel: 3 restaurants, room service, bars, tennis court, pool, gym, concierge, laundry service, parking (no fee) ⊟AE, DC, MC, V ⍩CP.

$$$ ⊞**Intercontinental Perth Burswood.** From the 10-story glass atrium atop
Fodor's Choice   its pyramid-shaped exterior to its 18-hole golf course, everything about
★   Burswood says "luxury." Spacious rooms have Japanese shoji screens between the bedrooms and bathrooms, as well as views of either the river or the city. Suites have hot tubs. The adjoining casino is one of the largest in the Southern Hemisphere, open around the clock for roulette, blackjack, baccarat, keno, and video games. Seven restaurants within the complex include upscale and buffet-style dining. ⌂Box 500, Victoria Park, Western Australia, 6979 ⊠Great Eastern Hwy. at Bolton Ave., Burswood, 6100 ☎08/9362–7777 or 1800/999667 ⌖reserve@ burswood.com.au ⊕www.burswood.com.au ⌦413 rooms, 16 suites ⌂In-room: ethernet. In-hotel: 7 restaurants, room service, bars, golf course, tennis courts, pools, gym, spa, concierge, laundry service, parking (fee and no fee), no smoking rooms ⊟AE, DC, MC, V.

$$$ ⊞**Parmelia Hilton Perth.** Although Perth's original five-star hotel is now dwarfed by adjacent steel-and-glass office buildings, which obstruct the once-excellent river views from many rooms, the opulence of this hotel is evident from the moment you enter the foyer; rich wood paneling, parquet floors, and many antiques—including Chinese silk tapestries and Mussolini's mirror (near the elevator)—immediately surround you. Many rooms have private balconies. Suites have crystal chandeliers, gilt mirrors, deep-pile carpeting, and luxurious marble bathrooms. There's personal service around the clock, and a 24-hour business center. ⊠14 Mill St., CBD, 6000 ☎08/9215–2000 ⊕www.perth.hilton. com ⌦220 rooms, 62 suites ⌂In-room: ethernet. In-hotel: 2 restaurants, room service, bars, pool, gym, public Wi-Fi, bicycles, concierge, laundry service, parking (fee) ⊟AE, DC, MC, V.

$$$ ⊞**Sheraton Perth Hotel.** Towering above the Swan River, this hotel is one of Perth's best-known five-star hotels. The lobby glitters with glass chandeliers, while the well-appointed rooms are furnished in Tasmanian oak and have sweeping river views. One of the two restaurants, Montereys Brasserie, has lavish breakfasts, and the Lobby Lounge is popular with locals for predinner and preshow drinks: Perth Concert Hall is just a short walk away. ⊠207 Adelaide Terr., CBD, 6000 ☎08/9224–7777 ⌖sheraton_perth@sheraton.com ⊕www.sheraton. com/perth ⌦368 rooms, 18 suites ⌂In-room: safe, dial-up. In-hotel: 2 restaurants, room service, bars, pool, gym, bicycles, concierge, laundry service, parking (fee) ⊟AE, DC, MC, V.

$$–$$$ ⊞**Joondalup Resort Hotel.** Although it's 30 km (19 mi) from Perth's busi-
★   ness district, this palm-shaded building—which resembles a southern plantation owner's mansion—is a comfortable place to relax for a few days, especially if you like golf. Spacious rooms, decorated in subdued pastels and warm tones, all have views over the lagoon or the 27-hole, Robert Trent Jones Jr.–designed golf course. A free shuttle runs daily to the Joondalup train station and Lakeside Shopping Centre. ⊠Country

Club Blvd., Connolly, 6027 ☎*08/9400–8888 or 1800/803488* ✉*hotel@ joondalupresort.com.au* ⊕*www.joondalupresort.com.au* ⇲*68 rooms, 4 suites* ♿*In-room: safe, VCR, Wi-Fi. In-hotel: 2 restaurants, bars, golf courses, tennis courts, pool, gym, laundry service, parking (no fee)* ▭*AE, DC, MC, V.*

$$ 🛏**Chifley on the Terrace.** Amenities at this bright, breezy business hotel— such as in-room Internet connections and spacious baths with aroma- therapy oils—are equal to those found at much pricier establishments. Rooms are furnished in earth tones, and executive suites have open- plan bathrooms with hot tubs. Casual alfresco dining is available at the Chifley Bar and Café, right off the lobby. ✉*185 St. George's Terr., CBD, 6000* ☎*08/9226–3355* ✉reservations.theterrace@chifleyhotels. com ⊕*www.constellationhotels.com* ⇲*73 rooms, 9 suites* ♿*In-room: ethernet. In-hotel: restaurant, bar, laundry service, public Wi-Fi, park- ing (fee)* ▭*AE, DC, MC, V.*

$$ 🛏**Rendezvous Observation City Hotel.** Watching the sun sink into the Indian Ocean from this beachside resort is a memorable experience. Elegant blues and golds decorate the stylish rooms, all of which have superb ocean views. The top three floors offer access to the Club Lounge with complimentary Continental breakfast and drinks at sun- set. You can dine at Savannahs Restaurant or have the buffet for break- fast, lunch, or dinner at Pines Grand Buffet and Carvery. The hotel is 30 minutes from the city center by free shuttle. ✉*Esplanade, Scar- borough Beach, 6019* ☎*08/9245–1000 or 1800/067680* ⊕*www.ren- dezvoushotels.com* ⇲*327 rooms, 6 suites* ♿*In-hotel: 2 restaurants, bars, tennis courts, pool, gym, spa, concierge, parking (no fee)* ▭*AE, DC, MC, V.*

$$ 🛏**Rydges Hotel.** Ultramodern furnishings in chrome, glass, and black leather fill the rooms at this 16-story hotel. Rooms above the 12th floor afford commanding views of the river and city. King executive rooms have floor-to-ceiling windows and goldfish tanks, and Executive Club floors include security-key access and oversize desks with printer, scanner, and fax capabilities. Complimentary membership passes are provided for a private fitness center nearby. ✉*Hay and King Sts., CBD, 6000* ☎*1800/063283* ✉reservations_perth@rydges.com/perth ⊕*www.rydges.com/perth* ⇲*245 rooms, 6 suites* ♿*In-room: ether- net. In-hotel: restaurant, room service, bar, pool, gym, laundry service, parking (fee)* ▭*AE, DC, MC, V.*

$ 🛏**Duxton Hotel.** Adjacent to the Perth Concert Hall, this elegant hotel is ★ within easy walking distance of the city center. Soothing autumn colors, paintings by local artists, and furniture crafted from Australian timber fill the comfortable rooms, some of which have views of the Swan River. The Grill, which opens on to a broad terrace, is open for breakfast, lunch, and dinner, serving an international cuisine, with many wines from Western Australia's premium wine regions. ✉*1 St. George's Terr., CBD, 6000* ☎*08/9261–8000 or 1800/681118* ✉res1@perth.duxton. com.au ⊕*www.duxton.com* ⇲*291 rooms, 15 suites* ♿*In-room: eth- ernet (some). In-hotel: restaurant, room service, bar, pool, gym, pub-*

lic Wi-Fi, *laundry service, parking (no fee)* =AE, DC, MC, V.

$ ⊞ **The Melbourne.** A restored 1890s building listed on the National Heritage Register houses this stylish boutique hotel. The Perth landmark retains all the original design elements of the era, including a grand staircase and elevator, along with contemporary accommodations and facilities. The elegant Melbourne Restaurant serves top-notch Australian cuisine; you can have a drink in the Melbourne Bar, or a snack and coffee at M Café. ⊠ *Hay and Milligan Sts., CBD, 6000* ☎ *08/9320–3333 or 1800/685671* ✎ *sales@melbournehotel.com.au* ⊕ *www.melbournehotel.com.au* ⇦ *34 rooms* ⚴ *In-room: ethernet. In-*

> **ROCKIN' IN PERTH**

Thanks in part to the example of pop, rock, and metal bands like Eskimo Joe, the John Butler Trio, the Waifs, Karnivool, Little Birdy, the Panda Band, and the Sleepy Jackson—who all started in Perth—the music scene here is thriving. Despite their isolation from the rest of Australia, Western Australian musos are turning out some top-notch material. Music commentators say there isn't a "Perth sound," as such, just a talented bunch of artists writing and performing original music. Check out ⊕ www.xpressmag.com.au for an up-to-date guide on live shows.

hotel: restaurant, room service, bar, tennis court, gym, laundry service, parking (no fee) =AE, DC, MC, V.

$ ⊞ **Sullivan's Hotel.** "The guest reigns supreme" seems to be the rule at this family-run hotel opposite waterfront parkland, and handy to the center of Perth and King's Park. The airport shuttle bus stops at the hotel and the city's free Cat buses pass the front door. There are also complimentary bicycles for guests. Rooms are brightly decorated, and the deluxe rooms have balconies with city and parkland views. ⊠ *166 Mounts Bay Rd., CBD, 6000* ☎ *08/9321–8022* ✎ *perth@sullivans.com.au* ⊕ *www.sullivans.com.au* ⇦ *70 rooms* ⚴ *In-hotel: restaurant, bar, pool, public Wi-Fi, bicycles, laundry facilities, parking (no fee)* =AE, DC, MC, V.

¢–$ ⊞ **Comfort Inn Wentworth Plaza Hotel.** This Federation-era inn is one
Fodor'sChoice   of Perth's most centrally located hotels; it's a block away from the
★   Perth Railway Station in one direction and a block from the Hay Street Mall in the other. The rooms here (there are also some two-room apartments) have period decor; downstairs, Bobby Dazzler's is a "true blue" Aussie pub, while Moon and Sixpence serves 30 different international and local beers in the atmosphere of a traditional British pub. ⊠ *300 Murray St., CBD, Perth, WA, 6000* ☎ *08/9481–1000 or 1800/355109* ⊕ *www.wentworthplazahotel.com.au* ⇦ *96 rooms* ⚴ *In-hotel: restaurant, room service, bars, laundry facilities, parking (no fee)* =AE, DC, MC, V.

12

NIGHTLIFE & THE ARTS

Details on cultural events in Perth are published in the comprehensive Saturday edition of the *West Australian*. A free weekly, *X-Press Magazine,* lists music, concerts, movies, entertainment reviews, and who's playing at pubs, clubs, and hotels. *SCOOP* magazine (⊕ *www.scooptraveller.com.au*), published quarterly, is an excellent guide to the essential Western Australian lifestyle.

THE ARTS

BOCS Ticketing (☎ *08/9484–1133*) is the main booking hotline in Perth for the performing arts.

Local talent dominates the arts scene in Perth, although the acclaimed **Perth International Arts Festival (PIAF)** (✉ *University of Western Australia, 3 Crawley Ave., Crawley, 6009* ☎ *08/6488–5555 for information, 9484–1133 for bookings* ⊕ *www.perthfestival.com.au*), held January and February in venues throughout the city, attracts international music, dance, and theater stars. This is Australia's oldest and biggest annual arts festival, and it's been running for more than 50 years. As part of the festival, the PIAF Sunset Cinema Season, adjacent to Winthrop Hall on Mounts Bay Road at the University of Western Australia, screens films outdoors December–March.

BALLET The **West Australian Ballet Company** (✉ *825 Hay St., CBD* ☎ *08/9481–0707* ⊕ *www.waballet.com.au*), one of just three ballet companies in Australia, focuses on classical ballet but also has contemporary ballet and dance in its diverse repertoire. Performances are at His Majesty's Theatre, although you can also see the 20-person troupe at such outdoor venues as the Quarry Amphitheatre (at City Beach) and on country tours. The company also tours nationally and internationally, and has performed in China, Japan, and the Philippines.

The **Perth Concert Hall** (✉ *5 St. George's Terr., CBD* ☎ *08/9231–9900* ⊕ *www.perthconcerthall.com.au*), a modern building overlooking the Swan River, stages regular recitals by the excellent West Australian Symphony Orchestra, as well as Australian and international performers. Adding to the appeal of the fine auditorium is the 3,000-pipe organ surrounded by a 160-person choir gallery.

OPERA The **West Australian Opera Company** (✉ *825 Hay St., CBD* ☎ *08/9278–8999* ⊕ *www.waopera.asn.au*) presents three seasons annually—in April, August, and November—at His Majesty's Theatre. They also perform Opera in the Park in Perth's Supreme Court Gardens each February. The company's repertoire includes classic opera, Gilbert and Sullivan operettas, and occasional musicals.

THEATER The opulent Edwardian **His Majesty's Theatre** (✉ *825 Hay St., CBD* ☎ *08/9494–1133* ⊕ *www.hismajestystheatre.com.au*), opened in 1904, is loved by all who step inside. Home to the West Australian Opera Company and the West Australian Ballet Company, it hosts most theatrical productions in Perth. The **Playhouse Theatre** (✉ *3 Pier St., CBD* ☎ *08/9325–3344* ⊕ *www.playhousetheatre.com.au*) stages local productions. For outdoor performances, the **Quarry Amphitheatre** (✉ *Ocean*

Dr., City Beach ☎ *08/9385–7144* ⊕ *www.quarryamphitheatre. com.au*) is popular, particularly during the Perth International Arts Festival. The **Regal Theatre** (✉ *474 Hay St., at Rokeby Rd., Subiaco* ☎ *08/9484–1133* ⊕ *www.regaltheatre.com.au*) hosts local performances. The **Burswood Theatre** (✉ *Great Eastern Hwy., Burswood* ☎ *08/9362–7777* ⊕ *www.burswood.com.au*) has regular theatrical and musical productions from around Australia.

12

NIGHTLIFE

Most luxury hotels in Perth have upscale nightclubs that appeal to the over-30 crowd. Apart from these, however, nightlife in the city center is virtually nonexistent. Twentysomethings most often head to North-bridge, Subiaco, or Fremantle. Pubs and bars generally close by 11 PM, which is when the crowds start arriving at the nightclubs; these tend to stay open until around 5 AM.

BARS The **Brass Monkey** (✉ *William and James Sts., Northbridge* ☎ *08/9227– 9596* ⊕ *www.thebrassmonkey.com.au*) is in a huge, old, crimson-painted building with potted plants flowing over the antique verandas. There's live stand-up comedy every Wednesday night. On Saturday nights a DJ keeps the music flowing. There's no cover charge. **Carnegie's** (✉ *356 Murray St., at King St., CBD* ☎ *08/9481–3222*), a relaxed, upscale café by day, turns into an attractive pub in the afternoon and then a disco late at night. With rock-and-roll decor, a raised dance floor, and DJs playing music from the 1960s to today's Top 40, the bar attracts an older clientele from the business and tourist sectors. On Tuesday nights, there's a quiz night with prizes, cheaper drinks, and free entry. The **Grosvenor Hotel** (✉ *339 Hay St., CBD* ☎ *08/9325– 3799*) has DJs who spin alternative music; it's popular with the younger crowd. **Lava Lounge** (✉ *1 Rokeby Rd., Subiaco* ☎ *08/9382–8889*) has excellent Mediterranean food and wine, with an alfresco courtyard in summer and a big fireplace for winter. **Queen's Tavern** (✉ *520 Beaufort St., Highgate* ☎ *08/9328–7267*) has an excellent outdoor beer garden. The upstairs bar has a relaxed lounge vibe, with DJs on Thursday and Sunday. The bar at the **Subiaco Hotel** (✉ *465 Hay St., Subiaco* ☎ *08/9381–3069*) attracts a lively after-work crowd during the week, with live rock bands on Thursday and Saturday in Bianca's Bar and live jazz on Wednesday and Saturday in the cocktail bar.

JAZZ & BLUES On Tuesday nights try the **Charles Hotel** (✉ *509 Charles St., North Perth* ☎ *08/9444–1051*) for live blues performances. The **Hyde Park Hotel** (✉ *331 Bulwer St., North Perth* ☎ *08/9328–6166*), a no-nonsense Aussie pub, hosts live entertainment every night, including contemporary jazz and rock bands, soloists, and comedy. The **Universal Bar** (✉ *221 William St., Northbridge* ☎ *08/9227–6771*) has live jazz and blues Wednesday–Sunday 5 PM to late.

NIGHTCLUBS **Club A** (✉ *Esplanade, next to the lookout, Scarborough* ☎ *08/9340– 5735*) is one of the city's top dance spots, attracting 18- to 35-year-olds. The **Hip-e Club** (✉ *663 Newcastle St., Leederville* ☎ *08/9227–8899*), a Perth legend, capitalizes on its hippy-era image with a neon kaleidoscope, 3-D color explosions, murals, and 1960s paraphernalia decorating the walls. Regular surf parties and backpacker nights take place monthly. **Margeaux's** (✉*Parmelia Hilton Perth, 14 Mill St., CBD* ☎*08/9215–2000*) is an upmarket, late-night drinking and dancing venue that's open Wednesday, Friday, and Saturday nights. The **Ruby Room** (✉*Intercontinental Perth Burswood, Great Eastern Hwy. at Bolton Ave., Burswood* ☎*08/9362–7777*) is a glitzy, two-story venue done up with stainless steel and retro fittings. Wednesday through Sunday, the four bars, cozy lounge areas, stage, and dance floor with sound-and-light show are packed with merrymakers. **Varga Lounge** (✉*161 James St., Northbridge* ☎*08/9328–7200*) mixes it up New York–style, with DJs who spin techno, rap, and hip-hop.

SPORTS & THE OUTDOORS

BICYCLING Perth and Fremantle have an extensive and expanding network of bike paths, which means you can ride along the rivers and coast without having to worry about traffic. Most freeways also have separate parallel cycle paths. Bicycle helmets are compulsory. Details on trails and free brochures are available from the **Western Australia Visitor Centre** (✉*Forrest Pl. at Wellington St., CBD* ☎*08/9483–1111, 1300/361351, 61/89483–1111 from outside Australia*). Maps are also available from **BikeWest** (✉*441 Murray St., CBD* ☎*08/9216–8000*).

Limotrikes Australia (✉*4 Rodgers St., Greenwood* ☎*08/9342–4424* ⊕*www.limotrikes.com.au*) offers tours in luxurious, enclosed motortrikes. Prices are from A$300 per hour (minimum one hour).

Outstanding Tours (✉*Box 712, South Perth, WA, 6951* ☎*08/9368–4949* 🖷*08/9367–8612* ⊕*www.outstandingtours.com.au*) has half-day and full-day personalized coach tours, as well as chauffeured rides aboard Harley-Davidson motorcycles from A$90 for one hour.

WATER SPORTS Parasailing is available from the Narrows Bridge on the South Perth shore every weekend from October to May, weather and winds permitting. It's A$80 for a single for 15 minutes and A$140 tandem. Contact **South Perth Parasailing** (✉*Narrows Bridge, South Perth* ☎*0408/382595*). If you want to enjoy the Swan River at a leisurely pace, rent a catamaran or a sailboard from **Funcats Surfcat Hire** (✉*Coode St. Jetty, South Perth* ☎*08/9387–4336 or 0408/926003*). It costs A$28 per hour; reservations are essential on weekends. Funcats operates from October to April.

CATCHING WAVES

Western Australians have a love affair with the beach. During the summer months, you'll find thousands of them lazing on sandy beaches, swimming, and surfing. There are popular beaches on Perth's doorstep, but serious board surfers will head south to the rugged coastline from Cape Naturaliste to Cape Leeuwin. Favorite surf breaks are Surfer's Point, Lefthanders, Three Bears, Grunters, the Bommie, Moses Rock, the Guillotine, the Farm, Barnyards, Suicides, and Supertubes. There are some 50 recognized surf breaks along this coast. Check out ⊕www.oceanoutlook.com.au for up-to-date surf reports.

SURFING Western Australians take to the surf from a young age—and with world-famous surfing beaches right on the city's doorstep, it's no wonder. The most popular year-round beaches for body and board surfing are Scarborough and Trigg, where swells usually reach 6–9 feet, and occasionally rear up to 12 feet. There are also more than a dozen beaches heading north from Leighton (near Fremantle), including the Cables Artificial Reef (near Leighton), and Watermans (in the northern suburbs of Perth).

If you venture outside the city, Rottnest also has good surf, and if you head south on the coast, you'll find more than 20 surf locations from Cape Naturaliste to Cape Leeuwin. The Main Break at Margaret River is the best known, where waves often roll in at more than 12–15 feet, setting the scene for the annual Margaret River Pro, a world-qualifying series event held in late March at Surfers Point. Western Australia's top board surfers head to Scarborough in August for the final round of the state competition. Wet suits are de rigueur for the winter months (May–September), when the surf is usually at its best.

SHOPPING

Shopping in Perth, with its pedestrian-friendly central business district, vehicle-free malls, and many covered arcades, is a delight. Hay Street Mall and Murray Street Mall are the main city shopping areas, linked by numerous arcades with small shops. In the suburbs, top retail strips include Napoleon Street in Cottesloe (for clothing and cooking items), Hampden Road in Nedlands (for crafts), and Beaufort Street in Mount Lawley (for antiques).

MALLS & ARCADES
Forrest Place, flanked by the post office and the Forrest Chase Shopping Plaza, is the largest mall area in the city. **David Jones** (☎ *08/9210–4000*) department store opens onto the Murray Street pedestrian mall. **Myer** (✉ *Murray St. Mall at Forrest Pl.* ☎ *08/9265–5600*) is a popular department store that carries goods and sundries. The **Hay Street Mall**, running parallel to Murray Street and linked by numerous arcades, is another extensive shopping area. Make sure you wander through the arcades that connect Hay and Murray streets, such as **Carillion Arcade**, which have many more shops.

AUSTRALIANA
Australian souvenirs and knickknacks are on sale at small shops throughout the city and suburbs. **Looking East** (✉ *Unit 3, 160 Hampden Rd., Nedlands* ☎ *08/9389–5569*) sells contemporary, minimalist Aussie clothing, furnishings, and pottery. **Purely Australian Clothing Company** (✉ *731 Hay St., CBD* ☎ *08/9321–4697* ✉ *38 London Ct., CBD* ☎ *08/9325–4328* ⊕ *www.purelyaustralian.com*) carries the most comprehensive selection of Oz-abilia in Perth, with stores in London Court and Hay Street Mall. **R. M. Williams** (✉ *Carillon Arcade, Hay St. Mall, CBD* ☎ *08/9321–7786* ⊕ *www.rmwilliams.com.au*) sells everything

for the Australian bushman, including moleskin pants, hand-tooled leather boots, and Akubra hats.

CRAFTS

FORM: Contemporary Craft and Design (⊠ *King St. Arts Centre, 357–365 Murray St., CBD* ☎*08/9226–2161*) carries a large selection of Western Australian crafts and giftware from established and emerging artists, including some Aboriginal art, jewelry, metal, ceramics, glass, textiles, and wood. You can find authentic Aboriginal artifacts at **Creative Native** (⊠*32 King St., CBD* ☎*08/9322–3398* ⊕*www.creativenative. com.au*); the Dreamtime Gallery, upstairs, is one of Australia's finest. Each piece of original artwork comes with a certificate of authenticity. A former car dealer's workshop has been transformed into the Outback at **Indigenart** (⊠*115 Hay St., Subiaco* ☎*08/9388–2899* ⊕*www. indigenart.com.au*), an art gallery–cum–Aboriginal culture center where you can view works and talk with the Aboriginal creators. They also have an **outlet** (⊠*82 High St., Fremantle* ☎*08/9335–2911*). **Maalia Mia** (⊠*10070 W. Swan Rd., Henley Brook* ☎*08/9296–0704* ⊕*www. maalimia.com.au*), an Aboriginal-owned and -operated cultural center, art gallery, and gift shop, sells art and artifacts purchased only from Aboriginal artists. Boomerangs, didgeridoos, and clapping sticks are made on-site.

GEMS

Opals from South Australia's Coober Pedy are available at **Costello's** (⊠*5–6 London Ct., CBD* ☎*08/9325–8588* ⊕*www.costellos.com.au*). **Linneys** (⊠*37 Rokeby Rd., Subiaco* ☎*08/9382–4077* ⊕*www.linneys. com.au*), whose designers and craftspeople have won national awards, carries an excellent selection of Broome pearls, Argyle diamonds, and Kalgoorlie gold, and will set the gems and pearls in the design of your choice. **Rosendorf's** (⊠*673 Hay St. Mall, CBD* ☎*08/9321–4015*), regarded as Perth's premier diamond jeweler, specializes in white and colored diamonds. They also have outlets in Karrinyup and Garden City shopping centers in the suburbs.

PERTH ESSENTIALS

TRANSPORTATION

BY AIR

Perth International Airport has two separate terminals. The domestic terminal is about 11 km (7 mi) from Perth, and the international terminal is about 16 km (10 mi) from the city. International airlines serving Perth International Airport include: Air New Zealand, Air Mauritius, Garuda Indonesia Airways, Qantas, Singapore Airlines, Cathay Pacific, Emirates, Malaysia Airline Systems, Thai Airways International, and South African Airlines. Qantas and Virgin Blue connect Perth to other Australian capital cities. Qantaslink and Skywest connect Perth with other towns in the state.

Taxis are available at the airport 24 hours a day. Trips to the city cost about A$33 and take around a half hour. Shuttle buses run

12

between terminals (A$8), as well as to hotels in Perth and nearby suburbs (A$15).

Airlines Air Mauritius (☎ 08/9486–9133 ⊕ www.airmauritius.com). **Air New Zealand** (☎ 1800/147332 ⊕ www.airnewzealand.com). **Cathay Pacific** (☎ 13–1747 ⊕ www.cathaypacific.com/au). **Emirates** (☎ 1300/303777 ⊕ www.emirates.com/au). **Garuda Indonesia Airways** (☎ 08/9214–5101 ⊕ www.garuda-indonesia.com). **Malaysia Airline Systems** (☎ 13–2627 ⊕ www.malaysiaairlines.com.au). **Qantas/Qantaslink** (☎ 13–1313 ⊕ www.qantas.com.au). **Singapore Airlines** (☎ 13–1011 ⊕ www.singaporeair.com.au). **Skywest** (☎ 1300/660088 ⊕ www.skywest.com.au). **South African Airways** (☎ 08/9216–2200 ⊕ www.flysaa.com). **Thai Airways International** (☎ 08/9488–9201 ⊕ www.thaiairways.com.au). **Tiger Airways** (⊕ www.tigerairways.com.au). **Virgin Blue** (☎ 13–6789 ⊕ www.virginblue.com.au).

Airport & Shuttles Airport City Shuttles (☎ 08/9277–7958) operates frequent coach services from both terminals to Perth city hotels, as well as between the airport terminals. The cost between terminals is A$8, and to downtown Perth is A$15 (unless prepaid with your air ticket).

BY BIKE

Perth's climate and its network of excellent trails make cycling a safe and enjoyable way to discover the city. But beware: summer temperatures can exceed 40°C (100°F) in the shade. A bicycle helmet is required by law, and carrying water is prudent. About Bike Hire, which rents bikes for A$30 a day or A$60 a week, is open Monday through Saturday 10–5 and Sunday 9–5. Free brochures detailing trails, including stops at historic spots, are available from the Western Australia Visitor Centre.

Contact About Bike Hire (⊠ Behind Causeway Car Park, Riverside Dr. ☎ 08/9221–2665 ⊕ www.aboutbikehire.com.au).

BOAT & FERRY TRAVEL

Transperth ferries make daily runs from 6:50 AM to 7:15 PM between Barrack Street Jetty in Perth to Mends Street, across the Swan River in South Perth. Reduced service runs on weekends and holidays.

Contact Transperth (☎ 13–6213 ⊕ www.transperth.wa.gov.au).

BY BUS

Greyhound Australia buses are routed through the Public Transport Authority terminal in East Perth. It's 60 hours to Darwin, 36 hours to Adelaide, 48 hours to Melbourne, and 60 hours to Sydney. TransWA has interstate train and bus services.

Contacts Greyhound Australia (☎ 1300/4739–46863 ⊕ www.greyhound.com.au). **Public Transport Authority** (⊠ W. Parade, East Perth ☎ 13–6213 ⊕ www.pta.wa.gov.au). **TransWA** (⊠ E. Perth Terminal, W. Parade, East Perth ☎ 1300/662205).

BUS TRAVEL WITHIN PERTH The Perth central business district and suburban areas are well connected by the Transperth line. The main terminals are at Perth Central Bus Station on Mounts Bay Road and at Wellington Street Bus Station.

Transperth tickets are valid for two hours and can be used on Transperth trains and ferries. Buses run daily 6 AM–11:30 PM, with reduced service on weekends and holidays. Rides within the city center are free. CAT (Central Area Transit) buses circle the city center, running approximately every 10 minutes weekdays 7–6 and Saturday 9–5. Routes and timetables are available from Transperth.

Contact **Transperth** (☏ 13–6213 ⊕ www.transperth.wa.gov.au).

BY CAR

The Eyre Highway crosses the continent from Port Augusta in South Australia to Western Australia's transportation gateway, Norseman. From there, take the Coolgardie–Esperance Highway north to Coolgardie, and the Great Eastern Highway on to Perth. Driving to Perth— 2,580 km (1,600 mi) and 30 hours from Adelaide, and 4,032 km (2,500 mi) and 56 hours from Sydney—is an arduous journey, which should be undertaken only with a car (and mental faculties) in top condition. Spare tires and drinking water are essential. Service stations and motels are spaced at regular intervals along the route.

Driving in Perth is relatively easy; just remember to stay on the left-hand side of the road. Peak traffic hours are 7:30 AM–9 AM heading into Perth and 4:30 PM–6 PM heading away from the city center. Country roads are generally well maintained and have little traffic. There are no freeways and few two-lane highways outside the Perth metropolitan area. "Self-Drive Tours Within WA," a free 72-page booklet that suggests itineraries around Perth, Fremantle, and the state, is available from the Western Australia Visitor Centre and major car-rental companies.

All major car-rental companies have branches at the international and domestic airport terminals. A good budget alternative is Network Car Rentals, which can arrange airport pickup and drop-off.

Contacts **Avis** (☏ 08/9325–7677 or 13–6333 ⊕ www.avis.com.au). **Budget Rent A Car** (☏ 1300/362848 ⊕ www.budgetwa.com.au). **Hertz** (☏ 13–3039 ⊕ www.hertz. com.au). **Network Car Rentals** (☏ 1800/736825 ⊕ www.1800rentals.com.au).

BY TAXI

Cab fare between 6 AM and 6 PM weekdays is an initial A$3.30 plus $A1.35 every 1 km (½ mi). From 6 PM to 6 AM and on weekends the rate rises to A$4.80 plus A$1.35 per 1 km (½ mi).

Contacts **Black & White** (☏ 13–1008). **Swan Taxis** (☏ 13–1330).

BY TRAIN

Crossing the Nullarbor Plain from the eastern states is one of the great rail journeys of the world. Great Southern Railways' *Indian Pacific* makes three-day runs from Sydney on Saturday and Wednesday and two-day runs from Adelaide on Sunday and Thursday.

TransWA trains cover routes in Western Australia, including the *Prospector* to Kalgoorlie, the *Australind* to Bunbury, and the *Avonlink* to Northam. Transperth trains provide a quick, easy way to get around the city. Fastrak trains run from Perth to Armadale, Clarkson, Fremantle, and Midland. The east–west line runs to Midland and Fremantle, while the north line runs to Joondalup, and the southeast line runs to Armadale. Perth to Fremantle takes about 30 minutes. All suburban trains stop at the station on Wellington Street in downtown Perth. Tickets must be purchased at vending machines before boarding.

Contacts Great Southern Railway (⊠ *422 King William St., Adelaide, SA, 5000* ☏ *13-2147* ⊕ *gsr.com.au*). **Transperth** (⊠ *E. Perth terminal, W. Parade, East Perth* ☏ *13-6213* ⊕ *www.transperth.wa.gov.au*). **TransWA** (⊠ *E. Perth Terminal, W. Parade, East Perth* ☏ *08/9326-2600* ⊕ *www.transwa.wa.gov.au*).

CONTACTS & RESOURCES

EMERGENCIES

In an emergency, dial **000** to reach an ambulance, the police, or the fire department.

Perth Dental Emergencies recommends private practitioners for emergency service. Royal Perth Hospital has a 24-hour emergency room.

Contacts Perth Dental Emergencies (⊠ *419 Wellington St., upper walkway level, Forrest Chase opposite Perth Railway Station, CBD* ☏ *08/9221-2777*). **Police** (☏ *13-1444 (assistance), 08/9222-1111 (general inquiries*). **Royal Perth Hospital** (⊠ *Victoria Sq., East Perth* ☏ *08/9224-2244*).

TOURS

Australian Pacific Touring, Australian Pinnacle Tours, and Feature Tours conduct day tours of Perth and its major attractions. You can also take a day tour of outer sights like Nambung National Park and the Pinnacles, Wave Rock near Hyden, and the Treetop Walk near Walpole.

Boat Torque runs excursions to Rottnest Island three times daily from Perth and five times daily from Fremantle; they also have Swan River cruises, and whale-watching trips between September and late November.

Captain Cook Cruises has trips on the Swan River, traveling from Perth to the Indian Ocean at Fremantle. Cruises cost A$18–A$130 and may include meals and wine. Oceanic Cruises runs several boat cruises, including tours of the Swan River with stops at wineries. Golden Sun Cruises also has tours upriver to the vineyards, as well as trips to Fremantle.

West Coast Rail and Coach uses trains and buses in conjunction with local operators to provide tours to such popular destinations as Margaret River, Bunbury, Busselton, Esperance, Walpole, Kalbarri, Albany, and Kalgoorlie.

Springtime in Western Australia (September–November) is synonymous with wildflowers, as 8,000 species blanket an area that stretches

645 km (400 mi) north and 403 km (250 mi) south of Perth. Tours of these areas, by companies such as Feature Tours, are popular, and early reservations are essential.

Orientation & Wildflower Tours Australian Pacific Touring (☎ *1300/655965* ⊕ *www.aptouring.com.au*). **Australian Pinnacle Tours** (☎ *08/9471–5555* ⊕ *www.pinnacletours.com.au*). **Feature Tours** (☎ *08/9475–2900* ⊕ *www.ft.com.au*).

Boat Tours Boat Torque (⊠ *Barrack St. Ferry Terminal, CBD* ☎ *08/9430–5844* ⊕ *www.boattorque.com.au*). **Captain Cook Cruises** (⊠ *Pier 3, Barrack Sq. Jetty, CBD* ☎ *08/9325–3341* ⊕ *www.captaincookcruises.com.au*). **Golden Sun Cruises** (⊠ *Pier 4, Barrack Sq. Jetty, CBD* ☎ *08/9325–9916* ⊕ *www.goldensuncruises.com.au*). **Oceanic Cruises** (⊠ *Pier 5, Barrack Sq. Jetty, CBD* ☎ *08/9325–1191* ⊕ *www.oceaniccruises.com.au*).

Bus Tour West Coast Rail and Coach (☎ *08/9221–9522*).

VISITOR INFORMATION
Contacts City of Perth Information Kiosk (⊠ *Murray St. Mall at Forrest Pl., CBD*). **Western Australia Visitor Centre** (⊠ *Forrest Pl. at Wellington St., CBD, 6000* ☎ *08/9483–1111, 1300/361351, 61/89483–1111 from outside Australia* ⊕ *www.westernaustralia.com*).

FREMANTLE & ROTTNEST ISLAND

The second-largest city on the west coast, Fremantle is also the jewel in Western Australia's crown. The major state port since Europeans first settled here in the early 1800s, the town basks in its maritime heritage. This is a city where locals know each other, and everyone smiles and says "hello" as they pass in the street. It's also a good jumping-off point for a day trip to Rottnest Island, where lovely beaches, rocky coves, and unique wallaby-like inhabitants called quokkas are among the charms.

FREMANTLE

About 19 km (12 mi) southwest of Perth.

Modern Fremantle is a far cry from the barren, sandy plain that greeted the first wave of English settlers back in 1829, at the newly constituted Swan River Colony. Most were city dwellers, and after five months at sea in sailing ships, they landed on salt-marsh flats that sorely tested their fortitude. Living in tents, with packing cases for chairs, they found no edible crops, and the nearest fresh water was a distant 51 km (32 mi)—and a tortuous trip up the salty waters of the

Swan. As a result they soon moved the settlement upriver to the vicinity of present-day Perth.

Fremantle remained the location of the seaport, however, and it is to this day Western Australia's premier port. Local architects have brought about a stunning transformation of the town without defacing the colonial streetscape or its fine limestone buildings. In the leafy suburbs nearly every other house is a restored 19th-century gem.

Like all great port cities, Freo (as the locals call it) is cosmopolitan, with mariners from all parts of the world strolling the streets—including 20,000 U.S. Navy personnel on rest and recreation throughout the year. There are plenty of interesting (and sometimes eccentric) residents, who find the mood of Freo much more interesting than the coastal suburbs north and south of the city.

An ideal place to start a leisurely stroll around town is South Terrace, known as the Fremantle cappuccino strip. Soak up the ambience as you wander alongside locals through sidewalk cafés or browse in bookstores, art galleries, and souvenir shops. No matter how aimlessly you meander, you'll invariably end up where you began.

Between Phillimore Street and Marine Terrace in the West End is a collection of some of the best-preserved heritage buildings in the state. The Fremantle Railway Station on Elder Place is another good place to start a walk.

Outside the port gates on the western end of town is **Arthur's Head,** a limestone cliff with cottages built to house employees of the Customs Department. Nearby **J-Shed** contains the workshop of perhaps the nation's foremost exponent of public art, the sculptor Greg James. His extraordinarily lifelike figures grace a number of Perth and metropolitan sites, including King's Square.

Seagulls squawk overhead, boat horns blare in the distance, and the tangy scent of the sea permeates the air along **Marine Terrace.** Walk across Esplanade Park to Mews Road where you can visit the **Kidogo Arthouse,** a gallery and arts center, or linger over fresh fish-and-chips as you watch the tide roll in from the old seawall. Or you can just dangle your feet from the wooden jetty that was rebuilt on the spot where it stood in the days of tall ships.

Like most of Fremantle, the fine, Gothic Revival **Fremantle Museum and Arts Centre** was built by convicts in the 19th century. First used as a lunatic asylum, by 1900 it was overcrowded and nearly shut down. It became a home for elderly women until 1942, when the U.S. Navy made it into its local headquarters. Artifacts trace the early days of Fremantle's settlement in one wing, while another wing houses the **Arts Centre.** The complex contains a restaurant and gift shop, and Sunday-afternoon courtyard concerts are a regular feature. ⊠ *Ord and Finnerty Sts.* ☎ *08/9430–7966, 08/9432–9555 Arts Centre* ✆ *Donation suggested in museum, Arts Centre free* ☉ *Museum Sun.–Fri. 10:30–4:30, Sat. 1–5. Arts Centre daily 10–5.*

The former **Fremantle Prison,** built in 1855, is where 44 inmates met their fate on the prison gallows between 1888 and 1964. Tours include the classic-art cell, where a superb collection of drawings by convict James Walsh decorates his quarters. Reservations are essential for the 90-minute Torchlight Tours (evening tours by flashlight). For the 2½-hour Tunnel Tour, visitors are provided with hard hats, overalls, boots, and headlamps before descending 65 feet into the labyrinthine tunnels which run beneath the prison. Reservations essential. ⊠*1 The Terr.* ☏*08/9336–9200* ⊕*www.fremantleprison.com* ✉*A$16, including a 75-min tour every 30 mins. Torchlight Tour A$20, Tunnel Tour A$55* ⊙*Daily 10–5; last tour at 5* PM. *Torchlight Tours Wed. and Fri., every 20 mins from 7* PM *on demand; last tour usually 9* PM. *Tunnel Tour every hr 9* AM*–3:20* PM.

The **Fremantle Market,** housed in a classic Victorian building, sells everything from potatoes to paintings, incense to antiques, and sausages to Chinese takeout from around 150 stalls. On weekends and public holidays the market can get crowded, but a small café and bar make it a wonderful place to refresh yourself while buskers and street musicians entertain. ⊠*South Terr. at Henderson St.* ☏*08/9335–2515* ⊕*www.fremantlemarkets.com.au* ⊙*Fri. 9–9, Sat. 9–5, Sun. and public holidays 10–5.*

For a glimpse of local color, wander through **High Street Mall,** in the center of the business district. This pedestrian mall is the haunt of people from all walks of Fremantle life, including retired Italian fishermen who now while away their days in conversation ⊠*High, Market, William, and Adelaide Sts..*

One of the oldest commercial heritage–listed structures in Western Australia is **Moores' Building,** an exhibition and performance space run by the Artist Foundation of WA. ⊠*46 Henry St.* ☏*08/9335–8366* ✉*Donation suggested* ⊙*Exhibitions daily 10–5.*

A landmark of early Fremantle atop the limestone cliff known as Arthur's Head, the **Round House** was built in 1831 by convicts to house other convicts. This curious, 12-sided building is the state's oldest surviving structure. From its ramparts there are great vistas of High Street out to the Indian Ocean. Underneath, a tunnel was carved through the cliffs in the mid-1800s to give ships lying at anchor offshore easy access from town. Volunteer guides are on duty during opening hours. ⊠*West end of High St.* ☏*08/9336–6897* ✉*Donation suggested* ⊙*Daily 10:30–3:30.*

Bounded by High, Queen, and William streets, **King's Square** is at the heart of the central business district. Shaded by 100-year-old Moreton Bay fig trees, it makes a perfect place for a rest. Medieval-style benches complete the picture of European elegance. Bordering the square are **St. John's Anglican Church** and the **town hall.**

C The **Spare Parts Puppet Theatre,** which stages imaginative productions for children several times a year, has an international reputation and regularly tours abroad. The foyer is a showplace for its puppetry. ⊠*1*

Short St., opposite railway station
☎*08/9335–5044* ⊕*www.sppt.
asn.au* ✉*Free* ☾*Daily 9–5.*

Fodor'sChoice The **Western Australian Maritime**
★ **Museum,** which resembles an
☾ upside-down boat, sits at the edge
of Fremantle Harbour. It houses
Australia 11, winner of the 1983
America's Cup, and the hands-
on exhibits are great fun for children. You can also take one-hour
guided tours of the adjacent submarine *Ovens,* a former Royal
Australian Navy World War II
submarine. The Shipwreck Gallery
houses the recovered remains of the
Dutch wrecks, including the *Bata-
via* (wrecked offshore in 1629),
and the 1872 SS *Xantho* steamer.
✉*Maritime Museum: west end of
Victoria Quay; Shipwreck Gallery:
Cliff St.* ☎*08/9431–8444 museum,
08/9431–8444 gallery* ⊕*www.
museum.wa.gov.au/maritime* ✉*Museum A$10 day pass, museum and
Ovens A$15, gallery free* ☾*Museum and gallery daily 9:30–5, Ovens
Fri.–Sun. and school holidays 10–4:30.*

WANDERING THROUGH FREMANTLE

The best way to experience Fremantle is on foot. Most of the
sights are clustered within a few
blocks in the west of the city. Get
yourself some fish-and-chips at
one of several outlets at the Fishing Boat Harbour, and sit along
the boardwalk to watch the waterfront activities. Then walk across
Esplanade Park to Marine Terrace,
and up Essex Street to South
Terrace—the city's cappuccino
strip and a great place to enjoy
Fremantle's Markets, craft shops,
trendy bars, and people watching.
Circle back westwards to the Maritime Museum, Roundhouse, and E
Shed Markets at Victoria Quay.

**OFF THE
BEATEN
PATH**

Mandurah. Just 94 km (59 mi) south of Fremantle is this charming city
set along the horseshoe-shaped Peel Inlet. Strolling along the scenic
boardwalk, dining at stylish restaurants, and cruising the more than
150 square km (60 square mi) of inland waterways are among the
attractions here. See **www.visitmandurah.com** for information about
Mandurah and the surrounding area.

WHERE TO EAT

$$–$$$ ✕**Joe's Fish Shack.** Fremantle's quirkiest restaurant looks like everyone's
vision of a run-down, weather-beaten Maine diner. With uninterrupted
harbor views, authentic nautical bric-a-brac, and great food, you can't
go wrong. Recommendations include the salt-and-pepper squid, stuffed
tiger prawns, and chili mussels. An outdoor dining area provides restaurant food at take-out prices. ✉*42 Mews Rd.* ☎*08/9336–7161*
⊕*www.joesfishshack.com.au* ⊟*AE, DC, MC, V.*

$–$$$ ✕**The Essex.** This 1886 cottage is one of the top places for upscale din-
★ ing in Western Australia. Its elegant dining room has flickering can-
dlelight, plush carpets, and antiques, and the fresh local seafood is
top-notch. Head chef Mark Spencer offers an extensive menu, includ-
ing grilled fillet of beef with local scallops, topped with garlic cream
sauce. Adventurous diners can opt for grilled Balmain bugs—not
insects but the delicious tails of rock-lobsterlike crustaceans caught in
ocean waters around Australia and New Zealand—a specialty of the

region. The extensive wine list includes some of Australia's best vintages. ✉*20 Essex St.* ☎*08/9335–5725* ⊕*www.essexrestaurant.com.au* ▭*AE, DC, MC, V.*

$–$$ ✕**Capri Restaurant.** You may need to wait for a table, but the complimentary minestrone and crusty bread will tide you over at this Fremantle institution. You'll likely get a warm welcome from the Pizzale family, who have owned and run the restaurant for more than 50 years, before you sit down to fried calamari, panfried scaloppine in white wine, rich spaghetti Bolognese, and fresh salads. Simple white-linen tablecloths, carafes of chilled water, and the sounds of laughter and clinking glasses round out the experience. This is old-style Fremantle at its best. ✉*21 South Terr.* ☎*08/9335–1399* ▭*MC, V.*

$–$$ ✕**Cicerello's.** No visit to Fremantle is complete without a stop at this locally famous and widely beloved fish-and-chip shop. Housed in a boathouse-style building fronting the famous Fishing Boat Harbour, this place serves the real thing: freshly caught oysters, mussels, crabs, fish, lobsters, and chips, all wrapped up in butcher paper (no cardboard boxes or plastic plates here). While you eat, you can check out the huge aquarium, where more than 50 species of Fremantle marine life are on display. ✉*Fisherman's Wharf, 44 Mews Rd.* ☎*08/9335–1911* ⊕*www.cicerellos.com.au* ▭*No credit cards.*

$–$$ ✕**Gino's Café.** There are 21 different ways to take your coffee at this hot, cappuccino-strip property with its alfresco terrace. Among the most popular drinks are the house coffee (Gino's Blend), and the Baby Chino—a froth of milk dusted with chocolate powder that young children love. Gino's opens at 6 AM to serve coffee, then cooked breakfasts from 7. Later in the day more than two dozen different pasta dishes are also available, including a superb Penne alla Vodka with chicken. ✉*South Terr. at Collie St.* ☎*08/9336–1464* ⊕*www.ginoscafe.com. au* ▭*MC, V.*

$ ✕**Istanbul Turkish Restaurant.** This bright, breezy street-front venue serves specialties from the Turkish cities of Samsun, Adana, and Iskendar. A secret of this restaurant's success is the fresh-baked Turkish flat bread that accompanies every meal. Start with one of the traditional dips— hummus, eggplant, or potato—then move on to delicacies like grilled lamb and *burek* (meat- or vegetable-stuffed pastries). Kavuma chicken, a house specialty, is grilled with peppers and served with tabbouleh and steamed rice. Save room for sweet, sticky baklava. Traditional music and belly dancing are performed Friday and Saturday nights. ✉*19B Essex St.* ☎*08/9335–6068* ▭*MC, V* 🍴*BYO* ⊘*Closed Mon.*

WHERE TO STAY

$$$$ ▥**Esplanade Hotel Fremantle.** Part of a colonial-era hotel, this establishment has provided accommodations (with sea views) for more than a century. The property is geared toward business travelers, and the stylish, bright pastel rooms have desks and in-room broadband. It's just a short walk to the heart of Fremantle's cappuccino strip and markets. Café Panache, right on the Esplanade, draws crowds all day, while the Atrium Garden Restaurant has a lavish buffet. ✉*Marine Terr. at*

Essex St., 6160 ☎*08/9432–4000 or 1800/998201* ✐*reservations@ ehf.com.au* ⊕*www.esplanade hotelfremantle.com.au* ⇥*293 rooms, 7 suites* ⎈*In-room: ethernet. In-hotel: 2 restaurants, pools, concierge, laundry service, parking (fee)* ▤*AE, DC, MC, V.*

$–$$ ▦**Fothergills of Fremantle.** Antiques and Italian pottery furnish this two-story, 1892 limestone terrace house opposite the old Fremantle prison. Food and service are excellent here, and although the house is some distance from the waterfront, the balconies afford harbor and sunset views. Breakfast in the elegant Provençal-style dining room is included. ✉*20–22 Ord St., 6160* ☎*08/9335–6784* ✐fotherg@iinet.net.au ⊕*www. babs.com.au/fothergills* ⇥*4 rooms* ⎈*In-room: refrigerator. In-hotel: restaurant, laundry facilities* ▤*AE, DC, MC, V* ⎊*BP.*

THE CUP

In 1848, Britain's Queen Victoria authorized the creation of a solid silver cup for a yacht race that would be "open to all nations." In 1851, the New York Yacht Club challenged 16 English yachts and won with the boat *America*. The U.S. continued to win for 132 years straight until the upstart *Australia 11* won 4–3 in sensational style, and the Cup came to Fremantle. Australia was euphoric. Fremantle spruced up for the defense of the Cup in 1987, but the fairy-tale ended in a 4–0 loss to the San Diego Yacht Club entrant. Today, *Australia 11* is a centerpiece display at the WA Maritime Museum.

12

$–$$ ▦**Fremantle Prison Cottages.** These restored colonial-style cottages are conveniently next to the old Fremantle prison, just a few minutes' walk from town. Rooms here are cozy, furnished in colonial style with lace curtains at the windows, eiderdown quilts on the antique wrought-iron beds, and Victorian-era lamp shades. Each has a kitchen and laundry facilities, with modern touches including TVs and microwave ovens. ✉*215 High St., 6160* ☎*08/9430–6568* ⊕*www.fremantlecolonialaccommodation.com.au* ⇥*3 cottages* ⎈*In-room: kitchen. In-hotel: laundry facilities, parking (no fee)* ▤*AE, DC, MC, V.*

$ ▦**Rosie O'Grady's Fremantle.** The restored heritage rooms of this Irish-theme, landmark Australian pub offer comfy lodging right in the middle of town. The deluxe rooms are spacious, and furnished with heavy pine furniture and floral print upholstery and bedspreads. Bars and a restaurant are right downstairs. ✉*23 William St., 6160* ☎*08/9335– 1645* ⊕*www.rosieogradys.com.au* ⇥*17 rooms* ⎈*In-hotel: restaurant, bars, no elevator* ▤*AE, DC, MC, V.*

NIGHTLIFE

There's nothing more pleasant than relaxing in the evening at one of the sidewalk tables on the cappuccino strip. This area, along South Terrace, opens at 6 AM and closes around 3 AM.

Dome Cafe (✉*13 South Terr.* ☎*08/9336–3040*) is a big, airy space that gets a little frantic at busy periods. **Little Creatures** (✉*40 Mews Rd.* ☎*08/9430–5555*) is a funky bar and restaurant surrounded by a gleaming state-of-the-art microbrewery. The industrial-style warehouse building, which overlooks Fremantle's busy harbor, spills into a courtyard. The Pale Ale was voted as Australia's best craft beer (microbrewery beer) in 2003 by members of Australia's liquor industry. It's open Monday–Friday 10 AM–midnight; Saturday and Sunday 9 AM–midnight.

Away from the waterfront, **Rosie O'Grady's** (⊠*23 William St.* ☎*08/9335–1645*) is as Irish as it gets in the heart of Fremantle. Locals come for the numerous draft beers and filling food, as well as nightly live music. Thanks to its selection of home-brewed beers, the **Sail and Anchor Pub–Brewery** (⊠*64 South Terr.* ☎*08/9335–8433*) is a popular watering hole. A shady courtyard beer garden makes a fair-weather gathering place.

Fremantle's classiest nightclub, the **Clink** (⊠*14–16 South Terr.* ☎*08/9336–1919*), caters to a well-dressed, sophisticated clientele Friday–Sunday. The industrial-style decor reflects the building's heritage— it used to be the police station with prison cells. Many local bands and soloists owe their big breaks to **Fly By Night Musicians Club** (⊠*1 Holdsworth St.* ☎*08/9430–5976* ⊕*www.flybynight.org*), a smoke-free venue.

The Harbourside (⊠*42 Mews Rd.* ☎*08/9433–3999*) has one of Fremantle's most spectacular waterfront views. The multilevel complex includes seven different areas of entertainment, including a sports bar, nightclub, beer garden, lounge, and live-music rooms featuring Perth's top DJs and musical artists six nights a week. In the heart of Fremantle's cappuccino strip, **Metropolis Concert Club Fremantle** (⊠*58 South Terr.* ☎*08/9336–1880* ⊕*www.metropolisfremantle.com.au*), a nonstop techno and funk dance venue, is a great place to go on Saturday night.

SHOPPING

At **Bannister Street Craftworks** (⊠*8–12 Bannister St.* ☎*08/9336–2035*), a restored 19th-century warehouse, craftspeople have gathered in their own workshops to turn out everything from woodwork to glass engraving, wildlife painting, textile printing, stained glass, and pottery. The artists, working as a cooperative, invite you to come in and watch as they demonstrate their skills, or just to browse among the exhibits. All of the crafts on display are for sale.

Into Camelot (⊠*Shop 9, South Terr. Piazza* ☎☎*08/9335–4698* ⊕*www. intocamelot.com.au*), a medieval-style dress shop, sells romantic wedding gowns and cloaks, street and evening wear, and peasant smocks for all occasions. Period boots, classic Saxon and Celtic jewelry, and masks (feathered and plain) are all available at affordable prices.

Kakulas Sisters (⊠*29–31 Market St.* ☎*08/9430–4445*), a unique produce shop, overflows with fragrances and sacks of goodies from across the globe, including Costa Rican coffee beans, Colorado black-eyed beans, Brazilian quince and guava pastries, and Japanese teas.

☾ A fairy theme pervades the **Pickled Fairy & Other Myths** (⊠*Shop 7B, South Terr. Piazza* ☎*08/9430–5827* ⊕*www.pickledfairy.com.au*), making it a delight for children (and children at heart). Celtic jewelry is sold here, along with books on magic and mythology.

ROTTNEST ISLAND

12

19 km (12 mi) west of Fremantle.

An easy cruise from Fremantle, or down the Swan River from Perth, sunny, quirky Rottnest Island makes an ideal day trip. The island has an interesting past. Though records of human occupation date back 6,500 years, when Aboriginal people inhabited the area, European settlement only dates back to 1829. Since then the island has been used for a variety of purposes, including attempts at agriculture, as a location to reform young boys who were in conflict with the law, and for military purposes in both the Great War and the Second World War. The Rottnest Museum is a great place to get the history of the place, and you can take a train trip and tour to the Oliver Hill fort to see gun emplacements from the Second World War.

Of course most West Australians go to the island for the beaches, the swimming, and the laid-back atmosphere on Perth's doorstep.

The most convenient way to get around Rottnest is by bicycle, as cars are not allowed on the island and bus service is infrequent. A bicycle tour of the island covers 26 km (16 mi) and can take as little as three hours, although you really need an entire day to enjoy the beautiful surroundings

Heading south from Thomson Bay, between Government House and Herschell lakes, is a quokka colony. Another colony lies down the road to the east, near the amphitheater at the civic center in sparkling Geordie Bay. Here tame quokkas eat right out of your hand.

Past the quokka colony are gun emplacements from World War II. As you continue south to Bickley Bay, you can spot the wreckage of ships—the oldest dates from 1842—that came to rest on Rottnest's rocky coastline.

Follow the main road past Porpoise, Salmon, Strickland, and Wilson bays to West End, the westernmost point on the island and another graveyard for unfortunate vessels. Heading back to Thomson Bay, the road passes a dozen rocky inlets and bays. Parakeet Bay, the prettiest, is at the northernmost tip of the island.

At the Thomson Bay settlement, visit the **Rottnest Museum** (✉*Digby Ave., Thomson Bay* ☎*08/9372–9732* ✆*Donation suggested*), which includes memorabilia recalling the island's long and turbulent past. Displays show local geology, natural history, and maritime lore; there's also a convict building and an Aboriginal prison. It's open daily 10:45–3:30. The **Wadjemup Lighthouse Tours**—providing 360-degree panoramic views of Rottnest—allow the public into the Heritage-status lighthouse building for the first time in more than a century. Tours depart daily at 9 AM.

The **Rottnest Island Railway Train** (✉ *Thomson Bay* ☎ *08/9372–9732*), known as the *Captain Hussey,* is an ideal way to see the island. The route from the Main Settlement to Oliver Hill is run daily at 12:30, 1:30, and 2:30, with extra services at 10:30 and 11:30 during summer months, and connects with a guided tour of the historic Oliver Hill gun battery. The fare is A$16.60 and includes the guided tour. The train fare without the guided tours is A$11.80. Tickets are available at the visitor information center.

The **Bayseeker Bus** (✉ *Thomson Bay* ☎ *08/9372–9732*), which runs a continuous hop-on, hop-off island circuit, picks up and drops off passengers at the most beautiful bays and beaches. Day tickets are A$7.50 and can be purchased from the driver.

You can also rent bikes at **Rottnest Bike Hire** (✉ *Thomson Bay* ☎ *08/9292–5105*) for A$17 per day, with a returnable deposit of A$25 per bike. Tandem bikes and pedal cars are also available for daily rental. Open daily 8:30–5.

> ## MARSUPIALS, NOT RATS
>
> Quokkas were one of the first Australian mammals ever seen by Europeans. In 1658, the Dutch Captain Willem De Vlamingh described them as rats, but in fact they are marsupials, carrying their young in a pouch. Once common around Perth, quokkas are now confined to isolated pockets on the mainland, but still thrive on their namesake Rottnest Island, where they are safe from predators (mainly foxes). Their cute, furry faces and small, round bodies make them very photogenic.

WHERE TO STAY & EAT

Accommodation on the island ranges from basic camping sites to self-contained holiday villas and hotels. Accommodation is at a premium during the summer months, Easter, and school holidays, and there is a ballot system, with the closing dates months in advance. Outside these times, accommodation is easier to find. Check ⊕ *www.rottnestisland. com* for details.

$$ ✕ ⌂ **Quokka Arms Hotel.** Previously known as the Rottnest Hotel, this property was once the official summer residence for the governors of Western Australia. Comfortable rooms, which overlook Thompson Bay or a grassy courtyard area, are motel-style, with cane furniture and neutral decor. As well as a popular beer garden, Hampton's Sportsmen's Bar and Chargrill ($–$$) is open every day for lunch and dinner, and features a charcoal grill with buffet salad bar. ✉ *Bedford Ave., Thomson Bay* ☎ *08/9292–5011* ✉ quokkaarms@rottnestisland.com ⊕ *www.rottnestisland.com* ⬎ *18 rooms* ⌂ *In-hotel: restaurant, bar, pool* ⊟ *AE, MC, V.*

$–$$ ✕ ⌂ **Rottnest Lodge.** Rooms at the island's largest hotel range from premium to budget. After a day of walking or biking around the island, you can take a dip in the pool or relax at the bar. The Marlin Restaurant ($$) serves up Thai seafood salad, chowder, and bruschetta with prawns and mango, and there's a buffet lunch from 11 to 2.

✉ *Kitson St.* ☎ *08/9292–5161* ⊕ *www.rottnestlodge.com.au* ⬦ *80 rooms* ⬧ *In-room: dial-up, refrigerator. In-hotel: restaurant, bar, pool* ⊟ *AE, DC, MC, V.*

⚠ **Allison Camping Area,** a major site for more than 50 years, has fresh water and washrooms, but no electricity. Bookings can be made up to 12 months in advance. ✉ *Thomson Bay* ☎ *08/9432–9111* ⊕ *www.rottnestisland.com* ⬦ *50 sites* ⬧ *Flush toilets, pit toilets, drinking water* ⊟ *AE, MC, V.*

FREMANTLE & ROTTNEST ISLAND ESSENTIALS

TRANSPORTATION

BY AIR

Speedy air service to Rottnest Island is available from Perth's domestic airport with Rottnest Air Taxi. Round-trip fare is from A$60 per person, and the service operates daily, weather permitting. Telephone for flight times.

Contact Rottnest Air Taxi (☎ *08/9292–5027 or 1800/500006*).

BY BOAT

Oceanic Cruises and Rottnest Express run ferries to Rottnest Island from Fremantle, as well as from Perth, and Hillarys Fast Ferries runs boats from Hillarys Boat Harbour. The ferries take approximately 25 minutes from Fremantle, 45 minutes from Hillarys, or an hour-plus from Perth—though the latter trip also includes a scenic cruise on the Swan River. Round-trip prices, including entry to Rottnest, are from A$51 per person from Fremantle and from A$66 per person from Perth and Hillarys.

Contacts Rottnest Express (☎ *08/9430–5844 in Fremantle, 08/9421–5888 in Perth* ⊕ *www.rottnestexpress.com.au*). **Hillarys Fast Ferries** (☎ *08/9246–1039* ⊕ *www.hillarysfastferries.com.au*). **Oceanic Cruises** (☎ *08/9335–2666 in Fremantle, 08/9325–1191 in Perth* ⊕ *www.oceaniccruises.com.au*).

BY BUS

Bus information for service from Perth is available from Transperth. Their Central Area Bus Service (CAT) provides free transportation around Fremantle in distinctive orange buses. The route begins and ends outside the Fremantle Bus/Train terminus, and stops include the Fremantle Museum and Arts Centre, the cappuccino strip, and the Fremantle Market. CAT buses run every 10 minutes weekdays 7:30–6:30, and 10–6:30 on weekends and public holidays.

Contact Transperth (☎ *13–6213* ⊕ *www.transperth.wa.gov.au*).

BY TRAIN

Trains bound for Fremantle depart from Perth approximately every 20–30 minutes from the Perth Central Station on Wellington Street. You can travel from Perth to Fremantle (or vice versa) in about 30 minutes. Tickets must be purchased prior to travel at the ticket vending machines. It is illegal to travel without a ticket.

Contact **Transperth** (☎ 13-6213 ⊕ www.transperth.wa.gov.au).

CONTACTS & RESOURCES

EMERGENCIES

The Rottnest Nursing Post, operated by qualified nurses, is open daily 8:30 to 5.

Contacts **Fremantle Hospital** (✉ Alma St. ☎ 08/9431-3333). **Rottnest Nursing Post** (✉ Thomson Bay ☎ 08/9292-5030).

Contacts **Rottnest Island Visitor Information Center** (✉ Adjacent to Dome Café, Thomson Bay beachfront ☎ 08/9372-9732 ⊕ www.rottnestisland.com). **Trams West** (✉ 39A Malsbury St., Bicton, 6157 ☎ 08/9339-8719 ⊕ www. tramswest.com.au).

VISITOR INFORMATION

The Fremantle Tourist Bureau on Kings Square is open weekdays 9–5, Saturday 10–3, and Sunday 11:30–2:30. The Rottnest Island Visitor Information Centre is open daily 7:30 AM–5:30 PM.

Contacts **Fremantle Visitor Centre** (✉ Kings Square at High St., Fremantle ☎ 08/9431-7878 🖨 08/9431-7755 ⊕ www.fremantlewesternaustralia.com). **Rottnest Island Visitor Information Centre** (✉ Adjacent to Dome Café, Thomson Bay beachfront ☎ 08/9372-9752 ⊕ www.rottnestisland.com).

THE SOUTH WEST

With a balmy Mediterranean climate, world-class wines, and pristine, white, sandy beaches, it's easy to see why the South West is Western Australia's most popular visitor destination. But it's not all coastal beauty—inland, rare hardwood forests make excellent hiking terrain. Add easy road and rail access from Perth and plenty of affordable, comfortable accommodations, and you have an ideal break from the city.

BUNBURY

184 km (114 mi) south of Perth, 109 km (68 mi) south of Mandurah.

As Western Australia's second-largest city and the major seaport of the South West, Bunbury provides a comfortable introduction to the region. The cappuccino strip, stretching down Victoria Street, and Marlston Waterfront, which overlooks the Outer Harbor and Koombana Bay, is a bustling area for cafés, restaurants, and bars.

♻ Around 100 bottlenose dolphins make their home in Koombana Bay, and a half dozen of them regularly visit the sandy beach in front of the excellent **Dolphin Discovery Centre.** Visitors here are permitted to wade into the water while the dolphins swim around them. There are some restrictions on actually swimming with the dolphins, but the helpful center volunteers explain all the rules, which are aimed at ensuring the dolphins aren't harmed by the human interaction. The center also conducts "Swim on the Wild Side" tours which allow you to swim

Australia's Strangest Animals

Australia's animals are among nature's oddest creations. So weird are the creatures that hop, burrow, slither, and amble across the Australian landmass that, until the 20th century, it was believed that the continent's fauna had a different evolutionary starting point from the rest of the Earth's species.

Australia's animal life was shaped by its plants, and they, in turn, were determined by the climate, which dramatically changed around 15 million years ago. Moist, rain-bearing winds that once irrigated the heart of the continent died, the great Inland sea dried up, and the inland rain forests vanished—flamingos and freshwater dolphins along with them.

The animals that did survive have evolved in strange and fascinating ways. For example, during droughts the water-holding frog locks itself away in an underground chamber, where it remains in a state of suspended animation waiting for rain for up to seven years. The ferocious looking thorny devil uses its heavy armor to collect water. Its exaggerated spikes and spines give the creature an enormous surface area. Dew condenses on the spines and is then channeled into its mouth.

The kangaroo is a superb example of adaptation. In the parched semidesert that covers most of central Australia, kangaroos must forage for food over a wide area. Their powerful hind legs act as springs, enabling them to travel long distances while using relatively little energy.

Kangaroos, wallabies, and their mid-size relations vary enormously in size, habitat, and location. Australia has everything from rat-size specimens to 6-foot, 200-pound red kangaroos from the cool, misty forests of Tasmania to the northern tip of Cape York.

One of the most fascinating groups of Australian animals is the monotremes, who lay eggs, as reptiles do, but are warm-blooded and suckle their young with milk. Only three species of monotremes survive: the platypus, a reclusive crustacean-eater found in freshwater streams in eastern Australia, and two species of echidna, a small, spiny termite-eater.

Best loved of all Australia's animals is the koala. A tree-dwelling herbivore, the koala eats a diet entirely of eucalyptus leaves, which are low in nutrients and high in toxins. As a result, koalas must restrict their energy level. Typically, a koala spend about 20 hours of each day dozing in a tree fork. Even the koala's brain has adapted to its harsh regimen. A human brain uses about 17% of the body's energy, but the koala saves on the wasteful expenditure by starting out with a brain the size of a small walnut.

However deficient in the cerebellum it may be, though, one thing that the koala will not tolerate is being called a bear. Cute and cuddly as it is—and despite its resemblance to every child's favorite bedmate—the koala is a marsupial, not a bear.

–Michael Gebicki

with wild dolphins in their natural environment. The tour is led by the center's own marine biologists and the cost of A\$125 per person includes entry to the interpretive center, instruction, equipment (mask, snorkel, fins, and wet suit), and light refreshments. Tours depart daily (weather permitting) at 9 AM and midday in November; at 8 AM and 11 AM from December to March; and at midday in April. ⊠*Koombana Dr.* ☎*08/9791–3088* ⊕*www.dolphindiscovery. com.au* ⊠*A\$6* ⊗*June–Aug., daily 9–3; Sept.–May, daily 8–4.*

Naturaliste Charters (☎*08/9755–2276* ⊕*www.whales-australia. com* ✉*info@whales-australia. com*) operates dolphin cruises on the bay year-round. From November to April the cruises

depart from in front of the Dolphin Discovery Centre, although from May to October departures are from the Yellow Jetty at the Marlston Waterfront. Departure times are 11 AM and 2 PM, with additional cruises during the busy summer months. The cruise costs A\$37.

Dardanup (⊕*www.dardanup.wa.gov.au*) is a small gathering of historic 19th-century buildings nestled at the entry point to the Ferguson Valley. If you take the winding Ferguson Valley Road up into the Darling Scarp, you'll discover wineries, art and crafts galleries, and farm-stay lodgings. The best time to come is between April and November, when the pastures are green from seasonal rains. **Willow Bridge Estate** (⊠*Lot 4, Gardincourt Dr.* ☎*08/9728–0055*) is open daily 11–5. **Ferguson Falls Wines** (⊠*Pile Rd., 2 km [1 mi] from Ferguson Valley Rd.* ☎*08/9728–1083*) is open weekends 10–5. Dardanup is 20 km (12 mi) inland from Bunbury.

WHERE TO STAY & EAT

\$–\$\$ ✕ **Vat 2.** A waterfront spot overlooking the Outer Harbour and marina
★ is the setting for this local favorite. Grown-ups can while away a lazy Sunday afternoon dining and wining alfresco to a live band while children frolic at the adjacent playground. Chef Danny Angove's menu includes lamb rump on a creamy white bean puree; steamed mussels with white wine, cream, and garlic; and Shark Bay whiting fillets with green chili dipping sauce. The extensive wine list taps the best of the region. If you love oysters, they're the Tuesday-night special. ⊠*2 Jetty Rd.* ☎*08/9791–8833* ⊕*www.vat2.com.au* ⊟*AE, DC, MC, V.*

\$\$ ✕▦ **Clifton Best Western.** With 42 tourism and restaurant awards since
Fodor'sChoice 1990, this small hotel is the most awarded lodging in the region. In
★

addition to the typical motel-style rooms, you can upgrade to one of four tastefully appointed suites furnished with antiques in the adjacent 1885 Grittleton Lodge. ✉ *15 Clifton St., Bunbury, WA, 6230* ☎ *08/9721–4300 hotel, 08/9721–9959 Louisa's Restaurant* ✆ *the-clifton@bestwestern.com.au* 🖳 *www.theclifton.com.au* 🛏 *48 rooms, 4 suites* ⬙ *In-hotel: pool, laundry facilities, parking (no fee)* ▭ *AE, DC, MC, V.*

12

$$$ 🏨 **Lord Forrest Hotel.** This central hotel is within walking distance of the cappuccino strip, cinemas, shops, and restaurants. Greenery dangles from garden beds around the eight-story atrium, where sunlight streams through clerestory windows. Rooms are pleasantly furnished and decorated in pastels; upper floors have city views. Spa at the Forrest offers massages and reflexology treatments, facials, and salt scrubs. ✉ *20 Symmons St., 6230* ☎ *08/9721–9966 or 1800/097811* ✆ *enquiries@lordforresthotel.com.au* 🖳 *www.lordforresthotel.com.au* 🛏 *102 rooms, 13 suites* ⬙ *In-hotel: 2 restaurants, bars, pool, parking (no fee)* ▭ *AE, DC, MC, V.*

NIGHTLIFE

Barbados (✉ *15 Bonnefoi Blvd., Marlston Waterfront* ☎ *08/9791–6555* 🖳 *www.barbados.com.au*), a second-story venue on the Marlston Waterfront, has views over Koombana Bay. There's standard Mod-Oz food plus wood-fired pizzas served in two dining areas, complemented by an extensive selection of regional wines. The energetic can migrate to the dance floor (DJs or live rock bands Friday, Saturday, and Sunday nights), while conversationalists can head to the quieter lounge area. It's open daily, Monday–Saturday 11 AM–midnight and Sunday until 10.

Fitzgerald's (✉ *22 Victoria St.* ☎ *08/9791–2295* ✆ *fitzgeralds@tpg.com.au*) is Bunbury's authentic Irish bar, housed in the historic Customs House Bond Store.

The lively **Reef Hotel** (✉ *12 Victoria St.* ☎ *08/9791–6677*) bar bustles from 8 PM into the wee hours. DJs spin rock, hip-hop, rhythm and blues, and heavy metal Sunday through Thursday, and there's live music Friday and Saturday nights. Admission is free.

EN ROUTE

From Bunbury to Busselton, take the scenic route through **Ludlow Forest,** the only natural tuart forest in the world. These magnificent tuart trees, a type of eucalyptus or gum tree that thrives in arid conditions, have been standing on this land for 400 years. Just south of Ludlow Forest is Wonnerup House, first settled by the Layman family in 1834. Wonnerup House is an important surviving example of early farm pioneering. The homestead (1859) and dairy (1837) are managed by the National Trust.

DUNSBOROUGH

21 km (13 mi) west of Busselton.

The attractive seaside town of Dunsborough is perfect for a few days of swimming, sunning, and fishing—which is why it's become a popular holiday destination for many Perth families. Onshore attractions include Meelup Beach, a protected cove with calm swimming water, and the nearby wineries of Margaret River. Offshore, you can dive on the wreck of the HMAS *Swan,* the former Royal Australian Navy ship deliberately sunk in Geographe Bay at the end of its useful life, or take a cruise to see migrating humpback and southern right whales September–December.

WHERE TO STAY & EAT

$$–$$$ ✕ **Wise Vineyard Restaurant.** Verdant bushland and a carefully manicured vineyard surround Heath Townsend's restaurant at the Wise winery. Simple, mostly locally sourced ingredients are transformed here into such culinary delights as twice-cooked duck with burnt orange sauce; lamb rump with eggplant puree, green beans, and almonds; and venison with gnocchi, diced tomato, oregano, and capers. Views of Eagle Bay complete the dining experience. Five homey chalets with names such as Teahouse, Potter's Cottage, and Doll House are also available for accommodation. Reservations for the restaurant are essential. ⊠ *80 Eagle Bay Rd.* ☎ *08/9755–3331 restaurant, 08/9756–8627 winery, 08/9756–8098 accommodations* ⊕ *www.wisefood.com* ☐ *AE, DC, MC, V* ⊗ *No dinner Mon.–Thurs.*

$$$ 🏨 **Broadwater Resort and Spa.** Sunny public areas and extensive sports facilities make this one of the best accommodation choices on the Geographe Bay beach strip. Romantic king rooms, done in pastel colors, have deluxe facilities, while the two- and three-bedroom apartments each have a lounge, dining room, and kitchen. Many rooms have superb ocean views. The casual, airy restaurant serves fusion cuisine using fresh local produce, cheeses, and olive oils. A selection of Margaret River wines is on hand to complement the meal. The resort has its own chapel in an attractive garden setting, which is often used for weddings. ⊠ *Caves and Holgate Rds., Marybrook, 6281* ☎ *08/9756–9777* ✉ *dunsborough@broadwaters.com.au* ⊕ *www.broadwaters.com.au* ⇨ *88 rooms* ♨ *In-hotel: restaurant, room service, bar, tennis courts, pool, spa, gym, beachfront, concierge, parking (no fee)* ☐ *AE, DC, MC, V.*

$$$ 🏨 **Quay West Bunker Bay Resort.** Sprawling down the hillside of the Cape Naturaliste Ridge in bushland, Bunker Bay Resort occupies a rare location with north-facing views of the calm blue waters of Geographe Bay. This villa property has one-, two-, and three-bedroom apartments, each with its own private courtyard. Villas are light, bright, and airy, with cathedral ceilings, and are finished in natural materials like limestone and Western Australia's famous jarrah timber. The property is also home to the award-winning restaurant, the Other Side of the Moon. ⊠ *Bunker Bay Rd. off Cape Naturaliste Rd., 6281* ☎ *1800/010449 or 08/9756–9100* ⊕ *www.mirvachotels.com. au* ⊅ *150 villas* ⌂ *In-room: ethernet, kitchen, DVD. In-hotel: restaurant, bar, concierge, tennis courts, pool, gym, spa, laundry service, parking (no fee)* ▤ *AE, DC, MC, V.*

¢–$ ▥ **Dunsborough Motel.** This motel for the dollar-conscious provides comfortable accommodations and proximity to town and the beach. Rooms are equipped with basic amenities, including electric kettles and supplies for making coffee and tea, while the property includes a restaurant, swimming pool, and barbecue area. ⊠ *Caves Rd. at Seymour Blvd., 6281* ☎ *08/9756–7711* ⊅ *48 rooms* ⌂ *In-hotel: restaurant, bar, pool* ▤ *AE, DC, MC, V.*

LEEUWIN–NATURALISTE NATIONAL PARK

Fodor's Choice *The northernmost part of the park is 266 km (165 mi) south of Perth,*
★ *25 km (16 mi) northwest of Dunsborough.*

This 150-km (93-mi) stretch of coastline on the southwest tip of the continent is one of Australia's most fascinating areas. The limestone Leeuwin–Naturaliste Ridge directly below the park contains more than 360 known caves. Evidence dates both human and animal habitation here to more than 40,000 years ago.

At the northern end of the park stands **Cape Naturaliste Lighthouse,** open daily 9:30–5 December to February, closing at 4 the rest of the year. Fully guided tours of the lighthouse cost A$10, with the last tour at 3:30. A 1½-km-long (1-mi-long) trail leads from Cape Naturaliste to Canal Rocks, passing rugged cliffs, quiet bays, and curving beaches. This is also the start of the 120-km (75-mi) Cape to Cape Walk. Four major cave systems are easily accessible. **Jewel** (☎ *08/9757–7411*), the southernmost of the system, has one of the longest straw stalactites to be found in any tourist cave in the world. It's open daily with tours every hour 9:30 AM–3:30 PM. **Lake** (☎ *08/9757–7411*), centered around a tranquil, eerie-looking underground lake, is also open daily with tours every hour 9:30–3:30. Tour cost at both Jewel and Lake caves is A$17. The **CaveWorks** (☎ *08/9757–7411* ✐ caveworks@margaretriver. com) display center at Lake Cave presents a good introduction to the whole cave system. **Mammoth** (☎ *08/9757–7411*), which has ancient fossil remains of extinct animals, is open daily 9–5:30, with the last entry at 4:30. Self-guided tours cost A$17. **Ngilgi** (☎ *08/9755–2152*), near Yallingup, is a main site for adventure caving. It's open daily 9:30–4:30, staying open to 5 PM during summer school holidays. Cave tours cost A$17 and run every half hour. Flashlight tours (where cave lights are turned off and the only light is from the flashlights) cost A$18, and adventure tours are A$70. Adventure caving and flashlight tours are available by prior arrangement only.

The view from the top of the **Cape Leeuwin Lighthouse** (☏ *08/9757–7411* ⊕ *www.margaretriver.com*), a 10-minute drive south of Augusta and the third-highest working lighthouse in Australia, allows you to witness the meeting of the Southern and the Indian oceans. In some places this alliance results in giant swells that crash against the rocks. In others, small coves are blessed with calm waters ideal for swimming. The lighthouse precinct is open daily 8:45–5. Guided tours to the top of the lighthouse cost A$10 and run every 30 minutes during September–April and every 40 minutes May–August. The last tour is at 4:30 PM. If you don't plan to camp, consider staying at Dunsborough or Margaret River. Campgrounds with toilets, showers, and an information center are north in Injidup. Campsites (including firewood) cost A$6 per adult per night. Facilities include toilets and barbecue facilities. For more information on camping in the state, visit www.naturebase.net.

MARGARET RIVER

★ *181 km (112 mi) south of Perth, 38 km (24 mi) south of Cape Naturaliste.*

The town of Margaret River is considered the center of the Southwest's wine region, though vineyards and wineries stretch from well north of Bunbury to the south coast. Nevertheless, close to Margaret River are some 80 wineries offering tastings and sales of some of the best wines in the world. The region, which is often compared to France's Bordeaux for its similar climate and soils, produces only around 1% of Australia's total wine grape crush, but this is spread into around 25% of the country's premium and ultrapremium wines. Both red and white vintages here are exceptional, the most notable labels toting chardonnay, sauvignon blanc, or sauvignon blanc–semillon and cabernet-merlot blends.

The **Margaret River Visitor Center** (✉ *100 Bussell Hwy.* ☏ *08/9780–5911* ⊕ *www.margaretriver.com*), open daily 9–5, has detailed brochures for individual cellars. You can also get information here on the World Masters Surf Circuit championships, which take place each March–April at Surfers Point, just 8 km (5 mi) outside Margaret River.

★ **Clairault Wines** (✉ *Henry Rd., Willyabrup* ☏ *08/9755–6225* ⊕ *www. clairault.com.au*) is one of the region's best wineries, known for its cabernet/merlot, cabernet sauvignon, and semillon. The property's manicured lawns and charming gardens are floodlighted after dark. The spacious restaurant has glass doors that swing back for expansive views in warm weather, while two huge stone fireplaces warm the tables in winter. The menus are innovative, and include duck and smoked chorizo terrine, with peach and fennel salad; gin-glazed pork belly, with tonic dressing, lime, and apple salad; and a local venison loin with parsnip and a crab ravioli.

Cape Mentelle (✉ *Wallcliffe Rd., 3 km [2 mi] west of Margaret River* ☏ *08/9757–0888*) was one of the first wineries in the area, and it's still one of the most notable. The adobe-style rammed-earth build-

12

ing and tasting rooms, so typical of the buildings in the Margaret River district, are as handsome and memorable as the wine. The winery produces chardonnay, sauvignon blanc, semillon, cabernet/merlot, cabernet sauvignon, shiraz, and zinfandel wines.

Winemaker Vanya Cullen produces one of Australia's best chardonnays and an outstanding cabernet/merlot at **Cullen Wines** (✉ *Caves and Harmans S Rds., Willyabrup* ☎ *08/9755–5277*), a family-run business.

★ **Leeuwin Estate** (✉ *Stevens Rd. off Gnarawary Rd.* ☎ *08/9757–9000* ⊕ *www.leeuwinestate.com.au*) is one of Australia's leading wineries. Their Art Series wines—especially the chardonnay and cabernet sauvignon—have a deserved reputation as some of the best in the country. Tastings and guided tours (A$9.90) are conducted on the property daily at 11 AM, 1 PM, and 3 PM, and the restaurant has daily lunch and Saturday dinner. In February the estate holds a series of concerts, and many international superstars—including John Farnham, Tom Jones, Diana Ross, Sting, and the late Ray Charles—have performed there against a backdrop of floodlighted karri trees.

Vasse Felix (✉ *Harmans S and Caves Rds., Cowaramup* ☎ *08/9756–5000*) has an excellent upstairs restaurant, a basement cellar, photogenic grounds, and an art gallery, which houses regular exhibitions from the celebrated Holmes à Court Collection, featuring works from Arthur Boyd, Sidney Nolan, Lloyd Rees, and other prominent Australian artists.

☾ **Eagle's Heritage** has the largest collection of birds of prey in Australia, all living in a natural bush environment. It is also a rehabilitation center for sick and injured birds of prey. The ancient art of falconry is shown in the free-flight display, with tours at 11 AM and 1:30 PM. ✉ *Boodjidup Rd., 5 km (3 mi) south west of Margaret River* ☎ *08/9757–2960* ⊕ *www.eaglesheritage.com.au* ⊠ *A$10* ☾ *Daily 10–5.*

WHERE TO STAY & EAT

$$ ✕ **Lamont's.** The signature dish at this lovely lakefront restaurant is the local marron—served grilled with roasted baby potatoes and a lime-and-chive beurre blanc. Another sure bet is the whole baked rainbow trout, with fennel bulb, asparagus, and tomoato buerre blanc. ✉ *Lot 1, Gunyulgup Valley Dr., Yallingup* ☎ *08/9755–2434* ⊕ *www.lamonts. com.au* ⊟ *AE, DC, MC, V* ☾ *No dinner Sun.–Fri.*

$$ ✕ **Vat 107.** This restaurant aims to bring city chic to the country, with its stylish decor, polished floorboards, and marble bars. A fre-

quently changing menu emphasizes seasonal fresh and locally supplied foods. Mains could include pancetta-wrapped salmon with spinach and raisins; sticky duck with pickled carrots and crisp scallions; and baby chicken with artichoke puree and organic walnut oil. The adjacent Vatini cocktail bar serves cocktails, beers on tap, and local wines in a Manhattan-style sophistication. Luxury studio apartments upstairs are available for overnight stays from A$180. ⊠ *107 Bussell Hwy.* ☎ *08/9758–8877* ⊕ *www.vat107.com.au* ⊟ *AE, DC, MC, V* ⊗ *Closed Mon.*

$–$$ ✕**Flutes Restaurant.** The pastoral setting here—over the dammed waters
★ of the Willyabrup Brook and encircled by olive groves in the midst of the Brookland Valley Vineyard—is almost as compelling as the food. The modern Australian cooking makes use of prime local produce. Margaret River venison, Pemberton marron, and Ferguson Valley chicken are all excellent, prepared simply yet with flair by executive chef François Morvan. ⊠ *Caves Rd., 5 km (3 mi) south of Metricup Rd.* ☎ *08/9755–6250* ⊕ *www.flutes.com.au* ⊗ *Reservations essential* ⊗ *Daily 12 noon–4* ⊟ *AE, DC, MC, V.*

$$$$ ▣**Cape Lodge.** The Cape Dutch architecture perfectly suits this elegant
Fodor'sChoice lodge in the midst of Margaret River wine country. Since undergo-
★ ing a A$3 million refurbishment in 2004, the property now offers 22 luxury suites, a lakeside restaurant with over-water alfresco dining, and a 14,000 bottle, temperature-controlled wine cellar stocked with premium vintage Margaret River wines. Several of the opulent, airy suites have their own balconies or terraces overlooking a private lake; others look out over woodlands or landscaped gardens. ⊠ *Caves Rd., Yallingup, WA, 6282* ☎ *08/9755–6311* ✎ stay@capelodge.com.au ⊕ *www.capelodge.com.au* ➾*22 suites* ⚷ *In-hotel: restaurant, room service, tennis court, pool, parking (no fee), no kids under 15* ⊟ *AE, DC, MC, V* ⊗*CP.*

$$$ ▣**Basildene Manor.** Each of the rooms in this grand, circa-1912 house has been lovingly refurbished. Rich lilac, gold, and red colors decorate the guest rooms. Breakfast—included in the rates—is served in the conservatory, where you can look out over the property's 14 beautifully landscaped acres. Special wedding packages are available. ⊠ *100 Wallcliffe Rd., 6285* ☎ *08/9757–3140* ⊕ *www.basildene.com.au* ➾*17 rooms* ⚷ *In-hotel: restaurant, pool, laundry facilities, parking (no fee)* ⊟ *AE, DC, MC, V* ⊗*BP.*

PEMBERTON'S CLIMBING TREES

Deep in the heart of the karri forest, the threat of summertime bushfires is all too imminent. During the 1930s and '40s, treetop lookouts were constructed and manned during the fire season so that telltale signs of smoke could be spotted early. Three of these fire lookouts are open for visitors—Gloucester, Dave Evans Bicentennial, and Diamond. But these climbs are not for the faint-hearted—ascend a spiral of steel spikes driven into the trunk of the tree and clamber onto one of the timber platforms. From here, enjoy the sweeping views of the forest canopy.

$$–$$$ **⊞Heritage Trail Lodge.** Nestled among the trees, this luxury retreat is only about ½-km (¼-mi) from Margaret River township. Spacious suites have hot tubs, king-size beds, and private balconies overlooking the forest. Walk the trails early, then enjoy a complimentary Continental breakfast of local produce in the conservatory. ☒ *31 Bussell Hwy., 6285* ☎ *08/9757–9595* ✉ enquiry@heritage-trail-lodge.com.au ⊕ *www.heritage-trail-lodge.com.au* ➪ *10 suites* ♿ *In-hotel: laundry facilities, parking (no fee)* ☰ *AE, DC, MC, V* ⦿*CP.*

$–$$$ **⊞Gilgara Retreat.** This stunning property, a replica of an 1870 station homestead, sits amid 23 gently rolling, bucolic acres. Antiques and lace furnish the romantic rooms, so it's no surprise that honeymooners frequently choose to stay here. A rose-covered veranda, open fireplaces, and a cozy lounge add to the charm. You might breakfast surrounded by spectacular blue wrens and sacred ibises, or catch a few kangaroos lounging near the front door. Rates include a Mediterranean-style breakfast. ☒ *Caves and Carter Rds., 6285* ☎ *08/9757–2705* ✉ stay@gilgara.com.au ⊕ *www.gilgara.com.au* ➪ *14 rooms* ♿ *In-room: no phone, no TV (some). In-hotel: laundry facilities, parking (no fee), no kids under 15* ☰ *AE, DC, MC, V* ⦿*BP.*

PEMBERTON

280 km (150 mi) southeast of Perth.

Pemberton is the heartland of the magnificent karri forest of Western Australia. These timber giants—said to be the third-tallest tree in the world behind mountain ash and Californian redwood—grow in their natural state only in this southern region of Western Australia.

The town was settled in 1913, and has relied on harvesting the karri trees since. If you take a walk through pristine forest in Warren National Park, you can climb to the top of the Dave Evans Bicentennial Tree, one of the tall karri trees used in summer by fire spotters on the lookout for bushfires. Just outside Pemberton is Gloucester Tree, another fire spotters' tree, which also allows you to climb to the top, 200 feet above the ground. Beedelup National Park has a gathering of 400-year-old karri trees.

Pemberton is the home of numerous woodworking artisans. A must-see is the **Fine Woodcraft Gallery,** which offers outstanding examples of wood as art, as well as more-practical pieces such as fine furniture. ☒ *Dickinson St.; follow signs from center of town* ☎ *08/9776–1399* ☉ *Daily 9–5.*

Pemberton is also expanding its reputation as the center of a premium wine region. **Gloucester Ridge Winery** was one of the first wineries in the area, and is now recognized for its excellent pinot noir. Sample a vintage or two at the cellar door. ☒ *Burma Rd.* ☎ *08/9776–1035* ☒*Free* ☉ *Daily 10–5.*

WHERE TO STAY

$$ 🏨 **Karri Valley Resort.** Built on the edge of a huge man-made lake, the resort has 55 rooms in one- and two-story timber buildings. The lakeside rooms, with private balconies overlooking the lake, are comfortably furnished in muted pastel tones; two- and three-bedroom chalets, with brightly colored cane and pine furniture, fireplaces, and kitchen facilities, are also scattered along the forested slopes surrounding the lake. There are more than 50 resort activities available, including canoeing, trout fishing, mini golf, craft classes, and mountain biking. The resort is about 20 minutes' drive from Pemberton. ⊠ *Vasse Hwy. south from Pemberton at 17-km (10-mi) mark* ☎ *08/9776–2020 or 1800/245757* ⊕ *www.karrivalleyresort.com.au* ⌒ *55 rooms, 10 chalets* ⚏ *In-room: no a/c. In-hotel: restaurant, laundry facilities, parking (no fee), no elevator* ⊟ *AE, DC, MC, V.*

EN ROUTE

🌀★ **Valley of the Giants.** Giant tingle trees, which grow only along the south coast near Walpole, are protected in this fascinating park. You can experience the environment of these trees from up in the canopy by taking the **Treetop Walk,** a 1,000-foot-long steel walkway that slopes gently upward and is suitable for children and wheelchairs. At 132 feet above the ground you have prime views of the forest, as well as of birdlife and flowers that most people never see. The ground-level **Ancient Empire Boardwalk** meanders through the park, occasionally winding through groves of veteran tingle trees. ⊠ *Valley of the Giants Rd., 13 km (8 mi) east on South Coast Hwy.* ☎ *08/9840–8263* ⊕ *www. naturebase.net* ⌖ *A$8* ⊙ *Daily 9–5, last admission 4:15; Dec. 26–Jan. 26, extended hrs 8* AM*–6* PM*, last admission 5:15.*

ALBANY

410 km (254 mi) southeast of Perth via Rte. 30, 377 km (234 mi) east of Margaret River.

Lying on the southernmost tip of Western Australia's rugged coastline, this sophisticated port city is a surprising find. The earliest settlement in Western Australia, it was founded in 1826 as a penal outpost—three years earlier than northern Swan River, which later became Perth. Originally named Frederickstown after Frederick, Duke of York and Albany, the town was renamed Albany in 1831 by Governor James Stirling. Its 1840s whaling fleet turned it into a boomtown, and though the whaling heyday ended in 1978, the town's heritage is still very much evident. Solid stone buildings clustered around the beautiful waterways of Princess Royal Harbour spread out around King George Sound.

🌀   Whalers brought huge numbers of sperm whales into Albany's harbor every season—the greatest number being 1,174, in 1975—until the practice was stopped in 1978. Today southern right whales and humpbacks are found in King George Sound during their migration between July and October. The old whaling station has been converted to the **Whaleworld** museum, which has memorable displays of cetaceans (whales and dolphins) and pinnipeds (seals and sea lions), as well as the restored whaling brig *Cheyne IV*. The museum lies 20 km (12 mi) from Albany along the shore of Frenchman's Bay. ✉ *Frenchman's Bay Rd.* ☎ *08/9844–4021* ⊕ *www.whaleworld.org* 🖃 *A\$18* ⊗ *Daily 9–5 (9–6 Dec. 26–Jan. 31); hrly guided tours 10–4.*

12

Built in 1851, the **Albany Convict Gaol** on Stirling Terrace served as the district jail from 1872 until it was closed in the 1930s. Restored by the Albany Historical Society in 1968, it now contains a collection of social and historical artifacts. Night tours are also available on Friday and Saturday evenings (A\$15). Nearby **Patrick Taylor Cottage**, a wattle-and-daub (twig-and-mud) dwelling built on Duke Street in 1832 is believed to be the oldest in the district. It contains more than 2,000 objects, including period costumes, old clocks, silverware, and kitchenware. ✉ *Stirling Terr. at Parade St.* ☎ *08/9841–5403* 🖃 *Gaol A\$4; Patrick Taylor Cottage, donation* ⊗ *Old Gaol, daily 10–4; Patrick Taylor Cottage, daily 11–3.*

The 1850 Residency building once accommodated government officials and later became offices. Since 1985 it has housed the **Western Australian Museum Albany**, one of the finest small museums in Australia and a focal point for both the social and natural history of the Albany region. Exhibits explore the local Noongar Aboriginal culture, as well as local geology, flora, and fauna. Also worth visiting are the adjoining saddlery and artisans' gallery. The lovely sandstone building affords sweeping views of the harbor. ✉ *Residency Rd. at Princess Royal Dr.* ☎ *08/9841–4844* 🖃 *Donation suggested* ⊗ *Daily 10–5.*

☺ Adjacent to the Residency Museum is a faithful replica of the brig *Amity*, on which Albany's original settlers arrived. Local artisans used timber from the surrounding forest to build the replica. If you board the ship, climb below deck and try to imagine how 45 men, plus livestock, could fit into such a small craft. ✉ *Parade Rd. off Princess Royal Dr.* ☎ *08/9841–5403* 🖃 *Free; guided tours A\$6, reservations essential* ⊗ *Daily 9:30–4.*

Created for snorkelers and divers, the **Albany Artificial Reef** is set on the former Royal Australian Navy ship HMAS *Perth*. Most of the original ship is intact, including the mast, forward gun, and the main radar dishes. It was scuttled in 100 feet of water in King George Sound; a scuba permit is required to dive at the site. **Albany Dive** (☎ *08/9842–6886*) has daily scuba dives to the reef (times depending on weather and demand) from A\$150, including full hire gear. ✉ *Frenchman's Bay Rd.* ☎ *08/9841–9333* 🖃 *A\$7.50* ⊗ *Daily, daylight hrs.*

OFF THE BEATEN PATH

Denmark. This charming old town 53 km (33 mi) west from Albany is nestled on a riverside—"where forest meets the sea," as the town motto goes. It's an ideal place to stop for a swim in the sparkling clear waters at Ocean Beach, or to browse through artisans' wares at the Old Butter Factory. If you want to stay a while, the **Chimes Spa Retreat** (☎ *08/9848–2255* ⊕ *www.chimes.com.au*) offers luxury accommodations and spa services on a secluded 60-acre property, while the **Cove** (☎ *08/9848–1770* ⊕ *www.thecovechalets.com*) has five craftsman-built chalets set in the forest with expansive views of the inlet.

Stirling Range National Park. The Stirling Ranges, together with the adjacent Porongurup National Park, 71 km (44 mi) north of Albany, are considered the only true mountain range in the South West. The highlight is a climb up the 3,541-foot Bluff Knoll for spectacular views of the largely flat surrounding countryside. Don't be fooled by the apparent short distance from the parking lot—the 3-km (2-mi) trek takes around three hours round-trip, and you need to bring plenty of water and wet-weather gear, as sudden storms can spring up, even in summer. The prettiest time to visit is during the wildflower season (September and October). Albany is close enough to serve as a base. If you want to stay overnight, **The Lily** (☎*08/9827–9205* ⊕*www.thelily.com.au*) offers double rooms adjacent to their restaurant, and an authentic Dutch windmill is on the premises. Freshly ground wholemeal flours are available for purchase.

WHERE TO STAY & EAT

$–$$$ ✕**Earl of Spencer Historic Inn.** There is plenty of history attached to this charming restaurant and bar. The first Spencer Inn was established in 1874, and operated as a lodging house and tavern until 1925. It was renovated in 1988 and re-opened as the Earl of Spencer Historic Inn and now serves an extensive range of snacks and main meals for lunch and dinner. Sit at the 120-year-old jarrah wood bar and enjoy some of the 15 different imported and local beers. ⊠*Earl and Spencer Sts.* ☎*08/9841–1322* ⊕*www.earlofspencer.com.au* ☐*MC, V.*

$–$$ ✕**Dylans on the Terrace.** Hearty meals are the watchword at this Albany landmark. Overlooking Princess Royal Harbour at the bottom end of town, Dylans serves breakfast, lunch, and dinner, and offers take-out. The menu includes grilled steak, lasagna, and marinated kebabs, or burgers and sandwiches if you're on the go. ⊠*82-84 Stirling Terr.CBD* ☎*08/9841–8720* ⊕*www.dylans.com.au* ☐*M,V.*

$–$$ ✕**Restaurant Rocks.** Possibly named for it's proximity to Albany's famous Dog Rock, this venue is a popular with the locals. Award-winning chef Greg Pepall uses regional seafood in his innovative menus. The fish of the day comes with eggplant rémoulade, skordalia potato, and a smoked mussel and saffron beurre blanc. Our favorite is the chermoula spiced lamb loin served with a cauliflower, new potato, and chickpea ragout with cucumber and coriander riata. ⊠*303 Middleton Rd.* ☎*08/9841–4422* ⊕*www.dogrockmotel.com.au* ☐*MC, V.*

$$$ ▦**The Beach House at Bayside.** With a style reminiscent of a Mediterranean villa, this property overlooks King George Sound at Middleton Beach. The rooms are furnished in mellow shades of yellow, blue, and tan and decorated with contemporary artworks by local and international artists. There are Jacuzzis in all rooms, a Mediterranean-style courtyard, colonnaded walkways, guest library, and complimentary afternoon tea and evening port. The hotel also offers guest bicycles, tour and golf bookings, and picnic hampers. ⊠*33 Barry Court, Bayside Links, 6330* ☎*08/9844–8844* ✐luxury@thebeachhouseatbayside. com.au ⊕*www.thebeachhouseatbayside.com.au* ⇦*6 rooms, 1 suite*

12

&In-room: ethernet. In-hotel: laundry service, parking (no fee), guest library, no elevator ☐AE, DC, MC, V ⭐IBP.

$$ 🏨**Balneaire Seaside Resort.** This property brings a bit of the south of France to the south of the state, just a short stroll from a prime stretch of Middleton Beach. Two- and three-bedroom villa-style apartments overlook lush gardens and a central courtyard designed to resemble a Provençal village square. Soft aquas, blues, and yellows decorate each fully-equipped villa. ✉*27 Adelaide Crescent, Middleton Beach, 6330* ☎*08/9842–2877* ✎enquiries@balneaire.com.au ⊕*www.balneaire. com.au* ⤴*28 apartments* &*In-room: kitchen. In-hotel: restaurant, beachfront, laundry facilities, parking (no fee)* ☐AE, DC, MC, V.

SOUTH WEST ESSENTIALS

TRANSPORTATION

BY AIR
Skywest provides daily service to the southern coastal town of Albany.

Contact Skywest (☎*1300/660088* ⊕*www.skywest.com.au*).

BY CAR
A comprehensive network of highways makes exploring the South West practical and easy. Take Highway 1 down the coast from Perth to Bunbury, switch to Route 10 through Busselton and Margaret River, Karridale, and finally Bridgetown, where you rejoin Highway 1 south to Albany via Manjimup.

From Perth you can reach Stirling Range National Park by traveling along the Albany Highway to Kojonup, proceeding east via Broome Hill and Gnowangerup, and then veering south through Borden onto the Albany Road. For a more scenic route, head south from Kojonup and then proceed east along the Stirling Range Drive.

CONTACTS & RESOURCES

EMERGENCIES
In case of an emergency, dial **000** to reach an ambulance, the police, or the fire department.

Contacts Albany Regional Hospital (✉*Warden Ave. at Hardie Rd., Albany* ☎*08/9892–2222*). **Peel Health Campus** (✉*110 Lakes Rd., Mandurah* ☎*08/9531– 8000*). **South West Health Campus** (✉*Bussell Hwy. at Robertson Dr., Bunbury* ☎*08/9722–1000*).

TOURS
Skywest provides three- to five-day packages throughout the South West that incorporate either coaches (buses) and hotels, self-drive hire cars or four-wheel-driving and camping. Westcoast Rail and Coach runs regular tours of the South West, with departures from Perth Central Station. You can go whale-watching with Naturaliste Charters, take four-wheel-drive tours into wilderness areas with Pemberton Dis-

covery Tours, and take a cruise on Walpole's inlets with WOW Wilderness Cruises.

Contacts Naturaliste Charters (☎ *08/9755–2276* ⊕ *www.whales-australia.com*). **Pemberton Discovery Tours** (☎ *08/9776–0484*). **Skywest** (☎ *1300/368168* ⊕ *www.skywestholidays.com.au*). **Westcoast Rail and Coach** (☎ *08/9221–9522*). **WOW Wilderness Cruises** (☎ *08/9840–1036* ⊕ *www.wowwilderness.com.au*).

VISITOR INFORMATION

The Western Australia Visitor Centre maintains an excellent library of free information for visitors, including accommodations and tours throughout the region. The center can book accommodations and tours.

Town and Country Accommodation Western Australia has extensive details of B&B and farm-stay accommodations throughout the state, from small holdings with rustic cottages to sheep stations of more than 654,000 acres where guests stay in sheep shearers' quarters and participate in station activities.

All major South West towns have visitor information centers that can arrange tours, book accommodations, and provide free information.

Contacts Albany Visitor Centre (✉ *Old Railway Station, Proudlove Parade, Albany* ☎ *08/9841–9290* ⊕ *www.albanytourist.com.au*). **Bunbury Visitor Information Centre** (✉ *Old Railway Station, Carmody Pl., Bunbury* ☎ *08/9792–7205 or 1800/286287* ⊕ *www.visitbunbury.com.au*). **Busselton Visitor Centre** (✉ *38 Peel Terr., Busselton* ☎ *08/9752–1288* ⊕ *www.geographebay.com*). **Denmark Visitor Centre** (✉ *60 Strickland St., Denmark* ☎ *08/9848–2055* ⊕ *www.denmark.com. au*). **Mandurah Visitor Centre** (✉ *75 Mandurah Terr., Mandurah* ☎ *08/9550–3999* ⊕ *www.visitmandurah.com.*). **Margaret River Visitor Centre** (✉ *100 Bussell Hwy., Margaret River* ☎ *08/9780–5911* ⊕ *www.margaretriver.com*). **Pemberton Visitor Centre** (✉ *Brockman St., Pemberton* ☎ *08/9776–1133* ⊕ *www.pembertontourist.com.au*). **Town and Country Accommodation Western Australia** (⊕ *www. towncountryaccommodationwa.com.au*). **Western Australia Visitor Centre** (✉ *Forrest Pl. at Wellington St., Perth* ☎ *1300/361351* ⊕ *www.wavisitorcentre.com*).

MONKEY MIA & NINGALOO REEF

Two marine wonders await in the northwestern corner of the state. At Monkey Mia, a World Heritage Site, dolphins interact freely with human beings. Ningaloo Reef Marine Park is a great spot to dive or snorkel among coral reefs, whale sharks, manta rays, and a wealth of other fabulous sea creatures.

MONKEY MIA

Fodor's Choice *985 km (611 mi) north of Perth, 450 km (280 mi) from Karijini*
★ *National Park.*

Monkey Mia is a World Heritage Site and the setting for one of the world's most extraordinary natural wonders; nowhere else do wild dolphins interact so freely with human beings. In 1964 a woman from one

CLOSE UP

The Goldfields

Gold has been the raison d'être for the remote twin-city area known as Kalgoorlie-Boulder—602 km (373 mi) east of Perth—for more than a century.

Paddy Hannan is credited with discovering gold in the region in 1893. In less than two years, more than 100,000 men and women made the arduous journey from Perth—some on foot—to work the ground with primitive implements. There was plenty of gold to be found, and the nickname the "Golden Mile" was given to a region now known to have one of the highest concentrations of gold in the world.

Today mining is big business, with massive machinery and huge open pits, yet the population of Kalgoorlie-Boulder is fewer than 30,000, and the surrounding communities are little more than ghost towns. Kalgoorlie-Boulder is a one-day journey from Perth by car, bus, or train. Flights from Perth take a little over an hour.

KALGOORLIE-BOULDER

"Kal," comprising the twin cities of Kalgoorlie and Boulder, is the major center in the goldfields. Although massive open-cut mines gouge the earth all around the town, including the massive Super Pit at 1,090 feet deep, 3 km (2 mi) long, and 1½ km (1 mi) wide and growing, the city still retains much of the heritage of the early gold-mining days and the atmosphere of a frontier town.

To get a sense of the area's history, you can visit **Hannan's Tourist Mine** and the **Mining Hall of Fame** (Goldfields Hwy., 3 km (2 mi) from Kalgoorlie towards Menzies, ☏08/9026–2700 ⊕www.mininghall.com). Here you'll find audiovisual displays, a reconstructed prospector's camp, historic buildings, opportunities to go underground, and the chance to see an authentic gold pour. Admission to both surface and underground attractions is A$24.

Hannan Street (named for Paddy Hannan) is the main thoroughfare of the area and contains the bulk of the hotels and places of interest, and it's a great place to wander on foot.

COOLGARDIE

Tiny Coolgardie (39 km [24 mi] west of Kalgoorlie) is probably the best-maintained ghost town in Australia. A great deal of effort has gone into preserving this historic gold-mining community where some 150 markers placed around town indicate important historic sights.

Among these sights is the Coolgardie **Railway Station Museum** (☏08/9026–6388), where the history of the area's rail transport is explained through exhibits, photographs, and artifacts. The **Coolgardie Cemetery** (1 km [½ mi] east of Coolgardie) with its stark weathered headstones, recalls stories of tragedy and the struggle for survival in a harsh environment. Many of the graves remain unmarked; the identities of their occupants were lost during the rush to the eastern goldfields.

More information on the goldfields is available at **The Kalgoorlie Goldfields Visitor Centre** (☏08/9021–1966 or 1800/004653 ⊕www.kalgoorlietourism.com) or the **Coolgardie Visitor Centre** (☏08/9026–6090).

of the makeshift fishing camps in the area hand-fed one of the dolphins that regularly followed the fishing boats home. Other dolphins followed that lead, and an extensive family of wild dolphins now comes of its own accord to be fed.

For many, standing in the shallow waters of Shark Bay to hand-feed a dolphin is the experience of a lifetime. There are no set feeding times. Dolphins show up at any hour of the day at the public beach, where park rangers feed them. Rangers share their food with people who want to get close to the sea creatures. The Monkey Mia Visitor Centre has videos and information. ⊠*Follow Hwy. 1 north from Perth for 806 km (500 mi) to Denham–Hamelin Rd., then follow signs* ☎*08/9944–1010 or 1300/135887* ☎*Free* ⊙*Information center daily 7–4:30.*

MEET THE DOLPHINS AT MONKEY MIA

Nicky, Surprise, Puck, and Piccolo are four female bottlenose dolphins who have been carefully hand-fed by government rangers at the beach at Monkey Mia. They generally turn up sometime between 7 AM and noon and often bring their calves, Sparky, Kiya, Burda, and Yadgalah. Under the supervision of the rangers, a few visitors are permitted to enter the shallows and assist in the hand-feeding, an experience to be treasured.

WHERE TO STAY

¢–$$$ 🏨 **Monkey Mia Dolphin Resort.** This resort has everything from unpowered tent sites to shared rooms and houses. Budget travelers sack out in the five- and seven-bed dorms, while groups can rent a private home or share one with other guests. Eight villas open straight onto Dolphin Beach, while other accommodations are surrounded by tropical gardens. Dolphin-watch cruises leave the resort's jetty daily at 10:30 AM. Several ecotours and cruises are escorted by a resident naturalist. ⌂*Box 119, Denham, 6537* ☎*08/9948–1320 or 1800/653611* ✎*enquire@ monkeymia.com.au* ⊕*www.monkeymia.com.au* ⇄*8 villas, 26 homes, 11 dorms with 78 beds, 200 campsites* ⌂*In-room: no phone (some), no TV. In-hotel: restaurants, bar, tennis court, pool, beachfront, laundry facilities, parking (no fee)* ▭*AE, DC, MC, V.*

■ EN ROUTE

Between Monkey Mia, 354 km (220 mi) south, and Ningaloo Reef Marine Park, 370 km (230 mi) north, the town of **Carnarvon** is a popular stopover. Stroll the Fascine, a palm-lined harborside boardwalk, where the Gascoyne River flows into the Indian Ocean. One Mile Jetty, built in 1899, is the longest jetty in the north of Western Australia, and you can walk to the end or take the Coffee Pot Ocean Tramway. It's a top local fishing spot, with mulloway, tailor, mackerel, trevally, and bream below year-round. From March to July you can watch locals catch blue manna crabs in drop nets. Drive 70 km (44 mi) north of Carnarvon to view the **Blow Holes,** where ocean swells force trapped air and streams of water up to 66 feet in the air.

NINGALOO REEF MARINE PARK

Fodor'sChoice *1,512 km (937 mi) north of Perth, 550 km (341 mi) from Monkey*
★ *Mia.*

Some of Australia's most pristine coral reef runs 251 km (156 mi) along
the coast of the Exmouth Peninsula, very far north of Perth. A happy
conjunction of migratory routes and accessibility makes it one of the
best places on Earth to see huge manta rays, giant whale sharks, humpback whales, nesting turtles, and the annual coral spawning. Exmouth
makes a good overnight base for exploring the marine park.

The beauty of Exmouth doesn't end at the seashore. Also worth seeing near Exmouth is the **Cape Range National Park,** including the Yardie
Creek Gorge, a ruggedly beautiful area that's excellent for an Outback holiday. Covering more than 123,000 acres, the national park
includes red-rock canyons, limestone ranges, and 50 km (31 mi) of
pristine beaches. The abundant wildlife includes emus and red kangaroos. A highlight of the winter season is the profusion of wildflowers,
which include the Sturt Desert Pea and the Bird Flower. ✉*Follow N.W.
Coastal Hwy. north 1,170 km (725 mi) to Minilya turnoff; Exmouth is
374 km (232 mi) farther north.*

**OFF THE
BEATEN
PATH**

Karijini National Park. About 1,411 km (875 mi) northeast of Perth and
450 km (280 mi) from Monkey Mia is the Western Australian Outback
as people imagine it: deep-red rock formations, and craggy, deep gorges
sheltering tranquil, pristine pools.

The huge rocks, crags, and gorges that make up the Hamersley Range
in the Pilbara region, northeast of Monkey Mia, are among the most
ancient land surfaces in the world. Sediments deposited by an inland
sea more than 2.5 billion years ago were forced up by movements in
the earth's crusts and slowly weathered by natural elements through
succeeding eons. The gorges are the most popular attractions in the
national park—unexpected deep gouges in a seemingly flat landscape
are relatively accessible, some, such as Fortescue Falls and Ferns pool,
just a short walk from parking lots throughout the park. Information
on all the park's attractions can be found at the **Karijini Visitor Centre**
(☎08/9189–8121 ⊕ www.naturebase.net).

There are also longer walks such as the popular, one-hour Dales Gorge
Trail hike. Some trails are challenging and require you to climb over
boulders and rock ledges, as well as wade through freezing waters—but
the reward of getting to Joffre, Knox, and Hancock gorges makes it
worthwhile. You must let park rangers know before attempting to hike
into any of the more-remote locations. Day trips to the park are available through **Lestok Tours** (☎08/9188–2032 ⊕ www.lestoktours.com.
au) from A$130 per person, departing daily from Tom Price.

WHERE TO STAY

The town of Exmouth, close to the tip of North West Cape at the
northernmost edge of Ningaloo Reef Marine Park, is the biggest center for lodging, dining, shopping, and tours. Coral Bay, the park's

Gentle Giants: The Whale Sharks of Ningaloo Reef

Whale sharks are the largest sharks on the planet, growing up to 40 feet in length and weighing more than 11 tons full grown. Surprisingly, little is known about these giant creatures other than the fact that their ancestors probably swam in prehistoric seas some 65 million years ago. By the mid-1980s fewer than 350 were known to roam the tropical and warm oceans of the world. Today the population is thought to be larger, though no one knows exactly how many remain, and the shark is still listed as "vulnerable" by several conservation organizations.

Every year around March, the whale sharks congregate in large numbers close to the shore along the Ningaloo Reef Marine Park, drawn by the annual mass spawning of coral. This gathering offers a rare treat for visitors, who can take a boat out into the calm waters and go overboard with mask, flippers, and snorkel while the whale sharks gently glide by, close to the surface. You don't need to be an

experienced diver to take the plunge (but you should be moderately fit and able to swim).

Though they're massive animals, and are known to float through the water with their enormous mouths wide open, there's no need to fear the sharks—they're not carnivorous. Rather, they are what's known as filter-feeders; like certain whales, they eat by sucking vast quantities of sea water into their mouths, to filter out the plankton, krill, and other small sea creatures.

Masks, flippers and snorkels are provided by tour operators who visit the sharks; these include **Ningaloo Blue Charters** (☎1800/811338 ⊕ *www. ningalooblue.com.au*), which has tours from A\$350 per person, and **Coral Bay Adventures** (☎08/9942–5955, ⊕ *www.coralbayadventures.com.au*), with all-inclusive tours from A\$330 per person.

–Graham Hodgson

southern gateway, has a laid-back setting that's ideal for getting close to nature.

¢–\$\$　▥**Bayview Coral Bay.** The beachfront overlooking Coral Bay makes this property especially appealing. Three-bedroom holiday units here sleep up to eight, while cabins sleep four. Most of the RV and camp sites have electricity. This is an ideal spot for families and those seeking a relaxing environment near the water. The on-site café serves basic pizza, pasta, steak, and fish-and-chips. ⊠*Robinson St., 6701* ☎*08/9385–6655* ☎*08/9385–6867* ✐bcb@coralbaywa.com ⊕*www.coralbaywa.com* ➳*8 holiday units, 12 cabins, 250 powered sites* ⚫*In-hotel: restaurant, tennis courts, pool, laundry facilities, parking (no fee)* ▤*MC, V.*

¢–\$\$　▥**Sea Breeze Resort.** This Best Western hotel 5 km (3 mi) north of Exmouth occupies the converted officers' quarters of the town's former U.S. Naval Base. The small "cyclone-proof" property has an à la carte restaurant and a bar. All rooms have queen-size beds (if you're tall and sleeping alone, you can also order an extra-long single bed). Daily dive trips and whale-shark tours are scheduled. ⊠*Harold E.*

Holt Naval Base, 116 North C St., 6707 ☎08/9949–1800 📠08/9949–1300 ✉info@seabreezeresort.com.au ⊕www.seabreezeresort.com.au ☞27 rooms ⚲In-room: ethernet. In-hotel: restaurant, room service, bar, pool, public Wi-Fi, laundry service, laundry facilities ▭MC, V.

12

MONKEY MIA & NINGALOO REEF ESSENTIALS

TRANSPORTATION

BY AIR
Skywest has daily flights from Perth to Learmonth Airport, 37 km (23 mi) from Exmouth and 120 km (75 mi) from Coral Bay. A shuttle bus meets every flight and for a fee you can catch a ride to Exmouth.

Contact Skywest (☎*1300/660088* ⊕*www.skywest.com.au*).

BY BUS
Greyhound Australia services Monkey Mia, Carnarvon, Coral Bay, and Exmouth. The Exmouth Visitor Centre on Murat Road is the booking agent and bus terminal. Ningaloo Reef Bus has a daily bus service from Exmouth to Ningaloo Reef, departing at 8:30 AM and returning at 4:30 PM.

Contacts Greyhound Australia (☎*13–1499* ⊕*www.greyhound.com.au*). **Ningaloo Reef Bus** (☎*1800/999941*).

CONTACTS & RESOURCES

BANKS & EXCHANGE SERVICES
There are limited places in this area where you can exchange money and cash travelers checks. In Exmouth the Westpac branch is open weekdays 9:30–4. There are also ATMs (which accept Cirrus, Plus, Visa, and MasterCard). Major credit cards are widely accepted at restaurants, lodgings, and shops, but having some cash is a good idea.

Contact Westpac (✉*Learmonth St. at Maidstone Crescent, Exmouth, 6707* ☎*13–1862* ⊕*www.westpac.com.au*).

EMERGENCIES
In an emergency, dial **000** to reach an ambulance, the police, or the fire department.

Contact Exmouth District Hospital (✉*Lyons St.* ☎*08/9949–3666*).

TOURS
Ningaloo Reef Marine National Park, accessible from both Exmouth and Coral Bay, has opportunities to mix with the local wildlife. Coral Bay Adventures takes small groups out to the reef to swim with the whale sharks from March to June. Their glass-bottom boat also allows you to view the coral and tropical fish life without getting wet. Monkey Mia Yacht Charters has daily cruises ranging from one to eight hours on board the *Aristocat 2* catamaran; passengers get to see dolphins, dugongs, turtles, sea snakes, and sharks in the wild. Wildsight Tours also offers daily cruises on board their 60-foot catamaran, including a Dugong Cruise to see these elusive sea creatures.

Exmouth Diving Centre and Ningaloo Reef Dive both offer dive tours to various sites on Ningaloo Reef, including diving with whale sharks. For anglers—both expert and neophyte—Sportfishing Safaris operates daily fishing trips from Monkey Mia. Black snapper, pink snapper, cobia, mack tuna, mackerel, bluebone groper, coral trout, trevally, tailor, sharks, and mulloway are among the species seasonally available here; the best time of the year to fish is between March and August. Half-day fishing trips around Monkey Mia cost A$100 per person. Coral Bay Ocean Game Fishing also offers half-day or full-day fishing tours.

Contacts **Coral Bay Adventures** (☎ *08/9942–5955* ⊕ *www.coralbayadventures.com.au*). **Coral Bay Ocean Game Fishing** (☎ *08/9942–5874* ⊕ *www.mahimahicoralbay.com.au*). **Exmouth Diving Centre** (☎ *08/9949–1201* ⊕ *www.exmouthdiving.com.au*). **Monkey Mia Yacht Charters** (☎ *08/9948–1446* ⊕ *www.monkey-mia.net*). **Ningaloo Reef Dive** (☎ *08/9942–5824* ⊕ *www.ningaloo reefdive.com*). **Sportfishing Safaris** (☎ *08/9948–1387* ⊕ *www.sportfish.com.au*). **Wildsight Tours** (☎ *1800/241481* ⊕ *www.monkeymiawildsights.com.au*).

VISITOR INFORMATION

Contacts **Carnarvon Visitor Centre** (✉ *11 Robinson St., Carnarvon, 6701* ☎ *08/9941–1146* ⊕ *www.carnarvon.org.au*). **Exmouth Visitor Centre** (✉ *Murat Rd., Exmouth* ☎ *08/9949–1176 or 1800/287328* ⊕ *www.exmouthwa.com.au*). **Denham and Monkey Mia Visitor Centre** (✉ *29 Knight Terr., Denham and 23 km (14 mi) east of Denham on the eastern shore of Peron Peninsula* ☎ *08/9948–1010 or 1300/135887* ⊕ *www.sharkbaywa.com.au*).

Adventure Vacations

WORD OF MOUTH

"We have fabulous wines and if you like hiking, you can walk the Bibbulum Track from Perth to Albany and there is also the tree top walk at Pemberton."

—albaaust

Updated
by Graham
Hodgson

YOU'LL MISS AN IMPORTANT ELEMENT of Australia if you don't get away from the cities to explore "the bush" that is so deeply ingrained in the Australian character. Many of the adventure vacations today were journeys of exploration only a generation ago.

Adventure vacations are commonly split into soft and hard adventures. A hard adventure requires a substantial degree of physical participation; in soft adventures the destination rather than the means of travel is often what makes it an adventure. With most companies, the adventure guides' knowledge of flora and fauna—and love of the bush—is matched by a level of competence that ensures your safety even in dangerous situations.

BICYCLING

Cycling is an excellent way to explore a small region, allowing you to cover more ground than on foot and to observe far more than you could from the window of a car or bus. Riding down quiet country lanes is a great way to relax and get fit at the same time. Cycling rates as a hard adventure because of the amount of exercise involved.

NEW SOUTH WALES
Season: Year-round.
Locations: Blue Mountains, Snowy Mountains, Southern Highlands.
Cost: From A$125 for a half day and A$185 for one day to about A$1,265 for six days.
Tour Operators: Blue Mountains Adventure Company, Boomerang Bicycle Tours.

Against the backdrop of Australia's highest peaks, Blue Mountains Adventure Company has several one-day rides on mountain bikes through the plunging walled valleys that border Sydney, including a spectacular ride along Narrow Neck and through a glowworm tunnel. Boomerang Bicycle Tours offers one- to six-day tours of the Hunter Valley (including the region's boutique wineries), Snowy Mountains, Southern Highlands, and Sydney. High-quality front-suspension mountain bikes, helmets, wind jackets, camping gear, and meals are all supplied. An air-conditioned support vehicle and all accommodation (from guesthouses and wilderness resorts to hotels) are included.

QUEENSLAND
Season: Year-round.
Location: Cape Tribulation.
Cost: From A$145.
Tour Operator: Adventure Company.

Pristine rain forests, clear-running rivers, and white sandy beaches comprise Daintree and Cape Tribulation national parks (both World Heritage sites), north of the coastal city of Cairns. You can go crocodile spotting on river cruises and take botanical walks on tours organized by the Adventure Company. Tours range from one to three days and leave from Cairns.

SOUTH AUSTRALIA

Season: April–October.
Locations: Barossa and Clare valleys, Flinders Ranges, Kangaroo Island.
Cost: From A$560 for a weekend to around A$2,955 for a 10-day Flinders Ranges safari.
Tour Operator: Ecotrek Bogong Jack Adventures.

South Australia affords gentle cycling on quiet country roads, particularly on Kangaroo Island and around the famous wine regions of the Barossa and Clare valleys, as well as more challenging mountain-bike expeditions into the rugged Flinders Ranges, far to the north of Adelaide. Ecotrek Bogong Jack Adventures has several such cycling trips, varying from weekends in the wine areas to one-week rides on Kangaroo Island and through the Flinders Ranges.

TASMANIA

Season: November–March.
Locations: Central Tasmania and the north and east coasts.
Cost: From A$600 for two days to A$2,200 for six days, including camping equipment or accommodation, support vehicle, bicycles, and all meals.
Tour Operators: Tasmanian Expeditions, World Expeditions.

The relatively small size of Tasmania makes cycling a great option for exploring. The classic tour is Tasmanian Expeditions' Cycle Tasmania, a six-day trip from Launceston that leads through pastoral lands down to the fishing villages of the east coast. Also consider the Heritage Cycle, which takes six days through the inland heart of the island, including overnight stops at heritage bed-and-breakfast accommodations. All of these tours are also sold by World Expeditions.

VICTORIA

Season: October–April.
Locations: Great Ocean Road, northeast Victoria.
Cost: From A$810 for a two-day tour of the northeast wineries to around A$1,615 for a six-day tour of the Alpine region.
Tour Operator: Ecotrek Bogong Jack Adventures.

The two main areas of interest in the state are the Great Ocean Road and the northeast. However, although it's a spectacular ride, the Great Ocean Road is fairly narrow and heavily used, and therefore best avoided during the peak December and January summer holidays. The northeast is a more varied experience, combining contemporary wineries, country towns that thrived during the gold boom, and the forests and hills of the Australian Alps.

BUSHWALKING (HIKING)

The Australian bush is unique. The olive-green foliage of the eucalyptus may seem drab at first, but when you walk into a clearing carpeted with thick grass and surrounded by stately blue gums, the appeal (and wonderful fragrance) of these trees becomes evident. Chances are good that you'll cross paths with kangaroos, wallabies, goannas, and lizards—but your success rate will be much higher if you travel with an expert guide. Depending on the type of trail, bushwalking can be a soft or hard adventure. Associated high-adrenaline hard adventures are abseiling (rappelling) and canyoning, forms of vertical bushwalking well suited to the Blue Mountains of New South Wales.

NEW SOUTH WALES

Season: Year-round.
Locations: Barrington Tops, Blue Mountains, Snowy Mountains.
Cost: Rates start at A$95 for a half day. Longer trips cost on average about A$135 per day, including packs, equipment, guide, and food.
Tour Operators: Australian Wild Escapes, Blue Mountains Adventure Company, Mountain Adventure Centre.

The scope for casual bushwalking in New South Wales is extensive. One of the finest one-day walks in the Blue Mountains begins in Blackheath and winds through Grand Canyon. The National Pass to Wentworth Falls is also stunning. The Snowy Mountains beyond Perisher are excellent for walking, as are the national parks to the north—especially Barrington Tops, a basalt-capped plateau with rushing streams that have carved deep chasms in the extensive rain forest. The same areas are ideal for longer treks, too.

Mountain Adventure Centre operates half-day and overnight trips in the Snowy Mountains between November and April. Australian Wild Escapes specializes in small-group tours (two-person minimum).

The deeply eroded sandstone canyons of the Blue Mountains provide exhilarating terrain for abseiling as well as bushwalking. There's intense competition among tour operators in this area, so a full day of canyoning in the spectacular Grand Canyon or the sublime Claustral Canyon costs less than A$135, including lunch. Blue Mountains Adventure Company has more than a dozen different canyoning, climbing, and abseiling programs around this area.

SOUTH AUSTRALIA

Season: April–October.
Locations: Flinders Ranges, Gammon Ranges, Kangaroo Island.
Cost: From A$1,460 for seven days.
Tour Operator: Ecotrek Bogong Jack Adventures.

The Flinders Ranges is Australia's most sensational Outback park. The arid sandstone hills are actually the stumps of eroded mountains, and they're a first-rate site for bushwalking, wildlife-watching, and photography. In several places the hills are sliced through by creeks lined with towering river red gums, making fine spots for camping. The Gammon Ranges, the northern extremity of the Flinders Ranges, are even more rugged and severe, and highly recommended for hikers who enjoy challenging terrain. In addition to those in the Flinders and Gammon ranges, Ecotrek Bogong Jack Adventures also operates walks on Kangaroo Island.

TASMANIA

Season: November–May.

Locations: Central highlands; south, east, and west coasts.

Cost: From about A$130 per day, including camping equipment and meals, to A$2,350 for the 6-day Cradle Mountain Huts walk, or about A$2,590 for a comprehensive 13-day tour of the island.

Tour Operators: Cradle Mountain Huts, Freycinet Experience, Tasmanian Expeditions, World Expeditions.

At one time some of the best overnight walks in Tasmania were major expeditions suitable only for the highly experienced and very fit. These days, this area is still plenty remote—you must either fly or take an overnight ferry—but all levels of trip difficulty are available. The nine-day South Coast Track Expedition operated by Tasmanian Expeditions will certainly satisfy the rugged adventurer in you. The trail includes some easy stretches along pristine, secluded beaches, as well as difficult legs through rugged coastal mountains. It's the combination of difficult trails, extreme isolation, and the likelihood of foul weather that gives this walk spice.

Much easier hiking terrain can be found on the Freycinet Peninsula, on the east coast about a three-hour drive north of Hobart. Much of the peninsula can be explored only on foot. The road ends at the pink granite domes of the Hazards, which form a rampart across the middle of the peninsula. Beyond lies a pristine seascape of white-sand coves and sparkling water edged with granite knuckles. The only guided hike is the four-day walk conducted by Freycinet Experience. The optional 18-km (11-mi) hike over Mt. Graham on the second day is just for experienced trekkers. Hikers carry light day packs and spend the first two nights in comfortable camps, complete with wooden platforms, beds, and pillows. The final night is in a Tasmanian hardwood lodge situated to take advantage of the best views.

The best-known walk in Tasmania is the trail from Cradle Mountain to Lake St. Clair. It's so popular that boardwalks have been placed along some sections to prevent the path from turning into a quagmire. The walk starts and finishes in dense forest, but much of it runs along exposed highland ridges. The construction of the Cradle Mountain Huts has made this trail far more accessible. However, these huts are available only to hikers on one of Cradle Mountain Huts' escorted walks. Huts are well heated and extensively supplied; there are even warm showers. Other operators continue to conduct camping tours along the trail as well as elsewhere in Tasmania.

VICTORIA

Season: October–May.

Locations: Alpine National Park and the Victorian Alps.

Cost: From about A$85 for a day walk to about A$2,745 for eight days.

Tour Operators: Ecotrek Bogong Jack Adventures, Walkabout Gourmet Adventures.

Victoria's Alpine region affords bushwalking vacations to suit every taste. Ecotrek Bogong Jack Adventures has several five- to eight-day guided walks, many of which focus on the region's abundant wildflowers. Tours are based in a comfortable lodge in the Alpine village of Dinner Plain. Optional activities include trout fishing and nocturnal tours. Walkabout Gourmet Adventures has an epicurean five-day bushwalking experience, where travelers stay in a country resort and eat good food and drink fine wine while seeing wildlife and relaxing.

CAMEL TREKKING

Strange as it may seem, a camel trek is an extremely pleasant way to spend a week or two in Australia; the experience beautifully recaptures desert travel as it was in the past. Camels were imported to Australia in the 19th century, when they formed the backbone of the heavy-duty transport industry of the Outback. The Indian cameleers who drove them were known as "Afghans" (hence the name of the *Ghan* train, which follows the old desert route of the Afghan camel trains from Adelaide to Alice Springs). Many camels now roam wild in the Outback.

NORTHERN TERRITORY–THE RED CENTRE
Season: April–September (weekly departures), October–March (every two weeks).
Locations: Alice Springs, Uluru (Ayers Rock).
Cost: From A$45 for a one-hour ride to about A$450 for three days or A$750 for five days.
Tour Operators: Camels Australia, Frontier Camel Tours.

From their camel farm 100 km (60 mi) south of Alice Springs, Neil and Jayne Waters of Camels Australia arrange several camel-riding experiences, from short yard rides to five-day camel camping safaris through Rainbow Valley National Park, remote gorge country that includes the oldest watercourse in the world and an ancient stand of palms. Safaris take place in the cooler months between March and October.

Frontier Camel Tours conducts popular "Take a Camel Out to Dinner" and "Take a Camel Out to Breakfast" tours from their headquarters near Alice Springs, as well as one-hour camel rides that operate every morning and afternoon. The company also runs the Camel Depot near Uluru (Ayers Rock) that arranges sunrise and sunset camel rides away from the tourist crowds.

CROSS-COUNTRY SKIING

Unlike the jagged peaks of alpine regions elsewhere in the world, the rounded summits of the Australian Alps are ideal for cross-country skiing. In stark contrast to downhill skiers on crowded slopes, cross-country skiers have a chance to get away from the hordes and experience the unforgettable sensation of skiing through forests of eucalyptus trees, with their spreading branches, pale leaves, and impressionistic bark patterns.

NEW SOUTH WALES

Season: July–September.
Location: Snowy Mountains.
Cost: From A$65 for a full day of instruction to A$1,100 for a five-day snow-camping tour.
Tour Operator: Mountain Adventure Centre.

Some 450 km (279 mi) south of Sydney, Jindabyne is the major gateway to the Snowy Mountains, and home to Mountain Adventure Centre, an offshoot of Australia's most respected outdoor-equipment retail store. It has a complete selection of ski tours and cross-country instructional programs, from half-day trips to two-, five-, or seven-day lodge-based trips and five-day snow-camping tours across the trails of the main range.

13

DIVING

Australia is one of the world's premier diving destinations. Much of the attention centers on Queensland's Great Barrier Reef, but there's very good diving elsewhere as well—including Tasmania, Western Australia, and Lord Howe Island. Australian diving operations are generally well run and regulated, and equipment is modern and well maintained. Since this is a competitive industry, prices are fairly low by world standards, and the warm waters off the Queensland coast are an ideal location to practice basic dive skills. Still, if you're planning on learning to dive in Australia you should closely examine each operator's dive package (especially equipment rental and the number of open-water dives) rather than basing a decision solely on cost.

QUEENSLAND

Season: Year-round.
Locations: All along the coast and Great Barrier Reef islands.
Cost: From around A$148 for a day trip that includes a boat cruise and two dives. Five-day certification courses start at around A$560.
Tour Operators: Dive Adventures, Mike Ball Dive Adventures, Pro Dive Travel.

The main diving centers in Queensland are the island resorts: Cairns, the Whitsunday Islands, and Port Douglas.

TASMANIA

Season: Mainly summer, but the best east-coast conditions are in winter.
Locations: Bicheno, King Island.
Cost: From A$140 per boat dive, including equipment.
Tour Operators: Bicheno Dive Centre, King Island Dive Charter.

Australia's southernmost state is not the obvious place to go diving. However, Tasmania's east coast has a remarkably sunny climate and some exceptional kelp forests, magnificent sponge gardens, and exquisite sea life that includes anemones, basket stars, squid, octopus, and butterfly perch. In winter there's a chance to dive with dolphins and whales that visit here on annual migration from Antarctica. And King

Island in Bass Strait, off the north coast, has some very good wreck diving. Overall, Tasmania has one of Australia's most wreck-strewn coastlines. There are more than 20 sites, including the 1845 wreck of the *Cataraqui,* the country's worst maritime disaster.

WESTERN AUSTRALIA
Season: Diving year-round; with whale sharks March–July.
Location: Exmouth.
Cost: From A$375, including all equipment, transfer to the boat, an optional dive on Ningaloo Reef, buffet lunch, and soft drinks. The cost also includes the spotter aircraft, the runabout to keep you in contact with the whale sharks, and the whale shark interaction license fee.
Tour Operator: Exmouth Diving Centre.

Whale sharks are the world's largest fish—they can weigh up to 40 tons and measure 50 feet from nose to tail. However, although whale sharks *are* members of the shark family, they're also completely harmless. Like many whales, these creatures live on tiny krill—not fish, seals, or people. From about March through July each year, more than 100 whale sharks can be found along the Western Australian coast near Exmouth. The exact season varies, depending on the time of the spawning of the coral on Ningaloo Reef. Exmouth is one of the few places in the world where you can be fairly certain of encountering whale sharks.

If you decide to swim with the sharks, it's as if you have adopted a puppy the size of a truck—or have your own pet submarine. Government regulations prohibit touching them or swimming closer to them than a yard or so. It's an expensive day of diving because you need a large boat to take you out to the sharks, a spotter plane to find them, and a runabout to drop you in their path. Although most of the day is spent with whale sharks, it begins with a dive on Ningaloo Reef. The diversity of coral and marine life here isn't as remarkable as at the Great Barrier Reef, but there is a spectacular juxtaposition of large open-water fish and huge schools of bait fish. Outside of whale-shark season you can encounter a passing parade of humpback whales (from July through September) and nesting turtles (from November through February). Non-divers who wish to go snorkeling may join the expedition for a slightly reduced fee.

DOWNHILL SKIING

Despite Australia's lack of high mountains, downhill skiing remains a popular winter sport with thousands of well-heeled urbanites from Melbourne, Canberra, and Sydney. To cater to the demand, Australia's Alpine region has a well-developed infrastructure of ski resorts and lift facilities. The Alpine skiing region is concentrated in the undulating hills that form the eastern border between Victoria and New South Wales. Tasmania has some skiing; however, facilities and accommodations are far less developed than on the mainland.

NEW SOUTH WALES
Season: July–September.
Location: Snowy Mountains.
Cost: Lift passes cost around A$87 per day.

The state's downhill ski areas are Thredbo and Perisher Blue, both within the borders of Kosciuszko National Park. With a total of 50 lifts giving access to an area of more than 4,000 acres, Perisher Blue is the largest ski area in the country, incorporating the adjacent resorts of Perisher, Smiggins, and Blue Cow. Vertical drop measures about 1,160 feet, and the resort has on-snow accommodation from luxurious to basic, as well as feisty nightlife. Access to Perisher Blue is via the Skitube from the parking area at Bullocks Flat, which is conveniently accessible by car from the subalpine town of Jindabyne. This allows skiers to take advantage of the less expensive accommodation options in Jindabyne. Thredbo has the greatest vertical drop of any ski resort in the country: a total of 2,240 feet. However, the low base elevation means that artificial snow must often be made to ensure top-to-bottom cover. The village at Thredbo has a European flavor, with ski-in ski-out accommodation available.

VICTORIA
Season: July–September.
Locations: Falls Creek, Mt. Buller, Mt. Hotham.
Cost: Lift passes cost around A$87 per day.

Mt. Buller is the largest ski resort in the state and the closest to Melbourne; accordingly, the slopes are especially crowded on weekends. It has the second-largest lifting capacity in Australia after Perisher Blue, and the resort contains extensive snowmaking facilities as well as ski-in ski-out accommodations. Set at the foot of a bowl surrounded by mountains, Falls Creek is the prettiest of the Victorian ski resorts. The vertical drop measures only 600 feet, yet the 1,000-acre resort combines vastly different types of terrain. Serious skiers who like a challenge can head to Mt. Hotham, where more than 40% of the runs are rated "advanced."

FOUR-WHEEL-DRIVE TOURS

Australia is a vast land with a small population, so many Outback roads are little more than desert tracks. Black soil that turns muddy and slick after rain, the ubiquitous red dust of the center, and the continent's great sandy deserts make a four-wheel-drive vehicle a necessity for exploring the more remote areas. Outback motoring has a real element of adventure—on some roads it's standard practice to call in at the few homesteads along the way so they can initiate search procedures if you fail to turn up at the next farm down the track. The laconic Aussies you meet in such places are a different breed from urban Australians, and time spent with them is often memorable.

NORTHERN TERRITORY

Season: April–October.
Locations: Throughout the Northern Territory, but mainly in Kakadu.
Cost: From about A$480 for three days to A$1,750 for seven days.
Tour Operators: Adventure Center, World Expeditions.

Although the number of tourists at Kakadu National Park has risen dramatically each year, some sites can still be reached only by a four-wheel-drive vehicle, including Jim Jim Falls and Twin Falls—two of Australia's most scenic attractions. At both of these falls the water plunges over the escarpment to the floodplains beneath. Below the falls are deep, cool pools and beautiful palm-shaded beaches. The Adventure Center has comprehensive tours of this remarkable area. World Expeditions conducts a one-week adventure safari into the wilderness of Kakadu that concludes with a canoe safari along the Katherine River. If you have a particular interest in Aboriginal culture, the seven-day (and longer) Kakadu trips, organized by World Expeditions, are recommended.

The **Northern Territory Tourist Commission** (✉ *43 Mitchell St., Darwin, NT, 0800* ☎*13–6110* 🖷*08/8951–8550* ⊕*www.travelnt.com.au*) can provide more information about the numerous tour operators based in Darwin.

QUEENSLAND

Season: Cooktown year-round; Cape York June–December.
Location: North of Cairns.
Cost: From A$285 for a one-day fly-drive Cooktown safari to A$2,595 for the 14-day Cape York Complete Camping Safari.
Tour Operator: Wilderness Challenge.

Every four-wheel-drive enthusiast in Australia seeks out Cape York, the most northerly point of the Australian mainland. After passing through the rain forest north of Port Douglas, the track travels through relatively dry vegetation the rest of the way. Several galleries of spectacular Aboriginal rock paintings are here, as are a historic telegraph station and the notorious Jardine River, whose shifting bottom made fording very tricky in the past. Until a few years ago, reaching the Cape was a major achievement; now a ferry service across the Jardine makes it easier, but Cape York is still frontier territory—a land of mining camps, Aboriginal settlements, and enormous cattle stations. For all intents and purposes, civilization stops at Cooktown, some 700 km (434 mi) from the tip of Cape York. From their base in Cairns, Wilderness Challenge arranges several four-wheel-drive experiences in the region, including a one-day fly-drive trip to Cooktown and the 14-day Cape York Complete Camping Safari: a four-wheel-drive trip to the tip of Cape York, including a fishing trip into the Torres Strait islands.

SOUTH AUSTRALIA

Season: Year-round.
Locations: Flinders Ranges, Kangaroo Island.
Cost: Kangaroo Island from about A$310 for a one-day tour to A$1,900 for a four-day nature retreat tour; Flinders Ranges from about A$195 for a one-day tour to A$1,055 for a four-day tour.

Tour Operators: Beyond Tours, Exceptional Kangaroo Island, Kangaroo Island Odysseys, Kangaroo Island Wilderness Tours.

Unless you have the time to walk, the rugged areas of South Australia are best explored by four-wheel-drive vehicle. Kangaroo Island is home to many Australian animals, including kangaroos, koalas, fur seals, fairy penguins, and sea lions, as well as such bizarre natural features as huge limestone arches and weatherworn rocks that resemble Henry Moore sculptures. Exceptional Kangaroo Island operates a series of tours, the most comprehensive being a three-day, two-night package. Kangaroo Island Odysseys has a similar program of tours lasting from one to four days, with short optional wildlife-based extension tours.

To the north of Adelaide, the rugged gorges, hills, and creeks of the Flinders Ranges provide an ideal backdrop for four-wheel-drive adventures. Beyond Tours operates two-, three-, and four-day trips from Adelaide to the Flinders Ranges, but be aware that the round-trip journey from Adelaide—485 km (300 mi) in each direction—absorbs much of the itinerary on the shorter trips.

WESTERN AUSTRALIA—THE KIMBERLEY

Season: May–November.
Location: The Kimberley.
Cost: About A$1,745 for a four-day safari; about A$945 for a two-day fly-drive Bungle Bungle tour, or A$775 for a one-day fly-in tour; about A$4,995 for a 13-day camping safari.
Tour Operators: Discover West Holidays, Kimberley Wilderness Adventures.

Most of the four-wheel-drive adventures in Western Australia take place in the Kimberley region in the far north. The only practical time to visit the Kimberley is during the Dry, May through November, because roads are very often flooded during the Wet.

Tour operators in the region are based either in Kununurra, at the eastern end of the Kimberley, or Broome, in the western end. Broome is also a resort center, a multicultural town with a wonderful beach and a number of hotel options—an ideal place to recover from the rigors of the Kimberley. Reaching Windjana Gorge, at the western end of the Kimberley, takes two days from Broome, while an absolute minimum of five days is required to experience some of the more remote parts of the region. Kununurra is the starting point for trips to the Bungle Bungle, spectacular beehive-stripe domes. A fly-drive safari to the Bungle Bungle takes a minimum of two days.

Kimberley Wilderness Adventures operates several tours from both Broome and Kununurra. Many of these tours use permanent campsites, which provide a reasonable level of comfort. Discover West Holidays has a one-day fly-in tour from Kununurra, with a combined four-wheel-drive and hiking tour of the highlights. The company also operates four-wheel-drive trips to the Bungle Bungle from Turkey Creek.

HORSEBACK RIDING

Trail bikes and four-wheel-drive vehicles have slowly been replacing horses on Australian farms and stations for the past two decades. On the plains and coastal lowlands the transformation is complete, but horses still remain a part of rural life in the highlands, and it's here that the best horseback adventures can be found. On a horse trek you come closer to the life of the pioneer Australian bushmen than in any other adventure pursuit. Indeed, the majority of treks are led by Australians with close links to the traditions of bush life.

Riding through alpine meadows, following mountain trails, and sleeping under the stars are excellent ways to see the Australian bush. A typical horseback vacation lasts several days, and the food and equipment for each night's camp is brought in by packhorse or four-wheel-drive vehicle. Although a cook, a guide, and all specialist equipment are provided, participants are expected to help look after the horses. An Australian saddle is a cross between the high Western saddle and the almost flat English one.

NEW SOUTH WALES
Season: Year-round, but mainly November–April.
Locations: Blue Mountains, New England Highlands, Snowy Mountains.
Cost: From A\$165 for a day ride to A\$325 for two days, and A\$1,650 for five days.
Tour Operators: Equitrek Australia, Megalong Australian Heritage Centre, Mountain Adventure Centre, Reynella Kosciuszko Rides.

The Great Dividing Range, which extends right through New South Wales, has some excellent trails for horseback riding. Almost every country town has a riding school with horses for rent, but a few long rides are particularly outstanding. In the Snowy Mountains high country, a six-day summer ride from Reynella homestead through Kosciuszko National Park covers terrain ranging from open plains to alpine forests. Riders camp out in some of the most beautiful valleys in the park—valleys not easily accessible except by horse. A hundred years ago this was the stuff of pioneer legend. From its base at the foot of the Blue Mountains just outside Sydney, Megalong Australian Heritage Centre conducts guided horse rides along forest trails. Mountain Adventure Centre organizes trail rides through the ranges of Kosciuszko National Park, from two hours to overnight camping treks.

In addition to its several New South Wales riding trips, Equitrek Australia arranges riding in South Australia, Queensland, Western Australia, and the Northern Territory.

VICTORIA
Season: October–May.
Location: Victorian high plains.
Cost: From about A\$70 for a two-hour ride, to A\$900 for three days, and A\$1,500 for five days.
Tour Operators: Bogong Horseback Adventures.

An important part of the Australian rural mythology is an A. B. (Banjo) Paterson 1895 poem entitled "The Man from Snowy River," based on the equestrian feats of riders in the Victorian high plains who rounded up stock and horses from seemingly inaccessible valleys. For those who wish to emulate the hero of that work, several operators, such as Bogong Horseback Adventures, have rides of 2 to 12 days in the area. Part of the journey is spent above the tree line, where, as Banjo Paterson said, "the horses' hooves strike firelight from the flintstones every stride." Accommodations are either in tents or in the original bushmen's huts that dot the high country.

13

RAFTING

The exhilaration of sweeping down into the foam-filled jaws of a rapid is always tinged with fear—white-water rafting is, after all, much like being tossed into a supersize washing machine. Although this sort of excitement appeals to many people, the attraction of rafting in Australia involves much more. As you drift downriver during the lulls between the white water, it's wonderful to sit back and watch the wilderness unfold, whether it's stately river gums overhanging the stream, towering cliffs, or forests of eucalyptus on the surrounding slopes. Rafting means camping by the river at night, drinking billy tea brewed over the campfire, letting the sound of the stream lull you to sleep at night, or spying an elusive platypus at dawn. Rivers here are smaller and trickier than the ones used for commercial rafting in North America, and rafts usually hold only four to six people. Rafting companies provide all rafting and camping equipment—you only need clothing that won't be damaged by water (cameras are carried in waterproof barrels), a sleeping bag (in some cases), and sunscreen.

NEW SOUTH WALES
Season: Generally September–May.
Locations: The Murray River in the southern part of New South Wales, the Gwydir River in the center, and the Nymboida River in the north.
Cost: From about A$160 for a one-day Nymboida trip to about A$360 for two days, including all camping and rafting equipment.
Tour Operator: Live Adrenalin.

The upper reaches of Australia's longest waterway, the Murray River, are open for rafting between September and November, when melting snow feeds the stream. The river is cold, but the rapids are challenging, and the Australian Alps are dressed in all their spring glory.

The Gwydir River is fed by a large dam, and the scenery downriver is mainly pastoral, but the river has a series of challenging rapids.

The Nymboida River is the premier white-water river in the state and also the warmest, flowing through beautiful subtropical rain forest near Coffs Harbour.

TASMANIA
Season: November–March.
Locations: Franklin River, west coast.
Cost: From about A$2,350 for 9 days to A$2,550 for 11 days.
Tour Operators: World Expeditions.

With deep rocky chasms, grand forested valleys, beautiful sandy beaches, and miles of untouched wilderness, the Franklin River has the most spectacular and rewarding rafting in Australia. The river leads through a truly remote area of Tasmania—there are few places where you can join or leave the river. You have the choice of exploring either the lower or upper parts of the Franklin, or the entire navigable length. By far the most rewarding option is covering the entire river. The combination of isolation, beauty, difficult rapids, and strenuous portages ensures that rafters finish the trip with a real feeling of achievement. It's a difficult and challenging journey that should be tackled only by travelers who are reasonably fit and comfortable in the bush.

SAILING

Australia has wonderful conditions for sailing, a population addicted to the water, and a climate that allows comfortable boating year-round. Take a cruise on Sydney Harbour to see just how eagerly Australians embrace their maritime tradition, in boats from sea kayaks to sailing yachts to vast luxury cruisers and the amazing 16-footers, the Formula 1 craft of the Australian sailing world.

NEW SOUTH WALES
Season: Year-round.
Location: Sydney Harbour.
Cost: Four-hour cruises cost from A$95 per person; skippered cruises on Beneteau yachts (classic French-designed sailboats) start at A$1,230 for four hours; bareboat Beneteau charters start at A$1,385 per day.
Tour Operators: Sail Australia, Sydney by Sail.

Sydney Harbour is the finest single sailing destination in the country, both in terms of its natural credentials and the selection of sailing options. Choices include small catamarans that can be rented by the hour, yachts that can be chartered by day, and sailboats that let you gain hands-on experience as a crew member. Summer weekends are the busiest time; however, the harbor is sufficiently large and diversified to offer quiet anchorages even in peak season.

QUEENSLAND
Season: Year-round.
Location: Whitsunday Islands.
Cost: From about A$465 to A$1,320 per day for a bareboat charter, about A$480 per person for a two-night, three-day cruise on a crewed vessel.
Tour Operators: ProSail Queensland, Sail Australia.

The state's premier sailing area is the Whitsunday Islands. Stretching off the mid-Queensland coast, these rugged, jigsaw-shape islands are encircled by bays that make marvelous natural marinas. Of the 100 islands in the group, at least half have comfortable anchorages.

There are several yacht charter specialists in the region with craft to suit most budgets and levels of nautical know-how. For experienced sailors bareboat charters are the best option; despite the name, a bareboat generally comes complete with such creature comforts as a barbecue, stereo system, hot showers, a well-equipped kitchen, and complete safety gear. You provide the crew and supplies for the cruise—you can even hire a skipper (for about A$200 a day) who can do the sailing for you. For solo travelers or couples looking to share a boat, several sailing vessels offer scheduled cruises through the Whitsundays, usually on a five- or seven-day itinerary. Passengers can either sleep in multiberth cabins or camp on the beach.

The most convenient starting points for Whitsunday cruising are the jet airports at Hamilton Island and Proserpine. Hamilton is linked to both Sydney and Melbourne via direct flights, but the choice of charter operators here is more restricted. Proserpine is about 25 km (15½ mi) inland from the marinas at Airlie Beach. Although sailing is possible year-round, the wettest months are January to March and the windiest are March to May.

ProSail Queensland operates crewed yachts exclusively, while Sail Australia operates both crewed yachts and bareboat charters.

VISITING ANTARCTICA

Australia competes with Argentina, Chile, and New Zealand as one of the major stepping-off points for trips to Antarctica. Indeed, Australia claims the largest share of Antarctica for administrative purposes, the Australian Antarctic Territory comprising 42% of the continent. Passenger ships specially adapted for the frozen continent depart for the Ross Sea from the Tasmanian port of Hobart between December and February.

Season: December–February.
Locations: Cruises from Hobart. Flights from Sydney and Melbourne, with connections from other Australian cities.
Cost: Flights from A$899 to A$5,199; cruises from A$7,680 for 11 days to A$15,600 for 19 days.
Tour Operators: Adventure Associates, Croydon Travel, World Expeditions.

A faster and cheaper option is to take a one-day Qantas overflight of Antarctica organized by Croydon Travel. Taking off from Sydney or Melbourne, you fly directly to the ice continent. You'll have good views of the mountains and ice, although you'll still be too high to see animals. It's worthwhile paying extra for a window seat not over the wing.

Tour Operators

There are far more adventure-tour operators in Australia than it's possible to include in this chapter. Most are small and receive little publicity outside their local areas; to get more information about them, you can either stop by their storefront locations (addresses for small-town tour offices are included below), or contact the relevant state tourist office.

Adventure Associates. Box 4414, Sydney, NSW, 2001 ⊠ 12–14 O'Connell St., Level 7, Sydney, NSW ☎ 02/8916–3000 for reservations, 800/222–141 ⊕ www.adventureassociates.com.

Adventure Center. ⊠ 1311 63rd St., Suite 200, Emeryville, CA, 94608, U.S. ☎ 510/654–1879 or 800/228–8747 ⊕ www.adventure-center.com.

Adventure Company. Box 2377, Cairns, QLD, 4870 ⊠ 287 Draper St., Cairns, QLD ☎ 07/4051–4777 ⊕ www.adventures.com.au.

Adventure Guides Australia. Box 548, Bright, VIC, 3741 ☎ 03/5755–1851, 04/1928–0614 (mobile) ⊕ www.adventureguidesaustralia.com.au.

Aurora Expeditions. 182 Cumberland St., The Rocks, NSW, 2000 ☎ 02/9252–1033 or 1800/637688 ⊕ www.auroraexpeditions.com.au.

Australian Wild Escapes. Box 42, Pennant Hills, NSW, 1715 ☎ 02/9980–8788 ⊕ www.australianwildescapes.com.

Back of Beyond Tours. ⊠ 316 The Terrace, Port Pirie, SA, 5540 ☎ 08/8632–1288 ⊕ www.backofbeyondtours.com.au.

Bicheno Dive Centre. ⊠ 2 Scuba Ct., Bicheno, TAS, 7215 ☎ 03/6375–1138 ⊕ www.bichenodive.com.au.

Blue Mountains Adventure Company. Box 242, Katoomba, NSW, 2780 ⊠ 84a Bathurst Rd., Katoomba, NSW ☎ 02/4782–1271 ⊕ www.bmac.com.au.

Bogong Horseback Adventures. Box 230, Mt. Beauty, VIC, 3699 ☎ 03/5754–4849 ⊕ www.bogonghorse.com.au.

Boomerang Bicycle Tours. Box 5054, Kingsdene, NSW, 2118 ☎ 02/9890–1996

Camels Australia. PMB 74 Stuarts Well, Alice Springs, NT, 0872 ☎ 08/8956–0925 ⊕ www.camels-australia.com.au.

Cradle Mountain Huts. Box 1879, Launceston, TAS, 7250 ⊠ Pleasant Banks, 170 Leighlands Rd., Evandale ☎ 03/6391–9339 ⊕ www.cradlehuts.com.au.

Croydon Travel. ⊠ 34 Main St., Croydon, VIC, 3136 ☎ 03/9725–8555 ⊕ www.croydontravel.com.au.

Discover West Holidays. Box 8073, Subiaco, WA, 6008 ☎ 08/6263–6410 ⊕ www.discoverwest.com.au.

Dive Adventures. ⊠ 32 York St., Level 9, Sydney, NSW, 2000 ☎ 02/9299–4633 ⊕ www.diveadventures.com.

Ecotrek Bogong Jack Adventures. Box 1020, Flinders Park, SA, 5025 ☎ 08/8346–4155 ⊕ www.ecotrek.com.au.

Equitrek Australia. ⊠ 5 King Rd., Ingleside, NSW, 2101 ☎ 02/9913–9408 ⊕ www.equitrek.com.au.

Exceptional Kangaroo Island. Box 169, Kingscote, Kangaroo Island, SA, 5223 ☎ 08/8553–9119 ⊕ www.adventurecharters.com.au.

Exmouth Diving Centre. ✉ *Payne St., Exmouth, WA, 6707* ☎ *08/9949– 1201* ⊕ *www.exmouthdiving.com.au.*

Freycinet Experience. ✍ *Box 43, Battery Point, TAS, 7004* ☎ *03/6223– 7565* ⊕ *www.freycinet.com.au.*

Frontier Camel Tours. ✍ *Box 8483, Alice Springs, NT, 0871* ☎ *08/8950– 3030* ⊕ *www.cameltours.com.au.*

Kangaroo Island Odysseys. ✉ *34 Addison St., Kingscote, Kangaroo Island, SA, 5223* ☎ *08/8553–0386* ⊕ *www.kiodysseys.com.au.*

Kangaroo Island Wilderness Tours. ✉ *42 Cook St., Parndana, Kangaroo Island, SA, 5220* ☎ *08/8559–5033* ⊕ *www.wildernesstours.com.au.*

Kimberley Wilderness Adventures. ✉ *475 Hampton St., Hampton, VIC, 3188* ☎ *03/9277–8444* ⊕ *www. kimberleywilderness.com.au.*

King Island Dive Charter. ✉ *15 Blackwood St., Grassy, TAS, 7256* ☎ *03/6461–1133* ⊕ *www. kingislanddivecharter.com.au.*

Live Adrenalin. ✉ *10/37 Nicholson St., Balmain East, NSW, 2041* ☎ *02/8755–3100* ⊕ *www. adrenalin.com.au.*

Megalong Australian Heritage Centre. ✉ *Megalong Rd., Megalong Valley, NSW, 2785* ☎ *02/4787–8188* ⊕ *www. megalong.cc.*

Mike Ball Dive Adventures. ✉ *143 Lake St., Cairns, QLD, 4870* ☎ *07/4053–0500, 800/952–4319 in U.S.* ⊕ *www.mikeball.com.*

Mountain Adventure Centre. ✉ *5 Kosciuszko Rd., Jindabyne, NSW, 2627* ☎ *02/6456–2922* ⊕ *www. mountainadventurecentre.com.au.*

Pro Dive Travel. ✉ *Shop 8, The Clock Tower, 35 Harrington St., The Rocks, NSW, 2000* ☎ *02/9255–0300* ⊕ *www. prodive.com.au.*

ProSail Queensland. ✍ *Box 973, Airlie Beach, QLD, 4802* ✉ *251 Shute Harbour Rd., Airlie Beach, QLD* ☎ *300/653–100* ⊕ *www. prosail.com.au.*

Reynella Kosciuszko Rides. ✉ *Reynella., Adaminaby, NSW, 2630* ☎ *02/6454–2386* ⊕ *www. reynellarides.com.au.*

Sail Australia. ✍ *Box 417, Cremorne, NSW, 2090* ☎ *02/4322– 8227* ⊕ *www.sailaustralia.com.au.*

Sydney by Sail. ✉ *National Maritime Museum, 2 Murray St., Darling Harbour, NSW, 2000* ☎ *02/9280–1110* ⊕ *sydneybysail.com.*

Tasmanian Expeditions. ✍ *Box 5010, Launceston, TAS, 7250* ☎ *03/6339–3999* ⊕ *www.tas-ex.com.*

Walkabout Gourmet Adventures. ✍ *Box 564, Beecroft, NSW, 2119* ☎ *02/9980–2928* ⊕ *www. walkaboutgourmet.com.*

Wilderness Challenge. ✍ *Box 254, Cairns, QLD, 4870* ☎ *07/4035–4488* ⊕ *www.wilderness-challenge.com.au.*

World Expeditions. ✉ *71 York St., Level 5, Sydney, NSW, 2000* ☎ *02/8270-8400* ⊕ *www. worldexpeditions.com.au.*

13

Australia
Essentials

PLANNING TOOLS, EXPERT INSIGHT, GREAT CONTACTS

There are planners and there are those who, excuse the pun, fly by the seat of their pants. We happily place ourselves among the planners. Our writers and editors try to anticipate all the issues you may face before and during any journey, and then they do their research. This section is the product of their efforts. Use it to get excited about your trip to Australia, to inform your travel planning, or to guide you on the road should the seat of your pants start to feel threadbare.

GETTING STARTED

We're really proud of our Web site: Fodors.com is a great place to begin any journey. Scan Travel Wire for suggested itineraries, travel deals, restaurant and hotel openings, and other up-to-the-minute info. Check out Booking to research prices and book plane tickets, hotel rooms, rental cars, and vacation packages. Head to Talk for on-the-ground pointers from travelers who frequent our message boards. You can also link to loads of other travel-related resources.

▮ RESOURCES

ONLINE TRAVEL TOOLS

ALL ABOUT AUSTRALIA

Australia.com (⊕ *www.australia.com*): the official site of the Australia Tourist Commission has information on every aspect of life and travel in Australia and is a great pre-trip resource. **Breakloose** (⊕ *www.breakloose.com.au*) is an adventure tourism portal—there's information on adrenalin hits Down Under and links to operators. **Walkabout** (⊕ *www.walkabout.com.au*) is a travel site with detailed information and maps for many destinations, organized thematically and regionally.

Aboriginal Culture Aboriginal Heritage (⊕ www.cultureandrecreation.gov.au/articles/indigenous) is a government-run Web site with good information on aboriginal art and culture. **Aboriginal Tourism Australia** (⊕ www.ataust.org.au) is a national organization aimed at protecting and developing Aboriginal tourism; it publishes a booklet with advice on buying indigenous art. **National Gallery of Australia Aboriginal and Torres Strait Islander Collection** (⊕ www.nga.gov.au): one of the best collections of indigenous Australian art. **Papunya Tula Artists** (⊕ www.papunyatula.com.au/): Australia's best-known Aboriginal artists' group.

Back to Nature Birds Australia (⊕ www.birdsaustralia.com.au): everything you need to know about Aussie feathered friends. **Confederation of Bushwalking Clubs of NSW** (⊕ www.bushwalking.org.au) is full of excellent advice on bushwalking—hiking in national parks and wilderness areas. **Department of the Environment and Water Resources** (⊕ www.environment.gov.au): a government page packed with information on natural Australia, including links to all national park Web sites. **Eco Tourism Australia** (⊕ www.ecotourism.org.au): this non-profit body oversees and approves eco-tourism ventures Down Under. **Great Barrier Reef Marine Park Authority** (⊕ www.gbrmpa.gov.au): the official site for Australia's most famous natural wonder.

Business Australian Financial Review (⊕ www.afr.com): the leading business daily. **business.gov.au** (⊕ www.business.gov.au): the Australian government's business portal is a wealth of online information about business resources Down Under. **U.S. Commercial Service Australia** (⊕ www.buyusa.gov/australia/en/): this U.S.–government site has great tips and links for business travelers to Australia.

Culture and Entertainment Australian Government Culture and Recreation Portal (⊕ www.cultureandrecreation.gov.au) is a one-stop information shop on all aspects of Australia culture, including links to organizations and events. **Australian Slang** (⊕ www.koalanet.com.au/australian-slang.html): a tongue-in-cheek glossary to help you understand Aussie English. **Collections Australia Network** (⊕ www.collectionsaustralia.net) is an official umbrella project with information on Australia's cultural heritage and links to museums, galleries, and libraries all over the country.

Currency Conversion Google (⊕ www.google.com) does currency conversion. Just type in the amount you want to convert and an explanation of how you want it converted (e.g., "14 Swiss francs in dollars"), and then voilà. **Oanda.com** (⊕ www.oanda.com) also allows you to print out a handy table with the current day's conversion rates. **XE.com** (⊕ *www.xe.com*) is a good currency conversion Web site.

Food and Wine **Australia Bushfood and Native Medicine Forum** (⊕ *www.bushfood. net*) is a searchable discussion forum about native Australian foods. **Australian Wine** (⊕ *www.wineaustralia.com*): the official industry site has a good overview of Australian wines by type and by region. **Best Restaurants of Australia** (⊕ *www.bestrestaurants. com.au*) has searchable reviews for eateries all over Oz. **Eat Australia** (⊕ *www.eataustralia. info*) has links to different aspects of Australian food and cooking.

Newspapers and Media **Australian Broadcasting Corporation (ABC)** (⊕ *www.abc.net. au*): Australia's main publicly funded media broadcaster. **News.com.au** (⊕ *www.news.com. au*) is an excellent online portal for all Australian news. **Sydney Morning Herald** (⊕ *www. smh.com.au*): a quality daily broadsheet favored by Australia's liberal intellectuals. **The Age** (⊕ *www.theage.com.au*): this Melbourne-based broadsheet is the city's favorite news source. **The Australian** (⊕ *www.theaustralian. news.com.au*) is a national broadsheet owned by Rupert Murdoch; it sits ideologically right of center.

Safety **Transportation Security Administration** (*TSA;* ⊕ *www.tsa.gov*).

Time Zones **Timeanddate.com** (⊕ *www. timeanddate.com/worldclock*) can help you figure out the correct time anywhere.

VISITOR INFORMATION

The Australian Tourist Commission Web site is one of the best places to start planning your trip. As well as general information, they have package deals and have searchable listings for U.S. travel agents who specialize in Australia.

For more specific information, visit the individual states' Web sites.

Countrywide Information **Australian Tourist Commission** (☎ *310/695–3200* ⊕ *www. australia.com*).

Regional Information Each Australian state has its own tourism Web site where you can find state-specific maps, thematically organized listings, travel information, and links to accommodation and transport. Some have free state travel guides that they'll send to you. In general, they handle queries online.

Contacts **Australian Capital Tourism** (⊕ *www.visitcanberra.com.au*). **Northern Territory** (⊕ *www.travelnt.com*). **South Australian Tourism Commission** (⊕ *www.southoz. com*). **Tourism New South Wales** (⊕ *www. sydneyaustralia.com*). **Tourism Queensland** (⊕ *www.queenslandholidays.com.au*). **Tourism Tasmania** (⊕ *www.discovertasmania.com. au*). **Tourism Western Australia** (⊕ *www. westernaustralia.com*). **Welcome to Victoria** (⊕ *www.visitvictoria.com.au*).

▌THINGS TO CONSIDER

GEAR

If Crocodile Dundee is your idea of an Aussie style icon, think again: Melbournites and Sydneysiders are as fashion-conscious as New Yorkers. In the big cities, slop around in shorts and you might as well wear an "I'm a tourist" badge. Instead, pack nicer jeans, Capri pants, skirts, or dress shorts for urban sightseeing. A jacket and tie or posh dress are only necessary if you plan on some seriously fine dining.

Things are a bit different out of town. No Aussie would be seen dead on the beach without their "thongs," as flip-flops are confusingly called here. Wherever you are, your accessories of choice are high-quality sunglasses and a hat with a brim—the sun is strong AND dangerous. Carry insect repellent and avoid lotions or perfume in the tropics, as they attract mosquitoes and other insects.

A light sweater or jacket will keep you comfy in autumn, but winter in the southern states demands a heavier coat—ideally a raincoat with a zip-out wool lining. You should pack sturdy walking boots if you're planning any bushwalking, otherwise sneakers or flats are fine.

Australian pharmacies stock all the usual hygiene products (including tampons and condoms) and toiletries, plus a whole lot of fabulous local brands often not available overseas. Grocery stores and supermarkets frown on you using too many plastic bags—carry a foldable canvas tote and you'll blend in perfectly.

PASSPORTS & VISAS

To enter Australia for up to 90 days, you need a valid passport and a visa (New Zealand nationals are the exception). These days, instead of a visa label or stamp in your passport, citizens of the U.S. (and many other countries) can get an Electronic Travel Authority (ETA). This is an electronically stored travel permit. It saves you time both when you apply—the process is all online—and when you arrive in Australia.

To obtain an ETA for Australia you must: 1) hold an ETA-eligible passport; 2) be visiting Australia for tourism, family, or business; 3) stay less than three months; 4) be in good health; and 5) have no criminal convictions. The Visitor ETA allows you as many visits of up to 90 days as you like within a 12-month period, but remember that no work in the country is allowed. If you're visiting Australia on business, a Short Validity Business ETA might be more appropriate. Technically, both are free of charge, but you need to pay a A$20 handling charge by credit card. Children traveling on a parent's passport also need an ETA. You can apply for the ETA yourself or your travel agent can do it for you.

At present, Australia doesn't require a notorized letter of permission if only one parent is traveling with a child, but it's always best to err on the side of caution and take along such a letter if you can.

Info Department of Immigration and Multicultural and Indigenous Affairs (⊕ *www.*

immi.gov.au). **Electronic Travel Authority (ETA) Applications** (⊕ *www.eta.immi.gov.au*).

PASSPORTS

We're always surprised at how few Americans have passports—only 25% at this writing. This number is expected to grow in coming years, when it becomes impossible to re-enter the United States from trips to neighboring Canada or Mexico without one. Remember this: A passport verifies both your identity and nationality—a great reason to have one.

U.S. passports are valid for 10 years. You must apply in person if you're getting a passport for the first time; if your previous passport was lost, stolen, or damaged; or if your previous passport has expired and was issued more than 15 years ago or when you were under 16. All children under 18 must appear in person to apply for or renew a passport. Both parents must accompany any child under 14 (or send a notarized statement with their permission) and provide proof of their relationship to the child.

■TIP➔ Before your trip, make two copies of your passport's data page (one for someone at home and another for you to carry separately). Or scan the page and e-mail it to someone at home and/or yourself.

There are 13 regional passport offices, as well as 7,000 passport acceptance facilities in post offices, public libraries, and other governmental offices. If you're renewing a passport, you can do so by mail. Forms are available at passport acceptance facilities and online.

The cost to apply for a new passport is $97 for adults, $82 for children under 16; renewals are $67. Allow six weeks for processing, both for first-time passports and renewals. For an expediting fee of $60 you can reduce this time to about two weeks. If your trip is less than two weeks away, you can get a passport even more rapidly by going to a passport office with the necessary documentation. Private expediters can get things done in as little as 48 hours, but charge hefty fees for their services.

U.S. Passport Information U.S. Department of State (☎ *877/487–2778* ⊕ *http://travel. state.gov/passport*).

U.S. Passport & Visa Expediters A. Briggs Passport & Visa Expeditors (☎ *800/806– 0581 or 202/464–3000* ⊕ *www.abriggs.com*). **American Passport Express** (☎ *800/455– 5166 or 603/559–9888* ⊕ *www.americanpassport.com*). **Passport Express** (☎ *800/362–6 or 401/272–4612* ⊕ *www.passportexpress.com*). **Travel Document Systems** (☎ *800/874–5100 or 202/638–3800* ⊕ *www.traveldocs.com*). **Travel the World Visas** (☎ *866/886–8472 or 301/495–7700* ⊕ *www.world-visa.com*).

GENERAL REQUIREMENTS FOR AUSTRALIA	
Passport	Must be valid for duration of visit
Visa	Electronic Travel Authority or visa required for Americans
Vaccinations	See shots and medications below
Driving	US drivers license accepted
Departure Tax	A$38, included in ticket price

SHOTS & MEDICATIONS

Unless you're arriving from an area that has been infected with yellow fever, typhoid, or cholera, you don't need to get any shots or carry medical certificates to enter Australia.

Australia is relatively free from diseases prevalent in many countries. In the far north there have been occasional localized outbreaks of dengue and Ross River fever—just take the usual precautions against mosquito bites (cover up your arms and legs and use ample repellent) and you should be fine.

For more information see Health under On the Ground in Australia, below.

Health Warnings National Centers for Disease Control & Prevention (*CDC* ☎ *877/394–8747 international travelers'*

health line ⊕ *www.cdc.gov/travel*). **World Health Organization** (*WHO* ⊕ *www.who.int*).

TRIP INSURANCE

What kind of coverage do you honestly need? Do you even need trip insurance at all? Take a deep breath and read on.

We believe that comprehensive trip insurance is especially valuable if you're booking a very expensive or complicated trip (particularly to an isolated region) or if you're booking far in advance. Who knows what could happen six months down the road? But whether or not you get insurance has more to do with how comfortable you are assuming all that risk yourself.

If you're going abroad, consider buying medical-only coverage at the very least. Neither Medicare nor some private insurers cover medical expenses anywhere outside of the United States besides Mexico and Canada (including time aboard a cruise ship, even if it leaves from a U.S. port). Medical-only policies typically reimburse you for medical care (excluding that related to pre-existing conditions) and hospitalization abroad, and provide for evacuation. You still have to pay the bills and await reimbursement from the insurer, though.

■TIP→ Australia has no reciprocal medical agreement with the U.S., so it's vital to have medical insurance. Be sure your insurance includes evacuation as it's routine for patients in a serious condition to be flown to the nearest state capital for treatment.

Expect comprehensive travel insurance policies to cost about 4% to 7% of the total price of your trip (it's more like 12% if you're over age 70). A medical-only policy may or may not be cheaper than a comprehensive policy. Always read the fine print of your policy to make sure that you are covered for the risks that are of most concern to you. Compare several policies to make sure you're getting the best price and range of coverage available.

BOOKING YOUR TRIP

Unless your cousin is a travel agent, you're probably among the millions of people who make most of their travel arrangements online.

But have you ever wondered just what the differences are between an online travel agent (a Web site through which you make reservations instead of going directly to the airline, hotel, or car-rental company), a discounter (a firm that does a high volume of business with a hotel chain or airline and accordingly gets good prices), a wholesaler (one that makes cheap reservations in bulk and then re-sells them to people like you), and an aggregator (one that compares all the offerings so you don't have to)?

Is it truly better to book directly on an airline or hotel Web site? And when does a real live travel agent come in handy?

Booking engines like Expedia, Travelocity, and Orbitz are actually travel agents, albeit high-volume, online ones. And airline travel packagers like American Airlines Vacations and Virgin Vacations—well, they're travel agents, too. But they may still not work with all the world's hotels.

An aggregator site will search many sites and pull the best prices for airfares, hotels, and rental cars from them. Most aggregators compare the major travel-booking sites such as Expedia, Travelocity, and Orbitz; some also look at airline Web sites, though rarely the sites of smaller budget airlines. Some aggregators also compare other travel products, including complex packages—a good thing, as you can sometimes get the best overall deal by booking an air-and-hotel package.

■ ONLINE

You really have to shop around. A travel wholesaler such as Hotels.com or Hotel-Club.net can be a source of good rates, as can discounters such as Hotwire or Priceline, particularly if you can bid for your hotel room or airfare. Indeed, such sites sometimes have deals that are unavailable elsewhere. They do, however, tend to work only with hotel chains (which makes them just plain useless for getting hotel reservations outside of major cities) or big airlines (so that often leaves out upstarts like jetBlue and some foreign carriers like Air India).

Also, with discounters and wholesalers you must generally prepay, and everything is nonrefundable. And before you fork over the dough, be sure to check the terms and conditions, so you know what a given company will do for you if there's a problem and what you'll have to deal with on your own.

■ WITH A TRAVEL AGENT

If you use an agent—brick-and-mortar or virtual—you'll pay a fee for the service. And know that the service you get from some online agents isn't comprehensive. For example, Expedia and Travelocity don't search for prices on budget airlines like jetBlue, Southwest, or small foreign carriers. That said, some agents (online or not) *do* have access to fares that are difficult to find otherwise, and the savings can more than make up for any surcharge.

A knowledgeable brick-and-mortar travel agent can be a godsend if you're booking a cruise, a package trip that's not available to you directly, an air pass, or a complicated itinerary including several overseas flights. What's more, travel agents that specialize in a destination may have exclusive access to certain deals and insider information on things such as charter flights. Agents who specialize in types of travelers (senior citizens, gays and lesbians, naturists) or types of trips (cruises, luxury travel, safaris) can also be invaluable.

■TIP→ Remember that Expedia, Travelocity, and Orbitz are travel agents, not just booking engines. To resolve any problems with a reservation made through these companies, contact them first.

A top-notch agent planning your trip to Russia will make sure you get the correct visa application and complete it on time; the one booking your cruise may get you a cabin upgrade or arrange to have bottle of champagne chilling in your cabin when you embark. And complain about the surcharges all you like, but when things don't work out the way you'd hoped, it's nice to have an agent to put things right.

Australia is a big, big country. If you're short on time, a travel agent can really help you to choose your destinations realistically, and book the most time-efficient way to get around. However, booking things for an Australia trip yourself—especially online—is also very easy, so if you're prepared to do the virtual legwork, a travel agent isn't really necessary. If you do decide to go with one, have a look at the "Aussie Specialists" agents recommended by the Australian Tourist Commisssion: they have agents all over the U.S.

Agent Resources American Society of Travel Agents (☎ *703/739–2782* ⊕ *www. travelsense.org*). **Australian Tourist Commission** (⊕ *www.australia.com*).

TRANSPORTATION

Australia is divided into seven states and Australian Capital Territory (ACT), similar to the District of Columbia. Tasmania, the smallest state, is an island off Australia's south-east point.

Sydney, Melbourne, and Canberra, Australia's most important cities, are bunched together in the south-east of the country and connected by the Prince's Highway. Sydney, the most northerly, is the biggest city in Australia, and capital of New South Wales. A short way inland are the Blue Mountains National Park and the Hunter Valley, a major wine-producing area. Canberra, Australia's purpose-built political capital, is southwest of Sydney in the landlocked Australian Capital Territory.

Melbourne, the capital of state of Victoria, also claims to be the country's capital of culture. To the east lie the Snowy Mountains, and to the west is the most famous stretch of the Prince's Highway or the Great Ocean Road, which runs alongside the Twelve Apostles—huge rock towers in the sea.

Due south from Melbourne, across a small stretch of sea called the Bass Strait, is the island of Tasmania. Hobart, the state capital, is on the southeast coast.

Most of South Australia is barren desert, but the fertile flank of land nearest the sea is home to Australia's best wine country, the Barossa Valley. Adelaide, the state capital, is on the coast near to the border with Victoria. Wildlife hotspot Kangaroo Island is a short boatride opposite it.

Western Australia, the largest state, takes up the whole left side of the country. Its capital, Perth, is on the southwest coast; nearby is the Margaret River wine region. The little-known Ningaloo Reef Marine Park, another barrier reef, is halfway up the coast.

The vast deserts that make up all of central Western Australia continue into Northern Territory. The area right in the middle of the country is known as the Red Centre—here you'll find Australia's most famous rock formations, Uluru and Kata Tjuta, and Alice Springs, the region's hub. The state capital, Darwin, is a long way away, atop the northern band of Australia imaginatively nicknamed "the Top End."

The capital of Queensland is Brisbane, a coastal city close to the state border with New South Wales. The Whitsunday Islands and the Great Barrier Reef are both off the northeastern Queensland coast. The area beyond Cairns—affectionately known as FNQ or Far North Queensland—is home to the Daintree rain forest.

Although it's true that Australia is a roadtripper's paradise, the sheer distances between points of interest mean that flying is usually the best way to get between the major hubs, especially if time is an issue.

TRAVEL TIMES FROM SYDNEY		
To	By Air	By Car
Melbourne	1 hour	11 hours
Brisbane	1¼ hours	13 hours
Canberra	½ hour	3¼ hours
Adelaide	2 hours	20 hours
Darwin	6¼ hours	71 hours
Perth	4 hours	55 hours
Alice Springs	3 hours	44 hours
Cairns	3 hours	38 hours

∎ BY AIR

Sydney is Australia's main international hub, though Melbourne, Brisbane, Cairns, and Perth are also easy to get direct international flights to. You can catch non-stop or one-stop flights to Australia from New York (21 hours via Los Angeles); Chicago (19 hours via Los Angeles); Los Angeles (14 hours nonstop); Vancouver (17 hours via Honolulu); Toronto (20 hours via Los Angeles); and London (20–24 hours via Hong Kong, Singapore, or Bangkok).

Since Pacific-route flights from the United States to Australia cross the international date line, you lose a day, but regain it on the journey home.

Airlines & Airports Airline and Airport Links.com (⊕ www.airlineandairportlinks. com) has links to many of the world's airlines and airports.

Airline Security Issues Transportation Security Administration (⊕ www.tsa.gov) has answers for almost every question that might come up.

AIRPORTS

Sydney's Kingsford-Smith Airport (SYD) is Australia's main air hub and the first port of call for more than half of the country's visitors. Terminal 1 is for all international flights, Qantas domestic flights operate out of Terminal 3, and Terminal 2 is for all other domestic flights (including Qantaslink and Qantas Jetstar). A rail link connects the terminals underground, and frequently shuttle buses run between them above ground. There is an excellent range of shops and restaurants in the international terminal.

Brisbane International Airport (BNE) is southern Queensland's main airport and rivals Sydney in quality and services. There are separate domestic and international terminals—the latter is currently being expanded (work is due to finish in mid-2008). Cairns International Airport (CNS), in north Queensland, is the hub for northern Queensland and visiting the Great Barrier Reef.

Melbourne Airport (MEL) is sometimes known as "Tullamarine," after a neighboring suburb. International flights leave

from Terminal 2; Qantas and Jetstar use Terminal 1 for their domestic operations. Virgin Blue makes up the bulk of the other domestic flights, which go from Terminal 3.

South Australia's main airport is Adelaide International (ADL). Domestic flights and a few services to nearby Asian cities land at Darwin International Airport (DRW) in Northern Territory. The hub for the Red Centre is Alice Springs Airport (ASP), which only receives domestic flights. Perth International Airport (PER) is the gateway to Western Australia. International flights operate from Terminal 1; Qantas domestic flights leave from Terminal 2; Terminal 3 is for Skywest and Virgin Blue.

Airport Information Adelaide Airport (☎ 08/8308–9211 ⊕ www.aal.com.au). **Alice Springs Airport** (☎ 08/8951–1211 ⊕ www. ntapl.com.au/ASIndex.htm). **Brisbane International Airport** (☎ 07/3406–3000 ⊕ www. brisbaneairport.com.au). **Cairns Airport** (☎ 07/4052–3888 ⊕ www.cairnsport.com.au). **Darwin International Airport** (☎ 08/8920– 1811 ⊕ www.ntapl.com.au/DIIndex.htm). **Kingsford-Smith International Airport, Sydney** (☎ 02/9667–9111 ⊕ www.sydneyairport. com). **Melbourne Airport** (☎ 03/9297–1600 ⊕ www.melair.com.au). **Perth International Airport** (☎ 08/9478–8888 ⊕ www. perthairport.com).

FLIGHTS

TO AUSTRALIA

Qantas is Australia's flagship carrier. It operates direct flights to Sydney from New York, San Francisco, Vancouver, and Los Angeles, from where flights to Melbourne and Brisbane also leave. There are connecting Qantas flights to many other North American cities, and direct flights from various Australian airports to many Asian and European destinations. It's part of the OneWorld alliance, and has excellent standards of safety and comfort. Qantas flights aren't always the cheapest, but their Aussie AirPass includes three stops within Australia for the same price as your ticket from North America.

United flies direct from LA and San Francisco to Sydney. Air New Zealand also flies direct between LA and Sydney, and has many other routes via Auckland. British Airways flies from Sydney to London. Cathay Pacific operates direct flights to Hong Kong and other Asian cities from Sydney, Melbourne, Perth, Darwin, Brisbane, Cairns, and Adelaide. Singapore Airlines has similar routes but to Singapore.

Jetstar is a low-cost local airline owned by Qantas, and has flights from Sydney, Melbourne, Brisbane, Cairns, and Darwin to Japan, Singapore, Thailand, Japan, and Honolulu. Another budget carrier, Virgin Blue, flies to Tonga, Samoa, Fiji, Vanuatu, New Zealand, and the Cook Islands.

Airline Contacts Air New Zealand (☎ *800/262–1234 in U.S., 132476 in Australia* ⊕ *www.airnz.com.au*). **British Airways** (☎ *800/AIRWAYS in U.S., 1300/767177 in Australia* ⊕ *www.britishairways.com*). **Cathay Pacific** (☎ *800/233–2742 in U.S., 02/9667–3816 in Australia* ⊕ *www.cathaypacific.com*). **Jetstar** (☎ *866/397–8170 in U.S., 13–1538 in Australia* ⊕ *www.jetstar.com*). **Qantas** (☎ *800/227–4603 in U.S., 13–1313 in Australia* ⊕ *www.qantas.com*). **Singapore Airlines** (☎ *800/742–3333 in U.S., 13–1011 in Australia* ⊕ *www.singaporeairlines.com*). **United** (☎ *800/538–2929 in U.S., 13–1777 in Australia* ⊕ *www.united.com*). **Virgin Blue** (☎ *13–6789 in Australia* ⊕ *www.virginblue.com.au*).

WITHIN AUSTRALIA

Australia's large distances mean that flying is the locals' favorite way of getting from one city to another. In general, safety standards on domestic flights are high, flight times are punctual, and there's plenty of timetabling choice. On routes between popular destinations like Sydney, Melbourne, and Brisbane, there are often several flights each hour.

Qantas, the national airline, has full-service flights and the most extensive

domestic routing, serving both major cities and regional towns. Australia's two budget airlines are Virgin Blue and Qantas-owned Jetstar. Both fly to cities both big and small, though Jetstar only serves the east coast. Regional Express, another budget carrier, serves New South Wales, South Australia, Tasmania, and Victoria.

Smaller regional airlines include Skywest (within Western Autralia) and Airnorth (in Northern Territory).

Airline Contacts Airnorth (☎ *1800/627–474* ⊕ *www.airnorth.com.au*). **Jetstar** (☎ *13–1538* ⊕ *www.jetstar.com*). **Qantas** (☎ *13–1313* ⊕ *www.qantas.com.au*). **Regional Express** (☎ *13–1713* ⊕ *www.rex.com.au*). **Skywest** (☎ *1300/660088* ⊕ *www.skywest.com.au*). **Virgin Blue** (☎ *13–6789* ⊕ *www.virginblue.com.au*).

∎ BY BOAT

Organized boat tours from the Queensland mainland are the only way to visit the Great Barrier Reef. Cairns is the number-one point of departure, but boats also leave from Mackay, Airlie Beach, Townsville, and Port Douglas. Boats also run between the Whitsunday Islands. The Great Barrier Reef Marine Park Authority Web site has helpful advice on how to choose a tour operator, and lists which companies are ecotourism-certified.

The daily *Spirit of Tasmania I* and *II* ferries take 10 hours to connect Melbourne with Devonport on Tasmania's north coast. Make reservations as early as possible, particularly during the busy December and January school holidays.

The Sealink Ferries transport passengers and vehicles between Cape Jervis on the South Australian coastline near Adelaide, and Penneshaw on Kangaroo Island.

You can find out about ferry and cruise schedules for these and other scenic rides at most state tourism offices and on their Web sites. All operators accept major credit cards and cash.

Information Great Barrier Reef Marine Park Authority (⊕ www.gbrmpa.gov.au). **Sealink Ferries** (☎13–1301 ⊕ www.sealink.com. au). **Spirit of Tasmania** (☎1800/634–906 ⊕ www.spiritoftasmania.com.au).

▌BY BUS

Bus travel in Australia is comfortable and well-organized. Long-distance buses, also called "coaches," have air-conditioning, on-board toilets, reclining seats, and even attendants and videos on longer routes. By law, all are required to provide seat belts, and you are required to use them. Smoking is prohibited on all buses.

Australia's national bus network is run by Greyhound Australia (no connection to Greyhound in the U.S.), which serves far more destinations than any plane or train services. However, Australia is a vast continent, and bus travel here requires plenty of time. The journey from Sydney to Melbourne takes 15 hours, Adelaide to Perth takes 39 hours, and Brisbane to Cairns takes 30 hours. If you plan to visit specific regions it could be worthwhile considering flying to a major hub, then using buses to explore the region when you get there.

Oz Experience is a private bus company aimed at budget travelers. They work in a similar way to Greyhound, and their routes take in both major cities and adventure destinations. They have a great selection of routes—you buy a pass, and then have unlimited stopovers along that route. You book onto each section by telephone as you travel. Oz Experience also has a hostel booking service, and will take you to the door of your hostel for no extra cost. For example, their Bruce Pass takes you along the coast between Melbourne and Cairns and costs A$735.

You can book passes and individual tickets on Greyhound and Oz Experience buses online through their Web sites, over the telephone, or in person at their desks in bus terminals.

Bus Information Greyhound Australia (☎13–1499 ⊕ www.greyhound.com.au). **Oz Experience** (☎61/2/9213–1766 ⊕ www. ozexperience.com.au).

▌BY CAR

Endless highways, fabulous scenery, bizarre little towns in the middle of nowhere: Australia is road-trip paradise. Even if you don't have time for major exploring, traveling by car can be a great way to explore a particular region at your own pace. Traffic in city centers can be terrible—so much so that in some capitals you have to pay a traffic charge—so keep the car for the open road.

Driving is generally easy in Australia, once you adjust to traveling on the left side of the road. Road conditions on busy coastal highways usually pose few problems, though remote roads (even big highways) and routes through the desert are often a different story. When you're preparing a driving itinerary, it's vital to bear in mind the huge distances involved and calculate travel time and stop-overs accordingly.

Most rental companies in Australia accept driving licenses from other countries, including the U.S., provided that the information on the license is clear and in English. Otherwise, an International Driver's Permit is required (but they'll still want to see your regular license, too).

GASOLINE

Gas is known in Australia as "petrol." Self-service petrol stations are plentiful near major cities and in rural towns. In remote regions they can be few and far between, so fill up whenever you can. In really out-of-the-way places, carrying a spare petrol can is a good idea. Smaller petrol stations often close at night and on Sundays, though in major cities and on main highways there are plenty of stations open round the clock.

PARKING

On-street parking is usually plentiful in Australia cities, except in the traffic-heavy CBD (downtown area) of the big capitals. Electronic meters are the norm—you pay in advance, and there's usually a maximum stay, which you should respect as Australian parking inspectors are very vigilant. Paid parking lots are also common and are usually clearly signposted. Outside of the capitals, on-street parking is usually free, as are the lots outside malls and supermarkets.

ROAD CONDITIONS

Except for some expressways in and around the major cities, most highways are two-lane roads with frequent passing lanes, but no barrier separating the two directions of traffic. Main roads are usually paved and well maintained, though lanes are narrower than in the United States.

Outside big urban areas roundabouts are far more common than traffic lights—some towns have dozens of them. Remember that when driving on the left you go around a roundabout clockwise and give way to traffic entering from the right and already on the roundabout.

Potential road hazards multiply in rural areas. Driving standards, which are generally high in Australia, become more lax. Road surfaces deteriorate, becoming potholed or uneven. Fine sand sometimes fills the holes, making them hard to see. Windshield cracks caused by small stones are practically routine. Flash floods are also common during the summer months in northern Australia: when in doubt, turn back or seek advice from the police before crossing.

Animals—kangaroos and livestock, primarily—are common causes of road accidents, especially at night. If you see an animal near the edge of the road, slow down immediately as they may just decide to step out in front of you. If they do, hitting the animal is generally preferable to swerving, as you can lose control of your car and roll. However, braking too suddenly into the animal can send it through your windshield. Ideally, you should report any livestock you kill to the nearest ranch, and should check dead kangaroos for joeys (babies carried in their pouches): if you find one, wrap it up and take it to the nearest vet.

"Road trains" are another Outback hazard: they're truck convoys made of several connected trailers, totaling up to 170 feet. They take a LONG time to brake, so keep your distance and overtake them only with extreme caution.

Outback driving can be very exhausting and potentially dangerous. Avoid driving alone and rest often. Carry plenty of water with you (4–5 liters per person per day)—high temperatures make dehydration a very common problem on the road. Don't count on your cell phone working in the middle of nowhere, and if an emergency occurs never ever leave your vehicle: it's visible and provides you shelter from the sun and cold. Stick by the side of the road: sooner or later, someone will come along.

ROADSIDE EMERGENCIES

If you have an emergency requiring an ambulance, the fire department, or the police, dial **000**. Many major highways now have telephones for breakdown assistance; you can also use your cell phone if you have one. Otherwise, flag down and ask a passing motorist to call the nearest motoring service organization for you. Most Australian drivers will be happy to assist, particularly in country areas.

Each state has its own motoring organization that provides assistance for vehicle breakdowns. When you rent a vehicle, check that you are entitled to assistance from the relevant motoring organization, free of charge. A toll-free nationwide number is available for roadside assistance.

Emergency Services Emergency Services
(☎ *000*). **Motoring Organization Hotline**
(☎ *13–1111*).

RULES OF THE ROAD

Speed limits vary from state to state. As a rough guide, 50–60 kilometers per hour (kph) is the maximum in populated areas, reduced to 25 kph near schools. On open roads limits range from 100–130 kph—the equivalent of 62–80 mph. Limits are usually signposted clearly and regularly, and are enforced by police speed checks and—in state capitals—by automatic cameras.

Drunk driving, once a big problem in Australia, is controlled obsessively. The legal limit is 0.05% blood-alcohol level, and penalties are so high that many Aussies just don't drink if they're driving. Seat belts are mandatory nationwide. Children must be restrained in a seat appropriate to their size. Car-rental agencies can install these for about A\$30 per week, with 24 hours' notice. It is illegal to use a mobile phone handset when driving.

Traffic circles, called "roundabouts," are widely used at intersections; cars that have already entered the circle have the right-of-way. At designated intersections in Melbourne's central business district you must get into the left lane to make a right-hand turn—this is to facilitate crossing streetcar lines. Watch for the sign RIGHT-HAND TURN FROM LEFT LANE ONLY. Everywhere, watch for sudden changes in speed limits.

The Australian Automobile Association has a branch in each state, known as the National Roads and Motorists Association (NRMA) in New South Wales and Canberra, the Automobile Association in the Northern Territory (AANT), and the Royal Automobile Club (RAC) in all other states. It's affiliated with AAA worldwide and offers reciprocal services to American members, including emergency road service, road maps, copies of each state and territory's Highway Code, and discounts on car rental and accommodations.

▌ BY TRAIN

Most long-distance trains are operated by various state-government-owned enterprises. The luxurious exceptions to the rule are the *Ghan, Indian Pacific,* and *Overland,* all run by the private company Great Southern Railway. Rail Australia is the umbrella organization for all of these services outside the country.

The state-owned trains are usually punctual and comfortable. Economy class has reclinable seats, and on longer routes there are sleeper classes. Second-class sleepers have shared bathrooms and sometimes you share your cabin with strangers, too. In first class you have the cabin to yourself and a small ensuite bathroom. Meals are sometimes included. Comfort levels increase in Gold Kangaroo class of the *Ghan, Indian Pacific,* and *Overland* and in the Queenslander class of the *Sunlander.* The high-speed Tilt Train is aimed at business travelers and has business-class-style reclinable seats.

Rail Australia offers several economy-class rail passes. Most are only available to foreign passport holders, and must be purchased before you get to Australia. You can usually pay a (hefty) supplement to upgrade to sleeper services.

Information Great Southern Railway
(☎ *13–2147* ⊕ *www.gsr.com.au*). **Queensland Rail** (☎ *13–1617* ⊕ *www.qr.com.au*). **Countrylink** (☎ *13–2323* ⊕ *www.countrylink.info*). **Rail Australia** (☎ *800/633–3404 in U.S., 13–4592 in Australia* ⊕ *www.railaustralia.com.au*).

ON THE GROUND

▌COMMUNICATIONS

INTERNET

Internet access is widely available to travelers in Australia. Top-end hotels always have some sort of in-room access for laptop users—Wi-Fi is becoming the norm, otherwise there are data ports. Note that sometimes you are charged a hefty premium for using this service. Hostels are also well-connected and charge reasonable rates. Many have free Wi-Fi, others have large on-site cybercafés, or, at worst, some terminals for guests to use.

Australia's main telephone network, Telstra, has wireless hotspots all over the country. McDonalds and Starbucks often have Telstra Wi-Fi—you pay A$5 for a software CD and 15 free minutes. Alternatively, you can pay using Telstra Phone-Away calling cards: there's no connection charge and time online costs A0.20¢ per minute. Connections can be slow, however. You can buy a card at newsagents, Australia Post, convenience stores, or online. Telstra's Web site also has hotspot listings.

Coin-operated terminals are also a common sight at airports and even in shopping malls. Cybercafés are very common in big cities; expect a high concentration in areas popular with backpackers. You can usually even find a machine or two in small outback towns. Expect to pay around A$2 for 15 minutes. Access at some public libraries can be free.

Australian phone jacks are different from American ones, so you'll need to buy a telephone cord (or ask your hotel for one) if you plan to use dial-up with your laptop.

Contacts Cybercafes (⊕ *www.cybercafes. com*) lists over 4,000 Internet cafés worldwide. **Telstra** (⊕ *www.telstra.com.au*).

PHONES

The good news is that you can now make a direct-dial telephone call from virtually any point on earth. The bad news? You can't always do so cheaply. Calling from a hotel is almost always the most expensive option; hotels usually add huge surcharges to all calls, particularly international ones. In some countries you can phone from call centers or even the post office. Calling cards usually keep costs to a minimum, but only if you purchase them locally. And then there are mobile phones (⇨ *below*), which are sometimes more prevalent—particularly in the developing world—than land lines; as expensive as mobile phone calls can be, they are still usually a much cheaper option than calling from your hotel.

The country code for Australia is 61. To call Australia from the United States, dial the international access code (011), followed by the country code (61), the area or city code without the initial zero (e.g., 2), and the eight-digit phone number.

CALLING WITHIN AUSTRALIA

Australia's phone system is efficient and reliable. You can make local and long-distance calls from your hotel—usually with a surcharge—or from any public phone. There are public phones in shopping areas, on suburban streets, at train stations, and outside rural post offices—basically, they're everywhere. You can use coins or phone cards in most public phones; credit card phones are common at airports.

All regular telephone numbers in Australia have eight digits. There are five area codes: 02 (for New South Wales, Australian Capital Territory, and northern Victoria), 03 (Victoria and Tasmania), 04 (for cell phones), 07 (for Queensland), and 08 (for Western Australia, South Australia, and Northern Territory). Toll-free numbers begin with 1800, and numbers starting with 13 or 1300 are charged at local rates anywhere in the country.

Calls within the same area code are charged as local: A50¢ for an unlimited amount of time. Long-distance call rates vary by distance, and are timed. When you're calling long-distance within Australia, remember to include the area code, even when you're calling from a number with the same area code. For example, when calling Canberra from Sydney, both of which have an 02 prefix, you still need to include the area code when you dial.

Directory Assistance Local Directory Assistance (☎1223).

CALLING OUTSIDE AUSTRALIA
To call overseas from Australia, dial 0011, then the country code and the number. Kiosks and groceries in major cities sell international calling cards. You can also use credit cards on public phones.

The country code for the United States is 1.

You can use AT&T, Sprint, and MCI services from Australian phones, though some pay phones require you to put coins in to make the call. Using a pre-paid calling card is generally cheaper.

Useful Numbers International Directory Assistance (☎1225). International Call Cost Information (☎1300/362–162).

Access Codes AT&T Direct (☎1800/881–011 from Telstra phones, 1800/551–155 from Optus phones). MCI WorldPhone (☎1800/881–100 from Telstra phones, 1800/551–111 from Optus phones). Sprint International Access (☎1800/881–877 from Telstra phones, 1800/551—110 from Optus phones).

CALLING CARDS
It's worth buying a phone card in Australia even if you plan on making just a few calls.

Telstra, Australia's main telephone company, has three different calling cards.

Their simply-named Phonecard is a prepaid card you can use for local, long-distance, or international calls from public pay phones. Another option is the Say G'day card, which is mainly for making international calls—you dial an access number and then enter your card number. Rates are much cheaper than using a regular Phonecard: calls to the U.S. cost around A4¢ per minute. You buy the card once, then can top it up online or over the phone, using a credit card. You can also use it to call landlines and mobiles, but the rates aren't good. The Super Buzz Global card is very similar, but is only for international calls, and is even cheaper—U.S. calls go for A1¢ per minute. You can buy any of these cards at newsagents, Australia Post offices, convenience stores, or online at Telstra's Web site.

Contacts Gotalk (⊕ www.gotalk.com.au). **onesuite.com** (⊕ www.onesuite.com). **Telstra** (⊕ www.telstra.com.au).

MOBILE PHONES
If you have a multiband phone (some countries use different frequencies from what's used in the United States) and your service provider uses the world-standard GSM network (as do T-Mobile, Cingular, and Verizon), you can probably use your phone abroad. Roaming fees can be steep, however: 99¢ a minute is considered reasonable. And overseas you normally pay the toll charges for incoming calls. It's almost always cheaper to send a text message than to make a call, since text messages have a very low set fee (often less than 5¢).

If you just want to make local calls, consider buying a new SIM card (note that your provider may have to unlock your phone for you to use a different SIM card) and a prepaid service plan in the destination. You'll then have a local number and can make local calls at local rates. If your trip is extensive, you could also simply buy a new cell phone in your destination, as the initial cost will be offset over time.

TIP→ If you travel internationally frequently, save one of your old mobile phones or buy a cheap one on the Internet; ask your cell phone company to unlock it for you, and take it with you as a travel phone, buying a new SIM card with pay-as-you-go service in each destination.

Nearly all Australian mobile phones use the GSM network. If you have an unlocked tri-band phone and intend to make calls to Australian numbers, it makes sense to buy a prepaid Australian SIM card on arrival—rates will be much better than using your U.S. network. Alternatively, you can rent a phone or a SIM card from companies like Vodarent. Rates start at A$5 per day for a handset and A$1 a day for a SIM. You can also buy a cheap, pay-as-you-go handset from Telstra, Virgin Mobile, or Optus. Cellphone stores are abundant, and staff are used to assessing tourists' needs.

Contacts Cellular Abroad (☎ 800/287 5072 ⊕ www.cellularabroad.com) rents and sells GMS phones and sells SIM cards that work in many countries. **Mobal** (☎ 888/888–9162 ⊕ www.mobalrental.com) rents mobiles and sells GSM phones (starting at $49) that will operate in 140 countries. Per-call rates vary throughout the world. **Optus** (⊕ www.optus.com.au). **Planet Fone** (☎ 888/988–4777 ⊕ www.planetfone.com) rents cell phones, but the per-minute rates are expensive. **Telstra** (⊕ www.telstra.com.au). **Virgin Mobile** (⊕ www.virginmobile.com.au). **Vodafone** (⊕ www.vodarent.com.au) rents phones from stands in many airports.

CUSTOMS & DUTIES

You're always allowed to bring goods of a certain value back home without having to pay any duty or import tax. But there's a limit on the amount of tobacco and liquor you can bring back duty-free, and some countries have separate limits for perfumes; for exact figures, check with your customs department. The values of so-called "duty-free" goods are included in these amounts. When you shop abroad, save all your receipts, as customs inspectors may ask to see them as well as the items you purchased. If the total value of your goods is more than the duty-free limit, you'll have to pay a tax (most often a flat percentage) on the value of everything beyond that limit.

Australian customs regulations are unlike any in the world. As an island long isolated from the rest of the world, Australia is free from many pests and diseases endemic in other places, and it wants to stay that way. Customs procedures are very thorough and it can take up to an hour to clear them.

All animals are subject to quarantine. Many foodstuffs and natural products are forbidden, including meat, dairy products, fresh fruit and vegetables, and all food served on aircraft. Most canned or preserved foods may be imported, but you have to declare them on your customs statement and have them inspected, along with wooden artifacts and seeds.

Airport sniffer dogs patrol arrivals area, and even an innocent dried flower forgotten between the pages of a book could incur a serious fine. If in doubt, declare something—the worst-case scenario is that it will be taken from you, without a fine.

Otherwise, non-residents over 18 may bring in 250 cigarettes (or 250 grams of cigars or tobacco) and 2¼ liters of alcohol. You can bring in other taxable goods (that is, luxury items like perfume) to the value of A$900, for adults.

Information Australian Customs Services (⊕ www.customs.gov.au): for information about duty-free allowances. **Australian Quarantine and Inspection Services** (⊕ www.daffa.gov.au/aqis/travel/entering-australia) tells you exactly what you can and cannot bring into Australia.

U.S. Information U.S. Customs and Border Protection (⊕ www.cbp.gov).

■ EATING OUT

Fresh ingredients, friendly service, innovative flavor combinations, and great value for your money mean that eating out Down Under is usually a happy experience.

Australia's British heritage is evident in the hearty food served in pubs, roadhouses, and country hotels. It all seems to taste much better than food in Britain, though. Roast meat and potatoes; fish and chips (french fries); pasties and pies swimming in gravy; flaky sausage rolls; sticky teacakes and fluffy scones—all these things are cheap and tasty counter staples. They give the big fast food franchises a serious run for their money.

These days, fusion food is what's putting Australia on the foodie map—indeed, many claim that the very term was invented Down Under. The huge Asian communities in cities like Sydney and Melbourne have brought their traditional condiments and cooking styles to bear on traditional local staples: the resulting combinations are what many of the country's most famous eateries specialize in.

Melbourne and Sydney also have huge immigrant communities from Mediterranean Europe, so expect to find really authentic Greek, Spanish, Italian, and Turkish dishes, both sweet and savory. These often form the backbone of the lunchtime fare Australian cafés do so well—huge salads, huge made-to-order sandwiches, specialty coffees, and massive wedges of freshly made cake.

At home, Australians love to barbecue. There are many restaurants where you can experience an Aussie barbie, or something like it. You choose from a range of raw meat cuts (anything from steak to kangaroo), pay for it, then have it cooked (or occasionally cook it yourself) at a large grill.

Bush tucker, or indigenous Australian food, was once something you only came across on bushwalking expeditions in the Outback. Suddenly, it's become fashionable, and uniquely Australian ingredients like lemon myrtle, wattle seed, and rosella (not to mention kangaroo meat) are appearing on fancy restaurant menus all over the country.

Food is an international language, but your English may fail you in Australian restaurants. "Entrée" means appetizer and "main courses" are what American entrées go by. The term "silver service" indicates upscale dining. French fries are called "chips," chickens are "chooks," sausages are known as "snags," and if you want ketchup, ask for "tomato sauce."

Vegetarianism is a popular lifestyle choice in Australia and there's always at least one menu option for ovo-lacto vegetarians—even McDonalds does a veggie burger. However, as many so-called Australian vegetarians actually eat seafood, the veggie dishes in many restaurants are often fish-based.

Some Australian restaurants serve prix-fixe dinners, but the majority are à la carte. The restaurants we list are the best in each price category. Properties indicated by a ✗⊞ are hotels with restaurants that deserve a special trip.

MEALS & MEALTIMES

Australians eat relatively early. Breakfast is usually between 7 and 10 AM and eating it out (usually at a café) is popular. Options range from toast, cereal through fruit and yogurt and muffins, pastries and hotcakes to a full fry-up—eggs, bacon, sausages, baked beans, hash browns, tomatoes, and mushrooms. Morning coffee and afternoon tea are popular in-between meals.

For most locals, lunch is usually lighter than dinner: a salad or a sandwich, say, usually between 11:30 AM and 2:30 PM. Dinner is the main meal and begins around 6:30. In the cities, dining options are available outside these hours, but the choices are far more restricted in the countryside and smaller towns, where even take-aways close at 8:30 PM.

Unless otherwise noted, the restaurants listed in this guide are open daily for lunch and dinner.

PAYING

At most restaurants you ask for the bill at the end of the meal. At sandwich bars, burger joints, and takeaways you pay upfront. Visa, MasterCard, and American Express are widely accepted in all but the simplest eateries.

For guidelines on tipping see Tipping below.

RESERVATIONS & DRESS

Regardless of where you are, it's a good idea to make a reservation if you can. In some places (Hong Kong, for example), it's expected. We only mention them specifically when reservations are essential (there's no other way you'll ever get a table) or when they are not accepted. For popular restaurants, book as far ahead as you can (often 30 days), and reconfirm as soon as you arrive. (Large parties should always call ahead to check the reservations policy.) We mention dress only when men are required to wear a jacket or a jacket and tie.

WINES, BEER & SPIRITS

Beer and wine are an important part of Australian life. Australia is the world's 10th-largest wine producer, and Australian wine is gaining considerable respect worldwide. Australia's most famous wine-producing areas are the Hunter Valley in New South Wales, the Barossa Valley in South Australia, and Western Australia's Margaret River region. Although there are no native grape varietals in Australia, Shiraz (also known as Syrah) is a local specialty. Cabernet Sauvignon and Pinot Noir are common reds; popular whites include Chardonnay, Sauvignon Blanc, and Pinot Grigio. Wolf Blass, Penfolds, Seppelt, Yalumba, Rosemount, and Hardy's are some of the big-name vineyards,

but there are plenty of boutique wine producers giving them a run for their money.

Australia produces a wide range of beers. As well as big national brands like Fosters, each state has its own brew: Victoria Bitter in Victoria or XXXX (called four-ex) in Queensland, for example. Lager is the most popular style, typically served ice cold from the tap, with a little head. Microbreweries are slowly gaining ground. There's a bewildering range of names for different size beer glasses—showing is usually easier than telling.

Most restaurants serve liquor. In some states, cafés also serve alcohol. Bottle shops, which sell beer, wine, and spirits for consumption off the premises, can be found in most shopping centers. In Australia the legal drinking age is 18. Bars usually close around 11 PM during the week, but close later on weekends. BYO (Bring Your Own bottle—usually limited to wine) restaurants are quite common throughout Australia. These usually have corkage charges.

If you're invited to an Australian's home, it's common—indeed, expected—practice to take a bottle of wine at dinner time, or a case of beer for a barbecue. When drinking at pubs, Australians always drink in rounds, British-style.

▌ ELECTRICITY

The electrical current in Australia is 240 volts, 50 cycles alternating current (AC), so most American appliances can't be used without a transformer. Wall outlets take slanted three-prong plugs and plugs with two flat prongs set in a V.

Consider making a small investment in a universal adapter, which has several types of plugs in one lightweight, compact unit. Most laptops and mobile phone chargers are dual voltage (i.e., they operate equally well on 110 and 220 volts), so require only an adapter. These days the same is true of small appliances such as hair dryers. Always check labels and manufacturer instructions to be sure. Don't use 110-volt outlets marked FOR SHAVERS ONLY for high-wattage appliances such as hair dryers.

Contacts **Steve Kropla's Help for World Traveler's** (⊕ www.kropla.com) has information on electrical and telephone plugs around the world. **Walkabout Travel Gear** (⊕ www.walkabouttravelgear.com) has a good coverage of electricity under "adapters."

▋ EMERGENCIES

Australian emergency services are extremely efficient. Local people usually help each other unquestioningly, too. For theft, wallet loss, small road accidents, and minor emergencies, contact the nearest police station. In a medical or dental emergency, ask your hotel staff for information on and directions to the nearest hospital or clinic; taxi drivers should also know how to find one.

Pack a basic first-aid kit, especially if you're venturing into more remote areas. If you'll be carrying any medication, bring your doctor's contact information and prescription authorizations. Most Australian pharmacies only fill prescriptions from Australian doctors, so bring enough medication for your trip.

Pharmacies usually open between 9 and 5, but most towns have a 24-hour pharmacy system so that one pharmacy is always open. In an emergency, the local police station can tell you which pharmacy is open, as can hospitals.

Embassies and consulates in Australia provide assistance to their nationals in case of lost or stolen passports and documents, major medical problems, and other travel emergencies.

U.S. Embassies **Consulate General** (⊠ *Level 6, 553 St. Kilda Rd., Melbourne, VIC, 3000* ☎ *03/9526–5900* ⊠ *16 St. George's Terr., 13th fl., Perth, WA, 6000* ☎ *08/9231–9400*

⊠ *MLC Centre, Level 59, 19–29 Martin Pl., Sydney, NSW, 2000* ☎ *02/9373–9200*). **U.S. Embassy** (⊠ *Moonah Pl., Yarralumla, ACT, 2600* ☎ *02/6214–5600*).

General Emergency Contacts Emergency Services (Police, Fire, Ambulance) (☎ *000*).

▋ HEALTH

The most common types of illnesses are caused by contaminated food and water. If you have problems, mild cases of traveler's diarrhea may respond to Imodium (known generically as loperamide) or Pepto-Bismol. Be sure to drink plenty of fluids; if you can't keep fluids down, seek medical help immediately.

Infectious diseases can be airborne or passed via mosquitoes and ticks and through direct or indirect physical contact with animals or people. Some, including Norwalk-like viruses that affect your digestive tract, can be passed along through contaminated food. Condoms can help prevent most sexually transmitted diseases, but they aren't absolutely reliable and their quality varies from country to country. Speak with your physician and/or check the CDC or World Health Organization Web sites for health alerts, particularly if you're pregnant, traveling with children, or have a chronic illness.

For information on travel insurance, shots and medications, and medical-assistance companies see Shots & Medications under Things to Consider in Before You Go, above.

SPECIFIC ISSUES IN AUSTRALIA

Australian health care is excellent, with highly trained medical professionals and well-equipped hospitals. Hygiene standards are also high and well-monitored, so you can drink tap water and eat fresh produce without worrying. You may take a four weeks' supply of prescribed medication into Australia (more with a doctor's certificate)—if you run out, pharmacies require a prescription from an Australian doctor. The quickest way to find one is to ask your hotel or look under "M" (for Medical Practitioner) in the Yellow Pages.

Sunburn and sunstroke are the greatest health hazards when visiting Australia. Remember that there's a big hole in the ozone layer over Australia, so even on cloudy days the rays of light coming through are harmful. Stay out of the sun at midday and, regardless of whether you normally burn, follow locals' example and slather on the sun cream. Protect your eyes with good-quality sun glasses, and try to cover up with a long-sleeve shirt, a hat, and pants or a beach wrap whenever possible. Keep in mind that you'll burn more easily at higher altitudes and in the water.

Dehydration is another serious danger, especially in the Outback. It's easy to avoid: carry plenty of water and drink it often.

Australia is free of malaria, but several cases of Ross River and Dengue fevers have been reported in recent years. The best way to prevent both is to avoid being bitten: cover up your arms and legs, and use ample repellent, especially during summer months and in the north of the country. No rural scene is complete without bush flies, a major annoyance. These tiny pests, found throughout Australia, are especially attracted to the eyes and mouth, in search of the fluids that are secreted there. Some travelers resort to wearing a face net, which can be suspended from a hat with a drawstring device.

Some of the world's deadliest creatures call Australia home. The chances of running into one are low, but wherever you go, pay close heed to any warnings given by hotel staff, tour operators, life guards, or locals in general. In the Outback, you need to worry about snakes and spiders. On the coast, there's everything from sharks through deadly octopi and stone-fish to jellyfish to reckon with. In northern Australia, rivers, lakes, billabongs, and even flooded streams are home to estuarine crocodiles, known to attack and kill humans. The best advice we can give you is to always be cautious, and check, check, and double-check the situation at each stop on your visit with the appropriate authority.

If deadly sea-critters weren't enough, Australian coastal waters are also home to seriously strong currents known as "rips." These kill tens of swimmers every year. Pay close attention to the flags raised on beaches, and only swim in areas patrolled by life guards. If you get caught in a rip, the standard advice is never to swim against it, as you rapidly become exhausted. Instead, try to relax and float parallel to the shore: eventually the current will subside and you will be able to swim back to the shore, albeit farther down the coast.

OVER-THE-COUNTER REMEDIES

Familiar brands of non-prescription medications are available in pharmacies. Note that Tylenol is usually called paracetomol in Australia.

HOLIDAYS

New Year's Day, January 1; **Australia Day,** January 26; **Good Friday,** March 21, 2008 and April 10, 2009; **Easter,** March 23, 2008 and April 12, 2009; **Easter Monday,** March 24, 2008 and April 13, 2009; **Anzac Day,** April 25; **Christmas,** December 25; **Boxing Day,** December 26. There are also several state- and territory-specific public holidays.

▌ MAIL

All regular mail services are run by the efficient Australia Post, which has offices all over the country. Post offices are usually only open during business hours Monday to Friday, but stamps are available from newsagents at other times. Post boxes for regular mail in Australia are usually bright red; express post boxes are yellow. Postage rates are A50¢ for domestic letters, A$1.95 per 50-gram (28.35 grams = 1 ounce) airmail letter, and A$1.25 for airmail postcards to North America—allow a week for letters and postcards to arrive.

When addressing mail to Australian addresses you need to include the four-digit Australian postal code (zip code). You can receive mail care of General Delivery (known as Poste Restante in Australia) at the General Post Office or any branch post office. The service is free and mail is held for one month; you need photo ID to collect mail. American Express also offers free mail collection at its main city offices for its cardholders.

Contacts Australia Post (⊕ www.auspost. com.au).

SHIPPING PACKAGES

Rates for large parcels shipped from Australia depend on their weight, shape, and contents. Printed papers (including books) are cheaper to send than clothes, for example. Sending parcels through Australia Post is usually reliable. It's worth paying the extra for recorded delivery, as you can track the parcel and claim insurance if it gets lost. Many stores—particularly upmarket ones—can ship your purchases for you, for a price.

Sending a 1-kilogram (2-pound) parcel to the United States with Australia Post costs A$16.96 by seamail, and A$24.70 by airmail. If you're shipping items in excess of 50 kilograms (110 pounds), it's often less expensive to send goods by sea via a shipping agent. Shipping time to the United States is 10–12 weeks.

Both DHL and Federal Express operate fast, reliable express courier services from Australia. Rates are around A$110 for a 1-kilogram (2-pound) parcel to the United States, including door-to-door service. Delivery time between Sydney and New York is approximately three days.

Express Services DHL Worldwide Express (☎ 13–1406 ⊕ www.dhl.com.au). **Federal Express** (☎ 13–2610 ⊕ www.fedex.com/au).

▌MONEY

The most expensive part of your trip to Australia will probably be getting there. Australian hotels are generally cheaper than similar establishments in North America, as is food.

Australians use debit cards wherever possible to pay for things—you can use your credit card, or pay cash, always in Australian dollars. ATMs are ubiquitous; it's very hard to change travelers' checks.

Prices for goods and services can be volatile at times. A 10% Goods and Services Tax (or GST—similar to V.A.T. in other countries) applies to most activities and goods, though some unprocessed foods are exempt.

Prices throughout this guide are given for adults. Substantially reduced fees are almost always available for children, students, and sometimes for senior citizens.

▐**TIP➔** Banks never have every foreign currency on hand, and it may take as long as a week to order. If you're planning to exchange funds before leaving home, don't wait until the last minute.

ATMS & BANKS

Your own bank will probably charge a fee for using ATMs abroad; the foreign bank you use may also charge a fee. Nevertheless, you'll usually get a better rate of exchange at an ATM than you will at a currency-exchange office or even when changing money in a bank. And extracting funds as you need them is a safer option than carrying around a large amount of cash.

▐**TIP➔** PIN numbers with more than four digits are not recognized at ATMs in many countries. If yours has five or more, remember to change it before you leave.

For most travelers to Australia, ATMs are the easiest—and often cheapest—way to obtain Australia dollars. Australia's biggest banks are Westpac, ANZ, the Commonwealth Bank of Australia, and the National Australia Bank. Their ATMs all accept Cirrus and Plus cards. Smaller state-based banks are also common but may not accept foreign cards. Major cities often have branches of international banks like Citibank or HSBC.

Before traveling, check if your bank has an agreement with any Australian banks for reduced ATM fees. For example, Bank of America customers can use Westpac ATMs to withdraw cash without incurring a fee.

CREDIT CARDS

Throughout this guide, the following abbreviations are used: **AE,** American Express; **DC,** Diners Club; **MC,** MasterCard; and **V,** Visa.

It's a good idea to inform your credit-card company before you travel, especially if you're going abroad and don't travel internationally very often. Otherwise, the credit-card company might put a hold on your card owing to unusual activity—not a good thing halfway through your trip. Record all your credit-card numbers—as well as the phone numbers to call if your cards are lost or stolen—in a safe place, so you're prepared should something go wrong. Both MasterCard and Visa have general numbers you can call (collect if you're abroad) if your card is lost, but you're better off calling the number of your issuing bank, since MasterCard and Visa usually just transfer you to your bank; your bank's number is usually printed on your card.

If you plan to use your credit card for cash advances, you'll need to apply for a PIN at least two weeks before your trip. Although it's usually cheaper (and safer) to use a credit card abroad for large purchases (so you can cancel payments or be reimbursed if there's a problem), note that some credit-card companies *and* the banks that issue them add substantial percentages to all foreign transactions, whether they're in a foreign currency or not. Check on these fees before leaving home, so there won't be any surprises when you get the bill.

■**TIP→** Before you charge something, ask the merchant whether or not he or she plans to do a dynamic currency conversion (DCC). In such a transaction the credit-card *processor* (shop, restaurant, or hotel, not Visa or MasterCard) converts the currency and charges you in dollars. In most cases you'll pay the merchant a 3% fee for this service in addition to any credit-card company and issuing-bank foreign-transaction surcharges.

Dynamic currency conversion programs are becoming increasingly widespread. Merchants who participate in them are supposed to ask whether you want to be charged in dollars or the local currency, but they don't always do so. And even if they do offer you a choice, they may well avoid mentioning the additional surcharges. The good news is that you *do* have a choice. And if this practice really gets your goat, you can avoid it entirely thanks to American Express; with its cards, DCC simply isn't an option.

Most Australian establishments take credit cards: Visa and MasterCard are the most widely accepted, American Express and Diners Club aren't always accepted outside the cities. Just in case, bring enough cash to cover your expenses if you're visiting a national park or a remote area.

Reporting Lost Cards American Express (☎ *800/992–3404 in the U.S. or 336/393–1111 collect from abroad, 1300/132639 in Australia* ⊕ *www.americanexpress.com*). **Diners Club** (☎ *800/234–6377 in the U.S. or 303/799–1504 collect from abroad, 1300/360060 in Australia* ⊕ *www.dinersclub. com*). **MasterCard** (☎ *800/622–7747 in the U.S. or 636/722–7111 collect from abroad, 1800/120113 in Australia* ⊕ *www.*

mastercard.com). Visa (☎ *800/847–2911 in the U.S. or 410/581–9994 collect from abroad, 1800/450346 in Australia* ⊕ *www.visa.com*).

CURRENCY & EXCHANGE

Australia has its own dollar—assume all prices you see in Australia are quoted in Australian dollars. The currency operates on a decimal system, with the dollar (A$) as the basic unit and 100 cents (¢) equaling $1. Bills, differentiated by color and size, come in $100, $50, $20, $10, and $5 denominations, and are made of plastic rather than paper—you can even take them swimming with you. Coins are minted in $2, $1, 50¢, 20¢, 10¢, and 5¢ denominations.

At this writing, the exchange rate was about A$1.21 to the U.S. dollar.

■ TIP➔ Even if a currency-exchange booth has a sign promising no commission, rest assured that there's some kind of huge, hidden fee. (Oh…that's right. The sign didn't say no *fee*.) And as for rates, you're almost always better off getting foreign currency at an ATM or exchanging money at a bank.

TRAVELER'S CHECKS & CARDS

Some consider this the currency of the cave man, and it's true that fewer establishments accept traveler's checks these days. Nevertheless, they're a cheap and secure way to carry extra money, particularly on trips to urban areas. Both Citibank (under the Visa brand) and American Express issue traveler's checks in the United States, but Amex is better known and more widely accepted; you can also avoid hefty surcharges by cashing Amex checks at Amex offices. Whatever you do, keep track of all the serial numbers in case the checks are lost or stolen.

Traveler's checks are increasingly hard to cash in Australia, even in major cities. Take some along as an emergency fallback option, but plan your trip around ATMs and credit cards—you'll save a whole lot of time and headaches, not to mention commission charges.

Contacts **American Express** (☎ *888/412–6945 in the U.S., 801/945–9450 collect outside of the U.S. to add value or speak to customer service* ⊕ *www.americanexpress.com*).

▌ SAFETY

Given Australia's relaxed lifestyle, it's easy to be seduced into believing that crime is nonexistent. In fact, Australia has its share of poverty, drugs, and crime, but rates aren't high by world standards, so be wary and you should have no problems. Wearing jewelry in public isn't a risk, and using ATMs in daylight hours is usually fine. Theft—especially pick-pocketing—is a problem only in major tourist areas such as Sydney's Bondi or Queensland's Gold Coast. Try to avoid leaving valuables on the beach when you go for a swim or in your car when you park. Australia has had enough cases of children going missing in public places for parents to want to be vigilant on beaches and in malls.

Traveling in Australia is generally safe for women, provided you follow a few common-sense precautions. Avoid isolated areas such as empty beaches; at night, avoid quiet streets. Single women usually receive attention entering pubs or clubs alone, but a few firm, polite words are usually enough to put a stop to it, if it's unwanted.

■ TIP➔ Distribute your cash, credit cards, IDs, and other valuables between a deep front pocket, an inside jacket or vest pocket, and a hidden money pouch. Don't reach for the money pouch once you're in public.

▌ TIME

Without daylight saving time, Sydney is 14 hours ahead of New York and Toronto; 15 hours ahead of Chicago and Dallas; and 17 hours ahead of Los Angeles.

Australia has three major time zones. Eastern Standard Time (EST) applies in Tasmania, Victoria, New South Wales, and

Queensland; Central Standard Time applies in South Australia and the Northern Territory; and Western Standard Time applies in Western Australia. Central Standard Time is ½ hour behind EST, and Western Standard Time is 2 hours behind EST.

Within the EST zone, each state chooses a slightly different date on which to commence or end daylight saving from its neighboring state—except for Queensland, where the powerful farm lobby has prevented the state from introducing daylight saving, since it would make the cows wake up an hour earlier. Western Australia and the Northern Territory also decline to recognize daylight saving, which means that at certain times of the year Australia can have as many as six different time zones.

▌ TIPPING

Australians don't tip nearly as much as North Americans. Wait staff are the exception: hotels and restaurants don't usually add service charges, so a 10%–15% tip for good service is normal. Room service and housemaids are only tipped for special services. Taxi drivers don't expect a tip, but leaving small change will get you a smile. Guides, tour bus drivers, and chauffeurs don't expect tips either, though they're grateful if someone in the group takes up a collection for them. No tipping is necessary—indeed, it would cause confusion—in hair salons or for theater ushers.

INDEX

PHOTO CREDITS

8, *Siobhan O'Hare.* 9 (left), *Gerry Pearce/Alamy.* 9 (right), *Johnny Stockshooter/age fotostock.* 10, *Jon Arnold/Agency Jon Arnold Images/age fotostock.* 11, *Sylvain Grandadam/age fotostock.* 14, *JTB Photo/ Alamy.* 15, *Danita Delimont/Alamy.* 16, *Bill Bachman/Alamy.* 18, *WorldFoto/Alamy.* 19 (left), *Georgie Holland/age fotostock.* 19 (right), *imagebroker/Alamy.* **Color Section:** *The sandstone mounds at Purnululu (Bungle Bungle) National Park, Western Australia: Elizabeth Czitronyi/Alamy. The perfect vineyard geometry of Coldstream Hills, located in Coldstream, Victoria: Cephas Picture Library/Alamy. Taking in the meticulously restored splendor of the Queen Victoria building in Sydney: John Henshall/Alamy. Beach bungalows in Melbourne, Victoria: Walter Bibikow/age fotostock.) Sydney Opera House, designed to look like sails in port: Ken Ross/viestiphoto.com. Aboriginal man playing the didgeridoo, a traditional instrument of Australia: Vidler/Mauritius/age fotostock. Palm Cove, Queensland, at dusk: ImageState/ Alamy. Two Red Kangaroos duke it out: Martin Rugner/age fotostock. A tourist in Tasmania surveys the scene at Cradle Mountain National Park: Worldfoto/Alamy. Remarkable Rocks, Flinders Chase National Park, Kangaroo Island: Woodfall Wild Images/Alamy. Frozen water in a stream in the Mossman Gorge rainforest, Queensland: Nic Cleave Photography/Alamy. A traditional aboriginal painted design: Suzy Bennett/Alamy. The monorail at Darling Harbour: Gonzalo Azumendi/age fotostock. Devil's Marbles, Northern Territory: Gonzalo Azumendi/age fotostock. Australia's national icon, the Koala bear: George Hunter/age fotostock. Lawn bowlers in Darwin: Kevin O'Hara/age fotostock. A school of Yellowfin goatfish, Great Barrier Reef: George Holland/age fotostock.*

NOTES

NOTES